AMERICA'S
GARDEN BOOK

AMERICA'S GARDEN BOOK

by

Louise and James Bush-Brown

Revised Edition by Howard S. Irwin

with the assistance of the Brooklyn Botanic Garden

MACMILLAN • USA

Editor: Pamela Hoenig

Project Editor: John Meils

Production Editors: Patricia Shaw Bozza and Cathy Felgar

Designer: Nick Anderson

Copyeditor: Candace Levy

Proofreader: Adaya Henis

Indexer: Mary Mortensen

With special thanks to all of the photographers:
David Cavagnaro
Christine Douglas
John Elsley
Elvin McDonald
Judy White
Cynthia Woodyard

*Thanks to all the photographers from the Brooklyn Botanic Garden,
including Anne L. Irwin and Howard S. Irwin.*

Line drawings by Dorothy Irwin

(Facing page) General editor Howard S. Irwin in his garden.

MACMILLAN
A Simon & Schuster Macmillan Company
1633 Broadway
New York, NY 10019

Library of Congress Cataloging-in-Publication Data
Bush-Brown, James.
    America's garden book / by Louise and James Bush-Brown. —Rev. ed. / by Howard S. Irwin,
        with the assistance of the Brooklyn Botanic Garden.
        p. cm.
    Includes index.
    ISBN 0-02-860995-6
        1. Gardening—United States. 2. Gardening. I. Bush-Brown, Louise. II. Irwin, Howard S.
        III. The Brooklyn Botanic Garden. IV. Title.
SB453.B9 1996   96-18752
635'.0973—dc20   CIP

Manufactured in the United States of America

10 9 8 7 6 5 4 3 2 1

I can enjoy a profounder peace there, more comfort, and fewer cares;
I need never wear a formal toga.... Everywhere there is peace and quiet.

—Pliny the Younger, writing of his Villa Tuscum

CONTENTS

IV. FLAVOR AND FRAGRANCE **621**

V. CULTURAL METHODS
AND PRACTICES **733**

FOREWORD

First published in 1939, *America's Garden Book* was the creation of Louise Bush-Brown, director of the Pennsylvania School of Horticulture, and her husband, James Bush-Brown, a noted landscape architect. The Bush-Browns revised and expanded the book in 1958 to place greater emphasis on the rising popularity of suburban gardening after World War II. In 1981, a third edition was published with the collaboration and sponsorship of the New York Botanical Garden, further expanding the book's comprehensiveness and utility in a wide range of areas. New information was included on the various soils and climates of the central and western regions of the United States, the increasing preference for informality in the design of home gardens, the intensifying popularity of outdoor "rooms" or landscaped spaces for outdoor living in warm seasons, and the ever-growing appeal of indoor gardening. The urgent need to incorporate recent advances in plant science into gardening practices was recognized, and the equally important need to revise the lists of recommended plants according to the results of horticultural and taxonomic research and the commercial availability of meritorious kinds was accomplished in the third edition.

To achieve these ends, the New York Botanical Garden was asked to review and revise the text and illustrations and to work with Charles Scribner's & Sons to make this edition even more useful than the earlier ones had been. As president of the New York Botanical Garden at the time, I appointed an editorial committee of staff horticulturists and outside collaborators to pursue the project. Through it all, however, I was personally frustrated that the press of other responsibilities kept me from doing more than organizing the project, proofreading contributor's copy, and keeping progress on schedule.

It was, therefore, a great pleasure to have the opportunity to again become involved with *America's Garden Book* and to prepare a fourth edition, this time without the constraints of a heavy administrative schedule. The institutional sponsor for the fourth edition is the Brooklyn Botanic Garden. The Garden's president, Judith Zuk, concurred with Dr. Albert Bush-Brown, son of the original authors, in asking me to take responsibility for preparing this edition and to involve myself as fully as I wished. Having the splendid bibliographic and technical resources of the Brooklyn Botanic Garden and Clark Botanic Garden at my disposal, I assembled extensive files of information, opted to do nearly all of the revisionary writing myself, and called on others for help as the need arose. The chapter on roses, for example was completely revised by Stephen Scanniello, rosarian at the Brooklyn Botanic Garden. Performance records of unusual annuals grown at Clark Botanic Garden were made available. Of the many photographs—all new in this edition— some were taken by Anne Irwin, my wife, some by me, some by staff members and volunteers at the Brooklyn Botanic Garden and Clark Botanic Garden, and still others were obtained from various sources by the publisher. The line drawings were prepared by Dorothy Irwin, my daughter.

Several new objectives are addressed in this edition. It is acknowledged that gardening is clearly America's most popular pastime, but because of the increase in two-income families, many enthusiasts find they have less time for it. Hence, the importance of time-saving garden design and maintenance procedures, such as substituting low-maintenance ground cover beds for high-maintenance lawns. Environmental awareness finds expression in the promotion of "organic" garden practices, water conservation measures, and integrated pest management. The book's geographic range of coverage has been extended to all regions of the United States except south Florida, southern California, and Hawaii, where the largely foreign cultivated flora is too extensive for inclusion. Much the same is also true in parts of the desertous Southwest. Plant names have been carefully checked for validity, and synonyms are given in cases where recent name changes in taxonomic literature might cause confusion. USDA hardiness zones are cited for all outdoor woody plants and perennials.

Throughout this revision, the basic organization of the previous editions has been retained while at the same time the scope of the book has been broadened, including a new chapter on seaside gardening, much-expanded plant lists, and various measures to eliminate or at least mitigate harmful environmental impact of certain fertilizers and pesticides.

When revising a work as venerable and durable as *America's Garden Book*, it is important to learn as much as possible about the original authors and especially to try to understand their purposes, their special interests, their biases, and their goals in undertaking such a vast work. In their foreword to the seminal edition, the Bush-Browns emphasized not only the importance of accurate, up-to-date information when creating and maintaining a garden, but stressed that the results should be *artistically* satisfying. These are ageless criteria, too often overlooked in how-to manuals, too often trivialized or omitted from specialist treatises.

Although I never met Louise Bush-Brown (she died in 1974), I enjoyed two all-too-brief encounters with James in his advanced years, one a stimulating repartee focused on the trees and shrubs we encountered as we strolled through the New York Botanical Garden on a warm spring day, the other an autumnal ramble through some dense oak-hickory woods on Long Island where he patted the trunks of admired trees with affection, pointing out the "muscles" in the limbs and trunks of ironwood and the "bold gauntness" of a leafless black locust. Then, with an impish glint in his eye, he even praised a big shrubby poison sumac for its "incomparably fiery fall foliage." James died in 1988.

Because Albert Bush-Brown made the arrangements for both the third edition and the present one, and because I was employed at Long Island University in the early 1980s when he was chancellor of that institution, I gained further familiarity with the work of the original authors and felt a vicarious kinship. A decade later, as I began work on this edition, Albert—or Bush, as he was known to friends—and I were in close touch, partly because he too was a knowledgeable and enthusiastic gardener. Until just weeks before his untimely death in 1995, we continued exchanging seeds, plants, and ideas.

Many others have also had a part in bringing this work to completion. Warm thanks are due to Donald Moore and Judith Zuk, successive presidents of the Brooklyn Botanic Garden, for their encouragement and support. I am also indebted to Dr. Stephen K-M Tim, vice president for science at the Brooklyn Botanic Garden, for reviewing the manuscript and referring appropriate parts to staff specialists for their input. Dr. Philip Waldman, owner of Roslyn Nursery in Dix Hills, NY, made many valuable additions to the sections on rhododendrons and azaleas. Two longtime wholesale nurserymen friends, now both passed away, allowed me to repeatedly pick their encyclopedic brains for useful information borne of their long experience and love of trees and shrubs: Bayer Lustgarten, founder of Lustgarden Farms and Nurseries of Middle Island, NY, and James Cross, founder of Environmentals of Cutchogue, NY. George Pouder, of Lieb's Greenhouses in New Rochelle, NY, has also conveyed much useful information over the years. Several hobby gardeners long familiar with previous editions of the book have pointed our errors and omissions that have been rectified in this edition. Especially helpful in this regard has been Nancy Sommer of Winston Salem, NC.

Most of all, I want to express my appreciation for the warm encouragement and consistent support of my wife, Anne, who went over every page of manuscript with a constructively critical eye and, being a lifelong gardener herself, made countless suggestions.

It is my hope, no less than that of the Brooklyn Botanic Garden, that this new edition of *America's Garden Book* will further the understanding of gardens and garden plants and thereby enrich the gardening experience of all who turn to it for guidance.

Howard S. Irwin
Truro, MA
1996

I
Garden Design

I

The Heritage of Gardening

THE FULL MEANING OF THE WORD *GARDEN* IN TODAY'S America is not always thoroughly understood. More often than not, it is used to refer to a piece of tilled or otherwise intensively cultivated land such as vegetable garden, rose garden, or a flower garden—the last, perhaps, no more than a small bed of petunias. As a verb, *to garden* implies the growing of plants, while *gardening* becomes a synonym for horticulture (from the Latin: *hortus,* "garden"). Yet the origins of the word derive from a larger and broader concept: that

Stately trees and a verdant bank informally crested with azaleas ablaze in spring glory invite ascent to a lovely home.

Informal and natural, a well-designed garden presents varied vistas both outdoors and from within.

of landscapes which have been altered or rearranged by humans to render them more useful, more pleasing, and more comfortable. Within this context, a garden is fine art.

In the history of gardens, we study not the culture of plants but the design of outdoor spaces for human habitat. The concept is clouded and complicated, however, by the fact that it deals with living materials as well as with abstract design. By their very nature, gardens change continually, moment by moment, with the hours, the days, and the seasons. A few years can bring awesome maturity or disappointing ruin to a garden. The success of the art, therefore, cannot be separated from the pure science of botany or biology, or from the applied science of horticulture.

The words *garden, yard, orchard,* and *paradise* all stem from a single concept: a more or less enclosed outdoor space, sheltered, leafy, refreshing, often bright with color and alive with fragrances, birdsong, the sounds of splashing water, and cooling breezes. History shows that the garden was the age-old training center in which the arts and sciences first blossomed. It was a sacred place, the fount of learning with horticulture and agriculture obvious derivations. Paleontology dates two basic gardening tools, the ax and the mattock, to at least 500,000 years ago. With this awareness of the great antiquity of gardening, its claim as the matrix of all culture becomes clear.

The most promising wild plants had to be propagated. Seeds had to be selected and saved for planting. The timing of garden operations—preparing land and tilling soil, ensuring sunlight and moisture, sowing seeds, suppressing weeds, fending off marauders, and harvesting and storing crops—had to be learned for each of the hundreds of kinds of food and medicinal plants being cultivated. Because human well-being depended on successful gardening, and much of that on forces beyond human control, gardens took on religious significance. The word *paradise* (derived from the Old Persian, *pairidaeza*, "enclosure") harkens to the sacred peace found in the ideal garden.

Pliny the Younger wrote of one of his villas (Tuscum): "I can enjoy a profounder peace there, more comfort, and fewer cares; I need never wear a formal toga. . . . Everywhere there is peace and quiet." Pliny had created his own paradise, that most beautiful and wonderful of gardens of Eastern philosophy to which the departed go in afterlife. In the medieval garden, the orchard was not a place for growing apples, but rather a grove of trees planted to provide cooling shade on hot summer days. So much was pleasure emphasized in these gardens that Sir Francis Bacon, sixteenth-century philosopher and statesman, referred to them as gardens of "pleasant delytes." Our own word *yard* stems directly from that medieval orchard. And in the pantheon of America's early leaders, it is no secret that Washington, Adams, Jefferson, and Franklin all had an abiding love of nature and a profound commitment to the land.

That the American backyard might be a cool and shady retreat is an appealing idea. Many homeowners already know that home can be a paradise; others, not so fortunate, continue to dash from place to place seeking it. With today's increasing concern over dwindling and costly energy supplies, it would make great sense if more of us turned to our own backyards to create oases at home. To do so, however, we must consider the backyard as living space rather than as vegetable plots and petunia patches. Within this larger concept, then, a garden becomes, by definition, outdoor space organized for our use, comfort, and pleasure. It is a place where family and friends can meet in relaxation and pleasure, where we need not always wear our best "togas."

While gardens have been a continuing source of inspiration for philosophers, poets, painters, and musicians, they take on added significance today as outposts of reality in this increasingly crowded and artificial world. A near renaissance in urban tree planting and in the creation of mini-parks, green spaces, plazas, garden shopping malls, and "vacant lot" gardening has taken place in recent decades. The ongoing boom of interest in houseplants, for example, is yet another expression of a basic human need: to have direct contact with reality as represented by the natural world. This is especially so in our modern, hard, artificial urban environ-

ments. We are, after all, creatures of nature, more related to trees than to machines. And while individual plants may help reassure us, the broader experience of unlimited landscape reveals a great deal more. As the world grows increasingly crowded, however, for many the opportunity to experience unlimited landscape inevitably diminishes.

Gardens, therefore—whether elaborate or minuscule or in-between—have come to symbolize the natural landscape that twentieth-century people are searching for. In other words, gardens have become more and more important to our survival as rational creatures.

Landscape can be organized for many purposes, to reach many goals—from the architectural sophistication of a city plaza to the biological sophistication of a country bog. Amos Bronson Alcott, famous nineteenth-century educator, mystic, and author, wrote in one of his essays: "Who loves a garden, still his Eden keeps; Perennial pleasures, plants, and wholesome harvests reaps." And, it should be added here, he also helps preserve a part of the total landscape. "Gardeners make extraordinarily good citizens," said Barbara Ward (Lady Jackson), eminent British economist and writer. We couldn't agree with her more.

In this time of intensifying environmental consciousness, we must find ways in gardening, as in all endeavors, to

Relating garden plants to literary passages can be a game, as might be played in this beautifully designed Shakespeare garden at the Brooklyn Botanic Garden.

conserve resources and discontinue environmentally harmful practices. For some, this may involve planting a tree or hedge not only for pleasing effect but also for casting shade on the roof in summer to reduce the need for air-conditioners, or to buffer our houses from harsh winter winds. For others, it will mean mulching to minimize summer watering. It will mean basing any fertilizer amendments on soil tests and forswearing use of biocides except in cases of clear need, and then only on specific targets. It will mean choosing garden plants—trees, shrubs, flowers, and food plants—that require minimal intervention.

*Trees such as these sugar maples (*Acer saccharum*) serve not only as ever-changing sentinels through the seasons, defining the setting as nothing else can, but, properly placed, cast welcome shade in summer.*

In essence, ours is an individual search for a satisfying, productive garden environment, one achieved without contributing to planetary degradation. Far from being a retrograde pursuit, it will require imagination and ingenuity, and involve a good deal of experimentation along the way, right in our own backyards. Our greatest need is for new ideas—

and the willingness to test them ourselves. Fortunately, more and more useful new ideas are reaching the garden marketplace. For example, low-maintenance expanses of ground cover or meadow are environmentally sound garden alternatives to high-maintenance lawn. Shrub plantings, perennial beds, and vegetable gardens mulched the year round are more nearly self-maintaining than the time-consuming, water-demanding bare-earth "clean-cultivation" standard that has so long been traditional.

In recent years, prolonged periods of drought in the West, especially in California, have led to water restrictions and, as a consequence, to an emphasis on water conservation in gardening. Called "xeriscaping," this approach to gardening emphasizes cultivating species and cultivars that thrive under drier than normal conditions yet perform to a desired standard, minimizing irrigation through soil improvement and the use of appropriate mulches, and designing gardens and maintaining them in ways that keep demands for supplemental water to a minimum.

Gardening is the best low-entropy activity we have. If designed and managed intelligently, a garden can efficiently convert natural wastes into living plants of extraordinary beauty and great utility. As an avocational activity, gardening not only is physically healthful but keeps us in touch with the ecological verities that may seem foreign to those who still eschew involvement with the soil. If in our gardens we decide to favor the simple over the complex, to produce more at home, to conserve and recycle nonrenewable resources, to minimize the use of polluting machinery and synthetic materials, to pursue a sustainable lifestyle that will benefit those coming after us, we will be happier and will also be making a contribution to the solution of serious local, regional, and worldwide problems.

THE HISTORY OF GARDENING

How it all began is a subject for conjecture. It is generally accepted that sometime after early hominids began walking upright, they began to feel the need for a "home place" from which they could go out and to which they could return, a place where they could gather and store their possessions and food, a place they would find familiar and comfortable. Perhaps this first home was no more than a small area cleared within a thicket or in the shelter of an overhanging bluff. When the first human organized that first bit of landscape, however, the first garden was created. Architecture, as we understand it, came much later.

Sir Francis Bacon is credited with saying: "Man comes to build stately sooner than to garden finely, as if the latter were the greater perfection." A civilization requires maturity before it can achieve great architecture or great gardens; these are not portable art forms like music, dance, poetry, and various other creative expressions. Fortunate are we, indeed, that this stability has provided us with a rich heritage of gardens, from ancient Persia and China, from classical Rome and Renaissance Italy, from the France of Louis XIV, and from the England of Capability Brown.

Anthropologists have found that in ancient hunting and gathering societies the beauty in flowers and other plant structures was reflected in crafts and adornments, that religious beliefs often involved a special respect for inexplicable phenomena about trees, and that subsistence itself depended on an intricate knowledge of the food and drug value of indigenous plants.

The ancient Egyptians, the Assyrians, and the Persians all developed gardens of majestic grandeur and opulence and incorporated plant forms in their architecture. The ancient Chinese, with their deep sensitivity to beauty, laid the foundations for a form of garden art that was eventually to have great influence on other lands. Bonsai, the miniaturization of idealized nature, seminally a Chinese art associated with Buddhism and subsequently elaborated by the Japanese, is a legacy of the period.

The Greeks also gave to the world a new concept of gardening. Their homes were adorned with flowers, but it was in their civic design and public buildings that they most skillfully applied their garden art. Their temples were surrounded by groves of trees, and trees graced the important streets and marketplaces in their principal cities.

Originating in ancient China and much elaborated upon in Japan, bonsai is the cultivation and training of miniaturized trees and shrubs in containers, often for decades, resulting in living art forms.

Much of the knowledge and skill in garden craft possessed by the Romans was acquired from the Greeks. In the second century A.D., the Romans began to build gardens on a tremendous scale, inspired by the precedent of the vast palace gardens of Mesopotamia, which they had conquered. They studied hydraulics and brought water from great distances by conduit to supply the ornamental fountains that adorned their villa gardens. These great villas were later to inspire the Italian garden architects to follow the Roman precedent.

During the Dark Ages, the art and practices of gardening were kept alive by monks in the monasteries. They made their work the interpretation of goodness and their study the means of gaining a deeper knowledge of life.

The geometric formality of a monastery garden bespeaks human control over nature, yet also the singular, almost sculptural, beauty of plants alone and in combination.

The gradual emergence of Europe into an era of revived culture and intellectual enlightenment; the spread of the study of the classics, brought about by the founding of the universities; the rise of an independent class of citizen craftspeople, unattached to the feudal system; the growing importance of the great free cities of Europe—all combined to usher in an age of increased prosperity and greater accomplishment in the arts. It was a remarkable era, destined to become known as the Renaissance, the time of rebirth of Western civilization.

It is only natural that while this great surge of rebuilding and rediscovery of learning fired the imaginations and ambitions of free citizens, experiments should be undertaken in many fields, each with the hope of capturing something of the unknown and mastering it. Painting, sculpture, architecture, garden design, music, and literature, all supported by the skilled crafts, were the outgrowths of the resurgent spirit of the times.

Gains in the arts were upheld by a firm economy based on a lively production of goods and an ever-expanding commerce. It was during this period that some of our most notable examples of garden art were created: the great villas of Italy, the palace gardens of Spain, the vast estates of the French *châteaux*, the careful *parterres* of the Dutch, and the beautiful manor-house gardens of England.

In the sixteenth century the Italians began to build palatial country villas after the manner of the Romans, and they designed and planted these gardens with all the artistic and poetic refinement of their sensitive natures. The results were marvelous essays of merged architecture, verdure, trees, sculpture, flowers, and watercourses, all woven into perfectly proportioned designs of subtle harmony. So beautiful were these visual compositions that they won the admiration and attention of the many visitors who flocked to Italy from all parts of Europe. Italian artists and architects were invited to France and Spain to practice their professions and to teach. Thus, the Italian Renaissance garden became the European Renaissance garden.

For 200 years this formal, architectural style of garden art prevailed throughout Europe. The artist-architects of each nation designed in this grand manner and modified the work of their predecessors to suit their times and their own countries. In all these gardens, formal shapes, symmetrically placed, predominated. The details expressed the basic character of the design, with emphasis placed on straight pathways, clipped hedges, balustrades, fountains, pools, and sculpture, symbolizing the supremacy of humankind over nature.

The Spaniards adopted the geometric patterns of the Moors and, later, the intricately ornamented details of the baroque Italian gardens. The French expanded the scale of garden building to a sweep of many tens of hundreds of acres in their far-spreading bosques and greenswards. The Dutch reduced the scale to fit their gardens compactly into the inevitably limited areas available to them in their comparatively small country. And the English gleaned from Italian, French, and Dutch styles in developing their formal gardens, adding notable touches of their own, such as the mount (an artificial hill constructed to afford a view), the

ha-ha (a deep, wide ditch that separates garden from surrounding countryside and excludes unwanted wildlife without imposing a visual barrier), and the sinuous perennial border.

In the sweeping grandeur of Versailles, a climbing rose lends charm and a note of warm intimacy.

In the early days of our own country, the colonists naturally drew their first inspiration from the familiar scenes of their natal homes in England. The villages of New England resembled the villages of old England, except that most of the houses here were built entirely of wood instead of stone or brick or half-timber and plaster. The plantations of Virginia, Maryland, and the Carolinas were set out in much the same arrangement as the manors of England. Their concept of garden art was that of seventeenth- and eighteenth-century England.

Thus precedent for garden design in the colonies was drawn from the English interpretation of the Renaissance spirit, just as the architecture we now describe as colonial was copied from the Georgian period in England, itself evolved from Italian Renaissance into English methods and materials. The gardens were rigidly geometric. Even in the small dooryard gardens of New England, Elizabethan patterns persisted. Prim, patterned flower beds, straight paths neatly edged with boxwood or with flowers, fruit trees in rows, turf squares bordered with flowers—these were typical features of the colonial garden. As architectural features and purely decorative ornaments were rarely included, the design was expressed almost entirely in plant materials, a medium that greatly softens the regularity and angularity of the formal style. The faithfully restored gardens at Williamsburg and Mount Vernon are fine examples of gardens of this period.

In the latter years of the eighteenth century, the Spanish tradition of the secluded patio was brought to New Orleans and southern California by the Spanish missionaries and early settlers, and with modifications, this has remained a feature of most modern gardens in those areas.

The Renaissance tradition in America lost its vitality during the early years of the Republic. To infuse new life into the thread of design, Greek forms were resorted to in architecture, as if contemporary design could go no further and must, therefore, return to the ultimate source of classic precedent. The Greek revival had its brief day during the early part of the nineteenth century. But it proved so utterly unsuited to domestic needs of the times in this country that it was soon abandoned, and for the next seventy years no serious attempt was made to derive inspiration from the classic monuments of architecture.

During the nineteenth century the attention and efforts of the American people were absorbed in the great tasks of winning the West, extending the railroads, and developing industries. To build a civilization in the wilderness was in itself a work that demanded the energies of several generations. It is small wonder, then, that until Americans finally achieved the leisure to travel in Europe and to see for themselves their art heritage, no great awareness of art developed in this country. The nineteenth century produced new and unfamiliar forms and expressions, and with the restoration of Colonial Williamsburg in the 1930s came a period of eighteenth-century revival. It was almost as if "good taste" ended in 1800. Much of our architectural heritage of the nineteenth century was destroyed, ersatz eighteenth-century flourished, and not until the 1960s did the nineteenth century come to be appreciated for what it was: a lively expression of a period in which the pioneering spirit excelled—in western expansion, in politics, in letters, and although belatedly recognized, in architecture and the other arts as well.

Through much of this period, the concept of a garden in Europe and America was that of a collection of plants, purely horticultural in purpose. There was great interest in botany, in the introduction of new plants collected in far-flung corners of the planet, and in the growing of fine horticultural specimens, and these interests completely occupied the minds of the gardeners of the period.

In England, control of the garden passed from the landscape gardener to the collector-horticulturist. Little attempt was made to produce examples of garden art of any significance.

During the last decades of the nineteenth century and the early decades of the twentieth, many educated Americans traveled widely in Europe, and in doing so, they renewed a

The formality conferred by straight lines and right angles is softened by bright spring colors and exuberant growth in this restored colonial garden.

close contact with that rich culture after a lapse of several generations. In the same period, the country home in America was assuming a more important aspect, and gardening was again looked on as a valid field of artistic expression. The garden styles of Italy, France, and England were diligently studied and copied here. English, Scots, Dutch, and Italian gardeners came to this country in great numbers to carry on their craft in a land of widening opportunities. Nurseries expanded and proliferated to meet the steadily increasing demands for choice plant materials. Yet, although garden art flourished as never before during this era of prosperity, no really new statements were made. Most gardens, however well planned, were reproductions of a past age. The estate, with its well-designed and superbly maintained garden surrounded by expansive lawns and embraced by protective woodland, was the part-time residence of only the person of wealth. These were gardens for the privileged few, cared for by professional gardeners.

After World War I, while the building of large and magnificent estates continued, a change gradually became perceptible. In the many small homes that were being built in rapidly spreading suburbs during that time, people began to take an interest in the development of their home grounds.

Seed companies and garden equipment suppliers gained prominence. Gardening was no longer for the few, but for the many. Each decade since then has witnessed an ever-increasing number of enthusiastic home gardeners, with new forms and variations coming steadily into favor—as with rooftop gardening, indoor "container" gardening, and so on.

These new gardens are of necessity different from the old. They frequently are more utilitarian; they are not limited by the tradition of formality and style. They require less maintenance, are more lived in, and are, more often than not, considered an extension or even an integral part of one's home. And this is as it should be. A garden should reflect the time in which it is built. It should not imitate styles of other lands. The very life of all arts is the power to rise, phoenixlike, from the past. People of the twentieth century are amply endowed with both tradition and precedent. Knowledge of what has been accomplished in past centuries is helpful and often inspiring, but it is a foundation, no longer the goal. Today, the purpose of garden design is to provide an environment for congenial living, according to one's needs. This is a do-it-yourself age, an ecologically aware age that is short on supplies of energy. Today's gardens are bound to reflect these times, just as the gardens of the past reflected

Suburban expansion after World War I led to the popularization of single-family dwellings surrounded by informal gardens, woodland remnants, and sweeping lawns.

theirs. All art forms demand honesty, and in that honesty lies the germ of distinction, whatever the age.

It is interesting to reflect on the gardens of history that were, by and large, the property of royalty, princes of the church, and the privileged landed gentry. In mid-twentieth-century America, new statements for small gardens began to emanate from California—a straightforward, almost sculptural approach that emphasized above all the need for family use, comfort, and pleasure. This concept for gardens proved so popular and successful that it soon set a new direction throughout the country for gardens as organized spaces. These gardens, in turn, not only revived ancient traditions but also influenced the design of larger gardens, industrial parks, shopping malls, and mini-parks. And while most of these new large gardens are privately owned in democratic America, they are open to all.

Simplicity and style emanate from this container planting in front of a shop, cheering passersby and welcoming them to the door.

Among the sources of authentic plant-related information for gardeners are botanic gardens. In this country such institutions number about 350 and offer labeled collections of trees, shrubs, climbers, and smaller garden plants so that the public may learn the plants' names and characteristics. In most,

the emphasis lies mainly on hardy outdoor plant materials, but many of these institutions maintain public greenhouses and conservatories in which tender (i.e., frost intolerant) ornamental plants are also exhibited. The larger gardens are botanical research centers and museums that focus on plant diversity around the world and possess extensive herbaria (study collections of pressed, dried, and labeled plant specimens) and associated libraries. Most botanic gardens are also training centers, both for the interested public and the aspiring professional, and are important disseminators of plant information. All are committed to the conservation of wild botanical resources and to promoting awareness of humankind's direct dependence on the plant world.

Many are the messages reflected in this late-season vegetable garden: moisture conservation, weed control, pest repulsion, bounteous crops, and the joie de vivre *lent by the bright colors of annuals.*

Today's increasing attention is given to the role of plants in human well-being and social development, recognizing that a deeper understanding of psychological, physiological, and social responses of people to plants can play a significant role in physical and mental health. As a group, gardeners tend to be active self-achievers. Gardens stimulate thought in a peaceful environment—your own thoughts, not those imposed by television or radio or other people. You can plan and act on your own. It is a place to hatch innovative thoughts. It can become a pleasant temple of the highest quality and deepest meaning, an enjoyable retreat in which to learn important lessons of far-reaching significance. For

Children's gardening programs, such as this one at the Brooklyn Botanic Garden, offer urban youngsters directed hands-on garden experience with peers and the satisfaction of taking home produce for the table.

Seed companies continuously develop and test new cultivars before offering them to home gardeners, thus assuring ongoing garden interest throughout the country, as by mixing flowering kale, pansies, and poppies in this display bed at the Burpee test headquarters in Santa Paula, California.

people of any age, a garden is a lens through which the world can be experienced in a new and hopeful way.

Today's concerns about environmental quality find ample expression in the garden. In recent years many once-common pesticides have been taken off the market. Excessive, careless use of fast-release synthetic fertilizers has been shown to threaten public water supplies. Increased emphasis is placed on minimal intervention in gardening, on fertilizing the soil only after its makeup is determined by a soil test, on choosing kinds of vegetables and flowers and landscaping materials that need the least attention, on cutting the ritual

use of water to irrigate lawns and gardens, on composting garden and other vegetable waste, on gardening more by thought-out plan and less by spur-of-the-moment impulse.

For some, plants and flowers are objects to be acquired, arranged, and rearranged, satisfying individual desires of the moment. To others they constitute subjective expressions of form, color, texture, and fragrance. To still others, flowers and plants are seen as organizations of cells to be studied, classified, and understood. Most recently, gardening has been employed as an instrument for healing in our troubled, stressful cities—a potent tool for human therapy and improvement, a symbol of order and beauty in chaos and ugliness, a sign of life in stagnating social systems.

There is wonder attached to the diversity of living forms, a wonder that captivates the child and gives the adult perspective in our often confusing world. By refreshing and stimulating the inner person, gardening helps us face life's problems creatively. As Lewis Mumford, American author and critic, put it, "How essential it now is to reclaim and extend the dominion of plants once more, if man's own survival is to be secured."

PLANT NAMES

In gardening, as in so many forms of human enterprise, initial intimidation yields to curiosity, and then to a feeling of kinship. In this relationship, plant names become critical to distinguish among the various kinds. Just as musicians have long had a uniform worldwide system of notation, botanists and horticulturists have their own basic, simplified, precise communication convention, and that consists of using two Latin terms to designate each plant species. Rules governing botanical names are laid out in the International Code of Botanical Nomenclature. Plants in horticulture are governed by a supplementary set of rules, the International Code of Nomenclature for Cultivated Plants, first issued in 1958 and under continuous revision since then.

Since the codes are internationally agreed on, a plant name, formally published according to code rules, has international currency: it applies to the same kind of plant wherever it occurs or is grown anywhere in the world. For example, *Rosa rugosa* refers to the same species of rose—and only that species—whether in its native Japan or in Italy, South Africa, Argentina, the United States, or anywhere else. Common or vernacular names, by contrast, are often applied to unlike plants and frequently vary from place to place. "Bluebell," for example, refers to one species (*Mertensia virginica*) in eastern United States, to another (*Eustoma grandiflorum*) in Texas, to still another (*Hyacinthoides non-scripta*) in England, and to yet another (*Campanula rotundifolia*) in Scotland—

Campanula rotundifolia

Mertensia virginiana

all unrelated. Other much-used common names, such as buttercup, lily, marigold, and daisy, are also associated with a wide diversity of mostly unrelated plants, even in the same region.

In addition to their precision, scientific or botanical names indicate relationship. All species of *Acer*, the maples, are fairly easily recognized by shared traits, as are those of *Quercus*, the oaks, and *Betula*, the birches. Each group comprises a genus, and each genus embraces a number of distinct species. True lilies also share many common characteristics and so are grouped in the genus *Lilium*. But other plants with "lily" in their common names, such as daylily, Amazon lily, ginger lily, water-lily, and lily-of-the-valley, are not sufficiently lilylike to be included in *Lilium*; indeed, most are completely unrelated to true lilies and to each other.

The botanical binomial term* for each species consists of a capitalized genus name and a lowercase species name, as in *Cornus florida* (which is known by at least two common names, flowering dogwood and eastern dogwood). The familiar pink-bracted type, which occurs in the wild, is considered a minor subentity or form and is formally designated *Cornus florida* form *rubra*. Form is usually abbreviated as f. Other variants, known only in cultivation, have either wholly Latin names (e.g., *Cornus florida* cultivar 'Xanthocarpa', for a yellow-fruited cultivar) or Latin and English names (e.g., *Cornus florida* 'Cherokee Chief', a cultivar with deep rosered bracts). Cultivar is abbreviated as cv. (or cvs. for the plural).

According to the rules of the codes, naturally occurring variants that are recognized within some species—that is, subspecies (abbreviated ssp.), variety (var.), and form (f.)—are given Latin names that begin with a lowercase letter. Cultivars, on the other hand, are given names that begin with a capital letter, are enclosed in single quotation marks, and are not italicized.

Many plants important in horticulture are hybrids, the results of cross-breeding two distinct but closely related kinds, usually species within a genus or variants within species, and are indicated by a multiplication sign × before the hybrid species' name. For example, *Platanus* × *acerifolia*, the London plane (the common sycamore, which is planted as a street and park tree in much of United States), is a hybrid of *Platanus occidentalis*, the American sycamore native to eastern North America, and *Platanus orientalis*, the Oriental plane native to Asia Minor and southeastern Europe. Like many hybrids, London plane does not occur in the wild, only in cultivation. In some plant families, such as the orchids and the cacti, two species of different genera may be induced to cross, resulting in an intergeneric hybrid whose new generic name (usually formed by combining those of the two parent genera) is preceded by a large multiplication sign as in × *Laeliocattleya*, the generic name for orchids resulting from crosses between species *Laelia* and *Cattleya*.

One sometimes disconcerting result of ongoing research into relationships among plants is that plant names may change. Contrary to the complaints of some gardeners, such changes are based on new information that has led to new interpretations by plant taxonomists (botanists specializing in plant diversity and relationships) that may call for combining once-separate genera or species or for separating variable ones into distinct subunits, often with new and unfamiliar names. For example, *Hyacinthoides non-scripta*, the bluebell of England, was until recently *Endymion non-scripus*, before which it was *Scilla non-scripta*. Far from being capricious, these changes improve precision and are formally published according to the provisions of the International Code of Nomenclature for Cultivated Plants.

The two-word name for most plants is in Latin; therefore, it is standard to set the genus and species names in italics.

2

Design

THE VISUAL APPEARANCE OF THE NATURAL LANDSCAPE IS the result of many gradual changes in its geologic formation, climate, and vegetation through the ages. Latterly, intensive use of land by humans has brought about further changes that have altered and sometimes even destroyed natural features. Farms, towns, cities, and highways replaced the forest and prairie; as a result, the natural landscape has been harmed and sometimes even irrevocably changed.

In the peaceful Japanese Garden at the Brooklyn Botanic Garden, emphasis lies more on complementary plant forms and their harmony with water and stone than on blazing floral colors.

Designing the landscape for human use requires a careful study of the natural conditions of a site. These conditions guide the modifications in the use and appearance of the land so that the resultant forms will be appropriate, pleasing, and convenient. The preservation of natural beauty and the development that best conserves and adapts a landscape to new uses is the function of landscape architecture or design.

A wooded embankment clothed with various rhododendrons can offer bright color for several months and foliar substance throughout the year. Acid, humusy soil and partial shade in summer favor most species and cultivars of Rhododendron.

Landscape design is a subtle art, involving a knowledge of plants, from both botanical and horticultural perspectives, as well as the exercise of imagination and good taste. It requires an understanding and an appreciation of natural conditions, imagination in foreseeing a site's possibilities, skill in creating pleasing compositions, taste in selecting living and nonliving materials, and ingenuity in adjusting to diverse requirements. Unless it is well designed, a landscape that is being modified is likely to become an inconvenient, unattractive arrangement of elements that lack comfort and beauty. A well-organized landscape not only will bring deeply rewarding satisfactions but will enhance your home, communicate pride, and make an aesthetic contribution to your community—to say nothing of raising the dollar value of your house and property.

HISTORIC STATEMENT AND STYLE

In architecture itself, as well as in landscape architecture, style is intimately connected with the social customs and economic and political structure of its time. Every historically important place has its own visual traits, reflective of cultural impact on natural conditions and especially of a sense of order and beauty. Habit and tradition tend to fix these expressions into styles, while changing social customs tend to bring about new treatments of the landscape.

Landscape architecture and design are more limited by local conditions than is architecture itself because they are more intimately involved with such natural elements as land forms, trees, sky, sunlight, and rainfall. In general, plant materials are best used in climatic zones that are similar to those of their place of origin. While an Italian villa can be built in New England and its design may be architecturally correct, it cannot be embellished by the cypresses, stone pines, and olive trees traditional in the Italian landscape; hardier substitutes must be found.

Style is as recognizable in garden art as it is in architecture. Our varied American heritage includes the simple dignity of the New England colonial village, the restricted, prim yards of the formal town houses in Philadelphia, the spacious formality of the southern plantation home, the secluded patios of New Orleans, and the early Spanish missions in California.

The precedents for these early gardens in America were the abundant gardens of England, both great and small, the stately architectural gardens of Italy, the measured formality of gardens in France, and the terraces and patios of Spain. All of these older styles were faithfully based on the formal plan: trees in balanced symmetry, straight paths paved and precisely edged, a flat terrace with a clipped hedge at the outer rim to provide transition between the formality of the garden and the naturalness of the outer landscape.

Whereas gardens in the West have long been designed to stimulate the primary senses, reflecting in some degree the fashion, economics, and tastes of the individual gardener, Oriental gardening has arisen from a religious-spiritual base, combining philosophy, religion, art, and poetry with horticulture. Originally the preserves of monasteries and the estates of nobles, the gardens of the East reflect the importance accorded form, control, predictability, and neatness in design. Primacy is given to water in motion and the solidity of stone. Plants are valued more for foliar textures than for exuberant floral display, the latter limited to subdued touches here and there.

The Oriental garden is thus a fusion of flora, art, water, and stone, restrained and subtly evocative rather than overt and direct in its effect. Each kind of plant has symbolic value, each individual specimen a structural role. The "mood of man" is evident in intricately clipped shrubs and carefully raked gravel. But a sense of intimacy with nature prevails. While Oriental gardens have great appeal to many Westerners, the complex aesthetic, philosophic, and spiritual concepts are beyond the ken of most, and the fastidious attention they require conflicts with Western lifestyles. Yet much can be learned from this form of garden art. Especially in this time of intensifying urbanization, we have a growing desire to create gardens that meet our needs for private sanctuary and union with the natural world, to remind us whence we have come and of the larger scheme of nature of which we are a part.

Most strongly rooted in today's American tradition is the naturalistic style of England. In this graceful, flowing style, symmetry is discarded in favor of sweeping curves and a balanced asymmetry of masses, of open lawns and meadows, flanked by groves of trees.

Contemporary garden design has broken away from much of the rigidity and formalism of the past, and is more respectful of nature. Most strongly rooted in today's American tradition is the naturalistic style of England— a graceful, flowing style that discards symmetry in favor of sweeping curves and a balanced asymmetry of masses, open lawns, and meadows flanked by groves of trees. This new approach affords one the freedom to shape the landscape

directly and offers interest in the selection and arrangement of materials, both living and nonliving. The designers of present-day gardens are more concerned with organizing garden space as a sculptural concept than as a pictorial composition. These new gardens are what can only be described as "hollow sculpture"—people containers— compositions to be experienced from within, rather than just to be looked at. Herein, then, lies the strength of this newer approach: to adapt landscape to meet our needs while at the same time recognizing and taking advantage of the demands, limitations, and opportunities of the site. At its best, nothing is forced on the landscape or superimposed; rather, the forms and shapes grow out of or are determined by that landscape.

The speed with which this functional approach to garden design has been accepted bears tribute to its validity. We see it everywhere: in shopping malls, new parks, and urban plazas; in corporate and industrial parks; and in private gardens, both vast and small. And as this approach has matured, it has become less rigid and more respectful of local tastes and preferences. Instead of copying the past or adopting a mechanistic formula approach to the arrangement of outdoor space for human purposes, we use our rich heritage to provide inspiration for refreshing new landscape designs in our home environments.

The gentle serpentine layout of a mixed perennial garden along a woodland border is enlivened with the bold forms and bright colors of many species carefully placed so that each is visible from the lawn.

GARDEN PLANNING

Except possibly for someone very skilled and talented, a plan is essential when creating a new garden—or even refurbishing an old one.

Planning on paper allows for an orderly process of thought and decision making to achieve a result that will meet your particular needs within the limitations of your site, budget, and interest. It is much less costly to make mistakes on paper, in the planning stage, than to try to correct them in the landscape itself. The planning process allows decisions to be made on interrelating factors. If a tree is needed to shade the west windows of a living room, for example, how does the same tree relate to shading an outdoor sitting area, to bedroom windows above, the neighbor's view, spring flowers, autumn color, or a septic tank leaching field where invading tree roots can cause problems?

Working on paper stimulates the kind of analysis that highlights and answers such practical as well as aesthetic questions. This is the function of a good landscape architect or designer; it is not the function of a nursery owner or landscape contractor. It is important to distinguish between organization of landscape in a spacial sense and the installation of plants, paving materials, fences, etc. It follows, then, that when selecting a landscape architect, designer, nursery owner, or contractor, you should ask to see other work he or she has done. You may decide to design your own property with or without assistance from an architect or designer. When consulting one or more good books on do-it-yourself landscape design, be sure to study them carefully to find the best approach for you.

*A grove of dawn redwood (*Metasequoia glyptostroboides*) makes an arresting sculptural impact against the autumn sky. The foliage turns bright yellow before dropping.*

Every site has its assets and its liabilities, some apparent, some cryptic or latent. The creative designer must be able to see beyond the actual conditions to arrive at possible solutions of the practical problems. One of the first steps in planning is the evaluation of these possibilities and the summing up of the practical facilities that must be provided. One must endeavor to plan for these necessary facilities in such a way as to preserve, as far as possible, the best qualities of the site. Major decisions come first; details later.

In developing a new piece of property, an early decision is where to position the house with respect to sunshine, prevailing winds, and views and its relationship to land forms and to other features of the landscape—these are all important considerations. Too often, suburban houses are placed on their lots with utter disregard for such factors. All too frequently a house is placed nearly in the center of a lot and the garage at the rear in the hope that the latter will be less conspicuous. This often means that the garage and driveway appropriate as much as 20 percent of all the land not occupied by the house and, if repeated by the neighbors, results in a panorama of unattractive garages as well. The most functional arrangement, and the most economical of space, is one in which the garage or carport along with other utilitarian spaces inside the house are grouped together facing toward the street. The other rooms thus occupy the more remote part of the house and look out on a comparatively secluded area that can be developed for satisfactory outdoor living.

While the architectural period or style of the house should be taken into consideration when determining scale, proportion, and materials (i.e., brick paving for a colonial house, terrazzo or precast blocks for a contemporary one), the garden design should grow out of the needs of the occupants. If the fundamentals cited above are adhered to and the existing character of the landscape respected, the garden need not repeat patterns of the past. Just because you live in a Cape Cod cottage, it is not necessary to have a dooryard garden any more than it is necessary to create boxwood parterres if you live in a reproduction of an Elizabethan manor.

The three major functional units of most properties are the approach (the driveway and front walk), the service area, and the area devoted to family living and recreational pursuits. In general, the approach should be reasonably direct; the service area convenient and accessible; and the living area ample, secluded, and attractive. Each of these units should be contiguous with the corresponding portion of the house. That is, the front walk should lead from the place for vehicle parking, whether on the street or in the driveway, directly to the front door. The service area should be convenient to the side or rear door and be designed to conceal waste containers. The outdoor living area not only should be convenient to one or more doors but should be visible from within. Local topographic conditions may dictate compromises, but wherever it is possible to adhere to this program, the plan should result in a convenient, economical, and functional arrangement.

Unsurpassed in stateliness of form and vividness of color, an accent group of tulips brightens the somber verdure of a groundcover bed.

After assigning different areas of the ground to certain uses, these areas must next be separated from one another and connected logically. This is best done by masses of foliage, trees, shrubs, hedges, fences, or walls. The designer should indicate on the plan the position of open lawn and of trees, the position of screen plantings to hide unsatisfactory views, the positions of viewpoints, and the directions of distant views. There is an element of the practical and of the aesthetic in each of these decisions.

On a small property, space must be very carefully planned and economically used. No amount of embellishment can overcome the inconvenience of an ill-adapted plan or make up for the loss of available space caused by an illogical arrangement of parts. The changing needs and desires of the family must be carefully considered, and one alternative weighed against another—whether a certain space would now be of more value if used as a play area rather than a vegetable garden, for example.

Stone steps, flanked by tubbed accent plants, and a dark opening in a massive ivy-clad wall comprise a mysterious portal, beckoning the visitor to pass through to the unknown.

On a very small lot dominated by straight property lines and the straight lines of the house, a rectilinear design is sometimes the most logical and most effective plan for a garden. This does not imply that the design must be symmetrical. A few well-chosen trees and one or two focal points on an imaginary line may be enough to make the plan harmonize with its restricted, geometric site. The planting of the shrubs and flowers may be incidental. Unity of design may be obtained by emphasizing the boundaries, by separating the property from adjoining neighbors, and by concentrating interest within the area. The boundary may take the form of a hedge or a fence or a wall that sets off and enhances the composition within.

That painters often succeed in designing great gardens is not surprising, for color and composition are the tools in both disciplines. By reducing lawn area, angling vistas, introducing sculptural accents, and choosing plant materials that will stay within bounds, one can fill even the smallest garden with multiple vistas, the effect on the visitor strolling through not unlike that of a picture gallery.

Casually splayed tulips growing out of informal azaleas in front of ivy-draped sculpture and trellis help impart added dimensions to a small setting.

An exposed natural outcrop enhanced with carefully placed rocks to create planting pockets makes an ideal environment for a diversity of low plants, access to which is facilitated by a stone path.

Because trees, shrubs, and flowers are so often planted in haphazard fashion without regard for the beauty of the composition as a whole or the eventual size of the plants, sorry results are legion. The same effort and money applied to carrying out a well-conceived plan would result in a much more satisfying, useful, and beautiful picture. Forethought helps create beautiful surroundings, and the small property deserves as much consideration as any, perhaps even more.

Improving an Existing Garden Design

Because of today's extraordinary mobility, most people live in homes they did not design and can find themselves dissatisfied dealing with gardens they did not create. Such gardens should be seen as opportunities rather than burdens, as a chance to choose what seems good, to discard the rest, and to make the garden your own creation, doing so as time becomes available, when the means are at hand, and desire dictates.

*Bold textural effects are achieved with hybrid cannas (*Canna × generalis*), backed by a tall screen of castor bean (*Ricinus communis*).*

While it is nearly always a love of plants that stimulates one to do gardening, few indulge their passion with a clear, comprehensive plan. The result is often disappointing and falls short in expressing the gardener's intention. Some gardeners are collectors, assiduously assembling representatives of all variations of a particular species or all species of a genus. Others, probably most, seek rich masses of color, the better in great sweeping borders. Still others grow plants for their floral and foliar perfumes. Botanists in the garden tend to promote diversity, often striving for representation of various plant families or ecological types. Each of these biases (and many others) can serve as a theme and lead to a beautiful, interesting garden, but each has limitations that require attention. Collector gardens often suffer from sameness, whether they contain roses, daylilies, lilacs, or hollies, as they are variations on a single narrow theme. Companion plants can help relieve the monotony. Gardens devoted entirely to color too often are transitory and lack the firm line, the satisfying architecture of a single plant seen alone. Gardens of botanists tend to reflect academic pursuits, often presenting plants as museum objects, but if embraced by an arresting, dramatic setting, as in many botanic gardens, the details of botany become enhancements of that larger entity.

Trees and Shrubs in the Landscape

Plantings of trees and shrubs form the dominant masses in most landscape plans. Not only are they important objects in themselves, interesting in outline, texture, and color, but they are one of the best means of marking the boundaries of a site and separating the various functional areas from each other. A mass of flowering shrubs, a hedge, or a vine-covered fence makes an excellent screen around service areas. Where a view is to be kept open, the most effective means of relating it to the foreground is to frame it within the branches of trees in the middle distance. This separates it from every other scene, fixes the attention on the distance, and contrasts the shadowy foreground with the light-filled surroundings. At the same time, trees afford shade that can make the house and its adjoining lawn or terrace more livable in summer. Trees and shrubs determine, by their position, the shapes of open areas in the design, contrasting the solid masses with the open spaces, the shade with the sunlight.

The owner should see that care is taken to protect the existing healthy trees on a piece of property that is to be developed. It is well to remember that the building of a house is apt adversely to affect nearby trees. Excavations frequently cut through the root system and change the water level of the subsoil, thus altering the tree's available water supply, and paved areas of driveway or terrace reduce the soil's normal supply of water and air. In many instances,

*A foundation planting of mixed azaleas flanked by dogwoods (*Cornus florida*) offers a few weeks of concentrated color in spring, but should be backed with other species that can carry interest through the rest of the year.*

mature trees become so adversely affected as a result of building operations that they go into irreversible decline and, after several years, die.

It is an obvious absurdity to compromise a house plan to save an existing tree and then have it die from lack of consideration of its needs. A new structure should be kept at a distance from any sizable tree you wish to save, so that no more than a fractional portion of the root system is disturbed in the course of construction.

Each new tree should be selected for the attributes it will offer at maturity, whether they be shade, flowers, fruit, or picturesque outline. To fulfill most completely the exacting requirements of the home property, trees should be chosen with certain criteria in mind: They should remain in scale with the surroundings; they should be deeply rooted, avoiding competition with lawns and gardens; they should be strong limbed, supple, and have relatively small deciduous organs (i.e., leaves, flowers, fruit, and bark bits), to minimize cleanup; they should be free of intense disease and insect infestations, obviating costly, often harmful chemical intervention; and they should be reproductively benign and not infest the grounds and neighborhood with myriad seedlings and saplings. Especially desirable are trees that possess well-shaped, symmetrical heads or attractive outlines, produce beautiful flowers or fruits, or whose leaves turn a striking hue in the fall.

For the small suburban property, the choice is necessarily limited, as the matter of scale must be given consideration. In most designs, a sense of proper scale is one of the most difficult qualities to preserve. For example, a small house with a massive chimney is made to appear even smaller than it really is, and so the chimney is considered to be "out of scale." In the same way, a small yard will seem smaller still if dwarfed by the presence of very large trees. On the other hand, this changing of the apparent scale may be just what we wish to accomplish. Certainly, there is no more homelike picture than a little New England farmhouse standing in the shelter of a great American elm. But most houses do not belong to this type of setting. Suburbs lack the expansive countryside to make the elm tree seem at home and appropriate. (And, alas, disease has so reduced the number of elms in our landscape that the sight is now a rare one.)

Today, typical residential lots are narrow, often too narrow for the houses on them; the street may be narrow in proportion to the amount of traffic it carries. In such a situation, smaller trees are better adapted. Trees, shrubs, and ground cover can be excellent investments. As they grow and mature over the years, the plants will continue to increase in value and to contribute, as nothing else can, to the value of the property.

*The annulated white and black bark of monarch birch (*Betula maximowicziana*) lends interest to the landscape at any time of year.*

If a new or revised landscape must be undertaken in stages, trees should be the first investment, once the final grading is completed and a temporary lawn grass has been planted to control dust and erosion. It is best to plant trees with a trunk diameter of 2½ to 3 inches. Larger sizes involve the use of costly machinery and the risk of failure is greater; smaller specimens require years to achieve a presence and in the meantime are vulnerable to injury and breakage.

Be slow to remove existing trees and shrubs, and resist the urge to plant grass extensively. A buffer strip of natural woodland or a woodland border edged with ornamental shrubs can be a far more suitable and less demanding enhancement than a vast sweep of high-maintenance lawn. A knowledgeable, experienced arborist can help select the trees and shrubs to be preserved and suggest a maintenance regimen. Keep in mind that a buffer strip of native and naturalized species usually does not require any fertilizer or other amendments and needs to be only occasionally purged of invasive saplings, shrublets, vines, and weeds.

If trucks, bulldozers, and other heavy machinery are to come onto the site, care should be taken if at all possible to keep them beyond the branch spread of existing trees. Tree roots extend at least as far as the overhead branches do, and substantial root breakage and soil compaction can start mature trees on that downward spiral of irreversible decline and premature death. Use of heavy planking can minimize damage where passage beneath trees is unavoidable. Building contractors should be required in advance to avoid such harmful practices as burying pieces of surplus drywall sheetrock on the site or emptying the toxically alkaline rinse water from mortar hods or plastering buckets onto the ground. If trenching for utility lines or piping must pass under large trees, it should be done by hand, to avoid severing or breaking large roots.

Where possible, place new trees near the property line, especially if their height at maturity will exceed 35 or 40 feet. In any case, it is best to place a tree of substantial mature dimensions no closer to the house than one-half the diameter of its ultimate branch spread. Moreover, one medium tree is often all that can be comfortably accommodated on the small suburban plot. A number of small trees (not exceeding 25 or 30 feet at maturity) and large shrubs will complete the "bones," or basic planting. Because trees are long-term investments that not only make the home

*Slow-growing dwarf evergreens, such as bushy mugo pine (*Pinus mugo*), with a blue spreading juniper (*Juniperus procumbens *'Nana'*) behind, embrace a boulder and provide a stable setting for other rockery plants.*

grounds more pleasing and enjoyable but enhance the value of the property, it is important to choose kinds that offer maximum virtue for the setting and involve minimal liability. Certain basics must be kept in mind: no one kind of tree will suit all circumstances, all trees do grow; and all trees eventually die. The information tabulated in Chapter 11 will help you choose those trees best suited to your site.

Shrubs in the home landscape are as important a design elements as are trees. Regretably, a narrow range of evergreen shrubs seems to have taken priority in today's landscapes, especially in front yards, contributing to much unnecessary monotony. Shrub plantings can be much more interesting if carefully chosen deciduous kinds are combined with evergreens, their floral display, foliar texture, and fruit color along with the architecture of the bare branches complementing the omnipresent green of the conifers. Shrubs should be planted in well-placed beds rather than scattered around the lawn, and are most effective when each kind is planted in groups of three, five, or more. Before making your shrub choices at the nursery or garden center, consider the attributes of the various kinds, discussed in Chapter 12.

Retail purveyors usually stock those shrubs known to sell well locally (especially the kinds with showy flowers in spring), but you may have to go to specialty nurseries to find less common but highly desirable kinds, such as the winter-flowering Oriental witch hazel (*Hamamelis mollis*) or the late-summer-flowering chaste bush (*Vitex agnus-castus*). Be careful not to plant shrub-size specimens of tree species in shrubbery plantings; all too often the charming and inexpensive 4-foot pine or spruce, mistakenly included in a foundation planting, grows on to become a towering leviathan, dwarfing the house it was meant to grace and casting year-long gloom within as well as beneath. Correcting such an unnecessary error is costly, yet left unremedied it is a liability that actually diminishes the value of the property.

In those parts of the grounds not planted in woody ornamentals or flowers and vegetables, consider ground covers, especially in those areas not required for foot traffic. Turf is still preferred where traffic is light to moderate; where heavy traffic leads to soil compaction and the thinning and eventual failure of turf, bricks or flagstones set in sand or a gravel path will suit most requirements without disrupting drainage to roots below.

Elsewhere, particularly among shrubs or in deep shade or on dry, sunny banks, ground covers are preferable. Not only are their maintenance needs minimal but they provide contrasts in color and texture, and offer seasonal interest as well. Beyond the well-known and overused pachysandra, creeping myrtle, and English ivy, there are at least 50 other easily grown kinds from which to choose (see Chapter 14).

Carefully chosen shrubs of varied hues and textures lend much visual interest to the building they adorn and provide a backdrop for perennials in the foreground.

Planting Design

By grouping and placing plants in a way that emphasizes their similarities and differences, it is possible to change an ordinary site that has no distinction and no natural advantages into one of rare beauty and much interest. The many forms, colors, and textures found in plants offer infinite possibilities.

One of the most important considerations in arranging plants in a landscape composition is to choreograph the experience that is intended. For example, a gate or trellis evokes a sense of entry. A wall, especially if bordered with low shrubs or bedding plants, encourages a journey of the eye and fosters a sense of physical passage. A focal point of special interest may be achieved with a specimen plant, a piece of sculpture, a fountain or pool, or a distant view. Small, delicate subjects should be placed for close view. Massed effects are best seen at a distance. Focal points should be placed to be evident from diverse vantages, for example, from a walkway, the patio, and the living room. Analysis of the site is critical when creating or developing a focal point.

A large built-in planter, benches interspersed with urns, and brick pavement of varied patterns help make a heavily traveled plaza a place of distinction and continuous interest.

The garden should be treated as an extension of the house and be an enhancement from several internal vantages.

Preparing a scaled plot plan at ¼ or ⅛ inch per foot is a valuable exercise, especially when the vista from each window and door is indicated and photographed. Each site presents its own challenges: how to make a small property seem larger, how to create a mood, how to entice people outside, how to make a shady site interesting, and which season(s) to emphasize.

Solutions will reflect individual tastes, priorities, and practicalities as well as the virtues and liabilities of the site. Select kinds of plants and individual specimens with an eye to the future. However perfectly suitable a tree or shrub may appear in a catalog photograph or at the nursery or garden center, its habit and mature dimensions will be determined largely by its genes, influenced in degree by location and care. Hence the importance of having factual information about your site (e.g., hardiness zone, soil pH, and regional soil traits, all obtainable from the local cooperative extension or botanic garden) as well as a predetermined list of suitable plants, with alternatives, before purchasing. For those knowledgeable of the local native and cultivated flora, reconnaissance of one's environs will reveal what grows well and, to some extent, what does not. For those lacking that basic knowledge, visits to botanic gardens, preferably at different seasons, can be illuminating. There one can gain three-dimensional year-round acquaintance with a wide diversity of hardy trees and shrubs and other garden plants, indigenous and exotic; and because the specimens are labeled, it is possible to obtain some objective data and subjective impressions when consulting literature for further background information.

One can recall example after example of the effect of viewpoint on the appearance and beauty of plants. But we must also remember that people move about in a landscape, so that while we may enjoy the sugar maple as an object to be seen from a distance, we may also walk under its sheltering canopy and experience sunlight shimmering through its golden autumn leaves.

The simplest aspect of a plant is its silhouette. In some situations, the shadowy trunks of trees contrasted with a sunny meadow against the wall of a building produce a picturesque composition in lines. In other instances, trees make a silhouette by spreading dark masses of foliage against the sky, the pines, for instance, being distinguished by their bold outlines. Another dramatic silhouette is made by white trunks of birch seen against a dark background.

A densely planted bed of shrubs and young trees, unless thinned or kept pruned, will soon threaten the attractive foreground planting with shade and root competition, and eventually require removal and replacement.

Any tree of distinctive outline, such as the littleleaf linden (*Tilia cordata*), white oak (*Quercus alba*), or European beech (*Fagus sylvatica*), is excellent in silhouette. Often a mist or a winter's snowstorm will bring into silhouette trees that at other times merge with those about them. Different species of native trees have typically characteristic outlines that make them recognizable by their silhouette alone. Hickory (*Carya* species), sugar maple (*Acer saccharum*), black walnut (*Juglans nigra*), tulip tree (*Liriodendron tulipifera*), American ash (*Fraxinus americana*), and Kentucky coffee tree (*Gymnocladus dioica*) are among those most easily distinguished from a distance.

From a design point of view, the three outstanding aspects of any plant are form, texture, and color. The outline of a tree seen as a silhouette is a print of its form, but the more subtle modeling is better appreciated by the play of light on the surface of the masses of foliage. The importance of form in design can hardly be overemphasized, as this gives balance and substance to the composition. And form is much more than outline. Whereas the outline of Pfitzer juniper (*Juniperus chinenis* 'Pfitzeriana') and Japanese yew (*Taxus cuspidata*) are very similar, their forms are quite different, because the branches of the yew are disposed in rather flat planes, while the many fine branches of the juniper are grouped in thick ascending masses.

Texture is a function of leaf size and distribution. The contribution that some trees and shrubs make to a landscape composition is largely in the texture of their foliage. Notable for this rather subtle beauty are the Katsura tree (*Cercidiphyllum japonicum*), the birches, the locusts, the English maple (*Acer campestre*), and the English oak (*Quercus robur*). Many of the azaleas have leaves grouped at the end of their branches, making beautiful patterns. The same effect on a larger scale is produced by the compound leaves of the horse chestnut (*Aesculus hippocastanum*). Trees and shrubs with compound leaves often have finer textures than those with simple leaves. The leaves of some plants are so large that adjusting them to the textures of other plants requires special care. In this group we find such plants as the castor bean (*Ricinus communis*), the elephant ear (*Alocasia macrorhiza*), and the big-leaf umbrella tree (*Magnolia macrophylla*).

*The elongated bed of even-sized azaleas and the horizontal branching pattern of the Japanese dogwood (*Cornus kousa*) are reflected in the storied branches of the pines that form a contrasting silhouetting backdrop for this attractive display.*

Plants provide the color scheme, and every plant contributes its facet of color to the whole mosaic. Most of the colors change with the seasons, the gray of winter merging into the green of spring, with a short period of brilliance at blossom time or the time of fruiting. Outline, form, mass, and texture are all important elements in the design, but in many compositions, particularly in the flower garden, color has the strongest appeal. However, it is not wise to make flower color your only consideration. Rather, it is better to plan for the more subtle and long-lasting basic greens and grays of the woody plants first, including any notable fall colors, before concentrating on the relatively brief color of annuals, perennials, and roses.

Foundation Planting

In most urban and suburban communities, foundation plantings are taken for granted. Indeed, they have become an unwritten—or in some communities, an explicit—dress code for houses, especially in the front. It is the garden area closest to the house, the one most visible to the public, the one that guides the visitor to and from the front door. Often, it is the only planting that receives attention—outside of the lawn. Nevertheless, one should consider whether a foundation planting is necessary or desirable. If brick or stone is the foundation material, the exposed faces may argue for no planting at all, or for the installation of a path.

Simplicity and parsimony are virtues in designing foundation plantings. It is very common for home owners to plant too many shrubs, too close to the house; individual shrubs soon overwhelm the setting, obscuring windows or crowding walks and doorways. Sometimes the shrubs grow to tree size, their foliage often crowded like mops atop poles, detracting from the setting they were intended to enhance.

Foundation plantings are usually shrub borders, but can also be gardens of colorful perennials and annuals or of foliage plants, such as ornamental grasses, perhaps in raised beds. In such cases, shrubs can be grouped elsewhere, as in islands, away from the house. If a more or less traditional planting is desired, it is especially important to choose shrubs that will remain within the bounds of the setting. This is especially critical near windows.

Thanks to the efforts of plant breeders, a wide variety of dwarf shrubs is now available, including conifers, broad-leaf evergreens, and deciduous species (see the table on page 271 for suggestions). Dwarf conifers have multiple growth points and thus tend to be more squat or spreading in habit than their full-size prototypes. Once quite esoteric and costly, they are now widely available and moderate in price. It is important to allow them space to grow, even if they are quite

diminutive when planted. The spaces in between may be planted with low bedding materials or minor bulbs, or covered with a attractive, moisture-conserving, weed-deterring mulch of bark chips.

A new slope planting of well-spaced dwarf evergreen shrubs, specimen trees, and flower beds makes generous use of shredded wood mulch in place of lawn or ground covers. Pleasing textures are lent by varied brick paving patterns and the three-tiered fence in the distance.

In the case of new houses, it is especially important to have the soil in the foundation planting area tested before planting. Acid-loving rhododendrons and azaleas, for example, suffer badly when planted in soil that has been alkalized from the leaching of new concrete or by buried remnants of drywall. Since backfill around foundations is usually subsoil that is deficient in organic matter, planting holes for new shrubs should be very generous in depth and width, allowing room for the addition of humus or compost at planting time. Be sure not to plant directly under unguttered roof driplines, as the soil will frequently be waterlogged—a fatal circumstance for most kinds of plants—and where winter snow avalanches can break and disfigure the staunchest subjects.

The planting in the foreground of the house should contain only such plants as harmonize with each other. This is more easily achieved with few kinds used in greater number than many diverse sorts. Yet variety does enrich and makes possible a succession of interests as the season advances. With care in the selection, it is possible to use diversity and yet keep to a fixed general character. This may be accomplished to a considerable extent by avoiding the use of plants that are conspicuous because they are unique in form or color. Also to be avoided is a soldierly row of same-size individuals of a single kind.

A beautiful house needs a beautifully designed setting, one that embraces the whole house as a dominant element in the composition and subordinates the details to their proper places. A planting that is simple and dignified will always be satisfying.

Built-in Planting Beds

A modification of the usual foundation planting area is the built-in, raised planting bed found in an increasing number of homes of contemporary design. This consists of a low retaining wall built about 3 or 4 feet out from the base of the house, and often of the same masonry as the house. If the house is of frame construction, treated landscape ties are often suitable.

Raised planting beds should be deep enough to provide a substantial bed of soil for root growth. The bed should have no bottom, i.e., the bed must be contiguous with the soil below. Thus the upward capillary movement of water in the soil will offset excessive evaporation of moisture, especially in summer, and will also facilitate drainage of surplus water.

An exposure of partial sun is ideal for most plants grown in raised planting beds. Beds exposed to full sun throughout the day in summer tend to dry out rapidly. Moreover, many plants are unable to withstand the combination of full sun and reflected heat from the wall of the building, which can be very intense during hot weather. For such an exposure, the choice of plant materials is definitely restricted.

The selection of plants for built-in beds needs careful consideration; you should note such points as hardiness, ultimate size, and good year-round appearance. Many evergreen and deciduous dwarf shrubs meet these requirements, and various perennials and bulbs may be used to add color and liveliness to the planting composition during the spring and summer months. For specific shrub recommendations, see Chapter 12.

As your garden is a private outdoor space around your home, it should be treated as an outdoor living area and be organized with the same attention to harmonious design as an indoor room, with careful thought given to both texture and color. Privacy may be achieved by creating outdoor "rooms," enclosing areas with hedges, fences, or walls as well as with small trees, flowering shrubs, and flower borders. Color displays of foliage, flowers, and fruit should be carefully planned, both compatibility for in synchronous displays as well as period of bloom and the succession of hues through the year. With good planning, an outdoor living space will be interesting in any season and from whatever vantage it is seen.

Architectural Features in the Garden

An architectual feature, placed at the end of an axis in the garden or used as a central motif, will serve to emphasize the major lines of the design that are so important in the often elaborate plantings that surround the house.

Pavements of flagstone and brick have an architectural function, as their regular pattern and outline give form to the overall plan. Walls, fences, and even hedges are essentially architectural, and as such, they can be very decorative with their rhythmic repetition of parts. The principal architectural embellishments of a garden are those structures that are functional as well as beautiful. The well-designed toolhouse at the corner of the garden and the rear or side wall of a garage offer infinite possibilities for pleasant treatment. Lattices, arbors, trellises, and pergolas not only provide practical support for vines but also contribute to the architectural enrichment of the garden. Fountains, sundials, sculptured seats, and benches may all be treated as incidental ornaments or as dominant features, but in either case they are architectural in character and give a sense of permanence to scenes made up largely of changing plant forms.

How and when these forms should relate to the architecture of the house can be difficult to determine. The most important relationship is that of scale—size, rather than period or style. Huge pieces of contemporary welded sculpture seem perfectly at home in some complex English landscapes of the eighteenth century, whereas ancient Japanese stone figures can fit equally well into compact contemporary gardens. Also important is appropriateness; the trite or cute may be amusing on first encounter but will soon pall and detract from the setting.

Garden Lighting

Since, for many people, the evening hours are the only time available for leisure and relaxation, lighting the garden makes possible more hours of outdoor living. Well-planned lighting extends the usefulness of the terrace, patio, and recreation areas. Such lighting dramatizes the beauty of the garden as viewed from the house or terrace, it highlights special points of interest, and it makes safe and pleasurable the use of garden paths and steps.

Light emphasizes the texture and pattern of foliage silhouetted against the darkness, and it brings out interesting details. A greater feeling of depth and form will be obtained if trees and flowers are lighted from the side rather than from the front; when dramatic effect is desired, it is usually best to concentrate on one or two points of interest, rather than illuminate too broad an area.

With the development of waterproof extension cords, moisture-proof outlets and connections, and attractively designed lamps, garden lighting has become a simple and comparatively inexpensive undertaking. There are fixtures of many types—lamps suitable for lighting outdoor dining areas and reading chairs; low, mushroom-type fixtures that direct the light downward, being specifically designed for lighting paths or steps; and spotlights of various types designed for general overall illumination or for highlighting some special group of plants or some garden feature.

For lighting paths and steps, ordinary bulbs are usually satisfactory. A 60-watt bulb in a mushroom-type fixture will light an area about 20 feet in diameter. For larger areas, or for creating dramatic effects at a distance, 150-watt bulbs, or PAR spot or floodlamps may be used. A 150-watt PAR bulb with a bullet-type reflector will illuminate a group of trees or a garden feature at a distance of 40 feet. Some fixtures are portable; others are stationary. Most spotlights are arranged so that they can be turned at any angle. All outdoor lighting fixtures should be of rugged construction and weatherproof.

It is important that the wiring and the laying of the cables meet the specifications of the local electical code, and it is advisable to have a well-qualified electrician do the work.

3

Grading

Whether planning a new home or modifying existing grounds, the process of arranging land for more intensified use is apt to involve changes in the grades and contours of ground surfaces. Such constructions as driveways, the immediate surroundings of the house, and play areas need to conform to certain standards of practicality and use. Local zoning ordinances also may dictate grade changes. Sloping surfaces too steep for convenient travel must be brought down to more gentle grades to accommodate new roads and

A low wall of boulders fitted without mortar moderates the slope and breaks up its expanse.

pedestrian access. Home patios and terraces usually demand flat surfaces.

GRADING FOR A NEW HOUSE

Grading the soil around a new house usually receives scant attention on the part of the owner or builder. The problems and challenges of landscape design tend to be postponed until house construction is completed. Meanwhile, the earth from the cellar excavation often has been dumped and spread over a considerable area, covering up much valuable topsoil. All too often, floor levels are fixed without regard for the design and contour of the surrounding ground areas.

Adjusting a new house to its site is difficult at best. When it has been complicated by postponing the task until the house has imposed a new set of conditions, it is even more difficult to reach a satisfactory solution. However, when a house and the surrounding areas are designed simultaneously, it is possible to compromise one to accommodate the other. For example, raising floor levels a few inches above those originally planned may be enough to save substantial expense in soil grading alone, to say nothing of easing the transition between architecture and landscape. Shifting the house several feet from the site originally selected may make possible a better grade and a more manageable curve in the driveway. These results are worth attaining and can be achieved by carefully designing a general landscape plan of the property, with a grading plan of the house site, *before* the house is built. All these considerations are part of overall design. But because there are certain factors such as maximum grade and minimum curve that limit road forms, the solution to grading problems may strongly influence the ultimate site design.

Planning changes in ground form requires careful measurement and the recording of existing grades. Such a record of the site is called a "topographic plan" because it represents the ground slopes and contours. The series of lines called "contour lines," each connecting all points on the earth's surface that are at an equal elevation, on the plan readily expresses the configuration of the ground. Where the lines are close together, the slope is steep; where they are far apart, the ground is more nearly level.

The finished grading plan represents the original ground form and the ground levels after they have been adjusted to new requirements. The plan then becomes the working drawing that controls the excavation and filling operations on the site. It is from this plan that earthwork quantities are computed and the new levels staked out.

Often, it is perfectly possible to grade land without benefit of a plan. Soil is excavated where necessary and deposited wherever it seems most needed or will do the least damage.

One serious difficulty with the ad hoc procedure is that there is no way of knowing in advance how much earth must be handled, whether there will be enough or too much to make the fills required, or even how far the fills will extend. It may also result in an uneven layer of topsoil that can cause uneven performance of whatever plantings are made later.

If the design is for the environs of a new house not yet built, the grading plan should be made to determine not merely the cuts and fills but the position and floor levels of the house. By adjusting the floor grade, the quantities of earth excavated and filled may be made to balance, thus reducing to a minimum the cost of grading. If too much earth is cut, the surplus must be hauled away. If not enough earth comes from the cuts, then additional earth must be hauled in to make the fills. In either case, more earth is handled than is necessary to do the job, thus imposing additional cost and, all too often, substantial environmental disruption and damage.

The suburban home site often abounds in valuable plant life that is unwittingly destroyed during excavation and grading. Large, valuable trees can frequently be saved by building walls or wells around them, and by providing proper drainage and aeration.

*A large white pine (*Pinus strobus*) is preserved at the base of a regraded slope by means of a wall that maintains the original grade over the tree's roots.*

The essential point to remember is that tree roots require air. A new overburden of heavy, compacted soil may exclude too much air, resulting in the slow decline of the affected tree. By spreading a 6-inch layer of coarse gravel on the soil beneath the tree, covering the area shaded by its branches, then placing a radiating pattern of perforated drainage tiles on top of the gravel, and finally raising the grade, using a sandy soil, air penetration is preserved. However, the situation is idiosyncratic at best. Some surface-rooting trees, such as the Norway maple, can usually survive 6 to 12 inches of added soil with no special measures taken. The willow and locust can withstand even more. In general, the older the tree, the more likely it is to react adversely to changes in grade.

Not so obviously salvageable are smaller trees, which many times can be transplanted to a safe location or even be temporarily heeled in and replanted once grading is finished. Even less often considered are shrubs, wildflowers, and grasses, which can similarly be saved and utilized. These seemingly dispensable plants may be particularly useful to the home owner who is interested in creating a natural landscape.

GRADING FOR LAWNS

If at all possible, all land should gently slope away from the house. If this cannot be achieved throughout, land sloping toward the house may be cut or excavated so that the finish grade near the house slopes away to a dip or depression, then rises beyond. Leave no low places where water can accumulate, as can happen when a winter rain falls on frozen ground.

Slopes for lawns are best if less than 1:4 (i.e., a 1-foot rise for each 4 lineal feet), and certainly not exceeding 1:3. Even at these ratios, surface erosion of topsoil will almost certainly occur over time, often impeding the establishment of dense turf and resulting in sediment buildup elsewhere. If steep slopes are unavoidable, consider planting a densely rooting ground cover in place of lawn or moderating the slope with one or more walled terraces (see Chapters 5 and 14).

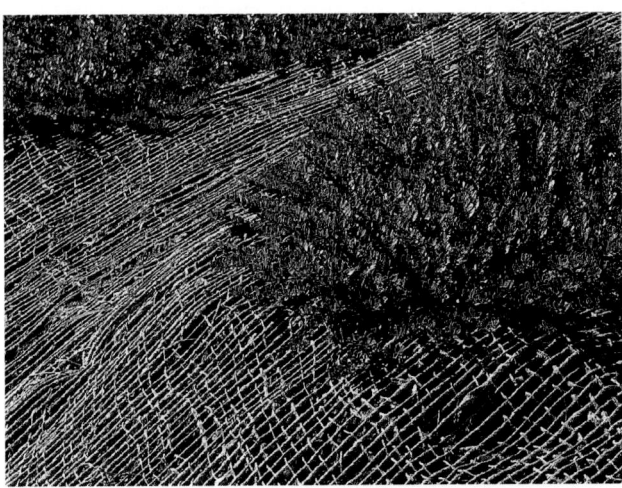

Jute netting or horticultural mesh, available in several grades of coarseness, may be spread over a sloping bank to stabilize the soil surface for a year or two while seeded materials or plants set through holes cut in the fabric become established. In time, the mesh deteriorates and disappears.

The importance of topsoil quality cannot be too strongly emphasized. Every finished surface of the open ground should have a top layer of at least 4 inches of loam for the support of plant life. Subsoil is not as productive and often will support only the toughest weeds. Even if much of the finished area of the property is to be converted to driveway, pavement, and house site, the topsoil originally on these areas should be scooped off and saved, and later added to the topsoil in areas devoted to garden, terrace, and lawn. In this way a natural topsoil only 6 inches in depth may be increased to 12 or even 24 inches in special places where extra depth will be an advantage. Garden flowers grow better, bloom better, and resist drought better in deep loam than in shallow soil. Fertilizer may be used to make up for the lack of proper depth in soil, but its desired effect is temporary at best, whereas a rich topsoil 15 inches deep, when carefully managed, becomes a permanent asset.

The base of a slope ends with a handsome drywall, its soil-filled chinks offering rootholds for such showy rockery plants as wall cress (Arabis caucasica), basket-of-gold (Aurinia saxatilis), and bergenia (Bergenia cordata).

Grading around an existing house is usually undertaken to correct poor drainage or to accommodate a new or realigned driveway, or other outdoor structure. The basic principles remain the same: drainage should be directed away from the dwelling, finished slopes should be gentle, and topsoil should not be mixed with or overspread by subsoil in the process. Special care should be exercised to keep heavy earth-moving or construction machinery away from existing trees and shrubs, both to prevent soil compaction and to avoid physical damage to roots, trunks, and branches. If substantial cutting or grade lowering is contemplated near a sizable tree that you want to save, an earth mound at original grade should be left around the trunk, its width equal to the branch spread above. If the resulting finish grade will exceed 1:4 or 1:3, the mound should be walled (see Chapter 5).

GRADING PROCEDURE

When grading begins, all the topsoil should be bulldozed or scooped from the area involved and piled conveniently near but outside the field of operations. Save all available topsoil, as any surplus will help make compost and topdressing and can be used to renew soil in containers and coldframes.

The next step is to excavate the foundations and any areas to be lowered. The earth thus removed should be placed, whenever possible, in its final position, handling it only once. The spreading of earth in areas of fill should be done in layers not deeper than 6 inches, and each layer should be rolled or tamped before the next is spread. Done carefully, this method compacts the earth so firmly that there will be practically no settling of subsoil. One caveat: soil should not be compacted near existing trees.

Failure to compact the earth while it is being filled will lead to a gradual, often uneven, settling of the surface during the next several years. In some places, this settling may be of no detriment, but in others, such as near paved walks or concrete steps, the settling can cause tilting or misalignment, a very awkward and even hazardous condition in the finished landscape.

The grades of the subsoil should be brought to levels below the proposed final grade equal to the thickness of topsoil or paving required in these various areas. Thus, if it is intended that a terrace should be furnished with 15 inches of topsoil, the subsoil should be smoothed off at a level 15 inches below final grades.

It is important to design the graded area so that no turf or pavement will be absolutely level, or so shaped that a concave surface will collect water. Though they should seem level to the eye, terraces should actually slope away from the building with a fall of at least 1 foot (preferably more) per 100 feet.

Where relatively flat areas are desired, lawns should be graded to a smooth, even surface but should not be absolutely level. This may be accomplished by sloping the ground away from one end to the opposite end, or away from a center line to the periphery, or away in all directions from a central high point.

DRAINAGE

Catch basins and drain inlets are important adjuncts to the driveway, walks, terrace, and flower garden. Properly placed and connected with a drain, they will remove surface water before it has a chance to flood flower beds or wash out banks. The drains should extend in straight lines from one basin to the next and should be at least 1 foot below the surface. The smallest diameter practicable for drains is 6 inches. Drains that take the outflow of three or more basins should measure 8 inches or more in diameter. Unless the town has separate storm water sewers, the outlet of drains usually must be accommodated on the property, by either being brought to the surface, distributed through a tile field, or emptied into a dry well or natural gulch.

A tile or drainage field is a series of perforated pipes, branching off from the main drain in parallel lines 10 feet or 15 feet apart and about 15 inches below the surface. The pipes are laid in trenches that are partly filled with crushed stone. The upper few inches of the trench are covered with topsoil. Drain water flowing through the pipes seeps out into the crushed stone and saturates the soil; grass roots absorb the water that does not evaporate from the soil surface. It is important to locate the field in open ground away from shrubs and trees. By promoting evaporation and uptake, sunshine keeps the soil in condition to absorb the water. Too often, tree roots invade drains and clog them.

The slope of the pipe is also important. It should fall at the rate of 1 percent ($\frac{1}{16}$ inch to the foot). A steep pitch in the pipes will cause the water to run to the end and oversaturate the soil.

A dry well is an excavation into the subsoil usually 6 feet to 8 feet deep and 4 feet to 6 feet in diameter, the sides of which are walled with perforated concrete block or a precast concrete structure. It receives rainwater, which then seeps away into the subsoil.

The back-filling of trenches and excavations must be done with great care. The earth should be filled in layers of 6 inches and each layer should be sprinkled with water and tamped into place. This method helps prevent future settling. Deep trenches of sewer and water lines should be thoroughly soaked, using a 4-foot length of pipe attached to a garden hose and inserted at intervals the length of the excavation. Do not mound soil over the excavation in anticipation of eventual settling, since it may take years to do so. Thorough compaction of backfill, using water, tamping, and rolling, is the better method.

If the grading has been in process for several months and the topsoil has been piled up during the house-building operation, fragments of roots and other debris will be more or less decomposed, but the pile may be covered with weeds, and in any case the soil will likely be full of weed seeds. Spreading the soil will induce at least some of the weed seeds to germinate. Then, if the ground is cultivated and allowed to dry, most of the weed seedlings can be eliminated. It is advantageous to allow at least three or four weeks to elapse between finish grading and sowing.

Keep in mind that most weed seeds germinate in the spring and the most favorable time to start a lawn is in late summer. Elsewhere, especially north of zone 6, spring is best. If topsoil has been spread in the autumn, too late for starting a lawn, then the ground should be stabilized through the winter with a cover crop of winter rye that can be sown in October (at the rate of 1½ bushels per acre) and turned under in the spring. Rye sown during the summer can be cut very short in mid-August or September; the ground is then shallowly scarified and overseeded with permanent lawn grasses.

WATER-SUPPLY SYSTEMS, UNDERGROUND PIPELINES, AND UNDERDRAINAGE

After subgrades are finished and, if possible, before the topsoil has been spread, the utility lines may be laid. House water supply pipes must be set in trenches at a depth greater than the maximum frost penetration for the region. House sewers and drains from catch basins and from the roofs need not be as deep, although 15 inches or 18 inches of soil over the pipes is advisable to keep them out of the way of planting operations.

Water supply pipes leading to garden hose connections need not be below frost line, if they are constructed in a way that permits the emptying of the pipe and faucets when the water is shut off for the winter. For this reason the pipes should slope to an outlet at the cutoff valve or at the spigot. An all-season outdoor water supply system must have pipes below the frost line and self-draining hydrants rather than faucets. Systems constructed of polyvinyl chloride (PVC) should be graded so that valves or taps are situated at the low points, to facilitate draining before the onset of freezing weather.

Gas pipes may be shallow, but they must also be graded so that there is a moisture outlet at each low point in the line.

Catch basins are constructed so that the outlet is well above the bottom. The sediment that collects should be removed periodically before it reaches the level of the outlet drain. Unmaintained catch basins are the principal cause of stoppages in the drainage system.

The size of the drain from the catch basin depends on the area of land it is to drain. The following table gives the pipe sizes and grades for draining areas of turf under conditions of rainfall prevailing in eastern North America.

The minimum grade for 6-inch tile drains is 1 percent, but 2 percent or more is better because the faster flowing water keeps the pipe clear. Increase in the grade of the pipe increases the flow and capacity.

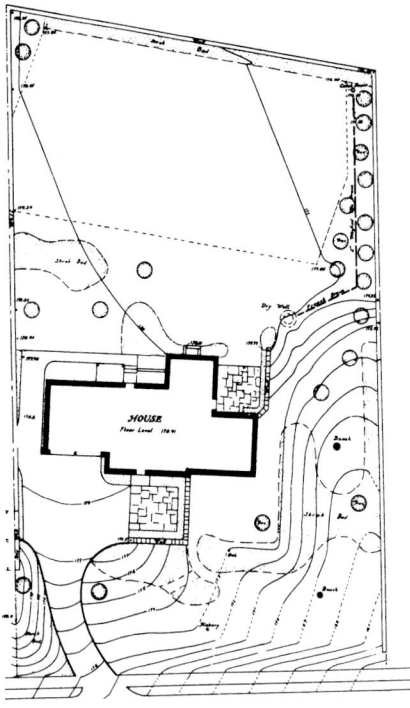

Grading plan of a suburban property. Contour lines indicate slopes.

		Area to Be Drained	
Size of Tile Pipe (inches)	Grade of Pipe (%)	In Turf (square feet)	In Pavement (square feet)
6	2	7,000	3,500
8	2	12,000	6,000
10	2	19,000	9,500
6	4	10,000	5,000
8	4	18,000	9,000
10	4	28,000	14,000

Land that contains too much moisture may be greatly improved by drainage lines. The pipes for draining land should be laid about 18 to 24 inches below the surface, and the ditch should be filled with crushed stone or gravel to within 8 inches of the surface. Strips of roofing paper on heavy polyethylene should be spread over the stone ballast and then covered with topsoil to bring the trench to an even grade. The pipes should be laid at a grade of about 2 percent in parallel lines 15 or 20 feet apart, and the outlet should be carried to a stream. The pipes most often used for this purpose are 3-inch agricultural drain pipes, but the main carrying off the outlet from several laterals should be 4- or 6-inch plastic piping, a suitable alternative to concrete or vitrified pipe, whose ease of installation renders it most practicable in many cases.

4

Terraces, Patios, and Sundecks

Aলthough the terms *terrace* and *patio* are often used interchangeably, it is best, from the gardening point of view, to distinguish them. A terrace is a flat area adjacent to or even surrounding the house, unprotected except perhaps by overhanging trees. A patio is usually smaller, often paved and characteristically enclosed, partly or entirely, by shrubs, fencing, or other screening. Sundecks evolved from porches and are most often wood-floored extensions of the house.

Colorful plants on and around this walled patio not only lend much interest but considerably soften the glare reflected from the paving slabs.

*A bleached wooden sundeck with substantial, compatibly styled table and benches to resist wind, bordered with sweet alyssum (*Lobularia maritima*), flowering cabbage (*Brassica oleracea *Acephala Group), and trained spherical standards, with specimen shrubs in mulched beds beyond, all components of an open, airy, sun-drenched environment.*

TERRACES

The terrace is an important feature of the modern home. It can be defined as a raised open level space, either square, rectangular, circular, or free-form, with one or more vertical or sloping sides. It usually marks the transition between house and garden.

In the great Italian villas, terraces commanded views over the surrounding countryside. They often extended across the whole garden scheme, and by the architectural treatment of their outlines with balustrades, they pleasantly combined architecture with plant forms. Often they were embellished with sculpture, fountains, potted plants, and patterned pavements and were usually shaded by large trees. Wherever garden art has felt the Italian influence, terraces have formed an important element in the landscape design.

Because of its architectural form, almost every house requires some degree of structure in its immediate surroundings; terraces, clipped hedges, parapets, balustrades, paving, and fences provide transition between the architectural and the natural landscape. The terrace makes a platform for the house and thereby adjusts it to its site in a graceful and easy transition. Furthermore, the terrace adds another room to the house, inviting when it is pleasant enough to sit out of doors. In this respect, the terrace should be arranged for varying weather, part of it being open to the breezes of summer and part hemmed in by the house so that, if possible, it is exposed to the warm sunlight of early spring mornings.

The size and proportions of a terrace are a matter of scale. The mass of the house, the size of the property, and the extent of the lawn are factors, and function is also to be considered. It is safe to say that one is more apt to make a terrace too narrow than too broad. The broad terrace has an air of spaciousness and offers a good foreground to a distant view. A narrow terrace is appropriate only on a restricted site where other elements, such as the lawn, are also compact or where a broader terrace might diminish a pleasant view. Unless conditions of the site dictate otherwise, the terrace should be at least as broad as the height of the house facade flanking it. It is usually better to build a terrace somewhat oversize to provide ample space for outdoor activities.

PLANTS FOR BORDERS AROUND A WINDY TERRACE

Name	Annual (A) or Perennial (P)	Zones	Height	Exposure*	Flower Color and Bloom Time
Achillea millefolium (yarrow)	P	4–8	1–1½'	S	White or pink; summer
Astilbe × arendsii	P	5–8	1–2'	PSh	Purple, lavender, pink, or white; summer
Coreopsis lanceolata 'Early Sunrise' (dwarf coreopsis)	P	4–8	10–14"	S to PSh	Yellow; spring and summer
C. verticillata 'Moonbeam' (Threadleaf coreopsis)	P	4–8	1½–2'	S to PSh	Cream; summer and fall
Dianthus spp. and cvs. (pinks)	P†	4–8	1–1½'	S	Red, pink, and/or white; spring and summer
Gypsophila repens (creeping baby's breath)	P	4–8	6–12"	S	White or pink; summer
Hemerocallis hybrids and cvs. (hybrid daylilies)	P	4–10	1¼–3'	S to PSh	Mostly orange and/or yellow, some red and/or purplish brown; summer
Lantana camara cvs.	A‡	—	1–2'	S	Yellow, orange, red, pink, and/or white; summer
Lavandula angustifolia cvs. (lavender)	P	5–8	1–2'	S	Purple, blue, lavender, rose, or white; summer
Lobelia erinus cvs. (annual lobelia)	A	—	4–6"	S	Blue, lavender, or white; summer
Pelargonium spp. and cvs. (geranium)	A‡	—	1–2'	S	Red, pink, or white; summer and fall
Phlox drummondii and cvs. (annual phlox)	A	—	6–14"	S	Red, purple, pink, or white; summer and fall
Salvia azurea, S. pratensis, and *S. × superba* (perennial sage)	P	4–8	2–4'	S	Blue; summer
Tagetes patula cvs. and *T. tenuifolia* cvs. (low marigolds)	A	—	6–12"	S	Orange, yellow, and/or mahogany brown; summer and fall
Yucca filamentosa	P	5–8	3–6'	S	Cream; summer
Zinnia angustifolia and *Z. elegans* low cvs. (low zinnias)	A	—	1–1½'	S	All but blue; summer

* S, full sun; Sh, shade (no direct sun); PSh, partial shade (sun exposure only part of the day); LSh, light shade (e.g., the shade of tall, open trees, with little or no exposure to direct sun).

† Also a few biennials and annuals.

‡ Shrubby in zone 10.

The house terrace may be raised above the surrounding land by a wall or bank; it may be level with the lawn, the separation being made merely by the edge of the pavement; or it may even be sunk below the adjacent ground. The grading will be suggested by the conditions of the site. The terrace floor, even if unpaved, should slope slightly away from the house and the surface water should be collected in drain inlets at the outer rim. Since foot traffic on a terrace often exceeds the endurance of turf, some sort of surfacing is desirable: pavement to accommodate the furniture, a small pebble surface, or what is usually better, a combination of materials. A broad expanse of stone paving just outside the house can be uncomfortably hot. If only a small part of the terrace is paved and if it is shaded by large trees, summer heat will be greatly mitigated. The less pavement used, the less reflected summer heat; the more turf, the greater the maintenance.

Built on the side of a hill, the terrace floor can be kept level by a masonry wall or by a smoothly graded bank. If the hill ascends above the terrace, it, too, must be retained, and the treatment of this wall may be made an interesting feature of the design. A long, unbroken masonry wall can be monotonous, but divided into bays by buttresses or pilasters, or surmounted by a balustrade, it becomes architectural, something in harmony with the artificiality of the house. Vines clinging to the wall or hanging down over it from above or fruit trees espaliered or pleached against it impart a softness of texture in pleasing contrast to the rugged masonry.

Because of the importance of ridding the terrace of rainwater promptly, drain inlets should be placed at frequent intervals. On a terrace 80 or 100 feet long, four drain inlets at the outer margin are sufficient to carry off the surplus rainwater. The terrace surface should slope toward the drain inlets. The inlet gratings may be small and inconspicuous, with 8 by 12 inches usually being ample. (For the construction of drains and inlets, see page 35.)

A very pleasant effect of stone paving is produced by growing diminutive flowering plants such as thyme and other herbs between the flagstones. Such a paving is not laid on a concrete base but on a cushion of sand, with pockets of soil for the plants in the crevices.

SMALL PERENNIALS TO GROW AMONG PAVING STONES

Name	Zones	Exposure*	Flower Color and Bloom Time
Allium caeruleum (dwarf blue onion)	7–9	S to PSh	Blue; summer
Arabis blepharophylla 'Spring Charm' (red rock cress)	7–9	S	Deep red; spring
A. ferdinandi–coburgi 'Variegata' (variegated rock cress)	7–9	S	White; spring to summer
A. muralis (rock cress)	6–8	S	Rose purple or white; summer
A. procurrens (rock cress)	5–8	S	White; spring to summer
Arenaria montana (sandwort)	4–8	S	White; summer
Armeria caespitosa dwarf cvs. (cushion pink)	8–9	S	Pink or white; spring to summer
A. maritima (sea pink)	4–7	S	Red, rose pink, or white; spring to summer
Dianthus plumarius cvs. (grass pink)	3–7	S to PSh	Pink or white, with red center; spring to summer
Gypsophila cerastioides (dwarf pink)	5–8	S	Pink or white; summer
G. repens dwarf cvs. (creeping pink)	4–7	S	Purplish pink to white; summer
Herniaria glabra (herniary, rupture plant)	5–8	S to PSh	White; spring to summer
Mazus reptans	3–7	S	Purple or white; summer
Minuartia verna (syn. *Arenaria verna*) (sandwort)	2–7	S	White; summer
Sagina subulata 'Aurea' (pearlwort)[†]	4–8	S	White; summer
Sedum acre (stone crop)	5–8	S	Yellow; spring to summer
S. sarmentosum (creeping sedum)	6–8	S to PSh	Yellow; spring to summer
Sempervivum tectorum (hen and chickens)	4–7	S	Dull rose pink; summer
Thymus praecox ssp. *arcticus* (mother of thyme)	5–7	S	Purple to white; spring to summer
T. pseudolanuginosus (woolly thyme)	6–8	S	Pale pink; summer
T. serpyllum (lemon thyme)	5–7	S	Purple or pink; summer
T. vulgaris (garden thyme)	7–8	S	Purple or white; summer

* S, full sun; Sh, shade (no direct sun); PSh, partial shade (sun exposure only part of the day); LSh, light shade (e.g., the shade of tall, open trees, with little or no exposure to direct sun).

[†] Often erroneously listed and sold as *Minuartia verna* 'Aurea'.

PATIOS

Although the term *patio* is from the Spanish, twentieth-century gardeners owe a debt of gratitude to the ancient Greek civilization, because it was that distant culture which contributed both the patio and the concept of pot gardening so familiar to us today.

The Greeks worshipped Adonis as the spirit of the green-growing world, and it was in the open inner courts of their dwellings dedicated to the god Adonis that baskets and pots, carefully filled with quickly sprouting seeds, were religiously nurtured. Much later, the patio or courtyard became one of the main architectural features in Spain, where it was introduced by the Moors during their conquest in the seventh century. These courts were enclosed within walls but were open to the sky and were enlivened with fountains and adorned with plants.

In the elegant homes built by members of the Spanish nobility and the wealthy aristocracy in Seville, Granada, and other cities of southern Spain in the sixteenth century, the protected patios became the center of family life, as they are even today. The central feature was usually a fountain around which potted plants were grouped; some special planting was usually featured in each patio and gave it its name—the patio of the orange trees, the patio of the box, or of the laurel, or of the myrtle. The white stucco walls that divided one patio from another were adorned with gracefully arched openings that had delicate, wrought-iron grills, or *rejas*, through which pleasant vistas were glimpsed. The walks were made of glazed tiles, river pebbles, or colored earth, such as bright ocher clay, firmly tamped. Vines or trees were intertwined against the walls, and there were low, clipped beds of ivy and myrtle, with pomegranate and pepper trees for accents; while in the spring, the patios were fragrant with the scent of orange blossoms. The rooms of the house opened on the various patios, and picturesque balconies looked down on the patterned walks and beds, with here and there a descending staircase, its graceful wrought-iron railing entwined with vines.

The early Spanish explorers and missionaries brought with them the memories of these lovely, secluded patios; when they built their homes and their missions in the New World, the enclosed patio was its central feature. This tradition has persisted for many years in some sections of Florida and in southern California—but mostly in New Orleans—and in these warm regions it has come to seem indigenous.

In contemporary garden design, the patio has assumed a variety of forms. It may be a paved area open to the sky and either partly or wholly enclosed by the walls of the house. It may be partly covered by a roof or by vines on a latticed support. It is usually adjacent to the house, serving as a transition between the house and the outdoors. Less commonly, it may be a paved area separated from the house with a supporting wall of its own and perhaps a roof.

A patio can be designed to fulfill a variety of functions. It may be an expanded entrance, separated from the street by a wall or fence. Small as such a patio must often be, it can possess great charm and provide a most attractive welcome to a home. A patterned pavement, a choice vine espaliered against the wall or a few well-chosen plants in pots and tubs can bring distinction to such an area.

An area may be designed as an intimate patio, entirely enclosed, and reached from only one room, such as the master bedroom. Here again, the treatment should be restrained and the planting composition handled with great sensitivity and skill, making such a secluded patio conducive to repose and quiet meditation. For a small child's patio adjoining a nursery, the treatment would be imaginative and playful.

Most usual, however, is the patio designed for the enjoyment of the family and for entertaining. Such a patio is generally of ample proportions and enhanced with plants in borders or in pots and tubs and hanging baskets. It has the pleasing aspect of partial enclosure, and if it is partly protected by a tree or two or a roof or awning, it affords a pleasant place for the enjoyment of social pleasures in sunshine or in shadow. If built adjacent to the recreational area—the pool, the outdoor grill, the sandpile—it becomes the center of family life in summer.

Patio furniture should be durable and substantial. Lightweight furniture, unless secured or stored, can become missiles in high winds.

Because of the enclosure and the regulation of sunshine and shade, conditions for plant growth may be made almost ideal on the patio. Shelter from the wind and exposure to sun from fall to spring tend to prolong the season and in winter make this a tranquil spot where it may be warm enough to grow tender plants without protection. On the other hand, protection from excessive sun in summer by

A sheltered brick patio graced with pots and tubs of brightly colored impatiens, begonias, and geraniums is a welcome retreat in summer with a cool woodsy outlook.

A massive, immovable planter serves as a partition separating one area from another, while at the same time livening both with welcome color.

vines on a lattice or by a louver roof, and the play of water in a fountain, make possible cooler conditions than would be attained on an open, sunny terrace. The patio has become, in the hands of a skillful designer, a versatile and charming adjunct to the modern home, one that contributes greatly to the comfort and enjoyment of outdoor living.

PAVEMENTS FOR TERRACES AND PATIOS

For pavements that are to be in constant use several months each year, the qualities most desired are firmness, smoothness, and watertightness. In cold climates it is also important that the pavement has a foundation that will be undisturbed by frost.

The paving materials generally used are brick, flagstone, wood block, and concrete. The construction of brick and flagstone pavings is described in Chapter 5.

Wood-block paving is laid in the same manner as brick, on a foundation of sand. The blocks, which are about the size of bricks, are set close together with the end grain forming the surface. Such a pavement will dry rapidly after a summer rain, the moisture draining down between the blocks to the sand beneath. Rot-resistant or treated wood is essential.

Most commonly used for pavements is concrete, which makes a firm, smooth, quick-drying surface, durable and therefore practical. Furthermore, it is economical, easily cast, and enduring. But ordinary concrete is not in the least interesting. It lacks pleasing color and texture, and it imparts a hard artificiality that is antithetic to the hand-wrought refinement of a garden or patio. On the other hand, concrete used with imagination can actually enhance the setting.

One of the most satisfactory methods of using concrete is to substitute small natural pebbles for the crushed stone in the mixture. Then, with a wire brush, remove the upper-most surface of the concrete before it has finished setting, exposing the pebble aggregate. The surface will be made up of the many irregular, rounded forms of the pebbles, which will impart their color and texture to the floor.

Broad expanses of this pavement may be divided into squares of 3- or 4-feet by 2-inch strips of treated wood set on edge in the concrete so that the wood and pebble surfaces are flush. Further variety may be made by using two or three sizes or colors of pebbles, each in a separate area. The result will be a pattern of several hues and an interesting sequence of textures, each catching the light in a different way.

POT PLANTS FOR TERRACES AND PATIOS

Few outdoor areas offer such dramatic opportunities for the use of different plants as do the terrace and patio.

Because the area is defined and intimate, each plant assumes an importance it would not have in a more expansive setting. The plants should, therefore, be chosen with special care.

There can be great variety and distinction in the planting. Plants may be grown in pots and tubs, in fixed or portable planting boxes, and in hanging baskets. There is wealth of material from which to choose.

With careful planning, a succession of bloom may be enjoyed from earliest spring, when the first diminutive blooms of the snowdrop and dwarf purple iris (*Iris reticulata*) unfold, to be followed by the starry flowers of the water-lily tulip, to late autumn when the last of the chrysanthemums are over.

To be of value for pot culture, a plant must meet certain requirements. It should thrive under the particular conditions that such culture imposes, it should be reasonably easy to grow, and it should flower over a long period. A surprising number of plants adapt well to pot culture. Among them we

ANNUALS WELL SUITED TO POT CULTURE*

Alonsoa warscewiczii (mask flower)
Browallia speciosa (bush violet)
Calendula officinalis
Catharanthus roseus (periwinkle, annual vinca)
Celosia cristata 'Plumosa' group (feather celosia)
Clarkia unguiculata (syn. *C. elegans*) (farewell-to-spring)
Coleus × hybridus
Heliophila longifolia (sun-lover)
Impatiens walleriana cvs.
Impatiens cvs. (New Guinea impatiens)
Lantana camara cvs. and *L. montevidensis*
Lobelia erinus (edging lobelia)
L. tenuior (Australian lobelia)
Lobularia maritima (sweet alyssum)
Nicotiana spp. and cvs. (flowering tobacco)
Pelargonium × domesticum cvs. and *P. × hortorum* cvs. (geranium)
Petunia × hybrida cvs.
Phlox drummondii and cvs. (annual phlox)
Salpiglossus sinuata cvs. (painted tongue)
Schizanthus spp. large-flowered cvs. (butterfly flower)
Tagetes patula cvs. and *T. tenuifolia* cvs. (low marigold)
Torenia fournieri (wishbone flower)

* See Chapter 17 for cultural details.

BIENNIALS WELL SUITED TO POT CULTURE*

Name	Zones	Height	Exposure[†]	Flower Color and Bloom Time
Campanula medium (Canterbury bell), including cv. 'Calycanthema' (cup-and-saucer plant)	7–9	2–3'	S	Purple, pink, white; summer
Digitalis × mertonensis, D. purpurea and cvs. (foxglove)	4–8	3–5'	S to PSh	Purple, pinkish lavender, or white; spring to summer
Erysimum cvs. (wallflower)	7–8	1–2'	S to PSh	Red-brown, red, orange, or yellow; spring
Myosotis alpestris cvs. and *M. sylvatica* (forget-me-not)	5–8	6–18"	S to PSh	Blue, pink, or white; spring
Viola tricolor (Johnny-jump-up) and *V. × wittrockiana* (pansy)	6–8	6–12"	S to PSh	Various; spring to summer

* See Chapter 18 for cultural details.

[†] S, full sun; Sh, shade (no direct sun); PSh, partial shade (sun exposure only part of the day); LSh, light shade (e.g., the shade of tall, open trees, with little or no exposure to direct sun).

PERENNIALS WELL SUITED TO POT CULTURE

Name	Zones	Height	Exposure*	Flower Color and Bloom Time
Chrysanthemum × morifolium[†] (hardy mum)	5–8	1–5'	S	Various; summer to fall
Dicentra eximia (fringed bleeding heart)	4–7	8–12"	PSh to LSh	Pink or white; spring to summer
D. spectabilis (old-fashioned bleeding heart)	4–7	2–3'	PSh to LSh	Pink and white or all-white; spring
Hosta spp. and cvs. (plantain lily)	4–8	1–2'	PSh to LSh	Lavender or white; summer or fall

* S, full sun; Sh, shade (no direct sun); PSh, partial shade (sun exposure only part of the day); LSh, light shade (e.g., the shade of tall, open trees, with little or no exposure to direct sun).

[†] See Chapter 15 for cultural details.

FLOWERING BULBS AND TUBERS WELL SUITED TO POT CULTURE*

Name	Zones	Height	Exposure†	Flower Color
SPRING-FLOWERING BULBS				
Crocus spp. and cvs.	3–8	3–6"	S to PSh	Purple, lavender, yellow, or white
Hyacinthus orientalis cvs. (hyacinth)	4–8	8–12"	S to PSh	Purple, blue, pink, yellow, or white
Iris danfordiae and *I. reticulata* (reticulate iris)	5–8	4–6"	S to PSh	Yellow and orange; purple, blue, or white and yellow
Iris hybrids and cvs. (dwarf bearded iris)	3–8	5–10"	S	Purple, blue, yellow, or white
Leucojum vernum (snowflake)	3–8	1–1½'	S to PSh	White and green
Muscari spp. (grape hyacinth)	3–8	6–9"	S to PSh	Purple or white
Narcissus spp. and cvs. (daffodil, jonquil)	4–8	6–15"	S to PSh	Yellow, orange, and/or white
Scilla siberica (Siberian squill)	5–8	3–6"	S to PSh	Deep blue-violet or white
Tulipa spp. and cvs. (tulip)	4–9	6–30"	S	Various
SUMMER-FLOWERING BULBS AND TUBERS				
Achimenes spp. and cvs. (Cupid's bower)	10	10–15"	PSh to LSh	Purple, red, pink, or white
Begonia × *tuberhybrida* cvs. (tuberous begonia)	10	6–15"	PSh to LSh	Red, pink, yellow, or white
Caladium × *hortulanum*	10	1–2'	PSh to LSh	Leaves variegated green and red or white; foliage only
Hippeastrum cvs. (amaryllis)	9–10	1–1½'	PSh	Red, pink, or white
Lilium spp. and cvs. (lily)	5–9	1–5'	S to PSh	Various
Polianthes tuberosa (tuberose)	9–10	2–3'	S	White
AUTUMN-FLOWERING BULBS				
Colchicum spp. and cvs. (autumn crocus)	3–9	4–8" flowers; 1–2' leaves	S to PSh	Purple, lavender, yellow, or white
Crocus spp. ‡ (fall-flowering crocus)	3–8	3–6"	S to PSh	Purple, lilac, yellow, or white

* See Chapter 16 for cultural details.

† S, full sun; Sh, shade (no direct sun); PSh, partial shade (sun exposure only part of the day); LSh, light shade (e.g., the shade of tall, open trees, with little or no exposure to direct sun).

‡ *C. byzantinus, C. laevigatus, C. longiflorus, C. medius, C. niveus, C. sativus* (meadow saffron), *C. serotinus* (syn. *C. asturicus*), and *C. speciosus*

find not only the usual pot plants such as geraniums, fuchsias, and begonias but many annuals; a number of very decorative biennials such as foxgloves and Canterbury bells, and a few of the herbaceous perennials, among them the lovely, old-fashioned bleeding hearts, sea lavenders (*Limonium latifolium*), and chrysanthemums.

A large number of bulbs and tubers, including the colorful tuberous begonias, the exotic lily of the Nile (*Agapanthus* hybrids), and many of the early spring bulbs may also be grown as potted plants.

In growing potted plants successfully, there are a number of points to be taken into consideration: the selection of the right type and size of pot, the soil mixture, watering, soil enhancement, and general care.

Selection of Pots

For centuries, plants have been grown very successfully in clay pots. However, clay pots are largely disdained in the nursery trade because of their fragility and weight. They are available at retail, however, for those who wish to use them. Today, plastic pots are favored in the trade because of their low cost, resistance to breakage, light weight, and compactness in storage.

There are both advantages and disadvantages to the plastic pot. Not only are such pots cheaper to produce, easier to clean and to handle in large quantities, and less subject to breakage but plants in plastic pots need watering less frequently. However, even if as many as five drainage holes are provided, there is a danger, especially during periods of heavy rain, that the soil in such pots will become waterlogged. The problem can be partially overcome by providing additional internal drainage with ½-inch gravel filled from the bottom up to a quarter of the height of the pot.

The quality and color of the plastic pot also are important. The pot should be strong and thick enough so that when planted the pot can readily be lifted with the thumb and index finger only, without breaking or cracking the rim. The very thin and soft plastic pots should be used only for shipping plants, not for growing them. A plastic pot should also be dark enough so that light will not penetrate it. In translucent, white, or light-colored pots, algae may form that can be harmful to some plants. However, many growers of epiphytic orchids prefer the translucent pot so that light *will* penetrate to the roots. Orchid growers reason that since in nature the roots of epiphytic orchids thrive in light, they will do best in cultivation if similarly treated.

The thin-walled plastic pot is especially practical for fast-growing, one-year crops and the growth of seedlings. But for slow-growing plants that are to remain in the same pot over extended periods, heavier opaque plastic is more enduring. For some, however, the old-fashioned clay pot is still preferred.

If one's garden budget will permit, beautiful handmade clay pots with fluted or rolled rims may be used. Pots of this type, skillfully molded by hand, lend great distinction and charm to the serried patios of southern Spain and the terraced gardens of Italy. They were the only type of flowerpot available in colonial days and have been reproduced in this country for use in the faithfully restored gardens at Mount Vernon and Williamsburg. Less costly versions are readily available, as are relatively inexpensive pots of terra-cotta and various ceramics and tubs made from halved whiskey barrels.

Sizes of Pots

Pots are obtainable in various styles and sizes. The standard type, the kind most generally used, is always as wide across the top as it is high. Standard pots come in sizes beginning at 1 inch and increasing up to 14 inches. The increase in the smaller sizes occurs at intervals of ½ inch, in the medium sizes at intervals of 1 inch, and in the larger sizes at intervals of 2 inches.

Pots commonly referred to as "pans" are one-half as high as they are wide, the smallest of this type being 5 inches in diameter. Pots known as "azalea" or "three-quarter" pots are three-quarters as high as they are wide. These pots are very popular for shallow-rooted plants, such as tuberous begonias, as they are broad at the base and cannot be easily tipped over.

Care of Pots

New clay pots should always be soaked overnight before they are used. If this is not done, the pot will draw from the soil water that is needed by the plant. Old pots should be soaked and washed to remove sediment before they are reused. Hot water and a small, stiff scrubbing brush will do a good job.

Providing Drainage

When you prepare the pots for planting, it is essential to provide adequate drainage. An inverted piece of broken crock placed over the one or more holes in the bottom of the pot will usually be sufficient. In the case of tuberous begonias, achimenes, and other plants that demand exceptionally good drainage, the pot sould be one-quarter filled with broken crocks or coarse gravel with a thin layer of sphagnum moss spread over this material before soil is added.

Potting Mixtures

It is well to stock a basic potting mixture that can be altered, when necessary, to meet the specific needs of certain plants. In general, such a mixture should be well supplied with humus and should be light, porous, and well drained, and consist of of good garden loam, well-decayed compost, a moderate amount of sand, and a small quantity of damp peat moss. For plants that thrive in a somewhat heavy soil, less sand and garden loam would be used. For plants requiring a soil exceptionally high in organic matter, an additional amount of compost or well-decomposed leaf mold would be added. For plants requiring soil of very high fertility, well-rotted manure or, if such manure is not available, a small amount of dried cow manure mixed with damp peat moss could be included. If the only garden soil available for use in the mixture is a very heavy clay loam, a soil conditioner such as perlite or vermiculite should be mixed in to lighten it up before it is used.

Potting

At the time of potting, the soil mixture should be damp but not in the least soggy. The usual test may be applied: a handful squeezed and dropped to the ground should crumble. If it retains its shape in the ball, it is too wet and sticky to use. The soil in the flats, trays, or pots in which the plants to be potted are growing should also be moderately moist but not saturated with water. If the soil is too wet at the time of potting, it is apt to form a solid mass through which the delicate feeding roots cannot penetrate, and the supply of oxygen will also be diminished. Consequently, the plants will fail to become well established and will not grow well. Overwatering of slow-growing seedlings can be avoided by transplanting them into clay pans, perforated plastic flats, or wooden flats. Fast-growing seedlings can be potted directly into small clay or plastic pots.

After plants have been potted, they should be watered and kept in semishade for a few days until their roots have become reestablished.

Repotting

Young, actively growing plants should be repotted as soon as their roots have filled the pot. This stage may be determined by knocking the plant out of the pot, which is a simple process. Turn the pot upside down, placing your left hand over the top of the pot, with the stem or crown of the plant held between your index and middle fingers. Tap the rim of the plant against a hard, wooden surface. The rootball will dislodge more easily if it is watered first. After one or two taps the plant will be dislodged from the pot. If no roots, or only a very few roots, are visible, the plant is not ready for repotting.

When plants are being shifted to larger pots, the pot next in size is usually adequate, although plants known to grow rapidly can be transferred to pots several sizes larger.

When old plants that have become badly potbound are being repotted, it is wise to rub off some of the soil on the surface so that the young feeding roots can come into contact with the fresh soil.

As plants reach maturity, they can be maintained for long periods without repotting, provided soil nutrients are maintained by periodic applications of fertilizer.

Watering

In general, the greater root density of potted plants causes soil in pots to dry out faster than in garden beds, and because of the porosity of bisqued clay, plants in clay pots dry out faster than those in plastic pots. The rapidity with which they dry out also depends on whether the plants are growing actively and whether the pots are in an exposed position in full sun or are shaded by other plants or structures. It is important to have in mind the requirements of the various plant groups and to try to meet their specific needs. Some plants, such as impatiens and tuberous begonias, transpire large amounts of water and suffer seriously if neglected, while most other plants thrive on a moderate amount of moisture and some, such as lantana, grow best if their soil is kept on the dry side.

If it is necessary to keep potted plants in a sunny location during very hot weather, it is possible to reduce the loss of moisture appreciably by digging the pots into the soil, peat, or sand, or by using the "pot-within-a-pot" method. The pot containing the plant may be set into another pot several sizes larger, the space between the two is then filled with wet sphagnum moss or damp peat moss. Potted plants thrive extraordinarily well when this practice is followed and seldom suffer from lack of sufficient moisture. A planter box or tub may be used to serve the same purpose. This procedure works best if the inner pot is of clay and the outer of plastic or some other impervious material. In any case, the outer container, should have drainage holes. Failing this, it is essential that the outer container be emptied of any excess water after a rain and even after an over-generous watering.

Maintenance

As plants in pots have a very restricted soil area from which to draw their nutrients, it is generally necessary to restore soil fertility periodically, especially during periods of active growth. Many exceptions exist, however, like geraniums, impatiens, and tuberous begonias, which perform best on a meager diet. For most, biweekly applications of manure tea or 5-10-5 soluble artificial fertilizer are sufficient. This is as important for houseplants brought outdoors as for those acquired specially for summer display.

Since a potted plant takes on much more individual importance than one in a bed of dozens or hundreds of the same kind, more individual care is usually needed. Beside the removal of spent flowers and yellowed leaves, it is usually advantageous, especially in plants having multiple or branched shoots, to pinch back growing tips to induce a denser, more compact form. Diseased or pest-ridden individuals should be isolated and treated or promptly discarded (not in the compost bin where their remains can infect the compost) rather than tolerated.

PLANTS IN TUBS AND VERY LARGE POTS

Some shrubs and trees are particularly well adapted to growing in tubs, while others will not thrive under such conditions. Some plants may be grown in tubs almost indefinitely; others, if not moved to a larger container, begin to deteriorate. In Italy, one occasionally sees orange trees or laurel trees that have been growing in tubs or huge pots for more than 100 years.

Initially at least, it is wise to choose plants known to grow well under the restricting conditions of pot and tub culture. Fortunately, a wealth of material is available from which selections may be made.

Unless shrubs are purchased as large specimen plants, they usually begin their sojourn on the terrace or patio in medium pots; they are then shifted into larger pots and eventually, as they mature, into tubs. Some trees and shrubs that normally grow to a considerable size will never attain their full development when grown in a tub and, with judicious pruning and wise handling, may be kept to almost any degree of dwarfness.

SHRUBS ADAPTED TO CULTURE IN TUBS

Name	Zones	Winter Care*	Height†	Comments
Abelia × grandiflora (glossy abelia)	6–9	A	4–6'	Evergreen to half-evergreen; white flowers from early summer to fall
Agapanthus hybrids‡ (lily of the Nile)	8–9	B	1–2'	Bulb with evergreen foliage, in clumps; violet, blue, or white flowers in summer
Aucuba japonica and cvs. (Japanese laurel)	7–10	A	3–6'	Evergreen; red berries (female only); in cv. 'Variegata' (gold-dust bush) leaves mottled or spotted yellow
Bougainvillea × buttiana, B. glabra, and cvs. (paper flower)	8–10	B	3–8'	Evergreen in frost-free areas; stems often thorny; floral bracts purple, red, pink, orange, yellow, or white in summer and fall
Bouvardia longiflora (white bouvardia) and *B. ternifolia* (red bouvardia)	10	C	1–2'	Evergreen; rounded habit; fragrant white or red flowers in summer; should be cut back after blooming
Brugmansia × candida, B. suaveolens (angel's trumpet tree)	10	C	5–8'	Evergreen; treelike habit; long, pendent, trumpet-shaped white to pinkish yellow flowers in summer
Buddleia davidii (butterfly bush)	6–9	A#	6–8'	Deciduous; often dying back in severe winters; long clusters of violet to white flowers in late summer
Buxus microphylla (littleleaf box)	5–9	A	1–3'	Evergreen; small, glossy, densely arranged leaves; in cvs. 'Green Gem', 'Green Mountain', 'Green Beauty', and 'Green Velvet' leaves retain green color through winter
B. sempervirens vars. and cvs. (common box)	6–9	A	6–12'	Evergreen; tends to winter kill in exposed locations in north; foliage emits distinctive odor
Citrus spp. and cvs. (lemon, orange, tangerine, etc.)	9–10	C	3–6'	Evergreen; glossy foliage; stems green, often thorny; fragrant white flowers in summer; yellow or orange aromatic fruit; dryish winter dormancy promotes bloom
Fatsia japonica and cvs. (rice tree, paper plant)	8–9	B	3–8'	Evergreen; large, glossy lobed leaves; clusters of small creamy flowers in summer; black berries in fall
Ficus carica dwarf cvs. (dwarf fig)	8–9	B#	3–5'	Deciduous; small, bushy, often treelike, greenish or purplish figs in summer
Fuchsia magellanica (Magellan fuchsia)	8–9	B#	2–5'	Deciduous or in zone 9 half-evergreen; nodding or pendent red-purple flowers in summer
F. spp. (except *F. magellanica*) hybrids and cvs.	9–10	C	1–3'	Evergreen; rounded, spreading habit; pendent purple, red, pink, white, or bicolored flowers spring to fall; best in partial shade; cut back before onset of new spring growth
Gardenia augusta (syn. *G. jasminoides*)	8–10	B	2–6'	Evergreen; rounded, with glossy foliage; flowers white, mostly double, intensely fragrant in summer and fall; requires high humidity and light shade
Hibiscus calyphyllus, H. rosa-sinensis, H. schizopetalus (Chinese hibiscus)	8–10	B	2–6'	Evergreen in zones 9 and 10; large, diurnal, continuously borne flowers red, pink, yellow, or white in spring to fall
Ilex aquifolium cvs. (English holly)	6–9	A	3–10'	Evergreen; glossy, spine-edged leaves; red berries in fall and winter (female only); many dwarf cultivars, often very hardy
Laburnum × watereri 'Vossii' (golden chain tree)	5–7	A	10–15'	Deciduous; small tree with greenish bark; pendent clusters of yellow flowers in spring
Lagerstroemia indica hardy cvs. (crape myrtle)	7–10	A	6–12'	Deciduous; purple, pink, or white flowers in summer and fall; may die back in winter in zone 7

(continues)

SHRUBS ADAPTED TO CULTURE IN TUBS (continued)

Name	Zones	Winter Care*	Height†	Comments
Lantana camara and cvs. and *L. montevidensis*	10	C	2–5'	Evergreen or half-evergreen; continuously borne flower heads of purple, red, lavender, yellow, or white, often changing shade with age; *L. camara* easily grown as a standard; *L. montevidensis* spreading in habit
Laurus nobilis (poet's laurel)	8–9	B	3–10'	Evergreen; leaves large, glossy; tolerates 5°F, but may lose leaves until spring
Ligustrum japonicum and cvs. (Japanese privet)	7–10	A	4–8'	Evergreen; glossy foliage; fragrant white flowers in summer; persistent black berries; easily trained hedge or specimen shrub
Mahonia aquifolium, *M. bealei*, *M. lomariifolia*, etc. (hollygrape, Oregon grape)	6–8	A	3–6'	Evergreen; glossy, spine-edged foliage; yellow flowers in spring; persistent blue-black fruit in fall
Myrtus communis (Greek myrtle)	8–9	B	2–6'	Evergreen; glossy, aromatic foliage; fragrant, white flowers in summer; good as espalier subject; cv. 'Tarantina' tolerates 5°F
Nandina domestica (heavenly bamboo)	6–9	A	4–8'	Evergreen in zones 8 and 9; white to pink flowers in spring; red berries in fall; many dwarf cultivars
Nerium oleander and cvs. (oleander)	9–10	C	6–12'	Evergreen; glossy foliage (poisonous if eaten); flowers single or double, purple, red, pink, yellow, copper orange, or white; flowers in summer; tolerates occasional brief lows to 15°F
Osmanthus heterophyllus (holly olive)	6–8	A	4–8'	Evergreen; glossy, hollylike foliage; good holly substitute, but seldom bears fruit
Pittosporum tobira (Australian laurel)	8–10	B	3–8'	Evergreen; glossy foliage; small, creamy, fragrant flowers in spring or summer; easily trained; tolerates occasional brief 15°F
Plumbago auriculata (Cape leadwort)	8–9	B	6–12'	Evergreen; stems long, arching, easily trained; pale blue flowers in summer and fall
Podocarpus elongatus (African yellowwood)	9–10	C	6–12'	Evergreen; round headed, horizontally branched, with spirally arranged dark leathery leaves; flourishes in summer heat
P. macrophyllus (southern yew; Buddhist pine)	8–9	B	6–12'	Evergreen; similar but hardier; var. *nakai* tolerates 5°F
Prunus laurocerasus (cherry laurel)	6–8	A	5–10'	Evergreen; firm, glossy dark foliage; erect spikes of white flowers in spring; purple-black fruit in late summer; cv. 'Otto Luyken' 3–4 feet high
Punica granatum and cvs. (pomegranate)	8–9	B#	3–6'	Deciduous; densely twiggy; foliage glossy; flowers red-orange in summer; fruit large, yellow-brown to red-violet; cv. 'Nana' 1½–3 feet tall, smaller in all traits
Pyracantha coccinea and cvs. (firethorn)	7–9	A	6–10'	Evergreen in zones 8 and 9; stems thorny; white flowers in spring; persistent orange to red-orange fruit in fall; cv. 'Lalandei' hardy to −15°F
Raphiolepis umbellata (Yedda hawthorn)	8–9	B	3–6'	Evergreen; leaves leathery; flowers clustered, white, fragrant, in spring
Rhododendron spp. and cvs. (azalea)	6–10††	A, B, C††	2–8'	Evergreen or deciduous**; flowers showy, in wide color range, in spring; protect from summer sun, especially in South
Rosa spp. and cvs. (rose)	4–9	A#	1–10'	Mostly deciduous; stems usually thorny; flowers in wide range of colors and size, borne mostly in late spring and early fall

Name	Zones	Winter Care*	Height†	Comments
Strelitzia reginae ‡ (bird-of-paradise)	8–10	B	2–4'	Evergreen; leaves numerous, erect, blue-green; flowers orange and blue in spring to summer; tolerates brief frost
Streptosolen jamesonii (marmalade bush)	8–9	B	3–6'	Evergreen; flowers clustered, yellow to rust orange in summer; tolerates occasional light frost
Viburnum tinus and cvs. (laurestinus)	8–9	B	4–8'	Evergreen; dense, rounded habit; flowers white to pink in spring; many cvs., some hardy to 10°F
Vitex agnus-castus (chaste bush)	7–9	A#	5–8'	Deciduous; long clusters of lilac flowers in late summer; may die back in winter in zone 7
Wisteria floribunda, W. × formosa, W. sinensis, and cvs., trained to tree form (tree wisteria)	5–8	A#	6–12'	Deciduous; drooping clusters of lilac purple or white flowers in spring; requires frequent pruning to discourage climbing

* A, usually requires no special care except protection from strong winter wind; B, tolerant of some frost but often suffers partial winter dieback (especially if exposed to wind or prolonged subfreezing cold), elsewhere best wintered in cool greenhouse or sunroom at 45 to 55°F; C, requires protection from all but the slightest occasional frost, elsewhere best wintered in a cool, dark basement; #, see p. 50 (Wintering Plants in Tubs).

† Height range for a plant in tub culture is usually less than in open ground.

‡ Stemless perennial.

** According to species.

†† See Chapter 12, Shrubs.

To grow plants in tubs, many practical points must be taken into consideration, such as the size and type of tub best suited to the needs of the plant, methods of shifting a plant from one tub to another, the choice of soil mixes, general maintenance requirements, and the wintering of plants in tubs.

Size and Type of Tub

Plant tubs may be purchased in a variety of types and sizes, or they may be constructed at home. Whether purchased or homemade, tubs should be made of treated wood or synthetic material that is resistant to decay. Such a tub will give years of service, whereas a tub constructed of cheap lumber that lacks the ability to resist rot will deteriorate rapidly and be worthless after a few years. The best and most durable woods are redwood, cypress, and cedar.

Tubs may be round, square, or hexagonal. The bottom of a tub should always be perforated, approximately five ½-inch holes per square foot, for drainage, and it should be raised slightly above the supporting surface to promote good air circulation and facilitate drainage. If the bottom is flush, the tub may be placed on small blocks of wood, or cleats may be used.

Ball-bearing casters placed on the bottom of a plant tub will greatly facilitate moving it from one location to another.

Commercially available types range in size from small tubs 8 to 12 inches in diameter, suitable for fuchsias and other small shrubs, to large tubs 20 to 30 inches in diameter, suitable for growing large shrubs or small trees. The depth of a tub will vary according to the needs of the plant for which it is to be used. Plants that are shallow rooted or that never attain great size, such as azaleas, bouvardias, fuchsias, and lantanas require tubs no more than 12 to 15 inches in depth, while larger plants such as camellias, poet's laurels, crape myrtles, and pittosporums require tubs 18 to 24 inches deep.

A very satisfactory type of tub that can be made by a good home carpenter is one square in shape, fastened together with removable bolts. This makes it possible to remove only one side, if desired, or all four sides, and greatly facilitates the shifting of a plant from one tub to another of larger size. It also makes easier such routine practices as root pruning and the addition of fresh soil or compost.

Methods of Shifting

When a plant is to be shifted from a pot into a tub, it is important to select a tub only slightly larger in size than the pot in which the plant has been growing. The same premise holds true in shifting a plant from a small tub into a larger tub. The increase in diameter should not exceed 1 or 2 inches. A plant in a 10-inch pot may be shifted into a 12-inch pot or tub; a plant in a 12-inch tub may be shifted into a 13- or 14-inch tub when its roots have begun to fill the smaller tub.

The size to which a plant develops can be controlled by regulating the size of the tub. If a plant normally reaches considerable size and you wish to maintain it at a size below the maximum, keep it in a small container. The procedure, therefore, is to continue shifting the plant from one tub to a slightly larger tub until it attains either its normal mature size or the smaller-than-normal size desired. There are instances in Italy where plants have been kept in the same size tubs or huge pots for 70 years or more and have retained their vigor and flowered regularly, although little or no increase in overall size has occurred.

Soil

The great majority of shrubs grown in tubs thrive on an ordinary soil mixture, such as two parts good garden loam, one part compost or leaf mold, and one part sharp sand. Some shrubs, such as the rhododendrons and many of the azaleas, require a definitely acid soil (see Chapter 12 for cutural information).

Maintenance

General maintenance includes such repetitive measures as watering, fertilizing, mulching, and pruning. Plants in wooden tubs do not dry out as rapidly as those in pots; and in hot weather, the soil remains at a cooler temperature, as wood is a poor conductor of heat. Water requirements vary, but most plants, when growing, require a constant and moderate amount of water. Frequent light waterings should be avoided as this tends to induce shallow rooting, which leaves the plant vulnerable to drought. It is best to water thoroughly once or twice a week, depending on the weather and the location of the tub (i.e., whether in full sun or shaded part of the day). In any case, watering should be delayed until the soil surface is dry. A mulch of peat moss, thick enough to remain constantly moist at the soil level, will help prevent soil moisture loss in hot, dry weather.

If a good soil mixture is used, three applications per year of a readily soluble, quick-release fertilizer will usually suffice. The first should be given early in the spring to encourage strong growth. If the plant indicates by the color of its leaves or its general appearance that it would benefit from more nutrients, additional applications may be given. If the plant normally lapses into dormancy for a winter rest period, no supplementary fertilizer should be applied after midsummer.

Pruning should be undertaken occasionally, especially at the close of the blooming period, to maintain an attractive shape and to remove dead wood or growth that is too twiggy.

Wintering Plants in Tubs

In mild climates (zones 8 to 10), it is possible for most tubbed plants to remain on the patio or terrace throughout the year, but where winters are severe, it is necessary to move them to some suitable area where they will be adequately protected from the cold and harsh wind. Success with many plants, shrubs especially, depends on being able to winter them well. A cool sun porch or a conservatory that can be maintained at a cool temperature provides ideal conditions, but when such a place is not available, a cool cellar may prove a good substitute, especially for deciduous shrubs, which, when out of leaf, require no light. Plants that retain their leaves should receive indirect low light. The temperature should range between 45° and 55°F. Warm temperatures in cellars are apt to prove disastrous, as the combination of high temperature, low humidity, and lack of light will often cause deadly desiccation or blanched premature growth.

Certain plants, such as fuchsias, require special pruning or other care at the time of winter storage; careful attention must be given to such details. Since some plants do not adapt well to a period of winter storage, one should keep this in mind when selecting plants to be grown in tubs in northern latitudes.

HANGING POTS AND BASKETS

Hanging pots and baskets cascading with bloom have a special charm and add much to the attractiveness of a terrace or patio. Flower baskets can be used with great distinction not only in private gardens but also along streets, at the doorways of shops, and in other public places. They are used on balconies and porches and hang from the beams of pergolas and arbors. For shady places, there are pendent types of tuberous begonias and fuchsias, both of which may be seen to best advantage in hanging pots or baskets. Indeed, a superbly grown basket of begonias is breathtaking and memorable. For hot, sunny situations, choices include trailing lantana, petunia, and verbena. On porches that get only a few hours of morning sun and then shade for the rest of the day, achimenes thrives, as do tuberous begonia and dwarf impatiens. In baskets of ample size, combinations are possible, such as wax begonia or petunia surrounded by sweet alyssum or trailing lobelia.

Types of Containers

Various types of containers may be used. Pots, wooden or plastic baskets, small wooden or plastic tubs, and wire baskets are all satisfactory. Plastic pots especially designed for hanging, complete with an attached saucer to reduce dripping after watering, have become extremely popular and, indeed, have helped to create a boom in the use of hanging plants. The light weight of these plastic hanging pots is a great advantage. A disadvantage is their color: the bright white pots especially are often more conspicuous than the

GARDEN PLANTS WELL SUITED TO CULTURE IN HANGING BASKETS

1. ANNUALS AND OTHER SPECIES GROWN FOR A SINGLE SEASON*

Begonia semperflorens × cultorum cvs. (wax begonia):
may be wintered over indoors

B. × tuberhybrida trailing cvs. (tuberous begonia):
dormant tubers may be stored dry away from frost

Browallia speciosa

Coleus × hybridus dwarf, branched

Fuchsia × hybrida

Heliotropium arborescens (garden heliotrope)

Impatiens walleriana dwarf cvs.

Lantana montevidensis (creeping lantana)

Lobelia erinus trailing (edging lobelia)

Lobularia maritima (sweet alyssum)

Nierembergia hippomanica var. *violacea* (cup flower)

Pelargonium peltatum hybrids (ivy-leaved geranium)

Petunia × hybrida

Phlox drummondii dwarf cvs. (annual phlox)

Sanvitalia procumbens (creeping zinnia)

Thunbergia alata (black-eyed Susan vine)

Tropaeolum majus (nasturtium)

Verbena × hybrida dwarf, spreading cvs.

Vinca major, especially with variegated leaves

Viola × wittrockiana (pansy)

2. TENDER PERENNIALS AND OTHER SPECIES GROWN IN PERMANANT BASKET PLANTINGS INDOORS WITH A SUMMER PERIOD OUTDOORS†

Abutilon megapotamicum (trailing flowering maple)

Achimenes cvs.

Aeschynanthus lobbianus (lipstick plant)

Asparagus densiflorus 'Sprengeri' group (asparagus fern)

Begonia spp., especially those of trailing or creeping habit

Bougainvillea spp. and cvs.

Campanula isophylla (star-of-Bethlehem)

Chlorophytum comosum (spider plant)

Cissus rhombifolia (grape ivy)

Columnea × banksii cvs.

Cymbalaria muralis (Kennilworth ivy)

Epiphyllum hybrids (orchid cactus) and other slender-stemmed,
diffusely branched epiphytic cacti such as *Lepismium* spp.
and *Rhipsalis* spp.

Epipremnum aureum (ivy arum, pothos)

Episcia cvs. (carpet plant) ferns, especially *Davallia fejeensis*
(rabbit's-foot fern), *Nephrolepis exaltata* (Boston fern),
and *Polypodium aureum* (bear's-foot fern)

Ficus pumila (creeping fig)

Gynura aurantiaca, G. procumbens (velvet plant)

Hatiora gaertneri (Easter cactus)

Hedera helix dwarf cvs. (English ivy)

Manettia luteo-rubra (firecracker vine)

Oxalis spp.

Pelargonium peltatum (ivy-leaved geranium)

Peperomia spp., especially *P. argyreia* (watermelon begonia)
and *P. obtusifolia* (baby rubber plant, radiator plant)

Philodendron cordatum (heart-leaved philodendron),
P. scandens var. *oxycardium* (glossy philodendron)

Plectranthus australis (Swedish ivy)

Schlumbergera × buckleyi (Christmas cactus),
S. truncata (Thanksgiving cactus)

Tolmiea menziesii (piggyback plant)

Tradescantia zebrina (wandering Jew)

Vinca major, especially cultivars with variegated leaves

* See Chapters 17, 18, and 26 for more information.

† See Chapters 38 and 40 for more information.

plants they contain. A small can of a gray green latex paint provides the remedy: simply paint the pot (even with the plant in place), and in a matter of minutes the paint dries and focus is back on the plant itself.

Especially constructed wire hangers are available that can be attached to the rim of any ordinary clay pot. These have a hook at the top, sometimes of a swivel type that greatly facilitates turning the pot. As clay pots are much heavier than plastic ones, size for size, more attention must be given to securing them to sufficiently strong hooks or hangers.

Baskets made of slats are available in various sizes and are attractive and durable if made of rot-resistant material. Small tubs or boxes are the best type in which to grow tuberous begonias and fuchsias, as they retain moisture better than any other type of hanging receptacle. They are made in various shapes: square with a tapered base, octagonal, and round, each in a range of sizes.

Open-mesh wire baskets are also obtainable in a great variety of shapes and sizes. They are considerably less expensive than the other types and work well for many plants if careful attention is given to the method of planting and watering. Copper wire is superior to galvanized wire, as it will not rust and will give more years of service. Similar baskets may be fashioned at home, if desired.

Pots, wire baskets, and other containers are also available with one flat side for use against walls, buildings, and fences.

Baskets of luxuriant, freely flowering geraniums are medallions of color on a busy, fenced patio.

Planting

Slatted and wire baskets should be lined either with sheets of wood moss or pieces of sphagnum moss. Osmunda fiber may also be used but is less satisfactory, as it is too diffuse to retain soil moisture. All of these materials are usually available from florist supply houses. Alternatively, burlap or even (plastic) wrap can be used, if perforated with a few holes to promote drainage.

The lining serves two purposes: it retains the soil within the basket and provides for good drainage of surplus water. Slatted and wire baskets tend to dry out rapidly, and if they are to be used in a sunny location it is advisable to place a flowerpot saucer in the bottom of the basket, covering it lightly with a layer of sphagnum moss. This will act as a reservoir for surplus water.

After the baskets are lined and about 1 inch of drainage material has been placed in the bottom, soil may be added. If you want to have plants growing out of the sides of wire baskets as well as dropping down from the top, the planting should be done when the basket is about half filled with soil. The plants should be placed on their sides, with the ball of earth around the roots kept intact. The moss lining should be temporarily pulled aside, and the leaves and stems worked carefully through the wires. The remaining soil should then be added. Growth habit of the plants selected and their size at maturity will govern the number placed in each container.

Watering

Hanging pots and baskets, particularly when placed in full sun, dry out rapidly and require faithful care. Daily watering is usually essential, and on days when there are hot, drying winds, it may be necessary to water twice. Pots and wire baskets dry out much more rapidly than solid wooden boxes. Glazed pots dry out less rapidly than pots of porous bisqued clay. If, however, a coat of varnish is applied to clay pots, evaporation will be reduced.

One of the most effective ways to overcome the loss of moisture is to employ the pot-within-a-pot method (see page 46) or some variation of it, such as a pot within a basket. Excellent growth is usually obtained with this method, other conditions being favorable.

If a number of baskets are to be watered, a hose attachment may be purchased that will greatly facilitate the task. This consists of a long, metal tube with a spray at the end, which is put on at a convenient angle for overhead watering.

PLANTS IN PORTABLE BOXES

Portable planting boxes are a recent innovation and have increased the opportunities for an ever-changing succession of bloom on the patio and terrace. Indeed, if they are skillfully planted and maintained, one may experience within a small paved area all the pleasures of a veritable garden.

Planting boxes of the portable type have great versatility. They are small enough to be moved easily from one location to another on the patio, and interesting effects may often be obtained by combining boxes of different sizes and shapes. They offer almost unlimited opportunities for dramatic and beautiful combinations of color, texture, and form, as plants may be removed as soon as they have completed their period of bloom and be replaced with other plants just coming into flower. Thus in the North a succession of bloom may be maintained from early spring, when the first bulbs come into flower, until late autumn; in mild climates, an unbroken cycle of bloom may be enjoyed. And special gems, such as some of the exquisite cyclamens and the precocious Christmas rose (*Helleborus niger*), which require special culture, may be grown in small boxes and used where their beauty will be most fully appreciated and enjoyed.

Planting boxes offer solutions to many practical problems, as they make it possible, in many instances, to provide conditions that approximate the ideal. Soil mixtures may be prepared that best meet the needs of special plants. One box may contain a rich, woodsy soil for tuberous begonia, while another may contain a lean, sandy mixture to restrain the often too rampant growth of lantanas, producing more abundant flowering. And in areas where nematodes are troublesome, sterilized, nematode-free soil may be used. Conditions involving exposure, humidity, watering, fertilizing, and the competition of other plants can be controlled more readily than is possible when plants are grown in the open ground.

Types of Boxes

The best materials for portable plant boxes are treated wood, fiberglass, and plastic.

In many areas, wooden boxes may be purchased ready-made, or they may be easily constructed at home by anyone who is handy with tools, as the making involves only very simple carpentry (see page 615). If durable lumber is used and the boxes are carefully made, they may last for ten years or more. Wooden boxes may be purchased in a wide variety of shapes and sizes and provide good growing conditions for plants.

Wooden plant boxes should always be made with cleats or blocks on the bottom to facilitate lifting and moving and to provide for air circulation and good drainage. Ball-bearing casters may be attached in place of cleats if desired and can greatly ease the shifting of boxes from place to place on smooth, hard surfaces.

Drainage

It is essential to provide good drainage in planting boxes. A narrow space may be left between the bottom boards or, if a solid board is used, drainage holes should be provided. In addition, it is advisable to place a 1-inch layer of broken crocks, bricks, or gravel on the bottom of the box over which a thin layer of moist sphagnum moss should be spread.

Soil

A soil mixture should be used that will meet the needs of the plants to be grown in the box. Unless plants have specific requirements, a general-purpose mixture that is light in texture and contains abundant humus will be the most satisfactory, as it will tend to drain well.

Maintenance

The usual good maintenance practices should be followed. The boxes should never be allowed to dry out completely but should be watered with care and good judgment, as over-watering can be as harmful as underwatering. Most plants will benefit from the application of a high-analysis, soluble fertilizer at intervals of two to four weeks.

For tuberous begonias and caladiums it may prove best to grow the plants in clay pots and sink the pots in peat moss rather than to fill the box with soil. Keeping the peat moss thoroughly damp will ensure a steady and even supply of moisture for plants rooted in such porous pots.

5

Garden Walls, Banks, Paths, and Steps

GARDEN WALLS

In ages past, high walls were built around gardens to protect them. Often a moat also surrounded the garden. In some cases the walls were built as much for shelter against winds as to exclude intruders. They also provided vertical surfaces for fruit trees that were trained against them. A south-facing wall surface stimulated spring growth in the espalier trees and induced earlier flowering and fruiting. Besides these practical functions, garden walls also served as a background

Generous but varied use of brick imparts an Italianate note to an otherwise carefree, informal display garden.

for flowers and foliage, in addition to providing both privacy and seclusion.

A broad, unbroken surface of masonry is not always interesting, but a wall divided into panels, interrupted by projecting buttresses, or built with a pleasing combination of materials has architectural significance. It is the link that unites the garden and the house as parts of one composition.

Freestanding Walls

It is essential that the top of a freestanding wall be watertight. One of the most practical means of preventing moisture from entering the masonry from above is to cover the wall with a coping of flagstones set in concrete mortar joints. In addition to its practical function, this definite edge also gives a finished appearance to the structure. A sharp-pitched roof of slate, brick, shingles, or painted boards is sometimes used. A brick coping is also frequently used for this purpose, and a wedge-shaped top built of brick courses in diminishing thicknesses is picturesque.

In the South, walls are sometimes built with some of the bricks omitted, leaving holes to allow for the passage of air currents. For obvious reasons, it is important not to exclude all the breezes in the warmer parts of our country, and the perforated wall serves as a practical screen but not an absolute barrier to circulating air.

A wall typical of South Carolina is brick with panels of stucco. The piers are thick, while the panels are only one brick in thickness. Thomas Jefferson's famous serpentine wall is only one brick thick. Structural strength comes from the serpentine construction.

During the last few decades the ornamental concrete block has found its way into the garden. These comparatively inexpensive blocks, which come in different designs, are usually 12 by 12 inches square and 4 to 5 inches thick. They are cemented between piers of 6- or 8-inch cement blocks and are plastered with white stucco. Like the perforated brick wall, these blocks prevent a complete view of the area behind, while at the same time allowing for the passage of air currents.

Retaining Walls

A retaining wall must hold its position against the pressure of the earth behind it. During seasons of alternate freezing and thawing, ground pressure is considerable. We see its effect when paved roads heave in early spring. If the wall is not adequate to hold, the pressure thus exerted may be translated into one of four kinds of movement:

1. The wall may be forced to bulge out of shape, opening cracks in the masonry; this is apt to happen in dry walls in which there is no mortar to hold the stones together.
2. The whole wall may slide away from the hill; this can happen if the footings of the wall are not deep enough to have a firm hold in the soil.
3. The wall can be forced to revolve about its baseline and thus be forced to lean forward out of position.
4. The wall may be lifted up vertically by the action of frost beneath the footings; this can happen when the foundations do not extend below the frost line of the region.

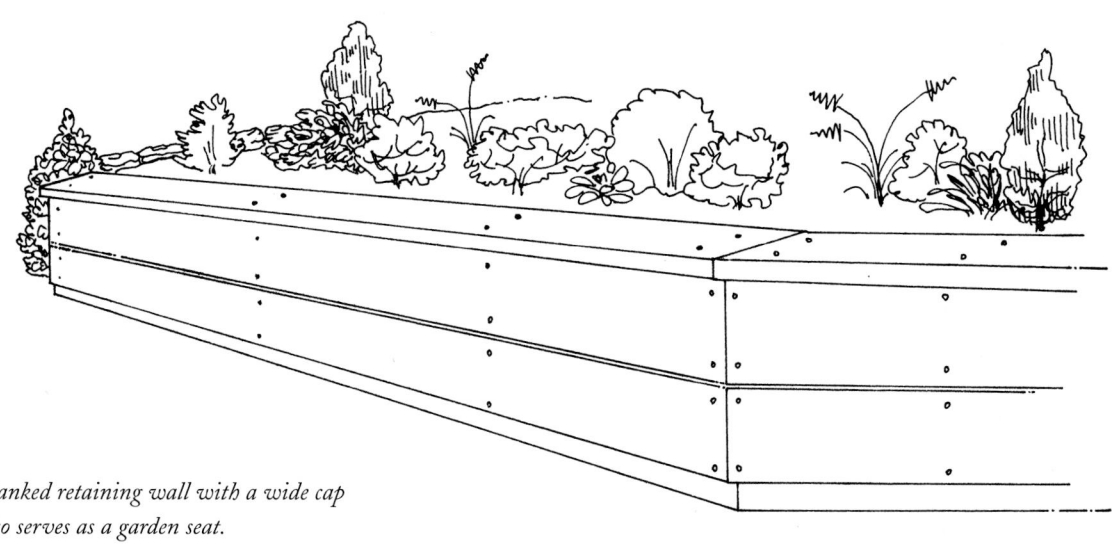

Planked retaining wall with a wide cap also serves as a garden seat.

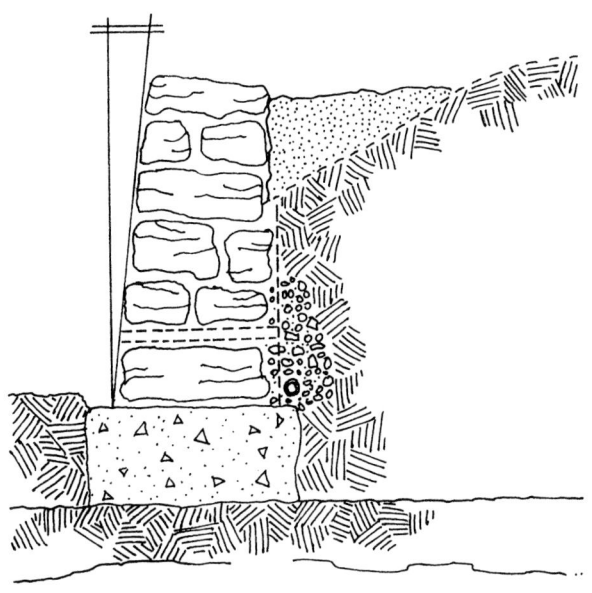

It has been found by long practice that the proportions shown in the sectional sketch are adequate to withstand the pressures in the soil. The footings are below frost line and slope down toward the rear. The thickness of the wall at the base equals one-third of the height measured from the lower ground level. The top of the wall is 18 inches thick. Special conditions, such as heavy traffic along or behind the top of the wall, will make necessary a greater bulk of masonry than for normal conditions.

By building projections or buttresses into the face of the wall at intervals of 10 or 12 feet, the effective base of the wall is widened, thus making the structure more resistant to the tendency to revolve about its base and hence more secure. The buttresses must be built with the wall as an integral part of the structure. The wider the projection of the base of the buttresses, the greater is the resistance to pressure. A buttressed wall may be built thinner than, and still be as strong as, a plain wall of the same height. Buttresses may be made a decorative element, dividing a long wall into bays.

Wet soil exerts greater pressure than dry soil. To prevent the soil behind a retaining wall from becoming saturated, or simply to permit the normal flow of water through the subsoil to continue uninterrupted by the wall, small holes should be left in the masonry near the base of the wall at intervals of 10 or 12 feet.

Stones should be laid into the wall in such a way as to form a strong bond. That is, the long dimension of the stone should be horizontal, and each stone should bridge over the joint between the two stones in the course below. In this way no long, vertical joint will appear. In any retaining wall, some stones should run from the front to the back face across the wall to tie the masonry more firmly together.

Very good retaining walls can be constructed of concrete rubble, the whole bonded together with a mortar of fresh concrete. The rubble is often easily obtained at little or no cost at construction sites. If the exposed surface is too coarse, it may be faced with stone, brick, or even pieces of rubble of similar thickness (as from a sidewalk) set at the same orientation (e.g., smooth side down).

The mortar should be a mixture of one part Portland cement and two parts sand. The well-built masonry wall is a structure of great strength and should serve as a permanent installation. The retaining walls of the great Italian villas, for example, have remained intact for 400 or 500 years.

Reinforced Concrete Walls

Another type of wall, known as the "cantilever" wall, holds together partly by the weight of earth on a broad projecting

A stepped, capped retaining wall of mortared brick with parallel beds of yellow marigolds and blue salvia makes a pleasing line of definition between two levels in the landscape.

footing. This is built of reinforced concrete and is, therefore, a monolith. Such walls are much lighter and thinner in construction than walls made of unbonded rocks held in place by gravity and are used especially in regions where sand is common and stone is scarce.

Concrete is made by mixing cement, gravel, and water; after it cures, the mixture turns into the equivalent of artificial stone. Because of its strength, permanence, and relatively low cost, concrete is one of the most important building materials used in modern construction. Though concrete is strong in compression, it is relatively weak in tension; that is, it tends to crack. Thus in applications in which the concrete is likely to be subject to tension, it should be reinforced with steel rods that can sustain such pressure.

The concrete used for reinforced walls is poured between temporary forms built of lumber. Steel reinforcing rods form a mesh of 12- or 15-inch squares, which gives the concrete great rigidity and prevents it from cracking under unequal pressure. The inner surface of a concrete wall should be sealed with an application of a waterproofing compound. Unless this is done, the concrete is likely to become porous and crack. With this protection from groundwater, a concrete retaining wall may be faced either with a coat of stucco or with brick. But unless the wall has been waterproofed as described above, the stucco will peel off and the brick will blossom out with rosettes of lime deposited by moisture coming through the bricks and then evaporating.

Timber Retaining Walls

If landscape ties treated with pentachlorophenol ("penta" in the trade) are used and if the usual precautions are taken to provide an adequate foundation and to anchor the ties securely for long-term stability, a timber retaining wall can be expected to last at least 25 years. Sections 5 by 6 inches wide and 8 feet long are the most economical and easiest to handle. The sometimes overwhelming expanse of a flat-faced wall can be mitigated by recessing each course of timbers ¾ inch back from the course below. Timbers should be lapped to avoid the weakness inherent in stacked joints. Lengths can be readily cut to size with a chain saw, and each timber should be anchored in place with a few heavy galvanized spikes driven through predrilled holes into the adjacent ties.

Additional interest can be developed by designing turns or jogs in what may otherwise become a massive surface. Stairs and recesses can be set in, and when completed, a timber wall makes a fine setting for plantings, above and below. In some cases, the chinks between ties may offer sites for such plants as Kennilworth ivy (*Cymbalaria muralis*) and various creeping sedums (*Sedum* species).

A gently stepped timber retaining wall defines not only two grades and two expansive areas but two distinct functions. The mulched shrub bed helps soften the transition.

GARDEN BANKS

In many cases, a simply treated, evenly sloping bank will be appropriate and will function as well as a retaining wall. The advantages of the wall are its architectural character, its economy of space, and its permanence. The advantages of the bank are its more natural character, its economy of construction, and its availability as a planting site. The bank that slopes either down or up from a terrace may be planted with various ground covers to add interest, prevent erosion, and to reduce maintenance. The bank may also rise from the top of a low retaining wall.

Turf Bank

Turf-clad banks have been used for many centuries, and with good reason. Nothing else presents such a finished effect as a carefully graded and well-maintained turf terrace bank, but such banks should not be graded to a steeper slope than 45° or 1 foot of rise per 2 lineal feet. Starting turf on a slope is more difficult than on level land. Unless the slope has been covered with protective mesh, a heavy rain will erode the newly seeded site, necessitating patching, regrading, and reseeding. Laying sod over the whole bank is the most certain method of starting grass. If the surface water from the hillside above the bank is diverted by turf gutters,

A wavelike terraced bank with concrete staircases is topped with a row of junipers and broken with scattered young spruces, which help make the transition from lawn to the tall trees beyond.

the bank grass may be started with seed sowing. In this case, strips of sod placed in horizontal lines along the banks at intervals of 4 feet or 6 feet will prevent the washing away of soil. This precaution is worth the additional cost and effort.

SHRUBBY GROUND COVERS FOR BANKS

Name	Zones	Foliage*	Height × Spread	Comments
Arctostaphylos uva-ursi (bearberry)	2–7	E	1 × 3'	Red fruit in fall
Calluna vulgaris cvs. (heather)	5–8	E	3 × 3'	Purplish pink to white flowers
Comptonia peregrina (sweet fern)	3–8	D	3 × 3'	Aromatic foliage
Cotoneaster horizontalis (rockspray cotoneaster)	6–8	D	2 × 6'	Red berries in late summer
Erica carnea (spring heath)	6–8	E	1 × 2'	Red, pink, or white flowers in early spring
Euonymus fortunei 'Colorata' (variegated winter creeper)	4 or 5–8 or 9	E	Climbs to 20'	Foliage turns purplish in winter
E. nana (Turkestan euonymus)	3–7	D	3 × 6'	Pink-and-orange fruit in late summer to fall
Jasminum nudiflorum (winter jasmine)	6–9	D	4 × 12'	Yellow flowers during mild periods in winter
Juniperus chinensis 'Pfitzerana' (Pfitzer juniper)	4–8	E	6 × 10'	Distinctive ascending habit, blue-green foliage
J. chinensis var. *procumbens* (procumbent juniper)	4–8	E	1 × 10'	Gray green foliage
J. communis var. *depressa* (ground juniper)	3–7	E	3 × 6'	Mat forming, various foliage colors in cultivars
J. conferta (shore juniper)	6–8	E	1 × 6'	Yellowish blue-green foliage
J. horizontalis 'Bar Harbor' (creeping juniper)	3–7	E	1 × 6'	Steel blue foliage
J. horizontalis 'Plumosa' (purple juniper)	3–7	E	1 × 6'	Purplish foliage in winter
Pachysandra terminalis	5–8	E	1 × ∞'	Mat forming, best in partial shade
Pinus mugo (mugo pine)	3–8	E	3 × 6'	Several cultivars lower in habit, e.g., 'Prostrata' and 'Slavinii' mature as mats 1 × 8'
Rosa rugosa and cvs. (rugosa rose)	2–7	D	3–6 × 10'	Pink or white flowers, red-orange fruit
Spiraea tomentosa (steeplebush)	5–8	D	4 × 4'	Purplish rose or white flowers in summer

* D, deciduous; E, evergreen.

PERENNIAL GROUND COVERS FOR BANKS

Name	Zones	Habit	Height × Spread	Comments
Ajuga reptans and cvs. (bugle)	5–8	Rhizomatous mats	3–6 × 18"	Blue-violet flowers in spring
Arabis alpina and cvs. (mountain rock cress)	5–7	Rosettes	6–12 × 15"	White flowers (pink to red in cultivars) in spring
Arenaria montana (mountain sandwort)	5–7	Mat forming	9–12 × 18"	White flowers in spring
Cerastium tomentosum (snow-in-summer)	4–7	Mat forming	6–12 × 24"	White flowers in summer; grayish foliage
Ceratostigma plumbaginoides (plumbago)	5–8	Mat forming	12–18 × 30"	Dark blue flowers in late summer
Convallaria majalis (lily-of-the-valley)	4–8	Rhizomatous mats	9 × 24"	Fragrant white flowers in spring
Hemerocallis fulva and cvs. (common daylily)	4–9	Rhizomatous mats	24–48 × 72"	Large orange flowers in early summer
Lysimachia nummularia (creeping Charlie)	5–7	Loose mats	2–3 × 18"	Yellow flowers in spring; best in damp partial shade
Nepeta mussinii (catmint)	5–8	Mat forming	12 × 24"	Blue flowers in spring
Phlox subulata and cvs. (mountain pink)	4–7	Mat forming	3–6 × 18"	Purple to pink or white flowers in spring
Sedum acre and *S. sarmentosum* (yellow creeping sedum)	4–8	Mat forming	3–6 × 24"	Yellow flowers in late spring
Thymus spp. (creeping thyme)	5–8	Mat forming	6–12 × 24"	Purple to white flowers; aromatic foliage

Planted Bank

A bank well furnished with topsoil and covered with densely spreading plants is perhaps the most satisfying and economical treatment of the change in levels. The slope should be no more than 1 foot of rise for every 2½ feet of horizontal dimension, and preferably less so. By a careful selection of plants, the bank may be made very beautiful. Conditions of soil and exposure may affect or even dictate a choice of plants, but a wide variety is readily available with which to attractively carpet difficult banks, including those with harsh exposures and the poorest of soils.

Arctostaphlos uva-ursi

Ceratostigma plumbaginoides

An interrupted, zigzag stairway, with pan lights and angular railings, is flanked by ribbons of procumbent and spreading junipers.

For a wholly or partially shaded bank, *Vinca minor* (periwinkle) and *Hedera helix* (English ivy) can be planted, with various spring and fall bulbs naturalized in groups throughout the area. These will provide welcome color in spring and fall in an otherwise year-round carpet of green. See the tables above.

GARDEN PATHS

The very words *garden path* bring to mind old brick walls bordered with boxwood, strips of turf between long flower borders, and flagstones interspersed with tiny herbs and shaded by arching branches of magnolias.

The path is one of the components of the garden plan that gives expression to the design: in some cases by making a pattern among the flower beds or by accenting the lines of symmetry, and in others by the use of a subtle turn or graceful curve.

Before designing and constructing a path, it is essential to be clear about what is to be accomplished by the chosen route. What is to be linked? What is the experience you will have while walking it? Clearly, a path linking your front lawn to the backyard serves a different purpose from one leading from a parking lot to the doctor's office. A garden path should be practical and clear in purpose while at the same time offering a pleasant, aesthetic experience derived from the combination of plants and architecture.

In considering the construction of paths, there are a number of matters that should be given careful thought— among them path width, selection and suitability of the materials to be used, the original cost, and the expense of upkeep.

Since shrubs and other garden plants adjacent to paths, even if frequently trimmed, tend to exceed their bounds

Mixed paving patterns can lend interest to walks.

and intrude, especially when wet or snow-laden, it is better to err on the side of greater breadth when planning a path. A 3-foot width is the absolute minimum for solitary passage, and a 5-foot width for two people walking together, as is sometimes essential when assisting the elderly. A 4-foot width will accommodate most garden carts and wheeled machinery.

While a straight path is the shortest route between two points, it will, especially if constructed of a single homogeneous material (e.g., concrete or asphalt), tend to narrow a garden; a gentle curve can obviate this illusion. On the other hand, excessive paving and complexity are to be avoided, especially on small properties, where space is at a premium

*A broad, open, turf-edged brick path leads past banked violaceous flower beds to a bright display in the distance. Contrasting foliar effects are achieved with bursts of tall grasses, the bold purple leaves of castor bean (*Ricinus communis *'Sanguineus'), and sheared conical evergreens.*

and priority should be given to the plantings. Illogical, fussy curves invite shortcutting. Constancy in width should be maintained except where function changes.

Often the suitability of one structural material over another will be the deciding factor. In an area where there is much activity, turf soon thins and develops bare patches. Within the confines of a garden, however, where there is comparatively little traffic, grass paths are entirely satisfactory. On the other hand, if one has a wooded tract developed along informal or naturalistic lines, a path of bark chips or wood chips would be suitable. In this kind of wooded setting, paths of brick or gravel would be out of harmony with the surroundings. For a pathway leading from the sidewalk to the door, where there is much activity, a durable material such as gravel, brick, or flagstones should be used.

The cost of materials varies considerably from place to place. In areas where there are natural outcrops and where rock is plentiful, flagstone paths might prove the most economical, while in other areas where such stone is scarce, they might be almost prohibitive in price because of the expense of shipping such heavy materials. For turf or bark or wood-chip paths, much of the work may be done by the average amateur gardener, and the costs may consequently be kept low. On the other hand, a turf path requires more upkeep than do most of the other types. It must be kept mowed and edged, for nothing detracts more from the trim and pleasing appearance of a garden than straggly grass and unkempt edges. This question of upkeep should be taken into careful consideration before the final decision is made on the type of garden path to construct.

Lines and Grades

In a formal garden, the lines and dimensions of paths must be laid out with great care. The best way to establish a straight line is to stretch a cord between two stakes. A steel tape or a heavy cloth tape is essential, and a surveyor's transit is a great help. Without a transit, any right-angle turns needed in the path may be marked off on the ground by the 3-4-5 method. This is most easily done by three people, using a tape and three stakes.

If one takes three sections of tape, the lengths of which are proportioned to one another as 3 is to 4 and as 4 is to 5, and places them end to end in a triangle, the angle between the "3" section and the "4" section will be a square angle, or 90°. The reason for this is the old geometric theorem "The square of the hypotenuse of a right-angled triangle is equal to the sum of the squares of the other two sides." Thus $3^2 + 4^2 = 5^2$ or $9 + 16 = 25$. If the lengths of the two lines are to extend some distance, it is best to use longer pieces of tape than 3, 4, and 5 feet, because a slight error in holding the tapes together would increase proportionately with the distance to the end of the line. Sections 9, 12, and 15 feet are convenient.

The most direct and best way of marking a "freehand" curve is to fling a section of garden hose or heavy rope on the ground. The hose may be adjusted until the desired alignment is reached, and it may then be marked by frequent stakes. However, avoid making curves in a walk just for the sake of having them. A natural obstacle, such as a tree, shrub, or boulder, should be the reason for a curve in a garden path.

Grades are important in path building. Surface water must be induced to run off promptly, and this can best be done by crowning or cambering, i.e., making the center of the path slightly higher than the sides. On a path 4 feet wide, whether made of brick, flagstone, or gravel, the crown should be about ¾ inch higher than the edges. A longitudinal slope of at least 1 percent (i.e., an elevational difference of 1 foot per 100 lineal feet) will further promote drainage.

Path Materials
Brick

Brick walks are usually very pleasant, and they age with an appealing mellowness and charm. The initial cost is comparatively high, but if good-quality brick is used and the walk is carefully laid, it should give service for many decades. In some of our old colonial gardens, we find paths laid two centuries or more ago that are still in good condition and attest to the worth of the fine craftsmanship of those masons.

In parts of the country where there is minimal frost action in winter and where there is a natural layer of sandy or gravelly soil, no additional foundation is needed for a brick path. If frost seldom penetrates more than 3 inches into the ground, it is possible to lay the bricks directly on a cushion of sand after the subgrades are determined. In sandy areas, bricks may be laid directly on the sand so long as the ground beneath is firm. Otherwise, and especially in colder regions (from zone 7 northward), a foundation course must be carefully prepared before the bricks are laid. Unless this is done properly, the alternation of freezing and thawing will gradually disarrange bricks, causing some to heave, crack, and break. Before many years have elapsed, the garden path will be not only unsightly but also unsafe.

Bricks may be laid either on a concrete base with a crushed stone or gravel foundation or on a cushion of sand above a gravel foundation. Gravel known as "pit gravel" is greatly preferred to washed gravel for the surfacing of walks and should be obtained whenever possible. If it is necessary to use washed gravel, limestone dust to the amount of approximately 15 percent should be mixed with it to help

*The lines of unmortared brick carry the eye to the curve ahead, past an overhanging border of late flowering mistflower or hardy ageratum (*Eupatorium coelestinum*).*

bind the surface. The particles of gravel or stone dust used for paths should be no larger than ¼ inch. If bricks are laid on sand with ½-inch soil-filled pockets between them, small plants can be grown, as on terraces (see the table on page 39 for plants suitable for this application).

Where the bricks are to be laid with mortar joints, the concrete base should be used. After the grades have been established and the earth has been excavated to a depth of 12 inches below the finished grade, a 6-inch layer of gravel should be spread in place. A 3-inch layer should first be spread, watered thoroughly, and then rolled or tamped. The second layer should be handled in the same manner. The base course of concrete should then be prepared and spread over the gravel to a depth of 3 inches. A mixture of one part cement, three parts sand, and five parts gravel is recommended for this purpose. After this concrete foundation has set for 24 hours, the bricks should be laid according to the desired pattern on a thin coat of mortar, which should consist of one part cement to three parts sand. When the

mortar has set and the bricks are firmly in place, the joints should be filled. This may be done in one of two ways. If the joints are ¼ inch or less in width, a dry mixture of cement and sand in the proportion of one part of cement to two parts of sand may be swept into the joints. After the bricks have been swept entirely free of cement, the walk should be watered with a fine, gentle spray until all the cement in the joints has become thoroughly wet. Where the joints are large, it is advisable to prepare a wet mixture of the same proportions and carefully pour it between the bricks until the joints are filled.

When a brick walk is to be laid on a sand cushion, a similar foundation course of gravel is used. On the surface of the gravel a 2-inch layer of fine sand should be spread, and it should be thoroughly rolled or tamped before the bricks are set in place. After the bricks are laid, the joints should be filled with sand. As the bricks are being laid, the surface of the walk should be kept at an even and uniform level. This may easily be done by placing a wide board crosswise to the path and tamping it until the surface is even. A curb should always be used when brick walks are laid in sand, because such walks have a tendency to creep, with the joints gradually becoming wider and wider as a result.

Bricks may be laid in various patterns, the running bond, herringbone, and basket-weave designs being the most usual.

Brick and Concrete in Combination

In France one often sees paths constructed of brick combined with concrete. A well-made path of this type is very pleasant and certainly possesses much more character and charm than a plain concrete walk. The construction is comparatively simple and the cost is not unduly high. After the grades have been established, the soil should be excavated to a depth of 10 inches. A 6-inch foundation course of gravel should then be laid in the same manner as that prescribed for brick walks. A very thin coat of concrete mortar, hardly more than 1 inch in thickness, should then be spread over the gravel; and on this foundation the bricks should be placed in any desired pattern. The spaces between the bricks should then be filled with mortar and the surface brought to an absolutely true level. A small quantity of terra-cotta dye mixed with the cement will give it a slightly reddish tone that harmonizes more pleasantly with the color of the bricks.

The bricks may be placed according to various patterns. When constructing a narrow path, the area of mortar between the patterned bricks should be relatively small, while in a path of more ample proportions, the scale could be increased accordingly.

In damp, shady locations, brick may support a growth of algae or moss, which can become dangerously slippery,

Brick walks

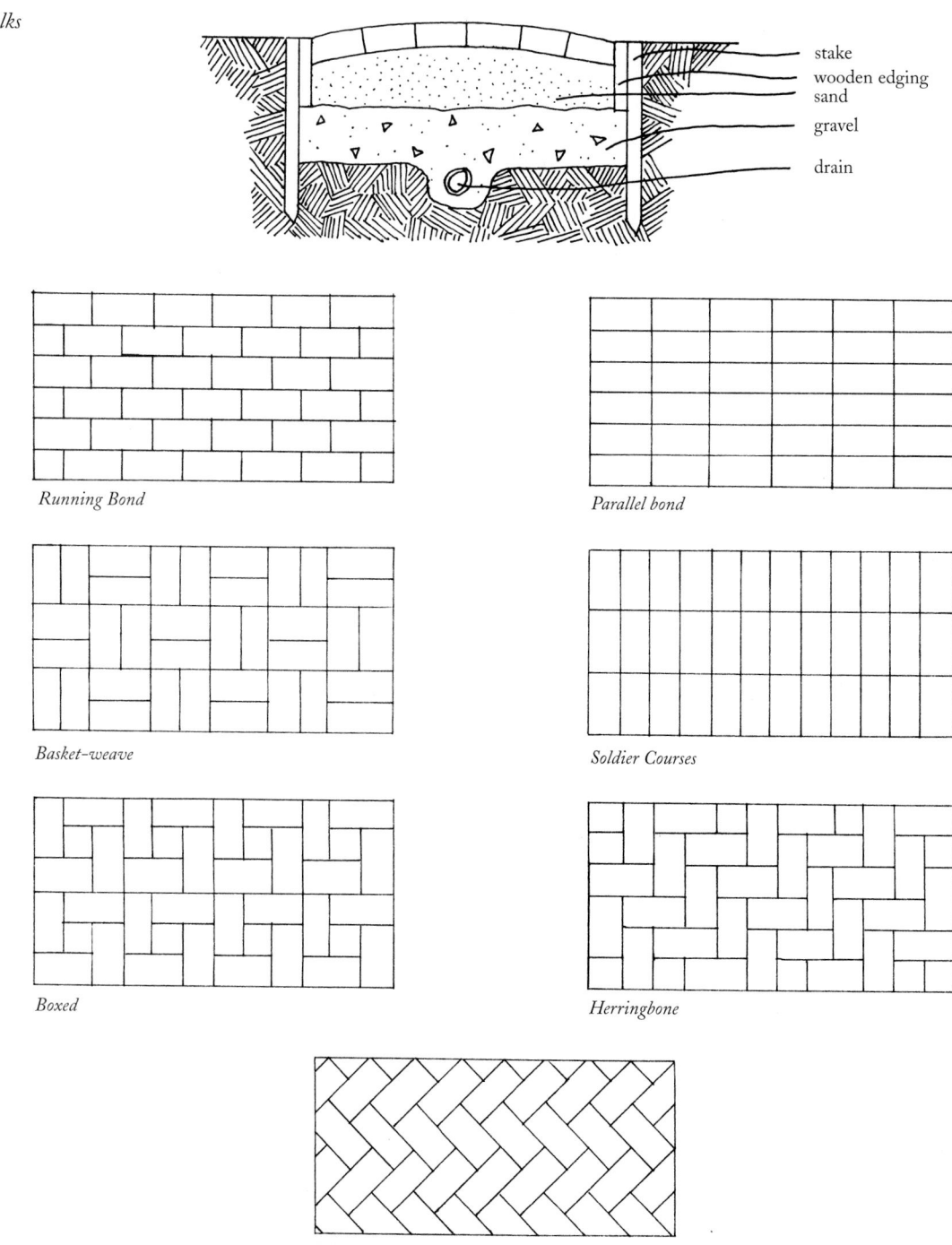

stake
wooden edging
sand
gravel

drain

Running Bond

Parallel bond

Basket-weave

Soldier Courses

Boxed

Herringbone

Diagonal herringbone

especially in wet weather. This film can be scrubbed off with soapy water or be treated with a swimming-pool algicide or be sprayed with the quickly degrading herbicide glyphosate (two brand names are Round-Up and Clean-up).

Flagstone

Flagstone paths have decided character and charm and are widely used. In sections of the country with an abundant supply of local stone, such paths are not expensive and are easily laid. There are various types: those made from stones of square or rectangular shape with cut edges are laid in a perfectly formal or symmetrical manner and those made from stones of more or less irregular shape are laid in a random pattern.

The stones may be laid either on a sand cushion with soil joints or on a concrete foundation with mortar joints. Laying them with earth joints makes possible the growing of turf or low-creeping plants between the stones, an attractive

Stone pavements

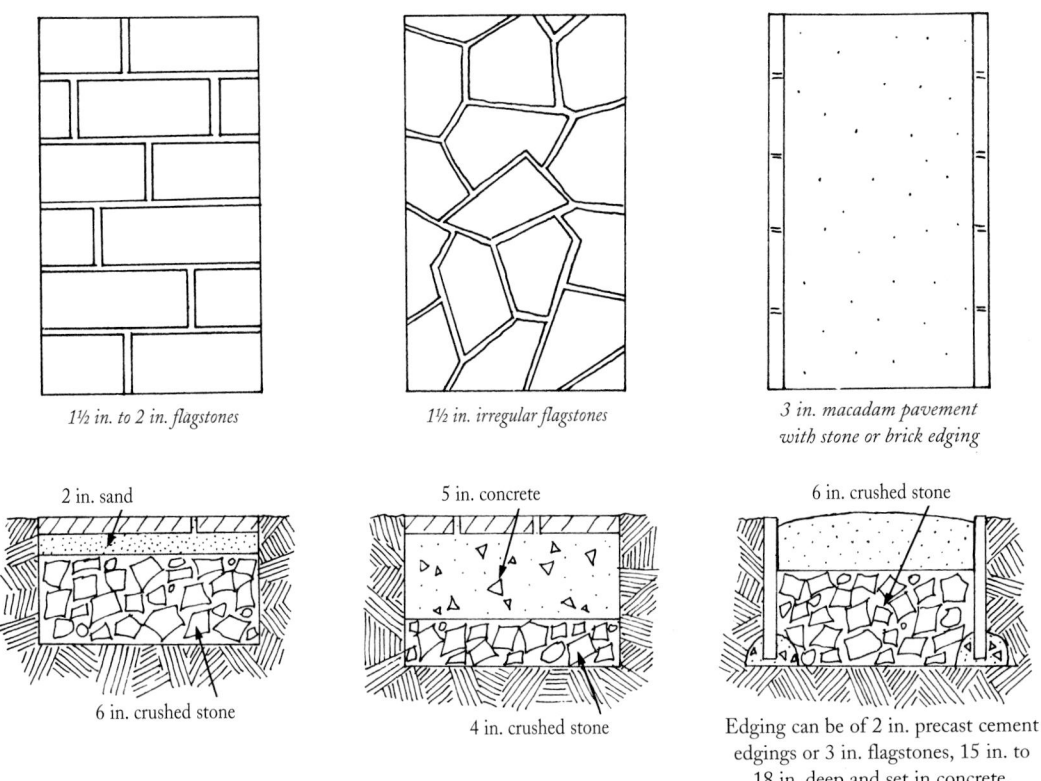

1½ in. to 2 in. flagstones   1½ in. irregular flagstones   3 in. macadam pavement
                                                                           with stone or brick edging

2 in. sand   5 in. concrete   6 in. crushed stone

6 in. crushed stone   4 in. crushed stone   Edging can be of 2 in. precast cement
                                                           edgings or 3 in. flagstones, 15 in. to
                                                           18 in. deep and set in concrete.

feature greatly to be desired. The laying of a flagstone path on a sand cushion is a simple matter and does not require a great amount of skill. The ground should be excavated only to a depth that will bring the stones to the desired level. A layer of fine sand about ½ inch in depth should then be spread over the surface of the soil. A 3- to 4-inch layer of crushed stones between soil and sand will prevent the accumulation of water, which, when frozen during the winter, will heave the flagstones. When the flagstones are in place, care should be taken to see that they are set firmly with no tendency to wobble or teeter. If the lower surface of the stone is uneven, it will be necessary to remove a portion of the soil directly under the protruding point to settle the stone more firmly into its bed. The surface of the path should be true to the desired grade, and as the stones are set in place, a carpenter's level should be used to check the surface. After the stones are properly positioned, sand should be spread over the surface of the path and swept into the joints, or if desired, the joints may be filled with small strips of turf. There are a number of low-creeping rock plants that are particularly suitable for planting between flagstones. *Thymus* species (creeping thymes) are fine textured and pleasing, as they emit a sweet, pungent fragrance when crushed underfoot. *Gypsophila repens* and its cultivars (creeping baby's breath) and *Veronica repens* and its cultivars

(creeping speedwell) are also excellent for this purpose. See page 40 for additional plants.

When flagstones are to be laid with mortar joints, they must be set in concrete. The soil should be excavated to a depth of 10 inches, and a 6-inch layer of crushed stone or gravel should be spread in two layers 3 inches thick, each layer being watered, then rolled or tamped. A 3-inch layer of concrete should be spread on this foundation course of gravel, being mixed in the proportions of one part cement, three parts sand, and five parts gravel. After the concrete has set for 24 hours, a thin coat of cement mortar should be spread over it, and the flagstones set in the mortar. When the stones have become firm, mortar should be carefully poured into the joints.

Gravel

Gravel walks were often used during colonial times, and they have maintained their popularity throughout the years. There are numerous methods of construction. If the walk will not have too much traffic, and if the ground is naturally well drained, the gravel may be laid directly on the soil after the subgrade has been established. However, a walk constructed in this manner will not withstand hard wear, and during wet weather it will have a tendency to become very soft and springy. A much better walk will result if a foundation

A formal path of white gravel, curbed with stone blocks, is edged with daffodils and a bank clothed with English ivy. The stone bench invites tarrying, yet adds to the angular formality.

course of slag or crushed stone is used. In the construction of a walk of this type, the soil should be excavated to a depth of 7 inches below the finished grade. A 5½-inch layer of slag or crushed stone with particles no larger than 2½ inches should then be spread and thoroughly tamped or rolled. The gravel should be spread on this surface, maintaining the crown, and then watered well and rolled.

As most of the traffic borne by any path is down the middle, wear causes loose gravel to shift to the edges, leaving the center thin and, in time, even lower than the margins. The puddling that eventually ensues can be avoided by occasionally raking gravel inward from the edges and restoring the crown.

Stepping-Stones

Stepping-stones laid in turf also make a very pleasant path. Because of their rather informal character, however, they may not conform to the gait of most adults. For that reason, such surfacing is perhaps more suitable for a casual or incidental path than for a walk that is rather heavily used.

The stones selected for a path of this type should be of comfortable size, at least 12 to 15 inches square, and the upper surface should be reasonably smooth. It is not necessary for the stones to be absolutely regular in shape, as very

nice effects may be obtained with stones of somewhat irregular outline. They should be placed at even intervals and spaced far enough apart to permit a pleasant, easy stride from one stone to the next, 18 inches being the usual comfortable distance.

Setting the stones is very simple. If a new walk is being made, they may be set at the same time that the surrounding area of grass is sown, or they may be easily set in a piece of established turf. Initially, the stones should be placed on the surface of the ground and their final position determined. The outline of each stone should then be marked with the edge of a trowel; after the stone has been lifted to one side, the soil within the prescribed area should be removed to the proper depth. A light layer of fine sand should be placed at the bottom of the excavation, as this makes a better bed on which to rest the stone and settle it into its final position. When placing the stones, you should make certain that they are perfectly firm and do not teeter from side to side. If the bottom of the stone is uneven, it may be necessary to remove it several times and cut one portion of the excavation or build up another until the stone is absolutely firm. The surface of the stone should be level with or slightly above the area of turf around it. Not only does this make a difference in the general appearance of the path but it greatly facilitates the use of the lawn mower. If, however, the stepping-stones are set too low, each will form a puddle of water after rain. To prevent this, the soil should be rammed in close around the edges after the stones have been set in place.

Turf

A turf path has a number of advantages. The initial cost of materials is comparatively low, and the construction requires no great degree of skill. And undoubtedly, green, luxuriant turf possesses a beauty and charm that are difficult to equal in other materials.

Turf paths may be readily established from seeding or, if immediate effect is desired and the much higher cost borne, sod may be laid. In either case the preliminary preparation of the ground is very much the same. If the soil is a medium or light sandy loam, no underdrainage will be necessary. If, however, the soil is of heavy clay texture or if the path is to be constructed in a low area that has poor natural drainage, some means of artificial drainage should be provided. A 6-inch perforated Polyvinyl Chloride (PVC) or tile drain laid 1 to 2 feet below the surface of the soil directly under the middle line of the path will usually prove entirely adequate. It will add greatly to the enjoyment of a turf walk that might otherwise be soggy and practically unusable after heavy rains or in the early spring when the frost is coming out of the ground. Instead of using drains, the channel can be filled with crushed stones or the soil may be excavated to a depth of 12 inches and a 6-inch layer of 2-inch crushed stones may be placed over the subsoil. A 6-inch layer of good topsoil should be placed above the crushed stones. This should be leveled off to the proper grade and then raked until it is finely pulverized. The first rolling will reveal any slight unevenness, which may then be corrected by subsequent rakings.

Where the path is to be seeded, approximately 1 pound of seed will be required per 30 square yards. Only seed of the highest quality should be used. Although clover has an unfortunate tendency to become rather slippery when it is wet, it resists wear and is very effective in stabilizing the crown; it is also drought tolerant and adds to soil fertility. If, however, grass alone is preferred, mixtures containing bluegrass, fescues, and redtop have proven useful and are more serviceable than bentgrass. The seed should be sown both lengthwise and crosswise on the path to get an even distribution. The ground should be rolled immediately after the seed is sown, as a firm seedbed is one of the secrets of success for this type of walk.

If the walk is sodded, great care should be taken to obtain sod of the best quality. The sod, which usually comes in long rolls, should be laid lengthwise with the path. After it is laid, the sod should be rolled and thoroughly soaked. It should not be allowed to dry out until it has become well established.

Interlocking Paving Stones

Interlocking paving stones for garden walks and driveways were first devised and produced in Europe in 1962. They proved so successful that many private and public garden administrators adopted them for use as a permanent outdoor floor covering. These stones are functional, are not slippery, and blend very well into the landscape.

The interlocking paving stones, which come in different colors, are made of compressed concrete and are manufactured in ordinary brick sizes. The evenly mixed aggregates produce a matte finish that prevents the stones from becoming slippery when wet. As a result, these paving stones are ideal for use on swimming pool decks and on sloping surfaces.

In the northeastern United States, the Z-shaped block paver has been increasingly used for malls, plazas, and sidewalks. The price range varies with the size, thickness, number, and color of edge units required. The 3¼-inch-thick stones

Interlocking concrete pavers

Surface view:

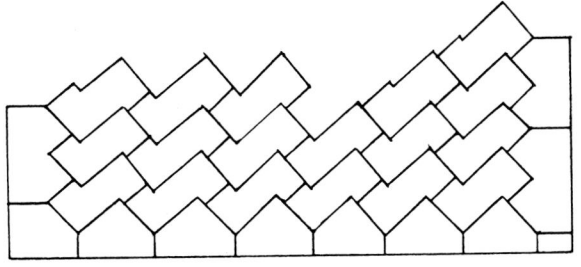

Cross section:

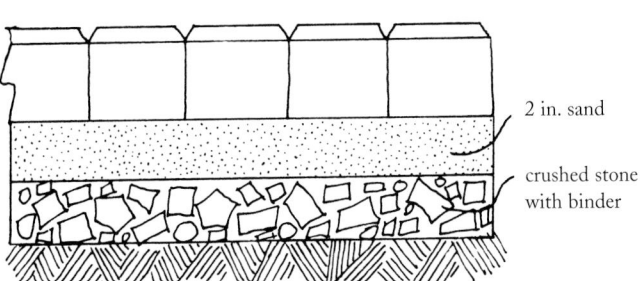

2 in. sand

crushed stone with binder

are especially good for vehicular traffic, while the 2½-inch-thick stones are adequate for pedestrian traffic. A paved area of this kind is frostproof if the underlying bed of sand and gravel is properly prepared to provide good drainage.

The ease with which **Z**-shaped blocks can be installed makes it feasible for the average homeowner to do this without professional help. To ensure a long-lasting paving job, however, the soil should be checked and the substructure designed in accordance with the ground conditions prevailing in the immediate area.

Construction of a path or drive with interlocking paving stones is straightforward. After excavating 6 inches below the intended finish grade, a 2-inch base of crushed stone and binder is spread, tamped, and wetted. This is overlaid with a 2-inch-thick layer of sand. The sand should be accurately sloped for desired pitches, and then it should be compacted. The brick-size pavers should then be laid directly on the sand, starting with the edging pieces. All interlocking pavers should be set at 45° angles to the path axis. They must be laid close-jointed, and their alignment should be checked periodically.

After the pavers are set, they should be about ¾ inch higher than required. At this point, they should be vibrated with a vibrator-compactor and worked down to the desired elevation. The joints of the pavers should be filled with sand that is first swept in and then hosed to settle.

Concrete

The familiar plain gray concrete of city sidewalks does not make for attractive garden paving; but with just a little additional effort and expense, concrete can become both useful and attractive. This can easily be accomplished if color, texture, and pattern are added to the basic mix. Earth colors are the safest, because greens and blues tend to fade and compete with foliage colors. New and different techniques can readily be combined with many styles of surface treatment today. For example, casting may be made with such patterns as burlap, reed mats, or the grain of weathered lumber. Sandblasting washed concrete with exposed aggregate surface, and plastering with pattern are other methods that can mellow the hard, dull look of concrete. These approaches to the use of concrete have gained wide acceptance among gardeners and landscape designers.

Several general requirements affect concrete surface finishes. The most important of these is the quality of the mix. For example, if the mix is too wet, the materials will tend to segregate, which leads to sand streaking, dusting, cracking, and discoloration. Conversely, too stiff a mix will impede workability at the corners and around patterns, and it may also result in undesirable honeycombing and roughness. The shape and thickness of the section, the complexity of the surface pattern, and the slope of the terrain all determine how workable the individual mix should be.

Paver patterns

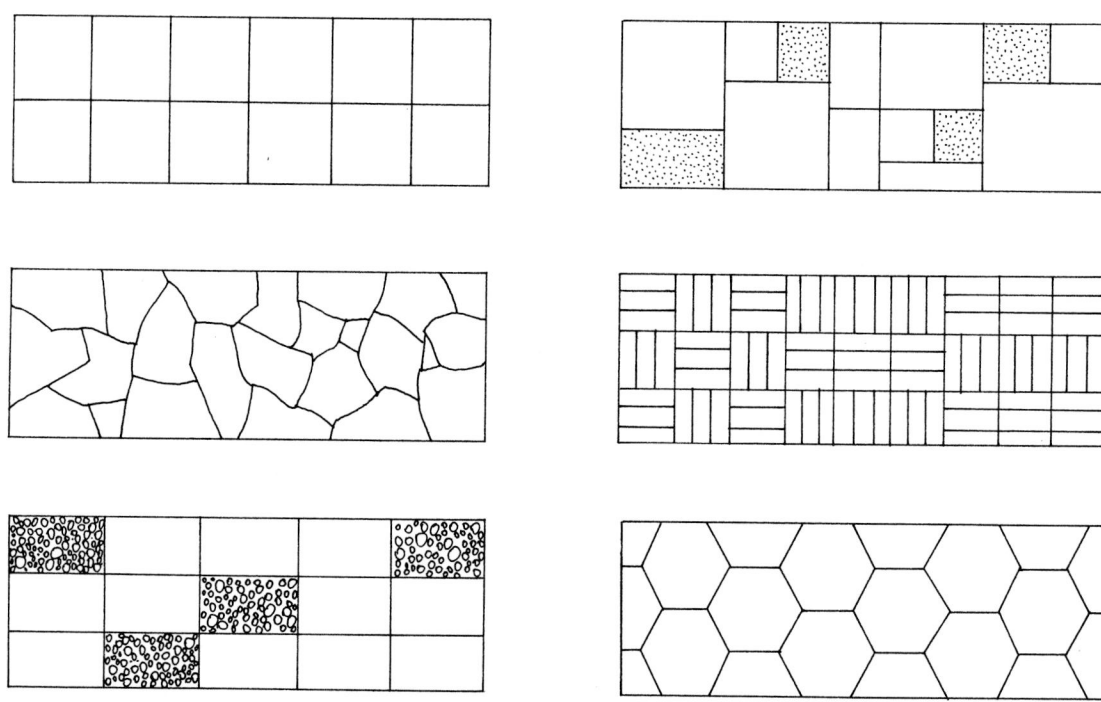

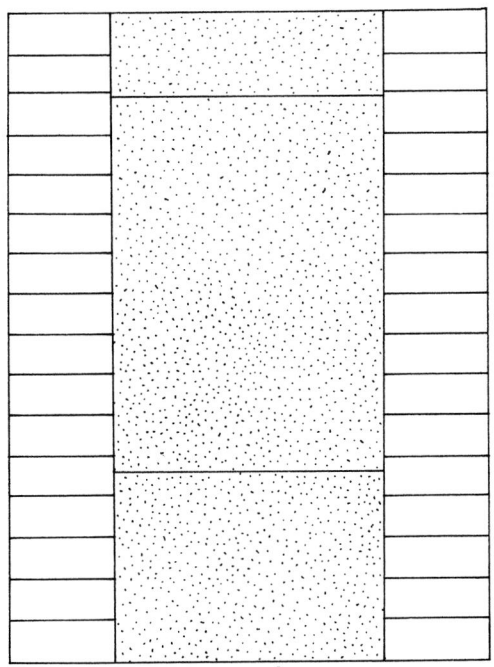

Concrete sidewalk widened with bricks

CONCRETE MIXES IN DIFFERENT PROPORTIONS FOR DIFFERENT PURPOSES

Purpose	Cement (parts)	Sand (parts)	Gravel (parts)
Foundations and footings	1	3	5
Walks	1	2½	4
Floors	1	2	4
Rough and smooth finishes	1	2	—

Edgings

The best method of keeping the margins of garden paths permanently neat is to build edgings or small curbs on each side of the path. Many materials may be used for marking the path and separating it from the garden beds. Bricks on edge, or on end, are appropriate for brick or gravel paths. The use of treated planks held at intervals with stakes is an effective method, particularly appropriate in an old-fashioned garden with gravel paths. Flagstones set on edge are appropriate with flagstone paving or gravel, while tile is interesting in an architectural garden. Metal strips are also sometimes used, and though not very attractive, they serve the purpose of keeping path edges neat and trim. Darkened zinc or aluminum is even more durable than steel and is unobtrusive. It is excellent for use between driveway and

lawn and also in geometric patterns of garden beds and paths.

Least expensive is plastic edging, which can prove satisfactory if well anchored at close intervals to prevent frost heaving and misalignment. However, as plastic becomes brittle at low temperatures and after long exposure to sun, it is less serviceable when subjected to frequent foot traffic. If heaved by frost, it is easily damaged by the lawnmower and other garden machinery.

GARDEN STEPS

As a change in levels in a garden necessitates a pleasant and easy transition from one level to another, garden steps may become an important landscape feature. Unless the steps are rustic in character, such as split logs, hewn landscape ties, or long heavy stones, they should rest on a foundation with footings below the frost line. The steps should be in harmony with the surrounding area and should be as broad as the path of which they are a part.

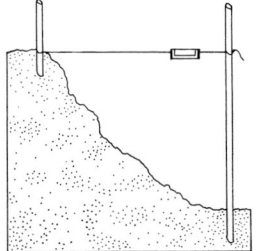

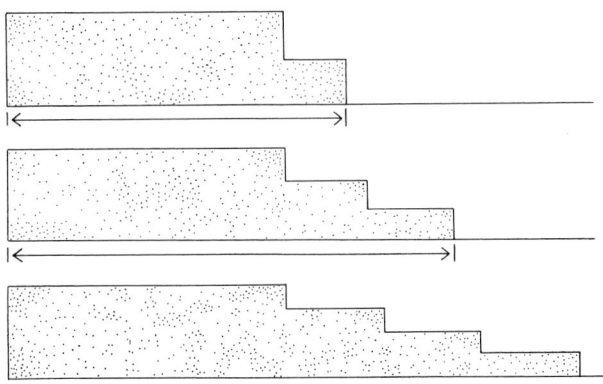

Tread and riser options

The angle of ascent of outdoor steps should be less steep than that of interior stairways. In general, the broader the tread, the lower the riser. In any case, treads should be constructed so that they pitch about ¼ inch toward the front so that the water will drain off readily after a rain.

Foundations

Foundations for stone or brick steps may be built of rubble masonry. Any irregular cast-off pieces of concrete or stone that are not easily used in finished masonry walls will be good enough for foundations. The stones are thrown in with enough mortar to hold them together. The footings must rest below the frost line. The foundation for concrete steps, or a wholly concrete foundation for stone or brick steps, need not be so solid. The concrete may be formed like a bridge and reinforced with steel rods. The top and bottom treads rest on footings below frost line, but the others are supported on the concrete slab cast between the supports. It is not necessary to excavate the earth between the supporting footings. On such a foundation, the stone, brick, or tile treads and risers are set on the concrete base with cement mortar.

The proper mixture for a concrete foundation is one part cement, two parts sand, and three parts aggregate—crushed stone in sizes from ¾ to 1 inch. The steel rods should be ⅝ inch in diameter, placed at intervals of 12 or 15 inches.

Step Arrangements

If at all possible, long, unbroken flights of steps should be avoided. If the difference in grade between the upper landing and the bottom is greater than 6 feet, a landing should be interposed. Do not use more than six steps between landings in a series of steps. Where feasible, a flight of steps should be recessed into a bank, as it will blend more harmoniously with the surrounding landscape and may not require handrails. Steps ascending a terrace held by a retaining wall may either project out from the wall or be recessed into the wall; or they may combine both of these arrangements, often with a landing at the wall itself. If the wall is high, the best arrangement is a flight of steps parallel to the wall, with landings near the top and bottom. Such a flight should have a hand railing of wrought iron, a balustrade, or a parapet.

Ramped Steps

Ramped steps are a series of gently sloping surfaces alternated with single steps. They are useful where the slope of the ascent is too steep for a path (10 percent or more), and not steep enough for a flight of steps. A 20 percent grade is about minimum for such steps. The risers are formed of narrow stones set on edge and sunk deeply into the ground. The treads or ramps are built of the same material as the pathways; flagstone or brick are most frequently used in this country. The narrow streets of hillside towns in Europe are often made into ramped steps, with stone risers and cobblestone ramps. A rustic path in a woodland is frequently stepped by placing logs across the path for the risers. Landscape ties are also good for this purpose.

The proper dimensions for ramped steps may be determined by establishing the distance between the risers at three normal paces, between 6 feet 3 inches and 8 feet, and

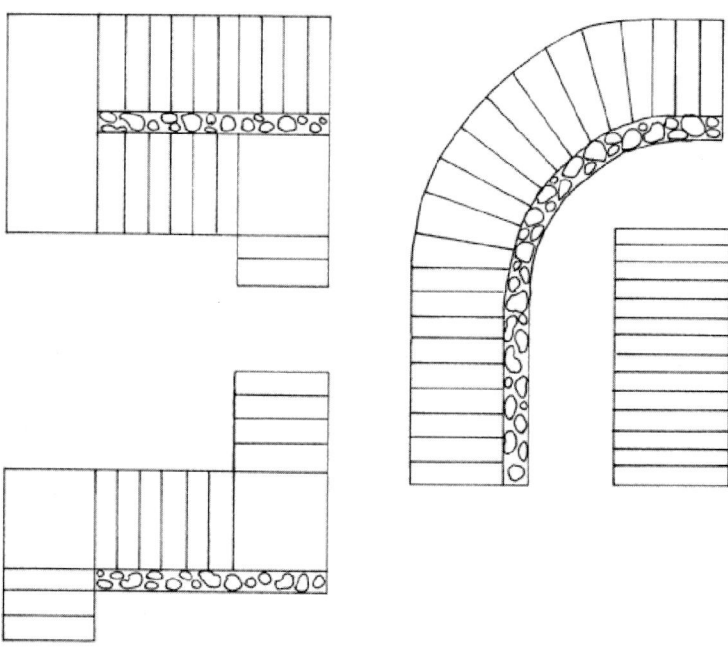

Making steps between levels on a steep slope.

the height of the riser from 3 to 5 inches. The slope of the ramp should not be greater than 20 percent. Obviously, the steeper the ramp and the higher the tread, the shorter the length of the ramp.

Construction of Garden Steps

> **Rule:** *All steps should be based on the length of the pace. Twice the riser plus tread is the length of a stride. For example, if your stride is 24 inches:*
>
> riser = 5 inches + 5 inches = 10 inches
> tread = 14 inches
> stride = 10 inches + 14 inches = 24 inches

1. Outdoor risers are usually lower than indoor ones and, therefore, have a wider tread than the steps within a building.
2. If the tread overhangs the riser by ½ to 1 inch, the steps create a neater appearance and also use less space; however, if the tread is set behind a riser of light-colored material, such as a dark bluestone tread behind a light gray Belgian block riser, the contrast helps define the limit of the step and thus is a help for those descending in dim light.
3. The riser of a step should rest on the tread of the preceding step; this is most important for steps built without the use of concrete.
4. Steps, like walks, should be built below ground level and should not protrude from the bank.
5. As previously mentioned, tread and landing should have a slight pitch to the front to ensure proper drainage of any surface water.
6. Riser and tread dimensions should remain the same throughout a series of steps. Varying dimensions upset the rhythm of one's gait and can be dangerous.
7. Steps should be sited and designed to avoid tight turns, which result in dangerous triangular treads.

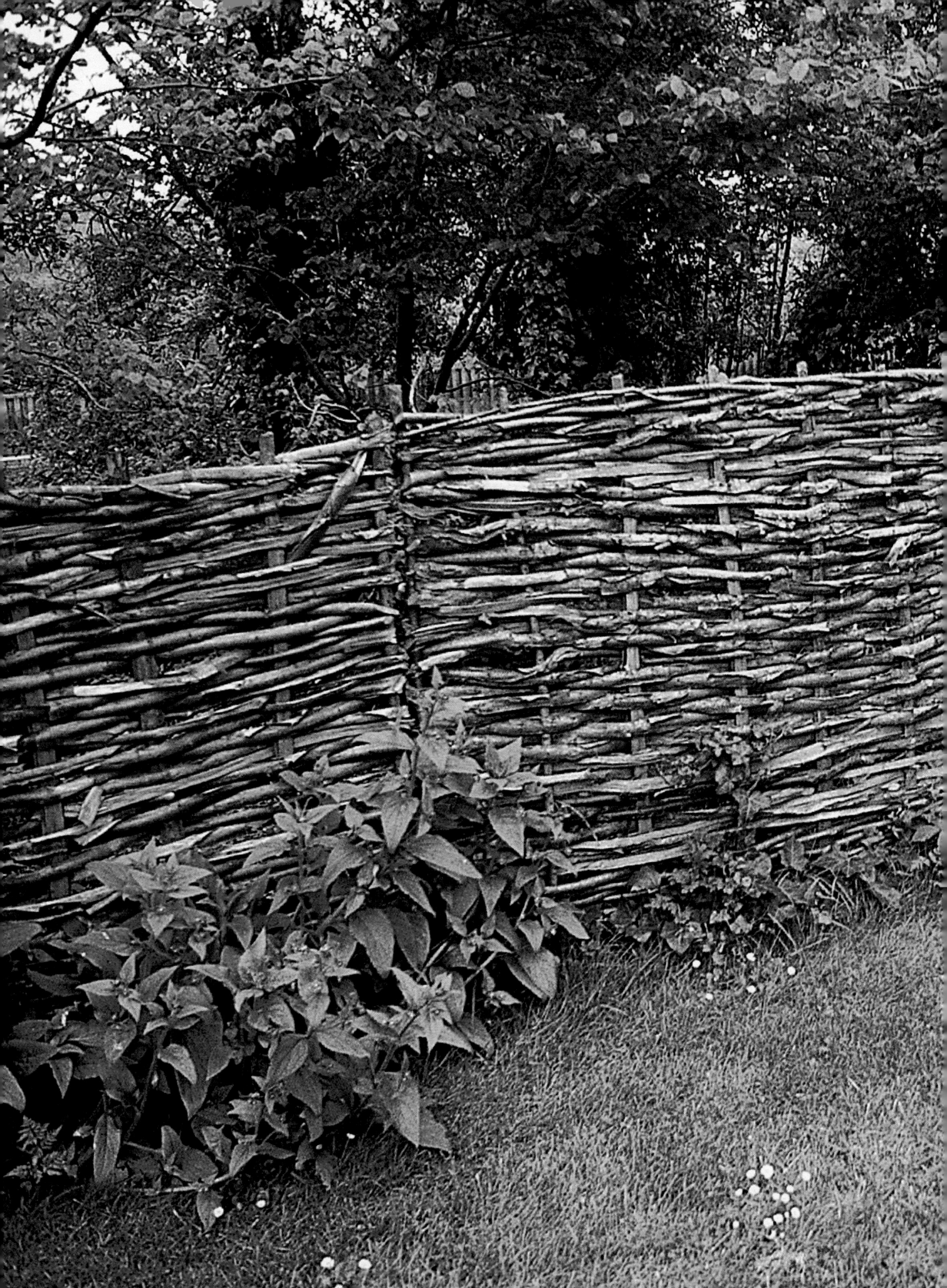

6

Fences

A FENCE IS AN ELEMENT OF THE LANDSCAPE CAPABLE of great variety of form and offers limitless possibilities for distinctive design. Today, fences have become backgrounds for much of our outdoor living.

Both as barriers and as ornaments, fences are conspicuous. As elements of design and as aids in the use of land, they are important and often indispensable. For the home owner who desires privacy, the fence provides a narrow linear screen and serves as a barrier against intrusion. Beyond these practical

In a wattle or basket-weave fence, slender flexible stems or strips of wood are woven in alternating courses between upright stakes, resulting in an opaque panel.

uses, a fence should be an expression of pure design, a frame for the grounds, and an architectural element that harmonizes with the house.

Materials and methods have brought about the designs of several distinctive types of fences. In certain regions the abundance of some good material has made a special type of fence structure typical of that locality. Thus the stone wall and the picket fence express New England; the zigzag rail fence, Virginia and Kentucky; the post-and-rail fence, Virginia; and the post-and-board fence, Pennsylvania and Maryland.

Today, transportation makes widely available materials other than those from local sources and has opened markets everywhere for the best materials, which in earlier times were used only in the regions of their origin. As a result, local tradition in fence design is no longer dominant. The decision as to the type of fence for a certain place is based primarily on considerations of strength, durability, appearance, and cost.

The practical attributes of a good fence are strength sufficient to hold its place against wind, durability (i.e., soundness after many years of exposure to weather), good appearance (the ability to remain neat and trim without much attention to maintenance), and economy of construction cost in relation to the life of the fence. A fence should be so firmly fixed in the ground that it will withstand many years of wind pressure and the effects of summer sun and winter freezing.

Posts should be set into the ground to a depth of 2½ to 3 feet for firm anchorage. In cold climates, the base of the post should be below the frost line to prevent heaving caused by freezing and thawing. Fences that are to serve as snow barriers should have an extra anchorage, such as a bracing second post slanting into the ground on the leeward side.

The backfilling of the earth around the posts, after they have been set in the hole, must be accompanied by firm tamping; any tendency to wiggle will be increased by the force of wind and weather. All fence corners should be cross-braced to provide additional strength.

Wood is the most generally available material for fences and is widely used for the enclosure of home properties. Metal is also used in the form of galvanized steel, wrought iron, and woven wire. For posts, wood, concrete, and steel are commonly used.

WOOD FENCES

There are many types of wood fences, some very simple in design and construction, others more elaborate. Regardless of the type, there are certain points that should be taken into

consideration: the durability of the wood selected, the setting of the posts, details of construction, and the upkeep of the fence.

When board fences or picket fences, except those of rustic type, are being constructed, the surfaces of the pickets and rails where they join one another and the surfaces of the rails and posts where they, in turn, join should be painted thoroughly before the fence is assembled. It is in these crevices that moisture is most apt to be retained, and the paint will provide protection against decay. At no later time can the painting of these particular spots be done so easily or so effectively. The extra labor required to do this will be more than repaid in the increased life of the fence.

Woods vary greatly in their durability. Some woods will give many years of service, while in certain climates other wood will last for only a few years under outdoor conditions. The durable woods are usually more expensive but prove to be the best investment in the end. It is poor economy to select a cheaper, less durable wood that will have to be replaced within a few years.

The decay of wood is caused principally by wood-destroying fungi. To live, these fungi must have favorable conditions, the important factors being moisture, air, warm temperature, and food. Food is supplied by the wood. If the temperature is too low, if the supply of air is inadequate, or if insufficient moisture is present, as in desert areas, the decay of wood is greatly retarded or does not occur. But in humid areas with mild climates, conditions are particularly favorable, and under certain circumstances, such as at the ground line, decay takes place rapidly. It is at this point that posts always decay, and only woods that are extremely rot resistant or that have been chemically treated should be used for fence posts.

Among the most durable woods are cypress, redwood, red cedar, arborvitae, white cedar, black locust, and sourgum. These woods contain oils that confer remarkable resistance to decomposition and are, therefore, recommended for posts. Because of very limited and diminishing supply, redwood should be resorted to in only the most extraordinary circumstances.

To increase its durability, wood may be treated with a chemical preservative. To be fully effective, the chemical should be applied under pressure so that deep penetration is obtained. In some cases, the entire post is treated; in other cases, the treatment extends only to well above the ground line, which is entirely satisfactory. In many cases, treated posts will sometimes prove the best choice, especially if the more durable woods are very costly or unobtainable.

For rails, pickets, palings, spindles, and panels, less durable woods may be used. Although redwood, cedar, and cypress will outlast them, such woods as pine, hemlock, spruce, and fir, even if untreated, will give many years of good service for these purposes, particularly if they are kept painted. For rustic fences black locust has few rivals, although cedar, redwood, and imported chestnut are sometimes used.

Split-Rail Fence

Split-rail fence

The "snake fence," or split-rail fence, is one of the most picturesque for open farmlands. It originated in Virginia in colonial times and is often called Virginia rail fence, though more properly Kentucky rail fence, because of its especially frequent use in that state. It is made of rails split from poles cut in the woods close at hand. Chestnut and ash were the favorite trees because their wood splits most easily. The rails were put together without nails or wire and were anchored only at the junctions by two slanting rails leaned against the junction of horizontal rails. A great deal of wood is required for the construction of this fence, but no other tool except the ax and no other materials are required. It is, therefore, the fence of the pioneer. As forests became depleted, various

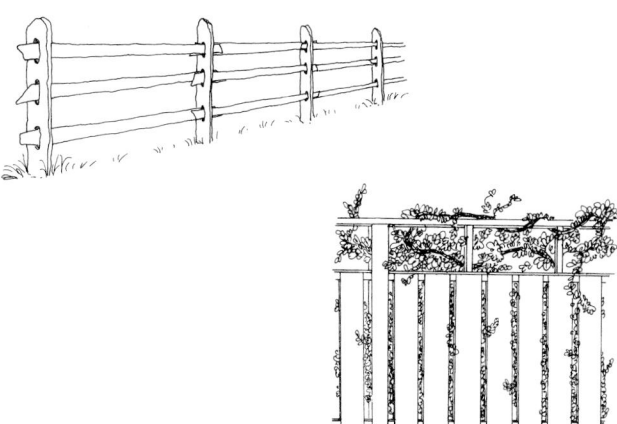

Top—*English hurdle fence*
Middle—*Post-and-rail fence*
Bottom—*Board fence*

Serpentine split-rail fence anchored with rocks

modifications of this fence were devised. One was the Virginia rail fence, with the rails laid end overlapping end in a straight line, their points of junction being kept upright by two posts set in the ground, one on each side, and wired together at the top. A later version of this is the post-and-rail fence, with three slots cut in the single post to receive the ends of the rails. Another was the stump fence, consisting of a row of pulled stumps and roots arranged as a crude barrier.

Post-and-Rail Fence

A very handsome pasture enclosure, the post-and-rail fence is suitable for the property lines of country residences. White cedar and black locust posts with large slots cut in them are erected at intervals of about 10 feet. The rails—half-round poles of the same wood as the posts, or a softer wood, and 11 feet long—are tapered to flat ends thrust through the slots in the posts. There are two sizes of posts, making two- or three-rail fences. It is an easy type of fence to erect and most satisfactory for its rugged appearance and durability. The weathering gives it a warm gray color, harmonizing well with the tones of the countryside.

Long-lasting reinforced concrete posts may be used instead of wood posts. When concrete posts are used, heavy planks are sometimes substituted for the split rails, contributing to a more finished appearance.

Hurdle Fence

Originally developed in England as a pasture fence, hurdle fencing is light, strong, and attractive and is excellent for use as a boundary fence on suburban properties of moderate size. It is picturesque, easily erected, and as easily moved; and it provides an excellent background for climbing roses and other vines. The panels come in 8-foot lengths at both 3- and 4-foot heights. They may be purchased already assembled or, at more moderate cost, in a knocked-down state ready for the home owner to put together. It is one of the quickest and easiest fences to erect. The sharpened posts are driven into the ground with a sledgehammer, and each panel is then pegged to the next. Longevity depends on the choice of wood.

Post-and-Board Fence

A post-and-board fence is framed on black locust, red cedar, or cypress posts erected at 10- or 12-foot intervals. Three or four horizontal rough boards 1 by 8 inches, or 1 by 6 inches, are nailed to the posts with wide spaces between them. A vertical 6-inch board covers the board ends against each post, and a 6-inch square board caps the post like a shed roof. Rough sawn pine boards are usually used. Whitewashed or, even better, painted white, this makes a very neat fence for a suburban property, especially one with a house of colonial architecture.

Post-and-board fence

A post-and-board fence with gate has squared pickets set at alternating heights. Painted white, it is especially suited to a colonial-style house on a small property.

Board Fence

With lattice top, the board fence is a very attractive type of fence and is appropriate for town yards, especially where the house is of colonial tradition; it may also be used as a garden enclosure. Many variations in design and proportion are possible. The posts are usually spaced about 10 feet apart, and several horizontal rails provide a framework to which the upright boards can be nailed. The lattice top, if strongly built, will provide a support for light, graceful vines, such as clematis and akebia. Wisteria should never be used for this purpose, as it is too rampant, and ultimately too heavy.

Louver Fence

The louver fence is a modification of the board fence, in which the boards are set at an angle to allow breezes through. It is used to achieve privacy and at the same time to provide for a good circulation of air. Fences of this type are very popular in hot climates, and they are also excellent for city gardens, where conditions are often not favorable for good air circulation. Sections of louver fences can be made so that they are adjustable and a slight push will control the breeze. Lightly constructed louver sections are often used as movable wind baffles and can be made into quite a decorative feature on a terrace or patio.

Woven Split Sapling Fence

The woven split sapling fence is rustic in character and makes an opaque screen. The construction is simple and strong. Posts are set at 10-foot intervals and are connected with two or three cedar rails. Panels of split saplings about

1½ inches wide, woven together with wire, are nailed to the rails, so that the finished fence is a continuous wall of rustic vertical lines. With the bark still on, the fence immediately has an old appearance, but with the bark stripped off, a year of mellowing will be required. Fences of this type are usually made of cedar, arborvitae, spruce, or imported French chestnut and are very durable. They may be obtained in various heights and provide an excellent barrier where complete privacy or protection is desired. They are manufactured at the mill and are shipped as panels with the requisite number of posts and rails.

Picket Fence

The picket fence has long been popular and has been used for the enclosure of town yards and gardens since colonial times. In the early New England villages, the white clapboard houses were grouped about the central green, and their dignified, spacious yards were always enclosed with picket fences. Within these enclosures flourished pleasant little flower gardens. Like the details of the houses, the fences were often designed with great distinction and gave an architectural expression to the house settings.

Picket fence with gate

The picket fence requires careful construction and the proper spacing of parts, as it expresses the qualities of rightness and precision. Great variation in design and proportion may be achieved.

The simplest type of picket fence has natural, round posts. The upper rail, a 2×4 set flat, rests on the top of the posts and is nailed to them. The lower rail, a 2×4 set on edge, is mortised into the face of the post and nailed. The pickets, ¾ by 3 inches or ¾ by 4 inches, are nailed to the outer side of the rails, and a picket covers each post.

Fences of more carefully studied design may have posts topped by turned finials. The shafts of such posts are of planed lumber, and the bases and caps have appropriate moldings. The pickets may also have specially designed tops. A fence of such finished carpentry should be supported by galvanized steel connectors mounted in concrete footings under the posts so that the base of the wood is several inches above the ground. This feature will greatly prolong the life of the fence, as there will be no ground rot. Fencing made of such materials may take on secondary, purely ornamental functions, such as supporting shelves for pots or planters of seasonally featured plants.

Rustic Picket Fence

The rustic picket fence has the same structural lines and general character as the picket fence but is less formal. Rustic pickets are made of split wood—usually arborvitae, cedar, or spruce—and the pickets should not be painted. In the popular stockade fence, the pickets are set in close order, forming a visual barrier.

Closely set natural pickets are wired together in this stockade fence, neatly capped with boards, to form a visual barrier and a backdrop for espaliered fruit trees.

Spindle Fence

The spindle fence is a refinement of the picket fence and is suitable for the formal dooryard or garden of a colonial mansion. The spindles are round in cross section, about 1¼ inches in diameter, and pass through holes in the rails at intervals of 5 to 7 inches. Variations from this are made by giving the fence a solid board base or even a third rail, 16 inches above the lower rail, and filling the space with a lattice of square bars in diamond pattern—the round spindles extend from the intermediate rail through the upper rail.

Such a fence with graceful fenceposts is in keeping with the careful carpentry required for ornamental cornices and pediments.

Snow Fence

The snow fence consists of lath pickets held in place by woven horizontal galvanized wires and fastened to metal posts driven into the ground. Used as a winter precaution, such fences are erected at a distance of 50 or 75 feet from the road, toward the prevailing wind; they create enough obstacles to cause snow or sand to form drifts in the lee close to the fence and not in the road. They may be used for various other temporary purposes, such as to surround play yards or dog runs. The life of the lath is usually about 10 years.

Lattice Fence

The lattice fence is most closely associated with the French style of garden art, for the French developed the intricate lattice patterns used in trellises. Very simple lattices were used in colonial gardens as supports for vines, particularly climbing roses. Painted white to harmonize with the frame house or the white trim of a brick or stone structure, the lattice is a fine-textured adjunct of formal design.

Lattice fencing imparts elegance to the garden and serves as a support for hanging baskets as well as a backdrop for tubbed specimens.

Chinese Lattice Fence

Used in California with much distinction, the Chinese lattice fence has large patterns of irregularly spaced rectangular openings. Only a few of the horizontal bars extend to both sides of the panel. The resulting design is balanced but informally asymmetrical. When used in combination with translucent plastic, it makes a pleasing background for flowering plants and also provides protection from the wind.

Grape Stake Fence

A rustic structure used around many small homes, especially in certain sections of California, the grape stake fence is reminiscent of early pioneer days. The stakes are driven into the ground close together, forming a sort of miniature stockade. The tops are cleated together with stakes placed horizontally, or a little on the slant. The tops of the stakes are not cut back to an even saw line, and the effect is very casual. Its great advantages are that the materials are inexpensive, its erection requires a minimum of skill, and it will last for many years. Locust, cedar, or treated pine are the woods most commonly used. The height may be varied to suit the desires of the owner.

Basket-weave Fence

The basket-weave fence is becoming increasingly popular and has much to recommend it. It consists of thin strips of wood woven horizontally between upright supports. The fencing is made up in panels of several heights, ranging from 4 to 8 feet. It is lightweight, easily erected, and comparatively inexpensive. It forms an excellent screen, providing complete privacy and protection, yet it permits some circulation of air. The modern basket-weave fence is made of

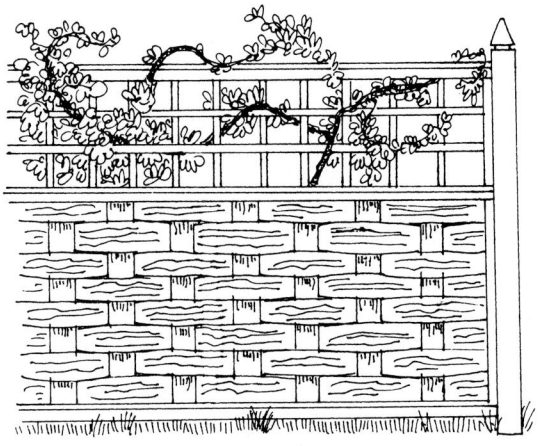

Basket-weave fence with lattice top

various woods and is available in preassembled sections of 8-foot lengths in both 6- and 8-foot heights. It is simple to install and very durable.

FENCES OF OTHER MATERIALS
Bamboo Fence

Bamboo fencing is versatile, durable, and pleasantly novel, whether of open or closed design, and employs cylindrical poles (or culms) and sometimes narrow slats set vertically and/or horizontally. Wires or dowel inserts join structural sections and ornamental ties fasten rails to posts, the latter supported by pipe set in concrete. The special texture imparted by bamboo makes it appealing throughout the year.

Plastic Fence

Post fences with top and bottom rails can be finished with sheets of translucent polyethylene plastic. This is one of the least attractive types of fence but is inexpensive and requires little skill in its erection.

Because the plastic soon sags and deteriorates and becomes tattered, even if made with a fiber reinforcement, this kind of fencing should be reserved for short-term applications. More substantial plastic mesh fencing, as is used around construction sites, is similarly unattractive, even if obtained in subdued colors, as the persistent gloss is intrusively conspicuous.

Canvas Fence

The canvas fence is best adapted to dry climates or for use where temporary protection from wind or from the public gaze is desired. The construction requires posts with top and bottom rails in between. The sheets of canvas are laced to the posts and rails. The ropes should be loosened in wet weather and tightened on sunny days. Such a fence has a certain novelty and charm when used in appropriate surroundings, as in the environs of an informal summer home.

Chain-link Fence

Made of galvanized steel and often used (in some cases required by local code) for swimming pool enclosures, the ubiquitous, undeniably sturdy, extremely durable chain-link fence is so utterly without aesthetic merit in the garden setting that a special effort should be made to disguise its presence. This may be accomplished by painting all parts flat black or brown (never green, which only renders it more conspicuous) or by encouraging adjacent hedging or other shrubs to grow through it, or by using it to support climbing roses or other woody climbers.

Woven-Wire Fence

The utilitarian woven-wire fence, whatever the mesh interval, may be the fence with the lowest initial cost, but unless it is pulled taut between posts and supported with a top wire of heavier gauge, it soon sags and deteriorates. Under the best of circumstances, such fencing, left unconcealed, detracts from the charm of the garden.

If it is necessary to use a woven-wire fence, its appearance can be greatly enhanced by training English ivy through the mesh. If this is faithfully pursued, the fence, if supported with steel stakes at 3-foot intervals, will eventually become a wall of solid dark green foliage and sufficiently rigid to support itself as an ivy hedge.

Temporary low fencing for seasonal exclusion of rodents and dogs can be removed and stacked for storage when no longer required. This fence usually consists of 18- to 24-inch sections of galvanized hardware cloth, which is mounted on light wood frames, 4 to 6 feet long, and wired to wood posts driven at requisite intervals. Such modular fencing is useful in spring for use around newly planted vegetable and flower gardens or simply to protect a specimen shrub or a newly seeded patch of lawn.

Live Basket-weave Fence

The live basket-weave fence is a "living" barrier, which is made of 4- to 5-foot long rooted saplings of hornbeam, hawthorn, willow, and the like. They are planted in a row 6 inches apart and woven into each other at a 45° angle. Eventually, the overlapping stems and branches will grow together to form a strong, impassable barrier. An annual pruning and shaping of the side branches will be necessary.

MAINTENANCE OF FENCES

Wood fences, except those of rustic character, require periodic painting.

All surfaces of new wood fences should have two primer coats of paint and one finish coat, preferably before assembly. Repainting should be done *before* the paint has worn off and the wood has become exposed to the weather. The intervals between paintings will depend somewhat on the climate and also on the quality of the paint and of the workmanship that goes into the job.

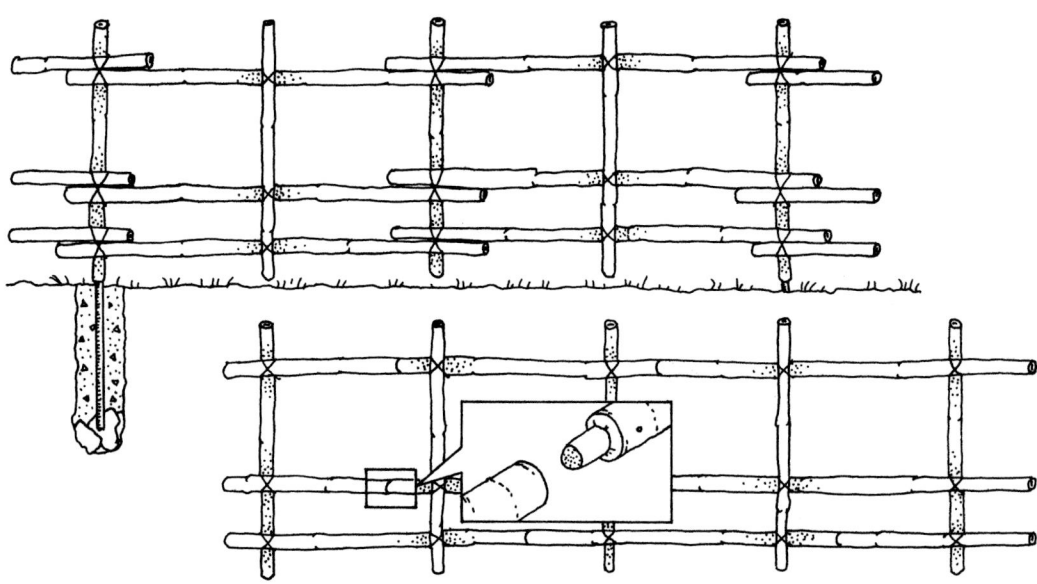

Methods of anchoring and joining bamboo fencing

All iron work should receive a coat of special rust-resisting paint before it is erected and should be repainted about every three years.

A periodic close inspection of fences is a good practice. One broken picket will spoil the appearance of a fence; a few minutes of work with a hammer, saw, and paintbrush will restore the rhythm and avoid the suggestion of shabbiness.

Posts occasionally weaken and should be tamped firmly into place, or if decay has set in, they should be replaced before the fence is allowed to sag out of place.

elements should be part of the gate's design and presentable in themselves. On a small property, gates should be treated as an important ornamental accessory. Their design requires care and attention to detail, not only with respect to the gate itself but also in regard to hinges, latches, and the gate stop.

As it can often be annoyingly inconvenient to close and latch a gate, various more or less automatic devices may be considered, ranging from a self-closing gravity gate mounted on slanting posts or hung on lift hinges to any of a number of more elaborate, often ingeniously idiosyncratic designs.

GATES

Gates provide access from one part of the property to another or into an adjoining parcel, or they may be part of a screen for a service area. In any case, gates should be attractive as well as functional. Their design should reflect the architecture of the house, the fence or enclosure of which they are a part, and of course, their specific purpose.

The material for construction of gates is essentially that of fences. Locust hinge-and-latch posts are among the longest lasting and, if set deeply enough or anchored in concrete, will resist the shock of repeated passage and closure. Usually the gate is enhanced and becomes more a part of the landscape if its posts are graced with an orb or ornamental finial.

Gates should be presentable from both sides, especially if passage is to be from either side. Ideally, the structural

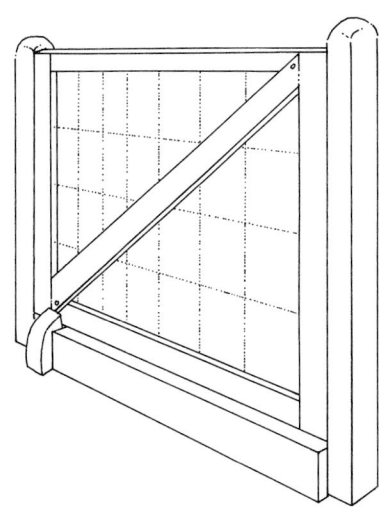

Lift gate, hinged on right, with wooden base catch on left

The ultimate material for elegant, long-lasting fences and gates, wrought iron is heavy but extremely durable and can be formed into delicate, graceful patterns. Here the elegance is enhanced with statuary busts atop the capped brick gateposts.

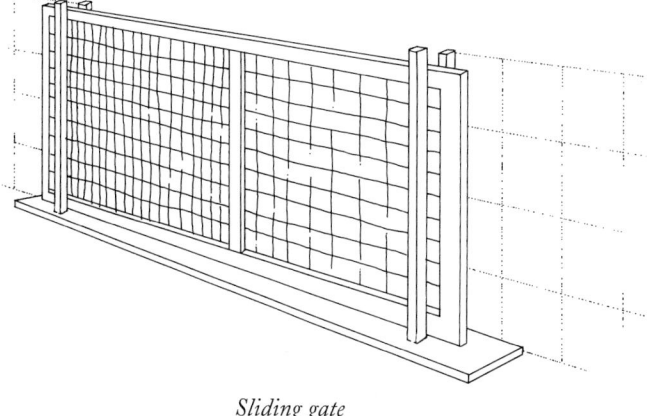

Sliding gate

Stile built as a wide stairway on both sides of fence

7

Hedges

T HE HEDGEROW HAS BEEN A FAMILIAR FEATURE OF THE landscape in Europe since medieval times. But the hedge itself antedates the medieval garden. The ancient Romans used hedges of myrtle, laurel, and box in their gardens. Indeed, so important a feature was the hedge in gardens of this period that the gardener who cared for it and kept it faithfully trimmed to the desired form and height was given the dignity of a special title, being known as "topiarius."

A low hedge, bevelled by shearing, frames the riotous exhuberance of this superlatively bright garden like a picture, cleanly separating it from the surrounding carpetlike lawn and providing horizontal contrast to the lofty trees beyond.

The designers of the Italian villas used hedges of holly, box, and cypress as great walls of green and made them architecturally important components of the design. The French gave the hedge even greater scale to conform to their vast estates by using large trees, such as elm, linden, hornbeam, and beech, trimming them to vertical form. In England, hedges played an important part in the design of the knot gardens, laid out in geometric patterns. Sometimes the spaces within the hedges were flower beds, but more often they were bits of turf. Herb gardens were frequently designed in this style, each plot being planted to a single herb, and the whole forming a pleasing pattern. In the gardens that surround the Elizabethan manor houses of England, there are magnificent yew hedges that were planted more than 400 years ago and that have been carefully tended throughout the years.

The primary purpose of a hedge is enclosure. The second is shelter from the wind, and the third is protection and privacy. In designing a landscape, the hedge is one of the best means of enclosing a formal area and separating it from the outer world. Not only does a hedge enclose and frame the garden but it may also frame the scenes within the garden and provide a background for flowering plants. It would be difficult indeed to find a more satisfying background for masses of bright flowers than the deep green of an evergreen hedge. The hedge is interesting enough in texture but is not conspicuous or obtrusive.

Tall, parallel slab-sided privet hedges form a corridor that directs attention to the vista beyond.

Furthermore, a hedge has the great attribute of permanence. It fixes the major lines of the design. It establishes the background for the garden, against which the succession of color and mass moves in ever-changing sequence. The hedge is not changeless in itself but grows in a slower cycle and thereby imparts an air of stability to the scene. It even invites confidence. By its continued existence, it links the past with the present. Season after season garden flowers come and go, generation after generation those who care for the garden come and go—but the hedge remains.

TYPES OF HEDGES

Hedges vary in size from small edging plants hardly 1 foot in height to towering trees. They may be extremely formal in outline, being trimmed to even surfaces and regular lines, or they may be natural in growth, with billowing masses of foliage and a profusion of flowers. Every kind of hedge has its own particular adaptation.

The width of a hedge is not always easy to predict. Theoretically, most hedges can be kept at any desired dimension of height or width. In actual practice, however, it is not always possible to do this, for the plants do grow and must be allowed to make some growth each year or they will suffer both in vigor and appearance. It is essential that adequate space be allowed for the eventual spread of a hedge. One occasionally sees box hedges, originally planted beside the garden paths to edge the flower beds, that have grown so wide that they entirely overshadow the path.

Hedge materials may be derived from many sources: from deciduous trees of naturally thick growth, branching close to the ground, from evergreen trees that have a fine texture and closely massed foliage, from deciduous shrubs that have dense foliage and make vigorous growth, from evergreen shrubs, from herbs, and from vines that may be trained to grow on a frame of any desired shape. But to be satisfactory as a hedge plant, a tree or shrub must meet certain very definite requirements. It must possess thick foliage of fine texture growing from numerous growth points or tips; it must be capable of even growth, it must produce branches and foliage close to the ground, and in the case of trimmed formal hedges, it must have the ability to withstand repeated cutting and regenerate growth from behind cut ends.

In places where high winds are frequent, as is the case shores and in mountains, the moderating effect of a windbreak established on the windward side of a plot can determine the kinds of plants one can grow successfully. While walls or solid fences can deflect wind near the ground, tall shrubs and densely branched low trees are more effective as high screens. A 12- to 15-foot barrier planting of autumn olive (*Eleagnus umbellata*) or sea buckthorn (*Hippophae rhamnoides*) will cut the wind velocity 50 percent or more up to 75 feet away on the leeward side. Such a reduction facilitates both flower and vegetable gardening by obviating desiccation and breakage.

PLANTING

As the roots of hedge plants are bound to be crowded, it is important to have the soil well prepared before planting. For soil of average fertility, the addition of well-rotted manure at the rate of 1 ton for 200 linear feet is recommended. If manure is not available, comparable amounts of compost, peat moss, or other well-decomposed organic matter should be worked into the soil. Since hedge plants are to form a dense wall of green, the individual plants should grow so closely that they are not distinguishable in the general mass. The plants are, therefore, set much closer together than in the usual shrub border. There should be good light and air on each side of the hedge to make up for this deficiency in the interior. A hedge placed too close to a wall not only looks out of place but seldom does well. Hedges under trees are rarely successful. When the inevitably crowded roots of a hedge must compete with tree roots, it is impossible for the hedge to obtain necessary light, water, and nutrients for vigorous growth and development. For example, privet hedges that thrive in the open become weak and spindly where they pass under trees, especially those species with dense, superficial root mats. A few hedge plants such as *Taxus cuspidata* (Japanese yew) and *Ilex glabra* (inkberry) can be exceptions, as they grow reasonably well in the shade of deeply rooted trees but do weaken if deprived of nutrients.

During the planting, a trench should be opened to a depth approximately equal to the depth of the balls of earth or, in the case of plants that are not balled, to the depth of the root system. After the plants have been spaced in the trench, each individual plant should be adjusted for depth and the earth should be filled in around it, as in any planting operation. A tape stretching along the side of the trench will aid in the correct spacing of the plants. Care should be taken to see that the plants are in an absolutely vertical position and in line with each other. The usual watering and trimming should follow planting.

PROTECTING THE GARDEN FROM ENCROACHING HEDGE ROOTS

Some of the more vigorous hedge plants have root systems that reach out long distances in search of the soil nutrients they require to sustain growth and abundant foliage. Privet is especially notorious in this respect, and for this reason it is a bad neighbor for the flower border. The bush honeysuckles, the viburnums, and the lilacs have similarly wide-ranging roots.

Although scarcely a hedge or topiary, evenly spaced pairs of clipped shrubs, even at a distance, introduce a note of formality and suggest the existence of a walk and stairs linking one level to the next.

If close proximity of such hedges to flower beds is unavoidable, then it is wise to interpose a barrier between them. One device is to dig a trench along the garden side of the hedge 18 inches deep and as wide as the spade. Fill the trench with rocks and a lean mixture of concrete—about one part cement, three parts sand, and five parts coarse aggregate (gravel or crushed stone). Alternatively, overlapping lengths of sheet aluminum or fiberglass can work effectively. Although such a barrier will keep the roots from intruding into the garden, it will be necessary to watch for surface roots hurdling over it through accumulating humus. A possible modification of this scheme, especially when on a slope, is to have the soil level within the enclosure higher than that outside. Generally, no precaution need be taken against the roots of box, arborvitae, or junipers because their roots are confined closely under the plant in a dense mat.

CARE

Untrimmed hedges require no more care than any ordinary planting of the same material. A hedge that is to be trained to a certain form, however, requires periodic care. In establishing a new hedge, it is advisable to cut back annual growth by about one-half until the ultimate desired height and width have been obtained. Such treatment encourages dense branching and the strongest possible structure for the new hedge. Formal hedges should have one clipping or more each year, depending the type of material used. Yew, arborvitae, and hemlock may be kept in excellent condition with one trimming a year, although two clippings are sometimes given. Privet should have three or four clippings a season, being trimmed whenever it has outgrown its prescribed size. Box and lilacs require but one clipping; beech, one clipping—never more.

Good hedge forms

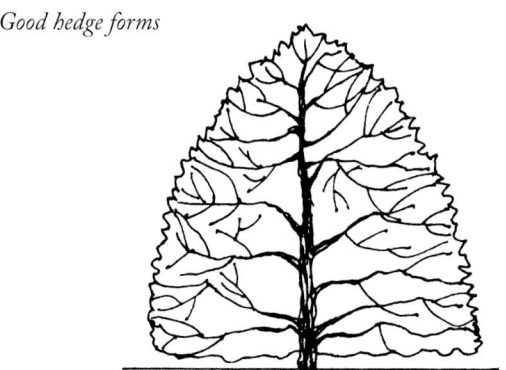

Hemlock, Japanese yew

Mugo pine, Japanese barberry

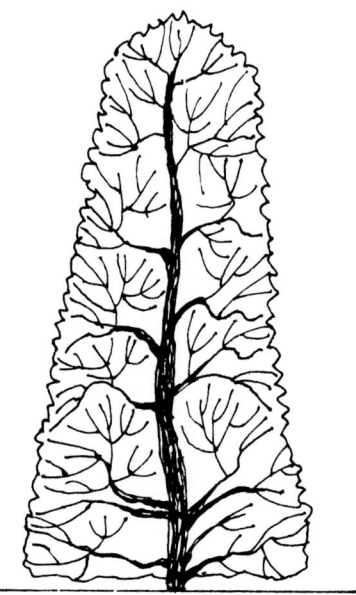

Beech, Hornbeam

Japanese yew (spreading form), Regel's privet

Privet form

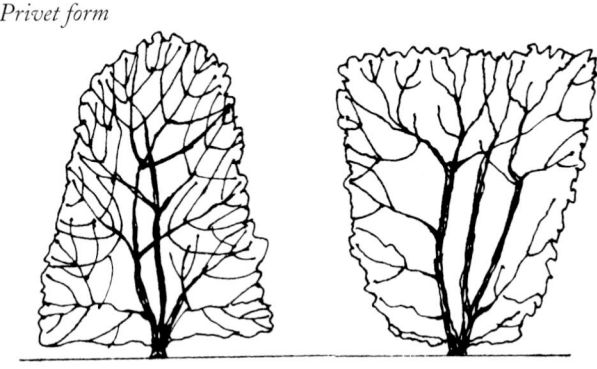

Good form: lower branches *Poor form: lower branches shaded*
get sunlight *by upper ones*

The purpose of trimming is to keep the hedge thick and neat and within bounds. Sometimes an informal hedge may be trimmed lightly to help thicken the mass of foliage. For most evergreen hedges, a summer trimming is usual. In this case, trimming should be done after growth has practically ceased. Lilac hedges should be trimmed in June, after flowering but before the next year's buds are set. Box hedges are best sheared in August.

As for tools, a number of excellent electric hedge trimmers are available; these are of great merit if extensive hedges are to be kept trimmed. The blades are set in a series, cutting much as do the blades of a hay mower, and the work can be done rapidly and efficiently. Ladders on wheels are a great aid to clipping high hedges; sometimes a scaffolding becomes necessary. For small, low hedge lines, the venerable manual hedge shears remains the tool of choice.

A taut line of string set at the desired height of the hedge and attached to stakes on either end will serve as a precise guide while clipping and will ensure a neat and straight planting. It is good to use a line level—a simple device available in hardware stores—to ensure that the string guide is level. It is important to avoid clipping a hedge to a shape that is narrow at the base and wider at the top; this will result in undue shading below and eventual weakening (or even drying) of the lower branches. The ideal shape is a base several inches wider than the top, with the sides sloping gradually in from the ground up.

Hedges of regular and geometric outline require more frequent clipping than do the simpler forms. The trimming of hedges into definite forms and shapes is very time-consuming and requires endless patience and much practice. Few things make a garden look more neglected than a formal hedge reverting to the wild state.

The general care of hedge plants does not differ appreciably from the usual gardening routine. An occasional cultivation is beneficial and prevents the intrusion of large weeds or sapling trees. Nothing spoils the beauty of a hedge more surely than seedling trees that have been allowed to grow up beside it, or within it. At first such seedlings are unnoticed, but by the time they emerge through the top of the hedge, they are difficult to get rid of, and their removal may create an unsightly gap in the hedge. If left unattended, such hedgerow intruders quickly overwhelm and eventually replace the hedge that protected them. Hence the strangely straight lines of mixed species of trees around old, long-neglected houses.

A yearly application of a mulch of well-rotted manure, preferably in the autumn, not only will increase the fertility of the soil but will afford protection to the roots during the winter. Box hedges respond remarkably well to an application of humus. This should be worked into the soil along the two sides of the hedge just outside of the readily evident mass of superficial roots. To rejuvenate an old box hedge that has suffered from neglect, the soil should be trenched along each side at the outer edge of the roots. The soil should be removed to a depth of about 15 inches and the trench refilled with a mixture of humus and topsoil. The amount of humus will depend on the quantity available; any proportion up to one part humus to one part topsoil will be satisfactory—the more humus the better.

Severe winter weather may kill back box and even privet, sometimes to the ground. However, such injury can often result in a lower, denser hedge, especially if care is taken in early spring to cut the entire hedge back to stubs so that all the shrubs rejuvenate together.

THE HA-HA

The ha-ha, a walled ditch, excludes large animals.

Where circumstances permit, especially when the visual barrier imposed by a hedge, fence, or wall is unwanted, but the intrusion of dogs and other large animals is also unwelcome, you might want to consider a ha-ha. This is essentially a ditch about 5 feet deep, dug around the area to be isolated, with a vertical face of stone, brick, or treated landscape ties on the side facing the tract to be protected. Once popular in England, the device was named for the exclamation supposedly emitted by one first encountering the recessed barrier. Unmarked, a ha-ha can indeed be hazardous, but a parallel planting, such as a very low hedge, can serve to warn those approaching the hidden drop.

A ha-ha, separating pasture from lawn and serving as a below-grade barrier to cows.

PLEACHING

Pleaching is the interweaving of branches of large shrubs or low trees to form a dense foliage mass or canopy. The process, which involves pruning, bending, tying, and interlacing, is sometimes called plashing. Especially suited for such directed growth are subjects with tough, elastic twigs and stems. Trunks or main stems are planted equidistant and are kept clean and as straight as possible. Branches are encouraged to grow in level planes and spread toward and intermingle with those of adjacent subjects, which are similarly treated. Wires or cords are sometimes used to hold young branches in place for a year or two. Trees that tend to grow too tall are topped to encourage lateral growth of trained branches. Often the intertwined branches of adjacent trees will form natural grafts, thus contributing to a continuous foliar ceiling. Although once popular in the grand gardens and estates of Europe, extensive pleaching is rarely seen today because of the time required to create and maintain the effect. However, if undertaken on a modest scale with relatively small, pliant material, the result can be a dramatic complement to the formal garden. Species especially suitable for this treatment include *Carpinus betulus* (European hornbeam), *Crataegus* species (especially *C. phaenopyrum*, Washington thorn), *Fagus sylvatica* (European beech), *Platanus × acerifolia* (London plane or sycamore), *Pyrus calleryana* (Callery pear), *Pyrus communis* (common pear), and *Tilia cordata* (littleleaf linden).

TOPIARY

Another specialty outgrowth of hedgework is topiary, which is the pruning and/or training of plant material into unnatural geometric or fantastic shapes. Still to be seen in some large formal gardens in England and Continental Europe, little is found in the United States, apart from the rather crude results of shearing fast-growing plants or inducing English ivy to grow over a preformed wire template.

In its simplest form, topiary consists of repetitively clipping and shaping the end plants of a hedge into globes, piers, or pyramids or of accenting a clipped hedge at intervals, perhaps to produce an orb on a squared base, thus breaking up an expanse of hedging.

More challenging topiary involves years of patiently pruning and guiding growth into cubes, balls, and pyramids or into such figures as chickens, rabbits, and dogs, or even giraffes and elephants. Such ambitious projects should be undertaken only if one has the considerable time required and has a formal garden setting necessary for the effective display of the resulting shapes and figures.

The best materials for topiary are *Buxus sempervirens* (box) and *Taxus* species and cultivars (yew). Also suitable, especially for large specimens, are *Carpinus betulus* (European hornbeam), *Crataegus* species (hawthorns), *Fagus sylvatica* (European beech), *Ligustrum* species (evergreen privets), and *Tsuga caroliniana* (Carolina hemlock).

A wide range of architectural and sculptural forms find expression in topiary.

Hedge shrubs of box trained into cubes, arches, orbs, and other shapes.

Great topiary specimens surround beds of summer annuals.

A tall spiral topiary, achieved through many years of careful clipping and shearing.

A great topiary dinosaur appears to saunter through flower beds to a fountain.

A topiary garden of yews trained into architectural forms.

ESPALIER

Espalier is a method of training woody plants, especially dwarf fruit trees, to regularly spaced or geometrically arranged supports. Usually, these supports are horizontal, vertical, or diagonal wires mounted on a wall or building. The term *espalier* may also be applied to the plant being trained or to the support.

The practice, which is much more common in Europe than in the United States, has the advantage of saving space, since the tree is essentially restricted to a single plane of development. Thus grown, espaliered trees require close and frequent attention, both to tie new growth to supports and to prune away unwanted stems. Since all parts of the espaliered tree have the same exposure to sunlight, fruit crops are usually generous. Fruit may be damaged, however, by chafing against supports or walls or by the high temperatures that may be radiated from the wall surface.

HEDGE SHRUBS OF SPECIAL MERIT

Name	Zones	Height Unpruned	Pruned	Spacing	Exposure*	Comments
Abelia × grandiflora (glossy abelia)	6–8	5–6'	3–4'	4'	S to PSh	Evergreen to half-evergreen; white flowers June to frost; may die back in severe northern winters; requires annual pruning of dead wood; best if used in natural unsheared form
Berberis × mentorensis (Mentor barberry)	5–8	5–6'	3–4'	3'	S to PSh	Half-evergreen, thorny, of even growth; yellow flowers in spring; sets no fruit; no special requirements
B. thunbergii (Japanese barberry)	4–8	5–7'	3–5'	3'	S	Deciduous; densely thorny; may be sheared low; yellow flowers in spring; conspicuous red berries persist in fall; tolerates urban conditions; becomes rangy and thin in shade; may be moved bare root; many purple-leaf and dwarf cultivars, the latter good for low hedges
Buxus sempervirens 'Suffruticosa' (dwarf or edging box)	6–8	3–6'	½–1½'	½–1½'	S to PSh	Evergreen; small glossy leaves; rounded, puffy habit; may be kept as low as 6 inches; best grown in acid soils of the East and South; may die back in severe winters
Cotoneaster divaricatus (spreading cotoneaster)	4–7	5–6'	3–4'	2½'	S to PSh	Deciduous to half-evergreen to evergreen; naturally spreading but easily trimmed to hedge habit; red berries in fall; thrives in average soil but tolerant of poor conditions
Euonymus alata 'Compacta' (burning bush)	4–8	5–10'	4–8'	3'	S to PSh	Deciduous; notable for brilliant red fall foliage, especially in full sun; twigs and stems often have conspicuous corky ridges; very adaptable
Ilex crenata 'Convexa' (compact Japanese holly)	5–7	6–8'	3–5'	3'	S to Sh	Evergreen; all plants bear black berries; suffers dieback at −20°F
I. crenata 'Microphylla' (littleleaf Japanese holly)	5–7	5–10'	2–3'	3'	S to Sh	Evergreen; fine-textured glossy foliage retained to base of shrub; slow growing and easily kept as low as 1 foot; cv. 'Helleri' is similar
Laurus nobilis (Grecian laurel)	7–10	20–30'	6–8'	4'	S to PSh	Evergreen; large glossy leaves impart coarse texture, hence not suitable for shearing or as low hedge
Ligustrum amurense (Amur privet)	3–7	8–12'	4–8'	3'	S to Sh	Deciduous to half-evergreen; glossy foliage; heavily fragrant white flowers in summer followed by black berries; as overused in the North as the similar but usually evergreen *L. sinense* (Chinese privet) is in the South
Pittosporum tobira (Japanese pittosporum)	8–10	10–12'	4–8'	4'	S to PSh	Evergreen; glossy dark green foliage (edged white in cv. 'Variegata'); best used as an informal unsheared hedge plant
Pyracantha coccinea (firethorn)	6–9	10–15'	4–8'	3'	S to PSh	Evergreen to half-evergreen; thorny; of diffuse, rangy habit unless sheared annually; clustered cream flowers in spring followed by persistent red-orange to yellow-orange fruit; the reliably hardy cv. 'Lalandei' is best in zones 6 and 7
Rosa rugosa (rugosa rose)	2–7	4–6'	2–3'	2'	S	Deciduous; thorny stems; rose purple to white flowers in summer, followed by red fruit (hips) 1 inch in diameter that persist into winter; best used as an informal unsheared hedge; good seaside plant; forms thickets
Sarcococca hookeriana (sweet box)	6–8	4–6'	1½–2'	1½'	PSh to S	Evergreen; glossy dark green foliage on green stems; var. *humilis* approximately 2 feet tall makes a superior low hedge in shade

(continues)

HEDGE SHRUBS OF SPECIAL MERIT (*continued*)

		Height				
Name	*Zones*	*Unpruned*	*Pruned*	*Spacing*	*Exposure**	*Comments*
Spiraea × vanhouttei (bridal wreath)	3–8	6–8'	6–8'	4'	S	Deciduous; arching, rounded, vaselike habit best left untrimmed; massed white flowers in spring; the similar *S. nipponica* 'Snowmound' is denser and neater
Taxus canadensis 'Stricta' (upright Canadian yew)	2–6	3–5'	3–5'	1½'	S to PSh	Evergreen; extremely hardy; deep green foliage; responds well to shearing but more graceful if left to grow untrimmed; subject to adelgid
T. × media 'Hatfieldii' (Hatfield yew)	4–7	6–10'	3–5'	2'	S to Sh	Evergreen; upright habit, with dense dark green foliage; one of the best evergreen hedge plants, hence overused; male clone (no red berries); cv. 'Hicksii' is similar
Thuja occidentalis (eastern arborvitae)	4–7	6–10'	3–5'	2'	S to Sh	Evergreen; spirelike natural habit, but responds well to shearing; medium green scalelike foliage disposed in flat sprays; in cv. 'Nigra' foliage remains rich green throughout winter

* S, full sun; Sh, shade (no direct sun); PSh, partial shade (sun exposure only part of the day); LSh, light shade (e.g., the shade of tall, open trees, with little or no exposure to direct sun).

Dwarf box (Buxus sempervirens *'Suffruticosa') makes a dense, neat hedge that can accept severe shearing.*

OTHER DECIDUOUS HEDGE SHRUBS

Name	Zones	Height Unpruned	Pruned	Spacing	Exposure*	Comments
Acanthopanax sieboldianus (five-leaf aralia)	4–8	8–10'	3–6'	2–3'	S to Sh	Prickly stems; rich green glossy foliage held until late fall; extremely tolerant of poor soil conditions
Caragana arborescens (Siberian pea shrub)	2–7	15–20'	5–10'	3–4'	S to PSh	Upright, stiffly twiggy, with light green foliage; yellow flowers in spring; one of the hardiest hedge shrubs, but rather gaunt when out of leaf
Chaenomeles speciosa (flowering quince)	4–8	6–10'	3–4'	2–3'	S to PSh	Open upright growth of thorny stems; red to pink or white flowers in spring, followed by greenish yellow fruit; numerous cultivars derived from hybrids of this species and the smaller *C. japonica*
Cornus mas (Cornelian cherry dogwood)	4–7	15–20'	5–10'	3–5'	S to PSh	Spreading habit but easily shaped; massed light yellow flowers appear before leaves (just before forsythia); underutilized as a hedge; numerous cultivars with variegated foliage
C. sericea (red-stem dogwood)	2–8	6–8'	3–5'	3–4'	S to PSh	Winter display of reddish stems is most effective in twigs regenerated after midsummer pruning; cv. 'Flaviramea' (yellow-stem dogwood) is similar but for yellowish winter twigs
Corylus avellana 'Fusco-rubra' (purple filbert)	4–7	10–15'	6–10'	3–5'	S to PSh	Purple-leaf shrub best used as a tall hedge; removal of old stems encourages dense, strongly upright growth
Cotoneaster adpressus var. *praecox* (littleleaf cotoneaster)	4–7	2–3'	2–3'	1½–2'	S to PSh	Stiffly ascending with glossy foliage; small white flowers in spring followed by attractive dark red berries; variable but useful in hedges; the similar *C. microphyllus* has very small leaves
Daphne × *burkwoodii* 'Somerset' (Somerset daphne)	4–8	3–4'	2–3'	1–2'	S to PSh	Foliage held until late fall or early winter; pinkish or cream flowers in spring followed by red berries; cv. 'Carol Mackie', a little smaller and hardier, bears white-edged foliage
Deutzia gracilis (slender deutzia)	4–8	2–4'	2–4'	1½–2'	S	Spreading, arching habit; showy white flowers in spring before the leaves; undistinguished except when in flower; best grown unclipped
D. × *lemoinei* (Lemoin deutzia)	2–8	5–7'	3–4'	1½–2'	S	Densely twiggy, with white flowers in spring; extremely hardy; best grown unclipped
Forsythia × *intermedia* (showy forsythia)	5–9	8–10'	4–6'	3–4'	S to PSh	Should be sheared in spring after flowering for best floral display the next year; flower buds may be killed by cold late-winter wind; cv. 'Lynwood' flowers especially well as a hedge plant
F. viridissima 'Bronxensis' (dwarf forsythia)	5–8	1–2'	1–2'	1–1½'	S to PSh	Compact, spreading, flat-topped habit; pale yellow flowers in spring best produced in full sun; makes low hedge with minimal care
Hibiscus syriacus (rose of Sharon)	5–8	8–12'	4–8'	3–4'	S to PSh	Vigorous upright habit, but seldom leafy to ground; foliage late to appear; flowers in late summer, lavender purple, pink, or white, up to 5 inches across in cultivars; noncultivar self-sows to the point of nuisance
Hydrangea arborescens 'Grandiflora' (hills-of-snow)	3–9	3–5'	3–4'	1½–2'	S to Sh	Forms a clump of unbranched stems, each topped with a large cluster of papery white flowers in summer; needs little or no shearing, but suckering roots should be cut occasionally to deter spreading
H. paniculata 'Grandiflora' (peegee hydrangea)	3–8	15–20'	6–10'	4–6'	S to PSh	Vigorous, upright, with 6- to 12- (sometimes 18-) inch clusters of creamy white flowers in summer that turn pink, then purplish and finally straw

(continues)

OTHER DECIDUOUS HEDGE SHRUBS (continued)

Name	Zones	Height Unpruned	Pruned	Spacing	Exposure*	Comments
						colored, persisting into fall; too rank and coarse for any but large settings, but if shrubs kept low with a few stems the flower show is most impressive
Hypericum frondosum (golden St. John'swort)	5–8	3–4'	2–3'	1–1½'	S	Narrow blue-green leaves, with bright yellow flowers in summer; winter stems with loose red-brown bark; cv. 'Sunburst' especially suitable as hedge; *H. kalmianum* also useful
Ligustrum ovalifolium (California privet)	5–10	15–20'	3–10'	1–1½'	S to PSh	Erect habit with glossy foliage held until late fall or even through winter; heavy-scented white flowers in summer; similar to other privets, easily grown, thrives on neglect, responds well to shearing
Lonicera fragrantissima (winter bush honeysuckle)	4–8	6–10'	3–6'	3–4'	S	Densely twiggy; foliage held until late fall; fragrant creamy white flowers in late winter or early spring, before leaves; not noteworthy hedge material except for flowering habit
L. maackii (Amur bush honeysuckle)	2–7	12–15'	5–8'	4–6'	S to PSh	Vigorous, fast growing; white flowers in spring, each turning yellow in age, followed by red berries; rather coarse and undistinguished; self-sows in the south; some cultivars (e.g., 'Rem Red') flower more amply
L. morrowii (Morrow bush honeysuckle)	3–8	6–8'	3–6'	3–5'	S to PSh	A dense twiggy mound, usually leafy to base; flowers in spring white, fading to yellow, followed by red berries; better than most shrubby honey-suckles for hedging
L. tatarica (Tatarian bush honeysuckle)	3–8	10–12'	5–8'	3–6'	S to PSh	Becomes a big wide-spreading shrub, but shears well; profusely borne white or pink flowers in spring are followed by paired red berries; subject to disfiguring, aphid-caused witches-broom; many cultivars with rose pink flowers and yellow berries; self-sowing can be a nuisance
Myrica pennsylvanica (northern bayberry)	2–6	6–12'	3–6'	2–3'	S to PSh	Diffusely branched, with aromatic semievergreen foliage; gray berries on female shrubs held into winter; tolerates poor soils, drought, high wind, and salt spray
Philadelphus coronarius (sweet mock orange)	4–8	10–12'	5–8'	3–5'	S to PSh	Showy white fragrant flowers in spring, double in many hybrids and cultivars; requires annual pruning out of dead wood; gaunt and gray in winter
Physocarpus opulifoliius (ninebark)	2–7	5–8'	3–5'	2–3'	S to PSh	Dense clusters of small white flowers in spring followed by small reddish fruit; reddish brown stems in winter; very tolerant of poor soils; too coarse in habit for small property; dwarf cultivars better
Poncirus trifoliata (hardy orange)	6–9	8–20'	5–8'	3–4'	S to PSh	Diffusely branched with thorny green twigs; fragrant white flowers in spring produce golfball-size fruit that matures yellow and persists into winter; usually devoid of lower branches
Potentilla fruticosa (shrubby cinquefoil)	2–7	2–4'	2–3'	1–2'	S to PSh	Rounded twiggy habit, with fine-textured three-part leaves; yellow or white flowers in early summer and sparingly to fall; thrives on poor soil, but becomes thin and wispy in shade
Rhamnus frangula (glossy buckthorn)	2–7	10–15'	5–8'	2–3'	S to PSh	Upright habit; inconspicuous flowers lead to small red fruit that mature black in late summer; rather rank, weedy, and undistinguished, but undeniably tough; self-sows; locally overused

Name	Zones	Height Unpruned	Height Pruned	Spacing	Exposure*	Comments
Rhodotypos scandens (jetbead)	4–8	4–6'	3–4'	2–3'	S to Sh	White flowers in early summer followed by tetrads of shiny black fruit; especially suited to shade, this is a tough, adaptable shrub that stays within bounds
Rhus aromatica (fragrant sumac)	3–9	4–6'	3–4'	1–2'	S to PSh	Bears downy three-part leaves and, on female plants, clusters of red-brown fruit that persist into winter; underused because of erroneous association with the poisonous white-fruited sumacs
Ribes alpinum (alpine currant)	2–7	4–8'	2–5'	1½–2'	S to Sh	Densely twiggy; early to leaf out; requires both male and female plants to set scarlet fruit; several dwarf cultivars require little or no pruning; a tough, thorny, drought-resistant shrub
Salix purpurea (purple osier willow)	3–8	6–10'	3–5'	2–3'	S to PSh	Upright, multistemmed, with narrow fine-textured blue-green foliage; becomes ragged and unkempt unless sheared several times each season
Spiraea × arguta (garland spiraea)	4–8	4–8'	3–6'	2–3'	S	Small, narrow leaves impart fine texture; white flowers appear before foliage; the very similar but smaller *S. thunbergii* flowers a bit earlier
S. × bumalda (Bumald spiraea)	3–8	2–3'	2–3'	1½–2'	S to PSh	Flat clusters of pink to white flowers in early summer; numerous cultivars available ('Anthony Waterer', 'Froebellii', 'Gold Flame', etc.); *S. japonica* is similar but taller
S. prunifolia 'Plena' (bridal wreath)	4–8	5–10'	3–5'	3–4'	S to PSh	Double white flowers in early spring before foliage; a one-time favorite that tends to straggly legginess unless severely pruned annually, now largely replaced by other spiraeas
Syringa meyeri 'Palibin' (Palibin lilac)	3–7	3–4'	3–4'	2–3'	S to PSh	A small-leaved, much-branched lilac, with compact clusters of pinkish lilac flowers in spring foliage; *S. microphylla* also good for hedges
S. × persica (Persian lilac)	3–7	4–8'	3–6'	2–3'	S to PSh	Fragrant pale lilac flowers open in spring as foliage expands; smaller and more graceful than the common lilac
S. vulgaris (common lilac)	3–7	8–15'	6–8'	2–3'	S	Very fragrant, showy flowers, single and double, in spring in a multitude of cultivars; tends to bare-stemmed gauntness in age and forms copses from root suckers; *S. chinensis* is similar, more graceful
Vaccinium corymbosum (highbush blueberry)	3–7	6–12'	4–6'	3–4'	S to PSh	Trains easily; glossy foliage turns red in fall; berry crops are diminished by shearing; requires acid soil, with sustained moisture through summer
Viburnum carlesii (Korean-spice viburnum)	4–8	5–6'	4–5'	2–3'	S	Dense, stiffly branched, with red buds opening to white in spring, the expanded flowers intensely fragrant; subject to leaf spot and powdery mildew, less so in cvs. 'Compactum' and 'Cayuga'
V. dilatatum (linden viburnum)	5–7	8–10'	4–6'	2–3'	S to PSh	Flat-topped clusters of white flowers in spring followed by scarlet fruit that persists into winter; several cultivars boast especially brilliant, long-retained fruit, most notably 'Erie' and 'Iroquois'
V. lantana (wayfaring tree)	3–7	10–15'	6–10'	3–4'	S to PSh	Clusters of whitish flowers in spring followed by fruit aging from green through yellow and red to black; responds well to hedge use, but coarse and gaunt when out of leaf

(continues)

OTHER DECIDUOUS HEDGE SHRUBS (continued)

Name	Zones	Height Unpruned	Pruned	Spacing	Exposure*	Comments
V. opulus (European cranberry viburnum)	3–8	8–12'	5–8'	2–3'	S	Pinwheel clusters of white flowers in spring followed by bright red fruit; easily grown, but best in damp sites; cv. 'Nanum' is half-size and seldom flowers, but good as a hedge
V. plicatum var. tomentosum (double-file viburnum)	5–8	8–12'	5–8'	3–5'	S to PSh	Flat clusters of showy white flowers in spring, followed by red fruit maturing to black; best left unsheared; cvs. 'Mariesii' and 'Shasta' are especially showy in bloom
V. prunifolium (black haw viburnum)	3–9	12–15'	6–12'	3–4'	S to Sh	Clusters of cream flowers in spring followed by pinkish fruit that matures black; rather stiff habit reminiscent of that of hawthorn; shears well and tolerates summer drought
V. sieboldii (Siebold viburnum)	2–8	15–25'	8–12'	3–5'	S to Sh	Clustered cream flowers in spring succeeded by red fruit that mature black (and are then often stripped by birds); foliage held through late fall, ill scented when crushed; best on moist soil; cv. 'Seneca' is a good hedge plant
V. trilobum (American cranberry viburnum)	2–8	8–12'	6–8'	3–4'	S to PSh	Flat-topped clusters of cream flowers in spring succeeded by red fruit that persist into winter; best used as an informal hedge; cv. 'Compactum' is half-size

* S, full sun; Sh, shade (no direct sun); PSh, partial shade (sun exposure only part of the day); LSh, light shade (e.g., the shade of tall, open trees, with little or no exposure to direct sun).

OTHER EVERGREEN HEDGE SHRUBS

Name	Zones	Height Unpruned	Pruned	Spacing	Exposure*	Comments
Ardisia japonica (Japanese ardisia)	8–9	1–2'	1–2'	6"–1'	PSh to Sh	Deep green foliage; red fruit persisting into winter; thrives on acid soil
Berberis julianae (wintergreen barberry)	5–8	6–8'	3–6'	1½–2'	S to PSh	Extremely thorny; foliage turns bronzy in winter; yellow flowers in spring, followed by black fruit held into fall; makes impenetrable barrier; cv. 'Nana' is about half-size
B. verruculosa (warty barberry)	5–8	3–5'	2–3'	1–1½'	S to PSh	Glossy leaves dark green above, grayish beneath; flowers yellow in spring, followed by black fruit; smaller dimensions overall and denser foliage distinguish this from B. julianae
Chamaecyparis obtusa 'Gracilis Compacta' (compact Hinoki cypress)	4–8	10–12'	3–7'	1½–2'	S to PSh	Lustrous deep green fine-textured foliage arranged in flat fans; requires minimal shearing; makes a hedge of high quality
C. obtusa 'Nana' (dwarf Hinoki cypress)	4–8	3–4'	1–2'	1–1½'	S to PSh	Similar to cv. 'Gracilis Compacta' but smaller and slower growing; good as low hedge
Euonymus fortunei var. radicans (wintercreeper)	5–8	3–5'	2–4'	2–2½'	S to PSh	Tends to form a low mound of dark green foliage; handsome but unpredictable in habit (may become erect or climb); cv. 'Vegetus' is similar
E. fortunei 'Minimus' (small-leaf wintercreeper)	5–8	2–3'	1–2'	1–1½'	S to PSh	Similar to var. radicans but smaller in all dimensions; has same variable traits
Ilex crenata (Japanese holly)	5–7	6–10'	3–6'	2–2½'	S to PSh	Dense lustrous foliage; black berries on female plants; shears well; leaf size variable

Name	Zones	Height Unpruned	Height Pruned	Spacing	Exposure*	Comments
Lonicera nitida (box-leaf bush honeysuckle)	7–9	5–8'	2–5'	1½–2'	S to Sh	Leafy, with small fragrant yellowish flowers in spring; confused in commerce with the somewhat hardier *L. pileata*; both may lose leaves in severe winters
Mahonia aquifolium (Oregon hollygrape)	5–9	3–6'	3–6'	2–2½'	PSh to Sh	Glossy deep green foliage; yellow flowers in spring, followed by blue-gray berries; best grown unsheared; harsh winter winds can cause browning or dieback
Paxistema canbyi (Canby paxistema)	3–8	½–1'	½–1'	6"	PSh	Lustrous dark green foliage; most effective as an edging, but requires annual pruning of horizontal shoots to be kept in bounds
Photinia glabra (Japanese photinia)	8–10	10–15'	5–8'	2–4'	S to PSh	Large leaves and bold habit make this unsuitable for shearing; best used in a tall informal hedge
Picea abies 'Maxwellii' (dwarf Norway spruce)	2–7	1½–2½'	1½–2½'	8"–1'	S to PSh	Of the several forms in commerce the erect multistemmed shrub is preferable for hedging
Pieris japonica (Japanese andromeda)	5–8	8–12'	4–6'	2–3'	S to PSh	Pendent clusters of whitish flowers in early spring contrast effectively with glossy foliage; very subject to damaging lacebug infestation, especially in the East; several cvs. have reddish foliage and flowers
Pinus mugo (mugo pine)	2–7	4–8'	3–5'	2–4'	S to PSh	Multiple upright stems with dense, dark green foliage and small cones; highly variable in habit; left unpruned it becomes a large shrub or small tree
Prunus laurocerasus (cherry laurel)	6–8	6–10'	4–6'	2–3'	PSh to Sh	Wide-spreading habit; large, glossy, dark green leaves; spikes of small white flowers in spring, followed by small black fruit; cv. 'Otto Luyken' less than 4 feet tall; harsh winter wind may cause dieback
Rhododendron spp. and cvs. (rhododendrons, azalea)	2–9	3–20'	3–12'	2–4'	S to Sh	Variation mainly in stature, leaf size, and flower color (lavender purple the commonest); most require acid, humusy soil with adequate summer moisture; large-leaved spp. and cvs. must be pruned rather than sheared in hedging
Santolina chamaecyparissus (lavender cotton)	6–9	1–2'	1–2'	8"–1'	S	Forms a rounded mound, with finely divided, aromatic, silver gray foliage; yellow flower heads in summer; tolerates the poorest, droughtiest soils; *S. virens* is green, otherwise similar; both good for edging
Teucrium chamaedrys (Germander)	7–9	1–1½'	¾–1'	1–1½'	S	Mounded habit; aromatic foliage; rose purple flowers in summer; makes a neat, fine-textured low hedge, but can be killed back by severe winter weather
Thuja occidentalis 'Holmstrupii' (Holmstrup arborvitae)	2–8	7–10'	2–4'	1½–2'	S to PSh	Compact, pyramidal, slow growing, with bright green foliage in flat fans; requires minimal attention
T. occidentalis 'Pumila' or 'Little Gem' (low arborvitae)	2–8	4–6'	3–4'	1½–2'	S to PSh	Slow growing; requires little shearing; does best with cool, moist summers; may brown in severe winters
T. occidentalis 'Techny' (Mission arborvitae)	2–8	8–12'	4–8'	2½–3'	S to PSh	Pyramidal, with dark green foliage year round; especially suited to northern conditions

* S, full sun; Sh, shade (no direct sun); PSh, partial shade (sun exposure only part of the day); LSh, light shade (e.g., the shade of tall, open trees, with little or no exposure to direct sun).

DECIDUOUS TREES FOR HEDGES

Name	Zones	Height Unpruned	Height Pruned	Spacing Unpruned	Spacing Pruned	Comments
Acer campestre (hedge maple)	4–8	25–30'	8–15'	10–12'	4–6'	Thrives in wide range of soils; endures drought; cv. 'Compactum' makes 4-foot hedge
A. ginnala (Amur maple)	2–7	10–20'	8–12'	5–7'	2–4'	Small fragrant flowers in spring, redwinged samaras; *A. tataricum* is similar
Carpinus betulus (European hornbeam)	4–7	20–30'	3–15'	8–10'	3–5'	Tough, enduring, amenable to severe pruning, shade tolerant; holds dead leaves over winter
C. caroliniana (American hornbeam)	2–9	20–30'	10–15'	8–10'	4–6'	Responds less well to hard pruning, otherwise similar to *C. betulus*
Crataegus crus-galli (cockspur thorn)	3–7	20–30'	6–15'	8–10'	3–5'	Rigid curved 3-inch thorns are formidable; white flowers in spring; foliage attacked by many insects
C. laevigata (syn. *C. oxycantha*) (English hawthorn)	4–7	15–20'	10–12'	10–12'	4–6'	Short thorns; single or double red to white flowers in spring often defoliated by pests; *C. monogyna* is similar
C. phaenopyrum (Washington thorn)	3–8	25–30'	10–15'	10–12'	4–6'	Thorny; white flowers in spring, then red fruit; foliage subject to rust; some cultivars bear heavy fruit crops
Eleagnus angustifolia (Russian olive)	2–7	12–20'	8–10'	5–7'	3–5'	Gray green foliage; yellowish fruit; very tolerant of poor droughty soil; shears well; subject to scale; self-sows
Fagus sylvatica (European beech)	4–7	50–60'	6–12'	12–20'	4–6'	Tolerates severe pruning; makes long-lived hedge; difficult to transplant; many cultivars with leaf variation
Maclura pomifera (osage orange)	4–9	20–40'	5–8'	10–15'	3–5'	Tough, adaptable; withstands severe pruning, but rather coarse; fruit rare in hedges
Ostrya virginiana (American hop hornbeam)	3–9	20–35'	6–10'	10–12'	3–5'	Birchlike foliage; shears well; thrives on drought; disease free; uncommon in nursery trade
Populus alba 'Pyramidalis' (Bolleana poplar)	3–8	40–60'	8–15'	2–3'	2–3'	Fast growing, columnar, with pale gray bark; weak wooded but superior to *P. nigra* 'Italica' (Lombardy poplar)
Quercus imbricaria (shingle oak)	4–8	50–60'	6–12'	12–20'	4–6'	Unlobed cherrylike foliage; shears well; holds dead leaves; *Q. phellos* (willow oak) similar but drops leaves in fall
Salix pentandra (laurel willow)	4–8	30–50'	6–10'	10–15'	3–5'	Glossy foliage; shears well; often defoliated and short lived
Tilia cordata (littleleaf linden)	3–7	50–60'	8–12'	12–20'	4–6'	Easily shaped; tolerant of hot dry urban conditions; often infested with aphids and sooty mold; *T. euchlora* (Crimean linden) also used for hedging
Ulmus pumila (Siberian elm)	4–9	50–60'	8–12'	12–20'	4–6'	Good as hedge, especially cv. 'Dropmore' with small leaves; brittle and self-sows if allowed to become tree

EVERGREEN TREES FOR HEDGES

Name	Zones	Height Unpruned	Height Pruned	Spacing Unpruned	Spacing Pruned	Comments
Calocedrus decurrens 'Columnaris' (California incense cedar)	5–8	30–50'	8–10'	6–12'	3–4'	Symmetrically columnar; heat tolerant; readily infested by mistletoe
Casuarina equisetifolia (Australian pine)	10	30–50'	6–12'	6–12'	2–4'	Forms dense mass of slender green shoots; tolerates poor soil and salt spray; self-sows
Cedrus atlantica var. *fastigiata* (upright Atlas cedar)	6–9	40–60'	6–12'	6–12'	3–4'	Blue-gray foliage very rich and conspicuous; expensive, difficult to transplant, slow to establish

| Name | Zones | Height | | Spacing | | Comments |
		Unpruned	Pruned	Unpruned	Pruned	
Cryptomeria japonica (Japanese cedar)	6–8	50–60'	8–12'	4–6'	2–4'	Graceful habit, with branches arching upward; best grown untrimmed, except for an occasional topping
Juniperus virginiana (eastern red cedar)	2–9	40–50'	6–12'	5–8'	2–4'	Scalelike deep green to blue-green foliage; subject to rust and bagworm; cultivars especially suited to hedging include 'Burkii' and 'Pyramidalis'
Picea glauca (white spruce)	2–6	40–50'	6–12'	6–12'	4–6'	Cv. 'Conica' (dwarf Alberta spruce) diminutive but very subject to spider mite injury
P. orientalis (Oriental spruce)	4–7	40–50'	6–12'	8–12'	4–6'	Easily shaped; may brown in harsh winter wind; uncommon in commerce
Pinus strobus (eastern white pine)	3–8	40–50'	10–15'	8–12'	5–8'	Makes good high hedge; cv. 'Fastigiata' especially good; sensitive to drought, urban pollution, and road salt
P. sylvestris (Scotch pine)	2–8	30–45'	10–12'	6–10'	5–6'	Shapes well; foliage blue- to yellow-green; becomes thin and wispy in shade; *P. virginiana* (Virginia scrub pine) also useful
Podocarpus macrophyllus (Maki or Chinese podocarpus)	8–10	20–30'	6–10'	6–8'	4–6'	Rigid habit; foliage yewlike, very heat and drought tolerant; foliage browns after prolonged frost
Pseudotsuga menziesii (Douglas fir)	4–7	50–75'	6–12'	8–12'	4–6'	Shears well; foliage deep to bluish green; best where cool humid summers prevail
Sciadopitys verticillata (umbrella pine)	4–8	20–30'	6–8'	6–8'	4–6'	Lustrous deep green leathery foliage; requires minimal shaping; slow growing; expensive; sensitive to cold wind in North and hot sun in South
T. canadensis (Canadian hemlock)	3–7	40–50'	6–10'	8–10'	3–5'	Soft two-ranked needles on slender twigs; shade tolerant; no longer recommended because of fatal woolly adelgid infestation over much of native range
T. caroliniana (Carolina hemlock)	4–7	25–35'	6–10'	6–8'	3–5'	Stiffer habit than *T. canadensis*; may be somewhat less subject to injury by woolly adelgid

A closely spaced hedgerow of somber white pines lends definition to a lively wildflower meadow.

A file of Colorado blue spruce (Picea pungens), though even-aged, often grows somewhat unevenly, but provides an effective year-round visual barrier.

8

Pools, Fountains, and Swimming Pools

Water traditionally has been the symbol of life, and with good reason. It makes all life possible. In parts of our Southwest, as in desertous parts of Africa where a garden is a highly developed oasis, an unfailing source of water is indispensable. The sound of a trickling fountain is refreshing indeed to those whose senses are accustomed to the barren dryness of the outer world.

While garden pools had their origin in warm countries and their primary purpose was to cool the atmosphere, the almost

An ornate dripping fountain on a tall, fluted pedestal in a formal octagonal pool contrasts with the exhuberant informality of the adjoining gardens with their traversing brick walks somewhat misaligned over time.

universal appeal of the sight and sound of water has made them equally appreciated in northern climes. The idea of a fountain or pool as a garden feature was first brought to Europe by the Crusaders after their contacts with the older and more highly developed culture of the Near East. Even in the comparatively damp climate of England and Scotland, the fountain idea has persisted, although with somewhat less elaboration and emphasis than it has received in Italy and Spain.

POOLS

Besides its original function of providing refreshment in hot weather by cooling the surrounding air, the garden pool serves a distinctly decorative purpose. Set in a frame of stone, the gleaming mirror of its surface becomes an object of admiration and attention. It may be used as the central feature of the garden, or it may be used as a terminal motive for a major or minor axis. It often provides a fitting foreground for a piece of sculpture, and its usefulness and charm can be heightened by making it the habitation of fish and water-loving plants. See Chapter 23 for plants that are suitable in and around pools.

In the design of a garden pool, the major decisions are the size, the shape, the material to be used for the coping, the depth of the water, and the color of the bottom. It is important for the pool to be in harmony with its surroundings and in scale as a detail of the garden design. Its setting, in patterned paving or in turf, should be carefully studied. The shape will largely depend on the general plan of the garden as well as on the personal preference of the owner. In some gardens a round pool would be the most logical and pleasing from a standpoint of design, while in other gardens a square or rectangular pool would be more in keeping with the general scheme. Increasingly, preference is shown for pools of natural, irregular form.

The material to be used in the construction of the coping is largely a matter of personal choice. A simple flagstone coping is always pleasant and is particularly suitable if the garden is small and informal. For gardens of more formal and elaborate design, a coping of cut stone might be preferred. Colored tiles are very decorative and lovely, and they can be used both as a coping and as a complete lining for the pool. While concrete may be used as a coping, it is decidedly less attractive and less interesting than most other materials unless suitably colored.

Special paints are available for use in the interior of concrete pools. If the bottom is painted black, it offers the illusion of much greater depth. Blue is the most popular color, as it seems to be a reflection of the sky, but care must be taken not to choose too harsh a tone, which would be artificial in the landscape.

A free-form garden pool, accessible by lawn and adjacent to informal flower beds, with curbed arbor, wall garden, and sitting nook along a path, all lending interest throughout the year.

When considering the construction of a pool, it must be borne in mind that the initial cost is usually the last. A well-constructed pool is a permanent feature of the garden, requiring little or no upkeep. When its construction has been completed, it will be a source of satisfaction for years to come. Fortunately for the home owner, a garden pool need not be elaborate or expensive. A small, simple pool may be constructed for a very modest sum, and most of the work can be done by the owner.

In constructing a garden pool, the major considerations are absolute watertightness; drainage; and water supply, including the control of inlet, outlet, and overflow. The walls of the pool are, essentially, retaining walls, and as such, they must be strong enough to withstand the soil pressure against them from the outside, that of the water from within, and also to resist the pressure of frost. There must be no heaving caused by the action of frost, as this will crack the walls and throw the coping out of level. A poorly constructed pool, which consequently is cracked by frost year after year, can become a source of constant annoyance. It is often difficult to permanently repair a pool that has developed a leak, and it is, therefore, a matter of sound economy to see that the pool is well constructed in the beginning.

The ground immediately surrounding the pool should be absolutely level. This is a matter of vital importance, which is sometimes overlooked by the amateur builder. If a pool is constructed on ground that is only slightly uneven, the result will be unsatisfactory. If there is no other alternative, and if a pool must be constructed on ground that is slightly sloping, it will be necessary to raise the coping on one side. If this is not done, the immediate surface may convey the distressing illusion of a tilted dish.

Construction Materials
Concrete

Concrete is one of the best materials to use for the construction of garden pools. For a pool of 100 square feet or less, the bottom should be 5 inches thick and the walls 8 inches thick. For very large pools, these figures should be slightly increased, while for very small pools they may be somewhat reduced. In constructing a small pool, it is not necessary to reinforce the sides. In a pool that is more than 5 feet in length, however, the sides, especially if straight and vertical, should be reinforced with steel rods to maintain the concrete as a crack-proof monolith against varying pressures.

The soil should be excavated to a depth of 12 to 18 inches below the proposed floor level of the pool. The sides of the excavation should be in line with the outside wall of the pool. A layer of gravel should be spread over the bottom of the excavation and tamped firmly into place. If the gravel is sprinkled with water, it will help the mass to settle into place. This layer will act as a drain and will keep the groundwater away from the undersurface of the concrete, thus reducing the danger of heaving caused by the action of the frost. The actual depth of the layer of gravel will depend somewhat on the character of the soil. In light, sandy soils a layer only a few inches in depth will be satisfactory, while in soils of a heavy clay texture, a layer at least 12 inches deep is advisable.

Clay Lined

A modification of the concrete pool is the pool with a clay bottom. The clay pool is similar to a natural pond in its formation. Spread evenly 2 or 3 inches thick and worked into the consistency of a mud pie, clay will hold water remarkably well. In regions where clay is obtainable, it has many advantages as a material for a large pool. No serious injury can come to the clay floor. No forms are required for building, and the actual labor of handling the material in construction is less than for concrete.

A large formal concrete pool, surrounded by brick coping, reflects sky as well as surrounding features. The statuary fountain adds visual interest and provides the soothing sound of flowing water.

Polyvinyl Chloride

Polyvinyl Chloride (PVC) can be used to make pools of almost any size and shape, provided this durable and flexible material is bedded in a firm base. The first step is to establish the outline of the pool, then to determine the size of the liner needed. To do so, measure a rectangle that will cover the ground area occupied by the pool as outlined. Then add twice the depth of the pool, plus another 1½ feet for the edge, to each side of the rectangle. If, for example, the outline of the pool on the ground is contained within a 3- by 5-foot rectangle and you are planning to have a pool 1 foot deep, you add twice the depth plus 1½ feet to each of the dimensions—the 3-foot dimension of the original rectangle becomes 6½ feet and the 5-foot dimension becomes 8½ feet.

After determining the outline of the pool and obtaining the liner, excavate to a depth of 1 foot or more, sloping the sides toward the center. Be sure to remove stones, sticks, roots, and other materials that might damage or puncture the liner. After the rough excavation has been completed, tamp all surfaces firmly. Then add 2 or 3 inches of damp builder's sand and tamp firmly into place. Spread the PVC sheet and carefully fold and tuck it into all corners and around all bends, allowing at least a 1-foot margin at grade around the periphery, onto which a coping of rocks and/or stepping-stones will be placed. To avoid the bright aqua color of the typical swimming pool, simply use the reverse side of the PVC, which is usually a dull gray-black. This dark bottom will add to the reflecting quality of the water.

After placing the liner in the excavation, fill with water to hold it in place and cut off any excess material on the edges, leaving a flap of about 1 foot. This then can be hidden under rocks and soil in the case of a natural-looking pool or bog, or you can have a more formal coping of stone slabs and concrete blocks set in the sand or soil.

Since no plumbing is ordinarily involved, a hose is used to add water as needed. When the pool must be drained, a bucket and siphon or pump may be used or, keeping things simple and economical, the garden hose used as a siphon may suffice.

Be sure not to place sharp stones and other sharp objects in the pool or use any sharp-edged tools in it, as these can puncture the lining. If a bucket or pot holding a water-lily or other plants or objects is desired, place a scrap of the plastic, or some similar material that will keep the hard edges from coming into direct contact with the liner, between the container and the pool bottom.

Fiberglass

Fiberglass is a light, durable material that is cast to size and shape at the factory and brought to the job in one piece. The floor and walls form a deep bowl with a smooth, curved surface. It is comparatively inexpensive. The excavation of the pit and the setting of the bowl in sand are the only tems of construction. It may be fitted with inlet, outlet, and overflow—as with any pool (see page 102)—and the joints may be sealed with liquid fiberglass, which hardens and is impermeable.

There are many prefabricated fiberglass pools available in shapes varying from the standard rounds, squares, and rectangles to irregular "natural" and free-form shapes.

To avoid structural stress and distortion, it is important to bed the fiberglass pool as firmly as possible in a layer of damp sand. This is accomplished by first covering the bottom of the excavation with sand deep enough to bring the pool flange to grade level, setting the pool on the sandy base, and then filling in the side spaces simultaneously from opposite sides. A spirit level should be used throughout construction to be sure the pool stays truly horizontal, since once filled the pool cannot be moved.

Maintenance

With adequate facilities for maintaining a flow of water through the pool and for emptying it, care and general upkeep are made easy. An occasional cleaning out of sediment and fallen leaves is practically all that is necessary. In northern regions, the concrete pool should be protected from the action of frost during the winter months. The water should be drained off before the onset of freezing weather, and a few sticks or boards placed in the bottom to absorb the thrust of any small amount of ice that may form after snow has melted.

A concrete pool may be arranged for winter with a water level just a little below normal by placing a few large floating logs or weighted blocks of Styrofoam in the water. These objects will absorb the thrust from the ice, thus relieving the pressure on the concrete walls. Another device is to build the pool with such sharply sloping sides that when the ice forms, it merely slides up the sides as it expands, and no pressure is transmitted to the structure.

Ways of Reducing Costs

Those who desire a garden pool but are deterred by the apparently high cost of installation may be interested in methods of reducing the expenses involved. Plumbing can be a major item, but it may be eliminated by using the garden hose to fill and empty the pool. Reinforcing rods comprise a big item. They may be omitted if the pool is small and of simple shape. Alternatively, discarded metal objects, such as pipe, steel tool handles, electrical conduit, and television antennae may be used in place of new reinforcing rods.

To facilitate cleaning and repairs or to prevent frost damage, it is sometimes necessary to remove the water from a pool. Emptying a pool with a garden hose is a simple trick, requiring only a place lower than the pool floor within reach of the hose, whence the water may flow off. To start the working of a siphon, place one end of the hose down the slope at this low point. Hold the other end near the edge of the pool and pour water into it out of a watering can. When the water begins to flow out of the lower end of the hose and while still pouring water into the upper end, plunge the end of the hose, together with the watering can, into the pool. The flow thus started will continue until the pool is practically empty. The watering can may be removed as soon as the flow from the pool has been established. The flow will continue until the water level reaches the end of the hose.

A small pool can be made of a half-barrel sunk into the ground. Alone, such a pool will last several years, or if surrounded with concrete, using the half barrel as a form, it will be permanent. A somewhat larger pool can be had using a discarded bathtub, whose true nature may be disguised by painting the interior black and, once sunk to its flanges, surrounding it with rocks or flagstones. If the excavation is made deeper than required and the tub is set on a bed of coarse gravel at least 1 foot thick, the pool may be drained simply by pulling the plug. A short section of PVC pipe, chosen to fit snugly in the drain hole, may serve as an overflow line; its upper end should be at the water line and covered with screening.

An Italianate fountain with a central gurgle and an ornate dripping edge, on a pedestal faced with spouting masks, all adding artful sights and sounds to a peaceful pool.

FOUNTAINS

In centuries past, a fountain was the most finely wrought and decorative feature of a garden. In dry climates where the presence of water was always highly prized, the fountain symbolized the life-giving power of water. Water was piped to the fountains at great expense and from the fountains it flowed in little canals throughout the garden to irrigate the soil and make possible the growing of plants.

During the Italian Renaissance the fountain became an elaborate work of art, combining spouting jets of water with architectural and sculptural forms. The Italian noblemen vied with each other in the display of animated water features in their villas. Water was often piped from streams several miles away to supply a series of fountains, which were so arranged that the overflow of one fountain supplied the next fountain on a lower terrace.

The fountain in most American gardens today is a much less complicated feature but is nonetheless important, and it is often the one note of architectural embellishment. The simplest type is the pool fountain with a single stream rising in a vertical jet from the center. The structure of such a fountain consists merely of a brass nozzle on the supply pipe at the water level. An elaboration of this arrangement is a central pedestal supporting a shallow basin, from the rim of which the water drips into the pool. In such a fountain, the central jet is sometimes replaced by a sculptured figure. Greater elaboration occasionally takes the form of minor jets of water near the rim. But as in so many other modern garden elements, simplicity is the keynote of a successful fountain.

The wall fountain as a terminal feature at the end of a garden walkway possesses infinite possibilities for artistic expression. Water coming from a spout or through a trough-shaped stone and falling in a narrow stream to the pool below is one of the most satisfactory arrangements for the inlet.

Since fountains are architectural in character, they may be used either as the dominating motif in a garden or as a mere incidental feature.

*A shallow pond border sports white pond lilies (*Nymphaea odorata*) with a sprinkling of fallen willow leaves and a file of stepping stones. The pond lilies may be kept from spreading by rooting them in sunken boxes, as in distance.*

A cascade made of harrow discs ornamented with coins dropped by passersby as a concealed recirculating pump keeps the small volume of water in constant motion.

In most fountains, it is necessary that small electric pumps be installed not only to create water sprays and jets but to recirculate the water, with allowance made for manual or automatic replacement of the portion lost to evaporation.

SWIMMING POOLS

A swimming pool that is well designed, carefully built, and conscientiously maintained can be a source of endless pleasure for many people. It can also be an investment in

*A small recirculating fountain is highlighted by a surrounding zone of white gravel within an expanse of darker gravel and backed by a pair of Alberta spruce (*Picea glauca *var.* albertiana*).*

healthful, wholesome recreation for the entire family and a contribution to happy living.

In the United States, the swimming pool first became a feature at country clubs and hotel resorts, and in some cities public pools were built as part of municipal recreational systems. Improvements in the methods of construction—particularly the vinyl-lined, steel-walled method for in-ground pools and the vinyl-lined wood and steel frame materials used for aboveground pools—and the perfection of filter systems combined to make the swimming pool increasingly popular and affordable.

Besides their comparatively low cost, the great advantage of the vinyl-lined, steel-walled swimming pools over cast concrete ones is that both the vinyl and the steel walls are flexible and can withstand the expansion and contraction caused by the freezing and thawing of the water in winter. It is necessary to put one or two logs or blocks of plastic foam into a concrete pool before freezing so that the wood may absorb the pressure of the ice; nonetheless, because of the rigidity of concrete, such pools are subject to cracking under severe stress, and leaks frequently occur. The vinyl liner can be punctured and may also develop leaks, but most of these can readily be repaired because patches can be applied underwater, thus obviating the necessity of draining the pool.

The decision to build a swimming pool is one that must be made with full recognition of a number of attendant conditions, especially that of an adequate water supply. In addition, the type of filtration system, the size and location of the pool, the choice of materials and methods, the overall construction costs, maintenance expenses, and finally, the duties and obligations of the owner, must be carefully considered before a final decision is made.

Water Supply and Filter Systems

A swimming pool must have clear, pure water. However, even pure water that remains standing will become clouded with algae in a few summer days. To overcome this condition, the water must be circulated by a pump through a filter. The advantages of the filter system are that the same water can be purified and used constantly while simultaneously maintaining a fairly even temperature.

There are two types of filters: the sand filter and the diatomite filter. The sand filter has been in use for many years and requires that the water be "backwashed," or periodically pumped back through the filter in the opposite direction. Such backwashing serves to wash out the impurities by discharging the flow into the drain. The diatomite filter makes use of a fine-grained or diatomaceous earth, which does not require rewashing but rather holds the impurities in the filter. In this method, the water passes through a series of bags of filter cloth, and the collected material is removed with the filter bags periodically. Because the filter bags expand as the sediment accumulates, long periods of operation are possible before changing or cleaning the filter elements becomes necessary. It is, therefore, an economical system to operate. But the schedule must be faithfully followed.

A regular schedule of vacuuming the pool and of testing and adding chlorine and other chemical purifiers when necessary is a very important part of pool maintenance. The process is simple, however, even when preparing the pool for the winter. If correct procedures have been followed, the water will be clear when the pool cover is removed in the

A constructed outcrop, sparingly planted, offers a jumping-off place into this informal in-ground swimming pool.

spring, and only the sediment in the bottom need be vacuumed away. Fine mesh covers are now available for winter protection; these are light and easy to use, and seem to work better than the solid vinyl plastic covers.

Size and Location

In general, the size of a pool should be in proportion to the number of people expected to use it. But there is a minimum size, fixed by the natural requirements of safety. For diving there should be a depth of at least 8½ feet at one end. Standard pools start at 12 by 32 feet. A larger one, 18 by 32 feet, of course, is better and is well worth the extra cost of construction. But a pool 20 or 25 feet wide and 40 or 50 feet long is a far more desirable size. For children and beginners there should be a shallow area at one end with the floor sloping from 3 to 4 feet, at which point it should slope steeply down to the deep diving area.

The placement of the pool in the landscape should be very carefully studied. Because the swimming pool is likely to be the most conspicuous element in the home landscape, it should be integrated with other landscape features. It should be convenient to use, private, and enclosed. The best location for a pool is in open sunshine, sheltered from the wind and unencumbered by nearby trees.

While in most neighborhoods fencing is required as a safety precaution for both children and adults, the fencing need not be immediately adjacent to the pool, thereby restricting the adjoining spaces. As long as the area containing the pool is adequately fenced and gated according to local codes, it can be either nearby or relatively far away from the pool itself. Since the pool invites active recreation, it is unwise to restrict space around it. And the fence does not need to be conspicuous to serve its purpose. Even a utilitarian chain-link fence can be made more attractive by the use of climbers, or it can be be rendered inconspicuous with a coat of dark paint, preferably flat black, and obscured with flowering shrubs or hedging allowed to grow through the mesh. The plantings will not only grace the setting, as much by being reflected from the water surface as directly, but also deflect unwanted wind.

To the extent possible, any shrubs and trees near the swimming pool should be chosen for their freedom from constantly dropping debris, especially during the swimming season, and absence of thorny stems and prickly foliage. Among the many conifers, Oriental spruce

Enclosed by a picket fence, this formal pool is surrounded by low gardens. Any tree litter is largely obviated by distance.

(*Picea orientalis*) is especially suitable. It thrives in zones 6 through 8, and although uncommon in horticultural commerce, its fine texture and neat appearance make it well worth seeking.

Other coniferous trees of note for this setting include Japanese cedar (*Cryptomeria japonica*) and Atlas cedar (*Cedrus libani* ssp. *atlantica*). Deciduous trees most suitable in the vicinity of a pool are the katsura (*Cercidophyllum japonicum*), ginkgo (*Ginkgo biloba*), seedless ash (*Fraxinus pennsylvanica* 'Marshall's Seedless'), thornless honey locust (*Gleditsia triacanthos* var. *inermis*), weeping willow (e.g., *Salix alba* 'Tristis' and *S.* × *pendulina*), and the deciduous conifer, dawn redwood (*Metasequoia glyptostroboides*). It should be borne in mind that any significant pool leakage, either through an ill-fitting drain plug or through structural cracks, will lead to heavy localized growth of tree roots and eventually to penetration and widening of the opening as the roots thicken.

Shrubs most congenial to the swimming pool environment include the following evergreens: Japanese laurel (*Aucuba japonica*), box (*Buxus* spp.), Japanese holly (*Ilex crenata*), inkberry (*Ilex glabra*), photinia (*Photinia* × *fraseri*), and andromeda (*Pieris japonica*). Deciduous shrubs include witch hazel (*Hamamelis* spp.), beauty-berry (*Callicarpa* spp.), smokebush (*Cotinus coggygria*), winter jasmine (*Jasminum nudiflorum*), peegee hydrangea (*Hydrangea paniculata* 'Grandiflora'), spicebush (*Lindera benzoin*), pussy willow (*Salix caprea, S. discolor, S. gracilistyla*, and *S. gracilistyla* var. *melanostachys*), and shrubby willow, e.g., *Salix purpurea*. Among other possible candidates, Russian olive (*Eleagnus angustifolia*), bush honeysuckle (e.g., *Lonicera fragrantissima* and *L. tatarica*), lilac (*Syringa* spp. and cvs.), and forsythia (*Forsythia* spp. and cvs.) all flower before the pool season, and if fruit is formed and dropped, it occurs in the fall, along with leaf drop. Among woody climbers, clematis and wisteria are good choices.

It is wise to place the deep end of the pool away from the major sitting area for at least two reasons: (1) small children can be easily supervised close at hand while they are in the pool, and (2) the splash made by divers should be away from people who may be sitting and relaxing beside the pool.

Obviously, a swimming pool is a great addition to the garden and to the quality of life for those who enjoy it. However, the obligations of maintenance—not only for appearance but also for health and safety—must be recognized and assiduously adhered to.

Equally important is the need to place the pool carefully and create congenial surroundings, both for its use in warm weather and to offset its inherent unattractiveness in winter. View lines outdoors and from within the house should be carefully determined and analyzed before construction. For example, it may be desirable to have the pool readily visible from the kitchen and living room, especially if children's activities in the pool are to be supervised, but hidden from view in the dining area where invited guests are hosted. As family needs and responsibilities change in time, the landscaping around the pool should be mutable enough to accommodate a corresponding change in design. For example, a lawn or a bed of low annuals or perennials that allows the pool to be visible from various indoor and outdoor vantages may eventually be changed to a shrub border or hedge that limits visibility and increases privacy. Generally, it is best to keep lawn at some distance from the pool edge, as grass clippings seem always to find their way into the water. Species that attract bees and other sometimes annoying insects during the pool season, such as linden (*Tilia* spp.), mesquite (*Prosopis juliflora*), oak (*Quercus* spp.), rose (*Rosa* spp.), sage (*Salvia* spp.), and clover (*Trifolium* spp.), are also best kept at a distance.

Before contracting for the construction of a swimming pool, it is well to investigate its likely effect on the value of your property. In many areas, pools are valuable assets—notwithstanding the tax increases they characteristically bring—but in others, acute water shortages or other factors make pools liabilities that may lower overall property value.

Once these issues are considered and the responsibilities of pool ownership and maintenance are accepted, the pleasure of a swimming pool is immeasurable.

9

City Gardens

No garden is more artificially situated than the garden in the city. Moreover, difficulties commonly abound. It is usually cramped for space. Neighboring buildings often deprive it of adequate sunshine and air circulation. And getting quite ordinary materials in and out of a city backyard garden (soil, mulch, new plants, pruning refuse) can be a tiresome, cumbersome, disruptive task.

If, by ingenious design, the space has been well utilized and, by technical skill, the cultural requirements for healthy

The feathery foliage of honey locust (Gleditsia triacanthos) in corner box planters suggests tree fern, complementing the classic elegance of a rectangular lily pool, trellised archway, and ornate urn.

plant growth have been provided, such a garden can bring real satisfaction to the owner. Even if the existing arrangement is not acceptable, a careful remedial effort will bring returns in utility and aesthetic gratification that nearly always justify the effort.

The surroundings of the city garden make an architectural approach to its design the most logical one. The garden site should be enclosed by a wall or fence, thus achieving definition and securing privacy. Axes should be considered as a framework of the design, giving it strength of form and harmonizing it with the adjoining architecture. However, exact symmetry may not necessarily be important in so small a space. Such architectural features as sculpture, a wall fountain, balustrades, a bench, wrought-iron grills, colored tiles, and pavement all are stylistic elements, and they add color and interest of detail to a garden in which flowering plants may not play a dominant part. The design should be simple, straightforward, small in scale, economical of space, and above all, not crowded.

As with so many gardens, the background is an important part of the composition. Walls 8 or 9 feet high are an effective means of blocking unwanted views, but in some situations they shut out too much sunshine and air circulation, and should be used with a careful regard for the points of the compass.

For permanence, brick, hollow tile with stucco surface, hollow tile with colored-tile surface, or combinations of these, are all satisfactory. The coping atop a wall—whether tile, flagstone, or brick—can be made a decorative color note. Climbers grown on walls not only soften the severity of masonry but reduce unwanted heat radiation in summer. Such hardy vines as English and Boston ivy cling to brick by rootlets, but clematis, silver-lace vine (*Polygonum aubertii*), and many others require wires or lattices on which to climb. Lattices of painted or weather-resistant wood can be of simple decorative patterns. Wood frames are good, especially if made of pretreated lumber, but galvanized pipe or wrought iron is preferred for wisteria, a climber whose thickening stems can break wood trellises in a few years. A well-proportioned low brick wall with high brick piers and fencing between them is especially handsome and the combination of materials makes it an interesting architectural feature.

Vertical lines direct eyes upward and evoke a sense of spaciousness over this secluded nook, surrounded by potted plants.

Late summer luxuriance abounds in this trellis-shaded outdoor room, elegant with glossy pavers.

There are numerous types of wood fences that may be used to good effect. The close-woven type of fence made of cedar pickets is available in various heights and affords excellent protection. The basket-weave type with a lattice top to provide support for vines is attractive, reasonable in price, and easily erected. Modern louver fences are excellent, as they provide for a good circulation of air and at the same time ensure privacy and protection. Well-designed board fences are also very good. Prefabricated units are readily available. See Chapters 5 and 6 for the design and construction of walls and fences.

PATHS

Concrete is permanent and the most practical and economic material for walks, but it is harsh and glaring and its use in the garden should be avoided if possible. Its combination with colored pebbles of a fairly uniform size may give pattern to an otherwise monotonous surface. In this type of pavement, the pebbles are pressed into the surface of the concrete while it is still wet and protrude above the surface, forming a knobby, rough floor. Such a pavement may be combined with flagstone. In areas where there is no winter heaving from freezes and thaws, "popple" stones, or small cobblestones, may be set on edge into the ground and firmed by tamping. The art of laying such a pavement is practiced in England, Spain, Portugal, and Brazil, where the passion for decoration is strong; these stones are placed in patterns of varied colors and sizes, especially in the enclosed courts or patios of town houses.

Brick and flagstone are the most satisfactory materials for paths in the city garden. They are in harmony with the architectural surroundings and are attractive and permanent. Paths of loose pebbles or crushed gravel are also appropriate in small formal schemes but do require raking and weeding. See Chapter 5 for more on garden paths.

Many a city-yard garden is also the means of access from street to kitchen. As a yard it must often accommodate receptacles for waste containers. An enclosure for rubbish cans may sometimes be concealed behind a low wall, the top of which is a broad shelf for potted plants. If the path to the alley is at a slightly lower level than the rest of the garden, this concealment is all the more easily accomplished.

PRACTICAL CONSIDERATIONS

Before designing a city garden, it is important to determine whether the ground will absorb rain without puddling. If the drainage of surface water is poor, it is advisable to plan

A mixed border of summer flowers, house plants, and lofty shrubs surrounds a bricked sitting area and lawn, creating an intimate backyard room.

for raised planting beds. Such beds may be held in place by narrow walls of brick, by flagstones set on end, by planks, or by landscape ties.

Soil is almost always a problem in city gardens. Usually it must be purchased and brought in by truck. However, it is wise to obtain a sample of the soil before the purchase is made, as there is a great difference in the quality of topsoil. The ideal soil is a good loam well supplied with humus, such as is found in old pastures or in well-managed fields. When highways are put through, or when areas are sold for development and roads are put in, such soil may become available, and one is fortunate to be able to obtain it. When purchasing soil, one should stipulate that it is not to be loaded and delivered when too wet. This is particularly important in the case of clay soils, as they can become extremely difficult to handle when saturated with water, and equally difficult when dried out and pavement hard. Such soil requires amendments of sand and compost.

Apart from any physical improvements made, soil in city gardens should be tested for heavy metals, especially lead, before any vegetables, fruits, or herbs are grown. Lead poses a medical hazard for young children and pregnant women. Testing for it is especially important if food plants are grown near old buildings, where particles of lead-based paints may have accumulated in the soil over the years, or near busy streets, where load is exhaust residues from cars and trucks may also have accumulated. If lead is present above a threshold amount, the upper 1 foot of soil should be removed and replaced or the food plants should be grown in elevated beds or containers.

Since plants are in a more or less restricted soil area in a city garden, special care must be taken to see that their nutrient requirements are met and that a pH is maintained that will meet their specific needs. The care of plants in a city garden sometimes poses special problems. All plants suffer in degree from the pollutants in city air. This is particularly true in the case of the broad-leaved evergreens. The best way to overcome the harmful effects of soot and other particulate residues is to spray the foliage at frequent intervals with a strong stream of water from a hose nozzle.

PLANT MATERIALS

Vines on walls; accent plants in containers; shrubs and small trees as background; bulbs heralding the arrival of spring in the city; roses in flower from June until late autumn; the colorful bloom of petunias, dahlias, and lantana; the dramatic coloring of fancy-leaved caladiums; hanging baskets of geraniums, impatiens, or achimenes with cascades of richly colored flowers—much of the beauty of gardens in the surrounding countryside may be enjoyed in the small city garden if, after preparing the site, the plants are selected with care. Although many plants do not flourish under urban conditions, many others will make themselves quite happily at home in a city garden, including, surprisingly, some wildlings.

Since a city garden is usually small, each individual plant assumes an importance it would not have in a large-scale planting. Instead of long beds filled with tulips or irises, there may be room for only one or two groupings, and the varieties to be used should be chosen with great care. Instead of a wealth of spring bloom from a variety of flowering trees, there may be room for but one tree, and the selection of that particular tree, whether a star magnolia, a Japanese flowering cherry, a dogwood, or a lilac, becomes a matter of great importance.

Since comparatively little space can be devoted to flower beds and borders in a city garden, plants in pots and tubs can be used effectively, and with careful planning a succession of bloom may be achieved from early spring until late autumn. Pots of early spring bulbs may be followed by tulips and bleeding hearts, foxgloves and Canterbury bells. And an array of tuberous begonias, fancy-leaved caladiums, geraniums, impatiens, and other annuals will carry on until the chrysanthemums come into flower in early autumn. For more on plants in containers, see Chapter 4.

The plants included in the following table will thrive under average urban conditions and are well suited to the small city garden. The table is not all-inclusive. It should be kept in mind that many trees will grow well in the city and are excellent as street trees but if planted in a garden would soon become too large, overwhelm the site, and rob the shrubs and flowers of light and nutrients.

Bright annuals and rampant ivy grace artful containers and lattice in a cozy outdoor corner.

WOODY ORNAMENTALS ESPECIALLY SUITABLE FOR URBAN CONDITIONS

Name	Zones	Height	Comments
SMALL DECIDUOUS TREES			
Acer buergeranum (trident maple)	4–8	20–25'	Drought tolerant; variable fall color
A. campestre (English maple)	4–8	25–35'	Succeeds in pH 5.0–7.5; pest and disease free
A. ginnala (Amur maple)	2–7	15–20'	Easily moved; often shrubby; red fall color
A. tataricum (Tatarian maple)	3–8	15–20'	Tolerates drought and neutral pH; yellow fall color
Carpinus caroliniana (American hornbeam)	2–9	20–25'	Drought and shade tolerant; red to orange fall color
Crataegus crus-galli (cockspur thorn)	3–7	20–25'	Tolerates drought and high pH; white flowers; purplish fall color; cv. 'Ohio Pioneer' lacks thorns
C. phaenopyrum (Washington hawthorn)	3–8	25–30'	Disease free; white flowers; persistent red fruit
C. viridis 'Winter King' (winter king hawthorn)	4–8	25–35'	Drought tolerant; disease free; white flowers; red fall color
Sorbus × thuringiaca 'Fastigiata' (columnar oak-leaf mountain ash)	5–8	20–25'	Narrow upright habit; orange fruit in fall
Syringa reticulata (Japanese tree lilac)	3–7	20–30'	Drought tolerant; large clusters of creamy flowers; cherrylike bark; good in tubs
MEDIUM DECIDUOUS TREES			
Acer pseudoplatanus (sycamore maple)	4–8	40–60'	Very adaptable; no fall color; yellow-green flowers; self-sows
Eucommia ulmoides (hardy rubber tree)	4–7	40–75'	Very adaptable but shade intolerant; secretes latex
Fraxinus pennsylvanica (green ash)	3–9	50–60'	Cv. 'Marshall's Seedless' good as street and park tree
Ginkgo biloba (ginkgo or maidenhair tree)	3–9	50–75'	Open habit; disease free; fruit malodorous (in female trees only)
Pyrus calleryana (Callery pear)	4–8	35–40'	Pyramidal habit; white flowers before leaves; cvs. 'Capitol' and 'White House' resistant to crotch breakage
Quercus phellos (willow oak)	5–9	40–60'	Pollution and drought tolerant; small, narrow leaves
Q. rubra (red oak)	4–8	50–75'	Very adaptable; *Q. velutina* similar, good in coastal areas
Tilia tomentosa (silver linden)	4–7	50–70'	Pyramidal habit; leaves silvery and hairy beneath
Ulmus × hollandica 'Groenveldt' (hybrid Dutch elm)	4–9	40–50'	Resistant to Dutch elm disease
U. parvifolia (Chinese elm)	4–9	35–40'	Drought tolerant; peeling mottled bark
Zelkova serrata (Japanese zelkova)	5–8	50–60'	Elm shaped; smooth gray bark; cv. 'Green Vase' superior in habit
DECIDUOUS SHRUBS			
Acanthopanax sieboldianus (five-leaf aralia)	4–8	8–10'	Pest and disease free; thorny stems; good hedge shrub
Berberis thunbergii (Japanese barberry)	4–8	3–6'	Very adaptable; thorny stems; red berries; good hedge shrub
Cotinus coggygria (smokebush)	4–8	10–15'	Finely branched fruit clusters impart "smoky" affect; pest and disease free; full sun best
Deutzia scabra (fuzzy deutzia)	5–8	6–10'	Wide spreading; white flowers; requires annual removal of dead stems
Exochorda racemosa (common pearlbush)	4–8	10–15'	Showy white flowers; adapts easily to diverse conditions
Forsythia × intermedia (common forsythia)	4–8	8–10'	Wide spreading; showy yellow flowers (especially in cv. 'Lynwood'); very adaptable
Hibiscus syriacus 'Diana' (large-flowered rose of Sharon)	5–8	8–10'	Drought tolerant; flowers in late summer
Lagerstroemia indica (crape myrtle)	7–9	10–15'	Often treelike in South; white or pink flowers in summer
Ligustrum ovalifolium (California privet)	5–9	10–15'	Very adaptable, often used for hedging; aromatic white flowers, then glossy black berries
Myrica pennsylvanica (northern bayberry)	2–7	5–10'	Semievergreen; female with gray berries
Philadelphus coronarius (sweet mock orange)	4–8	10–12'	Several species and equally useful, all with white flowers

(continues)

WOODY ORNAMENTALS ESPECIALLY SUITABLE FOR URBAN CONDITIONS (*continued*)

Name	Zones	Height	Comments
Physocarpus opulifolius (eastern ninebark)	2–8	8–10'	Widespreading habit; cv. 'Dart's Golden' more compact, with yellow-green leaves
Rhododendron spp. and cvs. (deciduous azalea): **see Chapter 12**			
Rhodotypos scandens (jetbead)	4–8	3–6'	Shade tolerant; white flowers; glossy black fruit
Rosa spp. and cvs. (rose): **see Chapter 19**			
Spiraea × vanhouttei (bridal wreath)	3–8	6–8'	Wide spreading; white flowers; performs best in full sun
Symphoricarpos albus (snowberry)	2–7	3–6'	Persistent white fruit best displayed in *S. × doorenbosii* 'White Hedge'
Syringa vulgaris (common lilac)	3–7	8–15'	Double-flowered cvs. less likely to sucker from roots; fragrant flowers, purple to white
Tamarix parviflora (tamarisk)	4–8	10–15'	Small pink flowers in large clusters; several other similarly useful
Vitex agnus-castus (chaste bush, summer lilac)	7–9	8–10'	Lilac blue flowers in late summer; stems may die back in severe winters; *V. negundo* is somewhat hardier (zone 6)
Weigela florida	5–8	6–9'	Red, pink, or white flowers; some cvs. with variegated leaves

EVERGREEN SHRUBS

Name	Zones	Height	Comments
Buxus microphylla var. *koreana* (Korean box)	4–8	3–4'	Hardiest box; cvs. 'Tide Hill' and 'Wintergreen' retain strong green color throughout year
Ilex crenata (Japanese holly)	5–7	5–10'	Shade tolerant; various dwarf small-leaved cvs. (e.g., 'Helleri')
Kalmia latifolia (mountain laurel)	4–9	8–10'	Shade tolerant; white to rose flowers; hybrid cvs. with red buds dubiously hardy
Pieris japonica (Japanese andromeda)	5–8	8–10'	Shade tolerant; waxy white flowers; numerous cvs. with red buds and/or leaves; attacked by lacebug in East
Pinus mugo (mugo pine)	2–7	5–8'	Low, rounded habit; retains low, ground-hugging branches
P. sylvestris 'Watereri' (dwarf Scotch pine)	2–7	6–10'	Wide spreading habit; blue-green foliage
Pyracantha coccinea (firethorn)	6–9	6–15'	Red-orange fruit persisting into winter; several cvs., mostly half-evergreen north of zone 8
Rhododendron spp. and cvs. (rhododendron, evergreen azalea): **see Chapter 12**			
Taxus spp. and cvs. (yew)	4–7	1–20'	Dark green foliage; males with red fruit; many cvs. of diverse habit; *T. baccata* cvs. hardy to zone 2
Thuja occidentalis (eastern arborvitae)	2–7	3–25'	Cvs. 'Nigra' and 'Techny' retain bright green color throughout winter

WOODY CLIMBERS

Name	Zones	Height	Comments
Hedera helix (English ivy)	4–9	to 50'	Bears unlobed leaves and black berries when climbing; numerous cvs. of varying hardiness and habit
Parthenocissus quinquefolia (Virginia creeper)	3–10	to 50'	Tenacious tendril climber with adhesive discs; red fall color; too rampant except in large trees or on high walls
P. tricuspidata (Boston ivy)	4–8	to 50'	Similar to *P. quinquefolia* but with smaller lobed leaves and less rampant habit
Polygonum aubertii (silver-lace vine)	4–7	to 30'	Twining, forming thickets in absence of tall support; creamy white flowers
Wisteria spp. and cvs.	5–9	to 40'	Vigorous twiners with pendent (nodding in *W. frutescens*) flower clusters in lilac purple to white

Name	Zones	Height	Comments
GROUND COVERS			
Hedera helix (English ivy)	4–9	6–12"	Spreads 100' or more, with lobed juvenile leaves; evergreen; stem rooting
Pachysandra terminalis	3–8	8–12"	Spreads by rhizomes; glossy evergreen foliage; best in partial shade, especially South
Vinca minor (creeping myrtle)	3–8	3–6"	Spreads by rooting stems; flowers blue-violet or white; evergreen
DECIDUOUS HEDGE SHRUBS			
Berberis thunbergii (Japanese barberry)	4–8	4–7'	Small leaves; stems thorny; red berries
Caragana arborescens (Siberian pea bush)	2–7	15–18'	Fine-textured foliage; yellow pealike flowers
Chaenomeles spp. and cvs. (flowering quince)	4–8	3–10'	Thorny stems; showy red to white flowers, followed by spotted fruit
Eleagnus angustifolia (Russian olive)	2–7	10–20'	Silvery foliage; yellowish fruit
E. umbellata (autumn olive)	3–8	12–15'	Similar to *E. angustifolia* but with red fruit
Euonymus alata (burning bush)	3–8	5–12'	Winged or ridged twigs; scarlet foliage in fall
Hibiscus syriacus (rose of Sharon)	5–8	10–12'	Showy flowers in late summer
Ligustrum spp. and cvs. (privet)	3–10	4–15'	Glossy often half-evergreen foliage; perfumed flowers; black fruit
Lonicera fragrantissima (winter bush honeysuckle)	4–8	6–10'	Fragrant white flowers before foliage
L. tatarica (Tatarian bush honeysuckle)	3–8	10–12'	Early to leaf out; white flowers age to yellow; red berries sought by birds
Rosa spp. and cvs. (rugosa, shrub rose)	2–7	3–20'	Thorny stems; pink or white flowers; showy red-orange fruit
Spiraea × vanhouttei (bridal wreath)	3–8	6–8'	Masses of small white flowers in spring; best left unpruned
Syringa vulgaris (common lilac)	3–7	10–18'	Fragrant lilac or white flowers sacrificed with late summer or fall pruning
Viburnum opulus (European cranberry viburnum)	3–8	8–10'	White flowers; red fruit held into winter
V. prunifolium (black haw)	3–9	10–15'	Cream flowers; black fruit held to fall
EVERGREEN HEDGE SHRUBS			
Berberis julianae (wintergreen barberry)	5–8	5–6'	Thorny stems, prickly leaves; yellow flowers, followed by black berries
Buxus microphylla var. *koreana* (Korean box)	4–9	1–3'	Foliage usually yellowish in winter; green in 'Tide Hill' and 'Wintergreen' cvs.
Ilex crenata 'Microphylla' (littleleaf Japanese holly)	5–8	2–4'	Small leathery leaves; female with black berries
Juniperus chinensis (Chinese juniper)	3–9	1–20'	Blue-green foliage; numerous cvs. of widely divergent habit
J. scopulorum (Rocky Mountain juniper)	3–7	10–20'	Green to steel blue foliage; numerous
J. virginiana (eastern red cedar)	2–9	15–30'	Dark green to blue-green foliage according to cv.
Taxus cuspidata (Japanese yew)	4–7	3–8'	Lustrous dark green foliage; upright cvs. 'Capitata' and 'Pyramidalis' very good as hedge shrubs
T. × media (hybrid yew)	4–7	3–8'	Lustrous dark green foliage; upright cvs. 'Hatfieldii' and 'Hicksii' very good as hedge shrubs
Thuja occidentalis (eastern arborvitae)	2–8	10–20'	Cv. 'Nigra' especially good, remaining green in winter
T. orientalis (Oriental arborvitae)	5–9	20–25'	Young foliage yellow-green, aging dark green
T. plicata (western arborvitae)	5–7	25–35'	Foliage dark green throughout year; cv. 'Atrovirens' good as hedge shrub
Tsuga caroliniana (Carolina hemlock)	4–7	15–25'	Superior to *T. canadensis* under city conditions

ROOF, TERRACE, AND BALCONY GARDENS

Apartment living has led to the development of roof or penthouse gardens as well as gardening on terraces and balconies high above the ground. The special problems inherent in gardening above grade are many and must be dealt with if success and satisfaction are to be had.

Before embarking on rooftop or terrace gardening at anything more than an incidental scale, whether atop a multistory apartment house or on the flat deck over an attached garage, two important factors must be considered: the load-bearing capacity of the roof and the availability and drainage of water. As soil-filled containers can quickly total tons of additional weight, the counsel of a structural engineer is usually advisable. Although the rapid evaporation of soil moisture, especially in warm, windy weather, makes for frequent watering, the ability to shed excess water after a deluge means that efficient drainage is equally critical.

No less important to planning, especially on roof terraces and balconies, is exposure: the number of hours and time of day the area receives direct sun during the growing season, the intensity of reflected light in areas not reached by the sun, the changes in sun exposure during the growing season, and the strength and direction of prevailing winds. In general, east or southeast exposures are best, west or southwest are hotter and windier, and northerly exposures are not only windy but receive less direct sun. Screening helps ameliorate both intense sun and high wind and thus can help reduce moisture loss.

Since a roof garden imposes distinct limitations in the use of plant materials, its charm depends to a considerable extent on its design and architectural embellishment. Because of the restrictions of the surroundings, design is best kept simple and formal. If at all possible, a pleasant sitting area and an attractive place for outdoor dining should be provided. Space and layout permitting, it is sometimes feasible to design a series of outdoor rooms separated by low hedges or fencing, reminiscent of Spanish patios. Such an arrangement affords a feeling of intimacy and can provide welcome protection from potentially damaging and often desiccating high winds.

Even on the most substantial roofs and terraces, the careful distribution and restriction of added weight is desirable. Tubs, half barrels, boxes, and other planters should be kept to the perimeter. Long boxes 14 to 18 inches deep, which distribute weight over a greater area, are preferable to deep tubs. Roof drains should be left uncovered and kept clean. Containers of lightweight cinder block, plastic, or metal are usually longer lasting than those of treated wood. All containers must have drainage holes or weep holes, and before any soil is added,

A free-standing trellis panel mirrors an adjacent French door, with the trellis motif carried onto planter boxes and furniture.

the bottom of each container should be covered with a 2-inch layer of pebbles, cinders, oyster shells, coke, or other coarse material to promote drainage. Each container should be raised about 1 inch above the roof. The soil mix should consist of one-quarter to one-third high-quality topsoil, with the rest being equal parts of peat moss and either perlite or vermiculite. The mix should include about 1 pound dolomite (ground limestone) or bonemeal per bushel of mix. Initially, and each spring thereafter, 1 inch of dried cow manure should be worked in, both to supply nutrients and to maintain good physical soil quality. Supplemental dolomite or bonemeal is best added in the fall to control the gradual acidification that usually takes place in containers. Soilless mixes are not suitable, as they afford poor root anchorage in high wind.

Well-placed architectural features, such as a wall fountain with a small pool below, ornamental pots, or a piece of sculpture, will contribute greatly to the charm of the roof garden. The areas devoted to outdoor living may be paved with tile, brick, or flagstone, or they may be carpeted with artificial turf. If, however, living turf is used, there should be at least 4 inches of good topsoil, and a good maintenance program is essential (see Chapter 10 for more information).

The greatest hazards with roof gardening are year-round wind and intense summer sunshine. Unprotected plants, especially if in small containers, quickly dry out and topple unless protected from winds—whose velocities at roof level far exceed those on the ground. Close-woven cedar picket fencing, available in prefabricated sections of varied dimensions, anchored securely to heavy soil-filled planter boxes is excellent for this purpose. Latticed Chinese fencing with translucent panels is both decorative and practical. Various types of wood-panel fencing are also suitable.

Particular attention should be given to the choice of furniture. It should be not only comfortable but also weather resistant and heavy enough to stay in place when the wind is gusty.

Selection of Plants

Plants for a roof garden must be selected with great care as many will not survive the rigors of strong wind and intense summer sun. The planting compositions should be carefully studied. Where feasible, there should be a few trees to give height and scale to the planting; shrubs with good evergreen foliage to provide year-round beauty; vines to adorn and soften the walls that provide enclosure for the garden; bulbs for the special joy they bring to any garden, especially in spring; and freely flowering plants throughout the season.

Trees

A number of trees have proved well adapted to the trying conditions of a roof garden and can be grown very satisfactorily in large tubs, casks, and planting boxes. When the root growth is thus restricted, the trees remain dwarfed, but this is usually an advantage in the roof garden setting. The fine-textured mimosa tree (*Albizia julibrissin*) does well in an eastern exposure, and its feathery, interesting foliage has unique charm. Its one disadvantage is that in the latitude of New York (zone 7) it is relatively short lived. Both the river birch (*Betula nigra*) and the gray or white birch (*Betula populifolia*) thrive and are decorative and graceful. The hardier hybrid hollies (*Ilex* spp. and cvs.) will do well if given a location in partial shade, and with deep green, glossy foliage and red berries, they are a thing of joy throughout the year. The Lombardy poplar (*Populus nigra* 'Italica') is best used as an accent against a high wall, where a tree of slender, tapering form is desired. Although not long lived even under the most favorable conditions, it will usually remain vigorous and attractive for some years on a rooftop terrace. Willows are among the easiest trees to grow, and they withstand the wind well. Graceful in form, they will often reach a height of 20 feet or more on a rooftop terrace, but may require

bracing in time. Also graceful in form and lovely when in flower are the Japanese cherries.

Some of the fruit trees, such as apples and pears, may be espaliered against walls, that is, trained to grow horizontally along regularly spaced supports. When trained in this way, they become a decorative feature of the roof garden and in time may bear a small quantity of delicious fruit. The ubiquitous ailanthus will thrive anywhere, under any conditions, but there are so many other superior trees that it is hardly deserving of space in a roof garden.

Shrubs

A number of very choice shrubs as well as many of the commoner types may be grown successfully in tubs and planting boxes in the roof garden. Many hardy azaleas thrive, especially if placed behind walls or away from harsh winds, and with their abundant and colorful bloom they add greatly to the charm of the garden in spring. Some of the hardiest species of the camellia, such as *Camellia sasanqua*, will thrive if grown in a protected corner where they can have partial

*With adequate light, hybrid purple clematis (*Clematis *Jackmannii Superba') blooms in late summer, contrasting effectively against the diagonal trellis.*

shade during the summer and some wind protection during the winter. They will come into flower in October and remain in bloom for a month or more. Forsythia may be allowed to assume its naturally graceful form, or it may be trained as an espalier against a wall where its branches will form a cascade of golden bloom in the spring. Among the evergreen shrubs particularly valued because of their beauty at all seasons are Japanese andromeda (*Pieris japonica*) and hardy firethorn (*Pyracantha coccinea* 'Lalandei'), which, with its brilliant orange berries, is one of the glories of autumn. *Pyracantha* may be easily trained to any desired form against a wall and is a most decorative feature in a planting composition. Both Regel's privet (*Ligustrum obtusifolium* var. *regelianum*) and the more common California privet (*Ligustrum ovalifolium*) also thrive under rooftop conditions, as does Japanese yew (*Taxus cuspidata*).

Climbers

Because of the great expanse of wall that often encloses a roof garden, climbers play an important part in the planting design. English ivy will usually thrive against a north or east wall but will be unable to endure the intensity of the sun on a wall with a southern or southwestern exposure. In the confinement of a tub or box, the otherwise invasive Japanese honeysuckle (*Lonicera japonica*) may be appreciated for its beloved fragrance and will give intermittent bloom from June to November, and the decorative silver-lace vine (*Polygonum aubertii*) will thrive under almost any conditions. Wisteria, one of nature's masterpieces, will also do well on rooftop terraces, making the weeks when it is in flower a memorable occasion. For rapid growth and quick shade, the Puerto Rican yam (*Dioscorea batatas*) is very good, and many of the annual climbers—such as moonflower (*Ipomoea alba*), morning glory (*Ipomoea nil*, *I. purpurea*, and *I. tricolor*), scarlet runner bean (*Phaseolus coccineus*), and cypress vine (*Ipomoea quamoclit*)—are also excellent and may be used very happily while the more permanent vines are becoming established.

Flowers

With careful planning, a succession of bloom may be achieved in the garden from early spring until late autumn. The spring bulbs, pansies, violas, and forget-me-nots, all of which may be purchased in pots or baskets, usher in the season of spring and are followed by greenhouse-grown annuals brought into early bloom. Perennials play a minor role in the rooftop garden. Their period of bloom is usually comparatively short and planting space is at such a premium that it cannot be spared. Some of the perennials, such as lovely old-fashioned bleeding heart, and some of the biennials, such as Canterbury bell and sweet William, can be purchased in large pots when just coming into bloom; they will continue to flower for many weeks. Among the sun-loving annuals there is a wide choice: the ever dependable petunias, which are available in enchanting colors and will give abundant bloom throughout the season; ageratum; alyssum, including the tetraploid giant variety 'Snowdrift', which will continue to flower until heavy frost; seedling dahlias in lovely colors; lantana, which thrives in intense heat; zinnias in pastel shades; and the marigolds, which never fail to be prolific with their blooms.

For fragrance there are nicotiana, night-blooming stock, heliotrope, and lavender, and for accents here and there, geraniums.

For shady areas there are the foliage plants such as coleus and named varieties of fancy-leaved caladiums. For north and west exposures, where they will receive good light but little direct sunshine, there are begonias and fuchsias as well as the ever-reliable impatiens.

In autumn, potted chrysanthemums may be used to replace some of the annuals that have begun to look a bit shabby, and a patch here and there of autumn crocus, which should be planted in August, will bring added interest.

Roses

Some roses, such as the lovely floribundas and the more stately grandifloras, grow extraordinarily well in the environs of a rooftop garden. In the latitude of New York they are often in full leaf by the middle of March and are in almost continuous bloom from June until late autumn. They may be grown in tubs, in planting boxes, or in specially prepared raised beds. Among the most dependable varieties for the roof garden are 'Betty Prior', which will reach a height of 4 to 5 feet and is never out of bloom; 'Carrousel'; 'Floradora'; 'Spartan'; and 'Vogue'.

*A clump of autumn crocus (*Colchicum speciosum *'Autumn Queen') provides a floral surprise in late summer when few other bulbs are blooming.*

*Rain forms beads on the waxy blades of fancy-leaf caladium (*Caladium × hortulanum *'Frieda Hemple'). Variegation in caladium ranges from green and red to white with green veins, according to cultivar.*

PLANTS SUITABLE FOR ROOF GARDENS

Name	Zones	Height	Exposure**	Comments
TREES*				
Albizia julibrissin 'E. H. Wilison' (hardy mimosa, silk tree)	5–9	—	S to PSh	Pink and white flowers in summer
Betula pendula 'Youngii' (dwarf weeping European birch)	3–7	—	S to PSh	White bark; weeping habit
B. populifolia (gray birch)	3–7	—	S to PSh	Whitish bark
Caragana arborescens (pea tree)	2–7	—	S to PSh	Yellow flowers in spring; low growing
Cataegus laevigata 'Crimson Cloud' (red hawthorn)	4–7	—	S to PSh	Red flowers in spring; thorny; requires deep tub
Ginkgo biloba (maidenhair tree)	3–8	—	S to PSh	Use male only as fruit is malodorous
Gleditsia triacanthos var. *inermis* (thornless honey locust)	3–9	—	S to PSh	Several cultivars
Malus cvs. (ornamental crab apple)	5–7	—	S to PSh	The following cultivars are disease resistant: 'Adams' (flowers: red aging to pink; fruit: red), 'Callaway' (flowers: pink aging to white; fruit: maroon), 'Centurion' (flowers: red aging to rose; fruit: red), 'Dolgo' (flowers: pink aging to white; fruit: red-violet), 'Evelyn' (flowers: deep rose; fruit: yellow and red), 'Harvest Gold' (flowers: white; fruit: yellow), 'Katherine' (flowers: pink; fruit: yellow and red), 'Molten Lava' (flowers: red aging to white; fruit: red-orange), 'Professor Sprenger' (flowers: pink aging to white; fruit: red-orange), 'White Cascade' (flowers: pink aging to white; fruit: yellow)
Prunus cerasifera cvs. 'Atropurpurea', 'Newport',	3–8	—	S to PSh	Purple leaves and 'Thundercloud' (purple plum)
P. serrulata cvs. (flowering cherry)	5–8	—	S to PSh	The following cultivars (with flower color) are recommended: 'Amanogawa' (semidouble pink), 'Sekiyama' (syn. 'Kwanzan') (double pink), 'Shirofugen' (pink aging to white), 'Shirotae' (syn. 'Mt. Fuji') (semidouble white)
P. subhirtella vars. (flowering cherry)	5–8	—	S to PSh	The following varieties (with flower color) are recommended: *pendula* (single to double, deep to pale pink), *autumnalis* (semidouble pink, some blooms in fall, the rest of the blooms in spring)

(continues)

PLANTS SUITABLE FOR ROOF GARDENS (*continued*)

Name	Zones	Height	Exposure**	Comments
P. yedoensis cvs. (flowering cherry)	5–8	—	S to PSh	The following cultivars (with flower color) are recommended: 'Akebono' (double pink), 'Hally Jolivette' (double pink aging to white) 'Pink Shell' (pink aging to pale pink), 'Yochino' (pale pink)
Pyrus calleryann (Callery pear)	4–8	—	S to PSh	White flowers; bronzy fall foliage; avoid cv. 'Bradford' as it is easily broken
P. ussuriensis (Chinese pear)	3–7	—	S to PSh	White flowers
Salix alba 'Tristis' (golden weeping willow)	2–8	—	S to PSh	Weeping habit; yellowish twigs
S. matsudana 'Tortuosa' (corkscrew willow)	4–8	—	S to PSh	Contorted twigs and leaves

DECIDUOUS SHRUBS[†]

Name	Zones	Height	Exposure**	Comments
Aronia arbutifolia 'Brilliantissima' (red chokeberry)	4–9	6–10'	S to PSh	White flowers in spring; red berries in fall
Berberis thunbergii (Japanese barberry)	4–8	4–7'	S to PSh	Yellow flowers in spring; red berries in fall
Buddleia davidii (butterfly bush)	5–9	8–12'	S to PSh	Purple to white flowers in summer; fruit inconspicuous
Calycanthus floridus (Carolina allspice, strawberry shrub)	4–9	6–8'	S to PSh to LSh	Dark red-brown flowers in spring or summer; brownish berries in fall
Cotoneaster horizontalis (rockspray cotoneaster)	4–8	1–2'	S to PSh to LSh	White flowers in spring; red berries in summer and fall
Deutzia scabra 'Candidissima' (double-white deutzia)	5–8	6–8'	S to PSh	White flowers in spring; fruit inconspicuous
Euonymus alata 'Compactus' (burning bush)	3–8	6–8'	S to PSh	Red fall foliage; corky ridges on twigs
Forsythia spp. and cvs.	6–9	4–10'[‡]	S to PSh	Yellow flowers in spring; fruit inconspicuous
Hamamelis mollis, H. japonica, H. × intermedia 'Arnold Promise' (Oriental witch hazel)	5–8	10–15'	S to PSh	Yellow or red-brown flowers in late winter to early spring; fruit inconspicuous
Hibiscus syriacus cvs. 'Diana' and 'Helene' (large-flowered rose of Sharon)	5–8	10–12'	S to PSh	Purplish to white flowers in summer; fruit inconspicuous
Hydrangea paniculata 'Grandiflora' (peegee hydrangea)	3–8	10–15'	S to PSh	White, then purplish pink, finally brown flowers in summer and fall; no fruit
Ligustrum spp. and cvs. (privet)	3–10	4–15'	S to PSh to LSh	White flowers in summer; black berries in summer and fall
Magnolia stellata cvs. (star magnolia)	3–8	8–15'	S to PSh	White or pink flowers in early spring; green fruit in summer
Philadelphus spp. and cvs. (mock orange)	4–8	6–8'	S to PSh	White flowers in spring and summer; fruit inconspicuous
Pyracantha coccinea 'Lalandei' (hardy firethorn)	5–9	8–10'	S to PSh	White flowers in spring; red-orange to yellow berries in fall and winter
Rosa spp. and cvs. (rose)	2–9[‡]	1–12'[‡]	S to PSh	Flowers of a wide color range in spring to fall; some cultivars have red-orange hips in fall
Tamarix ramosissima (tamarisk)	2–8	10–15'	S to PSh	Rose pink flowers in spring; fruit inconspicuous
Vaccinium corymbosum (highbush blueberry)	3–7	8–12'	S to PSh	Cream flowers in spring; dark purple, gray bloomy berries in summer
Viburnum carlesii 'Cayuga' (Korean spice viburnum)	4–7	6–8'	S to PSh	Pink buds and white flowers in spring; fruit inconspicuous
Weigela florida cvs.	5–8	6–9'	S to PSh	Red, pink, or white flowers in spring and summer; fruit inconspicuous

EVERGREEN SHRUBS

Name	Zones	Height	Exposure**	Comments
Aucuba japonica cvs. (Japanese laurel)	7–10	3–6'	PSh to LSh	Flowers inconspicuous; red berries (females only) in fall
Euonymus fortunei erect cvs. (shrubby wintercreeper)	5–8	4–5'	S to PSh to LSh	Flowers inconspicuous; red and orange fruit in fall

Name	Zones	Height	Exposure**	Comments
Ilex aquifolium cvs. (English holly)	6–9	3–12'‡	S to PSh to LSh	White flowers in spring; red berries (females only) in fall
I. crenata cvs. (Japanese holly)	5–7	2–10'‡	S to PSh to LSh	White flowers in spring; black berries (females only) in fall
I. opaca cvs. (American holly)	5–9	3–12'‡	S to PSh to LSh	White flowers in spring; red berries (females only) in fall
Juniperus spp. and cvs. (juniper)	2–9	1½–10'‡	S to PSh	Flowering cones inconspicuous; blue-gray berries (females only) in summer and fall
Leucothoë fontanesiana (drooping leucothoë)	4–7	4–5'	PSh to LSh	White flowers in spring; brown fruit in fall
Pieris japonica (andromeda)	5–8	8–12'	S to PSh	White flowers in early spring; brown fruit in fall
Pinus mugo (mugo pine)	2–7	3–6'	S to PSh	Woody cone
P. thunbergii (Japanese black pine)	5–7	6–15'	S to PSh	Woody cone
Prunus laurocerasus cvs. (cherry laurel)	5–9	10–15'	S to PSh to LSh	White flowers in spring; violet black fruit in summer and fall
Skimmia japonica (Japanese skimmia)	7–8	2–4'	PSh to LSh	Maroon buds and cream flowers in early spring; red fruit (females only) in summer to winter
Taxus spp. and cvs. (yew)	2–8‡	2–10'‡	S to PSh	Red fruit (females only) in summer
Thuja occidentalis cvs. (American arborvitae)	2–7	10–20'	S to PSh	Woody conelet
WOODY CLIMBERS				
Akebia quinata (five-leaf akebia)	4–8	20–40'	S to PSh to LSh	Purple flowers in spring; purple fruit (rarely seen) in summer
Aristolochia durior (Dutchman's-pipe)	4–8	20–30'	S to PSh to LSh	Green and purple flowers in summer; green fruit ripens brown in fall
Celastrus orbiculata and *C. scandens* (bittersweet)	3–8	20–30'	S to PSh	Green flowers in spring; orange and yellow fruit in fall
Hydrangea anomala (including ssp. *petiolaris*) (climbing hydrangea)	4–7	20–50'	S to PSh	White flowers in spring or summer; fruit inconspicuous
Lonicera × *heckrottii* (goldflame honeysuckle)	4–9	10–15'	S to PSh	Red and yellow flowers spring to fall; red fruit summer to fall
L. japonica (Japanese honeysuckle)	4–9	20–25'	S to PSh	White and yellow flowers in spring and summer; black fruit in summer and fall
L. sempervirens (trumpet honeysuckle)	4–9	10–15'	S to PSh	Red and yellow flowers in spring and summer; red fruit in summer and fall
Parthenocissus quinquefolia (Virginia creeper)	3–10	30–50'	S to PSh to LSh	Greenish flowers in summer; black fruit in fall
P. tricuspidata (Boston ivy)	4–8	25–35'	S to PSh to LSh	Greenish flowers in summer; black fruit in fall
Polygonum aubertii (silver-lace vine)	4–7	25–35'	S to PSh	White flowers in summer; greenish fruit in fall
Vitis spp. and cvs. (grape)	5–8‡	30–50'	S to PSh	Greenish flowers in spring; green or purple fruit (females only) in summer and fall
Wisteria spp. and cvs. (wisteria)	5–9	35–50'	S to PSh	Violet, lilac, or white flowers in spring; green pods ripen brown in fall
PERENNIALS§				
Achillea millefolium (pink yarrow)	4–9	18–24"	S to PSh	Flowers: pink or red; bloom time: M-L
Chrysanthemum × *morifolium* (hardy mum)	5–8	12–36"	S to PSh	Flowers: various colors; bloom time: L
Coreopsis lanceolata 'Early Sunrise' (dwarf coreopsis)	4–8	12–18"	S to PSh	Flowers: yellow; bloom time: E-M
C. verticillata 'Moonbeam' (threadleaf coreopsis)	4–8	18–24"	S to PSh	Flowers: cream; bloom time: E-L

(continues)

PLANTS SUITABLE FOR ROOF GARDENS (continued)

Name	Zones	Height	Exposure**	Comments
Geranium sanguineum (blood-red hardy geranium)	4–8	6–12"	S to PSh	Flowers: magenta; bloom time: E-M
Hemerocallis cvs. (hybrid daylily)	4–10	12–36"	S to PSh	Flowers: all colors but blue; bloom time: M; some cultivars (e.g., 'Stella d'Oro') will reflower through fall
Hosta plantaginea (fragrant plantain lily)	4–8	18–30"	PSh to LSh	Flowers: white; bloom time: L; requires midday shade, especially in the South
Iberis sempervirens (evergreen candytuft)	4–8	6–9"	S to PSh	Flowers: white; bloom time: E
Iris kaempferi cvs. (Japanese iris)	5–8	24–40"	S to PSh	Flowers: purple, lavender, or white; bloom time: E-M
Liatris scariosa (blazing star, gayfeather)	4–8	18–60"	S to PSh	Flowers: rose, lavender, or white; bloom time: M-L
Lysimachia nummularia (creeping Charlie)	4–8	2–4"	S to PSh	Flowers: yellow; bloom time: E-M
Sedum spectabile 'Ruby Glow'	4–8	6–8"	S to PSh	Flowers: dark ruby red; bloom time: L
S. spectabile 'Autumn Joy'	4–9	18–24"	S to PSh	Flowers: pink aging to rose red; bloom time: L

ANNUALS⌡

Name	Zones	Height	Exposure**	Comments
Ageratum houstonianum cvs. (dwarf ageratum)	—	4–6"	S to PSh	Flowers: lavender blue, pink, or white; bloom time: E-L
Begonia Semperflorens-Cultorum hybrids (fibrous-rooted begonia)	—	6–12"	S to PSh	Flowers: Red, pink, or white; bloom time: E-L
Calendula officinalis	—	12–18"	S	Flowers: orange, yellow; bloom time: E-L; flowering may diminish or cease in hot weather
Celosia cristata cvs. (cockscomb)	—	6–30"	S	Flowers: red, pink, orange, and/or yellow; bloom time: M-L
C. cristata 'Plumosa' group (plume cockscomb)	—	12–30"	S	Flowers: red, pink, orange, and/or yellow; bloom time: M-L
Dahlia cvs. (bedding dahlia)	—	12–24"	S to PSh	Flowers: all but blue; bloom time: M-L; flowering may diminish or cease in hot weather; tubers may be dug in fall and stored indoors for culture the next year
Heliotropium arborescens (heliotrope)	—	12–18"	S	Flowers: violet, blue, or lavender; bloom time: M-L
Impatiens walleriana cvs.	—	6–18"	PSh to LSh	Flowers: red, pink, orange, or white; bloom time: E-L
I. cvs. (New Guinea impatiens)	—	8–24"	S to PSh	Flowers: red, pink, lavender, or white; bloom time: E-L
Lobelia erinus cvs. (edging lobelia)	—	4–8"	S to PSh	Flowers: purple, magenta, blue, or white; bloom time: E-L; flowering may diminish or cease in hot weather
Lobularia maritima cvs. (sweet alyssum)	—	4–8"	S to PSh	Flowers: white, pink, or lavender; bloom time E-L
Petunia × hybrida cvs.	—	8–15"	S to PSh	Flowers: various; bloom time: E-L
Portulaca grandiflora cvs.	—	3–6"	S	Flowers: red, pink, yellow, or white; bloom time: M
Rudbeckia hirta var. *pulcherrima* 'Gloriosa' (gloriosa daisy)	—	24–36"	S	Flowers: yellow and brown; bloom time: M-L
Salvia farinacea cvs. (mealycup sage)	—	18–24"	S	Flowers: deep blue or white; bloom time: M-L
S. splendens cvs. (scarlet sage)	—	10–24"	S to PSh	Flowers: red, pink, purple, or white; bloom time: M-L
Scabiosa atropurpurea	—	12–26"	S	Flowers: purple, red, pink, yellow, or white; bloom time: M-L
Tagetes erecta cvs. (African marigold)	—	12–36"	S	Flowers: orange to yellow; bloom time: E-L
T. patula cvs. (French marigold)	—	6–18"	S	Flowers: orange, yellow, and/or red-brown; bloom time: E-L; flowering may diminish or cease in hot weather

Name	Zones	Height	Exposure**	Comments
Torenia fournierii cvs. (wishbone flower)	—	8–12"	PSh	Flowers: purple, blue, pink, or white; bloom time: M-L
Tropaeolum majus dwarf cvs. (nasturtium)	—	8–12"	S	Flowers: red, orange, yellow, or white; bloom time: M-L; flowering may diminish or cease in hot weather
Zinnia elegans cvs.	—	12–36"	S	Flowers: all but blue; bloom time: M-L
ANNUAL CLIMBERS				
Dolichos lablab (hyacinth bean)	—	10–12'	S	Flowers: lavender or white; bloom time: M-L
Ipomoea alba (moonflower)	—	10–15'	S	Flowers: white; bloom time: M-L; blooms at night
I. quamoclit (cardinal climber)	—	6–10'	S	Flowers: red or white; bloom time: M-L
I. spp. (morning glory)	—	10–15'	S	Flowers: red, purple, blue, or white; bloom time: M-L
Thunbergia alata (black-eyed Susan vine)	—	10–15'	S	Flowers: orange to white; bloom time: M-L
HARDY BULBS#				
Chionodoxa luciliae (glory-of-the-snow)	5–8	3–6"	S	Blue and white flowers in early spring
Crocus spp. and cvs.	4–9	4–6"	S	Purple, lavender, yellow, or white flowers in early spring
Galanthus elwesii (giant snowdrop)	5–8	10–12"	S to PSh	White and green flowers in late winter
G. nivalis (common snowdrop)	4–8	4–8"	S to PSh	White and green flowers in late winter to early spring
Hyacinthus orientalis cvs. (hyacinth)	5–8	10–14"	S	Various colors of flowers in spring
Muscari armeniacum (Armenian grape hyacinth)	5–8	6–9"	S	Blue flowers in early spring
M. botryoides (common grape hyacinth)	4–8	4–8"	S	Blue or white flowers in early spring
Narcissus spp. and cvs. (daffodil, jonquil)	5–9	6–24"	S	Pale yellow to deep red-orange flowers in early to mid spring
Ornithogalum umbellatum (star-of-Bethlehem)	4–8	8–12"	S to PSh	White flowers in spring
Scilla siberica (Siberian squill)	5–8	4–6"	S to PSh	Deep blue or white flowers in early spring
Tulipa spp. and cvs. (tulip)	5–7	6–30"	S	All flower colors except blue in early to late spring
TENDER BULBS				
Begonia × *tuberhybrida* (tuberous begonia)	—	8–15"	S to PSh	Flowers: red, pink, yellow, or white; bloom time: M-L
Caladium × *hortulanum* (fancy-leaf caladium)	—	12–24"	PSh	Leaves: variegated red, rose, salmon, white, and/or green; bloom time: M-L
Canna × *generalis*	—	18–72"	S	Flowers: red, pink, orange, or yellow; bloom time: M-L; some with bronzy leaves
Gladiolus × *hortulanus*	—	12–60"	S	Flowers: all but blue; bloom time: M-L

* No heights given, as they are determined by restriction in containers and by exposure.

† Height assumes adequate container and wind protection.

‡ Varies according to cultivar.

§ Full sun or partial shade is necessary for best flowering.

ʃ If E is indicated as bloom time, it is assumed that the plant was greenhouse grown.

All require maximum sun exposure to rebloom in successive years.

** S, full sun; Sh, shade (no direct sun); PSh, partial shade (sun exposure only part of the day); LSh, light shade (e.g., the shade of tall, open trees, with little or no exposure to direct sun).

Key: Bloom times: E, early (spring to early summer); M, mid (early to late summer); L, late (late summer to fall).

II

Plant Selection and Culture

LAWNS • TREES • SHRUBS • WOODY CLIMBERS • GROUND COVERS •

HERBACEOUS PERENNIALS • BULBS • ANNUALS • BIENNIALS • ROSES

10

Lawns

A LEGACY FROM FEUDAL TIMES, THE LAWN WAS originally an open pasture surrounding a castle that facilitated protective surveillance and afforded forage for horses and other stock animals. Today, lawns are a focus of home ownership. Their preparation and care consume scores of hours and hundreds of dollars annually as the home gardener strives to grow a sward that provides access to the grounds and demonstrates personal pride in the property. A dense green turf not only is a pleasure to behold but serves as a living self-renewing

Bold, parallel, uniform courses of contrasting shades of green bespeak the recent passage of a power mower and temporarily reinforce the simple horizontal lines of house architecture and foundation hedging.

129

A legacy of the past and commendably serving several purposes, this sward feeds sheep who simultaneously keep the orchard neat, weed-free, and accessible and the soil for both trees and grass fertilized.

carpet that withstands trampling, mowing, and the extremes of heat and cold as well as wind and drought. Anthropologists point out that in enjoying the lawn, especially one punctuated with medallions of floral color and patches of shade, we may be responding to a deeply seated genetic urge that drives us to seek or create such a habitat.

So important have lawns become in today's busy world that home owners often contract others to regularly mow and groom their lawns and to apply fertilizers and pesticides to keep them in optimal condition. This singular drive for turf perfection has become so intense that in some parts of the United States the negative environmental effects of lawn care have caused alarm. Studies of these effects have led to restrictions on the use of water, fertilizers, and pesticides in these areas. In densely settled suburban regions where water use for all purposes often overtaxes public water resources, questions have been raised not only about lawn sprinkling and the often ritual use of polluting fertilizers and pesticides but also about the desirability of committing large areas to turf rather than to other less demanding types of landscape vegetation.

Thus, in recent years, the thoughtful, responsible home gardener's first question regarding the lawn has shifted from how to get the best lawn for the least effort and expense to whether any lawn is desirable and, if so, how little will satisfy needs. Alternatives to the mowed lawn include wildflower meadows, ground cover beds, plantings of flowering shrubs and small trees, and of course, gardens of perennials and annuals—none of which is maintenance free or capable of withstanding repetitive foot traffic. But, if carefully designed and managed, they require far less work than lawn and are less likely to cause environmental harm.

Wherever lawn is desired, whether new or existing, it is important to choose kinds of turf grasses that are well suited to local conditions. The better suited lawn grasses are to the local idiosyncracies of soil, rainfall, temperature extremes, and exposure, the less care is required. In many areas, lawns can be maintained with no intervention whatever, save mowing. Indeed, this should be the goal for all. If substantial, regular applications of fertilizers, pesticides, fungicides, and water prove necessary to keep the lawn presentable, it is time to analyze the situation and ask whether the right kinds of grass have been chosen or whether lawn is the best treatment of the area in question.

Among the relatively few kinds of grasses that are favored for lawns, some thrive best under cool, moist growing

A neatly trimmed weed-free patch of Zoysia makes a pleasing transition between hard, gray concrete and a cheery flower border.

conditions, while others will withstand extreme heat and drought. Some grasses require a very high level of soil fertility, other types will grow on relatively poor soils; some will grow well in partial shade, other types must have full sun; some endure hard wear, while others need protection from heavy traffic.

It is, therefore, important to select a grass or a mixture of grasses that will be well adapted to the climate and will meet one's specific needs, whether it be exceptionally fine turf for a terrace, a rugged turf on which strenuous games will be played, or a good general-purpose lawn for family use and enjoyment.

Before reaching a final decision, it is wise to become familiar with the advantages and disadvantages of the various grasses that are adapted to one's locality. County extension agents and nearby botanic gardens can usually provide valuable authoritative information and guidance.

The quality of the seed is also important. In purchasing grass seed, it is poor economy to buy cheap or "bargain" seed. A lawn should be viewed as a long-term investment, and only the best quality of seed from a reliable source

should be considered. Cheap seed often tests low in germination and is apt to contain a high percentage of chaff and weed seeds or seeds of inferior grasses. State laws require that all grass seeds be labeled and that the following information be available on the tag: percentage of germination along with the name of each grass and its percentage by weight.

In purchasing grass seed, it is important to note the percentage of germination as stated on the tag. For high-quality seed, the germination percentage should run not lower than 80 percent; 90 percent or higher is preferable.

As lawn grasses differ in their tolerance of varying conditions of exposure, moisture, fertility, acidity, mowing height, and traffic, it is best to select a seed mix that includes several kinds known to be successful in your region. For example, a sun-shade mixture will contain one or more shade-tolerant strains along with the usual sun-loving kinds—all proven suited to the various soils and the climatic regimen in your area. It is also best to choose mixtures whose components have been accepted by the Lawn Institute as suitable for lawn use. Again, bargains in lawn grass seed mixtures often yield disappointing results, as the percentage of short-lived, coarse-textured grasses and nonliving chaff tends to be high.

When grass seed mixtures are selected, it is also important to make certain what types of grass are included in the mixture and the proportions in which they are represented. A mixture that includes a high percentage of such grasses as redtop, timothy, Canada bluegrass, sheep fescue, and meadow grass should not be considered, since those species are inferior as lawn grasses. Perennial ryegrass and redtop are used in mixtures as cover crops while permanent grasses are establishing; they are acceptable in small percentages.

A broad, well-sodded lawn extends the play area beyond its immediate zone of heaviest use and links home and patio to garden, fence, and the distant vista.

IMPORTANT LAWN GRASSES FOR THE CENTRAL AND NORTHERN UNITED STATES (ZONES 3 TO 8)

1. BLUEGRASS

Kentucky Bluegrass
(Poa pratensis)

The majority of home owners wish to have a lawn of luxuriant green turf that will withstand a reasonable amount of wear and can be easily maintained. If climate and soil conditions are favorable, Kentucky bluegrass will meet these requirements more completely than any other type of grass. There is no other lawn grass that can equal Kentucky bluegrass in its ability to produce a fine dense turf under average conditions of care and maintenance.

However, Kentucky bluegrass has some very definite requirements for satisfactory growth. It performs best in a cool climate, requires abundant moisture, thrives on loamy soil of better than average fertility, and requires a neutral or slightly acidic soil (pH 6.0 to 7.0). Kentucky bluegrass is not satisfactory in shady areas, it does not thrive well on sandy, droughty soils or on soils of low fertility, and it is intolerant of intense summer heat. Under such conditions, it soon develops into a thin, unsatisfactory turf and is eventually crowded out by inferior grasses and weeds. Kentucky bluegrass makes luxuriant growth during the cool, moist weather of early spring. It tends to go dormant when temperatures remain above 80°F for any length of time; and during prolonged periods of summer heat and drought, it makes little or no growth, often becoming parched and brown. However, with the onset of cooler weather, it revives and continues growth until late in the autumn.

Kentucky bluegrass germinates more slowly than many other lawn grasses and also requires a longer time to become established. It does not begin to form a dense, springy sod until the second year after sowing.

The results will usually be most satisfactory if Kentucky bluegrass is sown in combination with other good lawn grasses, but it should form 50 percent or more of the seed mixture. It is an extremely long-lived and persistent grass, and if conditions are favorable, it eventually will crowd out the other grasses and become completely dominant.

Merion Kentucky Bluegrass

Merion Kentucky bluegrass is the first improved strain of Kentucky bluegrass. This deep-rooting, somewhat creeping strain of bluegrass was first detected in 1936 at the Merion Golf Club in Ardmore, Pennsylvania, by Joseph Valentine. Merion Kentucky bluegrass has a wider climatic range than Kentucky bluegrass. It thrives in the more southern sections of the bluegrass region where Kentucky bluegrass is sometimes difficult to maintain, and it also thrives on the West Coast. It does not do well on very light, sandy soils.

Merion Kentucky bluegrass is a deeper green than Kentucky bluegrass, is more spreading in habit of growth, and is slightly coarser in texture. It has a deep root system and requires a nutrient-rich soil. It is more drought resistant than Kentucky bluegrass, red fescue, or the bentgrasses and will remain green during periods of heat and dry weather when most other grasses are brown and dormant. Merion Kentucky bluegrass does not go dormant in the summer until the temperature reaches the upper 90s. Merion Kentucky bluegrass also retains its green color during the winter better than almost any other grass. It is in active growth every day of the year when the temperature is above freezing. When planted alone, Merion Kentucky bluegrass forms a beautiful, dense turf that is reasonably resistant to wear. When grown under favorable conditions, it will produce a better turf than any other species of grass commonly used for home lawns. In a dense, well-managed Merion Kentucky bluegrass turf, there should be few, if any, weeds.

The seed of Merion Kentucky bluegrass is usually of high quality but is slow to germinate, and even under very favorable conditions, it sometimes requires 8 to 10 weeks to become established. The usual rate of seeding is considerably lower than for most other grasses, which helps to compensate for the higher cost of the seed. A rate of 1 to 2 pounds per 1,000 square feet is recommended.

Since the advent of Merion Kentucky bluegrass, additional high-bred bluegrass strains, such as K31, Delta, Pennstar, and others, have been introduced on the market. Although each has particular attributes, such as color or leaf texture, Merion Kentucky bluegrass is the oldest and most tested variety and probably remains the best Kentucky bluegrass hybrid choice for the home owner.

When a lawn area is to be seeded with Merion Kentucky bluegrass, the soil must be carefully prepared. A pH of 6.5 to 7.0 is considered optimum. (For preparation for seeding, see Chapters 3 and 30.) Merion Kentucky bluegrass should be seeded as soon after August 15 as possible. This is earlier than most autumn seedings but is advisable, as it will give the young grasses a chance to become established before winter. Seeding may also be done in very early spring, but because the results are usually far less satisfactory, autumn seeding is strongly recommended.

For best results, Merion Kentucky bluegrass should be seeded alone or in combination with some other grass known to be a good companion. However, as it has very slow starting habits, it sometimes fails to establish at all when part of an ordinary lawn grass mixture or when it is crowded out before the young seedlings become established. The fact that its cultural requirements differ from those of the more common lawn grasses also makes such a seeding inadvisable.

On the West Coast, an excellent turf that will remain green throughout all or most of the year can be obtained by seeding Merion Kentucky bluegrass and U3 Bermuda grass in combination. It is advisable, however, to use regular applications of fertilizer throughout the autumn months to encourage the growth of the Merion Kentucky bluegrass, which will dominate during the winter months while the U3 Bermuda is dormant.

When attempts are made to seed Merion Kentucky bluegrass in already established turf, the results are often disappointing, although under ideal conditions you may meet with success. The most favorable time for seeding Merion Kentucky bluegrass on established turf is during late winter, from the middle of February to the middle of March, when the soil is undergoing alternate freezing and thawing and is in a honeycomb condition. At this time no coverage is necessary. If an attempt is made to seed Merion Kentucky bluegrass on established turf in the autumn, the existing grass should be cut very close, ½ inch or less, and the soil should be thoroughly aerated. Lime and fertilizer should be added before the seed is sown. The seed should be worked into the soil with the back of an iron rake or with a rough fiber doormat, which may be used as a drag. The soil should be kept moist until germination has taken place and the young seedlings have become established. During this period, the existing grass should be cut very short. When

Merion Kentucky bluegrass is seeded on established turf, it may take two or three years before it begins to take hold and becomes at all evident.

Merion Kentucky bluegrass may also be established by the vegetative method, with either sprigs or plugs being planted.

In the management of a Merion Kentucky bluegrass turf, mowing, fertilization, and aeration all play important parts. Although Merion Kentucky bluegrass tolerates close cutting, the mower should be set to cut at a height of 2¼ to 3 inches. If turf density suffers at this height, it may be lowered provisionally to 1¾ to 2 inches. Mowing should begin as soon as it has reached a height at which there is anything to cut; the grass should not be mowed when wet, however. It must be borne in mind that close mowing is possible only in pure stands of Merion Kentucky bluegrass or when it is in mixture with bentgrasses, U3 Bermuda grass, or Meyer Zoysia. If a Merion Kentucky bluegrass turf is well fertilized and is mown closely, a dense turf will be formed that will resist the invasion of weeds and weedy grasses. However, short turf admits more sunlight to the soil surface and thus promotes surface evaporation, which, under hot, droughty summer conditions, soon

leads to lawn watering—a practice to be discouraged. Where soil conditions and the normal rainfall regimen routinely cause brown, dormant lawns in summer, other grasses, such as fescues, should be considered.

Merion Kentucky bluegrass requires more soil nutrients than many other grasses and particularly depends on an adequate supply of nitrate. It is important, however, to follow the guidelines offered by the local cooperative extension, botanic gardens, or other authoritative sources when applying fast-release high-nitrate fertilizers. Runoff nitrate has become a serious pollutant of drinking water in many areas.

It has been found that if too much water is applied to Merion Kentucky bluegrass, it tends to become shallow rooted and fails to do well. It requires a well-drained soil, rather infrequent watering, and a thorough soaking every 10 days or so during periods of prolonged dry weather.

It is recommended that Merion Kentucky bluegrass turf be aerated thoroughly in the spring and again in the early autumn. It is not advisable, however, to aerate the turf the first spring following fall planting.

While Merion Kentucky bluegrass is not immune to disease, it is highly resistant to leaf spot, a disease common to Kentucky bluegrass. Rust occasionally appears on Merion Kentucky bluegrass in autumn but is seldom serious. Merion Kentucky bluegrass possesses high sensitivity to phenylmercury compounds, and their use should be avoided in any program of disease control. As grubs make no distinction between the roots of Merion Kentucky bluegrass and other grasses, the usual precautions should be taken.

Rough-stalk Bluegrass
(P. trivialis)

Rough-stalk bluegrass is of value chiefly because it is one of the few lawn grasses that will grow in moist, shady locations. It is light green and forms a reasonably good turf under rather unfavorable conditions, although it is not drought resistant. Sometimes called rough-stalked meadow grass, it is often included in shade mixtures and spreads by above ground runners.

Early to awaken in spring, a rich green lawn invites survey of tulips and other early bloom and helps tie such landscape features as trees, shrubbery, walls, and curbing into a harmonious whole.

2. FESCUE
(*Festuca* spp.)

The fescues are among the most adaptable of lawn grasses, and while they do not form a turf of superior quality, they are valuable in specific lawn grass mixtures and for use under certain adverse conditions where better grasses would fail to thrive. The fescues will thrive almost equally well in sun or shade, and when used in a general-purpose mixture, they will usually become dominant in the shady areas beneath the trees on the lawn. Fescues are tolerant of both moist and dry conditions, and although appreciative of good fertility, they will grow surprisingly well on soils low in nutrients. A pH between 5.5 and 6.5 best meets their needs, but they will do reasonably well on more acidic soils. Except for tall fescues, these are cool-climate grasses that do not endure extreme heat well.

The turf formed by the fescues is deep green, dense, and fine in texture but somewhat stiff and wiry, imparting a ruggedness that makes it of special value in areas subject to heavy foot traffic and rough use, such as parks and playing fields. Fescues are also among the best grasses for dry slopes. They should not be mowed closer than 2 inches.

Fine or Red Fescue
(*F. rubra*)

Fine fescues tolerate acidic soils, low fertility, and shade. They do best in cool climates or elsewhere in cool seasons. Summer performance is not as good as with Kentucky bluegrass strains except in western Washington and Oregon, where summers are relatively cool.

Fine fescues are intolerant of high-nitrate fertilizers in warm weather and also fare poorly on heavy soils. Dollarspot disease can be very damaging to these grasses under conditions of even moderately poor drainage.

The fine fescues most successful in lawns can be divided into five major types. In the absence of a well-defined classification, they may be referred to as Chewings, creeping, spreading, hard, and tall fescues.

Chewings, creeping, and spreading fescues are considered variants of the species *Festuca rubra*. However, the three

The broad leaf blades of tall fescue help make a dense if somewhat coarse turf. As with all lawn grasses, cut ends bruise to a light brown unless mower blades are kept sharp.

are distinct in appearance, growth habit, management requirements, adaptability, and breeding behavior.

CHEWINGS FESCUE
(*F. rubra* var. *commutata*)

Chewings fescue is a fine-leaved, low-growing grass without rhizomes. When mowed, the plants spread slowly by basal tiller sprouts. In areas with cool summers, they tolerate close mowing, and under such conditions, they combine well with bentgrasses. Over much of the country, however, it is best not to mow Chewings fescue closely. The name Chewings is derived from the New Zealand merchant who first sold the seed in that country. Later grown commercially in Oregon, it was sold as the 'Cascade' strain. Improved strains of Chewings fescues now widely available include 'Jamestown' (developed at the University of Rhode Island) and 'Highlight' (developed in Holland). Both persist when mixed with Kentucky bluegrasses.

CREEPING FESCUE
(*F. rubra* var. *rubra*)

The creeping and spreading fescues are both considered minor variants of *Festuca rubra* var. *rubra*, but their differences are obvious and reflect distinct genetic traits. The creeping types, represented—most commonly by 'Cumberland Marsh', 'Dawson', 'Golfrood', and 'Oasis'—are

fine-leaved, low-growing grasses with short, thin rhizomes, and produce a turf similar in appearance to the 'Jamestown' and and 'Highlight' strains of Chewings fescue. 'Golfrood', in addition, is tolerant of salt and so finds use in littoral areas and along roadsides. Because creeping fescues are relatively infertile, their seed is costly. These fescues are also subject to dollarspot disease in some areas.

SPREADING FESCUE
(*F. rubra* var. *rubra*)

The spreading types of fine fescue have rather wide blades and long rhizomes. Although they show strong seedling vigor, they do not develop as dense a turf as the creeping and Chewings fescues and suffer when mowed close. Such representative strains as 'Fortress' and 'Ruby' mix well with Kentucky bluegrasses.

HARD FESCUE
(*F. longifolia*)

The hard fescues have attracted considerable attention since the Dutch strain 'Biljart' came onto the market. It and similar strains produce a turf comparable in growth habit and texture to Chewings fescues but are slower growing, better adapted to poor soils, and more resistant to turf diseases. Hard fescues spread only by basal tillering and are slow to recover from hard wear.

TALL FESCUE
(F. elatior)

Tall fescues are hardy, deep-rooting grasses that perform well on fully sun-exposed, drought-prone sites that receive little maintenance. In addition, they are not inclined to build up thatch. Several strains, such as 'Houndog', 'Maverick', 'Mustang', 'Rebel', 'Falcon', and 'Olympic', are very tolerant of shade. Where winters are especially severe, 'Brookston', 'Galway', and 'Mustang' are the most successful tall fescues.

3. ZOYSIA
(Zoysia japonica)

Although Zoysia is one of the most valuable lawn grasses in the South, it grows successfully as far north as Massachusetts, New York, Pennsylvania, Michigan, Iowa, Nebraska, and Colorado. It must be stressed, however, that Zoysia turns straw tan with the first heavy frost and does not become green again until the warm days of spring.

During a northern winter, the tan turf is conspicuous and emphasizes the fact that the bluegrasses remain green all winter.

Green dyes are available that may be sprayed on dormant Zoysia to make it less conspicuous. It is also possible seasonally to overseed established Zoysia with a fine winter rye, but considerable preparation is required. This includes a very low final mowing of the Zoysia, removal of all clippings, machine dethatching, and maintaining a constantly moist soil surface until the rye is established.

The principal advantages of Zoysia are its toughness, density, and low habit. But, as seed is impractical for large-scale propagation, Zoysia is established by planting rooted sprigs or plugs, which grow radially and eventually overlap. In the North, this process can take two years, especially if the planting interval is greater than 6 inches. Weed control is important until the continuous turf is established.

Beside the offseason color change and the tedium involved in establishing Zoysia,

annual dethatching is usually advisable, and controlling the invasion of node-rooting runners into adjacent plantings is a virtual certainty. The last may be achieved by trenching shrubbery borders and gardens that abut a Zoysia lawn and installing 6- or 8-inch-wide strips of aluminum or plastic edging.

For more information on Zoysia, see pp. 138–139.

4. BENTGRASS
(Agrostis spp.)

If you do not have to take into consideration the costs of establishment and maintenance, it is possible to achieve a lawn with turf of such supremely fine quality that it will resemble a putting green. It is sometimes possible to develop such a lawn in a small area—a house terrace or a grass panel in the flower garden—where it would not be practical to attempt it on a larger scale. For such a turf, the bentgrasses are the most desirable.

Zoysia foliage is killed by autumn frost and becomes yellow-brown until growth resumes with the arrival of warm spring weather.

Most of the bentgrasses are of low-growing, semicreeping habit, and if given proper care, they produce a turf of superior quality and beauty. All of the bents can tolerate considerable soil acidity and thrive best on soils with a pH between 5.5 and 6.5. They do well on moist soils, and since they also are extremely well adapted to close mowing, it is best to keep a bent lawn at a height of ¼ to ½ inch. The seeds of the bentgrasses are very fine, and they should be sown at the rate of not more than 2 pounds per 1,000 square feet.

In general, the bentgrasses are much more exacting in their demands than are most of the other lawn grasses. In addition to an adequate program of fertilization, watering, and mowing, it is necessary to apply frequent topdressings of rich compost to provide ideal conditions for vigorous growth. The bentgrasses are also more subject to attacks from various fungus diseases than are most other grasses. It is wise, therefore, not to attempt to develop a bentgrass lawn unless one is fully prepared to meet the additional requirements of labor and expense involved.

The three most desirable types of bentgrass are colonial bent, velvet bent, and creeping bent.

Colonial Bent
(A. tenuis)

Colonial bent produces an excellent quality of turf. It is not tolerant of shade but will grow on soils that vary widely in type, and it is moderately drought resistant. It is frequently used as a component of grass seed mixtures and may also be sown alone. A number of strains of colonial bent have been developed in various parts of the country to meet specific conditions, the most widely used being 'Astoria', 'Highland', 'New Zealand', 'Oregon', 'Penncross', and 'Rhode Island'. The 'Highland' strain is often used as a companion grass with Bermuda grass in the coastal areas of California, where it retains its green color throughout much of the winter. It is also recommended as a companion for Merion Kentucky bluegrass in the north-central and eastern states.

Velvet Bent
(A. canina)

The true aristocrat among lawn grasses, velvet bent is considered one of the most desirable of all the bentgrasses. Once well established, it is persistent, vigorous, and hardy, and it produces a remarkably fine-textured turf with a velvetlike quality. It is more tolerant of heat and is more drought resistant than the otherwise similar creeping bent (A. stolonifera), and it grows fairly well in light shade. In addition, it has the decided advantage of being more resistant to fungus diseases. Velvet bent may be grown either from seed or from stolons. It may be grown alone or in mixture with other grasses. As the seed germinates quickly, it does not require a nurse grass when sown alone.

Creeping Bent
(A. stolonifera, syn. A. palustris)

Finest in texture of the bentgrasses, creeping bent in used chiefly for professionally managed turfs as golf greens and bowling greens. It requires even more

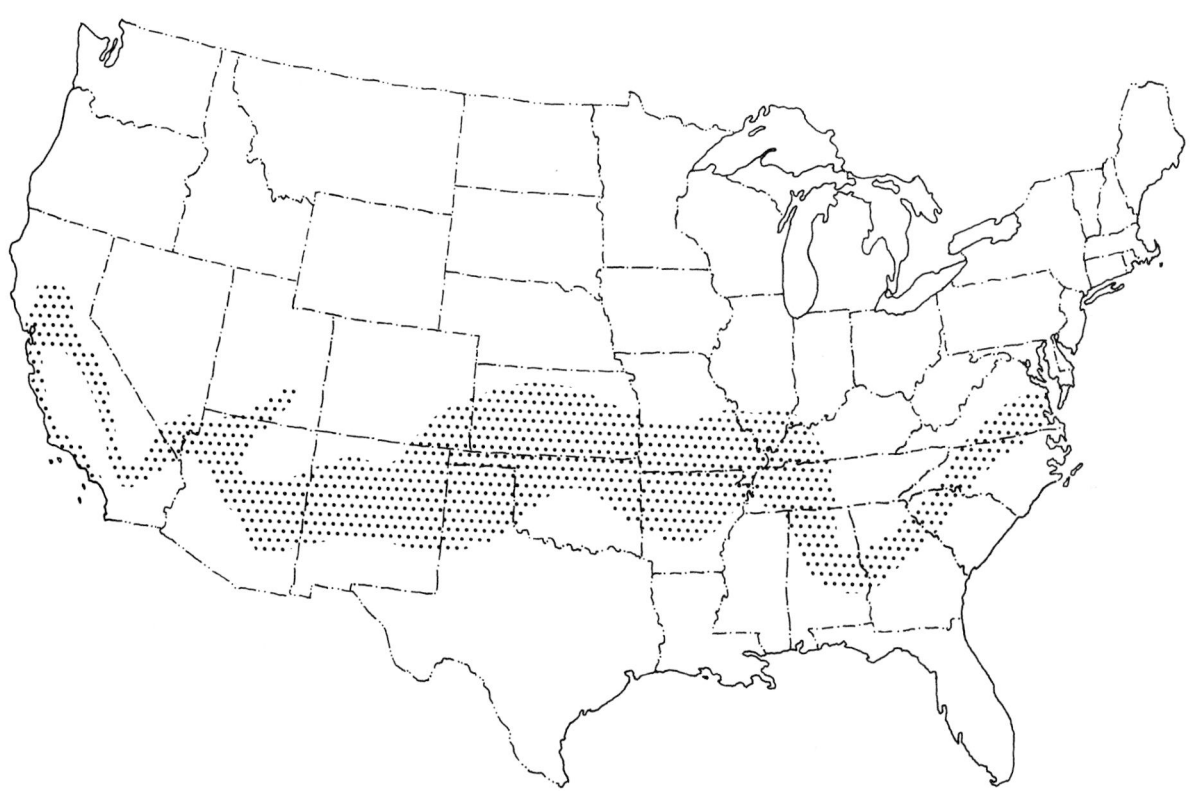

The stippled zone, roughly corresponding to USDA hardiness zone 8, is the region where both northern and southern lawn grasses may be grown.

intensive care than other bents and is therefore too troublesome for most home lawns. If, however, you must have the ultimate in fine-textured turf, Penncross is the most adaptable cultivar and is readily available as seed.

5. PERENNIAL RYE
(Lolium perenne)

Resembling Kentucky bluegrass, and almost as hardy, perennial rye is a non-spreading bunchgrass that is often included in seed mixtures. Its main virtues are its rapid germination and early site coverage. Planted alone, however, it results in a rather tufty turf, often with intervening bare spots.

6. REDTOP
(Agrostis alba)

A comparatively short-lived perennial, redtop is used principally as a nurse grass. It germinates very quickly, within a few days after sowing if conditions are

favorable, and gives a newly seeded lawn the appearance of green while the other more slowly germinating grasses are becoming established. It is fine textured when young but somewhat coarse when mature. When used in a mixture, it disappears as soon as the superior grasses have formed a good sod. The proportion of redtop in a general-purpose lawn mixture should not exceed 10 percent.

LAWN GRASS MIXTURES RECOMMENDED FOR USE IN ZONES 3–8	
SUPERIOR TURF MERION	
Kentucky bluegrass	65%
Creeping fescue	30%
Redtop	5%
GENERAL-PURPOSE MIXTURE	
Kentucky bluegrass	65%
Creeping fescue (e.g., 'Illahee' or 'Pennlawn')	25%
Redtop	10%
MIXTURE FOR MOIST SHADE	
Chewings fescue	50%
Rough-stalk bluegrass	40%
Kentucky bluegrass	10%
MIXTURE FOR DRY SHADE	
Chewings fescue	70%
Colonial bent	20%
Redtop	10%

IMPORTANT LAWN GRASSES FOR THE SOUTHERN AND SOUTHWESTERN UNITED STATES (ZONES 8 TO 10)

1. BERMUDA GRASS
(Cynodon dactylon)

Bermuda grass is one of the most widely used lawn grasses throughout the southern states and in the Southwest. It possesses many admirable qualities but also has very definite limitations. It is tolerant of intense summer heat and of drought conditions; it is comparatively free from pests and diseases; it is resistant to wear; and if well maintained, it makes an excellent and attractive turf with good summer color. Its chief disadvantages are that it is an extremely invasive grass and can become a serious pest in nearby plantings unless restrained; it does not thrive in shady areas; and in most areas where it is grown, it turns a dead-looking brown during the winter months.

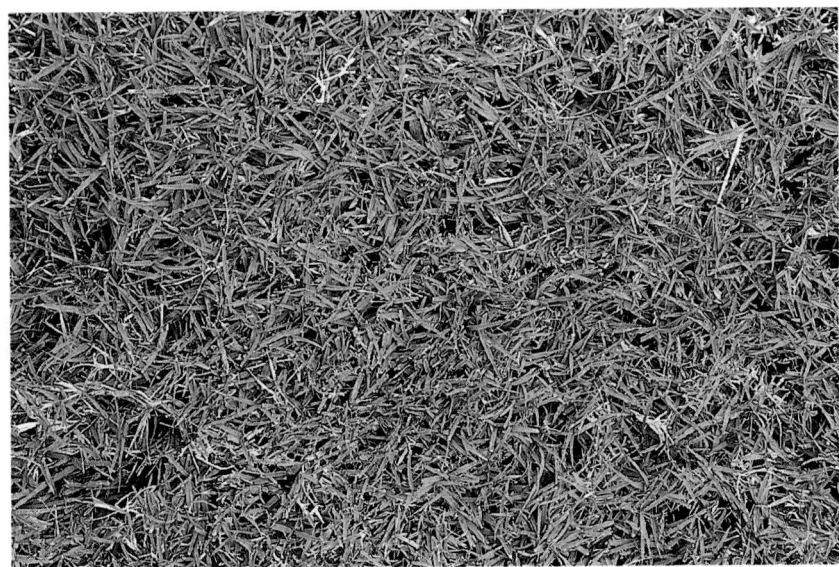

The Bermuda grass cultivar 'Tifton 57' makes a fine-textured, heat-tolerant lawn for the South, but in prolonged drought it forms considerable thatch.

Bermuda grass may be propagated either by seed sown at the rate of 1 pound per 1,000 square feet or by planting sprigs or plugs of sod. It makes the best turf when mowed very closely, being kept at almost putting-green height, not over ⅜ inch. At this height, it has less tendency to mat badly. If permitted to grow too tall before it is cut, the turf loses its green color and remains brown until new growth occurs.

Two applications of a complete lawn fertilizer—at the rate of 20 pounds per 1,000 square feet—are required for best results, one in early spring and another in early autumn. Additional nitrate may be applied during the early summer. The urea-based type slowly releases the nitrate over a long period and thus minimizes the water pollution potential.

During periods of prolonged dry weather, Bermuda grass should be watered thoroughly every week or 10 days. Among the improved strains of Bermuda grass, 'Ormond' and 'Tifton 57' are two that are popular in the Gulf states and will make a very satisfactory lawn under average conditions.

The Bermuda grass strain U3 is a fine-textured grass that produces a tight, velvety turf. The seed germinates quickly and makes rapid growth, forming a fairly good turf six weeks or more after sowing. U3 Bermuda grass is very hardy and will survive zero temperatures; it can, therefore, be grown as far north as zone 7. Like common Bermuda grass, it turns brown during the winter months but retains its green color for a longer period. On the West Coast, it produces a year-round green turf when grown in combination with Merion Kentucky bluegrass. 'U3' Bermuda grass requires very close mowing and liberal fertilizing for optimal results.

2. BUFFALO GRASS
(Bouteloua curtipendula)

Buffalo grass is one of the best grasses for the dry-land regions of the West. Few grasses can endure the difficult conditions found in these areas, but this native of the Great Plains will make a very satisfactory lawn if given good care. It is very adaptable, able to withstand extremes of heat and cold, and endures long periods of drought, growing vigorously under very

adverse conditions. It is low growing and produces a dense turf of soft gray-green.

Buffalo grass may be seeded in the spring at the rate of 1 pound per 1,000 square feet, or it may be established vegetatively through the use of plugs. The plugs should be set out during late spring 1 to 1½ feet apart. The soil should be well prepared and moist at the time of planting and should be kept well watered until the plugs have become established. Once established, the lawn will require no watering and little or no mowing. Its chief drawback is that it does not turn green until the weather warms, a characteristic that limits its applications.

3. ST. AUGUSTINE GRASS
(Stenotaphrum secundatum)

Adapted only to areas with mild winters (zones 8 to 10), St. Augustine grass is used extensively for lawns in Florida and the Gulf states. It thrives in either sun or shade, requiring abundant moisture and moderate fertility. The turf is coarse but, under good management, retains its deep green color throughout the year. It requires little mowing. St. Augustine sod does not withstand heavy wear. Since seed is not available, it must be planted vegetatively with plugs or sprigs.

4. ZOYSIA
(Zoysia japonica)

The Zoysia grasses, natives of Japan and Korea, are among the most valuable of all lawn grasses throughout the South.

An improved strain of the common Zoysia has been developed through the cooperative efforts of the U.S. Golf Association Green Section and the U.S. Department of Agriculture. This superior, fine-textured strain is known as Meyer (Z52) Zoysia and has gained rapid popularity as a desirable lawn grass. Another excellent strain, introduced under the name 'Emerald', has been developed by the Georgia Improvement Association.

Meyer Zoysia produces a firm, resilient turf with a pleasing texture and color, closely resembling a Kentucky bluegrass sod. A Zoysia lawn is durable and very resistant to wear when it is in active growth.

Grown under favorable conditions, Meyer Zoysia forms a very dense turf and has the ability to crowd out summer weeds and undesirable grasses.

Meyer Zoysia will grow on soils of almost any type, thriving equally well on very sandy soils and rather heavy clay soils. Exceptionally well adapted to sandy soils, it is widely used in coastal areas. It is also more tolerant of low soil fertility than most grasses. However, if a turf of superior quality is desired, regular and liberal applications of a high-nitrate fertilizer must be made.

Meyer Zoysia is deep rooted and extremely drought resistant. It is primarily a warm climate grass, being tolerant of extreme heat, and it thrives best during the heat of midsummer. In southern Florida, Meyer Zoysia remains green during the entire year, and throughout the lower South, it retains its green color during much of the year.

Meyer Zoysia must be grown vegetatively. Either plugs of sod or sprigs, the latter consisting of rooted stolons with no soil, may be used. Plug planting is preferred. Meyer Zoysia is sometimes rather slow to establish itself and may take several years to cover an area. If 2-inch plugs are planted 12 inches apart each way, a good solid turf may usually be obtained within two years. Plugs are removed from a pure stand of Meyer Zoysia sod with a simple tool designed for this purpose; the same tool is used to plug a freshly prepared lawn area or an existing lawn. Plugs may be purchased from a nursery, and for reasonably small areas, the cost is not excessive. A home owner may obtain a few packages of plugs and establish his or her own turf nursery, which can be drawn on later. Most nursery plugs measure about 2 inches in diameter. The plugs should be pressed firmly into the soil and should be kept watered until established, one or two soakings usually being sufficient except in very hot, dry weather. Plugs should be set 6 to 12 inches apart, usually being planted on 12-inch centers. Plug planting may be done at any time when the ground is not frozen or is not baked hard by drought.

Sprig planting is a simple process but is suited only to newly prepared lawn areas. If sprigs are planted on established turf, the competition of the other grasses is usually too great, and such a procedure is seldom successful. Plugs can be divided into sprigs having two to three joints each. The sprigs should be spaced 2 to 3 inches apart and pressed firmly into the soil. They should be only partially covered, with as much leaf growth left exposed as possible. The soil should be kept moist until the young sprigs have taken root. Sprigs may be planted at any time from early spring to midsummer.

Meyer Zoysia grows rather slowly and, therefore, requires mowing at less frequent intervals than most grasses. It forms the best quality of turf when a ½- to ¾-inch cut is maintained. When it is cut too high, it develops more slowly and produces an inferior turf that will permit the encroachment of weeds and undesirable grasses.

Since Meyer Zoysia makes its most active growth in midsummer, it profits from fertilization timed to offer nutrients at this season.

Meyer Zoysia seems to be unaffected by turf insects and the various diseases that affect other lawn grasses.

A high-quality Zoysia that is especially well adapted to the Deep South is emerald Manila grass (*Z. matrella* 'Emerald'). It is fast growing, fine textured, and deep green and makes an attractive turf. It is also tolerant of shade. Under favorable conditions, it becomes established rapidly and is one of the best cultivars for use in the Gulf states. It may also be grown successfully farther north.

5. OTHER GRASSES FOR ZONES 8 TO 10

Bahia Grass
(Paspalum notatum)

A coarse but low-maintenance grass from tropical America, Bahia grass is available as seed and, once established, spreads and thickens by runners. Hardy to zone 7b, Bahia grass—especially the cultivars 'Pensacola' and 'Wilmington'—is adaptable to a wide range of soils and tolerates some shade.

Carpet Grass
(Axonopus compressus)

Often confused with St. Augustine grass, carpet grass is somewhat less coarse and may be grown from either seed or sod. It thrives on heavy clay soils in locations where summer drought is not severe.

Centipede Grass
(Eremochloa ophiuroides)

An attractive but temperamental lawn grass from southeast Asia, centipede grass succeeds from South Carolina to Florida and west to eastern Texas, especially on thin, acidic and sandy soils. Started from seed or plugs, an established turf is easy to maintain.

LAWN GRASS SUBSTITUTES

Numerous low-growing plants are sometimes used as lawn grass substitutes, but many of these are best considered ground covers. To justify its use as a lawn grass substitute, a plant should be of extremely low growth, should have the general appearance of a green lawn, and should have at least some of the same attributes that the lawn grasses possess. To function as a lawn, it should be able to withstand at least moderate trampling and use, it should maintain a pleasing green color throughout the major portion of the year, it should not be unduly expensive to establish, and its maintenance requirements should be moderate.

If you prefer to grow a ground cover instead of having a lawn, there is a wide choice of material available. (See Chapter 14 for more information about ground covers.)

The following plants meet the requirements of a lawn grass substitute reasonably well, although each has certain limitations.

CHAMOMILE
(Chamaemelum nobile)

A low-growing herb of dense, compact growth, with finely cut foliage, chamomile thrives in full sun in a light, well-drained soil and is particularly well adapted to planting on sunny slopes where it is difficult to maintain a satisfactory stand of grass. It retains its beautiful green color throughout the year. It will withstand moderate use but is not well suited to areas that are subjected to constant wear. Under such conditions, it has a tendency to become shabby and die out, leaving bare, brown patches that require renovation. Its appearance is improved if it is cut and rolled once or twice a year. It is hardy in zones five to eight.

IRISH MOSS
(Arenaria verna var. *caespitosa)*

Irish moss is a mosslike perennial of dense, compact growth. Its color is a pleasing shade of bright green, and it bears tiny white flowers during the summer. It is hardy throughout the United States. It succeeds best in partial shade, but endures full sun, and requires a moist, friable soil well supplied with organic matter. It withstands some trampling and does not usually require any clipping. It has a tendency to become humpy, but this may be controlled by occasional thinning out. Plants may be obtained from nurseries and should be spaced 6 inches apart. It is best suited for small areas in partial shade where a very hardy bright green carpet is desired.

LAWN LEAF *OR* DICHONDRA
(Dichondra micrantha, D. repens)

Lawn leaf is one of the most widely grown and most satisfactory of the lawn grass substitutes, its chief limitation being its lack of hardiness. It suffers serious damage at temperatures below 20°F and is killed by sustained freezing. However, young self-sown seedlings sometimes replace the plants that have been killed. Dichondra is a very low, spreading, matlike plant with small rounded or heart-shaped leaves. It thrives in sun or partial shade, is as tolerant of traffic and wear as most lawn grasses, and has a pleasing appearance. It prefers a moist but well-drained fertile soil and can tolerate both acidic and alkaline conditions. It withstands intense summer heat well but must have ample moisture.

Weeds are often a problem until it has become established. It may be readily grown from seed, or plants may be obtained from nurseries. In areas where root-knot nematodes are prevalent, seeding is preferable, as there is danger of introducing the nematodes with purchased plants. Mowing is not necessary, but an occasional clipping will improve the appearance of the turf and will prevent bunching up.

Dichondra is well suited to the milder areas in California and to the Gulf Coast and the middle South (zones 9 and 10).

LIPPIA
(Phyla nodiflora vars.)

Lippia is a low-growing, matlike, subtropical plant that withstands extreme heat and thrives under desert conditions. The foliage is grayish in tone, and tiny, pinkish lilac flowers are borne during the summer. The plants appear shabby and dead looking for about two months in the winter. Lippia is tolerant of any type of soil, is highly drought resistant, and grows well in either sun or shade. No mowing is necessary, unless growth becomes too vigorous. It withstands hard wear well. New areas are established by setting out young plants in the spring, 4 to 6 inches apart. Occasional edging is advisable, as plants may spread into adjacent areas and become difficult to eradicate.

PREPARATION OF THE SOIL

For a first-rate lawn, 4 to 6 inches of high-quality topsoil are required. It is a far easier task to improve the condition of the soil before planting a lawn than it is to improve either soil texture or fertility afterward. Therefore the importance of adequate soil preparation before the seed is sown can hardly be overemphasized. The establishment of manageable grades, the provision of adequate drainage, and the preparation of the soil itself—physical texture, chemical reaction, pH, and nutrient content—must all be taken into consideration.

If grading is to be done, existing topsoil should be carefully removed and stockpiled; after the grading has been completed, it should be spread. This procedure will increase the cost of the grading but will prove to be a economically sound in the end. (For more on grading, see Chapter 3.)

If the area to be seeded includes low spots that are apt to be soggy at some seasons of the year, recontouring or underdrainage may be necessary. Frequently, such low spots can be eliminated with grading, but if this is not possible, they may be effectively drained with agricultural tile. The trenches are dug 15 to 24 inches deep and approximately 20 feet apart, with a slope of at least 3 inches for every 50 feet. The tile should be laid end to end and the joints covered with strips of tar paper or heavy plastic to keep the soil out.

Organic Matter

The physical texture of the soil plays a major role in establishing a fine turf. It may be improved to a very marked degree by the addition of organic matter. Most soils, with the exception of woodland and prairie soils, are deficient in humus. Soils with a marked deficiency of organic matter present very serious problems as they are low in water-retaining capacity, may be poorly aerated, often are readily compacted, tend to lose fertility, and generally provide a very poor medium for the healthy, vigorous growth of lawn grasses. It is an accepted fact that practically all of our better lawn grasses thrive best on a soil that is well supplied with organic matter to a depth of at least 6 inches.

Organic matter may be supplied in the form of well-rotted manure, spent mushroom soil, compost, cover crops, raw native peat, and commercial peat moss. Untreated manures have the disadvantage of introducing weed seeds into the lawn area, and in many communities are not readily available at a reasonable price. The great point in favor of manure is that it not only raises soil fertility but also adds water-holding organic matter. If it is applied several months before planting, most weed seeds will germinate and can be controlled by cultivation before the grass seed is sown. Spent mushroom soil is a mixture of rotted manure and soil that is particularly valuable in improving the texture of sandy and shaly soils. In areas of the country where mushrooms are grown commercially, such soil is readily available at a reasonable price and is one of the most satisfactory forms in which organic matter can be supplied. Screened garden compost is also an excellent source of organic matter. If it is possible to plan the program of work well in advance and to devote several months to the preparation of the soil, one or more cover crops may be grown, increasing and the organic content of the soil with comparatively little expense. When a new home is being built, it is frequently possible to do this in the course of construction.

The following cover crops are recommended.

Fall sowing. Sow in the late summer or early fall. For 1,000 square feet, use 1½ quarts rye and ½ pint winter vetch; per acre, 1 bushel rye and 1 peck vetch. Plow or spade the crop under in the spring or when it has attained a height of 12 inches.

Early spring sowing. Sow as early in spring as possible. For 1,000 square feet use 1½ quarts oats and ½ pint Canada field peas; per acre, 2 bushels oats and 1 peck Canada field peas. Plow or spade under before the onset of summer.

Late spring sowing. Sow between the middle of May and the middle of June. For 1,000 square feet, use 1 quart soybeans and 1 cup millet; per acre, 1 bushel soybeans and 1 peck millet. Inoculate the soybeans before planting to gain the full benefit of their nitrogen- fixing abilities. Buckwheat is also a satisfactory late-season cover crop. Plow or spade under at least one month before the time of lawn seeding.

Peat moss should always be thoroughly moistened before it is applied to the soil. If applied dry, it may actually do more harm than good, as it will take up the moisture from the soil. In areas where grass is to be sown, it should always be worked into the upper few inches of topsoil. Left on the surface, it quickly dries and impedes the penetration of rainwater.

The rate of application of organic matter depends on the character of the soil. Light, sandy soils will require liberal applications so that they may become more retentive of moisture. Soils of a dense, heavy texture will also be greatly improved and the drainage of the surface water facilitated if liberal quantities are applied. Manure should be applied at the rate of 1,000 to 1,500 pounds per 1,000 square feet of lawn area, or 20 to 30 tons per acre. Peat moss should be applied at the rate of 4 bales per 1,000 square feet of lawn area, or approximately 170 bales per acre. Native moist peat should be applied at the rate of 2 cubic yards per 1,000 square feet of area, or 86 yards per acre.

In whatever form it is applied, the organic matter should be thoroughly incorporated into the upper 5 or 6 inches of topsoil. The organic matter, particularly when applied in the form of peat moss, should never be allowed to form a definite layer, either on the surface of the soil or below, as such a zone deters plant growth. The organic matter should be thoroughly plowed, forked, or spaded into the upper 5 or 6 inches of topsoil. A rototiller is excellent for this purpose and leaves the soil in fine tilth.

Fertilizers

The fertility of the soil is one of the most important factors in establishing a new lawn. It is a widely accepted premise that all of our most desirable lawn grasses require a soil of fairly high fertility if they are to produce a fine quality of turf. It is well, therefore, to see that adequate nutrients are supplied before planting. The application of a well-balanced complete fertilizer will usually give the most satisfactory results; the amount required depends on the natural fertility of the soil. For soils of medium fertility, an application of 15 to 20 pounds per 1,000 square feet will usually be sufficient, or approximately 650 to 700 pounds per acre. For soils of low fertility, the application should be increased to 25 to 30 pounds per 1,000 square feet or 1,000 to 1,200 pounds per acre. (For soil tests and fertilizers, see Chapter 31.) To reduce the hazard of nitrate runoff or leaching, slow-release fertilizers are recommended.

Soil Acidity

The majority of the better-known lawn grasses are most successful if grown in an almost neutral or very slightly acidic soil. A few types, such as the bentgrasses and the fescues, are tolerant of rather strong acidity but make the strongest growth on soils that are more nearly neutral. Thus, for practically all types of desirable lawn grasses, it is advisable to have an acidity that does not fall below pH 5.5. The preferred range is pH 6 to 7. Soil tests should be made to determine the existing degree of acidity. Consult your local cooperative extension or state agricultural experiment station for instructions on preparing and sending soil samples for testing and interpretation. If the tests show that the soil is too acidic, the condition may be readily corrected by an adequate application of lime.

Lime may be applied in the form of hydrated lime or ground limestone, but hydrated lime acts more rapidly. Approximately 1 pound of a good-quality hydrated lime is equal in value to 1½ pounds of ground limestone. When the application is made, it is important that the lime be distributed uniformly over the surface of the soil and worked lightly into the upper few inches of topsoil. The lime will move slowly downward in the soil but not laterally; therefore, any soil areas not directly covered by the lime will receive no benefit from the application. There are various mechanisms on the market for the distribution of lime, but on very small areas where the use of machinery is not justified, one of the most satisfactory methods is to place the hydrated lime in a coarse, loosely woven burlap bag and to drag it back and forth over the area. If you prefer, the bag may be held a few inches above the soil and the lime shaken out onto the surface.

The importance of applying lime at the time the seedbed

is prepared can hardly be overstressed. If applications are delayed until after the sod has become established, it will require several years to correct any marked degree of acidity entirely, whereas this condition may be promptly and thoroughly overcome if an adequate application is made before or at the time of planting.

The rate of application depends entirely on the degree of soil acidity. On soils of extremely high acidity it is advisable to make several applications, as the heavy liming of strongly acidic soils is detrimental to normal plant growth. This extreme condition would be met only very occasionally. Soils testing over pH 6 require no application of lime. Soils testing between pH 5 and pH 6 should receive an application of 50 pounds of hydrated lime or 75 pounds of finely ground limestone per 1,000 square feet or 1 ton of hydrated lime per acre or 1½ tons of ground limestone. Soils testing between pH 4 and pH 5 or below should receive two or more applications, the total amount varying from 60 to 145 pounds per 1,000 square feet of hydrated lime, or 2¼ to 3 tons per acre. Only in very extreme cases would as much as 145 pounds per 1,000 square feet be necessary. In general, sandy soils of a given degree of acidity require lighter applications of lime than do heavy clay soils of the same pH value. Applications should, therefore, be slightly adjusted to meet the various soil types. Not more than 50 pounds or 60 pounds of hydrated lime or its equivalent in ground limestone should be applied at one time to 1,000 square feet. If heavier applications are necessary, the amount should be divided. It must be borne in mind that lime not only corrects conditions of soil acidity but serves other functions as well. It helps to improve the physical structure of the soil and consequently increases its water-absorbing capacity; it also provides both calcium and magnesium, which are essential elements for normal plant growth.

Lawn grass seed should be spread as evenly as possible, pressed into the surface with a roller, but left uncovered, because light is needed for germination.

Preparation of the Seedbed

After the organic matter, fertilizer, and lime have been thoroughly incorporated with the soil, the seedbed may be prepared for planting. In small areas, this may be easily accomplished with an iron hand rake. In large areas, it is done using spike-tooth and drag harrows and a smoothing board. The surface should be reasonably firm and absolutely even, with no hollows or small depressions.

Lawns for Poor Soils

When establishing a lawn on soil that is definitely deficient in fertility and cannot be immediately improved to a state that will support the better types of lawn grasses, it is wise to use some of the varieties that are less exacting in their demands. The fescues are the most satisfactory grasses under these conditions, as they thrive on poor, sandy soils; are tolerant of acidity; will endure considerable shade; and will withstand long periods of drought. The leaves of the fescues are tough and wirelike, and in habit of growth, the plants are low and inclined to be bunchy. It is advisable, therefore, to sow the fescues in mixture with other grasses to obtain a more even quality of turf. Of the many types, Chewings fescue and true creeping red fescue are the most desirable for lawn purposes. Because the seeds of the fescues soon lose viability, it is necessary to make rather heavy seedings. For a lawn on poor, sandy soil or on extremely acidic soil, the following mixture is recommended:

Chewings fescue	40%
Kentucky bluegrass	40%
Ryegrass	20%

Lawns for Shady Areas

For shady areas, it is necessary to choose grasses that are tolerant of such conditions. It must be borne in mind that all grasses require some sunlight for satisfactory growth, and if the shade is too dense, it is well to resort to an evergreen ground cover rather than to attempt to produce a lawn. Careful pruning will frequently mitigate the density of the shade sufficiently enough to make it possible to grow lawn grasses under large trees. If carried out in phases over several years, the pruning may be done without harming the form or beauty of the trees. The program consists of gradually removing the lower branches of the trees so that the morning and afternoon sun may reach the grass. The tree will put on additional growth at the top to compensate for what has been cut away and will continue to maintain its natural form. Between 2 and 3 feet of the lower branches may be cut away entirely each year, and at the end of five years, the foliage level will have been raised as much as 10 feet.

TEMPORARY LAWNS

Under some circumstances, you may wish to plant a purely temporary lawn. If, for example, you move into a new home late in the spring, it would be folly to attempt to plant a permanent lawn at a season of the year when it is most difficult for the better types of lawn grasses to establish themselves. Under such conditions, it is wise to resort to temporary measures. Within a few brief weeks it is possible to obtain a rich and almost luxuriant growth of turf, if the correct type of seed is used. Either the perennial ryegrass or the domestic ryegrass should be selected for this purpose. The growth is somewhat coarse and rank, but at least the grass will form a welcome covering of green on ground that might otherwise be bare. Before planting, a complete fertilizer (6-8-4 analysis) should be worked into the soil at the rate of 10 pounds per 1,000 square feet to stimulate growth. The seed should be sown at the rate of 6 pounds per 1,000 square feet. The soil should be kept moist until the seed has germinated, and the grass should be mown when it has reached a height of 2 inches. This temporary grass may be plowed or spaded under when the time approaches to prepare the seedbed for the permanent lawn, and it will benefit the soil by adding a small amount of organic matter.

SEEDING
Time of Sowing Grass Seed

The one point on which all authorities seem to agree is that the most desirable time for sowing lawn grasses in zones 6 to 8 is late August or early September. If it is not possible to do the work at this season, seed may be sown in *early* spring. Late spring and early summer sowings are not recommended, except in the case of purely temporary lawns. Early autumn sowing has several advantages over spring sowing. Practically all of the lawn grasses make their best growth

Rather than laboriously digging out a weedy, unsatisfactory parch of lawn in preparation for reseeding, sodding, or conversion to garden or ground cover bed, the area may be covered for some weeks with 5-mil black plastic to exclude light and water and promote heat buildup that will kill or weaken everything beneath.

during cool, moist weather, and the autumn months usually provide very favorable conditions for good germination of the seed and for the sturdy, vigorous growth of the young grass. There is comparatively little competition from weeds at this time of the year, and by the following summer, the autumn-sown turf should be so well established that it will not suffer seriously from drought or other adversities.

Method of Sowing

When sowing grass seed, the chief aim is to distribute the seed evenly over the lawn area. The seed may be cast by hand, but a hand-operated seeder or a mechanical seeder mounted on wheels will give best results, especially in large areas.

For small areas, sowing may be done satisfactorily by hand if care is taken to achieve even distribution. Hand sowing should be done on a calm day when there is little or no wind, as it is otherwise impossible to make an even sowing. It is wise to divide the quantity of seed in half and to sow in two directions, walking first north and south and the second time east and west, thus covering the area twice. Bulking the seed with cornmeal or another inert extender helps ensure even distribution.

Seeding with a hand-operated seeder is much more rapid than sowing by hand, and a fairly accurate distribution can usually be obtained. The most approved method, however, is to sow the seed with a mechanical distributor. Such a machine represents a small investment, and because it can also be used for periodical applications of fertilizer, its purchase is often justified even for lawns of moderate size. Such a machine can be adjusted to sow the seed at the desired rate.

RATE OF SEEDING
The quantity of seed required depends on the type of seed used.

Type of Grass	Seed Required per 1,000 Square Feet (pounds)
ZONES 3–8	
Kentucky bluegrass	4
Merion Kentucky bluegrass	1–2*
Rough-stalk bluegrass	3
Fescues	3–6*
Bentgrasses	2
General-purpose mixture	4
ZONES 8–10	
Bermuda grass	1

*Use the heavier seeding on thin, sandy soils.

After it has been sown, the seed should be raked into the soil *very* lightly with an iron rake; it should covered by not more than ⅛ inch. It is very important not to cover it too deeply, as poor germination will result. After the raking, the area should be lightly compressed with an empty roller to establish good contact between seed and soil.

From the time of sowing until the grass seed is well up, the area should be kept moist. Water should be applied in the form of a fine, mistlike spray. A fog nozzle is ideal for this purpose. A heavy spray will tend to cause a crust to form on the surface of the soil that may seriously interfere with germination.

MOWING NEW GRASS

Young, newly sown grass (with the exception of the bentgrasses, Bermuda grass, and Merion Kentucky bluegrass) should not be cut until the grass has reached a height of 2 inches. A lightweight unpowered reel mower will do the least damage at this stage. The mower blades should be carefully set so that the final cut will not be closer than 1½ inches. If young grass is mown too closely, it will prevent the formation of a vigorous root system and will seriously injure the quality of the turf.

SODDING NEW AREAS

Undoubtedly, the most rapid method of establishing turf is sodding. It consists of cutting strips of sod from an existing lawn, laying them carefully together on the new area and encouraging the grass roots to reestablish themselves in the soil. Under certain conditions this method may be preferable to starting grass from seed or stolons, because it has the advantage of being so quickly accomplished that there will be no opportunity for a hard rain to wash away the soil and ruin the surface of newly prepared ground. Banks and steep slopes can be prepared in this manner.

Turf selected for cutting and transplanting should be well-established grass growing in open ground and free from crab grass and weeds. The best source is a lawn grown from seed and composed of a mixture, bluegrass predominating over redtop and fescue. Pastures that have been well cared for also provide an excellent source of good sod. When purchasing sod, it is very important to make sure it is of good quality.

Sodding should be done when there will be at least four or five weeks of good growing weather before the onset of either winter or summer. Unless the roots become established well enough to supply moisture and nourishment, warm growing weather before the beginning of winter frosts will kill the grass altogether.

Before cutting sod, the area should be mown closely. The edges of the sod strips are then cut by a rotary blade or a spade held in a vertical position. The sod is thus divided by these vertical cuts into strips 12 or 15 inches wide and 10 feet or more long. If the job is a small one, cutting sod into squares may be more convenient. A specially built sod spade—the handle is at an angle to the blade—is forced under the sod, cutting off the lower roots and lifting up a mat of upper roots about 1½ inches thick. The strips are then rolled up and loaded onto a truck or wheelbarrow. It is important to keep the edges of the strips straight, parallel, and at a uniform distance apart. To facilitate this, a wide plank is laid on the sod with its edge at the last cut, and the new cut is made along the opposite side. This regularity will simplify the task of laying the sod.

The ground on which the sod is to be laid must be graded to an even surface, cultivated, raked smooth, rolled, and moistened.

Preparation for seeding or sodding includes carefully grading, raking, and rolling the soil surface to ensure rapid rooting and a smooth lawn surface.

The turf is then laid by unrolling a strip into place, and then firming it with blows of the back of the spade. Any irregularities caused by an uneven thickness of the sod should be adjusted at this time by rolling back the strip, and filling or cutting the soil below as required. This is the part of the work in which skill and patience are important and that will make the difference between an uneven turf and a smooth one. After rolling with a hand roller, the whole area should be watered until it is thoroughly soaked; it should not be allowed to dry out until it has become well established.

Over the last few decades, commercial sod farms have been established in virtually all large metropolitan areas, and the enterprise is highly mechanized and competitive. Sodding has become an increasingly attractive alternative for both the home owner and the commercial and industrial developer. Prices for sod are usually quoted on a per-square-foot or per-square-yard basis (1,000 square feet equals 111 square yards; 4840 square yards equals 1 acre). It is important that the period during which the sod is rolled up be as brief as possible, both to minimize drying and to prevent overheating.

MAINTENANCE OF EXISTING LAWNS

It is advisable for every home owner to work out a careful program of lawn maintenance and to adhere to it faithfully. The majority of the lawns in this country suffer sadly from neglect. After a lawn is established, the owner is all too apt to assume that the only subsequent care required is that of periodic mowing. Under such conditions of neglect, however, it does not take many years for a good lawn to deteriorate into a poor one. The fertility of the soil becomes gradually depleted to the point where it can no longer support the better types of lawn grasses, especially if clippings have been routinely caught and discarded. Inferior grasses consequently become more and more dominant; the soil becomes increasingly acidic, more compacted, and more impervious to water; the lawn becomes less resistant to injury from drought and insect attacks; and weeds creep in, which may, in time, almost entirely crowd out the grasses. It is, therefore, a matter of sound economy to follow a carefully planned program of lawn maintenance.

Lawn Rolling

The question of lawn rolling is much debated. It is undoubtedly true that rolling was greatly overdone in the past, and the present consensus seems to be in favor of one or two light rollings in the spring, mainly to eliminate air pockets caused by frost heaving and to ensure that all grass roots have soil contact. Rolling should not be done until all possibility of alternate thawing and freezing is past. It should be done when the soil is moderately moist—never when it is soggy. Too frequent rolling is apt to cause an undesirable compaction of the soil, which tends to interfere with the normal, thrifty growth of the turf. This danger is much greater on heavy soils than on soils of a sandier character. A water-ballast roller is the most desirable type for lawn use, as the weight may be adjusted to meet varying conditions. The roller should be just heavy enough to press the crowns back into the soil without making the soil unduly compact.

Soil Fertility

The maintenance of soil fertility is one of the major considerations in any program of lawn management. All of the most desirable lawn grasses require a soil of reasonably good fertility for satisfactory development. It is wiser, and better economy, to determine soil fertility year by year through soil tests and to make small corrective applications of compost or carefully selected slow-release commercial fertilizers than it is to allow the soil to become depleted.

The three most important elements of fertility needed by lawn grasses for satisfactory growth are nitrogen, phosphorus, and potassium. Nitrogen produces a vigorous growth of leaves and stems, phosphorus is needed for good root development, and potassium is valuable in promoting general vigor and resistance to disease. A complete commercial fertilizer contains these three essential elements. The true value of a commercial fertilizer, however, depends not only on the actual content of plant food but also on the form in which the nutrients are supplied. This point is of particular importance when fertilizing lawn grasses.

Nitrogen may be supplied in the form of ammonia compounds, nitrate compounds, urea-formaldehyde compounds, and various organic compounds. Ammonia compounds, such as sulfate of ammonia, are quickly available after application. When used year after year, sulfate of ammonia will tend to increase the acidity of the soil appreciably, but this may be overcome by sufficient application of lime. Nitrate compounds, such as nitrate of soda, are also quickly available but do not tend to increase the soil acidity. They have been preferred for use on soils that are strongly acidic or for grasses that require nearly neutral soil. However, runoff and downward percolation of highly soluble nitrate compounds, especially in areas that depend on underlying aquifers for drinking water, causes nitrate pollution, a rapidly intensifying problem. More acceptable are the urea-formaldehyde compounds, known as urea-form fertilizers, which release nitrogen very slowly over a period of many months. This is one of the best forms in which to supply nitrogen to lawn grasses, as there is no danger of burning and the nitrogen needs of the plants for the entire season can be supplied with one application—a matter of considerable importance in managing large areas of turf.

The various organic forms of nitrogen, such as cottonseed meal, soybean meal, dried blood, tankage, fish meal, and sludge, decompose slowly and are not active in releasing plant nutrients except under conditions of warmth and moisture. Although they may be applied in early spring, they supply very little nitrogen until the beginning of summer. If organic nitrogen is derived from but one source, it may cause delayed nitrogen burn when it is released during a period of hot, dry weather. Therefore, organic fertilizers applied to lawns should supply nitrogen from a number of sources so that it will be released more evenly over a period of time, avoiding the danger of delayed nitrogen burn. In general, the organic compounds are more valuable for use on sandy soils than on heavy, clay soils, since they are not lost through leaching as are some of the more readily available inorganic forms.

Phosphorus is usually supplied in the form of superphosphate. It is an important ingredient of a complete lawn fertilizer. Potash is commonly supplied in the form of muriate of potash, and is included in all complete fertilizer mixtures for turf areas.

Agricultural experiment stations and cooperative extension offices can advise you about which fertilizer formulations are most efficacious and least harmful under local conditions.

Even distribution of the fertilizer is essential, as areas not covered will receive little or no direct benefit from the application. If fertilizers are used in the dry form, they should be applied with a fertilizer distributor that can be adjusted to apply the material at the desired rate and that will make possible an even coverage. This is an essential piece of equipment for the establishment and maintenance of a good lawn, and if well cared for, it should last for many years. Fertilizer in the dry form should always be applied when the grass is dry to avoid the danger of burning the leaves.

It is both financially wasteful and environmentally irresponsible to exceed recommended amounts per unit area when applying commercial fertilizers. The excess simply leaches away beyond the reach of roots and contributes to the pollution of water supplies, wetlands, rivers, lakes, and coastal waters. Although ritual fertilizing of lawns was once encouraged, current emphasis is on using as little fertilizer as possible, and if conditions allow, even none at all. Allowing lawn clippings to remain in place will considerably diminish the need for supplementary fertilizer.

Planning a Fertilization Program
Soil Tests

The kind of fertilizer that should be applied and the amount required can be most accurately determined through soil tests. The advisability of having such tests made cannot be stressed enough. Unless this is done, you will be working in the dark. A reliable soil test will indicate not only whether lime is needed but the amount required to obtain the desired pH, which can also be readily figured, as shown on Chapter 31, page 762. Any deficiency of nitrogen, phosphorus, or potassium or any of the minor elements can also be accurately determined, and a fertilizing program can be worked out that will best meet specific needs.

Most state colleges and universities offer a soil testing service. In some states this service is free to residents, while in other states there is a nominal charge.

To confirm whether *regular* soil fertilizing is necessary, a portion of the lawn left untreated can serve as a check against the results of treating adjacent similar areas. The more similar the lawn on treated and untreated areas becomes, the less need there is for lawn fertilizing generally.

Requirements of a Lawn Fertilizer

To be effective, a lawn fertilizer should contain the essential elements of soil fertility—nitrogen, phosphorus, and potassium in the correct proportions. In general a ratio of 2:1:1 (2 parts nitrogen to 1 part phosphorus, to 1 part potassium) will best meet the needs of the average lawn. A fertilizer with an analysis of 10-5-5 (10 parts nitrogen, 5 parts phosphorus, and 5 parts potassium) is an example of a 2:1:1 ratio. If a heavier application of phosphorus than of potassium is needed, a ratio in which the sum of the phosphorus and potassium equals the amount of the nitrogen may be used, such as a 10-6-4 analysis. Adjustments of these ratios may be readily made if indicated as advisable by soil tests. However, they form a good basis on which to develop a program.

In addition to the above requirements, a good lawn fertilizer should contain nitrogen in several forms, derived from both quickly available and slowly available sources. The most favorable ratio is one to three, one part from quickly soluble sources and three parts from slowly available sources. This makes it possible to avoid the waste and environmental hazard of supplying more nitrogen initially than can be taken up, followed by a deficiency of nitrogen later in the season. And it also makes it possible to reduce the number of applications required per season.

Rate of Application

The rate of application depends on the analysis of the fertilizer used, the fertility status of the soil as indicated by soil tests, the kind of grasses that compose the turf, and to some extent, on the structure of the soil.

Since government regulations require not only disclosure of the content analysis of all prepared commercial fertilizers but also instructions about applying them, it behooves the gardener to read and implement the instructions carefully and to resist the all-too-common urge to double or triple the rate in the ill-founded hope that this augmentation will produce doubly or triply good results. Excessive amounts of fertilizer are at best wasted and at worst injurious or even lethal to the targeted plants, to say nothing of contributing to water pollution.

Without the benefit of soil tests, only very general recommendations can be made. The amount of fertilizer to apply can best be figured on the basis of the actual nitrogen required, the level of fertility, and the type of grass.

RATE OF FERTILIZER APPLICATION
According to grass type and soil fertility.

Type of Grass	Soil Fertility*	Annual Requirement per 1,000 Square Feet (pounds):	
		Nitrogen	5-10-5 or 10-6-4 Fertilizer
Kentucky bluegrass (alone or predominating in mixture)	High	2–3	20–30
	Medium	3–5	30–50
	Low	5–6	50–60
Merion Kentucky bluegrass (alone)	High	3–4	30–40
	Medium	4–5	40–50
	Low	6–6½	60–65
Fescues (alone or predominating in mixture)	High	1–1½	10–15
	Medium	1½–2	15–20
	Low	2½–3	25–30
Bermuda grass (alone)	High	1½–2	15–20
	Medium	3–4	30–40
	Low	4½–5	45–50
Zoysia (alone)	High	1½–2	15–20
	Medium	2½–3	25–30
	Low	3–4½	30–45

*As determined by soil analysis for principal nutrients.

The number of pounds of fertilizer that must be applied per 1,000 square feet to supply 1 pound of nitrogen may be determined by dividing 100 by the percent of nitrogen contained in the fertilizer. For example, for 5-10-5 fertilizer:

$$100 \div 5 = 20$$

Therefore, it would require 20 pounds of a 5-10-5 fertilizer to supply 1 pound of nitrogen per 1,000 square feet. For 10-5-10 fertilizer:

$$100 \div 10 = 10$$

Therefore, it would require 10 pounds of a 10-5-5 fertilizer to supply 1 pound of nitrogen per 1,000 square feet.

A fertilization program may be worked out for any type of grass, on soils of varying fertility, and with fertilizers of varied analyses if this procedure is followed and the proper ratio maintained.

A greater degree of precision can be achieved by having the soil tested before applying any soil amendments and by following the recommendations of the testing service.

Time of Application

The time of application depends on the type of grass, the fertility of the soil, and the kind of fertilizer used.

Bluegrass mixtures. On soils of high fertility, one application in the autumn (late August to mid-October) will be sufficient, provided the fertilizer contains two-thirds of its nitrogen in a slowly available form, such as urea-form. On soils of low fertility, it is advisable to make two applications of fertilizer of this type—two-thirds of the total amount in the autumn and one-third in late spring. If the fertilizer used does not contain slowly available forms of nitrogen, three applications should be made, the first very early in the spring, the second in early May, and the third in early autumn.

Bermuda grass. The first application should be made in early spring and the second application in early autumn. Additional application of nitrogen should be made in early summer if the need is indicated.

Zoysia. The first application should be made in early spring and the second in late spring or early summer.

Fescue mixtures. Follow the program outlined for bluegrass mixtures.

Topdressing

One method of supplying additional fertility to lawn areas and of improving the texture of the soil is through the use of topdressings. Topdressings in the form of rich topsoil, compost, or spent mushroom soil are widely used on many golf courses to keep the putting greens, which are composed largely of bentgrasses, in the best possible condition.

In using topsoil and compost for this purpose, it is extremely important that it be free of weed seeds. It is a disheartening experience to go to the labor and expense of applying a topdressing only to find that you have introduced new weeds into the lawn. It is, however, possible to destroy the weed seeds in the soil before it is spread so that there will be no danger of having this occur. The chemicals most satisfactory for this purpose are calcium cyanamide and Vapam. If any such preparations are used, instructions should be followed with great care.

The topdressing, which may be applied at any time during the growing season, should be spread as a thin layer over the surface of the lawn and worked into the turf with the back of an iron rake.

Liming

To promote a dense, vigorous growth of lawn grasses, the soil reaction (pH) should be kept as near to or within the pH 6.5 to 7.0 range as possible. While it is true that the bentgrasses and the fescues are decidedly tolerant of acidic soil, they do grow better on more nearly neutral soils.

Normally, grasses produce a new crop of roots each year. The old roots simply die, adding humus to the soil. In extremely acidic soil, however, these old roots fail to decay rapidly, and the soil tends to become seriously sod bound. Another point in favor of maintaining a nearly neutral soil reaction is that in highly acidic soils the grasses are less able to use nitrogen in the form of ammonium compounds. Under such conditions, the grass apparently absorbs the nitrogen but cannot assimilate it, and a toxic reaction occurs. It is also a well-established fact that when soils become highly acidic, the structure of the soil itself changes, and it gradually becomes less permeable to water. An adequate application of lime, therefore, not only neutralizes the acidity of the soil but also improves the soil structure and increases its water-absorbing capacity, as well as supplying small quantities of plant nutrients in the form of calcium and magnesium.

If soil tests indicate a degree of acidity below pH 6.0, an application of lime should be made, in the form of either hydrated lime or finely ground limestone. The most favorable seasons for applying lime are autumn, winter, and very early spring, when the alternate freezing and thawing of the ground will enable the lime to penetrate more deeply into the soil. It may, however, be applied at any season. Lime is slow in its reaction and no appreciable benefits will be noticed until five or six months after the application has been made.

However, the eventual beneficial effects of lime are of long duration and will be apparent for several years. Unless the soil is intensely acidic, which occurs infrequently, an application of lime once every two or three years will be sufficient to maintain the correct soil reaction. (For the rate of application, refer to the table on page 764.)

Mowing

The height at which a lawn should be maintained depends on the type of grass or grasses that compose the turf. Some grasses thrive best and present the most attractive appearance when they are cut very close, while other grasses must be maintained at a greater height in order to produce a healthy, vigorous turf.

In recent years, water conservation and other environmental concerns have lent favor to maintaining turf at greater heights. In the following table, the traditional height levels are followed by revised recommendations.

RECOMMENDED MOWING HEIGHTS FOR VARIOUS LAWN GRASSES

Type of Grass	Height after Mowing	
	Traditional	Revised
Kentucky bluegrass	1¼–2"	2¼–3"
Merion Kentucky bluegrass	1¼–2"	2¼–3"
Fescues	1¼–2"	2¼–3"
Bentgrasses	¼–½"	⅓–⅔"
Bermuda grass	3⁄16–⅜"	⅓–⅔"
Zoysia	½–¾"	⅔–1⅓"

Although the slender culms of most grasses gone to seed impart undeniable grace, it is best to keep lawn grasses regularly mowed the thickening and spreading of growth at ground level.

The lawn mower should be checked periodically and adjusted whenever necessary. To adjust a reel mower to cut at a given height, set the roller on the back of the mower so that the bedknife (the long, flat blade against which the blades on the revolving reel cut) is at the desired height. A change in the clearance of the blade of a rotary mower can be achieved by adjusting the wheels. In either case, the adjustment should be made with the mower set on a hard, level surface so that any change in mowing height can be measured.

Frequent, wisely regulated mowing tends to produce a fine-textured turf, as new leaf growth is stimulated. If a lawn is neglected and the grass is allowed to become too tall before it is cut, the results are unaesthetic, because growth becomes coarse and tough and the leaves lose their healthy deep green color. This is particularly true in the case of Bermuda grass.

In any case, it is unwise to cut a lawn by more than one-third of its premowing height at any one time. Thus a lawn standing at 4 inches should be cut no lower than 2⅔ inches and one at 5 inches, no lower than 3¼ inches. By mowing more frequently, say twice a week during periods of vigorous growth, the optimal height can be reached after two or three mowings and thereafter maintained.

Extremely early spring mowing should be avoided on lawns that are predominantly Kentucky bluegrass, as the root system is entirely renewed each spring, and if the grass is closely mown early in the season, there will be a decided reduction in root development. The quality of the turf will suffer considerably, and the grass will be less able to withstand the stresses of summer drought. To ensure vigorous root growth, the first spring mowing should not be done until the grass has reached a height of at least 3 inches.

Under normal conditions, grass clippings should be allowed to remain on the lawn, as they soon decay and help maintain the humus supply in the soil. If, because of a long period of wet weather or for some other unavoidable cause, the grass has become unusually long and rank in growth, the clippings will have a tendency to form clumpy mats on the surface of the newly mown lawn and may have a detrimental effect on the growth of the turf. If the clippings are heavy, they should be raked up with a light bamboo rake and composted. Of course, if the lawn mower is equipped with a grass catcher, the necessity of raking will be eliminated.

However, the ritual collection and removal of lawn clippings eventually leads to nutrient deficiency, which must be rectified if lawn quality is to be maintained. By mowing more frequently, the clippings will be fine and settle quickly to the ground, there to decay and return nutrients to the soil, thus averting the costly, time-consuming, and sometimes environmentally harmful application of supplemental fertilizer.

In selecting a power mower, it is advisable to avoid those that are unduly heavy, as they contribute to soil compaction—a common problem with heavy clay soils. Either rotary or reel-type mowers are acceptable for use on most home lawns. A small lawn can often be mowed easily with a nonmotorized reel mower. Power mowers may have either rotary or reel blades, the reel type providing a somewhat finer cut. The advantage of the rotary mower is that it can handle taller grass, but it is also the cause of frequent and serious injuries. Lawn mowers should *not* be used by careless or inexperienced persons. Although all rotary models have power-driven blades, they are available in either push-type or self-propelled styles, the choice depending on the size and terrain of the lawn. All gasoline power mowers are noisy, and rotary types are especially so. Electrical power rotaries are quieter but are seldom able to handle heavy outgrown turf. Estate lawns may require riding mowers, and the choice then widens to include flail-type and sickle-bar mowers. The flail cuts tall grass fairly well and is safer than rotary mower; the sickle-bar is suitable only for rough areas, such as roadsides, meadow edges, fence rows, or infrequently maintained lawns.

Aeration

Random foot traffic and repeated mowing often conspire to make many soils hard and compact, which is detrimental to the growth of turf. Clay and clay-loam soils are more subject to compaction than are soils of other types, but even sandy soils may become somewhat compact and crusted on the surface.

On lawns that are too compact, water fails to penetrate into the soil and there is apt to be considerable surface runoff. The grasses also suffer from inadequate oxygen, since sufficient air cannot penetrate the soil. Grasses on such soils tend to become shallow rooted, and the turf suffers seriously in time of drought. When fertilizers are applied, they often fail to reach the lower root levels where they are most needed.

Adequate aeration of lawn areas therefore serves many functions. It reduces surface runoff and, by permitting water to percolate down into the soil, encourages deeper and more vigorous roots. It makes it possible for fertilizers to penetrate to a depth where the roots can readily make use of the nutrients and provides for a better circulation of air in the soil, thus lessening the danger of oxygen starvation.

Aeration is usually done at the time when fertilizer is applied in the spring and again in the early autumn.

Many tools are suitable for the aeration of lawn areas. The simplest is an ordinary garden fork, practical only on very small lawns as it is laborious to use. The fork should be inserted into the turf at a 45° angle to a depth of 4 to 6 inches,

and a slight downward pressure should be exerted on the handle before it is withdrawn. This procedure should be repeated at distances of 1 foot. Forks specially designed for this purpose are available.

Another simple method of aeration is to drive spikes, several inches apart, through a board. The board is then placed on the turf, and by walking along it, you drive the spikes into the ground. This procedure is repeated over the area and is effective, but it also is practicable only on very small lawns. Flat wood sandals with spikes on the bottom can be strapped onto the feet, which can perform much the same function.

For larger lawn areas, there are numerous excellent spike-disc tools on the market that can be pushed along like a hand lawn mower. For extensive park and golf areas, power-driven machines are available.

Watering

Grasses are very efficient in extracting water from the soil for their life processes. Depending on the kind of grass, their roots may draw water from just a few inches below the surface to as much as 6 or 8 feet down. Grass roots will not grow in arid soil. Lawns receive water from natural rainfall and when this is insufficient to sustain growth or satisfactory appearance, from supplemental irrigation. The quantity and distribution of rainfall are highly variable, even in small areas. Among the factors that affect water uptake by lawns are the soil type, kind of grass, depth of rooting, height of cut, frequency of mowing, temperature, wind, humidity, and frequency and penetration of rainfall. Although much remains to be learned about how each factor affects water use, research has yielded several conclusions that are useful to the home gardener.

In general, there should be sufficient moisture in the soil to support satisfactory growth. Failing this, whatever has been lost through drainage, plant uptake, and evaporation should be replenished to the effective rooting depth of the grass. Irrigation to supplement rainfall should be applied only as demonstrably needed and not routinely. It is best to space irrigation periods as far apart as possible. Watering should be done in depth. Frequent light sprinklings encourage superficial root growth, and this does not prepare the lawn for protracted drought.

Since water drains through sandy soils faster than through clays, grasses rooted in sandy soils require more water, especially in hot summer weather. Intermediate loams, especially if underlain by sand, are very favorable to grasses because water retention is higher than in sand and aeration is better than in clay. A 12-inch depth of loam can hold the equivalent of about 1½ inches of rainfall (or irrigation water), whereas sand holds about half that amount and clay about twice as much.

Water is more effective if the soil is open and porous, thus soaking in rather than running off laterally. All but the sandiest soils become crusted and compacted at the surface as a result of traffic and repeated watering. When dry, such a surface may be totally impervious to water for a time and then allow only shallow penetration. When this occurs, there is considerable runoff, resulting in the waste of water, higher irrigation cost, and in time, deterioration of turf. Hence the importance of periodic aeration.

It is a basic principle of watering, then, to irrigate only as fast as the soil can absorb the water. If sprinklers or irrigation systems furnish water too rapidly, they should be moved or adjusted accordingly. Every system should be checked periodically for uniformity of application. This can be done quite simply by setting out low, straight-sided cans (such as cat food or tuna fish cans) at 5-foot intervals away from the sprinkler. Run the sprinkler for 10 or 15 minutes and then measure the depth of water in each can. In this manner you can determine not only the evenness of coverage but the time required to deliver 1 inch of water, the amount} generally required by lawns each week during the growing season.

Good soil aeration facilitates good drainage, which in turn promotes the development of deep root systems that can depend on moisture less subject to surface evaporation. Poor drainage makes it very difficult to grow good grass. When roots are deprived of oxygen by prolonged flooding or soil compaction, the blades turn yellow and die. Insufficient soil oxygen also excludes soil microorganisms whose activities help make nutrients available to grass roots. Because of excellent aeration, grasses develop deep, extensive root systems in light, sandy soils, but at the same time, nutrients tend to percolate downward and exceed root penetration. While this situation would seem to demand more frequent fertilizing, the addition of well-rotted manure, compost, and/or other organic matter will slow percolation and help the soil hold water.

Water Requirements of Various Lawn Grasses

The usual classification of lawn grasses into cool-season and warm-season types bears little relationship to the water requirements of the kinds of grasses involved, as the following table indicates.

Drought Tolerant	Intermediate	Drought Intolerant
Bahia grass	Colonial bent	Carpet grass
Bermuda grass	Fescue	Creeping bent
Buffalo grass	Kentucky bluegrass	Rough-stalk bluegrass
Tall fescue		St. Augustine grass

Deep-rooted grasses such as Bermuda grass utilize moisture in large volumes of soil and thus continue to grow for long periods between waterings. Some grasses curl their leaves during drought to reduce water loss (e.g., fescues and Zoysia); others hold water and nutrients in underground stems or rhizomes or in perennial root systems (e.g., Bermuda grass and buffalo grass).

Some grasses, most notably Kentucky bluegrass, bentgrass, Bermuda grass, and buffalo grass, slow their growth during hot weather. Overwatering lawns dominated by these grasses in midsummer simply stimulates weeds, crabgrass in particular. Other grasses, such as Bermuda grass and Zoysia, respond quickly to water and fertilizer in summer heat. Such behavior differentials are important considerations when choosing grasses for a lawn.

To maintain the best possible lawn through all kinds of weather, the following recommendations are germane.

1. Make sure the soil is in a condition to absorb the water, be it rainfall or irrigation, and aerate when necessary.
2. Maintain adequate soil fertility, as determined by periodic testing, and avoid unnecessary or excessive fertilizing.
3. Irrigate only when necessary, never ritually.
4. Allow irrigation water to soak in thoroughly to effective root depth, but interrupt irrigation or move sprinklers if the water puddles, indicating that the soil's absorption capacity has been exceeded.
5. Resume irrigation only when the need is clear, as may be determined by using a lawn probe that estimates soil moisture. Alternatively a small plug of sod may be dug with a narrow-bladed trowel for visual inspection.
6. Automatic, clock-driven irrigation systems should be overridden by moisture sensors to avert the waste and harm caused by irrigation during or shortly after a period of rain.

In-ground or Subirrigation Systems

Before the introduction of plastic piping, an in-ground irrigation system for the lawn was seldom within the range of home owners, due to the high cost not only of materials but also of installation. Today, however, there are a number of excellent products on the market that are moderate in price and may be installed by the do-it-yourself method.

Polyethylene plastic pipe has many advantages over the various types of metal pipe. It is light, pliable, and easy to handle; it will not rust, rot, or corrode; it does not need to be buried in a deep trench, as it will not freeze and crack; and it contains no substances that are toxic to plants. However, as plastic piping is subject to cuts and punctures by garden tools, it should be routed around—not through—garden beds, unless covered by at least 1 foot of soil.

Most of these products are equipped with noncorrosive plastic or brass fittings, and the sprinkler heads are set flush with the turf so that they will not interfere with lawn mowing. These are suited to both low- and high-pressure water systems, and they are obtainable in various sizes, covering from 1,000 square feet upward. The sprinkler heads deliver a spray similar to a gentle rainfall. The best of them minimize the generation of mist, which can waste a substantial percentage of the water delivered.

Since most lawn grasses depend heavily on an adequate supply of moisture to maintain an active, vigorous growth, it is a tremendous advantage to be able to supply water *when* it is needed. Although an irrigation system involves an initial outlay, it may be considered as a permanent investment, and the cost is relatively small when spread over a period of years. However, an irrigation system that is on a daily cycle, governed by a clock, will not only waste water but can so saturate the affected soil that the lawn and nearby plantings will be adversely affected and even killed. Soil-moisture sensors obviate this hazard.

PREPARING THE LAWN FOR WINTER

Contrary to popular belief, fall and early winter are good times to enhance the condition of the lawn. If the lawn was not reseeded in late summer or early fall, it is likely that bare spots will appear where annual crabgrass had grown. These areas may be dormant seeded and lightly covered with straw for the winter, with the expectation that germination will occur in early spring, long before heat-requiring, shade-intolerant crabgrass reappears. Furthermore, broad-leaf weeds such as dandelion and plantain are more easily pulled in fall or may be controlled with Trimec (a combination of 2,4D; MCPP; and Dicamba).

Once the lawn is definitely dormant (usually by Thanksgiving from zone 7 northward), but the soil surface remains unfrozen, supplemental fertilizing can be very beneficial. Root growth and rhizome extension begin in early spring, often well before new foliage appears, and will be augmented if nutrients are already in place. A complete fertilizer should be used, i.e., one containing nitrogen, phosphorus, and potassium. About 25 pounds of 10-6-4 per 1,000 square feet will suit in most areas, but it is best to check your local cooperative extension for its recommendations. Wherever groundwater pollution by nitrate is a problem, slow-release sources of nitrate are preferable to highly soluble fast-release forms. A topdressing of well-rotted manure or compost provides slowly released nitrate and other nutrients as well as a medium favored by earthworms and other beneficial soil organisms.

Fall is a good time to check soil pH and to add lime or ground limestone if necessary. By keeping the soil in the pH 6.5 to 7.0 range, maximal use will be made of any fertilizer that is applied. A pH check should be made every two years.

It is also important to rake the lawn clean of all fallen tree leaves before winter. The larger leaves are especially harmful, as they form canopies that exclude light and diminish water penetration

The lawn should be mowed in fall as long as it continues to grow and should go into winter not more than 2½ inches high. As in warmer weather, all clippings less than about 1 inch in length should be left to decompose. If clippings are longer, they usually accumulate on top of the turf and, if too deep, can smother the grass below, resulting in spotty dieout. Such accumulations should be removed and composted.

CONTROL OF LAWN PESTS AND DISEASES

Chemicals used to control lawn pests and diseases are poisons and must be handled with care. Special precautions should be taken to avoid inhaling the dusts and wettable powders and to wash off any materials that come into contact with the skin, since, in some cases, there is danger of absorption.

Not only are chlordane, DDT, and other chlorinated hydrocarbons prohibited for home use by law but the salts of heavy metals (such as lead arsenate) are also environmentally damaging and should be avoided. Research has led to the acceptance of various substitutes, but as this situation changes year by year, it is best to consult your local cooperative extension office for current recommendations.

In general, the best defense against lawn weeds, pests, and diseases is a strong, dense turf well provided with nutrients and made up of grass species best suited to the conditions at hand. Any symptoms of infestation should be analyzed and identified before corrective measures are considered. In many cases none need be taken.

Lawn Pests
Chinch Bug or Hairy Chinch Bug
Adult chinch bugs are about ⅛ inch long and have a black body with short white wings. Young nymphs are very small and bright red with a white cross-band. Enlarging as they mature, they turn brownish, then black. Adults and nymphs at all stages infest the base of grass blades near the ground, sucking juices from the plants. Infested turf develops irregular roundish dead patches margined by a yellowish zone of dying plants; it is in this zone that the insects are most

The Japanese beetle lays its eggs on the soil surface beneath turf in summer, and the burrowing grubs feed on grass roots over the winter and especially in spring before emerging as flying adults.

numerous. Because roots are unaffected, grass infested with chinch bugs cannot be rolled back like a piece of carpet, as in the case of beetle grub attacks.

Adult chinch bugs winter over in nearby tall grass and other vegetation. In the spring they migrate to the lawn, and the females lay their eggs at the grass roots. When the eggs hatch during June, the young nymphs begin feeding on the turf. They pass through several molts before becoming adults. A second brood, which is often more damaging than the first, appears in August, and the nymphs and adults continue to feed until well into autumn.

Any of several preparations will provide excellent control. When dusts are applied, they should be worked well into the turf with the back of an iron rake.

The first application of the chemical should be made in June. If there is still evidence of infestation, a second application should be made in August. Close cutting and a topdressing of fertilizer following treatment will aid the recovery of the injured turf.

Grubs

The grubs of several beetle species cause severe damage to lawns. Among them are those of the Asiatic beetle, the European lawn chafer, the Japanese beetle, the May beetle or June bug, the Oriental beetle, and the southern masked chafer. Grubs are C-shaped; whitish, with dark, yellowish brown heads; and have three pairs of legs. They vary from ¼ to 1½ inches long.

Grubs in lawns feed on the roots of grasses. If present in great numbers, they seriously impair the growth of turf, and if measures of control are not taken, they may kill the grass entirely. Badly infested turf appears brown and dead and can be rolled back like a carpet.

By cutting out 1 square foot of sod in the spring to a depth of 3 to 4 inches and examining it, one may readily determine whether the turf is seriously infested with grubs. The presence of 5 or 10 grubs indicates light infestation, but enough to warrant treatment. A count of 30 to 50 grubs indicates very heavy infestation.

The adult beetles lay their eggs in grass thatch during the summer months. The grubs hatch, burrow into the soils and begin feeding on the roots immediately. During the winter, they move downward in the soil below frost penetration and then move upward again in the spring, where they resume feeding, before passing into the pupa stage. Some types, such as the May beetle, require two years to complete their life cycle.

Although grubs can be completely controlled through the use of chemical insecticides, it is strongly recommended that to control Japanese beetle grubs milky spore disease powder be used. This is a slow-acting, specifically directed biological control that should be applied in warm weather. Once established, it remains effective for several years, but periodic reinoculation is advisable.

Any grub-proofing insecticides should be watered in with a heavy spray as soon after application as possible so they become immediately effective. Thus also lessens the danger to pets and wildlife.

Moles
Moles often cause severe damage to lawns. As beetle grubs are one of their chief sources of food, the best measure of control is to deprive moles of their food supply in the lawn area by eradicating the grubs.

Sod Webworm (Lawn Moth)
The sod webworms are most prevalent on bentgrass and bluegrass lawns and are more damaging in warm climates than in the North. There are a number of species that cause damage to lawns.

Although the adult months and the caterpillars differ somewhat in appearance, according to the species, they all have certain common characteristics. The small moths are usually seen at dusk, flying low over the grass where they drop eggs. The small, thick-bodied caterpillars, from ¼ to ¾ inch in length, make silk-lined tunnels among the grass blades near the ground.

When young, the caterpillars skeletonize the grass blades while feeding; but as they mature, they chew off the blades, causing the lawn to become ragged in appearance. If the infestation is heavy and measures of control are not taken, large areas of turf may be killed.

Control is usually difficult. Among the more effective agents, chlorpyrifos is less environmentally harmful than diazinon or carbaryl.

Cutworms
Cutworms are nocturnally active caterpillars that are usually gray or brown, hairless, and curled. They feed on young growth near the ground line in spring. Malathion will control them, but if the soil is drenched with this agent, all soil organisms contacted by it are likely to perish. Malathion soon becomes inert, however, and unless the drenched area is very large, the soil organisms soon recolonize from the untreated surroundings. Lawn grasses are unaffected by Malathion.

Leafhoppers
Leafhoppers are small green or brown wedge-shaped flying insects that feed most heavily in late summer and fall, sometimes causing patchy die-out. Malathion is the safest control, but kills all other insects and soil organisms contacted by it.

Nematodes
Nematodes are microscopic organisms that are present in nearly all soils. In drought and high temperatures, populations may expand to the point that their root feeding can cause wilting and patchy die-out of lawn grasses. Carefully maintained cutting height and periodic summer watering will help prevent nematode injury to strong turf. For control, which is often difficult, consult your cooperative extension agent.

Ants and Digger Wasps
Although ants and digger wasps are normal inhabitants of soil and seldom harm lawns, ants can be annoying and digger wasps can inflict painful stings. Carbaryl (Sevin) will control both but will also annihilate all other soil organisms it contacts. However, the potency of carbaryl, once applied, soon diminishes.

Lawn Diseases
Brownpatch
Brownpatch is a fungus disease caused by *Rhizoctonia solani*. Many species of lawn grasses are affected, the bentgrasses being particularly susceptible to injury. Some soils seem to be comparatively free from the fungus causing brownpatch, while other soils are badly infested. The disease is particularly prevalent during long periods of hot, humid weather. Excessive soil nitrogen, overwatering, poor drainage conditions, and high soil acidity are contributing factors in the spread of the disease.

When the turf first becomes affected, it turns very dark green, then gradually becomes light brown, imparting the appearance of dead, dried grass. The patches are roughly and irregularly circular and vary from a few inches to several feet in diameter.

There are a number of preventive measures that should be followed to lessen the occurrence of brownpatch.

1. Heavy applications of quick-release, high-nitrogen fertilizer should be avoided.
2. Watering should be done in the morning to minimize wet grass overnight.
3. Good air circulation should be provided for the lawn area, even if it means sacrificing some trees and shrubs.
4. Adequate drainage should be provided, especially in low areas.

Dollarspot
Dollarspot is a form of brownpatch that causes small, circular patches hardly more than 2 inches in diameter. The patches are of a somewhat lighter color than those typical of brownpatch.

Leaf Spots

The various leaf spots, which cause the diseases commonly known as melting-out and going-out, seriously damage lawns in some areas of the country. Kentucky, Canada, and annual bluegrasses are particularly susceptible; Merion Kentucky bluegrass, on the other hand, is highly resistant.

Going-out disease, sometimes called foot rot, occurs in the spring from March through May and occasionally recurs in autumn. The leaves attacked by the fungus shrivel, the crowns turn brown, and the rhizomes and roots rot away. Large areas of turf may become affected unless control measures are undertaken.

Copper Spot

Copper spot is a fungus disease that sometimes appears on bentgrass lawns after a prolonged rainy spell during the late spring or summer months. On close observation, salmon pink spores may be seen on the grass blades. Most other types of lawn grass are resistant.

Fading-out or Black Mold (Curvularia)

Fading-out is a fungus disease that usually occurs on bentgrasses fescues, and annual bluegrass. Velvet bent is particularly susceptible. Other grasses are resistant.

The injury is most severe during the heat of midsummer, but the disease may also appear in late spring or early autumn. Lawns affected with the fungus develop a yellowish green dappled appearance, similar in some respects to iron chlorosis, and the grass eventually dies out. On examination under a lens, a black mold may be observed on affected blades.

Snow Mold (Winter Scald)

When the last of a heavy snow has melted, patches of turf may be found that are covered with a grayish white or pinkish mold. This is caused by a fungus that thrives at low temperatures, and serious damage to the turf may occur. Low areas are particularly susceptible to attack.

Overfertilizing and overwatering are prime causes of disease, and a healthy, well-cared-for turf is the best insurance against such hazards. If fungicides must be used, a number of products are currently available, among them Acitidione, DuPont 1991, and Daconil. As with pesticides, fungicides must be applied specifically and carefully. The mercury compounds formerly used so widely are no longer available because of environmental hazards.

CONTROL OF LAWN WEEDS

In areas where correct turf management is faithfully practiced, weeds are usually not troublesome. Vigorous, rapidly growing grass is capable of crowding out many of the existing weeds and also of preventing new weeds from gaining a foothold. Many excellent lawns that are virtually free from weeds have been established and are maintained solely through the application of the fundamental practices of good lawn management. If, however, a lawn area has become badly infested with weeds through neglect, very definite measures of weed eradication can be adopted, along with a general improvement in the management of the lawn.

The basic source of weeds is the soil, which almost always contains a tremendous quantity of dormant seeds, often in great diversity. They are brought to the surface through annual freeze-thaw cycles in northern areas and through well-meant mechanical practices of turf dethatching and aeration. Every load of topsoil contains millions of weed seeds.

Elsewhere, weeds reproduce on site or are introduced from surrounding areas by wind, water, birds, pets, vehicles, and people. Relatively few are contained in commercial grass seed. Where there is space, as in a thin, patchy lawn, they quickly compete for light, moisture, nutrients, and more space.

It should also be remembered that in almost any weed-infested area allelopathy or mutual suppression often limits germination to only a small percentage of the seeds of any one species at a time, and that many weed species have extraordinarily long seed viability—as long as 20 years. Thus a heavily weed-infested lawn make take many seasons to restore.

On very small areas, weeding by hand produces excellent results. To keep the weed seed concentration from intensifying even more, weeds should be removed before seed has formed. After the weeding has been completed, all bare areas should be prepared for reseeding in accordance with the general principles involved in the seeding of new lawns.

While weeding by hand may be practical on small areas or where the infestation is very light, it is not feasible for large areas, as it is far too tedious and costly a method. In large areas, effective weed control may best be obtained through the use of various chemicals. A great deal of research has been completed by various institutions on the chemical control of weeds, and it has been proved conclusively that practically all of our common lawn weeds can be entirely eradicated by the proper and timely use of various chemicals. The factors contributing to the success of this method are the selection of the chemical most effective for the specific control of each particular weed or group of weeds, the method and time of application, the rate of application, the biodegradability of the control agent; and the subsequent method of revitalizing the turf.

Most lawn weeds may be divided into three classes, according to their general habit of growth. For each of these groups, there is one method of chemical control that will

1. *Creeping pennywort,* Hydrocotyle *spp., a lawn weed in moist places, chiefly in the South, is spread by birds who eat the seeds.*

2. *Naturalized from Eurasia, crab grass is an annual that infests lawns throughout the U.S.*

3. *Competition of roots and shade cast by the broad, rosetted leaves of the prodigiously seeding perennial English plantain weaken lawn grasses.*

4. *The taprooted dandelion is a long-lived perennial whose leaf rosettes crowd lawn grasses and whose flower heads soon liberate airborne seed.*

5. *Dandelion, crab grass, and field bindweed, all deeply rooted, continue growth in drought after most lawn grasses go dormant and turn brown.*

give the best results. It is, therefore, important to select the chemical most effective for the particular type of weed to be eradicated.

Weedy Grasses
Crab Grass (Digitaria sanguinalis)

Of the weedlike grasses that infest lawn areas, crab grass is by far the most troublesome. To eradicate it or to keep it under control, it is well to know something of its habit of growth. Crab grass is a tender subtropical annual, thriving in full sun and unable to endure shade. The seed germinates late in the spring, and the plants grow slowly during early summer. They then rapidly develop in the heat of July and August, reseed prolifically in late summer, and are killed by the first light frost. In controlling crab grass, we have three points of attack: to hand weed the young plants if the area is small, to encourage a luxuriant growth of desirable lawn grasses and to maintain the lawn at a sufficient height (1½ inches) so that the young crab grass seedlings cannot gain a foothold, or to use chemical intervention either to kill the crab grass or to prevent it from reseeding.

Preemergence weed killers (available under various trade names) have been used with varying success on lawns. The purpose is to prevent germination of crab grass seed and to kill small seedling plants before they have had time to make any growth. As crab grass seeds continue to germinate over a period of six weeks or more, from midspring to early summer, two to four applications are necessary. In some instances the preemergence materials have given excellent control, while in others they have been less satisfactory. The manufacturer's instructions should be followed carefully.

Other Weedy Grasses

Other weedy grasses sometimes troublesome in lawns include two annuals. Annual bluegrass (Poa annua) is a short-season annual common in thin, spotty lawns that soon liberates abundant seed. It yellows and dies at the onset of hot summer weather. Goosegrass (Eleusine indica) is a tufted annual of coarse appearance that persists through the summer but is killed by early frost. Both respond to the control procedures outlined for crab grass.

Among undesirable perennial grasses are quack or couch grass (Agropyron repens), a coarse invader of northern lawns that quickly spreads by rhizomes, and Johnsongrass (Sorghum halepense), a strong-growing rhizomatous species of even coarser habit, sometimes grown for forage but also a rampant lawn weed, especially in the South. Spot treatment with as benign an herbicide as possible is the only alternative to hand digging these invaders; on a large lawn, the cure can be worse than the problem.

Mat-forming Weeds

The mat-forming weeds include some species that can be very troublesome on lawns.

Common chickweed (Stellaria media) and mouse-ear chickweed (Cerastium spp.) may be controlled by spraying with potassium cyanate. Control is most effective when the application is made during moderately warm weather. If spraying is undertaken during the cooler months, it should be done on a warm, sunny day and hot water should be used when mixing the spray.

Potassium cyanate is also recommended as a control for crabgrass as well as for goosegrass, knotweed, and others. It possesses the additional advantages of having very low toxicity to human beings and animals and of having some fertilizing value. When potassium cyanate comes into contact with the soil, it is rapidly broken down into potash and nitrogen. Two or three applications are recommended, the first early in July, the last by mid-August. In large areas, applications may be made with a power sprayer, while in small areas a hand sprayer may be used very satisfactorily. Applications of potassium cyanate should be made only when lawn grasses are making active, vigorous growth. Under such conditions there will be little injury to most lawn grasses other than a slight and very temporary discoloration of the tips. However, if application is made during periods of extreme heat or when growth is stunted because of drought severe injury may result. The compound is not recommended for use on bentgrass lawns. Potassium cyanate may be combined with 2, 4-D, but when this is done, there is greater danger of injury to the turf.

Among other mat-forming broad-leaf weeds are such animals as knotweed (Polygonum aviculare), a blue-green, rather narrow-leaved annual with prostrate stems radiating from a deep taproot; spotted spurge (Euphorbia maculata), also a spreading annual, with milky sap and a purplish middle zone in each leaf; and purslane (Portulaca oleracea), a succulent, flat-to-the-ground annual with small yellow flowers. Perennials in this category include ground ivy (Glechoma hederacea), a rampant creeper, especially in damp semishade, with nearly circular, shallowly toothed leaves in pairs and lavender purple flowers in spring; heal-all (Prunella vulgaris), usually 8 inches tall or more but tolerant of mowing, and with paired leaves two to three times longer than wide and spikes of purple flowers in summer; mint (Mentha spp.), the familiar aromatic herb that can readily creep into lawns from adjacent gardens, as can bugle (Ajuga spp.), the well-known ground cover.

Unwisely shunned by many as a lawn weed, white clover (Trifolium repens) is beneficial as a lawn component, as its roots harbor nodules of nitrogen-fixing bacteria whose action contributes to soil fertility. A deeply rooting perennial creeper with spherical heads of white flowers, white clover endures foot traffic and drought better than most lawn grasses and blends inconspicuously into most turf. As clover is killed by most broad-leaf herbicides, this approach to weed control cannot be used if clover is to be retained in the lawn.

Rosette-forming Weeds
Dandelion (Taraxacum sp.)

Control at the dandelion may be obtained by spot spraying with glyphosate, available under the trade names Roundup and Cleanup. It is best used in late spring or early summer, after the leaves have fully expanded. Alternatively, 2, 4-D will kill dandelion if applied in early spring before flowering or in fall about the time of first frosts. Care is required with both substances. as they will harm or kill almost any plant they contact. Use them only on calm days. Most lawn grasses are resistant to 2, 4-D, if it is applied at the prescribed rate, but seedling grasses of all species are as likely to be killed by 2, 4-D as by glyphosate. If dandelion infestation is very localized or occasional, hand weeding is the safest approach.

Broad-leaf or English Plantain (Plantago major) and Narrow-leaf Plantain (P. lanceolata)

Both the broad- and narrow-leaf plantain may be effectively controlled with spot treatment using either glyphosate or 2, 4-D, as described for dandelion control.

Onion Grass or Wild Garlic (Allium canadense)

In many sections of the country onion grass, a relative of onion, garlic, and chives, is a serious lawn weed. Clumps of new growth appear in the fall, just as lawn grasses slow to dormancy. It becomes especially vigorous in early spring, well before the first mowing, and makes a lawn appear unkempt and shabby.

Hand digging the clumps is laborious but can be effective if care is taken to get all the associated bulblets. This is best done in early winter or earliest spring, when lawn grasses are dormant. Composting onion grass is not advisable, unless the clumps of bulblets are left buried under 1 foot or more of soil for at least one year.

RENOVATION OF OLD OR FAILED LAWNS
Old Lawns

Late summer or early fall is the best time to renovate an entire lawn or to reseed problem areas, especially in zone 8 and northward. Temperatures are usually cooler and rainfall

more plentiful and effective at this time. Renovated lawns have far less competition with weeds in fall than in spring.

Before getting under way, the cause of lawn failure should first be determined. If it is found that a disease such as fusarium blight had attacked the lawn, then a fusarium-resistant bluegrass, perennial rye, or bluegrass-rye mix should be used. Suitable bluegrass strains include 'Adelphi', 'Edmundi', 'Glade', 'Parade', 'Sydsport', 'Touchdown', 'Vantage', and 'Windsor'.

If the problem was poor drainage—which, left uncorrected, will doom a renovated lawn as certainly as it did the original one—it is possible that incorporation of 35 to 50 percent peat moss or other loose organic material into the top 6 to 8 inches may suffice. More likely, however, drainage tiles or regrading will be required or, alternatively, abandonment of lawn altogether in favor of shrubs and groundcovers that are tolerant of "wet feet."

If the lawn failed because it is difficult or impractical to supply adequate supplemental water, then drought-tolerant grasses should be chosen for the renovated lawn. Tall fescues do well in water-deficient situations, and although many of the old forms had rather coarse foliage, newer ones, such as 'Falcon', Hound Dog, and 'Rebel', have become well accepted as turf grasses. Tall fescues also have low fertilizer requirements and are tolerant of roadside and seaside salt.

In general, lawn grasses require several hours of direct sunlight daily. In heavily shaded locations, especially under large trees with a superficial root mat (such as Norway maple), even shade-enduring ground covers may prove disappointing, although a 3- to 6-inch layer of compost with well-rotted manure will usually allow a mat of fairy bells (*Disporum sessile* 'Variegatum') to become well established before the tree roots invade; English ivy (*Hedera helix*) is also very shade and root competition tolerant. Failing these, however, a layer of bark chips or even wood chips is more pleasing than the bare ground that often ensues when grass is attempted in heavy shade.

In moderate shade, several grasses have proven reliable, among them the bluegrass strains 'Bristol', 'Eclipse', 'Glade', 'Touchdown', and 'Warren's A-34'; the fescues 'Banner', 'Biljart', 'Highlight', and 'Jamestown'; and several perennial ryes. Of these, the fescues may fade and even vanish if the area is excessively fertilized and overwatered. As with new lawns, it is prudent to use a mix of two or more grasses, and one of the components should be a strain of perennial rye. Of the many perennial ryes available, 'Citation', 'Diplomat', 'Manhattan', 'Omega', and 'Yorktown' are used very widely.

The steps thereafter are as follows:

1. Check the soil pH with a soil testing kit and, if necessary, adjust the pH to 6.5 to 7.0.

2. Check the physical quality of the soil and, if excessively clayey or sandy, add compost, peat moss, and/or well-rooted manure.
3. Kill all residual grass and weeds with glyphosate.
4. Use a dethatcher to remove dead material.
5. Spread seed, preferably with a mechanical seeder, sowing one-half in a north-south direction and the rest in an east-west direction. Allow the soil surface to dry before sowing.
6. Drag an inverted bristly doormat over the surface or lightly rake the still-dry seeded surface to help bring the seed into contact with the soil.
7. Roll the still-dry surface with a light (empty) steel lawn roller to compact the surface soil gently.
8. Water the seeded area lightly but thoroughly. Heavy watering will float the seeds into low spots or, on sloping ground, completely off the site. Several successive light waterings are preferable to a single drenching.
9. Keep the soil surface evenly moist until the new grass is 1½ to 2 inches tall. This is especially critical, because if once-germinated seed is allowed to dry out, it dies.
10. Mow the new growth when it is 3 to 4 inches high, preferably with a lightweight hand mower.

Spotty, uneven germination is usually the result of uneven sowing, too much water before the seed sprouts, or too little water after the seed has begun sprouting.

Thatch in Lawns

Thatch is the normal spongy layer of dead plant parts that accumulates beneath the grass blades on top of the soil. If this layer is too thick and dense, it will impair the penetration of water to the roots below. In most lawns, a thatch layer thicker than ¾ in is excessive and may require dethatching and aerating so that water can get through. Not all lawn grasses are thatch producers: Kentucky bluegrass and most fescues are, but perennial ryes and tall fescues are not. Dethatching machines help pull some or most of the accumulated thatch but rarely all, especially if the spongy thatch layer is more than 1 inch thick. Machines with a fixed blade are preferable to those with spring tines, as the latter damage the lawn considerably in the process of extracting thatch. Core aeration may obviate dethatching in some cases, but the unrelieved buildup of thatch usually has a strangling effect on grass and results in the thinning of turf. Dethatching and core aeration are best carried out in spring or fall when the lawn can more readily recover than in summer. The use of well-rotted manure in place of synthetic fertilizers and of biological controls in place of synthetic biocides promotes the growth of the benign fungi and bacteria that accelerate the decomposition of plant remains and thus control the buildup of thatch.

Failed Lawns

Often a lawn is grown on whatever soil happens to be available. Even if such a lawn is fertilized and reseeded every year, the result can be disappointing. The most economical remedy in such circumstances is to begin over again and remove all grass and weeds during the summer, allowing sufficient time to upgrade the soil and undertake reseeding not later than early September.

Organic material such as screened compost, well-rotted manure, or peat moss should be worked into the soil at least 6 inches deep using a rototiller. The soil should be worked over several times in different directions so that the added material will be thoroughly and evenly incorporated. Heavy clay should be lightened with sand. Sandy soils prone to summer drought will be improved by the organic material, as it slows downward percolation and retains moisture. Procedure from this point on, i.e., establishing the seedbed and seeding, is the same as for new lawn.

Reconditioning a Weedy Lawn

The most important consideration when planning to improve an existing lawn is choice of season. For example, if crab grass is the problem, reseeding in spring will have no affect, as the crab grass, though late to germinate, will quickly outcompete young turf grass.

In most cases, it is best to deal with weed-infested lawns in the fall. The program must be well planned, however, with all needed materials on hand, so that work can be done when conditions are favorable—usually around mid to late August in zones 6 to 8.

First the lawn is mowed as closely as possible, with all clippings caught and removed. Then the surface is raked in all directions to raise weed runners and the lawn is mowed again. This is repeated as often as necessary to remove all seed heads. All clippings should be discarded, not composted.

The soil should be tested for acidity, and if the pH is lower than 6.5, ground limestone or lime should be added accordingly.

A complete fertlizer should be added, preferably formulated according to the results of a thorough soil analysis. If such a test is not undertaken, use a 10-6-4 fertilizer or a similar commercial preparation. A spiked roller will help get the fertilizer into the soil without seriously disturbing existing turf grass; alternatively, a garden fork may be thrust into the ground at close intervals and pulled out without levering the soil. The fertilizer should be spread when the grass

A thin, weedy lawn with patchy die-out is a candidate for renovation, once the causes of decline have been determined.

is dry, then lightly raked with a bamboo rake so that it all falls to the soil surface. Then water in the fertilizer.

Conditions will determine the type of grass, or preferably mixture, that is chosen. If in doubt, consult your local cooperative extension. Use only first-grade seed, as rapid germination is critical. Rake lightly with a grass rake and keep all seeded areas constantly moist as for new lawn.

Such a program should result in a dense stand of young turf by the onset of winter, which should thicken enough in the ensuing spring to deter crab grass and other lawn weeds.

Spot Renovation
Seeding
Although many home owners annually overseed entire lawns to effect renovation, this usually wastes much costly seed and results in minimal improvement, if any. It is much more effective to concentrate on thin and bare spots.

If weeds have replaced lawn in small areas, all weeds should be removed, the soil upgraded, and the area reseeded in early fall. If the lawn is thin but remains essentially weed free, the renovation may be done in early spring, with care taken to exclude traffic and to keep the treated area moist until the new turf is well developed. If the area to be treated

has suffered from too much foot traffic, it may require stepping-stones as well as turf restoration.

Sodding
Important small areas, for example, along an entry walk or a front sidewalk, sometimes become bare as a result of long-term trampling and soil compaction. If traffic can be kept to paths and walks, such worn spots are best restored by sodding. Suitable sod may be found at the edge of flower beds or other border areas. Once the area to be restored has been throughly forked and fertilized, the pieces of sod may be carefully set in place a bit higher than the adjacent lawn, tamped, and watered. If no suitable sod is available on site, rolls may be purchased at nurseries and garden centers.

Lawn Repair under Trees
Bare lawn areas often develop under shade trees. However, satisfactory turf can be grown under most such conditions if certain ameliorating or corrective measures are taken.

1. Depending on the size of the tree, spread one or more bales of peat moss and work it into the soil with a garden fork. The peat moss will retain moisture and

nutrients, facilitate the penetration of water, and soften the ground.

2. Test the soil for pH and adjust with ground limestone or lime to bring it into the pH 6.5 to 7.0 range.

3. Spread a complete fertilizer at the rate of 25 or 30 pounds per 1,000 square feet, using 10-6-4, 12-4-8, 23-7-7, or a similarly proportioned nitrate-rich mix on top of the peat moss, favoring slow-release nitrate in areas where nitrate pollution of water supplies is a problem.

4. Using a shovel or spade sharpened on a rotary grinding stone, dig in and mix the lime and fertilizer with the underlying peat moss-lightened soil, working backward from the periphery toward the trunk and digging as deeply as the tool blade will permit. This will cut the tree's mat of surface roots but leave major roots and all deeper root branches intact. It will also prepare the substrate for seeding.

5. Rake the prepared area level and proceed as for new lawn.

Be careful to choose a shade-tolerant grass, such as Chewings fescue, or a mix that includes shade-tolerant kinds. As in open areas, it is best to seed shaded areas in early fall, but care must be taken to remove fallen leaves promptly from the young turf. Routine aeration will usually be more important under trees than in open sites, because of the competition of underlying tree roots. A hand aerator or ordinary garden fork, used at least once a year, will help keep the soil adequately aerated.

Some trees, such as Norway maple and certain conifers, develop such dense root mats at the surface and cast such intense shade that turf often will not succeed. Under such conditions, an alternative solution should be sought. Certain highly tolerant plants, such as fairy bells (*Disporum sessile* 'Variegatum' or *D. flavum*) or English ivy (*Hedera helix*) cvs. have proven adaptable to such extreme conditions. Note that fairy bells, though perennial, dies to the ground in fall, and English ivy will climb the tree if allowed. A nonliving covering, such as bark chips or gravel, is another option.

II

Trees

Ever since the dawn of civilization, the forest and its products have affected the economics as well as the aesthetics of human life. A love and respect of trees has been characteristic of humankind since the beginning of our evolution. As the largest living objects we encounter, trees strongly influence the character of any setting of which they are a part.

Instinctively, we understand the importance of trees to our lives long before we are able to ascribe reasons for our

Acer japonicum *'Aureum'*

dependence on them. Today, the importance of trees to our well-being and happiness is a commonplace fact of daily life and one that is almost universally appreciated. In today's increasingly urban and suburban world, we remind ourselves of our primeval link with trees—as well as their physical and aesthetic value—by sheltering our homes whenever possible with the benevolent shade and symbolic strength of trees.

Trees are grown for many purposes. They may be grown for the sheer beauty of their form, foliage, or flowers. They may be grown to provide shelter from the wind, to provide shade, or to reduce unwanted noise. They may be grown for the production of fruits, nuts, timber, wood pulp, sugar, or turpentine. In addition to these many uses, trees fulfill other important functions. Though some trees in some places must be considered weeds or pests, even they make a valuable contribution in the appropriate setting. An acre of trees of most any kind produces enough oxygen to meet the needs of 18 people for a year and consumes all the carbon dioxide exhaled by the same number.

Beyond these considerations, it is clear that trees have idiosyncratic psychological values that can be realized in many ways. Whether in an ancient natural forest or in a carefully designed, well-maintained garden, trees touch something inside us. They provide sensory enjoyment and relaxation and help us experience our connection with our natural heritage and with our most deeply held cultural values. In short, trees have a way of making people feel good.

In a landscape composition, the trees native to a region are usually to be preferred to exotic trees that are alien to the immediate surroundings. In New England and other northern states, for example, the American elm, sugar maple, white oak, and white pine are typical trees dominant in the landscape, and their use in plantings in these areas is appropriate and satisfying. On the other hand, on the coastal plain, far from the Rocky Mountains where they are native, blue spruce, white fir, and ponderosa pine nearly always seem artificial and out of place.

This does not mean that nonnative trees should not be used, but rather that they should be used with discretion. As a matter of fact, in formal designs there is no such restriction. But if a naturalistic scene is desired, then the trees selected should either be native or have an appearance similar to those of native trees. For instance, the Chinese scholar tree (*Sophora japonica*), though it comes from the Orient, blends agreeably with the foliage of native deciduous trees and is pleasing as a specimen flowering tree or as a member

Trees not only serve as a backdrop for house and garden but cast welcome shade in summer.

of a grove. But the umbrella pine (*Sciadopitys verticillata*), another Oriental, unlike anything we have in this country, would seem an intrusion if placed in a naturalistic setting.

Trees are a very important, powerful element in landscape composition and are used for various purposes in design. Groups of them may form the masses in the design to contrast with an open area. Many trees together make a background for the structure and for the more intimate details of the design. Individual trees may serve as accents in the overall design or as incidental notes of the picturesque. By their shapes, trees express line as well as mass in the composition. Thus the famous group of spirelike cypresses at Villa Falconieri in Italy gives a dominant vertical line to the composition. The spreading, windswept Monterey cypresses of California make dramatic horizontal lines against the sky and sea.

Many trees produce showy or conspicuous flowers in profusion, thus lending the garden picture greater scale and variety and more richness of color. Still others are adorned with ornamental fruit, or with foliage that turns a glorious color in autumn, while some trees have attractive branching forms or bark texture and color that are particularly interesting in winter.

Trees, especially ornamental trees, should be considered a longtime, though continuous, crop. The mature trees immediately surrounding a house will eventually become aged and subject to decay, and home owners with forethought will plant young trees nearby to take over long before the old trees start to deteriorate. In this way the general form of the original landscape design will be maintained, although individual members of the group may change. Seedling trees frequently come up in places where they are not wanted. If these are not removed while young, they may spoil the appearance of the hedge or shrub border or rob the soil of nutrients in the flower bed, eventually overwhelming it.

When planting new trees, you must take into account their eventual dimensions; otherwise, within a few years, the inevitable crowding will occur, to the detriment of the overall design and of the individual trees. It is sometimes hard to cut down trees we enjoy. Although it is an advantage to plant woodland trees closely so that the young trees may benefit by mutual protection and be thinned out later, there is no justification for crowding specimen lawn trees.

Sometimes it is a great advantage to buy semimature trees. This shortens the waiting period. But in most cases, especially when the high cost of investment and the increased risk of failure is considered, smaller trees are better. On the other hand, it is a great mistake for an owner to postpone planting trees for several years. The money invested in small trees during the first year on a new property will greatly enhance the property's value. In addition, the trees themselves will increase in value, and a $100 tree may be worth $500 after only a few years of growing.

SELECTION OF TREES

It is important to recognize that when incorporated or planted in human environments, trees are inevitably subjected to stresses that can limit their full development. Such limitations include extensive pavement and other barriers to root growth, soil compaction, toxic pollutants in the soil and air, frequent injury by various chemical and mechanical agents, and especially when in a weakened physiological state, susceptibility to the depredations of pests and diseases. These limitations, when severe, reduce vigor, require inordinate maintenance, diminish aesthetic value, and shorten the life span of the tree. To live, any tree must have access to soil moisture, nutrients, and sunlight and must grow each year. In time, every tree dies, if not from trauma caused by a natural or unnatural event, then from protracted senility and decline.

When selecting trees for your property, there are many points to be considered in addition to the basic question of the size of the tree at maturity. Other factors of equal importance are the tree's hardiness in the climate; its resistance to wind; its adaptability to soil conditions; its habit and rapidity of growth; its production of attractive flowers or fruit; and its undesirable characteristics—such as the shedding of bark, the production of poisonous fruit, or its chronically serving as host to insect attacks. All these points should be taken into account.

If selection is being made for ornamental reasons, those kinds of trees having outstanding beauty during successive seasons of the year should be given preference, especially if the property is a small one. Trees form the backbone of any garden, and we must live with them for 52 weeks of the year, not just the brief period they are in flower. A tree that produces a good display of blossoms in spring, displays ornamental fruits in autumn, shows good autumnal leaf color, and presents a pleasing growth habit in winter is far more desirable than one that merely blossoms well in the spring and has no outstanding features throughout the rest of the year.

From a list of fairly dependable trees, a great variety may be selected for a large property, so that together they will produce bloom over a period from early spring to late summer, followed by a succession of ornamental fruit and rich autumn coloration. There are trees suitable for all purposes and for unusual growing conditions. There are trees for wet soil, dry gravelly soil, city atmosphere, wind, heat, and drought. And there are others that for one reason or another are not dependable or satisfactory in any human environment.

Trees for the small property should be chosen with particular care. Few features influence the surroundings of a home more than the flowering trees. And, fortunately, many of our most beautiful flowering trees do not grow large and are, therefore, well adapted to the small yard, as they will remain in scale and not outgrow the restrictions of the site. There are many to choose from: the bold saucer magnolia. (*Magnolia* × *soulangiana*), which greets spring with its display of waxy pink and white flowers; the various bracted dogwoods (*Cornus* spp.), with their wealth of ivory-tinted or pink bloom and their picturesque horizontal branches extending outward in rhythmic waves; the lovely silver bell tree (*Halesia carolina*), draped with myriad white hanging bells; the flowering crab apples (*Malus* spp.) and cherries (*Prunus* spp.), with their rosy buds and their profusion of bloom; the snowbell tree (*Styrax japonicus*) from Japan, with pendent white bells that open in early summer after the flowering period of most of the other trees has passed; and the sourwood (*Oxydendrum arboreum*), which in autumn brings to the small suburban home a touch of woodland glory, for there are few trees that have more beautiful fall coloring or retain it over so long a period. In addition to these, there are many other flowering trees from which selections may be made.

There are also a number of small trees that do not bear conspicuous flowers but, because of their picturesque form or other desirable characteristics, deserve to be considered. In this group are the English maple (*Acer campestre*) and the white-barked birches (*Betula* spp.). The English maple is a sturdy, compact tree that offers the traditional virtues of more familiar kinds of maple. A clump of white birches on the edge of the lawn area is always aesthetically pleasing, and when a planting of primroses and early spring bulbs is grouped beneath their branches, it makes a lovely composition.

If space permits, it is often desirable to have one or two larger trees for shade. Considerable thought should be given to the choice of such trees. A tree should be selected that will cast high shade and under which grass will grow well. The frequently planted Norway maple is an especially poor choice from this point of view because the dense shade it casts combined with its shallow, densely matted roots conspire to keep virtually any other plant from succeeding underneath it. The backyard shade tree should be graceful in form and modest in size. Trees with low spreading branches that sweep down to the ground are not suited to the small place, as year by year they diminish the area available for lawn and recreation. Gradually, the property becomes too heavily shaded. The backyard tree should be tidy, not one that sheds its bark or drops objectionable fruits on the lawn. Among the trees that are excellent as shade trees on the small home property are the familiar honey locust (*Gleditsia triacanthos*), sweet gum (*Liquidambar styraciflua*), male ginkgo (*Ginkgo biloba*), and littleleaf linden (*Tilia cordata*) as well as some less common kinds, such as the katsura (*Cercidiphyllum japonicum*), franklinia (*Franklinia alatamaha*), and stewartia (*Stewartia* spp.)

Other trees, set strategically on the property, can bring about long-term energy savings. By planting evergreens along north and west boundaries, the velocity of harsh winds, especially in winter, is much reduced—as much as 75 percent—which, in turn, can cut home heating costs up to 25 percent. Various pines and spruces are especially effective. As for summer protection, deciduous plantings to the south, southwest, and southeast will produce welcome shade, and in winter, when the leaves are down and the sun is low in the sky, they will admit warming sunshine. Maples and oaks come immediately to mind, but there are many other kinds to consider (see the tables later in this chapter).

Before choosing species for your yard, it is well to make an informal inventory of trees already growing in the surrounding community, to determine both the kinds that grow well and those that are underrepresented. In the environmentally stressed conditions that are rife in human habitats, especially in urban and suburban settings, diversity is to be promoted in all plantings.

In addition to exercising care in choosing the kinds of trees, it is equally important to be aesthetically discriminating. Choose one or more kinds that will truly grace the setting. See mature specimens in a nearby botanic garden, arboretum, or park to gain perspective on what time will bring.

Unless instant shade is essential, it is best to plant trees less than 10 feet tall. Even at that height, the tree's burlap-wrapped root ball will be 18 to 20 inches across and weigh 150 to 175 pounds. Specimens 12 to 15 feet tall will have balls weighing twice as much. Larger sizes inevitably involve the use of machinery, which greatly elevates the overall cost.

For the small property, it is best to choose trees with a maximum height no greater than 35 or 40 feet. The descriptions beginning on page 175 and the lists beginning on page 186 include height at maturity for all species. In general, actual maximum heights will be lower in seashore areas and windswept locations at high elevations than in protected valleys with deep soils.

PREPARATION OF SOIL FOR PLANTING

Trees growing in the woods often have a soil that is porous, rich in humus, and moist; in other words, they have natural built-in conditions that are most favorable to their growth. On the other hand, trees growing in lawn or field have a soil usually less rich in humus, less porous, and commonly matted with grass roots. Therefore, the careful preparation of the soil before trees are transplanted is one of the essentials to success. Rich, friable soil stimulates strong growth and helps make trees less subject to disease and less vulnerable to attack by insects. Undernourished trees start with a handicap in the battle for survival. The proper preparation of soil for tree planting should include the following: removal of all other potentially competing plants, deep hand digging if the area to be planted is comparatively small, the addition of humus or peat moss to lighten the soil and make it porous but moisture conserving; the addition of sand to lighten a soil that is too heavy with clay; and breaking up any clay subsoil with deep forking. Well-rotted manure may be added to improve the soil texture and moisture retention, and will, in addition, increase the available nutrients.

In preparing soil for the planting of large deciduous trees, the topsoil should be removed, the subsoil excavated to a depth of 18 to 24 inches below the final grade, and the hole filled with additional topsoil. The shock of transplanting is more severe to a mature tree than to a young one and the added depth of rich soil will contribute greatly in reestablishing the root system. The planting bed should be round and 3 feet wider than the diameter of the ball of earth that will come with the roots. If possible, this preparation should be done six months or a year in advance of planting to allow the soil to settle.

In preparing the soil for trees of any size, all shallow rock encountered at the site must be dealt with. One of three alternative procedures must be chosen. In some situations, especially in a depression, the grade of the ground may be raised by filling in topsoil over a wide area to a depth that will cover the rock by 18 inches of earth. In other cases, the position of the tree may be changed, without seriously affecting the pictorial composition, to a place where the underlying rock is set deeper. But if a tree must be planted at a certain position where rock is near the surface, the rock will have to be removed. Blasting a hole in the rock, removing the pieces, and filling in with soil is the best method. But if blasting is impracticable, jackhammering may be undertaken. A commercial excavator can use either method. Another method, now seemingly quaint, can, where permitted, nevertheless prove effective. On a cold day, build a wood fire on the rock, thus heating it. Rake away the ashes and pour cold water on the hot rock. The rapid and uneven change of temperature will crack the rock and the pieces can then be pried up with a crowbar and wedge.

TRANSPLANTING TREES
Digging and Transplanting Seasons
In most parts of the country, nursery-grown trees purchased in containers or with adequate balls of soil around their roots may be planted anytime during the growing season, but extra attention should be paid to watering if they are planted during hot periods in summer. In locations that have severe winters, as in Canada, northern New England, Michigan, Wisconsin, and west of Omaha, Nebraska, spring planting is preferable. The spring planting season begins as soon as the ground is dry enough to work, and continues until the buds of deciduous trees have sent forth their young leaves to ½ to 1 inch in length. Thus oaks, which leaf out late, should be transplanted later than horse chestnut trees.

The evergreen planting season is longer. Their fall planting season begins in late August in most areas and continues until hard-freezing weather. It is best not to move broad-leaf evergreens, however, after early or mid-October. Many evergreen trees and most deciduous trees may be transplanted with a frozen ball of earth during the winter, as described for transplanting large trees on page 172.

Some trees can be transplanted safely only at very specific times. Magnolias, for example, should be moved only in very early spring, before any growth is apparent. Their roots are easily broken, and since loss of root activity is to be expected after transplanting, it is wise to move these trees when compensatory root growth is most active, before flowering in the spring. Other trees that are best moved only in early spring include:

Betula spp.	Birch
Carpinus spp.	Hornbeam
Carya spp.	Hickory
Cladrastis lutea	Yellowwood
Cornus spp.	Dogwood
Gymnocladus dioica	Kentucky coffee tree
Juglans spp.	Walnut
Liquidambar styraciflua	Sweet gum
Liriodendron tulipifera	Tulip tree
Nyssa spp.	Tupelo
Ostrya spp.	Hop hornbeam
Quercus alba	White oak
Taxodium distichum	Bald cypress

Even with careful top pruning to help compensate for unavoidable root damage, trees of these species, when moved in autumn, run the risk of severe dieback because winter uptake of water fails to fully offset the water loss experienced through twigs and bark.

Because tree roots are difficult to see, misconceptions about them abound. The root systems of most trees are far more extensive and closer to the surface than is generally appreciated. Both pedestrian and vehicular traffic cause soil compaction, which diminishes water and air penetration.

Changes in grade and drainage also affect water relations, sometimes fatally. Especially relevant here is the fact that very little—often 25 percent or less—of a tree's original root system is moved when it is dug from the nursery. Hence the importance of preparing a hole large enough for the roots that remain to spread out, resume growth, and take in water and nutrients. Hence also the need to supplement rainfall during the first summer or two with irrigation. It is then that a recently transplanted tree is threatened not only by a severely diminished root system but also by the evaporation of soil moisture. A 2- to 3-inch blanket of woodchips or other mulch, spread well beyond the reach of the roots, will help conserve soil moisture at this critical time. Where mice and other gnawing rodents are common, it is advisable to keep the mulch several inches away from the trunk.

Plastic Sprays and Defoliation

The use of plastic antitranspirant sprays can appreciably reduce transplanting losses. Diluted in water, the plastic is sprayed over the entire tree so that all surfaces are covered with a thin, flexible, colorless, and long-lasting film that retards evaporation without arresting the natural process of transpiration. When used on deciduous stock in a dormant state, the need for pruning after planting is considerably reduced; it also provides better bark protection than wrapping the trunk with paper. One spraying is usually enough. Spraying should be done when the temperature is 50° F or warmer. In transplanting evergreen trees, the spraying of plastic before digging is an enormous help in retarding evaporation.

While the transplanting of deciduous trees in full leaf is not recommended, it may be done with some success if the whole plant is sprayed with plastic to cover both sides of the leaves. The use of these sprays not only reduces the need for severe pruning but also enables one to prolong the planting season into the late spring and to start it earlier in the autumn (with treatment), even in late summer.

Another method of preparing trees for transplanting is partial defoliation. All but about one-quarter of the leaves are cut off with shears (not pulled off from the twigs). This method is used particularly on both American and English holly when they are being transplanted in northern regions. New leaves usually reappear in weeks and meanwhile the tree will lose little moisture.

Methods of Transplanting
Bare-Root Transplanting

Bare-root transplanting is a popular method of moving many deciduous shrubs and young deciduous trees from the nursery to their permanent locations. It depends for its success on taking up a large proportion of the root system, keeping it moist, placing it in the ground again as soon as possible, and removing enough of the top (branches and foliage) to compensate for the temporary reduction of activity in the roots. This operation is best accomplished either in early spring, when the twigs are bare, or in the autumn when the plant is losing its leaves.

To transplant a bare-root tree, the gardener begins by digging into the ground in a circle at the outer ends of the roots—starting, say, 10 trunk diameters away—and works in toward the trunk, carefully forking the earth from the roots. Thus practically all the important main roots and a large portion of the fibrous roots remain intact. Any soil left clinging to the roots is carried with them, and is a great benefit to the plant while it is reestablishing itself in its new location. These little particles of soil held by the fine roots keep the contact and hence capillary action uninterrupted during transportation, and they continue to function unless they become very dry while out of the ground.

The time that elapses between digging in the nursery and planting in the new position should be reduced to a minimum. The new hole is best prepared and the soil enriched long before the tree is dug from its old location. The roots should never be exposed to the sun or wind during this interval, not even for a minute. If a group of plants must be kept out of the ground for several hours, as is usual on a large planting job, they should at least be set in the shade of a tree or building, their roots covered with burlap, damp leaves, or wet newspapers. A better precaution against the drying of the roots is to heel the trees in at once in a convenient place. Then if planting work is interrupted or delayed, the trees can wait until all is ready. This is also the best procedure to follow when bare-root trees are obtained from mail-order sources and time must elapse before they are properly planted. To heel in trees or shrubs, dig a trench large enough to accommodate the roots, throwing the soil to one side. Place the roots of the plants in the trench in such a way that the stems are inclined at an angle of 45° or lower to reduce possible wind whipping, and cover the roots with loose soil. If the roots are very dry when the plants are received, they should be soaked in a container of water for a half hour before being heeled in. The soil covering the roots should be kept wet. In such a situation, trees and shrubs may be kept safely for a few weeks.

When trees are dug in the nursery, they are bundled, labeled, and gathered for shipment. The risk of injury from chafing of the bark on the side of the truck may be minimized by placing a wad of burlap bagging where the trunk rests on the gate, rack, or other support.

Transplanting trees from the woods or from your own grounds entails more risk than transplanting from the

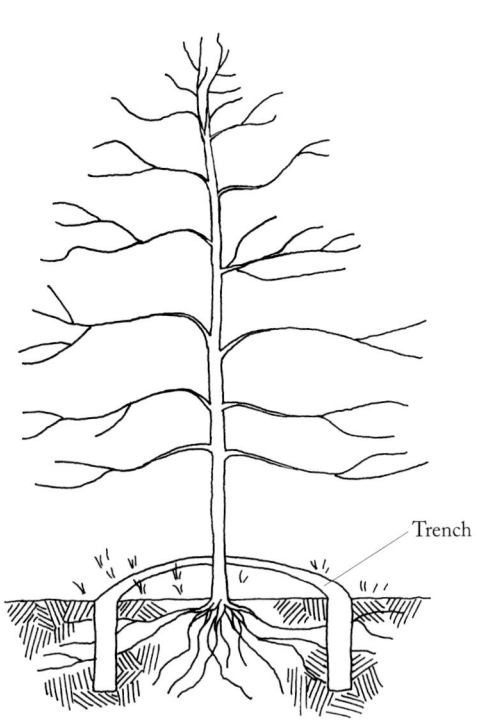

The effect of root pruning is to concentrate the roots in a ball.

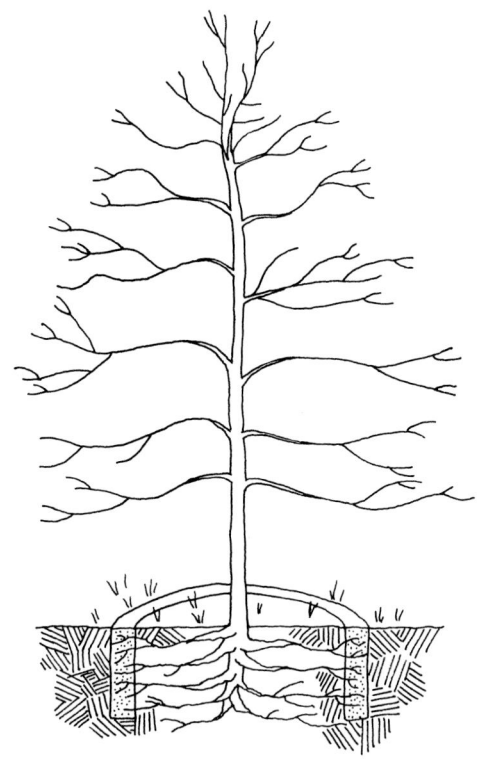

Topsoil fills trench.

nursery. In the nursery, each tree has been transplanted or root pruned once or twice to induce the growth of fibrous roots in a concentrated mass. On the other hand, the roots of forest-grown seedlings are rangy, and it is difficult to dig them up and make them stay together. If a tree is to be transplanted from the woods, it should be prepared for the change of location by pruning its roots a year in advance. assuming, of course, its removal is permissible. Root pruning is accomplished by digging a trench around the tree at a distance from the trunk equal in feet to the diameter of the trunk in inches. The trench need be no wider than the shovel's blade, but should be deep enough to cut through all the lateral roots, 18 to 24 inches, according to the size of the tree. The soil is then returned to the trench and new roots will develop within the circle and in the trench. When the tree is taken up, it should be done according to one of the methods of transplanting described in this chapter.

In placing the tree in its new location, make sure that the hole is large enough to accommodate the roots without bending them. The roots should be spread out evenly and the topsoil thrown in among the roots and allowed to settle. When the roots are covered with loose soil but the hole not yet filled, the earth should be settled in among the roots by watering. More soil is added and watered and the hole is thus filled. When adding soil, approximately one-third of the volume should be peat moss or compost, thoroughly

mixed in before backfilling. This will help promote moisture retention in the critical few years ahead. Deciduous trees should be planted 1 to 2 inches deeper than they were in the nursery. This better protects the roots from drying, pending the establishment of the plant, and is a measure of especial importance where soils are sandy and porous. Evergreens should be planted at the same level, never deeper than their former position. Deep planting of evergreens may deprive the roots of adequate air in the soil.

The top branches of the tree should be cut back quite severely to keep the rate of water loss within the absorptive capacity of the reduced root system. It should also be pruned the same day the tree is planted. This is particularly true of oaks and other slow-growing trees. Postponement of this part of the work results in loss of moisture and vitality for the entire plant. If delayed, the pruning will need to be even more severe and the results will not be as satisfactory. The extent of pruning required depends on the kind of tree and on the season, with early spring planting requiring less pruning than later plantings. As a general rule, about one-third of the growth should be removed. This should be done in such a way that the main shoot or leader is not interfered with, thus ensuring the best ultimate shape of the tree.

Before pruning is started, the pattern of lateral branches should be carefully studied. The aim is to eliminate some of the lateral branches entirely and cut others back by about one-half to one-third until the desired result is obtained (see the diagram below). If the tree has developed two leaders, one should be completely removed. This procedure will ensure that the tree develops a single trunk, eliminating the possibility of a weak crotch union later in the life of the tree.

The ground surrounding the newly planted tree should be shaped like a saucer to receive a generous supply of water from the first day onward. The function of the water at first is not so much to give the plant the extra moisture it needs but rather to settle the soil about the fine roots and to fill air pockets that inevitably remain in newly turned soil. The roots can take up only so much water, no matter how much is put on the soil, but the air in the soil can dry out the small roots before they become established. Water should be frequently given after planting and for the remainder of the growing season. But this watering should be intermittent, so that several days are allowed for drying and aeration of the soil.

Transplanted trees up to 8 or 10 feet tall should be secured with wires or nylon rope passed through sections of garden hose, linking the trunk to two stakes 5 to 8 feet tall that have been driven into the ground on opposite sides of the root mass and beyond its reach. This prevents the wind whipping and rocking that impedes establishment. Trees 10 to 18 feet tall are best steadied with three padded wires extending from the trunk to ground stakes driven at an angle outside the root mass. It is equally important to remove such temporary supports after two seasons of growth. Taller trees should be guyed with three to five heavy wires. In all cases, wires should be kept taut by twisting two strands about a peg or stick.

Transplanting with a Ball of Earth

Most evergreen trees, most deciduous trees 8 feet or more in height, and the majority of large shrubs require a more painstaking method of transplanting. For these specimens, transplanting is done with a ball of earth, wrapped tightly with burlap and tied securely with rope. The roots of such plants as box and hemlock form a dense mass in the soil, and it is easy to keep the earth together with burlap and hemp cord; but in moving plants with more loosely arranged roots, such as many of the junipers, it is harder to prevent the ball from cracking. A broken ball or crumbling earth is apt to lead to a dead tree. The ground must be in good condition before the trees are dug. If it is too dry, the earth will crack away from the roots in balling or while moving. This condition may be remedied by a thorough watering several days before transplanting. If it is too wet, though, the earth may cling to tools and be unworkable.

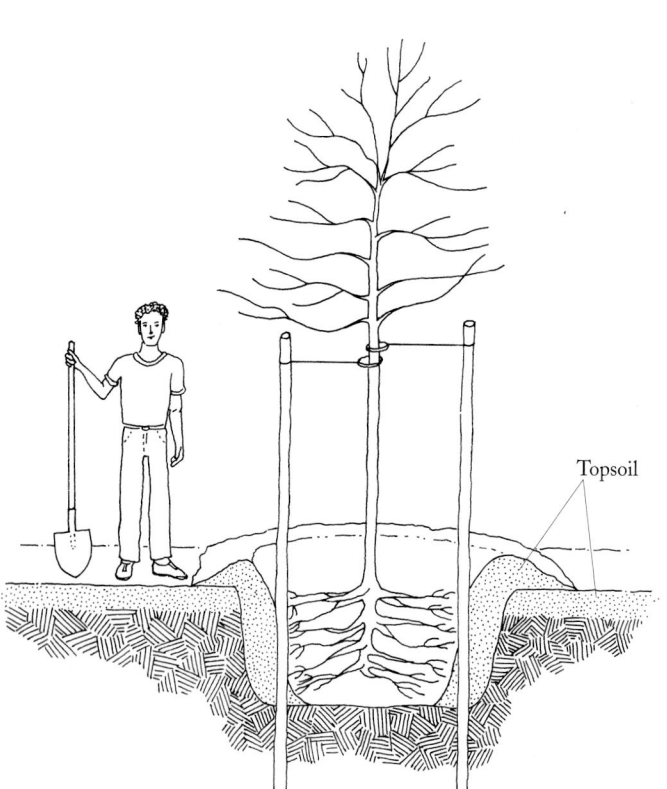

Topsoil

Transplanted tree, showing disposition of pruned roots.

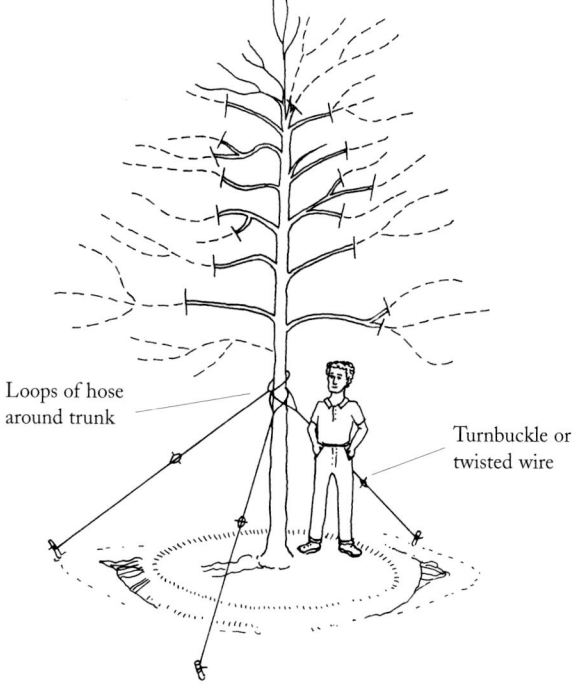

Loops of hose around trunk

Turnbuckle or twisted wire

After the loosening of burlap the tree should be backfilled with top-soil. The tree should be staked or guyed with wire and pruned. The soil should be graded in the form of a dish to conserve water. Support wires should pass through hose sections to protect the trunk from chafing.

Most trees are tough, however, and can survive well-intentioned but misinformed handling. But certain techniques will ensure successful transplanting and survival.

1. Transplant in early spring if possible, when soil moisture is usually high and a favorable growing season lies ahead for good root establishment. In regions like southern New England, and southward through the mid-Atlantic seaboard region, where the onset of severe winter weather is usually late, most trees can also be transplanted in the fall.

2. Move only healthy, vigorous plants with well-developed root systems. Plants with undersize root balls are more likely to fail.

3. If you are unable to plant a balled-and-burlapped tree immediately, keep the root ball moist, preferably covered; protected from the wind; and out of the sun. The best times to plant are in the early morning or late afternoon, or on a cloudy, overcast day, rather than in bright midday sun.

4. Dig a hole at least 8 to 10 inches wider than the root ball and deep enough to accommodate the roots without crowding. For small specimens, the hole should be dug 1 foot or more deep, regardless of the size of the root system. The hole should be as wide at the bottom as at the top so that the roots will be directed downward and outward, not upward. The soil at the bottom should be loosened with a fork and not left packed, thus facilitating root penetration.

5. Roots of other plants that project into the hole should be cut off, not merely bent out of the way. Left in place, they will soon compete with the roots of the transplanted tree.

6. If the soil removed from the hole contains a high proportion of clay or sand, improve its fertility and water retention by adding compost or humus, or at least peat moss. Predampen the peat moss before use. If the soil is very poor, it should be discarded entirely and replaced with topsoil conditioned with one or more amendments. This aids early establishment and resumption of vigorous growth.

7. Set the tree in the hole on enough soil so that the base of the trunk, where the roots first emerge, will be 1 to 2 inches below ground level. Partially backfill the space around the root ball, water well, then add more soil and water again.

8. If the tree is burlapped, untie the top of the burlap and fold it back into the hole before backfilling is completed. Be sure all the burlap is well below the surface, as any exposed corners or edges will act as a wick and draw water from the soil. Do not attempt to remove the burlap; it will soon decay. Similarly, if the ball is supported with a wire basket, leave it in place, as roots will soon grow through. If, on the other hand, the root ball is wrapped in plastic mesh, cut away as much of the plastic as possible once the ball is set in the hole and stabilized, since the plastic does not decay and will impede root growth. Mesh left under the ball is harmless. Any wire basketing used to firm the root ball may also be left. Roots will easily grow through the intervening spaces and the wire will eventually corrode and disappear.

9. Make a circular rim of soil around the outer margin of the filled hole, then puddle with water. Another technique, especially good for larger balled specimens, involves pushing a garden hose into the loose soil surrounding the root ball and allowing the water to saturate the soil. Guy wires should be in place and taut before this is begun.

Transplanting Trees Grown in Containers

It is common practice for nurseries to offer trees that have been grown entirely in plastic pots and tubs or field-grown material transplanted into such containers one or two seasons before sale. Such practices frequently reduce production and transportation costs for the nursery, are an efficient and attractive way to display and maintain the plants in retail garden centers, and offer greater convenience to the customer.

However, certain hazards and limitations are inherent with container cultivation of young trees. If the tree has been grown too long in its container, the root system may have become too crowded and major roots will have become entwined and entangled. In this case, the danger is that when the tree is planted and starts to mature, and the roots that were once crowded in the container expand in diameter, they will begin to choke each other out. Also, surface roots may have followed the periphery of the container, encircling the trunk and eventually girdling the tree completely. These conditions usually do not start to appear until the tree is several years old, and sometimes not until the tree is nearly mature. Symptoms may range from delayed growth after planting to a general decline in vigor later on or even the outright death of the tree caused by the reduced ability of the "choked" roots to transport water and nutrients. Sometimes a major root may completely encircle the base of the trunk and cause the tree to die for no readily visible reason.

In general, do not purchase container-grown trees from a nursery unless the plant shows signs of active, uninterrupted, healthy growth during the current season. If the leaves are few or appear undersize, pale green or brown edged, or otherwise discolored or drooping, the plant has probably dried out several times or nutrients have been leached out of the soil. If the tree appears quite large for its container, it probably has been in there far too long. Such trees will likely suffer root girdling and thus are no bargain at any price, even though the end-of-the-season sale is very tempting.

When removing a tree from its container just before planting, examine the root system thoroughly. If roots appear crowded or matted at the outer edges, they should be gently but thoroughly pried apart. If they are too densely entwined for this to be effective, several longitudinal cuts should be made with a sharp knife around the entire ball right through the outermost roots. Sometimes a spaghetti-like mass of thick roots will be seen at the base of the container. These too should either be pried apart or cut out. In each case, the aim is to break up the twining mass of roots and attempt to have as many roots as possible directed outward into the new soil in which the plant is placed.

If root disturbance or cutting is severe, then a corresponding amount of top growth should be pruned away.

Transplanting Large Trees

Transplanting large semimature trees is a job to be undertaken only by experienced nursery staff with adequate mechanical equipment. The same precautions must be taken with large trees as with smaller specimens. The roots must be kept shaded and moist while they are out of the ground, and they must be carefully placed and firmly packed about with soil. The amount of leafage (evaporation surface) must be reduced in proportion to the loss of roots. The task is made more difficult by the great weight of soil that must be moved with the roots and by the longer period of time that the tree is out of the ground, but the principles remain the same. The size of the ball of earth required for proper transplanting is proportionate to the size of the tree. It is almost impossible to take all the roots of a large deciduous tree, but for most species the diameter of the ball in feet should at least equal the diameter of the trunk in inches.

Moderately large trees with relatively compact branching are commonly moved by means of a hydraulic tree spade, which is actually a set of four or six very large shovel-like blades arranged on a steel frame in a circle and mounted on a truck chassis. After the hole has been dug for the tree at the new site, the truck is backed up to the tree and the blades adjusted around the trunk. They are driven one at a time into the ground by hydraulic pumps so that their tips converge beneath the root ball. The entire tree, with roots and soil intact, is lifted, tilted, and transported to the new site, where it is lowered into the already prepared hole. This procedure greatly shortens the time and lessens the hand labor involved in transplanting large specimens, minimizes shock (so long as the root mass is relatively compact), and is

especially suited to moving numbers of trees in a short period. It is unsuited, however, to steep, uneven terrain or to tightly confined sites. Use of a hydraulic tree spade frequently results in substantial damage to lawns and other nearby vegetation; and it is costly, especially if only one or a few trees are to be moved.

With trees of any size, transplanting is a shock, even under the best of circumstances. But for trees too large for the tree spade, shock must be mitigated as much as possible if there is to be any reasonable prospect of success. Planning is critical.

A year in advance of the transplanting, the circle of the ball should be marked out and a trench dug to a depth of 2 feet and as wide as a shovel's blade, cutting through existing roots. The trench should then be filled entirely with topsoil. During the year, the tree will form a dense mat of fibrous roots in the topsoil, which will be ready to grow out into a new layer of topsoil in the new location. When the tree is lifted, the new fibrous roots will help hold the soil firmly together.

The transplanting may be done in early autumn or in spring, and sometimes even in the winter when the ground is frozen solid. Winter transplanting is best done in a series of operations, beginning the previous year by preparing the ball as described before. In the late autumn the trench is dug and the tree ball twisted off its ground base. There it is left, with the open trench around it, until the ground is frozen. During the winter, the tree can be bound up with burlap and cord, tilted up and placed on a platform, removed to the new position, put into the hole, and left there still unplanted until spring weather thaws the ground. Then the space about the tree is filled with good topsoil.

In handling large trees, all the sliding, lifting, rolling on rollers, and skidding of the ball down into the hole should be done without sudden jostling or bumping. A block and tackle anchored to a "dead-man" will transmit the power of the winch and motor at a slow, steady motion. The descent into the hole by an inclined plane is the part most apt to bring disaster. Unless the power is strong enough to hold it back, the tree ball may roll with great force down the sloping planks and strike the earth side of the excavation, where it may crack. If the platform is on rollers, the tree ball can be gently eased down into the hole by slacking up slowly on the rope of the block and tackle.

In any case, moving very large trees should be undertaken with the awareness that even under ideal circumstances the shock of the operation may induce premature senility in the tree. Instead of establishment and continued growth, the tree may experience a gradual thinning of the top and the death of branches—one by one and often over a period of several years—culminating in death. The larger the tree, the greater the risk.

CARE OF TREES AFTER TRANSPLANTING

The shock of transplanting inevitably interrupts and possibly retards the life processes of any tree. Because the diminished vitality of a tree renders it more vulnerable to attack by insects and diseases and less able to withstand the effects of unusual weather conditions, it is obviously prudent to restore normalcy as soon as possible.

Moisture Requirements

The greatest danger to the tree both during and after transplanting is desiccation, or the excessive loss of moisture through natural transpiration of foliage, while the disturbed roots are unable to replace water and thus maintain a normal moisture content in the tissues. The function of pruning is to diminish the area of foliage and hence reduce the demand for water as well as the amount of water lost by the tree in a given period.

Watering the tree at intervals is a very important part of aftercare. The soil should be thoroughly soaked once a week if rain is insufficient; the soil around a newly transplanted tree should never be allowed to become really dry. On the other hand, in a soil kept constantly saturated, the water will exclude the air from the roots. Proper watering will enable the roots to take up the soil moisture rapidly and will encourage root growth. Evaporation through the bark and the danger of sun scald and splitting of the trunk during warm spells in winter is sometimes a problem, especially with larger trees. A method long in use by planters to retard this evaporation during the first year after transplanting is to wrap the trunk and larger branches with burlap, plastic, or paper strips. It is an effective procedure, especially against winter drying, but has the disadvantage of harboring insects, and may prove unsightly.

Mulches

To keep the soil moist about newly planted trees as well as to control weeds and moderate soil temperature, mulching is advisable. See Chapter 32 for more information about mulches. A 2- to 3-inch layer will suffice, and the mulch should not be heaped up on trunk bark to avoid possible damage inflicted by mice and other rodents.

Ground Covers as Root Protection

A treatment beneficial to trees, and one that may be used in certain situations where lawn is not essential, is a base planting of pachysandra, periwinkle, or English ivy. These plants have the ability to thrive even in dense shade, in many places

doing better than grass. But more important for the tree, they will collect fallen leaves, thus adding annually to the leaf mold in the soil, and will also protect the trunk from mechanical injury often caused by mowers, line trimmers, etc. This subject is more fully discussed in Chapter 14.

Fertilizing Trees

In their natural habitat in the forest, trees are nourished by a soil rich in organic material that is annually replenished by the decaying of fallen leaves and other debris. Under conditions where leaves and twigs are raked up, this renewal does not take place, which eventually leads to a nutrient deficit.

To compensate for insufficient soil fertility, solutions of salts of nitrates, phosphates, and potassium should be applied to the soil every three or four years. No commercial fertilizer should be placed in the hole in which a tree is to be planted, as the the roots may be further damaged by the concentration of salts.

Time of Application

Applications of fertilizer may be made a year after planting and at any time from early spring until midsummer and from the middle of September until late November. No applications should be made after midsummer as there is danger of stimulating a late, succulent growth that will be subject to winter killing. Tree roots take in nutrients most readily during the period of early spring growth, and they continue to absorb nutrients in the autumn long after the leaves have been shed.

Method of Application

The fine roots that absorb water and nutrients occur mostly in a zone that begins approximately one-third the distance from the trunk to the outer branches and extends beyond the limit of the outermost branches, often far beyond. Fertilizer should be applied over this entire area. Holes, varying in depth from 12 to 15 inches should be drilled with a soil auger; they should be spaced 15 to 18 inches apart. A mature tree will need about 100 holes. Into each hole place $1/10$ to $1/4$ pound of complete fertilizer, and then fill with water to dissolve the fertilizer.

Kind and Amount of Fertilizer

A 10-6-4 complete fertilizer is recommended for trees. It should be applied at the rate of 2 to 3 pounds per inch of trunk diameter. Trees with a trunk diameter less than 6 inches should receive about half this amount of fertilizer.

For a soil markedly deficient in phosphorus and potassium, a 4-8-7 mixture is recommended. The soil should be tested to determine what mixture to use, if any. If a tree is growing well in an already nutrient-rich soil, fertilizing is unnecessary.

Spraying to Diminish the Effects of City Soot and Gas

Sulfur dioxide, nitrous oxides, and other gases so prevalent today in the air in cities are detrimental to many trees. The accumulation of soot on the surface of leaves clogs the pores and retards respiration. These conditions are particularly hard on evergreen trees, the leaves of which remain active for several years. To help reduce the damage to trees from such atmospheric impurities, the foliage may be washed with a hose spray about once each rainless week during the growing season, assuming water use regulations permit. This treatment seems as beneficial to such evergreens as arborvitae and false cypress (*Chamaecyparis* spp.) as it is to deciduous trees.

Pruning

Well-positioned shade trees in good condition require comparatively little pruning. The removal of dead or diseased wood and the cutting out of crowded or interfering branches is usually all that is necessary. Pruning small dead branches may in some cases prevent the large branches or the trunk from rotting.

The cut should be made at the junction with the larger stem. When removing branches, first cut from below, partway through, then from above. The lower cut will prevent the weight of the branch, when falling, from ripping off a strip of bark below the branch just before the saw cuts through.

Larger and heavier branches need even more precaution to prevent this splitting of the bark. First cut partway through from below in the position of the final cut. Then cut through from above at a distance out from the crotch. After the limb is cut, a small stump will be left. Cut the stump off to a flat surface. Contrary to long-established practice, it is *not* advisable to paint tree cuts. Pruning paint not only does little to retard decay by preventing the entrance of fungi or other damaging organisms but can actually encourage decay. In living trees, all wood—even the heartwood—is normally damp. Thus the impermeable barrier formed by a coat of tree paint traps moisture along with the bacteria and fungal spores in ambient air, setting the stage for decomposition. The surface of a pruning wound, left unpainted, gradually dries. In most trees, fungicidal substances occurring naturally in the wood limit or at least slow the spread of any decay.

Similarly, the long-venerated practice of filling hollowed trunks of old storm-damaged shade trees with concrete is generally eschewed. Long experience has shown that decay accelerates between the concrete and adjacent wood, negating the entire effort. Current practice is to clean out all rotted wood, shape the cavity opening to promote drainage, and if necessary, cable the affected limb or tree to adjacent trunks for supplemental support.

For control of insect pests and diseases, see Chapter 34. For procedures in altering grades around trees, see Chapter 3.

Grading Around a Tree

If the grades around a tree are to be altered by filling soil over the original ground level, then special precautions should be taken to prevent the smothering of the roots. A fill of 4 inches of good topsoil over the roots of deciduous trees will usually do no damage, although it might affect evergreens unfavorably. A fill of 12 inches or more would usually be very harmful if not fatal. The quantity of air and water in the soil diminishes with the depth. Thus, when roots growing at a depth of 18 inches are covered so that they are 36 inches from the surface, they are deprived of their normal oxygen and water rations. To overcome this handicap, it is advisable to construct some device for maintaining a contact between the air and the root-containing soil. It is important to do this before the fill is made. First, the original soil is loosened by forking. Then a dry stone wall is built up around the tree, if possible at a distance of several feet from the base of the trunk and to the level of the new grade. Several 4-inch agricultural tile drains are laid in lines radiating from the inner surface of this wall. The entire area is then spread with a course of crushed stone or large gravel. This material is poured in to a depth of 6 inches, or to within 12 to 15 inches of the final grades. Above this is spread a layer of straw or, preferably, manure to prevent the soil above from sifting down through the stones or slag. Finally, a layer of topsoil is spread to a depth of 6 to 8 inches. This construction should cover the whole area of tree roots. The tile pipes may be used to conduct water to the roots and may be filled by a hose.

If soil has been washed away from the roots of large trees, as sometimes happens on steep slopes, or if the ground is worn down by pedestrian traffic, as in heavily traveled paths, the damage to the trees may eventually be fatal. Localized exclusion of all foot traffic is a vital first step. Restoration of the natural grade by applying a layer of topsoil to cover the roots and establishing a turf or a ground cover crop to retain the soil is the only permanent remedy for this situation.

DECIDUOUS TREES OF MERIT

ACER CAMPESTRE
(English maple, Hedge maple)

Height 25–35 feet; zones 4–8

The English maple is a pleasant shade tree, rather like a diminutive Norway maple (*A. platanoides*), and has dense, dark green foliage. It forms a broad dome, often with branches down to the ground, but these may readily be pruned to achieve clearance. The leaves are small, with five rounded lobes. Of the cultivars available, 'Leprechaun' is especially suited as a lawn tree for the small property, while 'Queen Elizabeth' grows fairly rapidly and has more upright branching.

ACER SACCHARUM
(Sugar maple)

Height 60–100 feet; zones 3–8

One of the noblest American trees, the sugar maple's dense habit of growth and its spectacular yellow-orange autumn color make it a tree to remember. This is one of the trees that has made New England famous for its fall foliage. It is much used as a street tree and shades many a New England village green. It cannot be surpassed as a shade tree on a broad home lawn or as a forest tree, but is sensitive to deicing salts and other pollutants as well as to soil compaction. The sugar maple is not a rapid grower, but it is long lived. Plant this tree for your children, and they will be able to pass it on to their grandchildren. The cultivar 'Bonfire' has red fall foliage, and cultivar 'Goldspire' is narrow in form and turns clear golden yellow.

BETULA PAPYRIFERA
(Canoe birch)

Height 50–70 feet; zones 2–7

One of our most picturesque native trees, canoe birch is adorned with bright, smooth, white stems and clear yellow foliage in autumn. Although less graceful than European white birch (*B. alba*), the canoe birch is much more resistant to borers. It is especially effective when grown as an accent and is at home among coniferous evergreen trees and mountain laurel. Asian white birch (*B. platyphylla* var. *japonica*) is similar and reputedly even more borer resistant.

Other birches, especially the river birch (*B. nigra* 'Heritage'), with its peeling creamy cinnamon bark, and Erman birch (*B. ermanii*), with pinkish cream bark, make handsome accents but are not as striking as the canoe birch.

CERCIDIPHYLLUM JAPONICUM
(Katsura tree)

Height 40–60 feet; zones 4–8

A native of Japan, planted for its beautiful foliage, katsura grows with one to several trunks which, in female trees, form a broad spreading dome. Male trees remain more upright. The paired heart-shaped leaves turn bright yellow and red in autumn. Although it is not the easiest tree to transplant (young container-grown stock is best) and it is not adaptable to heavy soils, Katsura is free of pests, diseases, and messy flower and fruit drop.

CERCIS CANADENSIS
(Eastern redbud)

Height 20–30 feet; zones (3) 4–9

Eastern redbud is an undergrowth tree common in the woods of Maryland and southward, where it blooms with the dogwood, but it is hardy to Canada. Its deep pink buds cling to the branches for several weeks before opening into rose pink, pealike blossoms.

Although it does best in the high shade of larger trees and in rich humusy soil, redbud is very adaptable. Other species of *Cercis* are similar. Among the several cultivars of *C. canadensis* are white-flowered forms and the unusual 'Forest Pansy', with leaves at first bright rosy purple, gradually maturing a more subdued red-violet.

CLADRASTIS LUTEA
(Yellowwood)*

Height 30–50 feet; zones 3–8

Native to a small region in the mountains of North Carolina to eastern Tennessee, but hardy throughout the nondesert United States, the yellowwood has a smooth, gray bark resembling that of a beech. The leaves are compound and turn a brilliant yellow in late September. Its glory is its large hanging panicles of creamy white fragrant flowers in June. A pink-flowered cultivar, 'Rosea', is also available.

CORNUS FLORIDA
(Flowering dogwood)

Height 20–30 feet; zones 5–9

A native of the understory of our eastern forests and one of the most

---

*Occasionally listed as C. kentukea.

beloved and most beautiful of our flowering trees, the flowering dogwood has been ravaged in recent years by dogwood anthracnose, a fungus disease that over several seasons causes the weakening and death of limbs from the base upward. Older trees are especially susceptible and recovery is rare. Although symptom intensity varies from year to year, it is presently inadvisable to plant this species, especially in areas of known infestation. In disease-free areas, flowering dogwood is a sturdy small tree with spreading branches. It bears quantities of white flowers, each with a central yellow head of florets surrounded by four notched spreading bracts. The blooms are particularly conspicuous because they precede the leaves. In fall, the foliage turns crimson, and for a time, the twigs are adorned with tight bunches of scarlet fruit. These are soon devoured by birds, but the promise of next spring's flowers lies in the button-like buds that are evident all winter.

Among many cultivars, 'Bay Beauty' continues in bloom until after its leaves have fully expanded. More popular are forms with pink bracts and variegated leaves.

CORNUS KOUSA
(Japanese dogwood)

Height 20–30 feet; zones 5–8

A native of Japan and Korea, the Japanese dogwood has a broad, spreading habit and dense foliage that make it an excellent tree for background and screen. Its chief beauty is its white blossoms, which cover the already leafy branches, usually in June. Unlike those in *C. florida*, the bracts are narrowly pointed. The large

pendent raspberry red fruits ripen in late summer and persist until leaf drop, if spared by the birds. Fall foliage is scarlet. In winter, the exfoliating bark results in an interesting mottling of gray, tan, and brown. *C. kousa* var. *chinensis* bears larger bracts. Among several cultivars are two weeping forms, of which 'Lustgarten Weeping' is the better, and 'Summer Stars', in which the bracts are retained through midsummer.

CRATAEGUS PHAENOPYRUM
(Washington hawthorn)

Height 25–30 feet; zones 3–8

Washington hawthorn is one of the best native hawthorns. It is excellent when used as an untrimmed hedge, as a windbreak, and as a specimen. Its horizontal branches and drooping twigs bear quantities of small, bright scarlet apple-like fruits in September, which hang on well into the winter. The leaves also turn scarlet and orange in the autumn. One caution: since the tree bristles with very sharp 2- to 3-inch-long rigid thorns, it should not be planted in high-traffic areas unless pruned up.

FAGUS SYLVATICA
(European beech)

Weeping European beech
(Fagus sylvatica 'Pendula')

Height 60–100 feet; zones 4–7

The European beech has a dignity and refinement deriving from its rugged form and smooth bark. The leaves are finely toothed; the buds long, sharp, and tapering; and the twigs small and wide spreading. Under optimal conditions, European

beech can reach 100 feet in height, yet have its lower branches sweeping the ground (a habit to be encouraged, since little will grow beneath beeches). The autumn color is at first clear yellow and then turns to rich brown, and many leaves hang on all winter.

Among scores of cultivars, the most frequently encountered are 'Cuprea' (copper beech), 'Atropunicea' (purple beech), 'Asplenifolia' (fern-leaf beech), and, pictured here, 'Pendula' (weeping beech), all highly variable and offered under various other cultivar names. Regardless of cultivar, European beech becomes a massive tree and can be recommended only for large properties.

FRANKLINIA ALATAMAHA
(Franklin tree)

Height 15–25 feet; zones 5–9

The Franklin tree is small and of slow growth. It is native to lowland Georgia, where it was discovered by John Bartram in 1777. It has not been found in the wild since 1790, and all the trees we have today are descended from the seedlings Bartram raised. It succeeds best in sheltered valleys in full sun, although it accepts the partial shade of large trees. Its lovely flower is a pure white cup of five petals with golden stamens, measuring about 3 inches across. The flowers appear in late summer and open in succession over a period of many weeks. The leaves turn crimson in the autumn. This is a rare and lovely small tree that deserves to be more widely grown.

FRAXINUS PENNSYLVANICA
(Green ash)

Height 50–60 feet; zones 3–9

At first pyramidal, the green ash develops a pleasingly irregular habit in maturity. An extremely adaptable, hardy tree, green ash is best known through one of its cultivars, 'Marshall's Seedless', a vigorous male form well suited to street and park use. It is especially favored in the Midwest.

Green ash (*Fraxinus pennsylvanica*)

GLEDITSIA TRIACANTHOS VAR. INERMIS
(Thornless honey locust)

Height 30–70 feet; zones 3–9

Valued for its rapid growth, lacy foliage, vaselike form, and freedom from disease, the thornless honey locust is well adapted for use as a street tree and on the home lawn. It thrives well in many types of soil and is best known through such popular cultivars as 'Moraine', 'Shademaster', 'Skyline', and 'Green Glory' (all podless) as well as 'Sunburst' (young foliage golden, eventually turning green).

HALESIA CAROLINA
(Carolina silver bell)

Height 30–40 feet; zones 4–8

The Carolina silver bell is a lovely small tree that is a native of the South. In late spring, it bears thousands of small, white, hanging bell-shaped flowers that are followed by four-winged fruits that are greatly relished by squirrels. Rapid in growth and free of diseases, this often shrublike tree is excellent for the small property. The leaves turn clear yellow in fall.

KOELREUTERIA PANICULATA
(Goldenrain tree)

Height 30–40 feet; zones 5–9

A most picturesque Oriental tree that is tolerant of drought and alkaline soil, goldenrain has rather wide-ranging, often twisted branches. Its light green foliage contrasts effectively with that of more familiar trees, but its great beauty bursts forth in early to mid summer, when the large panicles of bright yellow blossoms open. Later, when the blooms fall, they

GINKGO BILOBA
(Maidenhair tree)

Height 50–75 feet; zones 3–9

Brought from China more than two centuries ago and never known in the wild, the maidenhair tree has since been distributed widely in Europe and America. The growth is sparse, usually with relatively few upward-directed branches, giving it a rather angular but essentially pyramidal outline. The leaves are especially attractive. Each is a little fan with conspicuous, diverging veins and a wavy outer margin. In autumn, the maidenhair is a glorious clear yellow. Because of its hardiness, freedom from enemies, and pollution tolerance, it is often used as a street tree, but its value as a lawn tree is also well recognized. Sexes are on separate trees, and the fetid odor of the fruit is so objectionable that care should be taken to obtain male specimens. The cultivars 'Princeton Sentry', with a narrowly conical habit, and 'Autumn Gold', which is broadly spreading, are both male.

cover the ground with a carpet of yellow. The flowers are followed by conspicuous bladderlike pods that remain on the tree into early winter, thus greatly extending the season of ornamental interest. The autumn foliage is yellow. In the cultivar 'September', flowering is delayed until late summer.

LIQUIDAMBAR STYRACIFLUA
(Sweet gum)

Height 60–75 feet; zones 5–9

The sweet gum is a native forest tree that forms extensive stands in the lowlands of New Jersey and Maryland. As a young tree, it has a conspicuous central trunk and tapering crown, but in age it becomes wide spreading. Its star-shaped leaves usually turn to shades of yellow, orange, red, and purple in fall, often there are different colors on the same tree. The angular cork-ribbed branches provide added interest in winter, as do the hanging woody fruit balls that persist until spring.

LIRIODENDRON TULIPIFERA
(Tulip tree)

Height 75–90 feet; zones 4–9

A majestic tree, with a straight trunk often rising 30 feet or more to the first branch, the tulip tree is for the large, spacious property. It is a very fast grower, often achieving 50 feet in 15 years, partly because growth continues all summer. The large four-lobed leaves turn clear yellow in fall. The tulip-shaped blossoms, which appear in late spring and are greenish

yellow marked with an orange band, stand erect at the twig ends at the top of the tree where they are not easily seen. An excellent tree where space is adequate, because it casts high shade and permits grass to flourish beneath. The tulip tree is not a good street tree, however, as it soon outgrows the scale of most situations. Furthermore, it often rains honeydew —the product of harmless aphids—on cars parked beneath, and in dry summer spells, it prematurely drops its yellowing older leaves.

MAGNOLIA × *'ELIZABETH'*
(Yellow magnolia)

Height 40–50 feet; zones 4–9

Yellow-flowering trees are uncommon in temperate-zone latitudes, but the yellow magnolia, a true magnolia, is one such tree. It is the result of a cross between

the Asiatic early spring-blooming white-flowered yulan (*M. heptapeta*) with the native late spring-blooming greenish yellow-flowered cucumber tree (*M. acuminata*) performed in 1956 at the Brooklyn Botanic Garden. The clear primrose yellow flowers of 'Elizabeth' open as the leaves expand but, as is true with many hybrids, yield no viable seed. The tree's habit is neatly pyramidal, and its ultimate height, though not yet known, will likely approach that of the parent species.

MAGNOLIA × SOULANGIANA
(Saucer magnolia)

Height 20–30 feet; zones 4–9

One of the most spectacular of the small flowering trees, saucer magnolia is covered in early to mid spring with large, lavender, cup-shaped blossoms that

Saucer magnolia (*Magnolia × soulangiana* 'Speciosa')

Saucer magnolia (*Magnolia × soulangiana* 'Grace McDade' and 'Alba Superba')

MALUS FLORIBUNDA
(Japanese flowering crab apple)

Height 15–30 feet; zones 4–8

Of the dozens of species and hundreds of named cultivars of flowering crab apples grown for ornament, the Japanese crab apple is one of the finest and makes a most beautiful sight when in full bloom in midspring. Thousands of carmine pink buds open into pure white flowers, which resemble small apple blossoms and remain in bloom for several weeks. In September, the tree is covered with small, pale yellow apples about ⅓ inch in diameter. It will thrive for at least 50 years.

For other hardy crab apples, chosen not only for beauty of flower and fruit but also for resistance to the many pests and diseases that afflict the group, see the following table.

open before the leaves expand. The flower color is usually pinkish lavender outside and whitish within, but it varies from all-white to red-violet in many named cultivars. A late spring frost may occasionally damage or ruin the floral display. The bark is light gray and smooth, and the rich foliage is a medium green. The magnolias are remarkably free from disease and usually live for many years. They grow extremely well under city conditions if the soil is fairly rich and moisture retentive.

Malus 'Red Jade' crab apple

OTHER HARDY CRAB APPLES

Name	Height	Habit	Bud Color	Flower Color	Fruit Color and Persistence
M. × 'Adams'	25'	Rounded and dense	Red	Pink	Red; persistent
M. × 'Callaway'	20'	Rounded, graceful	Pink	White	Reddish maroon; persistent
M. × 'Donald Wyman'	20'	Spreading	Pink	White	Glossy red; persistent
M. halliana var. *parkmanii*	15'	Vase shaped	Rose	Pink	Dull red; not persistent
M. × 'Harvest Gold'	20'	Upright	Pink	White	Golden yellow; persistent
M. hupehensis 'Strawberry Parfait'	20'	Vase shaped	Rose	Pink	Yellow to red; not persistent
M. × 'Red Jade'	15'	Weeping	Pink	White	Glossy red; not persistent
M. × 'Red Jewel'	15'	Spreading	White	White	Bright red; persistent
M. × 'Sentinel'	20'	Narrowly upright	Pink	Pale pink	Red; persistent
M. × 'Snowdrift'	15'	Rounded and dense	Red	White	Red-orange; not persistent
M. × 'White Angel'	15'	Irregularly rounded	Pink	White	Glossy red; not persistent
M. × 'White Cascade'	12'	Weeping	Pink	White	Yellow; not persistent

METASEQUOIA GLYPTOSTROBOIDES
(Dawn redwood)

Height 60–75 feet; zones 4–8

A relatively recent arrival on the horticultural scene, having been discovered in China in 1941, the dawn redwood is a narrowly conical, fast-growing conifer. It bears feathery light green foliage that turns apricot orange before dropping in autumn, leaving its shaggy cinnamon brown bark and symmetrical architecture to grace the winter scene. As it reaches maturity, the tree develops a disproportionately massive lower trunk and buttressed base. The dawn redwood is especially well suited to the large property, where the full extent of its straight, clean form can be appreciated from a distance.

Weeping Higan cherry (*Prunus subhirtella* var. *pendula*)

OXYDENDRUM ARBOREUM
(Sourwood)

Height 25–40 feet; zones 5–9

The sourwood is a small, deciduous tree that is native to the forests in the Alleghenies from Pennsylvania southward. It is a member of that large family the Ericaceae and is thus related to the rhododendrons. Its blossoms, hanging in branched tassels in summer, resemble the white bells of andromeda (*Pieris japonica*), but its great glory is its fall foliage. By late summer the leaves begin to turn, and they remain yellow, purple, and bright crimson until midautumn, especially if grown in full sun. Sourwood, or sorrel tree, as some know it, is slow in growth, averaging less than 1 foot per year.

PRUNUS SUBHIRTELLA
(Higan cherry)

Height 20–30 feet; zones 5–8

The Higan cherry is one of the most disease resistant and long lived of the many Japanese flowering cherries, and it is a tree of graceful upright habit and great beauty. Pink buds and pale pink or white blossoms cover it in April. A pathway beneath a double row of these trees is very impressive. Best known by its pink-flowered weeping form, *P. subhirtella* var. *pendula*, Higan cherry also includes *P. subhirtella* var. *autumnalis*, which produces its pink semidouble flowers in spring and, though rather less generously, in fall, too.

QUERCUS COCCINEA
(Scarlet oak)

Height 50–70 feet; zones 4–8

A better choice than the overused, often chlorotic and pest-susceptible pin oak (*Q. palustris*), the fast-growing scarlet oak is broadly conical when young and becomes rounded in age. The glossy dark green leaves change to bright scarlet in fall. As yet uncommon in the nursery trade, this species is expected to gain popularity as a fine native oak for streets, parks, and the home grounds.

QUERCUS LAURIFOLIA
(Laurel oak)

Height 40–50 feet; zones 6–9

Handsome, adaptable, and fast growing, the laurel oak has unlobed semievergreen foliage. It is especially suited to the South and seems to thrive under less than ideal circumstances. Even faster growing but definitely deciduous is the cultivar 'Darlington'.

QUERCUS PHELLOS
(Willow oak)

Height 40–60 feet; zones 5–9

The willow oak is oaklike in architecture—though more finely branched than most—and willowlike in leaf form. This curious oak tolerates wide variation in soil moisture, and so is well suited for use at street side, in parks, and on the home grounds. It is especially suited for areas where pollution tolerance and ease of maintenance are important considerations.

QUERCUS RUBRA
(Red oak)

Height 50–70 feet; zones 4–8

The red oak is a highly valued and much used oak of fast growth (up to 2 feet per year). This adaptable species, stereotypically an oak in its characteristics, has found much favor in urban and suburban areas, much as the very similar black oak (*Q. velutina*) has. As oaks are generally rather difficult to transplant, it is usually prudent to purchase trees not more than 2 inches in diameter at the base.

Red oak (*Quercus rubra*)

SALIX ALBA *'TRISTIS'*
(Golden weeping willow)

Height 40–60 feet; zones (3) 4–8

Unlike the very rare Babylon weeping willow (*S. babylonica*), the golden weeping willow is very hardy and is widely planted throughout much of the United States. Even hardier is the Wisconsin, or Niobe, weeping willow (*S. × pendulina*, often listed as *S. × blanda*), and hardier still is the prairie cascade weeping willow (*S. × pendulina × S. pentandra*), developed in Manitoba. All have glossy foliage that persists into late fall and drooping yellow twigs that show to good advantage in winter.

SOPHORA JAPONICA
(Chinese scholar tree)

Height 50–75 feet; zones 4–8

Brought from China more than two centuries ago, the scholar tree is still not well enough known in this country. It is a graceful and wide-spreading tree when grown as a specimen. The leaves are compound and resemble those of the black locust. In late summer, great panicles of cream-colored pealike flowers are followed by drooping green pods. It is a very handsome shade tree suitable for the home lawn of spacious proportions. The cultivar 'Regent' is reliably upright in habit and precocious in flowering (reportedly when only six years old).

SORBUS ALNIFOLIA
(Korean mountain ash)

Height 40–50 feet; zones 3–7

The Korean mountain ash is a small tree with simple, undivided leaves and white blossoms in flat clusters in spring that are followed by showy pinkish red to orange or vermilion fruit in late summer. This is an excellent tree for the small property, graceful and distinctive, but it is slow to mature. Although its foliage is quite unlike that of the more common European mountain ash (*S. aucuparia*), the Korean tree is far more resistant to the trunk borers and fireblight that so often devastate mountain ashes, especially in urban and suburban environments.

STYRAX JAPONICUS
(Japanese snowbell)

Height 20–30 feet; zones 5–8

The Japanese snowbell is a compact tree with wide-spreading, horizontal branches and deep green leaves. In June and July, the branches are hung with little, white, fragrant, bell-like flowers; and in August, the oval green fruits appear, which turn brown as they ripen. This neat and attractive tree is excellent for the home grounds and is free of pests and diseases. In the cultivar 'Rosea' the flowers are pink.

SYRINGA RETICULATA
(Japanese tree lilac)

Height 20–30 feet; zones 3–7

The Japanese tree lilac is an attractive small tree that is well suited to the suburban home property. It is compact in habit of growth and in June bears large trusses of white flowers. It is remarkably free from pests and diseases and requires little maintenance. The cultivar 'Ivory Silk' is less rangy in habit and flowers when quite young; cultivar 'Summer Snow' is even more compact and bears larger flower clusters. In winter, the glossy cherrylike bark is distinctive.

TAXODIUM DISTICHUM
(Bald cypress)

Height 50–75 feet; zones 4–10

Although this deciduous conifer grows in the swamps of the South from Maryland to Louisiana, the bald cypress is nevertheless hardy in upland soil as far north as central New York State. One of the most beautiful sights of the southern spring is cypress trees with their new feathery leaves of pale green covering them like a mist. Contrary to popular belief, bald cypress will thrive in any reasonably moisture-retentive soil, and swampy conditions are not necessary for successful cultivation within its range of hardiness. Moreover, it appears adaptable to suburban and even urban conditions.

TILIA CORDATA
(Littleleaf linden)

Height 60–70 feet; zones 3–7

The littleleaf linden has been planted as a shade tree since ancient times. It has a broad, spreading base, with branches close to the ground, and a rounded head. The leaves are small, broad, and irregularly heart shaped. The cultivar 'Greenspire', along with several others, is reliably pyramidal and symmetrical with a single leader, and it has proven very tolerant of urban conditions.

TILIA TOMENTOSA
(Silver linden)

Height 50–70 feet; zones 4–7

Broadly pyramidal in form, the silver linden differs from most other lindens with its distinctively silvery lower leaf surface; the contrast with the deep green upper surface shows to best effect on breezy days. It is drought tolerant and, like all lindens, bears a plenitude of tiny, yellowish, intensely fragrant flowers in early summer.

ULMUS × HOLLANDICA 'GROENVELDT'
(Hybrid Dutch elm)

Height 40–50 feet; zones 4–9

A graceful, round-headed tree, usually with drooping twigs, the hybrid Dutch elm shows much more resistance to fatal elm pests and diseases than all other elms, except the small-leaf Siberian elm (*U. pumila*). None has the beloved vase form of the beleaguered American elm (*U. americana*), but this tree is well suited to urban and suburban street sides, parks, and home grounds.

Japanese zelkova (*Zelkova serrata*)

ZELKOVA SERRATA
(Japanese zelkova)

Height 50–60 feet; zones 5–8

Zelkova has received much publicity as an excellent substitute for the American elm. It is true that zelkova is fairly resistant to the ravages of Dutch elm disease, and it does possess an upright habit, many wide-spreading ascending branches, and leaves quite similar to those of the American elm. However, it is a short-trunked tree and does not grow to the majestic proportions of our native elm. Although it is being widely planted as a substitute, one should not expect the stately proportions and massive trunk of the American elm, once the most popular and handsome shade tree. It makes an excellent shade tree and is fairly rapid in growth.

The cultivar 'Green Vase' not only has the straight trunk of cultivar 'Village Green' but has branches arranged in such a way as to impart the wineglass shape of an elm.

EVERGREEN TREES OF MERIT

ABIES CONCOLOR
(White fir)

Height 50–60 feet; zones (3) 4–7

The white fir is one of those adaptable trees that seems to make itself at home in almost any situation. Native to the Rocky Mountains, it tolerates dry soil and windy exposures. Its great beauty is its majestic, broadly columnar form and soft, blue-green needles, which are long and waxy smooth. The white fir imparts a less formal effect than the blue-needled spruces.

CEDRUS LIBANI
SSP. ATLANTICA
(Atlas cedar)

Height 60–80 feet; zones 6–9

The Atlas cedar, the best known of the true cedars in cultivation, comes from the Atlas Mountains of North Africa. Because the needles are arranged

Atlas cedar (*Cedrus libani* spp. *atlantica*)

in starlike clusters covering the twigs nd branches with a fine pattern, this cedar is a beautiful symphony of line. At maturity, the tree's spread may exceed its height, with its massive trunk bearing branches to the ground. The cultivars 'Argentea' and 'Glauca' are the most frequently planted forms, both striking with silvery blue foliage.

Equally distinctive are cedar of Lebanon (*C. libani* ssp. *libani*) and deodar cedar (*C. deodara*), with longer needles but less cold hardiness, hence suited to only relatively mild climates (zones 7–9). Hardy cedar of Lebanon (*C. libani* var. *stenocoma*) is much more cold tolerant (zones 5–7), though only occasionally available commercially.

CHAMAECYPARIS PISIFERA
(Sawara cypress)

Height 40–50 feet; zones 3–8

Brought from Japan, the sawara cypress, along with its cultivars 'Plumosa' and 'Squarrosa', is used frequently in suburban plantings. It keeps a neat shape and density without shearing, though shearing will thicken the foliage. It should not be planted where it will outgrow a restricted space. It has a good, erect, tapering column of feathery evergreen foliage. Of the many cultivars, 'Plumosa' is very finely feathery in texture, and 'Squarrosa' has bluish scales that stand out as needles in fluffy masses. In Japan the sawara cypress is a lofty timber tree.

ILEX AQUIFOLIUM
(English holly)

Height 20–30 feet; zones 6–9

The European counterpart of our pest-afflicted American holly (*I. opaca*), English holly boasts highly lustrous foliage as well as the familiar fall display of clustered red berries (on female plants). Both species have spawned scores of hybrids and hundreds of cultivars, many of which are deservedly prominent in American horticulture. A rather diffusely branched understory tree in its native haunts, English holly adopts a broadly conical habit and lower height at maturity when grown in the open.

JUNIPERUS VIRGINIANA
(Eastern red cedar)

Height 35–80 feet; zones 2–9

The eastern red cedar is not in fact a cedar at all, but a juniper. It is familiar to all in the Northeast as a shaft of deep green colonizing old fields and open ground. Though much less lofty in the north than farther south, eastern red cedar is broadly pyramidal at maturity when grown in the open, whereas in woodland or crowded plantings the lower branches usually die, sometimes leaving only a tuft of foliage at the top, rather like a mop on a pole. The wood is very hard and resists decay for decades, hence trunks are much valued as fence posts.

Eastern red cedar
(Juniperus virginiana)

Many cultivars are available, offering wide variation in habit and foliage.

LAURUS NOBILIS
(Grecian laurel)

Height 20–30 feet; zones 7–9

The Grecian laurel is small evergreen tree with large glossy leaves, used as a specimen and in hedging in mild regions of Europe and on the Pacific Coast of the United States. Its picturesque branching and compact form produce a broadly tapering outline. It may be pruned into any formal shape. This is the laurel of history and poetry.

MAGNOLIA GRANDIFLORA
(Southern magnolia, Bull bay)

Height 35–70 feet; zones 7–9

The southern magnolia is the famous magnolia of the old plantations. Its height and its large, lustrous dark green leaves give it great distinction. But it is the great waxy white, cup-shaped blooms adorning the upper branches in spring through summer that are its most distinctive asset. Native throughout the lower South, it is grown in protected sites as far north as Cape Cod.

PINUS DENSIFLORA
(Japanese red pine)

Height 35–50 feet; zones 3–7

In many ways similar to the now pest-beleaguered Austrian pine (*P. nigra*), the

Japanese red pine is a very hardy species with decorative orange-brown bark. Its informal crooked or leaning habit suits it well to most home garden uses. One of the most attractive pines, it has numerous, mostly dwarf, cultivars.

PINUS STROBUS
(Eastern white pine)

Height 75–100 feet; zones 2–8

One of North America's handsomest trees, eastern white pine has been valued since earliest colonial times for its timber. As an ornamental tree for spacious suburban home grounds, it has few equals. One towering by the house can be a joy for every nature lover through winter and summer; it is the gathering place of warblers and finches, the shelter for juncos, and the home of nuthatches. In the carpet of its fallen needles in woodlands, the elusive pink lady slipper, Indian pipe, and yellow clintonia are sometimes found. Its soft needles clothe the twigs in a rich green verdure and sigh in the breeze.

Several other pines are of landscape value. Among them are Scots pine (*P. sylvestris*), a tree of picturesque habit and tolerant of excessively drained, nutrient-deficient soils. It usually matures to 30 to 60 feet high, and is hardy in zones 2 to 8. Japanese black pine (*P. thunbergii*) is irregular in habit and is often leaning. It is tolerant of salt spray and high wind, usually matures to 20 to 40 feet, and is hardy in zones 5 to 7.

PSEUDOTSUGA MENZIESII
(Douglas fir)

Height 60–75 feet; zones 4–8

Douglas fir occurs in two varieties. Coast Douglas fir (*P. menziesii* var. *menziesii*) is the extraordinarily lofty timber tree of the Pacific Northwest, also valued as a fast-growing ornamental in that region. Elsewhere, Rocky Mountain Douglas fir (*P. menziesii* var. *glauca*), with blue-green foliage and a much lower mature height, is the hardier and very adaptable form usually seen in cultivation. Its habit is less rigid than that of the spruces, and its adaptability is greater than that of the firs.

QUERCUS VIRGINIANA
(Live oak)

Height 40–50 feet; zones 7–9

The live oak was often planted along the avenues of southern homes, where it commonly becomes festooned with Spanish moss and can attain great age. The tree may achieve a horizontal limb spread more than twice its height. It is of rapid growth and will adjust itself to almost any soil. Although it is a forest tree, live oak makes a magnificent specimen for for the spacious lawn.

SCIADOPITYS VERTICILLATA
(Umbrella pine)

Height 20–30 feet; zones 4–8

One of the handsomest and most distinctive conifers, the umbrella pine has clustered glossy, leathery, deep green foliage of truly unusual effect. Slow growing, it gradually changes in form from broadly conical to irregularly globose. It is virtually free of pests and diseases.

THUJA OCCIDENTALIS
(American arborvitae)

Height 20–60 feet; zones 2–8

A tree for many climates and for a wide range of soil conditions, American arborvitae is normally a solid column of rich deep green and bears scalelike leaves arranged in broad fans that hang irregularly on the twigs. As an ornamental, it is best used in groups or as a single accent, but it is often used in hedges or windbreaks. Arborvitae is a hardy, persistent tree and grows equally well in heavy clays and light sandy soils, whether moist or dry. One caveat: It is often subject to bagworm infestation (see page 814). Of the many cultivars (mostly dwarf), 'Nigra' is full size and maintains dark foliage color throughout the winter months, instead of turning somewhat yellowish.

TSUGA CANADENSIS
(Canadian hemlock)

Height 50–75 feet; zones 3–7 (8)

In forests and glens, Canadian hemlock may rise above all other trees and develop a trunk 6 feet in diameter. Cultivated in suburban settings, however, it is valued as this country's most graceful conifer, and in time achieves impressive dimensions unless pruned. The slender nodding top and the drooping branches give it a gracefulness not seen in any other evergreen tree. The lower branches spread widely and may sweep the ground. It is important, therefore, to give it plenty of room. This makes an excellent background and is effective in clumps or scattered among white pines in a grove. It may be clipped into a very dense high hedge. It is sometimes wrongly planted next to a house, where in 10 years it outgrows the location. Its specimen beauty should not be compromised.

Over much of its range, especially in southern New England, southern New York, most of New Jersey, and eastern Pennsylvania, Canadian hemlock has been severely, often fatally, afflicted with the woolly adelgid, and so cannot be recommended for those areas. Wherever grown, it must be watered in dry summer weather for at least two years after planting.

Umbrella pine (*Sciadopitys verticillata*)

OTHER DECIDUOUS TREES

Name	Zones	Height	Soil Requirements	Flower Color and Bloom Time
Acer buergerianum (trident maple)	4–8 (9)	20–25'	Average	Greenish; spring
A. Davidii (David maple)	5–8	30–50'	Average	Yellowish; spring
A. ginnala (Amur maple)	2–7 (8)	15–20'	Average	Yellowish white; spring
A. griseum (paperbark maple)	4–7 (8)	20–25'	Average	Greenish; spring
A. japonicum (fullmoon maple)	5–8	20–25'	Rich, moist	Purplish; spring
A. miyabei (Miyabe maple)	4–8	30–35'	Average	Greenish yellow; spring
A. negundo (box elder)	2–9	50–60'	Any	Yellow-green; early spring
A. palmatum (Japanese maple)	(5) 6–8	15–20'	Rich, moist	Red or purple; spring
A. pensylvanicum (striped maple)	3–8	30–35'	Rich, moist	Yellow; spring
A. platanoides (Norway maple)	3–7	50–75'	Average	Yellow; spring
A. pseudoplatanus (sycamore maple)	4–8	40–60'	Average	Yellow-green; spring
A. rubrum (red maple)	3–9	60–75'	Wet to ordinary	Yellowish (males) or red (females); early spring
A. saccharinum (silver maple)	3–9	50–75'	Average	Greenish; early spring
A. saccharum ssp. *nigrum* (black maple)	3–8	50–75'	Average	Greenish; spring
A. tataricum (Tatarian maple)	3–8	15–20'	Average	Greenish white; spring
Aesculus × *carnea* (red horse chestnut)	3–7	30–40'	Average, moist	Pink to red; spring
A. flava, syn. *A. octandra* (yellow buckeye)	3–8	50–75'	Average	Yellow-green; spring
A. glabra (Ohio buckeye)	3–7	25–30'	Average, moist	Greenish yellow; spring
A. hippocastanum (common horse chestnut)	3–7	50–75'	Average, moist	White; late spring
Ailanthus altissima (tree of heaven)	4–9	50–60'	Any	Yellowish; late spring
Albizia julibrissin (mimosa, silk tree)	6–9	25–30'	Average	Pink and white heads; summer
Alnus glutinosa (European alder)	3–7	50–60'	Average, moist or dry	Reddish catkins; early spring
A. incana (white alder)	2–7	50–60'	Average, moist	Yellowish catkins; early spring
Amelanchier arborea (downy Juneberry)	4–9	25–30'	Average	White; spring
A. canadensis (shadblow, serviceberry)	3–7	15–20'	Average	White; spring
A. × *grandiflora* (apple serviceberry)	4–7	20–25'	Average	White; spring
Aralia elata (Japanese angelica tree)	3–9	15–30'	Any	White; summer

OTHER DECIDUOUS TREES

Fruit	Favorable Characteristics	Unfavorable Characteristics
Two-winged samara	Neat appearance; small leaves; disease free; underused shade tree	Fall foliage color varies
Two-winged samara	Unlobed dark green leaves; underused	Limited availability
Red two-winged samara	Brilliant scarlet fall foliage; shade tolerant; easily moved; disease free	Trunks often multiple
Two-winged samara	Very attractive peeling reddish brown bark; disease free	Slow growing; costly
Two-winged samara	Red fall foliage; several cultivars with interesting foliage variations	Usually low headed
Two-winged samara	Resembles small sugar maple; well suited to small property; leaves held late	Difficult to propagate, hence uncommon and expensive
Two-winged samara	Extremely adaptable; fast growing; good for screening	Brittle wood; limbs break easily in high wind
Two-winged samara	Many cultivars with purplish and dissected foliage; also several dwarf forms	Subject to stem canker
Two-winged samara	White-striped greenish bark effective in winter; shade tolerant	Relatively limited adaptability
Two-winged samara	Adaptable; long lived; fast growing	Casts very dense shade; roots shallow, heaves sidewalks; self-sows; subject to fatal verticillium disease
Two-winged samara	Adaptable to urban and seaside conditions	No fall color; self-sows
Red two-winged samara	Fall foliage scarlet and yellow	Shallow rooted, may heave sidewalks; intolerant of alkaline soils
Two-winged samara	Fast growing; develops graceful form; one cultivar with dissected leaves	Brittle wood, rots easily, often broken in high wind
Two-winged samara	But for leaf lobing, essentially similar to *A. saccharum*	Scarce in commerce
Two-winged samara	Tolerates drought and alkaline soils; disease free; fruit showy	Trunks often multiple
Smooth-shelled nut	Attractive in flower; cv. 'Briottii' has large scarlet flowers	Somewhat susceptible to leaf diseases
Light brown, without prickles	Pest and disease free; best of the horse chestnuts	Relatively scarce in commerce
Smooth-shelled nut	Only horse chestnut with showy (orange) fall foliage	Very subject to leaf diseases
Prickly shelled nut	Attractive flowers even showier in double-flowered horse chestnut (cv. 'Baumannii'), which also lacks fruit	Very subject to leaf diseases
Greenish or reddish samara	Fast growing; tolerates urban conditions; adaptable to seaside environments	Brittle wood, easily broken; self-sows; malodorous; invasive
Tan pod	Attractive finely divided foliage; handsome floral display through the summer	Short lived, mainly because of disease susceptibility
Small brown cone	Roots enrich soil; excellent in wet locations	Undistinguished appearance
Small brown cone	Roots enrich soil; excellent in wet locations	Undistinguished appearance
Red berry, ripening to purple	Attractive flowers in hanging clusters; useful in natural plantings	Leaf diseases can deform foliage
Red berry, ripening to maroon	Handsome light gray bark; yellow to red fall foliage; flowers held in erect clusters	Often confused with *A. arborea;* best treated as large shrub
Red berry, ripening to violet black	Handsome light gray bark; yellow to orange fall foliage	In all *Amelanchier* species flowers appear very briefly
Black berry	Very large much-divided leaves; large flower clusters; berries attract birds	Roots sucker freely; gaunt in winter; thorny stems

(continues)

OTHER DECIDUOUS TREES (*continued*)

Name	Zones	Height	Soil Requirements	Flower Color and Bloom Time
Asimina triloba (pawpaw)	5–8	20–25'	Rich; moist	Maroon; spring
Betula davurica (Dahurian birch)	4–8	50–60'	Average	Yellowish catkins; spring
B. ermanii (Erman birch)	4–9	25–30'	Average	Yellowish catkins; spring
B. lenta (cherry birch)	3–8	50–70'	Average	Yellowish catkins; spring
B. maximowicziana (monarch birch)	4–7	50–60'	Average	Yellowish catkins; spring
B. nigra (river birch)	4–9	50–60'	Average; moist	Yellowish catkins; spring
B. pendula (European white birch)	2–7	50–60'	Average	Yellowish catkins; spring
B. populifolia (Gray or white birch)	3–7	25–30'	Any	Yellowish catkins; spring
Broussonetia papyrifera (paper mulberry)	6–10	30–40'	Any	Greenish catkins; spring
Carpinus betulus (European hornbeam)	4–7	40–50'	Average	Brown-orange to red catkins; spring
C. caroliniana (American hornbeam, ironwood)	2–9	20–25'	Any; moist	Yellowish catkins; spring
Carya illinoensis (pecan)	5–9	50–75'	Rich; moist	Yellowish catkins (males); spring
C. ovata (shagbark hickory)	4–8	50–75'	Rich; moist	Yellowish catkins (males); spring
Castanea mollissima (Chinese chestnut)	4–8	40–50'	Well drained, acidic	Cream spikes (males); spring
Catalpa bignonioides (southern catalpa)	5–9	30–35'	Average; dryish	White with yellow and brown spots; early summer
C. speciosa (northern catalpa)	4–8	50–60'	Average; dryish	White with yellow and brown spots; early summer
Celtis australis (European hackberry)	6–8	40–60'	Average	Greenish, small; spring
C. occidentalis (common hackberry)	2–9	60–75'	Average; moist to dry	Inconspicuous
Cornus mas (cornelian cherry dogwood)	4–7 (8)	20–25'	Average	Yellow, before leaves; early spring
C. nuttallii (Pacific dogwood)	8–9	35–50'	Average; moist	Four to six pointed white bracts; spring
Corylus colurna (Turkish filbert)	4–7	40–50'	Average; dryish	Brownish catkins (males); early spring
Crataegus crus-galli (cockspur hawthorn)	3–7	20–25'	Average to poor	White; spring
C. laevigata 'Paulii' (Paul's scarlet hawthorn)	4–7	15–20'	Average to poor	Double red; spring
C. × lavallei (Lavalle hawthorn)	4–7	15–20'	Average to poor	White; spring
C. mollis (downy hawthorn)	5–8	25–30'	Average	White; spring
C. monogyna 'Stricta' (upright single-seeded hawthorn)	4–7	20–25'	Average	White; spring
C. nitida (glossy hawthorn)	4–7	25–30'	Average to poor	White; spring
Davidia involucrata var. *vilmoriniana* (Vilmorin dove tree)	5–8	25–30'	Rich; moist	Two white pendulous bracts; spring
Disopyros virginiana (common persimmon)	4–9	50–60'	Rich; moist	Greenish yellow; spring
Elaeagnus angustifolia (Russian olive)	2–7	15–20'	Poor; dry	Yellowish; late spring
Eucommia ulmoides (hardy rubber tree)	4–7	40–60'	Any	Inconspicuous
Euonymus europaeus (European spindle tree)	3–7	20–25'	Average to poor	Inconspicuous
E. hamiltonianus (Japanese spindle tree)	4–8	15–20'	Average	Greenish; spring
Fagus grandifolia (American beech)	3–9	50–75'	Rich; moist	Inconspicuous

OTHER DECIDUOUS TREES

Fruit	Favorable Characteristics	Unfavorable Characteristics
Yellow to brown, edible	Large drooping leaves; delicious fruit; disease free	Often suckers to form clumps; difficult to transplant
Small brown cone	Exfoliating reddish brown bark	No outstanding virtues except hardiness
Small brown cone	Striking pinkish cream bark	Scarce in commerce
Small brown cone	Cherrylike bark reddish brown to black, glossy; yellow fall foliage	Subject to disfiguring stem canker
Small brown cone	Exfoliating grayish to gray-orange bark; resistant to borers	Loses lower branches with age, leaving moplike head of foliage
Small brown cone	Exfoliating reddish brown to silver gray bark	Chlorotic on alkaline soils
Small brown cone	Graceful habit; exfoliating chalky white bark	Very susceptible to borers
Small brown cone	Fast growing; the usual multiple trunks whitening while still slender	Often shrubby; susceptible to borers
Inconspicuous	Succeeds in difficult locations	Often multistemmed and shrubby
Nutlet within three-lobed bract	Good foliage; responds well to shearing	Often suckers from the base; intolerant of alkaline soils
Nutlet within three-lobed bract	Smooth gray bark with bulging "muscled" effect; shade tolerant	Usually multistemmed and low headed
Edible nut	Fast growing; many cultivars developed for local conditions	Because of deep taproot only small trees can be planted
Edible nut	Bark exfoliates in long plates; excellent nuts	Deep taproot precludes planting any but seedlings
Edible nut	Good shade tree; excellent edible nuts	Resistant but not immune to chestnut blight
Pendent pod	Useful in drought-prone and seaside areas	Coarse, gaunt appearance in winter; late to leaf out
Pendent pod	Extremely adaptable to harsh conditions	As for *C. bignonioides*
Red, pea size	Very adaptable, drought resistant, long lived	Requires summer heat to thrive
Red-orange to dark purple berry	Smooth gray bark; thrives under dry adverse conditions	Subject to witches'-broom and many leaf diseases; intolerant of strongly alkaline soils
Red, cherrylike, in summer	Early flower display before leaves; pest and disease free	Too low headed for lawn use unless pruned up
Red or orange berry	Very handsome specimen tree	Suited only to the cool, moderate climate of the Pacific Northwest
Brown nut	Withstands drought, heat, and varied soil pH	Undistinguished appearance
Bright red berry	Makes impenetrable hedge; red to orange fall foliage	Sharp, rigid, 2-inch thorns hazardous (except in thornless var. *inermis*)
Deep red berry	One of the showiest hawthorns when in flower	Very subject to defoliating diseases
Red to orange berry	Ornamental fruit persists though winter	Hazardous 2-inch thorns
Dull red berry	Dense, twiggy habit; twigs and branches with 1- to 2-inch woody thorns	Many pests and diseases; thorns may cause injury; difficult to transplant
Dull red berry	Lustrous foliage; fruit persists all winter	Susceptible to fire blight
Dull red berry	Lustrous foliage; fruit persists all winter	Thorns hazardous if present
Green	Showy and unusual in flower	Requires many years to come into flower
Yellow-orange when ripe	Handsome specimen tree; ripe fruit very flavorful	Difficult to transplant; often remains shrubby
Yellow with silvery scales	Handsome silvery gray foliage	Subject to verticillium disease, especially in Midwest
Oblong winged capsule	Very adaptable; makes attractive specimen tree; latex sap a source of rubber	Intolerant of shade
Coral pink-and-orange capsule	Ornamental fruit display persists for several weeks	Not ornamental except in fruit
Orange or scarlet capsule	Conspicuous corky bark attractive in winter	Uncommon in commerce; little known
Three-angled nut	Smooth gray bark; yellow fall foliage	Suckers at base forming copses; dead foliage held in winter; difficult to move and establish

(continues)

OTHER DECIDUOUS TREES (continued)

Name	Zones	Height	Soil Requirements	Flower Color and Bloom Time
Franklinia alatamaha (Franklin tree)	6–8	10–20'	Average	White flowers in late summer; red-orange fall foliage
Fraxinus americana (American ash or white ash)	3–9	50–75'	Average	Inconspicuous
F. caroliniana (water ash)	6–8	25–35'	Wet, acidic	Inconspicuous; early spring
F. ornus (flowering ash)	5–6	35–40'	Average	Small white; fragrant; in clusters; early spring
F. velutina var. *glabra* (Arizona ash, Modesto ash)	5–8	40–45'	Alkaline	Inconspicuous
Gleditsia aquatica (water locust)	6–8	35–50'	Wet, acidic	Greenish; spring
Gymnocladus dioica (Kentucky coffee tree)	3–8	50–60'	Average	Inconspicuous
Halesia monticola (mountain silver bell)	5–8	50–60'	Rich; moist	White, bell shaped; spring
Hippophae rhamnoides (sea buckthorn)	3–7	15–20'	Average to poor	Inconspicuous
Juglans nigra (black walnut)	4–8	50–75'	Rich; moist	Inconspucuous catkins; spring
J. regia (English walnut)	5–8	35–50'	Rich; moist	Inconspicuous catkins; spring
Kalopanax pictus (castor aralia)	4–7	40–50'	Rich; moist	Small white; clustered; summer
Laburnum × *watereri* 'Vossii' (golden chain)	5–7	15–20'	Rich	Yellow; spring
Larix decidua (European larch)	2–6	50–75'	Average; moist	Inconspicuous
L. kaempferi (Japanese larch)	4–7	60–75'	Average	Inconspicuous
L. laricina (eastern larch)	1–5	35–50'	Average	Yellow (males) or red (females); spring
Maackia amurensis (Amur maackia)	3–7	20–25'	Average to poor	White; summer
Maclura pomifera (osage orange)	4–9	30–40'	Average to poor	Inconspicuous
Magnolia acuminata (cucumber tree)	3–8	50–60'	Rich; moist	Greenish yellow; late spring
M. heptapeta (yulan magnolia)	5–8	30–35'	Rich; moist	White; fragrant; early spring
M. × *loebneri* 'Merrill' (Merrill magnolia)	3–8	25–30'	Rich; moist	White; fragrant; spring
M. macrophylla (big-leaf magnolia)	5–8	35–40'	Rich; moist	Cream; fragrant; summer
M. tripetala (umbrella tree)	5–8	20–30'	Average	White; spring
M. virginiana (sweet bay)	5–9	25–50'	Rich; moist to wet	White; fragrant; early summer
Malus × *arnoldiana* (Arnold crab apple)	4–8	15–20'	Average	Buds rose, open pink, fade to white; spring
M. × *atrosanguinea* (carmine crab apple)	4–8	15–20'	Average	Buds red, open deep pink; spring
M. baccata (Siberian crab apple)	2–7	35–40'	Average	White; fragrant; spring
M. × 'Blanche Ames' (Blanche Ames crab apple)	4–7	15–20'	Average	Pink and white; semidouble; spring

OTHER DECIDUOUS TREES

Fruit	Favorable Characteristics	Unfavorable Characteristics
Inconspicuous	Small stature; large shiny flowers	Difficult to transplant and establish
Clustered green samaras (females)	Fast growing; fall foliage deep yellow to purple	Many serious pests and diseases in the Northeast and elsewhere
Clustered green samaras (females)	A good species for wet ground	Low crotches often split in storms
Clustered green samaras (females)	Ornamental flowers and fruit	Uncommon in commerce
Clustered green samaras (females)	Drought tolerant; excellent street and park tree	Little known outside the Southwest
Flat green pod maturing to brown	Useful on stream banks, pond borders, and other wet locations	Long (to 4 inches), branched, woody thorns potentially hazardous and may require removal from trunk
Thick brown pod in alternate years	Large, much-divided leaves; picturesque habit	Females have messy pod drop in fall
Dry winged pod	Valuable flowering tree, showier than the more common *H. carolina*	Chlorotic on alkaline soils
Orange berry (females)	Silvery gray-green foliage; very suitable for seaside use	Often fails to establish on rich soils
Large edible nut	Attractive black bark	Late to leaf out; leaves drop early in fall; taproot precludes planting anything but seedlings
Large edible nut	The cv. 'Carpathian' good nut producer in the North	Fails on poor or overmoist soils
Small, black berry	Large, bold foliage; disease free; seeds attract birds	Self-sows, sometimes annoyingly
Small tan pod	Very showy in flower; smooth green bark	Seeds poisonous
Brown cone, about 2 inches long	Fast growing; attractive habit in and out of leaf	Subject to borers and leaf pests
Brown cone, about 2 inches long	Fast growing; attractive habit in and out of leaf; young cones red	Subject to borers and leaf pests
Brown cone about ½ inch long	Attractive conical habit; young foliage light green; adaptable to wet soils	Intolerant of prolonged heat; sensitive to air pollution
Small pod	Attractive *erect* flower clusters; pest and disease free; drought tolerant	Very slow growing; slow to reach flowering size
Green, size of large orange	Good screen or hedge tree; var. *inermis* is thornless; unusual fruit	Except when in fruit, of little ornamental value; fruit drops in fall, a hazard over paths
Cucumber-shaped pod	Very pH adaptable; bold foliage; imposing habit at maturity	Fragile fleshy roots that require care when transplanting
Green pod opens to reveal red seeds	Very showy in flower	Flowers often damaged or killed by frost in the North
Green pod opens to reveal red seeds	Flowers when young; heavy floral display every year	Flowers sometimes damaged by frost
Green pod opens to reveal red seeds	The 20- to 30-inch leaves provide striking effect	Foliage effect too coarse except on large property
Red, conelike	Strikingly large, bunched leaves; fragrant, very large white flowers	Too coarse for use in small landscapes
Green pod opens to reveal red seeds	Deciduous in the North, evergreen in the South	Often remains shrubby in the North; chlorotic on alkaline soils
Yellow and red	Beautiful bud and flower contrast; flowers reliably every year	Highly susceptible to scab
Dark red	Showy in flower; resistant to scab	Fruits only minimally
Red or yellow	Good in tubs or containers; flowers annually	Susceptible to scab
Yellow	Graceful form; flowers annually; resistant to scab	Rare in commerce

(continues)

OTHER DECIDUOUS TREES (continued)

Name	Zones	Height	Soil Requirements	Flower Color and Bloom Time
M. × 'Bob White' (Bob White crab apple)	5–8	15–20'	Average	Buds pink, open white; spring
M. × 'Dolgo' (Dolgo crab apple)	3–7	30–35'	Average	White; fragrant; spring
M. × 'Dorothea' (Dorothea crab apple)	4–8	20–25'	Average	Buds rose, open deep pink; semidouble; spring
M. hupehensis (tea crab apple)	4–8	15–20'	Average	Buds deep pink, open white; spring
M. × 'Prince Georges' (Prince Georges crab apple)	4–8	15–20'	Average	Pink, double; spring
M. × purpurea 'Lemoinei' (Lemoine crab apple)	4–8	20–25'	Average	Deep magenta; spring
Morus alba (white mulberry)	4–8	35–40'	Any	Inconspicuous
Nyssa sylvatica (sour gum, black gum)	3–9	50–60'	Average; moist to wet	Inconspicuous
Ostrya virginiana (hop hornbeam)	3–9	35–50'	Average	Inconspicuous
Paulownia tomentosa (empress tree)	5–9	35–40'	Average to poor	Violet; spring
Phellodendron amurense (Amur cork tree)	3–8	30–45'	Average	Yellow-green; spring
Platanus × acerifolia (London plane, sycamore)	4–8	50–75'	Average to poor	Inconspicuous
P. occidentalis (American sycamore)	4–9	75–100'	Rich; moist to wet	Inconspicuous
Populus alba (white poplar)	3–8	50–60'	Average to poor	Inconspicuous catkins
P. alba 'Pyramidalis' (Bolleana poplar)	3–8	50–60'	Average to poor	Inconspicuous catkins
P. balsamifera (balsam poplar)	2–9	50–60'	Average to poor	Inconspicuous catkins
P. grandidentata (large-tooth aspen)	3–8	50–60'	Average to poor	Inconspicuous catkins
P. maximowiczii (Japanese poplar)	3–8	50–60'	Average to poor	Inconspicuous catkins
P. nigra 'Italica' (Lombardy poplar)	3–9	50–75'	Any	Greenish catkins; early spring
P. tremuloides (quaking aspen)	1–7	30–40'	Average to poor	Inconspicuous catkins
Prunus campanulata 'Okame' (Taiwan cherry)	6–9	20–25'	Average; well drained	Reddish pink; early spring
P. 'Hally Jolivette' (Hally Jolivette cherry)	5–8	10–15'	Average; well drained	Pink buds, open white; spring
P. maackii (Amur chokecherry)	2–6	25–30'	Average; well drained	White; spring
P. sargentii (Sargent cherry)	4–7	35–45'	Rich; moist	Deep pink; spring
P. serotina (black cherry)	3–9	50–75'	Average to poor	White, in spikes; late spring
P. serrulata (Oriental cherry)	5–8	20–25'	Average, moist	Pink to white; spring
P. × yedoensis (Yoshino cherry)	5–8	35–40'	Average, moist	White; spring

OTHER DECIDUOUS TREES

Fruit	Favorable Characteristics	Unfavorable Characteristics
Yellow	Fruit persists in winter	Tends to flower in alternate years; susceptible to fire blight
Bright red	Very hardy; useful in harsh climates	Flowers in alternate years
Bright yellow	Graceful in flower; blooms regularly every year	Susceptible to scab and fire blight
Greenish yellow	One of the most beautiful crab apples in flower	Susceptible to fire blight
No fruit	Flowers fragant, borne annually	Believed susceptible to rust; lacks fruit
Purplish red	Flowers annually; resistant to scab	Flower color deemed too strong by some; susceptible to fire blight
Whitish, pinkish, or purplish berry	Succeeds in very poor soils	Fruit drop messy; weedy, invasive
Small blue berry	Glossy foliage; scarlet fall foliage; good tree for wet ground	Slow growing; taproot precludes moving any but seedlings; rare in commerce
Hoplike cluster	Pest and disease free	Slow to establish after transplanting
Large brown persistent capsule	Showy flowers; attractive fruit persists all winter; fast growing	Late to leaf out; messy flower drop; soft wooded
Black (females)	Succeeds under difficult conditions; interesting corky bark	Offers thin shade; roots heave sidewalks; females self-sow, sometimes annoyingly
Light brown ball-shaped cluster	Fast growing; mottled bark; tolerant of urban conditions; cvs. 'Columbia' and 'Liberty' resist anthracnose and canker	Subject to defoliating anthracnose in wet springs; bark exfoliates in summer; overused
Light brown ball-shaped cluster	Long lived; majestic dimensions; smooth bark; good in wet locations	Very subject to defoliating and deforming anthracnose; too big for most suburban properties
Tiny, with cottony fluff	Thrives in littoral and other difficult locations	Roots sucker to form dense, invasive copses; limbs break in high wind
Tiny, with cottony fluff	An acceptable substitute for disease-prone *P. nigra* 'Italica'	Short lived; brittle wood
Tiny, with cottony fluff	Very adaptable; fast growing; leaves flutter in breeze	Short lived; sheds leaves in drought, twigs and branches in storms
Tiny, with cottony fluff	As for *P. balsamifera*	As for *P. balsamifera*
Tiny, with cottony fluff	Picturesque specimen tree; relatively disease free; fast growing	Coarse foliage unsuited to most suburban settings
None (a male clone)	Slender, strictly erect habit; fast growing	Soon deformed and killed by canker; substitutes include *Populus alba* 'Pyramidalis', *Quercus robur* 'Fastigiata', *Fagus sylvatica* 'Danwyk', and *Koelreuteria paniculata* 'Fastigiata'
Tiny, with cottony fluff	Leaves flutter in breeze; fall foliage clear yellow; bark greenish cream	Short lived; disease prone
Small, black	Attractive in flower and in fall foliage	Scarce in commerce
Sterile	One of the best flowering cherries	Scarce in commerce
Small, black	Flaking brownish yellow bark conspicuous in winter	Does not thrive in sustained summer heat
Dark violet; scant	Largest and one of the best flowering cherries; young leaves reddish; fall foliage bronzy	Eventual spread (equal to height) can overwhelm small settings
Black, pea size, often abundant; late summer	Lustrous foliage; fast growing; adaptable; fruit used in preserves and wine	Very subject to tent caterpillar; spreads invasively by bird-dropped seeds in much of the East
Mostly sterile	Many cultivars, flowers single or double, all showy in bloom; bark dark and glossy	Often short lived in East
Dark purple; scant	Some cultivars with pink flowers; very floriferous; long lived	Eventual spread (greater than height) can overwhelm small site

(continues)

OTHER DECIDUOUS TREES (*continued*)

Name	Zones	Height	Soil Requirements	Flower Color and Bloom Time
Pseudolarix amabilis (golden larch)	4–7	60–80'	Rich; moist	Inconspicuous
Ptelea trifoliata (hop tree)	3–9	15–20'	Average; well drained	Greenish white; spring
Pterocarya fraxinifolia (Caucasian wing nut)	5–8	50–60'	Rich; well drained	Greenish catkin; spring
Pterostyrax hispida (epaulette tree)	4–8	25–30'	Rich; moist	Cream; fragrant; late spring
Pyrus calleryana 'Bradford' (Bradford pear)	4–8	35–40'	Average	White; spring
P. ussuriensis (Chinese pear)	3–7	30–35'	Average	White; spring
Quercus acutissima (sawtooth oak)	(5) 6–9	35–40'	Average	Inconspicuous
Q. alba (white oak)	3–9	50–75'	Average	Inconspicuous
Q. bicolor (swamp white oak)	3–8	50–60'	Wet, acidic	Inconspicuous
Q. ilicifolia (scrub oak)	5–7	10–25'	Sandy, acidic	Inconspicuous
Q. imbricaria (shingle oak)	4–8	50–60'	Average	Inconspicuous
Q. marilandica (blackjack oak)	5–8	20–30'	Average	Inconspicuous
Q. muhlenbergii (yellow chestnut oak, chinkapin)	5–7	40–50'	Alkaline	Inconspicuous
Q. nigra (water oak)	6–9	50–60'	Average; moist to wet	Inconspicuous
Q. palustris (pin oak)	4–8 (9)	50–75'	Moist to wet	Inconspicuous
Q. prinus (chestnut oak)	4–8	50–60'	Average to poor	Inconspicuous
Q. robur 'Fastigiata' (upright English oak)	5–8	50–75'	Average to poor	Inconspicuous
Robinia pseudoacacia (black locust)	3–8	50–75'	Average to poor	White; late spring
Salix fragilis (crack willow)	5–7	40–60'	Wet, acidic	Green catkins; early spring
S. matsudana 'Tortuosa' (corkscrew willow)	4–9	25–30'	Average; wet	Yellow catkins; spring
S. pentandra (laurel willow)	4–8	50–60'	Average; wet	Yellow catkins; spring
Sassafras albidum	4–8	50–60'	Average	Small yellowish; spring
Sorbus aucuparia (European mountain ash)	3–7	25–30'	Average	White; spring
Stewartia pseudocamellia (Japanese stewartia)	4–8	25–30'	Rich, moist	White with yellow stamens; summer
Taxodium distichum (bald cypress)	4–10	50–75'	Average; wet, acidic	Drooping clusters of yellowish conelets; early spring
Tilia americana (American linden)	2–8	50–75'	Average	Small yellowish; fragrant; early summer
T. × euchlora (Crimean linden)	3–7	40–50'	Average	Small yellowish; fragrant; early summer
T. petiolaris (weeping silver linden)	5–8	50–60'	Average	Small yellowish; fragrant; early summer
Ulmus davidiana var. *japonica* (Japanese elm)	5–8	40–50'	Average	Inconspicuous
U. parvifolia (Chinese elm, lacebark elm)	4–9	35–40'	Average	Inconspicuous
U. pumila (Siberian elm)	3–9	50–60'	Average	Inconspicuous

OTHER DECIDUOUS TREES

Fruit	Favorable Characteristics	Unfavorable Characteristics
Pale green cone	Handsome conical habit; foliage golden yellow in fall	Slow growing, but requires substantial space
Winged, brown, persisting	Very tolerant of shade	Low headed; suckers from base
Small two-winged nut	Easily grown; disease free	Casts dense shade; tends to be low headed
Bristly, dry, persisting	Neat in habit; easily grown	Heat promotes flowering; scarce in commerce
Small, russet colored	Attractive in bloom; symmetrical form and absence of large fruit and leaves favors its use as a street tree	Susceptibility to crotch breakage reduced in cultivars 'Capital' and 'White House'; overused
Yellow 1½-inch edible pear	Hardiest of pears; disease free; much used as shade tree in Midwest	Little known outside of Midwest; uncommon in commerce
Acorn	Easily grown; distinctive foliage	Chlorotic on alkaline soils; most successful in the South
Acorn	Massive, very long-lived tree	Often fails as a lawn tree
Acorn	Good species for wet ground; a valued timber tree	Difficult to transplant; slow to establish
Acorn	Very tolerant of poor soil, high winds	Difficult to transplant; often remains shrubby in cultivation; scarce in commerce
Acorn	Lustrous, unlobed, laurel-like foliage retained until late fall	Afflicted by many pests and diseases, though few serious
Acorn	Tolerates poor soil, high winds	Slow to establish; slow growing
Acorn	Handsome tree, especially when mature	Difficult to transplant
Acorn	Good in wet places, although also successful as street tree, especially in the South	Rather slow growing in the North
Acorn	Handsome specimen tree with drooping branches; easily transplanted	Chlorotic on alkaline soils; subject to disfiguring thorn gall
Acorn	One of the best oaks for poor, dry soils	Form often unpredictably variable
Acorn	Narrow habit; useful in restricted locations	Not reliably long lived
Purple pod matures brown	Several interesting cultivars; best used on poor, dry soils	Subject to trunk borers; roots sucker; invasive, forming extensive copses
Tiny, with white fluff	Glossy foliage; handsome fissured bark; adaptable to wet conditions	Easily broken or toppled in storms; many pests and diseases of leaves
Tiny, with white fluff	Unusual habit; very early to leaf out	Often short lived; easily storm damaged
Tiny, with white fluff	Lustrous dark green foliage	Subject to serious leaf diseases
Blue, fleshy, one-seeded, ½-inch diameter, on red cuplike receptacle	Leaves occur in three shapes; foliage aromatic; free of pests and diseases	Often forms copses; difficult to transplant, hence little sold
Red to orange berry	Attractive small tree, especially in fruit	Often weakened and killed by borers
Green capsule	Showy flowers; smooth mottled bark	Variable in habit; not easily transplanted
Small greenish to brown cone	Stately, distinctive habit, with gracefully drooping twigs; very adaptable, especially to wet ground	Chlorotic on alkaline soils; *T. adscendens* is similar except for pale bark and upright twigs
Small green nut	Fast growing; pH tolerant; easily moved	Trunk suckers at base; coarse appearance; subject to many pests and diseases of leaves
Small green nut	Symmetrical habit when young; very adaptable to alkaline soils	Frequently suckers heavily beneath trunk graft
Small green nut	Symmetrical habit when young; yellow fall foliage	Trunk suckers
Small, winged	Disease resistant, substitute for *U. americana*, (American elm), especially in Midwest	Little known; rare in commerce
Small, winged	Attractive mottled exfoliating bark	Often and erroneously offered as *U. pumila* in commerce
Small, winged	Very adaptable; fast growing; resistant to Dutch elm disease	Soft wooded, hence easily storm damaged; self-sows

Japanese stewartia
(*Stewartia
pseudocamellia*)

European
spindle tree
(*Euonymus europaeus*)

David maple (*Acer davidii*)   **Yellow fullmoon maple** (*Acer japonicum* 'Aureum')

Franklin tree
(*Franklinia alatamaha*)

Northern catalpa
(*Catalpa speciosa*)

Upright English oak
(*Quercus robur* 'Fastigiata')

Empress tree
(*Paulownia tomentosa*)

Pacific dogwood
(*Comus nuttalli*)

Golden chain
(*Laburnum* × *watereri*
'Vossii')

Erman birch (*Betula ermanii*)   **Yoshino cherry** (*Prunus* × *yedoensis*)

Bradford Callery pear (*Pyrus calleryana* 'Bradford')

Sweet bay (*Magnolia virginiana*)

Hally jolivette cherry
(*Prunus* 'Hally Jolivette')

Yulan magnolia (*Magnolia heptapeta*)

TREES THAT THRIVE IN MOIST TO WET SOIL

DECIDUOUS

Acer negundo	Box elder	*Nyssa sylvatica*	Sour gum
A. rubrum	Red maple	*Platanus occidentalis*	Buttonwood
A. saccharinum	Silver maple	*Populus balsamifera*	Carolina cottonwood
Alnus spp.	Alder	*P. grandidentata*	Large-tooth aspen
Betula allegheniensis	Yellow birch	*Quercus bicolor*	Swamp white oak
B. nigra	River birch	*Q. palustris*	Pin oak
B. populifolia	Gray birch	*Q. phellos*	Willow oak
Carpinus caroliniana	American hornbeam	*Salix alba*	White willow
Carya ovata	Shagbark hickory	*S. alba* 'Vitellina'	Golden willow
Fraxinus caroliniana	Water ash	*S. × pendulina*	Weeping willow
F. pennsylvanica var. *lanceolata*	Green ash	*S. fragilis*	Brittle willow
Gleditsia aquatica	Water locust	*S. nigra*	Black willow
Larix laricina	American larch	*S. pentandra*	Laurel willow
Liquidambar styraciflua	Sweet gum	*Taxodium distichum*	Bald cypress
Magnolia virginiana	Sweet bay	*Tilia americana*	American linden

EVERGREEN

Abies balsamea	Balsam fir	*Picea mariana*	Black spruce
Calocedrus decurrens	California incense cedar	*P. rubra*	Red spruce
Casuarina spp.	Australian pine	*Thuja occidentalis*	American arborvitae
Chamaecyparis thyoides	Atlantic white cedar	*Tsuga canadensis*	Canadian hemlock
Ilex opaca	American holly		

OTHER EVERGREEN TREES

Names	Zones	Height	Soil Requirements
Abies balsamea (balsam fir)	3–5	50–70'	Average; moist
A. homolepis (Nikko fir)	4–7	50–60'	Average
A. koreana (Korean fir)	5–7	40–50'	Average
A. nordmanniana (Nordmann fir)	4–7	60–80'	Average
A. veitchii (Veitch fir)	3–6	50–60'	Average
Araucaria araucana (monkey puzzle)	(7) 8–10	50–75'	Average
A. bidwellii (bunya bunya)	9–10	50–75'	Average
Calocedrus decurrens (California incense cedar)	5–8	60–70'	Fertile; moist
Casuarina cunninghamiana (Australian pine)	9–10	30–50'	Average
C. equisetifolia (horsetail tree)	9–10	40–60'	Average
Chamaecyparis lawsoniana (Lawson cypress, Port Orford cedar)	5–7	50–75'	Fertile; moist
C. obtusa (Hinoki cypress)	4–8	40–50'	Average; moist
Cryptomeria japonica (Japanese cedar)	(5) 6–9	50–60'	Average
Cunninghamia lanceolata (China fir)	(6) 7–9	40–50'	Average
Cupressus macrocarpa (Monterey cypress)	8–9	50–75'	Stony
Eucalyptus gunnii (cider gum)	8–10	50–75'	Alkaline
E. pauciflora var. *niphophila* (snow gum)	8–10	15–20'	Alkaline
E. urnigera (urn gum)	8–10	20–30'	Alkaline
E. viminalis (ribbon gum)	8–10	50–75'	Alkaline
Ilex cassine (dahoon holly)	7–9	20–25'	Average
I. latifolia (lusterleaf holly)	7–9	30–40'	Average
I. opaca (American holly)	5–9	20–25'	Average
I. pedunculosa (longstalk holly)	4–9	15–20'	Average
Juniperus chinensis (Chinese juniper)	3–9	30–40'	Average
J. communis (common juniper)	2–7	15–20'	Average to poor
J. excelsa 'Stricta' (Greek juniper)	7–8	15–20'	Average
J. rigida (needle juniper)	5–7	20–25'	Average to poor
J. scopulorum (Rocky Mountain juniper)	3–7	25–30'	Average to poor
Ligustrum lucidum (wax-leaf privet)	7–10	30–40' (50')	Average
Magnolia grandiflora (evergreen magnolia)	6–9	30–50'	Average
Nothofagus antarctica (southern beech)	7–8	40–50'	Average
Photinia serrulata (Chinese photinia)	7–10	25–30'	Fertile; moist
Picea abies (Norway spruce)	2–8	50–75'	Average
P. engelmannii (Engelmann spruce)	2–7	50–60'	Average to poor
P. glauca (white spruce)	2–7	50–60'	Average
P. mariana (black spruce)	2–5 (7)	30–40'	Average
P. omorika (Serbian spruce)	4–7	40–50'	Average
P. orientalis (Oriental spruce)	4–7	40–50'	Average
P. pungens (Colorado spruce, blue spruce)	2–7	40–50'	Average
P. rubens (red spruce)	3–7	60–70'	Average
Pinus aristata (bristlecone pine)	4–7	25–40'	Average
P. banksiana (jack pine)	2–6	35–50'	Sandy, acidic
P. bungeana (lacebark pine)	4–8	30–40'	Fertile

OTHER EVERGREEN TREES

Characteristics	
Positive	*Negative*
Lustrous needles; conical form; aromatic	Intolerant of prolonged summer heat
Attractive foliage; conical habit	Loses symmetrical form with age
Formal conical habit when young	Formal appearance limits use
Glossy dark green foliage	Spirelike form limits use
Needles white underneath	Stiffly pyramidal form; heat intolerant
Unusual open habit; best in formal settings	Geometric form limits use
Useful specimen tree	Intolerant of sustained cold below 20°F
Distinctive narrow columnar habit	Very formal appearance limits use
Salt tolerant; useful near sea coast	Intolerant of sustained cold below 25°F
As for *C. cunninghamiana*	Invasive in frost-free coastal areas
Distinctive pyramidal habit	Intolerant of prolonged heat
Lustrous scale leaves arranged in fans; many varied cultivars	Very slow growing; difficult to transplant
Symmetrical when young; glossy foliage	Can suffer winter dieback in the North
Unusually wide needles confer distinctive appearance	Old, dead needles retained
Very adaptable, especially to coastal conditions	Shade intolerant; too low headed for lawn use unless pruned up
Hardy to 5°F; very adaptable; gray-green bark	Often rangy in habit; peeling bark messy
Hardy to 5°F; whitish bark	Slow growing; difficult to establish
Hardy to 15°F; very attractive foliage	Tends to be low headed or shrubby
Hardy to 15°F; reddish shreddy brown bark	Often very rangy in habit; peeling bark messy
Dense foliage; profuse red berries (females)	Uncommon in commerce (except cultivars)
Large leaved, no prickles	Often misused as a foundation shrub
Spiny foliage without luster; hardier than *I. aquifolium*	Leaf miner and other pests limit use
Lustrous leaves without prickles	Berry display often scant
Erect habit; scale foliage; many varied cultivars	Entire branches killed by twig disease (blight)
Very adaptable; many small cultivars	Subject to various diseases
Dense columnar habit; blue-green foliage	Suffers dieback in the North
Open habit; graceful hanging branches	Subject to twig blight
Upright habit; drought tolerant; many cultivars	Subject to twig blight
Adaptable; handsome foliage	Often confused with *L. japonicum*, a shrub
Large lustrous leaves; large fragrant white flowers mostly in spring	Needs space for wide crown
Graceful form, small lustrous leaves	Needs space for wide-spreading top
Lustrous foliage, red when young and old	Leaves turn brown in severe winters
Stiffly formal when young; good barrier tree	Overused; ragged with age; many pests
Blue-green foliage; dense upright habit	Foliage ages to dull blue-green
Pyramidal; tolerates heat and drought	Subject to spruce bagworm
Thrives in short growing season	Intolerant of prolonged summer heat
Narrow habit; pendent branches	Subject to aphids, budworms, and borers
Short glossy needles; pendent branches	Foliage may burn in severe winters
Many cultivars with intensely blue foliage	Stiff formal habit; often loses lower limbs in age
Very attractive habit and glossy foliage	Difficult to transplant and establish
Open picturesque habit	Extremely slow growing
Thrives on sterile soils in harsh environments	Gaunt with age; often of thin and open habit
Colorful exfoliating bark	Low headed, often with several trunks

(continues)

OTHER EVERGREEN TREES (*continued*)

Names	Zones	Height	Soil Requirements
P. cembra (Swiss stone pine)	3–7	30–35'	Average to poor
P. flexilis (limber pine)	3–7	30–40'	Average
P. koraiensis (Korean pine)	3–7	40–50'	Average
P. monticola (western white pine)	5–6	50–60'	Average
P. nigra (Austrian pine)	4–7 (8)	40–50'	Average to poor
P. parviflora (Japanese white pine)	4–7	30–40'	Average
P. pinaster (cluster pine)	8–9	50–70'	Stony, acidic
P. ponderosa (ponderosa pine)	3–7	50–75'	Stony, alkaline
P. resinosa (red pine)	2–6 (7)	50–60'	Average
P. rigida (pitch pine)	4–7	35–50'	Sandy, acidic
P. virginiana (Virginia scrub pine)	4–8	15–35'	Clay, acidic
P. wallichiana (Himalayan pine)	(6) 7–8	50–60'	Average
Sequoia sempervirens (redwood)	7	60–75'	Average
Sequoiadendron giganteum (giant sequoia)	6–7	60–75'	Average
Taxus baccata (English yew)	(5) 6–7	20–35'	Average
T. cuspidata (Japanese yew)	4–7	20–25'	Average
Thuja orientalis (Oriental arborvitae)	(5) 6–9	20–25'	Average
T. plicata (giant arborvitae)	5–7	50–60'	Average
Tsuga caroliniana (Carolina hemlock)	4–7	40–50'	Average

Carolina hemlock (*Tsuga caroliniana*)

Lusterleaf holly (*Ilex latifolia*)

Himalayan pine (*Pinus wallichiana*)

Chinese photinia (*Photinia serrulata*)

OTHER EVERGREEN TREES

Characteristics

Positive	Negative
Open picturesque habit	Very slow growing
Fine-textured appearance	Top requires room to spread
Looser habit than most pines	Very slow growing
Narrow symmetrical habit	Intolerant of acid soil and heat of the East
Fast growing; adaptable to harsh conditions	Afflicted by serious diseases
Short dark needles; very adaptable	Unpredictable habit
Succeeds in sterile soil, especially near coast	Difficult to transplant
Fast growing; open habit	Intolerant of soils and humidity of the East
Very adaptable; good for windbreaks	Disease prone and short lived south of zone 6
Thrives on sterile soils; rejuvenates after fire	Subject to tip moth; self-sows, often annoyingly
Thrives on heavy dry soils; grown as Christmas tree in the South	Intolerant of alkaline; foliage unattractive in winter; often low headed
Long, pendent, graceful needles	Suffers browning and dieback in severe winters
Fine-textured foliage; reddish brown shredded bark	Intolerant of temperature extremes and drought
Develops disproportionately thick trunk; fast growing	Requires generous space for trunk expansion
Deep green foliage; slow growing; many cultivars	Low headed, wide spreading
As for *T. baccata*	As for *T. baccata*
Columnar habit; many small cultivars	Often remains shrubby
Foliage remains green all year; good for screen	Slow growing in the East
Fine-textured foliage; resists adelgid attack	Less graceful than *T. canadensis*

California incense cedar
(*Calocedrus decurrens*)

Japanese cedar
(*Cryptomeria japonica*)

Longstalk holly
(*Ilex pedunculosa*)

Giant sequoia
(*Sequoiadendrom giganteum*)

White spruce (*Picea glauca*)

Evergreen magnolia
(*Magnolia grandiflora*)

TREES RELATIVELY FREE FROM INSECT PESTS AND DISEASES

DECIDUOUS

Ailanthus altissima	Tree of heaven	*Kalopanax pictus*	Castor aralia
Carpinus spp.	Hornbeam	*Koelreuteria paniculata*	Goldenrain tree
Celtis occidentalis	Hackberry	*Laburnum* spp.	Golden chain tree
Cercidiphyllum japonicum	Katsura tree	*Ligustrum lucidum*	Wax-leaf privet
Cornus mas	Cornelian cherry dogwood	*Liquidambar styraciflua*	Sweet gum
Corylus colurna	Turkish filbert	*Magnolia* spp.	Magnolia
Cotinus spp.	Smoke bush, smoke tree	*Nyssa sylvatica*	Sour gum
Elaeagnus angustifolia	Russian olive	*Ostrya* spp.	Hop hornbeam
Eucommia ulmoides	Hardy rubber tree	*Oxydendrum arboreum*	Sourwood
Franklinia alatamaha	Franklin tree	*Phellodendron* spp.	Cork tree
Ginkgo biloba	Maidenhair tree	*Sophora japonica*	Chinese scholar tree
Gleditsia triacanthos	Honey locust	*Stewartia* spp.	Stewartia
Gymnocladus dioicus	Kentucky coffee tree	*Styrax* spp.	Snowbell
Halesia carolina	Carolina silver bell		

EVERGREEN

Calocedrus decurrens	California incense cedar	*Juniperus* spp.	Juniper
Chamaecyparis spp.	False cypress	*Sciadopitys verticillata*	Umbrella pine

TREES FOR DRY, SANDY SOIL

DECIDUOUS

Acer negundo	Box elder	*Maclura pomifera*	Osage orange
Ailanthus altissima	Tree of heaven	*Populus alba*	White poplar
Albizia julibrissin	Mimosa, silk tree	*P. grandidentata*	Large-tooth aspen
Betula davurica	Dahurian birch	*P. tremuloides*	Quaking aspen
B. populifolia	Gray birch	*Quercus marilandica*	Blackjack oak
Broussonetia papyrifera	Paper mulberry	*Q. prinus*	Chestnut oak
Celtis australis	Hackberry	*Robinia pseudoacacia*	Black locust
Fraxinus velutina	Velvet ash	*Sassafras albidum*	Sassafras
Gleditsia triacanthos	Honey locust	*Sophora japonica*	Chinese scholar tree
Koelreuteria paniculata	Goldenrain tree	*Ulmus pumila*	Siberian elm

EVERGREEN

Cupressus macrocarpa	Monterey cypress	*Juniperus* spp.	Juniper
Eucalyptus spp., especially	Eucalyptus, gum	*Pinus banksiana*	Jack pine
E. camaldulensis,		*P. rigida*	Pitch pine
E. microtheca, and *E. rudis*		*P. virginiana*	Virginia scrub pine

TREES THAT MAKE GOOD WINDBREAKS

DECIDUOUS

Acer ginnala	Amur maple	*Crataegus mollis*	Downy hawthorn
A. negundo	Box elder	*C. phaenopyrum*	Washington hawthorn
A. platanoides	Norway maple	*Fagus* spp.	Beech
A. pseudoplatanus	Sycamore maple	*Fraxinus* spp.	Ash
A. rubrum	Red maple	*Maclura pomifera*	Osage orange
Carpinus betulus	European hornbeam	*Morus alba*	White mulberry

TREES THAT MAKE GOOD WINDBREAKS (continued)

DECIDUOUS

Populus alba	White poplar	*Q. phellos*	Willow oak
P. balsamifera	Balsam poplar	*Syringa reticulata*	Japanese tree lilac
P. tremuloides	Quaking aspen	*Tilia* spp.	Linden
Quercus imbricaria	Shingle oak	*Ulmus pumila*	Siberian elm
Q. palustris	Pin oak		

EVERGREEN

✕ *Cupressocyparis leylandii*	Leyland cypress	*Pinus nigra*	Austrian pine
Eucalyptus spp., especially	Eucalyptus, gum	*P. rigida*	Pitch pine
E. delegatensis ssp. *tasmanensis,*		*P. strobus*	Eastern white pine
E. eremophila, E. erythronema,		*P. sylvestris*	Scots pine
and *E. neglecta*		*P. thunbergii*	Japanese black pine
Juniperus virginiana	Eastern red cedar	*Thuja occidentalis*	American arborvitae
Picea abies	Norway spruce	*Tsuga canadensis*	Canada hemlock
P. glauca	White spruce	*T. caroliniana*	Carolina hemlock

TREES OF RAPID GROWTH

DECIDUOUS

Acer negundo	Box elder	*M. tripetala*	Umbrella magnolia
A. rubrum	Red maple	*Paulownia tomentosa*	Empress tree
A. saccharinum	Silver maple	*Platanus* ✕ *acerifolia*	London plane tree
Ailanthus altissima	Tree of heaven	*Populus alba*	White poplar
Betula maximowicziana	Monarch birch	*P. nigra* 'Italica'	Lombardy poplar
B. populifolia	Gray birch	*Prunus serotina*	Black cherry
Catalpa speciosa	Western catalpa	*Quercus palustris*	Pin oak
Fraxinus americana	White ash	*Robinia pseudoacacia*	Black locust
Ginkgo biloba	Maidenhair tree	*Salix alba*	White willow
Gleditsia triacanthos	Honey locust	*Sorbus aucuparia*	European mountain ash
Gymnocladus dioica	Kentucky coffee tree	*Syringa reticulata*	Japanese tree lilac
Larix decidua	European larch	*Tilia americana*	American linden
Liriodendron tulipifera	Tulip tree	*Ulmus pumila*	Siberian elm
Magnolia acuminata	Cucumber tree		

EVERGREEN

Eucalyptus spp.	Eucalyptus, gum	*P. resinosa*	Pitch pine
Picea abies	Norway spruce	*P. strobus*	White pine
Pinus rigida	Red pine		

SHADE TREES FOR STREETS

Many require special pruning while young to encourage an upright growth habit.
Many maples do not appear on this list because they heave sidewalks.

SMALL TREES (NOT EXCEEDING 30 FEET)

Acer campestre	English maple	*Halesia carolina*	Silver bell tree
A. ginnala	Amur maple	*Koelreuteria paniculata*	Goldenrain tree
Carpinus caroliniana	American hornbeam	*Syringa reticulata*	Japanese tree lilac
Crataegus phaeonopyrum	Washington hawthorn		

(continues)

SHADE TREES FOR STREETS (continued)

MEDIUM TREES (MATURING TO 30–50 FEET)

Betula nigra	River birch	*Gleditsia triacanthos* var. *inermis*	Thornless honey locust
Carpinus betulus	European hornbeam	*Ostrya virginiana*	Hop hornbeam
Cercidiphyllum japonicum	Katsura tree	*Phellodendron amurense*	Amur cork tree
Cladrastis lutea	Yellowwood	*Pyrus calleryana* 'Bradford'	Bradford callery pear
Corylus colurna	Turkish filbert	*Quercus phellos*	Willow oak
Eucommia ulmoides	Hardy rubber tree	*Sophora japonica*	Chinese scholar tree
Fraxinus pennsylvanica cv. 'Marshall's Seedless'	Seedless green ash		

TALL TREES (MATURING TALLER THAN 50 FEET)

Deciduous

Acer pseudoplatanus	Sycamore maple	*Metasequoia glyptostroboides*	Dawn redwood
Aesculus hippocastanum	Common horse chestnut	*Quercus coccinea*	Scarlet oak
A. flava (syn. *A. octandra*)	Yellow buckeye	*Q. rubra*	Red oak
Alnus glutinosa	European alder	*Taxodium distichum*	Bald cypress
Fagus sylvatica	European beech	*Tilia cordata*	Littleleaf linden
Gymnocladus dioicus	Kentucky coffee tree	*T.* × *euchlora*	Crimean linden
Liquidambar styraciflua	Sweet gum	*T. tomentosa*	Silver linden

Evergreen

Calocedrus decurrens	California incense cedar	*Eucalyptus* spp., especially *E. cinerea, E. macrandra,* and *E. platypus*	Eucalyptus, gum
Casuarina spp.	Australian pine		

DECIDUOUS TREES NOTABLE FOR FALL FOLIAGE COLORATION

PRIMARILY RED TO PURPLE

Acer palmatum	Japanese maple	*Nyssa sylvatica*	Black gum, tupelo
A. rubrum	Red maple, swamp maple	*Oxydendrum arboreum*	Sorrel tree, sourwood
A. saccharum	Sugar maple	*Parrotia persica*	Persian parrotia
A. tataricum	Tatarian maple	*Pistacia chinensis*	Chinese pistachio
Amelanchier spp.	Shadblow, serviceberry	*Prunus sargentii*	Sargent cherry
Carpinus caroliniana	Hornbeam	*Pyrus calleryana*	Callery pear
Cercidiphyllum japonicum	Katsura tree	*P. ussuriensis*	Chinese pear
Cornus florida	Flowering dogwood	*Quercus coccinea*	Scarlet oak
C. nuttallii	Pacific dogwood	*Q. palustris*	Pin oak
Crataegus × *lavallei*	Lavalle hawthorn	*Q. rubra*	Red oak
C. nitida	Glossy hawthorn	*Q. velutina*	Black oak
C. phaenopyrum	Washington thorn	*Sassafras albidum*	Sassafras
Franklinia alatamaha	Franklin tree	*Sorbus aucuparia*	European mountain ash
Liquidambar styraciflua	Sweet gum	*Stewartia* spp.	Stewartia

PRIMARILY YELLOW TO ORANGE

Acer macrophyllum	Oregon maple	*Fraxinus americana*	American ash
A. pennsylvanicum	Striped maple	*Ginkgo biloba*	Maidenhair tree
A. platanoides	Norway maple	*Halesia carolina*	Silver bell
Aesculus glabra	Ohio buckeye	*Koelreuteria paniculata*	Goldenrain tree
Asimina triloba	Pawpaw	*Liriodendron tulipifera*	Tulip tree
Betula spp.	Birch	*Metasequoia glyptostroboides*	Dawn redwood
Carya spp.	Hickory	*Populus tremuloides*	Quaking aspen
Castanea mollissima	Chinese chestnut	*Pseudolarix amabile*	Golden larch
Cercis spp.	Redbud	*Quercus alba*	White oak
Cladrastis lutea	Yellowwood	*Q. imbricaria*	Shingle oak
Fagus spp.	Beech	*Sorbus alnifolia*	Korean mountain ash

TREES FOR THE SEASHORE
Tolerant of strong wind and occasional salt spray

DECIDUOUS

Acer platanoides	Norway maple	*P. tremuloides*	Quaking aspen
A. pseudoplatanus	Sycamore maple	*Prunus maritima*	Beach plum
A. rubrum	Red maple	*P. serotina*	Black cherry
Aesculus hippocastanum	Horse chestnut	*Quercus ilicifolia*	Scrub oak
Ailanthus altissima	Tree of heaven	*Q. laurifolia*	Laurel oak
Amelanchier arborea	Shadblow, serviceberry	*Q. marilandica*	Blackjack oak
Carpinus betulus	European hornbeam	*Q. rubra*	Red oak
Crataegus crus-galli	Cockspur hawthorn	*Q. virginiana*	Live oak
C. laevigata	English hawthorn	*Robinia pseudoacacia*	Black locust
Elaeagnus angustifolia	Russian olive	*Salix alba*	White willow
Gleditsia triacanthos	Honey locust	*Sassafras albidum*	Sassafras
Nyssa sylvatica	Sour gum	*Tilia cordata*	Littleleaf linden
Platanus occidentalis	American plane tree	*T. × euchlora*	Crimean linden
Populus alba	White poplar	*Ulmus parvifolia*	Chinese elm
P. balsamifera	Carolina cottonwood	*U. pumila*	Siberian elm

EVERGREEN

Araucaria spp.	Norfolk Island pine	*P. pungens* var. *glauca*	Colorado blue spruce
Casuarina spp.	Australian pine	*Pinus nigra*	Austrian pine
Cryptomeria japonica	Japanese cedar	*P. pinaster*	Cluster pine
Cupressus macrocarpa	Monterey cypress	*P. rigida*	Pitch pine
Eucalyptus lehmannii	Lehmann mallee, bushy yate	*P. sylvestris*	Scots pine
Juniperus virginiana	Eastern red cedar	*P. thunbergii*	Japanese black pine
Magnolia grandiflora	Southern magnolia	*Quercus virginiana*	Live oak
Picea abies	Norway spruce	*Thuja occidentalis*	American arborvitae
P. glauca	White spruce		

Oregon maple (*Acer macrophyllum*)

Scots pine (*Pinus sylvestris*)

Japanese maple (*Acer palmatum*) in fall

Horse chestnut (*Aesculus hippocastanum*)

12

Shrubs

Second in importance only to trees, shrubs are a vital component of gardens and landscape plantings. Of the several thousand kinds of shrubs cultivated for ornament in temperate-zone regions around the world, only a small minority are available locally, and of those, just a relative handful dominate any local market and, therefore, our gardens, borders, foundation plantings, parks, street sides, and commercial areas.

*A clump of forsythia (*Forsythia × intermedia *'Lynwood'), its uppermost canes bending in the wind, is a traditional herald of spring.*

Considering the many purposes served by shrubs, the catalog should be much more diverse. More favored than deciduous kinds are broad-leaf and coniferous evergreens, especially for foundation plantings, even though the latter group is devoid of showy flowers and fruit and carries a high price tag.

Unfortunately, the common practice of impulsively buying flowering shrubs only in the spring when they are in bloom is reflected in our urban and suburban landscape scene: A great crescendo of forsythia and lilac, followed by rhododendron and azalea, reaches a climax in early to mid spring, to the exclusion of most other kinds, and with little else before or after. Yet with a little study and investigation, a plan can be devised that will offer a succession of ornamental shrubs in flower from winter through fall, some redolent in bright foliage in fall or retaining colored fruit through most of the winter, and many offering interesting architecture even in leafless dormancy.

Shrubs form the intermediate plantings on the home property. They are in scale with people. They may be used with restraint and distinction in the planting about the house; they may be used as low ornamental hedges to define the boundary of the property; they may be used as specimen plants where the beauty of their bloom or foliage can be enjoyed to advantage; and they may be planted in groups or as borders to bring a variety of form, bloom, and autumn coloring into the landscape picture. They also provide a nesting place and perhaps even some berries or other food for birds. They may be used as a background for tall perennials and lilies, and some of the smaller shrubs may be used in rock gardens to give character and form to the planting. Some types may be grown in tubs or planting boxes for decorative effect on the terrace or patio, and others, such as the firethorn (*Pyracantha coccinea*) and the wintercreeper (*Euonymus fortunei* var. *radicans*), can be trained to grow against masonry walls.

Although individual stems may die and be replaced, most shrubs are long lived and, like trees, are considered a permanent or longtime investment. However, most kinds mature in a very few years and thus begin early to pay dividends. Four or five years after planting, a shrub border or a boundary screen should usually be high and dense enough to conceal whatever lies behind it, and mature enough to bear blossoms and fruit in profusion.

Before winter is really over, some shrubs are already in bloom, followed by others that carry on through the season until autumn frosts or even later. However, the great majority of shrubs bloom in spring or early summer. From midsummer on it is rare to find more than the occasional shrub in flower. However, by careful selection, the gardener in all but the northernmost regions can have some shrubs in bloom almost every season except the coldest periods of winter. Shrubs with interesting fruit begin to produce it in late June or July, and the succession continues without intermission through midwinter and even early spring. Some of the fruits are striking in color—red, purple, orange, yellow, or blue—while others are only dry capsules but interesting nonetheless because of their form or texture. Fruits of many shrubs are frequently used for indoor flower arrangements. Color, form, texture, line—all the essentials of composition—are to be found in twigs and fruit as well as in leaves and blossoms of shrubs. The leaves of numerous shrubs turn brilliant colors in the autumn, with some of the viburnums, enkianthus, and euonymus rivaling the sugar maple.

Like any other type of plant, shrubs should be adapted to the soil and other conditions of the site. Some shrubs thrive in dry soil, others in wet, while the majority prefer a soil that is midway between the two. Some respond to cultivation and enrichment of the soil; others prefer a meager diet. Some are hardy on exposed summits; others require protection from the wind. Some grow well in shade, while most prefer plenty of sunshine. And then there is an easily satisfied group of shrubs that seems at home in any environment. All of these factors, while they may somewhat limit the use of some shrubs, also enlarge the possibilities of others.

SELECTION OF SHRUBS

The selection of shrubs for a garden site may be approached in various ways. Often the existing conditions of the site are (and very often must be) accepted, and only the shrubs that thrive in those conditions are used. Or existing conditions are modified to make possible a wider range in the use of shrubs. Sometimes conditions cannot be changed except at great expense. Sometimes it requires time to effect the change. But usually growing conditions may be improved by the application of organic matter and fertilizer, by cultivation and the removal of grass and weeds, by drainage or by irrigation. If the second method is used, shrubs may be selected solely for their quality and for their special contributions to the general composition. For methods of modifying acidity or alkalinity of the soil, altering drainage, and increasing fertility and organic matter content, see Chapter 31.

All too commonly, however, shrubs are selected uncritically and planted without regard for their adaptability or long-term suitability. A shrub so chosen may languish for lack of a key requirement, such as sun exposure or adequate soil moisture, or may soon overwhelm a small setting with exuberant growth. The latter condition frequently leads to ritual periodic shearing, usually at the sacrifice of graceful natural habit. Routine pruning or shearing to restrict a shrub's size betrays a poor choice for that particular location.

If we insist on having rhododendrons and azaleas on a bare open site with alkaline or neutral soil, then we will have to make changes: underdrain the soil, plant oak trees for shade and for acidity of soil add humus and leaf mold to the soil, and mulch, every year with a carpet of oak leaves. Only when these new conditions are established can we plant rhododendrons and laurel with any possibility of success.

If such changes will impose a high degree of repetitive maintenance or involve environmentally unsound practices, it is wise to consider alternative choices of shrubs.

If we accept existing conditions without making any changes, we must be content with the shrubs that grow under such conditions. So long as conditions are favorable, with an ordinary garden soil, some sun, not too much shade, and protection from wind, then the range of selection is very wide and our choice can be made entirely on climatic and aesthetic considerations.

Even if conditions seem a good deal less than optimal, it is safe to say that a surprising diversity of horticulturally useful kinds of shrubs is available commercially, providing time and care are taken to shop carefully in mail-order catalogs and at reputable nurseries.

The cultural requirements of all shrubs to be used in a planting scheme must be thoroughly understood before final selections can be determined or decisions made about the extent to which the site should be modified. The most critical factor is each shrub's ability to adapt to the existing or modified soil conditions. This includes tolerance of varying degrees of soil acidity or alkalinity (pH), availability or lack of moisture during various periods of the year (including whether the plant can withstand the extremes of these conditions), and the ability to grow well in various types of soil—sandy, gravelly, clayey, loamy, or any mixture of these. The manner in which a plant can adapt to varying degrees of sunlight and shade is equally important and will affect such characteristics as general vigor, height, habit or growth, heaviness of flowering and fruiting, and to some extent, hardiness. Other environmental and special site conditions to be considered include the resistance of the shrub to strong winds, glaring or reflected sunlight, snow or ice damage, and atmospheric pollution.

Matching a shrub's cultural requirements to existing or modified site conditions is only half the problem, however. No planting scheme will be ultimately successful if the shrubs fail to perform the function intended for them in the landscape. Prior knowledge of the habit of growth, height, and spread at maturity, and of flowering or fruiting characteristics, is essential and can save the home owner considerable disappointment or expense later on.

It is especially desirable, when space for planting is limited, to choose kinds that offer multiple benefits. Some shrubs, such as mock orange (*Philadelphus*), deutzia, and weigela, have very attractive flowers for a few weeks in the spring, but undistinguished foliage during the growing season and no ornamental fruits, autumn leaf color, handsome stems, or outstanding interest during the winter. On smaller properties we must live in intimate contact with shrubs the whole year round and those that possess ornamental features during two or more seasons are consequently much more rewarding. Interesting fruit, foliage, twig and bark characteristics, autumn color, and habit of growth are equally as important as heavy flowering. Few shrubs possess all these combinations, but the more combinations they do have, the greater will be their value in the landscape.

Knowledge of the various shrubs' ornamental characteristics will lead to further rewards when one is trying to select and combine shrubs that will provide pleasing seasonal or year-round contrasts. Interesting shapes may be juxtaposed one against another, attractive combinations of flower and fruit colors may be arranged, leaf shapes and textures may be used to create special effects, combinations of evergreen and deciduous shrubs may help liven the winter landscape, and shrubs with interesting or unique habits of growth may be used to create accents and focal points.

Selecting shrubs may be likened to selecting furnishings for a room. No one kind of shrub will suit all purposes or settings, and no one kind, however magnificent it may be at the moment of maximum display, is without certain attributes that can lessen its desirability. Shrubs under consideration should be seen and studied from all points of view and finally chosen with great care. Glowing descriptions in textbooks or nursery catalogs serve only as an introduction. Seldom are caveats or limitations pointed out. There is no substitute for actually seeing the plant beforehand, especially when it is at full maturity and preferably in as many seasons of the year as possible. Numerous opportunities for such studies exist. Examples of ornamental plantings in your own neighborhood make a good starting point. Conspicuous instances of successes and failures are easy to find. Local public parks, tours of private gardens and estates open to the public, and the display plantings of local nurseries and garden centers are good places to study various shrubs. Visits to botanic gardens, arboreta, and display gardens can be most rewarding, especially as the materials on display are usually labeled. In such gardens, shrubs may be planted among their close relatives, and opportunities exist to make comparisons between the ornamental value of the different kinds. Often, too, shrubs may be seen in such gardens at full maturity in uncrowded settings. The specimens displayed have withstood the test of time and climate and frequently represent the best species and cultivated varieties adapted to the local area.

PLANTING AND TRANSPLANTING SHRUBS

Each planting season has its advantages. Except for the very early spring-flowering shrubs, spring transplanting is preferred by many gardeners because it gives the plants increasingly good growing weather in which to reestablish themselves. However, spring is a busy time for all gardeners, and in apportioning the year's work, it often is advisable to plan the transplanting of new shrubs and trees in the autumn when such work may be spread over a longer period of good transplanting weather. In sections of the country from the shores of Chesapeake Bay southward through the coastal plains to Texas, in the central valley of California, and on the coast of Oregon, transplanting operations are safely carried on throughout the winter months because many parts of these regions have six months of continuous good transplanting weather. In colder portions of the Northeast, Midwest, and the Plains states, the seasons for transplanting are very short, September and May for evergreens and September through October and April and May for deciduous plants.

Shrubs that should be moved only in spring include *Buddleia*, *Abelia*, and *Magnolia* (very early). Shrubs that are best moved in the autumn include *Chaenomeles japonica*, *Cornus mas*, and *Hamamelis vernalis*.

Shrubs Balled and Burlapped

Shrubs that have been field grown in the nursery and purchased with balls of soil about the roots should be transplanted either in early spring, which is the more favorable time or, depending on the region and the kind of shrub, in the autumn. See "Transplanting Trees" on page 170 for procedures with balled-and-burlapped material.

Container-Grown Shrubs

It is standard practice for nurseries and garden centers to sell shrubs that have been raised in containers of various sorts. In many instances such plants have spent their entire life in the container but sometimes they have been field grown and transplanted into the container a season or two before sale. Shrubs obtained in this manner may be planted almost any time during the growing season, as the shock of transplanting can be reduced to a minimum. When selecting container-grown plants, be sure that plenty of healthy new vigorous growth is in evidence. This will indicate that the plant has not been kept in the container too long and that it has been well fed and continuously well watered in the nursery. Shrubs that have been kept in their containers too long, or those that have had their growth seriously checked by inadequate watering and fertilizing, often take one or more seasons to recover and grow vigorously when planted in their final site in the garden.

Water the plant thoroughly a few hours before it is removed from the container for planting. Upon removal, examine the root system carefully. If dense masses of roots are found at the perimeter of the soil mass, they should be pried gently apart before the plant is set into its hole. If the roots are especially dense and tangled, they should be cut with a knife. Make several slits no larger than ¼ inch into the root mass around the ball; each slit should run vertically from top to bottom and should be parallel to the next. Whether to separate the outermost roots by hand or to cut them with a knife depends on the severity of the crowding. This is a very important operation, however, as it will ensure that new roots grow out into the surrounding soil, rather than remain a tight, eventually strangling, knot of encircling roots. Planting methods for container-grown shrubs are otherwise similar to those for balled-and-burlapped shrubs and trees. Pruning need not be as severe, but if a considerable amount of root disturbance has been necessary, then the tops should be cut back correspondingly by one-fourth or one-third.

Bare-Root Shrubs

Shrubs that have been purchased with bare roots from nurseries or mail-order sources should be planted immediately on receipt. Delivery should be arranged so that the plants arrive in early spring, while they are still dormant and just before new growth commences. If the ground is still frozen when the plant arrives or if the weather does not permit immediate planting, then the plants should be stored indoors in a cool (35 to 45°F), shady place and the roots kept well covered and damp. Thoroughly moistened (but not soggy) burlap, peat, or sphagnum moss makes an ideal covering for this purpose. Soaking the roots for an hour or so in a bucket of water soon after receipt will help the plants to recover the moisture inevitably lost in shipping. If for any reason bare-rooted shrubs must be left longer than a week before planting, they should be placed in trenches out of doors and the roots covered with soil. This procedure, called heeling in (see photo on page 211 for more detailed instructions), should be done in a sheltered, shady place. A coldframe, if available, is ideal for this purpose.

Making the Move

Many shrubs may be moved from one location in the garden to another with bare roots, especially while young. Older, well-established plants with an extensive root system (especially broad-leaf evergreens and conifers) should be carefully dug and balled and burlapped. This method requires more time and effort but involves less risk than moving shrubs with bare roots. Early spring, just before the onset of new growth, is the best time for either of these procedures, with early autumn being a second preference.

The following shrubs are usually difficult to transplant and should be handled by the method recommended for each.

Ceanothus spp.	Balled and burlapped
Corylus spp.	Balled and burlapped
Cotoneaster spp.	Potted plants
Exochorda spp.	Balled and burlapped
Ilex spp.	Balled and burlapped
Magnolia spp.	Balled and burlapped
Myrica spp.	Balled and burlapped
Pyracantha coccinea	Potted plants
Rhamnus spp.	Balled and burlapped
Rhododendron spp. (including azaleas),	
Kalmia spp., and other broad-leaf evergreens	
small	Potted plants
large	Balled and burlapped
Tamarix spp.	Balled and burlapped
Viburnum spp.	Balled and burlapped

The procedures for digging, moving, planting, and transplanting bare-root shrubs and for balling and burlapping are the same as those for trees (see Chapter 11). The same general precautions as for trees are taken to get the plants into the ground as soon as possible, to water soon after planting and frequently thereafter, to prune back to compensate for root loss, to provide shade at first, and to mulch the ground about the more tender ones. Shrubs will stand even more pruning than seems necessary for trees. It is the roots that count most at first, and healthy roots will send up enough new shoots to balance the intake and evaporation of moisture. If the shrubs are not pruned enough when first transplanted, the tops will wilt and gradually die back. Much more severe pruning may then be required to save the plants. As a rule of thumb, approximately one-fourth to one-third of the branches and twigs should be removed; the exact amount depends on the severity of the root loss. Entire branches should be removed to ground level, rather than giving the plant a "haircut." Large shrubs that tend to form only a few main leaders, such as magnolias and hollies, should be pruned by thinning the side branches. Cutting back the leaders will ruin the habit of growth of these shrubs.

Some shrubs are much more subject to wilting after transplanting than others. The honeysuckles (*Lonicera* spp.) are particularly fast wilters and should not be transplanted while in leaf. Forsythia, on the other hand, is very tolerant and may be moved while in full flower.

The best days for transplanting are cloudy, cool days, with a high degree of humidity and no wind. Seldom are we able to pick ideal weather, however, and reasonable precautions against the rapid drying of stems and roots must be taken if satisfactory results are to be obtained.

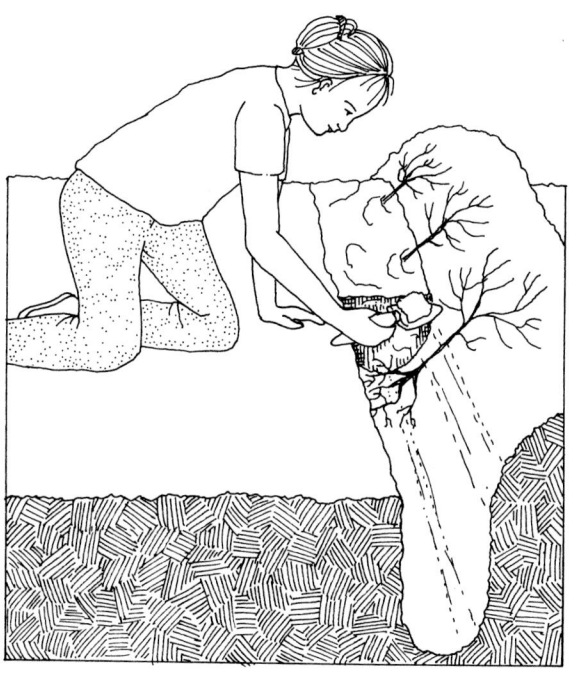

Heeling in

Transplanting is a shock to the plant, even if the person doing the job solemnly swears that "the thing will never know it has been moved." Unless the humidity of the air is 90 percent or more, the plant is losing moisture all the time it is out of the ground, not only through its stems and leaves but, what is more harmful, through its roots. Dried roots cause more failures after transplanting than any other factor. Whatever precaution we can take to prevent or retard this loss of moisture will reduce the effect of the shock on the recovery of the plant. With small boxwood (*Buxus* spp.), no trimming of stems and branches is necessary because of the dense mat of roots that have remained intact in the ball. The plant should be watered thoroughly at first and frequently throughout the remainder of the season, ending with a generous soaking in midautumn. This autumn watering is especially important for rhododendrons, azaleas, mountain laurels, and broad-leaf evergreens in general. These plants all continue to lose moisture through their leaves during the winter, and chances for survival are increased if they have a ready supply of water before the winter freezing of the soil surface about their roots sets in. Once the ground surface has frozen, rain or irrigation water will not penetrate.

Preparation of Beds for Planting

Areas to be planted with shrubs should be plowed or dug to a depth of 12 inches and the soil thoroughly broken up and loosened. Well-rotted manure should be worked into the soil by forking. Heavy soils may be improved by the addition of sandy loam to facilitate water penetration, and sandy soil should have an application of humus or decomposed vegetable matter to replace leached-out nutrients and increase moisture retention. The whole planting bed should thus be prepared, not merely little pockets where each shrub is to go. After all, this preparation and improvement of the soil is the last this area is likely to receive for many years and good soil well beyond the reach of existing roots is essential to the robust growth of any shrub.

The real test of success in transplanting shrubs that have been moved comes the second year after planting, following the winter. Providing the shrub is planted within its zones of hardiness and has regenerated enough of its root system the first summer to offset the inexorable loss of water through stems and any foliage that is retained in winter, second-year growth should be vigorous. Newly transplanted evergreens may be helped through the first winter with a baffle of burlap to mitigate cold, drying northwest winds; with a slatted A-frame to moderate the strong southern sun of late winter, or with a sprayed-on desiccation retardant. The importance of nutrient-rich soil around the roots of the newly planted shrub cannot be too strongly emphasized.

PRUNING

The primary purpose of pruning most shrubs is to keep them vigorous and to maintain their blooming ability. This is done by removing old wood, and with it the parts of the stems that no longer bloom freely. The healthy, active root system will then stimulate new top growth the following year and thus increase the quantity of stems that bear blossoms. This is particularly effective with spireas, lilacs, hydrangeas, mock oranges, shrub honeysuckles, and many other deciduous shrubs.

Many gardeners seem to think that the way to prune shrubs is to cut off all the branches to an even length. This

*Golden Bumald spirea (*Spirea × bumalda *'Gold Flame'), with youngest foliage coppery reds, fading to light yellow-green.*

"haircut" treatment ruins the grace of the shrub and frequently diminishes its vitality or flower production. Proper pruning technique calls for cutting weak, overcrowded, and dead branches to their bases and each year removing only about one-fifth or one-fourth of the entire mass. The purpose of this kind of pruning is to give new stems a better opportunity to develop from the base, thus maintaining the natural shape of the shrub.

If shrubs have to be pruned to keep them from growing too large for their specific location, then the wrong shrubs were selected for the planting scheme. If this is the case, such shrubs should then be transplanted to more ample surroundings and their place taken by suitably smaller ones.

In some shrubs, individual stems or canes may live only a few years, but are replaced successively by new growth arising from the base. Such shrubs need annual pruning to remove dead or dying stems. Included here are deutzia (*Deutzia* spp.), hydrangea (*Hydrangea* spp.), privet (*Ligustrum* spp.), mock orange (*Philadelphus* spp.) butterfly bush (*Buddleia davidii*), spiraea (*Spiraea* spp.), snowberry (*Symphoricarpos albus*), tamarisk (*Tamarix* spp.), kerria (*Kerria japonica*), and shrubby dogwoods (*Cornus* spp.).

Other shrubs frequently winter kill, especially in the north, and will need a spring clearing of dead stems. These include some of the shrubs listed above as well as glossy abelia (*Abelia* × *grandiflora*), beauty-berry (*Callicarpa* spp.), fringe bush (*Chionanthus* spp.), winter hazel (*Corylopsis* spp.), broom (*Cytisus* spp.), shrubby St. John'swort (*Hypericum* spp.), beauty-bush (*Kolkwitzia amabilis*), winter jasmine (*Jasminum nudiflorum*), hollygrape (*Mahonia* spp.), andromeda (*Pieris japonica*), and some azaleas (*Rhododendron* spp.).

Some shrubs benefit from removal of flower heads after blooming and before seeds are set. Whether this practice, traditionally known as "dead-heading," promotes increased growth and flowering for the next season is open to question, but in some cases, such as lilacs, there is an unquestioned aesthetic gain. Other kinds routinely dead-headed include rhododendron, mountain laurel, butterfly bush, and star magnolia.

A number of shrubs, such as red-osier dogwood (*Cornus sericea*) and coralberry (*Symphoricarpos orbiculatus*) sucker insistently from superficial runners or node-rooting horizontal trailing shoots, which should be removed as they appear if copse formation is to be prevented. Common lilac (*Syringa vulgaris*) is especially insistent in its formation of suckers from the roots. Maintaining a lilac in optimal flowering condition requires annual removal of suckers. In old lilacs, the oldest stems may show signs of failing, in which case one or two strong suckers may be allowed to develop and replace a dying stem.

Some shrubs may be cut to within a few inches of the ground and will regenerate stems from the roots. This should be done only when they have become hopelessly overgrown or leggy and are beyond restoration through less drastic pruning. In addition to lilac, sumac (*Rhus* spp.), shrubby honeysuckle (*Lonicera* spp.), privet (*Ligustrum* spp.), forsythia (*Forsythia* spp.), and bayberry (*Myrica pennsylvanica*) respond well to such treatment.

On the whole, shrubs show great vitality. Many will withstand utter neglect and even much abuse, living for years without attention. Those that are particularly self-reliant are the forsythias, shrubby honeysuckles, shrubby St. John'swort, and sumacs as well as the barberries (*Berberis* spp.), rugosa rose (*Rosa rugosa*), viburnums (*Viburnum* spp.), chokeberries (*Aronia* spp.), shrubby cinquefoil (*Potentilla fruticosa*), and broad-leaf evergreens in general.

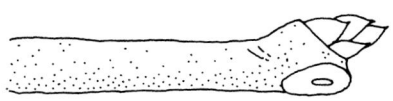

Correct cut

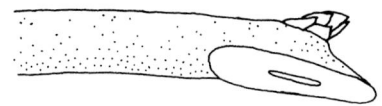

Too slanting

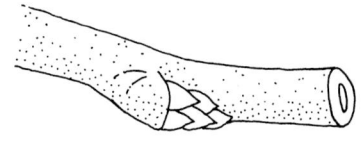

Too far

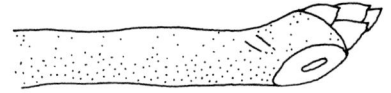

Too close

Twig pruning

Shrub in need of pruning

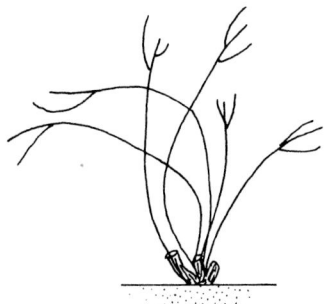

Correct pruning

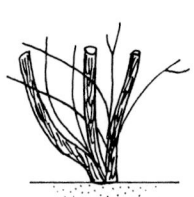

Incorrect pruning

Pruning an established shrub

Timing in the pruning of shrubs is vital. The best time to prune depends on individual flowering habits. Those shrubs that bear blossoms on *new* growth in late spring or summer should be pruned in early spring or during the last weeks of winter. In this category are the following genera:

Abelia (glossy abelia)
Berberis (barberry)
Buddleia (butterfly bush)
Callicarpa (beauty-berry)

Beauty-berry (*Callicarpa bodnieri* 'Profusion')

Caryopteris (bluebeard)
Ceanothus (New Jersey tea)
Clethra (sweet pepperbush)
Colutea (bladder senna)
Eleutherococcus (five-leaf aralia)
Hibiscus (rose of Sharon)
Hydrangea
Hypericum (shrubby St. John'swort)
Indigofera (shrubby indigo)
Kerria
Lagerstroemia (crape myrtle)
Lespedeza (bush clover)
Ligustrum (privet)

Lonicera (shrubby honeysuckle)
Neillia
Rhus (sumac)
Rosa (rose)
Salix (shrubby willow)
Spiraea (summer-flowering spiraea)
Staphylea (bladdernut)
Stephanandra
Tamarix (late-flowering tamarisk)
Vitex (chaste bush)

Shrubs that bear blossoms on *last year's* wood should be pruned soon after blooming. In this group, flower buds have been formed late in the previous growing season, and heavy winter or early spring pruning will remove many potential flowers that could otherwise be enjoyed during the spring. Pruning after flowering will not only prevent the formation of seed but in the case of some plants such pruning even improves their appearance. In this group are the following genera:

Caragana (pea tree, pea bush)
Cercis (redbud)
Chaenomeles (flowering quince)
Chionanthus (fringe bush)
Cytisus (broom)
Deutzia
Exochorda (pearlbush)
Forsythia
Magnolia (shrubby magnolia)
Philadelphus (mock orange)
Rhododendron (azalea)
Ribes (flowering currant)
Rosa (climbing rose)
Spiraea (spring-flowering spiraea)
Tamarix (spring-flowering tamarisk)
Viburnum

A few shrubs should be pruned lightly after blooming and again lightly in early spring. Some examples follow.

Cornus alba 'Sibirica' (red-stem dogwood)
C. racemosa (gray dogwood)
C. stolonifera 'Flaviramea' (yellow-stem dogwood)
Lonicera (shrubby honeysuckle)
Sambucus (elder)
Spiraea × bumalda (Bumald spiraea)
Symphoricarpos (snowberry, coralberry)
Viburnum opulus (European cranberry bush)
V. plicatum (double-file viburnum)
Weigela

Dwarf European Cranberry Bush
(*Viburnum opulus* 'Compactum')

WINTER PROTECTION

There are so many kinds of hardy shrubs from which to choose that there seems little justification in trying to maintain species that are not really hardy in your region. Those that may be induced to survive the winters by protecting them and that reward the gardener for this extra care are rare indeed, for an occasional exceptionally severe winter may make the protection of no avail.

The need for special winter protection is greatly reduced whenever broad-leaf evergreens can be planted in sites that do not experience excessive amounts of sunlight and wind in winter. Damage can be especially severe on such exposed sites during late February and March while the ground is still frozen and the sunlight is becoming more intense.

One of the most satisfactory methods of providing winter protection for broad-leaf evergreens or newly planted conifers is the use of plastic sprays known as antidesiccants (see page 168). The thin film of spray should be applied to the leaves and twigs between mid-November and early December. It is important to cover the undersurfaces of the leaves as thoroughly as possible because most moisture is lost by transpiration through the stomata, or pores, located in these areas. Roots cannot absorb enough moisture to replace the loss while the ground is frozen around them. The result of this imbalance is dieback, and it can be severe in newly transplanted shrubs with shallow roots.

For the protection of half-hardy shrubs, of broad-leaf evergreens in a very windy site, or of newly planted shrubs, some shelter from wind is advisable, and a windscreen should be constructed. This may be made of any material that will remain in place and not rot. Commercially manufactured straw mats are often used. These are usually available at garden centers, and they can be rolled up and put away at the end of the season and used year after year. Burlap tacked securely onto lath frames set about 1 foot out from the plant and surrounding it completely (but not covering it) is also very satisfactory, as is wire-mesh fencing made with an overlay of polyethylene plastic sheeting. Whatever method is chosen, it is important not to wrap protective material—particularly plastic—too tightly around the shrub. In such cases, winter sun will heat the shrub under the wrapping, creating a "greenhouse" effect. A sudden lowering of the temperature when the sun goes down can produce heavy damage to plant tissues, and plants "protected" by this method frequently are killed outright.

The winter screen should not be removed in the spring until all danger of a return to winter conditions has passed. In many regions, March and early April are especially trying, as brilliant sunshine, frozen ground, and frequent high wind create a water-supply stress that a well-designed, carefully placed shield can mitigate. It should be remembered that the purpose of such a measure is to conserve the moisture in the shrub's tissues, not to protect it from the cold.

Winter protection is often of great value for newly planted evergreen shrubs, such as rhododendrons, hollies, leucothoës, and hollygrapes, and as a general practice it is wise to provide some protection for two years following transplanting.

Some shrubs suffer seriously from the weight of heavy wet snow on their branches. Boxwood is particularly subject to such injury and suffers also from the action of sunshine on melted snow that has refrozen to form ice. In many parts of the country it is, therefore, wise to construct wood frames around the bushes and cover them with heavy canvas, burlap, chicken wire, or even cornstalks to prevent the snow from falling on the foliage and branches. If no covering is provided, careful vigilance should be practiced, and snow should be swept from branches as soon as it has fallen. A coating of ice on the branches, however, should be left alone. Attempts to remove it may only increase the chances of breaking the branches.

Breakage from heavy wet snow, ice, or a combination of these conditions—as, for example, when a load of snow and ice slides off a roof and crashes on the shrubbery below—accompanied by high winds can cause severe damage to the branches of large shrubs, or they are frequently bent or broken beyond redemption. To prevent this from happening, sloping roofs above shrub beds should be equipped with cleats to hold the snow.

Shrubs of Special Merit

ABELIA × GRANDIFLORA
(Glossy abelia)

Zones (6–9; less hardy to Zone 5)

Evergreen in zones 8 and 9 and semi-evergreen elsewhere, glossy abelia has a refined habit of growth. The foliage is glossy and becomes somewhat coppery in tone, especially in winter. The small, white, tubular flowers are borne in terminal clusters and continue from early summer through autumn. Densely twiggy in habit, glossy abelia at maturity will reach a height of about 6 feet. Scarcely exceeded for prolonged season of bloom, it is useful in shrub borders, in foundation plantings, or as a specimen. It also makes good unclipped hedge. Several hybrids and cultivars offer variations in habit and in color of foliage and flowers.

Glossy abelia does best on moist garden loam of average fertility in full sun to partial shade. It requires light pruning annually to remove dead wood and to maintain its naturally graceful form. The pruning is best done in late winter or early spring. The shrub is free of pests and diseases.

ACER GINNALA
(Amur maple)

Zones 2–8

The Amur maple is an extremely hardy and densely leafy large shrub or small tree that is especially useful for screening purposes or for specimen planting. It matures at 15 to 20 feet. The leaves are only 3 inches long and turn bright scarlet in the fall. The winged fruits (called samaras) redden in summer while the foliage is still green.

Amur maple grows well on virtually any soil so long as it is reasonably moist. It performs equally well in full sun or partial shade, is particularly resistant to high wind, and is largely free of pests and diseases. Topping young plants induces a denser, more shrubby habit. As maples in general tend to bleed sap profusely if cut in spring, it is best to do any pruning, including topping, in fall or early to midwinter, before sap flow resumes.

AUCUBA JAPONICA
(Japanese laurel)

Zones (6) 7–10

A reliable evergreen shrub maturing 6 to 10 feet tall, Japanese laurel is especially valued in the South for its thick, glossy 3- to 8-inch-long leaves (the length depending on the cultivar). The brilliant red berries are very effective in winter, but both male and female plants must be present for their production. The typical form has green leaves, while the leaves of the popular gold-dust bush (*A. japonica* 'Variegata') are mottled yellow. Several cultivars are available, differing in sex, size, leaf form, and degree of variegation. All are pest and disease free.

Average loam that retains moisture well and light to heavy shade suit Japanese laurel best. The leaves may blanch or burn in full sun and/or high wind in winter. It is easily transplanted, but requires consistent soil moisture. Pruning, if needed at all, is best restricted to the removal of dead or falling branches or to wayward, rangy shoots, which may be cut out anytime.

BERBERIS JULIANAE
(Wintergreen barberry)

Zones 5–8

One of the best of the hardy evergreen barberries, with dense glossy foliage and a height at maturity of 6 to 8 feet, the wintergreen barberry is a dependable background shrub. Its intensely thorny stems account for its use as a barrier hedge. Yellow flowers are borne in conspicuous clusters in spring. These are followed by black berries covered with a gray-blue bloom. This species is pest and disease free.

Wintergreen barberry adapts to most any soil of average fertility. Full sun is best, but it will perform satisfactorily in partial shade. Aside from the thorns complicating handling, this shrub is easily planted, quick to become established, and receptive to pruning in any season.

BERBERIS THUNBERGII
(Japanese barberry)

Zones 4–7 (8)

The Japanese barberry is one of the most rugged and versatile shrubs for the garden. It has a very dense habit of growth, thorny branches, and bright red berries that are retained throughout the winter. Nearly oblivious to soil conditions except in the extreme, it can be grown as a specimen plant, a clipped formal, or unclipped unformal hedge, in the shrub border, or as dense cover on banks that are difficult to maintain. The species attains heights of 4 to 7 feet, depending on location. There are many cultivars, including 'Atropurpurea', with reddish leaves (reddish green in shaded locations); 'Erecta', with an upright habit of growth; 'Aurea', with bright yellow leaves; and 'Crimson Pygmy', a red-leaf form that grows to only 2 or 2½ feet and is most useful as a woody ground cover or low hedge. Numerous other cultivars include further variations in foliage color and habit.

Japanese barberry grows at least satisfactorily in virtually any soil and is drought tolerant. Full sun yields the best results, especially for cultivars with purple, red, or yellow leaves, but the typical green-leaved form grows well in partial shade. Dense shade results in thin, wispy growth. When dormant, Japanese barberry may be moved bare root. Pruning may be done at any time of year.

BUDDLEIA DAVIDII
(Butterfly bush)

Zones (5) 6–9

The butterfly bush is a welcome addition to any planting, as it blooms during the summer months when few other shrubs are in flower. The foliage is a soft gray-green and the tall, slender wandlike branches are gracefully arched. The beautiful fragrant flowers are borne in terminal clusters and are violet purple (or white) with a small orange eye. The flowering period extends from early July well into the autumn. It can reach 12 feet in height and nearly as much in spread, but is easily kept smaller. The butterfly bush is excellent as a source of cut flowers. Among the numerous cultivars 'Charming', with pink flowers; 'Dubonnet', with dark purple flowers; and 'Empire Blue', with deep blue flowers are especially good.

North of zone 7, butterfly bush often dies to the ground in severe winters, but quickly rebounds, behaving very like a herbaceous perennial and flowering generously on growth of the season. Indeed, young plants often flower the first year from seed.

Butterfly bush succeeds on any moist but well-drained soil of average fertility. Full sun is essential for good flowering. The shrub is very easily raised from seed and readily transplanted. Pruning should be done in spring as it leafs out.

BUXUS MICROPHYLLA
(Littleleaf box)

Zones 5–9

Hardier than the more popular common box, littleleaf box is slow growing, has a compact habit, and seldom exceeds 3 feet in height. The cultivar 'Compacta' never grows over 1 foot high, but with age attains a spread of 2 to 4 feet. Pruning is optional; unpruned plants remain densely leafy and fairly symmetrical in form. Full sun to partial shade (especially in the South) and well-drained soil, preferably somewhat acid and mulched to retain moisture in summer and stabilize temperatures throughout the year, yield the best results.

Cultivars of *B. microphylla* var. *japonica* (e.g., 'Green Beauty', 'Green Gem', 'Green Velvet', and 'Green Mountain') maintain a rich green color through the winter and are useful alternatives to the often overused *Ilex crenata* (Japanese holly). Numerous dwarf cultivars are favorites for the rock garden. Littleleaf box is relatively free of pests and diseases.

BUXUS MICROPHYLLA VAR. KOREANA
(Korean box)

Zones 4–8

Hardiest of all the littleleaf boxes, Korean box has foliage that turns an unattractive yellowish brown in winter. However, several cultivars (e.g., 'Tide Hill' and 'Wintergreen') retain green foliage year round and are more compact in habit. These are the preferred cultivars to choose as low-maintenance edging plants in areas where hardiness is uncertain for other boxes. Unsheared, Korean box eventually reaches 3 feet, but it is easily kept as low as 1 foot with annual shearing in late spring or summer.

Korean box does best with moist, slightly acidic, well-drained sandy loam

in locations exposed to full sun or with partial shade. Extraordinarily tolerant of harsh winter wind, it requires little care, other than an annual grooming and adequate water during the first summer or two after planting.

BUXUS SEMPERVIRENS
(Common box, boxwood)

Zones (5) 6–9

Beloved and cherished in the gardens of our ancestors, common, or true, box is as highly appreciated now as it ever has been, especially in Virginia, Maryland, and the Carolinas, where the climate is particularly favorable for this shrub. Fine textured and evergreen, it retains its deep green color and freshness throughout the year. Under optimal conditions, heights of 15 to 20 feet may be seen, but most plantings are maintained much lower by annual shearing. The distinctive odor emitted by box foliage is disliked by some, but it is seldom truly objectionable.

Numerous cultivars are available, differing in habit, height, leaf color, leaf size, and hardiness. The following are some of the more popular ones.

'Handsworthiensis': an excellent hedge plant; dark green foliage; a wide upright habit of growth; slow growing.
'Newport Blue': very attractive bluish green foliage; a dense, rounded habit of growth.
'Suffruticosa': used for edging flower beds; very slow growing; compact; fragrant leaves.
'Vardar Valley': undoubtedly the hardiest cultivar of common box (suited to zone 5); very slow growing; does not exceed 2 to 2½ feet in height; much broader than tall.
'Pendula': tall growing, to 15 feet; pendulous branches.
'Argenteo-variegata': leaves variegated with white.
'Aureo-variegata': leaves variegated with yellow.

Common box grows best in rich, moist, humusy loam over a porous subsoil but is adaptable to other soil profiles. Partial shade is the best exposure in the North, with more shade in the South;

but full sun to fairly dense shade has yielded satisfactory performance throughout its range. Common box is easily transplanted and established, as it has a compact, fibrous root system. Pruning or shearing is best done in late spring or summer.

CALLICARPA DICHOTOMA
(Purple beauty-berry)

Zones 5–8

Purple beauty-berry is a low, twiggy shrub up to 4 feet tall. Its arching branches bear clusters of tiny pinkish cream flowers among the leaves in summer, which are followed by tight knots of glossy lilac-purple berries that persist long after leaf drop. The variety *albifructus* bears white fruit. Other cultivated beauty-berries are taller shrubs and bear looser fruit clusters.

Well-drained soil of average fertility suits best. Excessive nitrate promotes luxuriant foliage and diminished fruiting. Full sun is required for maximal fruit set. Purple beauty-berry may be pruned in early spring, as fruiting occurs on growth of the season. However, except to remove dead wood, pruning is not required.

CALYCANTHUS FLORIDUS
(Strawberry shrub, sweet shrub)

Zones 4–9

The strawberry shrub is particularly beloved because of its association with old-time gardens and the delightful and pungent fragrance of its flowers. It is rather coarse and open in its habit of growth and is, therefore, better adapted to mass plantings or backgrounds than for specimen purposes. It attains a maximum height of about 8 feet. The flowers, which appear in late spring or earliest summer, are dull red-brown and when crushed give off a very spicy fragrance. The branches also exude a strange, almost camphorlike odor. Strawberry shrub is free of pests and diseases.

It grows best on rich, moist loam but is very adaptable. In full sun, the shrub is more compact and floriferous than in shade. It is easily transplanted and reestablishes readily. Pruning, if required, is best done at the conclusion of flowering.

CAMELLIA JAPONICA
(Common camellia)

Zones 7–10

An increasingly popular (though in places overused) evergreen shrub or small tree with dark, glossy foliage, the common camellia offers several distinct types of flowers, all having a chaste and sculptured beauty that few other flowers possess. They range from singles and loose semidoubles to large peoniforms and imbricated sorts. The flowers range in color from white and cream through shades of pink to brilliant scarlet and deep red. In the South (zones 8 and 9), the camellia flowering season can be extended by including some cultivars of *C. reticulata*, which bloom in April and May. Height at maturity ranges from 8 to 15 feet.

Common camellia thrives best in regions with moderate temperatures and high humidity, as in much of the Southeast, from Florida to Texas, and along the coast to Virginia. It does not bloom well in southern Florida, but some of the hardier cultivars perform well in northern Georgia and Alabama and in Tennessee. If planted in sheltered locations, certain cultivars of exceptional hardiness may be grown as far north as eastern Pennsylvania; Long Island and Westchester County, New York; and the southern coast of New England to Cape Cod. Common camellia is especially well adapted to the Pacific Coast from California to Washington.

Although a few cultivars thrive in full sun, common camellia generally does best in the dappled partial shade of tall, open-headed, deeply rooted trees, protected from wind and, to the extent possible, from sudden changes in temperature. In the South, a northern or eastern exposure is usually best, but farther north a western exposure prevents the sometimes severe foliar damage caused when, after a frosty night, the morning sun induces a rapid thaw. The effect of a sudden temperature drop can be mitigated by directing a fine-mist spray over the shrub for several hours. Consistently adequate soil moisture is especially important during periods of growth and flowering.

As to soil, common camellia requires a light, acidic medium that is abundantly supplied with organic matter. Soils ranging from pH 4.5 to 6.5 are suitable, with pH 5.5 being considered optimal. Camellias are surprisingly adaptable, providing these requirements are adequately met.

In the camellia belt of the South, camellias are usually planted in the autumn. In zone 7 and parts of zone 8, spring planting is preferred. Year-round mulching is advisable as the root system is shallow. On the other hand, permanently soggy, water-logged soil is fatal.

Commercial fertilizer preparations specifically formulated for camellias are available from garden supply stores in the camellia belt, and may be purchased in small quantities by home owners who have only a few plants. However, over-fertilization of camellias should be guarded against, as the effects can be disastrous. No applications of a nitrate-rich fertilizer should be given after late spring so that the season's growth may harden well, thus reducing the danger of winter injury. An application of one part sulfate of potash to five parts superphosphate in late summer will be of benefit in hardening new growth and improving the quality of the flowers.

When applied in the dry form, the fertilizer may be spread as a topdressing on the mulch and watered in. The application should reach the outer spread of the branches. Pruning, if required, is best done after flowering is over.

CAMELLIA SASANQUA
(Sasanqua camellia)

Zones 7–10

Like other camellias, the Sasanqua is an evergreen shrub. The habit is more open than in *C. japonica*, and the lustrous leaves, borne on slender, fuzzy twigs, are smaller. The flowers are also smaller and more fragile in appearance than in the other species, but they are borne in profusion, are obtainable in a wide range of beautiful colors, and are delicately fragrant. The typical form of the flower is single, with wide-open petals and prominent stamens. There are also semidouble and fully double cultivars. The flowers of Sasanqua do not have the substance or the long-lasting qualities when cut that the blooms of common camellia possess, but for landscape effects, their value is unequaled. The flowers of Sasanqua range from white through various shades of pink to deep red, with some blendings in between. Cultivars of *C. sasanqua* vary considerably in growth habit, some being much more compact than others; they usually range from 6 to 10 feet high at maturity. The Sasanqua camellias are predominately autumn flowering, coming into bloom in September and continuing into December, by which time, in the Deep South, *C. japonica* has begun its show.

The Sasanqua camellia has great decorative value in the landscape scheme. It may be used as a specimen, in shrubery borders, and in foundation plantings. In California it is much favored in hedging.

Sasanqua camellia can be grown successfully throughout the same range as the common camellia. However, it withstands greater extremes of heat and cold and so is grown farther south and, some cultivars at least, farther north as well. In southern Florida it is far more satisfactory than *C. japonica*, and it has played an important part in extending the camellia belt northward. Within recent decades the hardier cultivars have been increasingly enjoyed in gardens in southeastern Pennsylvania, in New Jersey, on Long Island and adjacent southern New York State, in coastal southern New England, and in sheltered sites at least as far north as Cape Cod. For these northern areas, the earlier blooming cultivars should be selected.

Sasanqua camellia requires more sun exposure than the common camellia for best development and so thrives in full sun as well as in light shade. When grown in the North it should, however, be planted in a location where it will be protected from both full winter sun and harsh winds. Sasanqua camellia can also be grown successfully along the seacoasts, as it possesses considerable tolerance of salt spray and, indeed, can be planted within view of open water, provided other conditions are favorable.

Although Sasanqua camellia succeeds on poorer soil than common camellia, growth and flower production reach optimal levels only on well-prepared soil. In the North, spring planting is recommended. If compact growth is desired, as for a hedge, long shoots should be pruned back to induce branching, preferably when flowering is over.

CERCIS CHINENSIS
(Chinese redbud)

Zones (5) 6–9

Chinese redbud is an interesting and often showier relative of the larger eastern redbud. Chinese redbud seldom exceeds 12 feet. Beginning in March in the South, its numerous branches are clothed with rosy purple pealike flowers. It is seen to best advantage when used as a specimen plant on a smaller property or when planted in groups where its spread of 8 to 10 feet can be accommodated. It is especially effective when planted in groups against an evergreen backdrop or when combined with flowering dogwoods, silver bells, or azaleas of suitable floral shade. The flowers are followed by purplish pods.

Deep, loamy soil is best, but the shrub is quite adaptable, though intolerant of soggy conditions. Chinese redbud is easily moved and established in spring or fall, and for best flowering it should be placed in full sun. Flowering may be augmented by pruning out some leafy branches to admit light farther down in the canopy. This is best done in late spring at the conclusion of flowering.

CHAENOMELES JAPONICA
(Japanese flowering quince)

Zones 4–8

Japanese flowering quince is a less well-known close cousin of the Chinese flowering quince. It is a low-growing thorny shrub, seldom exceeding 3 feet, and presents a very picturesque outline of interlaced stems. The flowers, borne in spring in great profusion just as the leaves expand, are red-orange, scarlet, or carmine and are followed by fragrant greenish yellow quinces about ½ inch across that can be used to make preserves and jellies. It is a shrub of uncommon beauty and individuality and provides a note of brilliant color when included in a foundation planting.

Dwarf Japanese flowering quince (*Chaenomeles japonica* var. *alpina*), about 1 foot tall, is sometimes used as an edging or rock garden subject. Its flowers are orange.

Japanese flowering quince thrives in any reasonably well-drained, slightly acidic soil. For fullest flowering, it should be placed in a sunny position and may be planted in spring or fall. Although pruning is best deferred until after flowering, branches may be taken in late winter for forcing indoors.

CHAENOMELES SPECIOSA
(Chinese flowering quince)

Zones 4–8 (9)

Blooming in early to mid spring before its leaves appear, Chinese flowering quince is ablaze with very striking brilliant red blossoms. The shrub is of irregular, often picturesque habit, sometimes ascending vinelike through the lower branches of larger shrubs and small trees. Standing alone, it ranges from 5 to 10 feet tall. A shrub of great beauty when in flower, Chinese flowering quince also lends itself well to mass planting and makes a most attractive flowering hedge. Branches may be cut in late winter and readily forced into bloom indoors. The flowers are followed by attractive 2½-inch yellow-green, brown-speckled quinces that may be cooked for preserves and jellies.

Of the many cultivars, some of the better ones include 'Cameo', with double pink flowers; 'Texas Scarlet', with single watermelon red flowers; 'Nivalis', with single white flowers; and 'Toyo Nishiki', with flowers of red, pink, or white, or in combinations, all borne on the same branch.

Hybrid flowering quince
(*Chaenomeles* × *superba*)

Most any well-drained, slightly acidic soil suits this species. Planted equally safely in spring or fall, preferably in full sun, the shrubs will flower most prolifically if given an occasional severe pruning once the flowering period is over.

CHIONANTHUS VIRGINICUS
(*Fringe bush*)

Zones 3–9
One of the finest of our native species, fringe bush (or, in larger dimension, fringe tree) develops into a large multistemmed shrub or sometimes a small tree. It is particularly well suited as a lawn specimen or in a woodland border. It usually does not grow more than 10 to 12 feet tall, but it may grow considerably taller under prime conditions. In mid to late spring, it offers a glorious mass of bloom, the creamy white flowers borne in large, lacy, drooping clusters. Blue olivelike fruits

are borne singly or in clusters in late summer. Few shrubs exceed the beauty of a fringe bush in full flower. It is also decorative in form, and the ample foliage turns a clear bright yellow in fall. Fringe bush endures smoky, polluted air and thrives on wet ground.

Sandy, moist, fertile, acidic loam is ideal for fringe bush, but it adapts to a wide range of soil types. For fullest flowering, it should be planted in an open sunny position. It is easily established from containered or balled-and-burlapped stock, but older shrubs are not easily moved. Prolonged drought can be fatal. Pruning, if required, is best done after flowering.

CLETHRA ALNIFOLIA
(*Sweet pepperbush*)

Zones 3–9
Sweet pepperbush is valued for its fragrant white flowers borne in midsummer when few other shrubs are in bloom. A shrub of slender, erect habit, it reaches a height of 4 to 5 feet. It is free of serious pests and diseases. Prune in spring as the leaves appear. The cultivar 'Rosea' bears light pink flowers.

Sweet pepperbush thrives in moist to wet acidic soil. It should be kept well mulched with leaves or peat moss as it suffers under dry conditions. It luxuriates in partial shade, but also succeeds in full sun, as long as the soil is consistently moist.

CORNUS ALBA 'SIBIRICA'
(*Red-stem dogwood*)

Zones 2–8
Although not at all distinctive in leaf or flower, the red-stem dogwood is an exceptionally hardy shrub that bears conspicuous bluish white fruits. It is also a choice shrub for its effect in the winter landscape. It seldom exceeds 8 feet in height and spread. Young stems and twigs turn a bright coral red in the fall, and when seen either as a single specimen or massed,

they add a distinctly warm touch to even the coldest winter day. The effect is particularly charming against snow and can be enhanced if interplanted with yellow-stem dogwood (*C. sericea* 'Flaviramea'). As material sold as 'Sibirica' sometimes colors poorly, it is well to verify its winter color before purchasing.

Red-stem dogwood does well on most any soil but thrives and remains disease free on wet, acidic ground near water. Full sun ensures the most vivid winter show. Easily moved and established, it should have the oldest stems cut to the ground every few years in spring to encourage the fresh vigorous growth that provides the most vivid redness. Recovery from drastic pruning is very rapid.

CORNUS STOLONIFERA 'FLAVIRAMEA', SYN. C. SERICEA 'FLAVIRAMEA'
(*Yellow-stem dogwood*)

Zones 2–8
The stems and twigs of this shrub turn bright yellow in winter. See the discussion of *C. alba* 'Sibirica' for more information. The twigs of yellow-stem dogwood may become afflicted with disfiguring canker, especially in drought-prone areas.

COTINUS COGGYGRIA
(*Smoke bush*)

Zones (4) 5–8
The large pinkish to grayish plumelike fruiting panicles that cover the smoke bush in summer give a definitely "smoky" or hazy appearance. These may persist into early winter, thus creating a very long period of effectiveness. The shrubs grow large, up to 15 feet tall, and wide; they may be planted as single specimens or massed for spectacular effect on a larger property. Several cultivars, such as 'Purpureus', 'Flame', and 'Royal Red', have purplish to pinkish fruiting panicles and purple leaves. Smoke bush is virtually pest and disease free.

Smoke bush will produce acceptable results on most any soil. Full sun will ensure maximum fruiting and the strongest fall foliage color in the popular

Smoke bush (*Cotinus coggygria*)

wind, summer drought, and occasional salt spray, rock cotoneaster has a deep, rangy root system that makes transplanting difficult. For this reason, it is best to plant stock that has been raised in containers.

Other useful *Cotoneaster* species include the following.

> *C. apiculatus* (cranberry cotoneaster): resembles rock cotoneaster but bears much larger though usually fewer bright red fruit; red fall foliage; zones 4–7.
>
> *C. dammeri* (barberry cotoneaster): one of the best ground covers in this group; glossy, dark green foliage; ranges from evergreen to partly or wholly deciduous, depending on latitude and exposure; a sprinkling of deep red ¼-inch fruit in late summer; zones 4–7.
>
> *C. divaricatus* (spreading cotoneaster): diffuse; reaches 6 feet in height and more in spread; bears quantities of small red fruit in the fall; zones 4–7.
>
> *C. microphyllus* (littleleaf cotoneaster): evergreen to semievergreen; small leaved; spreading; seldom more than 3 feet high; bears scarlet fruit; zones 5–8.
>
> *C. salicifolius* (willow-leaf cotoneaster): open growth with arching stems; evergreen foliage; red fruit; ranges from 10 to 15 feet tall at maturity; zones 6–8.

DEUTZIA GRACILIS
(Slender deutzia)

Zones (4) 5–8

The slender deutzia is a diminutive shrub that seldom grows more than 3 feet tall and thus is particularly useful in foundation plantings. It is of dense, upright growth, with gracefully arching branches, which in midspring are festooned with clusters of pendulous white, bell-shaped flowers. As this species is not distinguished except when in flower, it is best used as a component in diversified plantings. It is free of pests and diseases.

Adaptable to virtually any soil, slender deutzia responds well to moderately moist, humus-rich locations. The shrub develops most fully and flowers best in full sun.

purple-leaf cultivars, but all endure some shade. Any pruning is best done in spring as the leaves appear.

The native American smoke tree or chittamwood (*C. obovatus*), a native of the Midwest, is similar but may reach 30 feet.

COTONEASTER HORIZONTALIS
(Rock cotoneaster)

Zones 5–9

One of the finest of this large, diverse, and aristocratic group, rock cotoneaster has prostrate or ascending branches with the twigs arranged in a distinctively flat, fishbone pattern. Seldom more than 2 feet high, a single shrub may reach 6 feet or more in spread. The foliage is small, dark green, and very glossy. In the North the leaves turn a brilliant red in the autumn and drop, while in the South they are practically evergreen. The flowers, which appear in spring and are white with a pinkish tinge, are small but surprisingly conspicuous and are followed by myriad bright red fruits that persist until fall and are very decorative.

Shrubs may be trained informally up a masonry wall for an interesting effect and make a delightful espalier in such a situation if appropriately pruned. Rock cotoneaster may also be used as a woody ground cover, especially on steep banks and spilling over walls.

As with nearly all *Cotoneaster* species, rock cotoneaster is adaptable to a wide range of soils so long as the substrate is well drained. Flowering and fruiting are best in sunny locations. Tolerant of high

As individual stems are not long lived, care should be taken to remove dead or dying stems after flowering, thus allowing new stems to grow and mature. Shearing should not be practiced on this shrub, as it encourages an excessively bushy or moplike, top-heavy appearance.

DEUTZIA × LEMOINEI
(Lemoine deutzia)

Zones 4–8

Lemoine deutzia is one of the beautiful hybrid deutzias and particularly desirable as a specimen shrub because of its graceful habit and its profusion of bloom. It seldom attains a height of more than 6 feet. The popular cultivar 'Compacta' is only 3 feet. It blooms in midspring, usually after *D. gracilis*, with masses of white flowers in dense clusters that are very showy. Culture is the same as for *D. gracilis*.

ELAEAGNUS ANGUSTIFOLIA
(Russian olive)

Zones 2–7

A fast-growing hardy shrub that endures extremely trying conditions, Russian olive is often used as a windbreak in the Great Plains and the West. The foliage is a soft gray green; the flowers, which are not showy, are borne in spring and are a silvery yellow-orange. The fruits are yellow-brown. Unpruned, Russian olive can reach 20 feet and become a small tree. Usually, however, it is periodically cut back to a lower height and becomes quite dense. Prune at any time.

Few shrubs are more easily established in difficult habitats, but several diseases, especially verticillium wilt, can be serious in the Midwest.

Russian olive is tolerant of almost any soil, but luxuriates on sandy, alkaline soils. The roots fix nitrogen, thus improving soil fertility. Full sun is best. Wind and drought are not problems.

ELAEAGNUS UMBELLATA
(Autumn olive)

Zones 3–8

Autumn olive is large, spreading, usually thorny shrub that grows to about 15 feet tall and wide. It has silvery foliage and fragrant silvery white flowers in spring followed by abundant ⅓-inch fruits that ripen red in late summer. Autumn olive is an excellent drought-tolerant soil stabilizer, especially on steep banks and other difficult terrain. However, bird-carried seeds spread this species far and wide in somes regions, often to the point of nuisance. The cultivar 'Cardinal' is especially attractive and very adaptable.

Autumn olive is very easily established on most any soil and thrives wherever it is in full sun. It may be pruned anytime.

ELEUTHEROCOCCUS SIEBOLDIANUS, SYN. ACANTHOPANAX SIEBOLDIANUS
(Five-leaf aralia)

Zones 4–8

Attractive compound leaves and the capacity to perform well under difficult urban conditions are the chief merits of five-leaf aralia, an infrequently used shrub. The flowers and fruit are rather inconspicuous. It can be clipped into an interesting hedge, used as a specimen plant, or used as a tall cover on steep banks. It can also be used to make a dense barrier plant if unclipped, evenually reaching a height of 8 to 10 feet, with an equal spread. The stems are prickly. Five-leaf aralia has no known pests or diseases.

This species adapts to most any soil and can withstand prolonged drought. It does equally well in full sun and heavy shade. It is easily transplanted, and pruning may be done anytime.

ENKIANTHUS CAMPANULATUS
(Redvein enkianthus)

Zones (4) 5–7

The redvein enkianthus is a handsome shrub, mostly because of its beautiful foliage, which is bronze through the early part of the season, turning a brilliant red in the autumn. In habit of growth, it is a refined and upright shrub, usually growing no taller than 10 feet, but it can be somewhat taller in optimal locations. The delicate drooping clusters of cream to pale orange, red-veined, bell-shaped flowers are borne at the ends of the branchlets in late spring.

Redvein enkianthus does best on moist, acidic, sandy-humusy soil in partial shade—essentially the same conditions that favor rhododendrons and azaleas, with which enkianthus is an aesthetic complement. Any pruning is best done at the conclusion of flowering in late spring.

Redvein enkianthus (*Enkianthus campanulatus*)

EUONYMUS ALATUS
(Burning bush, Winged spindle tree)

Zones 4–8

For either individual or group planting, the winged euonymus is a handsome subject. It is of regular, rather horizontal growth, 12 to 18 feet in height. The small, delicate flowers are borne in late spring and are followed by red fruits. The curious corky bark on the branches gives it a winged effect, hence the common name. The leaves are small and finely toothed, and in autumn they turn bright scarlet, especially in sunny sites.

E. alata 'Compacta' is more refined in habit—seldom exceeding 8 feet—and has a dense branching pattern. For these reasons, it makes good hedging material.

The winged spindle tree will succeed on most any reasonably moist soil and adapts to most any pH. Balled-and-burlapped stock is easily established. The winged twigs and stems, especially effective in the compact form, add considerable interest in winter. Pruning may be done anytime.

FORSYTHIA × INTERMEDIA 'LYNWOOD' OR 'LYNWOOD GOLD'
(Showy border forsythia)

Zones (4) 6–8 (9)

One of the best of this very popular group, the cultivar 'Lynwood' reaches a height of 8 to 10 feet, and in early spring, before the leaves unfold, it is a mass of glorious golden bloom. The flowers are larger and more open than in most of the other types; it also has the advantage of coming into bloom just late

Showy border forsythia (*Forsythia × intermedia* 'Lynwood')

enough in most areas to escape severe frost. Unquestionably overused and frequently badly sited, 'Lynwood' provides a welcome friendly show of golden yellow that is almost everyone's harbinger of real springtime. North of zone 6, buds are often winter killed, and flowering is sometimes meager in the Deep South.

As with all forsythias, the showy border forsythia succeeds on any but excessively wet or dry soils. It tolerates considerable shade, but for fullest flowering, it must be grown in full sun. It may be moved bare root.

Although well-placed forsythias will flower generously year after year with no care, a little attention each spring after flowering can result in a considerably augmented show the following spring. Cutting a few of the older stems at this time a few inches above ground level will stimulate new growth that in succeeding years will be far more floriferous than the old stems would have been. This method results in the shrub bearing its blossoms on gracefully arching branches. Wholly overgrown or outsized shrubs do far better in the long run if cut entirely back to the base rather than sheared annually to a predetermined height and width. It should be remembered that, even if given this recommended treatment, a full-grown showy border forsythia will

reach 8 or 10 feet in spread; sufficient space should be allotted for this dimension when planting. Except for dwarf forms, forsythias in general are really not suitable in foundation plantings, which seem so often to be their fate. Showy border forsythia, more than most other flowering shrubs, makes a reasonably acceptable hedge, especially if in full sun.

FORSYTHIA OVATA
(Early forsythia)

Zones 4–7

Early forsythia is a Korean species with ascending branches to 6 feet long that arch gracefully. The flowers are pale primrose yellow and are borne singly. This species flowers about 10 days before any other type. Its advantages are its early flowering and hardiness (without bud loss) in subzero winters.

The cultivars 'Ottawa' and 'Tetragold', even hardier and earlier flowering, are especially suited to northerly regions. Culture is the same as for *F. × intermedia*.

FORSYTHIA SUSPENSA *VAR.* SIEBOLDI
(Weeping forsythia)

Zones 5–8

Growing to 10 feet or more, weeping forsythia has long slender branches that often bend to the ground and root at the tips, thus tending to form thickets if left unattended. In time, the pendent branches can be used to clothe a wall or arbor or to trail over an outcrop or precipice. The flowers are pale yellow. Culture is the same as for *F. × intermedia*.

HAMAMELIS MOLLIS
(Chinese witch hazel)

Zones 5–8

A large shrub 10 to 15 feet tall and as wide, Chinese witch hazel is best kept smaller with a judicious annual pruning (not shearing) after the flowers fall. Of exceptional value for its showy eight-week display of spicily fragrant yellow flowers in February and March, it is often mistaken for a precocious forsythia. Each flower, however, has four strap-shaped petals that are variously crinkled and bent, each purplish at the base.

Hybrid witch hazel
(*Hamamelis × intermedia* 'Arnold Promise')

Similar and increasingly available is the slightly earlier-flowering hybrid *H. × intermedia* 'Arnold Promise'. All winter-flowering witch hazels show off best against a dark background, such as is created by yews or other evergreens. The large, velvety leaves turn clear yellow in fall.

Strong winter winds at temperatures below −10°F will kill flower buds, hence the need for protection, especially in zone 5. Otherwise, full sun yields the best results. A slightly acidic, well-drained soil of average fertility suits witch hazels generally. Pruning should be done in spring, as the foliage expands.

ILEX CRENATA
(Japanese holly)

Zones 5–7 (8)

The Japanese holly and several of its many cultivars are among our most useful evergreen shrubs. The leaves are small, dark green, and dense, its flowers and fruit inconspicuous. It combines well with other evergreens in the shrub border and may be used in foundation planting and for hedges. Japanese holly is very tolerant of city pollution and, except for nematodes in the South, is relatively pest and disease free. However, sudden severe freezes in autumn can be damaging and, on occasion, even fatal. Height and spread are usually 5 to 10 feet but may reach 15 feet.

Japanese holly succeeds under a wide range of conditions, from full sun to fairly dense shade, and from rich, well-drained, acidic loam to rather poor soils of nearly neutral pH. It is easily transplanted and established, but it requires irrigation during periods of drought. It ordinarily needs pruning only to thicken growth and for removal of dead wood, but it rebounds quickly from a severe cutting back. Early spring is the best time to prune.

Among the hundreds of named cultivars, the following are particularly important in the United States.

'Convexa': very hardy, densely branched female form; eventually reaches 4 to 6 feet tall and wide; channelled, convex leaves; often heavy crops of black berries on all shrubs.

'Compacta': dense globose mound to 6 feet; small, flat, shiny leaves; noticeably purplish young stems.

'Green Island' and 'Green Lustre': rather open, spreading shrubs; up to 3 feet tall and 6 feet across; handsome lustrous foliage.

'Helleri': dwarf in all dimensions; eventually reaches 4 feet; densely clothed with ½-inch, moderately lustrous leaves; better suited to the South than most forms.

'Hetzii': spreading mound; 4 feet tall and twice as broad; very attractive convex leaves.

ILEX VERTICILLATA
(Winterberry)

Zones 3–9

Winterberry is one of the most attractive native shrubs in the East. This is a deciduous member of the holly family, in most years producing quantities of red berries that remain

Dwarf Japanese holly (*Ilex crenata* 'Helleri')

throughout the early winter. A few twigs tucked into a Christmas wreath will brighten it with their sparkle. As a cultivated shrub, it is dense and handsome, usually maturing at a height of 6 to 8 feet.

Native to acidic swamps, winterberry is very adaptable to most garden soils and thrives in full sun or partial shade. It is easily established and is especially showy when massed. Male shrubs, preferably one for every six females, are required for fruit set. Prune in spring, as growth begins.

JASMINUM NUDIFLORUM
(Winter jasmine)

Zones (5) 6–10

Winter jasmine is a mounded shrub that may also trail or ascend in a vinelike manner. The long slender stems are green throughout the winter months; and during mild periods between January and March, even while snow remains, some of the red-tipped buds open into clear yellow flowers. They are flat salvers borne very close to the stem and appear intermittently until spring. Winter jasmine may be readily trained on a trellis as a vine and is often happily used in this way. Its habit of early flowering endears it to every home owner, for in its golden cup of bloom it seems to hold the very promise of spring.

A sunny, south-facing position in a reasonably fertile, well-drained soil yields the best results, especially in the North. Winter jasmine is very easily established and is readily propagated by tip-rooted branches. Pruning is best done in spring at the conclusion of flowering.

JUNIPERUS CHINENSIS
'PFITZERIANA'
(Pfitzer juniper)

Zones 3–9

The Pfitzer juniper is one of the larger of the spreading forms and one of the most popular junipers. It reaches 10 feet high and 15 feet across but is usually kept to smaller dimensions by pruning. It is very graceful in its ascending habit,

rather open and vase shaped. The dense foliage is a soft, cool green and retains its fresh coloring throughout the year. It is adaptable to any position where tenacity is important; it is considered one of the best of the spreading junipers. Not surprisingly, it is often used to excess.

Pfitzer juniper withstands extremely hard winter conditions, yet thrives in the South. It will grow perfectly well in sandy, dry soil of low fertility, but it is not suited to wet ground. It adapts to nearly any exposure but becomes thin and ragged unless it receives several hours of sun daily. It is most easily established from container or balled-and-burlapped stock and may be pruned anytime.

JUNIPERUS HORIZONTALIS
'PLUMOSA'
(Andorra juniper)

Zones 3–9

Of the scores of spreading juniper cultivars, the Andorra juniper is especially distinctive and one of the most frequently used. Hardy and compact yet graceful and long lived, Andorra juniper has a feathery texture and is especially pleasing in winter when the foliage takes on a purplish cast. At maturity it forms mats up to 10 feet across but not more than 18 inches high.

Almost any well-drained soil suits. Full sun is best, as plants become thin, ragged, and disease prone in shade.

KALMIA LATIFOLIA
(Mountain laurel)

Zones 4–9

One of the most beautiful of our native broad-leaf evergreens, mountain laurel is especially valuable in mass plantings and as an under planting in woodland settings. Though often included in foundation plantings, it usually becomes too large for such sites, as it approaches its usual maximum height of 8 to 10 feet. The handsome foliage is a dark, glossy green, and its lovely flower clusters open in late spring, varying from pure white to pinkish rose. Numerous pink-flowered cultivars, often red in bud, are increasingly available but seem less hardy than the wild type.

Grown on sandy, acidic soil in moist, partially shaded locations or in full sun with a moisture-retentive mulch, mountain laurel develops a compact fibrous root system that eases transplanting, so long as the root mass is kept moist. Rangy, oversize shrubs can be cut back in spring to 6- to 12-inch stubs that, in a few years' time, rejuvenate into attractive compact specimens.

KERRIA JAPONICA

Zones 4–9

Kerria is an attractive, useful deciduous shrub with slender wandlike branches that retain their green color throughout the year and are particularly appreciated in winter months. The single five-petaled flowers are a deep golden yellow and appear from early to mid spring. Kerria is especially good for foundation planting, because it is relatively open in habit and seldom exceeds 5 feet in height.

Kerria japonica 'Pleniflora', the popular double-flowered cultivar, reaches 8 feet or more and bears floral pompoms 1½ inches across not only in spring but again in early fall.

Although kerria is hardy to −25°F, the tops are killed back if exposed to strong wind at subzero temperatures. Partial shade helps prolong flowering and preserves the golden color from fading. Well-drained loamy soil of average fertility is best; excess nitrate encourages foliage but depresses flowering. Pruning, in early spring, is done for two reasons: (1) to prolong the length of bloom by cutting the branches back to various lengths and thus delaying the bloom on some and (2) to cut out any wood that was winter killed. This last should also be done in early spring, before the leaf buds swell. Kerria can be moved bare root, but balled-and-burlapped material recovers more quickly.

KOLKWITZIA AMABILIS
(Beauty-bush)

Zones 4–8

Beauty-bush is a very showy, decorative shrub when in flower. Of upright habit, with arching branches, it reaches a height of about 10 feet. The flower buds are deep pink, and the open blooms borne in such profusion in mid to late spring are somewhat paler, with delicate orange veins in the tubular throat. The weigela-like flowers are borne in pairs, with 25 to 50 in a single cluster. The light-colored bark exfoliates, or peels, from stems and twigs, thus offering added interest in winter.

Well-drained soil of low to moderate fertility results in the best flowering, particularly in shrubs growing in full sun. Beauty-bush is easily established and requires only an annual pruning out of dead and failing stems, ideally at the conclusion of flowering.

LEUCOTHOË FONTANESIANA
(Drooping leucothoë)

Zones 4–7

Leucothoë is a low, evergreen shrub with gracefully arching branches and glossy, dark green foliage that turns a rich bronze with purple tints in winter. It seldom grows more than 4 or 5 feet tall and is often broader than it is high. The little clusters of drooping, waxy, bell-shaped flowers appear in midspring

at the tips of the branches and are quite fragrant. Leucothoë is a very choice shrub, particularly useful as a filler between large evergreen shrubs, for foundation plantings, or in woodland settings. Several cultivars have leaf variegation and various winter foliage shades.

Rich, acidic loam that remains consistently moist through the summer yields the best results. Partial shade is ideal, but drooping leucothoë endures full sun as long as it is protected from severe winter wind. It transplants easily and quickly establishes in a new site if individuals are set about 4 feet apart. Outsize, leggy shrubs may be cut back to 6- to 12-inch stubs in the spring; these rejuvenate after a few years into compact, well-formed plants. Dead wood may be removed anytime.

LIGUSTRUM LUCIDUM
(Glossy privet)

Zones 8–10

Native to the Orient, glossy privet is a large evergreen shrub with lustrous leaves. Under favorable circumstances, it can become a tree up to 25 feet tall. Like most privets, it grows rapidly and is useful as a hedge and, left untrimmed, as a windbreak. It also makes an attractive specimen shrub. Clusters of white flowers appear in summer.

Glossy privet is often confused (and, for many purposes, is interchangeable) with Japanese privet (*L. japonicum*), but the latter is denser, smaller in most respects, and hardy to zone 7. Both species are disease free.

A sunny location with virtually any well-drained soil will suit glossy privet, but it is important to keep it away from the competing roots of shallow-rooted trees. This species is very easily established and withstands heavy pruning and frequent shearing anytime in the growing season.

LIGUSTRUM OBTUSIFOLIUM
(Border privet)

Zones 3–8

Left untrimmed, border privet grows to 12 feet tall and as wide, but it is nearly always sheared in hedging. The semi-

persistent foliage turns purplish in fall. The white, cloyingly perfumed flowers in summer are followed by black berries. Superior to the more common but overused Amur privet (*L. amurense*) and far better than the disease-prone European privet (*L. vulgare*), border privet, like the other two, is a popular hedge plant in the North.

Any well-drained soil is acceptable for this species, as is virtually any location—from full sun to partial shade—that is away from the roots of shallowly rooted trees, especially Norway maple. Border privet is easily moved bare root. Shearing may be done anytime in the growing season; severe pruning is best done in spring to allow time for regrowth.

LONICERA MORROWII
(Morrow bush honeysuckle)

Zones (3) 4–8

One of the loveliest of our bush honeysuckles, the Morrow bush honeysuckle is of wide, spreading habit. At maturity, it forms a mound of crooked, angular branches and ultimately reaches about 8 feet. The foliage is a soft gray green and the myriad paired flowers, which appear in midspring, open creamy white and age to yellow. These are followed by brilliant red berries (yellow in cultivar 'Xanthocarpa'). As the fruits are greatly relished by birds, Morrow honeysuckle is an especially desirable shrub in bird sanctuaries.

Average well-drained soil meets the needs of this shrub, as does a sunny location. Soils of low fertility may result in flowers subnormal in size and poor fruit set. A hard pruning at the time of planting (early spring or mid to late fall) will help encourage multiple stems rather than a single straggly one. Once established, shrubs need only have dead branches and sometimes the oldest, thickest branches removed after flowering.

MAGNOLIA STELLATA
(Star magnolia)

Zones 3–8

Although most magnolias are trees, the slow-growing star magnolia seldom exceeds 12 to 15 feet, and is characteristically

Star magnolia (*Magnolia stellata*)

branched to the ground. It is best used as a lawn specimen, where its generous display of fragrant white 3-inch multi-petaled flowers can be seen to full effect in early spring. But it is also useful in uncrowded groupings near buildings, especially if made of brick or a dark material.

Moist, deep, acidic loamy soil yields the best results. A south exposure will result in earlier flowering, but at risk of frost damage, which turns petals brown; protection from prolonged sun exposure at this time of year will delay flowering somewhat but lessen the risk. As with all magnolias, plant only in early spring, using well-wrapped balled-and-burlapped material, taking care to keep root disturbance at a minimum. Once established, star magnolia requires little care.

MAHONIA AQUIFOLIUM
(*Oregon hollygrape*)

Zones 5–8

Oregon hollygrape (sometimes simply called Oregon grape) is an evergreen shrub of rather low habit, seldom attaining a height of more than 4 to 5 feet. The handsome foliage is glossy, rather leathery in texture, and prickly. To the casual observer it resembles the foliage of our Christmas holly although it is much shinier. The young growth has a very characteristic bronze tint and the leaves turn a reddish bronze during the winter months. The flowers are yellow, borne in dense clusters at the ends of the branches in early to mid spring. The small blue-black fruits are covered in a gray bloom and ripen in late summer.

Oregon hollygrape succeeds in a wide range of slightly acidic to slightly alkaline soils and even tolerates dryish sandy conditions. It does best, however, in a moist, humusy soil of at least average fertility. Containered material is easiest to establish.

This shrub is best grown in partial or even dense shade, since the foliage becomes pale and eventually brown in strong sun. Protection from harsh winter winds is also advisable, as these too will cause leaf burn. Beyond removal of dead wood, which may be done anytime, pruning is seldom required.

MYRICA PENNSYLVANICA
(*Northern bayberry*)

Zones 2–7

Northern bayberry is very ornamental, especially when massed, and its merits are perhaps not fully appreciated. It grows 5 to 9 feet tall. The foliage is a medium green, smooth, glossy, and very attractive in appearance, and when bruised, it emits a delicious and pungent fragrance. The flowers are inconspicuous and the handsome gray fruits are borne in the fall (on female plants) in dense clusters close to the stem and remain in place throughout the winter months. To ensure fruit set, one or two male plants are necessary in any planting. The shrubs are pest and disease free as well as salt tolerant.

Northern bayberry is very adaptable as to soil, but performs best in a moist, peaty, acidic medium (pH 5.0 to 6.0). An open sunny position will maximize fruit display and also ensure compact growth. Balled-and-burlapped stock is the easiest to establish. Pruning, if required, is best done in the spring when growth begins. Tall, leggy shrubs may be cut back to stubs, with the expectation of rounded, rejuvenated specimens developing within a few years.

PAEONIA SUFFRUTICOSA
(Tree peony)

See page 339.

PHILADELPHUS × VIRGINALIS
(Virginal mock orange)

Zones 5–8

Virginal mock orange is a beautiful hybrid that was produced by the famous French hybridizer Victor Lemoine, and it is without doubt one of the most beautiful of the group. The white flowers, which are large and semidouble in form, are borne in profusion and are very fragrant. It blooms during midspring and occasional flowers are produced later in the season. The ultimate height varies from 6 to 8 feet. Like other hybrid mock oranges, it has the advantage of flowering while still quite small, but has little ornamental merit the rest of the year.

Virginal mock orange will succeed in almost any well-drained soil and tolerates shade better than most flowering shrubs, but a sunny position and moderately fertile soil ensure the fullest flowering. Pruning of weak or failing stems should be done after flowering. Leggy shrubs pruned to 6-inch stubs regenerate nicely.

PHOTINIA × FRASERI
(Fraser photinia)

Zones 7–9

The Fraser photinia is a very desirable evergreen shrub that is much used, sometimes to excess, for hedging in the South. Left unpruned, it becomes large and upright, reaching a height of 15 feet or more. The oval leaves are sharply toothed and lustrous. They are bright red when first expanding, and old leaves turn red again before dropping, a few at a time, during the growing season. The white flowers are small, like those of hawthorn, and somewhat malodorous. They appear in spring in rounded clusters and are followed by red berries that persist well into winter.

Planted in sandy, humusy soil in full sun, Fraser photinia is easily established, especially from container-grown stock. However, it performs reasonably well in partial shade. Annual spring pruning eventually leads to dense growth; otherwise Fraser photinia tends to be open in habit.

PIERIS JAPONICA
(Japanese andromeda)

Zones (4) 5–8

In the winter, Japanese andromeda is adorned with gracefully hanging tassels that are the flower buds. For six weeks in early to mid spring, it bears waxy white, bell-shaped blossoms; for the rest of the season, it carries picturesque seed capsules. Many cultivars feature red flower buds and/or leaves. The foliage is gracefully arranged in terminal clusters but has become increasingly subject to injury by lacebug, especially in the East, where affected andromeda foliage turns yellow or brownish.

Japanese andromeda thrives in organically rich soil that is neutral or slightly acidic and succeeds in full sun or partial shade, as long as it is protected from strong winter wind. It is very easily established from containered or balled-and-burlapped stock and requires little attention thereafter.

PITTOSPORUM TOBIRA
(Japanese pittosporum)

Zones (8) 9–10

Japanese pittosporum is widely used in the South and on the Pacific Coast, sometimes to excess, where it becomes a large evergreen shrub. It is well suited for use as an accent or in background plantings.

Virginal mock orange *(Philadelphus × virginalis)*

Often established in groupings around buildings, along walls, or beneath trees or sheared as hedges, Japanese pittosprum is naturally of spreading habit, reaching a height of about 15 feet. The foliage is thick, leathery, and dark green or, in the popular cultivar 'Variegata', edged with white. The creamy white flowers, which are borne in clusters in the spring, are fragrant.

It thrives in rich, humusy loam but adapts to many soils, it is unaffected by prolonged summer drought. Sun or partial shade suits it, and exposure to occasional salt spray causes no injury. It is best established from containered stock. Pruning is best undertaken once flowering is over.

PYRACANTHA COCCINEA 'LALANDEI'
(Hardy firethorn)

Zones 5–9

A shrub of striking beauty, the hardy scarlet firethorn reaches a height of 8 to 10 feet. The evergreen foliage (half-evergreen in the North) is dark and glossy, and the branches are thorny. The white flowers are borne in clusters in the spring and are followed by brilliant orange-scarlet fruits that last well into the winter. For its beautiful foliage, its flowers, and its highly ornamental fruits, this is a most desirable and

prized shrub. It may be used as an individual specimen and in group plantings, or it can be trained against a building or over a doorway or used as a hedge.

Other species and cultivars of *Pyracantha* are mostly less hardy in the North.

Any well-drained, nearly neutral (pH 6.0 to 8.0) soil of average fertility is adequate, and a location in full sun is necessary for ample flowering and a good fruit set. It is essential that new plantings be made from containered stock, as severe, usually fatal, root pruning is unavoidable when transplanting field-grown material. Pruning or shearing of branches may be undertaken after flowering, possibly at some sacrifice of fruit display, especially if severe.

RHODODENDRONS: EVERGREEN SPECIES AND CULTIVARS OF MERIT

More than most garden shrubs, rhododendrons are bold actors in the home landscape scene. They set whole gardens or woodlands—even hillsides—ablaze in midspring with trusses of lilac, pink, red, or white, sometimes even purple or yellow. Whether in bloom or out, their ample ever-present foliage, usually broadly oval and a glossy, deep green, often draws attention, even in the coldest winter weather when differential contraction of the upper and lower surfaces causes each leaf to roll up into a tight cylinder.

For a group of plants that was of little horticultural importance until the mid-1800s, rhododendrons have come a long way. Overall, there is hardly a more extensive or varied plant genus of horticultural gems than *Rhododendron*. Rhododendrons have a colorful history in the annals of plant exploration, especially in the 1800s, when so many of the more than 700 wild species were discovered as denizens of remote rocky ridges and craggy slopes of the Himalayas by such legendary adventures as Sir Joseph Hooker, George Forrest, Frank Kingdon-Ward, and E. H. Wilson.

Their living collections along with other contributions make up the world's most comprehensive rhododendron display, found at the Brodick Castle Garden on the Isle of Arran off the west coast of Scotland. There, with climate moderated by the northerly reaches of the Gulf Stream, hundreds of species and hybrids, from prostrate ground covers to sizable trees, combine to offer a continuous spectacle from May through August.

Here in the United States, most popular rhododendron cultivars are shrubby hybrids, with the hardy native Catawba and Carolina rhododendrons of the

southern Appalachians being two of the main parent species. Increasingly, however, other hardy kinds, both native and exotic, either pure or hybridized, are offered for the home landscape.

A rhododendron in bloom offers a touch of majesty, whether your focus is on an individual flower, on a well-formed shrub, or on an extensive planting. Flowering or not, a single plant or or a well-arranged group can become the focal point in the home landscape, thus calling for care in selection and placement. Planning is difficult, as most purchased plants are less than 2 feet tall and wide but grow 4 to 6 inches annually, reaching 6 feet or more in both dimensions.

Some rhododendrons are considered azaleas in the botanical sense not only because of their small, often deciduous leaves and singly borne massed flowers but for such less readily noticed characteristics as the presence of hairs, the absence of scales on stems and leaves, and the number of stamens in each flower. There are usually 5 stamens in azalea flowers, and 10 or more in those of rhododendrons. However, as more species become known, the differences break down, wreaking havoc on the traditional subgroup classifications. This is why today all rhododendron and azalea species are grouped in the the botanical genus *Rhododendron*.

A number of rhododendrons, such as the rosebay (*R. maximum*), are tolerant of rather dense shade, but the majority perform best in light or partial shade. In their native habitats, rhododendrons frequent open woodlands and forest margins. On the home property, the most favorable exposure is a location where they will be protected from hot afternoon sun in the summer and where early morning sun will not strike them in the winter. A northeastern exposure meets these requirements well. Such a location may be in the shelter of buildings or in an area protected by trees.

Where climatic conditions are not naturally favorable to the growth of rhododendrons, such as in the South and the Midwest, a northern exposure is always desirable so that the plants may have full protection from intense sunshine and searing winds. They will thrive well in areas where they receive good light, but no direct sun. In the Midwest, honey locusts afford an excellent overhead canopy for rhododendron plantings, and in the North and South pines and oaks provide favorable conditions, if the lowest branches are about 12 feet above the ground.

Never plant rhododendrons under trees that develop dense surface soil root systems and thereby deplete the soil of moisture and nutrients. Rhododendrons have shallow, very fibrous root systems and generally will not grow well under beeches or most maples. Although exposure to drying winter wind and hot summer sun can lead to disappointment, a substantial list of extraordinarily hardy cultivars known as "Ironclads" (see page 233) offers realistic options for difficult exposed sites.

To reduce ground-surface evaporation in periods of summer heat and to keep soil temperatures relatively stable both in the summer and in the winter, a 2- or 3-inch blanket of bark nuggets, wood chips, or pine needles will make a good protective mulch. By allowing the accumulation of fallen, windblown leaves trapped among the stems to remain, additional winter protection is gained.

For nearly all hardy rhododendrons, a setting with damp, sandy, humusy soil under high shade, preferably provided by deeply rooted oaks, is ideal. Most require pH 4.5 to 5.5 for optimal results, but a number are adaptable to less acidic conditions.

Although container-grown stock can be planted whenever the soil is workable, rhododendrons respond best when planted in very early spring, before growth starts, or in late summer, after growth has ceased but well before the onset of cold weather.

Plants that are at least 15 to 18 inches in height and well branched, with foliage low to the ground, are the most desirable for planting. If special soil preparation is required, an area of at least twice the depth and width of the ball of earth surrounding the plant should be prepared for each plant used as an individual specimen. If a mass planting is to be done, the entire area may be prepared at one time. In areas where the soil is definitely alkaline or where it is poorly drained and there is danger of its becoming waterlogged, it is advisable to plant rhododendrons in raised beds. This not only will provide for good drainage but will prevent surface water from seeping into the bed. This is the method followed so successfully in England when rhododendrons are grown in areas where the soil is highly alkaline.

Rhododendrons must always be planted at the same depth as they were growing in the nursery. After planting, they should be thoroughly watered, then mulched with dampened peat moss or acidic leaf mold.

The soil beneath rhododendrons should not be cultivated. Instead, it should be kept mulched at all times. During dry periods in the summer, a thorough soaking every 10 to 14 days is recommended. Heavy watering in August and September should be avoided, because the current season's growth is "hardening off" during this period and will be in better condition to survive low winter temperatures if not encouraged by too much water.

In severe climates, winter protection is advisable. A heavy 8-inch mulch of oak leaves may be applied in the fall or early winter, a portion of the mulch being removed in the spring and the rest left to decay. A snow fence or burlap protection should be provided in areas where winter winds are severe. Young plants, or even older ones in very windy sites, will benefit by winter application of an antidesiccant plastic spray (see page 168).

If seed capsules are not allowed to form, bloom may improve the following season. Such deadheading is practical only in small plantings.

Rhododendrons planted in soil that is rich in organic matter and quite acidic do not, in general, require significant applications of fertilizer to maintain healthy growth. Most of their nutritional requirements are obtained from the decomposition of the mulching material and humus in the soil. A 5-10-10 fertilizer spread at the rate of 3 pounds per 100 square feet yearly, or even every other year, is usually quite sufficient. This should be done as early in the growing season as possible (before midspring), and the fertilizer should be gently worked into the existing mulch, without disturbing the underlying roots, and left to percolate downward gradually. Later applications may stimulate new tender growth at the end of the season and result in considerable burning or winter kill. Cottonseed or soybean meal applied at the rate of 4 pounds per 100 square feet is also an excellent fertilizer to use with rhododendrons.

Because of the multiplicity of growth points, one at the end of each leafy twig, the low, slender-stemmed azaleas are amenable to annual pruning or even shearing at the conclusion of flowering each year. But because growth points are relatively few with the large-leaf, thick-stemmed rhododendrons, pruning must be undertaken with great care, if at all. Often outsize rhododendrons are best dug out and replaced, as severe pruning or cutting back usually leaves naked stubs that may refoliate here and there but too often unsatisfactorily.

For control of pests and diseases that afflict rhododendrons, see Chapter 34.

In each of the following seven categories of the genus *Rhododendron* are listed well-known, widely available species and cultivars that have proven most reliable, especially in the East and Pacific Northwest. Scores of other species and cultivars are offered, particularly by specialist growers. In areas less congenial to rhododendron culture, such as the South and Midwest, it is well to consult such specialists for guidance in selecting and growing.

I. Species Rhododendrons

Of the hundreds of *Rhododendron* species known, 50 or so are not only deserving of horticultural attention in their own right but are easy to grow. The species listed below are generally recognized as rhododendrons in the popular sense and are

most readily available commercially. Except where otherwise noted, all are evergreen and of rounded, rather open habit.

Blooming periods are necessarily relative, since they depend on latitude, elevation, and exposure. If the common hybrids of *R. catawbiense*, which in much of zone 7 flower in mid to late May, are taken to be midseason for rhododendrons generally, then the following bloom times can be specified. Those flowering in early to mid May are designated "early to mid season," early May bloomers are called "early season," and those blooming in April are deemed "very early." In the same zone, rhododendrons flowering from late May into early June are called "mid

to late season," those flowering in early to mid June are deemed "late," and those blooming in late June and early July are called "very late." By choosing species and cultivars with relative blooming periods in mind, it is possible to spread the period of bloom in your rhododendron display over several months. The sequencing of very early bloomers to very late ones will remain the same, no matter where rhododendrons are grown, but whereas midseason may be mid-May in zone 7, it will likely be late May in zone 6 and early May in zone 8, with all other blooming periods shifting accordingly.

The rhododendrons popularly known as azaleas are discussed on page 235.

SPECIES RHODODENDRONS

Name	Zones	Height	Characteristics*
R. adenopodum	(5) 6–8	6–8'	Leaves narrow, downy beneath; flowers rose pink, in rounded clusters; early to mid season
R. augustinii	5–7	6–8'	Habit compact, erect; leaves narrow, dark green; flowers light blue; early to mid season
R. brachycarpum (Fujiyama rhododendron)	4–7	6–10'	Habit dense; leaves 4 to 6 inches long, tan cottony beneath; flowers creamy white; late
R. bureavii	5–7	4–6'	Habit compact; slow growing; leaves dark green, with red-brown down; flowers light pink; midseason
R. bureavioides	5–7	4–6'	Similar to R. bureavii in habit and foliage; flowers white, flecked with rose pink; midseason
R. calostrotum	6–8	1–2'	Leaves small, blue-green; flowers rose violet, large; midseason
R. carolinianum (Carolina rhododendron)	5–8	5–8'	Habit diffuse; leaves dark green, glossy; flowers white to lilac rose, profuse; midseason
R. catawbiense (Catawba rhododendron)	4–8	6–10'	Leaves moderately glossy; flowers lilac to rosy purple; mid to late season
R. chartophyllum	6–8	6–9'	Leaves semideciduous, sharp pointed; flowers pale lavender pink; midseason
R. dauricum	5–8	4–6'	Habit compact; leaves semievergreen; flowers bright rose purple; very early
R. degronianum	5–7	3–5'	Habit compact; leaves narrow, glossy, brown cottony beneath; flowers pale pink; midseason
R. diaprepes, syn. R. decorum ssp. diaprepes	5–8	8–10' (20')	Habit rangy; leaves up to 1 foot long, reddish when young; flowers white, fragrant; late to very late
R. discolor, syn. R. fortunei ssp. discolor	5–8	6–10'	Leaves long, blue-green; flowers white, fragrant; very late
R. fastigiatum	6–7	1–2'	Leaves glossy, less than ½ inch long; lilac purple flowers, about ½ inch long; early
R. ferrugineum (alpen rose)	5–8	3–5'	Leaves small, glossy, rusty downy beneath; flowers rose pink; late
R. fortunei	6–8	8–12'	Leaves large, dark green; flowers pale pink; midseason
R. hyperythrum	6–8	6–10'	Leaves narrow, down turned, almost tubular; flowers pink in bud, opening white, bell shaped; early to mid season

(continues)

SPECIES RHODODENDRONS (*continued*)

Name	Zones	Height	Characteristics*
R. impeditum	6–8	1–1½'	Habit a cushionlike mound; leaves silvery blue-green; flowers purplish blue, about ½ inch long; early to mid season
R. keiskei	6–8	3–5'	Leaves small, narrow; flowers lemon yellow; early to mid season
R. keleticum	5–7	¾–1'	Leaves less than ½ inch long; flowers purplish red, about 1 inch across; midseason
R. makinoi	6–8	5–7'	Leaves long, very narrow, tawny woolly when young; flowers light pink; late midseason
R. maximum (rosebay rhododendron)	4–8	12–18'	Leaves long, dark green; flowers white to rose pink; very late
R. metternichii	6–8	2–3'	Habit compact; leaves glossy, with brown indument; flowers pink, bell shaped; midseason
R. minus	5–8	8–12'	Habit diffuse; leaves small, glossy; flowers pale pink to magenta; late
R. mucronulatum	5–8	4–7'	Habit upright; leaves deciduous; flowers appearing as leaves expand, pink to rose purple, or white; early
R. racemosum	5–8	2–4'	Leaves small, roundish, glossy; flowers white to rose pink; early to mid season
R. smirnowii (Smirnow rhododendron)	6–8	8–10'	Leaves dark green, with white felt aging brown; flowers pale rose pink; mid to late season
R. taliense	6–8	6–10'	Leaves dark green, glossy, tan felty beneath; flowers cream with rose spots; early to mid season
R. vernicosum	6–8	6–12'	Leaves smooth, hairless; flowers pinkish yellow to white; midseason
R. yakushimanum, syn. R. degronianum ssp. yakushimanum (Yakushima rhododendron)	5–8	2–4'	Habit often wider than high; slow growing; leaves down curved, brown woolly beneath; flowers deep rose pink in bud, opening pale pink, then white; early to mid season

* For an explanation of bloom times, see page 231.

Rhododendron mucronulatum

Rhododendron yakushimanum

II. Ironclad Hybrids

The Ironclads are the mainstays of the rhododendrons offered by nonspecialist nurseries, especially in the Northeast. They are easily capable of withstanding subzero lows (zones 4–7) and the drying effects of winter wind and sun as well as summer heat. As with all rhododendrons, however, soil moisture must be maintained during summer drought, most easily by permanent mulching.

III. Dexter Hybrids

Beginning in 1957, the long-neglected Cape Cod estate of rhododendron breeder Charles O. Dexter was gradually resurrected from two decades of abandonment and neglect following his death. The rhododendrons thereby saved are today the centerpiece of the Sandwich Heritage Plantation, the latter-day incarnation of Dexter's estate. Of these, and other hybrids since derived, the following Dexter hybrids have proved well suited to conditions in the East, zones 6–8. They are of rounded habit unless otherwise indicated.

IRONCLAD RHODODENDRONS

Names	Height	Characteristics*
'Album Novum'	5–6'	Upright, with large sun-tolerant leaves; large trusses of mauve flowers that age to white; late
'America'	5–6'	Extraordinarily hardy; red flowers held in dense trusses; mid to late season
'Boule de Neige'	5–6'	Slow growing; an old standby; a reliably generous display of pink buds that open white; earlier than most
'Catawbiense Album'	5–6'	Vigorous; upright and wide spreading; very hardy; blush-shaded buds that open white, held in large trusses; mid to late season
'Chionoides'	4–5'	Usually wider than tall; long flat leaves of a lighter green than usual; flowers white with a yellow eye; late midseason
'Cunningham's White'	3–4'	Compact habit; with pale pink buds opening white with a yellow-green blotch; late to mid season, often reflowering sparingly in early fall
'English Roseum'	5–6'	Very tolerant of cold and heat; superior to the otherwise similar 'Catawbiense Boursalt' and 'Catawbiense Grandiflorum'; flowers rosy lilac with pinkish tone; mid to late season
'Nova Zembla'	5–6'	Habit upright; very tolerant of cold and heat; the most reliable red-flowering rhododendron in the Northeast; midseason

* For an explanation of bloom times, see page 231.

Dexter hybrid rhododendron
(*Rhododendron* 'Scintillation')

DEXTER HYBRIDS

Names	Height	Characteristics*
'Ben Mosely'	5–6'	Rounded habit; handsome foliage; flowers pale lilac, darker at the margin, wine red in throats; midseason
'Gigi'	5–6'	An award-winning Dexter; flowers red spotted carmine within, in dense clusters of up to 18 blooms; late midseason
'Janet Blair'	5–7'	Habit vigorous, open; flowers pale pink blotched yellow; late midseason
'Parker's Pink'	5–6'	Flowers deep pink, the throat white with red spots; late midseason
'Scintillation'	5–6'	Leaves lustrous deep green; flowers pink with a paler throat and a bronzy area; midseason
'Tom Everett'	5–6'	Flowers pink, paler in throat and spotted light green; fragrant; midseason
'Wyandanch Pink'	5–6'	Performs well in full sun; flowers pink with darker spots; midseason

* For an explanation of bloom times, see page 231.

IV. Leach Hybrids

For many years the foremost rhododendron breeder in the United States, Dr. David Goheen Leach, has not only brought into being hundreds of hybrids but has taken pains to have the most promising of them test grown at least three years at six different locations across the country. Leach hybrids especially well suited to conditions in zones 6–8 include the following cultivars. They are all of rounded habit, about as wide as high, unless otherwise noted.

Leach hybrid rhododendron
(*Rhododendron* 'Party Pink')

V. Yakushimanum ("Yak") Hybrids

Since its introduction into horticulture in 1947, the Japanese species *Rhododendron yakushimanum* has become a mainstay in the breeding of freely flowering cultivars whose habit is generally low and broad. Superior hardiness and ease of cultivation further commend this group to the home gardener, especially in zones 6–8. Among the most reliable cultivars are the following.

Yakushimanum hybrids rhododendron
(*Rhododendron* 'Yaku Princess')

LEACH HYBRIDS

Name	Height	Characteristics*
'Anna M. Hall'	4–5'	Habit compact; with rose pink buds, opening white; midseason
'Burma'	5–6'	Broadly spreading habit; flowers intense red; late midseason
'Golden Gala'	3–4'	Leaves glossy; flowers light yellow; late midseason
'Normandy'	3–4'	Wider than high; deep green leaves; flowers pink marked tangerine; late midseason
'Party Pink'	5–6'	Flowers purplish pink, spotted yellow, 3 inches across, up to 18 blooms per truss; late midseason
'Rio'	2–3'	Twice as broad as tall; flowers salmon pink, red at margin, yellow in throat; midseason
'Swansdown'	5–6'	Foliage dense; flowers white to pale pink with a yellow highlight, held in large trusses; late midseason
'Trinidad'	5–6'	One of the first and hardiest bicolors; foliage dense; flowers rose pink with a paler center and a yellow flare; late midseason
'Vernus'	5–6'	Flowers bright pink with rose center; early

* For an explanation of bloom times, see page 231.

YAKUSHIMANUM HYBRIDS

Names	Height	Characteristics*
'Anita Gehnrich'	3–4'	Spreading, deep green leaves; flowers deep pink, frilled; midseason
'Dreamland'	3–4'	Similar to 'Anita Gehnrich', flowers pale pink with darker margins
'Gordon Jones'	2½–3'	Young foliage silvery; flowers lavender in bud, opening white with a purple flare; midseason
'Hoppy'	2–3'	Foliage dark green; flowers pale lilac in bud, opening white; midseason
'Percy Wiseman'	3–4'	Leaves glossy; flowers peach yellow, aging to white; midseason
'Sleepy'	2–3'	Flowers pale lavender pink, spotted light brown; midseason
'Solidarity'	3–4'	Flowers deep pink, borne in large clusters; midseason
'Tiana'	5–6'	Habit larger than most; flowers white with a burgundy blotch; midseason
'Yaku Princess'	3–4'	Flowers pale pink with green spots and a deeper pink throat; late midseason
'Yaku Queen'	3–4'	Similar to 'Yaku Princess'; flowers pale pink blotched yellow, deeper pink outside before fading to white

* For an explanation of bloom times, see page 231.

VI. Small-Leaf Rhododendrons

Of varied derivation, the small-leaf cultivars have in common smaller than usual leaves; the individual blades are often no longer than 3 inches. This trait, combined with a more finely branched habit, imparts a somewhat delicate effect, making these shrubs suitable where the boldness of the usual large-leaf types is not wanted. Some of the hardiest, most adaptable forms for zones 6–8 include the following:

Small-leaf rhododendron
(*Rhododendron* 'Olga Mezitt')

VII. Rhododendrons for Mild Climates

The following rhododendron cultivars have proven reliable in the Pacific Northwest, west of the Cascade Mountains, as well as in parts of the East where winter temperatures rarely fall below 0°F and sustained intense summer heat (90°F or higher) is uncommon. These rhododendrons are suitable for zones 7 and 8.

VIII. Azaleas

Azaleas are rhododendrons, botanically speaking, but most can be distinguished by their funnel-shaped flowers that are often solitary and have 5 stamens each and by their small, sometimes deciduous, leaves that are often hairy but never scaly. Rhododendrons, by contrast, frequently have bell-shaped flowers, each of which nearly always has 10 or more stamens. Rhododendron leaves are mostly evergreen, usually 3 inches long or longer, and commonly scaly, woolly, cottony, downy; or fine dotted on the undersurface. Still, there are numerous exceptions and

SMALL-LEAF RHODODENDRONS

Name	Height	Characteristics*
'Aglo'	5–6'	Fine textured; rounded in habit; foliage turns bronzy in fall; flowers light pink; early midseason
'Dora Amateis'	2–3'	Habit usually wider than tall; sun tolerant; flowers white; mid to late midseason
'Fairy Mary'	2–3'	Habit densely leafy; flowers cream tinged with pink and yellow-orange; early midseason
'Ginny Gee'	2–3'	Habit spreading; matlike; flowers opening pink, aging to white; early midseason
'Llenroc'	5–6'	Foliage semievergreen, turning orange in fall; flowers pink; early; the name is Cornell spelled backward
'Milestone'	5–6'	Habit bushy; semievergreen; flowers deep rosy pink; early
'Molly Fordham'	3–4'	Habit an upright mound; leaves lustrous, downy; flowers pale pink to white; early midseason
'Olga Mezitt'	3–4'	Habit upright; foliage bronzy in winter; also called 'Pink PJM'; flowers speckled with rust within; early midseason
'PJM'	5–6'	Habit upright; foliage greenish mahogany in winter; named for breeder's father, Peter J. Mezitt; flowers bright lavender pink; early
'Pioneer Silvery Pink'	3–4'	Habit upright; foliage reddish in fall; flowers pink; early
'Weston's Pink Diamond'	5–6'	Habit upright; vigorous; similar to 'PJM'; flowers pink, double-frilled, silvery throated; early

* For an explanation of bloom times, see page 231.

RHODODENDRONS FOR MILD CLIMATES

Names	Height	Characteristics*
'Anna Rose Whitney'	4–6'	Rounded, compact; glossy foliage; flowers pink, borne in ample trusses; midseason
'Blue Diamond'	2–3'	Rounded, densely compact; small leaved; flowers blue-lavender, abundant; early
'Cilpinense'	1½–2'	Spreading; small leaved; flowers pink, funnel shaped; early
'Cream Crest'	2–3'	Compact and spreading; small leaved; flowers light yellow; early
'David'	3–5'	Rounded, compact; upright; flowers blood red; midseason
'Fabia'	3–4'	Spreading; flowers orange to red-orange, bell shaped; late

(continues)

intermediate kinds, lending credence to all being grouped under the single generic name *Rhododendron*. Horticulturally, azaleas are treated separately not only because most of the commonly grown kinds are easily told apart from cultivated rhododendrons but also because their uses and cultural requirements are somewhat different.

Most azaleas, especially those with deciduous leaves, grow best in full sun, providing the soil is not allowed to dry out—a hazard in hot summer weather. A mulch of oak leaves or other acidifying, water-retaining medium is beneficial. If the characteristically shallow, finely ramified roots do dry out in summer heat, azaleas frequently fail to survive the ensuing winter; such a demise is often erroneously ascribed to winter tenderness.

Because of their generally lower growth and finer texture than that of true rhododendrons, azaleas are more readily used in foundation plantings, as facer material in front of taller leggy shrubs and in low mass plantings. Except to trim back an occasional errant shoot, they should not be pruned or shaped; such treatment not only frustrates their natural grace but diminishes the floral display—which is, after all, the main reason azaleas are grown.

Tender sorts (especially the Indian azaleas, *R. simsii* hybrids, often sold as seasonal decoration at Easter) may be grown as long-term houseplants; most flower during the winter or early spring if placed in a sunny window and benefit by being placed outdoors in a partly shaded position for the summer. As the floral display of a hardy, well-established azalea can be dazzling, care should be taken when selecting and placing various kinds that the flower colors of adjacent shrubs are harmonious.

SPECIES AZALEAS

Among the scores upon scores of *Rhododendron* species that are commonly called azaleas, those named in the following table are especially worthy of consideration for the home garden. All are of generally rounded habit, unless otherwise noted.

RHODODENDRONS FOR MILD CLIMATES (continued)

Names	Height	Characteristics*
'Loderi'	8–10'	Rounded; slow to reach blooming size; flowers pink to white, very large and showy; midseason (cvs. 'King George', 'Pink Diamond', and 'Venus' are similar)
'Loder's White'	4–5'	Rounded; blooms when small; flowers opening pink, aging to white, midseason
'Mars'	3–4'	Rounded; leaves glossy; flowers dark red; late
'Mrs. Charles E. Pearson'	4–5'	Rounded; leaves large, glossy; flowers opening bluish mauve, blotched orange-brown, aging to pale pink, held in large trusses; early
'Point Defiance'	4–6'	Rounded; leaves glossy; flowers white with pink edges; midseason
'Purple Spendour'	3–4'	Rounded; flowers deep purple with a black violet blotch; late
'Sappho'	8–12'	Rounded; requires pruning after flowering for compactness; flowers, white with purple blotch; midseason
'Spitfire'	4–6'	Rounded; leaves dark green; flowers very dark red; midseason
'Susan'	4–6'	Rounded; leaves glossy; buds rosy lavender, opening silvery lilac blue with the center paler and spotted red-brown; midseason
'Unique'	3–4'	Rounded, compact; buds red, opening peach or yellow; early

* For an explanation of bloom times, see page 231.

Royal azalea
(*Rhododendron schlippenbachii*)

Swamp azalea
(*Rhododendron viscosum*)

Flame azalea (*Rhododendron calendulaceum*)

SPECIES AZALEAS

Name	Zones	Height	Characteristics*
R. alabamense (Alabama azalea)	7–8	4–6'	Deciduous; flowers white with yellow blotches; fragrant; early midseason
R. albrechtii	5–8	4–5'	Deciduous; dark green foliage; flowers rose to rose violet, appearing just before leaves, bell shaped; early midseason
R. amagianum (Amagi azalea)	5–8	8–10'	Deciduous; leaves arranged in threes; flowers orange-red; late
R. arborescens (sweet azalea)	4–8	10–12'	Deciduous; diffuse habit; leaves lustrous, red in fall; flowers white with reddish stamens; late
R. atlanticum (Coast azalea)	5–8 (9)	4–6'	Deciduous; copse forming; leaves blue-green; flowers clustered, white to pink with purple inside, fragrant; midseason
R. austrinum (Florida azalea)	7–9	8–10'	Deciduous; diffuse; many stemmed; flowers clustered, light yellow to red, fragrant; early
R. bakeri (Cumberland azalea)	5–7	6–8'	Deciduous; flowers yellow-orange to red; probably a later-flowering variant of R. calendulaceum
R. calendulaceum (flame azalea)	5–8	8–10'	Similar to R. bakeri but larger (to 15 feet wide); late midseason
R. canadense (rhodora)	2–7	3–4'	Deciduous; twiggy; leaves gray green; flowers rose pink or purplish, held in small clusters; early
R. canescens (Piedmont azalea)	5–9	10–12'	Deciduous; forming; buds pink, opening white with pink inside, fragrant; curly midseason
R. flammeum (Oconee azalea)	5–8	4–6'	Deciduous; flowers red or orange (or yellow or pink in cultivars), held in clusters; midseason
R. × gandavense (Ghent hybrid azaleas): see page 238.			
R. japonicum (Japanese azalea)	5–8	6–8'	Deciduous; leaves large (to 4 inches); flowers salmon to orange or red; late midseason
R. kaempferi (torch azalea)	6–8	8–10'	Deciduous or half-evergreen; diffusely branched; leaves red in fall; flowers pink, orange, or red; midseason
R. kiusianum (Kyushu azalea)	(4) 5–8	2–3'	Semievergreen or fully evergreen; spreading; flowers purple or white, appearing even on very small plants; late midseason
R. linearifolium (spider azalea)	7–8	3–4'	Evergreen; leaves strap shaped, in whorls; flowers lavender, in radiating clusters; early midseason
R. luteum	5–8	8–10'	Deciduous; upright habit; flowers yellow, large, fragrant; late midseason
R. nakaharae	5–8	1– 1½'	Evergreen; spreading habit flowers red, pink, orange, yellow or white; midseason
R. oblongifolium (Texas azalea)	7–8	4–6'	Deciduous; one of the few azaleas suited to alkaline soil; leaves large (to 4 inches); flowers, white, clustered; late
R. obtusum (Hiryu or Kirishima azalea)	(5) 6–8	2–3'	Evergreen or semievergreen; spreading, intricately branched; leaves glossy; flowers reddish purple to deep red; midseason
R. ovatum	6–8	5–8'	Evergreen; foliage fine-textured, red when young; flowers white or pale pink spotted purple; late midseason
R. periclymenoides, syn. R. nudiflorum (pinxterbloom azalea)	3–8	4–6' (10')	Deciduous; flowers white or pale pink (rarely purple); midseason
R. prinophyllum (rose-shell azalea)	3–8	4–8'	Deciduous; flowers bright pink, spicily fragrant, appearing before leaves; early
R. prunifolium (plum-leaf azalea)	5–9	8–10'	Deciduous; flowers red-orange, opening wide; very late
R. reticulatum (three-leaf azalea)	6–8	10–15'	Deciduous; rangy, twiggy; leaves in twos or threes; flowers bright pink or rose purple, appearing before the leaves; early
R. schlippenbachii (Royal azalea)	4–7	6–8'	Deciduous; densely branched; flowers pale rose pink, 3 inches across, clustered, appearing with the leaves; early

(continues)

SPECIES AZALEAS (continued)

Name	Zones	Height	Characteristics*
R. serpyllifolium (wild thyme azalea)	6–8	2–3'	Evergreen; finely branched; leaves ⅔ to ¾ inch long; flowers lavender; early midseason
R. serrulatum	7–8	10–15'	Deciduous leaves finely toothed; flowers, white, fragrant; late
R. simsii (Sims' azalea)	8–10	3–5'	Evergreen or semievergreen; finely branched; flowers rose to red; midseason (when grown outdoors)
R. vaseyi (pink-shell azalea)	4–8	8–10'	Deciduous; rangy, irregular habit; leaves red in fall; flowers rose pink or white, appearing before the leaves; early
R. viscosum (swamp azalea)	3–9	3–8'	Deciduous; open, irregular habit; best grown on wet ground; flowers white, rarely pink, clove-scented
R. weyrichii	7–8	10–15'	Deciduous; leaves very late mostly in threes; flowers brick red or orange-red, appearing before the leaves; early
R. yedoense (Yodogawa azalea)	(4) 5–7	3–6'	Deciduous or semievergreen; flowers rose purple, double; midseason
R. yedoense var. *poukhanense* (Korean azalea)	(4) 5–7	3–6'	Similar to *R. yedoense*; flowers rose purple to lilac purple, 2 inches across, fragrant

* For an explanation of bloom times, see page 231.

AZALEA HYBRID GROUPS

The most frequently encountered azaleas are cultivars that belong to, or are derived from, one or more hybrid groups, each usually having a number of parent species. Some of the best-known hybrid groups are discussed below.

Gable Hybrids

Gable hybrids are very hardy (zones 5–8); were derived mainly from *Rhododendron kaempferi* and *R. yedoense* var. *poukhanense*; and were developed by Joseph Gable, a hybridizer in Pennsylvania. All are deciduous or half-evergreen, rounded in habit, and mature at 3 to 6 feet tall. Among the most widely grown cultivars are the following (see page 231 for explanation of bloom times).

'David Gable': flowers rose pink; early.
'Forest Fire': flowers deep red; midseason.
'Girard's Red': flowers red; midseason.
'Girard's Rose': flowers rose red; midseason.
'Louise Gable': flowers salmon pink; late.
'Purple Splendor': flowers purple; midseason.
'Rosebud': flowers pink; late.
'Rose Greeley': flowers white; early midseason.
'Stewartstonian': flowers red; early midseason.

Ghent Hybrids

Grouped under the binomial name *Rhododendron* × *gandavense*, the Ghent hybrids are derived from the American species *R. calendulaceum*, *R. flammeum*, *R. perclymenoides*, and *R. viscosum*; the Caucasian species *R. luteum*; and the Chinese species *R. molle*. Developed in Belgium, the derived cultivars show varied hardiness, but most are suited to areas with relatively cool summers and moderate winters (zones 5–7). All are deciduous, rounded in habit, and mature about 6 feet tall. Some of the better known cultivars are to listed below; for an explanation of bloom times, see page 231.

'Bouquet de Flore': flowers pink; midseason.
'Coccinea Speciosa': flowers orange; early to mid season.
'Daviesii': flowers creamy white; late.
'Gloria Mundi': flowers red, orange, or yellow; midseason.
'Narcissiflora': flowers double yellow; late.
'Pallas': flowers red-orange; midseason.

Glen Dale Hybrids

The Glen Dale hybrids make up a diverse and extensive group of evergreen cultivars varying greatly in habit, foliage, and flower traits. In some cultivars are found the largest flowers known among hardy azaleas, rivaling those of Indicum hybrids. Developed by B. Y. Morrison of the U.S. Department of Agriculture, the Glen Dale hybrids include as parents the Kaempferi and Kurume hybrids, which helps account for the hardiness of some of these large-flowered cultivars, all maturing to 3 to 5 feet tall and thriving in zones 7 and 8. Some of the better-known examples are listed below (see page 231 for an explanation of bloom times).

'Buccaneer': flowers red; midseason.
'Dayspring': flowers white with pink edge; early.
'Dimity': flowers white with red markings; early.
'Geisha': flowers white with purple markings; early.
'Helen Close': flowers white; midseason.
'Martha Hitchcock': flowers white with magenta edge; early midseason.
'Pink Ice': flowers double pink; midseason.
'Rosalie': flowers magenta; late.

Indicum Hybrids

The Indicum hybrids are tender evergreen azaleas, mostly suited to zones 8–10. They are derived from *R. mucronatum* of

Japan, *R. simsii* of China and Taiwan, and *R. pulchrum*, a species grown in China but unknown in the wild and possibly of hybrid origin. The derived cultivars are known for their generous production of often immense flowers (up to 4½ inches across), and for this reason, some are much favored in the florist trade as well as for outdoor use in the South and Southwest, where they mature to 3 to 6 feet tall. Better-known Indicum cultivars include the following (for an explanation of bloom times, see page 231).

'Duc de Rohan': flowers salmon pink; early midseason.
'Fielder's White': flowers white; early midseason.
'Flame Creeper': flowers red-orange; midseason; hardy to zone 7.
'Formosa': flowers red-violet; midseason to late midseason.
'George L. Taber': flowers pink; midseason to late midseason.
'Iveryana': flowers white with lavender markings; midseason.
'Pride of Dorking': flowers red; late.
'Prince of Wales': flowers rose red; midseason.

Kaempferi Hybrids

The Kaempferi hybrids are derived mainly from the torch azalea (*R. kaempferi*) and in varying degrees from the Hiryu azalea (*R. obtusum*), both of Japan. The many derivative cultivars, sometimes called Malvatica hybrids, are deciduous or semi-evergreen and vary in habit and flower color, although they tend to be of open and upright growth, 3 to 6 feet tall, with red flowers. The following cultivars are especially successful (see page 231 for an explanation of bloom times).

'Barbara': flowers pink; midseason.
'Fedora': flowers red; early.
'Herbert': flowers purple; midseason.
'Holland': flowers deep red; midseason.
'Mikado': flowers red; midseason.
'Othello': flowers red-orange; midseason.
'Palestrina'; syn. 'Wilhelmina Vuyk': flowers white; midseason to late midseason.

Knap Hill Hybrids

The Knap Hill hybrids are deciduous azaleas related to the Ghent and Molle hybrids, and to confuse matters further, some are separately grouped as Exbury hybrids, developed by Lionel de Rothschild in England. The parent species are *R. arborescens*, *R. calendulaceum*, *R. molle*, and *R. occidentale*. Most grow best in zones 5–7 and reach 4 to 6 feet tall. Habit and flower color vary. Of the many cultivars available, the following are especially desirable (see page 231 for an explanation of bloom times).

'Berry Rose': flowers rose pink; early midseason.
'Firefly': flowers red; midseason.
'Flamingo': flowers pink; midseason.
'Gibraltar': flowers orange; midseason.
'Golden Oriole': flowers yellow; late midseason.
'Sun Chariot': flowers yellow; midseason.
'White Swan': flowers white; midseason.
'White Throat': flowers double white; midseason.

Kurume Hybrids

Derived from the Japanese species *R. kaempferi*, *R. kiusianum*, *R. obtusum*, and *R. satense*, Kurume hybrids are mostly low (less than 3 or 4 feet tall), small-leaf, intricately branched evergreens with profusely produced flowers. Generally, the flowers are in shades of red and pink as well as white. Most cultivars are reliably hardy no farther north than zone 7. Some of the best cultivars are listed below (see page 231 for an explanation of bloom times).

'Broadleaf Double Red': flowers double red; midseason.
'Delicatissima': flowers white flushed pink; early midseason.
'Eureka': flowers double pink; late.
'Hershey's Red': flowers double red; midseason.
'Hino-Crimson': flowers red; midseason.
'Hinodegiri': flowers red; early midseason.
'Ho-Oden': flowers lilac with white and magenta; early midseason.
'King's Luminous Pink': flowers white with purplish pink; midseason.
'Komohana': flowers coral pink; early midseason.
'Polar Bear': flowers double white; midseason.
'Ruth May': flowers pink and white; early.

Molle Hybrids

The Molle hybrids are also known as Kosteranum hybrids. The origins of this group are not entirely clear, but

Kurume hybrid azalea (*Rhododendron* 'Hershey Red')

they are believed to be derived from *R. × kosteranum, R. molle, R. viscosum,* and perhaps others. The cultivars, mostly developed in Holland and best grown in zones 6–8; are deciduous; rather stiffly erect; and bear flowers in clusters of 7 to 13, mostly in shades of yellow, orange, red, and pink. Cultivars of particular importance, all flowering in midseason or a little later (see page 231), include the following.

'Adrian Koster': flowers yellow.
'Christopher Wren': flowers yellow.
'Consol Creole': flowers rose pink.
'Doctor Jacobi': flowers dark red.
'Koster's Brilliant': flowers red-orange.
'Snowdrift': flowers white.

Other Hybrid Groups

Of the several additional groups of azalea hybrids, most are of complex origin and are characterized by one or more physiological features that suit them for the relatively mild conditions that prevail in south-coastal California, the Gulf Coast, and Florida. Included here are Brooks hybrids, Rutherfordian hybrids, Gold Cup hybrids, Pericat hybrids, and Satsuki also known as (Gumpo, Macrantha, or Chugai) hybrids. Most of the derived cultivars were orginally developed for the heat tolerance, compact habit, and large flowers important in commercial greenhouse culture, but many of them have proven useful and desirable in outdoor landscapes where winter temperatures fall no lower than about 25°F. Some Satsuki and Pericat hybrids are hardy to 10°F or a bit lower. As with Indicum hybrids, these relatively tender azaleas can be grown in the North as houseplants, if given a sunny exposure indoors and placed outdoors in partial shade over the summer. With suitable fertilizing, flowers appear during the winter.

ROSA RUGOSA
(Rugosa rose, beach rose, Japanese rose)

Zones 2–7

Perhaps the most dependable of all the shrub roses for general use, the rugosa rose bears pink or white flowers in late spring and then sparingly or intermittently through the summer. The handsome brick red to orange fruits, about 1 inch across, are very ornamental and persist well into autumn. Rugosa rose is widely naturalized along the coast in the Northeast and is one of the best of all shrubs for seaside gardens. Normal height ranges from 5 to 6 feet, and this species adapts itself well to treatment as a hedge, either clipped or unclipped. There are many cultivars with single or double flowers, and colors range from white through pink and rose purple.

Rugosa rose succeeds in virtually any soil that is reasonably well drained, tolerates salt spray, and is free of pests and diseases. To flower satisfactorily, it must have full sun. Except for removal of dead or failing stems in the spring, no special care is required. See Chapter 19 for culture of hybrid roses.

SARCOCOCCA HOOKERIANA 'HUMILIS'
(Sweet box)

Zones (5) 6–8

Sweet box is a small, evergreen shrub that has proven itself of value in shaded locations. Its dark, glossy leaves, stoloniferous habit, and compact form make it an excellent ground cover in semishaded areas, and it may also be used very effectively as a foreground planting in an evergreen shrub bed or border. The flowers are white and inconspicuous. The leaves are 3 to 4 inches long and taper to a slender point. It is a shrub that grows slowly but eventually, after many years, can attain a height of about 2 feet. *Sarcococca confusa* and the typical form of *S. hookeriana* are similar but eventually grow to 6 feet.

Sweet box does best in loamy, well-drained soil of average fertility. Its shade tolerance suits it for use on the north side of buildings and walls. It is easily established but should be mulched with leaves and not subjected to soil cultivation.

SKIMMIA JAPONICA
(Japanese skimmia)

Zones (6) 7–8 (9)

Often overlooked and underused, Japanese skimmia is a slow-growing broad-leaf evergreen that reaches about 4 feet tall and 6 feet wide. It has handsome glossy foliage; maroon flower buds that open white in early spring, and in female plants, bright red, glossy pea-size fruit that persists through the winter. It is especially useful in shade where, with adequately moist soil, it thrives. One male shrub per six females usually results in good fruit display. It is free of pests and diseases.

Consistently moist soil, acidic in reaction and rich in organic matter, produces the best results. Shade is desirable for Japanese skimmia, especially from intense summer sun and bright sunlight in late winter and early spring. As it is usually available in containers, establishment is easily achieved. Except for removal of dead wood, pruning is not required.

SPIRAEA PRUNIFOLIA
(Bridal wreath)

Zones 4–8

A comparatively slender shrub, eventually growing 6 to 8 feet tall, bridal wreath is of upright, spreading habit, with graceful arching branches that are covered with bloom in early spring. The small, white, buttonlike flowers are double and borne in great abundance. As it has a tendency to become leggy near the ground, bridal wreath is best when massed, or included in foundation plantings, where it can be fronted with lower-growing materials. Its chief virtue is its delicacy, and when in flower it seems to convey the essence of spring.

This shrub will grow in any well-drained loamy soil, especially if kept moist over the summer. A sunny position ensures a generous flower display. Legginess can be minimized by cutting out all dead wood from the center that does not bear bloom, allowing new growth to come up. Pruning for this early spring-blooming type should take place after flowering, since flowers are borne only on the previous year's growth.

SPIRAEA THUNBERGII
(Thunberg spiraea)

Zones 4–8

Thunberg spiraea is a fine-textured shrub well adapted for the foreground of

Van houette spiraea (*Spiraea × vanhouttei*)

mass plantings as it rarely grows more than 4 feet tall. It is of bushy habit, with very slender, densely twiggy stems. The leaves are yellow-green, turning orange and red in the autumn. It blooms very early in the season, the myriad small white flowers appear before the leaves unfold.

Ordinary well-drained garden soil and a location exposed to full sun ensure good performance. Annual pruning of old, failing stems and, of course, of dead wood is desirable. It should be undertaken immediately after flowering.

SPIRAEA × VANHOUTTEI
(Vanhoutte spiraea, Bridal wreath)

Zones 3–8

A veritable fountain of bloom when it is in flower, Vanhoutte spiraea is of graceful form, 6 to 8 feet in height and as wide. The finely toothed, delicate foliage is an attractive blue-green throughout the season. The large white flower clusters are borne in lavish profusion during the month of May. It may be used as a specimen shrub, for both foundation and mass planting, and as a flowering hedge—but should be left unsheared.

As with *S. thunbergii*, average soil and a sunny position will ensure a lovely floral display year after year. Any pruning should take place directly after flowering, because bloom is borne on the previous year's growth. Pruning should be selective, since the divergent vaselike form of this shrub accounts for a great deal of its charm.

SYMPLOCOS PANICULATA
(Sapphire berry, Asiatic sweetleaf)

Zones 4–8

Sapphire berry is a large shrub, valued for its brilliant blue fruit, borne in hanging clusters in early autumn. The berries are highly attractive to birds, who often strip the fruit very soon after it changes color. The small white flowers, which appear in late spring, are borne in panicles. The height varies from 15 to 25 feet. The foliage, although small, is dense, and the shrub can be used either as a background or as an accent in a formal setting. It is free of pests and diseases.

Sapphire berry is easily grown, as long as adequate space is provided. It is best placed where the fruit display and the attracted birds can be seen to advantage.

Average well-drained soil and a position in full sun or partial shade are the basic requirements for success. Pruning, if required, is best done in early spring.

SYRINGA × CHINENSIS
(Chinese lilac)

Zones 5–8

The Chinese lilac is not a Chinese species at all but a hybrid between the Persian lilac (*S. × persica*) and common lilac (*S. vulgaris*). It first appeared in the nurseries of a French grower at Rouen about 1777 and was first supposed to be an imported species when it was named. Its blossoms are larger and more compact than those of *S. persica*, reddish purple, dark red, or white. The leaves are also larger and broader. Chinese lilac can reach 15 feet at maturity. Soil requirements, exposure, and culture are essentially the same as for common lilac (*S. vulgaris*) below.

SYRINGA MEYERI
(Meyer lilac)

Zones 3–8

A very handsome shrub, Meyer lilac is diminutive in all respects when compared with the common lilac (*S. vulgaris*) It ultimately reaches 6 feet but begins flowering when little more than 1 foot tall. The pinkish purple flowers appear in midspring. The leaves are free of the grayish powdery mildew that so often discolors the foliage of common lilac in summer. Meyer lilac is best known by the cultivar 'Palibin', a compact form usually less than 4 feet tall.

Soil requirements and exposure are the same as for common lilac, as is culture. Meyer lilacs, however, are free of suckers and powdery mildew.

SYRINGA MICROPHYLLA
(Littleleaf lilac)

Zones 5–8

A compact shrub to 6 feet, littleleaf lilac has mahogany red buds that open to light pink flowers. These appear in large clusters in midspring and are so abundant that the whole shrub resembles one large bouquet. Flowering may resume sporadically in late summer or early fall. The small leaves, between 1 and 1½ inches long, impart a fine texture to the shrub. Littleleaf lilac is best known by the very floriferous cultivar 'Superba' (Daphne lilac), in which the flowers are deep pink. Soil requirements, exposure, and culture are essentially the same as for common lilac (*S. vulgaris*).

SYRINGA PEKINENSIS
(Pekin lilac)

Zones 3–7

Although Pekin lilac may reach 15 to 20 feet at maturity, it is shrubby in habit. The yellow-brown bark peels like birch bark—a landscape asset. Large clusters of cream-colored flowers are borne in late spring. Although it was introduced from China in about 1880, Pekin lilac is regrettably still little known in this country. Soil requirements, exposure, and culture are the same as for common lilac (*S. vulgaris*).

SYRINGA × PERSICA
(Persian lilac)

Zones 3–7

Although for centuries thought to have originated in Persia (Iran), *S. × persica*, a graceful lilac, really comes from China. Many centuries ago, it was brought to Persia, where it was adopted for cultivation. From there it was introduced into Europe in the seventeenth century. The shrub is smaller than the common lilac (*S. vulgaris*), seldom exceeding 8 to 10 feet in height, and has smaller, narrower leaves. The small clusters of pink flowers are borne on lateral branches in late spring after the leaves have appeared. Soil requirements, exposure, and culture are the same as for common lilac.

Bicolor lilac (*Syringa patula*, syn. *S. velutina*), with flowers lilac and white within

SYRINGA VILLOSA
(Late lilac)

Zones 2–7

A very hardy bushy shrub 6 to 10 feet high, late lilac has broad leaves (often 7 inches long) and bears pale rose pink flowers in mid to late spring. To some people the odor of the bloom is disagreeable. It is one of the hardiest of all the lilacs and one of the last of the shrubby lilacs to blossom. Crossing this species with *S. reflexa* has resulted in a series of cultivars known collectively as the *S. × prestoniae* hybrids, which bloom even later and thus further extend the lilac season. Soil requirements, exposure, and culture are the same as for common lilac (*S. vulgaris*).

SYRINGA VULGARIS
(Common lilac)

Zones 3–7

A native of the mountainous regions of the Balkan Peninsula, common lilac was highly prized by the Turks, and from Constantinople it was introduced into Europe in about 1550. Its ability to naturalize and thrive caused it to run wild throughout Western Europe, so that by 1780 it was a common hedgerow shrub in parts of Italy and France. When or how it was brought to America is not known, but in all likelihood it reached the colonies before 1750. It was greatly appreciated by colonists because of its ability to survive severe winters, summer drought, and long periods of neglect.

It is a vigorous shrub, growing to a height of 15 to 18 feet, and bears its lavender or white flowers in large trusses, which are often paired at the ends of the upper branches. Early in the nineteenth century, horticulturists were experimenting with lilacs, producing new varieties and discovering some with distinctive characteristics. Hundreds of cultivars have been produced, in France, Belgium, Holland, Germany, Canada, and the United States, and many of these are now offered by American nurseries.

Common lilac will grow on any well-drained soil but performs best with rich garden loam that ranges from slightly acidic to slightly alkaline (pH 6.0 to 8.0). Although common lilac endures shade, it must have plenty of sun to bloom well. When well established, it withstands high wind, heavy snow, and prolonged cold.

Young shrubs should be trained to several main stems so that damage from borers is reduced to a minimum. If borers are detected in one stem (evident by piles of sawdust and serially dying branches), it should be removed and burned, and the borers with it, while the other stems carry on. Many lilacs have a habit of suckering from the roots. This should be checked by annual pruning down to the ground. Likewise the central or interior stems tend to become crowded and should be thinned out occasionally. When in bloom, the flowering stems may be cut long to include much foliage and may be used in decorating the house. Slitting or crushing the cut ends of the flowering branchlets prolongs the indoor display. This is one of the easy methods of pruning. If pruning is not done at this time, it may be undertaken directly after the flowering period, but no later, as the season's growth is completed within a few

SUPERIOR CULTIVARS OF COMMON LILAC (*S. VULGARIS*)

Flower Color	Single flowered	Double flowered
Blue	'Decaisne' 'President Lincoln' 'President Grevy'	'Ami Schott' 'Olivier de Serres'
Lilac	'Christophe Colomb' 'Leon Gambetta' 'Victor Lemoine'	'Alphonse Lavalle'
Magenta	'Capitaine Baltet' 'Congo' 'Mme. F. Morel'	'Charles Joly' 'Paul Thirion' 'President Poincaire'
Pink	'Lucie Baltet' 'Katherine Havemeyer' 'Montaigne'	'Belle de Nancy'
Purple	'Ludwig Spaeth' 'Monge' 'Mrs. W. E. Marshall'	'Adelaide Dunbar' 'Paul Hariot'
Violet	'De Miribel'	'Marechal Lannes'
White	'Jan Van Tol' 'Vestal'	'Edith Cavell' 'Miss Ellen Willmott'
Yellow	'Primrose'	

Single magenta common lilac (*Syringa vulgaris* 'Congo')

Double purple common lilac
(*Syringa vulgaris* 'Paul Hariot')

weeks and buds set for the next spring's bloom. Failure to bloom may be due to too severe pruning or no pruning the preceding season, to the accumulation of suckers, or to heavily shaded conditions.

With prolonged summer humidity, powdery mildew causes the leaves of common lilac to turn grayish, but this disease usually causes little harm. More serious are such pests as oyster shell scale and San Jose scale, both of which are damaging. Clusters on the twigs and branches results in the shriveling of leaves and general lack of vitality. Measures of control for borers and scales are described in Chapter 34.

VIBURNUM × BODNANTENSE 'DAWN'
(*Early pink viburnum*)

Zones 6–8
One of the very few early spring-blooming shrubs with a pink floral display, early pink viburnum offers red buds at about the change of seasons; these open pink and finally fade to near white. The berries that follow turn reddish, maturing to black. This viburnum eventually reaches 8 to 10 feet in height and is largely untroubled by pests and diseases.

Early pink viburnum is very adaptable to any well-drained site, but care should be taken to choose a sun-exposed site

away from frost pockets, such as the south side of buildings or walls, to avoid spring freezes, as frost damages the flowers. Flowering is sparse in sites that are shaded in summer. Culture is much the same as for *V. burkwoodii*.

VIBURNUM × BURKWOODII
(*Burkwood viburnum*)

Zones 3–8
A very attractive deciduous shrub to 10 feet tall, Burkwood viburnum has lustrous dark green foliage and rounded clusters of fragrant flowers in spring. It is especially suited to climates more severe than most viburnums can tolerate. Several cultivars (e.g., 'Anne Russell', 'Chenaultii', 'Fulbrook', and 'Mohawk') are available with more abundant pink- or red-budded flowers that emit a very sweet scent and gradually turn white. Burkwood viburnum is relatively disease and pest free.

Although this viburnum is pH adaptable, it performs best in well-drained, somewhat acidic, moderately moist soil in a location with full sun or partial shade. Burkwood viburnum is easily established from balled-and-burlapped stock or from container-grown material. Occasional selective pruning may be required for shaping. This is best done at the conclusion of flowering.

VIBURNUM CARLESII
(*Korean spice viburnum*)

Zones 4–7 (8)
Native to Korea and noted particularly for the sweet fragrance of its blossoms, Korean spice viburnum is a shrub of

somewhat rounded form, reaching 6 to 8 feet. The flowers, which form a close, compact head, are a delicate pink when they first open in early spring, gradually fading to white, and their fragrance is suggestive of that of daphne. Korean spice viburnum is largely pest and disease free.

As soil-adaptable as *V. × burkwoodii*, this species requires full sun for the best flower display. It is readily established from balled-and-burlapped and container-grown stock, preferably self-rooted rather than grafted. Any pruning is best done when flowers have passed.

VIBURNUM × CARLCEPHALUM
(*Fragrant snowball*)

Zones (5) 6–9
A hybrid of *V. carlesii* and *V. macrocephalum*, and possessing many of the best traits of both, fragrant snowball is vigorous in growth, though rather open and informal in habit, and reaches an ultimate height of 6 to 8 feet, sometimes even 10 feet. It combines the early bloom and intense fragrance of *V. carlesii* with the large rounded, white flowers of *V. macrocephalum*. The blooms are borne in great profusion, peaking in late spring. In the fall, the foliage turns a bright reddish violet.

Fragrant snowball thrives equally on acidic or neutral soil. Full sun or light shade is best. Culture is easier than and pruning is same as for *V. carlessii*.

VIBURNUM CASSINOIDES
(*Witherod viburnum*)

Zones 3–8
Witherod viburnum is a rounded, densely leafy native shrub that matures to 6 to 10 feet tall, It is deciduous or (in zone 8) semievergreen, with foliage that reddens attractively in fall. It bears flat-topped clusters of white flowers in the spring (often precociously in the fall in zone 8), followed by fruit that changes at varying rates from green through pink and red to blue before maturing to black. Although it is very handsome and relatively pest and disease free, this species remains little used.

Soil requirements are the same as for *V. × burkwoodii*. Full sun or light shade are important for maximal flower and fruit display. As with other viburnums, balled-and-burlapped and container-grown stock ensure easy establishment, while the transplanting of long-established shrubs is risky.

VIBURNUM DILATATUM
(Linden viburnum)

Zones (4) 5–7 (8)

Like most other viburnums, the linden viburnum is a vigorous shrub of dense habit. Decorative in three seasons, it is covered with clusters of white flowers in mid to late spring, and in early fall it bears masses of showy scarlet berries that hang on after leaf drop well into winter. An excellent component of the mixed shrub border, linden viburnum reaches 6 to 10 feet and is free of pests and diseases. Soil and other cultural requirements are the same as for *V. × burkwoodii*.

The cultivar 'Erie' offers a superior fruit display, and 'Xanthocarpum' has yellow berries but is somewhat less vigorous in growth. In this species, including its cultivars, the fruit displays are more effective at the cooler end of its range.

VIBURNUM PLICATUM F. TOMENTOSUM
(Double-file viburnum)

Zones (4) 5–8

The double-file viburnum is a strikingly handsome shrub in flower. In autumn, the dark green leaves take on a somber bronzy purple. It is initially of upright habit, to about 12 feet, and has wide-spreading branches that are gently ascending or horizontal. The white flowers, appearing at about the same time as those of the native dogwood (*Cornus florida*), are borne in flat 3-inch clusters, which are arranged on opposite sides of the twigs and line the upward side of the branches, producing an interesting layered effect. The small clustered fruits are red at first, then turn gradually to blue-black. This is one of the most desirable viburnums for specimen use and for mass planting. Double-file viburnum performs best

in full sun, but its culture is otherwise similar to *V. × burkwoodii*.

Among the numerous cultivars, the widely available 'Mariesii' and 'Shasta' are somewhat lower in habit but more heavily flowering. All are reliably pest and disease free.

VIBURNUM RHYTIDOPHYLLUM
(Leatherleaf viburnum)

Zones (5) 6–8

One of the few hardy members of this large group that is evergreen throughout its range, the leatherleaf viburnum is of vigorous growth with strong, stout branches. It ultimately reaches a height of 8 to 10 feet. The creamy white flowers open in late spring and are borne in broad heads well above the foliage. The fruits become red before changing to black. The large leaves are dark green, somewhat shiny, and are wrinkled or puckered in texture. In cold weather, they are pendent. Leatherleaf viburnum is free of pests and diseases.

This species is generally hardy but may lose some foliage or die back somewhat in exposed locations during windy subzero weather. Culture is the same as for *V. × burkwoodii*, except that partial shade is best in zone 8.

VIBURNUM SETIGERUM
(Tea-leaf viburnum)

Zones 5–7

Tea-leaf viburnum is a shrub for special consideration. Although its foliage is not especially dense and it tends to legginess in age, it has beautiful slender downward-pointing leaves and a profusion of white flowers in late spring or early summer, followed by heavy clusters of brilliant red, persistent berries. It is slow to mature but eventually reaches 10 to 12 feet. The cultivar 'Aurantiacum' has orange fruit.

Tea-leaf viburnum thrives on acidic or neutral soil but must have a well-drained site, preferably in full sun or at most partial shade. Because of eventual legginess, it should be fronted with lower shrubs. Pruning should be done after the fruit display is over.

Leatherleaf viburnum (*Viburnum rhytidophyllum*)

OTHER USEFUL SHRUBS

All are deciduous, unless indicated.

Name	Zones	Height	Exposure*
Abeliophyllum distichum (white forsythia)	5–8	4–5'	S to Sh
Abies concolor 'Green Globe' (dwarf fir)	(3) 4–7	2–3'	S
Acer tataricum (Tatarian maple)	3–8	15–20'	S to PSh
Aesculus parviflora (bottlebrush buckeye)	4–8 (9)	8–12'	S to Sh
Alnus rugosa (speckled alder)	4–8	15–25'	S to PSh
A. serrulata (tag alder)	4–8	15–25'	S to PSh
Amelanchier alnifolia (Saskatoon serviceberry)	4–6	6–18'	S to PSh
A. canadensis (shadbush)	3–7 (8)	6–20'	S to Sh
A. stolonifera (running serviceberry)	4–6	4–6'	S to PSh
Amorpha canescens (lead plant)	2–7	2–4'	S
A. fruticosa (false indigo)	4–9	6–20'	S
Andromeda polifolia (bog rosemary)	1–3	½–1'	S
Aralia spinosa (Hercules club)	4–9	10–20'	S to PSh
Arbutus unedo (strawberry bush, strawberry tree)	8–10	8–20'	S
Aronia arbutifolia (red chokeberry)	4–9	6–10'	S to PSh
A. melanocarpa (black chokeberry)	3–8 (9)	3–8'	S to PSh
A. prunifolia (purple chokeberry)	4–8	8–12'	S to PSh
Baccharis halimifolia (groundsel bush)	4–9	6–12'	S
Berberis × chenaultii (Chenault barberry)	5–8	3–4'	S to PSh
B. koreana (Korean barberry)	3–7	4–6'	S
B. × mentorensis (Mentor barberry)	5–8	5–7'	S
B. sargentiana (Sargent barberry)	6–9	6–7'	S
B. verruculosa (warty barberry)	5–8	3–6'	S
B. wilsoniae (Wilson barberry)	6–8	3–6'	S
B. wisleyensis (Wisley barberry)	7–9	3–4'	S
Betula pendula 'Trost Dwarf' (dwarf cutleaf birch)	2–7	3–4'	S
Bruckenthalia spiculifolia (spike heath)	6–8	½–1'	S
Buddleia alternifolia (fountain butterfly bush)	5–9	10–15'	S
Callicarpa americana (American beauty-berry, French mulberry)	7–10	3–8'	S to PSh
C. bodinieri (Bodinier beauty-berry)	6–8	6–10'	S
C. japonica (Japanese beauty-berry)	5–8	4–6'	S to PSh
Calluna vulgaris (heather)	4–6	½–2'	S to PSh
Caragana arborescens (Siberian pea bush)	2–7	15–18'	S
C. maximowicziana (Maximowicz pea bush)	2–7	3–6'	S
Caryopteris × clandonensis (blue-mist bush)	(6) 7–8	2–3'	S
C. incana (bluebeard)	(6) 7–8	3–5'	S
Ceanothus americanus (New Jersey tea)	4–8	3–4'	S
Cephalanthus occidentalis (buttonbush)	5–8	5–8'	S to PSh
Chamaecyparis lawsoniana (Lawson cypress dwarf cvs.)	5–7	2–8'	S
C. obtusa (Hinoki cypress dwarf cvs.)	4–8	2–8'	S to PSh
Chamaedaphne calyculatus (leatherleaf)	7–8	3–8'	PSh
Chimonanthus praecox (winter sweet)	(6) 7–9	8–12'	S to LSh
Chionanthus retusus (Chinese fringe bush)	6–9	8–12'	S to PSh
Clerodendrum trichotomum (harlequin glory-bower)	6–8	6–15'	S
Clethra barbinervis (Japanese clethra)	5–8	8–12'	S to PSh

OTHER USEFUL SHRUBS

Soil Requirements	Flower Color and Bloom Time	Comments
Sandy-humusy	White; early spring	Precedes true forsythias
Ordinary	Inconspicuous	Evergreen; dense, globular habit
Average	Greenish white; spring	Drought tolerant; disease free; red samaras in the fall
Loamy, moist	White; summer	Forms clump or copse
Wet, acidic	Yellow-brown; early spring	Good for stream banks and pond borders
Wet, acidic	Yellow-brown; early spring	Similar to *A. rugosa*
Average	White; spring	Purplish blue berries in late summer
Loamy, alkaline	White; before leaves appear	Fruit purple, edible
Average	White; early spring	Purplsh black berries in late summer
Poor, dry	Blue; late spring	Foliage gray green
Poor, dry	Purplish blue; late spring	Good on difficult sites
Porous, acidic	Pink; spring	Evergreen; soil-binding; good in rock gardens
Ordinary	White; late summer	Thorny stems; large cut leaves; black berries
Loamy, porous	White; late summer	Evergreen; red-and-yellow fruit
Ordinary to wet	White; spring	Red berries; red fall foliage
Ordinary to wet	White; spring	Black berries; purple fall foliage
Ordinary to wet	White; spring	Violet black berries; wine red fall foliage
Poor, dry	White; late summer	Tolerates salt spray
Average	Yellow, sparse; spring	Evergreen; similar to *B. julianae*; black fruit in the fall
Ordinary, well drained	Yellow; spring	Persistent red berries
Ordinary, well drained	Yellow; spring	Evergreen in the South; red berries
Ordinary, well drained	Yellow; spring	Evergreen, blue-black berries
Ordinary, well drained	Yellow; spring	Evergreen; purplish black berries
Ordinary, well drained	Yellow; spring	Half-evergreen; salmon berries
Ordinary, well drained	Red; spring	Black berries; heathlike habit
Sandy	Yellow catkins; early spring	Twiggy, fine textured
Sandy	Pink; late spring	Rock garden shrublet
Ordinary, well drained	Pale purple; late spring	Silvery foliage; weeping habit
Ordinary, well drained	Tiny pink; summer	Glossy violet berries
Ordinary, well drained	Tiny pink; summer	Glossy blue-violet berries, persistent
Ordinary, well drained	Tiny pink; summer	Violet or white berries, persistent
Sandy, humusy, moist	Rose pink; summer to early fall	Evergreen; fine textured
Poor, dry	Yellow; spring	Good in dry, windy sites
Poor, dry	Yellow; spring	Good hedging in difficult locations
Ordinary, well drained	Blue; late summer	Prune winter-killed stems in spring
Humusy, well drained	Blue-violet; late summer to fall	Cv. 'Candida' is white flowered
Sandy, dryish	White; late spring to early summer	Difficult to move; roots fix nitrogen
Muck, acidic	White; summer	Easy in wet places
Humusy, well drained	Inconspicuous	Cultivars offer color and texture combinations
Ordinary, well drained	Inconspicuous	As for *C. lawsoniana*
Wet, acidic	White; summer	Useful in wet, shaded places
Ordinary, well drained	Yellowish; fragrant; winter to very early spring	Winter-flowering curiosity
Moist, humusy	White; erect clusters; late spring	Useful in moist places
Ordinary, well drained	White; fragrant; late summer	Blue fruit with red calyx
Ordinary, well drained	White; summer	Attractive peeling bark

(continues)

OTHER USEFUL SHRUBS (continued)

Name	Zones	Height	Exposure*
Colutea arborescens (bladder senna)	5–7	6–8'	S
Comptonia peregrina (sweet fern)	2–5 (7)	2–4'	S to Sh
Cornus amomum (silky dogwood)	5–8	6–10'	S to PSh
C. mas (cornelian cherry dogwood)	4–8	10–20'	S to PSh
C. racemosa (gray dogwood)	4–8	10–15'	S to Sh
C. sanguinea (blood-twig dogwood)	4–7	6–15'	S to PSh
Corylopsis glabrescens (fragrant winter hazel)	5–8	8–15'	S to PSh
C. pauciflora (buttercup winter hazel)	6–8	4–6'	S to PSh
C. spicata (spike winter hazel)	5–8	4–6'	S to PSh
Cotinus coggygria (European smokebush)	(4) 5–8	10–15'	S to PSh
C. obovatus (American smoke bush, chittamwood)	4–8	15–20'	S to PSh
Cotoneaster adpressus (creeping cotoneaster)	4–7	1 × 1½ × 4–6'	S
C. apiculatus (cranberry cotoneaster)	4–7	2–3 × 3–6'	S
C. divaricatus (spreading cotoneaster)	4–7	5–6'	S
C. hupehensis (Hupeh cotoneaster)	5–8	4–6'	S
C. lucidus (hedge cotoneaster)	3–7	10–15'	S
C. microphyllus (littleleaf cotoneaster)	5–8	2–3'	S
C. simonsii (Simons' cotoneaster)	5–7	12–18'	S
Cyrilla racemiflora (leatherwood, swamp cyrilla)	6–10	10–15'	S
Cytisus × 'Hollandia' (pink broom)	5–8	3–5'	S
C. × *kewensis* (Kew broom)	5–8	about ½'	S
C. × *praecox* (Warminster broom)	5–8	6–10'	S
C. purpureus (purple broom)	6–8	1–1½'	S
C. scoparius (Scotch broom)	6–8	5–8'	S
Daphne × *burkwoodii* (Burkwood daphne)	4–8	3–4'	S
D. caucasica (Caucasus daphne)	5–8	4–5'	S
D. cneorum (rose daphne)	4–7	½–1'	S
D. genkwa (lilac daphne)	5–8	3–4'	S
D. mezereum (winter daphne)	5–8	3–5'	S
D. odora (winter daphne)	7–9	2–3'	PSh
D. retusa (Chinese daphne)	8–9	2–3'	PSh
Diervilla lonicera (dwarf bush honeysuckle)	4–7	3–4'	S to PSh
D. sessilifolia (southern bush honeysuckle)	4–8	3–5'	S to PSh
Dirca palustris (leatherwood)	4–9	3–6'	PSh to LSh
Disanthus cercidifolius	6–8	6–10'	PSh
Elaeagnus multiflora (cherry eleagnus)	5–7	6–10'	S
E. pungens (thorny eleagnus)	6–9	10–15'	S
Elsholtzia stauntonii (mintshrub)	4–8	3–5'	S
Enkianthus perulatus (white enkianthus)	5–8	4–6'	S to LSh
Erica carnea (winter heath, spring heath)	4–7	½–2'	S to PSh
E. cinerea (bell heath)	5–8	1–2'	S to PSh
E. × *darleyensis* (Darley Dale heath)	4–7	1–2'	S to PSh
E. tetralix (cross-leaved heath)	4–7	½–1'	S to PSh
E. vagans (Cornish heath)	5–8	1–2'	S to PSh
E. × *watsonii* (Watson's heath)	4–7	1–2'	S to PSh
E. × *williamsii* (Williams' heath)	4–7	½–1½'	S to PSh

OTHER USEFUL SHRUBS

Soil Requirements	Flower Color and Bloom Time	Comments
Ordinary, well drained	Yellow; summer	Bronzy red pods
Sandy or peaty	Inconspicuous	Aromatic foliage
Moist or wet	White; late spring	Blue berries
Ordinary, well drained	Yellow; early spring	Red fruit; with age becomes treelike
Ordinary, well drained	Cream; late spring	White or pale blue berries
Wet, acidic	White; malodorous; late spring	Greenish red twigs; useful screen in wet ground
Ordinary, well drained	Yellow; early spring	Flowers before leaves appear
Ordinary, well drained	Yellow; early spring	Of finer texture than *C. glabrescens*
Ordinary, well drained	Yellow; early spring	Very attractive, especially in flower
Ordinary, well drained	Inconspicuous	Pinkish gray fruiting plumes
Ordinary, well drained	Inconspicuous	Similar to *C. coggygria;* yellow, orange, and red fall foliage
Ordinary	White; spring	Useful to stabilize banks
Ordinary, well drained	Pale pink; late spring	Bronzy to purplish fall foliage; red berries
Ordinary, well drained	Rose pink; late spring	Red to dark red berries, persistent
Ordinary, well drained	White; spring	Red fruit; habit more graceful than in other species
Ordinary, well drained	Pale pink; spring	Black berry, persistent; stiff, upright habit
Ordinary, well drained	White; spring	Evergreen; tiny leaves (¼ to ½ inch long); red berries
Ordinary, well drained	White and pink; spring	Red berries; upright habit
Ordinary, wet, acidic	White; early summer	Especially useful in wet places; orange to red fall foliage
Ordinary, well drained	Pinkish purple; late spring	Unusual shade for brooms
Ordinary, well drained	Cream; late spring	Creeping habit
Ordinary, well drained	Pale yellow; spring	White to yellow cultivars exist
Ordinary, well drained	Purple; spring	Syn. *Chamaecytisus purpureus*
Sandy, dryish	Yellow to red; spring	Naturalized locally in Northeast and Northwest
Well drained, neutral pH	Pink; spring	Cultivar 'Carol Mackie' has cream-edged leaves
Well drained, neutral pH	White; fragrant; spring	Leaves deciduous
Sandy-peaty, neutral pH	Rose pink; spring, often late summer	Protect from summer sun and winter wind
Sandy-peaty, neutral pH	Lilac purple; spring	Flowers clustered along stems
Well drained, neutral pH	Pink to rose purple; late winter or early spring	Scarlet berries are poisonous
Well drained, pH 6.5 to 7.0	Rose purple or white; late winter or early spring	Flowers intensely fragrant
Well drained, neutral pH	Rose purple or white; spring	Flowers fragrant; berries red
Ordinary, well drained	Yellow; late spring to summer	Good in difficult sites
Ordinary, well drained	Yellow; late spring to summer	Extremely hardy
Moist to wet, acidic	Light yellow; early spring	Distinctive foliage, yellow fall color
Well drained, acidic	Dark purple; fall	Orange, dark red, and purple fall foliage; uncommon
Ordinary or sandy	Yellowish white; fragrant; spring	Red fruit
Ordinary or sandy	White; fragrant; spring	Evergreen; reddish fruit
Ordinary, well drained	Lilac purple; late summer to fall	Minty odor from leaves when crushed
Loam, acidic	White; spring	Red fall foliage
Sandy-humusy, acidic	Rose pink or white; winter to spring	Forms dense mats; many cultivars
Sandy-humusy, acidic	Pink to mauve; late spring to fall	Bushy open habit
Sandy-humusy, acidic	Lilac pink to white; fall to spring	Many cultivars; habit varies by cultivar
Sandy-humusy, acidic	Pink or white; late spring to fall	Gray-green foliage
Sandy-humusy, acidic	Pink or white; summer to fall	Glossy green foliage
Sandy-humusy, acidic	Lilac pink; summer to fall	Young foliage bright green
Sandy-humusy, acidic	Rosy or lilac pink; summer to fall	Young foliage goldtipped

(continues)

OTHER USEFUL SHRUBS (continued)

Name	Zones	Height	Exposure*
Euonymus americanus (strawberry bush)	6–9	6–10'	S to PSh
E. europaeus 'Aldenhamensis' (Aldenham spindle tree)	3–7	12–20'	S to PSh
E. fortunei 'Vegetus' (big-leaf wintercreeper)	(4) 5–8	4–5'	S to Sh
E. japonicus (Japanese spindle tree)	7–9	10–15'	S to PSh
E. kiautschoviicus syn. *E. patens* (spreading euonymus)	5–8	8–10'	S
Exochorda giraldii var. *wilsonii* (redbud pearlbush)	5–8	12–15'	S
E. racemosa (common pearlbush)	4–8	10–15'	S
Fatsia japonica (Japanese fatsia)	8–10	6–10'	PSh to Sh
Forsythia viridissima 'Bronxensis' (creeping forsythia)	5–8	1–3'	S to PSh
Fothergilla × *gardenii* (low fothergilla)	5–8	2–3'	PSh
F. major (tall fothergilla)	4–8	6–10'	PSh
Gaultheria shallon (salal)	(5) 6–8	3–5'	PSh to Sh
Gaylussacia brachycera (box huckleberry)	5–7	1–1½'	Psh
Genista tinctoria (dyer's greenwood, woadwaxen)	4–7	2–3'	S
Hamamelis × *intermedia* 'Arnold Promise' (winter witch hazel)	6–8	15–20'	S
H. japonica (Japanese witch hazel)	5–8	10–15'	S to PSh
H. vernalis (vernal witch hazel)	4–8	6–10'	S to PSh
H. virginiana (common witch hazel)	3–10	15–25'	PSh to Sh
Hedera helix 'Arborescens' (shrubby English ivy)	5–8	4–6'	S to Sh
Hibiscus syriacus (rose of Sharon)	5–8	10–12'	S
Hippophae rhamnoides (sea buckthorn)	3–7	10–15'	S
Hydrangea arborescens 'Grandiflora' (hills-of-snow)	3–9	3–5'	PSh
H. macrophylla (French hydrangea)	6–9	3–6'	S
H. paniculata 'Grandiflora' (peegee hydrangea)	3–8	10–25'	S to PSh
H. quercifolia (oakleaf hydrangea)	5–9	4–6'	S to PSh
Hypericum buckleyi (Blue Ridge St. John's wort)	5–7	½–1'	S to PSh
H. calycinum (Aaron's-beard, St. John's wort)	6–9	1–2'	S to PSh
H. frondosum (golden St. John's wort)	5–8	3–5'	S to PSh
H. × *moserianum* (goldflower St. John's wort)	5–7	1–1½'	S to PSh
H. patulum (golden cup St. John's wort)	6–7	2–3'	S to PSh
H. prolificum (shrubby St. John's wort)	3–8	4–5'	S to PSh
Ilex aquifolium (English holly)	7–9	15–25' (50')	S to PSh
I. aquipernyi (hybrid holly)	5–7	10–20'	S to PSh
I. cornuta (Chinese holly)	7–9	9–15'	S to PSh
I. glabra (inkberry)	4–9	6–8'	PSh to Sh
I. × *meservae* (Meserve holly)	(4) 5–8	8–12'	S to PSh
I. pedunculosa (long-stalk holly)	5–8	15–20'	S to PSh
I. vomitoria (yaupon)	7–10	15–25'	S to PSh
Illicium floridanum (Florida anise)	(7) 8–9	6–10'	S to Sh
Indigofera kirilowii (Kirilow indigo)	4–7	2–3'	S
Itea japonica (Japanese sweet spire)	5–9	2–2½'	S to Sh
I. virginica (Virginia sweet spire)	5–9	3–5'	S to Sh
Juniperus communis (common juniper)	2–6 (7)	5–10'	S

OTHER USEFUL SHRUBS

Soil Requirements	Flower Color and Bloom Time	Comments
Ordinary, well drained	Greenish purple; inconspicuous; spring	Showy pink and red fruit
Ordinary, well drained	Greenish; spring	Pink-and-orange fruit; purple fall foliage
Ordinary, well drained	Whitish; spring	Evergreen; pink-and-orange fruit; climbs if supported
Ordinary, well drained	Greenish; spring	Evergreen; pink-and-orange fruit
Ordinary, well drained	Greenish; summer	Semievergreen; pink-and-orange fruit
Humusy, moist	White; spring	Red-veined leaves
Ordinary, well drained	White; spring	Showy flowers; trouble free
Ordinary, well drained	White; fall	Evergreen; makes bold effect; foliage may burn in sun
Ordinary, well drained	Light yellow; early spring	Tip roots to form patches; often few flowered
Sandy loam, acidic	White; spring	Yellow to red fall foliage
Sandy loam, acidic	White; spring	Yellow to red fall foliage
Moist, acidic	White; late spring	Evergreen; good when massed; purple fruit
Sandy-humusy, dryish	White; late spring	Blue fruit; good under rhododendrons
Well drained, acidic	Yellow; summer	Thrives on poor, dry soil
Ordinary, well drained	Yellow with purple; late winter to early spring	Other cultivars, some with reddish flowers
Ordinary, well drained	Yellow; late winter to early spring	Flat-topped habit; yellow fall foliage
Ordinary, well drained	Light yellow; late winter to early spring	Hardiest winter-flowering species
Ordinary, well drained	Yellow; fall	Yellow fall foliage obscures flowers
Ordinary, well drained	Greenish; fall	Black fruit; nonvining; rounded habit
Ordinary, well drained	White, red, purple; late summer	Large-flowered cultivars showier
Sandy, poor	Yellowish; early spring	Persistent orange fruit (female)
Ordinary, well drained	White; summer	Flower heads dry tan
Humusy, well drained	Pink (soil pH 6.0 to 7.0) or blue (soil pH 5.0 to 5.5)	Many cultivars, in two cluster-form classes
Ordinary, well drained	White to pink to greenish bronze; persisting; summer	Flower heads dry tan; cv. 'Tardiva' has conical flower head
Ordinary, moist	Pinkish white to purplish; summer	Orange to purple fall foliage
Ordinary, well drained	Yellow; summer	Spreading habit; useful for stabilizing banks
Ordinary, well drained	Yellow; summer	Half-evergreen; spreads to form patches
Ordinary, well drained	Yellow; summer	Twiggy; rounded habit
Sandy, dryish	Yellow; summer to fall	May die to ground in winter
Ordinary, well drained	Yellow; summer	Semievergreen; useful in stabilizing banks
Sandy or gravelly	Yellow; summer	Flowers prolifically
Ordinary, well drained	White; spring	Evergreen; glossy, spine-edged foliage; red berries (females); becomes a tree with age
Ordinary, well drained	Whitish; inconspicuous; spring	Red berries; cv. 'San Jose' best known
Ordinary, well drained	Whitish, inconspicuous; spring	Red berries (female); many cultivars
Moist, acidic	Whitish; inconspicuous; spring	Black berries (female); open habit
Ordinary, moist	Whitish; inconspicuous; spring	Red berries (female); source of "blue" hollies
Ordinary, moist	Whitish; inconspicuous; spring	Red berries (female) on 1-inch stalks
Ordinary, well drained	Greenish white; spring	Useful evergreen shrub in South; red berries, persistent
Moist or wet, acidic	Maroon; spring	Whorled fruit; aromatic leaves
Well drained; alkaline	Rose pink; early summer	Thrives under dry conditions
Humusy, moist	White; fragrant; early summer	Purplish fall foliage, suckers
Humusy, moist	White; fragrant; early summer	Red fall foliage
Any well-drained soil	Inconspicuous	Evergreen; dark blue-green; many cultivars

(continues)

OTHER USEFUL SHRUBS (*continued*)

Name	Zones	Height	Exposure*
J. conferta (shore juniper)	6–8	1–1½ × 6–9'	S
J. horizontalis (creeping juniper)	3–9	1–2'	S
J. sabina var. *tamariscifolia* (savin juniper)	3–7	1½–10'	S
J. virginiana (eastern red cedar)	2–9	15–20'	S
Kalmia angustifolia (lambkill)	2–7	1–3'	S to PSh
Lagerstroemia indica (crape myrtle)	7–10	10–20'	S
Laurus nobilis (Grecian laurel, sweet bay)	(7) 8–9	12–30'	S to PSh
Lavandula angustifolia (English lavender)	5–9	1–2'	S
Ledum groenlandicum (Labrador tea)	2–5	2–4'	S to PSh
Leiophyllum buxifolium (box sandmyrtle)	5–7	1½–3'	S to PSh
Lespedeza bicolor (shrubby bush clover)	4–7	6–10'	S
Leucothoë axillaris (coast leucothoë)	5–9	2–4'	PSh
Leycesteria formosa (Himalaya bush honeysuckle)	(6) 7–8	4–6'	PSh to Sh
Ligustrum amurense (Amur privet)	3–7	12–15'	S to PSh
L. × ibolium (Ibolium privet)	3–7	12–15'	S to PSh
L. japonicum (Japanese privet)	7–10	6–12'	S to PSh
L. obtusifolium var. *regelianum* (Regel's privet)	3–7	4–5'	S to PSh
L. ovalifolium (California privet)	5–8	10–15'	S to PSh
L. sinense (Chinese privet)	7–10	8–15'	S to PSh
Lindera benzoin (spicebush)	4–9	6–12'	PSh to Sh
Lonicera fragrantissima (winter bush honeysuckle)	4–8	6–10'	S to PSh
L. korolkowii (blue-leaf bush honeysuckle)	4–8	12–15'	S to PSh
L. maackii (Amur bush honeysuckle)	2–7	10–15'	S
L. nitida (box-leaf bush honeysuckle)	7–9	5–7'	S to Sh
L. pileata (privet bush honeysuckle)	(5) 6–7	3–5'	S to Sh
L. tatarica (Tatarian bush honeysuckle)	3–7	10–12'	S to Sh
Loropetalum chinense (loropetalum)	7–9	6–10'	S to Sh
Lycium chinense (Chinese matrimony vine)	6–8	6–10'	S
Magnolia liliiflora (lily magnolia)	5–8	8–12'	S
Mahonia bealei (leatherleaf hollygrape)	6–7	6–12'	PSh to Sh
M. fortunei (Chinese mahonia)	8–9	5–6'	PSh
Malus 'Jewelberry' (jewelberry crab apple)	5–8	4–6'	S
M. sargentii (Sargent crab)	5–7	6–8'	S
Microbiota decussata (Siberian carpet)	2–7	1–1½'	PSh
Myrica cerifera (southern wax myrtle)	6–9	15–25'	S to PSh
M. gale (sweet gale)	(7) 8–9	10–15'	S to PSh
Nandina domestica (heavenly bamboo)	6–9	4–8'	S to Sh
Neillia sinensis (Chinese neillia)	5–7	5–6'	S to PSh
Nerium oleander (oleander)	8–10	6–12'	S to PSh
Neviusia alabamensis (snow wreath)	4–8	3–6'	S to PSh
Osmanthus heterophyllus (holly olive)	7–9	8–10'	S to PSh
Parrotiopsis jacquemontiana (parrotiopsis)	5–7	8–12'	S to PSh
Paxistima canbyi (cliff green)	3–8	½–1'	S to PSh
Philadelphus coronarius (sweet mock orange)	4–8	10–12'	S to PSh

OTHER USEFUL SHRUBS

Soil Requirements	Flower Color and Bloom Time	Comments
Sandy, poor	Inconspicuous	Evergreen; thrives under harsh coastal conditions
Any well-drained soil	Inconspicuous	Evergreen; blue-green; many cultivars
Any well-drained soil	Inconspicuous	Evergreen; mounded
Any well-drained soil	Inconspicuous	Dark green to blue-green; many low cultivars
Wet, acidic	Purple to rose red or white; early summer	Evergreen; useful in permanently wet sites
Ordinary, well drained	Purple to white; summer to fall	Many cultivars, some dwarf
Humusy, moist	Greenish; inconspicuous; spring	Evergreen; black berries
Dryish, alkaline	Violet, blue, pink, or white; early summer	Evergreen; useful as low hedge
Peaty sand, moist	White; spring	Naturalizes in wet places
Sandy, acid	White with pink; late spring	Attractive in flower; good as edging in front of taller shrubs
Ordinary to low fertility, dry	Rosy purple; summer	Open, airy habit; effective in masses
Humusy, moist, acidic	White; spring	Trouble free
Ordinary, moist	Purplish; late summer	Good facing shrub; needs spring pruning
Ordinary, well drained	White; late spring	Inconspicuous; good hedging plant
Ordinary, well drained	White; late spring	Persistent black berries; good hedging
Ordinary, well drained	White; spring	Evergreen; black berries
Ordinary, well drained	White; late spring to early summer	Black berries; horizontal branching
Ordinary, well drained	Whitish; late spring to early summer	Glossy black berries; good hedging
Ordinary, well drained	White; late spring	Claret berries
Humusy, moist	Yellow; early spring	Yellow to red berries (female); aromatic foliage
Ordinary, well drained	Whitish; very fragrant; late winter to early spring	Red berries
Ordinary, well drained	Pinkish rose; spring	Red berries; blue-green foliage
Ordinary, well drained	White, aging yellow; spring	Conspicuous red berries; invasive in South
Ordinary, well drained	Cream; late spring	Half-evergreen; bluish purple berries
Ordinary, well drained	Whitish; late spring	Semievergreen; purple berries
Ordinary, well drained	Pink to white; spring	Red berries; sought by birds; can be invasive
Well drained, acidic	Cream to white; early spring	Evergreen; tolerates deep shade
Ordinary, well drained	Purple; spring	Showy red berries; not climbing; useful for stabilizing banks
Ordinary, well drained	Purplish and white; spring	Many cultivars, most with purple flowers
Ordinary, well drained	Yellow; fragrant; spring	Blue-gray fruit
Ordinary, well drained	Yellow; spring	Evergreen; finer in texture than other *Mahonia* species
Ordinary, well drained	Pink in bud, opening white; spring	Dense and compact in habit; glossy red fruit
Ordinary, well drained	Red buds open to white; spring	Red fruit sought by birds
Ordinary, well drained	Inconspicuous	Evergreen; spreads to 5 feet or more
Ordinary, well drained	Inconspicuous	Waxy gray berries (female)
Ordinary, well drained	Inconspicuous	Gray berries (female); foliage fragrant
Humusy, moist	Pinkish to white; spring to summer	Evergreen; red berries; many dwarf cultivars
Ordinary, well drained	Pink; spring	Good for banks and as facing
Ordinary, well drained	Red, pink, or white; double or single; summer and fall	Cultivars with intermediate shades
Ordinary, well drained	White; spring	Showy flower lacks petals
Humusy, moist	White; late spring to early summer	Evergreen; flowers not showy but fragrant
Ordinary, well drained	White; spring	Attractive flowers; may become small tree
Humusy, moist	Reddish green; spring	Evergreen; ground cover shrublet
Ordinary, well drained	White; fragrant; late spring	Gaunt in winter

(continues)

OTHER USEFUL SHRUBS (*continued*)

Name	Zones	Height	Exposure*
P. inodorus var. *grandiflorus* (large-flowered mock orange)	4–8	10–12'	S to PSh
P. × *lemoinei* (Lemoine mock orange)	5–8	4–8'	S to PSh
Photinia serrulata (Chinese photinia)	7–9	15–20' (30')	S to PSh
P. villosa (oriental photinia)	(4) 5–7	10–15'	S to PSh
Physocarpus opulifolius (eastern ninebark)	2–8	8–10'	S to PSh
Pieris floribunda (mountain andromeda)	4–7	2–6'	PSh to Sh
Poncirus trifoliata (hardy orange)	(5) 6–9	8–15'	S
Potentilla fruticosa (shrubby cinquefoil)	2–7	3–4'	S
Prinsepia sinensis (cherry prinsepia)	3–7	6–10'	S
P. uniflora (hedge prinsepia)	3–7	4–5'	S
Prunus besseyi (western sand cherry)	3–6	4–6'	S
P. × *cistena* (purple-leaf sand cherry)	2–8	7–10'	S
P. glandulosa (dwarf flowering almond)	4–8	4–5'	S
P. laurocerasus (cherry laurel)	6–8	10–18'	S to Sh
P. maritima (beach plum)	3–8	4–8'	S
P. tenella (dwarf Russian almond)	2–7	2–5'	S
P. tomentosa (Nanking cherry)	2–7	6–10'	S
P. triloba var. *multiplex* (double-flowering plum)	3–8	12–15'	S
Pyracantha angustifolia (narrow-leaved firethorn)	7–9	10–12'	S to PSh
P. koidzumii (Formosa firethorn)	(7) 8–10	8–12'	S
Rhamnus cathartica (common buckthorn)	2–7	15–25'	S to PSh
R. frangula (glossy buckthorn)	2–7	10–12'	S to PSh
Rhaphiolepis umbellata (Yedda hawthorn)	8–10	6–10'	S to PSh
Rhodotypos scandens (jetbead)	4–8	3–6'	S to Sh
Rhus aromatica (fragrant sumac)	3–9	2–6'	S to Sh
R. copallina (shining sumac)	4–9	10–20'	S
R. glabra (smooth sumac)	2–9	9–15'	S
R. trilobata (skunkbush sumac)	4–8	3–6'	S
R. typhina (staghorn sumac)	3–8	15–25'	S
Ribes alpinum (alpine currant)	2–7	3–6'	S to Sh
R. odoratum (clove currant)	4–8	6–8'	S to Sh
R. sanguineum (red-flowering currant)	6–7	6–10'	PSh
Robinia hispida and *R. fertilis* (rose acacia)	5–8	6–10'	S
Rosa × *alba* 'Incarnata' (cottage rose)	7–8	4–6'	S
R. banksiae (Lady Banks' rose)	(7) 8	10–20'	S to PSh
R. blanda (meadow rose)	2–7	4–6'	S
R. carolina (pasture rose)	4–9	3–6'	S
R. centifolia (cabbage rose)	6–9	4–6'	S
R. cinnamomea (cinnamon rose)	5–8	4–6'	S
R. × *damascena* (damask rose)	5–8	6–8'	S
R. eglanteria (sweetbrier rose)	6–8	4–6'	S
R. foetida (Austrian brier rose)	5–8	8–10'	S
R. gallica (French rose)	6–8	4–5'	S
R. × *harisonii* (Harison's yellow rose)	5–7	4–6'	S

OTHER USEFUL SHRUBS

Soil Requirements	Flower Color and Bloom Time	Comments
Ordinary, well drained	White; late spring	Flowers large but scentless
Ordinary, well drained	White; fragrant; late spring	Many large-flowered cultivars
Ordinary, well drained	White; spring	Evergreen; persistent red berries; can become small tree
Ordinary, well drained	White; spring	Persistent red berries
Ordinary, well drained	White to pink; spring	Flaky bark; cv. 'Dart's Golden' good leaf color
Well drained, acidic	White; spring	Evergreen; good in place of *P. japonica*
Ordinary, well drained	White; spring	Yellow fruit 1½ inches; thorny green twigs
Ordinary, well drained	Yellow or white; summer	Many cultivars mostly yellow-flowered
Ordinary, well drained	Light yellow; early spring	Very early to leaf out; adaptable and reliable; red-orange fruit
Ordinary, well drained	White; early spring	Thorny stems; red-violet fruit
Ordinary, well drained	White; spring	Thrives in hot, dry conditions; black fruit
Ordinary, well drained	Pinkish; spring	Very hardy purple-leaf shrub
Ordinary; well drained	White or pink; spring	Best when grouped; straggly when alone
Humusy, moist	White; spring	Evergreen; purple-black fruit; dwarf cultivars
Sandy, dry	White; spring	Purple fruit; good shrub along coast
Ordinary, well drained	Rose red or white; spring	Short lived in prolonged heat
Ordinary, well drained	Pink to white; spring	Red fruit; good in shrub border
Ordinary, well drained	Pinkish; double; early spring	Early flowers subject to frost; no fruit
Ordinary, well drained	White; late spring	Ample red-orange fruit
Ordinary, well drained	White; spring	Persistent red fruit
Ordinary, well drained	Inconspicuous	Very adaptable; invasive in East
Ordinary, well drained	Greenish; spring	Red to black fruit; cv. 'Columnaris' good for hedges
Ordinary, well drained	White; spring	Evergreen; leathery leaves; black fruit
Ordinary, well drained	White; spring	Black fruit; good in difficult shady locations
Well drained, acid	Yellowish; spring	Good for stabilizing banks; orange to purple fall foliage
Ordinary, well drained	Greenish yellow; summer	Persistent purplish fruit; purple fall foliage
Any well-drained soil	Greenish; late spring or early summer	Persistent reddish fruit (female); scarlet fall foliage
Ordinary, well drained	Greenish; spring	Forms dense thickets; malodorous when bruised
Any well-drained soil	Greenish; late spring or early summer	Persistent reddish fruit (female); red fall foliage; cut-leaf cultivar
Ordinary, well drained	Greenish yellow; spring	Red berries (female); good as hedge; dwarf cultivars
Humusy, well drained	Yellow; fragrant; spring	Black fruit; suckers to form clump
Ordinary, well drained	Red; spring	Black fruit; intolerant of prolonged summer heat
Ordinary, dry	Rose pink; late spring	Bristly purplish pods; can be invasive
Ordinary, well drained	White tinged pink; double; late spring or early summer	Historic rose of York; many cultivars
Ordinary, well drained	White or yellow; spring to summer	Climber, more or less thornless; good near coast; many cultivars
Ordinary, well drained	Pink; single; spring	Red hips; naturalizes in open areas
Ordinary, well drained	Pink; late spring to early summer	Red hips; nearly thornless; thicket forming
Ordinary, well drained	Pink; double; late spring	Several cultivars
Ordinary, well drained	Pinkish purple; late spring	Red hips; forms dense thickets
Ordinary, well drained	Pale pink to red; double; late spring	Red hips; several cultivars, some double white
Ordinary, well drained	Pink; late spring	Red to orange hips; good hedging
Ordinary, well drained	Yellow; late spring	Red hips; several cultivars
Ordinary, well drained	Pink to red, solitary; late spring	Red hips
Ordinary, well drained	Yellow; double; late spring	Black hips

(continues)

OTHER USEFUL SHRUBS (*continued*)

Name	Zones	Height	Exposure*
R. hugonis (Father Hugo's rose)	5–7	4–6'	S
R. moschata var. *nastarana* (Persian musk rose)	7–8	6–8'	S
R. moyesii (Moyes' rose)	5–8	7–10'	S
R. multiflora (multiflora rose)	2–7	6–10'	S
R. nitida (bristly rose)	3–7	1½–2'	S
R. omeiensis (Omei rose)	4–8	10–15'	S
R. palustris (swamp rose)	5–8	4–6'	S
R. rubrifolia (redleaf rose)	2–7	5–7'	S
R. setigera (prairie rose)	4–7	10–15'	S
R. spinosissima (Scotch rose)	4–7	3–5'	S
R. virginiana (Virginia rose)	3–7	4–6'	S
R. wichuraiana (memorial rose)	5–8	Prostrate	S
Rosmarinus officinalis (rosemary)	8–10	2–4'	S
Rubus odoratus (flowering raspberry)	3–7	5–9'	S
Ruscus aculeatus (butcher's broom)	8	2–3'	Sh
Salix caprea (goat willow)	4–8	15–20' (25')	S
S. discolor (pussy willow)	2–8	10–20'	S
S. elaeagnos (hoary willow)	4–7	8–15'	S
S. gracilistyla (rose-gold pussy willow)	5–7	6–10'	S
S. gracilistyla var. *melanostachys* (black pussy willow)	5–7	6–10'	S
S. purpurea (purple osier)	3–7	6–10'	S
S. sachalinensis 'Sekka' (Japanese fantail willow)	4–8	10–15'	S to PSh
Sambucus canadensis (American black elder)	3–9	5–10'	S to Sh
S. nigra (European elder)	5–7	15–20'	S to PSh
S. pubens (Scarlet elder)	4–8	12–20'	S to PSh
S. racemosa (European red elder)	3–7	6–8'	S to Sh
Sarcococca confusa (intermediate sweet box)	(7) 8	4–6'	PSh
Senna corymbosa, syn. *Cassia c.* (Argentine senna)	8–9	6–10'	S
Shepherdia argentea (silver buffalo berry)	2–7	6–10'	S
S. canadensis (russet buffalo berry)	2–6	3–9'	S
Sorbaria tomentosa var. *angustifolia*, syn. *S. aitchisonii* (Kashmir false spiraea)	(5) 6–7	6–8'	S to PSh
S. sorbifolia (Ural false spiraea)	2–7	5–10'	S to PSh
Spartium junceum (Spanish broom)	8–9	5–9'	S
Spiraea alba (meadowsweet)	5–7	3–5'	S
S. × *arguta* (garland spiraea)	5–8	6–8'	S
S. × *billiardii* (Billiard spiraea)	3–7	4–6'	S
S. × *bumalda* (Bumald spiraea)	3–8	2–3'	S
S. japonica (Japanese spiraea)	3–8	4–5'	S to PSh
S. nipponica (Tosa spiraea)	3–8	6–8'	S to PSh
S. tomentosa (hardhack, steeplebush)	3–7	3–5'	S
S. trilobata (three-lobe spiraea)	3–8	4–5'	S to Sh
Staphylea colchica (Colchis bladdernut)	5–7	6–10'	Sh
S. trifolia (American bladdernut)	3–8	10–15'	PSh to Sh

OTHER USEFUL SHRUBS

Soil Requirements	Flower Color and Bloom Time	Comments
Ordinary, well drained	Yellow; spring	Dark red hips
Ordinary, well drained	Pink; late spring	Red hips; several cultivars
Ordinary, well drained	Deep red; late spring or early summer	Red hips; cv. 'Geranium' bright red flowers
Ordinary, well drained	White; late spring	Red hips; naturalizes; often invasive
Ordinary, well drained	Deep pink; late spring	Red hips; spreads by suckers
Ordinary, well drained	White; late spring	Red-orange hips; big red thorns ornamental
Constantly moist to wet	Pink; late spring to summer	Red hips; colonizes wet ground
Ordinary, well drained	Pink; late spring	Foliage coppery green
Ordinary, well drained	Pink or white; late spring to early summer	Red hips; good soil stabilizer
Ordinary, well drained	Yellow, pink, or white; late spring	Black hips; many cultivars
Ordinary, well drained	Pink; late spring to early summer	Red hips; good for hedging
Ordinary, well drained	White; fragrant; late spring to early summer	Red hips; wide-ranging ground cover
Ordinary, well drained	Blue; fall to spring	Evergreen; aromatic foliage; drought tolerant
Ordinary, well drained	Rosy purple or white; late spring to early summer	Red fruit (unpalatable)
Any well-drained soil	Dull white; early spring	Useful as cut holiday decoration
Constantly moist or wet	Gray catkins; early spring	More ornamental than *S. discolor*
Constantly moist or wet	Gray catkins; early spring	Stems susceptible to canker
Constantly moist or wet	Greenish catkins; spring	Narrow leaves turn yellow in fall
Ordinary, well drained	Pinkish gray catkins; early spring	Sold as French pussy willow
Ordinary, well drained	Black catkins, males with red stamens	Very distinctive floral display
Ordinary to wet	Greenish catkins; spring	Dense, erect stems used in basketry
Wet, acidic	Greenish catkins; early spring	Twisted, flattened twigs
Ordinary, wet to dry	White; late spring to early summer	Black berries; best used for naturalizing
Ordinary, well drained	Cream; late spring	Black berries; intolerant of sustained heat
Ordinary, well drained	Cream; spring	Red berries (yellow or white in some cultivars)
Ordinary, wet to dry	Cream; spring	Red berries; several cultivars
Ordinary, moist	Whitish; early spring	Evergreen; black berries
Ordinary, well drained	Yellow; summer	Evergreen; cigarlike pods
Dry, alkaline	Yellowish; spring	Very drought tolerant; thorny stems
Dry, alkaline	Yellowish; spring	Very drought tolerant; stems scaly
Ordinary, well drained	White; summer	Suckers freely; good as bank cover
Ordinary, well drained	White; late spring to early summer	Early to leaf out; good bank cover
Dry, alkaline	Yellow; summer	Very adaptable to harsh droughty conditions
Wet, acidic	White; summer	Clump forming; useful in wet places
Ordinary, well drained	White; spring	Like *S. thunbergii* but larger
Well drained, acidic	Rose pink; summer	Cv. 'Triumphans' fine late-blooming form
Ordinary, well drained	Pink to white; summer	Best known by cvs. 'A. Waterer' and 'Froebellii', among others
Ordinary, well drained	White to pink; late spring to early summer	Many colorful cultivars
Ordinary, well drained	White; spring	Cv. 'Snowmound' is lower
Wet, acidic	Rose to purplish pink; summer	Clump forming; useful in wet places
Ordinary, well drained	White; spring	Cv. 'Swan Lake' like a small *S. vanhouttei*
Humusy, well drained	Cream; spring	Bladderlike pods in late summer
Ordinary, well drained	Greenish white; spring	Attractive foliage; requires little care

(continues)

OTHER USEFUL SHRUBS (*continued*)

Name	Zones	Height	Exposure*
Stephanandra incisa (lace bush, cut-leaf stephanandra)	3–7	4–7'	S to PSh
Stewartia ovata (mountain stewartia)	5–9	10–15'	S to Sh
Stransvaesia davidiana, syn. *Photinia d.* (Chinese stransvaesia)	(5) 6–8	6–20'	S to Sh
Symphoricarpos albus (snowberry)	3–7	3–6'	S to PSh
S. orbiculatus (coralberry)	2–7	4–5'	S to PSh
Syringa laciniata (cut-leaf lilac)	4–8	6–8'	S
S. meyeri 'Palibin' (Palibin lilac): *see page 241.*			
S. microphylla (littleleaf lilac): *see page 242.*			
S. × *prestoniae* (Preston lilac)	4–8	8–10'	S to PSh
Tamarix gallica (French tamarisk, manna bush)	5–8	10–25'	S
T. parviflora (tamarisk)	4–8	10–15'	S
T. ramosissima, syn. *T. pentandra* (five-stamen tamarisk)	2–8	10–15'	S
Taxus baccata 'Repandens' (dwarf spreading English yew)	5–8	2–4'	S to Sh
T. cuspidata 'Densa' (dwarf Japanese yew)	4–7	3–4'	S to Sh
T. × *media* 'Hicksii' (Columnar yew)	4–7	10–20'	S to Sh
Ternstroemia japonica (Japanese cleyera)	(8) 9–10	10–12'	S to PSh
Thuja occidentalis 'Techny' (pyramidal arborvitae)	2–7 (8)	10–20'	S
Vaccinium arboreum (Farkleberry)	7–9	10–15'	S
V. corymbosum (highbush blueberry)	3–7 (8)	10–12'	S
Viburnum acerifolium (mapleleaf viburnum)	3–8	4–6'	LSh to Sh
V. davidii (David viburnum)	7–9	3–5'	S to PSh
V. dentatum (arrowwood viburnum)	2–8	8–10' (15')	S to PSh
V. japonicum (Japanese viburnum)	8–9	10–15'	S to PSh
V. × *juddii* (Judd viburnum)	4–7 (8)	6–8'	S
V. lantana (wayfaring bush)	3–7	10–15'	S to PSh
V. lantanoides (hobblebush)	3–7	8–12'	S
V. lentago (nannyberry, sheepberry)	2–8	12–20'	S to Sh
V. molle (Kentucky viburnum)	5–8	10–12'	S to PSh
V. opulus (European cranberry bush)	3–8	8–12'	S to Sh
V. prunifolium (black haw viburnum)	3–9	10–15'	S to Sh
V. sargentii (Sargent viburnum)	3–7	12–15'	S to PSh
V. sieboldii (Siebold viburnum)	4–7 (8)	10–20'	S to PSh
V. trilobum (American cranberry bush)	2–7	8–12'	S to PSh
V. wrightii (Wright viburnum)	5–8	8–10'	S to Sh
Vitex agnus-castus (chaste bush, summer lilac)	(6) 7–9	8–10'	S
Weigela florida (weigela)	5–8	6–9'	S
Xanthorhiza simplicissima (yellowroot)	3–9	2–3'	PSh to Sh
Yucca filamentosa (Adam's needle)	5–8	2–3'	S
Y. glauca (soapweed)	4–8	3–4'	S
Y. gloriosa (Spanish dagger)	6–9	6–8'	S
Zenobia pulverulenta (dusty zenobia)	5–8	2–3'	S to PSh

*S, full sun; Sh, shade (no direct sun); PSh, partial shade (sun exposure only part of the day); LSh, light shade (e.g., the shade of tall, open trees; little or no exposure to direct sun).

OTHER USEFUL SHRUBS

Soil Requirements	Flower Color and Bloom Time	Comments
Ordinary, well drained	White; spring	Useful as a densely leafy screen, hedge, or bank cover
Humusy, moist	White with purple stamens; summer	Smallest of stewartias
Ordinary, well drained	White; summer	Evergreen; red fruit; cv. 'Undulata' wavy leaved
Ordinary, well drained	Pinkish; summer	Persistent, white berries
Ordinary, well drained	Pinkish; late spring to early summer	Purplish red berries; thicket forming
Ordinary, well drained	Pale lilac; spring	Striking lacy foliage
Ordinary, well drained	Red-violet; spring	Several very good cultivars
Ordinary, well drained	Pink; summer	Thrives in dry, exposed locations; treelike with age
Acid, sandy, dryish, acidic	Pink; late spring to early summer	Other species very similar
Ordinary, well drained	Rose pink; late spring to early summer	Especially useful along the coast
Ordinary, well drained	Inconspicuous	Red fruit (female); spreads out to 8 or 10 feet
Ordinary, well drained	Inconspicuous	Red fruit (female); dark foliage; slow growing
Ordinary, well drained	Inconspicuous	Red fruit (female); good hedge shrub
Ordinary, well drained	White; spring	Foliage often variegated
Ordinary, well drained	Inconspicuous	Slow growing; hardy; good hedge plant
Well drained, acidic	White; spring	Black fruit (inedible)
Moist to wet, acidic	Pinkish white spring	Blue-black edible berries; bright fall foliage
Dryish, well drained	Cream; late spring to early summer	Black berry; open habit; copse-forming
Ordinary, well drained	Pink buds opening white; spring	Handsome blue fruit; several shrubs needed for cross-pollination
Ordinary, well drained	White; late spring	Black fruit; drought tolerant
Ordinary, well drained	White; spring	Evergreen; dense foliage; good as a low-maintenance screen
Ordinary, well drained	Red in bud, opening white; fragrant; spring	Hardy substitute for *V. carlesii* in the North
Ordinary, well drained	Cream; late spring to early summer	Fruit red, ripening to black
Ordinary, well drained	White; spring	Fruit red, ripening to black
Ordinary, moist to dry	Cream; spring	Black fruit; good for screening
Ordinary, well drained	White; spring	Showy black fruit
Ordinary, dryish to wet	White; spring	Persistent red fruit; cv. 'Nanum' good hedge plant
Ordinary, well drained	White; spring	Reddish to black fruit, edible
Ordinary, dryish to wet	White with purple stamens; spring	Persistent red fruit
Ordinary, moist	White; spring	Black fruit; lustrous foliage
Ordinary, well drained	White; spring	Persistent red fruit
Ordinary, well drained	White; spring	Red fruit; red fall foliage
Ordinary, well drained	Lilac; late summer	Stems may winter kill in the North
Ordinary, well drained	White, pink, or red; spring, sporadically after that	Many cultivars
Ordinary, well drained	Brown-violet; early spring	Suckers freely, forming dense mat; good bank stabilizer
Ordinary, well drained	Creamy white; late spring or early summer	Evergreen; flower stalk rises 4 to 6 feet; good in exposed places
Ordinary, well drained	Greenish white; summer	Evergreen; especially valued for narrow, rigid, blue-green foliage
Ordinary, well drained	White and purplish; summer	Evergreen; leaves spine-tipped as in all yuccas; especially effective in clumps
Well drained, acidic	White; spring	Attractive gray green foliage

Hardy orange (*Poncirus trifoliata*)

White forsythia
(*Abeliophyllum distichum*)

Littleleaf cotoneaster
(*Cotoneaster microphyllus*)

Oak-leaf hydrangea
(*Hydrangea quericifolia*
'Snow Queen')

Warminster broom (*Cytisus × praecox* 'All Gold')

Common witch hazel
(*Hamamelis virginiana*)

European cranberry bush
(*Viburnum opulus* 'Compactum')

Siberian carpet (*Microbiota decussata*)

Winter heath (*Erica carnea*)

Crape myrtle (*Lagerstroemia indica*)

Red-flowering currant
(*Ribes sanguineum*)

Cabbage rose
(*Rosa centifolia*)

Father Hugo's rose
(*Rosa hugonis*)

Tamarisk
(*Tamarix × ramosissima* 'Rosea')

Chaste bush (*Vitex agnus-castus*)

Buttercup witch hazel (*Corylopsis pauciflora*)

Aaron's-beard St. John's wort (*Hypericum calycinum*)

RELIABLE LOW-MAINTENANCE SHRUBS
Deciduous unless otherwise noted

Name	Zones	Height	Characteristics
Acer ginnala (Amur maple)	2–8	15–20'	Red samaras in fall
Aronia arbutifolia (red chokeberry)	4–9	6–10'	White flowers in spring; red berries in fall
A. melanocarpa (black chokeberry)	3–8 (9)	3–8'	White flowers in spring; black berries in fall
Berberis julianae (wintergreen barberry)	5–8	6–8'	Evergreen; yellow flowers in spring; black berries in fall
B. koreana (Korean barberry)	3–7	4–6'	Thorny stems; yellow flowers in spring
B. × mentorensis (Mentor barberry)	5–8	5–7'	Semievergreen; thorny stems; yellow flowers in spring; reddish brown berries in fall
B. thunbergii (Japanese barberry)	4–8	4–7'	Thorny stems; yellow flowers in spring; red berries in fall
Callicarpa dichotoma (purple beauty-berry)	5–8	3–4'	Pink flowers in spring and summer; purple berries in fall
Calycanthus floridus (Carolina allspice)	4–9	6–8'	Reddish brown flowers in spring
Caragana arborescens (Siberian pea shrub)	2–7	10–18'	Yellow flowers in spring
Cephalanthus occidentalis (buttonbush)	5–8	5–8'	White flowers in late summer
Clethra alnifolia (sweet pepperbush)	3–9	5–8'	White flowers in summer
Cornus alba 'Sibirica' (red-stem dogwood)	2–8	6–8'	White flowers in spring; gray berries in fall
C. mas (cornelian cherry dogwood)	4–8	10–20'	Yellow flowers in early spring; red berries in summer
C. stolonifera 'Flaviramea' (yellow-stem dogwood)	2–8	6–8'	White flowers in spring; whitish berries in fall
Cotinus coggygria (smokebush)	(4) 5–8	10–15'	Pinkish gray berries scattered in copiously hairy clusters in summer
Elaeagnus umbellata (autumn olive)	3–8	12–15'	White flowers in spring; red fruit in fall
Eleutherococcus sieboldianus (five-leaf aralia)	4–8	8–10'	Thorny stems; greenish flowers in spring
Euonymus alatus 'Compacta' (dwarf burning bush)	4–8	5–8'	Green flowers in spring; scarlet foliage in fall
Forsythia × intermedia cvs. (showy border forsythia)	(4) 6–8 (9)	8–10'	Yellow flowers in early spring
F. ovata (early forsythia)	4–7	5–6'	Yellow flowers in early spring
F. suspensa var. *sieboldii* (weeping forsythia)	5–8	8–10'	Yellow flowers in early spring
Hamamelis × intermedia cvs. (hybrid witch hazel)	5–8	10–15'	Yellow flowers in winter and early spring
H. mollis (Chinese witch hazel)	5–8	10–15'	Yellow flowers in winter and early spring
H. japonica (Japanese witch hazel)	5–8	10–15'	Yellow to bronzy flowers in winter and early spring
H. vernalis (vernal witch hazel)	4–8	6–10'	Yellow flowers in winter and early spring
H. virginiana (common witch hazel)	3–10	15–20'	Yellow flowers in fall
Hydrangea paniculata 'Grandiflora' (peegee hydrangea)	3–8	10–25'	White flowers in summer, drying tan and persisting
Kolkwitzia amabilis (beauty-bush)	4–8	8–10'	Pink to white flowers in late spring
Leucothoë fontanesiana (drooping leucothoë)	4–7	4–5'	Evergreen; white flowers in spring
Lindera benzoin (spicebush)	4–9	6–12'	Yellow flowers in early spring; red fruit in summer
Lonicera fragrantissima (winter bush honeysuckle)	4–8	6–10'	White flowers in early spring; red fruit in summer
L. korolkowii (blueleaf bush honeysuckle)	4–8	12–15'	Pink flowers in spring; red fruit in summer
L. maackii (Amur bush honeysuckle)	2–7	12–15'	White flowers in spring; black fruit in summer
L. morrowii (Morrow bush honeysuckle)	(3) 4–8	6–8'	White flowers in spring; red fruit in summer
L. nitida (box-leaf bush honeysuckle)	7–9	5–7'	Evergreen to half-evergreen; white flowers in spring; purple fruit in summer
L. pileata (privet bush honeysuckle)	(5) 6–7	3–5'	Evergreen to half-evergreen; white flowers in spring; purple fruit in summer
Myrica pensylvanica (northern bayberry)	2–7	5–9'	Half-evergreen to deciduous; gray aromatic berries in fall
Neillia sinensis (Chinese neillia)	5–7	5–6'	Pink flowers in spring
Neviusia alabamensis (snow wreath)	4–8	3–6'	White flowers in spring
Osmanthus heterophyllus (holly osmanthus)	7–9	8–10'	Evergreen; pink to white flowers in spring
Parrotiopsis jaquemontiana (parrotiopsis)	5–7	8–12'	White flowers in spring

Name	Zones	Height	Characteristics
Physocarpus opulifolius (eastern ninebark)	2–8	8–10'	White to pink flowers in spring; red fruit in fall
Potentilla fruticosa (shrubby cinquefoil)	2–7	3–4'	Yellow or white flowers in late spring and summer
Prinsepia sinensis (cherry prinsepia)	4–8	4–7'	Yellow flowers in early spring; red-violet fruit in late summer
Prunus maritima (beach plum)	3–8	4–8'	White flowers in spring; purple fruit in late summer and early fall
Rhododendron maximum (rosebay rhododendron)	4–8	12–18'	Evergreen; white to pink flowers in late spring and early summer
Rhodotypos scandens (jetbead)	4–8	3–6'	White flowers in spring; black fruit in fall and winter
Rosa rugosa (rugosa rose)	2–7	5–6'	Pink or white flowers in early summer; red-orange hips in fall
Spiraea × vanhouttei (Vanhoutte spiraea, bridal wreath)	3–8	6–8'	White flowers in spring
Staphylea trifolia (American bladdernut)	5–8	10–15'	White flowers in spring; green to brown capsule in late summer
Stephanandra incisa (lace bush)	3–7	4–7'	White flowers in spring
Symphoricarpos albus (common snowberry)	3–7	3–6'	Pink flowers in spring; white fruit in summer
Symplocos paniculata (Asiatic sweetleaf)	4–8	15–25'	White flowers in spring; blue fruit in fall
Vaccinium corymbosum (highbush blueberry)	3–7 (8)	10–12'	White flowers in spring; purplish black berries in summer
Viburnum dentatum (arrowwood viburnum)	2–8	8–10' (15')	White flowers in spring; black berries in fall
V. dilatatum (linden viburnum)	(4) 5–7 (8)	6–10'	White flowers in spring; red berries in fall
V. japonicum (Japanese viburnum)	7–9	3–5'	Evergreen; white flowers in spring; red berries in fall
V. lantana (wayfaring tree viburnum)	3–7 (8)	10–15'	White flowers in spring; red to black berries in late summer and fall
V. lentago (nannyberry, sheepberry)	2–8	12–20'	White flowers in spring; black berries in fall
V. opulus (European cranberry viburnum)	5–8	10–12'	White flowers in spring; red berries in fall
V. plicatum f. *tomentosum* (double-file viburnum)	(4) 5–8	10–12'	White flowers in spring; black berries in summer
V. prunifolium (black haw viburnum)	3–9	10–15'	White flowers in spring; blue-black berries in fall
V. rhytidophyllum (leatherleaf viburnum)	(5) 6–8	8–10'	Evergreen; white flowers in spring; black berries in fall
V. sargentii (Sargent viburnum)	3–7	12–15'	White flowers in spring; red berries in summer and fall
V. setigerum (tea viburnum)	5–7	10–12'	White flowers in spring; red berries in fall
V. sieboldii (Siebold viburnum)	4–7 (8)	10–20'	White flowers in spring; blue-black berries in summer and fall
V. tinus (laurustinus)	7–9	12–18'	Evergreen; white flowers in winter and early spring; black berries in summer
V. trilobum (American cranberry viburnum)	2–7	8–12'	White flowers in spring; red berries in fall
Yucca filamentosa (Adam's needle)	4–8	2–3' (6')	Evergreen; white flowers in summer
Y. glauca (soapweed)	4–7	2–3'	Evergreen; white flowers in summer
Y. gloriosa (Spanish dagger)	7–9	10–15'	Evergreen; white flowers in summer

SHRUBS WITH CONSPICUOUS FRUIT

Name	Fruit Color	Display Period
Amelanchier canadensis (shadbush)	Red to purple	Late summer to early fall
Aronia arbutifolia (red chokeberry)	Red	Fall to early winter
A. melanocarpa (black chokeberry)	Black	Fall to early winter
A. prunifolia (purple chokeberry)	Wine red	Fall to early winter
Baccharis halimifolia (groundsel bush)	White	Late summer to fall
Berberis koreana (Korean barberry)	Red	Fall to early winter
B. thunbergii (Japanese barberry)	Red	Fall to early winter
Callicarpa americana (American beauty-berry)	Purple	Fall to early winter

(continues)

SHRUBS WITH CONSPICUOUS FRUIT (*continued*)

Name	Fruit Color	Display Period
C. bodinieri (Bodinier beauty-berry)	Purple or white	Fall
C. dichotoma (purple beauty-berry)	Purple	Fall
C. japonica (Japanese beauty-berry)	Purple	Fall
Clerodendrum trichotomum (harlequin glory-bower)	Blue and red	Late summer to early fall
Cotoneaster apiculatus (cranberry cotoneaster)	Red	Late summer to early fall
C. divaricatus (spreading cotoneaster)	Red	Fall
C. hupehensis (Hupeh cotoneaster)	Red	Late summer to fall
C. simonsii (Simons cotoneaster)	Red	Late summer to fall
Eleagnus umbellata (autumn olive)	Red	Fall
Euonymus americanus (strawberry bush)	Red and orange	Fall
Hippophae rhamnoides (sea buckthorn)	Orange (female)	Fall to early spring
Ilex aquifolium (English holly)	Red (female)	Fall to winter
I. cornuta (Chinese holly)	Red (female)	Fall to winter
I. opaca (American holly)	Red (female)	Fall to winter
I. pedunculosa (long-stalk holly)	Red (female)	Fall to winter
I. verticillata (winterberry)	Red (female)	Fall to winter
I. vomitoria (yaupon)	Red (female)	Late summer to early spring
Leycesteria formosa (Himalaya honeysuckle)	Reddish purple	Fall
Ligustrum japonicum (Japanese privet)	Black	Fall to early spring
L. ovalifolium (California privet)	Black	Fall to early spring
Lonicera maackii (Amur bush honeysuckle)	Red	Fall
L. tatarica (Tatarian bush honeysuckle)	Red	Summer to fall
Mahonia aquifolium (Oregon hollygrape)	Gray black	Late summer to winter
M. bealei (Beal's hollygrape)	Bluish gray black	Late summer to winter
Malus 'Jewelberry' (Jewelberry crab apple)	Red	Late summer to fall
M. sargentii (Sargent crab apple)	Red	Late summer to fall
Myrica cerifera (southern wax myrtle)	Gray	Late summer to spring
M. pensylvanica (northern bayberry)	Gray (female)	Late summer to spring
Nandina domestica (heavenly bamboo)	Red	Fall to spring
Photinia spp. (photinia)	Red	Fall to spring
Poncirus trifoliata (hardy orange)	Yellow	Fall to winter
Prinsepia uniflora (hedge prinsepia)	Purplish red	Late summer to fall
Pyracantha coccinea (common firethorn)	Red-orange	Fall to winter
P. koidzumii (Formosa firethorn)	Red	Fall to late winter
Rhodotypos scandens (jetbead)	Black	Fall to early spring
Rhus copallina (shining sumac)	Dark red	Fall to early spring
R. glabra (smooth sumac)	Red	Fall to early spring
R. typhina (staghorn sumac)	Red	Fall to early spring
Rosa multiflora (multiflora rose)	Red	Late summer to winter
R. rugosa (rugosa rose)	Red-orange	Late summer to winter
Sambucus canadensis (eastern black elder)	Black	Late summer to early fall
S. nigra (European black elder)	Black	Early fall
S. pubens (American red elder)	Red	Early summer
S. racemosa (European red elder)	Red	Midsummer
Shepherdia canadensis (russet buffalo berry)	Yellowish red	Early summer
Skimmia japonica (Japanese skimmia)	Red (female)	Fall to spring
Symphoricarpos albus (snowberry)	White	Late summer to fall

Name	Fruit Color	Display Period
S. orbiculatus (coralberry)	Red	Fall
Symplocos paniculata (sweetleaf, sapphire berry)	Blue	Fall
Vaccinium corymbosum (highbush blueberry)	Blue-gray or black	Summer
Viburnum cassinoides (witherod viburnum)	Red to blue to black	Late summer
V. davidii (David viburnum)	Blue (female clones)	Late summer
V. dilatatum (linden viburnum)	Red	Fall to early winter
V. lantana (wayfaring tree viburnum)	Yellow to red to black	Late summer
V. lentago (nannyberry, sheepberry)	Blue-black	Early fall to early winter
V. molle (Kentucky viburnum)	Blue-black	Late summer
V. opulus (European cranberry viburnum)	Red	Fall to winter
V. plicatum f. *tomentosum* (double-file viburnum)	Red to black	Late summer
V. prunifolium (black haw viburnum)	Pinkish red to black	Fall
V. sargentii (Sargent viburnum)	Red	Late summer to early fall
V. setigerum (tea viburnum)	Red	Fall
V. trilobum (American cranberry viburnum)	Red	Fall to winter

SHRUBS FOR SHADY PLACES (DECIDUOUS SPECIES)
Many of the listed species include cultivars equally suited to shade.

Name	Zones	Height	Characteristics
	DECIDUOUS		
Abelia × grandiflora (glossy abelia)	6–9	5–6'	Evergreen in South; white flowers in early summer to frost
Amelanchier alnifolia (Saskatoon serviceberry)	2–7	8–12'	White flowers before leaves; purple fruit
A. canadensis (shadbush)	3–7	10–20'	White flowers before leaves; fruit red, ripening to purple
A. stolonifera (running serviceberry)	4–8	3–6'	Clump forming; flowers and fruit as for *A. canadensis*
Aronia arbutifolia (red chokeberry)	4–9	6–10'	White flowers; red berries; red fall foliage
A. melanocarpa (black chokeberry)	3–8	5–8'	White flowers; black berries; purple fall foliage
A. prunifolia (purple chokeberry)	4–8	8–12'	White flowers; purple-black berries; red-violet fall foliage
Berberis thunbergii (Japanese barberry)	4–8	4–7'	Thorny; red berries; orange, red, and purple fall foliage
Chionanthus virginicus (American fringe bush)	3–9	10–12'	Lacy flowers in late spring; yellow fall foliage
C. retusus (Chinese fringe bush)	6–9	6–10'	Flowers white, in erect clusters; yellow fall foliage
Clethra alnifolia (summersweet)	3–9	5–8'	Flowers white, fragrant, in late summer; yellow fall foliage
Cornus alba (Tatarian dogwood)	2–8	6–8'	Succeeds in shade but flowers best with some sun
C. amomum (silky dogwood)	5–8	6–10'	Porcelain blue fruit
C. mas (cornelian cherry dogwood)	4–8	10–20'	Abundant small yellow flowers in early spring before leaves
C. racemosa (gray dogwood)	4–8	10–15'	Gray to pale blue fruit
C. sanguinea (blood-twig dogwood)	5–8	8–12'	Reddish twigs; white flowers in spring; purple-black fruit
C. stolonifera 'Flaviramea' (yellow-twig dogwood)	2–8	6–8'	Stem color develops best with some sun exposure
Corylopsis pauciflora (buttercup winter hazel)	6–8	4–6'	Light yellow flowers in early spring before leaves
C. spicata (spiked winter hazel)	6–9	8–10'	Bright yellow flowers early before leaves
Daphne cneorum (rose daphne)	4–7	1–2'	Fragrant pink flowers in early spring
D. odora (winter daphne)	7–9	2–3'	Fragrant pink flowers in late winter
*Eleutherococcus sieboldianus** (five-leaf aralia)	4–8	8–10'	Attractive foliage; very adaptable
*Euonymus alatus** (burning bush)	4–8	6–8'	Winged twigs; bright red fall foliage

(continues)

SHRUBS FOR SHADY PLACES (DECIDUOUS SPECIES) (*continued*)

Name	Zones	Height	Characteristics
E. americanus* (strawberry bush)	6–9	6–10'	Fruit pink and red in fall
Forsythia × intermedia (common border forsythia)	6–8	8–10'	Tolerates shade but needs some sun to bloom creditably; flowers yellow, before leaves
F. suspensa var. *sieboldii* (weeping forsythia)	5–8	8–10'	As for *F. × intermedia* except stems slender, more or less trailing at ends
Fothergilla × gardenii (low fothergilla)	5–8	2–3'	White flowers early, before leaves; yellow fall foliage
Hamamelis virginiana* (common witch hazel)	3–10	15–25'	Yellow flowers and foliage in fall
Hydrangea arborescens (smooth hydrangea)	3–9	3–5'	Large persistent clusters of white flowers in summer
H. paniculata 'Grandiflora' (peegee hydrangea)	3–8	10–25'	Very large clusters of white flowers in summer turn purplish, then tan, persisting into winter
H. quercifolia (oak leaf hydrangea)	5–9	4–6'	White flowers in summer turn purplish, then brown; red, orange, and purple fall foliage
Hypericum calycinum (Aaron's-beard, St. John'swort)	6–9	1–2'	Spreading habit; large yellow flowers in summer; endures drought
H. frondosum (golden St. John'swort)	5–8	3–5'	Rounded habit; yellow flowers in summer
H. prolificum (shrubby St. John'swort)	3–8	4–5'	Erect habit; yellow flowers in summer
Ilex verticillata (winterberry)	3–9	6–8'	Bright red berries (female); best in wet locations
Kerria japonica (kerria)	4–9	4–6' (8')	Yellow flowers; green stems; double-flowered cultivar taller
Ligustrum japonicum (Japanese privet)	4–8	10–12'	Glossy foliage; good for hedging
L. sinense (Chinese privet)	7–10	8–15'	Fragrant white flowers; claret berries
Lindera benzoin* (spicebush)	4–9	6–12'	Yellow flowers before leaves; yellow berries ripen red (female); leaves aromatic when crushed
Lonicera fragrantissima (winter bush honeysuckle)	4–8	6–10'	Fragrant white flowers early before leaves
L. maackii (Amur bush honeysuckle)	2–7	12–15'	Flowers white to yellow in spring; red berries
L. tatarica (Tatarian bush honeysuckle)	3–7	10–12'	As for *L. maackii*; can be invasive
Myrica pensylvanica (northern bayberry)	2–7	5–9'	Aromatic foliage; gray berries (female)
Nandina domestica (ninebark)	6–9	4–8'	Bright red berries
Neviusia alabamensis (snow wreath)	4–8	3–6'	White flowers in spring
Rhamnus frangula (glossy buckthorn)	2–7	10–12'	Fruit red, ripening to black
Rhododendron spp. (native deciduous azaleas)	2–9	3–12'	Flowers various bright colors, mostly before leaves
Rhodotypos scandens (jetbead)	4–8	3–6'	White flowers in spring; black fruit
Rubus odoratus (flowering raspberry)	3–7	5–9'	Large rosy purple or white flowers in spring and summer
Stephanandra incisa (lace bush)	3–7	4–7'	White flowers in spring; fine-textured foliage
Symphoricarpos albus (snowberry)	3–7	4–7'	Persistent white berries
S. orbiculatus (coralberry, turkeyberry)	2–7	4–6'	Red-violet berries; can be invasive
Ternstroemia japonica (Japanese cleyera)	(8) 9–10	10–12'	White flowers in late spring; leaves often variegated
Vaccinium arboreum (farkleberry)	7–9	10–15'	White flowers in spring; black fruit (inedible)
V. corymbosum (highbush blueberry)	3–7	10–12'	Edible blue-black berries; red, orange, and yellow fall foliage suited to wet ground
Viburnum acerifolium (maple-leaf viburnum)	3–8	4–6'	Cream flowers in spring; black berries
V. cassinoides (witherod viburnum)	3–8	6–10'	White flowers in spring; fruit passes through several color phases
V. dentatum (arrowwood viburnum)	2–8	8–10'	White flowers in spring; black berries
V. lantanoides (hobblebush)	3–7	8–12'	White flowers in spring; red berries mature black
Xanthorhiza simplicissima (yellowroot)	3–9	2–3'	Good ground cover

EVERGREEN

Name	Zones	Height	Characteristics
Aucuba japonica (Japanese laurel)	7–10	5–6'	Best known by cv. 'Variegata' (gold-dust bush); red berries (female)
Berberis julianae (wintergreen barberry)	5–8	6–8'	Glossy foliage; yellow flowers in spring; gray black fruit; thorny stems

Name	Zones	Height	Characteristics
Buxus microphylla (littleleaf box)	5–9	1–3'	Glossy, fine-textured foliage
B. sempervirens (common box)	6–9	10–15'	Foliage emits mousy odor
Euonymus fortunei* (wintercreeper euonymus)	5–8	4–5' (or taller)	Can climb walls and trees by aerial rootlets
E. kiautschovicus (spreading euonymus)	5–8	8–10'	Semievergreen in the North; pink and orange fruit
Fatsia japonica (Japanese fatsia)	6–10	6–10'	Large, lobed leaves; white flowers in fall; black berries
Gaultheria shallon* (salal)	6–7	3–5'	White flowers in spring; black berries; best when massed; intolerant of hot summers
Ilex crenata* (Japanese holly)	5–7	5–10'	Small dark green leaves; black berries (female)
I. glabra* (inkberry)	4–9	6–8'	Open habit; black berries (female)
Kalmia angustifolia* (lambkill)	2–7	1–3'	Purplish pink flowers in late spring
K. latifolia* (mountain laurel)	4–9	8–10'	Glossy foliage; flowers white, purplish-spotted, in late spring
Laurus nobilis (Grecian laurel)	8–10	12–20'	Large glossy leaves; black berries (female)
Leucothoë fontanesiana (drooping leucothoë)	4–7	4–5'	Drooping stems; glossy foliage; white flowers in spring
Lonicera nitida (box-leaf bush honeysuckle)	7–9	5–7'	Often semievergreen; white flowers in spring; black-violet berries
L. pileata (privet bush honeysuckle)	6–7	3–5'	Often semievergreen; yellowish white flowers in spring; black fruit
Loropetalum chinense (evergreen witch hazel)	9–10	2–3'	Greenish white flowers in early spring
Mahonia aquifolium* (Oregon hollygrape)	5–8	4–5'	Glossy hollylike foliage; yellow flowers in spring; blue-black fruit
M. bealei* (leatherleaf hollygrape)	6–7	6–12'	As for *M. aquifolium*
M. fortunei* (Chinese hollygrape)	7–9	4–6'	Unbranched from base; yellow flowers profusely borne in spring
Myrica cerifera (southern wax myrtle)	6–9	15–25'	Large, wide-spreading shrub; gray berries (female)
Nerium oleander (oleander)	8–10	6–12'	Red, pink, or white flowers in summer and fall
Photinia × fraseri (Fraser photinia)	7–9	15–20'	New and old leaves reddish; red berries
Pieris japonica (andromeda, Japanese pieris)	5–8	8–12'	White flowers in spring
Rhaphiolepis umbellata (Yedda hawthorn)	8–10	6–10'	Leathery leaves; white flowers in spring; black fruit
Rhododendron spp. (evergreen azaleas)	3–8	3–10'	Shiny leaves; brightly colored flowers in spring
R. maximum* (rosebay rhododendron)	4–8	12–18'	Dark green leaves; white or pale pink flowers, early summer
Ruscus aculeatus (butcher's broom)	7–9	2–4'	Rigid leaflike cladodes replace leaves; red or yellow berries
Sarcococca hookeriana* (sweet box)	6–8	1–2'	Dark, glossy foliage; good for low hedging or edging
Skimmia japonica (Japanese skimmia)	7–8	3–4'	White flowers in spring; red berries (female); slow growing
Taxus spp. (yew)	4–7	3–8'	Many growth-form cultivars, all with dark foliage; red berries (female)

* Adaptable to fairly dense shade.

Hill's of snow
(*Hydrangea arborescens* 'Grandiflora')

Virginia sweetspire (*Itea virginica*)

Harlequin glory-bower
(*Clerodendrum trichotomum*)

SHRUBS FOR WET PLACES
Includes stream banks, pond borders, bogs, etc.

Name	Characteristics
Alnus rugosa (speckled alder)	Catkins in early spring before leaves
A. serrulata (tag alder)	Catkins in early spring before leaves
Amelanchier canadensis (shadbush)	White flowers in early spring before leaves; purple fruit; fall foliage yellow to red
Aronia arbutifolia (red chokeberry)	White flowers in spring; red fruit; red fall foliage
A. melanocarpa (black chokeberry)	White flowers in spring; black fruit; purple fall foliage
Calycanthus floridus (Carolina allspice)	Fragrant reddish flowers in spring
Cephalanthus occidentalis (buttonbush)	White flowers in late summer
Chamaedaphne calyculata (leatherleaf)	White flowers in spring; low habit
Clethra alnifolia (summersweet)	Fragrant white flowers in summer; yellow fall foliage
C. barbinervis (Japanese clethra)	Shredding bark; fragrant white flowers in summer; yellow fall foliage
Cornus alba (Tatarian dogwood)	Deep red stems; white flowers in spring; whitish berries
C. amomum (silky dogwood)	Red stems; cream flowers in spring; bluish berries
C. sanguinea (blood-twig dogwood)	Purplish red stems; white flowers in spring; black berries
C. sericea (red-osier dogwood)	Red or yellow stems; white flowers in spring; white berries
Cyrilla racemiflora (leatherwood)	White flowers in early summer; orange and red fall foliage
Dirca palustris (leatherwood)	Light yellow flowers in early spring; yellow fall foliage
Hypericum densiflorum (tall shrubby St. John'swort)	Yellow flowers in summer
Ilex glabra (inkberry)	Evergreen; black berries (females)
I. laevigata (smooth winterberry)	Red-orange berries (females)
I. verticillata (winterberry)	Red berries (females)
I. vomitoria (yaupon)	Evergreen; red berries (females)
Itea virginica (Virginia sweetspire)	White flowers in early summer; red fall foliage
Kalmia angustifolia (lambkill)	Evergreen; purplish rose flowers in late spring
Ledum groenlandicum (Labrador tea)	Evergreen; white flowers in spring
Lindera benzoin (spicebush)	Early yellow flowers (before leaves); aromatic foliage yellow in fall; yellow-and-red berries (females)
Magnolia virginiana (sweetbay magnolia)	Evergreen in the South; white flowers in spring
Myrica gale (sweet gale)	Aromatic foliage
M. pensylvanica (northern bayberry)	Gray berries; aromatic foliage
Rhododendron canadense (rhodora)	Rosy purple flowers in early spring
R. periclymenoides (pinxterbloom)	Fragrant white flowers in spring
R. vaseyi (pink-shell azalea)	Rose pink flowers in spring; light red fall foliage
R. viscosum (swamp azalea)	Fragrant white flowers in summer
Rosa palustris (swamp rose)	Pink flowers in late spring; red hips
Salix caprea (goat willow)	Gray to yellow catkins in early spring before leaves
S. discolor (pussy willow)	Gray to yellow catkins in early spring before leaves
S. gracilistyla (pink pussy willow)	Pinkish gray catkins in early spring before leaves; blue-green foliage
S. gracilistyla var. *melanostachys* (black pussy willow)	Black-and-red catkins in early spring before leaves
S. purpurea (purple osier)	Dense growth of slender, whiplike, upright stems
S. sachalinensis 'Sekka' (Japanese fantail willow)	Flattened twisted twigs
Sambucus canadensis (eastern black elder)	White flowers in early summer; black berries
S. pubens (American red elder)	White flowers in spring; red berries
Spiraea alba (summersweet)	White flowers in summer
S. tomentosa (steeplebush)	Pink flowers in summer
Vaccinium corymbosum (highbush blueberry)	Edible blue-black fruit; yellow, orange, and red fall foliage

Name	Characteristics
V. macrocarpon (cranberry)	Edible red fruit; fine-textured creeping habit
V. alnifolium (hobblebush)	White flowers in spring; reddish purple fall foliage
V. cassinoides (witherod viburnum)	White flowers in spring; red to blue to black berries; red to purplish fall foliage
V. dentatum (arrowwood viburnum)	White flowers in spring; blue-black fruit; red to purple fall foliage
V. lentago (nannyberry, sheepberry)	White flowers in spring; black fruit in fall
V. opulus (European cranberry viburnum)	White flowers in spring; red fruit in fall
V. trilobum (American cranberry viburnum)	White flowers in spring; red fruit in fall, persisting into winter

SHRUBS FOR FALL FOLIAGE COLOR

Name	Foliage Color	Name	Foliage Color
Acer ginnala (Amur maple)	Yellow and red	*Hydrangea quercifolia* (oakleaf hydrangea)	Orange, red, and purple
Amelanchier canadensis (shadbush)	Yellow, orange, and red	*Itea virginica* (Virginia sweet spire)	Red
Aronia arbutifolia (red chokeberry)	Red to red-violet	*Lagerstroemia indica* (crape myrtle)	Yellow, orange, and red
A. melanocarpa (black chokeberry)	Red	*Lindera benzoin* (spicebush)	Yellow
A. prunifolia (purple chokeberry)	Red-violet	*Photinia × fraseri* (Fraser photinia)	Red
Berberis koreana (Korean barberry)	Dark red-violet	*Rhododendron mucronulatum* (Korean rhododendron)	Yellow and red
B. × mentorensis (Mentor barberry)	Yellow, orange, and red		
B. thunbergii (Japanese barberry)	Orange, red, and purple	*R. schlippenbachii* (royal azalea)	Yellow, orange, and red
Chionanthus virginicus (fringe bush)	Yellow	*R. vaseyi* (pink-shell azalea)	Pink and red
Clethra alnifolia (sweet pepperbush)	Yellow	*Rhus aromatica* (fragrant sumac)	Orange, red, and purple
Cornus stolonifera (red-osier dogwood)	Red-violet	*R. copallina* (shining sumac)	Red and purple
Corylopsis glabrescens (fragrant winter hazel)	Yellow	*R. glabra* (smooth sumac)	Orange, red, and purple
		R. typhina (staghorn sumac)	Yellow, orange, and red
Cotinus coggygria (smokebush)	Yellow, red, and purple	*Rosa rugosa* (rugosa rose)	Yellow and orange
C. obovatus (chittamwood)	Yellow, orange, red, and purple	*R. virginiana* (Virginia rose)	Yellow, orange, red, and purple
Cotoneaster apiculatus (cranberry cotoneaster)	Red-bronze or purplish	*Stephanandra incisa* (cut-leaf stephanandra)	Orange, red, and purple
C. divaricatus (spreading cotoneaster)	Yellow, red, and purple	*Stewartia ovata* (mountain stewartia)	Orange and red
C. lucidus (hedge cotoneaster)	Yellow, orange, and red	*Ternstroemia japonica* (Japanese cleyera)	Reddish bronze
Cyrilla racemiflora (leatherwood)	Orange and red	*Vaccinium corymbosum* (highbush blueberry)	Yellow, orange, and red
Dirca palustris (leatherwood)	Yellow		
Disanthus cercidifolius (disanthus)	Red and purple	*Viburnum alnifolium* (hobblebush)	Purple
Enkianthus campanulatus (redvein enkianthus)	Yellow, orange, and red	*V. cassinoides* (witherod viburnum)	Orange, red, and purple
		V. dentatum (arrowwood viburnum)	Yellow, red, and purple
Euonymus alata (burning bush)	Red	*V. dilatatum* (linden viburnum)	Orange, red, and purple
Fothergilla gardenii (low fothergilla)	Yellow, orange, and red	*V. plicatum* f. *tomentosum* (double-file viburnum)	Red-violet
F. major (tall fothergilla)	Yellow, orange, and red		
Hamamelis × intermedia (hybrid witch hazel)	Yellow	*V. prunifolium* (black haw viburnum)	Red and purple
H. mollis (Chinese witch hazel)	Yellow	*V. trilobum* (American cranberry viburnum)	Yellow, orange, red, and purple
H. virginiana (eastern witch hazel)	Yellow	*Xanthorhiza simplicissima* (yellowroot)	Yellow and orange

SHRUBS FOR DRY PLACES

Names	Characteristics
Acer ginnala (Amur maple)	Red fruit (samaras); yellow and red fall foliage
A. tataricum (Tatarian maple)	Red fruit (samaras); yellow, red, and red-brown fall foliage
Amorpha fruticosa (false indigo)	Purple-and-orange flowers in late spring; extremely drought resistant
Arctostaphylos uva-ursi (bearberry)	Evergreen; glossy bronzy winter foliage; red berries
Baccharis halimifolia (groundsel bush)	Whitish fruiting heads; salt tolerant
Berberis thunbergii (Japanese barberry)	Red berries; red, orange, and yellow fall foliage; cultivars with purple leaves
Caragana arborescens (Siberian pea bush)	Yellow flowers in spring; green twigs in winter
Ceanothus americanus (New Jersey tea)	White flowers in early summer
Colutea arborescens (bladder senna)	Yellow flowers in early summer; inflated pods
Comptonia peregrina (sweet fern)	Decorative aromatic foliage
Cornus racemosa (gray dogwood)	White flowers in spring; white berries; purplish twigs
Cotinus coggygria (smoke bush)	Copiously hairy pinkish gray fruit clusters
Cytisus scoparius (Scotch broom)	Yellow flowers in spring; dense upright head of slender dark green twigs in winter
Elaeagnus angustifolia (Russian olive)	Yellow flowers in spring; yellow fruit; gray green foliage
E. umbellata (autumn olive)	White flowers in spring; red fruit; gray green foliage
Eleutherococcus sieboldianus (five-leaf aralia)	Rich bright green foliage; extremely tough and resistant
Hypericum prolificum (shrubby St. John'swort)	Yellow flowers in summer
Indigofera kirilowii (Kirilow indigo)	Rose pink flowers in early summer
Juniperus communis (common juniper)	Evergreen; many dwarf cultivars
J. conferta (shore juniper)	Evergreen; well suited to littoral sites
J. horizontalis (creeping juniper)	Evergreen; many low-growing cultivars
J. virginiana (red cedar)	Evergreen; upright, dark; many cultivars
Lavandula angustifolia (English lavender)	Blue, white, or pink flowers in summer; aromatic foliage
Lespedeza bicolor (bush clover)	Rose purple flowers in late summer
Ligustrum spp. (privets)	Some species evergreen; white flowers in summer; some species with black berries; lustrous foliage
Lonicera tatarica (Tatarian bush honeysuckle)	Pink or white flowers in spring; red berries
Myrica pennsylvanica (northern bayberry)	Gray berries (female); aromatic foliage
Physocarpus opulifolius (ninebark)	White flowers in spring; reddish fruit
Potentilla fruticosa (shrubby cinquefoil)	Yellow or white flowers in late spring and early summer
Prunus besseyi (western sand cherry)	White flowers in spring; purplish black fruit; gray green foliage
P. maritima (beach plum)	White flowers in spring; dark red to purple fruit
Rhamnus cathartica (common buckthorn)	Purple fruit (female)
R. frangula (glossy buckthorn)	Red to purple fruit
Rhus copallina (shining sumac)	Dark red fruit (female); purple fall foliage
R. glabra (smooth sumac)	Red fruit (female); scarlet fall foliage
*Robinia hispida** (rose acacia)	Rose purple flowers in spring; bristly purple pods
Rosa rugosa (rugosa rose)	Pink or white flowers in summer; red-orange fruit; yellow fall foliage
R. setigera (prairie rose)	Pink flowers in late spring; red fruit; purple to yellow fall foliage
R. spinosissima (Scotch rose)	Pink, white, or yellow flowers in late spring; brown-black fruit
R. virginiana (Virginia rose)	Pink flowers in late spring; red fruit; red canes in winter
Rosmarinus officinalis (rosemary)	Evergreen aromatic gray green foliage; blue flowers in fall
Shepherdia argentea (silver buffalo berry)	Reddish fruit; silver gray foliage
S. canadensis (russet buffalo berry)	Reddish fruit; gray green foliage
Spartium junceum (Spanish broom)	Yellow flowers in spring; green broomlike stems

Names	Characteristics
Tamarix ramosissima (five-stamen tamarisk)	Rose pink flowers in early summer; fine-textured foliage
Viburnum lentago (nannyberry, sheepberry)	Cream flowers in spring; blue-black fruit
Yucca filamentosa (Adam's needle)	Cream flowers in summer; rosetted evergreen foliage
Y. glauca (soapweed)	Greenish white flowers in summer; narrow evergreen foliage
Y. gloriosa (Spanish dagger)	Cream flowers in summer; evergreen foliage

* *R. boyntoni, R. elliottii, R. fertilis,* and possibly others are similar and sometimes offered as *R. nispida.*

SHRUBS OF RESTRICTED MAXIMUM HEIGHT*
Shrubs suitable for foundation plantings.

Name	Maximum Height and Spread	Name	Maximum Height and Spread
Abelia × *grandiflora* (glossy abelia)	6 × 6'	*R. dauricum* (Dahurian rhododendron)	6 × 6'
Abeliophyllum distichum (white forsythia)	5 × 5'	*R. flammeum* (Oconee azalea)	6 × 6'
Berberis × *chenaultii* (Chenault barberry)	4 × 4'	*R. keiskei* (Keiske rhododendron)	5 × 4'
Cotoneaster adpressus (creeping cotoneaster)	2 × 6'	*R. laetivirens* (Wilson rhododendron)	4 × 4'
C. apiculatus (cranberry cotoneaster)	3 × 6'	*R. obtusum* (Hiryu azalea)	6 × 6'
C. horizontalis (rockspray cotoneaster)	3 × 8'	*R. 'PJM'* (PJM rhododendron)	6 × 6'
Deutzia gracilis (slender deutzia)	4 × 4'	*R. yedoense* var. *poukanense* (Korean azalea)	6 × 6'
Enkianthus perulatus (white enkianthus)	6 × 6'	*Rhus aromatica* (fragrant sumac)	6 × 10'
Fothergilla × *gardenii* (dwarf fothergilla)	3 × 4'	*Ribes alpinum* (alpine currant)	6 × 8'
Gaylussacia brachycera (box huckleberry)	1½ × 5'	*Rosa rugosa* (rugosa rose)	6 × 6'
Genista tinctoria (dyer's greenwood)	3 × 3'	*Rosmarinus officinalis* (rosemary)	4 × 6'
Hypericum prolificum (shrubby St. John'swort)	4 × 4'	*Sarcococca hookeriana* (Himalayan sweet box)	4 × 6'
Ilex glabra (inkberry)	8 × 10'	*Skimmia japonica* (Japanese skimmia)	4 × 6'
Jasminum nudiflorum (winter jasmine)	4 × 8'	*Spiraea* × *arguta* (garland spiraea)	5 × 5'
Juniperus conferta (shore juniper)	1½ × 8'	*S.* × *billiardii* (billiard spiraea)	6 × 6'
J. horizontalis (creeping juniper)	2 × 8'	*S.* × *bumalda* (Bumald spiraea)	3 × 5'
J. sabina (savin juniper)	6 × 10'	*S. japonica* (Japanese spiraea)	5 × 4'
Lavandula angustifolia (English lavender)	2 × 5'	*S. prunifolia* (bridal wreath)	8 × 8'
Leiophyllum buxifolium (box sand myrtle)	3 × 5'	*S. thunbergii* (Thunberg spiraea)	5 × 5'
Leucothoë fontanesiana (drooping leucothoë)	6 × 6'	*S. trilobata* (three-lobe spiraea)	5 × 5'
Lonicera nitida (box-leaf bush honeysuckle)	6 × 6'	*S.* × *vanhouttei* (Vanhoutte spiraea)	6 × 10'
Mahonia aquifolium (Oregon hollygrape)	6 × 4'	*Stephanandra incisa* (lace bush)	7 × 7'
Myrica gale (sweet gale)	4 × 4'	*Symphoricarpos albus* (snowberry)	6 × 6'
Neillia sinensis (Chinese neillia)	6 × 6'	*Syringa meyeri* (Meyer lilac)	8 × 12'
Nevusia alabamensis (snow wreath)	6 × 6'	*S. microphylla* (littleleaf lilac)	6 × 10'
Pieris floribunda (mountain pieris)	6 × 8'	*S.* × *persica* (Persian lilac)	8 × 10'
Potentilla fruticosa (shrubby cinquefoil)	4 × 4'	*Taxus canadensis* (Canadian yew)	6 × 8'
Prunus glandulosa (dwarf flowering almond)	5 × 4'	*Viburnum carlesii* (Korean spice viburnum)	6 × 8'
P. tenella (dwarf Russian almond)	5 × 5'	*V. davidii* (David viburnum)	5 × 5'
Raphiolepis umbellata (Yedda hawthorn)	6 × 6'	*Yucca filamentosa* (Adam's needle)	2 (6) × 4'
Rhododendron carolinianum (Carolina rhododendron)	6 × 8'	*Zenobia pulverulenta* (dusty zenobia)	4 × 4'

* Many of these (and other, taller species) have dwarf cultivars.

SHRUBS FOR STABILIZING EMBANKMENTS

Name	Height and Spread	Name	Height and Spread
Arctostaphylos uva-ursi (bearberry)	1 × 6'	*Jasminum nudiflorum* (winter jasmine)	4 × 7'
Berberis koreana (Korean barberry)	6 × 6'	*Juniperus chinensis* var. *sargentii* (Sargent juniper)	2 × 8'
B. × *mentorensis* (mentor barberry)	5 × 8'	*J. chinensis* var. *procumbens* (creeping Chinese juniper)	2 × 12'
B. thunbergii (Japanese barberry)	6 × 6'	*J. conferta* (shore juniper)	1½ × 8'
Calluna vulgaris (heather)	2 × 2'	*J. horizontalis* (creeping juniper)	2 × 8'
Comptonia peregrina (sweet fern)	3 × 6'	*Leucothoë fontanesiana* (drooping leucothoë)	6 × 6'
Cornus alba (Tatarian dogwood)	5 × 8'	*L. axillaris* (coast leucothoë)	4 × 6'
C. racemosa (gray dogwood)	10 × 10'	*Lycium chinense* (Chinese matrimony vine)	6 × 10'
C. sanguinea (blood-twig dogwood)	8 × 8'	*Microbiota decussata* (Siberian carpet)	1 × 6'
C. stolonifera (red-osier dogwood)	8 × 8'	*Myrica gale* (sweet gale)	3 × 3'
C. stolonifera 'Flaviramea' (yellow-twig dogwood)	8 × 8'	*M. pensylvanica* (northern bayberry)	8 × 8'
Cotoneaster adpressus (creeping cotoneaster)	1 × 4'	*Neillia sinensis* (Chinese neillia)	6 × 6'
C. apiculatus (cranberry cotoneaster)	3 × 6'	*Physocarpus opulifolius* (ninebark)	7 × 10'
C. dammeri (bearberry cotoneaster)	1 × 6'	*Pieris floribunda* (mountain pieris)	5 × 7'
C. divaricatus (spreading cotoneaster)	6 × 6'	*Potentilla fruticosa* (shrubby cinquefoil)	4 × 6'
C. horizontalis (rockspray cotoneaster)	3 × 8'	*Prunus maritima* (beach plum)	6 × 6'
C. microphyllus (littleleaf cotoneaster)	2 × 4'	*Rhus aromatica* (fragrant sumac)	4 × 8'
C. × *praecox* (Warminster broom)	6 × 6'	*R. trilobata* (skunkbush)	4 × 6'
Cytisus scoparius (Scotch broom)	6 × 6'	*Robinia hispida** (rose acacia)	6 × 10'
Diervilla sessilifolia (southern bush honeysuckle)	4 × 4'	*Rosa multiflora* (multiflora rose)	6 × 10'
Forsythia 'Arnold Dwarf' (dwarf forsythia)	3 × 7'	*R. rugosa* (rugosa rose)	6 × 6'
F. suspensa var. *sieboldii* (weeping forsythia)	8 × 12'	*R. virginiana* (Virginia rose)	4 × 6'
F. viridissima 'Bronxensis' (creeping forsythia)	1 × 3'	*Sorbaria sorbifolia* (Ural false spiraea)	8 × 8'
Hydrangea arborescens 'Grandiflora' (hills-of-snow)	4 × 4'	*Spiraea* × *bumalda* (Bumald spiraea)	3 × 5'
Hypericum buckleyi (Blue Ridge St. John'swort)	1 × 2'	*Stephanandra incisa* 'Crispa' (dwarf lace bush)	3 × 6'
H. calycinum (Aaron's-beard, St. John'swort)	1½'	*Symphoricarpos albus* (snowberry)	6 × 6'
H. patulum (golden cup St. John'swort)	3 × 3'	*S.* × *chenaultii* (Chenault coralberry)	4 × 6'
H. prolificum (shrubby St. John'swort)	4 × 4'	*Vaccinium angustifolium* (lowbush blueberry)	2 × 3'
Indigofera kirilowii (Kirilow indigo)	3 × 8'	*Xanthorhiza simplicissima* (yellowroot)	3 × 8'

*R. boyntoni, R. elliottii, R. fertilis, and possibly others are similar and sometimes offered as *R. hispida.*

OLD-FASHIONED SHRUBS

Species appropriate for colonial gardens.

Names	Origin and Date of Introduction
Buxus sempervirens 'Suffruticosa' (box)	Southern Europe, Southwestern Asia, and Northern Africa; ancient selection from somewhere in natural range of *B. sempervirens*
Calycanthus floridus (Carolina allspice, sweet shrub)	Virginia to Florida; 1726
Chionanthus virginicus (American fringe bush)	Pennsylvania to Florida and Texas; 1736
Cotinus coggygria (smokebush)	Southern Europe to China; 1656
Hibiscus syriacus (rose of Sharon)	China to India; introduced in Europe before 1600, and then to the colonies
Ilex glabra (inkberry)	Nova Scotia to Florida; 1759
I. verticillata (winterberry)	Eastern Canada to Florida; 1736
Lagerstroemia (crape myrtle)	China; 1759
Ligustrum vulgare (common European privet)	Europe and Northern Africa; cultivated since classical times for hedging and topiary
Philadelphus coronarius (mock orange)	Southern Europe; 1560
Rosa × alba (cottage rose)	Ancient hybrid of disputed parentage
R. × centifolia (cabbage rose)	Ancient hybrid of disputed parentage
R. × damascena (summer damask rose)	Hybrid of *R. gallica* and *R. moschata* originated in Asia Minor; 1550
R. gallica (French rose)	Southern and Central Europe to Asia Minor; cultivated since classical times
R. majalis (cinnamon rose)	Northern and Central Europe to Siberia; cultivated in Europe since the 1500s
R. moschata (musk rose)	Western Europe, but unknown in the wild; cultivated since medieval times
R. palustris (swamp rose)	Eastern North America; 1726
Syringa vulgaris (common lilac)	Southeastern Europe; 1550
Tamarix gallica (tamarisk)	Mediterranean region; 1596

13

Woody Climbers

BY ITS PROPER BOTANIC DEFINITION, THE WORD *VINE* refers to grapes or members of the genus *Vitis*. Here we adopt the term *woody climber* to refer to slender-stemmed, woody plants that twine, scramble up, cling to, or in some other way attach themselves or become attached to supporting structures.

The vast majority of the world's woody climbers are native to the frost-free tropics. For obvious reasons, these cannot be included here. The focus in this chapter is on woody

*Japanese wisteria (*Wisteria floribunda*), in both of its popular color phases, when allowed to scramble over an outcrop, imparts incomparable grace to this rocky setting when in bloom.*

climbers that have merit in American gardens in zones 2 through 8.

Herbaceous climbers—those that die back to their roots in the fall or die altogether after a single season—are treated in the chapters devoted to perennials and annuals.

Climbers in the garden serve an important role because they are both decorative and functional. Probably the earliest use of them was for fruit and wine production, but the decorative value of the grapevine was so apparent that centuries ago the garden builders of Italy included grape arbors as part of their formal gardens.

Each climber possesses distinctive characteristics that suit it to certain locations in the landscape. Some are valued for the welcome shade they provide when trained on arbors or pergolas; others lend distinction to a planting when skillfully trained against the wall of a house or patio or when used to gracefully frame a doorway. Some climbers can be used to relieve the monotony of a large expanse of wall, as when trained to a definite pattern or allowed to clothe it completely with leafy green. With their blossoms and delicate tracery of leaf form, certain kinds can make an otherwise commonplace or ugly fence seem exciting and even exotically beautiful. Still others may form a cascade of bloom on rough, steep banks, while holding the soil in place.

Different climbers are admired and valued for many reasons: for their decorative habit of growth, for the fragrance or spectacular beauty of their flowers, for the graceful patterning of their supple stems, or for the beauty of their leaves and overall foliage texture. In the hands of the skillful designer and gardener, climbers offer a rich source of material with which to create compositions of striking beauty. Increasingly, climbers are finding favor in American gardens.

SUPPORTING CLIMBERS

Most climbers must have support. And since the various kinds differ in their habits of growth and climbing strategies, the support must be suitable to the type selected. Those that climb by stems twining around the support, such as wisteria, and those that have tendrils which reach out and grasp small objects in the manner of the grapevine need a lattice, arbor, or fence type of support. Those that cling to things by means of rootlets, rootlike "holdfasts" or tendrils with adhesive disks, need brick, stone, or masonry walls, or even great boulders as support. Boston ivy (*Parthenocissus tricuspidata*) and climbing hydrangea (*Hydrangea anomala* var. *petiolaris*) need this type of support.

Some climbers will grow without supports, but the amazing fact about many of them is that when grown in this manner they lose their vine characteristics and become shrublike in form. *Euonymus fortunei* var. *radicans* is an outstanding example of this modification. In some cases such shrubs will send out long straight stems along the surface in an effort to find a support. This is a tactic of the wisterias. Many others, such as Virginia creeper (*Parthenocissus quinquefolia*), memorial rose (*Rosa wichuraiana*), and English ivy (*Hedera helix*), are quite content to scramble on the ground and often make good ground covers. However, when they reach a support, up they go, for climbers are essentially opportunists in the plant kingdom; if they did not grow rapidly up and over their neighbors, they would not reach the light they need to flower and reproduce. The various kinds of climbers succeed biologically by rapidly growing up into the light without investing nutrients in the production of wood strong enough to support the leafy top growth. Instead, a climber depends on other objects (usually neighboring plants) for support, and some may even kill the very tree that offers support by smothering its foliage or constricting its trunk. Furthermore, the roots of some climbers range as widely and freely as their stems. This makes them bad neighbors for many plants. The home gardener should understand these tendencies in climbers and make provision for them.

The best type of support for climbers is the one that affords the required structural strength and stability and, at the same time, makes a neat appearance. In some gardens, the architectural arbor has its place, but in many cases the growth of climbers will so completely cover all but the posts that such embellishment seems unwarranted.

Woody climbers clambering up a trellis that is attached to a frame house are serious obstacles to the periodic painting the house requires. If rambler or climbing roses are trained on the trellis, the job of painting will be both difficult and uncomfortable. To overcome this trouble, the trellis should be built so that, together with the stems, it may be detached from the building. One of the best ways to accomplish this is to hinge the trellis at its base. When painting is needed, the top may be released, the trellis swung out and held in a slanting position by a strut. There will be sufficient pliancy in the stems of the climber to bend along with the hinge.

For the support of rather slender climbers against a stone or brick wall, special fasteners are available at most garden centers. These are attached to the wall by means of nails driven into plugs that fill holes drilled into the mortar. The plastic or soft metal fasteners are loosely bent around stems to prevent chafing and allow for growth. This is a most satisfactory means of training and supporting firethorn (*Pyracantha coccinea*), forsythia, and winter jasmine (*Jasminum nudiflorum*) against a masonry wall.

For the support of large stem-twining climbers against a masonry wall, metal frame lattices are best. Less expensive but equally effective is a large mesh network of wire cables fastened to expansion bolts, which project out about 8 inches from the face of the wall. The wires are made tight by turn buckles. This is suitable for such rampant climbers as wisteria and kiwi fruit (*Actinidia* spp.), and if the wires are placed 3 feet apart, forming squares, a very pleasing pattern of greenery and masonry will replace a large bare wall surface flanking a city garden.

MAINTAINING WOODY CLIMBERS

Pruning woody climbers to produce better bloom or to keep them within bounds is usually an annual task, requiring patience and skill. The removal of the old wood may involve several cuts to each stem so that they can be untangled. The same principles that guide the pruning of fruit trees also apply to woody climbers. Such pruning is done mainly to determine future growth. In the case of climbers whose flowers and/or fruit are valued, pruning should be timed according to the growth characteristics of each kind, as indicated in the plant descriptions that follow.

Climbers like wisteria and bittersweet (*Celastrus scandens*) develop large stems that tangle in grotesque knots. As the stems grow and expand, the knots become tighter, and in this way the vine is apt to strangle some of its own stems. This may be avoided in part by reducing the number of major stems when the climber is still young and by training the early growth in such a way as to prevent formation of heavy twisted ropes made up of several stems. If the central part of the plant is well branched, the formation of tangles in the outer parts is not so serious. They can be removed without spoiling the climber.

WOODY CLIMBERS OF MERIT

ACTINIDIA POLYGAMA
(Silver vine)

Zones 4–8

Silver vine is moderately vigorous twining species with handsome deciduous foliage and is remarkably free from insects pests and diseases. It bears small fragrant white flowers in clusters of three in the leaf axils in late spring to early summer. The edible fruit, which ripens in the fall, is a greenish yellow berry about 1 inch long. As the plant is sometimes dioecious, i.e., each plant is either male or female, an individual that does not bear fruit occasionally appears. This is of little consequence, however, as the nonbearing male plants tend to have more handsome silvery leaves. This species, like catnip, is extremely attractive to cats, and young plants may be mauled or completely destroyed by them if not protected.

Silver vine is very easily transplanted and established in most any well-drained soil of moderate fertility. It makes an attractive pattern on a trellis, fence, or wall in full sun or partial shade. It eventually reaches 10 to 15 feet in height. The only care required is an occasional thinning of the mass of stems, especially when the older ones begin to fail and die.

AMPELOPSIS BREVIPEDUNCULATA
(Porcelain berry)

Zones 4–8

A hardy, deciduous, tendril climber of rampant growth, porcelain berry has large, handsome three-lobed leaves. The inconspicuous flowers are followed by clusters of berries that change from pale lilac to yellow and ripen bright amethyst purple to blue—an unusual and most attractive combination of colors.

Like a wild grapevine in habit, porcelain berry does well on a trellis or arbor or sprawling over an outcrop. It is especially useful covering unattractive chain-link fences. Porcelain berry thrives in any well-drained soil and does equally well in sun or shade. It can eventually reach 25 feet on a vertical support.

ARISTOLOCHIA DURIOR
(Dutchman's-pipe)

Zones 4–8

Dutchman's-pipe, an old-fashioned favorite, is a vigorous twining climber with large heart-shaped leaves that thickly overlap one another. If grown on a series of horizontal slats or wires, it will form an opaque wall of green. The flowers, though inconspicuous and usually hidden, are very entertaining; appearing in late spring, they suggest a Dutch smoking pipe, and from this comes the common name. This species is native to the woodlands of eastern United States, from Pennsylvania and Minnesota southward to Georgia, and has long been in cultivation. Ultimate height is 20 to 30 feet.

Dutchman's-pipe grows well in any well-drained garden loam with a pH between 6.0 and 7.0. On a large arbor or trellis or on long wires, it casts dense shade and is often grown as a screen. Full sun or partial shade is best.

BIGNONIA CAPREOLATA
(Cross vine)

Zones (6) 7–8

A near relative of the trumpet creepers, cross vine is a tendril climber prized for its orange-red flowers in late spring and its evergreen foliage. It is fast growing, often develops many shoots from the roots, and needs plenty of space to mature. Care should be taken to plant it where it can achieve its full height of 35 to 50 feet or more. Pruning of living stems, if required, should be done after flowering has finished.

Cross vine thrives in most any well-drained, loamy soil in a location with full sun or partial shade. As its branched tendrils are persistent, this is an excellent choice to cover fences and walls and to climb rough-barked trees.

CAMPSIS GRANDIFLORA
(Chinese trumpet creeper)

Zones 7–9

Chinese trumpet creeper often has very few aerial rootlets, and it may be distinguished from other *Campsis* species by the fact that it generally has fewer leaflets (seven or nine) and bright scarlet flowers that are larger and open in late summer. Many gardeners consider Chinese trumpet creeper to be superior to the native species, partly because of its less vigorous habit of growth.

Chinese trumpet creeper is very easily grown and flourishes in full sun, especially if allowed to climb an arbor, trellis, fence, or wall. Given the chance, it can reach 20 to 25 feet.

CAMPSIS RADICANS
(American trumpet creeper)

Zones 4–9

American trumpet creeper has the easiest culture of the *Campsis* species. It bears orange to scarlet tubular blossoms in terminal clusters in the summer, each blossom 3 to 4 inches long. The coarse-textured foliage is very dense and consists of compound leaves of 9 or 11 leaflets. Native to forest borders from Pennsylvania to Texas, American trumpet creeper has been cultivated since colonial times. The cultivar

'Flava' has pure yellow flowers, and the hybrid *C. × tagliabuana* 'Madame Galen' has showy scarlet flowers.

Requiring virtually no attention and succeeding in most any soil, American trumpet creeper flowers best in full sun. It is most effective against brick, stucco, or stone walls, especially if allowed plenty of room. It clings by means of aerial roots, which grow wherever contact is made. It is best not to grow this climber against a building, as the rampant growth invades gutters and other structures, trapping litter and inducing rot. With annual pruning and shaping in the spring, it can be grown as a flowering hedge. It is advisable to grow American trumpet creeper away from garden beds and shrubbery as its roots generate suckers, often in profusion, which can complicate maintenance.

CELASTRUS SCANDENS
(American bittersweet)

Zones 3–8

American bittersweet, a native of our forests, is an old but still very popular favorite. This species should not be confused with the exceedingly rampant Chinese bittersweet (*C. orbiculatus*), which is similar in many respects and has escaped cultivation in much of the Northeast. Chinese bittersweet bears its fruit in small clusters positioned laterally in the angles between the leaf stalk and stem instead of in large terminal sprays.

American bittersweet is a high-climbing twiner that matures to 25 feet or more. It has rich green foliage of varying shape and stems that thicken year by year and, therefore, increasingly constrict and deform young trees and other living supports, sometimes fatally. The orange-and-red fruit, which ripens as the leaves drop in the fall, lasts all winter, even when brought into the house to decorate the mantel or table. The fruit is born in diffuse terminal clusters, which makes it conspicuous. Although American bittersweet will ascend the tops of trees and is at home in the shadiest forest glade, it is best to discourage its climbing specimen trees and scrambling over roofs. This species is dioecious, i.e., the male and female flowers are, for the most part,

borne on separate plants, with fruit developing only on female plants. Seeds are scattered by birds.

American bittersweet is best grown in full sun and adapts to any well-drained soil. It is most effective and least troublesome if grown on sturdy fences or arbors or encouraged to scramble over outcrops, stone walls, or embankments. Fruiting plants are best pruned in early spring; male plants may be pruned anytime.

CLEMATIS

The various species of *Clematis* include some of the world's most decorative and beautiful climbers. Some species are of vigorous growth and will do well under widely varying conditions, while others, and most hybrid sorts, are somewhat temperamental and will thrive only when their specific cultural requirements are met.

Three-flower clematis (*Clematis terniflora*, syn. *C. maximowicziana*), a semi-woody climber

Some species of *Clematis* have solitary or small clusters of bell-shaped or urn-shaped flowers; others bear masses of small blooms in loose clusters; and still others bear fewer, larger, more open, rather starlike flowers. Overall, the flowering season for clematis is long, beginning with the anemone clematis (*C. montana*) in midspring and ending with the large white blooms of the hybrid 'Duchess

Hybrid *Clematis* on tepee

of Edinburgh', which sheds its petals in late autumn.

Of the more than 200 species of *Clematis*, comparatively few are widely grown, but those that are add a special grace and charm to the garden composition.

Clematis armandii
(Armand clematis)
Zones 7–9

A lovely evergreen species that is much valued for both its foliage and flowers wherever it can be grown, Armand clematis has dark, glossy leaves and glistening, white, starlike flowers, which are borne in clusters in the spring. Pink-flowered cultivars are also available.

Armand clematis often takes a few years to become fully established, but then becomes a reliable performer year after year. In full sun, partial shade, or light shade, it is especially effective over doorways, along cornices, or outlining gables. With training and support, it can also be used along fence tops or on walls and, left unpruned, will grow to 20 feet or more. As the flowers are formed on the growth of the previous year, pruning should be done immediately after flowering. Humusy, well-drained soil is best.

Clematis crispa
(Marsh clematis, curly clematis)
Zones 5–9

Marsh clematis is a very attractive species that is native to swamps in the South, but it is hardy much farther north. The rather delicate steel blue flowers are bell or urn shaped and appear for several weeks in late summer.

Marsh clematis thrives on moist, humusy soil but also performs well on drier, well-drained sites, where, if trained on a trellis or arbor, it may be expected to reach 8 feet. Full sun, partial shade, or light shade are all satisfactory. Any pruning should be done in early spring when the foliage buds first expand.

CLEMATIS × JACKMANII *CVS.*
(Jackman clematis)
Zones (3) 4–8 (9)

The long-popular, large-flowered hybrid cultivars of the Jackman Clematises result

Jackman clematis
(Clematis × jackmanii)

mainly from the crossing of *C. lanuginosa* and *C. viticella*. Characteristically, Jackman clematis has wide open violet purple, four-petaled, star-shaped flowers, 5 to 7 inches in diameter. The cultivars, in both single and double forms, range from pure white through pink and wine red to purple; there are also bicolor forms. Heights range from 10 to 15 or even 20 feet. Cultural details are discussed under "Clematis Cultivars" on page 281.

CLEMATIS LANUGINOSA
(Woolly-leaved clematis)

Zones 6–9

Woolly-leaved clematis typically has very large white or lavender flowers that are borne in profusion throughout the summer. Its maximum height is about 10 feet, but height ranges from 6 to 15 feet in the various cultivars.

Woolly-leaved clematis shows to best effect when grown on an arbor, pergola, or trellis in full sun. Acidic, sandy-humusy, well-drained soil is best. As the flowers are borne on new growth, pruning should be carried out in early spring just as the new shoots appear.

CLEMATIS MACROPETALA
(Big-petal clematis)

Zones 5–9

Big-petal clematis is one of the most beautiful of all the clematis species. It flowers in mid to late spring, bearing azure blue blooms that range from 2½ to 4 inches across. The flowers are semi-double (i.e., with an incomplete circle of petals inside the complete outer whorl) and nod at the ends of their stalks. The stem rarely exceeds 10 feet in height.

Big-petal clematis responds best to full sun and is very decorative on an arbor, pergola, or trellis or, if supported, on a wall. Soil and pruning are the same as for *C. lanuginosa*.

CLEMATIS MONTANA
(Anemone clematis)

Zones 5–9

The anemone clematis is a vigorous climber that is completely covered with anemonelike flowers in late spring or early summer. The individual blooms are relatively small (about 2 inches across) and open white, aging to a pale pink. In pink anemone clematis (*C. montana* var. *rubens*), the flowers are a deep pink. Whatever their flower color, the plants mature at 10 to 15 feet high.

Plant in full sun or partial shade, in well-drained, humusy soil. Support should be provided, either an arbor, trellis, or fence. If wire or lattice is used, the plant can be trained up a wall. As flowers are borne on growth of the previous season, pruning should be minimal and limited to the removal of dead or weak stems in early spring, just as new growth begins.

CLEMATIS PANICULATA
(Sweet autumn clematis)

Zones 5–8

One of the most vigorous and easily grown of all clematis, sweet autumn clematis flowers abundantly in late summer or early fall, when it is virtually covered with small, white, fragrant flowers. These are followed by a profusion of feathery, twisted achenes, or seed pods, that turn tan and persist into winter. Left unsupported, sweet autumn clematis forms a dense thicket, but with access to a trellis or arbor, it can reach 10 feet or more.

Adaptable to most any well-drained soil in sun or partial shade, this species requires no regular care. Pruning, if needed, should be carried out in early spring, as flowers are borne on growth of the same season.

CLEMATIS TEXENSIS
(Scarlet clematis)

Zones 4–9

Scarlet clematis is a rangy, leafy climber, bearing ovoid, nodding, red or purplish flowers from midsummer to early fall on growth of the current season. Among the several derived cultivars, 'Dutchess of Albany', with spreading pink sepals, is especially attractive. For culture, see "Clematis Cultivars," below.

CLEMATIS VIRGINIANA
(Virgin's bower)

Zones 4–9

More suited to naturalizing along woodland borders or on rustic fences and walls, the native virgin's bower is fine textured but vigorous. It is especially beautiful when covered with masses of small white flowers in late summer. These are followed by persistent feathery seed heads. If allowed to climb, the vine reaches 15 to 20 feet.

This species is more tolerant of permanently moist or even wet sites than other clematises. Flowering is best in full sun or partial shade.

CLEMATIS VITALBA
(Traveler's joy)

Zones 4–8

One of the easiest of all clematis to grow, traveler's joy is a strong-growing climber from Europe, with very dense, rather coarse foliage. Clusters of small (1 inch in diameter), white, fragrant

---

CLEMATIS CULTIVARS OF MERIT

'Belle of Working' ('Florida' group): flowers pale mauve to silvery gray, double; spring; on the previous season's growth.

'Comptesse de Bouchard' ('Jackmanii' group): flowers satiny rose, summer to fall, on previous season's growth.

'Crimson King' ('Jackmanii' group): flowers crimson with brown anthers; summer, on previous season's growth.

'Dutchess of Edinburgh' ('Florida' group): flowers white, double, fragrant; spring, on previous season's growth.

'Henryi' ('Jackmanii' group): flowers very large, white with dark violet anthers; early summer, on current season's growth.

'Jackmanii Alba' ('Jackmanii' group): flowers white, single and double; summer, on both previous and current season's growth.

'Jackmani Rubra' ('Jackmanii' group): flowers dark red; summer, on both previous and current season's growth.

'Jackmanii Superba' ('Jackmanii' group): flowers dark purple; summer, on both previous and current season's growth.

'Lord Neville' ('Jackmanii' group): flowers dark purple; summer, on current season's growth.

'Nelly Moser' ('Patens' group): flowers mauve pink with deeper pink markings; spring, on previous season's growth.

Clematis
'Comptesse de Bouchard'
('Jackmanii' group)

Clematis
'Henryi'
('Jackmanii' group)

Clematis
'Nelly Moser'
('Patens' group)

flowers appear in late summer. High climbing if allowed to ascend trees, traveler's joy can reach 30 feet.

Best used to clothe a fence, arbor, or pergola, this species is adaptable to virtually any well-drained soil and flowers most fully in a sunny position.

Clematis Cultivars
Zones 5–8

The most beautiful and the most widely grown of the clematises are the large-flowered hybrids that have been developed from the various species. These lovely hybrids are both the joy and despair of many a gardener. They are so decorative that the gardener is driven to grow them to perfection; yet the plants are fastidious, and perfection is not easily achieved unless their cultural requirements are respected.

For convenience, the hybrids are usually separated into three groups according to growth characteristics and time of flowering. In the 'Patens' group (derived chiefly from *C. patens*), flowers are borne in the spring on stems of the previous season. In the 'Florida' group (originating with *C. florida* as one parent), flowers appear in late spring or summer on the previous year's growth. In the 'Jackmanii' group (with parentage of *C.* × *jackmanii, C. lanuginosa*, and/or *C. viticella*), flowers are borne in the summer and autumn, usually on the current season's growth but in some cultivars on the previous season's growth and in others on growth of both the current and previous season.

General Cultural Requirements

Exposure

Full sun should be provided wherever possible. Most clematises require maximum sunlight to produce the heaviest bloom. However, when planted in very lightly shaded locations, many of them will grow reasonably well and flower satisfactorily. They will not thrive in full shade or on the north side of buildings where they receive little direct sunlight. The location selected should be protected from strong winds.

Soil

Hybrid clematis grows best in a soil that is neutral or slightly alkaline (pH 7.0 to 7.5). A test for acidity should be made before planting, and lime should be applied if it is needed. A sandy loam well supplied with organic matter is considered ideal; heavy loam or clay soils do not provide favorable growing conditions. Good drainage is essential. However, the roots of clematis require cool, evenly moist soil conditions. Soils that tend to bake or dry out for long periods definitely are not suitable.

The soil should be carefully prepared before planting. A hole of generous size should be dug, from 18 to 24 inches deep. If drainage is likely to be a problem, a layer of gravel or rubble should be placed in the bottom of the hole. The soil that has been removed may be mixed with well-decomposed leaf mold, compost, and dampened peat moss, with a little superphosphate added to the mixture. If manure is used, it should be very well rotted and should not come into direct contact with the roots at the time of planting.

Planting

Early spring and autumn are considered the most favorable times for planting, although, as with container-grown material of any kind, the time of planting is determined not so much by the calendar as by the preparation of the site and by the need for follow-up care, especially in summer.

It is wise to purchase plants that have been grown on their own roots rather than grafted, as their performance and longevity are generally superior. Most nurseries supply young, vigorous own-root plants in pots. The crown of the plant should be set 2 to 3 inches below the level of the soil, and all plants should be watered thoroughly at the time of planting. Some type of support, such as a bamboo stake or a bit of wire mesh, must be provided immediately. It is important that this is done at the time of planting as the stems twist and break very easily. The young plant should also be protected at the base from possible injury. A circle of small stakes may be used.

Mulching

Regardless of its location, whether it be planted in full sun in an exposed situation or in light shade, it is essential that clematis be protected at the base so that the roots may be kept cool and moist. A mulch 2 inches deep and extending out at least 2 feet from the plant is recommended. Dampened peat moss or rotting leaf mold may be used. In some cases, a shallow-rooted ground cover or other low-growing plants near the base of the vine will give sufficient protection.

Fertilization

In early spring, a complete fertilizer, such as 5-10-5, may be applied at the rate of 1 tablespoon per square foot of area, and then watered in well. A small application of a high-analysis, soluble fertilizer may be made instead. Repeat every six weeks during the growing season, especially if the soil is deficient in nutrients.

Pruning

It is best to allow young clematis plants to become well established before any pruning is done. The amount of pruning advisable for established plants depends on the type. Cultivars that flower early on old wood produced during the previous year require only the removal of dead, weak, or crowding stems. Unless height is desired for some special purpose, the stems of late-flowering cultivars should be cut back to 12 to 18 inches to encourage vigorous growth and more abundant bloom. Pruning should be done in late winter or early spring. Maintaining six to eight vigorous stems will result in an attractive plant. Even if killed to the ground during a particularly severe winter clematis will usually renew itself.

Support

The stems of clematis require some type of support to prevent them from becoming a tangle. They should be encouraged to spread out on the trellis or wire so that all parts will receive maximum sunlight and also so that a pleasant pattern may be maintained. A light trellis, a fence, a post, or wire mesh will all make very satisfactory supports. Sometimes adjacent shrubs are used for this purpose. A brick or high stone wall furnished with adequate wire supports will form a handsome backdrop for most clematises.

Winter Protection

In cold climates where winter protection is needed, i.e., north of zone 7, soil, sand, peat moss, or coal ashes may be mounded about the base of the plant and covered with a layer of leaves or straw. The mounds should be leveled when the ground thaws in early spring.

Uses

Clematises are among the most versatile of climbing plants. They are lovely when trained on a trellis against the wall of a house or a patio, or when used to frame an entrance. Intermingled with not-too-rampant cultivars of climbing roses on a fence, they prolong the season of bloom; and when carefully trained on their own support, they lend added interest to a perennial border. Planted in large pots or tubs, they add distinction and charm to the planting on a patio or terrace. Such plants should be trained on bamboo stakes and the tips should be pinched out when the shoots are 2 feet high to encourage lateral branching. The soft, exquisite coloring and texture of the flowers; the delicate tracery of the stems and tendrils; and the long-lasting quality of the blooms make clematis a favorite among those who delight in arranging flowers.

In short, clematis cultivars are more demanding of the gardener than most ornamental climbers; but if properly planted, adequately supported, kept sufficiently moist, furnished with the requisite nutrients, and pruned correctly, they offer uncommon reward. The most frequent causes of failure are too shallow planting, excessive shade, overly acidic soil, heavy soil that is poorly drained, and soil that overheats and dries out in summer.

EUONYMUS FORTUNEI
(Wintercreeper euonymus)

Zones 4–8 (9)

Wintercreeper euonymus is an evergreen rootlet climber of exceptional merit. Hardy, vigorous, and handsome at all seasons of the year, the foliage is a fine, glossy green, and in autumn and winter the bright red berries add a note of welcome cheer to a planting composition.

E. fortunei var. *radicans* has rather thick, finely toothed, undulating leaves and sometimes bears persistent bright red or red-orange berries. Var. *vegeta* has leathery, coarsely toothed leaves and usually bears its fruit generously. If unsupported, var. *radicans* trails, whereas var. *vegeta* becomes an upright shrub, 4 to 5 feet tall. Whatever the variety, maximum climbing height is 20 to 30 feet, or sometimes more.

Extremely hardy and of the easiest culture, wintercreeper euonymus is often slow in starting but after the first year or so it makes vigorous growth. It tends to be semishrubby in habit, so that to train it to climb it must be given support when first planted and induced to grow upward. Otherwise, it will remain bushy or sprawl on the ground. Wintercreeper euonymus thrives in most any reasonably well-drained soil and grows equally well in full sun or dense shade. In some areas, it is attacked by oyster shell scale. Pruning is best done in early spring.

HEDERA CANARIENSIS
(Algerian ivy)

Zones (8) 9–10

Native to the Canary Islands, Algerian ivy is adapted only to mild climates. It is more tolerant of hot sun than English ivy and is, therefore, more satisfactory in southern areas, though not commonly used. The leaves are more widely spaced on the stems than are those of English ivy and are three to five lobed, measuring 5 to 8 inches in width. The cultivar 'Canary Cream' bears leaves edged with greenish white.

Valued for its ability to cling to brick, stone, and concrete, Algerian ivy grows well in full sun to moderate shade. It is easily established and requires little care beyond a occasional grooming. Any well-drained soil, acidic or alkaline, is suitable.

HEDERA HELIX
(English ivy)

Juvenile foliage of English Ivy

Zones 4–9

English ivy is a sturdy evergreen climber that has many uses and, not surprisingly, is widely grown. It clings by means of aerial rootlets, and the handsome, dark green, often whitish-veined, glossy foliage is attractive almost throughout the year when grown under favorable conditions.

There are many varieties and hundreds of cultivars of English ivy, each having distinctive characteristics of leaf form and habit of growth that make it suitable for specific uses. Those specially noted here as being extra hardy may be used in zones 4 and 5 wherever shelter from wind and winter sun can be provided.

'Baltica': noted for its hardiness; perfectly hardy as far north as Boston; the leaves are somewhat smaller than those of the typical form.

'Bulgaria': another hardy selection; has proven satisfactory in the Midwest, where winters may be particularly difficult on evergreens.

'Conglomerata': stiff upright stems; small leaves arranged in ranks of two along the stems.

'Minima': very small undulating leaves; shows a tendency to revert to type if the reverting shoots are not promptly pruned out.

'Rumania': similar to 'Bulgaria'; quite hardy.

'Thorndale': a very hardy form; white-veined leaves 3 to 4 inches long.

'238th Street': a selection of the New York Botanical Garden; quite hardy and resistant to burn by winter sun.

English ivy, like most rootlet and tendril climbers, ascends trees, but because the climber's stems grow longitudinally, they do not wrap around the trunk or outpace the the growth of a supporting tree. Hence, neither smothering nor strangulation ensues. In time, however, overlapping ivy stems self-graft and considerable additional weight becomes the tree's to bear.

English ivy may also be used as a ground cover (see Chapter 14) or as a fence or screen by weaving the shoots through a woven-wire livestock-type fence. In a season or two the wire will be completely covered and, in time, unneeded for support.

Humusy, acidic, well-drained soil is best, but English ivy grows satisfactorily on virtually any soil that is not waterlogged. Partial shade yields the densest foliage, but good results are had in dense shade and, in the North at least, in full sun. Pruning or shearing may be done anytime.

HYDRANGEA ANOMALA
VAR. PETIOLARIS
(Climbing hydrangea)

Zones 4–8

This climbing form of hydrangea clings by means of small rootlike "holdfasts" and is hardy and vigorous in growth. The deciduous leaves are heart shaped, and its creamy flowers are borne in early summer in wide, flat clusters and are very decorative. The peeling, reddish

Climbing hydrangea (*Hydrangea anomala* var. *petoiolaris*)

brown bark is another interesting feature that makes this climber particularly attractive in winter.

Climbing hydrangea is especially pleasing when grown against building walls. It clings equally well to stone, masonry, and wood. It can be dramatically effective as a climber on the trunk and major limbs of a large tree. In flower, its branches appear to be layered or tiered. It is also useful as a shrubby ground cover on steep embankments. In time it can reach 50 feet or more, or spread over 100 to 200 square feet of ground.

Requiring only a well-drained, reasonably fertile soil and full sun or partial shade, climbing hydrangea is one of the most interesting, versatile, and trouble-free climbers available and should be used much more than it is. Pruning is best done after flowering in late summer.

JASMINUM MESNYI
(Primrose jasmine)

Zones 8–9

A mounded, evergreen semiclimber with long, arching branches, primrose jasmine bears its bright lemon yellow flowers in late winter and early spring.

Its arching habit and relatively low maximum height of 8 to 10 feet lend it to use as a cascade over walls or berms.

Ordinary, well-drained soil and a position in full sun or partial shade are its only cultural requirements. Any pruning should be done in the spring, after flowering and before the onset of growth.

JASMINUM NUDIFLORUM
(Winter jasmine)

Zones (5) 6–10

If winter jasmine is given a support, it will become a graceful climber, with slender green branches that are especially effective in winter when the leaves have dropped. Winter jasmine is among the first woody plants to bloom, its red-tipped

buds emerging during mild spells in mid or late winter. The buds open to a clear yellow. Flowering is over by the time the new leaves appear. Trained against a wall, it can reach 10 to 15 feet.

For best effect, winter jasmine should be placed where it receives winter sun—for example, on the southern, southeastern, or southwestern side of a building or wall—and, preferably, where it may be seen from indoors. Occasional pruning is sometimes useful in thinning the tangle of stems that eventually develops. Almost any well-drained soil suits it. Pruning is the same as for *J. mesnyi*.

JASMINUM OFFICINALE
(Poet's jasmine)

Zones 7–10

Poet's jasmine is one of the most beloved of jasmines, ascending by growing up through shrubs and low trees, and bearing numerous small, intensely fragrant, white flowers from late spring to early fall. Semievergreen in zones 9 and 10, it is deciduous farther north and, if exposed to harsh winter winds, may be killed to the ground in zone 7 and fail to flower.

Best grown in a well-drained, loamy soil in sun or partial shade, poet's jasmine can reach 25 to 30 feet in trees, but it is most effective if provided a trellis, arbor, or pergola where its flowers can be enjoyed at close range. Prune at the conclusion of flowering in the fall or in early spring before new growth begins.

LONICERA × HECKROTTII
(Everblooming honeysuckle)

Zones (4) 5–9

A deciduous species of vigorous growth, everblooming honeysuckle has fragrant flowers that are creamy within and pink to rose on the outside. They are borne in profusion from midspring to early fall. Maximum height is 10 to 15 feet.

Everblooming honeysuckle, or gold-flame honeysuckle, as it is sometimes called, is one of the best twining honeysuckles to grow for flowers. It is especially effective on a trellis or arbor in full sun or partial shade with moderately fertile, well-drained, loamy soil. Pruning, if required, is ideally done in the spring but may be performed anytime without seriously diminishing flower production.

LONICERA SEMPERVIRENS
(Scarlet trumpet honeysuckle)

Zones 4–9

Scarlet trumpet honeysuckle is one of the showiest and most desirable of the twining honeysuckles. The leaves are semievergreen. The scarlet, yellow-throated flowers have very long tubes and are borne in long clusters of six; they are not fragrant. The period of bloom lasts from late spring to late summer. The flowers are followed by red berries that persist into midautumn. Cultivars include the following.

'Dropmore Scarlet': a vigorous hybrid; scarlet flowers.
'Sulphurea': yellow flowers.
'Superba': red-orange to scarlet flowers.

Any reasonably fertile, well-drained soil is suitable. A sunny position ensures generous flowering. With a maximum height of 10 to 15 feet, scarlet trumpet honeysuckle is well suited to climbing pergolas and trellises. It is also effective on fences and scrambling over outcrops.

PARTHENOCISSUS QUINQUEFOLIA
(Virginia creeper)

Zones 3–10

A well-known native species that carpets woodland areas, clambers over walls and fences, and ascends tall trees, Virginia creeper clings by tendrils, each branch of which has an adhesive disclike end. This special equipment for climbing enables it to cover masonry walls as readily as does English ivy, and it has been much used since colonial times. Its glossy compound leaves make a beautiful pattern and turn a brilliant crimson in the autumn. The bluish black fruit ripens in late summer or early fall. A very useful if exuberant foliage plant, Virginia creeper grows equally well in full sun or constant shade. It is common throughout eastern North America, from southern Ontario and Quebec and adjacent Maine south to Florida and the Bahamas. Depending on support, it will grow 30 to 50 feet or more and succeeds on virtually any soil.

P. quinquefolia var. *engelmannii*, with denser, finer-textured foliage, is especially well suited for clothing brick and masonry walls.

PARTHENOCISSUS TRICUSPIDATA
(Boston ivy, or Japanese creeper)

Zones 4–8

One of the strongest and most rapidly growing of climbers, Boston ivy can completely cover the entire facade of a large building within a few years. The leaves are glossy, three lobed, and long stalked. Young growth clings tenaciously to almost any surface by means of branched tendrils that end with adhesive discs and makes a very dense foliage pattern on a wall, even in shade. The foliage turns brilliant red in the fall.

Two cultivars are especially popular:

'Lowii': small leaves that are deeply three to seven lobed.
'Veitchii': small leaves, with purple juvenile foliage; tendrils cling even to glass.

Whatever the form, maximum height is upward of 30 feet.

Because of its fine foliar texture, Boston ivy is effective when clothing a low wall or a small building. It thrives in full sun or partial or light shade and accepts most any well-drained soil.

POLYGONUM AUBERTII
(Silver-lace vine)

Zones 4–7

Silver-lace vine is a rapidly growing twining climber that blooms abundantly from midsummer to early fall, producing an effect suggestive of sweet autumn clematis (*Clematis paniculata*). The flowers are creamy white and borne in long, threadlike panicles that completely cover the top of the plant. As it can be prolific in producing rhizomes and seedlings, silver-lace vine, or China fleece, as it is sometimes called, should be planted only where its vigorous growth will not become a threat to other plants. It can climb to 35 feet, given adequate support.

It adapts to virtually any soil and is tolerant of prolonged dry spells, but flowers best if grown in full sun. The best effect is achieved on fences and arbors, where, however, occasional severe pruning may be required. It does particularly well under adverse city conditions and does an admirable job of quickly covering the ugliness of tall chain-link fences.

ROSA *SPP. AND CVS.*
(Climbing roses)

See Chapter 19.

VITIS COIGNETIAE
(Crimson glory vine)

Zones 5–8

Probably the best of the numerous species of grape (*Vitis*) to grow for ornamental purposes, crimson glory vine grows very rapidly and can be counted upon to produce a screen more quickly than almost any other hardy climber. The leaves are up to 10 inches in diameter and impart a bold appearance. They turn a brilliant red in autumn. Like all grapes, this species was once seriously attacked by the Japanese beetle, but in most areas the depredations of this pest have diminished. Because the black grapes of crimson glory vine are not edible, the plant's main horticultural value is as a fast-growing ornamental screen.

It should be grown in full sun and adapts to most any reasonably well-drained soil. No special care is required except to keep it in bounds if space is restricted, as it can climb to 50 feet or more.

WISTERIA FLORIBUNDA
(Japanese wisteria)

Wisteria floribunda | *W. floribunda* 'Alba'

Zones 4–9

The wisterias are superbly beautiful twining climbers with great hanging clusters of flowers that are borne in profusion each spring. This and Chinese wisteria (*W. sinensis*) are vigorous, high-climbing, and remarkably long lived. Apart from floral traits, the two species may be distinguished by their twining habits: Japanese wisteria twines clockwise; Chinese wisteria, counterclockwise.

Often blooming a bit earlier than *W. sinensis*, Japanese wisteria opens the season of bloom for wisterias. Among the many cultivars in the trade, all with flowers opening in sequence from the cluster base to the tip, the following are especially of merit.

'Alba': flowers white, fragrant, densely arranged in clusters about 11 inches long.

'Issai': flowers violet or bluish violet, fragrant, in clusters about 12 inches long.

'Longissima Alba': similar to 'Alba', clusters about 15 inches long.

'Macrobotrys': flowers violet to red-violet, very fragrant, in clusters 18 to 36 inches long (sometimes reaching 48 inches).

'Rosea': flowers pale rose, tipped purple, in clusters about 18 inches long.

Japanese wisteria will grow 50 feet or more in trees but is best kept to lower supports where the flowers may be enjoyed close at hand. Exposure to sun is important. as flower-bud formation is scanty in shade.

When planted next to buildings, wisteria of any kind should be provided with a strong support, preferably constructed of pipe, and should be pruned back each year. This pruning helps to induce more bloom and exclude venturesome stems before they damage siding, gutters, shutters, or the roof. If neglected, wisteria will grow out over the roof and invade spaces between shingles and elsewhere. As the stems expand year by year, they separate structural elements and allow water to gain entrance as well as trap dead leaves and other debris that decay and hold moisture. Such damage can be very costly to repair. Nevertheless, wisteria is a horticultural treasure, and if grown on substantial, durable, freestanding arbors and pergolas, it confers a special quality to the setting while posing no threat to the structural integrity of buildings.

In addition to the annual top pruning, ground-hugging surface runners from the trunks should also be removed before they strike root and send up unwanted twining stems in places often distant from the original planting.

Plants that fail to bloom should be pruned severely during the summer, reducing the growth on any branch to about six buds. Newly acquired plants should be rooted cuttings or grafted from source plants known to flower. Do not use seed-grown specimens as they may take a decade or more to come into flower. Repeated applications of nitrate-rich fertilizer will stimulate exuberant foliage, often at the expense of flowering. Fall, winter, or early spring pruning accomplishes little besides ensuring still more verdure for the coming season. Root pruning is reputed to help, as is the application of superphosphate and ground limestone. If nothing produces the desired results, it may be necessary to dig out the nonflowering plant and start anew with fresh soil and known plant material from a reputable source. So long as sun exposure is generous, fertilizer is withheld (except to stimulate vegetative growth in a small plant), and watering is kept to a minimum, newly planted wisterias should flower within a few years in most any moderately fertile, well-drained soil.

Freestanding or tree wisterias may be grown in open sunny locations by tying the main stem to a stake and repeatedly limiting the length of side shoots. In time, a plant so restricted will stand unassisted and often flower lavishly.

WISTERIA SINENSIS
(Chinese wisteria)

Zones 5–8

Chinese wisteria differs from Japanese wisteria in its shorter flower clusters (6 to 12 inches long), usually borne after the leaves begin expanding, and by its counterclockwise twining habit. In both species, the flowers are succeeded by flat, velvety, few-seeded pods that become woody and persist into winter, eventually opening explosively and flinging the flat, lima bean–like seeds some distance away.

The hybrid *W. × formosa* is often sold in the United States as *W. sinensis*. Its parents are *W. sinensis* and *W. floribunda*, and it exhibits a mix of their traits.

Wisteria × formosa trained as a tree

The flowers open more or less simultaneously and each leaf consists of 7 to 13 leaflets, as in *W. sinensis;* its shoots twine clockwise and the flowers are noticeably fragrant, as in *W. floribunda*. It is likely that much if not most of what passes as *W. sinensis*, or just "wisteria" (species unspecified), in the U.S. horticultural trade is in fact this hybrid.

Besides a zone 5 limit of cold hardiness, *W. sinensis* and *W. × formosa* behave very much like *W. floribunda*, require the same care, and call for the same caveats.

WOODY CLIMBERS TO AVOID

*In addition to the caveats noted in the text concerning the possible invasiveness of certain kinds of climbers,
various other species are best avoided altogether, however attractive they may seem.*

Name	Unfavorable Characteristics
Celastrus orbiculatus (common Oriental bittersweet)	Rampant, high climbing, twiner; long-escaped from cultivation in the Northeast; clear yellow fall foliage; females have great quantities of orange-and-yellow pea-size fruit; annual expansion of tightly wound stems deforms and strangles supporting trees; seed spread by birds
Lonicera japonica (Japanese honeysuckle)	Fast-growing twiner; white flowers aging to yellow followed by black berries; entirely too rampant and invasive for the home landscape; forms dense thickets; difficult to eradicate
Pueraria lobata (kudzu)	Semiwoody twiner in Deep South; elsewhere to zone 7 a herbaceous perennial; stems growing 25 to 50 feet a season, smothering virtually all vegetation it encounters
Smilax spp. (greenbrier, bullbrier, catbrier, etc.)	Thorny tendril climbers; glossy, semievergreen foliage; females have clusters of black or red berries; spread by deep rhizomes; form dense impenetrable thickets, which are difficult to control or remove
Solanum dulcamara (nightshade vine, deadly nightshade)	Soft wooded twiner; attractive blue-and-yellow flowers followed by red berries; often found on fences and in shrubbery; although neither excessively vigorous nor highly poisonous (despite its common name), all parts are moderately poisonous if eaten raw; seeds freely spread by birds
Toxicodendron radicans (poison ivy)	Variously climbing by aerial rootlets; carpeting woods and roadsides as a ground cover; and in wet places, often growing as an erect shrub; this undeniably handsome plant is too much of a hazard for most to be allowed space in or even near the garden, the blaze of fall foliage notwithstanding; seeds in the clustered whitish berries are spread by birds; *T. diversiloba*, the thicket-forming western counterpart, should also be avoided

Kolomikta (*Actinidia kolomikta*)

Japanese hydrangea vine (*Schizophraga hydrangeoides*)

Carolina jessamine
(*Gelsemium sempervirens*)

Maypop
(*Passiflora incarnata*)

OTHER WOODY CLIMBERS SUITABLE FOR THE GARDEN

Names	Zones	Maximum Height	Deciduous or Evergreen	Flower Color and Bloom Time
Actinidia arguta (tara vine)	4–8	25–30'	Deciduous	Greenish white; early summer
A. chinensis (hardy kiwifruit)	7–9	15–20'	Deciduous	White; late spring to early summer
A. kolomikta (kolomikta)	4–8	20–30'	Deciduous	White; fragrant; late spring
Akebia quinata (five-leaf akebia)	4–8	20–40'	Deciduous in late fall or evergreen (in zone 8)	Purplish; spring
Ampelopsis arborea (pepper vine)	7–9	15–25'	Deciduous	Greenish; inconspicuous
Clematis apiifolia (October clematis)	5–8	10–15'	Deciduous	White; early fall
C. fusca (Stanavoi clematis)	5–8	10–15'	Deciduous	Purplish; summer
C. × jouiniana (Jouin clematis)	4–8	10–15'	Deciduous	White, aging to blue; late summer to early fall
C. ligusticifolia (western clematis)	5–8	15–20'	Deciduous	White; late summer
C. tangutica (golden clematis)	5–8	8–10'	Deciduous	Yellow; late summer
C. viticella (Italian clematis)	5–8	10–12'	Deciduous	Rose purple to deep violet; late summer
Gelsemium sempervirens (Carolina jessamine)	6–9	10–20'	Evergreen	Yellow; fragrant; late winter to spring
Hedera colchica (Colchis ivy)	6–9	50' or more	Evergreen	Greenish; fragrant; fall
Lonicera flava (yellow honeysuckle)	6–8	10–12'	Deciduous	Yellow to yellow-orange; spring
L. periclymenum (English woodbine)	5–8	15–20'	Deciduous	Yellowish white, tinged red outside; summer
L. × tellmanniana (Tellmann honeysuckle)	5–8	10–15'	Deciduous	Rosy pink in bud, opening to yellow; summer
L. tragophylla (Chinese honeysuckle)	6–8	25–50'	Deciduous	Yellow; late spring
Macfadyena unguis-cati (cat's-claw vine)	(8) 9–10	20–25'	Evergreen	Yellow; spring to early summer

OTHER WOODY CLIMBERS SUITABLE FOR THE GARDEN

Fruit	Exposure*	Soil Requirements	Pruning Time	Comments
Yellow-green (female), 1 inch across; insipid; early fall	S to PSh	Average to poor fertility, well drained	Anytime	Rampant twiner useful as a fast-growing cover; flowers hidden and fruit visually interesting but unpalatable to most; disease free
Yellow-brown (female), 1½ to 2 inches across, flavorful; fall	S	Moderate fertility, well drained	Anytime	Vigorous, trouble-free twiner with handsome foliage; best known for popular fruit; male and female plants needed for fruit set
Yellow-green (female), 1 inch across, edible; fall	S	Average, well drained, pH 7 or higher for foliage color	Anytime	Vigorous twiner, grown mainly for handsome foliage (purplish when young), blotched white or pink on male plants
Purple pod (female); late summer and early fall	S to Sh	Average, well drained	Anytime	Twining, with glossy five-parted leaves and fragrant flowers; an effective screen but often invasive, especially on fertile soils; best grown away from shrub beds
Varicolored, aging to black; late summer	S to PSh	Average, well drained	Early spring	Bushy tendril climber with ornamental berries; likely too rampant for most settings, especially in the South where it is an invasive and often pernicious pest; undeniably attractive when in fruit
Plumed achene; fall	S to PSh	Sandy-humusy, deeply prepared, well drained	Spring	Slender; drought tolerant; ascending by tendril-like winding of leaf stalks around supports; flowers borne massed in clusters; useful to cover and stabilize steep banks
Plumed achene; fall	S to PSh	Sandy-humusy, deeply prepared, well drained	Early spring	Slender stemmed; often dying back somewhat in winter; flowers nodding or hanging, bell shaped
Plumed achene; fall	S to PSh	Sandy-humusy, deeply prepared, well drained	Early spring	Rampant; sometimes bushy; semiclimber, often dying back in severe winters; flowers clustered, ranging to pink in cv. 'Oiseau Bleu' and silvery blue in 'Praecox'
Plumed achene; fall	S to PSh	Average, well-drained, pH 7.0 to 7.5	Spring	Essentially the western counterpart of *C. virginiana*
Silky plume; fall	S to PSh	Average, well drained	Spring	Slender; open habit; flowers solitary; var. *obtusiuscula* is especially beautiful
Plumed achene; fall	S to PSh	Average, well drained	Spring	Stems soft woody; usually dying back in winter but quickly growing back; bears long-stalked, hanging, bell-like flowers; cv. 'Kermesina' has deep wine red flowers
1½-inch capsule; spring to summer	S to PSh	Humusy, well drained, slightly acidic	Spring, after flowering	Funnel-shaped flowers, sometimes borne again in fall; good on poles or as a ground cover in partial shade; cv. 'Pride of Augusta' has double flowers; all parts poisonous to eat
Black berry; winter	S to Sh	Average, well drained	Anytime	Similar to *H. canariensis* but somewhat coarser; especially useful where summer drought is severe
Red berry; fall	S to PSh	Average, well drained	Spring, after flowering	Bushy twiner with the outermost pairs of leaves forming stem-encircling collars; flowers clustered
Red berry; late summer	S to PSh	Average, well drained	Summer or fall	Twiner with leaves blue-green beneath; var. *belgica* is bushier and its flowers are red-violet outside
Red berry; late summer	S to PSh	Average, well drained	Summer or fall	Open habit; weakly twining; outermost leaf pair collared; often sold as 'Redgold' honeysuckle
Red berry; summer	S to PSh	Any well-drained soil	Early summer, after flowering	Rampant twiner; outermost leaf pair collared; flowers showy
Pod 1 foot long; summer	S	Average, well drained	Summer, keeping stems more or less equal	Tendril climber; foliage often restricted to younger uppermost stems; flowers showy, trumpet shaped, 3 to 4 inches across

(continues)

OTHER WOODY CLIMBERS SUITABLE FOR THE GARDEN (continued)

Names	Zones	Maximum Height	Deciduous or Evergreen	Flower Color and Bloom Time
Menispermum canadense (moonseed)	4–8	10–15'	Deciduous	Greenish; inconspicuous
Muehlenbeckia complexa (wire vine)	6–9	3–4'	Deciduous	Greenish white; spring to summer
Parthenocissus henryana (silver-vein creeper)	(7) 8–9	15–20'	Deciduous	Greenish red; summer
Passiflora caerulea (blue passion flower)	7–10	10–20'	Deciduous	White, blue, and purple; summer
P. incarnata (maypop)	7–9	15–25'	Deciduous	White and pinkish purple; spring
Periploca graeca (silk vine)	7–9	20–40'	Deciduous or half-evergreen	Purplish; midsummer
Pileostegia viburnoides (tanglehead)	7–9	10–15'	Evergreen	Cream; early fall
Rosa laevigata (Cherokee rose): see Chapter 19				
R. wichuraiana (memorial rose): see Chapter 19				
Schisandra chinensis (Chinese magnolia vine)	(4) 5–8	20–25'	Deciduous	White or pinkish; fragrant; spring
S. propinqua (Himalayan magnolia vine)	8–9	20–25'	Deciduous	Orange; spring
Schizophragma hydrangeoides (Japanese hydrangea vine)	5–8	25–35'	Deciduous	Cream; summer
Thunbergia grandiflora (Bengal clock vine)	8–10	8–15'	Evergreen	Blue with yellow throat; summer
Trachelospermum asiaticum (Japanese star jasmine)	(7) 8–10	20–25'	Evergreen	Cream; summer
Tripterygium regelii (Regel's three-wing nut)	(4) 5–8	6–15'	Deciduous	Whitish; summer
Vitis aestivalis (summer grape)	4–8	25–50'	Deciduous	Greenish; spring
V. labrusca (fox grape)	5–8	20–40'	Deciduous	Greenish; spring
V. riparia (riverbank grape)	2–7	20–40'	Deciduous	Greenish; spring
V. vinifera (European wine grape)	6–8	50' or more; 6–12' in cultivation	Deciduous	Greenish; spring
V. vulpina (frost grape)	6–8	30–75'	Deciduous	Greenish; spring
Wisteria frutescens (American wisteria)	5–9	15–20' (#30)	Deciduous	Lilac purple with yellow; late spring to summer

* S, full sun; Sh, shade (no direct sun); PSh, partial shade (sun exposure only part of the day); LSh, light shade (e.g., the shade of tall, open trees, with little or no exposure to direct sun).

OTHER WOODY CLIMBERS SUITABLE FOR THE GARDEN

Fruit	Exposure*	Soil Requirements	Pruning Time	Comments
Black; summer	S to PSh	Any well-drained soil	Spring, severely if needed; quickly grows back	Twiner with overlapping ivylike foliage; useful in hiding cyclone fences; suckers from wide-ranging roots often invasive
White cup with black nutlets; summer to fall	S	Average, well drained	Anytime	Slender twiner with reddish stems forming ground-covering mats; easily trained up supports to hide stumps; often dies back to ground in winter in zones 6 to 7
Blue-black; fall	S to Sh	Any well-drained soil	Spring	Fast growing; tendril climber with white-and-pink-veined foliage that turns red to red-violet in fall
Yellow or orange; summer	S	Humusy, well drained	Anytime	Tendril climber with five-lobed leaves; stems often killed back to roots in zones 7 and 8
Yellow; late spring and summer	S to PSh	Humusy, well drained	Anytime	Fast growing; tendril climber with three-lobed leaves; wide-ranging roots sucker freely; often invasively
Green pod; late summer and fall	S	Average, well drained	Anytime	Twiner with glossy, deep green foliage; flowers somewhat malodorous; pods filled with silk-tasseled seeds; *P. sepium* is similar but smaller
Inconspicuous	S to PSh	Fertile, well drained	Anytime; seldom needed	Rangy; self-clinging; semiclimber; flowers borne in dense clusters; good against masonry, around rocks, or for hiding stumps
Red (female); summer	PSh	Fertile, well drained	Early spring	Twiner; lustrous reddish young growth; best in constantly moist locations
Red; summer	PSh	Fertile, well drained	Early spring	Similar to *S. chinensis*, but monoecious; *S. coccinea* has red flowers
Small capsule; fall	S to PSh	Fertile, constantly moist	Early spring	Climbs via stem-borne aerial rootlets; large, heart-shaped leaves; flowers borne in showy clusters; effective on walls, ascending trees, or scrambling over rocks or stumps; slow to establish
Leathery capsule; fall	S to PSh	Average, well drained	Spring	Vigorous twiner; leaves thickish, 8 inches long; flowers 3 inches across; var. *grandiflora* has larger white flowers
Paired podlike follicles; fall	PSh	Moist, well drained, acidic	Anytime	Twining with glossy foliage and milky sap; flowers borne in large clusters; *T. jasminoides*, hardy in zones 9 and 10, is similar but white flowered
Papery; three-winged; fall	S	Average, well drained	Early spring	Bushy scrambler with warty red-brown stems
Black-violet (female); late summer	S	Average, well drained	Fall or winter	Rampant tendril climber; three- to five-lobed leaves, 1 foot across; should be grown on arbors and not in trees or on buildings, where damage may result
Dark red to black-violet (female); late summer	S	Average; well drained	Fall or winter	Vigorous tendril climber; shallowly three-lobed leaves 10 inches across; edible thick-skinned fruit
Black-violet, bloomy (female); late summer	S	Moist to wet	Fall or winter	Rangy tendril climber; three-lobed, sharply toothed leaves, 10 inches across; clusters of edible bloomy fruit
Green to dark red, according to cultivars; summer to fall	S	Average, well drained	Fall or winter	Rampant tendril climber; three- to seven-lobed, bluntly toothed leaves, 8 inches across; ornamental cultivars with variously cut and colored foliage
Blue-black (female); late summer to fall	S	Average, well drained	Fall or winter	Vigorous, forked tendrils; faintly lobed, toothed leaves, 6 to 8 × 4 inches; fruit not sweet until after frost
Green velvety pod maturing to brown; fall	S to PSh	Average; well drained	Summer, after flowering	Twining; flowers clustered and nodding (not hanging); each with a yellow spot, good on fences and pergolas or trained as a treelet

14

Ground Covers

GROUND COVERS ARE LOW, SPREADING, OR MAT-FORMING plants, mostly perennials or small shrubs, that are used to stabilize and beautify areas where a low plant profile is desired and where there is to be little or no foot traffic.

Ideally, a species of ground cover would thrive in sun or shade, offer handsome evergreen foliage, bear attractive flowers and/or fruit, tolerate summer heat and drought as well as the rigors of winter, spread quickly to exclude weeds, and last indefinitely. No known plant meets all these

*Creeping myrtle (*Vinca minor*), including its white-flowered and variegated cultivars, is one of the most versatile evergreen ground covers, especially from zone 8 northward. The similar and equally useful but less cold-tolerant large Myrtle (*V. major*) is best grown outdoors in the South.*

criteria, but the hundred or more kinds known to grow well in this country's varied climates and soil conditions offer possibilities for most any situation.

Carefully chosen, properly planted, and prudently tended during the first year or two, ground covers can soon arrest and deter erosion on slopes that are difficult to mow or otherwise maintain. Some can convert bare root-ridged ground beneath densely shading trees into handsome verdant carpets, while others enliven hot, drought-prone stony slopes with a humus-generating, moisture-conserving leafy blanket. A well-established ground cover planting imparts a finished quality to any setting and usually reflects far more thoughtfulness and horticultural awareness than does biologically inefficient, labor-intensive lawn.

Before planting any ground cover, some basic information should be assembled and preparatory steps taken. First, the nature of the site should be analyzed: its exposure to sun and wind, the type and condition of soil (which is best tested to determine its chemical makeup), and its moisture retentiveness during the hottest and coldest times of year. It is equally important to decide on the effect you wish to achieve, which may be facilitated by consulting one or more books on landscape design or by checking nearby comparable sites on which ground covers have been planted.

It is nearly always beneficial to improve the soil with moisture-holding, nutrient-yielding humus or compost before making a planting, whether in the spring or fall. Sometimes it is necessary to add soil to fill in gullies or depressions resulting from erosion. Depending on the results of a soil test, and in the absence of well-rotted manure or other organic enhancement, an application of commercial fertilizer, such as 10-10-10 or 10-6-4, at 2 to 3 pounds per 100 square feet, will help stimulate initial growth. The spacing of plants depends on the nature of the site, the growth characteristics of the kind chosen, and the length of time you are willing to wait for massing to occur. Many clump-forming perennials are planted 6 to 12 inches apart, while stem-rooting, mat-forming creepers can be set out at greater intervals, unless on vulnerable erosion-prone slopes. The steepest slopes may require installation soil-stabilizing jute mesh to keep everything in place until the new ground cover has become established and its stems interlaced.

Weed control is important in the first year or two, before the new ground cover planting becomes dense enough to keep most invaders out. If heavy weed growth is likely, you may wish to consider applying a selectively acting preemergence herbicide such as DCPA (sold as Dachthal) or trifluralin (sold as Treflan) before planting, or to consult a trained professional at your local cooperative extension office. (See Chapter 33 for more information about weed control.)

After planting, add a weed-free mulch, such as wood chips, bark chips, or shredded leaves. In the first year or two it is vitally important to keep the ground cover bed adequately moist, especially during hot summer months when lawns and gardens require watering. Finally, no ground cover planting is entirely maintenance free. Weeds should be removed at frequent intervals, especially in the initial years, and even the densest of established beds will sprout tree seedlings. Removed promptly, these will do no harm; but left uncontrolled, weeds of any kind become unattractive and can soon overwhelm the entire planting and transform a beautiful setting into an unsightly thicket. At the same time, it is nearly always preferable to allow fallen leaves to remain and decompose, since the resulting humus improves soil quality and thus the planting itself, thereby lessening the need for supplemental fertilizers and water.

SELECTION OF GROUND COVER PLANTS

The selection of an attractive and suitable ground cover will depend on the area where it is to be used. There are ground covers that will grow well only in partial shade, others that require full sun, while some are tolerant of both sun and shade. Some require moist soils rich in humus, others are particularly well adapted to dry, shady soils. Some ground covers are low and matlike, hugging the soil closely, while others are somewhat tall and spreading, and of a shrubby character. Some are evergreen and lovely every season of the year, whereas others are deciduous and present pleasing contrasts from season to season.

It is, therefore, important that the ground cover best adapted to the particular location is chosen. Where a low evergreen ground cover is desired for a lightly shaded area, there are a number that meet the requirements. Among the best are English ivy (*Hedera helix*), pachysandra (*Pachysandra terminalis*), and creeping myrtle (*Vinca minor*). For clothing a sunny bank, some of the prostrate junipers or cotoneasters, with their spreading branches and interestingly texured foliage, would be a worthy choice. For use on the north side of buildings where there is continual shade, the choice is more limited. The most dependable species for such a location are ajuga (*Ajuga reptans*), lily-of-the-valley (*Convallaria majalis*), wintercreeper (*Euonymus fortunei*), and English ivy.

Occasionally, two ground covers can be grown as companions. One of the most pleasant associations is creeping myrtle and leadwort (*Ceratostigma plumbaginoides*). The soft, lavender blue flowers of the myrtle come in early or mid spring, and the brilliant blue flowers of the leadwort

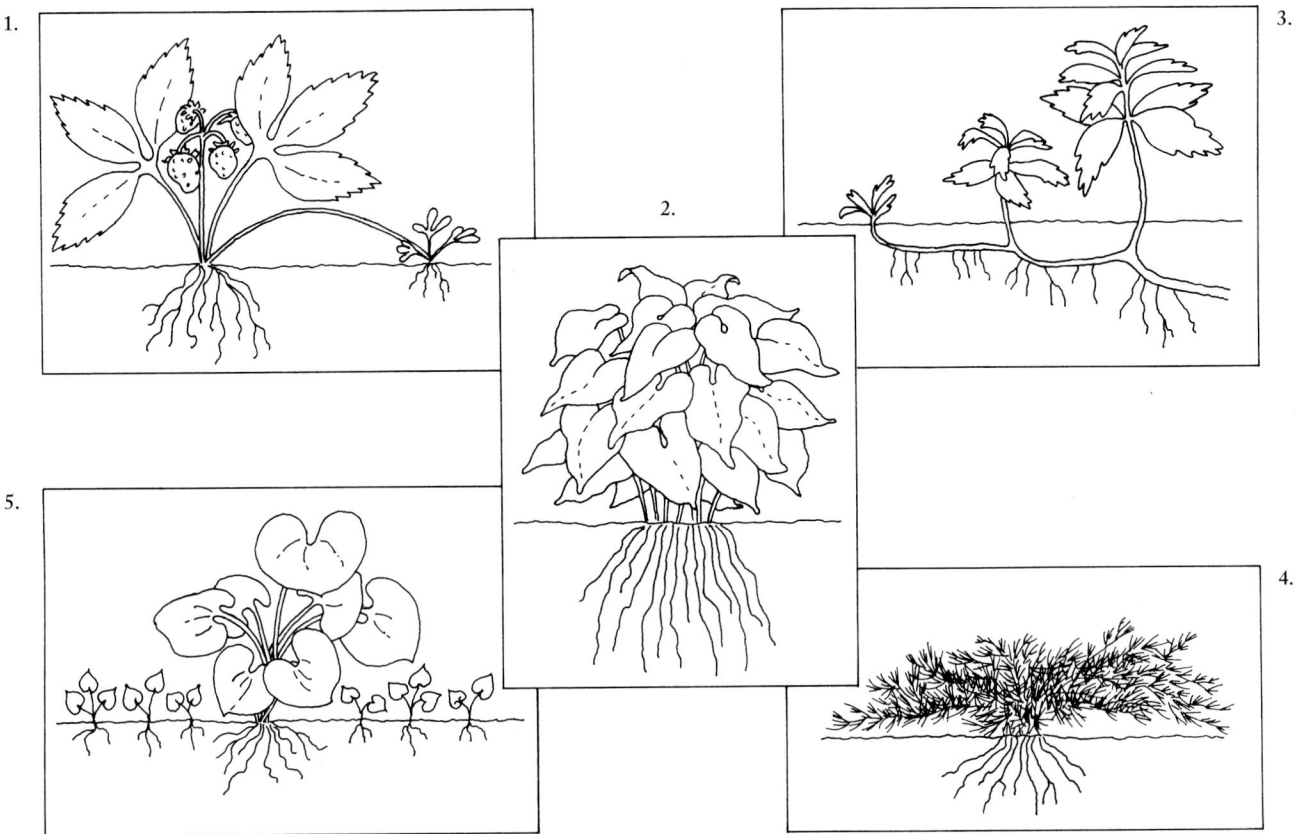

Five types of ground cover growth: 1. Stolons (strawberry); 2. Clump (hosta); 3. Underground stolons (paschysandra); 4. Creeping or spreading (juniper); 5. Self-seeding (violet).

carry the period of bloom well into the autumn. During the spring months, one is hardly aware that the leadwort forms a part of the planting; but in late summer it begins to assume a more important role, and by September it has become almost completely dominant.

Spring-flowering bulbs, such as snowdrops (*Galanthus nivalis*), bluebells (*Hyacinthoides* spp.), squills (*Scilla* spp.), and daffodils (*Narcissus* spp.), as well as autumn crocuses (*Colchicum* spp.), may be planted among some of the low-growing ground covers, such as creeping myrtle or English ivy, and are very effective.

Plantings that are slow to become established should be especially well mulched to retain moisture and deter encroachment by weeds. Hand weeding at frequent intervals is also important. If certain persistent weeds, such as Johnsongrass (*Sorghum halepensis*) or common mugwort or chrysanthemum weed (*Artemisia vulgaris*), successfully invade a ground cover planting, they may be difficult or impossible to eradicate, even after the cover becomes established.

TROUBLESOME GROUND COVER PLANTS

Some ground covers are usually too vigorous and invasive for use on the home grounds. Whatever virtues they may have in rapidly covering difficult sites or in uncommonly high endurance or in low cost, such species eventually present the gardener with unending problems of restraint and control, and in some cases, the need for complete eradication.

Ground covers to avoid include the following species.

Aegopodium podagraria (goutweed). A mat-forming deciduous perennial usually less than 1 foot high, with attractive divided leaves (sometimes variegated). Somewhat taller flowering stems bear flat-topped clusters of tiny greenish flowers in late spring or early summer. Goutweed spreads rapidly by way of branching underground stems, which are deterred only by continuous mechanical barriers, such as concrete curbing, paved walks, masonry walls, and asphalt drives.

English ivy clothes and softens angular masonry, rendering the beautifully ornamented newel in strong contrast.

Glechoma hederacea (ground ivy). A deciduous perennial creeper with paired, rounded leaves on fast-growing, node-rooting, prostrate stems. Bluish purple flowers appear in the spring. Ground ivy is not unattractive, but it so readily invades lawns and gardens that any virtues are soon forgotten. Once established, it is very difficult to completely remove, since any remaining bit of stem quickly roots and sprouts.

Lonicera japonica (Japanese honeysuckle). An aggressively twining woody climber that, in the absence of support, scrambles on the ground and makes an acceptable ground cover. It is deciduous to partly or wholly evergreen, depending on winter severity. It should be grown only if contained by frequently trod, well-maintained lawn or by pavement.

Lysimachia nummularia (creeping Charlie, creeping Jenny). A prostrate stem-rooting perennial forming leafy mats no more than 3 inches high and bearing attractive yellow flowers in the spring. The cv. 'Aurea' has yellow foliage. However diminutive this plant seems, it vigorously invades lawns and so should be limited to curbed beds, if used at all.

Polygonum cuspidatum (Japanese bamboo). Not a true bamboo but a giant form of knotweed, with rapidly spreading clumps of leafy, knobby jointed stems 6 to 8 feet tall that bear showy clusters of cream flowers in late summer. Extremely vigorous and tenacious, Japanese bamboo soon completely dominates any site planted to it and spreads relentlessly into adjacent areas. *P. cuspidatum* var. *compactum*, growing 1 to 1½ feet tall, is somewhat less exuberant, but it is best restricted to difficult areas where other ground covers cannot succeed. After frost, the dead stems of Japanese bamboo persist through the winter.

Pueraria lobata (kudzu). A fast-growing, soft-wooded or herbaceous twining climber that, in the absence of support, becomes a coarse, rampant ground cover. Introduced from China and Japan as a fodder plant and soil stabilizer, kudzu is now a pernicious smothering weed in much of the Southeast. Capable of growing as much as 50 feet in a season, kudzu usually far outruns the space available on the home grounds and should be assiduously avoided.

GROUND COVER PLANTS OF SPECIAL MERIT

AJUGA REPTANS
(Carpet bugle)

Zones 4–7 (8)

Carpet bugle is a semievergreen perennial, 4 inches high (6 to 12 inches when in flower), with dark green foliage. It grows rapidly and quickly forms a dense mat. Spikes of handsome blue, white, or purple flowers rise above the foliage in spring. One caveat: ajuga will readily invade lawns, so provide a barrier or do not plant near lawns.

The following cultivars are available.

'Alba' (white flowers).
'Atropurpurea' (bronzy purple leaves; dark purple flowers).
'Multicoloris' (leaves mottled red, white, and yellow on green).
'Variegata' (leaves mottled creamy white).

Geneva ajuga (*A. genevensis*) is of more upright habit, and crinkled ajuga (*A. pyramidalis* 'Metallica Crispa') has wrinkled purplish foliage.

Especially effective over large expanses, the ajugas should be planted in full sun or partial shade at the rate of 18 to 20 plants per square yard. Most any well-drained soil is suitable.

ARCTOSTAPHYLOS UVA-URSI
(Bearberry)

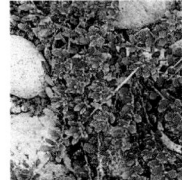

Zones 2–7

Bearberry is an evergreen creeping shrub that forms dense mats, 6 to 12 inches tall. Each plant spreads 2 to 4 feet or more. Small white flowers in the spring are followed by red berries that persist to early winter. Bearberry is one of the best evergreen ground covers for sandy soil and is one of the few that succeeds in littoral locations subject to sea spray.

It is very difficult to transplant and often slow to establish; for these reasons, purchase plants growing in pots and set out at the rate of four plants per square yard. A sunny location in perfectly drained acidic sandy soil is best; waterlogged clay is fatal.

ASARUM EUROPAEUM
(European ginger)

Zones 5–7

A handsome evergreen perennial, 4 to 6 inches high, with lustrous dark green leaves, European ginger is one of the best evergreen ground covers for shade—from partial or light shade to deep, constant shade. It can endure some sun exposure in the North, but it must have moist, loamy soil, preferably enriched with humus or compost. It is slow growing and never invasive. Set out at the rate of 12 to 16 plants per square yard.

Other species suitable for use as ground covers include the following.

A. canadense (wild ginger): native to the East; hardy to zone 4; deciduous leaves lack luster.
A. caudatum (Pacific ginger): hardy only to zone 7; dark green leaves, larger than those of *A. europaeum.*
A. shuttleworthii (mottled ginger): white-spotted; evergreen leaves.

CERATOSTIGMA PLUMBAGINOIDES
(Blue leadwort)

Zones 6–8

Frequently listed erroneously in catalogs as *Plumbago larpentiae*, blue leadwort, a spreading perennial, ranges from 6 to 12 inches high and bears dark blue flowers in late summer, after which the hairy-edged foliage turns a beautiful shade of reddish bronze. It is much valued for its effective bloom so late in the season. Although it appears quite late in the spring, with growth in the form of tufts, it combines well with other low-growing ground covers such as *Vinca minor*. Less rampant than many ground covers, blue leadwort can nevertheless invade lawns, and so it should be separated from turf areas with a barrier.

Thriving in sun or partial shade in moisture-retentive, well-drained soil, this species should be planted at the rate of nine plants per square yard.

The similar Chinese plumbago (*C. willmottianum*) has hairier leaves and is more drought resistant, but it is hardy only to zone 8.

CONVALLARIA MAJALIS
(Lily-of-the-valley)

Zones (2) 3–7 (8)

Lily-of-the-valley is a herbaceous perennial, 6 to 8 inches high, with fragrant white flowers in spring, followed by poisonous berries that ripen red-orange in fall. It adapts to a wide range of conditions, often persisting in open woods or along roadsides, but thrives on loamy, humusy soils in partial or light shade. On light soils in full sun, it can become unattractive toward the end of the growing season, especially in drought. The leaves die to the ground after frost, leaving the ground bare in winter.

Plant 12 to 15 rooted pips per square yard. If the soil is loosened and enriched with humus or compost, the plants will spread rapidly by underground rhizomes and soon carpet the area. As adjacent garden or lawn areas can be invaded, it is best to separate them from lily-of-the-valley with a curb or other barrier.

CORONILLA VARIA
(Crown vetch)

Zones (5) 6–8

An herbaceous perennial, crown vetch grows 1 to 2 feet high and freely produces pink pealike flowers in dense clusters in the summer. It grows best in full sun and average to poor, well-drained to droughty soils.

This is a very fast-growing ground cover, and is especially useful in clothing steep banks that have exposed subsoil. The cultivar 'Penngift' is particularly tough and favored for use on highway embankments. One or two plants per square yard soon provide complete coverage. Crown vetch dies to the ground each fall. In some regions, it has proven invasive and difficult to eradicate.

COTONEASTER DAMMERI
(Bearberry cotoneaster)

Zones 5–8

One of the best shrubby evergreen ground covers, bearberry cotoneaster makes a dark green carpet of dense, glossy foliage, to about 15 inches high. Each plant achieves a spread of 4 to 6 feet. Of the several cultivars available, 'Coral Beauty' is covered with red berries in late summer and 'Skogholm' is especially fast growing—reputedly the fastest of the prostrate cotoneasters.

Spacing of one or two plants per square yard in a sunny position on well-drained soil of average fertility yields best results.

COTONEASTER HORIZONTALIS
(Rockspray cotoneaster)

Zones 4–8

Rockspray cotoneaster is a spreading deciduous shrub with flat, nearly horizontal branches and a good show of persistent red berries from late summer into winter. Maximum height is about 3 feet; each plant eventually spreads 4 to 6 feet. Leaves may be held through mild winters in zone 8.

Effective on slopes as well as flat areas, rockspray cotoneaster thrives in loamy, moisture-retentive but well-drained soils and can survive considerable summer drought. Two plants per square yard is the correct planting interval. Full sun is preferable, especially in the North.

Other cotoneasters useful as ground covers include the deciduous creeping cotoneaster (*C. adpressus*) and the very similar cranberry cotoneaster (*C. apiculata*). Among evergreen or semievergreen kinds, littleleaf cotoneaster (*C. microphyllus*) is especially fine textured and has several cultivars of varied habit, all suitable as ground covers.

EPIMEDIUM GRANDIFLORUM
(Bishop's hat)

Zones 3–8

Bishop's hat is a deciduous perennial, 8 to 10 inches high, bearing red, purple, or white flowers in late spring. In time, bishop's hat forms very dense carpets and does well in the light to dense shade of deciduous trees. If feasible, old, winter-killed foliage should be removed before the flowers appear.

Slow to establish and spread, this plant is best used in relatively small areas, and should be set out at an interval of 12 to 15 plants per square yard. Well-drained, humusy soil hastens growth.

Other equally useful kinds include *E. alpinum*, *E. pinnatum*, and *E. rubrum*, all about 1 foot tall and bearing red-and-yellow flowers; *E. × versicolor* 'Sulphureum', also 1 foot tall, but evergreen in the South and bearing yellow flowers; and *E. × youngianum* 'Niveum', not over 8 inches high and producing white flowers.

EUONYMUS FORTUNEI
(Wintercreeper euonymus)

Zones (4) 5–8

Wintercreeper euonymus, an evergreen creeper (or, with support, a climber by aerial rootlets), forms a mat of rooting branches 6 inches to 2 feet high. It is especially suited to moist, shady locations.

One of the hardiest and most adaptable ground covers, wintercreeper euonymus may be planted one plant per square yard, or more densely if rapid cover is desired, and succeeds in all but the driest or most sodden locations. It can, however, be seriously affected by euonymus scale (see page 820), especially in the South. Also excellent as ground covers are several *E. fortunei* cultivars.

'Coloratus': a vigorous form; does well in full sun; turns bronzy or purplish in winter.
'Minimus': leaves not over ⅝ inch long.
'Dart's Blanket': good resistance to salt spray from road deicers and ocean storms.

E. fortunei var. *radicans* and its cultivar 'Vegetus' are also much used as ground covers, the latter favored for its wavy leaves and production of attractive pink-and-orange pea-size fruit in the fall.

FORSYTHIA VIRIDISSIMA 'BRONXENSIS'
(Creeping forsythia)

Zones 5–7

A shrub 1½ to 3 feet tall with arching branches that root at the tip wherever in contact with the ground, creeping forsythia eventually forms a dense spreading thicket. The light yellow flowers, borne in early spring, are relatively sparse, even in full sun. Creeping forsythia thrives in sandy-humusy soils but succeeds in most any medium.

This species is an excellent choice for covering steep embankments. Aside from an occasional grooming, it requires little care once established. Four plants per square yard will ensure rapid coverage.

The hybrid *Forsythia* 'Arnold Dwarf' is somewhat larger (3 to 7 feet tall) and flowers more generously, but it shows little or no tendency to tip root.

HEDERA HELIX
(English ivy)

Zones 4–9

English ivy is an evergreen creeper widely used as a ground cover because of its adaptibility to a wide range of conditions—from full sun to deep shade (even beneath shallow-rooted trees), from moist, rich soil to droughty, nutrient-poor sand. It makes a good background for spring bulbs and clumps of ferns. Of the hundreds of cultivars, some are especially cold tolerant: 'Baltica', 'Bulgaria', 'Hibernica', 'Rumania', and '238th Street'.

Similar but larger leaved and, therefore, somewhat coarser are Colchis ivy (*H. colchica*), hardy in zones 6 to 9; and Algerian ivy (*H. canariensis*), hardy only in zones 9 and 10.

Three rooted cuttings per square yard is the usual planting interval, but for faster coverage this density can be doubled.

HEMEROCALLIS FULVA
(Orange daylily)

Zones 3–10

A herbaceous, tuberous-rooted perennial, orange daylily is more or less evergreen in the Deep South. It has scapes 2 to 3 feet tall in early summer, bearing clusters of large orange flowers, each lasting a day. Naturalized throughout the eastern United States, orange daylily thrives on neglect, forming extensive colonies by means of rhizomes. The cultivar 'Kwanso' has double flowers.

Ease of hybridization between this and several other species has resulted in many thousands of named cultivars. Among the cultivars are wide variation's in plant traits, including scape height (from 6 inches to more than 5 feet), flowering period (mostly early or mid summer, but some beginning in mid-spring with flushes continuing until frost), size of flower parts, and flower color (from cream through yellow, orange, and red to deep brown-violet, with some bicolors). Cultivars are less forgiving of poor conditions and neglect, most requiring average to moderately rich, well-drained soil and exposure to full sun to flower well.

Orange daylily is useful in stabilizing steep embankments as well as carpeting flat areas. A spacing of three or four plants per square yard is adequate on level sites, ranging up to twice that frequency on steeper, erosion-prone slopes. Nonrhizomatous species and cultivars are best kept to relatively level locations and may be spaced four to six plants per square yard, depending on ultimate clump size. Scapes should be cut to the base after blooming.

HOSTA *SPP.*
(Plantain lily)

Zones (3) 4–8

Hostas are herbaceous, clump-forming perennials, with 2- to 3-foot-tall scapes, bearing horizontal or pendent flowers of lavender or white in the summer or early fall. All are valued highly for their large, rosetted, ribbed foliage, which varies in length and width and is often variegated, forming leafy mounds of varying shades and textures. Flower stalks should be removed after blooming. Leaves die to the ground after frost. For traits of the several *Hosta* species in cultivation and some of the hundreds of cultivars available, see page 329.

Plantain lilies thrive on loamy, moisture-retentive soil and do better in partial shade or light shade than in full sun or deep shade. Planting interval ranges from one to four plants per square yard, depending on eventual clump size of the kind chosen.

Siebold plataiin lily (*Hosta sieboldiana* 'Elegans')

HYDRANGEA ANOMALA SSP. PETIOLARIS
(Climbing hydrangea)

Zones 4–7

Climbing hydrangea is a deciduous climbing shrub and, in the absence of support, scrambles widely, tending to form irregular mounds up to 3 feet high. It strikes root here and there where stems become buried in humus. It makes an especially handsome ground cover on slopes, bearing creamy white flowers in clusters in early summer. Once the lustrous, deep green leaves fall, the papery peeling cinnamon brown bark of the stems is revealed.

A planting interval of one per square yard is recommended, but as this ground cover is slow to become established, interplanting with short-lived herbaceous perennials—columbine (*Aquilegia* spp. and cvs.), for example—will help fill gaps temporarily. Because it may eventually spread 8 to 10 feet or more, climbing hydrangea is not recommended for small sites.

HYPERICUM CALYCINUM
(Aaron's-beard, St. John's-wort)

Zones (5) 6–8

Aaron's-beard, an evergreen or semi-evergreen shrub 1 to 1½ feet tall, spreads widely by way of stolons and bears golden yellow flowers in the summer. Stem tips often die back after severe winter weather, but regeneration in the spring is rapid, and flowering is unaffected.

One of the best ground covers for showy summer bloom, Aaron's-beard thrives on sandy soils in full sun. However, it adapts well to heavier soils, as long as they are well drained, and succeeds in partial shade, though with less generous bloom. Four plants per square yard is a good planting interval.

JUNIPERUS HORIZONTALIS
(Creeping juniper)

Zones 3–9

A creeping coniferous evergreen shrub 1 to 2 feet high, creeping juniper eventually spreads to 12 feet or more. It is one of the best plants for covering steep, droughty slopes, but it does equally well on level sites. Creeping juniper requires no attention once established, except to limit its spread over pavement or into other garden areas. The blue-green foliage develops bronzy tints in winter.

Among many cultivars, those proving especially reliable and versatile include the following:

'Douglasii' (Waukegan juniper): fast growing; steel blue foliage, becoming purplish in winter.
'Plumosa' (Andorra juniper): lighter green, rather feathery foliage, turning purplish in winter.
'Wiltonii' (blue-rug juniper): slower growing; similar to 'Douglasii'.

Other very satisfactory junipers for ground cover use include Sargent juniper (*J. chinensis* var. *sargentii*), a dense moundlike shrub to 1 foot tall and up to 8 feet across; shore juniper (*J. conferta*), also 1 by 8 feet but especially tolerant of salt spray; Japanese juniper (*J. procumbens*), a dense shrub of stiff habit 1 to 2 feet high by 10 to 15 feet across, with attractive blue-green color throughout the winter; and tamarisk juniper (*J. sabina* var. *tamariscifolia*), 1½ feet high by 10 to 15 feet across, usually mounded, tolerant of urban conditions and successful on limestone soils.

With all these junipers, one or two plants per square yard is a good planting interval. Full sun is advisable, and dryish sandy soils are best.

LEUCOTHOË FONTANESIANA
(Drooping leucothoë)

Zones 4–7 (8)

A broad-leaf evergreen shrub, 3 to 6 feet high and wide, drooping leucothoë has long, gracefully arching stems and lustrous downward-pointing leaves. If planted in light to dense shade and acidic, well-drained soil, it proves reliable and trouble free. But in sun or on drought-prone soils, the foliage often burns.

Among the cultivars available, some—such as 'Nana' and 'Scarletta'—are small, maturing to only 2 to 3 feet tall and wide; others—such as 'Folia Multicolor', 'Girard's Rainbow', and 'Trivar'—feature varicolored foliage. All bear whitish flowers in drooping clusters in spring.

One shrub per square yard ensures dense coverage, except for the dwarf forms, which should be planted two to four per square yard, according to ultimate size.

LONICERA SPP.
(Climbing honeysuckle)

Zones 4–9

Several deciduous or semievergreen climbing honeysuckles make useful, if exuberant, ground covers in the absence of support. Henry honeysuckle (*L. henryi*), for example, forms a semievergreen mat about 6 inches deep, with yellowish red to purplish flowers in late spring or early summer, followed by black berries that are held until winter. Hall's Japanese honeysuckle (*L. japonica* 'Halliana') is a rampant, often invasive form with white flowers, aging to yellow. Both should be restricted to beds without trees, shrubs, or other climbing supports and surrounded by lawn or pavement. Other twining species, such as goldflame honeysuckle (*L.* × *heckrottii*) and trumpet honeysuckle (*L. sempervirens*), are less successful as ground covers.

A planting interval of two or three per square yard on sites with well-drained soil and in full sun or partial shade ensure rapid coverage.

PACHYSANDRA TERMINALIS
(Common pachysandra, Japanese pachysandra)

Zones (3) 4–8

Pachysandra is a lustrous broad-leaf evergreen creeper that forms dense mats, 6 to 9 inches high, with inconspicuous whitish flowers in the spring. The most popular and versatile ground cover in the United States, pachysandra is undoubtedly overused. In suitable soils, it spreads rapidly by underground stolons and succeeds in the dense shade of such surface-rooted trees as Norway maple and European beech.

Although it survives in poor soils, pachysandra requires a moist, humusy soil to truly thrive. Similarly, a position in full sun, especially if in combination with a nutrient-deficient soil, usually results in unattractively bleached foliage.

The cultivar 'Green Carpet' forms a dense, deep green cover 4 to 6 inches high. Less adaptable is 'Variegata', or 'Silver Edge', which, if grown in partial (not full) shade, has white-edged or -mottled leaves and a tendency toward spare, less dense cover.

Under ideal conditions, a planting interval of one rooted cutting per square foot is suitable, but under less favorable conditions, especially on slopes, denser planting is advisable.

POTENTILLA TRIDENTATA
(Wine-leaf cinquefoil)

Zones 2–7

An evergreen mat-forming creeper with lustrous leaves, wine-leaf cinquefoil bears white flowers in the summer. A fine-textured perennial, it grows best in full sun or partial shade, making a carpet 3 to 9 inches high. Acidic, well-drained soil is required, and even then it is slow to establish.

The cultivar 'Minima' forms a refined carpet no more than 2 inches high. Creeping cinquefoil (*P. aurea* 'Verna'); similar in habit, is yellow flowered.

Any of these cinquefoils should be planted one per square foot.

RHUS AROMATICA
(Fragrant sumac)

Zones 3–9

Fragrant sumac is a deciduous shrub, about 3 feet tall, with aromatic three-parted leaves (somewhat suggestive of poison ivy, but harmless). In late summer, female plants display red berries. Fall foliage varies from yellow and red to purplish.

Fragrant sumac spreads by underground stems and makes a dense stand that especially suits it for use on embankments. It adapts well to poor soil in full sun or partial shade.

The cultivar 'Gro-low' remains lower than 2 feet but spreads 6 to 8 feet.

Planting interval for fragrant sumac is one shrub per square yard.

ROSA WICHURAIANA
(Memorial rose)

Zones 5–8

The memorial rose is a trailing, semi-evergreen, thorny-stemmed rose with glossy foliage. Its stems are prostrate or gently arching to 1 foot high and grow to 10 or 12 feet long. The 2-inch flowers are single, white, and borne in late spring or early summer. They are followed by small red hips.

This is the most trouble-free rose for ground cover use. It is very vigorous and does especially well on embankments. But, as its cover is fairly open, especially the first few years, an area planted to memorial rose will require some weeding or mulching until the mat of branches thickens.

The cultivar 'Poteriifolia' is more compact in habit. Two recently introduced ground cover roses are *Rosa* 'Lavender Dream', with lavender pink flowers all summer, and *R.* 'Ralph's Creeper', also everblooming, with single red flowers.

One plant per square yard will soon lead to a mat of tenaciously interlocking stems.

SEDUM ACRE
(Creeping sedum, gold moss)

Zones 3–8

A succulent evergreen perennial, 2 inches high, with minute leaves, creeping sedum bears bright yellow flowers in the spring. It is attractive, especially in flower, and very vigorous, particularly on sunny, droughty sites. Creeping sedum, however, is often invasive, if bits of stem are carelessly strewn about, as when raking a lawn or other garden area adjacent to a bed of this plant. Every little snippet seems to strike root and proliferate.

One cutting, rooted or not, per square foot will soon confer complete coverage.

VINCA MINOR
(Creeping myrtle)

Zones 3–8

Creeping myrtle, a glossy, evergreen, trailing perennial, about 6 inches high, has lavender blue flowers in the spring. It vies with pachysandra as the most popular ground cover, but in less than ideal circumstances, it can become spotty in coverage. Moist, acidic, humusy soil in partial or light shade will yield best results, but full sun or dense shade is suitable, as long as soil requirements are met.

Cultivars of creeping myrtle include the following.

'Alba': spreading; white flowers.
'Flore Pleno': spreading; double purplish blue flowers.
'Atropurpurea': spreading; deep purple flowers.
'Bowlesii': clump forming; large dark sky blue flowers.

There are several cultivars with variegated foliage.

Large periwinkle (*Vinca major*), a popular ground cover in the South and well known elsewhere by its variegated cultivars, which are much used as basket plants, is reliably hardy only from zone 8 south.

Creeping myrtle is often slow to become established, but rooted cuttings that have begun to spread, planted nine per square yard, will soon blanket the area.

XANTHORHIZA SIMPLICISSIMA
(Yellowroot)

Zones 3–8

A deciduous mat-forming shrub, 2 to 3 feet high, yellowroot has inconspicuous flowers and fruit. It is valued chiefly for its handsome foliage, which turns yellowish to purplish orange in the fall, and its capacity to grow for years with no attention whatever. In moist, humusy soil, it thrives in full sun or partial to light shade and is free of pests and diseases.

Yellowroot should be planted at the rate of nine per square yard. Spread is soon achieved by underground stolons.

OTHER GROUND COVERS

The following species are mostly suited to special uses and habitats.

ACHILLEA TOMENTOSA
(Woolly yarrow)

Zones 4–7

A mat-forming perennial, 6 to 12 inches high, woolly yarrow has finely divided white woolly foliage and dense clusters of small yellow flower heads in early summer. It is very easily established in hot, dry, sunny places and can tolerate some foot traffic. A planting of 6 to 12 per square yard soon provides continuous cover.

ADIANTUM PEDATUM
(Northern maidenhair fern)

Zones 3–8

Northern maidenhair fern is a fine-textured, deciduous perennial with more or less palmately divided foliage. It is closely related to southern maidenhair fern (*A. capillis-veneris*) of the Southeast in zones 7 to 9. Both are denizens of damp, shady woods and require such conditions to succeed in cultivation. Between 12 and 15 plants per square yard are needed to compensate for the slow rate of spread.

ALCHEMILLA MOLLIS
(Lady's mantle)

Zones 4–7 (8)

A clump-forming deciduous perennial, lady's mantle has silky leaves, 8 to 12 inches high. Its flower stalks reach 18 inches and bear loose clusters of small yellow-green flowers in late spring. It grows best in cool, partly shaded locations away from prolonged heat and drought. Because clumps expand slowly, six to eight plants per square yard is the recommended planting rate.

AMMOPHILA BREVILIGULATA
(American beach grass)

Zones 6–8

A coarse, mat-forming grass, 1½ to 2½ feet high, American beach grass has glossy, arching leaves that are more or less evergreen and occasional somewhat higher flower heads in summer. It is valued chiefly for its rhizomatous habit and capacity to thrive under sandy, littoral conditions, where it is much used to stabilize coastal dunes and embankments. From 12 to 18 plants per square yard is the recommended planting rate on slopes; half that rate can be used in level areas. Planting is best done during dormancy, from late fall until early spring. Full sun is a must.

ARISARUM PROBOSCIDIUM
(Mouse plant)

Zones 7–8

The mouse plant is a rhizomatous perennial, about 6 inches tall, with glossy arrow-shaped leaves and curiously appendaged brown-and-white flowers in the spring. It does best in damp shade on humusy soil.

ARMERIA MARITIMA
(Sea pink, thrift)

Zones 4–7

A tufted, fine-textured, evergreen perennial, 3 or 4 inches tall, sea pink has 12-inch-high heads of pink or white flowers in the spring. Plant on dry, infertile soil in full sun or partial shade. Patchy die-out often occurs on moist, fertile soils.

ARTEMISIA SCHMIDTIANA
(Angel's-hair wormwood)

Zones 4–7

Angel's-hair wormwood is a perennial with finely cut, silvery foliage arranged in a rounded mound, 1 to 1½ feet high. It thrives on poor, droughty soil in full sun. This species is excellent when massed.

ATHYRIUM GOERINGIANUM 'PICTUM'
(Japanese painted fern)

Zones 5–7

A deciduous perennial, Japanese painted fern has triangular leaves that are attractively metallic gray to purplish It ranges from 9 to 18 inches high. Use this species in consistently moist, shady sites. It is very dramatic when combined with bolder clump-forming shade plants, such as *Hosta* spp. Planted alone, 12 to 18 plants per square yard are required for a good, continuous cover.

AURINIA SAXATILIS
(Basket-of-gold)

Zones 4–7 (8)

A clumped perennial with silvery gray semievergreen foliage, basket-of-gold bears loose sprays of small yellow flowers in the spring. The flowers are often produced in great abundance. It is best on rocky banks in full sun, but it is often short lived, requiring replenishment. Six plants per square yard is a good planting interval.

BERGENIA CILIATA F. LIGULATA

Zones (4) 5–7

Bergenia is a bright green, more or less evergreen perennial that grows to about 1 foot. It forms cabbagelike rosettes that turn coppery in the winter. Its flowers are pink, dark red, or white, according to cultivar. Bergenia is best grown in partial shade on moist, humusy soil. It tends to winter kill under severe, exposed, or droughty conditions. From 12 to 15 plants per square yard are required for good cover.

BERGENIA CORDIFOLIA

Zones 3–8

B. cordifolia is similar to *B. ciliata* f. *ligulata* but is larger, with roundish evergreen leaves up to 16 inches long. This species turns bronzy purplish in the winter. Its flowers are pink, borne in early spring. It is slow to spread but is hardy.

Bergenia cordifolia in foreground

CAMPANULA ELATINES
(Adriatic bellflower)

Zones 5–7

A deciduous perennial, 6 to 12 inches tall, Adriatic bellflower forms loose mats up to 3 feet across. It bears blue-violet or white flowers in early summer. It is highly variable with numerous forms and cultivars, some of which can be invasive. Adriatic bellflower is best in sun or partial shade and succeeds on any reasonably moist, well-drained soil. Serbian bellflower (*C. poscharskyana*) is similar, but it is semievergreen and has larger flowers. Three to six plants per square yard will provide continuous cover in a year or two.

CERASTIUM TOMENTOSUM
(Snow-in-summer)

Zones 4–8

A deciduous, mat-forming perennial, about 6 inches high and up to 3 feet across, snow-in-summer has silvery downy foliage and a generous display of white flowers in late spring and early summer. Rather rampant, especially in fertile ground, this species is most successful on sandy, droughty soil of low fertility in full sun. Use 12 plants per square yard to provide full cover.

CHAMAEMELUM NOBILE
(Roman chamomile)

Zones 4–8

Roman chamomile is a creeping, mat-forming, much-branched perennial with finely divided aromatic foliage and yellow daisylike flowers in the summer. It succeeds especially well in dry, sunny locations that are too harsh for lawn grass. Space plants 6 inches apart.

CHIASTOPHYLLUM OPPOSITIFOLIUM
(Creeping crassula)

Zones 7–9

Creeping crassula is a succulent perennial with prostrate stems, spreading by way of rhizomes. Small cream flowers are borne on stalks up to 1 foot tall in the summer. The cultivar 'Tropfichen' is somewhat smaller and has yellow flowers. Moist, gravelly or rocky soil in light shade is best. Plant at the rate of six to eight plants per square yard.

CHRYSOGONUM VIRGINIANUM
(Golden star)

Zones (4) 5–8

A fast-growing, more or less prostrate evergreen perennial, 6 to 10 inches high and up to 2 feet across, golden star has bright yellow five-rayed daisylike flowers from spring to late summer. It thrives in sunny or partially shaded locations on fertile, humusy soils. Plant four to six individuals per square yard.

CORYDALIS LUTEA
(Yellow corydalis)

Zones 5–7

A prolifically self-sowing perennial, 6 to 12 inches tall, yellow corydalis forms a lacy mound of gray-green foliage, topped by clusters of yellow flowers from late spring to early fall. It succeeds best in partial to light shade on average, well-drained soil. As few as four plants per square yard will self-sow freely enough to provide full cover in two years.

CORNUS CANADENSIS
(Bunchberry)

Zones 2–6 (7)

A deciduous, mat-forming perennial that spreads via woody rhizomes, bunchberry has glossy, dark green foliage that turns wine red in the fall. Its dogwood-like flowers appear in late spring to early summer, each consisting of a buttonlike head of tiny yellow florets surrounded by four white pointed bracts. Only 3 to 9 inches high, bunchberry thrives in cool partial shade in humusy, acidic soil beneath conifers. It is not easily established. From 6 to 12 plants per square yard is the recommended planting rate.

CYTISUS × KEWENSIS
(Creeping broom)

Zones 6–7

Creeping broom is a green-stemmed shrub with sparse foliage, less than 1 foot high. It bears showy masses of creamy yellow flowers in the spring. *C. decumbens* has gray green stems and leaves, and bears clear yellow flowers. Both thrive in full sun on sandy, well-drained soil of low fertility. Use six plants per square yard for good coverage.

Warminster broom (*Cytisus × praecox* 'Warminster')

CYTISUS PURPUREUS
(Spreading broom)

Zones 6–8

Spreading broom is a deciduous shrub with divergent horizontal stems and green twigs, up to 2 feet tall and 5 feet across. The purple, pink, or white flowers are borne in the spring. It requires full sun, preferably on dryish, sandy soil. One or two plants per square yard is usually sufficient.

DAPHNE CNEORUM
(Rose daphne)

Zones 4–7

An evergreen shrub, about 1 foot high and up to 2 feet across, rose daphne has trailing upturned branches and delightfully fragrant bright rose pink flowers in the spring and sometimes again in early fall. Partial shade and well-drained, nearly neutral soil bring best results, but it is often difficult to establish. Six to eight plants per square yard are required for good initial coverage.

DICENTRA EXIMIA
(Fringed bleeding heart)

Zones 4–8

Fringed bleeding heart is a deciduous, clump-forming perennial with finely dissected gray green foliage and nodding clusters of pinkish purple flowers from spring to fall. It does best in partial or light shade with moist, humusy soil, where it often self-sows. Between 12 and 15 plants per square yard is a good planting rate for full coverage.

DIERVILLA LONICERA
(Dwarf bush honeysuckle)

Zones 4–8

A fast-growing, deciduous shrub, quick to reach its maximum height of 2 to 3 feet, dwarf bush honeysuckle bears yellow flowers in the spring. It is best used to clothe rocky banks in full sun. Southern bush honeysuckle (*D. sessilifolia*) is similar, but slightly larger, and has conspicuously reddish young growth. Four plants per square yard will soon lead to complete cover.

DRYOPTERIS ERYTHROSORA
(Japanese sword fern)

Zones 5–8

Japanese sword fern is a deciduous fern whose young growth is coppery. It is usually 1½ to 2 feet tall and spreads slowly by rhizomes. It is a handsome ground cover for moist, shady locations. Plant in moist, humusy soil at the rate of 8 to 12 plants per square yard.

EUPHORBIA AMYGDALOIDES VAR. ROBBIAE
(Wood spurge)

Zones 7–9

A deciduous perennial that forms clumps to 2½ feet tall and spreads by way of rhizomes, wood spurge has leathery, deep green leaves and yellow-green flowers in the spring. Plant in any well-drained, moderately fertile soil in full sun at the rate of six to eight plants per square yard.

EUPHORBIA CYPARISSIAS
(Cypress spurge)

Zones 4–8

Cypress spurge is a deciduous rhizomatous perennial, 1 foot high, with narrow blue-green leaves. Its showy yellow flowers are borne in the spring, and age to red and finally purplish. It is best in full sun on dry banks where, if planted at the rate of 8 to 12 plants per square yard, it soon becomes a continuous carpet.

FESTUCA OVINA VAR. GLAUCA
(Blue fescue)

Zones 3–8

Blue fescue forms striking blue-green tufts that are especially attractive in formal rows or beds or as an edging along walks. Dryish, sandy soil in full sun or partial shade is necessary if spotty die-out of this perennial grass is to be avoided. Easily started from seed, blue fescue should be planted at the rate of about 12 plants per square yard.

GALIUM ODORATUM
(Sweet woodruff)

Zones 5–8

A semievergreen, mat-forming perennial, sweet woodruff has loose sprays of small white flowers in late spring. It succeeds best in partial or light shade on moist, loamy soil. A total of 12 plants per square yard will soon lead to a continuous carpet.

GAULTHERIA PROCUMBENS
(Checkerberry, creeping wintergreen)

Zones 3–7

Checkerberry is an evergreen creeper, 6 inches high, with glossy, dark green leaves that turn reddish in the fall and nodding pinkish white flowers in the spring. Red berries follow. It thrives on moist, acidic, humusy soil in partial or light shade. Slow to establish and spread, checkerberry should be planted at the rate of 12 to 18 plants per square yard.

GERANIUM MACRORRHIZUM
(Bigroot geranium)

Zones 4–8

A deciduous perennial, bigroot geranium grows into a rapidly wide-spreading mound that smothers competition. Clusters of pink flowers are borne in late spring. Sun or partial shade with ordinary loamy soil is suitable. Six to eight plants per square yard is a good planting interval.

GERANIUM × OXONIANUM 'ROSE CLAIR'
(Oxford geranium)

Zones 5–8

A 3-foot-high, deciduous perennial, the Oxford geranium has rose pink flowers

in the summer and early fall. It is drought tolerant and readily self-sows. Use six to eight plants per square yard in ordinary soil in full sun.

GERANIUM SANGUINEUM
(Blood-red geranium)

Zones 4–8

The blood-red geranium is a spreading deciduous perennial, 6 to 12 inches high and up to 2 feet across. The lobed circular leaves turn reddish after frost. Magenta (or pink or white) flowers are borne in late spring. It thrives in full sun to partial shade on ordinary, well-drained soil. Four to six plants per square yard will provide complete cover in a year or two.

GERANIUM WALLICHIANUM
(Prostrate geranium)

Zones 7–8

A matlike deciduous perennial, 6 to 8 inches high, prostrate geranium has stems spreading in all directions and eventually will cover 2 square feet. The cultivar 'Buxton's Blue' is equally useful and bears blue flowers with white centers in summer. Four to six plants per square yard is the recommended planting interval. Full sun ensures generous flowering.

GLYCERIA MAXIMA 'VARIEGATA'
(Striped manna grass)

Zones 5–8

A vigorous, perennial, reedlike grass, 6 to 8 feet tall, stripped manna grass has creeping rhizomes and forms extensive dense stands in permanently moist sites. It is useful in controlling erosion on sunny streambanks and riverbanks. Two or three plants per square yard usually suffice.

HELIANTHEMUM NUMMULARIUM
(Sunrose, Rockrose)

Zones 4–7

A semievergreen, clump-forming perennial, sunrose has spreading stems,

12 inches high and about as wide, that bear pink, red, orange, yellow, and bicolor flowers in late spring and early summer. It requires alkaline soil in full sun or partial shade and winter mulch.

HELLEBORUS FOETIDUS
(Setterwort hellebore)

Zones 6–8

A large 3-foot-tall, erect, perennial, Setterwort hellebore has bold upswept foliage and clusters of reddish green, usually fragrant flowers in the summer. It freely self-sows to establish large colonies in either sun or shade. Although it is drought tolerant, it does best on moist, humusy soil. Four plants per square yard are recommended.

HEUCHERA SANGUINEA
(Coralbells)

Zones 4–8

Coralbells form clumps of more or less evergreen foliage, 3 to 6 inches high. Slender flower stalks arise from the foliage in late spring to about 2 feet, bearing pendent bells, about ⅓ inch long, in red, pink, or white. Of the various cultivars, the 'Bressingham' hybrids are especially floriferous and 'Matin' extends its show of coral red bloom to late summer. All are best in partial shade, especially in the South, and in humusy, well-drained soil. As clumps develop slowly, 12 to 18 plants per square yard are are required for continuous cover.

HYPERICUM BUCKLEYI
(Blue Ridge St. John'swort)

Zones (5) 6–7

A spreading deciduous shrub, about 1 foot high and 3 feet across, Blue Ridge St. John'swort has erect twigs that bear bright yellow flowers in the summer. It is trouble free in full sun, even on poor soils, but is subject to some die-back in severe winters. Two or three plants per square yard will provide continuous cover within a few years; a closer interval is necessary for immediate results.

IBERIS SEMPERVIRENS
(Evergreen candytuft)

Zones 4–8 (9)

Evergreen candytuft is a dwarf shrublet, 6 to 9 inches high and spreading to 3 feet, that forms dense mats with glossy, leathery foliage, which is covered with white flowers in the spring. Very adaptable, it does best in full sun on loose, sandy soil of low fertility. Between 6 and 12 plants per square yard are needed if a blanket is to develop within a few years.

INDIGOFERA DECONA
(Chinese indigo)

Zones 5–8

Formerly known as *I. incarnata*, Chinese indigo is a fast-growing, more or less spreading, deciduous shrub, 2 to 3 feet tall. It bears long clusters of rose pink or white flowers in the spring and summer. The plant often dies back somewhat in severe winters. Full sun is advised as is a well-drained, fertile soil. Six to eight plants per square yard are required for continuous cover.

IRIS CRISTATA
(Crested iris)

Zones 4–8

A semievergreen perennial, crested iris has gray green, spear-shaped leaves arising from shallow, thickened rhizomes. It bears large, showy, purple flowers in late spring. It grows well in partial shade on damp, humusy soil of average fertility. Foliage is usually 6 to 9 inches high, and flower scapes rise to about 1 foot. From 10 to 15 plants per square yard are recommended.

LAMIASTRUM GALEOBDOLON *VAR.* VARIEGATUM
(Yellow dead nettle, yellow archangel)

Zones 5–8

Yellow dead nettle is a durable, easily grown, semievergreen creeper, 6 to 12 inches high. It has silvery mottled leaves and erect 1- to 1½-foot-high clusters of yellow flowers in the spring. It does best in partial shade on average soil, but it endures summer drought. Wide-spreading stems can arch into or even over small shrubs and can invade adjacent garden beds and borders. Six to eight plants per square yard will result in complete cover within a year or two.

LAMIUM MACULATUM
(Spotted dead nettle)

Zones 4–7

A wide-spreading, stem-rooting, deciduous creeper, 6 to 10 inches high, spotted dead nettle has variously mottled foliage and clusters of pink or white flowers in the spring. It does best in partial shade on moist soil of average fertility. Use six to eight plants per square yard.

LAVANDULA ANGUSTIFOLIA
(English lavender)

Zones 5–8

A fragrant, semievergreen perennial that forms rounded clumps 1 to 2 feet high by 2 to 3 feet wide, English lavender bears spikes of lavender or purple flowers in summer. Fall pruning promotes vigorous spring growth and generous summer bloom, especially in full sun. Plant 8 to 12 per square yard, preferably in sandy, humusy soil.

LIRIOPE MUSCARI
(Tall lilyturf)

Zones 6–9

Tall lilyturf is an evergreen perennial that forms a dense, slowly spreading mound of strap-shaped leaves, 15 to 20 inches high, from which spikes of bluish purple, lavender, or white flowers emerge in the summer. It endures full sun but is best in partial or light shade on most any well-drained soil. Use 10 to 15 plants per square yard.

LIRIOPE SPICATA
(Creeping lilyturf)

Zones (4) 5–8

An evergreen, grasslike perennial creeping lilyturf forms rapidly spreading mats, 8 to 10 inches high and 2 feet or more across, and bears spikes of small lilac-colored flowers in the summer. It competes well with tree roots in dry shade but performs best in partial shade. It endures occasional foot traffic and mowing. Four to six plants will eventually clothe a square yard; double the number for more rapid coverage.

LOTUS CORNICULATUS
(Bird's-foot trefoil)

Zones 5–8

Bird's-foot trefoil is a deeply rooted, deciduous perennial with prostrate stems. It forms a low mat, 1½ to 2 feet across, and bears clusters of bright yellow flowers in late spring and early summer. It is frequently used to stabilize droughty roadside banks. Plant in full sun in any well-drained soil. Use six to eight plants per square yard.

LUZULA MAXIMA
(Greater wood rush)

Zones 6–8

Greater wood rush (formerly known as *L. sylvatica*) is a deciduous perennial that forms bright green tussocks and spreads by stolons. It bears brown flower

Creeping Lilyturf (*Liriope spicata*)

heads in the summer. Reaching 2 feet or more, it is useful beneath mature rhododendrons as well as for stabilizing exposed banks. Use four to six plants per square yard on average, somewhat acidic, moisture-retentive soil.

MAHONIA REPENS
(Creeping hollygrape)

Zones 5–7

A low, creeping, evergreen shrublet of rigid habit, creeping hollygrape has glossy leaves that turn purplish in winter and a modest display of clustered yellow flowers in early spring, which are followed by gray black berries. It is best in sun or partial shade on moist, humusy soils. It is slow to establish, especially where summer drought occurs. Creeping hollygrape should be planted 8 to 12 plants per square yard.

MAZUS REPTANS
(Creeping mazus)

Zones 3–7

A node-rooting perennial, creeping mazus forms tough, bright green mats, with violet-blue tubular flowers borne in spring. A white-flowered form also exists. It is best on moist ground in partial shade, where light foot traffic and occasional mowing are possible. Six plants per square yard in sandy-humusy soil soon results in complete cover.

MENTHA REQUIENII
(Corsican mint)

Zones 6–8

A prostrate, creeping, deciduous perennial, 1 to 2 inches high and 1 to 2 feet across, Corsican mint has fine-textured, fragrant foliage and small clusters of lavender flowers in the summer. It is useful among stepping-stones, but it vanishes in winter. Six or eight plants per square yard will give complete coverage in a year or two, especially if in full sun or partial shade and in sandy-humusy, moisture-retentive soil.

MICROBIOTA DECUSSATA
(Siberian carpet)

Zones 3–7

Siberian carpet is a spreading juniper-like evergreen shrub, 1 to 2 feet high and 3 to 6 feet across. It has green scale-leaves that turn purplish in the winter. It performs best in partial shade and tolerates both summer heat and winter severity. Plant in sandy soil of no more than average fertility. Indeed, it may fail to establish and die out on heavily fertilized or excessively moist ground. Two to four plants per square yard soon cover the surface.

MITCHELLA REPENS
(Partridgeberry)

Zones 3–9

A very low, creeping evergreen, not more than 2 inches high, partridgeberry has paired white or purplish flowers in late spring to early summer, followed by red berries. It requires moist, acidic, well-drained soil in light to fairly dense shade. It is not easily grown. Between 12 and 18 plants are required to cover a square yard.

NEPETA RACEMOSA
(Persian catmint)

Zones 4–8

Persian catmint (often listed as *N. mussinii*) is a deciduous, mat-forming

perennial, 6 to 18 inches high and 1 to 2 feet across. It has aromatic gray green foliage and loose clusters of lavender flowers in the summer. It does best in full sun on average soils, but it is attractive to cats, who can damage or even destroy a planting. Six or eight plants soon cover a square yard, both by clump expansion and self-sowing.

OENOTHERA FRUTICOSA
(Sundrops)

Zones 3–8

A mat-forming, deciduous perennial, sundrops has erect stems that in early summer bear bright yellow flowers. Its semievergreen foliage turns reddish in late summer. Because it is invasive in adjacent beds and lawns, it should be kept to enclosed areas. It does best in sun or partial shade on any well-drained soil. *O. perennis*, *O. pilosella*, and *O. tetragona* are similar and equally useful. In any case, 8 to 12 plants per square yard soon provide full cover.

OPHIOPOGON JAPONICUS
(Mondo grass)

Zones 7–10

An evergreen perennial, similar to *Liriope*, mondo grass forms a thick mat of narrow leathery leaves, 8 to 12 inches high, and spreads by underground stolons. Its nodding flowers are pale lilac to white and are borne in the summer. It thrives in partial to full shade. Plant four to six plants per square yard, or more for more rapid cover, in average soil.

OSMUNDA CINNAMOMEA
(Cinnamon fern)

Zones 3–9

Deciduous and clump forming, the cinnamon fern has divergently arching foliage, 3 to 4 feet high and produces erect, cinnamon brown spore-bearing stalks in the summer. It thrives in wet, boggy ground but is adaptable to drier settings. Similar but somewhat smaller is the interrupted fern (*O. claytoniana*). Both are useful in moist, open, partially shaded woodland areas. Use four to six plants per square yard.

PARONYCHIA KAPELA
(Nailwort)

Zones 7–8

Nailwort is a silvery gray, mat-forming perennial with attractive papery floral bracts. It makes a good carpet for small spring bulbs and succeeds well in full sun and summer drought. Use 12 to 15 plants per square yard to achieve good coverage. Note that on heavily fertilized soil, nailwort can become invasive.

PARTHENOCISSUS QUINQUEFOLIA
(Virginia creeper)

Zones 3–10

A rampant, deciduous, woody creeper, Virginia creeper has glossy five-parted leaves and will climb any support by means of tendrils with adhesive discs. Its ground-hugging growth does not flower. Virginia creeper is too coarse and vigorous for small areas, but its red fall foliage is often spectacular. It succeeds in sun to deep shade and on most any soil. For early cover, use four plants per square yard.

PAXISTIMA CANBYI
(Rat-stripper)

Zones 3–8

A dwarf evergreen shrub about 1 foot high, rat-stripper has horizontal, soil-rooting branches; shiny, boxlike foliage that turns bronzy in winter; and inconspicuous red-brown flowers. It does best on neutral or alkaline soils of low fertility in full sun or partial shade. Fertilizer can be fatal. Plant 8 to 12 plants per square yard.

PHALARIS ARUNDINACEA VAR. PICTA
(Ribbon grass)

Zones 5–8

Ribbon grass is a rapidly spreading perennial grass, 2 to 3 feet high. It has green-and-white longitudinally striped leaf blades and forms a tough, soil-binding, ever-expanding but ornamental patch. Unless it is contained, it can be tenaciously invasive. Four plants per square yard in full sun or partial shade, on most any soil, dry or wet, will soon completely cover the ground.

PHLOX STOLONIFERA
(Creeping phlox)

Zones 4–7

A mat-forming, deciduous perennial, creeping phlox has hairy foliage and, in the spring, erect flower stalks 6 to 12 inches high that bear pink to reddish purple blooms. A white-flowered form also exists. It thrives in partial shade on moist, humusy soil. Plant 8 to 12 plants per square yard.

PHLOX SUBULATA
(Mountain pink)

Zones 4–7

A dense perennial mat, mountain pink has linear evergreen leaves and masses of red-violet, purple, pink, or white flowers in the spring. Scarcely more than 3 inches high, it will spread to 2 feet or more in full sun on sandy, near-neutral soil. Relatively slow to spread, mountain pink should be planted six to eight plants per square yard for early coverage.

PLEIOBLASTUS VARIEGATUS
(Dwarf white-striped bamboo)

Zones 7–8

Dwarf white-striped bamboo is a vigorous, clump-forming, more or less evergreen bamboo, no taller than 3 feet. Its leaves are longitudinally cream striped. It is easily grown, shade tolerant, and noninvasive. Use six to eight plants per square yard in any well-drained soil.

POLYSTICHUM ACROSTICHOIDES
(Christmas fern)

Zones 3–9

Evergreen and clump forming, Christmas fern is a perennial with lustrous foliage that holds up well in winter until flattened by heavy snow. It is long lived in partial, light, or heavy shade in consistently moist ground. Rosettes of emerging silvery gray spring leaves contrast

effectively with the dark, shiny, older foliage. Plant four to six plants per square yard, preferably in sandy-humusy soil.

POLYSTICHUM MUNITUM
(Western sword fern)

Zones 4–7

A coarse evergreen, western sword fern has lustrous leaves, 3 to 4 feet high, and forms majestic clumps. It does best in deep, moist shade on humusy soil. Between four and six plants per square yard offer good cover.

PULMONARIA SACCHARATA
(Bethlehem sage)

Zones 4–8

A compact, clumped perennial, Bethlehem sage has attractive, white-flecked, deciduous foliage and clusters of whitish or red-violet flowers in the spring. It is effective when massed in

partial to light shade on moist, loamy soil. Use 8 to 12 plants per square yard to carpet the ground.

RHODODENDRON IMPEDITUM
(Cloudland rhododendron)

Zones 5–6

Cloudland rhododendron is a spreading, small-leaf, cushionlike evergreen shrub 1 to 1½ feet tall. It displays bluish violet flowers in the spring. It does best in partial shade on acidic, humusy soil. Six to eight plants per square yard will provide continuous cover.

SAGINA SUBULATA
(Irish moss, Corsican pearlwort)

Zones 5–7

Irish moss is a mat-forming perennial with very narrow leaves and small, white, solitary flowers in the summer. It is

Irish moss or pearlwort *(Sagina subulata)*

especially useful as a living carpet among stepping-stones in full sun. The cultivar 'Aurea' has yellow-green foliage. Moss 12 to 15 plants per square yard for early carpet effect. Sandy-humusy, well-drained soil is best.

SANTOLINA CHAMAECYPARISSUS
(Lavender cotton)

Zones 7–8 (9)

An evergreen shrublet, lavender cotton has finely cut aromatic silvery gray leaves and yellow, buttonlike flowers in the summer. The very similar *S. virens* is green leaved. Both thrive in full sun on sandy, infertile soils and grow 1 to 2 feet tall and 2 to 3 feet wide. Plant four to six plants per square yard.

SAPONARIA OCYMOIDES
(Rock soapwort)

Zones 4–8

A trailing, much-branched perennial, rock soapwort has generous display of deep rose pink flowers in late spring. It reaches 6 inches in height and is 3 feet across. The best results are had in full sun on dryish, relatively poor soils. Four plants soon cover a square yard.

SAXIFRAGA STOLONIFERA
(Strawberry geranium, mother-of-thousands)

Zones 6–9

The strawberry geranium is a perennial, 10 inches high, and has round leaves that are red-violet beneath. It displays loose, open clusters of cream flowers in the summer. It spreads by threadlike stolons, forming dense patches. Strawberry geranium is a popular houseplant. Partial shade on sandy-humusy soil is best. Four to six plants per square yard will carpet the surface within a year or two.

SAXIFRAGA × URBIUM
(London pride)

Zones 6–8

A perennial, London pride has thick, scalloped leaves. It remains low, spreading by way of stolons. It displays clusters of white or pink flowers, 10 to 14 inches high, in the summer. London pride is a traditional ground cover beneath roses in full sun to partial shade. Use six to eight plants per square yard.

SEDUM SPURIUM
(Red creeping stonecrop)

Zones 5–8

A semi-evergreen succulent, red creeping stonecrop has prostrate rooting stems that form a mat 3 to 6 inches high and 1 foot or more across. Its red to white flowers are borne in the summer. In the cultivar 'Dragon Blood', the flowers are crimson. This and several other *Sedum* species, many yellow flowered, are drought tolerant, sun-loving ground covers. Plant 8 to 12 plants per square yard in sandy-humusy soil for best results.

STACHYS BYZANTINA
(Lamb's ears)

Zones 4–8

An evergreen, mat-forming perennial, 3 to 6 inches high, lamb's ears has light gray, felty foliage. It displays erect spikes, 1 to 1½ feet tall, of small purplish pink flowers in the summer. Distinctive, hardy, and drought tolerant, lamb's ears is rather coarse and can be invasive, espe-

cially in rich soils. Plant in full sun, preferably in well-drained, relatively infertile soil, at the rate of six to eight plants per square yard.

STEPHANANDRA INCISA 'CRISPA'
(Dwarf lace bush)

Zones 3–7

Dwarf lace bush is a mounded, tip-rooting deciduous shrub, 2 to 3 feet high and up to 6 feet across, and has finely divided leaves that often turn reddish in fall. Its loose clusters of small white flowers are borne in late spring. It forms a low, dense tangle in full sun to light shade. Any well-drained, moderately fertile soil is suitable; use one plant per 2 square yards.

SYMPHYTUM GRANDIFLORUM
(Spreading comfrey)

Zones 5–8

A bristly hairy perennial, spreading comfrey forms a mound up to 1 foot high and twice as wide. It bears pendent yellowish or pink flowers in the spring. This species is a very useful ground cover in dry shade on moderately fertile soils. Four to six plants per square yard soon provide cover.

Lamb's ears (*Stachys byzantina*)

TEUCRIUM CHAMAEDRYS
(Wall germander)

Zones 5–9

Wall germander, an evergreen shrublet, has dark green foliage and rose purple flowers in the summer. With a maximum height of 15 inches, it is especially effective as an edging plant, but it also serves as a ground cover when mass planted in full sun or partial shade. It may suffer dieback in severe winters. Use four to six plants per square yard in ordinary, well-drained soil.

THYMUS SERPYLLUM
(Mother of thyme)

Zones 6–8

A spreading, deciduous, aromatic, mother of thyme has wiry stems, 3 to 6 inches high and up to 2 feet across. Its spikes of small purple (or red, pink, or white) flowers are borne in late spring. This variable (likely the result of confusion with several related species) thyme tends to die back after severe cold unless mulched. In woolly thyme (*T. pseudolanuginosus*), the leaves are gray woolly on both sides. All require full sun and do best on sandy or gritty, humusy soils. Plant six to eight plants per square yard.

TIARELLA CORDIFOLIA
(Foamflower)

Zones 5–7

A compact, deciduous perennial, 6 to 12 inches high, foamflower spreads by underground stems and has hairy maple-like foliage and erect clusters of cream flowers in the spring. It is best grown in moist, shady locations on humusy, well-drained soil. Use 12 to 15 plants per square yard.

TOLMIEA MENZIESII
(Piggyback plant)

Zones 6–9

Piggyback plant, a clump-forming, deciduous perennial, forms new plants at the bases of older leaf blades and bears spikes of purplish flowers in the summer. It effectively carpets moist, partly or lightly shaded ground, especially where summer temperatures are moderate. Plant 10 to 12 plants per square yard on average, well-drained soil.

VANCOUVERIA HEXANDRA
(American barrenwort)

Zones 5–7

American barrenwort is a fine-textured, deciduous perennial, 1½ to 2 feet tall, that forms spreading clumps. It displays sprays of tiny white flowers in the spring. It is easily grown on damp ground in partial or light shade. Between 8 and 12 plants per square yard provide good cover, especially if in moist, sandy-humusy soil.

VERONICA CHAMAEDRYS
(Angel's-eye veronica)

Zones 4–8

A creeping, stem-rooting, deciduous perennial, angel's-eye veronica forms mats, 3 to 6 inches high, and has erect clusters of blue white-centered flowers in the spring. It spreads rapidly, invading lawns and garden beds; hence it should be kept within curbing. Angel's-eye veronica flowers best in partial shade on most any reasonably moist soil. Four plants per square yard soon provide complete cover.

VERONICA OFFICINALIS
(Common speedwell)

Zones 3–8

A fast-growing, mat-forming, deciduous perennial, three to six inches high, common speedwell has 12- to 18-inch-high clusters of sky blue flowers in the spring. Four plants per square yard in full sun to partial shade on average, loamy soil soon take hold and require no special care.

VERONICA REPENS
(Creeping veronica)

Zones 6–9

A creeping, mat-forming, mosslike perennial, about 2 inches high, creeping veronica has blue white-edged flowers borne in small clusters in the spring. It makes a good ground cover in bulb beds. Use 8 to 12 plants per square yard in any well-drained garden soil. It thrives in full sun or partial shade.

VIOLA ODORATA
(Garden violet)

Zones 5–8

Garden violet is a clump-forming, deciduous perennial. Its purple flowers are borne in the spring and are followed by separately formed capsules that explosively fling abundant seed in late summer, thus forming dense ground-covering colonies. This and numerous other *Viola* species—variously with purple, lavender, white, yellow, or bicolor flowers, produced mostly in the spring—thrive in partial, light, or dense shade. It may prove invasive. Four to six plants per square yard in average, well-drained soil will blanket the area within a year or two.

WALDSTEINIA FRAGARIOIDES
(Barren strawberry)

Zones 5–8

A tufted, deciduous perennial, 4 to 8 inches high, barren strawberry spreads 3 to 6 feet by creeping rhizomes. It has three-parted strawberrylike leaves and solitary or small clusters of yellow flowers in the spring. Six to eight plants per square yard on average, well-drained soil, especially if constantly moist, will soon develop a continuous mat. Barren strawberry thrives in full sun to light shade.

15

Herbaceous Perennials

THE LARGE GROUP KNOWN AS HERBACEOUS PERENNIALS includes many of our most beloved garden flowers. Although very diverse in form and habit of growth, there is one characteristic they share. They are nonwoody plants that live more than two years and die down to the ground in the winter and renew their growth again in the spring. Some herbaceous perennials live on almost indefinitely, while others may die out after a few years.

Hybrid daylilies, astilbe, and hybrid loosestrife make a colorful early summer display in a garden of mixed perennials.

All of these common and familiar garden flowers originally came from wildflowers. They were brought into cultivation because of their beauty, and through selection and hybridization many of them have been developed and "improved" to such an extent that their relationship to their ancestors is difficult to recognize today. Indeed, with some flowers it is impossible to determine the place of origin or line of descent, so long have they been cultivated and so dissimilar are they to the wild species.

Most of these domesticated plants are more vigorous in growth, and the flowers larger and more varied, than those of their wild counterparts. In some instances, such as double-flowered chrysanthemums, the blossoms have become so modified that they no longer set seed.

Some perennials have been in cultivation for many centuries, even since ancient times, while others have come into gardens more recently, especially following the era of extensive exploration. Those plants that have been cultivated in gardens since ancient times were first grown in the countries of their origin. Plants cultivated in regions where they originated were later introduced into Europe by the returning Crusaders or by explorers or travelers. Thus the flowers that were originally gathered together in the monastery gardens, and then displayed in public botanic gardens, gradually became the familiar ornamentals of the European flower garden.

The early colonists in the New World brought with them many of the perennial flowers they had known and loved in their homelands. Qualities of hardiness, long life, and success under adverse and widely varying conditions made these perennials particularly welcome to the European settlers of this country, and these same sturdy qualities make them just as valuable today.

Many of the old favorites constitute the core of an informal, practical category called low-maintenance perennials. To be low maintenance, a perennial must meet certain criteria: it must perform well under a wide range of soil conditions; it must live at least five years without needing to be replaced; it must be staunch enough not to require staking; it must be so immune to or tolerant of diseases and pests that spraying will not be needed; it must thrive in ordinary garden conditions for at least four or five years before requiring lifting and dividing; it must not be invasive; and its spent flowers must be shed and not detract from garden quality if left untended. It is surprising to some that several hundred of the thousands of kinds of herbaceous perennials cultivated in America meet these standards. In the descriptions and lists of perennials that follow, species that are low maintenance are so indicated.

SITE CONSIDERATIONS

The ideal site for a perennial garden is one that (1) receives direct sunlight for as many hours during the day as possible (a minimum of four or five, preferably at least six to eight) but also has a partially shaded corner or two, as might be provided by nearby trees; (2) is sheltered from strong winds; (3) possesses deep, fertile, well-drained, loamy, and neutral soil, rich in organic matter; (4) is on flat or only slightly sloping land; and (5) occupies a conspicuous location on the property. Few gardeners are blessed with such a site! Fortunately, poor soil can be enriched and improved. By proper selection, plants that tolerate a fairly wide range of soil or light conditions may be chosen, and some species adapt to special situations with very poor soil or heavy shade. The further one departs from the ideal conditions outlined above, however, the more limited the choices will be.

The worst site for a perennial garden is one where the soil is poorly drained, especially during the winter. In such conditions, the hardiness of many perennials is considerably reduced; plants tend to be heaved out of the ground during

Mixed perennials

periods of alternate freezing and thawing, and the choice of suitable plants for such a situation is thus very restricted. Unless considerable time and expense can be spent to drain the site extensively or to raise the ground level by installing landscape ties or other structural materials, a garden of perennials should not be attempted in such a location. Alternatively, you may choose to accept the wetness and design a garden using species specially adapted to such conditions (see Chapter 23).

Another limiting location for a perennial garden is one that receives less than four hours of direct sunlight a day. The choice of plants for such a situation is again restricted, though admittedly not so limited as in wet locations. Although many sun-loving perennials tolerate partial shade, the greater the degree of shade, the more slender the growth and, therefore, the greater the need for staking. Moreover, such gardens are often subject to attack from fungi and other disease organisms, since plants grown under less than ideal circumstances are stressed and constitutionally weaker than those whose cultural requirements are more adequately met.

In general, perennial plantings are most effective against a backdrop, such as a hedge or wall. Good hedge plants for this purpose include yew or privet. Wood fences, or even chain-link fences (especially if painted flat back), are also appropriate. Indeed, a well-planned perennial border can mask the ugliness of a chain-link fence as effectively as it complements the beauty of a wood fence or screen. Many other backdrops are possible, including the walls of the house itself, a mixed shrub border, or outbuildings on the property.

In contemporary gardens, the perennial border is frequently liberated from the prescribed, often stereotyped backdrop. It may be an insular planting in the lawn, independent of any single feature or structure, yet be in complete harmony with the overall landscape plan. The shape may be symmetrical in outline or free-form. It may be defined by gently curving lines or be raised or contoured in elevation. In such situations, use of shrubs with contrasting shapes, leaf colors, and textures will complement the perennials and add interest during both the growing season and the winter months when perennial gardens usually are least interesting.

Other sites on the average home property may present possibilities as good locations for a perennial garden. These include areas along driveways, parallel to walks within or partially surrounding vegetable gardens, around existing specimen shrubs or small trees, mixed into annual borders, adjacent to terraces or patios, at the base of an outcrop, near a fence or hedge, or among the shrubs of the foundation planting or shrub border. The possibilities are almost equal to the myriad sites to be found or created on any property.

Perennials are especially effective when complementary in habit, sequential in flowering, and arranged before a backdrop such as a tall hedge.

PLANNING THE PERENNIAL BORDER

No planting problem is more diverse and intricate than that of the perennial flower border. No planting plan requires more careful thought, more detailed study, or more creative skill. It should be the aim of the designer to produce a succession of color harmonies that will merge imperceptibly, one into the other, as the season advances. No other type of plant material offers such infinite possibilities for color compositions as do perennials, and the gardener finds in this ever-changing medium wide scope for his or her artistic skill and creativity.

It must be borne in mind, however, that perennials alone will not produce as full an effect of bloom and color throughout the season as will perennials supplemented with spring- and summer-flowering bulbs and with annuals, biennials, and shrubs. Therefore, in planning the border for continuous bloom, it is an advantage to include plants from these other valuable groups as well.

With spatial definition provided by the distant hedge and access afforded on a transversely planked path, this white garden is as effective at night as in daylight.

When designing a perennial garden, the entire life cycle of each plant must be taken into consideration to determine its position—its period of growth, blossoming, and retrogression. In selecting and arranging plant material, the most important factors are the ultimate height of the plants, the color range, and the season of bloom. But other factors must also be taken into consideration: the texture and color of the foliage, the longevity of the plant, and its particular cultural requirements. All of these considerations may at first seem confusing, especially to the novice, but they need not be so if the decisions are made in logical sequence.

The usual procedure in preparing a planting plan for a perennial garden is first to draw to scale a diagram showing the outline of the various beds or borders. A scale of ½ inch equals 1 foot will usually provide for a plan of workable size, unless the garden is unusually large, in which case the scale may be reduced to ¼ inch equals 1 foot. The next step is to compile a list of the plants and bulbs one wishes to include in the planting plan. The plant names may either be jotted down quite at random as they come to mind, listed alphabetically, or listed in some other logical order such as blooming sequence. Here's an example of such a list, arranged alphabetically.

Anemone × hybrida (Japanese anemone)
Aquilegia spp. (columbine)
Artemisia lactiflora (white mugwort)
Aster novae-angliae (New England aster)
Chrysanthemum × morifolium hybrids (hardy mum)
Delphinium spp.
Dicentra spectabilis (old-fashioned bleeding heart)
Hemerocallis hybrids (hybrid daylily)
Heuchera sanguinea (Coralbells)
Iris hybrids (bearded iris)
Linum perenne (blue flax)
Lupinus Russell hybrids (perennial lupine)
Paeonia lactiflora (peony)
Phlox divaricata (wild sweet William)
Phlox paniculata (summer phlox)
Thalictrum aquilegifolium (meadow rue)
Viola spp. (violet)

When this tentative list has been completed, it should be broken up into a number of subgroupings, according to (1) season of bloom, (2) color, and (3) height. Biennials, bulbs, and annuals may be selected and added to the list to provide more abundant bloom at certain seasons or because they are particularly good companions. Thus the original alphabetical list could be rearranged and augmented as shown in the following lists.

PERENNIALS AND COMPANION PLANTS ARRANGED BY SEASON OF BLOOM

SPRING

Perennials

Aquilegia spp. (columbine)
Dicentra spectabilis (old-fashioned bleeding heart)
Iris hybrids (bearded iris)
Paeonia lactiflora (peony)
Phlox divaricata (wild sweet William)
Thalictrum aquilegifolium (meadow rue)

Biennials

Bellis perennis (English daisy)
Viola × wittrockiana (pansy)

Bulbs

Narcissus spp. (daffodil, jonquil)
Tulipa spp. and cvs. (tulip)

EARLY SUMMER

Perennials

Delphinium elatum
Hemerocallis hybrids (hybrid daylily)
Heuchera sanguinea (coralbells)
Linum perenne (blue flax)
Paeonia lactiflora (peony)
Phlox paniculata (summer phlox)

Biennials

Campanula medium (Canterbury bells)
Digitalis purpurea (foxglove)
Dianthus barbatus (sweet William)

Bulbs

Lilium spp. and cvs. (lily)

MID TO LATE SUMMER

Perennials

Artemisia lactiflora (white mugwort)
Aster × frikartii 'Wonder of Stafa' (Wonder of Stafa aster)
Hemerocallis hybrids (hybrid daylily)
Lupinus 'Russell Hybrids' (perennial lupine)
Phlox paniculata (summer phlox)

Bulbs and corms

Gladiolus × hortulanus
Lilium spp. and cvs. (lily)

Annuals

Ageratum houstonianum
Antirrhinum majus (snapdragon)*
Cleome hassleriana (cleome)
Cosmos bipinnatus (tall cosmos)
Cosmos sulphureus (orange cosmos)

Nicotiana spp. and cvs. (flowering tobacco)
Petunia × hybrida
Salvia farinacea (mealycup sage)*
Tagetes spp. and cvs. (marigold)
Torenia fournieri (wishbone flower)
Verbena × hybrida
Zinnia elegans (common zinnia)

FALL

Perennials

Anemone × hybrida (Japanese anemone)
Aster novae-angliae (New England aster)
A. novi-belgii (New York aster)
Chrysanthemum × morifolium (hardy mum)

Annuals

Ageratum houstonianum
Antirrhinum majus (snapdragon)**
Cleome hassleriana (cleome)
Cosmos bipinnatus (tall cosmos)
Nicotiana spp. and cvs. (flowering tobacco)
Petunia × hybrida
Tagetes spp. and cvs. (marigold)
Torenia fournieri (wishbone flower)
Verbena × hybrida
Zinnia elegans (common zinnia)

* Perennial from zone 8 southward

** Perennial in zones 9 and 10

PERENNIALS AND COMPANION PLANTS ARRANGED ACCORDING TO HEIGHT

SHORT (LESS THAN 2 FEET)

Perennials

Aster × frikartii 'Wonder of Stafa' (Wonder of Stafa aster)
A. novi-belgii cvs. 'Jenny' and 'Snowball' (dwarf New York aster)
Linum perenne (blue flax)
Phlox divaricata (wild sweet William)

Biennials

Bellis perennis (English daisy)
Dianthus barbatus (sweet William)
Viola × wittrockiana (pansy)

Bulbs

Narcissus spp. and cvs. (daffodil, jonquil)
Scilla spp. and cvs. (squill)
Tulipa spp. and cvs. (tulip)

Annuals

Ageratum houstonianum
Petunia × hybrida
Tagetes patula (French marigold)
Verbena × hybrida

MEDIUM (2 TO 4 FEET)

Perennials

Anemone × hybrida (Japanese anemone)
Aquilegia spp. and cvs. (columbine)

(continues)

PERENNIALS AND COMPANION PLANTS ARRANGED ACCORDING TO HEIGHT (*continued*)

Chrysanthemum × morifolium (hardy mum)
Dientra spectabilis (old-fashioned bleeding heart)
Hemerocallis hybrids (hybrid daylily)
Heuchera sanguinea (coralbells)
Iris hybrids
Lupinus 'Russell Hybrids' (perennial lupine)
Paeonia lactiflora (peony)
Phlox paniculata (summer phlox)

Biennials
Campanula medium (Canterbury bells)

Bulbs and corms
Gladiolus × hortulanus
Lillium spp. and cvs. (lily)
Tulipa cvs. (tulip)

Annuals
Antirrhinum majus (snapdragon)*
Cleome hassleriana (cleome)
Nicotinana spp. and cvs. (flowering tobacco)
Salvia farinacea (mealycup sage)**
Tagetes erecta cvs. (African marigold, American marigold)
Zinnia elegans cvs. (common zinnia)

TALL (MORE THAN 4 FEET)
Perennials
Artemisia lactiflora (white mugwort)
A. novae-angliae (New England aster)
A. novi-belgii (New York aster)
Delphinium elatum
Hemerocallis hybrids (hybrid daylily)
Thalictrum aquilegifolium (meadow rue)

Biennials
Digitalis purpurea (foxglove)

Bulbs
Lilium spp. and cvs. (lily)

Annuals
Cosmos bipinnatus (tall cosmos)
Tagetes erecta cvs. (African marigold, American marigold)
Zinnia elegans cvs. (common zinnia)

* Perennial from zone 8 southward

** Perennial in zones 9 and 10

PERENNIALS AND COMPANION PLANTS ARRANGED BY FLOWER COLOR

WHITE
Perennials
Anemone × hybrida (Japanese anemone)
Aquilegia, white cvs. (columbine)
Artemisia lactiflora (white mugwort)
Aster novae-angliae 'Albus' (white New England aster)
A. novi-belgii 'Snowball' (white New York aster)
Chrysanthemum × morifolium, white cvs. (hardy mum)

Delphinium elatum, white cvs.
Iris, white hybrids (bearded iris)
Paeonia lactiflora, white cvs. (peony)
Phlox paniculata, white cvs. (summer phlox)

Biennials
Bellis perennis, white cvs. (English daisy)
Campanula medium 'Alba' (white Canterbury bells)
Dianthus barbatus 'Albus' (white sweet William)
Digitalis purpurea, white cvs. (foxglove)
Viola × wittrockianna, white cvs. (pansy)

Bulbs, corms, and tubers
Dahlia, white hybrids
Gladiolus × hortulanus, white cvs.
Lilium, white spp. and cvs. (lily)
Narcissus, white spp. and cvs. (daffodil, jonquil)
Tulipa, white cvs. (tulip)

Annuals
Antirrhinum majus, white cvs. (snapdragon)*
Cleome hassleriana 'Helen Campbell' (white cleome)
Cosmos bipinnatus 'Purity' (white tall cosmos)
Nicotiana alata, white cvs. (flowering tobacco)
N. sylvestris (starburst tobacco)
Torenia fournieri 'Alba' (white wishbone flower)
Verbena × hybrida 'Crystal' (white verbena)
Zinnia elegans, white cvs. (common zinnia)

BLUE, LAVENDER, PURPLE, OR MAUVE
Perennials
Aquilegia spp. and cvs. (columbine)
Aster × frikartii 'Wonder of Stafa' (Wonder of Stafa aster)
A. novae-angliae (New England aster)
A. novi-belgii (New York aster)
Chrysanthemum × morifolium (hardy mum)
Delphinum elatum
Iris hybrids (bearded iris)
Linum perenne (blue flax)
Phlox divaricata (wild sweet William)
P. paniculata (summer phlox)
Thalictrum aquilegiifolium (meadow rue)

Biennials
Campanula medium (Canterbury bells)
Digitalis purpurea (foxglove)
Viola × wittrockianna (pansy)

Bulbs and corms
Gladiolus × hortulanus
Scilla sibirica (Siberian squill)
Tulipa cvs. (tulip)

Annuals
Ageratum houstonianum
Antirrhinum majus cvs. (snapdragon)*
Nicotiana alata (flowering tobacco)
Petunia × hybrida
Torenia fournieri Salvia farinacea (mealycup sage)**
(wishbone flower)
Verbena × hybrida 'Amethyst' (purple verbena)
Zinnia elegans cvs. (common zinnia)

PINK, SALMON, ROSE, OR RED

Perennials

Anemone × hybrida cvs. (pink Japanese anemone)
Aquilegia spp. and cvs. (columbine)
Aster novae-angliae 'Roseus' (pink New England aster)
A. novi-belgii 'Jenny' (red New York aster)
Chrysanthemum × morifolium cvs. (hardy mum)
Dicentra spectabilis (old-fashioned bleeding heart)
Heuchera sanguinea (coralbells)
Iris hybrids (bearded iris)
Lupinus 'Russell Hybrids' (perennial lupine)
Paeonia lactiflora (peony)

Biennials

Bellis perennis (English daisy)
Campanula medium (Canterbury bells)
Dianthus barbatus (sweet William)
Viola × wittrockianna (pansy)

Bulbs, corms, and tubers

Dahlia hybrids
Gladiolus × hortulanus
Lilium spp. and cvs. (lily)
Tulipa spp. and cvs. (tulip)

Annuals

Antirrhinum majus (snapdragon)*
Cleome hassleriana (cleome)
Cosmos bipinnatus (tall cosmos)
Nicotiana alata cvs. (flowering tobacco)
Petunia × hybrida
Verbena × hybrida (verbena)
Zinnia elegans (common zinnia)

YELLOW, ORANGE, OR BRONZE

Perennials

Aquilegia spp. and cvs. (columbine)
Chrysanthemum × morifolium cvs. (hardy mum)
Hemerocallis spp. and cvs. (daylily)
Iris hybrids (bearded iris)
Lupinus 'Russell Hybrids' (perennial lupine)
Paeonia lactiflora (peony)

Biennials

Digitalis purpurea cvs. (foxglove)†
Viola × wittrockianna (pansy)

Bulbs, corms, and tubers

Dahlia hybrids
Gladiolus × hortulanus cvs.
Lilium spp. and cvs. (lily)
Tulipa spp. and cvs. (tulip)

Annuals

Antirrhinum majus cvs. (snapdragon)*
Cosmos sulphureus (orange cosmos)
Tagetes spp. and cvs. (marigold)
Zinnia elegans cvs. (common zinnia)

---

* Perennial from zone 8 southward

** Perennial in zones 9 and 10

† Rare color

With such lists at hand, you are ready to select the plant material for your overall plan. A piece of tracing paper may be laid over the outline plan, which was carefully drawn to scale, and the notation of the plant names can be made on this rough sketch sheet. The most orderly and logical sequence is to begin with spring bloom and to place the names of the plants on the plan in the approximate positions they are to occupy. In this early stage of the design, the exact outline of the clumps need not be indicated, nor should the quantity of each group be considered. At this point, you are concerned only with color harmonies, the sequence of bloom, and height.

The selection of plants for early summer, mid and late summer, and autumn bloom is then made, and the names are noted on the plan. If it is not possible to indicate the interplanting of annuals because of lack of space, those names may be written outside the area of the border with an arrow pointing to the spot each kind will occupy.

After the color harmonies and the sequence of bloom have been determined, and the sketch plans and all final decisions have been made, the plant names should be placed on the final plan, the outline of each clump should be indicated, and notation should be made of the number of plants to be used in each group. The groups should be large enough to give an effective display and avoid spottiness. Low-growing plants, such as English daisy (*Bellis perennis*) and wild sweet William (*Phlox divaricata*), may be used in long edging drifts along the front of the border; the taller plants may be used in groups of 5 to 10, depending on the size of the garden. An occasional plant, such as old-fashioned bleeding heart (*Dicentra spectabilis*), should be used as an accent and planted alone, rather than in a group.

In general, the overall plan of the border should be to place lower-growing species toward the front and taller ones at the rear. You can create even more interest, while at the same time giving the border a feeling of greater depth, if occasionally a group of taller perennials is brought out into the middle, and groups of plants of medium height are brought toward the front of the border. The reverse, however, should not be attempted, as low perennials would definitely appear out of place in the middle of the border or those of medium height at the rear.

Herbaceous perennials may be propagated in various ways: by seed, cuttings, division of old clumps, layering, division of tubers and rhizomes, and in some relatively few cases where traditional methods are unsatisfactory, by tissue culture or even grafting. Some perennials may be propagated by several methods, some by only one method; but seed and division are the commonest practices. For detailed directions concerning seed sowing, division, and the various other methods of propagation, see Chapter 36. Purchasing enough plants to establish a large perennial garden can be quite expensive. The gardener who is familiar with the above-listed, relatively simple methods of increasing his or her perennials has a big advantage over the novice. Only one or two plants of each species need be purchased when the border is first established. During the year or two required for these to increase in size and be used for propagation, the gaps in the garden may be filled in with less expensive annuals.

PREPARATION OF THE SOIL

Since perennial beds and borders constitute a long-term or even permanent type of planting, the soil should be adequately prepared. Most herbaceous perennials attain their maximum perfection in a fertile, well-drained loam that is high in organic content, is slightly acidic to neutral in pH, and has been deeply and thoroughly prepared before planting.

Since many perennials are deep rooted, and as it is well to induce the more shallow-rooted types to develop roots downward, the soil should be prepared to a depth of at least 12 to 18 inches. Trenching and double-digging have long been the most approved traditional methods of soil preparation, but deep rototilling may work equally well, especially in light, sandy soils. Deep preparation is especially important in heavy clay soils. These should be lightened by the addition of sand, compost, and/or well-rotted manure. If the site is poorly drained—a circumstance that can be fatal to many favorite perennials—it should be remedied first, before any soil amendments are added and well before any planting takes place.

Light, sandy soils that drain excessively and require much summer watering can be improved both in water retention and nutrient level by the incorporation of compost and well-rotted manure and by the use of a summer mulch, such as shredded or roughly ground pine bark, buckwheat hulls, or well-rotted manure. For detailed information on mulching and soil preparation consult Chapters 32 and 37.

SOIL pH

A few kinds of perennials thrive only in soil that is slightly alkaline (pH 7.0 to 7.5), while most perform best in a somewhat acidic medium. Many kinds, however, show broad amplitude in this respect and seem indifferent to soil pH. As a general guide, a soil pH of 6.5 to 7.0 will suit the vast majority of garden perennials. In preparing the soil for perennial beds, samples from different garden areas should be tested for pH. If the results show a pH below 6.5, an application of lime should be made after the beds have been

prepared for planting. The lime should be sprinkled over the surface of the bed and then cultivated lightly into the soil. To meet the needs of those perennials that clearly do best in a slightly alkaline soil, a sufficient quantity of lime should be applied over the area where they are to be planted in order to bring the reaction to a pH of approximately 7.5.

PERENNIALS THAT GROW BEST IN A SLIGHTLY ALKALINE SOIL (pH 7.0–7.5)

Anemone × hybrida (Japanese anemone)
Clematis integrifolia and other spp.
  (herbaceous nonclimbing clematis)
Delphinium elatum
Dictamnus albus (gas plant)
Gypsophila paniculata (perennial baby's breath)

GENERAL MAINTENANCE

A garden of perennials requires consistent care and maintenance throughout the season. In the spring a general inspection of the garden should be made. Any plants that have been partially heaved out of the soil during the winter should be gently pressed back into place, and notations should be made of any plants that have failed to survive the winter. During this first spring reconnaisance, the condition of each individual group of plants should be carefully studied, their needs assessed, and the plans for spring work outlined. Some plants will require division, others will need to be replaced with younger, more vigorous stock, and plans must be made for the spring feeding (see the index for details on maintenance of fertility). It is also wise to make a few soil tests at this time to determine whether an application of lime is advisable. During the early spring, any remaining dead leaves should be turned under, stalks removed and composted, and the beds and borders edged, so that the garden looks neat and trim from the very beginning of the season.

An initial cultivation should be given as soon as the soil is dry enough to be workable, both to promote aeration and to kill off any weed seedlings or perennial weeds that survived the winter. Soil should not be cultivated when it is unworkably wet, especially if heavy with clay, as hard lumps will form that, when dry, are very difficult to break up and reincorporate. An excellent way to test the workability of the soil is to take a small amount and squeeze it tightly in your hand. If it crumbles when it falls to the ground, it is in good condition to be cultivated. If, however, it remains in a firm, compact lump, it contains too much moisture and should not be worked until it has become drier. Cultivation maintains the upper soil stratum in a loose, friable state, and thus facilitates the penetration of water and air and eases the removal of weeds. Every effort should be made to keep from walking among the plantings as this soon leads to damaging soil compaction. In a large garden, paths or stepping-stones promote easy access. A summer mulch obviates the need for repeated cultivation and deters most weeds. Any weeding should be performed as much as possible from existing lawns, paths, and stepping-stones. Use of a plank will prevent serious soil compaction when it is necessary to enter a planted area. A small weeder with three flexible prongs is one of the most convenient and efficient tools for cultivating perennial beds.

Carefully chosen, well-planted, adequately tended perennials grown with appropriate exposure to sunlight and in fertile, friable, moist soil of correct pH should perform optimally and be relatively free of pests and diseases. If insects or fungi do strike, and especially when a certain kind of perennial proves chronically subject to serious depredation, it is best to make a substitution of kind rather than embark on endless intervention with sprays, dusts, and other biocides. (For control of pests and diseases see Chapters 34 and 37.) If all or most kinds of perennials aredisappointing in performance, the underlying cause may be a general soil-nutrient deficiency, wrong pH, too much or too little soil moisture, or insufficient sun. The soil should be tested and appropriate amendments added, or moisture withheld or added. It may be necessary to prune or remove one or more nearby trees, or to relocate the garden elsewhere.

Throughout the season, all flower stalks should be cut down once the blooms have faded. Not only will this improve the overall appearance of the garden, but depending on the species, it will also help to conserve the vigor of the plants, as the production of seed can be the most energy-intensive function the plant performs, yet one that contributes little or nothing to its role as an ornamental in the garden. There are other advantages to be gained from deadheading: with some plants, such as cultivars of yarrow (*Achillea millefolium*) and fringed bleeding heart (*Dicentra eximia*), the blooming period can be considerably extended if seed is prevented from forming; with others, such as delphinium (*Delphinium elatum*) and milky bellflower (*Campanula lactiflora*), it is possible to induce a second round of flowering. In still others, as with rose campion (*Lychnis coronaria*) and European columbine (*Aquilegia vulgaris*), it will prevent unwanted self-seeding. In most cases, however—with *Hemerocallis* hybrids being an outstanding example—the removal of spent flowers each day adds immeasurably to the overall appearance of the planting and promotes daily intimate enjoyment of the garden.

Included also in general maintenance are such tasks as watering, staking, feeding, and the occasional division and replanting of established plants.

Watering

For their best development, most perennials require an adequate but not overabundant supply of moisture throughout the season. A few perennials thrive on very dry soils, and there are others that grow optimally under extremely moist conditions, but the vast majority flourish with a moderate and fairly constant supply of moisture. In most areas of the country, these requirements are met by normal rainfall. If, however, rainfall fails temporarily to meet the garden's needs, it is time to turn to artificial watering. Frequent, light waterings are of little value and may do far more harm than good as they tend to encourage roots toward the surface. A very thorough watering should be given once every 5 to 10 days, depending on weather conditions, making sure that about 1 inch has been delivered (as can be determined by placing an empty cat-food tin under the sprinkler). Late afternoon and early evening are the most favorable times for watering as there is less evaporation and the soil retains the moisture more readily then. There are a number of excellent sprinkling attachments for an ordinary garden hose that make it possible to cover a considerable area simultaneously. For more information on watering, see Chapter 37. If the garden is large, it is possible to water a section each evening and thus an entire area can be watered with comparatively little effort.

Staking

Staking appears to be such a very simple operation, yet it is seldom done in an entirely satisfactory manner. Staking is necessary for two purposes: either to provide support for weak and floppy stems or to protect tall flower spikes from being bent and broken by winds and heavy storms. Whatever the purpose, staking should be done in such a way that the natural form and beauty of the plant are preserved and the stakes themselves are as inconspicuous as possible.

Some perennials produce a quantity of small stems that have a tendency to flop and consequently need some support. In this group are sneezewort (*Achillea ptarmica*), coreopsis (*Coreopsis grandiflora*), balloon flower (*Platycodon grandiflorus*), and spiked speedwell (*Veronica spicata*). For such plants, twiggy tree or shrub branches may be used very successfully. Birch and alder are particularly good for this purpose. While the plants are still young, the twigs may be stuck into the ground close beside them, and as the foliage develops, the twigs will be entirely concealed. Such twigs offer a very good framework for the support of weak stems.

Plants such as delphinium, New England aster (*Aster novae-angliae*), and Maximilian sunflower (*Helianthus maximiliani*), among many others, require tall, strong stakes. Bamboo stakes can be obtained in a variety of sizes and work very well. Those stained a soft green become almost invisible after they are in place. Strong wire stakes are also satisfactory and can be purchased in various styles and sizes. The type with spiral turns is particularly valuable for supporting individual flower stalks. Wood stakes are often used, and if painted a dull green, they are reasonably unobtrusive in appearance. However, they lack the suppleness of bamboo and wire and may have a tendency to snap off. It is wise to keep a variety of stakes on hand to be prepared for every need. Some plants require stout stakes for adequate support, while for others more slender ones suffice.

When staking large clumps, it is advisable to use more than one stake. When tall flower stalks are to be staked, they should be tied to the stake at several points. The wired tape should first be wound firmly about the stake and then about the stalk, being brought back and tied to the stake rather loosely. A flower stalk should never be tied tightly to a stake lest the beauty and grace of the plant be impaired. When a large clump is to be staked, the tape may first be attached to one of the stakes and then woven through the clump, being wound about each individual stalk until it reaches the far side of the clump, where it is attached to the opposite stake. Clumps of peonies may be supported by special wire hoops that may be placed about the entire plant, the legs resting on the soil. For beds of peonies, tall chrysanthemums, or other moderately tall, leafy, clump-forming perennials, a section of coarse 4- to 6-inch mesh wire fencing can be laid horizontally and stapled atop 3-foot stakes already hammered in around the periphery of the bed. With this structure in place in early spring, the shoots rapidly grow through the mesh and hide it while they are supported the rest of the season.

The material to be used in tying must be chosen carefully. Stems that are hollow and brittle must be tied with some very soft material that will not cut or bruise the stalk. Various types of plastic tape are available that are excellent for this purpose. These tapes are an inconspicuous green, are soft in texture, strong and durable, and have much to recommend them. Equally useful are strips of polyethylene plastic cut from ordinary plastic bags or cross-sectional strips cut from discarded pantyhose.

Enhancing Soil Fertility

To maintain the perennial border at its best from year to year, nutrient levels should be kept at a reasonably high level. Depending on the results of soil tests, an early springtime application of supplemental fertilizer, such as well-rotted manure spread as a 2-inch topdressing, can be beneficial for most perennials. Those species with high nutrient uptake, such as monkshood (*Aconitum* spp.), delphinium, and peony (*Paeonia lactiflora*), benefit from a second application in early summer.

Failing a supply of manure, a complete commercial fertilizer with an analysis of 5-10-5, 4-12-4, or 4-8-6 may be applied at the rate of 1½ to 3 ounces per square yard or 1 to 2 pounds per 100 square feet; use the lower amounts for sandy, porous soils, to which a second similarly reduced application may be made four to six weeks later.

Applying excessive amounts of synthetic, highly soluble fertilizer is not only wasteful but (as much of the excess leaches away, especially in sandy soils) may contribute to nitrate pollution of streams, ponds, and groundwater. If not applied evenly and raked in, pockets of concentrated fertilizer can actually harm or kill the very plants to be benefited. By contrast, a springtime topdressing of well-rotted manure will slowly release nutrients well into the growing season in addition to conserving soil moisture and deterring weeds.

During periods of prolonged rain it may be necessary to supply additional amounts of nitrate, as the available supply in the soil can be rapidly leached out under such conditions. A soil test will tell. If restoration is indicated, it may be achieved quickly by applying sodium nitrate or ammonium sulfate, or for more lasting results, by renewing the topdressing of manure.

Division and Replanting

At some point, perhaps every five or six years, it is usually advisable to lift all plants and rearrange the perennial garden entirely. Groups of plants become too crowded, many of the original clumps require division, and the fertility of deep soil layers requires restoration by incorporation of compost or well-rotted manure. If the garden is large, successive portions may be renovated year by year. It is preferable to do this work in the autumn, not only because there is usually more leisure time to undertake such work but also because at the same time new bulbs may be planted and clumps of established bulbs (marked earlier in the season in case their tops die down in summer) may be divided.

Once all plant materials have been lifted, the bed should be deeply rototilled or forked and liberal quantities of manure or or compost added and worked in. Such long-lived plants as old-fashioned bleeding heart (*Dicentra spectabilis*), gas plant (*Dictamnus albus*), peony, and balloon flower, which do not readily transplant, may be worked around and left undisturbed during this process of garden rejuvenation without serious interference to the work. If possible, choose a period of calm, damp, overcast weather for the project. Otherwise, dug-up plants should be placed in the shade in pots or plastic bags or wrapped in wet burlap.

RENEWING PERENNIAL PLANTS

When applied to plants, the term *perennial* denotes "permanence." It cannot be assumed, however, that once perennial plants have become established they will bloom on year after year without further thought or care on the part of the gardener. A few of the exceedingly robust types, such as peony or gas plant, might measure up to such an expectation, but the vast majority of our more desirable perennials do require a reasonable amount of care if they are to grow well and provide an abundance of bloom.

Some perennials are comparatively short lived, and new plants should be grown to replace those that have served their period of usefulness in the garden. In this group are the beautiful hybrid columbines, which have a tendency to die out after several years of luxuriant bloom; the stately lupines; the glorious hybrid delphiniums, which often fail to carry on over a period of many years unless conditions are extremely favorable for their growth; blue flax (*Linum perenne*), Italian alkanet (*Anchusa azurea*), primrose (*Primula* spp.), and many others. As some of our most choice perennials are to be found in this group, it is well to recognize the fact that these plants are more or less transient in the garden and that new specimens should be propagated at intervals of every few years.

Other perennials will thrive well for a year or two after they are planted, then may deteriorate rapidly unless the clumps are divided. In this group are hardy mum (*Chrysanthemum* × *morifolium* cvs.), obedient plant (*Physostegia virginiana*), New England aster (*Aster novae-angliae*), New York aster (*A. novi-belgii*), bearded iris (*Iris* hybrids), and summer phlox (*Phlox paniculata*). Hardy mums should be lifted and divided each year, or new plants should be started from cuttings, as the old clumps usually produce inferior blooms. Obedient plant should also be lifted and divided annually, not only for the sake of better bloom but also to prevent it from encroaching on its neighbors and becoming a pest. Hardy asters should be lifted and divided every two or three years. Bearded iris should be divided every three or four years, and summer phlox every five or six years.

There are a few perennials that will thrive for many years without being divided and replanted; in fact, in some cases

A large clump of daylilies dug in late summer and divided into fans, each a single shoot with roots. Fans are planted and become established in the remainder of the season.

such plants are harmed by being disturbed. In this group are old-fashioned bleeding heart, peony, Oriental poppy (*Papaver orientale*), gas plant, and balloon flower.

In maintaining a perennial garden, it is good to know the requirements of each individual group and to meet these needs as adequately as possible. But it must be remembered that no plant is immortal; perennials of all kinds eventually die. Hence the wisdom of maintaining a small area as a nursery for perennials: a place for seedlings, divisions, and cuttings to grow on and serve as a reserve of backup plants in case of some unforeseen failure, or to offer to friends, perhaps in exchange for some other long-sought kind. (See Chapter 36 for the most reliable propagation methods for perennials.)

PERENNIALS OF SPECIAL MERIT

Each of these following perennials is extraordinary in one or more respects, whether it be floral beauty, foliar boldness, architectural intricacy, textural refinement, or a combination of these or other memorable traits. Some are low-maintenance perennials, but most require some degree of regular care—repaid with a special contribution to garden quality.

ACONITUM × BICOLOR
(Hybrid aconite)

Zones 5–8

Derived from *A. carmichaelii* and *A. napellus*, hybrid aconite forms clumps of erect stems, 3 to 4 feet tall, and bears clusters of blue-and-white flowers in late summer. The individual blooms are hooded or helmet shaped. Like most aconites, this kind grows best in partial or light shade and requires consistently moist soil of at least average fertility. Once planted, aconites of any sort should be left undisturbed. All parts are poisonous to eat. Several cultivars of this hybrid have flower colors ranging from all white to deep blue-violet.

ACONITUM CARMICHAELII
(Azure aconite)

Zones 4–8

Azure aconite reaches 2½ to 3½ feet and bears pale blue flowers in long wand-like clusters in late summer or early fall. Tall aconite (*A. carmichaelii* var. *wilsonii*) may exceed 6 feet and produces deep purple flowers in late fall. Both forms are often offered incorrectly as *A. fischeri*.

ACONITUM NAPELLUS
(Garden monkshood, helmet flower)

Zones 4–8

Growing to 3 or 4 feet tall and clothed with finely divided, deep green foliage, garden monkshood bears spikes of deep blue-violet flowers in late summer.

ANCHUSA AZUREA
(Italian alkanet)

Zones 4–8

A large, erect, bristly, hairy plant, 3 to 5 feet tall and at least half as wide, Italian alkanet has loose clusters of intensely blue flowers in early summer. Full sun and average, well-drained soil yield good results. Often surviving only a few years, Italian alkanet should be replaced often. It is difficult to transplant mature individuals but it is readily grown from seed. Of the several cultivars available, 'Dropmore' has gentian blue flowers; 'Little Gem', a compact form to 18 inches, bears deep blue flowers; and 'Loddon Royalist', 3 feet tall, has royal blue flowers.

ANEMONE × HYBRIDA
(Japanese anemone)

Zones 5–7

A clump-forming perennial, with three-parted leaves, Japanese anemone has open, white or pink, yellow-centered flowers, 2 to 3 inches across, on branched stems, 2 to 3 feet tall, borne in early fall. A good cut flower, it grows best in partial shade protected from strong wind and in moist, well-drained, humusy soil, ideally between pH 6.5 and 7.0; but it flowers creditably up to pH 7.5. Except to occasionally divide clumps, it is best to leave established plants undisturbed. The cultivar 'Honorine Jobert' is the best of single white-flowered forms; others have single or semidouble flowers ranging from white through pink to rose.

AQUILEGIA CAERULEA
(Rocky Mountain columbine)

Zones 4–8

The state flower of Colorado, Rocky Mountain columbine grows to about 2½ feet and bears clear blue flowers, each with a white cup and golden stamens. Often short lived in eastern gardens, it is easily grown from seed and does best in sandy, moderately fertile, slightly acidic soils in full sun or partial shade. Many single-colored cultivars, such as 'Candidissima' (pure white), and hybrid strains, such as 'Music Hybrids' (compact growth and loose, open flowers), have been developed. Foliage is susceptible to leaf miner.

As with all columbines, the removal of faded blooms will induce the formation of additional flowers along the same stems, extending the flowering period for a month or more. Columbines are especially effective when grown in combination with lupines (*Lupinus* spp.), blue flax (*Linum perenne*), catmint (*Nepeta* × *faassenii*) and meadow rue (*Thalictrum* spp.)—the groupings generating exquisite color harmonies. Flowering begins in midspring. All columbines are easily transplanted and need no special winter protection except in the most severe climates, where dry leaves or salt hay may serve.

AQUILEGIA CANADENSIS
(Wild columbine, rock columbine)

Zones 4–8

Slender, 1 to 1½ feet tall, with nodding red and yellow flowers in mid to late spring, wild columbine is a denizen of dry, rocky, partly shaded ledges and banks with neutral soil. It seldom does well in the usual garden setting. Instead, it is best grown in a woodland border or shaded portion of the rock garden, protected from competition.

AQUILEGIA CHRYSANTHA
(Golden columbine)

Zones 3–8

Golden columbine grows to 3 feet or more, has leaf miner–resistant foliage, and bears long-spurred yellow flowers, often tinged with pink, in mid to late spring. Several cultivars feature double flowers, and numerous hybrids with other species (these often erroneously named *A. longissima*) are distinguished by long spurs. It is best grown in the partial shade of a woodland border in sandy, slightly acidic soil.

AQUILEGIA × HYBRIDA
(Hybrid columbine)

Zones 4–7

Hybrid columbine includes a varied assemblage of types with diverse parentage. All the hybrid columbines are characterized by pendent, long-spurred flowers of various colors, in mid to late spring, borne on 1- to 3-foot stems above three-parted gray green leaves. Since it is characteristically short lived, hybrid columbine is best interplanted every year or two with new material grown from purchased seed, rather be allowed to self-sow, as the latter tend to be dominated by pastel monotones instead of the vibrant color combinations available in named cultivars. It grows best in full sun or partial shade on sandy-humusy, well-drained soil. Leaf miner commonly afflicts the foliage after flowering but causes no substantial harm.

Among the most popular cultivars are the following.

'McKana Giant' hybrids: 3 feet tall; flowers in various bitone combinations of red, pink, yellow, blue, purple, and white.

'Nora Barlow': 2 to 2½ feet tall; flowers double, pink-and-red, tinged with green.

'Biedermeyer Strain': stiffly upright; about 1 foot tall; flowers upward facing, short spurred, purple, pink, or white.

AQUILEGIA VULGARIS
(European columbine)

Zones 4–8

Clump forming, European columbine grows 1½- to 2-feet-tall, This species is distinguished by its generous production of nodding, short-spurred, usually single-colored flowers of purple, blue, red, pink, or white, which open in late spring. It readily self-sows, sometimes to the point of nuisance. A parent of many strains grouped under *A. × hybrida*.

ARTEMISIA LACTIFLORA
(White mugwort, ghost plant)

Zones 4–8

A strongly erect, clump-forming perennial, 6 feet tall, white mugwort has large, diffusely branched sprays of multitudes of tiny cream-colored flower heads in late summer. The soft tone of the flowers is a pleasant foil for blossoms of a more brilliant tone, such as dahlias, gladioluses, or mealycup sages. Full sun and adequate space (15 inches apart) are required, as is a moist, well-drained, fertile soil. Staking is usually not necessary.

ASCLEPIAS TUBEROSA
(Butterfly weed)

Zones 3–8

Butterfly weed is hardly a weed in any sense. This choice native milkweed produces several to many erect or ascending stems, 1½ to 3 feet tall, from the top of a deep, carrotlike root. It bears tight clusters of intensely orange flowers in midsummer. Essential to long-term

success are full sun and sandy, well-drained (even dryish), moderately fertile, slightly acidic soil. The deep taproot makes transplanting risky, but culture from seed is easy, if each seedling is grown in a separate container before being carefully transferred to a permanent location. In the cultivar 'Gay Butterflies', flower color ranges from red-orange to yellow. Plants in the garden should be marked, as late shoot emergence in spring may lead to inadvertant damage by tools.

ASTER × FRIKARTII
(Frikart aster)

Zones 5–6 (8)

A many-stemmed, much-branched, clump-forming perennial, 2 to 2½ feet tall and as wide, Frikart aster has violet blue, yellow-centered flowers which are borne in late summer and early fall. Average, well-drained, loamy soil in full sun yields ideal results, but in zone 5 winter mulch is advisable. The best known cultivar is the easily grown 'Wonder of Stafa' ('Wunder von Staffa'), which can reach 4 feet tall, with profusely borne lavender blue flowers from mid to late summer; This cultivar blooms the first year and is hardy to zone 4.

ASTER NOVAE-ANGLIAE
(New England aster)

Zones 2–8

New England aster, strongly erect, clump forming, and hardy, reaches 3 to 6 feet tall. Its upper stems branch in midsummer and bear clusters of deep purple, yellow-centered flowers from late summer to early fall. Full sun and moist, loamy soil ensure ample bloom. Staking is usually necessary. Scores of cultivars exist, most of them color variants, ranging from lavender-purple through red and pink to white. Best known are 'Alma Potschke', compact with salmon red flowers, and 'September Ruby', tall with rose pink flowers.

ASTER NOVI-BELGII
(New York aster, Michaelmas daisy)

Zones 2–8

Variable in habit and sometimes exceeding 6 feet, New York aster has spreading rhizomatous roots and diffusely branched clusters of violet blue, yellow-centered flower heads from late summer well into fall. Average, loamy soils in full sun are best. Among the several hundred cultivars may be seen wide variations in height (8 inches to 8 feet), flower color (claret and red through pink and white), and amplitude (singles to full doubles). Among the best known are 'Crimson Brocade', about 3 feet tall with deep red, semidouble flowers, and 'Professor Kippenburg', just a little more than 1 foot tall with lavender blue flowers.

ASTILBE × ARENDSII
(Astilbe, False spiraea)

Zones 5–8

The false spiraeas includes numerous hybrids by the German breeder Georg Arends and derive from several species. There are at least 60 named, commercially available cultivars of false spiraea. They range from 1½ to 4 feet, rising from a basal clump of compound leaves, which are often coppery when young. It produces erect, much-branched clusters and bears masses of tiny flowers from late spring into summer. Flower color is usually pinkish purple or rose lavender, but it ranges from deep red to white. Partial shade and sandy-humusy, moderately fertile, acidic soil (pH 5 to 6) yield best results. A summer mulch of compost or well-rotted manure augments flowering and helps avert fatal drought. Among the most popular cultivars are the following.

'Bridal Veil' ('Brautschleier'): 2½ feet tall; white flowers.
'Cattleya': 3½ feet tall; lilac pink flowers
'Deutschland': compact form; 2 feet tall; white flowers.
'Fanal', 2½ feet tall; dark foliage; deep red flowers.

CAMPANULA CARPATICA
(Carpathian harebell)

Zones 4–8

A low, leafy mound, 6 inches high, Carpathian harebell is overtopped by flower stalks twice as high. The blue or lilac blue bell-shaped flowers are borne singly, mostly in late spring and early summer and sparingly thereafter. Sun or partial shade and average, well-drained, loamy soil in the front of the perennial border are best. Protection from slugs and snails is often required (see Chapter 34). The cultivars 'Alba' and 'White Clips' bear white flowers, 'China Doll' lavender flowers, and 'Blue Clips' large blue flowers.

Carpathian harebell, like most bell-flowers, may be raised from seed, by cuttings made from young growth in spring, or by the division of old clumps. Seedlings raised to partial growth by autumn are carried over the winter in cold frames and transplanted to the garden in the spring.

CAMPANULA PERSICIFOLIA
(Peach-leaf bellflower)

Zones 4–8

Erect and little branched, the 2-to-3-foot-tall peach-leaf bellflower has narrow, glossy leaves. It bears an elongated cluster of blue-violet or white bell-shaped flowers in early summer and often reflowers later, especially if deadheaded. It is easily grown and long lived when provided a sunny location with well-drained soil of average fertility. Among the several dozen cultivars are the following.

'Alba': single white flowers.
'Fleur de Neige': fully double white flowers.

'Moerheimei': semidouble white flowers.
'Telham Beauty': 4 feet tall; exceptionally large, single porcelain blue flowers.

CAMPANULA ROTUNDIFOLIA
(Bluebell, harebell)

Zones 3–8

Bluebell, famous as the bluebells of Scotland, is in fact a highly variable species. It typically produces a low, compact mound of foliage from which slender flowering shoots rise 3 to 18 inches high, each bearing one to several pendent, bell-shaped flowers of deep blue or white from late spring to late summer. Of the popular cultivars, 'Alba' is consistently white flowered; 'Purple Gem' has deep purple flowers, and 'Olympica', a tall form, has conspicuously toothed, deep green foliage.

CHRYSANTHEMUM ×
MORIFOLIUM
(Hardy mum)*

Zones 5–8

The hardy mum, a very variable hybrid of uncertain origin, has many thousands of derivative cultivars specialized for the florist trade and greenhouse exhibition as well as those—the focus here—bred for garden culture. The hardy mum is clump forming; grows to 1 to 5 feet tall; and has thick, aromatic foliage. From late summer to hard frost, its stems are topped with clusters of yellow, orange, red, bronze, lavender, or white flower heads, single to fully double. The size and number of

* Sometimes listed as *Dendranthema × grandiflorum*

Chrysanthemum × morifolium ('Redcoat')

Well-rooted cuttings, sold as small pot-grown plants, should be purchased in the spring from a reliable nursery. After a selection of desirable cultivars has been obtained, it is possible to maintain or increase the stock by propagating new plants each spring. This may be done either by the division of old clumps or by cuttings taken from the young shoots as they start into growth in the spring (see Chapter 36 for more on propagation).

DELPHINIUM ELATUM
(Tall perennial delphinium)

Zones 4–7

The principal parent of a varied group of hybrids commonly but erroneously labeled *D. decorum*, tall perennial delphinium is characterized by erect stems up to 6 feet tall, growing from a woody crown, which are topped by elongated spikelike clusters of usually blue to purple or white flowers. The 1-inch flowers are borne primarily in late spring and early summer, but the plant often reflowers sporadically through the summer. Not easily grown, delphinium requires full sun (but suffers in high heat and humidity) in consistently moist, humusy, highly fertile, well-drained, slightly alkaline (pH 7.5) soil. Staking is usually essential, and protection from strong wind is advisable. Young growth is poisonous to eat.

Delphinium elatum
'New Century Hybrids'

flowers depend in part on the practice of repeatedly decapitating ("pinching") the stems as they grow. Best results are obtained in full sun on fertile, humusy, consistently moist but well-drained soils with pH 6.5. Supplementary applications of liquid manure every two weeks promote optimal flowering. It is easily transplanted but often short lived; hence the practice of wintering choice plants in cold frames. The numerous cultivars suitable for garden use fall into several categories based on flower form and growth habit.

Cushion mum: forms a dense, rounded clump, 1 to 1½ feet tall, 1½ to 2½ feet across; relatively small flower heads; often blooms as early as mid-summer.

Decorative type: taller and more diffuse in growth (usually requiring stakes for support); flower heads 1½ to 3 inches or more in diameter; usually blooms in very late summer and early fall.
Pompon type: dense, spherical flower heads.
Spoon type: with each floral ray ("petal") is spoon shaped.
Single or daisy-flowered type: the central yellow disc is surrounded by one to five rows of rays.

Whatever forms are chosen, hardy mums are indispensible end-of-the-season subjects in the sunny garden. Care should be taken to choose cultivars suited to both summer and winter conditions; few grow equally well in zone 5 and zone 8.

Even under ideal conditions, delphinium is pest and disease prone (see Chapter 34 for control). Supplemental topdressings to maintain high soil fertility (especially necessary for tall types) are made with liquid manure or synthetic fertilizer, as the usually favored well-rotted manure promotes some of the diseases that afflict delphinium. Disease entry is facilitated by the hollow stubs of cut stems, which can trap water and initiate crown rot; stems should be cut back to the crown.

Despite the many obstacles, delphinium offers the reward of uncommon distinction in its stately form and wide-open blooms of clear sky blue and other shades and can greatly complement a simultaneous display of roses. Of the hybrid strains that are readily available commercially (derived from *D. elatum* and at least four other species), the most desirable are the following.

'Belladonna' hybrids: 3 to 4 feet tall; flowers light blue, dark blue, purple, or white, held in loose spikes through much of the summer.
'Connecticut Yankee': about 2½ feet tall; flowers blue, purple, lavender, or white.
'Dwarf Pacific hybrids': 2 feet tall; flowers mostly in shades of blue; often grown as an annual; do not confuse with the delphiniumlike annual larkspur (*Consolida ambigua*).
'Pacific Giant' hybrids: 6 feet tall or more; flowers mostly double, in blue, purple, maroon, lavender, pink, or white.

Named 'Pacific Giant' cultivars of special merit include the following.

'Astolat': flowers lavender or pink with a black or gold bee*.
'Black Night'; flowers deep purple with a black bee*.
'Blue Bird': flowers medium blue with a white bee*.
'Blue Jay': flowers dark blue (no bee*).
'Galahad': flowers white (no bee*).
'Guinevere': flowers lavender and blue with a white bee*.
'Summer Skies': flowers soft blue with a white bee*.

Delphiniums are best grown from containered material grown by a reputable nursery or from seed obtained from a well-known seed house. Genetic instability makes the use of garden-grown seed unwise and usually disappointing.

* The bee is the central blotch.

The tendency to crown rot makes root division risky.

DICENTRA SPECTABILIS
(Old-fashioned bleeding heart)

Zones 4–7

Growing 2 to 3 feet tall and as wide, old-fashioned bleeding heart has an open habit and deeply cut blue-green foliage. It bears strings of hanging heart-shaped flowers of pink and white in mid to late spring. An old favorite of undiminished popularity, this species thrives in partly shaded sites with moist, fertile, well-drained soil. It makes a good accompaniment for tulips and other spring bulbs, but as the foliage yellows and vanishes by late summer, it is best grown through a permanent ground cover. It is also effective either as a solitary accent or in small groups. It is easily grown, but as the roots are rangy and brittle, it is hard to transplant when mature. In the cultivar 'Alba', the flowers are entirely white.

GYPSOPHILA PANICULATA
(Perennial baby's breath)

Zones 4–8

Diffusely branched, 2 to 3 feet tall and broad, perennial baby's breath has wiry, jointed stems, sparse foliage; and myriad small white flowers in the spring and early summer. Undemanding as to soil, it performs best on a well-drained, consistently moist, sandy medium that is slightly alkaline (pH 7.5). Soggy soil in the winter is fatal. It must have full sun to flower effectively and will reflower if cut back before going to seed. Of the many culti-

vars available, the following are especially suited to varying conditions.

'Bristol Fairy': flowers large, long lasting, double white.
'Double Snowflake': flowers double and single, all white.
'Perfecta': flowers larger than those of 'Bristol Fairy', double, white.
'Pink Fairy': 1½ to 2 feet tall, flowers double pink.

GYPSOPHILA REPENS
(Creeping baby's breath)

Zones 4–8

Mat forming, creeping baby's breath has trailing stems that produce erect flowering shoots, about 6 inches tall, each bearing loose open clusters of small, white flowers from late spring to early fall. A first-rate, trouble-free edging plant, it thrives in full sun with average, slightly alkaline, well-drained soil. In *G. repens* var. *rosea*, the flower buds are rose red, opening pink.

HEMEROCALLIS HYBRIDS
(Hybrid daylily)

Zones 2–10

The hybrid daylily, clump forming and long lived, has tuberous roots and dense tufts ("fans") of long, narrow leaves, from among which flowering scapes, 1 to 5 (mostly 1½ to 2½) feet tall, arise. There are five to nine (exceptionally, as many as 30) flowers per scape, opening serially, each lasting a single day. They bloom mostly in early to mid summer and range in color from cream through yellow, orange, pink, and red to deep brown-violet, with a number of bicolors. There is no blue or pure white hybrid daylily.

Developed originally from 11 species native to China and Japan, some 20,000 cultivars have been listed by the International Registration Authority and twice that number with the American Hemerocallis Society, the latter adding 1,000 new cultivars each year. Variation occurs mostly in the color, dimensions, and amplitude of floral components; in the height of the scape; and in the flowering period. Easily hybridized, daylilies now present a plethora of variants, few of which can be confidently identified if unlabeled.

Labeled or not, a selection of hybrid daylilies, if chosen according to flowering period, can reliably provide striking color and boldness in the border year after year from early summer to frost. Full sun brings the best results, especially in the North, if the soil is well drained and also augmented every year or two with compost or well-rotted manure. Excess nitrate, however, leads to rank foliage and poor flowering. Tetraploid forms (having double the normal number of chromosomes) often seem more robust and do bear larger flowers than the commoner, stauncher diploids.

HEUCHERA SANGUINEA
(Coralbells)

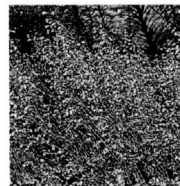

Zones 3–8

A low, rounded, semievergreen, clump-forming perennial, coralbells has rounded leaves and slender stems, 1½ to 2 feet tall, each bearing numerous small, hanging, coral red, bell-shaped flowers in late spring or early summer. This species adapts to various soils as long as they are well drained, especially in winter. Locations in full sun are best, but partial shade is tolerable. Removal of spent flower stalks to prevent seed set will extend the bloom, especially in the North. Spring planting is preferable, as plants set in the fall tend to be heaved out of the ground by frost. A light winter mulch helps to diminish the severity of freeze-thaw cycling. Of the many cultivars available, the following are especially desirable.

'Chatterbox': flowers deep rose pink.
'June Bride': flowers white; larger than average.
'Queen of Hearts': flowers bright coral.
'Rosamundi': flowers bright coral pink, profuse, borne over several months.
'White Cloud': flowers creamy white.

HOSTA *SPP. AND CVS.*
(Plantain lily)

Zones 4–8

Since the generic traits for the 40-some species and many cultivars of *Hosta* in cultivation are quite distinctive and because culture for them varies little, the following summary applies to all types. Hosta is valued for its ribbed, often wavy, sometimes bloomy foliage and for its lavender or white flowers, borne on erect or ascending scapes in late summer (or exceptionally, in fall). Plantain lily is an easily grown, low-maintenance, clump-forming plant that performs best in light or partial shade. Shade is essential in the South.

It does well in any ordinary garden soil, but thrives if the medium is consistently moist (not saturated) and well supplied with organic matter. To allow for the spread of the large, overlapping leaves, spacing of 2 to 4 feet between plants is advisable, depending on kind. As there is considerable variation in the names of the botanical varieties and horticultural cultivars in the literature, alternative names or synonyms are given here, if known.

Hosta fortunei
(Common plantain lily)

H. fortunei includes a rather varied group of hybrid plantain lilies, developed

in Europe. Material offered in the United States forms clumps about 30 inches across, with oval, pale green leaves, about 1 foot long. The 2½- to 3-foot scapes bear pale purple flowers in late summer. A number of foliar variants are popular.

'Albo-marginata' ('Marginato-alba'): leaves 1 foot long or more, irregularly edged in white (material sold under this name is often *H. crispula*, which is superficially similar).
'Albo-picta', syn. *H. fortunei* var. *albopicta*: young leaves pale yellow edged green, aging to all green.
'Aurea': young leaves cream, aging to green.
'Aureo-marginata', syn. *H. fortunei* var. *rugosa*: leaves edged yellow to cream.
'Gold Standard': leaves pale yellow-green, aging to creamy yellow, with green border.

Hosta plantaginea
(August lily, fragrant plantain lily)

A robust, rounded plant 1½ feet tall and 2½ feet across, August lily has shiny pale green foliage and bears white, sweetly fragrant, horizontally held, trumpet-shaped flowers on 1½- to 2½-foot-tall scapes, in late summer. It performs as well in full shade as in partially shaded sites throughout its range of cultivation. Two hybrid cultivars are especially favored.

'Honeybells': large lilac lavender flowers on 3-foot scapes.
'Royal Standard': especially fragrant white flowers on 2-foot scapes.

Hosta sieboldiana
(Siebold plantain lily)

The Siebold plantain lily has very large, puckered leaves, up to 15 inches long, and forms a bold mound, 2 to 3 feet high and up to 4 feet across. It produces low scapes of pale lilac or white flowers, which are often partly hidden in the foliage. Especially effective is the cultivar 'Frances Williams' which has blue-green leaves edged in yellow and white flowers.

Hosta undulata
(Wavy-leaf plantain lily)

H. undulata is varied group of clones, all characterized by more or less wavy-edged,

Wavy-leaf plantain lily *Hosta undulata*

somewhat twisted leaves that are variously variegated, mostly with green margins surrounding the cream midportion. It forms moundlike clumps about 1 foot high and up to 1½ feet across. In midsummer, the scapes rise to about 15 inches, bearing numerous 2-inch funnel-shaped flowers of pale lavender. Among the numerous cultivars are the following.

'Albo-marginata', syn. *H. undulata* var. *albo-marginata*: leaves flat or only slightly wavy, green with a cream border.

'Erronema', syn. *H. undulata* var. *erronema*: leaves all green, thrives in deep shade.

'Univittata', syn. *H. undulata* var. *univittata*: leaves have distinctively broad but variable stripe like central cream zone.

IRIS

The genus *Iris* includes a large assemblage of diverse species, some of which have been intensively hybridized. Irises have been important garden flowers for many centuries, and with their grace, delicacy of form, and luminous colors, they impart a radiance to the garden that is hardly equaled by any other flower.

In medieval times, the iris was so beloved by the people of France that it was given a special distinction and became the symbol of the royal house and hence of the entire realm. It appears in many illuminated manuscripts; and in the heraldy, architecture, and jewelry of the early Renaissance in France it was affectionately called *fleur-de-lis* ("flower of the lily").

Not only are irises valued today for the rare quality they contribute to a planting composition but they are also greatly prized for their decorative qualities as cut flowers.

During the last several decades, remarkable progress has been made in breeding new and superbly beautiful iris hybrids. The color range has been extended from purple, blue, yellow, and white to include dramatically lovely shades of pink, many subtle and muted tones of rose, and tawny sunset reds and violets as well as exquisite blends and combinations.

Each year, new cultivars of *Iris* are introduced. Medals and certificates of merit are awarded by the American Iris Society to forms considered worthy of these coveted honors. Thus, over the years, a great number of cultivars of exceptional merit, vigorous in growth, and indescribably beautiful in floral form and color have gradually replaced the older types. When new varieties are first introduced they are often very high in price, but within a few years, when stock has become more plentiful, they become available at a more modest cost that is well within the means of the interested gardener.

There are many species, groups, and subgroups of *Iris,* each endowed with a special charm. Some are stately and majestic, others diminutive; some prefer dry situations, others are at their best when grown by the waterside; some grace the spring garden with their bloom, others bring dramatic beauty to the garden in midsummer, and the lesser-known fall-blooming irises are often in flower until late in the autumn.

With careful selection and planning, many months of iris bloom may be obtained in the garden. This succession of bloom can be achieved, however, only by planting various species and cultivars, representing the groups and subgroups discussed below. For example, the diminutive *I. reticulata* and *I. danfordiae*, both appearing in very early spring, are heralds among the irises. They are followed in due succession by the Dutch iris and then the Dwarf Bearded, Intermediate Bearded, and Tall Bearded groups. During the summer months, the Siberian, Spuria, Louisiana, and Japanese groups carry on the gay pageantry of bloom; and the fall-blooming irises often continue to flower until cut down by heavy frosts.

Irises are classified into several groups, according to their root characteristics and flower forms. Most of the more commonly cultivated types have thickened fleshy underground stems known as rhizomes, while some types are cormous and a few have fibrous root systems.

Many of our garden irises, which originally came from central Europe, have a fuzzy zone or tongue on the lower flower petals. These comprise the Bearded group. Others completely lack the bearded zone and are part of the Beardless group. Still others have a channeled ridge instead of the beard and make up the Crested group.

Because so many new cultivars of dwarf, intermediate, and tall bearded iris are introduced and marketed each year, displacing older forms, any list soon becomes obsolete. Current lists of the most popular cultivars may be obtained from the American Iris Society.

Bearded Group
Zones 3–8

DWARF BEARDED IRIS
The Dwarf Bearded group includes miniature dwarf bearded and standard dwarf bearded irises as well as several species, such as *I. pumila*, and many hybrid forms. Some types are miniature in size, hardly more than 3 or 4 inches high, while others reach a height of 10 inches. Flowers range widely in color and vary in form from exquisitely delicate to the full and voluptuous blooms of the tall bearded types.

Dwarf irises are especially suited to well-drained pockets in the rock garden. They are also very effective when planted in drifts along a path or when used as an edging in a sunny flower border, particularly when combined with primroses, small narcissus, and species tulips. They make a stunning display alone or in combination with various low rock garden plants. Most dwarf irises bloom early in the spring, several weeks before the tall bearded types, and there are also several autumn-blooming cultivars.

The culture of dwarf bearded irises is similar to that of the Tall Bearded groups. Good drainage and a position in full sun are essential to their success. If conditions are favorable, they increase very rapidly, and a single plant will develop into a large clump within a few years. To prevent crowding, they should be divided and replanted about every three years in late summer.

INTERMEDIATE BEARDED IRIS
The Intermediate Bearded group includes miniature tall bearded and border bearded irises. Many of the cultivars in this group have been developed by hybridizing some of the Dwarf bearded with the tall bearded types. The flowers are lovely in form, possessing many of the characteristics of the Tall Bearded group, but are smaller and more delicate. Some have ruffled or frilled petals, giving them distinction no less than that of the midspring tulips. Less top heavy and more effective in groupings than the tall bearded types, these irises are rapidly becoming low-maintenance favorites in the spring-blooming perennial border. There are also several fall-blooming forms within this group.

TALL BEARDED IRIS

Tall bearded iris

The decorative landscape value of the tall bearded irises remains unchallenged through the years. It is in this ever-expanding group that we find many of our most magnificent garden irises, superb in form and indescribably beautiful in color. No garden is complete without them, and in the spring they bring dramatic beauty to many a planting composition.

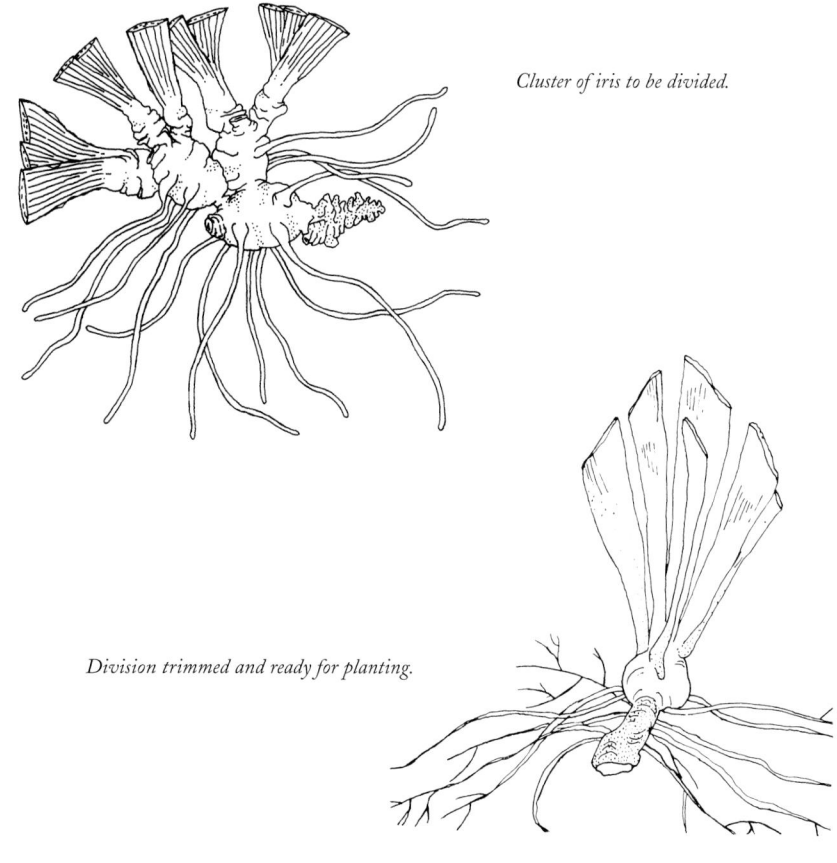

Cluster of iris to be divided.

Division trimmed and ready for planting.

Although tall bearded iris are easily grown in average garden soils in full sun, they do demand some care to be at their best. Staking is often necessary. Prompt removal of spent flowers helps preserve the high aesthetic quality of an iris planting throughout its relatively brief blooming period, but this entails designing the planting with ready access in mind. Because of their bold, distinctive majesty, tall bearded irises do not mix gracefully with most other perennials; yet, if grown massed in extensive iris-only beds, they can become subject to serious pests, such as rhizome borers. Hence their appeal to the ardent devotees of irisdom willing to minister to their weaknesses to bring forth floral glory.

AUTUMN-FLOWERING IRIS, REMONTANT IRIS

After years of patient effort on the part of plant hybridizers, a number of iris cultivars have been introduced that reflower in late summer or early fall. These remontant irises usually have two or more distinct flowering periods, blooming in the spring and, after growing vegetatively in summer, flowering again, sometimes right up to killing frosts. Although hardy in northern gardens, these reflowering irises are specially recommended for the South, where the fall-blooming season may extend over many months. The plants vary in height from 15 to 30 inches. In addition to hybrid cultivars, several *Iris* species also exhibit the reflowering trait.

Culture of Bearded Iris

Bearded irises of all groups adapt successfully to widely varying soil types, from sandy loam to heavy clay, as long as the soil is well drained. Although many irises do reasonably well on nutrient-deficient soils, prolific bloom requires soil of good fertility. To reflower reliably, remontant types may require supplemental fertilizing at the close of the spring bloom. Special beds or areas devoted to irises are best prepared before planting or while rhizomes are lifted for division. Well-rotted manure, compost, or humus should be generously applied and worked to a depth of at least 1 foot to encourage

deep root growth. Alternatively, a complete commercial fertilizer, proportioned at 5-10-5, applied at the rate of ½ pound per square yard, may be used, but it lacks the soil-conditioning, moisture-retaining effect of an organic supplement.

Although bearded irises tolerate a fairly wide range of soil pH, from midly acidic (pH 6.5) to quite alkaline (pH 8.0), they flower best on soil that is neutral (pH 7.0)—this despite their being traditionally classified as lime-loving plants. A soil pH test is advisable before preparing the planting area.

Dwarf bearded irises may be planted from 5 to 6 inches apart if the effect of a large clump is desired. The intermediate and tall types should be planted 15 to 18 inches apart. Crowding should be avoided, as clumps soon compete for space and nutrients at the price of reduced vigor, disappointing bloom, and increased susceptibility to disease. When planting bearded irises—preferably in late summer—each rhizome should be placed horizontally, with its top surface exposed (in the North) or covered with no more than ½ inch of soil (in the South); and the

roots, which should not be trimmed off, should be directed downward and outward in a well-prepared hole. Rhizomes that are improperly prepared and badly planted may rot, especially if set too deep, or be heaved out by frost, if roots have been trimmed or have been planted too late for additional roots to grow and provide anchorage.

The cultural requirements of the bearded iris are not exacting. The plants need an abundance of moisture during the blooming season but are able to endure long periods of drought at other periods. The best bloom is usually produced the second, third, and fourth years after planting. As soon as the rhizomes show evidence of becoming crowded, the clumps should be lifted and divided. Most iris plantings will continue to bloom well and remain in good condition for about five years. After this time, the rhizomes in the center of the clump usually become so crowded that the plants begin to detiorate.

Each spring, the soil about the clumps should be lightly cultivated, and if it seems advisable to improve the fertility of the soil, a thin layer of screened manure

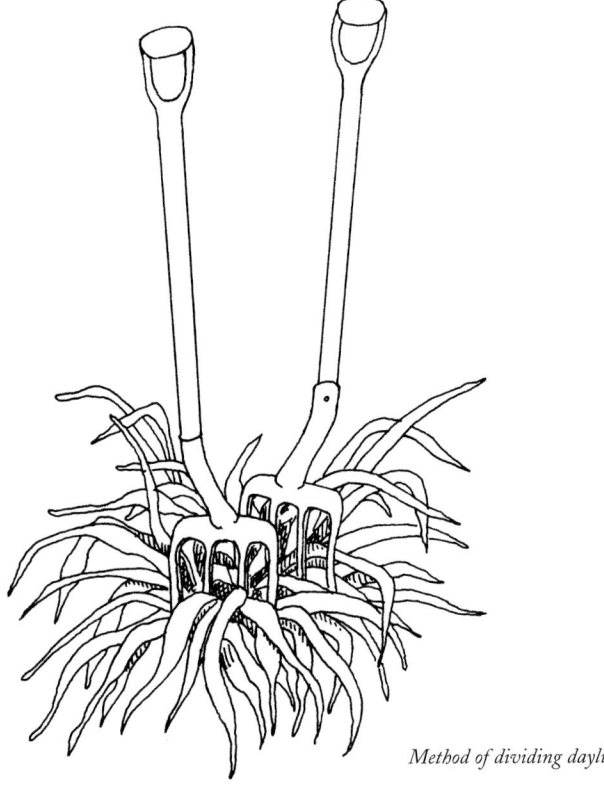

Method of dividing daylily clump.

or commercial fertilizer (about ¼ pound per square yard) should be sprinkled around the plants, but not on top of the rhizomes, and lightly worked in and watered. It is important to keep weeds under control; this especially applies to perennial grasses, which may invade from an adjacent lawn, as they soon develop tenacious mats that cannot be removed successfully unless the iris rhizomes are dug up.

In the fall, iris foliage often browns toward the tip. All foliage should be cut back to within 4 or 5 inches of the rhizome, and all dead or shriveled leaves should be removed. Winter protection is not necessary, except in areas where the winters are of extreme severity. Mulching iris rhizomes is generally inadvisable. In regions with particularly severe, often snowless winters (colder than zone 4), a covering of evergreen boughs will help, especially where soils are heavy with clay, by moderating the heaving damage that can occur in the freeze-thaw cycles of early spring.

Throughout the season, the gardener should be contantly alert for signs of insect infestation or disease. Iris borers are a serious problem in some areas and should be controlled as soon as they are noticed (see Chapter 34).

Beardless Iris

Less coherent than the Bearded groups, beardless irises are actually a series of distinct species and their derivative cultivars.

IRIS ENSATA *(Japanese iris)*
Zones 5–8

Often listed incorrectly as *I. kaempferi*, Japanese iris has become increasingly popular because of its great beauty and distinctive dignity. The flowers are characteristically flat and broad—as much as 6 inches across—the standards and falls being horizontal rather than ascending and descending. The flowers possess colors predominantly in the red-purple, purple, lavender, and blue sector of the color scale. Some are a mahogany red and a few have a gray background tone with deep purple, violet, or wine red markings. The leaves are narrow and reedlike; and the blooms, with their broad, crepelike

Japanese iris (*Iris ensata*)

petals, are borne on tall, erect stems that attain a height of 2½ to 5 feet. With the exception of the reflowering fall-blooming bearded varieties, they are among the last of the irises to flower, blooming in early to mid summer.

Japanese iris requires full sun for optimal flowering and an abundance of moisture during its flowering season. It is then able to withstand considerable drought, although it should never be allowed to dry out completely. During the winter months, the soil should not be soggy or puddly. It is almost the universal custom in Japan to flood iris plantings when the plants are in bud and in bloom, but during the balance of the year, water is withdrawn and the soil is kept comparatively dry. Japanese iris should never be planted in a location where the water table rises to the surface of the ground during the winter months.

Japanese iris grows best in a rich, highly fertile soil, well supplied with organic matter and definitely acidic (pH 6.5 or lower). In preparing the soil, liberal quantities of leaf mold (preferably oak), peat moss, and well-rotted cow manure (if obtainable) should be used. Lime should never be used where Japanese iris is growing.

As with bearded irises, old clumps of Japanese irises may be dug and divided, the ideal time being late summer or very early fall. If the divisions are made at this season, the young plants will reestablish themselves quickly and may provide some bloom the following summer. Clumps may also be divided early in the spring, but the results are not as satisfactory, because many of the divisions may fail to grow and only a small percentage will flower the following year. An entire clump may be lifted and divided, being pried apart with two strong spading forks until it is sufficiently loosened to fall into many natural divisions. Large pieces may also be removed from established clumps without lifting them. It requires a stout spading fork with considerable pressure behind it to accomplish this feat. The rhizomes should not be allowed to dry out before planting. If immediate effect is desired in the garden, the divisions should consist of three fans of leaves. If, however, rapid increase of stock is desired, single fans may be planted. The foliage should be cut back to about 6 inches.

Japanese iris may also be propagated by seed. If the seed is sown outdoors in the autumn as soon as it is ripe, it will germinate in the spring and will bloom in two to three years. The various cultivars do not, however, come true from seed.

The rhizome of the Japanese iris is very slender, with many fibrous roots. At the time divisions are planted, these roots should be shortened to 5 or 6 inches. Since the new roots will develop from the base of the leaf fans, the crowns should be planted 2 inches below the surface of the soil to enable these new roots to gain anchorage. For mass plantings that will remain undisturbed for many years, plants should be spaced 1½ to 2 feet apart. If clumps of Japanese irises are to be used in herbaceous borders or in other similar locations, more immediate effect may be obtained if three, four, or five divisions are planted about 10 inches apart.

With the exception of newly planted divisions, the Japanese iris requires no winter protection. Young plants that have not had an opportunity to become established are liable to suffer severely from the effects of heaving, especially on heavy soils. It is, therefore, wise to protect them during the first winter. Oak leaves are excellent as a mulch, if they are held in place by a layer of twigs or evergreen boughs. Well-rotted stable manure may also be used. The Japanese iris is one of the very few members of the iris family for which a mulch of rotted manure can be used with impunity.

Among the several popular cultivars, the white-flowered 'Great White Heron' and the deep purple 'Summer Storm' are especially attractive. In areas with winter cold more severe than in zone 5, use Arctic iris *(I. setosa)*, which is hardy to zone 2 and has bluish violet flowers (2 to 3½ inches across) that resemble those of Japanese iris.

IRIS SIBIRICA *(Siberian iris)*
Zones 4–8

The Siberian iris is of great decorative value in the garden and is enchantingly lovely as a cut flower. Properly grown, it is lavish with its bloom, a well-established clump sometimes producing more than 50 flowers. The blooms are borne well above the narrow, swordlike leaves, each slender stalk bearing 5 to 10 graceful flowers on branching pedicels. Cultivars vary from 2 to 3 or even 4 feet in height and offer a wide range of colors.

For best results, Siberian iris must have full sun and a highly fertile, fairly moist, consistently well-drained soil. Before planting, the soil should be enriched with well-rotted manure, rich compost, or leaf

Siberian iris (*Iris sibirica* cv.)

mold. The plant is acid tolerant but does best in a soil near neutral (pH 7.0). Although Siberian iris responds best to fertile soil, it makes a remarkably good showing on rather poor soils. This is particularly true of some of the old cultivars such as 'Snow Queen', which will thrive under the most adverse conditions.

Old, oversize clumps should be lifted and divided in late summer, as with other irises. The rhizomes should be

Siberian iris (*Iris sibirica*) enhances an informal planting

planted 2 inches deep and set 15 to 18 inches apart. To achieve a clump effect as quickly as possible in the garden, a small section containing five to seven slender rhizomes should be selected for planting. If, however, rapid increase in stock is desired, smaller sections should be used. The Siberian iris has long, fibrous roots, and when planting the divisions, it is important to make the hole large enough so the roots will not be cramped. Long-established clumps are sometimes very difficult to divide, as their roots have often formed a very dense interlocking mass. Siberian iris may be propagated by seed but wide variation is found among the seedlings, and it is a method seldom employed except by hybridizers.

Siberian iris is among the easiest of perennials to grow and is almost certain to do well under average conditions. It does require ample moisture before and during the flowering period if maximum bloom is to be obtained, but beyond this, little care is needed. It is rarely attacked by pests or diseases, and the clumps may be left undisturbed for many years. No winter protection is necessary, except in very cold climates or in the case of young plants that have not become established. Under such conditions a light mulch of salt hay or some similar material will prove helpful.

A sampling of the most popular cultivars includes the following.

'Caesar's Brother': purple.
'Cambridge': pale blue.
'Dreaming Spires': lavender and royal blue.
'Ego': medium blue.
'Eric the Red': deep red.
'Sea Shadows': blue and turquoise.
'White Swirl': white with yellow.

IRIS HYBRID COMPLEX DERIVED FROM SEVERAL SOUTHEASTERN SPECIES
(Louisiana iris)
Zones 4–9

The beautiful Louisiana iris, derived from *I. brevicaulis, I. giganticaerulea, I. fulva,* and other species native to the swamps and bayous of the lower Mississippi River, has proved so extraordinarily hardy and adaptable that it is widely grown in all but the coldest sections of the country.

Crested iris *(Iris cristata* 'Abbey's violet')

Exceptional in color and form, many of these species and their hybrids are startling in their beauty. They range in height from 2 to 4 feet. Many of the flowers are flat in form, while others have flaring or hanging segments. In color the blooms range through velvety tones of deep garnet, rosy apricot, rose petal pink, deep pansy violet, pale lavender, and ivory white. They are very useful as cut flowers.

Thriving in sun or partial shade, members of this complex do best on acidic soil and must have moist ground during flowering. Before planting, the soil should be well and deeply prepared. Liberal quantities of coarse peat moss, leaf mold, unscreened compost, and rotted cow manure, if available, should be thoroughly worked into the soil to a depth of 12 inches or even 18 inches. Although the Louisiana iris can hardly be supplied with too much water during the growing season, care must be taken when it is being planted in a northern garden not to select a location where water would freeze about its roots during the winter, as this can prove fatal to the plant.

In addition to the species themselves, several cultivars are especially attractive.

'Gold Reserve': orange, veined red.
'May Roy': pink and purplish.
'Roll Call': violet-and-green.
'Sea Wisp': 4 feet tall; blue-and-yellow.

IRIS CRISTATA *(Crested iris)*
Zones 4–8

Native to moist, thinly wooded hillsides and streambanks from Virginia to Missouri and southward, crested iris succeeds best when cultivated under similar conditions. It is exquisite, though hardly more than 4 inches in height. The diminutive flowers, their lavender petals touched with crested gold, spread their bloom above the carpet of soft green leaves in late spring. Sun-splashed patches of crested iris along a woodland path hold joy for all who pass.

Although partial shade is best, crested iris does reasonably well in full sun as long as the soil remains moist. A gravelly, well-drained soil, rich in humus, is ideal, although crested iris will perform satisfactorily in almost any consistently well-drained soil of moderate fertility.

White crested iris *(Iris cristata* 'Alba')

This species is readily propagated by division of the small rhizomes. This may be accomplished anytime during the growing season but, in contrast to most irises, very early spring is preferable. The rhizomes should be barely covered with soil and planted 5 to 6 inches apart. When the clumps become too crowded, the plants should be lifted and divided. Careful weeding must be done throughout the season to prevent alien growth from crowding out the small, delicate rhizomes.

In its native haunts, crested iris receives an annual cover of leaf litter, and if grown where leaf drop does not provide such a covering, it has a tendency to grow itself out of the ground. In such locations, it should be given an annual topdressing of screened compost or leaf mold.

As slugs have a special fondness for members of the iris family and are capable of destroying large clumps of this species in an incredibly short time, one should be on the alert to detect the first signs of infestation. Fortunately, with simple precautions, damage from slugs can usually be prevented (see Chapter 34).

The cultivar 'Alba' is a beautiful white-flowering iris.

IRIS TECTORUM *(Japanese roof iris)*
Zones 5–8

I. tectorum is the roof iris of China and Japan, so famed in song and story. The flowers are a clear blue and are borne on stalks, 12 to 15 inches tall, above the broad, heavily ribbed leaves that, in zone 8, are evergreen.

Japanese roof iris grows best in full sun or partial shade on alkaline soils (pH 7.0 to 7.5, or even higher), but it adapts reasonably well to acidic, sandy soil as

Japanese roof iris *(Iris tectorum* 'Alba')

long as it is humusy and unfailingly well drained. Clumps are best divided just after flowering.

Although seemingly temperamental, roof iris thrives where summers are hot, winters moderately cold, and rainfall fairly well distributed through the year. One of the most shallow-rooting of all irises, it requires frequent enrichment of the soil. It is most effective in patches or drifts, the rhizomes spaced 6 to 8 inches apart; but it often wanes unless lifted and divided every other year. Where the winters are severe, it should be given the protection of leaves and brush.

The cultivar 'Alba' is considered one of the most exquisite of flowers. Anyone who has once seen it will never forget the chaste perfection of its bloom, which resembles a magnified snowflake. The flowers are fragile and suffer from wind and rain, but during periods of unfavorable weather they may be cut in the bud and allowed to open in the house. The white form is somewhat less hardy than the blue type.

Bulbous (cormous) iris is discussed in Chapter 16.

LINUM PERENNE
(Perennial blue flax)

Zones 5–8

Blue flax, which reflects the blue of soft spring skies, is valued in the perennial border for its airy grace and long period of bloom. The fine foliage is a pale bluish green, and the lovely single flowers of soft azure blue are borne in great profusion on slender, graceful stems, 1 to 1½ feet tall. On days of brilliant sunshine, the petals fall before evening, but in cloudy weather they remain throughout the day.

A position in full sun and in light, sandy, well-drained loam of moderate fertility is ideal. This species roots shallowly in heavy, saturated soils, hence tends to be heaved in the freeze-thaw cycles of late winter and early spring. Light soils obviate the need for winter protection.

Easily grown from seed and flowering reliably the second year, perennial blue flax is readily transplanted in the spring. If flower stalks are cut back halfway just after flowering, secondary branches will

produce another round of bloom, thus greatly prolonging the display, often until late summer.

The cultivar 'Alba' has white flowers. The blue-flowered *L. perenne* ssp. *lewisii* is adapted to the alkaline soils of the West.

LUPINUS *'RUSSELL HYBRIDS'*
(Perennial lupine)

Zones 4–7

Few of the many species of *Lupinus* are suited to garden culture, but the 'Russell' hybrid strain makes a delightful show in areas where summers are relatively cool, such as coastal New England, parts of the Great Lakes region, and the Pacific Northwest. Rising 3 or 4 feet above a mound of attractive palmately compound leaves in late spring and early summer are densely flowering spikes of pealike flowers, ranging from purple and blue through red, pink, orange, and yellow to white. The flowers can be either single shades or bicolors.

Full sun in a somewhat sheltered position on a light, well-drained, but moist soil of good fertility and pH around 6.5 constitute ideal conditions. Lupines should be spaced about 1 foot apart. The soil around each plant should be topdressed with well-rotted manure or rich compost in the spring, both to supply additional nutrients and to conserve moisture. Long, hot summers or protracted winter cold shorten longevity. Lupine is easily grown from seed. Mature, well-established plants have long, rangy roots, which make transplanting risky.

LYTHRUM SALICARIA *CVS.*
(Garden loosestrife)

Zones 4–8

Because of their long season of bloom and their showy flower spikes, *Lythrum* cultivars are an asset in the perennial garden during the summer months. A dozen or more flower spikes often will be produced on a single plant, and they make a brilliant note of color in the midsummer garden, blooming from late June well into September. There are several varieties that reach a height of 3 to 4 feet, while some are more dwarf in form, not exceeding 1½ feet. Care should be taken to avoid the wild purple loosestrife found along streams and in other open, wet places, because this species (naturalized from Europe) self-sows so freely, dominating such habitats, that in some states its cultivation is prohibited. Check with your local cooperative extension office. Fortunately, the cultivars are not invasive, although they, too, are proscribed in certain states.

Garden loosestrife thrives in full sun but also does well in partial shade. Although any garden soil will yield good results, even in dry summers, the various cultivars reach perfection in moist to wet soil that is well supplied with organic matter. Large, oversize clumps are easily divided, either in early spring or in early fall. Tall forms should be spaced 2 to 3 feet apart, small ones 1½ to 2 feet apart.

Among the many cultivars, some derived from related species, the following are particularly attractive.

'Dropmore Purple': 4 feet tall; rich violet purple flowers.
'Firecandle': 3 feet tall; intense rosy flowers red.
'Happy': 1½ feet tall; deep pink flowers.
'Marden's Pink': 4 feet tall; clear pink flowers.
'Marden's Rose': 3 feet tall; bright rosy red flowers.
'Purple Spires': 4 feet tall; rose purple flowers.
'Robert': 2 feet tall; bright rosy red flowers.

PAEONIA LACTIFLORA *HYBRIDS*
(Hybrid peony)

P. lactiflora consists of the soft-stemmed or herbaceous peonies that die to the ground in the fall and grow anew from the long-lived root each spring. The tree peony (*P. suffruticosa*) is discussed on page 339. The peony has long been a favorite among gardeners, and it is one of the hardiest and most easily grown of any of the perennials. Once established, hybrid peonies are virtually immortal, flowering year after year. Indeed, some of the old-fashioned types are still blooming in gardens where they were planted more than 100 years ago.

In a small garden, peonies are often out of scale. The blooms are so large and the plants themselves require so much room that they should be used sparingly, if at all. However, in a large garden where quantity of bloom and mass effect are desired, peonies may play an important part in the planting composition. They are lovely when planted in groups along the front of a shrubbery border, or when used as specimen or accent plants. They may also be used very effectively as a low, herbaceous hedge. With the selection of early, mid, and late season varieties, six weeks of bloom may be enjoyed.

The hybrid peony does best in full sun but grows reasonably well in partial shade, especially in the South. It seems to thrive in almost any soil that is nearly neutral (pH 7.0) but luxuriates in well-drained, clay loam. The soil should be deeply prepared and well enriched at the time of planting. At no future time will it be possible to supply fertility so effectively, and the plant will derive benefit from it for years to come. A hole of generous proportions should be dug. Well-rotted manure or rich compost should be mixed with the topsoil and placed in the bottom of the hole and firmed well to prevent too much settling later on. Over this a few inches of good topsoil should be spread to prevent the roots of the plants from coming into direct contact with the manure before they have become established.

Hybrid peony should be planted in early to mid autumn. Spring planting is much more of a shock for this plant and is not recommended. Planting depth is critical; more failures are due to planting them too deeply than to any other cause. Each root division—containing at least three buds—should be placed in the hole so that the tip of the buds will be 1 to 2 inches below the surface of the soil. If planted too deeply, it may never bloom. Good topsoil should be filled in about the roots and firmed well, and the plant should be watered thoroughly immediately after planting. It is wise to allow the plant ample room for full development. Peonies should be spaced approximately 3 feet apart.

In successive years, an annual application of well-rotted manure, topdressed around the crown but not directly over it, augments soil nutrients and conserves moisture. Alternatively, two applications of high-phosphate fertilizer, such as 5-10-5, may be used, the first made in the spring when the new shoots are about 1 foot high and the second made after flowering is over. Apply approximately ¼ cup per clump, sprinkling it on the soil surface and working it in lightly with a small hand weeder. The ground should then be watered well.

It should be kept in mind that hybrid peony is slow to recover from transplanting, sometimes not flowering for several years thereafter. If at all possible, an established plants should be left undisturbed indefinitely.

In some cultivars with large, fully double flowers, the stems may bend to the ground under the weight of the bloom. For a few such plants, slender stakes, carefully set to avert root damage, may suffice. For a large bed, however, more support may be needed. Use a section of steel 6-inch mason's reinforcing mesh or wide-interval wire mesh fencing cut to the dimensions of the bed; spread it horizontally and staple it to the tops of 2 × 2-inch stakes that have been driven into the ground to stand about 2 feet high. Such a structure will allow the shoots to grow through and will provide complete support for the rest of the season. If painted flat black, the entire installation disappears from view and may be left in place indefinitely.

For general garden effect, peonies are not usually disbudded. However, if exhibition blooms are desired, all of the side buds on the flower stems should be removed, leaving only the large central bud.

When cutting blooms for indoor use, leave as much foliage on the plant as possible, since no new leaves will grow and their photosynthetic activity through the summer is essential for the next season's flowering. More for aesthetic than physiological reasons, it is best to remove all flowers as they fade and prevent formation of the follicular seed capsules.

After the foliage has died down in the autumn, the stems should be carefully cut off just below the ground level, raked up, bagged, and disposed of as a precaution against the spread of botrytis blight, a serious disease of peonies.

Ants on peony buds are a perfectly natural phenomenon and should not be a cause for alarm. They are merely seeking nectar produced on the buds. They neither harm the plant in any way nor do they affect the opening of the flower. For control of pests and diseases, see Chapter 34.

Peony Classification

The considerable variation in the flower form of hybrid peonies has led to a number of classifications, some quite elaborate and mainly of interest to specialists, but most garden cultivars fall into one of the following five classes.

Single: a ring of a few broad petals, the center filled with pollen-bearing stamens and seed-bearing carpels.

Japanese: the beginnings of doubling; outer ring or guard petals like those in the single but some filaments have become petaloid; presence of anthers.

Anemone: next step in doubling; no anthers; central petaloids narrow and short, distinct from the outer collar of true petals.

HYBRID PEONY CULTIVARS OF MERIT

Of the hundreds of hybrid peony cultivars on the market, those with fully double flowers are clearly preferred. The cultivars listed have been available for many years and, for the beginner, are proven candidates for garden use.

Double red
'Burma Ruby'
'Chocolate Soldier'
'Felix Crousse'
'Francis Ortigot'
'Longfellow'
'Mary Brand'

Double pink
'Auguste Dessert'
'Moonstone'
'President Roosevelt'
'Sarah Bernhardt'

Double white
'Festiva Maxima'
'Kelway's Glorious'

Japanese (semidouble) red
'Mikado'

Japanese (semidouble) pink
'Bowl of Beauty'
'Kathalo'
'Nippon Gold'

Japanese (semidouble) white
'Lotus Queen'
'Toro-no-maki'

Single red
'Nippon Beauty'
'Philippe Rivoire'
'President Lincoln'

Single white
'Krinkled White'
'LeJour'
'Mildred May'

Hybrid peony (*Paeonia lactiflora* 'Felix Crousse')

Semidouble: similar to the anemone but petaloids occur in all stages of transformation; formation is loose.

Rose (or double): fully double; all stamens and carpels nearly or completely transformed; more or less evenly arranged petaloids, not distinguishable from the surrounding guard petals.

PAEONIA SUFFRUTICOSA
(Tree peony)

Zones 7–9

Somewhat shrubby and far from tree-like, tree peonies usually mature around 3 feet high, with some forms rising to 5 or 6 feet. Long treasured in the gardens of China and Japan, tree peonies have come to the attention of American gardeners only in this century. Because they are often grown with hybrid peonies, although they have distinct cultural requirements, tree peonies are treated in this chapter rather than in Chapter 12.

Tree peonies have an ornamental value throughout the year and lend distinction to any garden. The deciduous foliage is deeply cut, soft in tone and texture, and very decorative; the shrublike, woody stems have a striking quality in the winter landscape picture, and the flowers are of superb beauty. The blooms exhibit a silky sheen that imparts both delicacy and elegance. Measuring 6 to 10 inches across, the flowers also vary in form in much the way hybrid peonies do: from single to semidouble to fully double. Colors range from red and pink to white and also include mahogany, maroon, lilac, purple, and yellow. Small, young plants usually bear only a few flowers, but mature specimens offer as many as 50.

Very tolerant of summer heat, tree peonies do well in full sun or partial shade on sandy-humusy, well-drained soil of slightly acidic pH (6.5 to 7.0). As their roots are deep and subsequent transplanting is inadvisable, site preparation should be thorough, down to about 2 feet. Planting may be done in either spring or fall, but only when the plants are dormant. Small, pot-grown plants are more easily established than larger balled-and-burlapped or bare-root specimens. Plants should be set deep, with the crowns about 4 inches below the surface in heavy soils, to about 6 inches below in lighter, sandy soils. Annual applications of well-rotted manure or rich compost are beneficial. The use of summer mulch, such as sawdust, wood chips, or buckwheat hulls, helps conserve soil moisture and moderate soil temperature and is recommended in regions having hot, dry summers.

Beyond removal of dead wood, little pruning is required. Leggy, rangy plants may be cut back severely to encourage denser, lower growth. This is best done in the fall.

Among the many cultivars, most of which originated in China and Japan, are the following.

'Godaishu': semidouble white.
'Kintei': single yellow, streaked deeper yellow.
'Renkaku': double white.
'Yae-kazura': double pink.

PAPAVER ORIENTALE
(Oriental poppy)

Zones 3–7

One of the most striking perennials in late spring or early summer, the Oriental poppy has long been a very popular garden subject. Although its flowering period is brief, few can match it for boldness of bloom or intensity of hue. The old-fashioned cultivars vary from deep red-orange to scarlet, but many of the newer hybrids offer subtle pastel tones of pink and salmon.

Oriental poppies thrive in full sun in any well-drained garden loam, be it heavy clay or light and sandy. Transplanting is best done during the period of summer dormancy, when the poppy's leaves have vanished. Plants to be moved should be marked while in flower with stake labels. Soon after the flowers drop, the foliage yellows and disappears. The roots, which resemble small, slender carrots, may then be dug bare root and quickly transferred to a predug hole. It is best to use a long, narrow-bladed tree spade, as any bits of root left in place will generate new plants. Oriental poppies may also be moved in early fall when new foliage appears, but then care must be taken to move a soil ball with the roots and to shade the plants for at least a week thereafter.

Established clumps may occupy as much as a square yard. Noncompeting filler plants, such as perennial baby's

Oriental poppy (*Papaver orientiale*)

breath *(Gypsophila paniculata)*, may be interplanted to provide attractive cover during the poppy's summer dormancy.

As Oriental poppy self-sows readily, it is usual to cut down the flower stalk before the seed pod forms. If this is not done in the case of the hybrid cultivars, the resultant colonies of young plants will revert to the brilliant flame orange of the old-fashioned type. However, dormant roots cut into 2-inch sections and planted will exactly replicate the plants from which they were taken.

Because the usual tall Oriental poppy sprawls when in flower, unless staked, and bears fragile, easily damaged blooms, the shorter, multiflowered, long-blooming 'Minicap' hybrids are especially welcome.

Among the many commercially available cultivars, the following are especially meritorious:

'Beauty of Livermore': deep red with black basal spots.
'Bonfire': red-orange with crinkled petals.
'Carnival': red-orange with the lower half of each petal white.
'China Boy': orange and white.
'Crimson Pompon': deep red, double.
'Dubloon': orange, double.
'Glowing Rose': watermelon pink.
'Harvest Moon': yellow-orange.
'Helen Elizabeth': light pink, reddish at base of petals.
'May Curtis': rose red.
'Raspberry Queen': raspberry red;
'Warlord': deep red.

PHLOX PANICULATA
(Tall summer phlox)

Zones 4–8

An important, easily grown mainstay of the mid and late summer garden, tall summer phlox succeeds under a wide range of conditions, but it makes its fullest contribution in full sun on moist, well-drained soil of moderate fertility. Winter cold is a necessity. Under such conditions, it forms dense clumps of stiffly erect stems, rising 3 or 4 feet tall, topped with dense clusters of flat tubular flowers. Flower color ranges from purple through a near red, lavender, and pink to salmon and white (no blue or yellow); the lighter

shades often have a darker center ("eye"). Cool summers result in a longer period of bloom, but where summers are hot, the phlox season can be extended by including the similar but earlier-flowering Carolina phlox *(P. carolina)*, of which the cultivars 'Miss Lingard' (white) and 'Rosalinde' (pink) are widely available. In prolonged humid weather, the older, lower foliage of tall summer phlox often turns gray with relatively harmless powdery mildew and prematurely withers. The unsightliness of this condition can be shielded by fronting the phlox planting with somewhat lower-growing perennials, such as hardy ageratum *(Eupatorium coelestinum)*. As tall summer phlox can self-sow to the point of nuisance—the offspring usually reverting to magenta, pinkish lavender, or white flowers— it is best to remove flower clusters as the blooms fade. This has the further benefit of stimulating the growth of side shoots and extending the flowering period, often into fall.

For maximum growth and prolific bloom, tall summer phlox requires a rich, well-drained garden loam, high in organic content and very slightly acidic. It is important that nutrients be readily available to the plant in the upper 8 inches of topsoil, as phlox is shallow rooted. It responds well to heavy applications of potash, so a fertilizer should be used that has a high potash content. An application of wood ashes worked into the soil about the plant is very beneficial. A summer mulch of rotted manure or rich compost will supply additional nutrients and keep the roots cool and moist.

During the growing season, phlox requires an abundance of moisture and suffers seriously from the effects of drought.

However, extremely wet soil and poor air circulation are also very injurious.

Old, oversize clumps should be lifted in early fall or early spring and split apart. The outer portions should be replanted 1 to 1½ feet apart. The woody, inner cores of the clumps may be discarded.

Tall summer phlox *(Phlox paniculata)*

Among the hundred or more cultivars available commercially, many of which were developed the former Soviet Union, the following are outstanding.

'Blue Boy': deep lavender blue.
'Blue Ice': opening pinkish blue, aging to white.
'Bright Eyes': pale pink, edged red.
'Dodo Hanbury Forbes': clear pink, in large clusters.
'Dresden China': shell pink, with a darker eye.
'Fairest One': pale salmon.
'Juliet': pale pink.
'Lilac Time': lilac blue.
'Mount Fujiyama': white.
'Orange Perfection': salmon.
'Pinafore Pink': pink with a red eye; dwarf form, 4 inches high.
'Rembrandt': white.
'Russian Violet': violet purple.
'Sir John Falstaff': salmon pink with red eye.
'Starfire': bright near red.
'World Peace': white; late flowering.

SALVIA × SUPERBA
(Perennial salvia)

Zones (4) 5–8

S. × superba, the most reliable salvia for the North, embraces several cultivars of varied origin. All are clump forming with blue-violet, purple, or pink flowers borne in numerous spikes, 1 to 2½ feet

Perennial salvia (*Salvia* × *superba* 'May Night')

Columbine meadow rue
(*Thalictrum aquilegifolium*)

tall. All require full sun and a well-drained soil of average fertility for best results. Summer drought is readily tolerated, but soggy soil in the winter is fatal. Perennial salvia will not flower well in the shade. Container-grown plants are easiest to establish, as the long, rangy roots of established specimens make transplanting risky.

Among the meritorious cultivars available commercially are the following.

'Blue Queen': 1 to 1½ feet tall; violet blue flowers.
'East Friesland': 1½ to 2 feet tall, violet flowers.
'May Night': 1½ to 2 feet tall; deep violet blue flowers.
'Rose Queen': 2 to 2½ feet tall; rose pink flowers.

THALICTRUM AQUILEGIFOLIUM
(Columbine meadow rue)

Zones 5–7

Graceful and fine textured, columbine meadow rue forms a basal clump of columbinelike foliage and produces branched stems, 2 to 3 feet tall, that bear fluffy tufts of pink or white flowers in late spring and early summer. Sexes are on separate plants, and the male flowers are somewhat showier. Partial shade and moist, well-drained soil yield best results; although in coastal and montane areas with cool summers, full sun is acceptable as long as the soil remains moist.

As with all meadow rues, clumps may be divided in early spring. Columbine meadow rue is also easily grown from seed.

In the cultivar 'Purpureum', the flowers are purple, and in 'Thundercloud', they are rose purple.

THALICTRUM ROCHEBRUNIANUM
(Lavender-mist meadow rue)

Zones 5–7

The most striking of the meadow rues, lavender-mist meadow rue produces 4- to 6-foot-tall stems in late summer and bears loose clusters of lavender-purple flowers, each with a central tuft of yellow stamens. If grown without nearby supporting vegetation, staking is required. The similar *T. dipterocarpum* (syn. *T. delavayi*) flowers a bit earlier but is more difficult to establish in most areas. In both cases, partial shade and moist, humusy soil suit best.

THALICTRUM SPECIOSISSIMUM
(Yellow meadow rue)

Zones 5–7

A tall meadow rue, up to 6 feet high, yellow meadow rue has blue-green foliage and dense clusters of tufted light yellow flowers in early summer. Forming a compact leafy clump, each plant produces a small group of closely spaced, stiffly erect stems. It is useful in the back of the perennial border or in the woodland garden. If grown alone, staking is usually essential. Moist, well-drained soil is required, and partial shade is preferable.

OTHER USEFUL PERENNIALS

Name	Zones	Height	Exposure*	Soil Requirements	Flower Color and Bloom Time	Comments
Acanthus mollis (bear's-breech)	8–9	2–3'	S	Ordinary, well drained	Lilac or rose; summer	Attractively cut foliage
A. spinosus (spiny bear's-breech)	5–8	3–4'	S	Ordinary, well drained	Purple or white; summer	Good as a specimen
Achillea filipendulina (fern-leaf yarrow)	2–9	3–4'	S	Ordinary, well drained	Yellow; early summer	Finely cut foliage; good cut flowers
A. filipendulina cvs.	2–9	1½–2'	S	Ordinary, well drained	Pink to red; summer	Can spread invasively
A. × lewisii (tufted yarrow)	3–7	4–6"	S	Ordinary, well drained	Pale yellow; summer	Semievergreen
A. millefolium (common yarrow)	2–9	1½–2'	S	Ordinary, well drained	White to red; summer	Can become invasive
A. × 'Moonshine' (hybrid yarrow)	2–9	1½–2'	S	Ordinary, well drained	Yellow; early summer	One of the best yarrows
A. ptarmica cvs. (sneezewort)	2–9	1½–2'	S	Ordinary, well drained	White; summer	Tolerates poor soil
A. tomenosa cvs. (woolly yarrow)	2–9	6–12"	S	Ordinary, well drained	Canary yellow; summer	Spreads rapidly
Aconitum henryi (large-flowered monkshood)	3–7	3–4'	S to PSh	Fertile, well drained	Dark blue; late summer to early fall	Slow to establish; poisonous to eat
Actaea spp. (baneberry): **see Chapter 22**						
Adenophora confusa (Farrer's ladybell)	4–8	2½–3'	S	Ordinary, well drained	Deep blue; summer	Not easily moved
A. liliifolia (lily-leaf ladybell)	4–8	1½–2'	S	Ordinary, well drained	Blue; summer	Not easily moved
Adonis amurensis (Amur adonis)	4–8	1'	S to PSh	Ordinary, well drained	Yellow; early spring	Finely dissected foliage
A. vernalis (yellow adonis)	5–8	1'	S to PSh	Ordinary, well drained	Yellow; spring	Finely dissected foliage
Aethionema grandiflorum (Persian stonecress)	5–8	1'	S	Sandy-humusy	Pink; spring	Useful among rocks
Ajuga genevensis (Geneva bugle)	4–7	6–8"	S to PSh	Ordinary, well drained	Blue; spring	Invasive in lawns
A. reptans (carpet bugle)	4–7	3–6"	S to PSh	Ordinary, well drained	Blue; spring	Invasive in lawns
Alchemilla vulgaris (lady's mantle)	3–7	1–1½'	PSh to LSh	Sandy-humusy	Yellow; spring	Attractive foliage
Aloysia triphylla (lemon verbena)	8–10	5–10'	S to PSh	Ordinary, well drained	White; summer	Lemon-scented foliage
Amsonia tabernaemontana (bluestar)	3–7	1½–2'	S, PSh, LSh	Ordinary, well drained	Light blue; late spring to early summer	Trouble free
Anaphalis margaritacea (pearly everlasting)	3–8	1–1½'	S to PSh	Sandy, poor	Yellowish; late spring to early summer	Woolly gray foliage
Anemone sylvestris (snowdrop windflower)	4–7	1–1½'	PSh	Gritty, well drained	White; early summer	Forms spreading patches
A. vitifolia (grape-leaf anemone)	4–8	2–3'	S to PSh	Ordinary to poor	Light pink; early fall	Tolerates poor conditions
Antennaria dioica (pussy toes)	4–7	8–10"	S	Ordinary, well drained	Pinkish white; summer	Mat forming; foliage silvery
Anthemis sancti-johannis (orange marguerite)	3–7	2–3'	S	Ordinary, well drained	Orange; summer to fall	Often short lived
A. tinctoria (golden marguerite)	2–8	2–3'	S	Sandy, poor	Yellow; late spring	Self-sows

Name	Zones	Height	Exposure*	Soil Requirements	Flower Color and Bloom Time	Comments
Aquilegia alpina (alpine columbine)	5–7	1–2'	S	Ordinary, well drained	Blue; spring	Also white and purple cultivars
A. flabellata (fan columbine)	5–7	1–1½'	S to PSh	Ordinary, well drained	Lilac or white; late spring	Good edging plant or in rockery; dwarf cultivars
A. skinneri (Mexican columbine)	8–9	1½–3'	S to PSh	Humusy, dryish	Yellow and red; spring	Suited to Southwest
Arabis alpina (alpine rockcress)	5–7	6–12"	S	Ordinary, well drained	White; spring	Forms a carpet
A. caucasica (wallcress)	5–7	6–12"	S	Ordinary, well drained	White; spring	Forms a carpet
A. procurrens (wallcress)	4–7	6–12"	S	Ordinary, well drained	White; spring	More robust than *A. caucasica*
Arctotheca calendula (capeweed)	9–10	8–12"	S	Ordinary, well drained	Yellow; early summer	Forms dense mounds
Arenaria montana (mountain sandwort)	4–7	6–8"	S	Ordinary, well drained	White; spring	Requires summer irrigation
A. verna, syn. *Minuartia verna* (moss sandwort)	5–7	2–4"	S	Ordinary, well drained	White; spring	Mossy foliage
Armeria maritima (thrift)	4–7	6–12"	S	Sandy, dryish	Pink or white; late spring to early summer	Clumps; good near seashore
Artemisia abrotanum (Southernwood, old man)	5–8	2–3'	S to PSh	Ordinary	Yellow; late summer	Shrubby in South; aromatic foliage
A. absinthium (absinthe)	3–7	2–4'	S to PSh	Ordinary, well drained	Pale yellow; late summer	Shrubby in South; aromatic foliage
A. lactiflora (white mugwort)	3–7	4–6'	S to PSh	Ordinary, well drained	White; late summer	Cv. 'Variegata' has bicolored leaves
A. ludoviciana var. *albula* (silver king)	4–8	2–3'	S	Sandy, dryish	White; summer	Gray foliage; good everlasting
A. schmidtiana 'Nana' (silver mound)	3–7	1½–2'	S	Sandy, dryish	Grown for foliage	Silvery leaves all season
A. stelleriana (dusty miller)	3–7	1–1½'	S to PSh	Sandy, dryish	White; late spring to early summer	Silvery leaves; can be invasive
Arum italicum 'Pictum' (painted arum)	5–8	1–1½'	PSh to LSh	Rich, moist	Greenish white; early summer	Variegated leaves; red berries
Aruncus dioicus (goatsbeard)	4–7	4–6'	S to PSh	Ordinary, well drained	White; late spring to early summer	Good background plant
Asclepias incarnata (pink milkweed)	3–8	2–4'	S to PSh	Ordinary, well drained	Pink; mid to late summer	Flowers fragrant; large pods
Asphodeline lutea (asphodel)	6–9	2–3'	S to PSh	Ordinary, well drained	Yellow; spring	Flowers fragrant; grayish grasslike foliage
Aster alpinus (alpine aster)	3–7	8–12"	S	Ordinary, well drained	Violet; late spring	Blue, pink, and white cultivars
A. amellus (Italian aster)	5–8	1½–2½'	S	Ordinary, well drained	Purple; mid to late summer	Pink cultivars
Astilbe chinensis 'Pumila' (dwarf Chinese astilbe)	5–7	8–12"	PSh	Ordinary, well drained	Pink; mid to late summer	Tolerates some drought
Astrantia major (masterwort)	5–8	2–3'	S to PSh	Ordinary, well drained	Silvery pink; spring	Good foliage plant
Aubrieta deltoidea (purple rockcress)	5–6 (7)	3–6"	S	Ordinary, well drained	Purple or white; spring	Forms mats; intolerant of prolonged heat
Aurinia saxatilis (basket-of-gold, yellow alyssum)	4–7	1–1½'	S	Ordinary, well drained	Yellow; spring	Also dwarf cultivar; others with pale flowers

(continues)

OTHER USEFUL PERENNIALS (*continued*)

Name	Zones	Height	Exposure*	Soil Requirements	Flower Color and Bloom Time	Comments
Baptisia australis (blue indigo, false indigo)	4–8	2½–4'	S to PSh	Ordinary, well drained	Indigo blue; late spring	Lupinelike flowers; black pods
Begonia grandis, syn. *B. evansiana* (hardy begonia)	6–8	1½–2'	PSh to LSh	Ordinary, well drained	Pink; late summer	Self-reproduces by bulbils
Belamcanda chinensis (blackberry lily)	5–8	2–4'	S to PSh	Ordinary, well drained	Orange; late summer	Bunched black seeds in early fall
Bellis perennis (English daisy)	4–7	3–6"	S to PSh	Ordinary, well drained	White, red, or purple; spring to early summer	Short lived; self-sows
Bergenia cordifolia (heart-leaf bergenia)	2–8	1'	S to PSh	Ordinary, well drained	Rose purple; spring	Evergreen, bold foliage
B. crassifolia (leatherleaf bergenia)	3–9	1'	S to PSh	Ordinary, well drained	Lavender pink; spring	Evergreen, bold foliage
Boltonia asteroides 'Snowbank' (white boltonia)	4–9	5–7'	S to PSh	Ordinary, well drained	Cream; late summer or early fall	Grayish foliage; good background plant
Brunnera macrophylla (Siberian bugloss)	4–8	1–1½'	S to LSh	Ordinary, well drained	Blue; mid to late spring	Large leaves; forget-me-not flowers
Buphthalmum salicifolium (sun wheel)	4–8	2–2½'	S to PSh	Ordinary, well drained	Yellow; summer	*B. speciosum* larger but similar
Calceolaria biflora 'John Innes' (dwarf calceolaria)	6–7	4–6"	S to PSh	Ordinary, well drained	Yellow; summer	Leaves basal; flower stalk rises 12 to 15 inches
Callirhoë involucrata (winecups)	4–8	6–12"	S	Ordinary, well drained	Red-violet; spring and summer	Long, creeping stems; drought tolerant
Caltha palustris (marsh marigold)	3–7	6–12"	S to LSh	Moist to wet	Yellow; spring	Dies back to ground in summer
Campanula elatines (Adriatic bellflower)	6–8	6–12"	S to PSh	Ordinary, well drained	Blue or white; late spring to early fall	Sprawling, rapidly spreading
C. latifolia 'Macrantha' (giant bellflower)	3–7	3–5'	S to PSh	Ordinary, well drained	Purple; late spring to summer	Tallest bellflower; requires staking
C. porscharskyana (Serbian bellflower)	5–8	4–8"	S to PSh	Ordinary, well drained	Lavender purple; mid to late summer	Trailing, can be invasive
C. portenschlagiana (dalmatian bellflower)	5–8	4–8"	S to PSh	Ordinary, well drained	Lilac blue; late spring to early summer	Creeping, mat forming
C. takesimana (Korean bellflower)	4–8	1½–2'	S to PSh	Ordinary, well drained	Lavender, spotted maroon within	Mat forming, self sows
Canna × generalis (hybrid canna)	8–10	2–7'	S	Ordinary, well drained	Various colors; summer to fall	Winter mulch in zone 8
Carlina acaulis (Carline thistle)	6–9	6–8"	S to PSh	Ordinary, well drained	Reddish or white; summer	Spiny foliage; good edging plant
Catananche caerulea (cupid's dart)	6–8	1½–2'	S	Sandy, dryish	Blue; late summer to early fall	Everlasting
Celmisia spectabilis (New Zealand daisy)	7–9	9–12"	S to PSh	Ordinary, well drained	White; early summer	Forms spreading mats
Centaurea dealbata 'Sternbergii' (Persian cornflower)	3–8	2–3'	S	Sandy, dryish	Purple-and-white; summer	Tolerates summer drought
C. macrocephala (globe centaurea)	3–8	3–4'	S	Ordinary, well drained	Yellow; late spring to early summer	Bold effect; rather coarse
C. montana (mountain bluet)	4–8	1½–2'	S	Ordinary, well drained	Blue-violet; late spring to early summer	Tolerates summer drought
Centranthus ruber (red valerian)	4–8	2–3'	S to PSh	Ordinary, well drained	Pink or white; summer	Self-sows freely
Cerastium tomentosum (snow-in-summer)	4–7	6–9"	S	Sandy, dryish	White; late spring to early summer	Spreading; can be invasive

Name	Zones	Height	Exposure*	Soil Requirements	Flower Color and Bloom Time	Comments
Ceratostigma plumbaginoides (blue leadwort)	6–9	9–12"	PSh to LSh	Ordinary, well drained	Deep blue; late summer to early fall	Spreading; appears late in spring
Chelone glabra (turtlehead)	3–8	2–3'	S to PSh	Moist, humusy	Pinkish to white; summer	Good on wet ground
C. lyonii (pink turtlehead)	3–8	2–3'	S to PSh	Moist, humusy	Deep rose; late summer to early fall	Good on wet ground
Chrysanthemum coccineum (pyrethrum, painted daisy)	4–8	2–3'	S to PSh	Ordinary, well drained	Red to white; late spring to early summer	Good cut flower
C. nipponicum (Nippon daisy)	5–7	1½–2½'	S to PSh	Ordinary, well drained	White; late summer to early fall	Requires cutting back to base in spring
C. serotinum, syn. *Leucanthemella serontinum* (hairy-stemmed daisy)	7–9	3–5'	S to PSh	Ordinary, well drained	Red or white; late spring to summer	Cv. 'Herbstern' has white flowers with yellow centers
C. × superbum (Shasta daisy)	5–8	1–3'	S to PSh	Ordinary, well drained	White; summer	Numerous cultivars, some double flowered
Chrysogonum virginianum (golden star)	5–8	9–12"	PSh to LSh	Ordinary, well drained	Yellow; summer	Good ground cover
Cimicifuga foetida (Kamchatka bugbane)	3–7	3–5'	S to PSh	Ordinary, well drained	White; late summer to early fall	Good background plant
C. racemosa (black cohosh)	3–7	5–8'	S to PSh	Ordinary, well drained	White; late summer to early fall	Good background plant
C. simplex (snakeroot)	4–7	2–4'	S to PSh	Ordinary, well drained	White; early fall	Good backdrop for mums
Clematis heracleifolia var. *davidiana* (blue tube clematis)	3–8	3–4'	S to PSh	Ordinary, well drained	Deep blue; late summer	Difficult to transplant; fragrant flowers
C. integrifolia 'Coerulea' (porcelain clematis)	3–8	1½–2'	S to PSh	Ordinary, well drained	Light blue; late spring to early fall	Difficult to transplant
C. recta 'Grandiflora' (ground clematis)	3–8	3–4'	S to PSh	Ordinary, well drained	White; early summer	Difficult to transplant
Convallaria majalis (lily-of-the-valley)	4–7	6–9"	PSh to LSh	Ordinary, well drained	White; spring	Fragrant, spreads; pink cultivars; red berry is poisonous
Coreopsis auriculata 'Nana' (dwarf earlobed coreopsis)	5–8	4–6"	S	Ordinary, well drained	Yellow-orange; summer	Drought tolerant
C. grandiflora (common coreopsis)	5–8	2–3'	S to PSh	Ordinary, well drained	Yellow; late spring to summer	Drought tolerant; good cut flower
C. lanceolata 'Sunburst' (double coreopsis)	5–8	1½–2'	S to PSh	Ordinary, well drained	Yellow; summer	Drought tolerant; good cut flower; flowers semidouble
C. verticillata (threadleaf coreopsis)	3–7	1½–2'	S to PSh	Ordinary, well drained	Yellow to cream; summer	Moundlike habit
Coronilla varia (crown vetch)	6–8	1–3'	S	Infertile, well drained	White, purple, or pink; summer	Useful in stabilizing banks
Corydalis lutea (golden corydalis)	5–7	6–12"	S, PSh or LSh	Humusy, well drained	Yellow; spring	Self-sows freely
Crambe cordifolia (colewort)	6–8	5–7'	S to PSh	Ordinary, well drained	White; summer	Striking habit; for large gardens
Cynoglossum nervosum (great hound's-tongue)	5–8	1½–2'	S	Sandy, dry	Blue; summer	Heat and drought tolerant
Darmera peltata, syn. *Peltiphyllum peltatum* (Indian rhubarb)	7–8	3–5'	S to PSh	Marshy or muddy	Pink; spring	Cv. 'Nana' is 1½ to 2 feet tall

(continues)

OTHER USEFUL PERENNIALS *(continued)*

Name	Zones	Height	Exposure*	Soil Requirements	Flower Color and Bloom Time	Comments
Delphinium 'Connecticut Yankees' (Connecticut Yankee delphinium)	4–7	2–2½'	S to PSh	Humusy, moist	Purple to white; summer	Good cut flower
D. nudicaule (orange delphinium)	8–9	1–1½'	S to PSh	Ordinary, well drained	Orange; summer	Intolerant of sustained winter cold
D. semibarbatum (yellow delphinium)	6–8	1–2'	S to PSh	Ordinary, well drained	Yellow; late spring to early summer	Tuberous roots
Dianthus deltoides cvs. (maiden pink)	4–6 (7)	6–9"	S to PSh	Ordinary, well drained	Pale to deep pink; late spring	Best on alkaline soil
D. gratianopolitanus (cheddar pink)	5–8	9–12"	S to PSh	Ordinary, well drained	Pale to deep pink; late spring to early summer	Forms mounds or mats; good edging plant
D. knappii (yellow dianthus)	3–8	9–12"	S to PSh	Ordinary, well drained	Pale yellow; late spring to early summer	Good edging plant
D. plumarius cvs. (cottage pink)	4–7	1'–1½'	S to PSh	Ordinary, well drained	Pink to white, often red centered; late spring	Bluish foliage; source of 'Allwood' hybrids
Dicentra cucullaria (Dutchman's-breeches)	4–7	5–8"	PSh to LSh	Humusy, well drained	White and yellow; spring	Self-sows freely
D. eximia (fringed bleeding heart)	2–8	8–9"	PSh to LSh	Sandy-humusy	Pink to rose or white; spring to early fall	Summer dampness sustains flowering
Dictamnus albus (gas plant)	4–8	2–3'	S to PSh	Ordinary, well drained	White or rose; spring	Flowers emit flammable vapor
Digitalis ferruginea (rusty foxglove)	6–8	3–5'	PSh	Ordinary, well drained	Rusty yellow-brown; late spring to early summer	Often short lived
D. grandiflora (yellow foxglove)	5–8	2–3'	S to PSh	Ordinary, well drained	Pale yellow; late spring to early summer	Forms clumps
D. lanata (Grecian foxglove)	5–8	2–3'	PSh	Ordinary, well drained	Cream to yellow-brown; summer	Effective in large clumps
D. lutea (straw foxglove)	5–8	2–3'	PSh	Ordinary, well drained	Cream to yellow; late spring to early summer	Effective in large clumps
D. × mertonensis (pink foxglove)	5–8	2–3'	S to PSh	Ordinary, well drained	Rose pink; late spring to early summer	Often short lived
D. parviflora (small-flowered foxglove)	5–8	1½–2½'	S to PSh	Ordinary, well drained	Pale red-brown; late spring to early summer	Effective in large clumps
Disporum flavum (fairy bell)	4–8	2–3'	PSh to LSh	Sandy-humusy	Yellow; spring	Thrives in dry shade
D. sessile 'Variegatum' (striped fairy bell)	4–8	1–2'	PSh to LSh	Sandy-humusy	Greenish white; spring	Cream-striped foliage
Dodecatheon meadia (shooting star)	5–8	1–2'	PSh to LSh	Humusy, well drained	Magenta to white; spring	Foliage dies back in summer
Doronicum columnae (leopard's-bane)	3–7	1½–2'	S to PSh	Ordinary, well drained	Yellow; spring	Earliest of yellow daisies
D. orientale 'Magnificum' (leopard's-bane)	3–7	1–2'	S to PSh	Ordinary, well drained	Yellow; spring	Very early
D. pardalianches, syn. *D. cordatum* (great leopard's-bane)	5–7	2–4'	PSh	Ordinary, well drained	Yellow; early spring	Cv. 'Goldstrauss' is especially floriferous
Dracocephalum argunense (dragonhead)	4–7	2–2½'	PSh	Ordinary, well drained	Deep blue to purplish; summer	*D. ruyschiana* is very similar
Duchesnea indica (barren strawberry)	4–8	3–6"	S to PSh	Ordinary, well drained	Yellow; spring	Habit of strawberry; red fruit not palatable
Echinacea purpurea (purple coneflower)	4–8	2–4'	S to PSh	Ordinary, well drained	Rosy purple; summer	Cv. 'White Swan' has white flowers

Name	Zones	Height	Exposure*	Soil Requirements	Flower Color and Bloom Time	Comments
Echinops ritro 'Taplow Blue' (small globe thistle)	4–8	3–5'	S	Ordinary, well drained	Steel blue; summer	Spiny foliage
E. sphaerocephalus (great globe thistle)	4–8	4–7'	S	Ordinary, well drained	Pale blue to whitish; summer	Coarse, spiny foliage
Epilobium angustifolium (fireweed)	5–7	3–5'	S	Ordinary, moist to wet	Rose pink; summer	Forms extensive stands; can be invasive
Epimedium alpinum (bishop's hat)	5–7	9–12"	PSh to LSh	Ordinary, well drained	Red and yellow; spring	Good ground cover in shade
E. grandiflorum (bishop's hat)	5–7	1–1½'	PSh to LSh	Ordinary, well drained	Red, violet, and white; spring	As for *E. alpinum*
E. pinnatum (bishop's hat)	5–7	1–2'	PSh to LSh	Ordinary, well drained	Yellow and red; spring	As for *E. alpinum*
E. × *rubrum* (bishop's hat)	5–7	9–12"	PSh to LSh	Ordinary, well drained	Red and yellow; spring	As for *E. alpinum*
E. × *versicolor* 'Sulphureum' (bishop's hat)	5–7	9–12"	PSh to LSh	Ordinary, well drained	Pale yellow; spring	As for *E. alpinum*
E. × *youngianum* 'Niveum' (bishop's hat)	5–7	6–9"	PSh to LSh	Ordinary, well drained	White; spring	As for *E. alpinum*
Eremurus himalaicus (foxtail lily, desert candle)	3–7	4–7'	S	Sandy-humusy	White; spring	Spikelike flower clusters
E. robustus (giant foxtail lily)	6–8	4–8'	S	Sandy-humusy	Pink; spring	Usually requires staking
Erigeron aurantiacus (double orange daisy)	6–8	9–15"	S	Ordinary, well drained	Double orange; summer	Mounded habit
E. hybridus cvs. (hybrid fleabane)	4–8	1½–2'	S	Ordinary, well drained	Orange to rose purple; summer	Varied hybrid group
E. speciosus (Oregon fleabane)	3–7	1½–2'	S	Ordinary, well drained	Violet blue, yellow centered; early summer	Clump forming
Eryngium alpinum 'Superbum' (blue-top sea holly)	4–8	1½–2'	S	Ordinary, well drained	Silvery blue; late summer	Spiny foliage; hard to transplant
E. amethystinum (amethyst sea holly)	4–8	2–3'	S	Ordinary, well drained	Steel gray to amethyst; summer	Spiny foliage; hard to transplant
E. bourgatii (Mediterranean sea holly)	3–8	1½–2'	S	Ordinary, well drained	Steel blue; summer	Spiny foliage; hard to transplant
E. planum (flatleaf sea holly)	4–8	3–4'	S	Ordinary, well drained	Steel blue; summer	Broad, somewhat spiny foliage
Eupatorium coelestinum (hardy ageratum)	5–8	2–3'	S to PSh	Ordinary, well drained	Blue; late summer to early fall	Late to start in spring; forms spreading clumps
E. maculatum (lesser joe-pye weed)	3–8	4–6'	S to PSh	Humusy, moist	Purplish to pinkish mauve; late summer	Pinching induces bushier growth
E. purpureum (joe-pye weed)	5–8	6–10'	S	Moist to wet, acidic	Pinkish purple; late summer	Forms large clumps
E. rugosum, syn. *Ageratina altissima* (white snakeroot)	5–8	3–4'	S to PSh	Ordinary, well drained	White; late summer	Freely self-sows
Euphorbia characias ssp. *wulfenii* (Dalmatian spurge)	8–9	3–4'	S	Sandy, dryish	Yellow; spring	Drought tolerant
E. corollata (flowering spurge)	4–7	1–3'	S	Sandy, dryish	White; summer	Drought tolerant
E. cyparissias (cypress spurge)	4–7	9–12"	S	Sandy, dryish	Yellow aging to red-orange; spring	Invasive in rich soil

(continues)

OTHER USEFUL PERENNIALS (continued)

Name	Zones	Height	Exposure*	Soil Requirements	Flower Color and Bloom Time	Comments
E. epithymoides (cushion spurge)	5–8	1–1½'	S	Ordinary, well drained	Yellow; spring	Mounded habit
E. myrsinites (myrtle spurge)	4–8	6–9"	S	Sandy, dryish	Yellow; spring	Evergreen; creeping; blue-green foliage
Filipendula rubra (queen of the prairie)	2–8	4–7'	S to PSh	Ordinary, well drained	Pink; late spring to early summer	Forms clumps
F. ulmaria (queen of the meadow)	2–8	3–4'	S to PSh	Ordinary, well drained	White; late spring to early summer	Fragrant
F. vulgaris (dropwort)	4–8	1½–2'	S	Sandy, dryish	Cream; late spring	Cv. 'Flore Pleno' is double flowered
Fuchsia magellanica (hardy fuchsia)	7–8	2–3'	S to PSh	Ordinary, well drained	Red; summer	Shrub grown as perennial
Gaillardia × grandiflora cvs. (blanketflower)	4–8	6–36"	S to PSh	Ordinary, well drained	Red and yellow; late spring to early fall	Cream to deep red flowers in cultivars
Galega officinalis (goat's rue)	4–8	2–3'	S to PSh	Ordinary, well drained	Blue-violet; summer	Long blooming period
Galium odoratum (sweet woodruff)	5–7	9–12"	PSh to LSh	Ordinary, well drained	White; spring	Useful edging plant
Gaura lindheimeri (white gaura)	6–9	3–5'	S to PSh	Ordinary, well drained	White to pink; summer to early fall	Diffuse habit; drought tolerant
Gentiana andrewsii (bottle gentian)	5–8	1½–2'	S	Moist, acidic	Bluish purple; summer	Flowers stay closed
G. asclepiadea (willow gentian)	6–8	1½–2'	S to PSh	Moist, acidic	Deep blue; summer	Effective if grouped
G. lagodechiana (dwarf blue gentian)	6–8	9–12"	S to PSh	Moist, acidic	Blue-violet; summer	Mat forming
G. septemfida (crested gentian)	5–8	4–6"	S to PSh	Moist, acidic	Deep blue; summer	Good edging plant
Geranium cinereum cvs. (alpine geranium)	5–7	4–6"	S to PSh	Ordinary, well drained	Lilac to magenta; summer	Long blooming period
G. dalmaticum (Dalmatian geranium)	5–7	4–6"	S to PSh	Ordinary, well drained	Pale pink to white; late spring	Good edging plant
G. endressii cvs. (Pyrenees cranesbill)	4–7	1–1½'	S to PSh	Ordinary, well drained	Blue, pink, or white; late spring to late summer	Long blooming period
G. himalayense (lilac cranesbill)	4–7	1½–2'	S to PSh	Ordinary, well drained	Magenta; late spring	Long blooming period; spreads rapidly
G. ibericum (Iberian cranesbill)	6–8	1½–2'	S to PSh	Ordinary, well drained	Violet blue; late spring to early summer	Large, deeply cut basal leaves
G. macrorhizum (big-root geranium)	4–7	9–12"	S to PSh	Ordinary, well drained	Pink; late spring to early summer	Dense; aromatic; mat forming; edging plant
G. maculatum (hardy geranium, cranesbill)	4–7	1½–2'	S to PSh	Ordinary, well drained	Pinkish purple; spring	Forms large clumps
G. sanguineum (blood-red geranium)	4–7	9–12"	S to PSh	Ordinary, well drained	Purplish red; spring to late summer	Long blooming period
G. sanguineum var. *prostratum* (spreading cranesbill)	4–7	4–6"	S to PSh	Ordinary, well drained	Bright pink; late spring to late summer	Compact; mat forming
Gerbera jamesonii	8–10	1–1½'	S to PSh	Ordinary, well drained	Yellow to red; summer to early fall	Winter mulch needed in zone 8
Geum × borisii (Werner Arends avens)	3–7	6–9"	S to PSh	Ordinary, well drained	Red-orange; summer	Not always reliable north of zone 5
G. coccineum (garden avens)	5–8	2–½'	S to PSh	Ordinary, well drained	Various colors; late spring to late summer	*G. quellyon* is similar

Name	Zones	Height	Exposure*	Soil Requirements	Flower Color and Bloom Time	Comments
G. reptans (creeping avens)	6–8	6–9"	S to PSh	Ordinary, well drained	Yellow-orange; summer	Spreads by runners
Gillenia trifoliata	4–7	2–3'	S to PSh	Ordinary, well drained	White; summer	Easily grown
Hedychium coronarium (white ginger lily)	8–10	3–6'	S to PSh	Moist, acidic	White; summer	Fragrant; mulch in zone 8
H. gardnerianum (yellow ginger lily)	9–10	6–8'	S to PSh	Moist, acidic	Yellow-and-red; summer	Fragrant
Hedysarum coronarium (French honeysuckle)	3–7	3–4'	S to PSh	Ordinary, well drained	Red; early summer	Good in mass plantings
Helenium autumnale cvs. (sneezeweed)	3–8	2–6'	S	Ordinary, well drained	Yellow to reddish bronze; early to mid autumn	Height varies according to cultivar
H. hoopesii (summer sneezeweed)	4–8	2–2½'	S	Ordinary, well drained	Orange; late spring to early summer	Flower heads to 3 inches across; foliage toxic to animals
Helianthemum nummularium (rockrose)	4–7	6–12"	S to PSh	Ordinary, well drained	Pink, orange; yellow, or white; early summer	Numerous flower-color cultivars
Helianthus angustifolius (swamp sunflower)	4–8	3–4'	S to PSh	Humusy, moist	Yellow; late summer to early fall	Good background plant; good cut flower
H. decapetalus (thinleaf sunflower)	5–8	5–7'	S to PSh	Ordinary, well drained	Yellow; late summer	Good background plant; good cut flower
H. maximiliani (Maximilian sunflower)	4–8	6–10'	S to PSh	Ordinary, well drained	Yellow; late summer to early fall	Good background plant; forms large clumps
H. multiflorus (perennial sunflower)	3–7	3–5'	S to PSh	Ordinary, well drained	Yellow; summer	Some cultivars with double flowers
Heliopsis helianthoides (orange sunflower)	4–8	3–4'	S to PSh	Ordinary, well drained	Yellow-orange; summer	Often attacked by aphids
Helleborus foetidus (setterwort)	6–7	2–2½'	PSh to LSh	Ordinary, well drained	Greenish to purplish; early to mid spring	Several sweet-scented cultivars
H. lividus var. corsicus (Corsican hellebore)	8–9	2–3'	S to PSh	Ordinary, well drained	Pale green; late winter to spring	Tolerant of full sun and summer heat
H. niger (Christmas rose)	4–8	9–12"	PSh to LSh	Well drained, pH 7.5	White, aging to pink or green; late winter to early spring	Shade essential in South
H. orientalis (Lenten rose)	5–8	1–1½'	PSh to LSh	Well drained, pH 7.5	White, aging to purple or brown; late winter to early spring	Shade essential in South
Hemerocallis aurantiaca (orange daylily)	6–9	2½–3'	S to PSh	Ordinary, well drained	Orange; late spring to early summer	Good ground cover
H. dumortieri (Dumortier's daylily)	4–8	1–1½'	S to PSh	Ordinary, well drained	Orange; late spring to early summer	Good ground cover
H. fulva (common daylily, tawny daylily)	2–8	2½–3½'	S to PSh	Ordinary, well drained	Rusty orange; early summer	Spreads rapidly, can be invasive
H. lilioasphodelus (lemon daylily)	4–8	2–2½'	S to PSh	Ordinary, well drained	Lemon yellow; early summer	Fragrant; good ground cover
H. middendorffii (Amur daylily)	5–8	1½–2'	S to PSh	Ordinary, well drained	Yellow-orange; late spring to early summer	Good ground cover
H. minor (dwarf yellow daylily)	4–8	1–1½'	S to PSh	Ordinary, well drained	Yellow; early summer	Useful edging plant

(continues)

OTHER USEFUL PERENNIALS (*continued*)

Name	Zones	Height	Exposure*	Soil Requirements	Flower Color and Bloom Time	Comments
H. thunbergii (Thunberg's daylily)	4–8	3–4'	S to PSh	Ordinary, well drained	Canary yellow; early summer	Good ground cover
Hesperis matronalis (dame's rocket)	6–8	3–4'	S to PSh	Ordinary, well drained	Lilac or white; late spring to early summer	Fragrant; self-sows
× *Heucherella tiarelloides* (Bridget bloom)	3–7	1–1½'	S to PSh	Ordinary, well drained	Pink; late spring to early summer	Combines well with *Heuchera sanguinea*
Hibiscus coccineus (scarlet rose mallow)	7–9	6–8'	S to PSh	Moist to wet	Deep red; mid to late summer	Tolerant of ordinary garden conditions
H. moscheutos hybrids and cvs. (garden rose mallow)	5–8	3–8'	S to PSh	Ordinary, well drained	Red, pink, or white; late summer	Summer moisture augments flowering
Hosta decorata (blunt-leaf plantain lily)	4–8	1–2'	PSh to LSh	Moist, well drained	Purple or white; late summer	Spreads by stolons
H. lancifolia (narrow-leaf plantain lily)	4–8	1–2'	PSh to LSh	Moist, well drained	Lavender purple; late summer	Leaves all green; forms dense clumps
H. montana f. *aureo-marginata* (yellow-edge plantain lily)	4–8	1–2'	PSh to LSh	Moist, well drained	Gray lavender or white; late summer	Leaves wavy, yellow edged
H. tardiflora (late plantain lily)	4–8	1–1½'	PSh to LSh	Moist, well drained	Purplish mauve; early fall	Last hosta to flower
H. ventricosa (blue plantain lily)	4–8	1–3'	PSh to LSh	Moist, well drained	Bluish lilac; late summer	Several cultivars with leaf-color variations
H. venusta (dwarf plantain lily)	4–8	3–6"	PSh to LSh	Moist, well drained	Pale violet; late summer	Smallest hosta
Iberis sempervirens (evergreen candytuft)	4–8	9–12"	S to PSh	Ordinary, well drained	White; spring	Evergreen; forms mats to 3 feet across
Incarvillea delavayi (hardy gloxinia)	6–8	1–1½'	S to PSh	Ordinary, well drained	Rose pink; mid to late spring	Winter mulch advisable
Inula ensifolia (swordleaf inula)	4–7	9–12"	S to PSh	Ordinary, well drained	Yellow; summer	Makes a large rounded clump
I. helenium (elecampane)	5–7	4–6'	S to PSh	Ordinary, well drained	Yellow; summer	Root used medicinally
Iris pallida var. *dalmatica* (orris)	6–8	2–3'	S to PSh	Ordinary, well drained	Blue-violet; late spring to early summer	Several cultivars with variegated leaves
I. pseudacorus (yellow flag)	5–8	4–6'	S to PSh	Moist to wet	Yellow; summer	Effective at pond borders
I. spuria (butterfly, spuria iris)	6–8	1½–2'	S to PSh	Ordinary, well drained	Blue-violet, yellow, or white; late spring to early summer	Variable; many cultivars
I. versicolor (blue flag)	3–7	2–3'	S	Moist to wet	Violet-and-yellow; summer	Good at pond borders
Jasione perennis (shepherd's scabious)	5–8	9–12"	S to PSh	Ordinary to poor	Steel blue; late, spring to early summer	Thrives on poor soils
Kniphofia cvs. (red-hot poker, torch lily)	6–9	2–6'	S	Ordinary, well drained	Red, orange, yellow, or white; summer	Height varies with cultivar
Lathyrus grandiflorus (two-flowered sweet pea)	6–8	4–6'	S to PSh	Ordinary, well drained	Rose purple; summer	Flowers borne in pairs; requires support
L. latifolius (perennial sweet pea)	4–7	4–8'	S to PSh	Ordinary, well drained	Pink or white; summer	Effective on a pole
Lavandula angustifolia (English lavender)	5–8	1–3'	S to PSh	Ordinary, well drained	Lavender to purple; summer	Cultivars vary in height and flower color
Leontopodium alpinum (edelweiss)	4–7	6–12"	S	Sandy, dryish	Silvery; late spring to early summer	Requires excellent drainage

Name	Zones	Height	Exposure*	Soil Requirements	Flower Color and Bloom Time	Comments
Liatris pycnostachya (cattail gayfeather)	2–8	4–6'	S to PSh	Moist, well drained	Pinkish lavender; late summer	Spikes bloom from top down
L. scariosa (tall gayfeather)	2–8	2–5'	S to PSh	Moist, well drained	Purple; summer	Summer moisture augments flowering
L. spicata (spike gayfeather)	2–8	1½–3'	S to PSh	Moist, well drained	Pink to purple; late summer	Numerous cultivars
Ligularia dentata (ragwort)	3–8	3–4'	S to PSh	Ordinary, well drained	Yellow; late summer	Bold foliage; wilts under summer sun
L. przewalskii (tall ragwort)	3–8	4–6'	S to PSh	Ordinary, well drained	Yellow; summer	*L.* 'The Rocket' is similar
L. tussilaginea 'Aureo-maculata' (leopard plant)	6–8	1½–2'	S to PSh	Ordinary, well drained	Yellow; summer	Evergreen; yellow-spotted foliage
Limonium latifolium (sea lavender)	4–8	1½–2'	S	Ordinary, well drained	Lavender blue; late summer	Everlasting; not easily transplanted
L. perezii (Canary statice)	8–9	1½–2'	S	Ordinary, well drained	White; summer	Valued ornamental in the Southwest
Linum flavum (golden flax)	5–8	1–1½'	S	Ordinary, well drained	Yellow-orange; summer	Plants heaved on heavy soil
L. narbonense (Narbonne flax)	5–8	1½–2'	S	Ordinary, well drained	Light blue; late spring	As for *L. flavum*
Liriope muscari (big blue lilyturf)	7–10	1–1½'	PSh to LSh	Ordinary, well drained	Violet to lilac or white; summer	Evergreen; good edging plant
L. spicata (creeping lilyturf)	5–9	9–12"	S to Sh	Moist, well drained	Pale lilac or white; summer	Spreads by stolons
Lobelia cardinalis (cardinal flower)	3–7	2–3'	PSh to LSh	Moist, well drained	Scarlet; late summer to early fall	Short lived; self-sows
L. siphilitica (great blue lobelia)	4–7	2–3'	S to PSh	Ordinary, well drained	Blue or white; summer	Summer moisture augments flowering
Lychnis chalcedonica (Maltese cross)	2–8	2–3'	S to PSh	Ordinary, well drained	Red, pink, or white; summer	Usually requires staking
L. coronaria (mullein pink)	4–8	2–3'	S to PSh	Ordinary, well drained	Red or white; summer	Gray, felty foliage; short lived; self-sows freely
L. viscaria (German catchfly)	4–8	1–1½'	S to PSh	Ordinary, well drained	Magenta; late spring to early summer	Can be invasive by self-sowing
Lysimachia clethroides (gooseneck loosestrife)	4–8	2–3'	S to PSh or LSh	Ordinary, well drained	White; summer	Forms extensive clumps
L. punctata (yellow loosestrife)	4–8	2–3'	S to PSh	Ordinary, well drained	Yellow; late spring to early summer	Forms large clumps
Macleaya cordata (plume poppy)	4–8	5–8'	S to PSh	Ordinary, well drained	Cream; summer	Forms large clumps; can be invasive
Malva alcea 'Fastigiata' (hollyhock mallow)	5–8	3–4'	S to PSh	Ordinary, well drained	Pink; late spring to summer	Short-lived; self-sows freely
M. moschata (musk mallow)	3–8	2–3'	S to PSh	Ordinary, well drained	Pink or white; late spring to early summer	As for *M. alcea* 'Fastigiata'
Marrubium incanum (horehound)	4–8	2–3'	S to PSh	Ordinary, well drained	White; summer	Silvery foliage; heat tolerant
Meconopsis cambrica (Welsh poppy)	6–8	1½–2'	PSh	Moist, well drained	Yellow or orange; late spring to summer	Intolerant of drought

(continues)

OTHER USEFUL PERENNIALS (*continued*)

Name	Zones	Height	Exposure*	Soil Requirements	Flower Color and Bloom Time	Comments
Melissa officinalis (lemon balm)	6–8	1–2'	S to PSh	Ordinary, well drained	White; summer	Forms clumps; aromatic foliage; self-sows
Mertensia virginica (Virginia bluebell)	3–7	1–2'	PSh to LSh	Ordinary, well drained	Blue; spring	Dies to ground in early summer
Mirabilis jalapa (four o'clock)	(7) 8–9	1½–3'	S	Ordinary, well drained	Various; summer	Nocturnal flowers open in late afternoon; grown as annual in North
Monarda didyma (bee balm)	5–8	2–3'	S to PSh	Moist, well drained	Red; summer	Pink and white flowered cultivars forms spreading mats
M. fistulosa (wild bergamot)	3–7	2–5'	S to PSh	Ordinary, well drained	Pinkish lavender; summer	Best at back of garden
Myosotis scorpioides 'Semperflorens' (perennial forget-me-not)	5–8	1–2'	S to PSh	Moist, well drained	Blue; spring to summer	Long blooming period
Nepeta × faassenii (catmint)	4–7	1½–3'	S to PSh	Ordinary, well drained	Blue-violet to lavender; late spring to early summer	Sterile; propagated by division
N. racemosa (mauve catmint)	4–7	9–12"	S to PSh	Ordinary, well drained	Blue or white; late spring to early summer	Good for edging; usually listed as *N. mussinii*
Oenothera fruticosa 'Youngii' (large-flowered sundrops)	4–8	1½–2'	S	Ordinary, well drained	Bright yellow; late spring to early summer	A day-flowering evening primrose
O. missouriensis (Ozark sundrops)	3–7	9–18"	S	Ordinary, well drained	Yellow; summer	Sprawling habit; flowers 3 to 4 inches across
O. pilosella (common sundrops)	4–8	1–1½'	S to PSh	Ordinary, well drained	Yellow; late spring to early summer	Spreads rapidly, but easily controlled
O. speciosa (creeping evening primrose)	5–8	6–12"	S	Ordinary, well drained	Pink or white; late spring to early summer	Very invasive; grow in confined bed
Omphalodes cappadocica (navelwort)	6–8	8–12"	PSh, LSh, or Sh	Sandy, dryish	Blue; late spring	Shade required; drought tolerant
O. verna (creeping forget-me-not, blue-eyed Mary)	6–9	6–8"	PSh, LSh, or Sh	Humusy, well drained	Blue or white; late spring	Useful as a carpet beneath shrubs
Opuntia humifusa (hardy prickly pear)	6–7	9–12"	S	Sandy, dryish	Yellow; late spring to early summer	Clumps; pads shrivel in winter
Origanum majorana (sweet marjoram)	8–9	1–2'	S to PSh	Ordinary, well drained	Purplish; summer	Aromatic foliage; usually grown as herb
Papaver nudicaule (Iceland poppy)	2–7	1–2'	S	Ordinary, well drained	Various colors; early summer	Fails in hot weather; often biennial
Patrinia scabiosifolia	5–7	2–3'	S to PSh	Ordinary, well drained	Yellow; early summer	Intolerant of summer heat
Penstemon barbatus (common beardtongue)	5–8	2½–3'	S	Ordinary, well drained	Red to salmon; late spring to early summer	Often blooms first year; winter mulch advisable
P. cobaea (purple beardtongue)	5–7	1½–2'	S to PSh	Ordinary, well drained	Purple to white; summer	Flowers large for this group
P. gloxinioides (gloxinia beardtongue)	8–9	2–3'	S to PSh	Ordinary, well drained	Red or white; summer	Intolerant of summer heat; best on West Coast
P. heterophyllus ssp. *purdyi* (foothills beardtongue)	8–9	1–1½'	S to PSh	Ordinary, well drained	Blue; summer	Intolerant of summer heat; best on West Coast
P. hirsutus (sticky beardtongue)	4–7	1–1½'	S to PSh	Ordinary, well drained	Mauve; summer	Sticky, hairy stems; glossy foliage
P. smallii (Small's beardtongue)	6–8	2–3'	S to PSh	Ordinary, well drained	Pinkish purple and white; summer	Adaptable species from the Southeast

Name	Zones	Height	Exposure*	Soil Requirements	Flower Color and Bloom Time	Comments
Perovskia atriplicifolia (Russian sage)	5–8	3–4'	S to PSh	Ordinary, well drained	Lavender blue; late summer	Grayish aromatic foliage
Petrorhagia saxifraga (tunic flower)	5–8	6–9"	S to PSh	Ordinary, well drained	Pink; summer	Soil drainage essential
Phlomis russelliana (sticky Jerusalem sage)	7–9	3–4'	S to PSh	Ordinary, well drained	Yellow; summer	Attractive gray green foliage
Phlox divaricata (blue phlox)	3–7	9–12"	S to PSh	Ordinary, well drained	Lavender blue; spring	Good with spring bulbs and primroses
P. × *procumbens* (hairy phlox)	5–8	9–12"	S	Ordinary, well drained	Purple; spring	Clump forming; spreading
P. stolonifera (creeping phlox)	5–8	6–12"	PSh to LSh	Ordinary, well drained	Purple; late spring	Mat forming; some shade required
P. subulata (mountain pink)	2–7	3"	S	Ordinary, well drained	Bluish purple, red, pink, or white; spring	Forms dense mats
Physalis alkekengi (Chinese lantern)	4–7	1½–2'	S to PSh	Ordinary, well drained	White flowers early to mid summer; fruit late to develop conspicuous orange color	Grown for everlasting inflated orange fruit calyx
Physostegia virginiana (false dragonhead, obedience)	4–9	1½–3'	S to PSh	Moist, well drained	Rose purple or white; late summer	Forms clumps; can be invasive
Platycodon grandiflorus (balloon flower)	4–8	2–3'	S to PSh	Ordinary, well drained	Blue or white; late spring to early summer	Large plants not easily moved; *P. grandiflorus* var. *mariesii* is a dwarf form
Polemonium caeruleum (Jacob's ladder)	4–7	1–1½'	PSh to LSh	Ordinary, well drained	Blue or white; late spring	Requires summer shade
P. reptans (Greek valerian)	4–7	9–12"	PSh to LSh	Ordinary, well drained	Blue-and-white; spring	Requires summer shade
Polygonatum commutatum (great Solomon's seal)	4–7	2–5'	PSh to LSh	Humusy; moist	Cream; spring	Forms clumps with arching stems
P. odoratum var. *thunbergii* 'Variegatum' (variegated Solomon's seal)	4–7	2–3'	PSh to LSh	Humusy, moist	Cream; spring	Grown for variegated foliage
Polygonum affine (Himalayan fleeceflower)	4–7	6–9"	S to PSh	Ordinary, well drained	Rose pink; summer	Mat forming
P. amplexicaule (mountain fleece)	4–7	2–3'	S to PSh	Ordinary, well drained	Rose red or white; early fall	Small flowers in dense clusters
P. bistorta 'Superbum' (European bistort)	4–6	2–3'	S to PSh	Ordinary, well drained	Pink; late spring to early summer	Clump forming; best where summers are cool
P. japonicum var. *compactum* (Raynoutria fleeceflower)	5–8	1–1½'	S to PSh	Ordinary, well drained	Pink to red-brown; late summer	Good for stabilizing steep dry slopes
P. sachalinense (giant knotweed)	4–8	8–12'	S to PSh	Ordinary, well drained	Greenish white late summer to early fall	Tenacious; can be invasive
Potentilla atrosanguinea (ruby cinquefoil)	5–8	1–1½'	S to PSh	Ordinary, well drained	Red to yellow; late spring to early summer	Sprawling habit
P. nepalensis (Nepal cinquefoil)	5–8	1–1½'	S to PSh	Ordinary, well drained	Rose; summer	Cv. 'Miss Willmott' especially ornamental
P. neumanniana (spring cinquefoil)	3–7	3"	S to PSh	Ordinary, well drained	Yellow; late spring	Rhizomatous; mat forming
P. recta 'Warrenii' (sulfur cinquefoil)	3–7	1½–2'	S to PSh	Ordinary, well drained	Yellow; late spring	Well suited to hot areas

(continues)

OTHER USEFUL PERENNIALS (continued)

Name	Zones	Height	Exposure*	Soil Requirements	Flower Color and Bloom Time	Comments
P. × *tonguei* (orange cinquefoil)	6–8	3"	S to PSh	Ordinary, well drained	Orange-and-red; late spring to early summer	Spreads by runners
P. tridentata (three-tooth cinquefoil)	3–7	3–6"	S to PSh	Ordinary, well drained	White; late spring to early summer	Vigorous ground cover
Primula denticulata (Himalayan primrose)	5–7	9–12"	PSh to LSh	Moist, well drained	Lilac pink or white; spring	Intolerant of summer heat
P. japonica (Japanese primrose)	5–7	1½–2'	PSh to LSh	Moist, well drained	Red to white; late spring	As for *P. denticulata*
P. × *polyantha* (polyanthus)	2–7	6–12"	PSh to LSh	Moist, well drained	Various colors and combinations; spring	As for *P. demticulata*
P. sieboldii (Japanese star primrose)	4–7	9–15"	PSh to LSh	Moist, well drained	Purple, rose, or white; late spring	As for *P. denticulata*
P. yeris (cowslip primrose)	5–7	9–12"	PSh to LSh	Moist, well drained	Yellow; spring	As for *P. denticulata*
P. vulgaris cvs. (English primrose)	6–7	6–9"	PSh to LSh	Moist, well drained	Various colors and combinations; spring	As for *P. denticulata*
Prunella grandiflora (self heal)	4–7	9–12"	PSh to LSh	Ordinary, well drained	Pale violet, red-violet, or white; summer	Summer shade desirable
Pulmonaria angustifolia (blue lungwort)	3–8	9–12"	PSh to LSh	Ordinary, well drained	Blue to pink; early spring	Clump forming; shade essential in summer
P. montana (red lungwort)	5–8	6–12"	PSh to LSh	Ordinary, well drained	Rose pink or white; spring	Semievergreen unspotted foliage
P. officinalis (Jerusalem sage, lungwort)	2–8	6–12"	PSh to LSh	Ordinary, well drained	Purple, blue, or white; spring	Spotted foliage
P. saccharata (Bethlehem sage)	2–8	6–12"	PSh to LSh	Ordinary, well drained	Reddish violet, pink, or white; spring	Spotted foliage
Ranunculus aconitifolius 'Flore Pleno' (double-white buttercup)	5–8	1½–2'	S to PSh	Ordinary, well drained	White; spring	Clump forming; not invasive
R. acris 'Flore Pleno' (tall double buttercup)	4–7	2–3'	S to PSh	Ordinary, well drained	Yellow; spring	As for *R. aconitifolius* 'Flore Pleno'
R. repens 'Flore Pleno' (creeping double buttercup)	3–7	1–1½'	S to PSh	Ordinary, well drained	Yellow; mid to late spring	Spreads by node-rooting stolons; can be invasive
Ratibida columnifera (prairie coneflower)	3–8	2–3'	S to PSh	Ordinary, well drained	Yellow-and-reddish green; summer	Best grown in masses
Rodgersia aesculifolia (tall rodgersia)	4–8	5–7'	S to PSh	Moist to wet	Cream to pink; late spring to early summer	Bold foliage; best on boggy ground
R. pinnata (featherleaf rodgersia)	5–8	3–4'	S to PSh	Moist to wet	Red to white; late spring to early summer	Foliage turns bronzy in late summer
Romneya coulteri (Matilija poppy)	7–8	6–8'	S	Ordinary, well drained	White; late summer to mid fall	Start in pots; root disturbance fatal
Roscoea cautleoides (hardy ginger)	7–8	1½–2'	S to PSh	Ordinary, well drained	Pale yellow; summer	Roots intolerant of frost; other species with pink or blue flowers
R. purpurea syn. *R. procera* (purple ginger)	6–9	6–12"	S to PSh	Ordinary, well drained	Purple or white; summer	Plant crowns 6 inches deep; mulch in winter
Rosmarinus officinalis (rosemary): *see Chapter 29*						
Rudbeckia fulgida var. *sullivantii* 'Goldsturm' (coneflower)	4–8	2–2½'	S	Ordinary, well drained	Yellow with brown-black center; summer	Large-flowered
R. hirta var. *pulcherrima* (black-eyed Susan)	4–8	2–4'	S to PSh	Ordinary, well drained	Yellow with brown-black center; summer	Often biennial; flowers first year, hence commonly treated as annual

Name	Zones	Height	Exposure*	Soil Requirements	Flower Color and Bloom Time	Comments
R. laciniata 'Golden Glow' (golden glow)	4–9	4–5'	S	Ordinary, well drained	Yellow; summer	Double flowers profusely borne
R. nitida (coneflower)	4–8	2–4 (7)'	S	Ordinary, well drained	Yellow with greenish center; summer	Some cultivars tall, others double flowered
Salvia argentea (silver sage)	5–8	3–4'	S to PSh	Ordinary, well drained	Purple or cream; summer	Short-lived; often grown as biennial or annual
S. azurea var. *grandiflora* (azure sage)	6–9	4–5'	S	Ordinary, well drained	Light blue; late summer to early fall	Often listed as *S. pitcheri*
S. elegans (pineapple sage)	8–10	4–6'	S to PSh	Ordinary, well drained	Red; late summer to fall	Roots survive mild winters if mulched
S. farinacea (blue sage, mealycup sage)	8–10	2–3'	S to PSh	Ordinary, well drained	Blue or gray white; late summer to fall	As for *S. elegans*; often grown in the North as an annual
S. pratensis (meadow clary)	6–8	2½–3'	S	Ordinary, well drained	Pink to purple; summer	Often short lived
Sanguisorba canadensis (great burnet)	3–7	3–6'	S to PSh	Ordinary, well drained	Cream; fall	One of the best late-blooming perennials
S. obtusa (Japanese burnet)	4–7	2–3'	S to PSh	Ordinary, well drained	Rose pink; fall	Grayish foliage; arching flower spikes
Santolina chamaecyparis (lavender cotton)	6–8	1–2'	S	Ordinary, well drained	Yellow; early summer	Shrubby; silvery gray aromatic foliage
S. virens (green lavender cotton)	6–8	1–2'	S	Ordinary, well drained	Yellow; early summer	Similar to *S. chamaecyparis* but has green foliage
Saponaria ocymoides (rock soapwort)	4–7	4–12"	S	Ordinary, well drained	Deep pink; late spring, sporadically to fall	Trailing, mat forming
Saxifraga × *arendsii* (mossy saxifrage)	4–7	4–6"	PSh to LSh	Humusy, moist	Pink to red; late spring	Best in damp, shaded wall gardens
S. paniculata (aizoon saxifrage)	4–7	3–12"	PSh to LSh	Humusy, moist	White to rose; late spring to early summer	Continuous moisture required
S. stolonifera (strawberry geranium)	6–8	9–12"	PSh to LSh	Humusy, moist	White; late spring	Spreads by slender runners
S. × *urbium* (London pride)	6–8	9–12"	PSh to LSh	Humusy, moist	Pink; late spring	Suited to the Pacific Northwest
Scabiosa caucasica (perennial scabiosa)	4–7	1½–2'	S to PSh	Ordinary, well drained	White, blue, or lilac; summer	Intolerant of summer heat; numerous cultivars
Schizostylis coccinea (crimson flag, African lily)	6–8	1½–2'	S to PSh	Moist, well drained	Red; summer to early fall	Requires constant soil moisture
Sedum acre (stonecrop, wall pepper)	5–8	2–4"	S	Ordinary, well drained	Yellow; late spring	Forms carpet; often invasive in the East
S. 'Autumn Joy'	3–8	1½–2'	S to PSh	Ordinary, well drained	Pink; late summer to early fall	Superior late-season perennial
S. sarmentosum (creeping sedum)	7–8	2–4"	S to PSh	Ordinary, well drained	Yellow; late spring	Forms carpet; stems root freely
S. spectabile (showy sedum)	4–8	1½–2'	S to PSh	Ordinary, well drained	Pink; late summer to early fall	Flowers red to white in cultivars
S. telephium var. *maximum* 'Atropurpureum' (purple leaf sedum)	3–8	1½–2'	S to PSh	Ordinary, well drained	Pink; late summer to early fall	Foliage maroon purple
Sempervivum spp. (hen and chickens, houseleek, live-forever)	(4) 6–8	3–6" (12" in flower)	S	Sandy or gritty	Pink or purplish; summer	Form dense fleshy rosettes; many cultivars

(continues)

OTHER USEFUL PERENNIALS (continued)

Name	Zones	Height	Exposure*	Soil Requirements	Flower Color and Bloom Time	Comments
Senecio cineraria (dusty miller)	8–10	1–2'	S to PSh	Ordinary, well drained	Yellowish; late summer	Grown for silver gray foliage
Senna hebecarpa (hardy senna)	5–8	3–6'	S to PSh	Ordinary, well drained	Yellow; summer	Formerly *Cassia; S. marilandica* is similar
Sidalcea malviflora (checkerbloom)	5–8	2–3'	S to PSh	Ordinary, well drained	Pink, purplish, or white; late spring to early summer	Looks like a small hollyhock; short lived
Silene dioica (red campion)	6–8	1½–2½'	S to PSh	Ordinary, well drained	Reddish purple; spring	Sexes on separate plants
S. schafta (moss campion)	6–8	½–¾"	S to PSh	Ordinary, well drained	Pink or purple; late summer to fall	Mat forming; good edging plant
Silphium perfoliatum (cup plant, rosinweed)	4–8	6–8'	S to PSh	Ordinary, well drained	Yellow; late summer	Paired leaves joined at base
Smilacina racemosa (false Solomon's seal)	3–8	2–3'	S to PSh, or Lsh	Ordinary, well drained	Cream; spring	Showy red berries in fall on arching stems
Solidago cvs. (goldenrod)	5–9	1½–4'	S to PSh	Ordinary, well drained	Yellow; late summer	Good cut flower
Spigelia marilandica (pinkroot)	5–8	1–1½'	PSh to LSh	Ordinary, well drained	Red-and-yellow; early summer	Requires shade, especially in the South
Stachys byzantina (lamb's ears)	4–7	1–1½'	S	Ordinary, well drained	Purple; summer	White woolly; forms rapidly spreading mat
S. grandiflora (big betony)	4–7	1½–2'	S to PSh	Ordinary, well drained	Purple; late spring	Good cut flower
Stellaria pubera (starwort)	5–7	9–12"	S to PSh	Ordinary, well drained	White; spring	*S. holostea* is similar
Stokesia laevis (Stokes aster)	5–10	1–2'	S to PSh	Ordinary, well drained	Blue; late summer	Cultivars have lilac or white flowers
Strobilanthes atropurpureus (Mexican petunia)	5–8	3–4'	S to PSh	Ordinary, well drained	Blue-violet; late summer	Winter mulch advisable
Symphytum grandiflorum (yellow lungwort)	5–7	8–12"	PSh to LSh	Ordinary, well drained	Pale yellow; late spring to early summer	Forms dense mats in dry shade
S. × rubrum (comfrey)	5–7	1½–2'	S to PSh	Ordinary, well drained	Red; late spring to early summer	Forms clumps; long lived
S. × uplandicum (Russian comfrey)	5–7	2–3'	S to PSh	Ordinary, well drained	Blue-and-purple; summer	Cv. 'Variegatum' has attractive foliage
Telekia speciosa, syn. *Buphthalmum speciosa* (sun wheel)	6–8	5–6'	S to PSh	Ordinary, constantly moist	Yellow; summer	Large, coarse, clump forming
Teucrium chamaedrys (germander)	5–8	1–2'	S to PSh	Ordinary, well drained	Violet; late spring to early summer	Evergreen; useful as low hedge
Thermopsis caroliniana (false lupine)	4–8	3–5'	S to PSh	Ordinary, well drained	Yellow; late spring to early summer	Especially effective when massed
Thymus pseudolanuginosus (woolly thyme)	6–8	3"	S	Ordinary, well drained	Pale pink; late spring	Forms woolly gray green mat
T. serpyllum (mother of thyme)	5–7	3–6"	S	Ordinary, well drained	Purple; late spring to early summer	Fragrant; mat forming; creeper
Tiarella cordifolia (foamflower)	5–8	6–12"	PSh to LSh	Humusy, moist	White; spring	Creeper; *T. wherryi* forms clumps

Name	Zones	Height	Exposure*	Soil Requirements	Flower Color and Bloom Time	Comments
Tradescantia hirsuticaulis (hairy spiderwort)	5–8	9–12"	S to PSh	Ordinary, well drained	Purplish blue, pink, or white spring to summer	Forms large clumps
T. virginiana hybrids, syn. *T. × andersoniana* (garden spiderwort)	5–8	1½–2'	S to PSh	Ordinary, well drained	Purple, pink, or white; spring to summer	Variable, of diverse parentage; some self-sow
Tricyrtis hirta (toad lily)	5–7	2–3'	PSh to LSh	Ordinary, well drained	White and purple; early to mid fall	Flowers effective at close range
Trillium spp. (wake robin): *see Chapter 22*						
Trollius × cultorum (hybrid globeflower)	5–7	1½–2'	S to PSh	Humusy, moist to wet	Cream to orange; late spring to early summer	Requires consistently moist soil
T. europaeus (European globeflower)	5–7	1½–2'	S to PSh	Humusy, moist to wet	Lemon yellow; late spring to early summer	As for *T. × cultorum*
T. ledebourii (late globeflower)	5–7	2–3'	S to PSh	Humusy, moist to wet	Orange; late summer	As for *T. × cultorum*
Uvularia grandiflora (bellwort)	5–9	1½–3'	PSh, LSh, or Sh	Humusy, moist	Yellow; late spring	Clump forming
Valeriana officinalis (common valerian)	5–8	5'	S to PSh	Ordinary, well drained	Lavender, pink, or white; summer	Best in informal border
Verbena canadensis (rose vervain)	5–7	1½–3'	S to PSh	Ordinary, well drained	Rose purple or white; spring to summer	Clump forming; spreading; stem rooting
V. rigida (veiny verbena)	7–9	1–1½'	S to PSh	Ordinary, well drained	Red-violet; summer	Spreads by stolons; often used as annual
V. tenuisecta (moss verbena)	7–8	9–12"	S to PSh	Ordinary, well drained	Purple to pink or white; summer	Branched; spreading; stem rooting
Vernonia noveboracensis (ironweed)	6–8	4–6'	S to PSh	Constantly moist	Purple; summer	Clump forming
Veronica austriaca (Hungarian speedwell)	4–8	1–1½'	S	Ordinary, well drained	Blue; summer	Mat forming; often listed as *V. latifolia*
V. grandis var. *holophylla* (Japanese speedwell)	4–8	2–3'	S	Ordinary, well drained	Bright blue; late summer to fall	Latest flowering of this group
V. incana (woolly speedwell)	3–7	1–1½'	S	Ordinary, well drained	Blue; late spring to early summer	White woolly foliage
V. longifolia (beach speedwell)	4–8	2–4'	S	Ordinary, well drained	Lilac blue; late summer	Often listed as *V. maritima*
V. prostrata (hairbell speedwell)	4–8	8–10"	S	Ordinary, well drained	Blue; late spring to summer	Soon carpets the ground
V. spicata (spike speedwell)	5–8	1–2'	S to PSh	Ordinary, well drained	Blue or white; late summer	Cultivars have red or purple flowers
Veronicastrum virginicum (Culver's root)	4–8	3–6'	S to PSh	Ordinary, well drained	White or pale lavender; late summer	Tall spikes effective at rear of garden
Viola cornuta (horned violet, viola)	5–7	6–9"	S to PSh	Ordinary, well drained	Various; spring to summer	Usually short lived
V. odorata (sweet violet)	5–8	4–8"	PSh to LSh	Ordinary, well drained	Violet, rose, or white; spring	Many cultivars, varying in flower size and color
Yucca filamentosa (Adam's needle, eastern yucca)	5–8	4–6'	S	Sandy or gravelly	Cream; summer	Evergreen; rigid, spine-tipped leaves in big rosettes

* S, full sun; Sh, shade (no direct sun); PSh, partial shade (sun exposure only part of the day); LSh, light shade (e.g., the shade of tall, open trees, with little or no exposure to direct sun).

Blue indigo (*Baptisia australis*)

Garden avens (*Geum coccineum*)

Veronica 'Minuet'

Evergreen candytuft (*Iberis sempervirens*)

Blue phlox (*Phlox divaricata*)

Garden rose mallow (*Hibiscus moscheutos*)

Large-flowered sundrops (*Oenothera fruticosa*)

Balloon flower (*Platycodon grandiflorus*)

Gooseneck loosestrife (*Lysimachia clethroides*)

Sneezeweed (*Helenium autumnale*)

Yellow foxglove (*Digitalis grandiflora*)

Silver king (*Artemisia ludoviciana*)

Cattail gayfeather (*Liatris pycnostachya*)

Maltese cross
(*Lychnis chalcedonica*)

Coneflower
(*Rudbeckia fulgida*
'Goldsturm')

Toad lily
(*Tricyrtis hirta*)

Tall ragwort (*Ligularia* 'The Rocket')

Adam's needle (*Yucca filamentosa*)

Basket-of-gold
(*Aurinia saxatilis*)

Musk mallow
(*Malva moschata*)

Small globe thistle
(*Echinops ritro*
'Taplow Blue')

Variegated
Solomon's seal
(*Polygonatum
falcatum* 'Variegatum')

Great burnet (*Sanguisorba canadensis*)

Myrtle spurge (*Euphorbia myrsinites*)

Stokes aster
(*Stokesia laevis*)

Perennial scabiosa
(*Scabiosa caucasica*)

Hardy fuchsia
(*Fuchsia megellanica*)

Red valerian
(*Centranthus ruber*)

Golden glow
(*Rudbeckia laciniata*
'Golden Glow')

Lavender cotton
(*Santolina
chamaecyparis*)

Amethyst sea holly
(*Eryngium
amethystinum*
'Jos Elking')

Hardy senna
(*Senna hebecarlpa*)

Black cohosh
(*Cimicifuga racemosa*)

'Disco Belle', a dwarf, large-flowered cultivar of *Hibiscus moscheutos*

Sedum 'Autumn Joy'

Bluestar (*Amsonia tabermaemontana*)

Fern-leaf yarrow (*Achillea aquilegifolium*)

Red-hot poker (*Kniphofia hybrid*)

Prairie coneflower
(*Ratibida columnifera*)

Nippon daisy
(*Chrysanthemum
nipponicum*)

Maximilian sunflower
(*Helianthus maximiliani*)

Blood-red geranium
(*Geranium
sanguineum*)

Leopard's-bane
(*Doronicum orientale* 'Mrs. Mason')

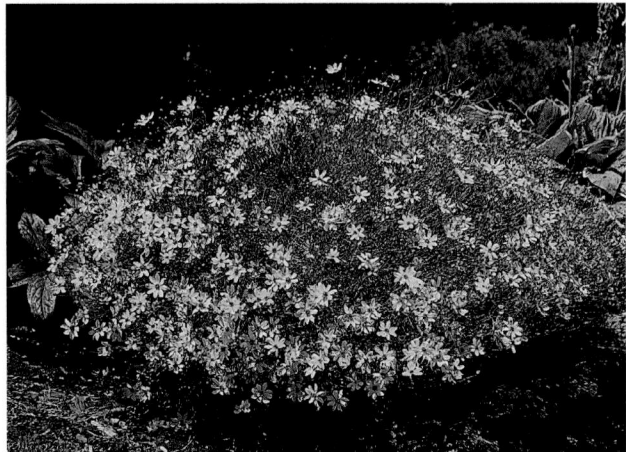

Thread-leaf coreopsis (*Coreopsis verticillata* 'Moonbeam')

Bellwort
(*Uvularia grandiflora*)

Hardy prickly pear
(*Opuntia humifusa*)

Great blue lobelia
(*Lobelia siphilitica*)

PERENNIALS FOR POOR, NUTRIENT-DEFICIENT SOIL

Name	Zones	Height	Exposure*	Flower and Foliage Color and Bloom Time
Achillea millefolium (common yarrow)	2–9	1½–2'	S	Flowers white, some cultivars pink to red; summer
Anaphalis margaritacea (pearly everlasting)	3–8	1–1½'	S to PSh	Flowers yellowish; foliage gray; late spring to early summer
Anchusa azurea (Italian bugloss)	3–7	3–5'	S to PSh	Flowers blue; late spring to early summer
Anthemis tinctoria (golden marguerite)	2–8	2–3'	S	Flowers yellow; late spring
Arabis caucasica (wallcress)	5–7	6–12"	S	Flowers white; spring
Artemisia ludoviciana (silver king)	4–8	2–3'	S	Foliage gray
A. schmidtiana (silvermound)	3–7	1½–2'	S	Foliage silvery
A. stelleriana (dusty miller)	3–7	1–1½'	S to PSh	Foliage silvery
Asclepias tuberosa (butterfly weed)	3–8	1½–3'	S	Flowers orange; summer
Aurinia saxatilis (basket-of-gold)	4–7	1–1½'	S	Flowers yellow; spring
Baptisia australis (blue indigo)	4–8	2½–4'	S to PSh	Flowers indigo blue; late spring
Callirhoë involucrata (winecups)	4–8	6–12"	S	Flowers red-violet; spring and summer
Centaurea macrocephala (globe centaurea, yellow knapweed)	3–8	3–4'	S	Flowers yellow; spring to early summer
Cerastium tomentosum (snow-in-summer)	4–7	6–9"	S	Flowers white; late spring to early summer
Coreopsis grandiflora (common coreopsis, tickseed)	5–8	2–3'	S to PSh	Flowers yellow; late spring to summer
Dianthus deltoides (maiden pink)	4–6	9–12"	S to PSh	Flowers pink; late spring
D. plumarius (cottage pink)	4–7	1–1½'	S to PSh	Flowers pink; late spring
Eryngium amethystinum (amethyst sea holly)	4–8	2–3'	S	Flowers bluish; summer
Euphorbia myrsinites (myrtle spurge, creeping spurge)	4–8	6–9"	S	Flowers yellow; spring
Gaillardia × grandiflora (blanketflower)	4–8	2–2½'	S to PSh	Flowers red-and-yellow; late spring to early fall
Gaura lindheimeri (white gaura)	6–8	3–5'	S to PSh	Flowers white to pink; summer to early fall
Geranium maculatum (hardy geranium)	4–7	1½–2'	S to PSh	Flowers pinkish purple; spring
G. sanguineum (blood-red geranium)	4–7	9–12"	S to PSh	Flowers purplish red; spring to late summer
Hemerocallis fulva (common daylily)	2–8	2½–3½'	S to PSh	Flowers rusty orange; early summer
Iberis sempervirens (evergreen candytuft)	4–8	9–12"	S to PSh	Flowers white; spring
Iris hybrids (tall bearded iris)	3–8	2–4'	S	Flowers various colors; spring, some again in fall
Linum perenne (perennial flax)	5–8	1½–2'	S	Flowers blue; spring and summer
Oenothera missouriensis (Ozark sundrops)	3–7	9–12"	S	Flowers yellow; summer
Phlox subulata (mountain pink)	2–7	3"	S	Flowers bluish purple, red, pink, or white; spring
Potentilla tridentata (three-tooth cinquefoil)	3–7	3–6"	S to PSh	Flowers white; late spring to early summer
Rudbeckia fulgida (perennial black-eyed Susan, coneflower)	4–8	2–2½'	S	Flowers yellow and brown-black; summer
Salvia azurea (blue sage, azure sage)	6–9	4–5'	S	Flowers blue; late summer to early fall
Sedum spp. (creeping stonecrop)	3–7	3–9"	S	Flowers yellow, pink, or white; late spring to summer
Sedum spp. (clump sedum)	3–8	1–2'	S to PSh	Flowers pink to reddish purple; late summer to early fall
Sempervivum spp. (hen and chickens)	5–8	3–4"	S	Flowers reddish purple; summer

* S, full sun; Sh, shade (no direct sun); PSh, partial shade (sun exposure only part of the day); LSh, light shade (e.g., the shade of tall, open trees, with little or no exposure to direct sun).

PERENNIALS FOR DRY, SANDY SOIL

Name	Zones	Height	Exposure*	Flower and Foliage Color and Bloom Time
Achillea millefolium (common yarrow)	2–9	1½–2'	S	Flowers white, same cultivars pink to red; summer
A. ptarmica (sneezewort)	2–9	1½–2'	S	Flowers white; summer
Ajuga reptans (carpet bugle)	4–7	3–6"	S to PSh	Flowers blue; spring
Anthemis tinctoria (golden marguerite)	2–8	2–3'	S	Flowers yellow; late spring
Artemisia ludoviciana (silver king)	4–8	2–3'	S	Foliage gray
A. schmidtiana (silvermound)	3–7	1½–2'	S	Foliage silvery
A. stelleriana (dusty miller)	3–7	1–1½'	S	Foliage silvery
Asclepias tuberosa (butterfly weed)	3–8	1½–3'	S	Flowers orange; summer
Aster novae-angliae (New England aster)	2–8	3–6'	S to PSh	Flowers purple and yellow; early fall
Callirho involucrata (winecups)	4–8	6–12"	S	Flowers red-violet; spring and summer
Coreopsis grandiflora (common coreopsis, tickseed)	5–8	2–3'	S to PSh	Flowers yellow; late spring to summer
Dianthus plumerius (cottage pink)	4–7	1–1½'	S to PSh	Flowers pink; late spring
Echinops ritro (globe thistle)	4–8	3–5'	S	Flowers blue; summer
Eryngium amethystinum (amethyst sea holly)	4–8	2–3'	S	Flowers bluish; summer
Eupatorium coelestinum (hardy ageratum, mist flower)	5–8	2–3'	S to PSh	Flowers blue; late summer to early fall
Gaillardia × *grandiflora* (blanketflower)	4–8	2–2½'	S to PSh	Flowers red and yellow; late spring to early fall
Helianthus × *multiflorus* (perennial sunflower)	3–7	3–5'	S to PSh	Flowers yellow; summer
Iris hybrids (tall bearded iris)	3–8	2–4'	S	Flowers various colors; spring
Liatris pycnostachya (cattail gayfeather, Kansas gayfeather)	2–8	4–6'	S to PSh	Flowers pinkish lavender; late summer
Papaver nudicaule (Iceland poppy)	2–7	1–2'	S	Flowers various colors; early summer
Senna hebecarpa (hardy senna)	5–8	3–6'	S to PSh	Flowers yellow; summer

* S, full sun; Sh, shade (no direct sun); PSh, partial shade (sun exposure only part of the day); LSh, light shade (e.g., the shade of tall, open trees, with little or no exposure to direct sun).

PERENNIALS FOR WET GROUND

Name	Zones	Height	Exposure*	Moisture†	Flower Color and Bloom Time
Anemone × *hybrida* (Japanese anemone)	5–7	2–3'	S to PSh	Moist	White to pink late summer
Aruncus dioicus (goatsbeard)	4–7	4–6'	S to PSh	Moist	White; late spring to early summer
Astilbe × *arendsii*	5–7	9–12"	PSh	Moist	Pink, some cultivars red or white; late spring to summer
Astrantia major (masterwort)	5–7	2–3'	S to PSh	Wet	Pink; spring
Brunnera macrophylla (Siberian bugloss)	4–8	1–1½'	S, PSh, or LSh	Moist	Blue; mid to late spring
Caltha palustris (marsh marigold)	3–7	6–12"	S to PSh	Moist to wet	Yellow; spring
Chelone glabra (turtlehead)	3–8	2–3'	S to PSh	Wet	Pinkish to white; summer
C. lyonii (pink turtlehead)	3–8	2–3'	S to PSh	Wet	Pinkish to white; late summer to early fall
Chrysanthemum serotinum (giant daisy)	5–8	4–7'	S	Wet	White-and-yellow; summer
Cimicifuga racemosa (black cohosh)	2–7	5–8'	S to PSh	Moist	White; summer to early fall
Epilobium angustifolium (fireweed)	5–7 (8)	3–5'	S	Moist to wet	Rose pink; summer

(continues)

PERENNIALS FOR WET GROUND (continued)

Name	Zones	Height	Exposure*	Moisture†	Flower Color and Bloom Time
Epimedium spp. (bishop's hat)	5–7	1'	PSh	Moist	Red, pink, yellow and/or white; spring
Eupatorium purpureum (joe-pye weed)	5–8	6–10'	S	Moist to wet	Pinkish purple; late summer
Filipendula spp. ‡ (queen of the prairie)	2–7	4–6'	PSh	Wet	Pink or cream; late spring to early summer
Gentiana andrewsii (bottle gentian)	5–8	1½– 2'	S	Wet	Bluish purple; summer
Hemerocallis hybrids (hybrid daylily)	2–10	1–5'	S to PSh	Moist	Various colors; early summer, a few reflowering
Hibiscus moscheutos (rose mallow)	5–8	3–8'	S	Moist to wet	Red, pink, or white; late summer
Hosta spp. and cvs. (plantain lily)	4–8	1½–3'	PSh	Moist	Lavender or white; late summer and early fall
Iris cristata (crested iris)	4–8	3–4"	PSh	Moist	Lavender-and-yellow; late spring
I. ensata (Japanese iris)	5–8	2½–5'	S to PSh	Moist	Reddish purple to blue; early to mid summer
I. hybrids (bearded iris)	3–8	1–4'	S	Moist	Various colors; spring
I. pseudacorus (yellow flag)	5–8	3–4'	S to PSh	Wet	Yellow; summer
I. sibirica (Siberian iris)	4–8	2–3'	S	Moist	Purple, blue, or white; late spring
I. versicolor (blue flag)	4–7	2–4'	S	Moist to wet	Lavender purple and yellow; summer
Ligularia dentata (bigleaf goldenray, ragwort)	3–8	3–4'	PSh	Moist to wet	Yellow; late summer
Lobelia cardinalis (cardinal flower)	3–7	2–3'	PSh	Moist to wet	Red; late summer to early fall
L. siphilitica (great blue lobelia)	4–7	2–3'	S to PSh	Moist	Blue or white; summer
Lysimachia clethroides (gooseneck loosestrife)	4–8	2–3'	S to PSh	Moist	White; summer
L. punctata (yellow loosestrife)	4–8	2–3'	S to PSh	Moist to wet	Yellow; late spring to early summer
Lythrum salicaria hybrids (hybrid loosestrife)	4–8	3–4'	S to PSh	Moist to wet	Rose pink to white; summer
Monarda didyma (bee balm)	5–8	2–3'	S to PSh	Moist	Red; summer
Myosotis scorpioides (perennial forget-me-not)	5–8	1–2'	S to PSh	Moist to wet	Blue; spring to summer
Ranunculus acris 'Flore Pleno' (tall double buttercup)	4–7	2–3'	S to PSh	Moist	Yellow; spring
Ranunculus repens 'Flore Pleno' (creeping double buttercup)	3–7	1–1½'	S to PSh	Moist	Yellow; spring
Tradescantia virginiana hybrids, syn. *T.* × *andersoniana* (spiderwort)	5–8	1½–2'	S to PSh	Moist	Purple, pink, or white; spring to early summer
Trollius × *cultorum* (hybrid globeflower)	5–7	1½–2'	S to PSh	Moist to wet	Yellow; late spring to early summer
Vernonia noveboracensis (ironweed)	6–8	4–6'	S to PSh	Moist	Purple; summer

* S, full sun; Sh, shade (no direct sun); PSh, partial shade (sun exposure only part of the day); LSh, light shade (e.g., the shade of tall, open trees, with little or no exposure to direct sun).

† Moist, constantly damp, never drying out; wet, mostly saturated, but occasionally only damp during prolonged dry periods.

‡ Except *F. vulgaris*

PERENNIALS WITH ESPECIALLY FRAGRANT FLOWERS OR FOLIAGE
The abbreviation fol. *indicates fragrant foliage.*

Name	Zones	Height	Exposure*	Flower Color and Bloom Time
Aloysia triphylla (lemon verbena)	8–10	5–10'	S to PSh	White; summer; fol.
Arabis spp. (rock cress)	5–7	6–12"	S	White; spring
Artemisia abrotanum (Southernwood)	5–8	2–4'	S to PSh	Yellowish; late summer; fol.
A. lactiflora (white mugwort)	3–7	4–6'	S to PSh	Cream; late summer; fol.

Name	Zones	Height	Exposure*	Flower Color and Bloom Time
Centranthus ruber (red valerian)	4–8	2–3'	S to PSh	Pink or white; summer
Convallaria majalis (lily-of-the-valley)	4–7	6–9"	PSh to LSh	White; spring
Dianthus plumarius (cottage pink)	4–7	1–1½'	S to PSh	Pink to white; late spring
Dictamnus albus (gas plant)	4–8	2–3'	S to PSh	Rose pink or white; spring
Hemerocallis lilioasphodelus (lemon daylily)	4–8	2–2½'	S to PSh	Yellow; early summer
Hesperis matronalis (dame's rocket)	6–8	3–4'	S to PSh	Lilac or white; late spring to early summer
Hosta plantaginea (fragrant plantain lily)	4–8	1½–2½'	PSh to Sh	White; late summer
Lathyrus grandiflorus (two-flowered sweet pea)	6–8	4–6'	S to PSh	Rose purple; summer
Lavandula angustifolia (English lavender)	5–8	1–3'	S to PSh	Lavender to purple; summer; fol.
Lychnis viscaria (German catchfly)	4–8	1–1½'	S to PSh	Magenta; late spring to early summer
Melissa officinalis (lemon balm)	6–8	1–2'	S to PSh	White; summer; fol.
Monarda didyma (bee balm)	5–8	2–3'	S to PSh	Red; summer
Origanum majorana (sweet marjoram)	8–9	1–2'	S to PSh	Purplish; summer; fol.
Paeonia lactiflora hybrids (hybrid peony)	2–7	2–4'	S to PSh	Various colors; late spring
Phlox paniculata (tall summer phlox)	4–8	2–4'	S to PSh	Pink, red, or white; summer
Thymus spp. (thyme)	5–8	3–4"	S to PSh	Purple to white; spring and summer; fol.
Valeriana officinalis (common valerian)	4–7	3–4'	S to PSh	White, pink, or lavender; late spring to early summer
Viola cornuta (horned violet)	5–7	6–9"	S to PSh	Various colors; spring and summer
V. odorata (sweet violet)	5–8	4–8"	PSh to LSh	Violet, rose, or white; spring

* S, full sun; Sh, shade (no direct sun); PSh, partial shade (sun exposure only part of the day); LSh, light shade (e.g., the shade of tall, open trees, with little or no exposure to direct sun).

LOW-GROWING PERENNIALS FOR EDGING

Name	Zones	Height	Exposure*	Flower Color and Bloom Time
Achillea × *lewisii* (tufted yarrow)	3–7	4–6"	S	Pale yellow; summer
A. tomentosa (woolly yarrow)	2–9	6–12"	S	Yellow; summer
Adonis amurensis (Amur adonis)	4–8	8–12"	S to PSh	Yellow; early spring
Ajuga reptans (carpet bugle)	4–7	3–6"	S to PSh	Blue; spring
Alchemilla vulgaris (lady's mantle)	3–8	1–1½'	PSh to LSh	Yellow; spring
Anemone pulsatilla (pasque flower)	5–8	8–12"	S to PSh	Bluish purple; spring
Antennaria dioica (pussy toes)	4–7	8–10"	S	Pinkish white; summer
Aquilegia flabellata (fan columbine)	5–7	1–1½'	S to PSh	Lilac or white; late spring
Arabis caucasica (wallcress)	5–7	6–12"	S	White; spring
A. procurrens (wallcress)	4–7	6–12"	S	White; spring
Arctotheca calendula (capeweed)	9–10	8–12"	S	Yellow; early summer
Arenaria montana (mountain sandwort)	4–7	6–8"	S	White; spring
A. verna (moss sandwort)	5–7	2–4"	S	White; spring
Armeria maritima (thrift)	4–7	6–12"	S	Pink or white; late spring to early summer
Astilbe chinensis 'Pumila' (dwarf Chinese astilbe)	5–7	8–12"	PSh	Pink; mid to late summer
Aubrieta deltoidea (purple rock cress)	5–7	4–6"	S	Purple or white; spring
Aurinia saxatilis 'Compactum' (dwarf basket-of-gold)	4–7	8–10"	S	Yellow; spring

(continues)

LOW-GROWING PERENNIALS FOR EDGING (continued)

Name	Zones	Height	Exposure*	Flower Color and Bloom Time
Bellis perennis (English daisy)	4–7	3–6"	S to PSh	Red, pink, or white; spring to early summer
Calceolaria biflora 'John Innes' (dwarf calceolaria)	6–7	4–6"	S to PSh	Yellow; summer
Campanula carpatica (Carpathian harebell)	4–8	6–12"	S to PSh	Bluish lilac, purple, or white; late spring to early summer
Cerastium tomentosum (snow-in-summer)	4–7	6–9"	S	White; late spring early summer
Ceratostigma plumbaginoides (blue leadwort)	6–9	9–12"	PSh to LSh	Deep blue; late summer to early fall
Chrysogonum virginianum (golden star)	5–8	9–12"	PSh to LSh	Yellow; summer
Corydalis lutea (yellow corydalis)	5–7	6–12"	S to LSh	Yellow; spring to summer
Dianthus deltoides (maiden pink)	4–7	6–9"	S to PSh	Pink; late spring
D. gratianopolitanus (cheddar pink)	5–8	9–12"	S to PSh	Pink; late spring to early summer
D. plumarius (cottage pink)	4–8	1–1½'	S to PSh	Pink to white; late spring
Dicentra cucullaria (Dutchman's-breeches)	4–7	5–8"	PSh to LSh	White and yellow; spring
Duchesnea indica (barren strawberry)	4–8	3–6"	S to PSh	Yellow; spring
Epimedium spp. (bishop's hat)	5–7	9–12"	PSh to LSh	Red, pink, yellow, or white; spring
Euphorbia epithymoides (cushion spurge)	5–8	1–1½'	S	Yellow; spring
E. myrsinites (myrtle spurge)	4–8	6–9"	S	Yellow; spring
Festuca ovina var. *glauca* (blue fescue)	5–8	6–10"	S	Silvery foliage
Galium odoratum (sweet woodruff)	5–7	9–12"	PSh to LSh	White; spring
Geranium dalmaticum (dalmatian geranium)	5–7	4–6"	S to PSh	Pink to white; late spring
Geum reptans (creeping avens)	6–8	6–9"	S to PSh	Yellow-orange; summer
Gypsophila repens (creeping baby's breath)	4–8	4–6"	S	White or pink; spring to fall
Helianthemum nummularium (rockrose)	4–7	6–12"	S to PSh	Various colors; early summer
Heuchera sanguinea (coralbells)	3–8	1–2'	S to PSh	Coral red, pink, or white; late spring to early summer
Iberis sempervirens (evergreen candytuft)	4–8	9–12"	S to PSh	White; spring
Inula ensifolia (sword-leaf inula)	3–7	9–12"	S to PSh	Yellow; summer
Iris cristata (crested iris)	4–8	4–6"	S to PSh	Lavender and yellow; late spring to early summer
I. hybrids (dwarf bearded iris)	5–8	10–15"	S to PSh	Various colors; spring
Leontopodium alpinum (edelweiss)	4–7	6–12"	S	Silvery; late spring to early summer
Nepeta racemosa (mauve catmint)	4–7	9–12"	S to PSh	Blue-violet; late spring to early summer
Oenothera missouriensis (Ozark sundrop)	5–8	4–6"	S	Yellow; late spring to early summer
Omphalodes cappadocica (navelwort)	6–8	8–12"	PSh, LSh, or Sh	Blue; late spring
O. verna (creeping forget-me-not)	6–9	6–8"	PSh, LSh, or Sh	Blue; late spring
Opuntia humifusa (hardy prickly pear)	6–7	6–12"	S	Yellow; late spring to early summer
Petrorhagia saxifraga (tunic flower)	5–8	6–10"	S to PSh	Pink; summer
Phlox × procumbens (hairy phlox)	5–8	9–12"	S	Purple; spring
P. stolonifera (creeping phlox)	5–8	6–12"	PSh to LSh	Purple; spring
P. subulata (mountain pink)	2–7	2–3"	S	Bluish purple, red, pink, or white; spring
Polemonium reptans (Greek valerian)	4–7	9–12"	PSh to LSh	Blue and white; late spring
Potentilla neumanniana (spring cinquefoil)	3–7	2–3"	S to PSh	Yellow; spring
P. × tonguei (orange cinquefoil)	6–8	2–3"	S to PSh	Orange and red; late spring to early summer
P. tridentata (three-tooth cinquefoil)	3–7	3–6"	S to PSh	White; late spring to early summer
Primula sieboldii (Japanese star primrose)	4–7	9–15"	PSh to LSh	Purple, rose, or white; late spring
P. veris (cowslip primrose)	5–7	9–12"	PSh to LSh	Yellow; spring
P. vulgaris (English primrose)	6–7	6–9"	PSh to LSh	Various colors and combinations; spring
Prunella grandiflora (self heal)	4–7	9–12"	PSh to LSh	Violet or white; summer

Name	Zones	Height	Exposure*	Flower Color and Bloom Time
Pulmonaria angustifolia (blue lungwort)	3–8	9–12"	PSh to LSh	Blue to pink; early spring
P. officinalis (Bethlehem sage)	2–8	6–12"	PSh to LSh	Purple, blue, or white; spring
P. saccharata (Bethlehem sage)	2–8	6–12"	PSh to LSh	Reddish violet, pink, or white; spring
Roscoea purpurea	6–9	6–12"	S to PSh	Violet; summer
Saponaria ocymoides (rock soapwort)	4–7	4–12"	S	Pink; spring to fall
Saxifraga × urbium (London pride)	6–8	9–12"	PSh to LSh	Pink; spring
Sedum spp. (creeping sedum, stonecrop)	3–8	3–6"	S	Yellow, pink, or white; late spring to summer
Silene schafta (moss campion)	6–8	6–9"	S to PSh	Pink or purple; late summer to fall
Stellaria pubera (starwort)	5–7	9–12"	S to PSh	White; spring to early summer
Symphytum grandiflorum (yellow lungwort)	5–7	8–12"	PSh to LSh	Light yellow; late spring to early summer
Tradescantia hirsuticaulis (hairy spiderwort)	5–8	9–12"	S to PSh	Purplish blue; spring to summer
Verbena tenuisecta (moss verbena)	7–8	9–12"	S to PSh	Purple to blue; summer
Veronica austriaca (Hungarian speedwell)	4–8	1–1½'	S	Blue; summer
V. incana (woolly speedwell)	3–7	1–1½'	S	Blue; late spring to early summer
V. prostrata (hairbell speedwell)	4–7	8–10"	S	Blue; late spring to summer
Viola spp. (violet)	3–8	6–12"	S to PSh, or LSh	Purple, yellow, or white; spring

* S, full sun; Sh, shade (no direct sun); PSh, partial shade (sun exposure only part of the day); LSh, light shade (e.g., the shade of tall, open trees, with little or no exposure to direct sun).

PERENNIALS WITH A LONG PERIOD OF BLOOM

Name	Zones	Height	Exposure*	Flower Color and Bloom Time
Achillea filipendula (fern-leaf yarrow)	2–9	3–4'	S	Yellow; spring to summer
Anchusa azurea (bugloss)	4–8	3–5'	S	Blue; spring to summer
Anthemis sancti-johannis (orange marguerite)	3–7	2–3'	S	Orange; summer to fall
A. tinctoria (golden marguerite)	2–8	2–3'	S	Yellow; summer to fall
Aquilegia chrysantha (golden columbine)	3–8	2–3'	PSh	Yellow; spring to summer
Armeria maritima (thrift)	4–7	6–12"	S	Pink or spring to summer white
Aster × frikartii (Frikart aster)	5–8	2–2½'	S	Lavender blue; summer to fall
Callirhoë involucrata (winecups)	4–8	6–12"	S	Red-violet; spring to summer
Campanula carpatica (Carpathian harebell)	4–8	4–6'	S to PSh	Blue or white; spring to summer
C. elatines (Adriatic bellflower)	6–8	6–12'	S to PSh	Blue or white; spring to summer
C. rotundifolia (bluebell, harebell)	3–8	3–18'	S to PSh	Blue or white; spring to summer
Centaurea montana (mountain bluet)	4–8	1½–2'	S	Blue; spring to summer
Chrysanthemum × morifolium (cushion mum)	5–8	1–2'	S	Various colors; summer to fall
C. × superbum (shasta daisy)	5–8	1–3'	S to PSh	White; summer
Coreopsis auriculata 'Nana' (dwarf earlobed coreopsis)	5–8	4–6"	S	Yellow; summer
C. grandiflora (common coreopsis)	5–8	2–3'	S to PSh	Yellow; summer
C. lanceolata 'Sunburst' (double coreopsis)	5–8	1½–2'	S to PSh	Yellow; summer
C. verticillata (threadleaf coreopsis)	3–7	1½–2'	S to PSh	Yellow to cream; summer
Coronilla varia (crown vetch)	4–7	1–2'	S	Pink and white; summer

(continues)

PERENNIALS WITH A LONG PERIOD OF BLOOM (continued)

Name	Zones	Height	Exposure*	Flower Color and Bloom Time
Delphinium elatum hybrids	4–7	4–6'	S to PSh	Various colors; summer
Dicentra eximia (fringed bleeding heart)	2–8	9–18"	PSh to LSh	Pink or white; spring to fall
Gaillardia × grandiflora (blanketflower)	4–8	6–36"	S to PSh	Red and yellow; spring to fall
Galega officinalis (goat's rue)	4–8	2–3'	S to PSh	Blue-violet; summer
Gaura lindheimeri (white gaura)	6–9	3–5'	S to PSh	White to pink; summer to fall
Geranium endressii (Pyreness cranesbill)	4–7	1–1½'	S to PSh	Blue, pink, or white; spring to summer
Gerbera jamesonii (Transvaal daisy)	8–10	1–1½'	S to PSh	Yellow to red; summer to fall
Geum × borisii (Werner Arends avens, dwarf avens)	3–7	6–9"	S to PSh	Orange; summer
Gypsophila paniculata (perennial baby's breath)	3–7	2–3'	S	White or pink; summer
Heliopsis helianthoides (orange sunflower)	4–8	3–4'	S to PSh	Yellow-orange; summer
Heuchera sanguinea (coralbells)	3–8	1½–2'	S to PSh	Red, pink, or white; spring to summer
Hibiscus moscheutos (rose mallow)	5–8	3–8'	S to PSh	Red, pink, or white; summer
Lathyrus latifolius (perennial sweet pea)	4–7	4–8	S to PSh	Pink or white; summer
Linum perenne (perennial flax)	5–8	1–1½'	S	Blue; spring to summer
Lychnis coronaria (mullein pink)	4–8	2–3'	S to PSh	Red, pink, or white; summer
Lythrum salicaria cvs. (garden loosestrife)	4–8	1½–4'	S to PSh	Purple, pink, or white; summer
Malva moschata (musk mallow)	3–8	2–3'	S to PSh	Pink or white; spring to summer
Nepeta racemosa (mauve catmint)	4–7	9–12"	S to PSh	Blue or white; spring to summer
Oenothera missouriensis (Ozark sundrops)	4–8	3"	S	Yellow; summer
Papaver nudicaule (Iceland poppy)	2–7	1–2'	S	Various colors; summer
Petrorhagia saxifraga (tunic flower)	5–8	6–9"	S to PSh	Pink; summer
Phlox paniculata (tall summer phlox)	4–8	3–4'	S to PSh	Red, pink, or white; summer to fall
Physostegia virginiana (obedience)	4–9	1½–3'	S to PSh	Rose purple or white; summer
Platycodon grandiflorus (balloon flower)	4–8	2–3'	S to PSh	Blue or white; spring to summer
Rudbeckia hirta cvs. (black-eyed Susan)	4–8	2–4'	S to PSh	Yellow-and-brown; summer
Salvia azurea var. grandiflora (azure sage)	6–9	4–5'	S	Blue; summer to fall
Scabiosa caucasica cvs. (perennial scabiosa)	4–7	1½–2'	S to PSh	Blue or white; summer
Sidalcea malviflora (checkerbloom)	5–8	2–3'	S to PSh	Pink or white; spring to summer
Tradescantia virginiana hybrids and cvs. (spiderwort)	5–8	1½–2'	S to PSh	Purple, pink, or white; spring to summer
Trollius spp. (globeflower)	5–7	1½–3'	S to PSh	Yellow; spring to summer
Verbena canadensis (rose verbena)	6–8	1–1½'	S to PSh	Pinkish purple to white; summer
Veronica longifolia (beach speedwell)	4–8	2–4'	S	Lilac blue; summer
V. spicata (spike speedwell)	5–8	1–2'	S to PSh	Blue or white; summer
Viola cornuta (horned violet, viola)	5–7	6–9"	S to PSh	Various colors; spring to fall

* S, full sun; Sh, shade (no direct sun); PSh, partial shade (sun exposure only part of the day); LSh, light shade (e.g., the shade of tall, open trees, with little or no exposure to direct sun).

PERENNIALS FOR SHADE

Name	Zones	Height	Exposure*	Flower and Foliage Color and Bloom Time
Aconitum spp. (monkshood)	3–7	3–5'	PSh	Flowers blue-violet; late summer to early fall
Actaea spp. (baneberry)	3–7	1–2'	LSh	Flowers white or red berry; fall

Name	Zones	Height	Exposure*	Flower and Foliage Color and Bloom Time
Ajuga spp. (bugle)	4–7	6–9'	PSh to LSh	Flowers blue-violet; spring
Anemone × hybrida (Japanese anemone)	5–7	2–3'	PSh	Flowers pink; early fall
A. sylvestris (snowdrop windflower)	4–7	1–1½'	PSh	Flowers white; early summer
A. vitifolia 'Robustissima' (grape-leaf anemone)	4–8	2–3'	PSh	Flowers pink; early fall
Arum italicum 'Pictum' (painted arum)	5–8	1–1½'	LSh	Foliage variegated
Aquilegia spp. (columbine)	4–8	†	PSh	Flowers various colors; spring
Aruncus dioicus (goatsbeard)	4–7	4–6'	PSh	Flowers white; late spring to early summer
Astilbe × arendsii	5–8	2–3'	PSh	Flowers red, pink, lavender, or white; mid to late summer
Brunnera macrophylla (Siberian bugloss)	4–8	1–1½'	PSh to LSh	Flowers blue; mid to late spring
Caltha palustris (marsh marigold)	3–7	6–12"	PSh to LSh	Flowers yellow; spring
Campanula spp. (bellflower)	3–8	†	PSh	Flowers purple or white; spring to fall
Chelone spp. (turtlehead)	3–8	2–3'	PSh	Flowers pink or white; summer to early fall
Cimicifuga spp. (bugbane, cohosh)	3–8	3–8'	PSh to LSh	Flowers white; late summer to early fall
Convallaria majalis (lily-of-the-valley)	4–7	6–9"	PSh to LSh	Flowers white; spring
Corydalis lutea (golden corydalis)	5–7	6–12"	PSh	Flowers yellow; spring to summer
Dicentra spp. (bleeding heart)	2–8	6–36"	PSh to LSh	Flowers white, pink, or yellow; spring to early fall
Digitalis spp. (perennial foxglove)	5–8	2–4'	PSh	Flowers yellow, cream, white, or pink; late spring to summer
Disporum spp. (fairy bell)	4–8	1–3'	PSh to LSh	Flowers yellowish; spring
Dodecatheon meadia (shooting star)	5–8	1–2'	PSh	Flowers magenta to white; spring
Doronicum cordatum (leopard's bane)	5–7	4–24"	PSh	Flowers yellow; early spring
Dracocephalum spp. (dragonhead)	4–7	†	PSh	Flowers reddish purple or white; summer
Epilobium angustifolium (fireweed)	5–7	3–5'	PSh	Flowers rose pink; summer
Epimedium spp. (bishop's hat)	5–7	9–12"	PSh to LSh	Flowers yellow, red, or white; spring
Eupatorium coelestinum (hardy ageratum)	6–8	2–3'	PSh	Flowers blue; late summer to early fall
E. rugosum, syn. *Ageratina altissima* (white snakeroot)	5–8	3–4'	PSh	Flowers white; late summer to early fall
Filipendula spp. (queen of the prairie)	2–7	†	PSh	Flowers pink or white; late spring to early summer
Galium odoratum (sweet woodruff)	5–7	9–12"	PSh to LSh	Flowers white; spring
Geranium spp. (hardy geranium)	4–8	6–24"	PSh	Flowers magenta, purple, pink, or white; late spring to late summer
Helleborus spp. (hellebore)	4–9	9–36"	PSh to LSh	Flowers white to purplish; late winter to spring
Hemerocallis hybrids (hybrid daylily)	4–9	1–5'	PSh	Flowers various colors; early summer, some reflowering
Heuchera sanguinea (coralbells)	3–8	1½–2'	PSh	Flowers pink or white; late spring to early summer
× H. tiarelloides (Bridget bloom)	3–7	1–1½'	PSh	Flowers pink; late spring to early summer
Hosta spp. (plantain lily)	4–8	1–3'	PSh to LSh	Flowers lavender or white; late summer to fall
Lobelia cardinalis (cardinal flower)	3–7	2–3'	PSh to LSh	Flowers red; late summer to early fall
L. siphilitica (great blue lobelia)	4–7	2–3'	PSh to LSh	Flowers blue or white; summer
Mertensia virginica (Virginia bluebell)	3–7	1–2'	PSh to LSh	Flowers blue; spring
Monarda didyma (bee balm)	5–8	2–3'	PSh	Flowers red; summer
Phlox divaricata (blue phlox)	3–7	9–12"	PSh to LSh	Flowers blue; spring
P. paniculata (tall summer phlox)	4–8	3–4'	PSh	Flowers pink, red, or white; summer to fall
P. stolonifera (creeping phlox)	5–8	6–12"	PSh to LSh	Flowers purple; late spring
Platycodon grandiflorus (balloon flower)	4–8	2–3'	PSh	Flowers blue or white; late spring to early summer

(continues)

PERENNIALS FOR SHADE (*continued*)

Name	Zones	Height	Exposure*	Flower and Foliage Color and Bloom Time
Polemohium spp. (Jacob's ladder, Greek valerian)	4–7	9–18"	PSh to LSh	Flowers blue or white; spring
Polygonatum spp. (Solomon's seal)	4–8	1–4'	PSh to LSh	Flowers white; spring
Primula spp. (primrose)	5–8	6–24"	PSh	Flowers various colors; spring
Pulmonaria spp. (lungwort)	2–8	6–12"	PSh to LSh	Flowers blue to pink, or white; spring
Smilacina racemosa (false Solomon's seal)	3–8	2–3'	PSh to LSh	Flowers white; spring
Thalictrum spp. (meadow rue)	5–8	2–7'	PSh	Flowers mauve or yellow; late spring to early summer
Tradescantia virginiana hybrids and cvs. (spiderwort)	5–8	1½– 2'	PSh	Flowers purple, pink, or white; spring to summer
Tricyrtis hirta (toad lily)	5–7	2–3'	PSh to LSh	Flowers white and purple; early to mid fall
Trillium spp.	4–8	6–30"	PSh to LSh	Flowers purple, pink, or white; spring
Trollius spp. (globeflower)	5–7	1½–3'	PSh	Flowers yellow; late spring to early summer
Uvularia grandiflora (bellwort)	5–9	1½–3'	PSh to LSh	Flowers yellow; late spring
Viola spp. (violet)	4–8	6–12"	PSh to LSh	Flowers purple, yellow, or white; spring

* S, full sun; Sh, shade (no direct sun); PSh, partial shade (sun exposure only part of the day); LSh, light shade (e.g., the shade of tall, open trees, with little or no exposure to direct sun).

† Height varies according to species and cultivar.

Christmas rose (*Helleborus niger*)

'Baths Pink' (*Dianthus*)

Fern-leaf yarrow (*Achillea filipendula*)

PERENNIALS AND BIENNIALS FOR BOLD EFFECTS

The abbreviation bi. *indicates that the species is biennial.*

Name	Zones	Height	Exposure*	Comments
Acanthus mollis var. *latifolius* (bear's-breeches)	8–9	3–4'	S	Large leaves
A. spinosus (spiny bear's-breech)	5–8	3–4'	S	Large, spiny-edged leaves
Aruncus dioicus (goatsbeard)	4–7	4–6'	S to PSh	Large clusters of small flowers; rangy habit
Canna × *generalis* (hybrid canna)	8–10	2–7'	S	Large, broad leaves; large, irregular flowers
Cimicifuga racemosa (black cohosh)	3–7	5–8'	S to PSh	Tall, wandlike flower spikes
Dipsacus fullonum (teasel)	4–8	4–7'	S to PSh	Large leaves; cylindrical flower spikes; bi.
Echinops spp. (globe thistle)	4–8	3–7'	S	Large leaves; spherical flower heads
Helianthus × *multiflorus* (perennial sunflower)	3–7	3–5'	S to PSh	Large leaves and flowers
Heracleum spp. (cow parsnip)	5–7	4–10'	S to PSh	Immense leaves and flower clusters; bi- or triennial
Macleaya cordata (plume poppy)	4–8	5–8'	S to PSh	Tall clumps of plumed flowers
Onopordum acanthium (Scotch thistle)	4–7	6–9'	S to PSh	Large, silvery woolly, spiny leaves; bi.
Polygonum sachalinense (giant knotweed)	4–8	8–12'	S to PSh	Large heart-shaped leaves
Silphium perforatum (cup plant, rosin weed)	4–8	6–8'	S	Large leaves cupped around stems
Telekia speciosa (sun wheel)	6–8	5–6'	S to PSh	Large, aromatic leaves; yellow daisylike flowers; also listed as *Buphthalmum speciosum*
Verbascum olympicum (Olympic mullein)	5–8	5–7'	S to PSh	Large white woolly leaves; lofty-branched spikes of yellow flowers; bi.
Yucca filamentosa (Adam's needle, eastern yucca)	5–8	4–6'	S	Evergreen; long, narrow rosetted leaves; tall flower scapes

* S, full sun; Sh, shade (no direct sun); PSh, partial shade (sun exposure only part of the day); LSh, light shade (e.g., the shade of tall, open trees, with little or no exposure to direct sun).

TALL PERENNIALS FOR BACKGROUNDS

Name	Zones	Height	Exposure*	Flower Color and Bloom Time
Aconitum carmichaelii var. *wilsonii* (giant aconite)	4–8	5–7'	S to PSh	Deep purple; late summer to early fall
Aruncus dioicus (goatsbeard)	4–7	4–6'	S to PSh	White; late spring to early summer
Aster novae-angliae (New England aster)	2–8	3–6'	S	Red-violet to white
Boltonia asteroides	4–9	5–7'	S to PSh	Purple to white; late summer to early fall
Campanula latifolia 'Macrantha' (giant bellflower)	3–7	3–5'	S to PSh	Purple; late spring to summer
Cimicifuga racemosa (black cohosh)	3–7	5–8'	S to PSh	White; late summer to early fall
Delphinium elatum hybrids (tall hybrid delphinium)	4–7	4–7'	S to PSh	Blue, purple, or white; late spring to early summer
Echinops spp. (globe thistle)	4–8	3–7'	S	Steel blue; summer
Helenium autumnale (sneezeweed)	3–8	2–6'	S	Yellow to reddish bronze; fall
Helianthus maximiliani (Maximilian sunflower)	4–8	6–10'	S to PSh	Yellow; summer to early fall
Hibiscus moscheutos (rose mallow)	5–8	5–8'	S to PSh	Red, pink, or white; late summer
Macleaya cordata (plume poppy)	4–8	5–8'	S to PSh	White; summer
Rudbeckia laciniata 'Golden Glow' (golden glow)	4–8	5–7'	S	Yellow; summer
Senna hebecarpa (hardy senna)	5–8	3–6'	S to PSh	Yellow; summer
Valeriana officinalis (common valerian)	5–8	4–5'	S to PSh	Lavender, pink, or white; summer

* S, full sun; Sh, shade (no direct sun); PSh, partial shade (sun exposure only part of the day); LSh, light shade (e.g., the shade of tall, open trees, with little or no exposure to direct sun).

ORNAMENTAL PERENNIAL GRASSES AND SEDGES

All require full sun or partial shade (sun exposure at least several hours each day) unless otherwise noted.

Name	Zones	Height	Habit
Alopecurus pratensis 'Aureus' (golden foxtail grass)	6–9	1–1 ½'	Dense, rounded clump
Arrhenantherum elatius 'Variegatum' (variegated oat grass)	5–9	9–12"	Low, open clump
Arundo donax (giant reed)	(5) 6–9	12–16'	Upright, cornlike
A. donax 'Variegata' (striped reed)	7–9	12–16'	As for *A. donax*
Briza media (quaking grass)	4–8	2–2 ½'	Upright clump
Calamagrostis acutiflora 'Stricta' (feather reed grass)	5–9	3–4'	Slender, upright clump
Carex conica 'Variegata' (white-striped sedge)	7–9	1–1 ½'	Tufted clump
C. marrowii 'Aureovariegata' (variegated Japanese sedge)	7–9	1–1 ½'	Tufted clump
Chasmanthium latifolium (northern sea oats)	5–9	2 ½–3'	Upright, arching
Cortaderia selloana (pampas grass)	8–10	5–10'	Large, dense clump
Deschampsia caespitosa (tufted hair grass)	4–9	2–3'	Mounded clump
Elymus arenarius (blue lyme grass)	6–8	3–5'	Spreads by creeping cordlike rootstocks
Erianthus ravennae (plume grass)	5–9	10–14'	Large, dense clump
Festuca ovina var. *glauca* (blue fescue)	5–10	9–12"	Dense, tufted clump
Hakonechloa macra 'Aureola' (golden variegated hakonechloa)	(5) 6–9	1–1 ½'	Dense, mounded clump
Helictotrichon sempervirens (blue oat grass)	5–9	2–3'	Rounded clump
Holcus mollis 'Variegatus' (variegated velvet grass)	5–9	6–12"	Open, spreading clump
Hordeum jubatum (squirrel-tail grass)	5–9	1–2 ½'	Open, tufted clump
Imperata cylindrica var. *rubra* 'Red Baron' (Japanese blood grass)	6–9	1 ½–2'	Upright clumps
Koeleria glauca (blue June grass)	5–9	1–1½'	Open, upright clump
Melica ciliata (pearl grass)	6–9	2–3'	Dense, tufted clump
Milium effusum 'Aureum' (Bowle's golden grass)	6–9	1–2'	Dense clump
Miscanthus floridulus (giant Chinese silver grass)	5–9	2–15'	Upright clump
M. sacchariflorus var. *robustus* (giant silver banner grass)	5–9	5–8'	Upright clump
M. sinensis (eulalia, or Chinese or Japanese silver grass)	5–9	6–8'	Upright clump
Molina caerulea 'Variegata' (variegated purple moor grass)	(4) 5–9	1½–2'	Broad clump
Panicum virgatum (switch grass)	5–9	2–3'	Broad, rounded clump
Pennisteum alopecuroides (tall fountain grass)	5–9	3–4'	Broad, rounded clump
P. setaceum (low fountain grass)	5–9	2–4'	Upright clump
Phalaris arundinacea var. *picta* (ribbon grass)	5–9	1½–2	Rapidly spreading mat
Sorghastrum avenaceum (Indian grass)	5–9	4–6	Upright, open clump
Spartina pectinata (prairie cord grass)	5–9	4–5	Spreading clump
Stipa pennata (feather grass)	5–9	2–3	Rounded clump
S. gigantea (giant feather grass)	6–9	5–6	Rounded clump

ORNAMENTAL PERENNIAL GRASSES AND SEDGES

All require full sun or partial shade (sun exposure at least several hours each day) unless otherwise noted.

Foliage	Flowers	Comments
Yellow-and-green striped	Flower heads not ornamental	Showy foliage
Spreading; blue-green with white	Flower heads not ornamental	Showy foliage
Drooping; 3–4 feet long	Tassels red-brown, aging to whitish; 2 feet	Imposing; persistent tassels
Variegated with white	As for *A. donax*	Showy foliage
Mostly on stems	Drooping; swinging; green to tan	Graceful flower heads
Coarse, reflexed	Spikes greenish pink, aging to tan; erect	Showy flower clusters
Longitudinally white striped	Flower heads not ornamental	Showy foliage; good in shade
Longitudinally yellow striped	Flower heads not ornamental	Showy foliage; good in shade
Stem borne; diverging	Short; dense; flat; drooping	Open, airy flower clusters
Arching; saw edged	Dense white or pink plumes	Flowers most effective on females
Arching; often curled	Large; open; erect; tan panicles	Some cultivars with yellow flower clusters
To ¾-inch wide	Held in stiff dense clusters above foliage	Good sand binder in seaside areas
With central longitudinal white stripe	Silvery gray plumes	Northern substitute for pampas grass
Narrow; numerous; silvery blue	Flower heads not ornamental	Popular ground cover
Arching; with yellow longitudinal bands	Flower heads not ornamental	Showy foliage
Light silvery blue; upright or arching	Loose; open; drooping; one-sided clusters	Attractive flower clusters
Green with white edges	Flower heads not ornamental	Showy foliage
Scattered along unbranched stem	Spikes with long, silvery bristles	Usually grown as annual
Reddish, aging to burgundy; erect or arching	Flower heads not ornamental	Showy foliage
Narrow; diverging; more or less evergreen	Spikes dense; silvery white	Conspicuous flower spikes
Threadlike; gray green	Nodding; purplish spike	Striking
Arching; yellow	Yellow spikes	Showy
As for *M. effusum* but larger	As for *M. effusum* but larger	Showier than *M. sinensis*
Similar to *M. sinensis*	Similar to *M. sinensis*	Requires wet soil
Diverging or drooping; mostly basal	Pink to dark red spikes	Showy flower spikes
Longitudinally white-striped	Mostly purplish but variable	Showy foliage
Long; arching; ends drooping	Reddish aging to tan; erect and branched	Cultivars, have red leaves
Strongly arching	Dense, like bottlebrush	Attractive form
Arching; green or variously colored	Pink or purplish spikes	Several color cultivars
Arching; white-striped	Flower spikes not ornamental	Invasive; useful as bank stabilizer
Ascending; rough surfaced	Yellowish plumes 1 foot long	Several color cultivars
Erect or arching	Branched; one-sided twisted spikes	Best in wet ground
Arching; basal	Long-stalked feathery clusters	Attractive flower clusters
Arching; basal	Long-stalked yellowish clusters	Attractive flower clusters

16

Bulbs

Iɴ ᴛʜᴇ ᴘᴀɢᴇᴀɴᴛʀʏ ᴏғ ᴛʜᴇ sᴇᴀsᴏɴs, ʙᴜʟʙs ᴘʟᴀʏ ᴀɴ important part. From the first flowers of the diminutive snowdrops in late winter to the last lingering blooms of the autumn crocuses, there is an ever-changing succession. The fleeting beauty of the spring crocuses, squills, and grape hyacinths gives way to the far-flung loveliness of the daffodils and their kin. As the season advances, the tulips, with their clean, sculptured beauty, hold center stage, then surrender

In a massed planting, the unusually rich purple of the Triumph tulip *'Negrita' contrasts with the foliage, whether the flowers are closed in dim light or open in the sun.*

it to the summer display of lilies, gladioluses, dahlias, and tuberous begonias.

There are few flowers that give so generously of their bloom and beauty as do the bulbs. Many of the spring-flowering bulbs, when once established, will increase rapidly and form large colonies. This is particularly true of the early bulbs, such as the snowdrops, squills, grape hyacinths, and varied daffodils and other narcissus. Wide-spreading clumps of snowdrops along a woodland path in very early spring, the intense blue of a carpet of squills beneath the spreading branches of a great European beech, a meadow alive with myriad grape hyacinths in bloom, a bank clothed with hundreds of daffodils swaying in a gentle breeze—these are among the joys of spring.

In the broadest anatomical sense, bulbs are underground food-storage organs that enable certain plants to survive unfavorable periods during the year and respond appropriately—sometimes very quickly—to the resumption of growing conditions. In general, bulb-producing plants have evolved in parts of the world having relatively brief periods of warmth or adequate rain or both, example on alpine slopes or tropical savannas.

Mixed planting of hardy spring bulbs.

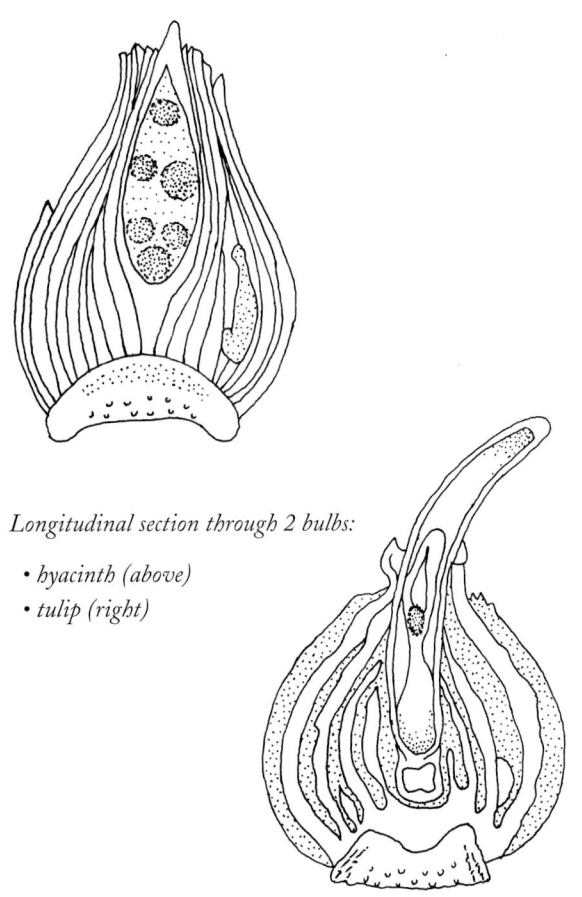

Longitudinal section through 2 bulbs:

• *hyacinth (above)*
• *tulip (right)*

What are collectively and loosely referred to as bulbs actually fall into four principal categories: true bulbs (such as onions, lilies, and amaryllises), consisting of concentric or overlapping scales or layers, which are in fact the food-storing bases of leaves; corms (crocuses and gladioluses), consisting of a dense, thickened bit of underground stem, usually clad in dry, parchmentlike scale leaves; tubers (tuberous begonias and dahlias), consisting of a thickened, naked portion of stem or root that bears buds ("eyes") from which the next season's growth develops; and rhizomes (cannas and bearded irises), consisting of thickened, underground, horizontal stems, usually bearing scalelike leaf rudiments and annually producing upright flowering shoots.

All plants with such specialized storage organs are perennials in the wild, flowering year after year, but because they have evolved elsewhere under widely varying climatic and soil conditions, they require differing treatments when grown in the garden. Wherever possible, gardeners strive not only for the spectacular floral display that most bulbs offer but also the conditions favorable for bulb regeneration and successive seasons of growth and flowering.

For convenience of reference, bulbs useful in horticulture are grouped into several major categories and subcategories, regardless of the true anatomical nature of the bulb.

LATE WINTER TO EARLY SPRING BULBS (HARDY)

Narcissus spp. and cvs. (dwarf daffodil)
Crocus spp.
Chionodoxa luciliae (glory-of-the-snow)
Eranthis hyemalis (winter aconite)
Iris reticulata, I. danfordiae (reticulate iris)
Galanthus spp. (snowdrop)
Tulipa spp. (tulip)
Scilla spp. (squill)

EARLY TO LATE SPRING BULBS (HARDY)

Allium spp. (flowering onion)
Fritillaria imperialis (crown imperial)
Muscari spp. (grape hyacinth)
Hyacinthus orientalis cvs. (true hyacinth)
Tulipa hybrids (tulip)
Iris spp.* (bearded iris)

SUMMER BULBS

Hardy

Iris tingitana × *I. xiphium* (Dutch iris)
Kniphofia hybrids (red-hot poker)
Lilium spp. and hybrids (true lily)
Hemerocallis spp. and cvs. (daylilies)

Tender

Caladium bicolor cvs.
Dahlia hybrids
Gladiolus × *hortulanus* cvs.
Begonia × *tuberhydrida* cvs. (tuberous begonia)

AUTUMN BULBS

Hardy

Colchicum spp. (autumn crocus)
Crocus laevigatus, C. speciosus (fall-flowering true crocus)

Tender

Crocosmia × *crocosmiiflora*

Indoor bulbs

Indoor bulbs include tender types grown as house plants (e.g. paper-white narcissus, *Narcissus tazetta* cvs., treated in Chapter 38), and hardy kinds suitable for forcing (e.g., crocuses, hyacinths, and certain daffodils and tulips).

Outdoor gardening styles suitable for bulbs are widely varied and include formal, geometric beds; informal borders in front of shrubbery or along walls or fences; naturalized massings in open woodland or along woodland margins; clumps or small groups in rock gardens; and informal groupings in lawns.

CULTURE OF HARDY SPRING AND SUMMER BULBS

Except where noted, hardy bulbs should be planted in late summer or fall. It is best for soil temperatures to be no higher than 60°F when dormant bulbs are planted. Actual planting time will vary according to plant hardiness zone and the vagaries of the season, but the following list can be used as a guide.

Zones 2–3: mid-September
Zones 4–5: late September to early October
Zones 6–7: mid-October to early November
Zone 8: mid-November to early December
Zone 9: early to mid-December

As a rule, the top of the bulb should lie two to three times its height below the surface; plant deeper in light, sandy soil; shallower in heavy, clay soil.

In addition to planting different kinds of bulbs to heighten interest and extend the blooming season, it should be borne in mind, especially where space is limited, that bulbs can be layered. For example, in beds where Darwin tulips are set 8 inches deep, crocuses may be planted 4 inches deep over them. The crocuses will finish their blooming cycle before the tulips open, and their roots will not compete.

Before planting, dig the bed at least one-third deeper than the bulb size requires and add a generous layer of well-rotted manure or compost for easy root penetration and maximum nutrient uptake. Keep in mind that the bulb growth period is in most cases brief and that root growth precedes the production of leaves and flowers. Where possible, choose a site shaded from warm afternoon sun to extend the flowering period. Cool, cloudy weather also lengthens flowering.

Since the flowers and foliage of spring-flowering bulbs usually die back and vanish by midsummer, spring is a good time to take note of what needs to be replenished or planted anew in fall. A rough sketch of the garden with present bulb plantings indicated will prove invaluable at planting time. List the kinds to be purchased or mark the catalog from which orders will be made, and then mark the planting sites or areas in the garden with wood or plastic labels.

*See Chapter 15.

These preparations will greatly facilitate bulb planting later on and eliminate the risk of disappointment the following spring. By leaving the labels in place after planting, bulbs will be protected from accidental disturbance and the flower displays will be identified as they emerge. Moreover, labels can be used to flag tight, overgrown clumps that should be lifted and divided when dormant.

Besides ordinary garden tools, a soil-coring bulb planter, either hand held or foot driven, is useful when setting large numbers of bulbs in prepared beds and borders.

It is especially important in bulb culture to be sure of soil fertility and to have the soil tested before applying any fertilizer. This is best done before planting so that, if needed, a suitable amount of the correct formulation can be worked in as the bulbs are planted. Seldom are more than 5 pounds of 5-10-5 fertilizer required, followed perhaps by 1 pound of ammonium sulfate for the same area in early spring each successive year. Where available, however, well-rotted manure is preferable and should be worked into the soil before planting and topdressed on bulb beds annually to help maintain soil nutrient levels and conserve soil moisture. This regimen helps ensure reflowering in successive years and promotes bulb propagation.

Although many gardeners believe it advantageous to add lime to soil in which bulbs are to be planted, there is no need if a soil test shows the pH lies between 6.5 and 7.0, since in this range soil nutrients are fully available. Soils below pH 6.5 should be alkalized or "sweetened" by adding some form of lime (calcium carbonate), preferably dolomitic limestone at the rate of about 6 ounces per square yard if the soil is sandy, or 7 to 8 ounces per square yard if the soil is a heavier clay. Bonemeal is less effective than dolomite for this purpose and is far more expensive. Bonemeal is best used to increase a soil's potassium level, should that be needed.

Most bulbs are relatively free of pests and diseases. However, shallowly planted bulbs may be dug up and eaten by rodents. An inverted basket made from ½ inch-mesh hardware cloth set beneath the surface and over the bulbs is usually sufficient deterrent. Where rodent infestation is especially severe, tulips and daffodils may be planted in large black plastic pots sunk to their rims and then covered with hardware cloth. Any bulbs apparently diseased in storage should be discarded to prevent spread of infection. Dusting lifted bulbs with sulfur helps prevent bulb rot.

All bulbs should be purchased from reputable dealers who certify that all bulbs for sale are from cultivated stock and not collected in the wild, as called for by international agreement among growers, exporters, and environmental organizations.

HARDY SPRING-FLOWERING BULBS

NARCISSUS *SPP. AND CVS.*
(Daffodil, Jonquil)

The genus *Narcissus*, with its wealth of beautiful, welcome flowers, is rich in species and cultivars that are among the most adaptable among hardy bulbs and should be represented in every garden. They are dependable, demand little care, and continue to bloom year after year, whether arranged in long drifts, in masses bordering wooded areas, or in clumps on grassy slopes. They are seldom menaced by garden wildlife.

The members of the genus *Narcissus* are classified mainly according to flower structure and how the blooms are borne on the scape, or flower stalk. There are essentially two flower parts that are used for classification purposes: a central trumpet, or corona, and a surrounding perianth, or saucerlike ring of petals. Those with a large, projecting, trumpet-shaped corona are popularly called daffodils.

Nearly all of the 26 species of *Narcissus* are in cultivation, and a great number of hybrids have enriched this diversity. Except for the nonhardy *N. tazetta* and its well-known 'Paper White' and 'Soleil d'Or' hybrids, all should be planted in late summer or early fall, according to hardiness zone, to promote early root development, which is essential for generous and timely flowering. Most are best planted in groups of six or more of a kind. Dig the planting area about 1 foot deep, fill the bottom 3 or 4 inches with humusy compost, mixed with well-rotted manure if available. On this surface, bulbs should be set 6 to 8 inches apart if large, or 3 or 4 inches apart if small. Fill the hole to grade with friable topsoil. If needed, ground limestone or bonemeal (½ pound per 25 square feet) may be worked in at the surface.

In planning any planting of *Narcissus*, it should be remembered that the flowers nod toward the sun, so any shade should be behind the bed. The large-flowered types (Divisions I–IV) are most effective when massed informally, as in naturalized areas in open woods or beneath tall, deep-rooted deciduous lawn trees. Unless they are to be succeeded by summer annuals, daffodil and narcissus beds should be mulched with wood or bark chips to stabilize winter temperatures and retain moisture in late spring and early summer. Ground cover beds make an excellent site for these bulbs. In addition to creeping myrtle (*Vinca minor*) and ajuga (*Ajuga reptans*), such species as spotted dead nettle (*Lamium maculatum*) and rock cress (*Arabis caucasica*) provide lovely backdrops. Companion plantings of Bethlehem sage (*Pulmonaria saccharata*), striped squill (*Puschkinia scilloides*), and purple trillium (*Trillium erectum*) complement daffodils and other tall narcissus handsomely. Smaller sorts (Divisions V–VII and IX–XI) are best in the rock garden or in intimate groupings among dwarf evergreens or in wild gardens. Mixtures, though less expensive, are usually not as satisfactory as single-type groupings.

It is important not to cut or remove daffodil foliage sooner than six weeks after flowering or, preferably, until the leaves have begun to yellow. If the splayed foliage becomes unsightly, the leaves may be rolled and tied into a compact bun or be braided, in either case leaving some leaf area exposed to the sun while allowing room for seedling annuals or other successor plants. Removal of seed capsules is beneficial, but not essential for the next year's flowering. When tight clumps have formed after several years' natural propagation, lift the mass after the foliage has yellowed, separate the bulbs, and reset at appropriate intervals, either immediately or in late summer or fall, preparing the planting sites as for new bulbs.

Division I. Daffodil or Trumpet Narcissus
Zones 4–8 (9)

Daffodils are large-flowered hybrids with one flower per scape. The trumpet is as long as or longer than the six perianth segments.

Yellow daffodil or trumpet narcissus (*Narcissus* 'King Alfred')

White daffodil or trumpet narcissus (*Narcissus* 'Mount Hood')

DIVISION I CULTIVARS OF MERIT

Yellow

'Arctic Gold'	'King Alfred'
'Dutch Master'	'Kingscourt'
'Golden Harvest'	'Unsurpassable'
'Golden Rapture'	

Pink

'Mrs. R. O. Backhouse'
'Pink Glory'

White

'Beersheba'	'Empress of Ireland'
'Broughshane'	'Mount Hood'
'Cantatrice'	'Vigil'

Bicolor

'Bravoure'	'Spellbinder'
'Foresight'	'Spring Glory'
'Lunar Sea'	'Trousseau'
'Queen of the Bicolor'	

Division II. Large-Cupped Narcissus
Zones 4–8 (9)

Large-cupped narcissuses have one flower per scape. The cup, or corona, is more than one-third but less than the length, of the perianth segments.

Yellow large-cupped narcissus (*Narcissus* 'Carlton')

White large-cupped narcissus (*Narcissus* 'Ice Follies')

Division III. Small-Cupped Narcissus
Zones 4–8

Small-cupped narcissuses have one flower per scape. The cup, or corona, is not more than one-third the length of the perianth segments.

Division IV. Double-Flowered Narcissus
Zones 4–8

Double-flowered narcissuses have flowers with multiple perianth segments.

Yellow double-flowered narcissus (*Narcissus* 'Golden Ducat')

DIVISION II CULTIVARS OF MERIT

Perianth, yellow; corona, the same or another shade of yellow to red-orange

'Armada'	'Gigantic Star'
'Binkie'	'Juanita'
'Butterscotch'	'St. Keverne'
'Carbineer'	'Scarlet O'Hara'
'Carlton'	'Standard Value'
'Delibes'	

Perianth, white; corona, white

'Easter Moon'
'Ice Follies'
'Stainless'

Perianth, white; corona, yellow to red-orange

'Amor'	'Professor Einstein'
'Duke of Windsor'	'Red Hill'
'Early Bride'	'Royal Orange'
'Festivity'	'St. Patrick's Day'
'Flower Record'	'Spring Queen'
'Peaches and Cream'	

Perianth, white; corona, pink or pink edged

'Accent'	'Rosy Sunrise'
'Louise de Coligny'	'Salmon Trout'
'Passionale'	'Salomé'
'Pink Charm'	'Toscanini'

DIVISION III CULTIVARS OF MERIT

Perianth, yellow; corona, usually darker than perianth

'Apricot Distinction'	'Edward Buxton'
'Barrett Browning'	'Fortissimo'

Perianth, white; corona, colored

'Roseworthy'
'Verger'

Perianth, white; corona, white

'Ice King'
'Polar Imp'
'Portrush'

DIVISION IV CULTIVARS OF MERIT

Yellow

'Golden Ducat'	'Meeting'
'Inglescombe'	'Yellow Cheerfulness'

White

'Cheerfulness'	'White Lion'
'Obdam'	'White Marvel'

Bicolor

'Irene Copeland'	'Tahiti'
'Mary Copeland'	'Texas'

Division V. Triandrus Narcissus
Zones 5–8

Triandrus narcissuses have two to six flowers per scape. The flower is white or yellow, usually pendent, and fragrant. Its six perianth segments are swept back behind the cup; and the cup is usually about half as long as the perianth segments.

DIVISION V
CULTIVARS OF MERIT

Yellow
  'Hawera'
  'Liberty Bells'

White
  'Ice Wings'
  'Shot Silk'
  'Silver Chimes'
  'Thalia'
  'Tresamble'

Division VI. Cyclamineus Narcissus
Zones 6–8

Cyclamineus narcissuses have one flower per scape. The flower is yellow and pendent, and each of its six perianth segments is swept back behind the cup. The cup is at least as long as the perianth segments.

Yellow cyclamineus narcissus (*Narcissus* 'Peeping Tom')

Yellow cyclamineus narcissus (*Narcissus* 'Tête-à-tête')

DIVISION VI
CULTIVARS OF MERIT

'Charity May'   'Jumblie'
'February Gold'   'March Sunshine'
'Jack Snipe'   'Peeping Tom'
'Jenny'   'Tête-à-tête'
'Jetfire'

White triandrus narcissus (*Narcissus* 'Thalia')

Division VII. Jonquil
Zones 4–8

Jonquils have two to six flowers per scape. The flower is yellow, upward facing, and sweetly fragrant, with a tubular base about 1 inch long. The cup is less than half as long as the perianth segments.

DIVISION VII
CULTIVARS OF MERIT

'Cherie'
'Lintie'
'Pipit'
'Suzy'
'Trevithian'

Division VIII. Tazetta Narcissus
Zones 8–9

Tazetta narcissuses have three to eight flowers per scape. The flower is white or yellow, upward or outward facing, and intensely fragrant. The cup is much shorter than the perianth segments.

DIVISION VIII
CULTIVARS OF MERIT

Yellow
  'Early Perfection'
  'Scarlet Gem'
  'Yellow Cheerfulness'

White
  'Bridal Crown'
  'White Cheerfulness'

Bicolor
  'Cragford'
  'Geranium'
  'Laurens Koster'
  'Minnow'

Bicolor tazetta narcissus (*Narcissus* 'Geranium')

Division IX. Poeticus Narcissus
Zones 5–8

Poeticus narcissuses have one flower per scape. The fragrant flower has a white perianth and a very flat cup, which is yellow to red or red rimmed.

**DIVISION IX
CULTIVARS OF MERIT**

'Actaea'
'Cantabile'
'Pheasant's Eye'
'Red Rim'

Division X. Species Narcissus and Wild Varieties and Hybrids
Zones (4) 5–7 (9)

Division X *Narcissus* includes numerous, mostly small, species, varieties, and natural hybrids that are often best grown in the rock garden where they can be protected from encroachment and enjoyed for their delicacy of floral detail. Not all are readily obtainable commercially, and those that are should be certified as grown from nursery-propagated stock. Indiscriminant collection of wild narcissus has threatened some forms with extinction. Included here are such species as *N. asturiensis, N. bulbocodium, N. cyclamineus,*

and *N. juncifolius* which are described in the table on page 416.

Hoop-petticoat daffodil
(*Narcissus bulbocodium*)

Division XI. Split-Corona Narcissus
Zones 4–8

The corona of Division XI *Narcissus* is split into three or more segments at least one-third of its length back from the rim. The segments are often spread and flattened against the perianth.

**DIVISION XI
CULTIVARS OF MERIT**

'Marie José'
'Palmares'
'Tricollet'

Narcissus asturiensis

Division XII. Miscellaneous Narcissus

The miscellaneous narcissuses include any form not confidently classifiable in the first 11 divisions.

TULIPA *SPP. AND CVS.*
(*Tulip*)

There are few flowers that offer the gardener so great an opportunity for color harmonies as the tulips. In the skillful hands of the artist, they may be used to create the most subtle and beautiful compositions in the spring garden. Tulips are highly favored because of their intense colors, uniform growth, and the high position of the flowers, usually well above the foliage. The perianth segments ("petals") open according to the intensity of the sun, hence exterior coloration is as important as interior. Many of the 45 wild species are in cultivation, but most of the popular cultivars are derived from just one species, *T. gesneriana.* Making use of species and hybrid tulips, a succession of bloom may be had extending from very early spring, when *T. kaufmanniana,* the exquisite water-lily tulip, opens its graceful flowers, to late May and early June when the last of the stately Darwin and lily-flowered tulips bring the season to a close.

Plant tulips where four to six hours of direct sun is ensured on sunny days, preferably morning sun. Although tulip flowers open only in the sun, protection from warm afternoon sun will extend flowering. Tulip bulbs must have four to six months of cold dormancy (35° to 45°F) to flower. Commercially sold bulbs will often have been pretreated. Plant them so that the top of the bulb is 6 to 9 inches below the surface, or somewhat shallower if the soil is heavy clay. Deep planting helps obviate the mining of bulbs by rodents and reduces damage from hot soil in summer. It also helps to keep the bulbs out of contact with the roots of voracious annuals, gladioluses, and other shallowly rooted plants. Soil drainage must be good throughout the year, as water-logged earth is fatal. Mulching tulips, planting them in a sunny bed of low ground cover, or following them with a succession planting of summer annuals keeps the soil cool in summer and diminishes the unsightliness of their yellowing ripened foliage.

Thorough soil preparation helps ensure reflowering in successive years. The bed should be dug 14 to 16 inches deep and lined with 4 to 6 inches of porous, fluffy compost. Bulbs should be set 6 to 8 inches apart and then covered with humusy topsoil which, in acidic soils should be neutralized with ground limestone (25 pounds per 100 square feet). If mice and other rodents are a problem, cover the bulbs with ½-inch-mesh hardware cloth before backfilling. Alternatively, the tulip bed may be prepared by deep rototilling, and the bulbs planted using a soil-boring bulb planter. This procedure, however, makes it difficult to place the hardware cloth.

Plant tulip bulbs in the fall after the soil has begun to cool but well before hard freezing. If planted earlier, bulbs may push out buds in the fall, only to be destroyed by frost; if later, root development may be too scant to ensure a uniform show of optimal-size flowers in spring.

Even with the best of preparation, tulips usually vanish a few at a time, year by year, and seldom reproduce in the garden. Hence the advisability of planting them in informal groupings or drifts, so that the failure of a few scattered tulips will not upset the display as much as in a formal, geometric planting. In informal beds, the annual planting of supplemental bulbs of the same cultivar helps maintain the display year after year.

Tulips for Southern Gardens

It was long a matter of regret to southern gardeners that tulips would not thrive for them. For generations, those who gardened in the South had to be content with miserably weak and floppy specimens or had to forgo the beauty of tulips entirely.

Today, tulips may be grown as successfully in the South as in the North, provided that the bulbs are placed in cold storage for several months before they are planted. Excellent results may be obtained if the bulbs are held in storage at a temperature of 45°F for about six months before actual planting.

Lady tulip (*Tulipa clusiana* var. *chrysantha*)

Obviously, this time span means that the southern gardener who wants an impressive tulip display must have the foresight to order bulbs well in advance of planting time or be certain that the tulips chosen for purchase have been cold treated.

Bulbs usually may be planted anytime from December through early February, though in the case of later plantings, active growth will probably begin almost immediately. If this method is followed, an abundance of tall, strong-stemmed blooms may be had.

As soon as the foliage has died down and the bulbs have ripened, they should be lifted and placed in cold storage. Some bulbs will flower well for several seasons if accorded this treatment, while others deteriorate rapidly and must be replaced by new stock that has been specially treated for southern planting.

Tulip Cultivars of Merit, Arranged by Class

Most hybrid garden tulips are the products of many years of complex breeding and selection, a process that began in Europe in the late 1500s, when wild kinds were first brought from Turkey. It continues to this day, especially in Holland, historically the world center of the horticultural bulb industry, where from 1634 to 1637 the craze for rare, bizarrely colored variants (actually caused by a virus) led to "tulipmania" and fabulous prices for individual bulbs.

The hundreds of commercially available cultivars now available are grouped into 11 classes, according to season of bloom and floral form. In addition, there are four groupings of species tulips, most of which are smaller and earlier flowering than the cultivars.

I. SINGLE EARLY

Single early tulips have solitary flowers that are white to deep purple, some with colored margins or flecks or a secondary exterior shade ("flame"). The flowers are borne on stalks, 6 to 18 inches tall, in early to mid spring.

Red
'Brilliant Star'
'Couleur Cardinal'

Pink
'Christmas Marvel'
'Ibis'

White
'Diana'

Yellow
'Bellona'

Orange
'Dr. Plesman'
'General De Wet'
'Princess Irene'

Bicolor (yellow and red)
'Keizerkroom'

II. DOUBLE EARLY

Double early tulips have fully double, bowl-shaped, solitary flowers. Flower color is white through yellow to red, some with colored margins or flecks. The flowers are borne on on stalks, 12 to 18 inches tall, in early to mid spring.

Red
'Electra'

Pink
'Peach Blossom'

White
'Schoonoord'

Yellow-orange
'Orange Nassau'

Yellow-orange double early tulip
(*Tulipa* 'Orange Nassau')

Yellow and red single early tulip (*Tulipa* 'Keizerkroom')

III. TRIUMPH

Triumph tulips have single, solitary flowers that are white through yellow, orange, pink, red, and deep purple, some with colored edges or flecks. The flowers are borne on stalks, 18 to 24 inches tall, mostly in midspring. This group includes cultivars formerly classified as Mendel tulips.

Red
'Ambassador'
'Cheerleader'
'Garden Party'
'Lucky Strike'
'Paul Richter'
'Prominence'

White
'Hibernia'
'White Dream'

Pink
'Don Quichotte'

'Dreaming Maid'
'Gander's Rhapsody'

Purple
'Attila'
'First Lady'
'Negrita'
'Purple Star'
'Victor H. Ries'

Yellow to orange
'Bestseller'
'Kees Nelis'

Pink triumph tulip
(*Tulipa*
'Don Quichotte')

Purple triumph tulip
(*Tulipa* 'Negrita')

'Makassar'
'Orange Wonder'
'Yellow President'

Bicolored
'Abu Hassan' (red, edged yellow)
'Anna José' (pink and yellow)
'Broadway' (red and white)
'Douglas Baader' (pink and white)
'Dreamland' (pink and white)
'Indian Girl' (red-brown and yellow)
'New Design' (yellow and pink)
'Shirley' (white and magenta)

IV AND V. LATE SINGLE (DARWIN HYBRID, DARWIN TULIP, AND COTTAGE TULIP)

The flowers of the late single tulips are mostly solitary and display the full color range. They are borne on stalks, 24 to 36 inches tall, in mid to late spring. Darwin tulips are mostly late season and are deeply cup shaped. 'Darwin' Hybrids are mostly midseason and result from crosses between Darwin tulips and various species, especially *T. fosteriana*. Cottage tulips are late season. The usually egg-shaped flowers are, in some cultivars, borne in clusters of four to six, which are known as bunching, multiflowering, or bouquet forms. These three very popular tulips are combined here because, as a result of hybridization, many cultivars cannot be assigned to a specific category with certainty.

Red
'Apeldoorn'
'Apeldoorn Elite'
'Flying Dutchman'
'Hollands Glory'
'Oxford'
'Parade'
'Spring Song'

Yellow
'Beauty of Apeldoorn'
'Golden Age'
'Gudoshnik'
'Jewel of Spring'
'President Kennedy'
'Sweet Harmony'
'Yellow Dover'

Purple to purple-black
'Queen of Night'
'Scotch Lassie'
'The Bishop'

Purple-black late single tulip
(*Tulipa* 'Queen of Night')

Mauve to lilac
'Bleu Aimable'
'Insurpassable'

Orange
'Daydream'
'Elizabeth Arden'
'Orange Sun'

Pink to Rose
'Aristocrat'
'Big Chief'
'Clara Butt'
'Pink Impression'
'Queen of Bartigons'

White
'Duke of Willington'

Bicolor
'Françoise' (yellow and white)
'Magier' (white and red-violet)
'Olympic Flame' (yellow and red)
'Silverstream' (yellow and red)
'Sorbet' (white and red)

Orange
late single tulip
(*Tulipa*
'Daydream')

Yellow and red
late single tulip
(*Tulipa*
'Olympic Flame')

VI. LILY-FLOWERED

Lily-flowered tulips have solitary, single flowers that are white to deep purple, some with colored margins. The flower segments diverge or curve outward at the tip. The flowers are borne on stalks, 18 to 26 inches tall, in mid to late spring.

Red
'Queen of Sheba'
'Red Shine'

Yellow
lily-flowered tulip
(*Tulipa*
'West Point')

White
lily-flowered tulip
(*Tulipa*
'White Triumphator')

Red lily-flowered tulip (*Tulipa* 'Queen of Sheba')

Yellow
'Alaska'
'West Point'

White
'White Triumphator'

Rose pink
'China Pink'

Violet
'Maytime'

VII. FRINGED

Fringed tulips are similar to the late single tulips, except that the flower segments have fringed margins, sometimes of a contrasting color.

Red
'Redwing'

Yellow
'Maja'

Red fringed tulip
(*Tulipa* 'Redwing')

Yellow fringed tulip
(*Tulipa* 'Maja')

Pink
'Bellflower'

Violet to red-violet
'Blue Heron'

Bicolor
'Fancy Frills' (pink with white fringe)
'Burgandy Lace' (claret with white fringe)

VIII. VIRIDIFLORA

The Viridiflora tulips are similar to the late single tulips, except the flower segments are streaked or blotched with green.

'Angel' (green with off white)
'Artist' (green with deep rose)
'Golden Artist' (green with yellow and red)
'Greenland' (green with pink)
'Hummingbird' (green with yellow)
'Pimpernel' (green with claret)
'Spring Green' (green with ivory)

IX. REMBRANDT

The flowers of the Rembrandt tulips are irregularly bicolored or have "broken" patterns, caused by an aphid-transmitted virus. These tulips were much prized by early tulip fanciers and painters. This group is mentioned here for historical interest; it is little known or grown today.

X. PARROT

Parrot tulips have large, single, and solitary flowers, with slashed or deeply cut margins and ruffled surfaces. Often bicolored, the flowers are borne on weak stalks, 22 to 28 inches tall, in mid to late spring. This is a group of mutants so named because the flower segments in bud curl around each other, suggesting a parrot's beak.

Red
'Estella Rijnveld'
'Firebird'
'Parrot Wonder'

Red parrot tulip
Tulipa 'Estella Rijnveld')

Yellow
'Karel Diorman'
'Texas Gold'

Pink
'Fantasy'

Orange
'Apricot Parrot'
'Orange Favorite'

Purple
'Black Parrot'
'Blue Parrot'
'Lilac Perfection'

XI. PEONY-FLOWERED, DOUBLE LATE

The peony-flowered tulips have flowers that are more or less double (with more than six flower segments). The large, solitary flowers usually resemble fully doubled peonies or roses and are borne on stalks, 24 to 30 inches tall, in mid to late spring.

Red
'Bonanza'
'Uncle Tom'

White
'Carnival de Nice'
'Marilyn'
'Mount Tacoma'
'White Swallow'

Pink
'Angelique'
'Elegant Lady'
'Eros'
'May Wonder'

Yellow
'Gold Medal'

Orange
'Orange Triumph'

XII. KAUFMANNIANA

The flowers of the Kaufmanniana tulips are single and solitary, with strap-shaped segments that open wide in direct sunlight, hence they are often called "waterlily tulips." The flowers are borne on stalks, 6 to 12 inches tall, in early spring.

'Dance' (red and white)
'Fritz Kreisler' (pale peach)
'Johann Strauss' (yellow and red)
'Shakespeare' (salmon with yellow and red)
'Stresa' (orange and red)
'Sweet Lady' (orange-pink)
'Waterlily' (light yellow)

Orange and red kaufmanniana tulip
(*Tulipa Kaufmanniana* 'Stresa')

XIII. FOSTERIANA

The Fosteriana tulips have single, solitary flowers that are oval to oblong. The flowers are white through yellow to red, sometimes with colored margins, and the foliage is often purple streaked or mottled. The flowers are borne on stalks, 6 to 18 inches tall, in very early spring.

Red fosteriana tulip
(*Tulipa fosteriana* 'Red Emperor')

Red
  'Red Emperor'

Yellow
  'Yellow Empress'

White
  'Concerto'
  'Purissima'
  'White Emperor'

Pink
  'Pink Emperor'

XIV. GREIGII

The flowers of Greigii tulips are single and can be solitary or in clusters of four to six. They are yellow to red, often multicolored, and the foliage is variously streaked or mottled brown-violet. The flowers are borne on stalks, 6 to 10 inches and even up to 18 inches tall, in early spring.

Multicolored single greigii tulip
(*Tulipa greigii* 'Cape Cod')

Multicolored clustered greigii tulip
(*Tulipa greigii* 'Toronto')

'Cape Cod' (orange with yellow, red, and black)
'Corsage' (orange-pink edged yellow)
'Golden Tango' (yellow)
'Plaisir' (cream with red and yellow)
'Red Riding Hood' (red with yellow and black)
'Sparkling Fire' (red)
'Toronto' (salmon pink with yellow, red, and green, clustered)

XV. OTHER SPECIES AND HYBRIDS

Miscellaneous tulips, mostly small kinds, make up the last class. These tulips are suited to rock gardens with gritty, very well-drained soil. They should be planted away from competition.

Species

  T. batalinii (pale orange)
  T. biflora (white and yellow with red and green)

Tulipa pulchella

Tulipa turkestanica

T. clusiana (cream and red)
T. linifolia (red and black)
T. pulchella (red-violet)
T. saxatilis (lilac and yellow-orange)
T. sylvestris (yellow with green and red)
T. tarda (cream and yellow)
T. turkestanica (white and yellow)
T. wilsoniana (red and black)

Hybrids

  'Fusilier' (red; a bunching tulip derived from *T. praestans*)
  'Peppermint Stick' (red and white)
  'Unicum' (red; a bunching tulip derived from *T. praestans*)
  'Van Tubergen' (red; a bunching tulip derived from *T. praestans*)

Tulipa tarda

Tulipa saxatilis

CROCUS *SPP. AND CVS.*
(Crocus)

Zones 3–8

Among the most beloved and most widely grown of the small spring-flowering bulbs are the crocuses. The "Dutch" hybrid crocus is the garden type most commonly grown, and when planted in masses, it gives a lavish display of color. The jaunty, erect, cuplike flowers come in a variety of colors—white, deep violet, porcelain blue, dark lilac, and golden yellow. They open only in sunlight.

Lovely as the Dutch crocuses are, any gardener who has never grown some of the smaller species crocuses has missed one of the greatest joys of very early spring. They come into flower soon after the snowdrops are over and possess a sprightliness and a piquant charm that is very endearing. A little patch of species crocuses near the house, in some sheltered corner where they will catch the first warm rays of spring sunshine, will be a source of joy year after year. They may be tucked into all sorts of places: along a path, on a bank, and in front of shrub plantings (preferably with a southern exposure) and where they can be left undisturbed after they have flowered.

All the crocuses are of easy culture. They perform best in a light, sandy-humusy, moderately fertile soil and an exposure in full sun or partial shade. Corms of the Dutch hybrid crocuses should be planted about 4 inches deep, and those of the species crocuses about 3 inches deep. All should be spaced 2 to 3 inches apart. Plant in the fall.

If crocuses are planted in the lawn, they should be closely grouped for maximum effect and the grass should be left uncut in these groupings until the crocus foliage has yellowed in late spring.

As the yellow-flowered hybrids are sterile, and therefore produce no seed, their numbers increase less rapidly and may require supplemental plantings of new corms.

In areas where mice and other rodents are common, crocus plantings should be protected with ½-inch wire mesh or netting, laid flat over the bed and turned down several inches into the soil at the edges. Even when crocuses are so protected, rodents may shred the flowers in their attempt to reach the corms. Squirrels and chipmunks are particularly assiduous at finding, digging up, and eating newly planted crocus.

HYACINTHUS ORIENTALIS *CVS.*
(Hyacinth)

Zones 4–8

Hyacinths are rather stiff and formal but effective when grown in groups or masses, especially as a foreground to a shrub border. They are prized not only for their clear colors but also for their sweet fragrance. Both attributes make them popular for forcing indoors.

Hyacinth bulbs are disproportionately large. To ensure good performance in successive years, thorough soil preparation is important. If new, the bed should be dug out to a depth of 1 foot and the bottom 3 inches filled with loose compost, preferably mixed with well-rotted manure. Bulbs should be set 6 to 8 inches apart and covered with humusy topsoil, which, depending on soil-test results, may be neutralized with ground limestone or bonemeal (25 pounds per 100 square feet). Planting should be done in late summer or early fall. It is

---

CROCUS SPECIES AND CULTIVARS OF MERIT

DUTCH HYBRID CULTIVARS

Purple to lilac

'Enchantress'	'Queen of the Blues'
'Flower Record'	'Remembrance'
'Paulus Potter'	'Striped Beauty'
'Pickwick'	

White

'Jeanne d'Arc'
'Peter Pan'
'Snowstorm'

Yellow

'Golden Yellow'
'Yellow Mammoth'

CROCUS SPP. AND CVS.

Purple to lilac

C. biflorus	*C. medius*
C. chrysanthus 'Blue Pearl'	*C. sieberi* and cvs.
C. etruscus 'Zwanenburg'	*C. tomasinianus* and cvs.
C. goulimyi	*C. vernus* 'Early Perfection'
C. imperati ssp. *suaveolens*	*C. versicolor**

White

C. chrysanthus 'Snow Bunting'	*C. vernus* ssp. *albiflorus*
C. fleischeri	*C. versicolor* [†]
C. niveus	

Yellow

C. chrysanthus and cvs.	*C. korolkowii*
C. flavus	*C. susianus* (syn. *C. angustifolius*)
C. imperati ssp. *imperati*	*C. vernus* ssp. *vernus*

Red-violet

C. tommasinianus 'Ruby Giant'
C. tommasinianus 'Whitewell Purple'

*White with purple stripes.
[†]All white.

important that the planting site have at least six hours of sun exposure each day, especially for good performance in successive years.

"Dutch" hyacinths, as hybrids of *H. orientalis* are called in catalogs, are classed by bulb size. "Exhibition" bulbs are the largest, and "bedding" bulbs are somewhat smaller. "Prepared" bulbs have been cold treated for forcing. "Roman" hyacinth is a smaller-flowered type, less hardy, and usually earlier to bloom. For ordinary purposes, bedding hyacinths are satisfactory and considerably less expensive than exhibition bulbs. It is advisable to avoid color mixtures; hyacinths are best displayed in single-color groups.

Ordinarily, hyacinths persist many years, but the density of flowers on the scape diminishes after the first year, with older plantings acquiring grace in place of the initial dramatic grandeur. Hence, it is best not to mix new bulbs into established hyacinth beds.

After the bulbs have flowered, the foliage should be left undisturbed until it yellows. Hyacinths do well in sun-exposed plantings of low ground covers or may be succeeded by shallow-rooted annuals.

HYACINTH CULTIVARS OF MERIT

Purple to blue
- 'Amethyst' (lilac)
- 'Blue Blazer' (violet blue)
- 'Blue Giant' (light blue)
- 'Blue Jacket' (blue and purple)
- 'Delft Blue' (blue)
- 'Distinction' (deep red-violet)
- 'Myosotis' (pale blue)
- 'Ostara' (blue-violet)
- 'Violet Pearl' (lilac purple)

Yellow to orange
- 'City of Haarlem' (yellow)
- 'Gypsy Queen' (salmon orange)

Red to pink
- 'Anna Marie' (light pink)
- 'Hollyhock' (double red)
- 'Jan Bos' (cherry red)
- 'Lady Derby' (pink)
- 'Pink Pearl' (deep pink)
- 'Pink Perfection' (medium pink)

White
- 'Carnegie'
- 'L' Innocence'
- 'Queen of the Whites'
- 'White Pearl'

Pink hyacinth
(*Hyacinthus orientalis* 'Anna Marie')

Violet blue hyacinth
(*Hyacinthus orientalis* 'Blue Blazer')

White hyacinth
(*Hyacinthus orientalis* 'Queen of the Whites')

OTHER HARDY SPRING-FLOWERING BULBS

Just as a bed of annuals limited to one or two species lacks the special interest that diversity confers, so it is with spring bulbs. The main actors in the garden drama are usually daffodils and tulips, but there is an enticing list of supporting players, each with a special contribution to make. Some, such as the giant onion (*Allium giganteum*) and crown imperial (*Fritillaria imperialis*), are bold and commanding, while others, like Grecian windflower (*Anemone blanda*) and Siberian squill (*Scilla sibirica*), are individually diminutive but offer a colored carpet if massed in drifts and allowed to naturalize.

As with the daffodils, tulips, and hyacinths, soil preparation is no less important when growing the following spring-flowering bulbs. Newly purchased bulbs will flower most anywhere given water, light, and warmth, but the rewards of good planning and careful preparation come in successive years, with repeated and augmented performances spring after spring, reflective of the gardener having chosen a site knowledgeably and managed the garden environment with each species requirements in mind.

ALLIUM SPP.
(Flowering onion)

Zones 4–10

Of the 400 species of *Allium*, perhaps 150 and some hybrids are in horticultural commerce, all with small flowers arranged in tight, usually spherical clusters held well above the basal foliage. Although the various species most often cultivated are adaptable to a range of garden conditions, most thrive in full sun on sandy, well-drained soil of moderate fertility.

Allium giganteum

Among the small kinds, chives (*A. schoenoprasum*) is as ornamental as it is a useful herb, producing 1-inch-wide red-violet heads on 1-foot scapes in late spring to early summer among tubular aromatic leaves. Golden garlic, or lily leek (*A. moly*), 8 to 12 inches tall, bears loose heads of yellow flowers in late spring above flat leaves. *A. oreophilum*, also with flat leaves, produces scapes only 6 inches tall with purplish pink flowers in late spring. Rather similar but up to 1 foot tall is the species *A. ostrowskianum*. One of the most striking of the small species is the Turkestan onion (*A. karataviense*), which has strap-shaped leaves, 4 to 5 inches wide, and pale purplish flowers in spring, held in clusters 3 to 4 inches across. Ramsons (*A. ursinum*),

also wide leaved, grows up to 18 inches tall, bearing loose clusters of white flowers in spring. *A. neapolitanum* is similar but has narrow foliage.

Of the taller spring-flowering species, star of Persia (*A. christophii*) produces a rosette of flat leaves and a stout 1½- to 2½-foot scape in late spring. It bears a remarkably large sphere of lilac flowers that are firm in texture and dry in place without dropping, making the entire scape useful in dry bouquets. This species has long been hybridized with *A. elatum*, and one cross has yielded the cultivar 'Globemaster', which has dense globular clusters, 9 inches across, of bright violet flowers atop 3-foot scapes. The late spring display lasts about a month.

Star of Persia (*Allium christophii*)

The tallest of the flowering onions are *A. aflatunense*, 3 to 5 feet, with a dense 3- to 4-inch ball of purple flowers opening in late spring, and *A. giganteum*, about as tall, with a 6-inch globular cluster of purple flowers, also appearing from late spring to early summer. The latter is suited to zones 5 to 10. In both of these species, the large strap-shaped basal leaves usually wither at blooming time.

ANEMONE BLANDA
(*Grecian windflower*)

Zones 5–8
Grecian windflower, a sprightly little anemone with blue, pink, or white flowers, comes into bloom in early spring, just after snowdrop (*Galanthus* spp.) and winter aconite (*Eranthis hyemalis*). Hardly more than 3 inches in height, with daisylike flowers among the finely cut leaves, this diminutive plant self-sows and, if left undisturbed, soon forms dense patches that intensify in effectiveness year after year. The flowers open in the sun.

Grecian windflower grows best in partial or light shade and is especially lovely as a carpet around or beneath shrubs such as early flowering rhododendrons. Since the tuber-corms are sold very dry and shriveled, it helps to soak them in water for an hour or two before planting. They should be set about 3 inches deep and 2 inches apart and are most effective in single-color groupings of a dozen or more. Fall is the best planting time. It is wise to label plantings and thus avoid accidentally disturbing them during dormancy.

CAMASSIA *SPP.*
(*Camass lily*)

The several commercially available species of *Camassia* are all similar in habit and culture, but differ somewhat in hardiness.

In each, a single bulb produces a clump of grasslike leaves topped, in late spring, by a 2½- to 4-foot spike of blue

Chives (*Allium schoenoprasum*)

to purple or white flowers, about 1 inch across. Camass lily performs best on deeply prepared, fertile, slightly acidic soils in full sun. It is most effective in clumps of six or more. The four most frequently grown species vary in hardiness.

Species	Zones
C. cusickii	5–8
C. leichtlinii	3–8
C. quamash	5–8
C. scilloides	7–9

CHIONODOXA LUCILIAE
(Glory-of-the-snow)

Zones 3–8

Blooming in late winter or early spring, glory-of-the-snow grows 4 or 5 inches high and presents several upward-facing blue flowers, about 1 inch across, each with a white center. Because its flowering overlaps with the even earlier blooming snowdrop and the early narcissus and species tulips that soon follow, this species is worthy of much wider use. Mass plantings, if left undisturbed, will become carpets, the result of both the bulbs naturally dividing and the seeds being shed in place.

Plant bulbs in the fall about 3 inches deep and 2 inches apart. Sunny positions with ordinary well-drained soil are best. The foliage vanishes soon after flowering is finished.

Cultivars include 'Alba', with white flowers; 'Rosea', with pink flowers; and 'Gigantea', with larger, more numerous blue flowers.

CONVALLARIA MAJALIS
(Lily-of-the-valley)

Zones 4–8

Lily-of-the-valley, a diminutive member of the lily family, is an old-time favorite. Rising 6 to 9 inches in mid-spring, the one-sided stalks of nodding creamy white bells emit an exquisite fragrance. The bud-tipped rhizomes, or pips, should be planted in fall 2 to 4 inches apart, with the tips not more than 1 inch below the surface and the roots directed downward. Lily-of-the-valley thrives in sandy-humusy soil of average fertility that stays consistently moist through the growing season. Flowering is most generous in partial or light shade. In dense shade, the plants will grow but flowers are sparse. In the South, light shade is required if premature yellowing of foliage is to be prevented.

Since thick, dense clumps flower less freely year by year, it is best to lift them every few years and divide them into smaller clumps for replanting. Unless allowed adequate space to spread, lily-of-the-valley can become invasive as the rhizomes radiate from the original planting. Plastic or metal curbing, or other continuous barriers, set about 8 inches deep will help limit rhizome extension.

Among the several cultivars are 'Fortunei', with larger flowers and leaves; 'Rosea', with pink flowers; and 'Aureo-variegata', with yellow variegated foliage.

ENDYMION

See Hyacinthoides.

ERANTHIS HYEMALIS
(Winter aconite)

Zones 3–8

Blooming with the snowdrop, winter aconite, an endearing little flower, seems to hold within its golden cup the very promise of spring. Borne on a stalk hardly more than 2 or 3 inches tall in late winter to early spring, each flower is upward facing and surrounded by an Elizabethan ruff of green leaves. Winter aconite self-sows readily, and large colonies eventually develop from a small planting, as long as the site is left undisturbed. Since the foliage disappears in early summer, it is best to grow winter aconite with a low, relatively benign ground cover, such as Himalayan mazus (*Mazus reptans*).

Patches of winter aconite are especially effective in open woodland, on an embankment, or in the easily seen foreground of a shrub planting. It does well in full sun or partial shade, but in zones 7 and 8 light shade in summer is beneficial. The small tubers, usually sold dry and shriveled, should be soaked in water for an hour or two before planting, which should be done in the fall. Plant about 2 inches deep and 2 to 3 inches apart.

ERYTHRONIUM *SPP.*
(Dogtooth violet)

Zones (3) 4–8 (9)

Dogtooth violet is also called adder's tongue, avalanche lily, fawn lily, and trout lily. The dozen or so mostly native species and several hybrids in cultivation range, according to kind, from 4 inches to 2 feet tall and bear yellow, pinkish purple, rose pink, or white flowers in the spring.

E. dens-canis of Europe and *E. albidum*, *E. americanum*, and *E. propullans* of the eastern United States are the hardiest species. Western species are less hardy, with the possible exception of *E. hendersonii*. All have pointed whitish corms (the "dog's tooth") that should be planted point up in the fall in moist, partially shaded, humusy soil. Mass plantings give the most effective results. Care should be taken to keep the corms moist while planting. The hybrid cultivars 'Pagoda' (yellow) and 'White Beauty' (white) are especially attractive when naturalized in informal woodland settings. Plant the bulbs in the fall about 6 inches deep, spacing them 3 to 4 inches apart.

FRITILLARIA IMPERIALIS
(Crown imperial)

Zones 4–8

Crown imperial is a striking plant, especially, when grown in groups of 6 to

12, and never fails to command attention. The stout stem rises 2 to 4 feet, bears numerous light green leaves about 6 inches long, and terminates in a leafy tuft beneath which hang 6 to 12 red-orange bell-shaped flowers about 2 inches long. All parts emit a mild skunky odor. The flowers appear in early to mid spring and the foliage usually dies down by early summer.

If crown imperial is to reflower, the planting site must be carefully chosen and well prepared. The location should receive full sun during the relatively brief growing period and, if possible, be sheltered from strong wind. The south or southeastern side of a building, wall, or evergreen hedge is usually ideal. At fall planting time, the soil should be dug out to a depth of 18 inches by about 1 square foot per bulb. For example, for a planting of six bulbs, an area roughly 2 by 3 feet should be excavated to a depth of 18 inches and cleared of any tree roots. In the bottom of the hole, spread a 4- to 6-inch layer of well-rotted manure mixed with rich compost. The bulbs are set on this layer, tilted or on their sides to prevent water from collecting in the top depression, and spaced 6 to 8 inches apart. The planted hole should be filled with a light, moisture retaining, humusy soil and settled with water. Shallow-rooted annuals or ground covers may be planted as seasonal successors.

Color variants include the cultivars 'Lutea Maxima', with yellow flowers, and 'Rubra Maxima', with red flowers.

FRITILLARIA MELEAGRIS
(Checker lily, Guinea hen flower)

Zones 4–8

The flower of the checker lily is borne on a slender 1-foot-tall stem. The single, sometimes two or three, hanging, 2-inch maroon violet bells open in early to mid spring, their colors mottled or streaked. Interest can be heightened by massing a few dozen plants in a square yard or two of sun-exposed garden with consistently moist, well-drained, humusy soil. Smaller groupings are effective in rock gardens.

As with all fritillaries, the soil beneath the bulbs should be enriched, and the individual bulbs should be set on their sides. Planting depth is about 4 inches, and spacing about 3 inches. Planting time is in the fall.

Among the several color-variant cultivars, 'Alba', with white flowers, is particularly effective.

GALANTHUS NIVALIS
(Snowdrop)

Zones 3–8

Because the snowdrop is the true floral harbinger of spring, often coming into flower in mid or late winter while there is still snow on the ground, it is especially cherished and beloved. Though only 4 to 6 inches tall, it easily survives a heavy snowfall quite unharmed and even a prolonged spell of frigid weather, blooming on when conditions moderate. The long-lasting 1-inch flowers, each pendent on a slender, threadlike stalk, are white with green spots and open in bright sunlight. Thriving in partial shade and moist, sandy soil of average fertility, snowdrop increases over the years, both by seed and bulb division, forming large, dense clumps. Snowdrop bulbs should be planted in the fall 2 to 3 inches deep and about 2 inches apart. It is especially effective when massed and naturalized in open woodland or grouped around the base of trees in the lawn or in patches in front of evergreen shrubs along a requently traveled walk. As the flowers are small, snowdrop should be planted where it will be visible at close range, especially in small plantings. When combined with patches of species crocus, winter aconite, and Siberian squill, it is especially appealing.

Among the few cultivars available, 'Flore Pleno' is probably the most distinctive, with puffy double flowers. Giant snowdrop (*G. elwesii*), hardy in zones 5–8, is larger in all respects, with its paired leaves up to 8 inches long and nearly 1 inch wide. Its flowers are 1½ to 1¾ inches across. Often flowering a bit

earlier than *G. nivalis* and of equally easy culture, it can be used together with the other species to extend the snowdrop display. The foliage of snowdrops yellows and disappears by the onset of summer.

GLADIOLUS COMMUNIS SSP. BYZANTINUS
(Hardy gladiolus)

Zones 6–8

Resembling a slender summer-flowering hybrid gladiolus, but blooming in late spring, hardy gladiolus bears one or two spikes, each with 10 to 20 flowers. The individual blooms are about 1½ inches across and mostly in shades of red-violet or cerise but also white. Unless the corms are planted in sandy-humusy soil in a sunny location, flowering will eventually diminish and cease over the years.

It is best to plant hardy gladioluses in groups of one or two dozen at a depth of 4 to 6 inches and 3 or 4 inches apart. If possible, plant the corms in the fall. Spring-planted corms will flower in early summer the first year, and then revert to their normal spring-flowering period in successive years. It is essential for future flowering that the foliage continue to receive direct sunlight after flowering is over and until the end of the growing season.

HYACINTHOIDES HISPANICA
(Wood hyacinth)

Zones 3–8

Wood hyacinth is also listed in catalogs under *Endymion hispanicus*, *Scilla hispanica*, and *Scilla campanulata*. It flowers with the late tulips and makes a fine companion plant in an informal tulip bed. It naturalizes freely, especially in partial shade, and so can be established along woodland paths and under lightly shading trees. From the clumps of reflexed strap-shaped leaves, erect clusters of ¾-inch bluish lavender flowers rise to 1 foot or more.

Most successful on sandy-humusy soil of average fertility, wood hyacinth bulbs should be planted in the fall 4 to 6 inches deep and 3 to 4 inches apart. This species often naturalizes and reproduces by both

Wood hyacinth (*Hyacinthoides hispanica*)

bulb division and seed. Large, dense, long-established clumps can be lifted after the foliage yellows and dies back in early summer; the bulbs are then separated and replanted immediately or stored for fall planting.

Numerous cultivars exist, some of them hybrids with English bluebell (*H. non-scripta*).

'Alba Maxima': white flowers.
'Excelsior': 2 feet tall; large violet blue flowers.
'Rosabella': pink flowers.
'Rosea': purplish pink flowers.

IRIS SPP.
(Early dwarf bulbous iris)

The genus *Iris* is a very large and diverse group. Garden irises for the most part bloom in the spring, and fall into two categories: very early dwarf bulbous kinds (described here) and early to late, dwarf to tall rhizomatous kinds (described in Chapter 15). The larger bulbous iris are discussed later in this chapter.

Few of the small bulbous irises are in cultivation. The best known is netted iris (*I. reticulata*), 6 to 9 inches tall, with

Iris reticulata

grass like four-angled foliage. Its purple, yellow-crested, fragrant flowers are borne in very early spring. Scarcely 4 inches tall and slightly earlier is *I. danfordiae*, which bears yellow flowers marked with olive and orange. Both are hardy to zone 5.

Iris danfordiae

Unless grouped at least 12 together in a highly visible location, as along a frequently traversed walk, netted iris is easily overlooked, so well do its dark-toned flowers blend in with the subdued browns and tans of the soil and leafy mulch that prevail on the surface in early spring. Lighter shades—as in cultivars such as 'Joyce' (pale blue) and 'Natascha' (ivory)—are more conspicuous. Although it is smaller, *I. danfordiae* is quite showy and truly brightens the scene.

Full sun and a soil pH of 7.0 to 7.5 are important for both species, especially for reflowering in successive years. Plant the bulbs 4 to 6 inches deep in the fall, spacing them about 3 inches apart. If the planting depth is shallower, each bulb tends to fragment into numerous bulblets, none of which will flower for several years.

LEUCOJUM VERNUM
(Spring snowflake)

Zones 3–8

Spring snowflake resembles the snow-drop, having pendent, bell-shaped, white flowers, with segments tipped green. It blooms later than snow-drop, however, and is taller and more robust. Naturalized in a woodland planting, grouped in the foreground of a shrub border, or even placed among tulips, it is most effective when massed. Spring snowflake is very long lived and, once established, will continue to bloom on year after year, requiring only an occasional digging.

The bulbs should be planted in the autumn about 3 inches deep and spaced 4 to 5 inches apart. There are several types and varieties, some blooming earlier than others. For a succession of snowflake blooms, spring through fall, two later-flowering species are available. Summer snowflake (*L. aestivum*) reaches 12 to 14 inches tall and has three or four flowers per scape. It blooms in late spring to early summer, and autumn snowflake (*L. autumnale*) is 9 to 12 inches tall, and bears paired flowers in early fall (see page 415).

MUSCARI *SPP.*
(*Grape hyacinth*)

Zones 3–8

Of the dozen species of grape hyacinth known, four are cultivated. All are low in habit, bearing spikes of tiny globular blue or blue-violet flowers in the spring. The grape hyacinths have thick, linear leaves that radiate away from the flower stalk. Grape hyacinths thrive in partial shade on sandy-humusy soil but are very adaptable and frequently naturalize, reproducing by bulb offsets and seed. Once established, they require no special care. Bulbs should be planted in the fall 3 to 4 inches deep and about as far apart.

Most frequently seen is common grape hyacinth; *M. botryoides* is 6 to 9 inches tall and has a compact spike that appears with the hybrid crocuses. Among its several cultivars are 'Caeruleum', with bright blue flowers; 'Carneum', with pink flowers; and 'White Beauty', with white flowers. Least common but a bit earlier to flower and lower in habit is sky blue grape hyancinth *M. azureum*.

The tallest of the four species is Armenian grape hyacinth *M. armeniacum,* which is about 1 foot tall. Each flower is tipped white. Its foliage appears in September and carpets the ground all winter, setting the scene for the flowers, which appear with the daffodils. Thus Armenian grape hyacinth makes a good ground cover and color complement for the daffodil. Several cultivars are available.

Armenian grape hyacinth
(*Muscari armeniacum* 'Blue Spike')

'Blue Spike': double blue flowers.
'Heavenly Blue': intense blue flowers.
'Saphir': sterile, long-lasting, deep blue-violet flowers.

Most distinctive of the four species is *M. comosum* (tassel hyacinth), which is usually listed as *M. plumosum* in catalogs. It produces a terminal tuft of sterile flowers above the hanging fertile ones. In the cultivar 'Monstrosum' (also called feather hyacinth), all the flowers are sterile and are cut into fine shreds, conferring a feathery appearance to the spike.

ORNITHOGALUM *SPP.*
(*Star-of-Bethlehem*)

In southern gardens, i.e., those in zones 8 and 9, tall star-of-Bethlehem (*O. arabicum*) and chincherinchee (*O. thyrsoides*) bear clustered white or cream flowers on 15- to 24-inch-tall stalks in the spring. In the North, these, and other South African species, may be grown in pots or in the garden as tender bulbs, to be brought indoors in the fall for frost-free storage.

Star of Bethlehem
(*Ornithogalum umbellatum*)

Two hardy lower-growing European species, *O. nutans* (zones 6 to 8) and *O. umbellatum* (zones 5 to 8), have naturalized in many northern areas, even to the point of invasiveness. The commoner *O. umbellatum* reaches 6 inches and bears flat-topped clusters of intensely white flowers in mid to late spring. The flowers open only in direct sun. *O. nutans* bears its green-and-white flowers, nodding or drooping, on erect 12- to 15-inch-tall spikes.

All are of easy culture, having no special soil requirements except good drainage and adequate moisture while growing and flowering. The bulbs are usually planted in the fall about 4 inches deep and 4 to 6 inches apart for *O. umbellatum*; plant 10 to 12 inches apart for *O. arabicum*, *O. nutans*, and *O. thyrsoides*.

PUSCHKINIA SCILLOIDES
(*Striped squill*)

Zones 3–10

Striped squill is regrettably little known, but it is as deserving of garden culture as the closely related glory-of-the-snow (*Chionodoxa* spp.) and squill (*Scilla* spp.). Striped squill blooms about the time of the early daffodils, making a charming display of upward-facing pale blue flowers on short spikes. Most any well-drained soil suits it; a location in full sun at flowering time yields the most bounteous results.

Striped squill (*Puschkinia scilloides*)

Mass planting intensifies the display. Care should be taken to protect the shallow bulbs from disturbance once the foliage yellows and vanishes. Otherwise, no attention is required. The bulbs should be planted in the fall about 3 inches deep and 2 to 3 inches apart.

SCILLA SIBERICA
(Siberian squill)

Zones 5–8

The various squills are among the loveliest of the small spring-flowering bulbs. Once established, they increase rapidly, especially from self-sown seed, and readily naturalize. They are particularly effective along paths in open woodland or on shady banks, thriving in partial or light shade but also performing well in full sun. Plant the bulbs in the fall 2 to 3 inches deep and about as far apart.

Siberian squill is the smallest of the dozen or so *Scilla* species in cultivation and is the first to come into flower. The color is a very intense, bright blue to blue-violet, and the bell-like drooping flowers are borne singly or in small clusters 3-to 4-inch-tall stalks.

Among the cultivars available are 'Spring Beauty', which readily self-sows and thus easily naturalizes, and 'Alba', with white flowers.

Siberian squill (*Scilla siberica*) with pansies

HARDY SUMMER-FLOWERING BULBS

ALLIUM *SPP.*
(Flowering onion)

Zones 3–8 (9)

The several species of flowering onion that bloom during the summer months are less well known than the spring-flowering types. Most are rather low and thus are suited to the front of the garden or in beds of low-growing plants. All perform best in full sun and well-drained, moderately fertile soil. The bulbs should be planted in the fall, with the necks twice to three times as deep as the height of the bulb (e.g., a 2-inch-high bulb should be 4 to 6 inches deep) and spaced two to three times the diameter of the bulb.

A. flavum: tubular leaves; 15 to 18 inches tall; yellow flowers, with whiskerlike bracts beneath each head; midsummer.
A. pulchellum: threadlike foliage; 12 to 18 inches tall; pinkish purple flowers, which are at first erect but later droop; late summer.

A. senescens var. *glaucum:* short, flat, slightly twisted, gray green leaves; 18 to 24 inches tall; pinkish purple flowers, borne in loose, open clusters; late summer.
A. sphaerocephalum (drumstick onion): slender, hollow leaves; 2½ to 3 feet tall; reddish purple flowers, in dense or somewhat elongated heads; early to mid summer.

Garlic chive
(*Allium tuberosum*)

A. stellatum (prairie onion): flat leaves; native to Midwest; slender scapes; 18 inches tall; pinkish rose flowers; late summer.
A. tuberosum (garlic chive): flattish, mildly garlic-scented leaves, in dense clumps; 18 inches tall; self-sows; flattish scapes; white flowers, borne in loose clusters; late summer.

BEGONIA GRANDIS
(Hardy begonia)

Zones 6–8

Often listed in catalogs as *B. evansiana*; hardy begonia is one of the few species of the immense, largely tropical genus *Begonia* that thrives outdoors year round in temperate latitudes. Hardy begonia bears large leaves that are often red beneath and, in late summer, loose clusters of pink flowers on 1½-

to 2½-foot-tall stems. It should be grown in partial shade or light shade in humusy, well-drained soil. Because the shoots are late to appear (in some locations not until June), it requires protection from springtime cultivation. Permanent metal labels make an ever-present reminder.

Hardy begonia propagates naturally from ¼-inch reddish bulbils that form on the stems in late summer and drop to the ground, surviving the winter and helping develop large clumps in due course. As the tubers and bulbils are very small, it is best to use the easily transplanted growing plants to establish them. Winter mulch is beneficial in zones 6 and 7.

BELAMCANDA CHINENSIS
(Blackberry lily)

Blackberry lily
(Belamcanda chinensis)
in flower

Pods of blackberry lily and *Iris sibirica*

Zones 5–10

Blackberry lily, an iris relative, bears narrow sword-shaped leaves and branched stems, 2½ to 4 feet tall. From early to midsummer it displays flat, 2-inch flowers of orange with maroon or purple spots, each opening for one day. The flowers are followed by a green seed capsule, which eventually splits open to reveal numerous round, shiny black seeds in a tight group, suggestive of a blackberry. In the fall, the fruiting stalks can be dried for use in winter bouquets. Seeds that drop often supplement the planting. *B. flabellata* is very similar, but has yellow flowers.

Blackberry lily grows best in full sun on sandy-humusy soil. The fleshy rhizomatous roots should be planted in the spring. The crowns should be set just below the surface and the roots spread outward and downward. Alternatively, seed may be germinated in the spring indoors, grown on in a coldframe, and the seedlings transferred to the garden in late summer.

BLETILLA STRIATA
(Hardy orchid)

Zones (6) 7–9

Although the foot-long foliage at the hardy orchid seems irislike, the flowers tell the story: this is a true orchid. Unlike most native terrestrial orchids, hardy orchid is relatively easy to grow in the garden. The scapes, each bearing three to seven flowers in early to mid summer, rise 18 to 24 inches. In typical orchid fashion, each flower has five radiating petal-like members, in this case colored pink, surrounding a central tubular structure, also pink but with purple markings.

Bletilla striata

The key to success with hardy orchid is the soil, which should be humusy and consistently moist through the growing season. Roots should be planted in the spring about 4 inches deep and 8 to 12 inches apart. Mulch well in the winter to avert sustained deep freezing. Partial shade helps reduce the effects of extreme summer heat.

EREMURUS SPP.
(Foxtail lily)

Zones 5–9

Of the 40 to 50 species in the genus *Eremurus*, perhaps one-third are in cultivation, but none is common. This is a pity, as the lofty spikes of foxtail lily make dramatic accents for a month or more in mid to late summer.

E. stenophyllus (syn. *E. bungei*) grows 3 to 4 feet tall and bears yellow flowers. *E. himalaicus*, the hardiest species, can reach 8 feet and has white flowers. In two hybrid groups—Cathedral and Shelford, each with several named cultivars—the

flowers are yellow, orange, pink, or white, on plants ranging from 3½ to 5 feet high.

Foxtail lilies require full sun, well-drained soil of average fertility, and staking when in flower. Winter mulching is advisable in zone 7 and essential in zones 5 and 6. The mulch should be left in place in the spring until danger of frost has passed. The thick, radiating, rhizomatous roots should be planted in the spring in holes large enough to allow the easily broken roots to spread fully and deep enough so that the crowns lie about 6 inches beneath the surface. The distance between plants is determined principally by leaf length of the species or cultivar at hand. For example, the leaves of *E. himalaicus* spread about 1½ feet, so to prevent undue shading, plants should be set 2½ to 3 feet apart. Transplanting established plants is seldom successful.

KNIPHOFIA *HYBRIDS*
(Red-hot poker)

Zones (6) 7–10
Several of the many species of the South African *Kniphofia* have been crossed, leading to a moderately hardy assemblage of garden cultivars that bear bold spikes of drooping, densely arranged, tubular flowers in colors ranging from pale yellow to red, mostly appearing in mid to late summer. Foliage consists of a basal clump of linear, grasslike leaves.

Often slow to become established, red-hot poker responds best to sandy-humusy soil. Full sun stimulates the best floral display. In zone 6 and in exposed locations in zone 7, winter mulch is required. Elsewhere, the foliage can be tied up in the fall to form a protective hood or tent over the root crown. Planting small bare-root material or potted individuals is best done in the spring, with an interval of 1 to 1½ feet between plants. It is not advisable to attempt moving established clumps as the system of thickened roots is diffuse and wide ranging.

Among the 20 or so commercially available named hybrids are the following.

'Earliest of All'; the most reliably hardy form in the North; 2 to 2½

feet tall; coral pink to orange flowers;
early to mid summer;
'Primrose Beauty'; 2 to 2½ feet tall;
yellow flowers.
'Royal Standard': 3 feet tall; red and
yellow flowers.
'Springtime': 2 to 2½ feet tall; red to
white flowers.
'White Fairy': 2 feet tall; cream flowers.

LILIUM
(Lily)

Zones (4) 5–9

A large and varied group, the true
lilies make excellent summer accents in
the garden. Of the 80 species and hundreds of hybrids, many are reliable and
easily grown, but others have little adap-
tive amplitude and seldom succeed under
garden conditions, however carefully
they have been altered.

Among the easiest species to grow is
tiger lily (*L. lancifolium*), with few to many
nodding, orange, black-spotted flowers
borne on 4- to 6-foot stems in midsummer.
Its numerous hybrids have pendent to
upward-facing flowers, in colors ranging
from cream to deep purplish red, borne
on 2- to 5-foot stems, usually in early
summer. Turk's-cap lily (*L. martagon*) has
6 to 40 pendent, purple, black-spotted,
rather malodorous flowers on 4- to 6-foot
stems. It is especially easy to grow. Its most
popular cultivars are grouped in the strain
called 'Paisley' hybrids, characterized by
lower height and scentless flowers in late
spring ranging from deep purple to white.

Another popular species is madonna lily
(*L. candidum*), which bears 5 to 20 waxy
white, hanging flowers on 3- to 5-foot
stems in midsummer. Regal lily (*L. regale*)
is similar in dimensions, but its 1 to 25
white flowers are usually borne horizontally and appear in early to mid summer.

Although the Easter lily (*L. longifolorum*)
is best known as a potted flowering bulb
in the spring as a result of greenhouse
forcing, it is perfectly hardy and readily
adapts to the garden, bearing its white,
horizontal trumpets on 2- to 3-foot
stems year after year in the summer. The
Japanese lily (*L. speciosum*) blooms in late
summer and has sweetly scented, white
or pale pink, purple-spotted and -warted

Regal lily (*Lilium regale*)

flowers. There are usually 3 to 13 flowers
on the 3- to 4-foot-tall stems.

In recent years, the many hybrid lilies
on the horticultural market have gained
favor over *Lilium* species. Most are easily
cultured and, left to themselves, prove
reliable over many seasons, often developing sizable clumps. Seven main classes of
hybrids are presently recognized, distinguished by the characteristics of the parent
species. By selecting cultivars from several
of these classes, you can maintain a long
season of bloom and enjoy much of the
diversity to be found in the genus *Lilium*.

Because of their usually narrow ecological amplitudes ("fussiness" in gardening parlance), native lilies are best left
undisturbed in the wild. In exceptional
cases, as, for example, when a garden
habitat closely approximates one in which
wild lilies grow, a trial cultivation may
be attempted, providing laws allow, as,
for example, when a wild area is to be
preempted for other purposes. Regrettably,
such attempts seldom succeed.

With hybrid cultivars and amenable
species, thoughtful site choice, thorough
soil preparation, and careful handling of

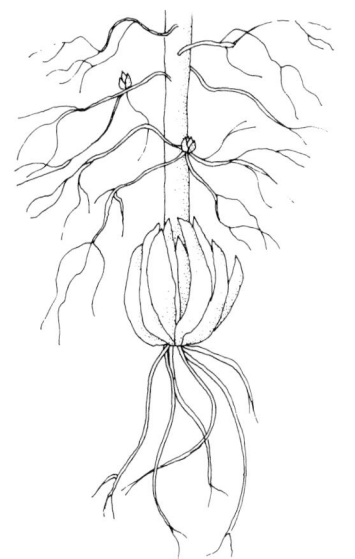
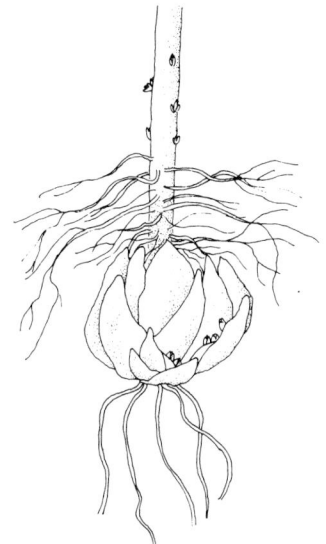

Rooting patterns in regal lily (Lilium regale) *and gold-banded lily* (L. auratum), *with
roots produced at bulb bases and along stem.*

the bulbs help lilies become established as long-term garden assets. The site should be sunny or only briefly or lightly shaded, away from strong winds, isolated from such herbivorous wildlife as rabbits, and free from puddling or flooding. Soil should be prepared deeply, keeping in mind that, in general, the top of the bulb should be set at a depth equal to three times the bulb's height if the soil is sandy, or two times in heavier, clayish soil. Since many lilies are stem rooting (i.e., developing roots along the subterranean portion of the stem as well as at the base of the bulb), the soil should be prepared to a depth of at least 1 foot.

Lilies that are base rooting (i.e., forming no roots along the stem and only from the bulb base) may be planted at a depth 1½ to 2 times the bulb height, or in the case of *L. candidum* and its hybrids, bulb tops need be no deeper than 2 inches below the surface. Most lilies should be planted 8 to 12 inches apart. Very tall

'Enchantment' cultivar of tiger lily
(*Lilium lancifolium*)

Japanese lily (*Lilium speciosum*)

HYBRID LILIES OF MERIT

1. HYBRIDS DERIVED FROM *L. LANCIFOLIUM* AND SEVERAL OTHER SPECIES (ALL STEM ROOTING)*

   Flowers upward facing; early summer
   'Connecticut King' (yellow)
   'Cote d'Azur' (pink)
   'Enchantment' (red)
   'Mont Blanc' (white)

   Flowers horizontal; early to mid summer
   'Corsage' (pale pink, spotted purple, yellow exterior)
   'Fire King' (red-orange, spotted purple)
   'Sterling Star' (cream, spotted brown)

   Flowers pendent; early to mid summer
   'Black Butterfly' (deep red-violet)
   'Citronella' (yellow, spotted black)
   'Connecticut Yankee' (red-orange)
   'Fiesta' hybrids (yellow to red)
   'Harlequin' hybrids (salmon with various other shades)

2. HYBRIDS OF *L. MARTAGON* (TURK'S-CAP LILY) OR *L. HANSONII* (JAPANESE TURK'S-CAP LILY) (ALL STEM ROOTING; SUMMER BLOOMING)

   'Backhouse' hybrids (ivory, yellow, pink, burgundy)
   'Marhan' (orange, spotted reddish, yellow, spotted brown-violet)

3. HYBRIDS DERIVED FROM *L. CANDIDUM* (MADONNA LILY), *L. CHALCEDONICUM* (SCARLET TURK'S-CAP LILY), AND OTHER SPECIES OF EUROPE, EXCLUDING *L. MARTAGON* (ALL BASE ROOTING; SUMMER BLOOMING)

   'Ares' (bright red-orange)
   'Artemis' (pale pink to yellow-orange)
   'Prelude' (red-orange, tipped dark red)

4. HYBRIDS DERIVED FROM SEVERAL SPECIES NATIVE TO NORTH AMERICA (SOME STEM ROOTING; ALL SUMMER BLOOMING)

   'Bellingham' hybrids (yellow-orange; red, spotted brown)
   'Bellmaid' hybrids (yellow, tinged orange, aging to red)

5. HYBRIDS DERIVED FROM *L. LONGIFLORUM* (EASTER LILY) AND *L. FORMOSANUM* (FORMOSA LILY) (ALL STEM ROOTING; SUMMER BLOOMING)

   'Formobel' (white, yellow throat)
   'Formolongi' (all white)

6. HYBRIDS DERIVED FROM *L. HENRYI* (HENRY LILY) AND SEVERAL OTHER ASIATIC SPECIES (ALL STEM ROOTING; SUMMER BLOOMING)

   Flowers trumpet shaped
   'African Queen' (orange)
   'Black Dragon' (purplish red, white inside)
   'Golden Splendor' (yellow, striped purple)
   'Pink Perfection' (purplish pink)

   Flowers bowl shaped
   'First Love' (yellow, edged pink, pale green throat)
   'Heart's Desire' (yellow to white)

species, such as *L. columbianum*, which may exceed 6 feet, are best spaced 12 to 18 inches apart.

Ideally, the soil should be a consistently moist, sandy loam, with much compost incorporated. Lily bulbs consist of fleshy scales that quickly desiccate in a dry atmosphere. Hence the importance of prior preparation of the site, including the digging of planting holes, before the bulbs are unpacked and the prompt placement and covering of them once the packaging has been opened. Cloudy, calm, even misty weather in the fall is ideal for planting lilies.

As with other hardy bulbs, it is advisable to take measures to prevent the accidental disturbance of dormant lilies. A low, nonaggressive ground cover, such as creeping myrtle (*Vinca minor*) or wine-leaf cinquefoil (*Potentilla tridentata*) makes a useful companion for lilies and helps keep the soil cool and moist in summer.

Madonna lily (*Lilium candidum*)

Turk's-cap lily (*Lilium martagon*)

Flowers flat, or only one petal curved back
 'Golden Showers' (brown, yellow inside)
 'Summer Song' (all yellow)

Flowers recurved
 'Bright Star' (ivory and orange)
 'Golden Sunburst' (yellow, green veins outside)
 'White Henryi' (white and orange)

7. HYBRIDS DERIVED FROM *L. AURATUM*, *L. JAPONICUM*, *L. RUBELLUM*, AND *L. SPECIOSUM* (ALL JAPANESE; STEM ROOTING; AND MID TO LATE SUMMER BLOOMING)

Flowers trumpet shaped
 'Green Magic' (white)

Flowers bowl shaped
 'Casablanca' (white)
 'Empress of Japan' (white, banded yellow, spotted purple)

Flowers flat
 'Imperial Pink' (pink)
 'Imperial Silver' (white, spotted purple)

Flowers recurved
 'Jamboree' (deep red, spotted dark, edged white)
 'Journey's End' (deep red, tipped and edged white)
 'Pink Solace' (pale pink, aging to red, pale green throat)

* I.e., producing roots not only from the base of the bulb but also along the stem between the top of the bulb and the soil surface.

BASE-ROOTING *LILIUM* SPECIES, HYBRIDS, AND CULTIVARS

Name	Native to	Zones
L. bolanderi (Bolander lily)	Northwest United States	5–8
L. canadense (meadow lily)	Eastern North America	5–8
L. candidum (madonna lily)*	Balkans	6–8
L. chalcedonicum (red Turk's-cap lily)	Greece	5–8
L. columbianum (Oregon lily)	Northwest United States	5–8
L. grayi (Allegheny lily)	Eastern United States	5–8
L. humboldtii (Humboldt lily)	California	5–8
L. kelloggii (Siskiyou lily)	Northwest United States	5–8
L. maritimum (coast lily)	Northwestern California	4–8
L. martagon (Turk's-cap lily)	Eurasia	4–7
L. monadelphum (Caucasus lily)	Caucasus	5–8
L. pardalinum (leopard lily)	Northwest United States	5–8
L. pomponium (alpine lily)	Maritime Alps of Europe	4–7
L. pyrenaicum (Yellow Turk's-cap lily)	Pyrenees to Turkey	3–7
L. superbum (American Turk's-cap lily)	Eastern United States	3–7
L. × testaceum (Nankeen lily)	†	6–8
L. washingtonianum (Washington lily)	California	4–7

* Requires shallow planting, with the top of the bulb not more than 2 inches below the surface.
† Garden hybrid.

LYCORIS *SPP.*
(Hardy amaryllis)

Two species of hardy amaryllis have long been cultivated in American gardens. Magic lily (*L. squamigera*), hardy in zones 5 to 8, has strap-shaped leaves that fade by midsummer; then, usually after a late summer rain, scapes rise 1½ to 3 feet high, each usually bearing 6 to 8 large, pink or rosy lilac amaryllislike flowers, each 3 to 4 inches across. The scapes may bear as few as 4 and up to 12 flowers.

Because of the gap between the foliar and flowering stages, it is advisable to mark the site with stakes or to have interplanted compatible perennials, such as Japanese anemones (*Anemone* × *hybrida*) or peonies (*Paeonia lactiflora* hybrids) to prevent damaging the emerging scapes. Newly planted bulbs may not flower until the second year. Once planted, bulbs should not be disturbed, as their roots are permanent.

Red spider lily (*L. radiata*), hardy in zones 7 to 9, has narrow grasslike foliage that is retained through the summer.

From the 12- to 14-inch-tall scapes, four to six deep pink to red or white flowers arise. The 1½-inch flowers are borne in late summer or early fall.

Both species do best in sunny or lightly shaded locations in well-drained soil of average fertility. Bulbs should be planted with their tops 4 to 6 inches below the surface. They are especially effective when grouped, with three to six bulbs set 6 inches apart, and groups spaced 2 to 3 feet apart. Planting may be done in early spring, before the leaves develop, or late fall, after flowering is over.

TENDER SUMMER-FLOWERING BULBS AND TUBERS

ACHIMENES *CULTIVARS*
(Cupid's bower)

Zone 10

Cupid's bower, a gesneriad, offers brightly colored flowers of unusual distinction. Its habit suits it to window boxes, hanging pots and baskets, and small containers on the terrace or patio. It is especially effective on low walls, along the edge of terraced beds, or at the edge of raised planting beds around the house.

Among *Achimenes* cultivars, there is variation in the size and shape of the blooms as well as in their coloring and general habit of growth. Some types are dwarf and compact, others taller and more robust, reaching a height of 10 to 12 inches; most types are definitely trailing in habit. Most Cupid's bowers have a curved floral tube, with the petals opening into pansy-faced or petunialike flowers. The colors range from white through mauve, violet, and pale lavender blue to deep purple, with a few pink and scarlet types.

After the plants come into bloom, they will bear continuously until the onset of cool weather, often flowering over a period of four or five months.

The most important cultural requirements of Cupid's bower are moderate temperatures (a range of 55° to 80°F is optimal) and light shade. Direct sun is suitable in the early morning and late afternoon, but sun exposure between 9:00 A.M. and 5:00 P.M. can be seriously damaging or even fatal. Locations with high winds or heavy downpours should also be avoided. A coarse, loose, fertile soil is best, and good drainage is essential. The scaly tubercles may be planted between February and May, outdoors in the South but indoors north of zone 8. In outdoor beds, the tubercles should be spaced 3 to 4 inches apart and at a depth of about 1 inch. In containers, spacing may be cut by one-half. Alternatively, tubercles may be sprouted on damp paper toweling in a closed glass or clear plastic container and then transplanted to beds or containers, or they may be started in seed flats or cell packs. High humidity is desirable throughout the growing season; dry soil causes premature dormancy. Tepid water is best when irrigating containers. The discoloration and shriveling of leaves in late summer or early fall signals approaching dormancy. Once the tops have died back and dried, they may be cut off and the containers stored in a cool, dry place away from frost, with the tubercles left in place. The same treatment should be followed even in frost-free areas. With the onset of spring, the containers should be brought into light and given water to stimulate growth for the approaching summer. After a few season's growth in the same container, tubercles should be removed, thinned, and replanted in fresh soil.

ACIDANTHERA BICOLOR
(Peacock orchid)

Zones (7) 8–10

Sometimes listed in catalogs as *Gladiolus callianthus*, peacock orchid has the foliage of gladiolus, but bears side-facing or drooping, long-tubed, white flowers about 3 inches across, each with a central blotch of deep red-violet or violet-brown. The scapes reach 3 to 3½ feet, and the blooming period is late summer. Corms should be planted in groups of a dozen or more in a sunny location, 2 to 3 inches deep and 4 to 5 inches apart, preferably in sandy-humusy soil. Handle the corms in fall as for gladiolus or, where hardy, leave in place for reflowering in successive seasons. In zone 7, it is advisable to provide a substantial winter mulch to prevent the corms from freezing.

AGAPHANTUS *HYBRIDS*
(African lily)

Zones (7) 8–10

Stately whether grown alone or in groupings, several species of African lily, especially *A. africanus*, are much used in the South and Southwest. *A. campanulatus* and the hardier hybrids, however, can be grown with some care in most of zone

7 (i.e., where winter temperatures are no lower than about 5°F) with winter mulch and protection from strong winter winds. Scapes rise gracefully from a mound of arching, strap-shaped leaves to about 3 feet, and each bears a large, loose, globular cluster of blue, violet, or white flowers in mid to late summer. Especially valuable are the Headbourne hybrids, which include a number of named flower-color cultivars.

Plant the thickened fleshy roots in moist, humusy soil in full sun or partial shade. Choice of location is important, as the root system becomes extensive and, once established, is best not disturbed. African lily is most effective in clumps; four to six small plants may be planted in 1 square foot, with a few inches between individuals. The crowns are set just beneath the soil surface, and the roots are directed outward and downward. If planted individually, spacing should be 1 foot, allowing for the eventual development of each plant into a clump. In time, spacing may be increased by removing alternate clumps. From zone 7 northward, tub culture is advisable; the containers should be brought into a cool, well-lighted place in the fall.

ALSTROEMERIA *SPP.*
(Peruvian lily)

Zones (7) 8–10

Idiosyncratic and unpredictable, the Peruvian lily is a garden challenge but worth the effort. It has deep, fleshy tubers or rhizomes that often produce separate leafy and flowering shoots, the latter rising 2 to 3 feet high and bearing clusters of 1½- to 2-inch flowers, mostly yellow, orange, or salmon, and variously spotted and streaked. Most flower in early to mid summer.

With adequate mulch, *A. aurea* (syn. *A. aurantica*), *A. haemantha*, and their hybrids (such as Ligtu hybrids) are hardy down to about 10°F. Other kinds are hardy to 20°F.

As they are late to appear and quick to go dormant, Peruvian lily should be interplanted with a lightly blanketing ground cover and left undisturbed. The soil should be sandy-humusy and deeply prepared, to at least 1 foot deep. Dormant tubers or rhizomes should be planted about 8 inches deep and about 1 foot apart. Planting is best done in the spring. In zone 7, a heavy protective blanket of leaves, salt hay, and/or evergreen branches should be put over the plants to a depth of at least 6 inches after frost has penetrated the uppermost 1 or 2 inches of soil.

In areas too cold for outdoor culture, Peruvian lily is very attractive grown in tubs or urns in the summer. The containers are brought indoors in the fall and allowed to dry out somewhat, but never completely. When returned outdoors in mid to late spring, normal watering is resumed. The planting interval in containers is usually a few inches. Flowering stems usually require staking.

AMARYLLIS BELLADONNA
(Naked lady, belladonna lily)

Zones 8–10

Not to be confused with *Hippeastrum*, the popular amaryllis grown indoors for its immense flowers, naked lady is usually grown outdoors. It does not easily reflower year after year, however, where winter temperatures fall below 20°F because the straplike leaves, which appear after the flowers and promote bulb growth, are held all winter and are damaged or destroyed at lower temperatures. Between 6 and 12 pink or white lilylike flowers, about 3½ inches across, are borne atop a solid scape (not hollow as in *Hippeastrum*) in late summer.

Well-drained soil of average fertility suits this bulb. Plant in the spring 6 to 8 inches deep and 8 to 12 inches apart in a sunny location that is not subject to deep cultivation or other disturbance.

AMORPHOPHALLUS RIVIERI
(Devil's tongue, snake palm)

Devil's tongue in flower

Zones (8) 9–10

Devil's tongue, a striking tropical plant, once mature, goes through two distinct phases each year. The flowering phase, often forced indoors in late winter or early spring, especially in the North, is heralded by a single, stout, olive green, purple-spotted stalk. The stalk quickly rises to 2 to 4 feet high; elongates, and thickens at the tip; then it splits open to reveal a long, deep brown-violet, cigar-like spadix whose base is clothed with light yellow ill-scented florets. The whole is enveloped in a glossy, deep claret, collar-like spathe. If placed outdoors in mild weather during its most malodorous day or two, devil's tongue will attract carrion-seeking flies (which are, in fact, its pollinating agents).

There is a brief resumption of dormancy after flowering, during which the container may be set outdoors (only after all danger of frost has passed) or the corm may be planted (4 to 6 inches deep in the garden). Then another stout, similarly mottled stalk arises to about the same height and opens into a large, three-parted, much-dissected, parasol-like leaf (the "snake palm"). In this leafy phase, the plant should be in full sun or partial shade to charge the corm in preparation for the next flowering phase. When the leaf yellows in the fall, it should be cut off, and the potatolike corm and its often numerous subsidiary cormlets should be stored in dry peat moss away from frost. Before potting-up time in late winter, the cormlets will have separated and may be grown separately. Several seasons are required for them to reach flowering size. In zone 8, the corms can be left outdoors, but a substantial winter mulch is required to protect them from freezing.

Because the roots develop from the top of the corm, devil's tongue should be planted—indoors or out—so that the single large pink bud is pointed up and set 4 to 6 inches deep. Sandy-humusy soil and unfailing moisture help ensure maximum development in both phases.

Voodoo lily
(*Sauromatum venosum*) in flower

Closely related are voodoo lily (*Sauromatum venosum*), zones 8 to 10, and dragon arum (*Dracunculus vulgaris*), zones 8 to 10. Both have smaller floral structures that are briefer in duration and even more ill scented. The flowers are followed by a single, mottled, 2- to 4-foot-tall stalk, which bears 7 to 15 large leaflets, arranged in a crescent. Culture is the same as for devil's tongue. All are exceptionally attractive foliage plants and do best in pots or tubs in full sun to partial shade.

ANEMONE CORONARIA
(*Florist's anemone, poppy anemone*)

Zones 7–9
Venerated as the biblical "lily of the field," the tuberous poppy anemone thrives in regions having cool, moist winters and hot, dry summers, as in parts of the Southwest. The mostly basal leaves are much divided, and the striking 1½- to 2½-inch flowers are borne on 6- to 15-inch-tall stems in spring and early summer. Colors range from purple through red and pink to blue and white, always with a central tuft

of dark blue anthers. Principal cultivars include the following.

'DeCaen' group large, single flowers; various colors
'His Excellency': large, single flowers; scarlet with white center
'The Bride': single flowers; white
'Mona Lisa': single, abundantly produced 4-inch flowers; wide color range
'St. Bridgit' group: semidouble flowers; color range

North of zone 7, all may be planted in the spring for summer bloom. Alternatively, the tubers may be planted indoors in late winter and transferred outdoors in the spring after the frost threat has passed, for late spring to early summer bloom. In zones 8 and 9, the tubers should be planted in the fall. Set the tubers, whether in the ground or in containers, about

3 inches deep and 5 to 6 inches apart in rich humusy, consistently moist soil. Protection from hot afternoon sun extends the flowering period.

BEGONIA × TUBERHYBRIDA
(*Tuberous begonia*)

Zones 9–10
The tuberous begonias make up an extensive and varied group of highly decorative hybrids derived from several Andean species and arranged in 13 classes, according to flower form and complexity. The flowers, which are from 1 to 6 inches across, vary in color from deep red through pink to white, yellow, and orange, with various bicolors. Single flowers have four flat tepals (a term for the two petals and two similar but slightly smaller sepals), and in some of the double flowers, the

---

CLASSES OF TUBEROUS BEGONIAS

1. *Single.* Large, single flowers with flat tepals.
2. *Frilled, or Crispa.* Large, single flowers with frilled or ruffled tepals. In 'Pin-up' the tepals are white, edged red.
3. *Crested, or Cristata.* Large, single flowers, each tepal with a frilled outgrowth.
4. *Daffodil-flowered, or Narcissiflora.* Large, double flowers in which the inner tepals are upright and spreading.
5. *Camellia-flowered, or Camelliiflora.* Large, double flowers in which all tepals are the same size and more or less flat, resembling a double camellia. Cultivars of merit in this most popular class include 'Allan Langdon' (dark red), 'Bernat Klein' (white), and 'Buttermilk' (cream, flushed apricot). Notable hybrid series include 'Clips' hybrids (mixed colors, blooming in about 3½ months from seed) and 'Midnight Beauty' hybrids (very dark green leaves, mixed colors).
6. *Ruffled camellia.* Similar to the camellia-flowered begonias, but all the tepals are ruffled.
7. *Rosebud, or Rosiflora.* Large, double flowers, with the innermost tepals tightly clustered, resembling a rosebud.
8. *Carnation, or Fimbriata plena.* Large, double flowers, each tepal with finely cut edges.
9. *Picotee.* Large, double flowers, the tepals finely edged with a contrasting color. Among the numerous cultivars are 'Bridesmaid' (white with red edge), 'Fairy Light' (white with pink edge), 'Jean Blair' and 'Prima Donna' (yellow with red edge), and 'Lace Red' (red with white edge).
10. *Margined, or Marginata.* Similar to the Picotee begonias, but each tepal is bordered with a band of contrasting color. The distinction between class 9 and 10 is often difficult.
11. *Marbled, or Marmorata.* Large, double flowers, pink marbled white. Best exemplified by the 'Marmorata' hybrids.
12. *Hanging basket, or Pendula.* Horizontal or pendulous stems, bearing numerous single or double flowers, mostly 1 to 2 inches across. Cultivars of merit include 'Bridal Cascade' (white), 'Crimson Cascade' (red), 'Gold Cascade' (yellow), and 'Orange Cascade' (orange).
13. *Multiflora.* Low, bushy, compactly branched plants, with numerous small single or double flowers.

yellow stamens or pistils have been converted to additional tepals.

Although tuberous begonias may be obtained by cultivar name, many vendors list them simply by class name and color. Some so-called hybrids, such as Nonstop hybrids, are mixtures of cultivars from various classes. Hybridization between classes has resulted in intermediates. Some classes are not well represented in the cultivars commercially available.

North of zones 9 and 10, start tuberous begonias indoors roughly three months before setout time in warm spring weather, first placing the tubers upside down (i.e., hollow side down) in pans or flats in a warm, moist, covered terrarium until occasional inspection reveals that the stem buds are about ½ inch long. Then turn the tubers upright and sink in moist potting soil with the buds exposed to subdued light. When the roots reach a length of about 1 inch, plant individually in 6- to 7-inch clay pots with loose, friable compost or soil mix, and once the weather has warmed, sink the pots in a partly shaded location outdoors, preferably away from strong wind. Tuberous begonias may also be grown in window boxes or, if the garden soil is sandy and humusy, in the ground. In the fall, before hard frost, lift, dry, and store the tubers in dry peat moss in a frost-free place.

To grow tuberous begonias from seed, follow the instructions for wax begonia (*Begonia* Semperflorens-Cultorum hybrids) in Chapter 17.

CALADIUM BICOLOR
(Fancy-leaf caladium)

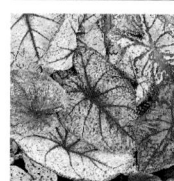

Zones 9–10

A large group of cultivars (sometimes listed collectively as *C. × hortulanum*) has been derived from the fancy-leaf caladiums, a highly varied species and a denizen of tropical rain-forest shade. All are grown for the large, beautifully varicolored leaves held 1 to 2 feet high, with red, pink, or white variegation. Caladium requires warm, humid conditions (soil temperature no lower than 60°F) for growth and protection from

sustained, direct sun and from strong winds to succeed. Well-drained, humusy, moderately fertile soil that is constantly moist ensures the largest leaves.

North of zones 9 and 10, corms are best started indoors four to six weeks before the night temperatures are no lower than 55°F. They should be planted with the corm tops about 2 inches deep and transplanted outdoors with the corms set 3 or 4 inches deep and spaced 8 to 12 inches apart. In the fall, when nights become cool, usually well before frost, the foliage quickly fades and vanishes. Corms should be lifted as the foliage dies, dried, and stored in dry peat moss in a cool location away from freezing temperatures.

Of the many cultivars, the following are especially striking; they are arranged according to their dominant color.

White
'Aaron' (bright green border)
'Candidum' (green border; green veins)
'June Bride' (fine green veins)
'Mrs. F. M. Joyner' (red veins; some pink shading)
'White Christmas' (distinct green veins)

Red
'Blaze' (green border; scarlet veins)
'Frieda Hemple' (green border)
'John Reed' (green border)
'Postman Joyner' (green border; deep red veins)

Red and green fancy-leaf caladium
(Caladium bicolor 'Frieda Hemple')

Pink
'Carolyn Wharton' (green border; rose veins)
'Fannie Munson' (green border)

Green
'Gypsy Rose' (rose veins; pink mottling)
'Pink Beauty' (red veins; pink marbling)
'Red Flash' (red veins; red center area)

CALOCHORTUS *SPP.*
(Mariposa lily)

Zones (5) 6–10

The genus *Calochortus* consists of a group of attractive, slender-stemmed plants, 2 to 2½ feet tall. The mariposa lily has two to six open, upward-facing, tuliplike flowers in bright colors, mostly yellows, purples, and white. Little-known natives of the Far West, all species do best in somewhat alkaline soils (pH about 7.5) and are effective if planted in groups of 8 or 12 or more.

In colder zones, they may be treated as gladiolus, the bulbs lifted in fall or just after the foliage yellows in summer and stored away from frost and wetness. The bulbs are replanted in sunny places in the spring. Plant them 6 to 8 inches deep and 4 to 6 inches apart. From zone 6 south, the bulbs may be left in the ground, but it is essential that the soil drain freely. As alternating frost and thawing are especially damaging, plantings of mariposa lily should be generously mulched where these conditions occur in the spring, and the mulch left in place until growth appears.

Of the 60 species, white globe lily (*C. albus*), with white flowers in spring, sego lily (*C. gunnisonii*), with purple-and-green or white-and-green flowers in late spring, and green-banded mariposa (*C. macrocarpus*), with pinkish purple, green-striped flowers in early to mid summer, seem more amenable to garden conditions than most.

CANNA × GENERALIS
(Hybrid canna)

Zones 8–10

Of the 50 wild species of *Canna*, all natives of tropical America, three are the parents of most large-flowered hybrids. All have thick, horizontal rhizomes and very large green, bronzy or purplish bananalike leaves that clasp the 2- to 8-foot stems, imparting a bold effect. Canna is best grown alone in lawn "islands" or as accent clumps against buildings or walls. The flowers of the hybrids are 3 to 4 inches across, asymmetric, and brightly colored—usually shades of red or yellow. Several recently

Hybrid canna (*Canna × generalis*)

developed dwarf hybrids, some no higher than 18 inches, may be flowered from seed the same season as sown. A number of other cultivars have spotted or bicolored flowers. The flowers are borne from midsummer to frost.

North of zone 8, stems should be cut to the base after the first killing frost. Then the rhizomes should be lifted, freed of soil, dried for a day or two, and stored in cartons of dry peat moss kept at 40° to 60°F. Higher temperatures can cause rhizomes to dry excessively and die. In the spring, the rhizomes should be divided into pieces, each bearing one or two buds, or growth points. These may be planted shallowly in pots or flats with soil mix in a sunny window 4 to 6 weeks before transfer to the garden (at about tomato-planting time). Cannas will not grow outdoors until the soil temperature is at least 60°F. When set in the garden, the rhizomes should be 4 to 6 inches deep and 8 to 12 inches apart: Friable, consistently moist, humusy soil of average fertility is best, as are full sun and high temperatures. Cannas may be wintered in place in zone 8 as long as frost does not penetrate to the rhizomes. Heaped mulch usually prevents damage. Seeds should be notch filed (i.e., held with tweezers or pliers and a notch filed through the hard seed coat) and soaked a day in water before sowing, so that germination will be prompt and even.

The following cultivars are especially recommended.

Tall; grown from rhizomes.
'City of Portland': 3 to 4 feet; green foliage; rosy pink flowers.
'Cleopatra': 3 to 4 feet; green foliage, mottled deep purple; red-and-yellow flowers.
'Pfitzer' series: 3 feet; green foliage; yellow, yellow-orange, pink, or red flowers.
'Red King Humbert': 5 to 7 feet; bronze foliage; red-orange flowers.
'Richard Wallace': 5 to 7 feet; green foliage; yellow flowers.
'Rosamond Cole': 3 to 4 feet; green foliage; red flowers with yellow border.
'The President': 5 to 7 feet; green foliage; scarlet flowers

Dwarf; grown from seed; all with green foliage.
'Doc': red flowers.
'Grumpy': pink flowers.
'Happy': yellow flowers.
'Seven Dwarfs' hybrids: red, pink, yellow, or orange flowers.

CRINUM BULBISPERMUM
(*Crinum lily*)

Zones (7) 8–10
Frequently listed in catalogs as *C. capensis* or *C. longifolium*, crinum lily is the hardiest of a large group of mostly tropical plants closely related to the popular amaryllis (*Hippeastrum*). It is suited to garden cultivation in sheltered settings, where it should be left undisturbed year after year. The long-necked bulb produces a rosette of long, broad, strap-shaped leaves and, in late spring or early summer, a 3-foot scape bearing about a dozen pink or white flowers, each about 4 inches wide and as long. Similar and nearly as hardy is *C. × powellii*. In zones 7 and 8, a thick winter mulch of straw or wood chips is required, preferably mixed with manure.

Bulbs should be planted 2 to 3 feet apart and deep enough so that the tip of the neck is at the surface. Planting is done in the fall or spring. Crinum lily is best grown in clumps in full sun or partial shade, free of competing vegetation, in well-drained soil generously supplied with compost or well-rotted manure. It makes a magnificent ornamental as long as the roots remain undisturbed. Such disturbance often results in the cessation of flowering for several years.

In northern areas, crinum lily is should be grown in pots or tubs, which are wintered over dry and indoors away from frost; the soil is left undisturbed from year to year.

CROCOSMIA *CULTIVARS*
(*Montbretia*)

Zones (6) 7–10
Montbretia is a colorful relative of gladiolus, with sword-shaped foliage. It has numerous, usually orange, star-shaped flowers, measuring 1 by 2 inches, clustered on 3- to 4-foot-tall scapes. The flowers are borne through much of the summer. Montbretia is most effective if grown in clumps of a dozen or more. Corms should be planted in the spring after threat of frost 3 to 5 inches deep and 6 to 8 inches apart in a sunny position in well-drained soil of average fertility. North of zone 7, corms should be lifted in the fall and stored indoors, as for gladiolus.

Among the many cultivars available, the following are especially desirable.

'Emberglow' (orange-brown)
'Emily MacKenzie' (orange and red)
'Lucifer' (red)
'Solfaterre' (orange)

Orange and red montbretia
(*Crocosmia* cv. 'Emily MacKenzie')

CYCLAMEN PERSICUM
(Common cyclamen, florist's cyclamen)

Zones 9–10

Blooming in cool spring weather and dormant in summer when grown outdoors, cyclamen grows 6 to 9 inches high from a large, flat-topped tuber that succumbs at temperatures below 25°F. The rosette of round leaves surrounds the 2-inch flowers, which range from white with a purple basal blotch to all red.

Absolutely essential to success is free soil drainage; rot quickly consumes tubers in soggy soil. Similarly, cool, humid conditions are necessary during the dormant period. To meet both conditions, many gardeners prefer to grow cyclamen in pots, even in frost-free regions, and to have the freedom to move the plants to the most advantageous location from season to season. Where hardy outdoors, corms may be planted at any time, but wherever planted, the corm top should be set even with the soil surface. Space the corms 6 inches apart. Flowering normally begins in early spring.

In northern latitudes, cyclamen is grown in pots and summered outdoors in light shade. Pots are brought indoors well before frost and placed in a well-lighted location but out of direct sunlight and away from cold drafts. Flowering occurs in winter.

Among the numerous cultivars, the following are distinctive.

'Boheme' (flowers fuchsia red)
'Dwarf Fragrance' hybrids (flowers small, numerous, fragrant)
'Flamenco Frills' (flowers white, 3 inches across, feathery edged)
'Gabi' (flowers deep salmon; small plant)
'Kati' (flowers lilac; foliage silvery)
'Lightfire' (flowers white; foliage silvery veined)
'Little Dresden' hybrids (flowers various; foliage variegated)
'Mirabelle' mix (flowers various; foliage dark green)
'Victoria' (flowers white with red border and blotch)

DAHLIA *HYBRIDS*

Zones (7) 8–10

Derived from two tropical species, the tuberous-rooted dahlia is a superb garden subject well beyond its zone of hardiness. It offers a wide range of flower color, form, and size. Heights range from 1 to 5 feet or more. Indeed, dahlias bring a richness to the late summer garden that is scarcely equaled. The tall-growing, large-flowered cultivars may be used very effectively at the rear of the border, while the dwarf sorts are more suitable in bedding. All are invaluable for the cutting garden.

Dahlias are grouped into classes according to flower traits. The classification adopted by the International Registration Authority is as follows.

1. *Single flowered.* Open-centered flowers, 3 to 4 inches across; one or two complete outer rows of rays ("petals"); bedding plants seldom exceeding 15 inches.
2. *Anemone flowered.* Flowers 3 to 4 inches across; one to a few rows of rays, surrounding a dense central tuft of erect tubular florets; 3 to 4 feet tall.
3. *Collarette.* Open-centered flowers, 4 to 6 inches across; an inner ring of short, rudimentary rays (the collar) and one or two outermost' rows of full-size rays; 3 to 5 feet tall.
4. *Water-lily flowered.* Fully double flowers (no central disc) but relatively flat, 4 to 6 inches across; relatively few rays, wide and sometimes incurved or curled; 3½ to 4½ feet tall.

5. *Decorative.* Fully double flowers; rays usually blunt tipped and more or less alike; 4 to 6 feet tall.
6. *Ball.* Somewhat flattened globelike flowers, 4 to 6 inches across; rays cupped with blunt or rounded tips; mostly 3 to 5 feet tall.
7. *Pompon.* Fully double flowers, small (to 2 inches across), ball shaped; rays with inrolled edges; 3 to 4 feet tall.
8. *Cactus flowered.* Fully double flowers, 5 to 8 inches across; long quill-like rays; mostly 3 to 5 feet tall, some shorter forms.
9. *Semicactus flowered.* Similar to cactus-flowered dahlia; rays narrow and quill-like only at the tips.
10. *Miscellaneous.* Includes several small, unrelated groups: orchid (single flowers; rays with down-rolled edges), star (single flowers; two or three rows of incurved rays), chrysanthemum (double flowers; incurved rays), lilliput (similar but flowers only 1 inch across), and peony flowered (two or three rows of flat rays surrounding a central disc, sometimes bearing twisted rudimentary rays).

Although dahlias are native to Mexico and luxuriate in hot, damp conditions, they are remarkably adaptable and may be grown in almost any section of the United States. For optimal performance, they require full sun and consistently available soil moisture in a sandy-humusy loam. With inadequate sun, the plants become spindly and produce undersize flowers. Insufficient moisture and nutrients result in undersize plants that flower little, if at all. Heavy, poorly drained clay soils must be lightened with sand, compost, and well-rotted manure if dahlias are to thrive. High-nitrate, quick-release fertilizers stimulate foliage but little flowering and hence should be avoided in favor of phosphate- and potassium-rich, slow-release preparations. Each location for planting should be dug out to a depth of at least 8 (preferably 12) inches, and the soil beneath that level loosened with a garden fork. The backfill should be prepared in advance of planting and consist of sandy loam with compost and well-rotted manure added.

Dahlia tubers are swollen roots that grow in tight clumps. If an entire clump is planted, growth is often a tangle of slender, overcrowded stems with substandard flowers. Tuber clumps are, therefore, divided before planting; but new shoots develop not on the tuber itself but at the base of the previous season's stems. For this reason, it is important to stimulate dormant tuber clumps into rudimentary shoot formation before planting them in the garden. This can be done in early spring by placing dormant tuber clumps in flats or shallow pans, covering them with damp peat moss. Place the containers in a warm place for 7 to 10 days. Under these conditions, initial growth will be stimulated, and the tuber clumps can be divided so that each rudimentary shoot will be attached to one or a few tubers. Tubers without shoots will not grow; neither will shoots detached from tubers (unless treated as cuttings and rooted in a medium of damp sand). With planting sites in the garden already prepared, the divided tubers can be planted, assuming danger of frost has passed. To ensure prompt development of leaves, the planting holes are only half-filled with backfill soil. Later, when the shoots are above ground level, they may be filled to grade. The tubers should then be about 8 inches deep in sandy soil, or a bit shallower in heavier soils, and spaced 2 to 3 feet apart for tall cultivars and 1 to 1½ feet for bedding dahlias.

Small bedding dahlias (especially those cultivars in groups one and three) are often grown from seed. Although hybrid dahlias do not come true from seed, the mixture of bright, harmonious colors makes a most decorative display. Seeds sown indoors six or eight weeks before the average last spring frost produce seedlings (especially if grown in cell packs) that flower by early summer. Tubers of especially fine-flowered individuals may be dug in fall for winter storage, and the rest discarded. South of zone 7, it is important to dig out tubers of any unwanted dahlias, as those left in the ground are often forgotten and then resprout the following spring, perhaps intruding on a planting subsequently devoted to other materials.

If the largest possible blooms are desired, only one stalk should be allowed

Dahlia division

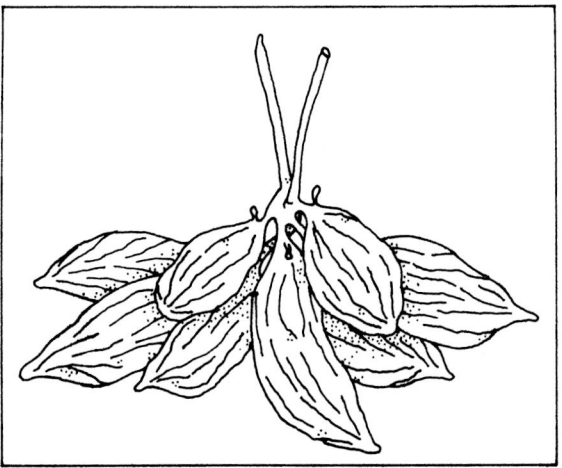

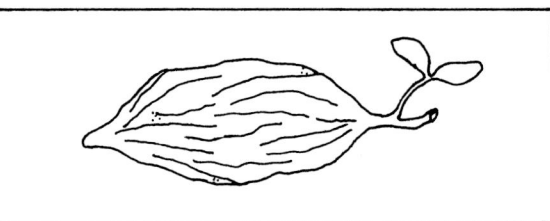

Top: Dahlia clump to be divided.
Bottom: Division including shoot, ready for planting.

DAHLIA CULTIVARS OF MERIT*

LOW (MOSTLY 1 TO 2½ FEET TALL)

Red

'Arnhem' (5)	'Indian Girl' (7)
'Bell Boy' (7)	'Little William' (7)
'Dandy' (3)	'Nelly Geerlings' (5)
'Ellen Houston' (5)	'Venice' (5)
'Fabel' (2)	'Winner's Pride' (5)

Yellow to orange

'Alstergruss' (2)	'Munich' (5)
'Autumn Fairy' (9)	'Potgieter' (7)
'Banting' (7)	'Sisa' (5)
'Brio' (2)	'Summer Souvenir' (7)
'Flashlight' (8)	'Sungold' (7)
'Irene Van der Zwet' (5)	'Yellow Cheer' (5)

Pink and rose

'Ace of Hearts' (2)	'Murillo' (1)
'Betty Ann' (7)	'Park Princess' (9)
'Fascination' (10, peony flowered)	'Preference' (8)
'Gerry Hoek' (4)	'Pride of Berlin' (7)
'Honey' (5)	'Siemon Doorents' (5)

Purple to lavender

'Andrew Lockwood' (7)	'Cheerio' (8)
'Berliner Kleene' (5)	'Rosa Bella' (5)

White
'Albino' (7)	'Little Willow' (7)
'All Triumph' (9)	'Sneezy' (1)
'Celestia' (7)	'Snowflake' (7)
'Doxy' (7)	'Wittem' (5)

Mixed colors
'Bambino' (10, peony flowered)	'Figaro' (5)
'Collarette Dandy' (3)	'Redskin' (5)
'Coltness' (1)	'Rigoletto' (5)
'Dapper' (10, peony flowered)	'Showpiece' (5)

TALL (MOSTLY 3 TO 5 FEET)

Red
'Arabian Night' (5)	'Helga' (8)
'Arthur Godfrey' (5)	'Mary Elizabeth' (5)
'Autumn Blaze' (5)	'Miramar' (5)
'Deutschland' (5)	'Mujaba' (5)
'Duet' (5)	'Thomas Edison' (5)
'Envy' (5)	

Yellow to orange
'À la Mode' (5)	'House of Orange' (5)
'Apeldoorn' (8)	'Kelvin Floodlight' (5)
'Bach' (8)	'Orange Julius' (5)
'Croydon Ace' (5)	'Playboy' (5)
'Croydon Masterpiece' (5)	'Procyon' (5)
'Diamond' (5)	'Trendy' (5)
'Glory of Heemstede' (5)	

Pink to rose
'Alfred Grill' (10, star)	'Jersey Beauty' (5)
'Canby Charm' (5)	'Otto's Thrill' (5)
'D-Day' (5)	'Rosella' (5)
'Good Earth' (5)	'Smokey' (5)

Purple to Lavender
'City of Wellston' (5)	'Lilac Time' (5)
'Lavender Perfection' (5)	'Lilac Veil' (8)
'Lawrence Welk' (5)	'Purple Gem' (8)
'Lilac Shadow' (5)	

White
'Alabaster' (5)	'My Love' (9)
'Eveline' (5)	'Snow Country' (5)
'Lula Pattie' (5)	'White Perfection' (5)

Mixed colors (from seed) and bicolors
'Flying Saucer' (8)	'Octopus' (10, star)
'Grand Prix' (5)	'Tartan' (5)
'Holland's Festival' (5)	

*The number following the cultivar name indicates its International Registration Authority class, described on page 405. For class 10, miscellaneous, the specific group name is provided.

to develop from each tuber and only the first or terminal flower bud allowed to mature. Frequent topdressings of well-rotted manure (which also serves as a moisture-conserving mulch) or 2-10-6 or 4-8-6 commercial fertilizer will further ensure very large flowers.

Dahlia foliage is killed by the first frost in the fall. Stems should then be cut to within 6 inches of the ground and tubers left in the ground for 7 to 10 days to mature fully. Tubers should be lifted carefully to minimize bruising and breakage. This is done by thrusting a

garden fork into the soil about 1 foot from the stem stubs and gently rocking it back to pry the tuber clump upward. The clump should be freed of as much soil as possible and allowed to dry for several hours in direct sun. The tubers are best stored for winter if they are dipped in a mixture of one part Wilt-Pruf and four parts water; allowed to dry; buried in dry peat moss; and placed in a cool, dry, frost-free area, preferably where the temperature range is 45° to 50°F. Higher temperatures may result in shriveled, mummified tubers that often die.

South of zone 7, where frost seldom penetrates the soil to the depth of the tubers, dahlias may be grown as hardy perennials, especially if protected with adequate winter mulch, but even here it is desirable to lift the clumps in earliest spring and divide them in the interest of achieving maximum floral development.

Some 20,000 dahlia cultivars have been developed and registered over the years and new ones continue to appear in horticultural commerce. Of those commercially available, a number have been offered for many years, attesting to their sustained popularity. The most widely available cultivars are listed here, arranged by plant size and flower color (or the dominant color in the case of bicolors).

EUCOMIS COMOSA
(Pineapple lily)

Zones (7) 8–10

Pineapple lily forms a rosette of purple-flecked, daylilylike foliage, from which one or more purple-spotted spikes rise 2 to 3 feet. Each spike is clothed with masses of small, starry, purplish flowers and topped with a tuft of leaflike bracts. Flowering is in early to mid summer.

Plant the large bulbs in the fall about 6 inches apart in humusy, well-drained soil so that the tops are 3 to 4 inches below the surface. A location in full sun or in the high, thin shade of the southern or eastern side of a building or wall is best. In zone 7, a substantial winter mulch is necessary.

E. bicolor is similar but hardy only to zone 8. Its cultivar 'Alba' has uniformly greenish white flowers. In marginal areas,

Bulb planting depth chart

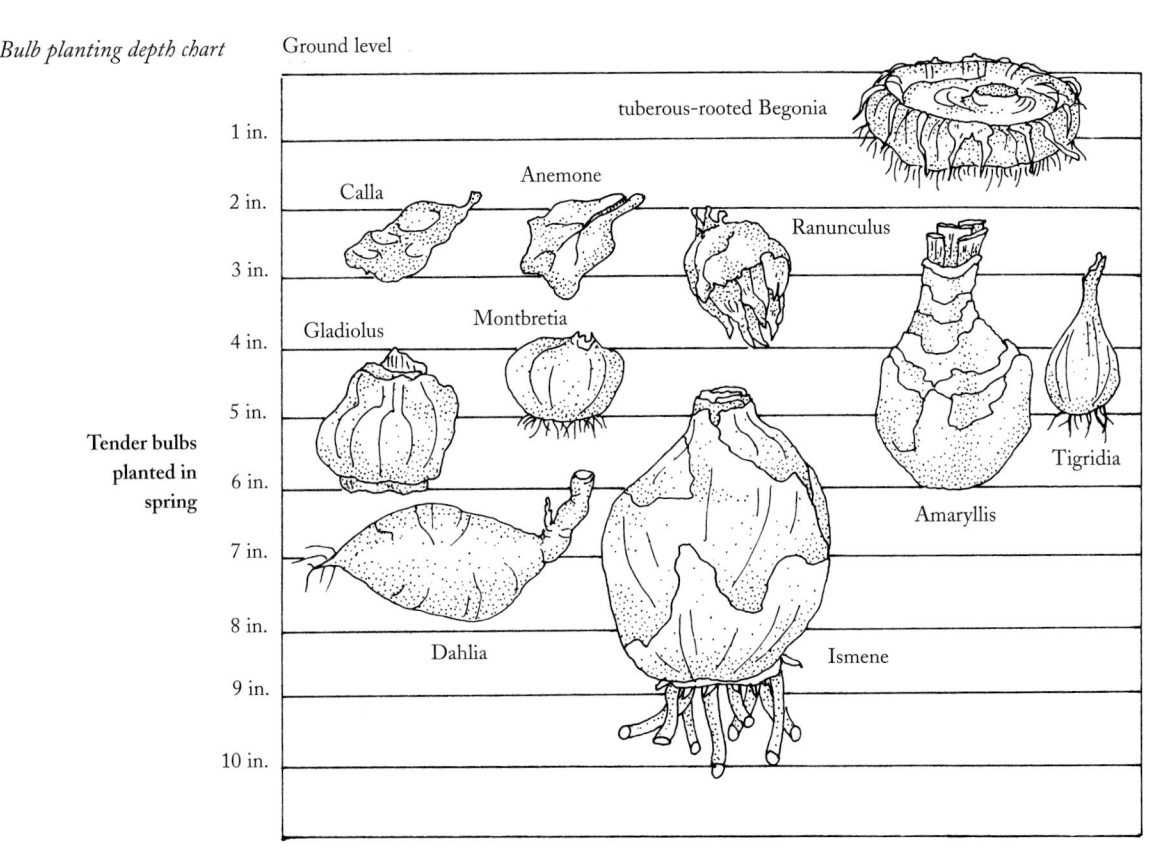

Ground level

1 in.
2 in.
3 in.
4 in.
5 in.
6 in.
7 in.
8 in.
9 in.
10 in.

Tender bulbs planted in spring

tuberous-rooted Begonia

Calla   Anemone   Ranunculus

Gladiolus   Montbretia   Tigridia

Amaryllis

Dahlia   Ismene

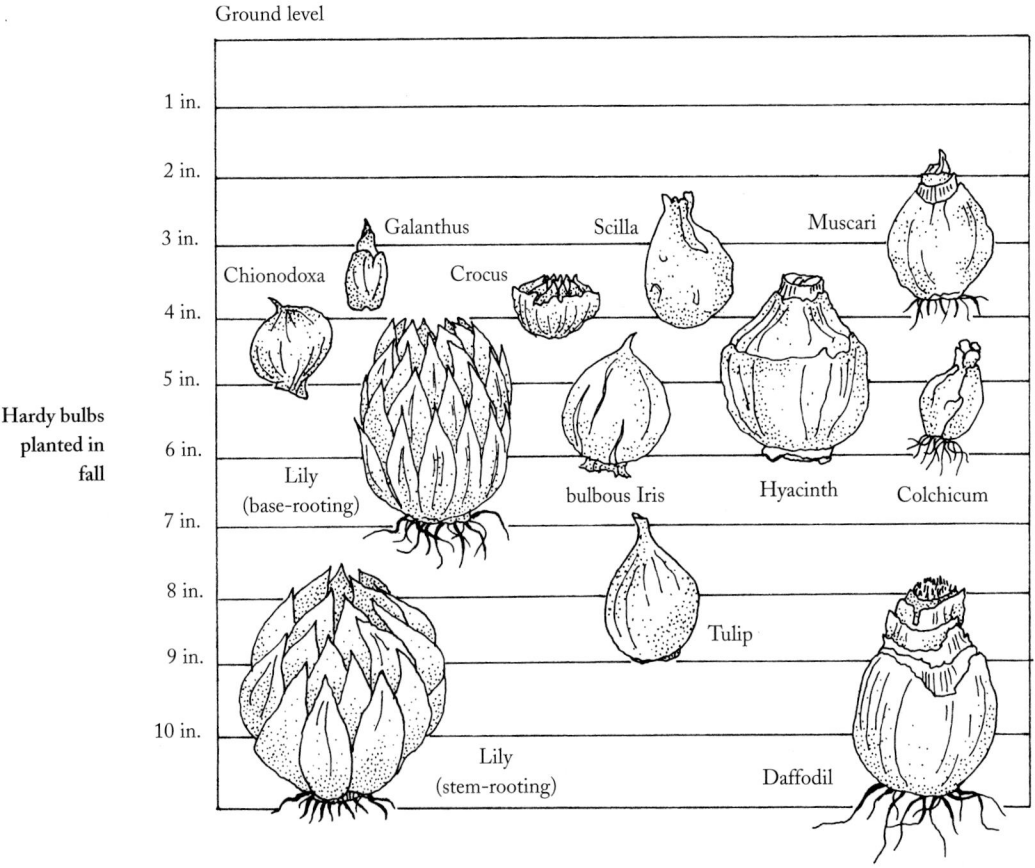

Ground level

1 in.
2 in.
3 in.
4 in.
5 in.
6 in.
7 in.
8 in.
9 in.
10 in.

Hardy bulbs planted in fall

Galanthus   Scilla   Muscari

Chionodoxa   Crocus

Lily (base-rooting)   bulbous Iris   Hyacinth   Colchicum

Tulip

Lily (stem-rooting)   Daffodil

a substantial winter mulch will help protect the bulbs from frost penetration.

GALTONIA CANDICANS
(Summer hyacinth)

Zones (7) 8–10

The creamy white, bell-shaped flowers of summer hyacinth, a native of South Africa, are decorative and especially effective when planted against a backdrop of deep green shrubs, such as yews. The flowers appear in late summer and often continue until frost. The flower scapes usually attain a height of 18 inches and, under ideal conditions, may rise to 4 feet.

The bulbs may be planted in the spring in ordinary garden soil about 6 inches deep and 8 to 12 inches apart. A location in full sun ensures the best results. Unless planted on the southern or southeastern side of a protective wall or building and mulched generously in winter, the bulbs seldom survive in zone 7, and almost never farther north. Thus the bulbs should be lifted in the fall, allowed to dry, and stored in dry peat moss in a cool but frostproof place. As lifted bulbs frequently fail to bloom in the successive season, it is advisable to replenish the stock frequently.

GLADIOLUS × HORTULANUS

Zones (7) 8–10

Gladiolus demands so little care and gives so generously of its bloom and beauty that it is looked on as one of our most useful summer flowers. It is invaluable for cutting and may be had in flower every month of the year—albeit with the help of a greenhouse in the north. Especially prized for its decorative value in the garden, gladiolus may be planted in great drifts through garden beds and borders, and thus become the dominant note in a planting composition from midsummer on, or it may be used in an incidental way, filling an occasional gap here and there.

Gladiolus thrives in a pH range of 6 to 7 on almost any soil of moderate fertility.

GLADIOLUS CULTIVARS OF MERIT

LARGE FLOWERED, TALL (4 TO 6 FEET)

Red

'Intrepid'	'St. George's'
'Oscar'	'St. Peter's'
'Peter Pears'	'Sans Souci'
'Red Beauty'	'Summer Sunrise'
'Red Sky'	'Tradehorn'

Yellow to orange

'Canary Bird'	'Nova Lux'
'Dreaming Spires Orange'	'Princes Margaret Rose'
'Esta Bonita'	'Sundown'
'Gold Coin'	'Sun Tan'
'Harvest King'	'Yester'
'Jacksonville Gold'	

Pink to salmon

'Daybreak'	'Spic and Span'
'Dreaming Spires Pink'	'True Love'
'First Kiss'	'Veerle'
'Fond Memory'	'Windsong'
'Glorianda'	'Wine and Roses'

Violet

'Plum Tart'
'Purple Gem'
'Zigeunerbaron'

Lavender

'Blue Bird'	'Royal Dutch'
'Canterbury'	'Storm Clouds'
'Her Majesty'	

White to cream

'America'	'Prince Carnaval'
'Day Dream'	'Sacred Heart'
'Easter Time'	'St. Mary's'
'Glacier'	'White Friendship'
'My Love'	'White Prosperity'
'Pink Attraction'	

Green

'Green Bay'
'Green Woodpecker'
'St. Patrick's'

Multicolored

'Priscilla'

MINIATURE (LESS THAN 3½ FEET TALL)

Red

'Amanda Mahy'

Pink

'Rubinette'

White

'Impressive'
'The Bride'

With heavy soils, the flowers are outstanding, but relatively few cormlets form around the large corms. On light, sandy soils, the flowers are somewhat smaller but cormlets are produced in quantities. Superphosphate, applied at the rate of 5 pounds to every 100 feet of row, stimulates early, generous bloom. To ensure a succession of bloom, gladioluses should be planted every two weeks once the danger of frost has passed until mid-summer. Flowers appear eight to 10 weeks after planting.

Gladiolus corms are graded by vendors according to size. Sizes 1, 2, and 3 are of flowering size, while size 4 may not bloom until the second year. Sizes 2 and 3 are considerably less expensive than size 1 and usually give equally good results. In beds and borders, the corms should be placed about 6 inches apart. In light, sandy soil, the planting depth should be about 6 inches; in heavier clay soils, about 4 inches. The more deeply the corms are planted, the less staking will be required for the flower scapes and, in zones 7 and 8, the less likely frost will damage or kill the corms in winter.

If grown in rows in the cutting garden, gladioluses should be planted 4 inches apart in rows spaced 18 inches apart. Scapes should be cut when only one or two of the flowers have opened, and the rest will follow successively when the scape is set in water. All foliage should be left attached to the plant to facilitate the development of the new corm and any cormlets.

North of zone 7, corms should be dug once the foliage has yellowed—usually about six weeks after flowering. If this should occur sooner than the first fall frost, and before such disturbance is wanted in the garden, each gladiolus should be marked with a label thrust in the soil, as the foliage soon deteriorates and vanishes. After frost, the corms should be gently lifted with a garden fork, with care taken to collect the cormlets. All the corms should be placed in flats and stored indoors for several weeks to mature. If the corms are dug before killing frost and still have green leaves, these should be left attached until they yellow. Once corm ripening is complete, stalks and leaf bases should be cut back to 1 inch and any roots trimmed off. The old mother corm that had been planted in the spring or early summer will have shriveled. It should be removed from the base of the new corm. New corms and cormlets should be spread in flats or shallow trays in a cool, well-ventilated basement, ideally with a temperature of about 45°F and humidity of 80 percent. If flats or trays are stacked, they should be spaced to allow ventilation. In less than ideal storage conditions, at least some corms are liable to shrivel or rot. If cormlets are carefully stored, they will produce flowering-size corms the second or third year.

In zone 8 and south, corms need not be lifted for winter, although it is advisable to do so on alternate years to remove cormlets for planting elsewhere. This occasion can be used for adding compost or well-rotted manure to the soil.

In zone 7, a gladiolus planting on the south side of a wall or house may survive most winters if mulched. If in doubt initially, leave a few corms in marked locations over the winter and check their growth the following spring.

GLORIOSA SUPERBA
(Climbing lily)

Zone (9) 10

Climbing lily is a slender, tuberous-rooted climber that ascends 6 to 8 feet by means of leaf tendrils and bears beautiful downward-facing red-and-yellow lilylike flowers, 5 to 8 inches across, from midsummer to frost. In zone 8 and north, tubers should be started indoors in large clay pots in late winter or earliest spring, set about 6 inches deep in a pot twice that depth, and plunged to the rim outdoors in spring in full sun once night temperatures remain above 45°F. If more than one vine is grown, space them about 2 feet apart. It is preferable that the soil surface be shaded, and thus cooled, with a ground cover or other low growth. In the fall, as the foliage yellows, lift the pots with the tubers and allow the soil to dry. With the tubers still in the soil-filled pots, store in cool, dry conditions, away from frost. The tubers are brittle and easily broken, hence should be left undisturbed for several seasons before dividing and repotting. In protected positions, and with generous winter mulch, the tubers of climbing lily may survive the winter in the ground in zone 9. The most common cultivar in cultivation is 'Rothschildiana', which has red-and-yellow flowers that age to all red.

HEDYCHIUM CORONARIUM
(Ginger lily)

Zones 9–10

The ginger lily is a bold cannalike plant that grows from rhizomes. It reaches 8 feet and bears large, showy, fragrant, white flowers with green centers. A denizen of swampy places in the tropics, ginger lily is best grown in large tubs partly immersed at the edge of a pond or stream. The tub should be at least 1 foot deep, and a cluster of three rhizomes should be planted about 6 inches deep. The soil should be enriched with well-rotted manure. In the fall, the tops should be cut back and the tubs, with soil and rhizomes in place, stored dry in a frost-free place. In the spring, when night temperatures remain above 50°F, the tubs may be returned outdoors. Storage in a cool greenhouse permits retention of foliage over the winter, which stimulates earlier flowering the following season.

HIPPEASTRUM *HYBRIDS*
(Amaryllis)

Zone (9) 10

Although generally forced as a winter-flowering pot plant, amaryllis performs equally well as a garden subject. In frost-free areas and in protected locations in zone 9, where beds should be generously straw mulched for winter, amaryllis may be left in place year after year. Elsewhere, bulbs are best grown in porous 6- to 8-inch pots, using a mixture of two parts potting soil and one part perlite over a layer of pebbles and pot chips (known as "crock"). Pots should be deep to allow for the amaryllis's large system of thick, permanent roots, but need be no more than 1 or 2 inches wider than the bulb diameter. The bulb should be planted with the top half out of the soil. Once night temperatures in the spring fall no lower than 55°F, the pots should be plunged to the rim in a partially shaded, well-drained location. The stout, hollow scapes rise 12 to 18 inches high, and each bears two to six (up to eight) immense (up to 8 inches across), horizontal, trumpet-shaped flowers of red, pink, white, or combinations. Usually, the large, strap-shaped leaves appear with or just after the flowers. In the fall, before a killing frost, the pots should be lifted with their foliage, bulbs, and soil intact and allowed to dry out in a well-lighted, frost-free place. When the foliage yellows, it should be cut off, and the pot (with soil and bulb still in place undisturbed) should be stored at 55° to 60°F. Higher temperatures may trigger premature flowering. After two months' dormancy, the bulbs may be forced for indoor bloom (see page 948). In the spring, the leafy bulb should be transferred from the usual indoor plastic pot to a similar size clay pot and plunged for the summer. In general, bulbs forced into bloom during the winter indoors will not reflower outdoors the following summer; likewise, it is best to keep summer-flowering bulbs dormant over the winter rather than attempt to force them into flower indoors. Occasionally, this can be done, but the energy required usually exceeds stored reserves and results in diminished or fragmented bulbs that may not reflower for several years.

When a bulb has grown to nearly fill the pot diameter, it should be transferred to the next larger size, preferably when the soil is dry and easily shaken off the roots. It is important that the roots, which in amaryllis are permanent and not transitory structures, should be preserved intact and not trimmed off. With each change of pots, fresh soil mix should be used.

Of the several dozen amaryllis cultivars in commerce, the following are especially meritorious and exemplify the floral diversity achieved.

AMARYLLIS CULTIVARS OF MERIT

SINGLE, LARGE FLOWERED
'Apple Blossom' (white, red lines and pink blush)
'Bouquet' (salmon pink)
'Cantate' (rose pink)
'Christmas Gift' (white)
'Masai' (white, fine red lines)
'Minerva' (red, broad white bands and green throat)
'Orange Sovereign' (red-orange)
'Oscar' (red)
'Picotee' (white, fine red border)
'Red Lion' (red)
'Rilona' (peach pink)
'Valentine' (lavender pink and white)
'Vlammenspiel' (red, narrow white bands)
'White Dazzler' (white)

DOUBLE, LARGE FLOWERED
'Double Picotee' (white, fine red border and pink blush)
'Lady Jane' (rose pink, faint white bands)
'Pasadena' (red, white bands)

SINGLE, SMALL FLOWERED
'Charm' (orange, yellow-green throat)
'Germa' (yellow)
'Scarlet Baby' (red)
'Spotty' (red-brown, greenish white lines)

HYMENOCALLIS NARCISSIFLORA
(Peruvian daffodil)

Zones (8) 9–10
Peruvian daffodil is a showy, tender, summer-flowering bulb (often listed in catalogs as *H. calathina* or *Ismene calathina*) that has long been a popular garden subject. The large, fragrant, white flowers have a 4-inch-long interior funnel, which is surrounded by six fringed petallike segments, 2 inches long. The glossy strap-shaped, amaryllis-like foliage remains a decorative feature long after bloom is over and often persists until the bulbs are lifted. Whether in flower or just in leaf, Peruvian daffodil adds a special note of interest to the summer garden composition. The flower scape reaches a height of 15 inches to as much as 3 feet.

Peruvian daffodil should be grown in full sun, and it adapts to most any garden soil. From zone 8 north, the bulbs should be planted in the spring 4 to 5 inches deep and 8 to 10 inches apart. In the fall, once the foliage has yellowed or after the first frost, the bulbs should be carefully lifted, with care taken to preserve the fleshy roots; dried; and stored separate from each other (i.e., not touching) at 60° to 70°F. In zones 9 and 10, the bulbs are best left in place until overcrowding justifies their being lifted in the fall, divided, and replanted immediately in the manner indicated above.

IRIS *SPP.*
(Summer-flowering bulbous iris)

Zones (7) 8–10
Of the several larger, hardy kinds of bulbous iris, those most suitable for garden use are Spanish iris, English iris, and Dutch iris. Spanish iris (*I. xiphium*) is a species that has long been cultivated in Europe and includes many cultivars. This is also true for English iris (*I. xiphioides*). The derivative Dutch irises, named after the country in which they were originally bred, are commercially grown and are hybrids of *I. xiphium* and other species. Their heavier stems bear larger blooms

DUTCH IRIS CULTIVARS OF MERIT

'Blue Ribbon' (blue and bronze)   'Romano' (blue and yellow)
'Bronze Queen' (blue and bronze)   'Rosalie' (lavender blue and yellow)
'Golden Emperor' (yellow)   'Silvery Beauty' (blue, white, and yellow)
'Golden Harvest' (yellow)   'Wedgewood' (porcelain blue)
'H. C. van Vliet' (dark violet blue)   'White Perfection' (white)
'Oriental Beauty'   'White Superior' (white)
    (lavender and yellow-orange)   'Yellow Beauty' (yellow)
'Purple Sensation' (purple and yellow)

than the Spanish parent, and so it is Dutch irises that are commonly sold as cut flowers by florists. Of these three irises, the Dutch hybrids are best suited for garden use. Their showy flowers suggest orchids in form and color range, with many fine porcelain blues among them.

Dutch iris produces rather thick, single-flowered stems, 1½ to 2 feet tall. Although the bulbs are usually sold in the United States as mixtures, it is worth checking catalogs of Dutch suppliers dealing in this country for the distinctive named cultivars. Planted in the fall, Dutch iris will flower in late spring. Simultaneous plantings of Dutch, Spanish, and English irises will result in a sequence of bloom.

For all three, a position in full sun is essential if the bulbs are to be adequately nourished for reflowering in successive seasons. An average, moderately fertile, well-drained soil suits Dutch iris; its bulbs should be planted 6 to 8 inches apart and 4 to 5 inches deep. Active root growth begins soon after the bulbs are planted, and most will send up several green, spearlike shoots during the autumn. After the flowering period is over in late June, the foliage should be allowed to ripen, and it is essential that it be exposed to full sun during this period. When the leaves have become brown, the bulbs may be lifted. They should be placed on shallow trays, covered with dry sand, and stored in the hottest attic available, where conditions will approximate as nearly as possible the conditions found in their native habitat. If the bulbs are not lifted but are instead left undisturbed after the foliage has died down, some few varieties will persist for several years, but most will fail to reappear after the first season of bloom. Replanting of lifted bulbs may take place in the fall from zone 8 south;

elsewhere, plant in the spring. If the flowers are used for cutting, the foliage will be reduced to such an extent that the vigor and vitality of the bulb will be impaired, and new bulbs should, therefore, be planted the following year.

In areas north of zone 8, should you choose to leave bulbs in the ground, a layer of pine needles and/or evergreen branches applied as a winter mulch after the onset of hard freezing will help deter the penetration of the deep frost that can damage or kill iris bulbs. Under even the most ideal circumstances, however, supplemental bulbs will be needed to maintain a planting of these irises year after year.

IXIA *CULTIVARS*
(Corn bells)

Zones (7) 8–10

Among the most beautiful South African iris relatives, corn bells are successfully grown outdoors in the South and along the Pacific Coast. In zone 7, they may survive winters if planted on the southern side of a building or wall or are mulched loosely after the ground surface freezes. Corms are set 4 to 6 inches deep and as far apart, in average well-drained soil. Plant corn bells in full sun or partial shade in late summer or early fall.

The narrow, grasslike foliage appears in the fall and should be left exposed through the winter, although protection from harsh wind is advisable. The bell-shaped bicolored or tricolored flowers that appear in the spring and early summer are about 1 inch long and borne in clusters atop 10- to 14-inch-tall scapes. Foliage fades after the flowers; hence the need to mark plantings or interplant with ground cover or low annuals as protection against accidental disturbance.

Among the most colorful cultivars are the following.

'Afterglow': red, green, and black flowers.
'Giant': ivory and purple flowers.
'Mabel': red-violet and red-brown flowers.
'Uranus': deep yellow and red flowers.

POLIANTHES TUBEROSA
(Tuberose)

Zones 9–10

With grasslike foliage from a tuberous root, the tuberose produces a spike 2 to 3 feet tall, studded with highly perfumed white, tubular, six-parted flowers, about 2½ inches long, each bent at the base. Long, hot summers are needed for success.

The thickened bulblike tubers and their offsets should be planted in the spring, 2 to 3 inches deep and 4 to 6 inches apart in humusy, well-drained soil in full sun. Frequently, no flowers are borne the first year, even with adequate soil moisture and fertility. From zone 8 north the tubers should be dug up in the fall and stored in dry peat moss or sand at about 60°F. After a few months' dormancy, they may be forced in pots for indoor bloom or left to be planted for another season of garden cultivation. The form most commonly grown is the double-flowered cultivar 'Excelsior Double Pearl'.

TIGRIDIA PAVONIA
(Tiger flower)

Zones 9–10
The showy blooms of tiger flower, a native of tropical America, are unusual in form, and their colors, are brilliant, ranging from flame red through orange and yellow to buff, with spotted centers. The corms are generally available in assorted colors only. Although the individual flowers last only a day each, the blooms are produced in succession over a period of nearly two months, from late summer to midfall, and are borne on 1- to 2-foot scapes.

The bulbs should be planted in spring 6 to 8 inches apart and 4 to 6 inches deep in sandy-humusy soil or shallower in heavy soil or if undersize. Warm temperatures, a position in full sun, and generous soil moisture are required during the growing season. In zones 9 and 10, they may be left undisturbed and will provide a beautiful display year after year. From zone 8 north, the bulbs should be dug up before the ground freezes; allowed to dry; and stored in a cool, frost-free place, preferably spread out in a mesh flat or hung by their bunched and tied tops. Two caveats: The bulbs are very attractive to rodents, and they are liable to rot if subject to dampness during dormant storage.

TRITONIA CROCATA
(Montbretia)

Zones (8) 9–10

A member of the iris family, montbretia is a half-hardy cormous plant similar to *Crocosmia*. Its brilliant, colorful flowers make it an uncommonly decorative summer-flowering bulb. The flowers are borne on tall, graceful spikes, varying in height from 2 to 4 feet. The flowers are lovely for cutting as they last extremely well, often remaining fresh for two weeks or more. Some of the Earlham culitvars are of striking beauty, with wide, flaring flowers in tones of orange and apricot.

Montbretia grows best in full sun in sandy-humusy soil. In zones 9 and 10, the corms may be planted in the fall. From zone 8 north, where temperatures drop below 15°F, it is best to plant the corms in the spring. They should be set 3 to 4 inches deep and spaced 5 to 6 inches apart. Plantings in zone 8 on the southern side of buildings or walls may survive winter conditions if well mulched. In zone 8 and north, after the first frost, the corms may be lifted and stored for the winter in the same manner as are gladiolus corms.

ZANTEDESCHIA *SPP.*
(Calla lily)

Zones (7) 8–10
Of the half dozen species of *Zantedeschia*, all African, three are universally popular

greenhouse material and also make interesting garden subjects in the South. Outdoor culture farther north involves protecting the rhizomes from frost.

White calla (*Z. aethiopica*) grows best in full sun or partial shade under moist or wet, rather cool conditions, such as a pond or pool border or near a brook. It is a sturdy plant, 2 to 2½ feet tall, with large arrow-shaped leaves. During the summer, it bears a succession of pointed, flared, white or creamy spathes surrounding the yellow, stalklike spadixes. Each spadix is studded with minute florets.

From zone 7 north, the rhizomes should be lifted in the fall and allowed at least two months' dormancy at 40° to 50°F in damp peat moss. They may then be forced in pots filled with rich soil for early spring bloom indoors, followed by another dormant period before being planted outdoors. From zone 8 south and in well-protected locations

in zone 7, the rhizomes may be left in the ground but must be protected from frost with a blanket of loose, nonmatting mulch, such as straw covered with evergreen boughs.

Yellow calla (*Z. elliottiana*) and pink calla (*Z. rehmannii*) also do best in partial shade but require drier, warmer conditions and are hardy only in zones 9 and 10. Elsewhere, the rhizomes should be lifted in the fall, allowed to dry, and stored in dry peat moss.

With all species, the rhizomes should be planted so that the tip is just at or slightly below the soil surface. The soil should be prepared about 1 foot deep and include a generous supplement of well-rotted manure and/or compost. For the best effect, grow callas in single-color groups of 6 to 12 each, spacing the rhizomes about 1 foot apart in each group. Wait until night temperatures are no lower than 50°F before replanting.

Pink calla (*Zantedeschia rehmannii*)

HARDY AUTUMN-FLOWERING BULBS

COLCHICUM SPP.
(Autumn crocus)

Zones 3–9

The crocuslike blooms of *Colchicum* bring a bright touch to the end of the gardening season. Although usually pale lavender, the colors vary according to species and cultivar and range from purple to white and even yellow. Most autumn crocuses bloom in early to mid fall. Since the flowers appear without foliage, they are at their best when planted in a bed of low ground cover, such as creeping myrtle (*Vinca minor*). They are especially effective in the foreground of dark evergreens, such as yews, or in rock gardens. A patch near a frequently used entrance lends interest and surprise to the setting.

Corms are usually shipped in late summer and should be planted immediately on arrival. Indeed, if held only a few days, the flowers may expand and open in the package. Whatever the stage of growth, the corms should be planted 4 to 6 inches deep and 6 to 8 inches apart in well-drained soil of average fertility. The foliage of autumn crocus does not appear until the following spring. It is important that the corms be planted in a site that affords the lush spring foliage full sun and that it be allowed to mature and die down naturally. The foliage may reach 18 inches in height and usually vanishes by late spring. To prevent inadvertently disturbing dormant corms in the summer, the site should be labeled.

Although a dozen or more species of *Colchicum* are in cultivation, the autumn crocuses of greatest distinction for garden use are hybrid cultivars, among which the following are especially meritorious.

'Autumn Queen': rosy lilac; often appears in late summer.
'Giant', 'The Giant': lilac pink, large.
'Lilac Wonder': pale lilac, fading to white; narrow segments.
'Violet Queen': pinkish lilac, speckled purple, large; opens as late as midfall.
'Waterlily': deep rose pink, white at base, double (up to 20 segments).

Autumn crocus
(*Colchicum autumnale* 'Waterlily')

In addition to the commonly grown *C. autumnale*, species of special merit include *C. bornmuelleri*, with 5-inch flowers of rosy lilac and a white base, aging to purple; *C. speciosum*, especially its white-flowered form; and as a curiosity, *C. luteum*, with yellow flowers borne in spring.

CROCUS SPP.
(Fall-flowering crocus)

Zones 3–9

Although crocuses are usually thought of as heralds of spring, a number of species flower in the fall, and once established in suitable places, they will bloom year after year. Because the fall-blooming crocus is diminutive, even when massed, and appears at a time when the garden may still be lush with late-season growth, care must be taken to place it away from competition, as in an opening in the rock garden; along the edge of the shrub border; in little patches at the base of lightly shading trees such as honey locust (*Gleditsia triacanthos*); or along a well-traveled walk.

The corms should be planted as soon as they are received, usually in late summer, and set 2 to 4 inches deep and as far apart in a sandy-humusy soil. Full sun to partial shade yields the best results. As with the more familiar spring-flowering crocus, care must be taken to protect the foliage—which appears in spring also—from excessive shade and premature removal. By planting fall-flowering crocus in a bed of low ground cover, such as creeping myrtle (*Vinca minor*) or creeping sedum (*Sedum* spp.), the possibility of accidentally disturbing dormant corms is minimized.

CYCLAMEN HEDERIFOLIUM
(Hardy cyclamen, or sowbread)

Zones (6) 7–9
Sometimes still listed in catalogs as *C. neapolitanum*, hardy cyclamen reaches 3 to 6 inches in height and bears 1-inch pink or white, red-blotched flowers in early fall. It requires protection from competing vegetation and, later, from excessive, sustained hard frost. Because of the plant's small size, partially shaded rock gardens are favorite locations, but, here especially, substantial winter mulch is usually advisable, particularly if in snowless periods the temperature descends below 10°F.

The corms should be planted flat side up, with the top just beneath the surface, in sandy, well-drained soil in the light shade of trees or tall shrubs. They should be planted in the spring and spaced 6 to 9 inches apart. Patches of six or more make an effective display.

FALL-FLOWERING CROCUSES OF MERIT

C. byzantinus (deep purple)
C. laevigatus (white, with mauve and yellow)
C. longiflorus (yellow, striped with violet)
C. medius (bluish mauve and white)
C. niveus (white)
C. sativus (meadow saffron), (mauve, lilac, or white)
C. serotinus (syn. *C. asturicus*) (mauve to lilac blue)
C. speciosus (pale mauve to white)

Crocus longiflorus

GALANTHUS PLICATUS
(Fall snowdrop)

Zones 6–8

Generally suggesting a vigorous form of the familiar spring snowdrop (*G. nivalis*), fall snowdrop, a little-known bulb, makes its modest floral show in early fall. Since so many other larger garden subjects are still in flower at this time, fall snowdrop should be grown in the rock garden or in other sunny, uncrowded places, preferably near a walk or patio where it can be seen at close range. The pendent 1-inch white-and-green flowers are borne on 8- to 10-inch-tall scapes.

Plant the bulbs with their tops 3 to 4 inches deep and 2 to 3 inches apart. Spring planting results in good first-year blooming; if done later, flowering is often out of season and disappointing or may fail to occur until the second year. Massing is advised for an effective display.

LEUCOJUM AUTUMNALE
(Autumn snowflake)

Zones (6) 7–8

Resembling the spring-blooming kinds of *Leucojum*, autumn snowflake bears its narrow leaves in spring and summer, followed by one to three drooping white snowdroplike flowers held on slender scapes in early fall. Best when massed in small groups, it should be grown away from competing growth, as in a bed of low ground cover, in a rock garden, or among dwarf conifers.

Culture is the same that of spring and summer snowflakes, except that bulbs may be planted in the spring or fall. Winter mulch is advised in exposed sites, especially in zone 6.

STERNBERGIA LUTEA
(Winter daffodil)

Zones 3–9

Winter daffodil, a little-known bulb, brings a touch of bright color to the autumn garden. The crocuslike flowers, surrounded by glossy foliage, are clear, golden yellow and remain showy for several weeks. Winter daffodil is especially attractive when planted in patches in the rock garden or along a walk, and if left undisturbed, it will flower bountifully year after year.

The bulbs should be planted in the spring or summer at a depth of about 4 inches and spaced 4 to 6 inches apart. It thrives in a neutral or slightly alkaline (pH 7.0 to 7.5), well-drained soil and should have full sun or, at most, partial shade.

OTHER BULBS FOR GARDEN CULTURE

Nearly all do best in well-drained, moderately fertile soil at pH 6.5. The only exception is Dierama pulcherrimum, *which tolerates wet soil.*

Name	Zones†	Height	Exposure*	Flower Color and Bloom Time
Albuca nelsonii	10	5"	S to PSh	White; spring
Allium acuminatum	4–8	8–12"	S to PSh	Rose purple; late spring
A. cyaneum	5–8	6–12"	S to PSh	Bluish violet; summer
A. cyathophorum	5–8	10–15"	S to PSh	Bluish violet; late spring
A. narcissiflorum	5–8	4–10"	S to PSh	Rose pink; summer
A. rosenbachianum	5–8	2–2½"	S to PSh	Pinkish; late spring
A. roseum (rosy garlic)	5–8	1–2"	S to PSh	Pink to white; late spring
Anemone appennina	6–9	6–8"	S to PSh	Blue; early spring
A. pavonina	8–10	12–15"	S to PSh	Red, pink, or purple; early spring
Bellevalia pycnantha, syn. *Muscari paradoxum*	7–9	1½–2½"	S to PSh	Blue-black and yellow-green; spring
Brimeura amethystinus	5–8	4–10"	S to PSh	Light blue; spring
Brodiaea coronaria (triplet lily)	(7) 8–9	12–18"	S to PSh	Violet; summer
Cardiocrinum giganteum	7–9	10–12"	PSh to LSh	White with green and purple; summer
Chlidanthus fragrans (sea daffodil)	9–10	12–18"	S to PSh	Yellow; spring
Chlorogalum pomeridianum (soap plant)	8–9	2–3"	S to PSh	White; summer
Crocosmia × crocosmiiflora	7–9	3–4"	S to PSh	Orange-yellow; summer to fall
C. masoniorum	7–9	2–4"	S to PSh	Orange-red; summer
Cyclamen cilicium	7–9	6–9"	PSh to LSh	Pink or white and red; summer to fall
Cypella herbertii	9–10	1–1½"	S to PSh	Bronzy orange; late spring
Cyrtanthus elatus (Scarborough lily)	10	2–3"	S to PSh	Red-orange; summer to fall
Dichelostemma pulchellum (blue dicks)	5–8	1½–2"	S to PSh	Violet or white; early spring
Dierama pulcherrimum (wandflower)	7–10	5–6"	S to PSh	Magenta or white; summer

(continues)

OTHER BULBS FOR GARDEN CULTURE (*continued*)

Name	Zones†	Height	Exposure*	Flower Color and Bloom Time
Dietes bicolor (butterfly iris)	9–10	2–3"	S to PSh	Yellow and maroon; spring to fall
Eucharis × grandiflora (Amazon lily)	10	1–2"	S to PSh	White; summer
Eucrosia bicolor	10	2–2½"	S to PSh	Red and green; summer
Habranthus tubispathus	9–10	6–9"	S to PSh	Rose pink; summer to fall
Haemanthus katharinae (blood lily)	9–10	1½–2"	S to PSh	Red; summer
Hermodactylus tuberosus (snake's-head iris)	6–9	1–1½"	S to PSh	Purple and green; early spring
Homeria collina syn. *H. breyniana*	9–10	1–1½"	S to PSh	Orange and yellow; late spring
Ipheion uniflorum (spring starflower)	6–9	6–8"	PSh to LSh	White and blue; early spring
Iris histrioides 'Major'	5–8	4–9"	S to PSh	Purple and white; early spring
Ixiolirion tataricum (Siberian lily)	7–9	12–15"	S to PSh	Blue to purple; summer
Lachenalia aloides (cape cowslip)	9–10	8–12"	PSh	Yellow with green and red; early spring
Lapeirousia laxa, syn. *Anomatheca laxa*	7–9	6–10"	S to PSh	Red; summer
Ledebouria socialis	10	4–6"	S to PSh	Green and white; late spring
Lilium amabile	4–8	2–3"	S to PSh	Red-orange; late spring
L. auratum (gold-banded lily of Japan)	5–8	3–8"	S to PSh	White, red, and yellow; summer
L. concolor (star lily)	5–7	3–4"	S to PSh	Red; summer
L. formosanum (Formosa lily)	6–8	5–7"	S to PSh	White and purplish red; summer to fall
L. hansonii (Japanese Turk's-cap lily)	4–7	4–5"	S to PSh	Yellow-orange; late spring
L. henryi (Henry lily)	5–8	7–9"	S to PSh	Orange; summer
L. × hollandicum (candlestick lily)	5–8	2–2½"	S to PSh	Yellow to red; summer
L. michiganense	5–7	4–5"	S to PSh	Red-orange; summer
L. parryi (lemon lily)	7–9	4–6"	S to PSh	Yellow; summer
Lloydia serotina	5–7	2–6"	LSh	White; spring
Milla biflora (Mexican star)	9–10	6–12"	PSh to LSh	White; summer
Moraea polystachya	9–10	2–3"	S to PSh	Blue and yellow; spring
Muscari aucheri; syn. *M. tubergenianum*	6–8	4–8"	S to PSh	Blue to white; spring
Narcissus asturiensis	5–8	4–5"	S to PSh	Yellow; early spring
N. bulbocodium (hoop-petticoat daffodil)	6–8	6–15"	S to PSh	Yellow; early spring
N. cyclamineus	6–8	6–12"	S to PSh	Yellow-orange; early spring
N. jonquilia (jonquil)	4–8	1–1½"	S to PSh	Yellow; spring
N. juncifolius	6–8	4–6"	S to PSh	Yellow; early spring
N. minor	5–8	4–6"	S to PSh	Yellow; early spring
N. obvaliaris (Tenby daffodil)	6–8	8–12"	S to PSh	Yellow; early spring
N. × odorus (Campernelle jonquil)	6–8	8–12"	S to PSh	Yellow; early spring
N. poeticus (pheasant's-eye daffodil)	5–8	1–1½"	S to PSh	White and red-brown; spring
N. rupicola	6–8	4–6"	S to PSh	Yellow; early spring
N. triandrus (angel's tears)	5–8	8–12"	S to PSh	White; early spring
Neomarica caerulea (twelve apostles)	10	2–3"	S to PSh	Blue and purple; summer
N. gracilis (walking iris)	10	2–3"	S to PSh	White and maroon; summer
Nerine bowdenii	9–10	1–2"	S to PSh	Pink; fall
Notholirion thomsonianum	7–9	3–4"	PSh to LSh	Purplish pink; early spring
Ornithogalum saundersiae (giant chincherinchee)	7–9	3–4"	S to PSh	White; summer
Oxalis adenophylla	8–10	4–6"	S to PSh	Pink; summer
O. bowiei	8–10	8–12"	S to PSh	Rose to purple; summer
O. braziliensis	8–10	5–10"	S to PSh	Magenta and yellow; summer
O. deppei (good-luck plant)	8–10	6–12"	S to PSh	Red-violet; summer

Name	Zones[†]	Height	Exposure*	Flower Color and Bloom Time
O. lasiandra	9–10	8–12"	S to PSh	Pinkish red; summer
O. pes-caprae (Bermuda buttercup)	9–10	8–12"	S to PSh	Yellow; early spring
O. purpurea	9–10	4–6"	S to PSh	Pink, violet, or white; fall
O. regnellii	9–10	6–12	S to PSh	Pink to white; spring to summer
O. rubra	8–10	6–12"	S to PSh	Rose pink; late winter to early spring
O. violacea (purple wood sorrel)	5–9	5–10"	S to PSh	Pinkish; late spring
Sprekelia formosissima (Aztec lily)	9–10	8–12"	S to PSh	Red; summer
Stenomesson miniatum	9–10	10–14"	S to PSh	Orange or red; summer
Streptanthera cuprea	9–10	6–9"	S to PSh	Purple; late spring
Triteleia hyacinthina (wild hyacinth)	6–9	15–20"	S to PSh	Lilac or white; summer
Tulipa acuminata (Turkish tulip)	4–8	1–1½"	S to PSh	Yellow and red; late spring
T. aucheriana	4–8	6–8"	S to PSh	Pink and yellow-brown; early spring
T. hageri	4–8	4–6"	S to PSh	Yellow to red; early spring
T. kolpakowskiana	4–8	4–6"	S to PSh	Yellow and red; early spring
T. orphanidea	5–8	8–12"	S to PSh	Yellow to yellow-brown; early spring
T. praestans	4–8	8–12"	S to PSh	Red; early spring
T. sprengeri	5–8	8–12"	S to PSh	Red-orange; late spring
T. undulatifolia, syn. *T. eichleri*	5–8	6–8"	S to PSh	Red with yellow and black; spring
Urceolina urceolata	9–10	10–14"	S to PSh	Green and cream; summer
Veltheimia bracteata (unicorn plant)	9–10	1½–2"	PSh to LSh	Pinkish purple; early spring
Watsonia cvs.	8–10	3–4"	PSh	Red, pink, or white; late summer
Zephyranthes atamasco (Atamasco lily)	7–9	8–12"	S to PSh	White or pale lilac; early spring
Z. candida	9–10	8–12"	S to PSh	White or pale pink; summer to fall
Z. citrina	9–10	8–12"	S to PSh	Yellow and green; fall
Z. grandiflora (zephyr lily)	9–10	8–12"	S to PSh	Pink or red; spring to summer

* S, full sun; Sh, shade (no direct sun); PSh, partial shade (sun exposure only part of the day); LSh, light shade (e.g., the shade of tall, open trees, with little or no exposure to direct sun).

[†] Bulbs of most species that aren't hardy north of zone 9 may be lifted in fall for cool but frost-free storage or grown in winter as pot plants indoors or in a greenhouse.

Atamasco lily (*Zephyranthes atamasco*)

Purple-leaf oxalis (*Oxalis regnelli*)

Spring starflower (*Ipheion uniflorum*)

Turkish tulip (*Tulipa acuminata*)

17

Annuals

Annuals are plants that complete their life cycles within one growing season. In this group are such popular, though sometimes overused, flowering plants as impatiens (*Impatiens walleriana* cvs.), marigolds (*Tagetes* spp. and cvs.), petunias (*Petunia* × *hybrida* cvs.), and zinnias (*Zinnia elegans* cvs.). Other plants, such as snapdragons (*Antirrhinum majus* cvs.) and geraniums (*Pelargonium* spp. and cvs.), for example, are not true annuals but are handled as

Twisted buds opening at dawn are transformed into the membranous funnels of blue morning glory (Ipomoea tricolor *'Heavenly Blue'), usually closing by noon but remaining open until dusk on cloudy, cool days.*

Border of tall colorful annuals.

such because they come to flower quickly and are not winter hardy in most areas of the country.

Annuals have a multitude of uses. Many give a wealth of bloom throughout the summer and early fall. Some are indispensable for cutting. They are useful in the beds and borders of perennials, where they extend color into the summer and early fall when perennial bloom is largely over. If a garden is new or only temporary, as with rental property, annuals may form the core of the planting. For window boxes and terrace planters, for porch pots and hanging baskets, for the indoor window garden, and for winter bloom in a small greenhouse, selected annuals can hardly be equaled.

In both form and color, these flowers offer an extraordinarily wide range, which makes them useful in many ways. For edging beds and other plantings or for solid low carpets of color, there are edging lobelia (*Lobelia erinus*), wax begonia (*Begonia* Semperflorens-Cultorum hybrids), verbena (*Verbena × hybrida*), sweet alyssum (*Lobularia maritima*), annual phlox (*Phlox drummondii*), and petunia. For border plants of medium height, there is a wealth of material from which to choose, including China aster (*Callistephus chinensis*), African marigold (*Tagetes erecta*), Shirley poppy (*Papaver rhoeas*), larkspur (*Consolida* spp.), and zinnia. Feathery cosmos (*Cosmos bipinnatus*), lofty Mexican hat

(*Tithonia rotundifolia*), and bold castor bean (*Ricinus communis*) are excellent for use as tall background plants.

The terms *tender annual, half-hardy annual, hardy annual*, and *winter annual* are used in some catalogs and reference works to indicate various qualities. Tender annuals cannot withstand even the slightest frost; impatiens is such a plant. Hardy annuals withstand some frost, the degree varying according to the kind and age of the plant. Mature sweet alyssum endures several degrees of frost, as does young larkspur, whose fall-germinated seedlings often survive winter in zones 7 and 8 and then quickly come to flower in the spring. Half-hardy annuals are generally frost intolerant as seedlings, becoming more cold tolerant as they mature and even surviving a few degrees of frost in the fall; petunia is an example. Winter annuals such as calendula are plants that, in zone 9 particularly, are planted in the fall and flower in mild periods during the winter.

Tremendous advances have been made in developing superior strains among many of the more widely grown annuals. Plant breeders have succeeded in doubling the chromosomes of some annuals, with the result that these plants have greater vigor, larger flowers, longer stems, and more luxuriant foliage. Popular examples include the giant ruffled tetraploid petunias and the tall, large-flowered snapdragons. Through careful breeding and controlled pollination, new cultivars of petunia, begonia, snapdragon, impatiens, and other annuals are now abundantly available. The plant breeder inbreeds to get two lines that, when crossed, give predictable and superb results. This is known as the F_1 generation, the seeds of which produce superior flowers.

Most annuals perform best when grown in full sun. Relatively few, such as impatiens and wax begonia, thrive in partial shade or in the light dappled shade of tall trees. The ideal site for a garden of annuals, therefore, will be open to direct sunlight all or most of the day. In general, annuals thrive in a soil of average fertility that is amply supplied with moisture-retaining organic matter and falls between pH 6.5 and 7.5. A few grow on extremely poor soil; some do well on strongly acidic soils, others on strongly alkaline soils; and many seem indifferent to pH. Nearly all, however, require good soil drainage.

Good soil preparation is essential to optimal performance. Since most annuals are shallow rooted, deep tillage is not as important as for perennials or woody plants. Well-rotted manure or rich compost spread about 2 inches thick

Especially effective in groups, spider flower (Cleome hasslerana) takes its name from the long protruding stamens and pistil, and also from the even longer seed pods, radiating from the stems.

over the surface and forked or rototilled in to a depth of 8 inches makes an ideal growing medium for most annuals. If prepared in the autumn, the surface of the soil should be left rough during the winter to deter sheet erosion and improve aeration. However, if the surface of the bed is prepared in the spring, it should be carefully leveled with an iron rake until the soil is of fine tilth.

If successive soil tests show the need for higher fertility, a summer topdressing of well-rotted manure or loose compost will not only release nutrients but also conserve soil moisture. Alternatively, a light topdressing of commercial fertilizer may be applied in early summer and again about a month later. A 4-12-4 or a 5-10-5 complete fertilizer will yield good results but should be applied with restraint, i.e., spread at the rate of no more than 2 pounds to every 100 square feet. When greater amounts are used, the excess can injure the very plants targeted for help and may drain or leach away beyond the reach of roots, contributing to water pollution. In applying commercial fertilizer, care should be taken not to get any of the fertilizer on the foliage of the plants as it might cause burning. It should be sprinkled lightly on the surface of the soil and watered in.

The same caution applies to high-analysis, quickly soluble fertilizers, however great their value. They may be applied lightly as a booster application at the time of transplanting and again in midsummer when the plants are flowering heavily. If the soil tests below a pH of 6.5, lime should be applied. (For more information on soils and soil improvement see Chapter 31.) In places where soil drainage is marginal or poor, particularly where deep clay soils prevail, it may be necessary to take remedial measures, such as laying a subsurface gravel zone drained by perforated plastic pipe or constructing raised beds.

Since in nature the prototypes of our garden annuals survive the cold or dry season of each year as seeds only, it follows that most annuals are propagated by seed. However, sowing seed of annuals in open ground is generally risky practice, because the soil usually contains many insects and disease organisms that may consume the seeds (which are, after all, little pills of concentrated food) or infest or consume the small seedlings. Better results are had by sowing seed in sterilized, weed-free growing media (such as potting soil mixed with perlite or a peat-based mix with vermiculite), using pots, flats, or cell packs and controlling the light, moisture, and temperature. For detailed directions on seed sowing, both in open ground and in containers, see Chapter 36.

Some annuals self-sow, i.e., some of their seeds survive the winter to germinate in the spring (California poppy, for example); in others (such as dwarf impatiens) successive generations revert to tall wild types of inferior ornamental value. When self-sowing occurs, the seedlings frequently require thinning or transplanting, as it is essential that each individual plant be allowed ample space for its full development if good bloom is to be obtained. The ultimate space required by the plants should be determined, and the thinning should be done before the plants start becoming overcrowded. In some cases, as with cosmos and cleome, the plants that are thinned out may be planted in another part of the garden. In the case of seedlings that do not transplant readily (such as poppy and mignonette) it is best to discard those that have been thinned out. If thinning and transplanting are done on a calm, cloudy day when the ground is moist, the affected plants will suffer little shock and soon recover. The seedlings should be handled gently to minimize root damage and should be watered immediately. An extra boost can be given the plants at this time by watering them with a weak starter solution of a water-soluble fertilizer, after which they should be covered with newspaper tents, inverted baskets, or some similar loose covering for a few days, especially if the sun and heat are intense.

Most annuals should be allowed to develop their natural habits of growth and will either produce a spire of bloom or will branch quite freely if they are given ample space for their full development. There are a number of annuals, however, that definitely benefit from judicious pinching back. Snapdragon is a good example. Left to its own devices, a plant tends to make tall, narrow, or even spindly growth. It is advisable, therefore, to pinch out the tip of the growth when the plant has reached a few inches in height, encouraging bushiness and often more generous flowering.

GARDEN ANNUALS THAT BENEFIT FROM PINCHING

Abutilon × hybridum (flowering maple)
Anoda cristata (opal cup)
Bupleurum rotundifolium (green gold)
Cosmos bipinnatus (tall cosmos)
Hypoestes phyllostachya (polka-dot plant)
Malope trifida (mallowwort)
Malva sylvestris (purple mallow, striped mallow)
Nicandra physaloides (shoofly plant)
Oenothera biennis var. *grandiflora* (southern evening primrose)
O. glazioviana (orange-flowered evening primrose)
Oxypetalum caeruleum (blue milkweed)
Salvia coccinea (hairy red sage)
Solanum sisymbrifolium (sticky nightshade)

Once established in the garden, annuals usually require weeding, as most do not compete effectively with intruders. However, the long-venerated practice of surface cultivation is not advised. If the soil has been correctly prepared, i.e., with well-rotted manure or compost incorporated and later also spread as a supplemental topdressing, there is no need for cultivation. Indeed, cultivators inevitably damage surface roots. Soil compaction can be reduced by using planks or stepping-stones for any weeding, staking, flower-picking, or deadheading that is out of reach.

Although some annuals, such as California poppy, portulaca, and annual phlox, are unaffected by high soil temperatures and minimal soil moisture, many others, such as zinnia, marigold, and snapdragon, are greatly benefited by a summer mulch, 2 or 3 inches thick, not only to moderate soil temperature but also to conserve needed moisture and deter weeds.

The flowering period of most annuals is prolonged, sometimes greatly, if fading flowers are regularly removed. In fact, this maintenance detail, called deadheading, is more important for annuals than it is for any other group of flowers. The chief function of an annual plant is to blossom and produce seed; having fulfilled this function, it has no further reason for existence. The prevention of seed formation, therefore, stimulates additional flowering. In the case of low border plants such as sweet alyssum, it is sometimes wise to shear the plants back if they become somewhat rangy or straggly, and vigorous compact new growth will thus be induced. Some cool-weather annuals such as calendula can be cut back severely in the heat of August to stimulate new growth and a good autumn crop of flowers.

Specific recommendations for the treatment of diseases and pests of annuals are given in Chapter 34.

SELECTION OF CULTIVARS

From the long lists of annuals in seed catalogs, it is difficult to make wise selections for your own gardening needs unless you have had an opportunity to become familiar with the plants. They are all listed in the voluminous catalogs—the dependable ones and the fickle ones; the sturdy ones and the temperamental ones; those with flowers of exquisite daintiness and those that have a bold form or hue; those that are planted for their fragrance and those that may have an objectionable odor but nevertheless would serve to fill in a particularly troublesome spot. The seed catalogs from several leading seedhouses should be studied carefully for a range of flowers from which to choose for your specific purposes. It should be borne in mind, however, that seed catalogs are sales media, and thus present their offerings in the best possible light, often omitting the caveats that help the gardener make an informed selection. Some of the more significant reservations are included in the descriptions and listings of plants that follow.

It is obviously impossible to discuss every annual. The species discussed here have been selected for some particular characteristic of merit. A nice aspect about growing annuals is that new ones can be tried each year, while at the same time repeating old favorites.

ANNUALS OF EXCEPTIONAL MERIT

The following annuals are treated in detail because they perform well under a wide range of garden conditions; are relatively (in some cases, quite) easy to grow from seed or are locally available as seedlings, often in a wide range of cultivars; and have become traditional mainstays in the summer garden.

ANTIRRHINUM MAJUS
(Snapdragon)

Few annuals are more versatile than the snapdragon. Beyond its staple importance as a greenhouse-grown flower in the florist trade, snapdragon is indispensable in flower beds and borders and is equally valuable in the cutting garden. It tolerates heat, yet bears bloom—most prolifically in the fall—until temperatures drop below 30°F. It is lovely in form, and its colors vary widely, ranging from delicate apple-blossom pink through shades of salmon and apricot, to tawny yellow and deep wine red. The intermediate type, reaching a height of about 18 inches, is the most popular, but for the rear of the flower border the giant types are preferable, since they often reach a height of 3 feet or more. Snapdragon is also available in a dwarf form with shortened flower clusters, but for many gardeners, the tall, stately spires are still most appealing. The flower forms range from the familiar "snapping dragon" to double and bellflower forms in which the flowers are open and resemble those of gloxinia.

For early spring bloom, seed may be sown in late summer, and the young plants wintered over in a coldframe. They should be set out in the garden as soon as the soil can be worked, spaced 6 to 12 inches apart, according to the ultimate height of the cultivar. For summer bloom, sow seed under lights or in a cool greenhouse in late winter, or in hotbeds in very early spring (see Chapter 36). Wherever sown, the seed must have light to germinate and hence should be left on the surface and covered with nothing more than a little dust. As soon as they are large enough, the seedlings should be pricked out and planted in cell packs, one to a cell, and pinched back to encourage bushiness.

Young plants, whether grown or purchased, should be set in the garden after danger of hard frost. Exposure to full sun or, at most, brief partial shade, is necessary for optimal flowering. Most any well-drained soil suffices, although the incorporation of well-rotted manure or compost not only ensures supplemental nutrients for enhanced bloom but also conserves necessary soil moisture.

If faded flowers are removed regularly, thus precluding seed-capsule formation, and if the plantings are watered and weeded, they will provide generous bloom over a period of four months or more. The tallest cultivars usually require staking. Although snapdragon is usually grown as an annual, plants commonly live through the winter from zone 7 south (though not reliably in zone 7 unless mulched) and thus may be regarded as a perennial or, in zone 9, as a shrub.

Nearly all snapdragon cultivars now available are resistant to rust fungus, which formerly took a heavy toll and seriously diminished the popularity of this flower. The hundreds of named cultivars now available fall into three height classes; some notable selections are listed below for each.

Tall (30 to 36 inches)
'Butterfly': open, symmetrical (peloric), penstemonlike flowers; single-color cultivars ('Butterfly Bronze, 2-foot' and 'Butterfly White 3-foot'), mixtures ('Bright Butterflies' and 'Madame Butterfly Mixed').
'Rocket': normal snapdragon flowers; the highest tolerance of summer heat; single-color cultivars ('Red Rocket' and 'White Rocket'), mixtures ('Rocket' hybrids).

Intermediate (14 to 24 inches)
'Coronette' hybrids: mixed colors.
'Princess White with a Purple Eye': white with a red-violet center; more winter hardy than most.
'Sprite' hybrids: mixed colors.

Dwarf (6 to 12 inches)
'Floral Carpet' hybrids: mixed colors; very floriferous.
'Kolibri' hybrids: mixed colors; early flowering.
'Little Darling' hybrids: peloric (symmetrical) flowers; mixed colors.
'Pixie' hybrids: peloric flowers; mixed colors.
'Royal Carpet' hybrids: mixed colors; spreading habit; long period of bloom.
'Sweetheart' hybrids: double flowers in short spikes, mixed colors.

BEGONIA SEMPERFLORENS-CULTORUM HYBRIDS
(Wax begonia)

The wax begonia, waxy leaved and fibrous rooted, was once limited to the houseplant or Memorial Day "cemetery basket" kind of gardening, but today's plant breeders have created one of the most useful of garden plants with an impressive array of new hybrids. These neat, mound-shaped plants bloom continuously from late spring or early summer, beginning while still quite small, until frost. They are very adaptable and will even take full sun in cooler locations (where temperatures seldom exceed 90°F). They perform best, however, in partial or light shade. The glossy, succulent foliage is bright green in most strains but is bronzy in some.

Flower color is red, pink, or white; in some white-flowered cultivars, the petals are red or pink bordered. As in all begonias, the flowers are borne in loose clusters and the first to open are male, with a tuft of yellow stamens in the center, followed by the female flowers, each opening at the end of a three-angled ovary. The ripened ovary eventually liberates the dustlike seed.

Of the two principal size classes, dwarf begonias grow no taller than 6 or 8 inches and, if massed, make tight carpets of color. Some strains are available in any combination of foliage and flower color. Intermediate begonias, which grow 10 to 12 inches tall, are just as compact in habit and are available in color-specific cultivars as well as in mixed colors. Tall wax begonias, a third class, are seldom grown outdoors. Plant breeders have developed forms with large flowers, which in some cultivars (such as 'Wings' and 'Glamour' hybrids) reach 2 inches across, making these strains especially suitable for pots, window boxes, and hanging baskets.

Wax begonias are well adapted to culture under lights and require about four months from seed to bloom, hence the need to start seed in late winter for the longest period of outdoor bloom. The dustlike seed should be sown very thinly on the surface of finely prepared potting mix; the container should be bottom watered and covered with a pane of glass or clear plastic. The seedlings are at first minute and grow more horizontally than vertically as the successively larger leaves develop, underscoring the importance of sowing thinly and of pricking out the seedlings as soon as possible into cell packs or small pots; toothpicks or other small tools can be used for this. If you pay attention to these details, you can raise large numbers of plants from a mere pinch of seed. If only a small number of plants is required, however, it is better to purchase them.

In the garden, wax begonias grow well on any moderately fertile, well-drained soil as long as it provides adequate moisture. Flowering diminishes or ceases altogether in drought.

Of the many cultivars available, the following readily available ones are especially meritorious.

Dwarf (6 to 8 inches)
'Cocktail' hybrids: a series of cultivars, each with a specific leaf- and flower-color combination.
  'Brandy': bronze leaves; pink flowers.
  'Gin': bronze leaves, deep pink flowers.
  'Rum': bronze leaves, white flowers with a red broder.
  'Vodka': green leaves, red flowers.

'Whisky': bronze leaves, white flowers.
'Coco' hybrids: bronzy foliage; red, pink, white, or bicolored flowers.
'Linda': green leaves; rose red flowers.
'Lucia': green leaves; red, pink or white flowers; compact in habit; more heat tolerant than most.
'Thousand Wonders': bronze leaves and red flowers or green leaves and white flowers; very floriferous.
'Viva': green leaves, white flowers.

Intermediate or Tall (10 to 12 inches)
'Calla Queen': variegated green and white leaves; pink flowers.
'Danica Scarlet': bronze leaves; red flowers, 2 inches across.
'Frilly Dilly' hybrids: green leaves; red or pink flowers, wavy petals.
'Pink and White Avalanche': green leaves; pink or white flowers; pendulous habit.
'Wings' hybrids: green leaves; red, pink, white, or bicolor flowers 2 inches across; unusually showy.

COLEUS × HYBRIDUS, *SYN.* SOLENOSTEMON SCUTELLARIOIDES
(Coleus)

Like begonia, geranium, and impatiens, coleus used to be limited to baskets, boxes, and window sills. Plant breeders, however, have exploited its genetic plasticity so that today many cultivars are available that can be grown easily from seed with predictably good results. The ornamental leaf variegation ranges from creamy white leaves with green edges (cv. 'Candidum') to solid deep crimson ('Red Velvet'). There are large-leaf and small-leaf cultivars, large bushy plants, and compact dwarfs. Partial or light shade intensifies the foliar colors and the variegation contrasts. All coleuses are grown as tender annuals, but they may be treated as perennials or even small shrubs in frost-free areas.

Seed sown indoors should be started under lights, in a warm, sunny window; or in the greenhouse about two months before set-out time. Rich, humusy soil and continuously moist conditions favor rapid growth. Coleus does not thrive under hot, dry conditions or in poor soil. Some shade is advisable, especially for

seedlings and young plants. Flower spikes should be removed as they form, since flowering tends to result in loss of older leaves. At the end of the season, cuttings of especially attractive plants can be rooted in water or wet sand and grown for indoor display. In addition to its value as a bedding plant, coleus is also excellent in outdoor containers.

Of the 60 or more hybrids and cultivars in commerce, some reaching 3 feet, the following, mostly much shorter, are quite distinct and readily available.

'Brilliant' hybrids: 1½ to 2 feet tall; large single color, bicolor, or tricolor leaves; red, rose, pink, bronze, copper, chartreuse, ivory, and/or purple.
'Carefree' hybrids: 6 to 8 inches tall; small lobed leaves; amber, brown, bronze, red, green, ivory, and mahogany, in various combinations.
'Dragon' hybrids: 9 to 12 inches tall; variously lobed leaves; several colors, mostly with a yellow-green border.
'Fairway' hybrids: 8 to 10 inches tall; small, shallowly toothed leaves; various color combinations; branching from the ground; compact habit.
'Fashion Parade': 9 to 12 inches tall; variously lobed and patterned leaves (oak leaf, saber leaf, laced, fringed, etc.); varicolored.
'Fiji' hybrids: 10 to 15 inches tall; fringed and frilled leaves; striped and mottled in various colors.
'Mini-coral' hybrids: 4 to 6 inches tall; small, variously lobed, bicolor and tricolor leaves.
'Molten Lava': 8 to 10 inches tall; black-violet and red.
'Old Laced' hybrids: 15 to 18 inches tall; intricately lace-patterned leaves; lilac, pink, red, rose, salmon, or white with pale green or yellow edging.
'Rainbow' hybrids: 12 to 15 inches tall; medium leaves, striped and mottled in various colors.
'Red Velvet': 12 to 15 inches tall; deep red, darkening with age.
'Saber' hybrids: 8 to 10 inches tall; long, saber-shaped leaves; variously colored; basally branched.
'Scarlet Poncho': 10 to 12 inches tall; red with green flecks, edged yellow-green.

'Volcano': 9 to 12 inches tall; deeply lobed leaves; red with yellow border.

'Wizard' hybrids: 8 to 10 inches tall; large heart-shaped leaves; combinations of red, pink, violet-black, and ivory; basally branched.

IMPATIENS WALLERIANA

As a result of intense hybridization efforts by plant breeders, impatiens has become a primary bedding annual, especially in locations that are partly or mostly shaded. Impatiens is particularly valued for its continuous and abundant production of flowers in bright, clear colors. Ranging from nearly 3 feet tall down to tiny dwarfs, impatiens cultivars offer a wide assortment of colors, from scarlet through red, rose, salmon, orange, and pink to white. Bicolors are also available in various patterns as well as forms with purplish or bronzy foliage.

Although commonly purchased as young plants in flower in cell packs or flats, impatiens, a tender annual, can be grown from seed if started indoors under lights or in a greenhouse 8 to 10 weeks before set-out time. If, in a mixture, a particular plant is considered choice, it can be wintered over as a houseplant and propagated by cuttings for use in the next year's garden.

In addition to *I. walleriana*, two other open- or flat-flowered species are horticulturally important. *I. hawkeri* is the source of the 'New Guinea' hybrids, which typically have stouter stems; longer, narrower, and often variegated leaves; and scarlet, red, pink, purple, or white flowers, 2 inches or more in diameter. In cultivation, 'New Guinea' hybrids require greater exposure to direct sunlight than *I. walleriana* to flower fully. A partially shaded (half a day of sun) location is usually optimal.

I. platypetala generally resembles *I. walleriana* except for its tendency to lankiness. It has distinct flowers, which are an intense orange with a deep red center (best expressed in the cultivar 'Tangerine'). It prospers in light or partial shade.

Seed of impatiens requires light to germinate, hence it should not be covered

---

SELECTED HYBRID SERIES OF *I. WALLERIANA*
Each has a full range of colors, unless otherwise noted.

'Accent' hybrids: 6 to 8 inches tall; rounded habit; early flowering; flowers 1½ to 2 inches in diameter.

'Blitz' hybrids: 14 to 16 inches tall; dense habit; flowers 2 to 2½ inches in diameter.

'Cinderalla Variegated' hybrids: 8 to 12 inches tall; a central longitudinal white stripe on each petal.

'Cleopatra' hybrids: 6 to 10 inches tall; compact habit; early flowering; more tolerant of direct sun than most; well suited to container culture.

'Dazzler' hybrids: 8 to 10 inches tall; basally branching; flowers 1½ to 2 inches in diameter, often with a darker central spot in the lighter shades.

'Fantasia' hybrids: 10 to 12 inches tall; basally branching.

'Futura' hybrids: 8 to 10 inches tall; basally branching, usually wider than tall; very floriferous.

'Gem' hybrids: 8 to 10 inches tall; flowers relatively small (about 1½ inches in diameter) but abundantly produced; more tolerant of direct sun than most.

'King Kong' hybrids: 9 to 12 inches tall; flowers 2 to 2½ inches in diameter, often obscuring foliage.

'Mini' hybrids: 6 to 8 inches tall; very compact habit, does not spread; very effective when massed.

'Novette' hybrids: similar to 'Super Elfin' but shorter and earlier flowering.

'Pastel' hybrids: 9 to 12 inches tall; very early to flower, mostly in pastel shades.

'Princess' hybrids: 8 to 10 inches tall; flowers 2 to 2½ inches in diameter, in strong colors.

'Rosette' hybrids: 18 to 20 inches tall; flowers mostly semidouble or fully double.

'Starbright' hybrids: 6 to 8 inches tall; flowers mostly in shades of red or pink, a longitudinal white stripe or zone on each petal.

'Super Elfin' hybrids: 8 to 12 inches tall; basally branching; amply floriferous; the standard dwarf impatiens.

'Tempo' hybrids: 8 to 10 inches tall; early flowering, colors include a burgundy shade and various pastels.

'Twinkles' hybrids: 8 to 10 inches tall; early flowering, mostly bicolor.

SELECTED HYBRIDS AND CULTIVARS OF NEW GUINEA IMPATIENS
All are 12 to 18 inches tall with green leaves, unless otherwise noted.

'Apple Blossom': flowers semidouble, pink, abundantly produced.

'Big Top': flowers single, white.

'Damask Rose': foliage deep purplish green; flowers double, deep red.

'Double Salmon': flowers 2½ to 2¾ inches in diameter, salmon orange, frilled, abundantly produced.

'Firelake' hybrids*: leaves variously variegated with red and cream; flowers about 2 inches in diameter, red, pink, purple, orange, or white.

'Headliner': flowers coral pink.

'Showboat': flowers raspberry red.

'Spectra' hybrids: foliage in some plants variously variegated; flowers 2 to 3 inches in diameter, in shades of red and pink, or white, or bicolor.

'Star Dancer': foliage striped; flowers lavender.

'Sweet Sue'*: flowers 2 to 2½ inches in diameter, deep orange.

'Tango'*: 18 to 24 inches tall; foliage bronzy green; flowers orange.

* Available as seed.

with soil. To keep the seed-bed medium moist, cover it with a pane of glass or clear plastic. To facilitate pricking out, the seed should be distributed thinly on top of the medium. Seedlings should be transplanted to cell packs before crowding causes legginess. Pinching back seedlings induces basal branching. In the garden, its normal shallow rooting and a high rate of transpiration result in leaf wiltin direct summer sun. High soil nitrate levels and abundant moisture can cause dwarf cultivars to exceed stated maximum heights considerably. Seed pod formation and seed production are generous in late summer, and in zones 9 and 10 self-sown seedlings can abound, but such plants tend to revert to prototypic characteristics, such as tall habit, large leaves, and modest production of mostly rose pink flowers.

LOBELIA ERINUS
(Edging lobelia)

The intensity of the blue found in the flowers of edging lobelia is equaled in few other annuals. The many cultivars now available have greatly increased the popularity of these much-valued edging and basket plants.

A tender annual, edging lobelia is often purchased in cell packs, especially if only a small number of plants is needed. If grown from seed, however, it should be started indoors under lights or in the greenhouse at 70° to 75°F about 10 weeks before set-out time. The very fine seed requires light to germinate and so should not be covered. Moist conditions can be maintained by covering the seed pan with glass or clear plastic until the seeds have sprouted. Bottom watering is advised until germination. Transplant the tiny seedlings, individually or in small clumps, to cell packs for continued growth. Sow the seed thinly to facilitate transplanting.

In the garden, edging lobelia is of simple culture in full sun or partial shade if planted in ordinary, well-drained garden loam 4 to 6 inches apart. Best performance is had in relatively cool summer weather, i.e., in temperatures below 90°F.

Although the prototype or wild form grows to 1 foot tall or more, the emphasis in breeding has been toward dwarf compact forms suitable for edging and trailing forms for container culture. Cultivars offer various shades of blue, pink, and red, as well as white flowers.

LOBULARIA MARITIMA
(Sweet alyssum)

Sweet alyssum has long been one of the most popular of the annual edging plants. Several of the exceedingly dwarf forms attain a height of hardly more than 3 inches, while some of the larger types are fully 12 inches tall. The plants begin to flower when still very small, and they generate a profusion of distinctly fragrant bloom throughout the summer and on past frost, attesting to this species' hardy-annual status. The cultivars most commonly grown are white flowered, but there are several strains bearing other colors. Within any cultivar, the plants are usually uniform in height and habit.

Seed of sweet alyssum may be sown outdoors as soon as the soil is free of frost. As sweet alyssum seed requires light to germinate, it should simply be spread on the surface of the soil and pressed into contact with soil granules with a block of wood, then moistened with a fine spray. Seedlings should be thinned or transplanted to stand 4 to 6 inches apart. Ordinarily, flowering begins about six weeks after sowing. Seed may also be sown indoors or in coldframes about six weeks before set-out time, thus ensuring very early flowering. Bloom often diminishes in hot weather but resumes when temperatures moderate and is often most abundant in fall. Sweet alyssum may naturalize from zone 7 south.

COMPACT HYBRIDS AND CULTIVARS OF EDGING LOBELIA

'Blue Moon': 4 to 6 inches tall; flowers dark violet blue.
'Blue Stone': 5 to 9 inches tall; flowers intense sky blue.
'Cambridge Blue': 3 to 4 inches tall; tufted habit; flowers sky blue.
'Crystal Palace': 3 to 4 inches tall; foliage bronzy green; flowers deep blue.
'Emperor William': 4 to 6 inches tall; flowers bright blue.
'Mrs. Clibran Improved': 4 to 6 inches tall; flowers deep blue with white center.
'Rosamund': 4 to 6 inches tall; flowers deep carmine red with white center.
'Royal' hybrids: 6 to 8 inches tall; somewhat spreading; flowers blue or white.
'Snowball': 4 to 6 inches tall; flowers white or occasionally pale blue.
'String of Pearls': 3 to 4 inches tall; flowers deep blue, medium blue, carmine, or rose.
'White Lady': 4 to 6 inches tall; flowers white.

TRAILING LOBELIA HYBRIDS AND CULTIVARS
Sometimes called pendula lobelia.

'Cascade' hybrids: long, slender, trailing, or pendulous stems; flowers vary with cultivar.
  'Blue Cascade': light blue.
  'Lilac Cascade': lavender blue.
  'Red Cascade': deep purplish red.
  'Ruby Cascade': purplish carmine.
  'White Cascade': white.
'Sapphire': lax, trailing habit; flowers deep blue with white center.

'Color Carpet': a mixture of white-, rose-, and purplish-flowered strains.

'Little Dorrit': about 4 inches tall; flowers white.

'Navy Blue': 3 to 4 inches tall; flowers deep purple.

'New Carpet of Snow': 3 to 4 inches tall; flowers white, profusely borne.

'Oriental Night': about 4 inches tall; flowers purple, very fragrant.

'Rosie O'Day': 3 to 4 inches tall; flowers rose pink.

'Royal Carpet': 3 to 4 inches tall; flowers purple, profusely borne.

'Snowcloth Improved': 3 to 4 inches tall; wide spreading; flowers white.

'Snow Crystal': 3 to 4 inches tall; wide spreading; flowers white, twice the usual size (tetraploid).

'Sweet White': 3 to 4 inches tall; flowers white, very fragrant.

'Wonderland' hybrids: 3 to 4 inches tall; wide spreading; flowers deep purple, rosy red, or white, appearing about five weeks from seed.

PELARGONIUM *SPP. AND CVS.*
(Geranium)

Geraniums, widely used in horticulture, are divided into several classes, of which three are important in the home flower garden. Far and away the most common are the zonal geraniums, grouped within *P. × hortorum*, which are mostly complex hybrids derived from two South African species. They are tender aromatic shrubs, often reaching 4 to 6 feet in zone 10, but are usually grown as hardy annuals. They have round leaves, often with a dark central zone, and bear round-topped or flattened clusters of single or double red, pink, salmon, white, or streaked flowers, each bloom 1 to 2½ inches in diameter.

While zonal geraniums have traditionally been purchased as potted plants propagated by cuttings, it is also possible to grow them from seed. The seed is costly, however, and is best used as a means of growing cultivars not otherwise obtainable, from which cuttings may be taken in due course. The most desirable cultivars are self-branching, compact, and profusely flowering. The seed must be started indoors about 10 weeks (preferably four months) before set-out time and is best germinated under lights or in a greenhouse. Bottom heat of 70° to 75°F facilitates germination. Seedlings should be carefully transplanted into pots to allow maximum opportunity for each to branch. In the garden, spacing of 1 foot is usually sufficent. Intense summer heat and high humidity in zones 8 to 10 can cause plants to weaken and die.

Similarly, prolonged wet, cold conditions can also be fatal. Dry heat and well-drained soils of average fertility result in the best performance, but many cultivars are remarkably tolerant of adverse conditions. Zonal geraniums may be wintered as ordinary houseplants or left in pots unwatered in a cool sunny window. Resumption of watering in spring will initiate new growth.

Among the dozens of hybrid groups and hundreds of cultivars of zonal geraniums, the following especially meritorious ones are also available as seed. Heights represent one season's growth.

'Border' hybrids: 14 to 16 inches tall; flowers in clusters 4 to 5 inches across, in various shades—'Cherry Border', 'Deep Rose Border', and 'Scarlet Border'.

'Breakaway' hybrids: 12 to 14 inches tall; well-branched and diffuse in habit; flowers red to white; good for basket culture.

'Dolly Vardon': 12 to 14 inches tall; leaves green and rose with a white margin; flowers single red; grown primarily for its decorative foliage.

'Earliana' series: 14 to 16 inches tall; foliage green or zoned; flowers in clusters 3 to 4 inches across, red to white; early to bloom.

'Elite' hybrids: 8 to 10 inches tall; mostly; unzoned foliage; numerous flowers in clusters 3 to 4 inches across, red to white, long-stalked (to 3 inches above the highest leaves), early to bloom.

'Fantasia': 4 to 6 inches tall; double flowers held in tight clusters; white.

'Freckles': 12 to 15 inches tall; unzoned foliage; flowers in clusters 3 to 4½ inches across, rose pink, a deep rose basal spot on each petal, early to bloom (about 15 weeks from seed); tetraploid.

'Hollywood' hybrids: 10 to 15 inches tall; well-zoned foliage; flowers in clusters 3 to 4 inches across, red to white.

'L'Amour' hybrids: 10 to 12 inches tall; lightly zoned foliage; flowers in clusters 3 to 4 inches across, red to white with a silvery sheen.

'Lucky Break' hybrids: 10 to 12 inches tall; mostly zoned foliage; flowers in clusters 3 to 4 inches across, red to white, all in each cluster opening almost simultaneously, early to bloom.

'Masquerade' hybrids: 12 to 15 inches tall; lightly zoned foliage; flowers in clusters 3 to 4 inches across, bicolored (petals red to pink with a white base) or all white.

'Multibloom' hybrids: 8 to 10 inches tall; strongly purple zoned foliage; flowers in red to white, some bicolor, clusters 3 to 4 inches across, numerous and dense, early to bloom (12 to 14 weeks from seed).

'New Dawn': 12 to 15 inches tall; lightly zoned foliage; flowers in clusters 4 to 4½ inches across, salmon pink, a white base on each petal.

'Orbit' hybrids: 12 to 14 inches tall; strongly zoned foliage; flowers in clusters 4 to 5 inches across, red to white, including purplish red.

'Picasso': 12 to 15 inches tall; lightly zoned foliage; flowers in clusters 4 to 5 inches across, violet cerise, two of the petals marked orange.

'Pinto' hybrids: 16 to 18 inches tall; strongly zoned foliage; flowers in clusters 3 to 4 inches across, mostly red to pinkish orange, early to bloom.

'Playboy Speckles': 10 to 15 inches tall; zoned or unzoned foliage; flowers in clusters 3 to 4 inches across, salmon to white, flecked or streaked red to pink, early to bloom (14 to 15 weeks from seed).

'Ringo' hybrids: 12 to 14 inches tall; mostly zoned foliage; flowers in clusters 3 to 4 inches across, red to white; seed has a higher germination rate than most.

'Startel' hybrids: 12 to 14 inches tall; zoned foliage with pointed lobes; flowers in clusters 3 to 4 inches across, red to white, each petal distinctively pointed.

'Tetra Scarlet': 10 to 14 inches tall; lightly zoned foliage; flowers in clusters 4 to 5 inches across, deep red; remains in flower longer in hot weather; tetraploid.

'Video' hybrids: 8 to 10 inches tall; bronzy zoned foliage; flowers in clusters 3 to 4 inches across, red to white, numerous.

Also useful, especially in window boxes and hanging baskets, or wherever their sprawling or rangily pendulous growth habit is desired, are the ivy-leaved geraniums. Derived largely from *P. peltatum*, the older ivy-leaved hybrids are characterized by slender, brittle stems; by leaves that are similar to those of English ivy (i.e., five-lobed and leathery), often glossy and/or aromatic; and by open clusters of flowers in shades of purple, pink, or white. Superior hybrids feature relatively pliant stems, compact growth, and dense flower clusters. Among the particularly meritorious cultivars are the following.

'Crocodile': cream-veined leaves; single, rose pink flowers.

'Galilee': flowers rose pink, double.

'La France': flowers purple-and-white with mauve veins, semidouble.

'Rouletta': white flowers with red stripes, semidouble.

'Summer Showers': glossy, unzoned foliage; flower cluster 4 to 5 inches across, ranging from burgundy red to near white; one of the few ivy-leaved hybrids available as seed (flowers in 16 to 18 weeks).

The third class of *Pelargonium* hybrids popular in home gardening is the 'Regal', or 'Martha Washington', geranium, derived mainly from *P. cucullatum*. These geraniums grow as bushy subshrubs with five-lobed, upswept or cup-shaped leaves. The flower clusters have relatively few but quite large flowers, usually in shades of purple and pink with white, and nearly always streaked, striped, or blotched. Because Martha Washington geraniums tend to flower in the spring and early summer, they are less suited to summer bedding than zonal geraniums. Propagation is mostly by cuttings. Meritorious cultivars include the following.

'Atomic Snowflake': flowers white.

'Grand Slam': flowers rose red with purplish markings.

'Pompeii': flowers violet black with narrow pale pink border.

For information about scented geraniums, see Chapter 29.

PETUNIA × HYBRIDA

Long the focus of plant hybridizers, the petunia is one of our most useful and popular annual flowers and is surpassed in favor only by impatiens. Some 200 cultivars are in horticultural commerce, and new ones are added each year. Always dependable, demanding very little care, thriving under adverse conditions of soil and summer weather, hybrid petunias offer an abundance of bloom and beauty throughout the warm months. For porch and window boxes, hanging baskets, or masses of bloom in the border, the petunia is indispensable.

With single or double and ruffled or fluted flowers, it offers a wider range of floral color than almost any other annual. Shades of velvety purple, pale rose, and deep wine red are especially effective when used in combination with other annuals. The multiflora petunias are extremely prolific, while the grandiflora have fewer but larger flowers, often elaborately ruffled and striped or veined in contrasting colors. All are extraordinarily reliable and offer a perfection of bloom that places them in a class by themselves.

For early bloom, seeds should be sown indoors under lights or in a greenhouse 8 to 10 weeks before set-out time. The seed is very fine and should be spread thinly on the moistened medium and covered very lightly with dry, powdery or dusty soil that, once in place, should be gently moistened. The seedlings should be pricked out as soon as they can be handled and be transplanted singly into cell packs. Young plants may be set out in the garden when danger of frost is past. The tall, spreading cultivars that grow 1 to 2 feet tall should be spaced about 1 foot apart, while the dwarf

---

PETUNIA HYBRIDS AND CULTIVARS OF MERIT

SINGLE MULTIFLORA
Flowers mostly 2 to 2½ inches across, each a single funnel, abundantly borne, and unspotted by rain. Good bedding plants.

'Plum Pudding' hybrids: 10 to 12 inches tall; flowers red, pink, lilac, or yellow, with darker throat.

'Polo' hybrids: 12 to 15 inches tall; mounded habit; heat tolerant; flowers mostly shades of red-violet ('Burgundy Star') or pinkish ornage ('Salmon').

'Rainbow': 10 to 12 inches tall; flowers shades of red, pink, purple, blue, or yellow, or white.

'Sails' hybrids: 10 to 12 inches tall; flowers mostly pastel shades with dark veins ('Lacy Sails', blue with violet veins).

DOUBLE MULTIFLORA
Flowers 2 to 2½ inches across, fully double and ruffled, abundant, and unspotted by rain. Best grown in window boxes, tubs, and hanging baskets.

'Delight' hybrids: 10 to 12 inches tall; flowers red, pink, blue, white, and bicolor.

'Sweet Tart' hybrids: 10 to 12 inches tall; flowers red to white and bicolor, somewhat more fragrant than most.

FLORIBUNDA

Flowers mostly 2½ to 3 inches across, single, and otherwise similar to (and not always distinguishable from) single multiflora petunias. Useful as bedding plants and in containers.

'Celebrity' hybrids: 8 to 10 inches tall; very compact, heat tolerant; flowers red, white, blue, burgundy, and salmon, including pastels, early to bloom.

'Ice' hybrids: 8 to 10 inches tall; very compact; flowers rose pink to off white with darker veins, especially in throat.

'Madness' hybrids: 10 to 12 inches tall; spreading to 16 inches; flowers red to white, including red-violet, some with contrasting veins, borne prolifically.

'Picotee' hybrids: 10 to 12 inches tall; flowers about 3 inches across, red to purple with white border; 'Hoolahoop' (red with white border), is especially effective.

'Starship' hybrids: 9 to 12 inches tall; flowers red to purple, each with five radiating white bands.

SINGLE GRANDIFLORA

Flowers 3½ to 5½ inches or more across, single but often ruffled, and more or less subject to rain spotting. Not as prolific as multiflora types, but their larger size compensates. Useful as bedding plants and in containers.

'Apple Blossom': 8 to 10 inches tall; flowers light pink, fringed.

'California Girl': 10 to 12 inches tall; flowers yellow.

'Cascade' hybrids: 8 to 10 inches tall; compact; flowers red, pink, or lilac.

'Cloud' hybrids: 9 to 12 inches tall; spreading; flowers red to white, also purple.

'Countdown' hybrids: 10 to 12 inches tall; flowers 3 to 4½ inches across, red to white, purple, some bicolors, early to bloom (50 days from seed).

'Daddy' hybrids: 12 to 14 inches tall; flowers red to white, lavender, with darker veins, early to bloom.

'Flair' hybrids: 10 to 14 inches tall; spreading to 2 feet; flowers 3½ to 4 inches across, red to white, blue, salmon.

'Fluffy Ruffles': 15 to 18 inches tall; flowers 5 to 6 inches across, heavily ruffled, mostly red to white, often bicolor or tricolor, with dark veining in throat.

'Master' hybrids: 9 to 12 inches tall; flowers mostly shades of red, relatively less subject to rain spotting than others single grandifloras.

'Prio' hybrids: 8 to 9 inches tall; flowers red to white, purple; relatively less subject to rain spotting than other single grandifloras.

'Razzle Dazzle' hybrids: 8 to 10 inches tall; compact in habit; flowers 4 to 5 inches across, red to white, salmon, violet, relatively abundant.

'Ultra' hybrids: 10 to 12 inches tall; compact habit; flowers early to appear, red to white, salmon, purple, early to bloom; relatively less subject to rain spotting than other single grandifloras.

DOUBLE GRANDIFLORA

Flowers 3½ to 4 (exceptionally to 5) inches across, fully double and fringed, sometimes relatively few but usually very conspicuous nonetheless, and suffer in heavy rain. Best used in containers.

'Blue Danube': 10 to 12 inches tall; flowers light blue, veined purple.

'Bouquet' hybrids: 10 to 12 inches tall; compact habit; flowers red to white, purple, some bicolor, very full, early to bloom.

'Purple Pirouette': 10 to 12 inches tall; flowers purple with white border.

'Red and White Double Empress': 8 to 10 inches tall; flowers red and white.

'Sonata': 10 to 12 inches tall; flowers white.

'Think Pink': 10 to 12 inches tall; flowers 4 to 5 inches across, pink.

'Valentine': 10 to 12 inches tall; flowers red.

'White Swan': 8 to 9 inches tall; flowers about 4 inches across, white, amply fringed.

forms, reaching no more than 10 or 12 inches, should be set about 6 inches apart.

Having a longer season of bloom than most annuals, petunias may become spindly in late summer; by cutting them back, new growth will soon branch out from the base. Hybrid petunias may survive winters in zones 9 and 10, but as survival is usually erratic and uncertain, it is best to begin with fresh material each spring.

PHLOX DRUMMONDII
(Annual phlox)

The several wild progenitor species of the annual garden phlox are native to Texas. Long hybridized, the resultant cultivars are all grouped under *P. drummondii.* Since its introduction into cultivation, this complex has become one of our most useful edging and low border annuals. It is especially well adapted to regions with cool summers. There are many variations in flower form and color which, taken together, provide an interesting carpet of bright, jewel-like tones. Colors are red, pink, salmon, purple, pale yellow, and white, sometimes occurring as bicolors.

In the South, annual phlox is often started in the fall and grown as a winter annual, since it can endure temperatures in the 20s (°F) and bloom on. South of zone 7, seed may be planted in the fall or in earliest spring in the open, with flowering beginning in mid to late spring. Elsewhere, sowing indoors under lights or in a greenhouse is advisable. Seedlings are readily transplanted; those of dwarf cultivars, which seldom exceed 6 or 7 inches in height, should be planted about 6 inches apart, while taller types are best spaced about 9 inches apart. Annual phlox thrives in open, sunny locations and does better on poor, sandy soil than on rich loam. If plants are not allowed to reseed, especially in hot weather, flowering will continue into fall.

Hybrids and cultivars of *P. drummondii* are characterized primarily by plant size and petal form. The most meritorious are the following.

'Brilliant': 12 to 18 inches tall; flowers in wide color range, long season of bloom (but cease in mid and late summer heat, resuming in milder weather).

'Dwarf Beauty' hybrids: 6 to 7 inches tall; flowers in wide color range.

'Globe' hybrids: 7 to 8 inches tall; similar to 'Dwarf Beauty' hybrids.

'Petticoat' hybrids: 4 to 6 inches tall; flowers in wide color range; somewhat more heat tolerant than taller cultivars.

'Twinkle': 6 to 8 inches tall; flowers in wide color range; petals fringed or pointed.

TAGETES *SPP.*
(Marigold)

Although the terms *French, African, Mexican,* and *American* have been applied to hybrid marigolds, all of their prototypic species are native to tropical America. Over the years, hybridizers have performed near miracles in developing these showy, dependable flowers. Today's cultivars include carnation-flowered and chrysanthemum-flowered and small singles to very large and full doubles, with colors mainly yellow and orange, but ranging from mahogany brown to creamy white. Plants mature at only a few inches tall or rise to 4 feet or more, varying in habit from wide spreading to narrowly erect.

Beyond their aesthetic value, marigolds, both wild and cultivated, are of utilitarian

African marigold
(*Tagetes erecta* 'Jubilee Yellow')

French marigold
(*Tagetes patula*)

HYBRIDS AND CULTIVARS OF MERIT OF THE AFRICAN, AZTEC, OR AMERICAN MARIGOLD (*T. ERECTA*)
Upright habit and double flowers.

'Climax' hybrids: 2½ to 3 feet tall; flowers 3½ to 4½ inches across, very double, ruffled, light yellow.
　'Primrose Climax': light yellow, medium yellow.
　'Yellow Climax': medium yellow.
　'Golden Climax': deep yellow.
　'Toreador': deep orange.
'Crackerjack' hybrids: about 2 feet tall; foliage deeply dissected; flowers 3 to 4 inches across, yellow, gold, or orange.
'Crush' hybrids: 8 to 9 inches tall; flowers about 4 inches across, yellow or orange, early to bloom.
'Discovery' hybrids: 8 to 10 inches tall; flowers 4 to 5 inches across, yellow or orange, heat resistant.
'Dwarf Dolly' hybrids: 10 to 12 inches tall; flowers 3½ to 4 inches across, yellow, gold, or orange.
'Galore' hybrids: 16 to 18 inches tall; flowers 3½ to 4½ inches across, yellow or gold, prolific.
'Giant Fluffy' hybrids: 2 to 2½ feet tall; flowers 3 to 3½ inches across, yellow or orange.
'Gold Coin' hybrids: 2½ to 3 feet tall; flowers 3 to 4 inches across, yellow, gold, or orange.
'Inca' hybrids: 16 to 18 inches tall; flowers 4 to 5 inches across, yellow, gold, or orange, early to bloom; heat resistant.
'Jubilee' hybrids: 1½ to 2 feet tall; flowers 4 to 5 inches across, spherical, yellow, gold, or orange, early to bloom.
'Lady' hybrids: 18 to 20 inches tall; flowers 3 to 3½ inches across, yellow, gold, or orange.
'Merrymum' hybrids: 18 to 20 inches tall; flowers 2 to 2½ inches across, divided petals, yellow, gold, or orange.
'Odorless' hybrids: 1½ to 2 feet tall; nearly odorless foliage; flowers 3½ to 4 inches across, yellow, gold, or orange.
'Snowbird' and 'Snowdrift': 1½ to 2 feet tall; flowers 2½ to 3½ inches across, creamy white; less staunch and with a briefer blooming period than most.
'Space Age' hybrids: 12 to 14 inches tall; flowers early to appear, about 3 inches across, early to bloom.
　'Moonshot': yellow.
　'Viking': gold.
　'Apollo': orange.
'Sugar and Spice': 18 to 20 inches tall; flowers 3 to 3½ inches across, yellow, gold, orange, or cream.
'Sweet 'n Yellow': 20 to 24 inches tall; foliage nearly odorless; flowers 3½ to 3¾ inches across, densely double, yellow.

TRIPLOID OR TETRAPLOID HYBRIDS (*T. ERECTA* × *T. PATULA*) OF MERIT

'Fireworks' hybrids: 12 to 14 inches tall; flowers about 2¾ inches across, double, yellow, deep yellow, orange, or red-brown with yellow, prolific.
'Nugget' hybrids: 10 to 12 inches tall; flowers about 2 inches across, double, yellow, deep yellow, orange, or red-brown, prolific.
'Superstar Orange' hybrids: 14 to 16 inches tall; flowers 2½ to 3 inches across, double, orange, prolific.
'Zenith' hybrids: 10 to 12 inches tall; flowers early to appear 2½ to 3 inches across, crested (i.e., outer petals surround a densely doubled and raised center), yellow, orange, or red-brown with yellow, prolific, early to bloom (seven to eight weeks from seed).

HYBRIDS AND CULTIVARS OF MERIT
OF THE FRENCH MARIGOLD (*T. PATULA*)
Low, spreading habit, unless otherwise noted.

'Aurora' hybrids: 10 to 12 inches tall; flowers 2½ to 3 inches across, double, yellow, light yellow, or red-brown with orange edge, profilic, early to bloom (about seven weeks from seed).

'Bolero': 12 to 14 inches tall; flowers mahogany red and yellow.

'Bonita' hybrids: 10 to 12 inches tall; flowers 2½ to 3 inches across, double, yellow, orange, or red-brown.

'Boy' hybrids: 6 to 8 inches tall; flowers 2½ to 3 inches across, crested,* yellow, gold, orange, or red-brown, early to bloom (six to seven weeks from seed).

'Burgundy Ripple': 12 to 14 inches tall; flowers 2 to 2½ inches across, single, maroon with yellow edge.

'Cheerful' hybrids: 8 to 10 inches tall; flowers 2 to 2½ inches across, crested,* yellow, gold, orange, or red-brown with orange center.

'Cinnabar': 12 to 14 inches tall; flowers 2 to 2½ inches across, single, maroon with orange center.

'Disco' hybrids: 8 to 10 inches tall; flowers about 2 inches across, double, yellow, orange, red-brown, or red-brown with yellow with yellow edge, prolific.

'Fireflame': 8 to 10 inches tall; flowers 2 to 2½ inches across, crested,* red-brown and yellow.

'Golden Gate': 8 to 10 inches tall; flowers 2 to 2½ inches across, double, deep yellow with red-brown at base, early to bloom (six to seven weeks from seed).

'Gypsy Sunshine': 6 to 8 inches tall; flowers 2 to 2½ inches across, crested,* yellow, prolific.

'Happy Days' hybrids: 8 to 10 inches tall; flowers about 2 inches across, double, yellow, orange, or red-brown.

'Hero' hybrids: 10 to 12 inches tall; flowers 2½ to 2¾ inches across, crested,* yellow, orange, red-brown, or red-brown with orange crest; heat resistant.

'Holiday Crested' hybrids: 10 to 12 inches tall; flowers 2 to 2½ inches across, crested,* yellow, orange, or red-brown, early to bloom (six to seven weeks from seed).

'Honeycomb': 10 to 12 inches tall; flowers about 2 inches across, double, deep red-brown edged with orange.

'Janie' hybrids: 6 to 8 inches tall; flowers 1½ to 1¾ inches across, crested,* light yellow, medium yellow, orange, or red-brown with orange edge, prolific, early to bloom (six to seven weeks from seed).

'Lemon Drop Improved': 6 to 8 inches tall; flowers 2 to 2½ inches across, double, yellow.

'Little Nell': 10 to 12 inches tall; flowers 3 to 3½ inches across, single, red-brown and yellow.

'Marietta' hybrids: 8 to 10 inches tall; flowers 2 to 2½ inches across, single, yellow with red-brown base.

'Pretty Joy' hybrids: 5 to 7 inches tall; flowers about 1½ inches across, double, yellow, yellow-orange, or red-brown, early to bloom (seven weeks from seed).

'Queen Sophia': 12 to 14 inches tall; flowers 2 to 2½ inches across, semidouble (i.e., low crested* or anemone flowered), red-brown edged with bronzy orange.

'Safari': 10 to 12 inches tall; flowers about 3 inches across, double, yellow, orange, or red-brown, early to bloom (seven to eight weeks from seed); heat resistant.

'Scarlet Sophie': 10 to 12 inches tall; flowers 2 to 2½ inches across, double, red-brown with faint orange border.

'Sophia' hybrids: 10 to 12 inches tall; flowers about 2½ inches across, double, yellow, orange, red-brown, or red-brown with yellow edge.

'Susie Wong': 10 to 12 inches tall; flowers 3 to 3½ inches across, single, yellow.

'Teeny Weeny': 4 to 5 inches tall; flowers 2 to 2½ inches across, single, red-brown mottled with yellow; wide spreading.

'Tiger Eyes': 12 to 14 inches tall; flowers 2 to 2½ inches across, red-brown with yellow crest.*

* Outer petals surround a densely doubled and raised center.

interest because of the biocidal substances that mature plants of certain kinds secrete from their roots. Varying degrees of control over slugs and nematodes have been reported. Marigolds may also control a number of important weeds as well: ground ivy (*Glechoma hederacea*), bindweed (*Calystegia sepium*), and couch grass (*Agropyron* spp.). Rabbits are repelled by marigold's aromatic foliage. Plants intended for such purposes should be started indoors at least eight weeks before set-out time.

In sunny locations, marigolds provide more color for effort expended than almost any other annual. From midsummer, marigolds may be counted on for generous bloom. They may be used as the dominant note in the late summer garden, or they may play a minor role by filling in an occasional gap here and there. In the cutting garden, they are equally valuable. They are so profligate with their bloom that they may be cut with lavish abandon and great bowls of them will carry the rich yellow and orange tones of late summer into the house, until first frost.

Hybrid marigolds are of the easiest culture. The seed is manageably large and germinates readily, and seedlings are easily transplanted. Indeed, they may be moved into the garden while in full flower. They are tolerant of poor soil and will thrive under almost any condition, in full sun or partial shade, in wet or dry ground. Ideal, however, is a location in full sun with moist well-drained soil of at least average fertility. Once the threat of frost is past, seed may be sown in the open where the plants are to grow. Or sow indoors in a sunny window or under lights 8 to 10 weeks before set-out time for dwarf hybrids, or about 7 weeks for the faster-growing tall sorts. It is important that seedlings of the tall hybrids not become pot bound and arrested in cell packs, as they will often not resume growth or flower satisfactorily, even if transplanted to optimal garden conditions. In many cultivars, intense summer heat may suspend flowering, but triploid or "mule" types are less heat senstive.

Hybrid marigolds, for the most part, comprise two classes, each derived from a different wild species.

ZINNIA ELEGANS
(Common zinnia)

Zinnias are among the most popular of the annuals, and they have much to recommend them. They offer wide variations in form and coloring, they bloom over a long period, they will endure drought and succeed when all else fails, and the brilliantly colored flowers add immeasurably to the beauty of gardens, from midsummer through early autumn. In size, zinnias range from the tiny 'Thumbelina' strain, suitable for edging, to the so-called giant cultivars that reach 3 feet high and bear flowers 6 inches or more across. Flowers may be single, crested, or double, and some have curled or quilled petals.

As a midsummer cut flower, zinnia is difficult to surpass. It is even superior to the marigold, because it has the added advantage of a much wider color range and the capacity to flourish in hot weather. In addition to reds, pinks, oranges, yellows (including one approaching green), and creamy white, multicolored blooms are also available.

Less commonly grown is the narrow-leaf zinnia (*Z. angustifolia*), a slender-stemmed, medium plant, with a generous and continuous production of single orange or white flowers. Its foliage is free of the powdery mildew that often attacks *Z. elegans* in hot, humid weather. The 'Pinwheel' hybrids of *Z. angustifolia* and *Z. elegans* are similar and have red, pink, or white flowers.

Another species, *Z. haageana*, is best known by its bicolor cultivars 'Old Mexico' and 'Persian Carpet'. Many popular zinnia cultivars have resulted from crosses between *Z. haageana* and *Z. elegans*.

Z. ELEGANS HYBRIDS AND CULTIVARS OF MERIT
All with double flowers (dahlia flowered) in red, pink, orange, yellow, lilac, or white, unless otherwise noted.

TALL (2 TO 3½ FEET)
'Big Red': flowers 5 to 6 inches across, deep red, early to bloom (seven weeks from seed).
'Big Tetra' hybrids: 2 to 2½ feet tall; flowers 5 to 6 inches across, in all colors but lilac purple; tetraploid.
'Big Top' hybrids: flowers 6 to 8 inches across, cactus flowered.*
'Envy Double' hybrids: flowers 3 to 4 inches across, chartreuse or pale yellow-green.
'Fruit Bowl' hybrids: flowers 6 to 8 inches across, cactus flowered.*
'Giant-flowered', syn. 'California Giants': flowers 4 to 5 inches across.
　　'Scarlet Queen': red.
　　'Exquisite': pink.
　　'Canary Bird': yellow.
　　'Purity': white.
'Peppermint-stick' hybrids: flowers 3 to 4 inches across, cream streaked or striped with red, orange, or red-violet.
'Ruffles' hybrids: flowers 6 to 7 inches across, ruffled, in all colors but lilac purple.
'Scabious-flowered' hybrids: flowers 3 to 3½ inches across, crested, red, orange, yellow, or cream.
'State Fair' hybrids: flowers 5 to 6 inches across; tetraploid.
'Sunshine' hybrids: flowers 4 to 5 inches across.
'Zenith' hybrids: flowers 5½ to 6 inches across, cactus flowered.*
　　'Firecracker': red.
　　'Goddess': salmon.
　　'Rosy Future': rose pink.
　　'Torch': orange.
　　'Yellow Zenith': yellow.

MEDIUM (1½ TO 2 FEET)
'Border Beauty' hybrids: flowers 3 to 4 inches across, double or semidouble, red, rose pink, salmon, orange, yellow, or cream.
'Bouquet' hybrids: flowers 3 to 3½ inches across, somewhat ruffled, red, rose pink, pink, orange, yellow, or white, prolific.
'Burpeana' hybrids: flowers 5 to 5½ inches across, cactus flowered.*
　　'Red Mom': red.
　　'Big Snowman': white.
'Candy Cane' hybrids: flowers 3½ to 4 inches across, double or semidouble, white or yellow flecked or striped pink or red.
'Chippendale': flowers 3 to 3½ inches across, single, dark red with yellow tips.
'Cut and Come Again': flowers about 2½ inches across, prolific.
'Lilliput' hybrids: flowers 1½ to 2 inches across, prolific.
'Splendor' hybrids: flowers 4 to 5 inches across, somewhat ruffled, red, pink, orange, or yellow.
'Sun' hybrids: flowers about 4 inches across.
　　'Red Sun': red.
　　'Yellow Sun': yellow.
'Whirligig' hybrids: flowers 3 to 4½ inches across.
'Yellow Marvel': flowers about 2½ inches across, yellow.

SHORT (6 TO 15 INCHES)
'Button Box' hybrids: flowers about 1½ inches across, red, rose, pink, or yellow.
'Dasher' hybrids: flowers 3 to 3½ inches across, double and semidouble, early to bloom.
'Fantastic Light Pink': flowers 3 to 4 inches across, pink.

'Marvel' hybrids: flowers 3 to 4 inches across.

'Parasol' hybrids: flowers 2½ to 3½ inches across; grows and blooms well in cool temperatures.

'Peter Pan' hybrids: flowers 3 to 5 inches across.

'Pulcino Double' hybrids: flowers about 2½ inches across.

'Red Lollipop': flowers about 2½ inches across, deep red.

'Scarlet Parasol': flowers 3½ to 4 inches across, red.

'Small World' hybrids: flowers 2 to 2½ inches across, prolific.

'Sombrero': flowers 2 to 2½ inches across, single, red with yellow tips.

'Starlight', syn. 'Starlet': flowers 3 to 3½ inches across, double and semidouble.

'Thumbelina' hybrids: flowers 1 to 1½ inches across.

* The rays ("petals") are irregularly rolled in.

OTHER ZINNIA SPECIES, HYBRIDS, AND CULTIVARS OF MERIT

Z. *ANGUSTIFOLIA*, SYN. *Z. LINEARIS*

'Classic': 8 to 10 inches tall; flowers about 1½ inches across, single, orange, prolific.

'Linearis': 6 to 8 inches tall; flowers about 2 inches across, single, orange with yellow band, prolific.

'Orange Star': 6 to 8 inches tall; flowers about 1½ inches across, single, orange, prolific.

'Pinwheel': 10 to 12 inches tall; flowers 2½ to 3 inches across, single, red, rose pink, salmon, orange, or white with yellow-orange center.

Z. *HAAGEANA*

'Old Mexico': 12 to 15 inches tall; flowers 2 to 2½ inches across, red-brown tipped yellow, red tipped yellow, or yellow tipped red.

'Persian Carpet': 10 to 12 inches tall; flowers 1½ to 2 inches across, double or semidouble, orange tipped yellow or red tipped orange.

Whatever the species or cultivar, zinnias are of easiest culture and thrive under widely varying conditions, as long as sun exposure is generous and extended and the soil is well drained. The seed of these tender annuals may be sown indoors under lights or in a greenhouse six to eight weeks before set-out time. Or sow directly in the garden after danger of frost is past. Seed should be firmly covered with ¼ inch of soil or oil mix, as the seed must be in the dark to germinate.

Transplanting may be undertaken at any stage, even when plants are in full flower. The dwarf cultivars, maturing at no more than 1½ feet, should be spaced about 9 inches apart, while the tall sorts should stand about 1 foot apart.

Zinnia elegans 'Big Red'

Narrow-leaf zinnia (*Zinnia linearis*)

OTHER ANNUALS OF MERIT

To add special interest to the garden, it is a good idea to include some annuals that are less commonly seen, though, in most cases, no more difficult to grow and maintain than the ubiquitous favorites. Some of the following were once highly prized but in time slipped from favor, often for unknown reasons. They continue to offer much decorative value and deserve consideration.

ABELMOSCHUS *SPP.*
(Flowering okra)

There are two dissimilar species of flowering okra. Both are rather hibiscus-like and easily grown. Sometimes still listed under *Hibiscus*, the stately yellow flowering okra (*A. manihot*) reaches 6 to 8 feet and from mid to late summer begins to bear a long series of huge, light yellow, mallowlike flowers 6 to 8 inches across, each with a deep purple center. Each flower lasts one day, but the numerous buds produce bloom that lasts for weeks, much as in the related hollyhock. Perennial where native in tropical Asia, yellow flowering okra survives winters in zones 9 and 10 and may elsewhere, if roots and stem bases are protected from frost. Although it performs best in hot summer weather, direct sun causes the leaves to noticeably but harmlessly wilt. Variable in the wild as to leaf lobing, blooming period, and flower size, the yellow flowering okra available commercially is large leafed, large flowered, and blooms mostly in late summer when day and night length are about equal. Flower size diminishes when night temperatures fall below 50°F. Although some catalogs list 'Cream Cup' and 'Golden Bowl' as cultivars, these are merely large-flowered extremes of wild plants. Seed is produced abundantly in the large, bristly (and inedible) pods, and self-sowing occurs as far north as zone 7.

Lower, more branched and smaller in leaf and flower is red flowering okra (*A. moschatus*). It, too, requires hot summer

Red-flowering okra (*Abelmoschus moschatus*)

weather to flourish and usually grows 1½ to 2 feet tall. The 4- to 5-inch flowers are usually all red, but some may be pink or have white-based petals. Performing best in zones 8 to 10, where it readily self-sows, red flowering okra may prove disappointing farther north, where cool nights depress bud formation. The cultivar series 'Pacific' hybrids consists of compact plants (12 to 15 inches tall) and includes 'Pacific Light Pink' and 'Pacific Orange Scarlet' (syn. 'Oriental Red' and 'Mischief'), both with white petal bases.

Both species are best started from seed sown indoors under lights or in a greenhouse, especially from zone 8 north, about eight weeks before set-out time. Full sun and a continuously moist, well-drained soil of average fertility yield best results. If grown in large pots or tubs, the plants may be moved into a greenhouse with the approach of frost and wintered over in a semidormant state. In the garden, yellow flowering okra should be planted about 1½ feet apart and red flowering okra about 1 foot.

ABUTILON × HYBRIDUM
(Flowering maple)

Although usually treated as a houseplant north of zone 9, flowering maple is easily grown from seed, and if placed so that the hanging bell-like flowers may be seen beneath the leaves, it makes a charming contribution to the garden. The handsome lobed leaves are ornamental in their own right.

Seed-grown plants may reach 2 feet by summer's end, but careful pinching of terminal shoots keeps them lower, more compact, and better suited to potting up in fall for indoor display. Exposure to strong afternoon sun causes temporary wilting and, if soil moisture is inadequate, loss of the oldest leaves, resulting in legginess. As flower-color transmission by seed is unpredictable, flowering maple is offered as a mixture, with colors ranging from purple through red, pink, salmon to yellow, and white, often with contrasting veins. Propagation by cuttings is easily achieved and ensures color integrity. Seed should be started indoors under lights or in a greenhouse eight to 10 weeks before set-out time. A 70° to 80°F soil temperature is required for germination. Flowering usually begins about 100 days after sowing. Ordinary, well-drained soil in a location exposed to morning sun brings best results. Plants should be planted 1 to 1½ feet apart in the garden.

Several flower-color cultivar selections are available as living plants or cuttings, any of which may turn up in seed-grown mixtures.

'Albus' (white).
'Luteus' (yellow).
'Nabob' (burgundy).
'Roseus' (pale pink with dark veins).
'Tangerine' (orange with pink veins).
'Vesuvius Red' (scarlet).

Some cultivars have leaves variegated white or yellow. A number of other species, all of which become shrubs south of zone 8, are sometimes grown, including the following.

A. megapotamicum: long-stalked, pendent flowers, usually red, sometimes with yellow.
A. pictum: usually yellow-variegated foliage; pinkish orange flowers.
A. vitifolium, syn. *Corynabutilon vitifolium*: lavender or white flowers.

AGERATUM HOUSTONIANUM

Ageratum varies in size from the familiar very dwarf, compact types (sometimes no taller than 6 inches) to tall, branching cultivars that may reach 2 feet or more. The pale lavender blue flowers are always welcome in the garden and, in the taller forms, are also excellent for cutting. White, pink, and dark blue cultivars are also obtainable, but these colors are often dull or flat. Extraordinarily dwarf ageratums bear witness to assiduous efforts by plant breeders to improve compactness and flower color, durability, and showiness.

Ageratum is a tender annual. For early bloom, the seed should be sown indoors under lights, in a sunny window, or in a greenhouse, six to eight weeks before set-out time. Sowings made outdoors in late spring will ensure end-of-season bloom. As ageratum seed requires light to germinate, it should not be covered with anything but the merest layer of fine dust. Ageratum self-sows so abundantly that it often reestablishes itself in the garden year after year, especially from zone 8 south. If faded blooms are removed and the plants not allowed to form seed, the planting will look neater and remain in full bloom right up until frost. The dwarf cultivars are traditional edging material and the plants should be spaced 4 to 6 inches apart. Taller sorts, best arranged in groups, should be set 10 to 14 inches apart.

Among the many cultivars in commerce are the following.

'Adriatic Improved': 6 to 8 inches tall; uniformly compact; flowers early to bloom, medium blue.

'Bavaria': 18 to 20 inches tall; flowers blue tipped with deep blue.

'Blue Blazer': 6 to 8 inches tall; flowers bluish mauve.

'Blue Danube': 5 to 6 inches tall; flowers lavender blue.

'Blue Horizon': 18 to 30 inches tall; flowers held in 3-inch clusters; medium blue.

'Blue Lagoon': 6 to 8 inches tall; flowers early to bloom, medium blue.

'Blue Mink': 8 to 10 inches tall; flowers prolific, lavender blue.

'Blue Ribbon': 6 to 8 inches tall; wide spreading; flowers cover the entire plant, medium blue.

'Capri': 8 to 12 inches tall; flowers medium blue with white centers.

'Hawaii' hybrids: 6 to 8 inches tall; flowers prolific, blue, lavender, or white.

'North Sea': 6 to 8 inches tall; red-violet buds opening blue-violet.

'Pink Powderpuffs': 7 to 9 inches tall; flowers slow to lose color; rose pink.

'Royal Delft': 5 to 7 inches tall; flowers deep violet blue.

'Southern Cross': 8 to 12 inches tall; flowers blue with pale centers.

'Summer Show': 4 to 6 inches tall; flowers white.

'White Cushion': 9 to 12 inches tall; flowers white.

AMARANTHUS SPP.
(Amaranth)

Although the foliage is coarse and the habit weedy, *Amaranthus* includes three very ornamental annuals worthy of inclusion in any garden, as long as there is adequate space. All three are native to the tropics, hence they require long, hot summers to perform well in the garden. The actual flowers are minute, but are borne in dense, colorful clusters or among brightly colored leaves.

North of zone 8, it is best to start seedlings indoors under lights or in a greenhouse six to eight weeks before set-out time. It is important to take care to sow the seed thinly and to provide 75° to 80°F daytime temperatures (no lower than 60°F at night). Seedlings should be transplanted to cell packs or individual pots, given bright light, and have a growing medium that is constantly moist but not soggy. If growth is slowed or interrupted in the initial weeks, stunted plants of substandard ornamental value often result.

Love-lies-bleeding or tassel flower (*A. caudatus*) grows 4 to 5 feet high and produces very long, drooping, blood red tassels that reach the ground and last all summer. The tassels, however, soon lose their color if picked and dried. Staking is required. Lower-growing (1½ to 2 feet) and equally ornamental with erect tassels is the cultivar 'Green Thumb', with spikes ranging from emerald green to cream. *A. hypochondriacus* 'Pygmy Torch' is similar in habit, but the tassels are maroon.

Prince's feather (*A. cruentus*), a cereal grain in tropical America, grows 3 to 6 feet tall and is decorative with reddish or purplish foliage and large reddish plumed flower clusters. Staking is usually necessary. Fountain plant (*A. tricolor*), 3 to 6 feet tall, bears large bicolor or tricolor leaves. In some forms, the uppermost leaves are brilliant shades of red. Staking is necessary. In addition to *A. tricolor* var. *salicifolius*, with narrow, drooping leaves, the following cultivars are of merit.

'Early Splendor': 3 to 5 feet tall; greenish purple stems and lower foliage, uppermost leaves large and scarlet, persist for weeks.

'Flaming Fountains': 3 to 5 feet tall; narrow-leaf form, uppermost foliage carmine, scarlet, and bronze.

Love-lies-bleeding (*Amaranthus caudatus*)

'Illumination': 3 to 4 feet tall; similar to 'Early Splendor' but with touches of yellow on the uppermost scarlet leaves.

'Joseph's Coat': 4 to 6 feet tall; lower foliage chocolate, yellow, and green, the uppermost leaves upright and light red with golden yellow.

'Molten Fire': 3 to 5 feet tall; lower leaves deep red-violet, uppermost leaves scarlet.

'Perfecta' or 'Splendens Perfecta': 3 to 4 feet tall; all leaves red, yellow, and green.

ARCTOTIS VENUSTA
(Blue-eyed African daisy)

Blue-eyed African daisy is classed among the worthy annuals because of the simple beauty of its flower, which resembles a white daisy with long point-ed petals, lavender on the under side, and a steel blue center. Each flower is borne in summer on a long, graceful, almost leafless stem and is excellent for cutting as it lasts extremely well. Blue-eyed African daisy reaches a height of 15 to 18 inches and will continue to bloom throughout the summer if the fading blooms are removed. It is very tolerant of poor soil and drought, which makes it particularly valuable for the gardener who must struggle against such handicaps. In fact, rich, moist soil encourages lank, floppy growth and a paucity of flowers.

Blue-eyed African daisy is a half-hardy annual. The seed should be sown indoors under lights or in a greenhouse six to eight weeks before set-out time, or later in the season either in coldframes or directly in the garden where they are to flower. Sow thinly and cover with about ⅛ inch of fine soil. Plants should be spaced 10 to 12 inches apart in the garden. It is remarkably free from pests and diseases, and since it is so modest in its demands regarding soil and moisture, it may be classed among the most easily grown annu-als. In zones 9 and 10 it may overwinter.

ASCLEPIAS CURASSAVICA
(Bloodflower milkweed)

Bloodflower, a tropical perennial grown as an annual north of zone 9, in bloom superficially resembles the native perennial butterfly weed (A. tuberosa), but it is upright in habit (3 to 4 feet tall) and comes into flower about 5 months from seed. When examined closely, it is seen that the bloodflower's petals are cinnabar red and its inner corona orange (both are orange in butterfly weed). If the pods are kept from maturing, flower-ing continues until night temperatures dip below 50°F.

Bloodflower milkweed
(Asclepias curassavica)

Seed should be started indoors under lights or in a greenhouse 8 to 10 weeks before set-out time. Sow the seed thinly and cover with about ¼ inch of soil mix. Transfer the seedlings to cell packs. Rich, moist soil and full sun are requisite for abundant bloom. Plants should be spaced 1 to 1½ feet apart in the garden. Bloodflower is especially effective in regions having long, hot, humid summers.

BROWALLIA SPECIOSA

Blue is a color that is found none too frequently among the annuals, and for this reason, browallia is especially prized for its abundant bloom throughout the summer. The wide-open, tubular flowers are violet blue or white and are decora-tive not only in the garden but perhaps even more so in containers, especially if seen at close range. Browallia grows 8 to 14 inches tall and wide and produces flowers that range from 1½ to 2 inches across. Less commonly grown is the similar B. americana (syn. B. elata), with somewhat viscid foliage and smaller flowers.

Browallia seed should be started 10 to 12 weeks before set-out time indoors under lights or in a greenhouse. The seed is very fine and should be scattered thinly on the surface and lightly pressed into the soil mix, which, if kept moist and at 70°F, will yield seedlings in about a week. These should be transferred to cell packs in about a month to continue slow growth. Plants should be pinched back when 4 to 6 inches tall to induce branching.

Browallia performs best when grown in partial shade in well-drained soil of average fertility. Excessive moisture or fertilizer results in much foliage and little bloom. Spacing should roughly equal the expected height. Dwarf cultivars are especially useful as edging material.

The following cultivars are meritorious both for garden beds and for culture in pots, window boxes, and hanging baskets.

'Blue Bells Improved': 12 to 18 inches tall; self-branching; flowers about 1½ inches across, opening violet blue, aging to powder blue.

'Blue Troll': 8 to 10 inches tall; flowers about 1½ inches across, blue-violet.

'Dawn Blue': 15 to 20 inches tall; flowers about 1½ inches across, pale lilac blue.

'Heavenly Bells': 9 to 12 inches tall; flowers about 2 inches across, pale sky blue.

'Jingle Bells' hybrids: 9 to 14 inches tall; flowers about 1½ inches across, blue, lavender, or white.

'Major': 10 to 14 inches tall; flowers 2 inches across, lavender blue.

'Marine Bells': 8 to 10 inches tall; flowers about 1½ inches across, indigo blue.

'Powder Blue': 10 to 14 inches tall; flowers about 1½ inches across, blue.

'Silver Bells': 10 to 14 inches tall; flowers about 1½ inches across, white.

'Sky Bells': 8 to 10 inches tall; flowers about 1½ inches across, powder blue.

'Vanja': 10 to 14 inches tall; flowers about 2 inches across, blue with white center.

'White Bells': 6 to 8 inches tall; flowers about 1½ inches across, white.

'White Troll': 10 to 12 inches tall; slower growing than most; flowers about 1½ inches across, white, abundant.

Calendula officinalis

CALENDULA OFFICINALIS

There is a clean, simple quality in the yellow or orange blooms of calendula that is very appealing. A hardy annual tolerant of considerable frost, calendula may be grown in the garden throughout the winter in zones 9 and 10. In the North, calendula is grown mostly as a summer annual, but it is also popular as a greenhouse plant to supply flowers for cutting during the winter. Although calendula performs best where summer temperatures are relatively cool (60° to 80°F), a number of cultivars show heat tolerance by flowering more or less continuously through the summer.

In much of zone 9 and in zone 10, fall-sown seed will yield flowers through all but the coldest periods of winter. In zones 7 and 8, fall-sown seed will produce flowering plants by mid to late spring. Elsewhere, seed may be sown outdoors from spring through midsummer, with the expectation of bloom beginning in about eight weeks. For early bloom in the North, seed may be sown indoors under lights, in a sunny window, or in a greenhouse. Seed must be covered to exclude light. Seedlings should be transplanted 8 to 12 inches apart for standard cultivars, which grow 12 to 18 inches tall, or 6 to 8 inches apart for dwarf types. Calendula is not only good border material but is valuable in the cutting garden. Most any reasonably well-drained, moderately fertile soil is suitable.

Among the many hybrids and cultivars available, the following are distinctive.

'Art Shades' hybrids: 18 to 24 inches tall; flowers 2 to 2½ inches across, cream to deep orange, most with contrasting centers.

'Bon Bon' hybrids: 10 to 12 inches tall; more heat tolerant than most; flowers about 3 inches across, yellow or orange.

'Coronet' hybrids: 10 to 12 inches tall; more heat tolerant than most; flowers 3 to 4 inches across, yellow or orange.

'Crested' hybrids: 18 to 24 inches tall; flowers 3 inches across, yellow or orange, crested centers.

'Dwarf Gem' hybrids, 10 to 12 inches tall; flowers 2½ to 3 inches across, yellow to deep orange, double.

'Fiesta Gitana' hybrids: 10 to 12 inches tall; flowers 2½ to 3 inches across, cream to deep orange.

'Geisha Girl': 18 to 24 inches tall; flowers about 3 inches across, orange, incurved rays.

'Hen and Chicks': 18 to 24 inches tall; flowers 2 to 2½ inches across, orange, a circle of small secondary flowers develops from the base of each normal flower head as it fades.

'Indian Song': 18 to 24 inches tall; flowers about 2½ inches across, yellow with a dark center.

'Kablouna' hybrids: 15 to 20 inches tall; flowers about 2½ inches across, yellow or orange, a quilled crest in the center.

'Mandarin Flower' hybrids: 12 to 18 inches tall; flowers 2½ to 3 inches across, orange, early to bloom.

'Pacific Beauty' hybrids: 12 to 15 inches tall; more heat tolerant than most; flowers 4 to 5 inches across, pale cream to deep red-orange.

'Prince' hybrids: 18 to 30 inches tall; flowers 2½ to 3 inches across, yellow or orange, double, rays more deeply colored on under surface.

'Radio Extra Selected': 16 to 20 inches tall; flowers 2½ to 3 inches across, orange, rays rolled downward along the edges (i.e., cactus flowered).

'Sunglow': 10 to 12 inches tall; flowers about 1 inch across, yellow, single, abundant.

CALLISTEPHUS CHINENSIS
(China aster)

Long an important source of cut flowers for florists and popular as a summer annual as well, the China aster is obtainable in a wide range of forms and colors and offers abundant bloom throughout the summer if early, midseason, and late-blooming cultivars are chosen. Flower forms vary from formal powder-puff types to curled, fluffy forms and wide-eyed singles. Colors range from deep purple through lavender and pink to white.

China aster thrives best in fertile, well-drained, humusy soil and full sun. From zone 7 north, seed should be sown indoors under lights or in a greenhouse about six weeks before set-out time. Sow the seed thinly, cover with about ⅛ inch of fine soil, and transplant seedlings to cell packs. As China aster is shallow rooted, cultivation should be avoided. To keep moisture levels up to their needs, summer mulch is advisable. Cultivars resistant to fusarium wilt and to stem rot should be selected. To further minimize the ravages of fusarium wilt, it is best to avoid planting China aster two successive years in the same location. If any plants fail during the season, they should be pulled and discarded off-site, not in the compost.

CATHARANTHUS ROSEUS
(Periwinkle, annual vinca)

Periwinkle, a tropical perennial, tolerates no frost and so is grown as a tender annual in all but zone 10. The glossy, dark green foliage contrasts handsomely with the wide-open red, pink, or white, often red-eyed flowers, which are borne singly and measure about 1½ inches across. Flowering is at its height in hot, humid summer weather; flower size diminishes with the onset of cool autumn nights. Plants range from erect and about 2 feet tall to prostrate.

Seed should be sown indoors under lights or in a greenhouse 8 to 10 weeks

HYBRIDS AND CULTIVARS OF CHINA ASTER
All bear double flowers unless otherwise indicated. Tall China asters should be spaced about 1 foot apart, medium sorts about 8 inches, and dwarfs about 6 inches.

TALL (18 TO 30 INCHES)
'Burpeeana Extra Early': flowers early to bloom, 2 to 2½ inches across, shades of purple and red, and white.

'Duchess' hybrids: wilt resistant; flowers 4 to 5 inches across, purple, red, peach, or yellow.

'Family Silvery Blue': flowers about 2½ inches across, white suffused with lavender, rays incurved.

'Giant Single Andrella': flowers 3 to 3½ inches across, single (daisylike), shades of purple and red and white, with yellow center.

'King Size Apricot': flowers 3 to 3½ inches across, yellowish salmon.

'Operetta' hybrids: flowers 3 to 3½ inches across, shades of purple and red, and white, chrysanthemum flowered.*

'Pastel' hybrids: wilt resistant; flowers 3 to 3½ inches across, pink, pale orange, yellow, lilac, rose cerise, or white.

'Pompon Splendid' hybrids: flowers early to bloom (90 days from seed), 2 to 2¼ inches across, red to lavender.

'Powderpuff' hybrids: wilt resistant; flowers 2 to 2½ inches across, quilled.†

'Seastar': flowers 4 to 5 inches across, shades of purple and red, also white, quilled,† curved rays.

'Super Princess Symphonie': flowers 3 to 3½ inches across, purple, red, or yellow, some with pale centers, tightly quilled.†

'Totem Pole Mixed': long stalked; flowers 4½ to 5 inches across, shades of purple or red, and white.

MEDIUM (12 TO 18 INCHES)
'Early Ostrich Plume' hybrids: branched from base; flowers 3½ to 4 inches across, shades of purple or red, and white, rays long and lax.

'Fluffy Ruffles' hybrids: flowers 4 to 5 inches across, shades of purple or red, and white.

'Gusford Supreme': wilt resistant; flowers 3 to 3½ inches across, red with large white center.

'Pompon' hybrids: flowers 1¾ to 2 inches across, shades of purple or red, and white, quilled† centers.

'Red Mound': flowers 3 to 3½ inches across, cinnabar red, rays relatively short.

DWARF (6 TO 12 INCHES)
'Blue Skies': flowers 2½ to 3 inches across, lavender blue, prolific.

'Carpet Ball' hybrids: flowers 2 to 2½ inches across, shades of purple or red, and white, form tight balls.

'Color Carpet' hybrids: flowers 3½ to 4 inches across, shades of purple or red, and white.

'Contraster' hybrids: flowers 2½ to 3 inches across, white, each ray longitudinally striped in shades of purple or red.

'Crimson Sunset': flowers 2 to 2½ inches across, dark red.

'Dwarf Queen' hybrids: wilt resistant; flowers early to bloom, 2½ to 3 inches across, purple to white.

'Gem' hybrids: wilt resistant; heat tolerant; flowers 2½ to 3 inches across, shades of purple or red, and white.

'Milady' hybrids: wilt resistant; flowers 2 to 2½ inches across, shades of purple or red, and white; long period of bloom.

'Pinocchio' hybrids: flowers 1½ to 2 inches across, shades of purple, red, or yellow, and white.

'Pot 'n Patio' hybrids: flowers early to bloom; require short days of early spring (in zones 8 and 9) and in late summer and fall (farther north) to bloom; shades of purple or red, and white.

'Ribbon hybrids': flowers early to bloom, 3 to 3½ inches across, violet blue or pink, rays strap shaped or ribbonlike.

'Pixie Princess' hybrids: flowers early to bloom, shades of blue or red, and white.

* The rays are rolled downward and are incurved.
† The petals are rolled downward along their edges.

before set-out time. Sow thinly and cover with about ⅛ inch of fine soil. The seed requires temperature of 70° to 80°F to germinate. Seedlings should be transferred to cell packs when they are large enough to handle. In the garden, a well-drained, sandy loam is ideal, but periwinkle adjusts to a wide range of soils. Full sun is required for optimal flowering. Spacing of erect, tall-growing forms should be equal to one-half to three-quarters of expected height or, in the case of prostrate or low-growing ones, the same fraction of expected spread.

Among the diverse cultivars available are the following.

'Bright Eyes' hybrids: 15 to 18 inches tall; flowers 1¼ to 1½ inches across, white with rose center or rose with red center.

'Cooler' hybrids: 6 to 8 inches tall; flowers 1¾ to 2¼ inches across, abundantly borne.

'Grape Cooler': rose with red center.

'Peppermint Cooler': white with red center.

'Blush': rose.

'Little' hybrids: 8 to 10 inches tall; flowers 1¾ to 2¼ inches across.

'Little Orchid': purplish pink.

'Little Pinkie': rose pink.

'Little Bright Eye': white with red center.

'Little Blanche': white.

'Magic Carpet' hybrids: 3 to 4 inches tall; spreads to 24 inches; flowers 2 to 2½ inches across, rose, pink, salmon, white, or bicolor.

'Morning Mist': 12 to 16 inches tall; flowers 2 to 2¼ inches across, white with rose center.

'Parasol': 10 to 12 inches tall; flowers 2¼ to 2½ inches across, profusely borne, white with rose center.

'Pink Carousel': 3 to 5 inches tall; spreads to 20 inches; flowers 2 to 2¼ inches across, pink.

'Pink Panther': 6 to 8 inches tall; flowers 1¾ to 2 inches across, profusely borne, pink.

'Polka Dot': 4 to 6 inches tall; spreads to 24 inches; flowers 2 to 2¼ inches across, white with red center.

'Pretty in Pink': 10 to 12 inches tall; flowers 1¾ to 2 inches across, rose pink.

'Sahara White with Red Eye': 6 to 8 inches tall; flowers 1¾ to 2 inches across, profusely borne, white with red center.

'Snowflakes': 8 to 10 inches flowers 1¾ to 2 inches across, white.

CELOSIA ARGENTEA
(Plumed celosia),
C. ARGENTEA *VAR.* CRISTATA
(Cockscomb)

The celosias enjoyed great popularity some decades ago, then fell into disfavor, and now are enjoying something of a resurgence. Especially valued are the tall plumed celosias for providing masses of color, mostly in shades of red, orange, and yellow; in some, hints of flower color are found in the stems and leaves. The cockscomb is a tetraploid variety in which the flowers are condensed in a flattened or serpentine fasciated comb, rather like broccoli. It is available in tall cultivars (staking required) that bear massive combs, 8 to 10 inches across, and in diminutive forms that bear smaller but still disproportionately large combs. Both plumed and comb types are superb

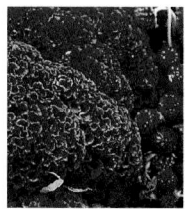

Plumed celosia
(*Celosia argentea*
'Apricot Brandy')

Cockscomb
(*Celosia argentea*
var. *cristata*)

PLUMED CELOSIA CULTIVARS OF MERIT

'Apricot Brandy': 14 to 16 inches tall; flowers early to bloom; plumes orange.

'Castle' hybrids: about 12 inches tall and wide; flowers early to bloom; plumes red, pink, or yellow, densely conical.

'Century' hybrids: 24 to 28 inches tall; 15 to 18 inches wide; flowers early to bloom (seven weeks from seed); plumes red, rose, yellow, or cream.

'Fairy Fountains': 10 to 12 inches tall; plumes 4 to 6 inches long, deep red, scarlet, rose, pink, yellow-orange, or yellow.

'Fiery Feather': 10 to 12 inches tall; plumes red, densely pyramidal.

'Fire Dragon': 18 to 20 inches tall and wide; plumes red.

'Forest Fire': 20 to 24 inches tall; foliage bronzy green; plumes red-orange.

'Geisha' hybrids: 6 to 10 inches tall; plumes red, orange, or yellow.

'Golden Triumph': 24 to 30 inches tall; plumes yellow.

'Kimono' hybrids: 6 to 8 inches tall; heat tolerant; plumes red, orange, or yellow, short but dense; successor to the slightly larger 'Kewpie' hybrids.

'New Look': 8 to 10 inches tall; foliage bronze green; plumes deep red.

'Red Fox': 20 to 24 inches tall; plumes deep red.

COCKSCOMB CULTIVARS OF MERIT

'Chief' hybrids: 36 to 40 inches tall; combs 6 to 8 inches across, deep red, scarlet, rose, pink, yellow, or bicolor, globular.

'Empress': 10 to 12 inches tall; foliage deep reddish green; combs 8 to 10 inches across, deep red.

'Fireglow': 20 to 24 inches tall; combs 4 to 6 inches across, red-orange, globular.

'Floradale' hybrids: 14 to 16 inches tall; combs 4 to 6 inches across, lateral ones smaller, deep red, scarlet, rose pink, or yellow.

'Jewel Box Dwarf' hybrids: 5 to 6 inches tall; combs deep red, scarlet, pink, or yellow.

'Kardinal Improved': 8 to 10 inches tall; combs 4 to 6 inches across, red.

'Red Velvet': 24 to 30 inches tall; combs 10 by 6 inches, red.

'Toreador': 18 to 20 inches tall; combs 10 to 12 inches across, red.

'Treasure Chest': 8 to 10 inches tall; combs 8 to 10 inches across, deep red, scarlet, pink, salmon, yellow-orange, or yellow.

for cutting fresh and, as the colors are retained, also for drying. Bloom extends through summer to frost.

Celosia is easy to grow from seed sown outdoors after danger of frost. Sow a few seeds together in a depression about the width and depth of a quarter, cover with fine soil, and in the ensuing weeks pinch off the weaker seedlings, leaving the strongest to grow and flower. For earlier bloom, seed may be started indoors under lights or in a greenhouse. It is important, however, to sow the seed very thinly to avoid overcrowding, to transplant seedlings to cell packs as soon as possible, to provide bright light, and to keep the soil consistently moist but not soggy. Any slowdown or check in early growth may result in undersize plants that flower poorly, if at all. In the garden, both kinds grow best in well-drained, humusy loam, but they tolerate poor soil as long as it remains moist through the summer. Full sun is a necessity.

CLEOME HASSLERIANA
(Spider flower)

Spider flower is a tender, bushy annual that reaches 3 to 6 feet tall. It has somewhat sticky, aromatic, palmately divided leaves and dense, ever-lengthening clusters of purplish to pink or white flowers with very long stamens and pistils, which are followed by slender, long-stalked pods. The flowers open in late afternoon and persist through the next day; the color turns paler through out the day. The flowering period is midsummer to frost.

Cleome salvia

From zone 7 south, seed can be sown outdoors in early spring, and the seedlings transplanted to at least 1 foot apart. If spider flower has been grown previously, self-sown seedlings are often abundant. Elsewhere, or for early bloom anywhere, seed may be started indoors under lights or in a greenhouse 8 to 10 weeks before set-out time. Sow thinly and cover seed with about ⅛ inch of fine soil. Seedlings are best grown individually in pots, to allow for ample root development. In the garden, average soil fertility is fine. Spider flower grows best in hot weather and flowers optimally if grown in full sun and kept well watered.

Cultivars with distinctive flower colors (at time of opening) include the following.

'Cherry Queen' (cherry rose).
'Helen Campbell' (white).
'Pink Queen' (light pink).
'Rose Queen' (rose pink).
'Ruby Queen' (red-violet).
'Violet Queen' (purple).

CONVOLVULUS TRICOLOR
(Dwarf morning glory)

Dwarf morning glory is a low, spreading, nonclimbing member of the morning glory clan. It seldom exceeds 1 foot in height or spread, and bears a succession of wide-open, funnel-shaped, upward-facing flowers, 1¼ inches across, that open at dawn and generally close by midday. The usual color is blue-violet with a white throat grading to a yellow center. Bloom period is through the summer, especially in the warmest six to eight weeks.

From zone 8 south, seed is best sown outdoors once the ground has warmed, Cover seed with ¼ inch of fine soil, and as soon as possible after germination, transplant the seedlings to 6 to 8 inches apart. Elsewhere, seed may be started indoors under lights or in a greenhouse six to eight weeks before set-out time. Soaking seeds several hours in weak detergent solution or notching the seed coat with an artist's file will help ensure prompt, even germination. In regions where rabbits are troublesome, care should be taken to protect the seedlings, as dwarf morning glory seems irresistible

to them. Flowering is most generous in full sun.

Cultivars of merit include the following, all of whose flowers have white throats and yellow centers.

'Blue Ensign' (pale blue).
'Cambridge Blue' (pale blue).
'Crimson Monarch' (shades of red).
'Lavender Rosette' (lavender pink).
'Rainbow Flash' (various colors).
'Royal Ensign' (dark blue).

COREOPSIS TINCTORIA
(Calliopsis, annual coreopsis)

Calliopsis is a fast-growing, slender, much-branched, hardy annual, typically 2½ to 3 feet tall. It has sparse, finely dissected foliage and long-stalked, daisylike flowers, about 1¼ inches across. The flower's rays are yellow and often have a red-brown base; they surround a red-brown or purplish brown central disc. Deadheading spent flowers is necessary if succession of bloom is to be maintained.

Seed is best sown directly in the garden in early spring, even before the last spring frosts. North of zone 6, to ensure early bloom, it may be started indoors under lights or in a greenhouse about six weeks before set-out time. Flowering begins in early summer, usually with a heavy flush. In hot weather, flowering often ceases after the first flush of bloom and plants may die out, especially if not deadheaded and not adequately watered. A second sowing at that time will provide another round of bloom in early fall. Some late-season plants often form dense foliage rosettes for the winter, then flower early and bounteously the next spring. Plants will flower best if crowded, with only 3 or

4 inches between individuals. Calliopsis often self-sows, especially on sandy soils south of zone 6. Good performance is had on most any well-drained soil, however, especially in full sun.

Besides the dwarf form, 'Nana', which grows 6 to 12 inches tall, cultivars, such as one with multiple rows of floral rays and another with all reddish brown rays, are generally available only in mixtures.

COSMOS BIPINNATUS
(Tall cosmos),
C. SULPHUREUS
(Orange cosmos)

Tall cosmos is of particular value in the garden because of its height, the larger cultivars often reaching 6 feet or more, its gracefully dissected foliage, and its large, showy flowers. If both early- and late-blooming cultivars are planted, the floral display may extend from early summer to frost. As tall cosmos tends to be rather spindly in habit, it is best planted at the rear of the garden. It is also a valuable component of the cutting garden. In any case, staking is often required. Flowers are typically red (paler beneath), pink, or white with yellow centers; are mildly fragrant; and measure 3 to 5 inches across.

Quite different in habit, foliage, and flower color, orange cosmos seldom exceeds 3 feet, has foliage strikingly similar to that of common ragweed (*Ambrosia artemisiifolia*), and bears 1½- to 2½-inch flowers that are prototypically orange (but cultivars range from lemon yellow to deep red-orange).

Both tall and orange cosmos are tender annuals. Seed may be sown outdoors once danger of frost is over or, for earlier bloom, may be started indoors under lights or in a greenhouse about six weeks before set-out time, and grown in cell packs. Seed should be sown thinly about ¼ inch deep and the seedlings soon separated to avert root competition and stunted growth. Plentiful light and space are required if lankiness is to be avoided. In the garden, sandy-humusy, well-drained soil in a sunny location yields

TALL COSMOS CULTIVARS OF MERIT

'Anemone-flowered': 4 to 5 feet tall; flower 3 to 3½ inches across, crested, semidouble center, red, pink, or white.

'Candy Stripe'; 5 to 6 feet tall; flowers 3½ to 4 inches across, white or pale pink with red longitudinal stripes and edges.

'Daydream': 4 to 6 feet tall; flowers 3½ to 4 inches across, white or pale pink with a deep pink base.

'Early Wonder': 3 to 4 feet tall; flowers 3½ to 4 inches across, red, pink, or white, profuse, early to bloom.

'Gazebo': 3 to 3½ feet tall; flowers 3½ to 4 inches across, red, pink, or white, early to bloom.

'Gloria': 4 to 6 feet tall; flowers 4½ to 5 inches across, pink with red base.

'Imperial Pink': 4 to 5 feet tall; flowers 3½ to 4 inches across, lilac pink with a purplish base.

'Purity': 4 to 6 feet tall; flowers 4 to 4½ inches across, white.

'Sea Shells': 5 to 6 feet tall; flowers 4 to 4½ inches across, rays ("petals") cupped or quilled upward into flared tubes, red (with the whitish underside in striking contrast), pink, or white.

'Sensation' hybrids: 4 to 6 feet tall; flowers 3 to 3½ inches across, red, pink, or white.

'Sonata': 3 to 4 feet tall; flowers, about 3 inches across, red, pink, or white, profuse, early to bloom.

'Versailles Tetra', syn. 'Red Versailles': 4 to 6 feet tall; flowers 3½ to 4 inches across, deep red with purplish base.

ORANGE COSMOS CULTIVARS OF MERIT

'Bright Lights'; 2½ to 3 feet tall; flowers 2 inches across, semidouble, red-orange, medium orange, yellow-orange, or yellow.

'Diablo': 2 to 2½ feet tall; flowers 2 inches across, semidouble, red-orange.

'Goldcrest': 2 to 2½ feet tall; flowers 2 inches across, semidouble, yellow-orange.

'Klondyke Sunset': 1½ to 2 feet tall; flowers 2 inches across, semidouble, deep red-orange.

'Ladybird': 10 to 12 inches tall; flowers 1¾ to 2 inches across, semidouble, orange or yellow.

'Lemon Twist': 2 to 2½ feet tall; flowers 2 inches across, semidouble, yellow.

'Sunny' hybrids: 1 to 1½ feet tall; flowers 2 inches across, single and semidouble, red-orange, medium orange, or yellow.

best results. Cultivars of tall cosmos should be planted 1½ to 2 feet apart, and those of orange cosmos 1 to 1½ feet apart. Excess soil nitrate promotes giant, leafy plants that flower late and often poorly. Tall cosmos often self-sows from zone 7 south and orange cosmos from zone 8 south.

DAHLIA *HYBRIDS*
(Low-bedding dahlia)

Bedding dahlias form low, rounded, much-branched plants, seldom exceeding 2 feet. They bear large numbers of single, semidouble, or fully double flowers, 2 to 3 inches across, in all colors but blue,

usually within seven weeks from seed. These dahlias are grown as annuals from seed. Some have ornamental bronzy or reddish foliage. Most bloom copiously until the onset of intensely hot summer weather; they then resume flowering as the nights cool in late summer and continue until frost. Tubers may be dug after frost and stored in dry peat moss in a cool (40° to 50°F) place, but very small tubers often fail to survive.

Seed is best started indoors under lights or in a greenhouse six to eight weeks before set-out time. Sow thinly and cover with ¼ inch of fine soil to exclude light; penetration of light to dahlia seeds inhibits germination. The seedlings should be grown in cell packs or, preferably, in 3-inch pots to allow early tuber development. In the garden, a sunny position in fertile, well-drained loam is necessary for optimal results. Bedding dahlia is excellent when massed or used for edging. Plant 1 to 1½ feet apart.

Among the many cultivars of bedding dahlia, the following, all in mixed colors, are especially desirable.

'Bambino': 12 to 18 inches tall; flowers semidouble (peony flowered).

'Collarette': 20 to 24 inches tall; flowers single, an inner ring ("collarette") of small, quilled rays, usually in a lighter, contrasting color.

'Coltness': 18 to 24 inches tall; flowers single.

'Dapper', 18 to 20 inches tall; flowers mostly double, early to bloom (seven or eight weeks from seed).

'Figaro': 10 to 12 inches tall; flowers semidouble and fully double, early to bloom.

'Piccolo': 8 to 12 inches tall; flowers single, some bicolor, early to bloom.

'Redskin', 12 to 15 inches tall; foliage bronzy green or purplish; flowers double.

'Rigoletto': 12 to 14 inches tall; flowers semidouble and fully double, early to bloom.

DIANTHUS *SPP.*
(Annual pinks, annual carnation)

Although most *Dianthus* species are perennial or biennial, the annual forms have long been garden favorites, since they produce generous bloom throughout the summer months. Both single- and double-flowered cultivars are available in various shades and combinations of red, pink, and white. The plants usually develop as branched cushions or tufts and reach a height of about 1 foot, making them especially useful in the front of the border.

From zone 7 south, seed may be sown in a coldframe or directly in the garden in the spring after the ground has warmed. For early bloom, seed should be started indoors under lights or in a greenhouse 8 to 10 weeks before set-out time. Sow thinly and cover with ⅛ inch

of fine soil. Seedlings require bright light and do best with night temperatures of 55° to 60°F. In the garden, a fertile, humusy, well-drained soil and a sunny location result in optimal bloom. Plants should be spaced 8 to 10 inches apart.

Best known as a greenhouse flower, the carnation (*D. caryophyllus*) may also be grown in the garden, and certain small-flowered, heat-resistant hybrids with fragrant blooms are especially well adapted. These include the following.

'Chabaud's Giant Improved': 15 to 20 inches tall; flowers long-lasting, double, about 2½ inches across, mixed colors.

'Dwarf Fragrance' hybrids: 12 to 15 inches tall; flowers decidedly fragrant, mixed colors, on sturdy stems.

'Knight Series' hybrids: 10 to 12 inches tall; flowers double, 2 inches across, through red, pink, salmon, yellow, and white, self-supporting stems.

Several other species and hybrids are grown as annuals. Deptford pink (*D. armeria*) has narrow, grasslike foliage and clusters of rose pink flowers, ¾ inch across, held atop 12- to 16-inch-tall stems. It is best grown in dense patches and thrives on dry soil. Deptford pink readily self-sows and, from zone 7 south, may persist as a biennial.

Sweet William (*D. barbatus*) is best known as a biennial, but most cultivars bloom the first year if seed is sown early. The flowers are ¾ inch across; single or double; and borne in large, flat clusters on 6- to 15-inch tall stems, which arise from a basal tuft of foliage. Of the Sweet William hybrids especially good as annuals, 'Indian Carpet' and 'Roundabout' are 6-inch dwarfs, while 'Summer Beauty' reaches 1 foot or more. Sweet William tolerates partial shade.

China pink (*D. chinensis*) forms mounds or clumps, 8 to 15 inches tall, which are usually covered with single red, pink, white, or bicolor flowers. Hybrids and cultivars of merit include the following.

'Double Gaiety': flowers double, 1¼ to 1½ inches across, each petal is fringed.

'Magic Charms': flowers single, 1½ to 1¾ inches across, each petal is fringed.

Dianthus 'Lacy Loveliness', a perennial hybrid that blooms in the first year, hence often grown as an annual

'Snowfire': 8 to 10 inches tall; flowers white with a red center.

'Telstar Picotee': 6 to 8 inches tall; flowers red, finely edged with white.

DIMORPHOTHECA SINUATA
(Cape marigold)

Cape marigold is also known as Cape daisy, African daisy, and star of the veldt and is sometimes listed as *D. aurantiaca* or *Osteospermum sinuatum*. It resembles a bright orange daisy and deserves a place both in the flower border and in the cutting garden. In the garden, plants seldom exceed 1 foot in height but may spread considerably. The flowers have long, slender, somewhat pointed petals that seem to shimmer in sunlight. Their colors range from light yellow through salmon pink to deep orange.

Seed may be started directly in the garden once the ground warms in the spring or, for earlier bloom, indoors under lights or in a greenhouse six to eight weeks before set-out time. Sow thinly and cover with ⅛ inch of fine soil. Cape marigold does best in full sun and on relatively infertile, dryish soil. Overly moist conditions with excess nitrate result in sprawling, weak-stemmed growth and minimal flowering. Drought tolerance is higher than with most garden annuals. The plants should be spaced 8 to 10 inches apart. Successive sowing four to six weeks apart will help maintain a succession of bloom, as Cape marigold tends to bloom heavily for several weeks and then subside and die out, even if deadheaded. Bloom begins in early or midsummer and continues to hard frost.

Of the several cultivars available, the following single-color forms are of merit.

'Glistening White': 6 to 8 inches tall; flowers 3½ inches, shiny black centers.
'Orange Improved': 10 to 12 inches tall; flowers 3 inches, deep orange.
'Salmon Beauty': similar to 'Orange Impoved', salmon pink flowers.
'Tetra Goliath': 12 to 15 inches tall; flowers 3 to 3½ inches, orange.
'Tetra Pole Star': 12 to 15 inches tall; spreads to 18 inches; flowers white with violet centers.

The best mixed-color hybrid is 'Starshine', which has an abundance of 2- to 3-inch flowers, ranging from deep red through rose and pink to white.

ESCHSCHOLZIA CALIFORNICA
(California poppy)

California poppy is one of the brightest of our summer-flowering annuals and beloved by many a gardener. A spring-flowering perennial in its native habitat, it is not able to survive the extreme cold of northern winters and is, therefore, usually grown as an annual. The foliage is soft gray green and finely cut. The flowers are borne above the foliage on slender, upright, 8- to 15-inch-tall stems. During the night and on cloudy days, the petals remain closed, but in direct sun, they open fully. In the wild, California poppy varies from deep orange to cream, but hybrid cultivars offer a much wider color range, from brown-violet, crimson, scarlet, and various shades of orange to salmon, pink, and ivory.

California poppy is of easy culture. Although it thrives on light, sandy soil, it performs well on soil of almost any type but must have full sun to flower maximally. From zone 7 south, seed may be sown in the garden in late fall, shortly before the onset of hard freezes, or in early spring before the last spring frosts. The plants make their strongest growth in cool, moist spring weather. Flowering ceases and the plants begin to die out in hot, humid weather. Seed should be sown thinly where the plants are to flower, since California poppy, like most poppies of any kind, is not easily transplanted. To make the spreading of the very fine seed even and spare, the contents of the seed packet may be mixed with a cupful of vermiculite or sand. For more northerly zones, and to have early bloom anywhere (especially where spring quickly passes to summer heat), seeds may be sown indoors under lights or in a greenhouse six to eight weeks before set-out time, using cell packs instead of germination pans or flats. Sow just a few seeds per cell, lightly cover with fine soil, and thin the seedlings to one or two. Transferring seedlings to the garden should be done very carefully, preferably in cloudy, cool weather, with the soil mix in the cells thoroughly wetted beforehand to keep it from falling away and exposing the roots. Use of peat pots helps minimize this problem. Spacing should be about 6 inches. Flower size will be greatest with the first blooms and then will gradually decrease as the season advances.

Hybrids and cultivars of merit include the following.

'Aurantiaca': 10 to 12 inches tall; flowers 2½ to 3 inches across, single, orange. 'Orange King' is similar.
'Ballerina': 8 to 10 inches tall; flowers 2½ to 3 inches across, double, orange, fluted petals.
'Carmine King': 12 to 15 inches tall; flowers 2¼ to 2½ inches across, single, deep red.
'Milky White': 12 to 15 inches tall; flowers 2¼ to 2½ inches across, cream with yellow center.
'Mission Bells': 10 to 12 inches tall; flowers 2½ to 3 inches across, semi-double and fully double, mixed colors.

'Monarch' hybrids: 7 to 9 inches tall; flowers 2¼ to 2½ inches across, single and semidouble, mixed colors.
'Purple Gleam': 12 to 15 inches tall; flowers 2¼ to 2½ inches across, single, purple. 'Purple Violet' is similar.
'Thai Silk' hybrids: 8 to 10 inches tall; flowers 2¼ to 2½ inches across, semidouble, mixed colors, fluted petals with wavy edges.

The tufted California poppy (*E. caespitosa*) is also cultivated and is best known by the cultivar 'Sundew', which forms compact tufts of finely divided, blue-green foliage topped with slender, 6- to 10-inch-tall stalks. Each stalk bears a bright lemon yellow flower, 1 to 1½ inches in diameter. Culture is the same as for *E. californica*.

EUSTOMA GRANDIFLORUM
(Prairie gentian, lisianthus)

Long known as the native prairie bluebell from Nebraska to Mexico, prairie gentian, a short-lived perennial, has found much favor in horticulture in recent decades, first as a greenhouse cut flower and then as a garden annual. Of slender habit, garden forms of prairie gentian grow 18 to 30 inches tall; have smooth, gray green foliage; and bear showy, 2- to 3-inch wide, bell-shaped flowers in small clusters. Colors are shades and combinations of blue-violet, pink, and creamy white. The flowers are long lasting, whether left in place or cut for indoor use. Bloom begins in mid-summer and continues until night temperatures fall below 40°F.

To grow prairie gentian from seed requires care and patience, as the seed is dust fine, the seedlings minute, and growth in the initial weeks is very slow. Care should be taken to avoid overwatering and to protect the seedlings from cold drafts. For these reasons, starting seeds indoors under lights about 12 weeks before set-out time is de rigueur, keeping in mind that 20 weeks elapse between seed sowing and first flowers. Sow on the surface of very fine soil mix and barely cover with a sprinkling of fine, dry dust. Water gently with a fine spray or mist. Seedlings should be transplanted to cell packs while they are in the two-leaf stage, with care taken to avoid breaking the fine, disproportionately long roots. In the garden, any well-drained, moderately fertile soil suits prairie gentian, but full sun is necessary for optimal bloom. Flowering plants usually require pinching back, staking, or the support of lower plants such as ageratum. Space 6 to 8 inches apart.

From zone 8 south, prairie gentian cultivars may survive the winter, but they are not reliably hardy. Some so-called cultivars are naturally occuring variants; others have been developed or selected by breeders.

Among the many hybrids and cultivars available are the following.

'Double Eagle' hybrids: 18 to 24 inches tall; flowers 2½ to 3 inches across, double, purple, blue, claret, rose, pink, cream, white, or bicolor.

'Echo' hybrids: 12 to 14 inches tall; flowers 3 to 3½ inches across, double, purple, blue, claret, rose, pink, cream, or white.

'Heidi Yellow': 18 to 24 inches tall; flowers 2½ to 3 inches across, single, light yellow.

'Lisa': 6 to 8 inches tall; flowers 3 to 3½ inches across, single, purple, blue, claret, rose, pink, cream, white, or bicolor.

'Little Bell': 7 to 9 inches tall; flowers 3 to 3½ inches across, double, violet, lilac, rose, pink, or white.

'Red Gloss': 18 to 24 inches tall; flowers 2½ to 3 inches across, single, rose red.

'Striped Beauty': 12 to 18 inches tall; flowers 2½ to 3 inches across, blue marbled and striped with white.

'Yodel' hybrids: 18 to 30 inches tall; flowers about 2 inches across, single, purple, rose, pale pink with a rose center, or white.

HELIANTHUS ANNUUS
(Sunflower)

Although the sunflower is generally thought to be of such coarse and ungainly growth that it is ill-suited to the flower border, many cultivars produce outstanding

---

SUNFLOWER HYBRIDS AND CULTIVARS OF MERIT
FOR THE FLOWER GARDEN
Flowers are 3 to 4 inches across, unless otherwise noted.

'Autumn Beauty': 5 to 6 feet tall; flowers single, 5 to 6 inches cross, yellow, bronze, or mahogany with a darker basal zone.

'Color Fashion' hybrids: 4 to 5 feet tall; flowers single, yellow, bronze, red, purple, bicolor.

'Dwarf Sungold': 12 to 15 inches tall; flowers semidouble.

'Italian White': 4 to 6 feet tall; flowers single, cream with light yellow at base.

'Lemon Queen', 'Luna': 4 to 5 feet tall; flowers single, light yellow with deeper yellow base.

'Music Box': 2½ to 3 feet tall; flowers single, 4 to 5 inches across, cream, yellow, bronze, or mahogany.

'Orange Sun': 3 to 3½ feet tall; flowers double, orange, rays ("petals") very narrow and numerous.

'Piccolo': 3 to 4 feet tall; flowers single, yellow with dark base.

'Purpureus': 4 to 5 feet tall; flowers single, deep red-brown.

'Sunburst' hybrids: 3 to 4 feet tall; flowers single, yellow, bronze, or mahogany, most with darker basal zone, borne well above the foliage.

'Sunspot': 1½ to 2 feet tall; flowers single, 8 to 10 inches across, yellow.

'Taiyo': 4 to 5 feet tall; flowers single, 5 to 6 inches across, yellow with large brown central disc.

'Teddy Bear': 1½ to 2 feet tall; flowers double, crested, yellow.

'Velvet Queen': 4 to 5 feet tall; flowers single, deep mahogany red.

---

cut flowers or serve as effective background plants in a country garden. Some are sufficiently dwarf to be harmonious in the flower border. Flowers range from the immense solitary heads of 'Russian Mammoth' in the vegetable garden to a profusion of 3- or 4-inch blooms in colors that range from cream to deep red-brown, and mature plants may surpass 8 feet or stay as low as 18 inches.

Bloom begins in midsummer and, in all but the smallest cultivars, continues until fall. The flowering period in dwarfs tends to be brief, even with deadheading. For early bloom, seed may be sown indoors under lights, in a greenhouse, or in a coldframe six to eight weeks before set-out time, or it may be sown directly in the garden after all danger of frost is over. Sow seed 1 to 1½ inches apart and about ½ inch deep. In the garden, soil quality and drought are of little importance in sunflower culture, but full sun is essential for flower production. The plants should be spaced 15 to 20 inches apart. Tall cultivars may require staking or, in the case of many-branched types, encirclement with twine to prevent branches breaking in high winds.

Sunflower
(*Helianthus annuus* 'Piccolo')

HELICHRYSUM BRACTEATUM
(Strawflower)

The strawflower offers double, daisy-like flowers, 1½ to 2 inches across, in bright solid shades and combinations of red, orange, and yellow as well as white. It is much prized as an everlasting, because when dried the flowers retain their colors and shape exactly as in life. Indeed, their strawlike texture makes them seem nearly dry on the living plant. Ranging from 1 to 3 feet in height according to cultivar, strawflower is easily grown in full sun on average, well-drained soil and tolerates several degrees of frost in the fall. Taller forms usually require staking. Bloom time is from midsummer to frost.

Seed may be sown directly in the garden from zone 7 south or started indoors under lights or in a coldframe about six weeks before set-out time. Sow seed thinly and cover with ⅛ inch of fine soil or soil mix. Space plants about 1 foot apart.

Of the numerous named hybrid strains, 'Monstrosum' is especially meritorious, standing 2½ to 3 feet tall, its flowers are 2½ to 3 inches across in mixed colors. Cultivars include the following, each of a self-evident color.

'Candy Pink'
'Crimson Sky'
'Golden'
'Orange One'
'Rose'
'Salmon Rose'
'Silver Rose'
'Snow White'
'Straw Gold'
'Terracotta'

'Bikini' hybrids are 12 to 15 inches tall and bear 2- to 2½-inch flowers in various colors.

Among the many other species of *Helichrysum*, most native to Australia and South Africa. *H. subulifolium* is valued for its prolific production of yellow flowers, about 1½ inches across. It is best known by the especially floriferous cultivar 'Golden Star'.

HUNNEMANNIA FUMARIIFOLIA
(Mexican tulip poppy)

Somewhat taller (1½ to 2 feet) than California poppy (*Eschscholzia california*), to which it is closely related, Mexican tulip poppy produces clear yellow flowers, 2 to 3 inches across, which are held well above the much-divided grayish foliage. Although perennial in zone 10 and in protected places in zone 9, it is usually treated as an annual and cultivated in the manner indicated for California poppy.

Mexican tulip poppy seems less affected by summer heat than California poppy and often blooms throughout the summer. The flowers open in bright sunlight and otherwise remain closed, much as tulips do. The only cultivar, 'Sunlite', has intensely gray blue foliage and flowers up to 3 inches across.

IMPATIENS BALSAMINA
(Garden balsam, lady's slipper)

An easily grown relative of the popular flat-flowered impatiens, garden balsam is upright in habit, bears single or double 1- to 2-inch snapdragonlike flowers all summer, and does best in full sun or light shade (especially in the South) on well-drained, moisture-retentive soil. Height at maturity varies from 6 to 30 inches, according to cultivar. Flowers are borne singly or grouped along the stems, and colors range from purple through red, pink, and yellow to white, in some cases mottled or spotted. Garden balsam self-sows readily, especially from zone 6 south, sometimes to the point of nuisance.

Seed is best sown directly in the garden in the spring, even before the last spring frost, from zone 7 south. Farther north, it may be started indoors under lights or in a greenhouse six to eight weeks before set-out time. Seed should be pressed into the soil but not covered, as light is required for germination. Sandy-humusy soil is best in the garden, and spacing should be 6 to 8 inches.

Hybrids and cultivars of merit include the following.

'Blackberry Ice': 15 to 30 inches tall; flowers double, red-violet mottled with white.
'Camellia-flowered' hybrids: 15 to 30 inches tall; flowers double, red, rose, or white, sometimes spotted or mottled.
'Carambole' hybrids: 12 to 14 inches tall; rounded habit; flowers double, violet, red, pink, or white, held above foliage.
'Strawberry Ice': 15 to 30 inches tall; flowers double, pink mottled with white.
'Tom Thumb' hybrids: 8 to 10 inches tall; compact habit; flowers double, mixed colors.

LAVATERA TRIMESTRIS
(Bush mallow)

Usually rounded in habit, bush mallow bears single 3-inch flowers in rose pink, pale pink, or white. The flowers occur singly along the leafy stems and, in typical mallow fashion, each lasts a day or two, beginning in early summer. The succession of bloom continues until the summer weather turns intensely hot.

Seed may be sown directly in the garden in the fall from zone 7 south or in the spring, even before the last spring frosts, farther north. For early bloom from zone 7 north, seed may be started indoors under lights or in a greenhouse six to eight weeks before set-out time. Sow seed thinly and cover with about ¼ inch of soil or soil mix. Seedlings should be transferred to cell packs for growing. A second sowing in early summer often results in a second round of flowering toward summer's end. In the garden, bush mallow is adaptable to various well-drained soils of average fertility. Droughty conditions will foreshorten flowering. Full sun is required for full flowering.

Notable cultivars include the following.

'Loveliness': 3 to 4 feet tall; flowers 3 to 3½ inches across, deep rose pink.
'Mont Blanc': 18 to 21 inches tall; flowers about 4 inches across, white.
'Mont Rose': 18 to 21 inches tall; flowers about 4 inches across, rose pink.
'Pink Beauty': 20 to 24 inches tall; flowers about 4 inches across, pale pink.
'Ruby Regis': 20 to 24 inches tall; flowers about 4 inches across, bright cerise pink.
'Silvercup': 20 to 24 inches tall; more heat resistant than most, flowers about 4 inches across, rose pink.

LINARIA *SPP.*
(Toad flax)

The genus *Linaria* includes two diminutive annuals that are useful as edging plants or when massed in the front of the border. Both are slender, much-branched plants that produce a succession of small snapdragonlike flowers in many colors and combinations. Bloom begins in early summer and if cut back at the onset of hot weather, there is rebloom often from late summer to frost. Seed may be sown directly in the garden in the fall from zone 8 south or in early spring elsewhere, even before the last spring frosts. For earlier flowering, seed may also be started indoors under lights or in a greenhouse six to eight weeks before set-out time. Seed should be sown thinly and very lightly covered with fine soil or soil mix. Most any well-drained, moderately fertile soil suits toadflax in the garden, where full sun or a little partial shade is best. Spacing is 2 to 3 inches.

L. maroccana is known through two cultivars: 'Fairy Lights' grows 10 to 12 inches tall and bears flowers from red-violet to white, mostly in pastel bicolors. 'Northern Lights' grows 24 inches tall and bears flowers in the same color range. *L. reticulata* 'Crown Jewels' grows 8 to 15 inches tall and bears a multitude of purple-and-orange flowers, creating a truly eye-catching display when mass planted.

MELAMPODIUM CINEREUM
(Medallion daisy)

Native to the lower Midwest, medallion daisy is a bushy, much-branched, tender annual, 15 to 18 inches tall, with a generous summer-long display of yellow to cream 1- to 1½-inch daisylike blooms. With the advance of summer, successive leaves become smaller and flowers more numerous, heightening the display. Two of the signal virtues of this plant are its extraordinary heat tolerance and its freedom from pests and diseases.

From zone 7 south, seed is best sown directly in the garden in the spring, even before the last spring frosts. The seedlings are easily transplanted and should stand about 1 foot apart. Farther north, seed may be started indoors under lights or in a greenhouse six to eight weeks before set-out time. Sow the seed thinly and cover with about ¼ inch of fine soil or soil mix; shift seedlings to cell packs to grow. Most any well-drained soil is satisfactory in the garden; and the more sun, the better the display.

Melampodium paludosum

The cultivar 'Medallion' has yellow-orange rays and bronzy centers.

MIRABILIS JALAPA
(Four o'clock)

Four o'clock is a bushy tropical perennial usually grown as an annual north of zone 7, but the deep tuberous roots survive the winter farther south, especially in protected locations, such as the southern or eastern side of a building or wall in sandy, well-drained soils, producing ever-larger plants in successive years. The 1-inch trumpet-shaped flowers are borne at the ends of the knobby, leafy stems from midsummer to fall, each opening in late afternoon and lasting until struck by sun the following day. Often flowers on the same plant are differently colored, especially if streaked or mottled. If to be seen at night, as from a patio or path, four o'clocks with white or pale yellow flowers should be favored over those with red or purple. Self-sowing is common south of zone 6, but in successive generations special flower colors and patterns are lost to the prototypic red-violet, red, yellow, or white.

From zone 7 south, the relatively large seed is best sown directly in the garden in the spring, even before the last spring frosts. Elsewhere, or for earlier bloom anywhere, seed may be started indoors under lights or in a greenhouse six to eight weeks before set-out time. Sow the seed 1 inch apart and about ½ inch deep. To accommodate the taproot that soon forms, seedlings should be grown in large cell packs or in separate pots. Where winters are severe, the carrotlike tubers may be dug up after the first killing frost and stored like those of dahlia (see page 441). Four o'clock will perform well in most any well-drained soil and flowers most generously if located in a sunny position. It is extraordinarily tolerant of heat and drought.

Of the several cultivars available, the most notable are 'Four O'clock Special', which grows to 2 feet and has 1½- to 2-inch flowers in various colors (many variously mottled and streaked), and 'Jingles', which grows to 2½ feet and has generously spotted and flecked flowers.

NICOTIANA *SPP. AND HYBRIDS*
(Flowering tobacco)

The flowering tobacco group includes some of the most valuable hardy annuals, ranging in height from 1 to 6 feet. There is a diverse assemblage of cultivars well suited to a variety of planting compositions. In the evening, when the beautiful white, tubular flowers of *N. alata* recede into the twilight, their delicate fragrance pervades the stillness, luring night moths in the dusk. Unfortunately, many of the other species and most hybrids lack this lovely perfume, but a wide range of colors is available, including lavender, coral, soft pink, rose mahogany, crimson, and lime green. Flowering extends from early or mid summer to frost.

Flowering tobacco is easily grown from seed, and once established in the garden, it self-sows very readily, year after year. Unfortunately, the various garden sorts are not distinguishable as seedlings, so care must be taken to label plantings, especially if two or more kinds are grown simultaneously. The seed is extremely fine and is best started indoors under lights or in a greenhouse six to eight weeks before set-out time. As the seed requires light for germination, it should be peppered thinly on the soil surface and pressed into the medium with a wood block before being moistened. The fast-growing, wide-spreading, flat foliage soon causes crowding in the seed bed, so young seedlings are best transplanted as soon as possible to individual pots. Transplanting to the garden is easily accomplished; once in the garden, even flowering specimens can be moved safely. As the plants bloom over a long period, they make useful replacements for early-blooming biennials, such as Canterbury bells and foxglove. Sandy-humusy soil is ideal in the garden, but flowering tobacco succeeds in a wide range of well-drained soils. Full sun to partial or even light shade will result in a full floral display. Spacing ranges from 8 to 12 inches for smaller cultivars to 2 feet or more for the tall species. Self-sown seedlings appearing in fall may be potted up before heavy frost for indoor culture, often yielding generous bloom over the winter.

Meritorious cultivars of *N. alata* (often listed as *N. affinis* or *N. grandiflora* in catalogs) include the following.

'Breakthrough': 10 to 12 inches tall; flowers early to bloom, red, pink, or white, fragrant.
'Domino' hybrids: 10 to 12 inches tall; basally branching; flowers rose purple, red, pink, lime green, white, or bicolor, fragrant, open all day.
'Dwarf White Bedder': 14 to 16 inches tall; flowers white, fragrant.
'Fragrant Cloud': 2½ to 3 feet tall; flowers white, strongly fragrant.
'Lime Green': 2 to 2½ feet tall; flowers pale green, prolific.
'Nicki' hybrids: 10 to 12 inches tall; flowers in wide color range, prolific, especially early in season, reblooms later if deadheaded.

Flowering tobacco
(*Nicotiana alata* 'Nicki Red')

'Sensation' hybrids: 2 to 3 feet tall; flowers in wide color range, fragrant, open all day.

Two additional species are especially worthy of cultivation. Bellflower tobacco (*N. langsdorffii*) grows 3 to 4 feet tall and bears long sprays of drooping, bell-shaped, greenish yellow flowers. It is especially effective against a dark background, such as a yew hedge. Starburst tobacco (*N. sylvestris*) grows 4 to 6 feet tall. Its leaves, up to 15 inches long, clothe a stout stem that terminates with dense clusters of drooping, long-tubed, trumpet-shaped, white flowers about 4 inches long and 1 inch across. It is a striking subject for a lawn island or at the rear of the garden, but it must have plenty of room for leaf spread. In neither species are the flowers fragrant.

Bellflower tobacco
(*Nicotiana langsdorffii*)

Starburst tobacco
(*Nicotiana sylvestris*)

NIEREMBERGIA HIPPOMANICA *VAR.* VIOLACEA
(*Cupflower*)

Cupflower is a short-lived perennial grown as a hardy annual north of zone 9. Its habit is low and spreading; its foliage fine textured; and it bears a long succession of blue-violet, upward-facing, cup-shaped flowers from midsummer to frost. Partial shade facilitates sustained flowering and color retention in regions prone to hot summer weather.

From zone 7 and north, plants may be lifted in the fall and wintered in a coldframe. Seed should be started indoors under lights or in a greenhouse 8 to 10 weeks before set-out time. Sow thinly and lightly cover with fine soil or soil mix. Transfer the seedlings to cell packs and then plant them in the garden 6 inches apart. In the garden, ordinary well-drained soil will suit but supplemental irrigation is required during periods of summer drought.

Cupflower is best known by the cultivar 'Purple Robe', which produces 1-inch purple flowers in abundance on plants not exceeding 6 inches in height and often spreading about 1 foot. The cultivar 'Mont Blanc' is white flowered. Both are suited as edging plants or in the rock garden.

PAPAVER RHOEAS
(*Shirley poppy*)

Of all annuals, Shirley poppy is among the most striking. Its flowers are of exquisite delicacy and are extremely showy in the garden and dramatic as a cut flower. Derived from the red-flowered Flanders poppy or corn poppy of Europe, Shirley poppy is somewhat branching, reaching a height of 2 feet or more. It bears a profusion of beautifully formed flowers, 2 to 3 inches across, usually most generously in early to mid summer but on through late summer into early fall if deadheaded. Both single- and double-flowered cultivars are available, in shades of crimson through rose, salmon, apricot, and pink to white.

Seed may be sown directly in the garden from zone 7 south either in the fall or in early spring. Care must be taken to sow the seed very thinly where the plants are to flower, as transplanting seedlings in the garden is almost never successful. Alternatively, seed may be started indoors under lights or in a greenhouse using cell packs, a few seeds per cell very lightly covered with fine soil and later thinned to two or three plants. This should be done six to eight weeks before set-out time. Transfer from cell pack to the garden should be done very carefully to minimize disturbance to seedling roots. Use of peat pots reduces the likelihood of root disturbance. Once in place and established, only the strongest plant from each cell should be allowed to grow and flower; others should be pinched off at ground level (not pulled, to avoid root damage). The young plants should stand 6 to 8 inches apart. Shirley poppies grow best in cool or mild weather, hence should be sown in the garden or transferred from cell packs as soon as danger of frost has passed. This is especially important in regions where summer heat is intense. In periods of sustained wet weather, some of the flower buds may abort.

Hybrids and cultivars of merit include the following.

'Mother of Pearl': 10 to 14 inches tall; flowers 2 to 3 inches across, single, mostly pastel shades, some streaked or bicolor.

'Reselected Double' hybrids: 20 to 24 inches tall; flowers about 3 inches across, double, red, pink, salmon, or white.

'Reverend Wilkes' hybrids: 18 to 24 inches tall, flowers 2 to 3 inches across, semidouble and double, mixed colors (no yellow).

'Single Shirley' hybrids: 20 to 30 inches tall, flowers 2 to 3 inches across, single, mixed colors (no yellow).

PORTULACA GRANDIFLORA
(Garden portulaca)

Portulaca, also known as rose moss, sun rose, eleven o'clock, and wax pink, is a low, wide-spreading (3 inches tall by 12 inches across) annual with narrow, succulent foliage and bright 1- to 1½-inch flowers that open at dawn and close by noon on sunny days. It blooms from early or mid summer to early fall. Single- and double-flowered cultivars offer colors from purple and red to pink and yellow as well as white, some marked with spatters or streaks.

The fine seed is best sown thinly and covered lightly in garden locations where the plants are to remain. Early to mid spring is best. In northerly regions, or for earlier bloom, seed may be started indoors under lights or in a greenhouse six to eight weeks before set-out time. Bright light is essential to prevent legginess in seedlings. These should be grown in cell packs, two or three plants per cell, before transfer to the garden, where spacing should be about 4 inches. Ordinary, well-drained garden soil kept on the dry side in a sunny location yields best results. Portulaca is well suited for edging, rock garden, and container culture.

Notable hybrids and cultivars include the following.

'Afternoon Delight': flowers 1½ to 1¾ inches across, double, mixed colors, open until late afternoon.

'Aztec Double': flowers double, yellow-and-rose pink.

'Calypso' hybrids: flowers fully double, wide color range; F_2 hybrid.

'Cloudbeater' hybrids: flowers 1½ to 1¾ inches across, double, mixed colors, open until late afternoon.

'Dwarf Double Minilaca' hybrids: tufted and nontrailing habit; flowers double, mostly red or yellow.

'Extra Double' hybrids: flowers mostly double, mixed colors; F_2 hybrid.

'Magic Carpet' hybrids: 6 inches tall; spreads 12 inches; flowers double, mixed colors.

'Peppermint Candy': flowers single, red and white.

'Sundance' hybrids: flowers semidouble, mixed colors, open until late afternoon.

'Sundial' hybrids: flowers single, mixed colors.

'Sunnyboy' hybrids: flowers semidouble, mixed colors.

'Swan Lake': flowers 2 inches across, double, white.

'Wildfire' hybrids: spreads 15 to 20 inches; flowers single, mixed colors, early to bloom (eight to 10 weeks from seed).

RHUDBECKIA HIRTA
(Black-eyed Susan)

A biennial or short-lived perennial to zone 4 in nature, black-eyed Susan can easily be brought to bloom the first year by starting seed in early spring, either outdoors in the South or indoors under lights or in a greenhouse in the North (from zone 7) about eight weeks before set-out time. Sow the seed thinly and cover lightly with fine soil or soil mix. Seedlings should be grown on in cell packs.

The various large-flowered and double-flowered tetraploids are preferred for garden use. All grow 2 to 3 (up to 4) feet tall and bear daisylike flowers up to 6 inches across, mostly with yellow rays and a raised, cone-shaped, brown-black disc. The bloom period extends from early or mid summer until night temperatures fall below 45°F. Black-eyed Susan and its variants all thrive in summer heat on moderately fertile, well-drained soil and do best in full sun. Spacing of 12 to 18 inches promotes basal branching.

Hybrid and tetraploid cultivars of merit include the following.

'Autumn Leaves': 2½ to 3 feet tall; flowers 4 to 5 inches across, single, rays yellow with orange, red, or red-brown at the base, disc brown.

'Double Gold': 2 to 3 feet tall; flowers 4 to 4½ inches across, double, rays yellow, disc brown.

'Gloriosa Daisy': 2½ to 3 feet tall; flowers 5 to 6 inches across, rays yellow, sometimes with red or red-brown at base, disc dark brown.

Rudbeckia hirta hybrid 'Gloriosa Daisy'

'Gloriosa Daisy Double': similar to 'Gloriosa Daisy', flowers semidouble or double.

'Goldilocks': 8 to 10 inches tall; flowers 2½ to 3½ (up to 4) inches across, semidouble or double, rays yellow-orange, disc brown.

'Green Eyes', 'Irish Eyes': 24 to 30 inches tall; flowers 4 to 5 inches across, rays yellow, disc olive green.

'Marmalade': 1½ to 2 feet tall; flowers 3 to 4 inches across, rays yellow-orange disc brown, abundant.

'Nutmeg': 2 to 2½ feet tall; flowers 3½ to 4 inches across, double, rays yellow, basal zone red to red-brown, disc brown.

'Rustic Color' hybrids, 'Rustic Dwarf' hybrids: 1½ to 2 feet tall; flowers 3 to 4 inches across, rays bronze, orange, or orange-brown, solid or bicolor.

'Sputnik': 3 to 4 feet tall; flowers 3½ to 4 inches across, rays wider and fewer than usual, yellow with brown-orange base, disc brown.

SALVIA FARINACEA
(Mealycup sage)

Also known as blue sage, Texas sage, or salvia, mealycup sage is a perennial or subshrub in zone 9 but is widely grown as a hardy annual bedding plant farther north. It is everywhere prized for its spikes of rich blue or white flowers—colors that are retained when the spikes are dried for winter bouquets. Because the individual flowers are small, mealycup sage is most effective when massed. Flowering usually begins in mid to late summer but may be advanced by starting seed earlier indoors. Height ranges from 1 to 2 feet, according to cultivar.

Although mealycup sage can be started from seed sown in the garden in much of zone 8, earliest flowering is had by starting it under lights indoors or in a greenhouse. Seed should be germinated 8 to 10 weeks before set-out time. Seeds require a soil temperature of 70° to 75°F to sprout. Seedlings should be transferred to cell packs for growing on before being set out in the garden. Plant individuals 1 to 1½ feet apart. Mature plants can survive occasional frost to 25°F. In colder areas, roots may be dug, potted up, and stored in a cold frame. Average,

well-drained soil suits, and full sun ensures maximum flowering.

Cultivars of mealycup sage are listed below.

'Alba': 18 to 24 inches tall; flowers white.

'Argent': 15 to 18 inches tall; flowers early to bloom, white.

'Blue Bedder': 12 to 15 inches tall; flowers violet blue.

'Catima': 18 to 24 inches tall; flowers deep blue.

'Delft': 15 to 18 inches tall; flowers light blue.

'Regal Purple', 'Royal Purple': 18 to 24 inches tall; flowers deep violet blue.

'Rhea': 10 to 12 inches tall; flowers early to bloom (about 15 weeks from seed), dark blue.

'Silver', 'Silver White': 15 to 18 inches tall; flowers early to bloom, white.

'Victoria': 15 to 18 inches tall; flowers early to bloom (about 15 weeks from seed), deep blue; spikes prolific.

'Warwick': 15 to 18 inches tall; flowers dark blue.

'White Porcelain': 12 to 15 inches tall; flowers silvery white.

SANVITALIA PROCUMBENS
(Creeping zinnia)

Creeping zinnia is a spreading, mat-forming, tender annual that does not exceed 6 inches in height but spreads to 12 to 15 inches. It bears a profusion of miniature zinnialike flowers from early summer to frost. The individual heads are ½ to ¾ inch across, and the rays are in shades of yellow and orange, surrounding a purplish brown central disc. Excellent for edging, creeping zinnia is also well suited to window boxes.

Seed may be sown directly in the garden from zone 8 south in early spring. Elsewhere it is best to start seed indoors under lights or in a greenhouse at about 70°F 8 to 10 weeks before set-out time, growing the seedlings on in cell packs. In the garden, sandy-humusy soil is ideal, but any well-drained, loamy soil suffices. Creeping zinnia thrives in summer heat

and high humidity, but if the mats become too thick and dense, spotty die-out can ensue. Hence the advisability of spacing plants 10 to 12 inches apart. Floral abundance depends on adequacy of sun exposure, with full sun yielding best results.

The relatively few cultivars include the following.

'Gold Braid' (double yellow-orange flowers).

'Golden Carpet' (single yellow flowers).

'Mandarin Orange' (semidouble orange flowers, ¾ to 1 inch across).

'Yellow Carpet' (dark green foliage; single yellow flowers).

SCHIZANTHUS SPP.
(Butterfly flower)

Sometimes called the poor man's orchid because of the delicacy of its violet, pink, or white flowers and its ease of cultivation, butterfly flower presents a pyramid of bloom above the finely cut, very ornamental foliage. Plants grow 1 to 4 feet tall, depending on species or cultivar.

Seed may be started directly in the garden in the spring after danger of frost or indoors under lights or in a greenhouse six to eight weeks before set-out time. Sow seed thinly and cover lightly; transfer seedlings to cell packs. In the garden, most any well-drained, loamy soil of moderate fertility is adequate, and plants come into flower early, often only six weeks after germination. Usually, the period of bloom is limited to relatively cool weather in late spring and early summer, when night temperatures are below 65°F. Butterfly flower is thus best used as an interplanting in the transitional period between spring bulbs and summer annuals. Along the Pacific Coast and in other regions enjoying relatively cool summer nights, butterfly flower will perform creditably over several months. Spacing will vary from 12 to 18 inches for tall types and 6 to 9 inches for dwarfs.

Most garden hybrids and cultivars are derived in part from S. × wisetonensis. The cultivars listed below grow 10 to 15 inches tall, unless otherwise noted.

'Angel Wings': more resistant than most to summer heat; flowers purple, red, pink, or salmon, all with yellow centers.

'Cherry Shades': 1 to 2 feet tall; flowers red with purple or maroon marbling.

'Disco': compact habit; flowers violet, pink, or white.

'Dwarf Bouquet': flowers red, pink, salmon, or yellow-orange.

'Hit Parade': flowers shades of pink and pinkish violet.

'Star Parade': 6 to 9 inches tall; very heat sensitive; flowers violet, red, pink, salmon, or white.

TITHONIA ROTUNDIFOLIA
(Mexican sunflower)

Also known by the common names Mexican hat and torch flower, Mexican sunflower is valued as a tall accent in the rear of the garden. It produces a long succession of striking red-orange or yellow flowers, 3 to 3½ inches across, that resemble single dahlias. Height ranges from 4 to 8 feet, depending on cultivar. The taller sorts usually require staking, but even when supported, they may break apart in summer storms. If plants are spaced 1½ to 2 feet apart, such damage is usually minimized.

Seed may be started directly in the garden from zone 8 south after all danger of frost. In the North, bloom from midsummer to frost is ensured by starting seed indoors under lights or in a greenhouse at 70° to 75°F six to eight weeks before set-out time. Plant seeds about ¾ inch apart and ¼ inch deep; grow seedlings in small pots in a sandy soil mix, as sogginess can be fatal. Mexican sunflower is a tender, large-leaved annual that thrives in heat and humidity, and grows quickly in average

or even substandard well-drained soil if placed in full sun. As the lower, older foliage may succumb to powdery mildew in late summer, it is well to front Mexican sunflower with somewhat lower plants, such as tall cosmos or marigold.

Mexican sunflower cultivars include the following.

'Goldfinger': 2 to 3 feet tall; flowers 2½ to 3 inches across, red-orange.

'Sundance': 3 to 4 feet tall; flowers 2½ to 3 inches across, red-orange.

'Torch': 4 to 6 (up to 8) feet tall; flowers 3 to 4 inches across, red-orange.

'Yellow Torch': 3½ to 5 feet tall; flowers 2½ to 3½ inches across; yellow.

TORENIA FOURNIERII
(Wishbone flower)

The little trumpetlike flowers of wishbone flower are borne in profusion over most of the summer, heat notwithstanding, as long as soil moisture is adequate. Attaining hardly more than 1 foot in height, wishbone flower is an excellent edging plant or border subject, especially if planted in large patches or drifts. The usual flower colors are lavender and deep violet with a yellow blotch, but forms with pink or white flowers also exist. A tender annual, wishbone flower tolerates no frost, but often self-sows.

Seed may be sown indoors under lights or in a greenhouse 8 to 10 weeks before set-out time, with the seedlings grown in cell packs. Alternatively, seed may be started somewhat later in a coldframe. Scatter the seed thinly and cover very lightly with fine, dry, dusty soil or soil mix. Moisten with a fine spray or mister. The seedlings are easily transplanted and should be spaced 6 to 8 inches apart in

moderately fertile, well-drained soil, preferably in partial shade.

Cultivars include 'Clown Hybrids', 6 to 9 inches tall with 1-inch flowers in combinations of purple, lilac, rose pink, pale pink, and white, all yellow-blotched; and 'Compacta', 6 to 8 inches, with the prototypic lavender and purple flowers, each with a yellow blotch.

TROPAEOLUM MAJUS
(Nasturtium)

Garden nasturtiums are a group of mounded or trailing cultivars derived mainly from the climbing wild type and are among the easiest annuals to grow. The leaves are circular and waxy, and the solitary, irregular, spurred, side-facing flowers are large and showy—about 2½ inches across, in shades of yellow or red. Bloom begins in midsummer, but the flowers become more abundant as the summer wanes, days shorten, and heat is less intense.

Seed should be sown in the spring after danger of frost where the plants are to grow, as nasturtium does not transplant easily. Simply push one or two seeds together 1 or 2 inches into the soil. For early bloom, especially north of zone 6, they may be started indoors under lights or in a greenhouse four to six weeks before set-out time, using peat pots. In the garden, these can be planted, pot included, thus averting root disturbance. Poor soil is an advantage with nasturtium; it results in smaller plants and more flowers than does ordinary garden loam. Rich soil stimulates a great growth of oversize foliage, which is undeniably attractive in its own right, but few flowers. Full sun is also requisite for maximal bloom. Spacing of dwarf forms is about 1 foot, of larger ones 2 feet or more, depending on habit.

Among the many hybrids and cultivars available, the following are meritorious.

'Alaska' hybrids: 12 to 18 inches tall; 3 to 4 feet wide; leaves small, variegated with white; flowers single, many shades, from cream through yellow, orange, and red to red-brown.

'Cherry Rose': 9 to 12 inches tall; flowers semidouble, rosy cerise, borne above foliage.

'Double Gleam' hybrids: trails to 3 feet; flowers semidouble or fully double, mixed colors.

'Dwarf Compact' hybrids: 6 to 8 inches tall; flowers single, mixed colors, borne above foliage.

'Empress of India': 7 to 9 inches tall; flowers single, deep red.

'Fiery Festival': 4 to 6 inches tall; flowers single, red, fragrant.

'Fordhook Favorites': trails to 6 feet; flowers single, mixed colors.

'Gleam' hybrids: trails to 1½ feet; flowers semidouble, mixed colors.

'Jewel' hybrids: 10 to 12 inches tall; flowers double, red-brown, red, or yellow.

'Salmon Baby': 9 to 12 inches tall; flowers deep salmon pink, fringed.

'Strawberries and Cream': 9 to 12 inches tall; flowers single, cream with red basal spots.

'Tom Thumb' hybrids: 6 to 9 inches tall; flowers single, mixed colors.

'Whirlybird' hybrids: 10 to 12 inches tall; flowers early to bloom, mixed colors, borne above foliage, spurless, upward facing.

VERBENA × HYBRIDA
(Garden verbena)

Garden verbena is a perennial from zone 9 south but is widely grown as an annual and valued everywhere for its wide range of bright floral colors and diverse habit. Most popular today are the dwarf, spreading cultivars, seldom exceeding 1 foot in height, and flowering generously in all but the hottest summer weather. Supplemental irrigation and deadheading at such times help restore flowering when the heat moderates.

The seed of verbena is sometimes resistant to breaking dormancy, but chilling the seed in the refrigerator for a week or so before sowing seems to help, as does limiting soil moisture in the seed bed to mere dampness. In the latter case, the soil mix should be thoroughly wetted one day, the seed planted the next day, the bed covered with clear plastic and watered no further until seedlings appear. At this point, the plastic cover should be removed but the seedlings watered only

when the soil surface appears dry. A temperature of 60° to 70°F is required throughout. Sow seed thinly and cover with ¼ inch of fine soil or soil mix well tamped down, as the seeds must be shielded from light to germinate. As it takes about 2½ months for verbena to come into flower from seed, seed should be started indoors under lights or in a greenhouse six to eight weeks before set-out time, and the seedlings grown on in cell packs. Ordinary, well-drained, loamy soil in full sun yields best results. Dwarf

---

GARDEN VERBENA HYBRIDS AND CULTIVARS OF MERIT

DWARF, SPREADING FORMS (8 TO 12 INCHES TALL, UNLESS OTHERWISE INDICATED)
'Amethyst': flowers 2½-inch clusters, sky blue with white base.
'Blaze': flowers red with white base.
'Crystal': flowers white.
'Dwarf Jewels': flowers mixed colors.
'Marbella': flowers white.
'Peaches and Cream': 6 to 8 inches tall; spreads to 12 inches; flowers salmon, rose pink, and white.
'Romance' hybrids: 6 to 8 inches tall; spreads to 12 inches; flowers early to bloom mixed colors.
'Showtime' hybrids: spreads to 15 inches; flowers mixed colors.
'Sparkle' hybrids: flowers mixed colors with white base.
'Springtime' hybrids: spreading habit; flowers mixed colors.
'Tropic': flowers solid deep red (without white base).

TALL, UPRIGHT FORMS (12 TO 18 INCHES TALL)
'Amour' hybrids: flowers mixed colors.
'Limbo': flowers magenta.
'Petite' hybrids: compactly branched; flowers mixed colors.
'Trinidad': compactly branched; flowers rose pink.

Garden verbena
(*Verbena × hybrida* 'Blaze')

VIOLA HYBRIDS AND CULTIVARS OF SPECIAL MERIT
All 4 to 8 inches tall.

'Admiration': flowers deep violet with yellow center.
'Arkwright Ruby': flowers red with dark red blotch, fragrant.
'Bambini' hybrids: flowers small, mixed colors, mostly bicolor.
'Chantreyland': flowers apricot-orange.
'Cuty': flowers 1½ to 1¾ inches across, upper petals violet, lower petals cream with violet smudge.
'Jersey Gem': flowers blue.
'Lord Nelson': flowers deep violet.
'Lutea Splendens': flowers yellow.
'Maroon Picotee': flowers red-brown with other colors.
'Pretty': upper petals purple with yellow edge, lower petals all yellow.
'Princess Blue': flowers 1 inch across, violet blue, early to bloom (10 weeks from seed).
'Rubin': flowers reddish claret.
'Scottish' hybrids: flowers 1½ to 2 inches across, solid colors and bicolor.
'White Perfection': flowers all white.
'Yellow Charm': flowers all yellow, prolific.

strains should be spaced 6 to 10 inches apart, tall ones 12 to 15 inches.

VIOLA *SPP.*
(Pansy, viola)

Pansy and other violas are hardy annuals or short-lived perennials treated as annuals and are derived from several species that are closely related to various wild violets. All are low plants that bear their solitary flowers most freely in spring and early summer, and sometimes again in fall.

In zones 6 through 8, seed may be sown in the fall in a coldframe and the plants set out in the spring. Alternatively, seed may be started indoors under lights or in a greenhouse 10 to 12 weeks before the average date of the last spring frost. The seedlings should be grown in cell packs and hardened off in a coldframe before being set out. It should be kept in mind that the seed of pansies and violas requires light to germinate, hence should be sown thinly and pressed into the soil or soil mix with a block of wood before being moistened gently to prevent the seed floating away. Ordinary, well-drained soil in full sun or partial shade promotes bountiful bloom. Spacing should be 6 to 8 inches. Afternoon shade from zone 7 south helps prolong flowering into summer, which, however, normally ceases as daytime temperatures approach 90°F. If plants are cut back and the soil kept moist, some may rejuvenate and reflower in the fall. Pansies will survive most winters from zone 7 south, especially if mulched loosely with straw or pine needles in late fall.

Garden pansies are a complex of hybrids included under the species *V. × wittrockiana*, characterized by large (2 to 4 inches or more in diameter), single, flat flowers in a great range of colors (mostly bicolor and tricolor) and patterns. Garden violas are a separate complex of hybrids, derived by crossing one or more species (chiefly *V. cornuta*) with various pansies. Violas bear 1- to 1½-inch flowers in nearly as wide a color range but are mostly bicolor. Violas flower later into the summer, but unless given afternoon shade from zone 7 south, they cease flowering and largely die out.

PANSY HYBRIDS AND CULTIVARS OF SPECIAL MERIT
All are 5 to 7 inches tall, except where otherwise indicated.

'Accord': flowers 3 to 3½ inches across, mixed colors, mostly with contrasting blotch, prolific.

'Azure Blue': flowers sky blue.

'Beaconsfield': petals pale blue, lower petals dark blue; blooms in fall and early spring (all winter in zone 9).

'Black Devil': flowers 2 inches across, black-violet, with yellow eye.

'Black Prince': flowers 3 to 3½ inches across, black with yellow eye.

'Colossal' hybrids: flowers 4 to 4½ inches across, mixed colors.

'Crown' hybrids:* flowers 3¾ to 4 inches across, bicolor or solid.

'Crystal Bowl' hybrids:* flowers, 2¼ to 2½ inches across, solid mixed colors (no blotch), early to bloom.

'Flame Princess':* 5 to 8 inches tall; flowers yellow to cream with red to mahogany blotch, early to bloom.

'Floral Dance' hybrids: 6 to 9 inches tall; flowers mixed colors, blooms in fall, winter, and early spring in zone 9.

'Glacier Ice': 6 to 9 inches tall; flowers deep blue, white toward base, purple central blotch.

'Imperial' hybrids:* spreads to 12 inches; flowers 3¾ to 4 inches across, mixed colors, long period of bloom.

'Joker' hybrids: flowers bicolor and tricolor, strong color contrasts (e.g., 'Jolly Joker' has deep violet-and-orange flowers).

'Love Duet' hybrids: flowers white with rose pink to red-brown central blotch.

'Lyric' hybrids:* flowers 3 to 3½ inches across, mixed colors, blotched.

'Majestic Giants' hybrids:* flowers 3¾ to 4 inches across, wide range of colors, mostly bicolor, early to bloom.

'Maxim' hybrids:* flowers mostly tricolor, prolific.

'Moody Blues': flowers 2¾ to 3 inches across, deep blue-violet, white toward base, deep violet central blotch.

'Rippling Waters': 6 to 9 inches tall; flowers deep violet with white border.

'Padparadja': flowers 1½ to 2 inches across, deep orange.

'Shades of Blue': 6 to 8 inches tall; flowers various shades and patterns of blue and white.

'Silver Bride': flowers white with violet central botch.

'Spring Magic' hybrids:* 6 to 9 inches tall; flowers sometimes solid colors (e.g., 'Spring Magic Moonlight' has pale yellow flowers).

'Super Majestic' hybrids: flowers 4 to 4½ inches across, mixed, bicolor and tricolor.

'Swiss Giants' hybrids: syn. 'Roggli' hybrids: flowers mostly bicolor, bloom later than most.

'Universal' hybrids: flowers about 2 inches across, mixed colors, various patterns, prolific, early to bloom.

'Viking' hybrids:* flowers 3¾ to 4 inches across, mixed colors, various patterns.

'Wine Fashion': flowers white with burgundy blotch.

* An F_1, heat-tolerant cultivar.

Pansy (*Viola × wittrockiana*)

OTHER GARDEN ANNUALS

Name	Height	Spacing	Flower (or Foliage) Color	Sowing*	Comments
Abronia umbellata (sand verbena)	6–10"	8–12"	Rose pink	I 6	Best where summers are cool
Acroclinium roseum (rose everlasting)	1–1½'	4–6"	Rose pink	I 6–8 or O spring	Good everlasting
Actinotus helianthi (flannel flower)	1½–2'	8–12"	White	I 8–10 or O spring	Perennial in zones 9 and 10; elsewhere grown as an annual
Adonis aestivalis (summer adonis)	1–1½'	6–8"	Red and black	I 6–8 or O early spring	Blooms in spring if sown in fall
A. annua (pheasant's-eye)	1⅓–1⅔'	6–8"	Red and black	I 6–8 or O early spring	Blooms in spring if sown in fall
Agrostemma githago 'Milas' (corn cockle)	3–4'	8–12"	Rose lavender	I 6 or O spring	Dies at onset of hot weather
Alcea rosea annual cvs. (annual hollyhock)	2–6'	1–1¼'	All but blue	I 6–8 or O early spring	Some plants may overwinter
Alonsoa linearis (mask flower)	1¼–1½'	6–8"	Brick red	I 6–8	Thrives in cool summer weather
A. warscewiczii (mask flower)	1½–2'	6–8"	Orange	I 6–8	Thrives in cool summer weather
Alternanthera ficoidea (parrot leaf)	2–3⅓'	8–12"	Variegated foliage	Grown from cuttings	Cultivars with white, rose, red, or orange variegation
Ammi majus (bishop's flower)	1–3'	8–12"	Cream	O spring	Sow seed where plants will grow
Ammobium alatum var. *grandiflorum* (winged everlasting)	2–3'	8–12"	White or yellow	I 6–8	Perennial in zones 9 and 10
Anagalis arvensis var. *caerulea* (blue pimpernel)	6–8"	8–10"	Blue	O spring	Spreads; cool weather best
A. monelli var. *linifolia* (flax leaf pimpernel)	10–18"	4–6"	Blue, purple, or red	I 6–8	Seedlings tolerate light frost
Anchusa capensis 'Blue Bird' (blue bird alkanet)	1–1½'	6–9"	Bright blue	I 6–8 O spring, or O fall (zones 9 and 10)	One of the best blue-flowered annuals
Androsace lactiflora (Siberian rock jasmine)	6–8"	4–6"	White	O spring	Tufted habit
A. macrantha (dwarf rock jasmine)	1½–2"	3–4"	White	O spring	Good for rock gardens
Anoda cristata (opal cup)	3–4'	1–1½'	Lavender	I 6–8 or O spring	Requires staking; self-sows
Arctotis × *hybrida* (African daisy)	1–1½'	6–8"	Yellow, red, or purple	I 6–8	Best in cool summers
Argemone grandiflora (prickly poppy)	3–3⅓'	10–12"	White	I 8–10 or O spring (zones 9 and 10)	Requires summer heat to perform optimally
A. mexicana (Mexican poppy)	2–3'	10–12"	Yellow or orange	I 8–10 or O spring (zones 9 and 10)	Requires summer heat to perform optimally
Asperula orientalis (blue woodruff)	9–12"	4–6"	Lavender blue	I 6–8	Does well on poor soil and in partial shade
Atriplex hortensis (garden orache)	2–3'	10–15"	Colored foliage	O spring	Leaves edible
Baileya multiradiata (desert marigold)	1¼–1⅔'	6–8"	Yellow	O spring or O fall (zone 9 and 10)	Performs best in cool summers
Beta vulgaris var. *flavescens* 'Dracaenifolia' (ornamental red chard)	10–14"	8–10"	Red foliage	I 6–8 in peat pots or O spring	Ornamental foliage
Borago officinalis (borage)	1½–2'	10–12"	Blue	O early spring	Successive sowing advisable
Bassia scoparia f. *trichophylla* (kochia, summer cypress)	2–5'	8–15"	Red foliage in fall	I 6–8 or O spring	Neat, pyramidal habit; self-sows in zones 8 to 10
Brachycome iberidifolia (Swan River daisy)	9–14"	4–6"	Blue, pink, or white	I 4–6 or O spring	Good edging plant; successive sowings advisable

(continues)

OTHER GARDEN ANNUALS (continued)

Name	Height	Spacing	Flower (or Foliage) Color	Sowing*	Comments
Brassica oleracea cvs. (flowering cabbage, flowering kale)	1–1¼'	1–1¼'	White, pink, or rose foliage	I 8–10 or O spring	Leaf variegation best in fall and early winter
Bupleurum rotundifolium (green gold)	1–1½'	3–6"	Yellow	I 4–6 or O spring	Good filler plant; attractive leaves
Calandrinia ciliata (red maids)	9–12"	6–8"	Red	I 4–6 or O spring	Performs best in cool summers; often biennial
C. grandiflora (rock purslane)	1½–2'	10–12"	Rose	I 4–6 or O spring	Performs best in cool summers; often biennial
C. umbellata (rock purslane)	6–8"	4–6"	Magenta	I 4–6 or O spring	Gray green foliage
Calceolaria crenatiflora (slipperwort)	1–2'	8–10"	Yellow with dark spots	I 4–6 or O early spring	Performs best in cool summers
C. integrifolia, syn. *c. rugosa* (little sweeties)	2–5'	1–1½'	Yellow to red-brown	I 4–6 or O early spring	Performs best in cool summers
C. mexicana (slipper flower)	1–1½'	8–10"	Yellow	I 4–6 or O early spring	Performs best in cool summers
C. tripartita (lemon drops)	9–24"	6–8"	Yellow	I 4–6 or O early spring	Performs best in cool summers
Campanula macrostyla (annual Canterbury bells)	1–2'	10–12"	Blue, pink, or white	I 6–8 or O spring	Blooms in late summer and early fall
C. medium (Canterbury bells)	2–3'	8–12"	Purple, lavender, pink, or white	I 10–12	Normally biennial but flowers first year from sown very early indoors
C. ramosissima (bluestar bellflower)	8–12"	4–6"	Blue	I 6–8	Mound forming
Capsicum annuum (ornamental pepper)	8–24"	6–12"	Red or black fruit	I 8–10	Requires sustained heat; hot edible fruit
Catananche caerulea (Cupid's dart)	1½–2'	1–1½'	Blue and/or white	I 6–8	Easily dried everlasting
Centaurea americana (basket flower)	3–4'	1–1½'	Lavender	O spring or O fall (zones 8 and 9)	Performs best in cool summers
C. cineraria (dusty miller)	1½–2'	9–15"	Purple rose	I 6–8	Grown for gray foliage
C. cyanus (cornflower, bachelor button)	1½–3'	8–12"	Blue, pink, or white	O early spring or O fall (zones 8 and 9)	Cool weather and poor soil yield best results
C. moschata (sweet sultan)	1½–2'	8–12"	Blue, pink, or white	I 6–8 or O spring	Best in cool summers; also listed as *Amberboa moschata*
C. moschata var. *imperialis* (royal sweet sultan)	1½–2½'	8–12"	Blue, pink, or white	I 6–8 or O spring	Larger-flowered form of *C. moschata*
Centaurium pulchellum (centaury)	6–15"	3–6"	Pink	O early spring or O fall (zones 9 and 10)	Performs best in cool summers
Ceratotheca triloba (southern foxglove)	5–6'	1½–2'	White	I 6–8 or O early spring (zones 8–10)	Performs best in hot summers
Chamaecrista fasciculata (partridge pea)	2–4'	8–12"	Yellow	O spring	Best in hot summers; also listed as *Cassia fasciculata*
Chrysanthemum carinatum (annual chrysanthemum)	2–2½'	9–10"	Various bicolors	O early spring	Performs best in cool summers
C. coronarium (crown daisy)	2–4'	1–1½'	Yellow	O early spring	Performs best in cool summers
C. parthenium (feverfew)	1–2½'	9–12"	White and yellow	I 6–8 or O spring	Flowers best in late spring and early fall
C. segetum (corn marigold)	1–2'	8–12"	Yellow	I 6–8 or O spring	Performs best in cool summers
Cirsium japonicum (Japanese thistle)	1½–2½'	6–8"	Red-violet	I 6–8 or O spring	Foliage relatively thorn free

Name	Height	Spacing	Flower (or Foliage) Color	Sowing*	Comments
Clarkia amoena (farewell-to-spring; godetia)	1½–2½ (5)'	10–12"	Red, pink, lilac, or white	I 6–8 or O spring	Thrives in cool summer weather; seed requires light to germinate, hence is surface sown
C. pulchella	1–1½'	8–10"	Lilac	I 6–8 or O spring	Thrives in cool summer weather; treat seed as for *C. amoena*
C. unguiculata	2–4 (6)'	10–12"	Pink, rose purple, or white	I 6–8 or O spring	Thrives in cool summer weather; treat seed as for *C. amoena*
Collinsia bicolor (Chinese houses)	1½–2'	6–8"	Blue, pink, or white	I 6–8 or O spring	Best in cool summers; listed as *C. heterophylla* in some catalogs
Collomia cavanillesii (Chilean gilia)	1½–2'	6–8"	Red	I 6–8 or O spring	Performs best in cool summers
Consolida ambigua (rocket larkspur)	2–3'	9–12"	Purple, blue, pink, or white	O early spring or O fall	Sow seed where plants will grow, cover well to shield from light; listed as *Delphinium ajacis* in some catalogs
C. regalis (field larkspur)	1½–2'	9–12"	Violet or blue	O early spring or O fall	Sow seed where plants will grow, treat seed as for *C. ambigua*; listed as *Delphinium consolida* in some catalogs
Coreopsis bigelovii (Bigelow coreopsis)	1¼–1½'	10–15"	Yellow	O spring	Incorrectly listed as *C. stillmanii* in some catalogs
C. grandiflora 'Early Sunrise' (double coreopsis)	1¼–2'	8–12"	Yellow	I 6–8	Perennial; reliably flowering the first year
C. maritima (sea dahlia)	2–3'	9–12"	Yellow	O spring	Often perennial in zones 9 and 10
Crepis rubra (hawk's beard)	1–2'	6–10"	Red to pink	I 6–8 or O spring	Thrives in cool summer weather
Crotalaria juncea (rattlebox)	3–4'	1–1½'	Yellow	I 8–10	Performs best in hot summers
C. retusa (rattlebox)	1–1½'	6–12"	Yellow	I 8–10	Performs best in hot summers
C. spectabilis (rattlebox)	2–4'	1–1½'	Yellow	I 8–10	Performs best in hot summers
Cuphea ignea (firecracker plant)	1–1½'	8–12"	Red, black and white	I 8–10	Performs best in hot summers
C. × purpurea (cigar flower)	8–12"	6–8"	Red or cerise	I 8–10	Good edging plant
C. viscosissima (clammy cuphea)	1½–2'	8–12"	Magenta and white	I 8–10	Covered with sticky hairs
Cynoglossum amabile (hound's-tongue)	1½–2'	6–9"	Blue, pink, or white	I 6–8, O spring, or O fall (zones 9 and 10)	Performs best in cool summers
C. officinale (hound's-tongue)	1½–2'	9–12"	Purplish red	I 6–8, O spring or O fall (zones 9 and 10)	Performs best in cool summers
Datura inoxia (angel's trumpet)	2–3'	1–1½'	White to pale lavender	I 8–10	Large flowers nocturnal, fragrant; perennial from zone 7 south
D. metel (horn of plenty)	3–5'	1½–2'	White, yellow, lavender, and/or purple	I 8–10	Flowers single or double; all *Datura* spp. poisonous to eat
Diascia barberae (twinspur)	10–18"	4–6"	Pink and purple	I 6–8	Performs best in cool summers
Digitalis grandiflora 'Temple Bells' (white annual foxglove)	1½–2'	8–10"	Cream	I 8–10, O early spring, or O fall (zones 7–9)	Flowers in summer; sometimes over-winters and reflowers
D. purpurea 'Foxy' (purple annual foxglove)	2–3'	10–15"	Magenta and white, spotted	I 8–10	Branching habit; flowers in summer; sometimes overwinters

(continues)

OTHER GARDEN ANNUALS (continued)

Name	Height	Spacing	Flower (or Foliage) Color	Sowing*	Comments
Dorotheanthus bellidiformis (Livingston daisy)	2–3"	4–6"	Lavender, pink, or yellow	I 8–10 or O spring	Performs best in cool summers
Dyssodia tenuiloba (Dahlberg daisy)	6–8"	3–6"	Yellow	I 6–8 or O early spring	Performs best in cool summers; blooms 15 weeks from seed
Echium plantagineum (viper's bugloss)	1½–2'	1–1¼'	Purple, pink, or white	I 6–8, O spring, or O fall (zones 9 and 10)	Excellent border plant
E. vulgare (viper's bugloss)	1–1½'	8–12"	Purple, pink, or white	I 6–8, O spring, or O fall (zones 9 and 10)	Several cultivars in various shades
Emilia javanica (tassel flower)	1½–2'	6–9"	Red, orange, or yellow	I 6–8, O spring, or O fall (zones 9 and 10)	Second sowing in midsummer advisable; often self-sows
Erysimum hybrids (double-flowered annual wallflower)	8–12"	4–6"	Red, yellow, or mahogany	I 8–10 or O early spring	Performs best in cool summers
Euphorbia cyathophora (painted spurge)	2–3'	8–12"	Upper foliage red at base	I 6–8 or O spring	Red leaf bases appear in late summer; often self-sows
E. marginata (snow-on-the-mountain)	3–4'	1–1¼'	Upper foliage white edged	O early spring	Milky juice poisonous; often self-sows
Exacum affine (Persian violet)	8–18"	6–8"	Blue, purple, and yellow	I 8–10	Requires light shade and warmth to flower; good pot plant
Felicia amelloides (blue marguerite)	1–2½'	1–1½'	Blue to purple or white	I 6–8	Performs best in cool summers
F. bergeriana (kingfisher daisy)	4–8"	4–6"	Blue with yellow disc	I 6–8	Good for edging or window boxes
Gaillardia amblyodon (maroon gaillardia)	1½–2'	6–9"	Red-brown to maroon	I 6–8 or O spring	Cool summers and deadheading extend bloom
G. × grandiflora (hybrid gaillardia)	1½–2½'	1–1¼'	Yellow and red	I 6–8	Perennial, flowering first year if started early
G. pulchella (rose-ring gaillardia, Indian blanket)	1½–2'	6–9"	Yellow and rose purple	I 6–8 or O spring	Bloom extended in cool summers
Gaura lindheimeri (Texas gaura)	2–5'	1½–2'	White, aging to pink	I 6–8 or O spring	Perennial (zones 7 to 9), flowering first year
Gazania hybrids (treasure flower)	8–16"	6–10"	Red to yellow, darker at base	I 6–8	Flowers open in sun; intolerant of high humidity
Gerbera jamesonii (Transvaal daisy)	10–24"	8–12"	Red to yellow pastels	I 10–12	Slow growing; perennial in zones 9 and 10
Gilia capitata (globe gilia)	2–3'	9–12"	Blue	I 6–8 or O spring	Performs best in cool summers
G. tricolor (bird's-eye gilia)	1½–2½'	9–12"	Purple and white	I 6–8 or O spring	Performs best in cool summers
Gomphrena globosa (globe amaranth)	10–24"	6–12"	Magenta	I 6–8 or O spring	Makes a good everlasting
Gypsophila elegans (annual baby's breath)	1–1½'	6–8"	White or pink	O spring, or O fall (zones 9 and 10)	Profusion of small flowers; resow for succession of bloom
G. muralis (cushion gypsophila)	4–6"	4–6"	Rose	O spring, or O fall (zones 9 and 10)	Good edging plant or for rock gardens
Helianthus debilis (cucumber-leaf sunflower)	1–4'	1–2'	Yellow or red-brown	O spring	Best for cut flowers; several dwarf cultivars
Heliophila leptophylla (Cape stock)	1–1½'	8–10"	Blue and white	I 6–8 or O spring	Performs best in cool summers; *H. longifolia* is similar
Heliotropium arborescens (heliotrope)	10–15"	8–12"	Purple to lavender	I 10–12	Performs best in warm summers; rich soil

Name	Height	Spacing	Flower (or Foliage) Color	Sowing*	Comments
Helipterum spp. (everlasting)	1–2'	8–12"	Yellow or white	I 6–8 or O spring	Flowers easily dried
Hibiscus acetosella (purple-leaf hibiscus)	4–8'	1–2'	Deep purple foliage	I 6–8 or O spring	Flowers relatively inconspicuous
H. trionum 'Sunny Day' (flower-of-a-day)	1½–3'	8–12"	Pale yellow with purple center	I 6–8 or O spring	Each flower opens for one day; often self-sows
Hypoestes phyllostachya (polka-dot plant)	1–2'	10–15"	Leaves red-, pink-, or white-spotted foliage	I 10–12	Flowers inconspicuous; several color-specific cultivars
Iberis amara (annual candytuft)	6–12"	4–6"	Red-violet to white	O spring, or O fall (zones 7–10)	Flowers usually fragrant
I. umbellata (globe candytuft)	9–16"	6–8"	Purple, red, or pink	O spring	Deadheading prolongs flowering
Impatiens balfourii (pink touch-me-not)	1½–2'	6–8"	Pink and white	O early spring	Seed requires cold to germinate; often self-sows
I. cristata (Himalayan touch-me-not)	2–3'	10–12"	Light yellow	I 6–8, O spring, or O fall (zones 7–9)	Best in light shade; often self-sows
I. glandulifera (orchid impatiens)	3–5'	1–1½'	Red, pink, and/or white	O early spring	Seed requires cold to germinate; often self-sows
I. noli-tangere (European touch-me-not)	1½–2'	6–8"	Yellow spotted red	I 6–8 or O spring	Best in partial or light shade on damp ground
Ionopsidium acaule (violet cress, diamond flower)	2–3"	4–6"	Lilac	O spring or O fall (zones 9 and 10)	Rosette plant; performs best in cool summers
Ipomopsis aggregata (skyrocket)	1½–2½'	10–15"	Red, pink, or yellow	I 6–8, O spring, or O fall (zones 9 and 10)	Performs best in cool summers
I. rubra (standing cypress, Texas plume)	2–5'	9–12"	Red and yellow	I 6–8, O spring, or O fall (zones 9 and 10)	Performs best in cool summers
Lathyrus odoratus dwarf cvs. (dwarf sweet pea)	6–12"	6–12"	All but blue	O early spring or O fall (zones 8–10)	Several cultivars good edging plants or in baskets; best in cool summers
L. odoratus var. *nanellus* 'Snoopea' (bush sweet pea)	2–2½'	1–1½'	All but blue	O early spring or O fall (zones 8–10)	Mounding, nonclimbing form; best in cool summers
Layia platyglossa (tidytips)	1–1½'	8–10"	Yellow tipped white	O spring or O fall (zones 10)	Performs best in cool summers
Leonitis nepetifolia (prince's flag)	4–6 (8)'	1–1½'	Orange	I 6–8 or O spring	Usually unbranched; serial balls of flowers
Limnanthes douglasii (meadow foam)	4–8"	3–4"	White and yellow	O spring or O fall (zones 9 and 10)	Performs best in cool summers
Limonium sinuatum (notchleaf sea lavender)	1½–2'	10–15"	Violet to white	I 6–8	Good everlasting; includes *L. bonduellii*
L. suworowii: **see Psylliostachys**					
Linaria bipartita (cloven-tip toadflax)	1½–2'	10–15"	Purple, pink, white, with yellow	O spring or O fall (zones 9 and 10)	Performs best in cool summers
Linum grandiflorum (flowering flax)	8–12"	6–9"	Red, pink, blue, or ivory	O spring or O fall (zones 9 and 10)	Several color-specific cultivars; best in cool summers

(continues)

OTHER GARDEN ANNUALS (*continued*)

Name	Height	Spacing	Flower (or Foliage) Color	Sowing*	Comments
Lobelia tenuior (Australian lobelia)	1–1½'	6–8"	Blue or white	I 6–8 or O spring	Perennial in zone 10
Lopezia racemosa syn. *L. hirsuta* (mosquito flower)	1–2½'	6–8"	Red, pink, or white	I 8–10	Requires summer heat; flowers resemble mosquitoes
Lupinus hartwegii (Hartweg lupine)	2–3'	1–1½'	Purple, yellow, and pink	I 6–8 or O spring	Performs best in cool summers
L. hirsutus (blue annual lupine)	1½–2'	8–12"	Blue	O spring	Cv. 'Sunrise' makes superior display
L. luteus (European yellow lupine)	1½–2'	10–12"	Yellow	I 6–8 or O spring	Performs best in cool summers
L. texensis (Texas bluebonnet)	10–12"	6–9"	Dark blue and white	I 6–8 or O spring	Best in alkaline soil; best in cool summers
Lychnis coeli-rosa (rose of heaven)	1–1½'	6–8"	Rose pink	I 6–8 or O spring	Thrives in summer heat
Machaeranthera tanacetifolia (Tahoka daisy)	1–2'	8–12"	Lavender blue	I 4–6 or O spring	Seed requires three weeks at 40°F to germinate; best in cool summers
Malcolmia maritima (Virginia stock)	6–12"	3–6"	Purple, pink, or white	O spring (or fall in zones 9 and 10)	Flowers fragrant
Malope trifida (mallowwort)	2–4'	10–12"	Rose red	O spring	Performs best in cool summers
M. sylvestris 'Mauritiana' (purple mallow)	3–6'	1–1½'	Purple	O spring	Blooms best in early fall; self-sows
M. sylvestris 'Zebrina' (striped mallow)	2–4'	8–12"	Lavender with purple stripes	O spring	Hardy to 20°F; often biennial; self-sows
M. verticillata 'Crispa' (curled mallow)	4–6'	1–1½'	Purple	O spring	Wavy leaves; self-sows
Martynia annua (unicorn plant)	3–4'	1½–2'	Purple to white, spotted	I 6–8 or O spring	Grown for long, curved capsule with two diverging horns
Matricaria recutita (German camomile)	1–2½'	1–1¼'	White and yellow	O spring	Performs best in cool summers
Matthiola incana (stock)	1–2½'	4–10"	Rose or purple or white	I 8–10, O early spring, or O fall (zones 9 and 10)	Very fragrant; dwarf and tall cultivars; best in cool summers
M. longipetala (evening stock)	1–1½'	6–8"	Purple or white	I 8–10, O early spring, or O fall (zones 9 and 10)	Night blooming; grown for fragrance
Mentzelia lindleyi (annual blazing star, bartonia)	1½–2½'	1–1¼'	White or yellow	O spring	Night blooming; fragrant; best in cool summers
Mesembryanthemum crystallinum (ice plant)	3–4"	10–12"	Pink or white	I 6–8 or O early spring (zones 9 and 10)	Brief flowering period; best in cool summers; spreads 18 to 24 inches
Mimosa pudica (sensitive plant)	9–12"	6–8"	Pink	I 8–10	Grown for touch-sensitive foliage; thrives in heat
Mimulus cupreus (monkey flower)	9–15"	6–9"	Red, yellow, or mottled	I 6–8	Usually short lived; best in cool summers; numerous cultivars
M. × hybridus (monkey flower)	1–1½'	6–9"	Purple, red, and/or yellow	I 6–8	See *M. cupreus*
Molucella laevis (bells of Ireland)	1½–2½'	8–12"	Green	O spring	Seeds require light to germinate; best in cool summers
Myosotis sylvatica (annual forget-me-not)	6–15"	4–6"	Blue, pink, or white	I 6–8 or O fall	Good edging plant; best in cool summers; self-sows
Nemesia strumosa (funfair)	9–18"	6–9"	Purple, red, orange, yellow, or white	I 6–8	Performs best in cool summers
Nemophila maculata (five-spot)	4–6"	6–8"	White with purple spots	I 6–8 or fall (zones 9 and 10)	Good edging plant; best in cool summers; spreads 10 to 12 inches

Name	Height	Spacing	Flower (or Foliage) Color	Sowing*	Comments
N. menziesii	9–12"	10–12"	Blue and/or white	I 6–8 or O fall (zones 9 and 10)	Performs best in cool summers
Nicandra physalodes (shoofly plant)	3–5'	1–1½'	Lilac blue and white	I 6–8	Papery five-winged pods used in dry arrangements
Nigella damascena (love-in-a-mist, devil-in-a-bush)	1–1½'	6–9"	Purple, blue, pink, or white	O spring	Brief blooming period; pods used in dry arrangements
Nolana paradoxa (blue bird)	3–6"	6–8"	Blue and white	I 6–8	Good edging plant; best in cool summers; spreads 10 to 15 inches
Ocimum basilicum (purple basil)	1–2'	6–8"	White or pink	I 8–10	Aromatic foliage; 'Dark Opal' best known cultivar
Oenothera biennis var. *grandiflora* (southern evening primrose)	3–6'	1½–2'	Yellow, aging to orange	I 8–10 or O spring	Night blooming; flowers larger than in common weedy form
O. deltoides (desert evening primrose)	2–10"	6–8"	White, aging to pink	I 8–10 or O spring	Night blooming; basally branched; spreading
O. drummondii (Drummond evening primrose)	6–12"	6–8"	Yellow	I 8–10 or O spring	Night blooming; spreading
O. glazioviana (orange-flowered evening primrose)	2–6'	1–1½'	Yellow aging to orange or red	I 8–10 or O spring	Night blooming; often sold as *O. erythrosepala*
O. laciniata (red-flowered evening primrose)	6–24"	4–8"	Yellow aging to red	I 8–10 or O spring	Night blooming; widely naturalized
O. macrocarpa (Ozark sundrops)	4–6"	6–8"	Yellow aging to red	I 8–10 or O spring	Night blooming, flowers 4 to 5 inches cross; spreading 10 to 15 inches; often sold as *O. missouriensis*
O. speciosa (showy evening primrose)	1–1½'	10–15"	White or pink	I 8–10 or O spring	Perennial, blooming first year; invasive by rhizomes
Omphalodes linifolia (navelwort)	1–1½'	6–8"	White	I 6–8	Performs best in cool summers; good cut flower
Orthocarpus purpurascens (owl clover)	6–12"	6–12"	Red-violet	O spring or fall (zones 9 and 10)	Attractive red stems
Osteospermum ecklonis (African daisy)	2–2⅓'	1–1½'	White with blue center	I 8–10 or O spring	Flowering extended by deadheading
Oxypetalum caeruleum (blue milkweed)	1½–3'	6–12"	Light blue	I 6–8	Often weakly twining; syn. *Tweedia caeruleum*
Penstemon cvs. (beardtongue)	1½–3'	6–8"	Purple, red, blue, or white	I 10–12	Performs best in cool summers; perennial, blooms first year if sown early
Perilla frutescens (purple basil, beefsteak plant)	2–3'	1–1¼'	Purplish	I 6–8 or O spring	Grown for odorless purple foliage; self-sows in zones 7 to 10
Phacelia campanularia (California bluebell)	8–12"	6–9"	Dark blue	I 6–8, O spring, or O fall (zones 9 and 10)	Performs best in cool summers; effective when massed
P. tanacetifolia (fiddleneck)	2–3'	8–12"	Blue to purple	O spring	Good bee plant; thrives in clay soils
P. viscida (sticky bluebell)	1–1½'	6–9"	Dark blue	O spring	Performs best in cool summers
Pimpinella anisum (anise)	1½–2½'	1⅔–2'	Light yellow	O spring	Useful herb; attracts dogs
Platystemon californicus (cream cups)	4–10"	4–6"	Light yellow	O early spring or O fall (zones 9 and 10)	Good edging plant
Polygonum capitatum 'Magic Carpet' (creeping knotweed)	1–3"	8–12"	Pink	I 6–8 or O spring	Good temporary ground cover

(continues)

OTHER GARDEN ANNUALS (*continued*)

Name	Height	Spacing	Flower (or Foliage) Color	Sowing*	Comment
Proboscidea fragrans (unicorn plant)	1½–2'	8–12"	Mauve	I 6–8 or O spring	Similar to *Martynia*
Psylliostachys suworowii (pink statice, Suworow sea lavender)	1½–2'	10–12"	Pink	I 8–10 or O spring	Thrives in heat, dryish soil
Rehmannia elata (Chinese foxglove)	1½–2'	8–12"	Rose pink	I 10–12	Perennial in zones 8 and 9, treated as annual elsewhere
Rhodanthe maglesii (Swan River everlasting)	1–2'	6–10"	Rose pink or white	I 6–8 or O spring	Flowers useful as everlastings
Ricinus communis (castor bean)	4–10'	2–3'	Yellow or red	I 6–8 or O spring	Grown for foliage; seeds toxic; best in heat and humidity
Sabatia spp. (marsh pink)	9–30"	6–12"	Pink	O summer (in coldframe)	Winter in coldframe for bloom in spring; most need moist to wet soil
Salpiglossus sinuata (painted tongue)	1½–2'	6–9"	Purple and/or yellow	I 8–10	Seed requires light to germinate; best in cool summers
Salvia coccinea (hairy red sage)	1½–3 (5)'	10–12"	Red, pink, and/or white	I 6–8 or O spring	Several cultivars, some tall and/or bicolored
S. elegans (pineapple sage)	2–4'	1–1½'	Red	I 10–12	Flowers in early fall
S. patens (gentian sage)	1½–2½'	10–12"	Dark blue	I 6–8 or O spring	Intense blue color; thrives in heat
S. sclarea (clary)	2–3'	10–12"	Purple and blue or white	I 6–8 or O spring	Aromatic foliage
S. splendens (scarlet sage)	1–2½'	8–12"	Red, pink, purple, or white	I 6–8 or O spring	Effective when massed; several color-specific cultivars
S. uliginosa (bog sage)	4–6'	1–1½'	Blue	I 6–8 or O spring	Requires moist soil
Saponaria calabrica (Calabrian soapwort)	1–1½'	8–10"	Purple, rose, or white	I 6–8 or O spring	Much branched; flowers abundant
Scabiosa atropurpurea (pincushion flower)	2–3'	8–12"	Purple, blue, red-brown, rose, or white	I 6–8, O spring, or O fall (zones 8 and 9)	Cover seed well to shield from light; thrives in heat; usually requires staking; attracts hummingbirds
Schizopetalon walkeri (fringed mustard)	8–18"	3–6"	White	I 6–8 (in pots)	Flowers almond scented, finely dissected; best in cool summers
Senecio cineraria (dusty miller)	1–2½'	8–12"	Gray white leaves	I 6–8	Excellent foliage plant; light needed for germination; perennial in zones 8 to 10
S. elegans (purple groundsel)	1½–2'	6–8"	Purple, rose, or white	I 6–8 or O fall (zones 8 and 9)	Performs best in cool summers
Silene armeria (sweet William campion)	1–1½'	6–8"	Rose pink	O spring	Sow seed where plants will grow
Silybum marianum (holy thistle)	3–4'	1–1½'	Purple	I 6–8	Thorny white-veined foliage; biennial, flowering first year if started early
Solanum integrifolium (tomato eggplant)	2–3'	1½–2'	White	I 8–10	Grown for decorative red-orange fruit
S. melongena cvs. (white eggplant)	1–2'	1–1½'	Lavender	I 12–16	Grown for decorative white, egglike fruit
S. sisymbrifolium (mustard-leaf nightshade)	2–4'	1½–2'	Lavender	I 6–8	Thorny stems; red berries in late summer; hardy to 20°F; self-sows
Tagetes tenuifolia var. *pumila* (dwarf signet marigold)	6–12"	6–12"	Yellow or orange	I 6–8 or O spring	Finely divided foliage; small, abundant bloom
Talinum paniculatum (jewels of Opar)	1–2'	6–8"	Red to yellow	I 6–8	Abundant beadlike flowers; perennial in zone 10
Thelesperma burridgeanum	1–1½'	6–8"	Brown-orange and yellow	O spring	Thrives in heat
Tolpis barbata (yellow hawkweed)	1–2'	6–12"	Yellow	I 6–8	Daisylike flowers late summer to frost

Name	Height	Spacing	Flower (or Foliage) Color	Sowing*	Comments
Trachymene caerulea (blue lace flower)	2–2½'	6–9"	Blue	I 6–8	Performs best in cool summers
Tweedia caerulea: see **Oxypetalum caeruleum**					
Ursinia anthemoides (sunshine daisy)	1–1½'	6–8"	Orange and red-violet	I 6–8	Performs best in cool summers in full sun
Vaccaria hispanica (sow cockle)	1–2'	8–12"	Pinkish purple	I 6–8 or O spring	Often self-sows
Venidium fastuosum (Cape daisy)	2–3'	8–12"	Orange and yellowish brown	I 6–8 or O spring	Showy flowers; attractive foliage
Verbena rigida (veiny verbena)	1–2'	1–1½'	Purple	I 6–8	Perennial in zones 8 and 9; can be invasive by underground stems
V. tenuisecta (moss verbena)	1–1¼'	8–10"	Purple	I 6–8	Stems mostly prostrate
Xeranthemum annuum (immortelle)	2–3'	6–9"	Purple	I 6–8	Performs best in cool summers; useful everlasting

* I, sow indoors the recommended number of weeks before set-out time. For example, "I 6–8" means sow indoors six to eight weeks before set-out time. O, sow outdoors in the recommended season. For example, "O spring" means sow outdoors in the spring.

Pincushion flower (*Scabiosa atropurpurea*)

Snow-on-the-mountain (*Euphorbia marginata*)

Corn cockle (*Agrostemma githago*)

Blue milkweed (*Oxypetalum caeruleum*)

Blue marguerite (*Felicia amelloides*)

Maroon gaillardia (*Gaillardia amblyodon*)

Flowering kale (*Brassica oleracea*)

Veiny verbena
(*Verbena rigida*)

Funfair
(*Nemesia strumosa*)

Hairy red sage
(*Salvia coccinea*)

Heliotrope
(*Heliotropium arborescens*)

**Notchleaf
sea lavender**
(*Limonium sinuatum*)

Castor bean
(*Ricinus communis*)

Striped mallow
(*Malva sylvestris* 'Zebrina')

Farewell-to-spring
(*Clarkia amoena*)

Ornamental pepper
(*Capsicum annuum*)

Love-in-a-mist (*Nigella damascena*)

Tassel flower (*Emilia javanica*)—background

ANNUAL CLIMBERS

All of the annual climbers discussed here perform best in full sun or partial shade. They flower from midsummer to frost, unless otherwise noted.

ASARINA ANTIRRHINIFLORA
(Climbing snapdragon)

4–8 feet

Climbing by leaf stalks that hook around supports, this slender climber has 1-inch leaves and solitary purple flowers, 1 inch long. Named cultivars have red, yellow, or white flowers. Climbing snapdragon endures cold to 25° F and is adaptable to most any soil, as long as moisture is adequate.

A. BARCLAIANA
(Climbing snapdragon)

8–12 feet

A. barclaiana is similar to *A. antirrhiniflora*, but it climbs by way of twining stems as well as hooking leaf stalks. Flowers range from pinkish lavender to purple.

A. SCANDENS
(Climbing snapdragon)

8–12 feet

A. sandens is similar to *A. antirrhiniflora*, but its flowers are about 1½ inches long. The blooms are purple, blue, pink, or white.

CAIOPHORA LATERITIA
(Froth flower)

4–6 feet

With twining stems and foliage partly clothed with stinging hairs, froth flower's blooms are 3 to 3½ inches across, opening orange and aging to white. Froth flower is an interesting curiosity and is best grown on sandy-humusy soil and supported with a wire mesh tomato cage.

CARDIOSPERMUM HALICACABUM
(Balloon vine)

6–10 feet

A tendril climber with divided leaves, balloon vine bears clusters of small white flowers followed by inflated, membranous, three-chambered seed capsules, about 1 inch across. The capsules may be dried and used in arrangements of everlastings. Balloon vine thrives in summer heat. Most any well-drained soil is suitable.

CENTROSEMA VIRGINIANA
(Butterfly pea)

6–8 feet

A slender twiner with three-parted leaves, butterfly pea bears lavender flowers, 2 inches across, that resemble large, inverted sweet peas. Long, slender, pointed, purple-edged pods follow. Sandy-humusy soil and long, hot summers produce best results.

CLITORIA TERNATEA
(Butterfly pea)

6–8 feet

A slender twiner with three-parted leaves, butterfly pea has flowers that are an intense deep blue and measure about 1½ inches across. The cultivar 'Blue Sails'

has double flowers. Grow in ordinary, well-drained soil.

COBAEA SCANDENS
(Cathedral bells, Cup-and-saucer vine)

10–20 feet

Climbing by leaf tendrils, cathedral bells bears nodding, bell-shaped, purple or greenish white flowers, each with a saucerlike base, from late summer to hard frost. It is a perennial in zones 9 and 10. Cathedral bells performs well on ordinary, well-drained soil.

CUCUMIS METULIFERUS
(African horned cucumber)

10–12 feet

A tendril climber with attractive yellow flowers 1 to 1½ inches across, African horned cucumber bears edible cucumber-like fruit, 3 to 5 inches long, that ripen bright red. Sandy-humusy soil is best.

CUCURBITA PEPO
VAR. OVIFERA
(Yellow-flowered gourd)

10–15 feet

Yellow-flowered gourd is a fast-growing tendril climber with large leaves. Its yellow-

Cathedral bells (*Cobaea scandens*)

orange flowers are 3 to 4 inches across. Variously colored, globose, ovoid, or bottle-shaped fruit, some conspicuously patterned or warted, follow. If allowed to mature before picking, it may be dried for use in autumn arrangements. Rich, humusy soil and plenty of compost and/or well-rotted manure are needed for maximum fruit production.

DOLICHOS LABLAB
(Hyacinth bean)

10–15 feet

Hyacinth bean is a fast-growing twiner with large, three-parted leaves and ¾-inch, lilac purple, pealike flowers borne on 6-inch spikes. Short, thick, horizontal pods follow, which are edible when young. Sandy-humusy soil yields best results both with flowers and pods.

ECCREMOCARPUS SCABER
(Glory flower)

6–10 feet

Glory flower is a tendril climber with divided leaves and 1-inch bell-shaped flowers of red, orange, or yellow. Perennial in zones 9 and 10, it blooms anywhere the first year if started indoors under lights six to eight weeks before set-out time. Ordinary, well-drained soil is suitable.

HUMULUS JAPONICUS
(Japanese hop)

10–20 feet

Japanese hop is a fast-growing twiner with long-stalked leaves and clusters of greenish flowers. In the cultivar 'Variegatus', the foliage is streaked and blotched white. Nitrate-rich, well-drained soil encourages large, well-developed leaves.

IPOMOEA ALBA
(Moonflower)

10–15 feet

A heat-loving twiner, moonflower has heart-shaped leaves and large, white, trumpet-shaped flowers, 4 to 6 inches across, that open quickly at dusk. Moonflower is perennial in zone 10. Sandy-humusy, well-drained soil yields the heaviest flowering.

I. NIL
(Hairy morning glory)

8–10 feet

A bristly twiner, hairy morning glory bears 3- to 4-inch trumpet flowers, ranging from purple to pale pink, and also white and some bicolors. Among named color-specific cultivars are the following.

'Chocolate' (pale pinkish brown).
'Early Call' (purple to pink with a white throat).
'Flying Saucers' (blue and white).
'Limbata' (purple with a white border).
'Scarlet O'Hara' (red).
'Spice Islands' (creeping, nonclimbing habit; variegated foliage; sparse red or pink flowers).

Grow on sandy-humusy soil enriched with superphosphate for abundant flowers.

I. PURPUREA
(Common morning glory)

6–10 feet

In common morning glory, the stems and foliage are downy hairy. The 2½- to 3-inch trumpet-shaped, day-opening flowers occur in shades of blue, purple, and red, or white, often streaked, sometimes double. Soil is the same as for *I. nil*.

I. QUAMOCLIT
(Cypress vine)

6–10 feet

Cypress vine is a slender twiner with finely divided leaves and red, pink, or white day-opening flowers, about ¾ inch across. It is especially effective if grown on a tall wire mesh tomato cage. Soil is the same as for *I. nil*.

I. TRICOLOR
(Smooth morning glory)

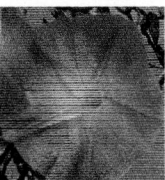

10–15 feet

A hairless twiner, smooth morning glory has heart-shaped leaves and blue, day-opening, trumpet-shaped flowers with a white tube and yellow base. The best-known cultivars are 'Heavenly Blue', with flowers 4 to 5 inches across, and 'Pearly Gates', with white flowers. Soil is the same as for *I. nil*.

LAGENARIA SICERARIA
(White-flowered gourd)

15–30 feet

A vigorous, fast-growing tendril climber, white-flowered gourd has velvety, musk-scented leaves, 8 to 10 inches across. Its white nocturnal flowers are 1½ to 2½ inches across and are followed by cylindrical or bottle-shaped fruit, 1 to 4 feet long and up to 1 foot in diameter, that matures light green and dries tan. White-flowered gourd is a perennial in zone 10. Rich, humusy soil and plenty of compost and/or well-rotted manure are need for maximum fruit production.

LATHYRUS ODORATUS
(Sweet pea)

6–8 feet

Sweet pea is a tendril climber with blue-green foliage and small, long-stalked clusters of 1½-inch flowers in all colors but blue. It grows best in cool weather in deep, richly prepared soil. Deadheading can prolong bloom into summer. Seed should be planted in early spring.

LUFFA CYLINDRICA
(Dishcloth gourd)

10–20 feet

Dishcloth gourd, a fast-growing tendril climber, is a gourd relative. It has yellow flowers, 2 to 3 inches across, and cucumberlike fruit (edible when small and unripe) that matures 1 to 2 feet long. Once dry, the fruit has a removable fibrous interior that is useful for scrubbing. Rich, humusy soil and plenty of compost and/or well-rotted manure are best for dishcloth gourd.

MINA LOBATA

8–10 feet

A purple-stemmed twiner, mina has purplish green leaves and paired horizontal or arching one-sided spikes of small curved flowers that open red and age to white on the same spike. Mina is especially effective if grown on a tall wire mesh tomato cage. Mina does best on sandy-humusy soil enriched with superphosphate.

PHASEOLUS CARACALLA
(Snail bean)

8–12 feet

Snail bean is a twining climber with three-parted leaves. It bears hanging clusters of purple and white pealike flowers with long spiral keel petals. Snail bean requires a long, hot summer. It is best from zone 8 south and is perennial in zone 10. Sandy-humusy soil yields best results.

P. COCCINEUS
(Scarlet runner bean)

8–12 feet

A vigorous twiner with three-parted leaves, scarlet runner bean bears erect clusters of red pealike flowers, followed by broad pods (edible when young) that mature 10 to 12 inches long. It is peren-

nial in zone 10. Ordinary, well-drained soil meets its needs.

RHODOCHITON ATROSANGUINEUM
(Purple bell vine)

12–18 feet

Purple bell vine, a twiner with heart-shaped leaves, has deep red tubular flowers, each with a pink, saucer-shaped calyx. It needs hot weather to flower and is perennial in zone 10. Rich, humusy soil is best.

THUNBERGIA ALATA
(Black-eyed Susan vine)

4–6 feet

A slender, branched twiner with paired leaves, black-eyed Susan vine bears showy, solitary, cream to orange flowers, about 1¼ inches across, usually with a brown throat. It is perennial in zone 10. Most any well-drained soil is suitable.

T. FRAGRANS
(Angel wings)

6–8 feet

Angel wings is similar to the *T. alata*, but its flowers are white and about 2 inches across. It requires a long growing season (zone 7 south) and is perennial in zone 10. Soil is the same as for *T. alata*.

TROPAEOLUM MAJUS
(Climbing nasturtium)

4–6 feet

Climbing nasturtium is the wild prototype of the dwarf, bushy, or creeping nasturtium and is best grown on wire mesh fencing. Among the circular leaves appear solitary flowers, 1½ to 2 inches across, in shades of red, orange, and yellow. It blooms best from late summer to fall, as days shorten and nights turn cool. Sandy-humusy soil of no more than average fertility is best.

T. PELTOPHORUM, *SYN.* T. LOBBIANUM
(Colombian nasturtium)

6–8 feet

A trailing plant, Colombian nasturtium can be induced to climb wire mesh fencing. The cup-shaped, long-spurred flowers are yellow or red-orange. It is perennial in zone 10. Soil is the same as for *T. majus*.

T. PEREGRINUM
(Canary vine)

4–8 feet

Canary vine, a slender twiner, has five-lobed leaves and 1-inch yellow flowers, mostly borne in late summer and fall. It is perennial in zone 10. Soil is the same as for *T. majus*.

Climbing nasturtium (*Tropaeolum majus*)

ORNAMENTAL ANNUAL GRASSES

All require full sun and thrive in ordinary, well-drained garden soil.

Name	Height	Habit	Flowers
Agrostis nebulosa (cloud grass)	10–12"	Clump of short, narrow leaves	Diffuse clusters of persistent spikes
Avena sterilis (animated oat)	2½–3'	Tufted foliage	Large, erect panicles
Briza maxima (quaking oat)	1¼–2'	Clump of upright foliage	Spikes short; thick, nodding, or drooping
B. minor (little quaking grass)	6–15"	Dense clump or tuft of foliage	Erect, broadly pyramidal heads
Coix lacryma-jobi (Job's tears)	3–5'	Broad leaves, both basal and stem, up to 24 inches long; sometimes yellowish	Beads white to bluish; formed in hot weather
Hordeum jubatum (squirrel-tail grass)	1¼–2½'	Leaves scattered on unbranched stems	Spikes densely long pointed; silky or golden
Lagurus ovatus (hare's-tail grass)	10–12"	Foliage in upright tuft	Heads flattened; woolly; off white
Lamarkia aurea (golden-topgrass)	1¼–1½'	Foliage in dense tuft	Spikes one sided; yellow or violet
Panicum capillare (switch grass)	2½–3'	Clumped, upright, or spreading	Tassels green or purple; nodding
Pennisetum setaceum (annual fountain grass)	3–4'	Foliage usually reddish or purplish	Spikes plumed
P. villosum (dwarf feather grass)	1½–2½'	Leaves reflexed	Spikes feathery; off white
Phalaris canariensis (canary grass)	1½–2 (5)'	Usually clumped; variegated leaves	Heads variegated
Polypogon monspeliensis (rabbit's foot grass)	2–2½'	Leaf blades drooping	Spikes densely furry; green to pale yellow
Setaria glauca (foxtail grass)	2–3'	Pleated leaves, palmlike	Spikes cylindrical; drying reddish gold
S. italica (foxtail millet)	3–5'	Arching leaves	Spikes green to purple, then brown; nodding
Triticum aestivum (wheat)	3–4'	Foliage upswept	Heads dense; large seeded

Quaking Oat (*Briza maxima*)

Annual Fountain Grass (*Pennisetum setaceum*)

SPECIALIZED LISTS

ANNUALS FOR SPECIAL HABITATS

ANNUALS THRIVING IN PARTIAL OR LIGHT SHADE

Abronia umbellata (sand verbena)
Abutilon × hybridum (flowering maple)
Begonia Semperflorens-Cultorum hybrids
  (wax begonia)
Calceolaria spp. (slipperwort)
Campanula spp. (annual bellflower)
Centaurea americana (basket flower)
Chrysanthemum carinatum
  (annual chrysanthemum)
C. coronarium (crown daisy)
Cirsium japonicum (Japanese thistle)
Coleus × hybridus

Collinsia bicolor (Chinese houses)
Consolida ambigua (rocket larkspur)
C. regalis (field larkspur)
Cuphea ignea (firecracker plant)
Cynoglossum officinale (hound's-tongue)
Dianthus barbatus (sweet William)
Digitalis purpurea 'Foxy' (annual foxglove)
Impatiens spp.
Ionopsidium acaule (violet cress)
Lobularia maritima (sweet alyssum)
Machaeranthera tanacetifolia (Tahoka daisy)
Malcolmia maritima (Virginia stock)

Matthiola longipetala (evening stock)
Mimulus spp. (monkey flower)
Myosotis sylvatica (annual forget-me-not)
Nemophila maculata (five-spot)
N. menziesii (baby blue eyes)
Penstemon cvs. (beardtongue)
Rudbeckia hirta cvs. (black-eyed Susan)
Sabatia angularis (rose pink)
Schizanthus spp. (butterfly flower)
Seneccio elegans (purple groundsel)
Tanacetum parthenium (feverfew)

ANNUALS THRIVING IN LIGHT TO MODERATE SHADE

Begonia Semperflorens-Cultorum hybrids
  (wax begonia)
Catharanthus roseus (periwinkle)
Celosia argentea (plumed celosia, cockscomb)
Clarkia amoena (satin flower, godetia)

Coleus × hybridus
Coreopsis tinctoria (calliopsis, annual coreopsis)
Exacum affine (Persian violet)
Impatiens spp.
Lobelia erinus (edging lobelia)

Malcomia maritima (Virginia stock)
Mimulus spp. (monkey flower)
Nicotiana spp. (flowering tobacco)
Torenia fournierii (wishbone flower)

ANNUALS THAT ENDURE HEAT AND DROUGHT

Actinotus helianthi (flannel flower)
Argemone grandiflora (prickly poppy)
Centaurea cyanus (cornflower)
Chamaecrista fasciculata (partridge pea)
Convolvulus tricolor (dwarf morning glory)
Consolida ambigua (rocket larkspur)
Coreopsis tinctoria (calliopsis, annual coreopsis)
Euphorbia cyathophora (painted spurge)
E. marginata (snow-on-the-mountain)

Gaillardia pulchella (rose-ring gaillardia)
Gazania hybrids (treasure flower)
Gomphrena globosa (globe amaranth)
Helianthus annuus (sunflower)
Helichrysum bracteatum (strawflower)
Helipterum roseum (everlasting)
Hunnemannia fumariifolia (tulip poppy)
Mirabilis jalapa (four o'clock)
Oenothera deltoides (desert evening primrose)

Osteospermum ecklonis (African daisy)
Perilla frutescens (purple basil)
Portulaca grandiflora
Rudbeckia hirta 'Gloriosa Daisy' (gloriosa daisy)
Salvia splendens (scarlet sage)
Sanvitalia procumbens (creeping zinnia)
Zinnia elegans (common zinnia)

ANNUALS ESPECIALLY SUITED TO ALKALINE SOILS
pH higher than 7.0

Abutilon hybridum (flowering maple)
Antirrhinum majus (snapdragon)
Asclepias curassavica (bloodflower milkweed)
Asperula orientalis (blue woodruff)
Begonia Semperflorens-Cultorum hybrids
  (wax begonia)
Bellis perennis (English daisy)
Browallia spp.
Calceolaria spp. (slipper flower)
Campanula medium (Canterbury bells)
Capsicum annuum (ornamental pepper)
Coleus × hybridum
Dahlia hybrids

Datura spp. (angel's trumpet, horn of plenty)
Eustoma grandiflorum (lisianthus)
Exacum affine (Persian violet)
Iberis amara (annual candytuft)
Impatiens spp.
Limnanthes douglasii (meadow foam)
Lobelia erinus (edging lobelia)
Lopezia hirsuta (mosquito flower)
Moluccella laevis (bells of Ireland)
Myosotis sylvatica (annual forget-me-not)
Nemesia strumosa
Nierembergia hippomanica var. *violacea*
  (cup flower)

Omphalodes linifolia (navelwort)
Papaver rhoeas (Shirley poppy)
Phlox drummondii (annual phlox)
Platystemon californicus (cream cups)
Ricinus communis (castor bean)
Sabatia angularis (rose pink)
Salvia uliginosa (bog sage)
Schizanthus spp. (butterfly flower)
Solanum melongena cvs. (white eggplant)
Torenia fournierii (wishbone flower)
Tropaeolum majus (nasturtium)
Viola cornuta (garden viola)
Zinnia spp.

(continues)

ANNUALS FOR SPECIAL HABITATS (continued)

ANNUALS TOLERANT OF NUTRIENT-DEFICIENT SOILS

Amaranthus caudatus (love-lies-bleeding)
Celosia argentea (plumed celosia, cockscomb)
Centaurea moschata (sweet sultan)
Clarkia amoena (farewell-to-spring)
Cleome hassleriana (spider flower)
Coreopsis tinctoria (calliopsis)

Eschscholzia californica (California poppy)
Gaillardia pulchella (rose gaillardia)
Impatiens balsamina (garden balsam)
Lobularia maritima (sweet alyssum)
Mentzelia lindleyi (annual blazing star)
Mirabilis jalapa (four o'clock)

Papaver rhoeas (Shirley poppy)
Petunia × hybrida
Portulaca grandiflora
Tropaeolum majus (nasturtium)

ANNUALS THAT THRIVE IN COOL SUMMERS
Temperatures above 80°F are infrequent or not sustained.

Alonsoa spp. (mask flower)
Anagallis arvensis var. *caerulea* (blue pimpernel)
Anchusa capensis (alkanet)
Androsace spp. (rock jasmine)
Antirrhinum majus (snapdragon)
Baileya multiradiata (desert marigold)
Bellis perennis (English daisy)
Calceolaria spp. (slipper flower)
Calendula officinalis
Campanula medium (Canterbury bells)
Centaurea cyanus (cornflower)
Chrysanthemum carinatum
  (annual chrysanthemum)
Cirsium japonicum (Japanese thistle)
Clarkia amoena (farewell-to-spring)
Collinsia bicolor (Chinese houses)
Consolida spp. (larkspur)
Cosmos spp.
Cynoglossum amabile (hound's-tongue)
Dianthus spp. (pink)
Dyssodia tenuiloba (Dahlberg-daisy)
Echium vulgare (viper's bugloss)

Emilia javanica (tassel flower)
Erysimum spp. (wallflower)
Eschscholzia californica (California poppy)
Felicia spp. (blue marguerite, kingfisher daisy)
Gilia spp.
Iberis amara (annual candytuft)
Ionopsidium acaule (violet cress)
Ipomopsis spp. (skyrocket, standing cypress)
Lavatera trimestris (bush mallow)
Layia platyglossa (tidytips)
Limnanthes douglasii (meadow foam)
Linaria spp. (toadflax)
Lobelia erinus (edging lobelia)
Lobularia maritima (sweet alyssum)
Lonas annua (yellow ageratum)
Lupinus spp. (lupine, bluebonnet)
Machaeranthera tanacetifolia (Tahoka daisy)
Malcolmia maritima (Virginia stock)
Matthiola spp. (stock)
Mentzelia lindleyi (annual blazing star)
Mesembryanthemum crystalinum (ice plant)
Mimulus spp. (monkey flower)

Molucella laevis (bells of Ireland)
Myosotis sylvatica (annual forget-me-not)
Nemesia strumosa
Nemophila spp. (five-spot, baby blue eyes)
Nigella damascena (love-in-a-mist)
Oxypetalum caeruleum (blue milkweed)
Papaver rhoeas (Shirley poppy)
Penstemon cvs. (beardtongue)
Phacelia campanularia (California bluebell)
Phlox drummondii (annual phlox)
Pimpinella anisum (anise)
Platystemon californicus (cream cups)
Salpiglossis sinuata (painted tongue)
Saponaria calabrica (Calabrian soapwort)
Scabiosa atropurpurea (pincushion flower)
Schizanthus spp. (butterfly flower)
Silybum marianum (holy thistle)
Trachymene caerulea (blue lace flower)
Tropaeolum majus (nasturtium)
Ursinia anthemoides (sunshine daisy)
Venidium fastuosum (Cape daisy)
Viola spp. (pansy viola)

ANNUALS FOR SPECIAL PURPOSES

ANNUALS FOR CUT FLOWERS

Amaranthus caudatus (love-lies-bleeding)
Antirrhinum majus (snapdragon)
Arctotis × hybrida (African daisy)
Argemone spp. (prickly poppy)
Browallia speciosa
Calendula officinalis
Callistephus chinensis (China aster)
Centaurea spp. (cornflower, sweet sultan)
Chrysanthemum spp. (annual chrysanthemum)
Clarkia amoena (farewell-to-spring)
Consolida ambigua (larkspur)
Coreopsis spp. (annual coreopsis, calliopsis)

Cosmos spp.
Dianthus chinensis (China pink)
Emilia javanica (tassel flower)
Eschscholzia californica (California poppy)
Gaillardia spp. (annual gaillardia)
Gypsophila elegans (annual baby's breath)
Helianthus annuus (sunflower)
Lathyrus odoratus (sweet pea)
Lavatera trimestris (bush mallow)
Lupinus spp. (annual lupine)
Matthiola spp. (stock)
Nicotiana spp. (flowering tobacco)

Osteospermum ecklonis (African daisy)
Papaver spp. (annual poppy)
Phacelia spp. (annual bluebell)
Phlox drummondii (annual phlox)
Psylliostachys spp. (annual statice)
Salpiglossis sinuata (painted tongue)
Scabiosa atropurpurea (pincushion flower)
Senecio elegans (purple groundsel)
Tagetes spp. (marigold)
Verbena × hybrida (garden verbena)
Zinnia spp.

ANNUALS FOR SPECIAL PURPOSES (continued)

ANNUALS FOR EDGING

Ageratum houstonianum*
Anagallis arvensis var. *caerulea* (blue pimpernel)
Antirrhinum majus* (dwarf snapdragon)
Asperula orientalis (blue woodruff)
Calendula officinalis* (dwarf calendula)
Celosia argentea*
  (dwarf celosia, dwarf cockscomb)
Collinsia bicolor (Chinese houses)
Coreopsis tinctoria* (dwarf calliopsis)
Dianthus chinensis (China pink)
Eschscholzia californica (California poppy)
Iberis amara* (annual candytuft)
Linum grandiflorum (flowering flax)
Lobelia erinus (edging lobelia)

Lobularia maritima (sweet alyssum)
Mesembryanthemum crystallinum (ice plant)
Nemophila maculata (five-spot)
N. menziesii (baby blue eyes)
Nolana paradoxa (blue bird)
Phacelia campanularia (California bluebell)
Phlox drummondii* (annual phlox)
Sanvitalia procumbens (creeping zinnia)
Saponaria calabrica (Calabrian soapwort)
Tagetes patula (French marigold)
T. signata (signet marigold)
Torenia fournierii (wishbone flower)
Tropaeolum majus* (nasturtium)
Verbena × *hybrida* (garden verbena)

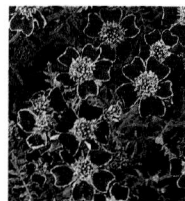

Orange signet marigold
(*Tagetes signata* 'Tangerine Gem')

Yellow signet marigold
(*T. signata* 'Lemon Gem')

ANNUALS FOR WINDOW BOXES, HANGING BASKETS, AND OTHER SMALL CONTAINERS

Ageratum houstonianum*
Begonia Semperflorens-Cultorum hybrids
  (wax begonia)
Browallia speciosa
Catharanthus roseus* (periwinkle)
Centaurea cineraria (dusty miller)

Impatiens walleriana*
Lobelia erinus (edging lobelia)
Lobularia maritima (sweet alyssum)
Pelargonium × *hortorum** (geranium)
Petunia × *hybrida*
Phlox drummondii* (annual phlox)

Portulaca grandiflora
Tagetes patula (French marigold)
T. signata (signet marigold)
Tropaeolum majus* (nasturtium)
Verbena × *hybrida* (garden verbena)
Zinnia elegans* (common zinnia)

ANNUALS FOR TEMPORARY HEDGES

Bassia scoparia f. *trichophylla*
  (summer sypress, kochia)
Helianthus debilis (cucumber-leaf sunflower)

Helichrysum bracteatum (strawflower)
Impatiens balsamina (garden balsam)
Mirabilis jalapa (four o'clock)

Pennisetum setaceum (annual fountain grass)
Ricinus communis (castor bean)

ANNUALS WITH DECORATIVE FOLIAGE

Beta vulgaris var. *flavescens*
  'Dracaenifolia' (ruby chard)
Atriplex hortensis (garden orache)

Euphorbia cyathophora (painted spurge)
E. marginata (snow-on-the-mountain)
Hibiscus acetosella (purple-leaf hibiscus)

Perilla frutescens (purple basil, beefsteak plant)
Ricinus communis (castor bean)
Senecio cineraria (dusty miller)

ANNUALS USEFUL AS EVERLASTINGS

Acroclinium roseum (everlasting)
Actinotis helianthi (flannel flower)
Alcea rosea 'Majorette' (dwarf double hollyhock)
Agrostis nebulosa (cloud grass)
Amaranthus cruentus (prince's feather)
Ammobium alatum var. *grandiflorum*
  (winged everlasting)
Baileya multiradiata (desert marigold)
Briza maxima (quaking oat)
Catananche caerulea (Cupid's dart)
Celosia argentea (plumed celosia)
C. argentea var. *cristata* (cockscomb)
Clarkia amoena (farewell-to-spring)

Coix lacrymi-jobi (Job's tears)
Consolida spp. (larkspur)
Cynara cardunculus (cardoon)
Cynoglossum amabile (hound's-tongue)
Gomphrena globosa (globe amaranth)
Helichrysum bracteatum (strawflower)
Hordeum jubatum (squirrel-tail grass)
Lagurus ovatus (hare's tail grass)
Limonium sinuatum (notchleaf sea lavender)
Lonas annua (yellow ageratum)
Molucella laevis (bells of Ireland)
Nicandra physaloides (shoofly plant)
Nigella damascena (love-in-a-mist)

Oenothera biennis var. *grandiflora*
  (southern evening primrose)
Orthocarpus purpurascens (escobita)
Panicum capillare (switch grass)
Pennisetum setaceum (annual fountain grass)
P. villosum (dwarf feather grass)
Phalaris canariensis (canary grass)
Polypogon monspeliensis (rabbit's foot grass)
Psyliostachys spp. (annual statice)
Scabiosa stellata (scabious)
Setaria italica (foxtail millet)
Triticum aestivum (wheat)
Xeranthemum annuum (immortelle)

* Dwarf cultivars of taller species.

ANNUALS WITH SPECIAL ATTRIBUTES

FRAGRANT ANNUALS

Ageratum houstonianum
Antirrhinum majus (snapdragon)
Calendula officinalis
Centaurea moschata (sweet sultan)
*Datura inoxia** (angel's trumpet)
Dianthus spp. (pink)

Heliotropium arborescens (heliotrope)
Iberis amara (annual candytuft)
Lobularia maritima (sweet alyssum)
Lupinus luteus (European yellow lupine)
Matthiola spp.* (stock)
Nicotiana alata (flowering tobacco)

Petunia × hybrida
Scabiosa atropurpurea (pincushion flower)
Tagetes spp. (marigold)
Trachymene caerulea (blue lace flower)

ANNUALS WITH A BRIEF SEASON OF BLOOM

All require two or more sowings for a season-long succession of continuous bloom.

Centaurea cyanus (cornflower)
Coreopsis tinctoria (calliopsis)
Iberis amara (annual candytuft)
Gypsophila elegans (annual baby's breath)

Lobularia maritima (sweet alyssum)
Myosotis sylvatica (annual forget-me-not)
Nigella damascena (love-in-a-mist)
Osteospermum ecklonis (African daisy)

Papaver rhoeas (Shirley poppy)
Phlox drummondii (annual phlox)

ANNUALS THAT BENEFIT FROM PINCHING BACK

Ageratum houstonianum
Antirrhinum majus (snapdragon)
Browallia speciosa
Calendula officinalis
Chrysanthemum carinatum
  (annual chrysanthemum)

Dianthus chinensis (China pink)
Petunia × hybrida
Phacelia spp. (annual bluebell)
Phlox drummondii (annual phlox)
Salpiglossis sinuata (painted tongue)
Schizanthus pinnatus (butterfly flower)

Verbena × hybrida (garden verbena)
Zinnia elegans (common zinnia)

SLOW-GROWING ANNUALS

All require a long season to reach bloom from seed.

Ammobium alatum var. *grandiflorum*
  (winged everlasting)
Antirrhinum majus (snapdragon)
Callistephus chinensis (China aster)
Centaurea americana (basket flower)
C. moschata (sweet sultan)

Helichrysum bracteatum (strawflower)
Helipterum humboldtianum (rhodanthe)
Hunnemannia fumariifolia (tulip poppy)
Linum grandiflorum (flowering flax)
Lobelia erinus (edging lobelia)
Petunia × hybrida

Salpiglossis sinuata (painted tongue)
Scabiosa atropurpurea (pincushion flower)
Verbena × hybrida (garden verbena)
Xeranthemum annuum (immortelle)

ANNUALS THAT ARE DIFFICULT TO TRANSPLANT

Sow seed where plants are to grow or start in peat pots or cell packs.

Argemone grandiflora (prickly poppy)
Eschscholzia californica (California poppy)
Gypsophila elegans (annual baby's breath)
Helianthus annuus (sunflower)
Lathyrus odoratus (sweet pea)

Lupinus spp. (annual lupine)
Nigella damascena (love-in-a-mist)
Oenothera drummondii
  (Drummond evening primrose)
Papaver rhoeas (Shirley poppy)

Phaseolus coccineus (scarlet runner bean)
Portulaca grandiflora
Trachymene caerulea (blue lace flower)
Tropaeolum majus (nasturtium)

ANNUALS THAT FREQUENTLY SELF-SOW

Especially from zone 7 south

Browallia speciosa
Calendula officinalis
Centaurea cyanus (cornflower)
Cleome hassleriana (spider flower)
Consolida ambigua (larkspur)
Coreopsis tinctoria (calliopsis)

Cosmos bipinnatus (tall cosmos)
Eschscholzia californica (California poppy)
Euphorbia marginata (snow-on-the-mountain)
Gypsophila elegans (annual baby's breath)
Ipomoea purpurea (common morning glory)
Lobularia maritima (sweet alyssum)

Mirabilis jalapa (four o'clock)
Nicotiana spp. (flowering tobacco)
Petunia × hybrida
Portulaca grandiflora
Salvia farinacea (mealycup sage)

ANNUALS THAT MAY BE SOWN IN THE GARDEN IN THE FALL
From zones 7 or 8 south

Antirrhinum majus (snapdragon)
Calendula officinalis
Centaurea cyanus (cornflower)
Clarkia amoena (farewell-to-spring)
Consolida ambigua (larkspur)
Coreopsis tinctoria (calliopsis)

Cosmos bipinnatus (tall cosmos)
Dianthus chinensis (china pink)
Eschscholzia california (California poppy)
Gypsophila elegans (annual baby's breath)
Iberis amara (annual candytuft)
Lathyrus odoratus (sweet pea)

Lavatera trimestris (bush mallow)
Lobularia maritima (sweet alyssum)
Nigella damascena (love-in-a-mist)
Papaver rhoeas (Shirley poppy)
Vaccaria hispanica (cow cockle)
Viola tricolor (pansy)

* Night scented.

ANNUALS BY FLOWER COLOR

WHITE OR NEAR WHITE

Actinotus helianthi (flannel flower)
Ageratum houstonianum (ageratum)
Ammobium alatum (winged everlasting)
Androsace spp. (rock jasmine)
Arctotis × hybrida (African daisy)
Argemone grandiflora (prickly poppy)
Browallia speciosa cvs.
Campanula spp. (annual Canterbury bells)
Catharanthus roseus (periwinkle)
Centaurea spp. (cornflower, sweet sultan)
Ceratotheca triloba (southern foxglove)
Clarkia amoena (farewell-to-spring)
Cleome hasslerana 'Helen Campbell'
   (spider flower)
Collinsia bicolor (Chinese houses)
Consolida ambigua (rocket larkspur)
Cosmos bipinnatus (tall cosmos)
Datura inoxia (angel's trumpet)
Echium vulgare cvs. (viper's bugloss)
Gaura lindheimeri (Texas gaura)
Gilia tricolor (bird's eye gilia)

Gypsophila elegans (annual baby's breath)
Helianthus annuus 'Italian White'
   (white sunflower)
Helichrysum bracteatum (strawflower)
Iberis amara (annual candytuft)
Impatiens balsamina (garden balsam)
I. walleriana
Lathyrus odoratus (sweet pea)
Lavatera trimestris 'Mont Blanc'
   (white bush mallow)
Limonium sinuatum (notchleaf sea lavender)
Lobelia erinus, L. tenuior (annual lobelia)
Lobularia maritima (sweet alyssum)
Lopezia hirsuta (mosquito flower)
Malcolmia maritima (Virginia stock)
Martynia annua (unicorn plant)
Matricaria recutita (German camomile)
Matthiola incana (stock)
M. longipetala (evening stock)
Mentzelia lindleyi (annual blazing star)
Mesembryanthemum crystallinum (ice plant)

Mirabilis jalapa (four o'clock)
Myosotis sylvatica (annual forget-me-not)
Nemesia strumosa
Nemophila maculata (five-spot)
Nicotina alata (flowering tobacco)
N. sylvestris (starburst tobacco)
Nigella damascena (love-in-a-mist)
Oenothera speciosa (showy evening primrose)
Omphalodes linifolia (navelwort)
Osteospermum ecklonis (African daisy)
Penstemon cvs. (beardtongue)
Sabatia angularis (rose pink)
Salvia spp. (annual sage)
Saponaria calabrica (Calabrian soapwort)
Scabiosa atropurpurea (pincushion flower)
Senecio elegans (purple groundsel)
Tanacetum parthenium (feverfew)
Viola cornuta
Zinnia angustifolia (narrow-leaf zinnia)
Z. elegans (common zinnia)

RED, ROSE, OR PINK

Abelmoschus moschata (red flowering okra)	Red	*Catharanthus roseus* (periwinkle)	Rose
Abronia umbellata (sand verbena)	Rose pink	*Centaurea* spp. (cornflower, sweet sultan)	Red, rose, pink
Adonis spp. (pheasant's eye)	Red (and black)	*Centaurium pulchellum* (centaury)	Pink
Agrostemma githago (corn cockle)	Rose lavender	*Clarkia amoena* (farewell-to-spring)	Rose, pink
Alcea rosea annual cvs. (annual hollyhock)	Red, rose, pink	*Cleome hassleriana* (spider flower)	Pink
Amaranthus caudatus (love-lies-bleeding)	Red	*Collinsia bicolor* (Chinese houses)	Pink
Antirrhinum majus (snapdragon)	Red, rose, pink	*Collomia cavanillesi* (Chilean gilia)	Red
Arctotis × hybrida (African daisy)	Red	*Consolida ambigua* (rocket larkspur)	Pink
Begonia Semperflorens-Cultorum hybrids (wax begonia)	Red, pink	*Cosmos bipinnatus* (tall cosmos)	Red, pink
		Crepis rubra (red hawk's beard)	Red
Bellis perennis (English daisy)	Red, rose, pink	*Cuphea* spp. (cigar flower)	Red
Brachycome iberidifolia (Swan River daisy)	Pink	*Cynoglossum* spp. (hound's-tongue)	Pink
Calandrinia spp. (red maids, rock purslane)	Red	*Dahlia* hybrids	Red, rose, pink
Callistephus chinensis (China aster)	Red, rose, pink	*Dianthus* spp. (annual pink)	Red, pink
Campanula spp. (annual bellflower)	Pink	*Diascia barberae* (twinspur)	Pink

(continues)

ANNUALS BY FLOWER COLOR (continued)

Dorotheanthus bellidiformis (Livingston daisy)	Pink	*Mimulus* spp. (monkey flower)	Red
Echium spp. (viper's bugloss)	Pink	*Mirabilis jalapa* (four o'clock)	Red, pink
Emilia javanica (tassel flower)	Red	*Myosotis sylvatica* (annual forget-me-not)	Pink
Eschscholzia californica (California poppy)	Red, pink	*Nemesia strumosa*	Red, pink
Gerbera jamesonii (Transvaal daisy)	Red, rose, pink	*Nicotiana alata* (flowering tobacco)	Red, rose, pink
Gypsophila elegans (annual baby's breath)	Pink	*Oenothera speciosa* (showy evening primrose)	Pink
G. muralis (cushion gypsophila)	Rose	*Orthocarpus purpurascens* (owl clover)	Pink
Helichrysum bracteatum (strawflower)	Red, pink	*Pelargonium* × *hortorum* (geranium)	Red, rose, pink
Helipterum spp. (everlasting)	Rose, pink	*Papaver rhoeas* (Shirley poppy)	Red, rose, pink
Iberis amara (annual candytuft)	Dark red, pink	*Petunia* × *hybrida*	Red, rose, pink
Impatiens balsamina (garden balsam)	Red, rose, pink	*Phlox drummondii* (annual phlox)	Red, rose, pink
I. walleriana	Red, rose, pink	*Polygonum capitatum* 'Magic Carpet' (creeping knotweed)	Pink
Ipomopsis aggregata (skyrocket)	Red, pink	*Portulaca grandiflora*	Red, rose, pink
Lantana montevidensis (pink lantana)	Pink	*Psylliostachys* spp. (annual statice)	Rose
Lathyrus odorata (sweet pea)	Red, rose, pink	*Salvia sclarea* (clary)	Rose
Lavatera trimestris (bush mallow)	Rose	*S. splendens* (scarlet sage)	Red, rose
Limonium suworowii (Suworow sea lavender)	Rose pink	*Saponaria calabrica* (Calabrian soapwort)	Rose
Linaria spp. (toadflax)	Red, pink	*Scabiosa atropurpurea* (pincushion flower)	Rose, pink
Linum grandiflorum (flowering flax)	Red	*Schizanthus pinnatus* (butterfly flower)	Rose, pink
Lopezia hirsuta (mosquito flower)	Red	*Senecio elegans* (purple groundsel)	Rose, pink
Lychnis coeli-rosa (rose of heaven)	Rose pink	*Silene armeria* (sweet William campion)	Rose pink
Malcolmia maritima (Virginia stock)	Pink	*Tropaeolum majus* (nasturtium)	Red, rose, pink
Malope trifida (mallowwort)	Rose red	*Verbena* × *hybrida* (garden verbena)	Red, rose, pink
Matthiola incana (stock)	Rose, pink	*Zinnia elegans* (common zinnia)	Red, rose, pink
Mesembryanthemum crystallium (ice plant)	Pink		

BLUE, LAVENDER, PURPLE, AND MAUVE

Ageratum houstonianum	Blue, lavender	*Dorotheanthus bellidiformis* (Livingston daisy)	Lavender
Agrostemma githago 'Milas' (corn cockle)	Rosy lavender	*Echium* spp. (viper's bugloss)	Purple
Alcea rosea annual cvs. (annual hollyhock)	Lavender, purple	*Eustoma grandiflora* (lisianthus, prairie gentian)	Lavender, purple
Anagallis arvensis var. *caerulea* (blue pimpernel)	Blue	*Exacum affine* (Persian violet)	Blue, purple
A. monellii var. *linifolia* (flax-leaf pimpernel)	Blue, purple	*Felicia amelloides* (blue marguerite)	Blue, purple
Anchusa capensis 'Blue Bird' (bluebird alkanet)	Blue	*F. bergeriana* (kingfisher daisy)	Blue
Anoda cristata (opal cup)	Lavender	*Gilia* spp.	Blue, purple
Arctotis × *hybrida* (African daisy)	Purple	*Heliophila leptophylla* (Cape stock)	Blue
Asperula orientalis (blue woodruff)	Lavender blue	*Heliotropium arborescens* (heliotrope)	Lavender, purple
Borago officinalis (borage)	Blue	*Hibiscus acetosella* (purple-leaf hibiscus)	Purple (foliage)
Brachycome iberidifolia (Swan River daisy)	Blue	*Iberis amara* (annual candytuft)	Lavender, purple
Browallia spp.	Lavender purple	*I. umbellata* (globe candytuft)	Purple
Callistephus chinensis (China aster)	Blue, lavender, purple	*Impatiens balsamina* (garden balsam)	Lavender, purple
Campanula spp. (annual bellflower)	Blue, lavender, purple	*Ionopsidium acaule* (violet cress)	Lavender
Catananche caerulea (Cupid's dart)	Blue	*Lathyrus odoratus* (sweet pea)	Lavender, purple, mauve
Centaurea americana (basket flower)	Lavender		
C. cyanus (cornflower)	Blue	*Limonium sinuatum* (notchleaf sea lavender)	Lavender
C. moschata (sweet sultan)	Blue	*Linaria maroccana* (toadflax)	Lavender, mauve
Clarkia amoena (farewell-to-spring)	Lavender, purple	*Linum grandiflorum* (flowering flax)	Blue
Collinsia bicolor (Chinese houses)	Blue	*Lobelia erinus* (edging lobelia)	Blue, purple
Consolida spp. (larkspur)	Blue, lavender, purple, mauve	*L. tenuior* (Australian lobelia)	Blue
		Lupinus spp. (annual lupine)	Blue, lavender, purple
Convolvulus tricolor (dwarf morning glory)	Blue-violet, lavender	*Machaeranthera tanacetifolia* (Tahoka daisy)	Lavender blue
Cynoglossum amabile (hound's-tongue)	Blue	*Malcolmia maritima* (Virginia stock)	Purple
Datura metel (horn of plenty)	Lavender, purple	*Martynia annua* (unicorn plant)	Lavender, purple
Digitalis purpurea 'Foxy' (annual foxglove)	Lavender purple	*Matthiola* spp. (stock)	Purple

Mimulus × *hybridus* (monkey flower)	Purple	*S. sclarea* (clary)	Blue, purple
Myosotis sylvatica (annual forget-me-not)	Blue	*S. splendens* (scarlet sage)	Purple
Nemisia strumosa	Purple	*S. uliginosa* (bog sage)	Blue
Nemophilia menziesii (baby blue eyes)	Blue	*Saponaria calabrica* (Calabrian soapwort)	Purple
Nicandra physaloides (shoofly plant)	Lavender	*Scabiosa atropurpurea* (pincushion flower)	Blue, lavender, purple
Nigella damascena (love-in-a-mist)	Lavender, purple	*Schizanthus pinnatus* (butterfly flower)	Lavender, purple, mauve
Nolana paradoxa (blue bird)	Blue		
Oxypetalum caeruleum (blue milkweed)	Blue	*Senecio elegans* (purple groundsel)	Purple
Penstemon cvs. (beardtongue)	Blue, purple	*Silybum marianum* (holy thistle)	Purple
Perilla frutescens (purple basil)	Purple (foliage)	*Torenia fournierii* (wishbone flower)	Lavender and purple
Petunia × *hybrida*	Lavender purple	*Trachelium caeruleum* (blue lace flower)	Blue
Phacelia spp. (annual bluebell)	Blue, purple	*Vaccaria hispanica* (cow cockle)	Pinkish purple
Proboscidea fragrans (unicorn plant)	Mauve	*Verbena* × *hybrida* (garden verbena)	Lavender, purple
Phlox drummondii (annual phlox)	Lavender purple	*V. rigida* (veiny verbena)	Purple
Salpiglossis sinuata (painted tongue)	Purple	*V. tenuisecta* (moss verbena)	Purple
Salvia patens (gentian sage)	Blue	*Xeranthemum annuum* (immortelle)	Purple

YELLOW AND ORANGE

Abelmoschus manihot (yellow flowering okra)	Yellow (with purple center)	*I. noli-tangere* (European touch-me-not)	Yellow (with red spots)
Abutilon hybridum (flowering maple)	Yellow, salmon orange	*Lantana camara*	Yellow, orange
Alonsoa warscewiczii (mask flower)	Orange	*Lathyrus odoratus* (sweet pea)	Yellow, orange
Ammobium alatum var. *grandiflorum* (winged everlasting)	Light yellow	*Layia platyglossa* (tidytips)	Yellow
		Leonitis nepetifolia (prince's flag)	Orange
Antirrhinum majus (snapdragon)	Yellow, orange	*Limnanthes douglasii* (meadow foam)	Yellow
Argemone mexicanum (Mexican prickly poppy)	Yellow to orange	*Lonas annua* (yellow ageratum)	Yellow
Asclepias curassavica (bloodflower milkweed)	Orange	*Lupinus luteus* (European yellow lupine)	Yellow
Baileya multiradiata (desert marigold)	Yellow	*Mentzelia lindleyi* (annual blazing star)	Yellow
Bupleurum rotundifolium (green gold)	Yellow	*Mimulus* × *hybridus* (monkey flower)	Yellow
Calceolaria spp. (slipperwort)	Yellow	*Nemesia strumosa*	Yellow, orange
Calendula officinalis	Yellow, orange	*Oenothera* spp. (evening primrose, sundrops)	Yellow, orange
Callistephus chinensis (China aster)	Light yellow, orange	*Papaver rhoeas* (Shirley poppy)	Orange
Celosia argentea (plumed celosia, cockscomb)	Yellow, orange	*Petunia* × *hybrida*	Yellow
Cerinthe major (cerinthe)	Yellow	*Pimpinella anisum* (anise)	Light yellow
Chamaecrista fasciculata (partridge pea)	Yellow	*Platystemon californicus* (cream cups)	Light yellow
Chrysanthemum spp. (annual chrysanthemum)	Yellow	*Portulaca grandiflora*	Yellow, orange
Coreopsis spp. (calliopsis, annual coreopsis)	Yellow	*Rudbeckia* spp. (coneflower)	Yellow to orange
Cosmos sulphureus (orange cosmos)	Yellow, orange	*Salpiglossis sinuata* (painted tongue)	Yellow
Dahlia hybrids	Yellow, orange	*Sanvitalia procumbens* (creeping zinnia)	Yellow, orange
Datura metel (horn of plenty)	Light yellow	*Tagetes* spp. (marigold)	Yellow, orange
Diascia barbarae (twinspur)	Orange	*Talinum paniculatum* (jewels of Opar)	Yellow
Dimorphotheca sinuata (Cape marigold)	Yellow, orange	*Thelesperma burridgeanum*	Yellow and orange
Dyssodia tenuiloba (Dahlberg daisy)	Yellow	*Thunbergia alata* (black-eyed Susan vine)	Orange
Emilia javanica (tassel flower)	Orange	*Tithonia rotundifolia* (Mexican sunflower)	Yellow, orange
Gaillardia × *grandiflora* (hybrid gaillardia)	Yellow (and red)	*Tolpis barbata* (yellow hawkweed)	Yellow
Gazania hybrids (treasure flower)	Yellow, orange	*Tropaeolum majus* (nasturtium)	Yellow, orange
Gerbera jamesonii (Transvaal daisy)	Yellow	*Ursinia anthemoides* (sunshine daisy)	Orange
Helianthus annuus (sunflower)	Yellow	*Venidium fastuosum* (Cape daisy)	Orange
Helichrysum bracteatum (strawflower)	Yellow, orange	*Viola cornuta*	Yellow, orange
Hibiscus trionum 'Sunny Day' (flower-of-a-day)	Light yellow (with purple center)	*V. wittrockiana* (pansy)	Yellow
		Zinnia angustifolia (narrow-leaf zinnia)	Orange
Hunnemannia fumariifolia (tulip poppy)	Yellow	*Z. elegans* (common zinnia)	Yellow, orange
Impatiens cristata (Himalayan impatiens)	Light yellow		

18

Biennials

A BIENNIAL IS A PLANT THAT COMPLETES ITS LIFE CYCLE within two years. During the first year, leafy vegetative growth is produced at ground level; and during the second year, the plant blooms, produces seed, and dies.

As with so many generalizations, this definition is subject to many exceptions. For example, some biennials, such as hollyhock (*Alcea rosea*), as indeed not a few perennials, may flower the first year, especially if the seed is sown early. Others, such as English daisy (*Bellis perennis*), are short-lived

Floral spikes of common biennial foxglove complement the vertical pickets of the rustic fence.

475

perennials in their native haunts, but are customarily grown as biennials. And, not uncommonly, a garden biennial such as hollyhock or sweet William (*Dianthus barbatus*) may linger on through a third or fourth year, and thus qualify as a short-lived perennial. These variations notwithstanding, most biennials most of the time follow the two-year life cycle.

In this group we find some of our most beautiful garden flowers, and yet, because the individual plants are not permanent residents of the garden, we are inclined to underestimate their potential. It is true that they are but transients in the flower border—that few, if any of them, may be counted on for even one full season of bloom; yet during the space of the few or several weeks when they are in flower, biennials contribute a full measure of beauty to any planting.

It is this transient quality of biennials that may be considered one of their primary assets, for it eases planning a long succession of bloom. Whereas perennials such as Siberian iris (*Iris sibirica*), tall summer phlox (*Phlox paniculata*), and peony (*Paeonia lactiflora*) are best left undisturbed in the border throughout the season, year after year, spending most of their time *not* in bloom, biennials may be raised in a nursery bed, moved into the garden a few weeks before they are to flower, and then, once their bloom is past, taken away, leaving space for annuals, summer-flowering bulbs, and perennials: For example, foxglove (*Digitalis purpurea*) may be followed by hardy mums (*Chrysanthemum × morifolium*); gladiolus (*Gladiolus × hortulanus*) may be planted as soon as the Canterbury bells (*Campanula medium*) have finished; and pansy (*Viola × wittrockiana*) and English daisy, which make the spring border exceptionally colorful, may be followed later on by such low-growing annuals as annual phlox (*Phlox drummondii*), edging lobelia (*Lobelia erinus*), and wishbone flowers (*Torenia fournierii*).

So, while perennials continue as the mainstays of our flower gardens, and while some annuals, particularly those that offer a long season of bloom, are equally invaluable, we should not overlook the special attributes, of biennials, as they have much to offer.

Almost all biennials are propagated by seed, sown usually in late spring or early summer (see Chapter 36). Because they usually consist of a rosette of ever larger leaves the first year and require much sun at this stage, it is best to raise most biennials in a separate bed and not attempt to start them among annuals and perennials. On the other hand, a few, such as the white-felty mullein (*Verbascum bombyciferum*), have such bold, attractive foliage that they deserve space among perennials, even in their first year.

Most biennials are very easy to transplant. It is best to do the transplanting on a cloudy day, and the plants should be moved with as much soil about the roots as possible. A generous forkful of well-rotted manure or rich compost, or an application of high-analysis synthetic fertilizer, will help minimize any transplanting shock or setback. When weather conditions are not favorable for transplanting (during periods of intense sunshine and in hot, drying winds), when transplanting hollyhocks and other biennials that are difficult to move, or when transplanting large plants already in flower, cover them with shade cloth, inverted baskets, or newspaper tents for a day or two after transplanting to help reduce wilting.

As hollyhock not only has long rangy roots but develops a dense clump of large circular leaves, it is best to grow this biennial in large pots plunged in the seedbeds, and then, in early spring of the second year, to transplant it from the pots into the desired blooming position in the garden. Iceland poppy (*Papaver nudicaule*) is also not easily dug up and moved; hence it also benefits from initial pot culture and careful setting out the second spring.

Digitalis × mertonensis (hybrid pink foxglove)

BIENNIALS OF MERIT

ALCEA ROSEA
(Hollyhock)

Zones (6) 7–9

Picturesque and highly ornamental, hollyhock is reminiscent of old-time gardens, and it seems equally at home beside a modest cottage doorway or in the long herbaceous borders of a formal garden. There are both single and double forms, and a wide range of colors—white, rose, salmon, scarlet, crimson, purple, and black-violet as well as yellow (which often has narrowly lobed leaves and is listed as *A. ficifolia*). Hollyhock is among our most useful background plants, attaining a height of 6 to 8 feet. It is particularly lovely when planted against an old wall or picket fence. The period of bloom extends from early summer to early fall.

While hollyhock is mostly biennial, some plants survive for more than one blooming period, and because it self-sows so liberally, it often creates patches or colonies in a garden that are perennial in effect. Some of the dwarf cultivars bloom the first year, especially if started early, and are often treated as annuals.

Thriving in full sun, but also doing reasonably well in partial shade, hollyhock is a reliable performer under most garden conditions as long as the soil does not become saturated and soggy in the winter. It responds well to high fertility but makes satisfactory growth and a creditable display on poor soils.

Hollyhock may be grown very easily from seed. If the seed is sown by midsummer, ¼ inch deep and 1 inch apart, bloom may be expected the following season. Because of their long rangy roots, the seedlings should be moved to their blooming position while still quite small or, better yet, grown in large sunken pots in the nursery and planted in the garden in the fall or early spring. Once established, hollyhock self-sows so readily that it is seldom necessary to make additional sowings. If even a few stalks are allowed to produce seed, the resultant seedlings are usually numerous and should be thinned or transplanted to stand 1½ to 2 feet apart. Transplanting is best done in early fall or very early spring. Except for cultivars less than 3 feet tall, staking is usually required. Unless seed is wanted, flower stalks should be cut as soon as bloom has ceased.

Although many cultivars and seed races are available, most with double flowers, the single-flowered hollyhock has a special grace and clarity still preferred by many. Cultivars of merit include the following.

'Chaters Double': 3 to 4 feet tall; flowers fully double.
'Nigra': flowers single, deep chocolate maroon.
'Pompadour': flowers double, crinkled, single row of outer petals surround central tuft or half-ball of shorter petals, full color range.
'Powderpuff' hybrids: 5 to 8 feet tall; flowers fully double.

A. rugosa is similar to *A. rosea* but bears single yellow-orange flowers and is more resistant to the rust fungus that often disfigures the foliage of other hollyhocks.

BELLIS PERENNIS
(English daisy)

Zones (4) 5–8

In Scotland, the tufted 2- to 4-inch English daisy selfsows so freely that it invades lawns and is frequently regarded as a pest. However, the double, large-flowered strains offered in the horticultural trade come in shades of pink, deep rose, and white and make good springtime companions for pansies (*Viola × wittrockiana*), violas (*V. cornuta*), and forget-me-nots (*Myosotis sylvatica*).

Although English daisy is actually a perennial, and in regions with mild summers may be so treated, it is best grown as a biennial and discarded after flowering. If this is not done, it may self-sow and soon revert to the small-flowered, single white form.

English daisy is of the easiest culture and thrives under cool, damp conditions, such as prevail in the Pacific Northwest and in places along the Northeast coast. Seed should be sown by midsummer, preferably in flats sheltered in coldframes, and the seedlings set 4 to 6 inches apart in early fall. Seed sown in the spring may result in flowering plants in late summer of the same year; usually such plants flower more generously the following spring. North of zone 7, a light winter mulch is advisable to stabilize soil temperature and avert frost heaving in late winter and early spring. In any location, they must be protected from summer drought, which can be fatal. Partial shade is an advantage, especially in the South. Because of its compact, fibrous root system, English daisy may be transplanted even when in full flower. Aside from constant soil moisture, it has no special needs and harbors no pests and diseases.

Among the many double-flowered cultivar strains available are the following.

'Bright Carpet': dwarf in all respects, flowers red to white.
'Dresden China': flowers light pink.
'Goliath': flowers 2½ to 3 inches across, red, pink, or white.
'Habañera': flowers 2 to 2½ inches across, narrow, filamentous rays.
'Kito': flowers cherry red, incurved rays.
'Morgenrote' or 'Morning Blush': 12 to 18 inches tall: flowers pink.
'Pomponette': flowers 1½ inches across, red, pink, or white, borne in profusion.

CAMPANULA MEDIUM
(Canterbury bells)

Zones (6) 7–9

Canterbury bells is among the most beautiful and showy of biennials. In the South (zones 8 and 9), it comes into bloom in early spring, while in the North it reaches its peak as spring merges into summer, just after the columbines (*Aquilegia* spp.) and bearded irises are over and while common foxglove (*Digitalis purpurea*) is in its prime. Canterbury bells may used as a major component in the garden or simply to fill an occasional gap here and there. It may be expected to reach 2 to 3 feet (or exceptionally 4 feet) in height.

Easily grown from seed, Canterbury bells should be started in late spring, preferably in flats protected in a cold-frame. The seed, which is very fine, should be sown thinly and barely covered with very fine soil. The bed should be kept constantly moist. Seedlings should be transplanted to stand 4 to 6 inches apart to grow a vigorous rosette of foliage. Young plants may be placed in the garden in early fall or early the following spring, just before bloom. The compact, fibrous root system eases transplanting.

If the fading blooms are pinched off at the base, smaller auxiliary buds will form and extend the flowering, period, some-times through the summer. Canterbury bells thrives in almost any soil, provided it is well drained, but makes the best display when soil fertility is high. In locations subject to harsh winter winds, an inverted flower pot over each plant will help prevent excessive drying of foliage. A winter mulch that can mat may cause crown rot.

Canterbury bells exists in both single- and double-flowered forms, the latter listed as the cultivar 'Calycanthema', popularly called cup-and-saucer flower. Both occur in a wide range of colors: purple, lavender, rose, pink, and white. In addition to the cup-and-saucer variant, several dwarf forms exist, of which 'Dwarf Musical Bells', 12 to 18 inches tall and prolifically blooming, is especially showy.

Some mail-order vendors offer year-old plants ready to bloom. Gardeners wishing only a few plants may find these plants to be an attractive alternative to raising their own from seed.

DIANTHUS BARBATUS
(Sweet William)

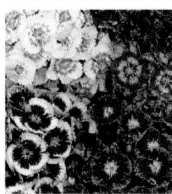

Zones 5–8

Although it is actually a short-lived perennial, sweet William is best treated as a biennial for garden purposes. Its pleasing form and wide range of flower colors make it an important part of the garden palette in late spring. It grows 1 to 1½ feet tall and presents its broad, flat clusters of flowers—often double and bicolor—in shades and combinations of red, pink, and white.

Seed should be sown no later than late spring, planted about ¼ inch deep and ½ inch apart. The seedlings should be thinned to grow on about 4 inches apart, so that the young plants will be staunch enough to survive the winter and flower freely the following spring. From zone 7 north, a loose winter mulch or protection in a coldframe is advisable. Spacing in the garden of 6 to 9 inches allows sufficient room to spread while at the same time ensuring the density that is necessary to keep the flowering stems from toppling. A location in full sun or partial shade is best; flowering is diminished in sustained shade.

Single-flowered, self-colored cultivars include 'Crimson Beauty', 'Pink Beauty', 'Pure White', and 'Scarlet Beauty'. 'Indian Carpet' is a dwarf (5 to 8 inches tall) with single flowers both self-colored and bicolor. Among the double-flowered cultivars is 'Excelsior', which includes mixed colors, some single, most double, some bicolor. 'Harlequin' has rounded clusters of pink-and-white flowers.

DIGITALIS PURPUREA
(Common foxglove)

Zones 4–8

Although most species of *Digitalis* are true perennials, the most commonly grown foxglove is biennial. No other garden plant is quite like it. It is among the first flowers of spring to give height and substance to the garden composition. The stately, one-sided spires of bloom, 3 to 5 feet (exceptionally 8 feet) high, especially when backed by a hedge or wall, add distinction to any planting. Foxglove reaches peak bloom just as many spring-flowering perennials subside and just before roses come forth, thus serving as a valued link.

As the seed of foxglove is very fine, the seed bed should be well prepared with screened sandy soil. Seed sown in late spring will yield many young seedlings. The seedlings should be carefully transplanted, kept moist, and grown in partial shade—preferably in a coldframe—to develop into large, vigorous plants by fall and provide generous bloom the following spring. Seedlings soon crowd each other to death if left untransplanted, thus diminishing the display potential.

From zone 7 south, foxglove may be wintered over in open ground, but to the North it is advisable to keep it in a cold-frame or other protective enclosure to reduce the loss of leaves by desiccation. Also important for foxglove culture is well-drained soil. The thick, fleshy leaf stalks and dense crowns rot very easily if the soil remains soggy during winter dormancy. Spacing in the coldframe, ideally 6 to 9 inches, should be increased to 10 to 14 inches when the plants are set in the garden in early spring. A sandy

Digitalis purpurea

Common foxglove (*Digitalis purpurea*)

soil enriched with well-rotted manure or rich compost yields best results. Under favorable conditions, foxglove self-sows and maintains its presence in the garden, much as does hollyhock.

Common foxglove is a highly variable species with numerous geographical races, some of which have found favor as garden cultivars. Among the more notable are the following.

'Alba': flowers white.

'Apricot': flowers pale orange, unspotted.

'Campanulata': uppermost flowers united to form a large segmented bloom.

'Dwarf Sensation': less than 3 feet tall; flowers large, open, held horizontally or upswept.

'Excelsior' hybrids: flowers borne all around the spike instead of on one side, mostly pastel mauve through pink and yellowish to white.

'Foxy' hybrids: less than 3 feet tall; flowers deep red through pink and cream to white, heavily spotted brown-violet; often flowers the first year from spring-sown seed, may rebloom again the following spring.

'Giant Shirley': flowers very large, mostly pink with purple spots.

'Gloxinioides' or 'Gloxiniiflora': 5 to 7 feet tall; flowers very large and open.

'Heywoodii': flowers pale pinkish cream, spotted red-violet.

'Sutton's Apricot': flowers pinkish orange.

ERYSIMUM *CVS.*
(*Wallflower*)

Zones (6) 7–8

The wallflowers make up a rather heterogeneous group, derived in part from *E. cheiri. (syn. Cheiranthus cheiri*), Siberian wallflower (*E. cellionii*), *E. hieraciifolium* (syn. *E. alpinum*), and western wallflower (*E. asperum*). Wallflower cultivars are among the most effective spring-flowering plants for the low border, and their brightly colored blooms provide pleasant contrast with those of subtler hues. Usually growing 1 to 2 feet tall, they may be used very successfully in combination with late-blooming narcissuses, mid- to late-season tulips, and such spring-flowering perennials as blue phlox (*Phlox divaricata*) and Virginia bluebell (*Mertensia virginica*).

Seed should be sown in late spring to early summer, and the seedlings transplanted to stand 3 to 4 inches apart. In zones 7 and 8, young plants may be wintered over in the open but north of zone 7, the protection of a coldframe is advisable. In early spring, they may be moved to stand 8 to 12 inches apart in a sunny or partially shaded spot in the garden. Soil quality is not critical, but the site must be well drained.

Among the many cultivars available, the following are especially distinctive.

'Blood Red': flowers deep red.

'Cloth of Gold': flowers yellow, fragrant.

'Double Dwarf' mixed: about 15 inches tall; flowers double, ranging from deep red to cream.

'Eastern Queen': flowers salmon red.

'Fire King': flowers red-orange.

'Glasnost' mixed: about 1 foot tall: flowers fragrant, from deep red-brown to cream.

'Jubilee Gold': flowers yellow.

'Moonlight': about 6 inches tall and 12 inches wide; red buds open to yellow.

'Orange Bedder': about 15 inches tall; flowers orange.

'Primrose Bedder': 15 inches tall; flowers light yellow.

'Scarlet Bedder': 15 inches tall; flowers red.

'Sprite': 1 foot tall; flowers pale yellow.

'Tom Thumb' mixed: 6 to 9 inches tall; flowers various colors.

'White Dame': flowers cream.

'Yellow Bedder': 1 foot tall; flowers yellow.

'Biennial Forget-me-not' (*Myosotis*)

MYOSOTIS ALPESTRIS, M. SYLVATICA
(Biennial forget-me-not)

Zones 5–8

Some species of forget-me-not, such as *M. scorpioides*, are perennials, while others, such as *M. stricta*, are annuals. The two biennial species make excellent additions to the spring border, although in their wild forms they self-sow so freely as to become nuisances. It is for this reason that named cultivars are preferable. Not only is their seed set more modestly but they offer colors from deep blue through lavender and pink to white.

For spring bloom, seed should be sown in midsummer, and the seedlings transplanted to winter over in coldframes, especially north of zone 7, or in the open. As seedlings are very susceptible to damping off, it is advisable to incorporate a fungicide in the irrigation water (see Chapter 36). Young plants are readily moved, owing to a compact, fibrous root system, and may be set 6 to 8 inches apart in early spring. *M. alpestris* reaches 6 to 12 inches in height; *M. sylvatica*, 12 to 18 inches. The former makes a good underplanting for tulips, the pale blue contrasting pleasingly with the tulips' strong colors.

Meritorious cultivars of *M. alpestris* include the following.

'Blue Ball': about 6 inches tall; very compact; bright blue flowers.
'Carmine King': about 8 inches tall; rosy red flowers.
'Royal Blue': about 1 foot tall; deep indigo blue flowers.
'White Ball': 6 inches tall; white flowers.

Cultivars of the typically taller *M. sylvatica* include the following.

'Alba': white flowers.
'Blue Bird': 1 ½ to 2 feet tall; deep blue flowers.
'Compacta': 6 to 9 inches tall; blue flowers.
'Fischeri': 6 to 9 inches tall; blue flowers, showing a pink tint.
'Rosea': pink flowers.

PAPAVER NUDICAULE
(Iceland poppy)

Zones 2–8

Although Iceland poppy is a true perennial in its native subarctic habitat, it takes on all the characteristics of a biennial when grown in the garden and is best treated as such. That is, it blooms luxuriantly the year following sowing, and then usually dies, with only an occasional individual surviving to the next year.

The soft, gray green leaves form a basal rosette, and the delicate, tissuelike flowers are presaged by nodding buds that open upward. The flowers are borne on leafless stalks, 1 to 2 feet tall. As many as 50 blooms are produced by a single plant. The finely crinkled petals range from deep red to yellow and white and are sometimes double. Flowering coincides with that of late narcissuses and early tulips. If the seed capsules are removed, flowering will continue through most of the summer.

Seed should be sown in late summer or under lights indoors in the winter. Young plants from summer-sown seed are best wintered over in coldframes north of zone 7. Regardless of when it is done, the seed should be sown in small pots or cell packs, a few seeds per container, and not in the ground, as the long, slender taproots make transplanting very risky. Seedlings should be thinned to two or three individuals per container. In early spring, they should be planted in the garden about 1 foot apart. In the case of self-sown seedlings, flower color usually reverts to pastel shades.

Cultivars of merit include the following.

'Champagne Bubbles': 2 feet tall; flowers 6 inches across, various colors.
'Garden Gnome' hybrids: 12 to 15 inches tall; flowers various colors.
'Hamlet': flowers 4 to 6 inches across, various colors.
'Matador': flowers red.
'Oregon Rainbows': 1½ to 2 feet tall; flowers various colors, some individual blooms multicolor.
'Pacino': 12 to 15 inches tall; flowers yellow.
'Sparkling Bubbles': flowers 4 to 6 inches across, various colors.
'Unwin's Giant Coonara': 2 feet tall; flowers various colors.
'Wonderland' hybrids: mostly under 1 foot tall; flowers various colors.

VERBASCUM SPP.
(Mullein)

Zone (5) 6–8

As a group, mulleins are not as well known as other biennials, but several are worthy garden subjects. They are often dismissed because of the weedy nature of the common great mullein (*V. thapsus*), a denizen of roadsides, railroad embankments, and other disturbed places. This is regrettable, as a number of other mullein species and their hybrids and cultivars make colorful additions and often stately accents.

Olympic mullein
(*Verbascum olympicum*)

All may be grown from seed best sown in late spring. If a dozen seeds are sown and barely covered in each compartment of a cell pack, kept constantly moist, and the seedlings thinned to two or three per cell, then shifted to a 5- or 6-inch pot in which only the strongest is allowed to grow on, the others pinched off, strong plants will be ready to go into the garden in the fall. Such measures are advisable because if the deep, slender taproot is broken in transplanting, flowering is seriously diminished. If grown in locations subject to wind, the taller sorts usually require staking. Except for *V. blattaria* and *V. phoeniceum*, dryish conditions yield best results. Deep, fertile soil results in more luxuriant foliage and great floral spires, but most kinds flower as well and are less leafy on average or even poor soils.

One of the most easily grown is purple mullein (*V. phoeniceum*), a relatively diminutive species, usually not more than 2½ feet tall. It bears slender, often branched, spikes of purple, pinkish lilac, lavender, or white flowers in late spring and early summer. Somewhat taller and a bit more robust is moth mullein (*V. blattaria*), which has yellow or white flowers. The central tuft of the stamens is often purple. Moth mullein can be found naturalized in the eastern United States. Both species respond well to average garden conditions and tolerate partial shade.

Of the taller sorts, all yellow-flowered, felty mullein (*V. bombyciferum*) is much branched, rises to 8 feet or more, and produces erect spires studded with 1-inch flowers. All parts but the flowers are densely clothed in white felt. The cultivar 'Silver Lining' is especially felty. Lower, to about 4 feet, slenderer, and less woolly is *V. chaixii*, with its ¾- to 1-inch-wide flowers arranged along the erect, few-branched spikes. Occasional plants have white flowers. Olympic mullein (*V. olympicum*) is gray downy throughout, with branched, densely flowered spikes 6 to 8 feet tall. All three develop large leaf rosettes the first year, often reaching 3 feet across, and thus require ample spacing to flower optimally the second year.

In addition to the *Verbascum* species are a number of hybrids and cultivars, the following are among the most distinctive.

'Cotswold Gem': 6 feet tall; flowers bronzy with purple stamens.
'Cotswold Queen': 6 feet tall; flowers salmon to bronzy, lilac stamens.
'Pink Domino': 5 feet tall; flowers rosy pink, with a darker center.
'Royal Highland': about 5 feet tall; flowers yellow-orange.

Felty mullein (*Verbascum bombyciferum*)

OTHER BIENNIALS FOR GARDEN CULTURE
All require well-drained, moderately fertile soil at pH 6.5 to 7.0.

Name	Zones	Height	Exposure*	Flower Color and Bloom Time	Comments
Anagallis monellii (blue pimpernel)	7–9	1½–2'	S to PSh	Blue and pink; summer	May flower first year; cv. 'Gentian Blue' 6 to 9 inches tall
Anchusa capensis 'Blue Angel'	9–10	8–10"	S to PSh	Blue; spring to early summer	Cv. 'Blue Bird' 15 to 18 inches tall; flowers indigo blue
Arabis serpillifolia	6–8	9–12"	S	White; spring	*A. turrita* matures at 3 feet tall; flowers yellow
Campanula americana (tall bellflower)	4–8	5–7'	S to PSh	Violet blue or white; late spring to summer	Often performs as an annual
C. barbata (bearded bellflower)	6–8	1½–2'	S to PSh	Lavender blue; summer	Flowers pendulous on one-sided spikes
C. longistyla	6–8	1½–2'	S to PSh	Violet or blue; summer	Flowers nodding on branched spikes
C. pyramidalis (chimney bellflower)	7–9	4–6'	S to PSh	Violet blue or white; late spring to summer	Spectacular in flower
C. spicata	6–8	1½–2½'	S to PSh	Violet or blue; summer	Flowers many, small, on long spikes
C. thyrsoides	5–8	2–3'	S to PSh	Light yellow; summer	Cv. 'Carniolica' has flowers in narrow spikes
Chelidonium majus (greater celandine)	6–8	2–3'	PSh to LSh	Yellow; spring	Self-sows readily; cv. 'Flore Pleno' is double flowered
Digitalis ferruginea (rusty foxglove)	6–8	3–5'	S to PSh	Rusty yellow-brown; late spring to summer	Often a short-lived perennial
D. grandiflora (yellow foxglove)	5–8	2–3'	S to PSh	Pale yellow; late spring to summer	Often a short-lived perennial
D. lanata (Grecian foxglove)	5–8	2–3'	S to PSh	Cream to yellow-brown; late spring to summer	Often a short-lived perennial
D. lutea (straw foxglove)	5–8	2–3'	S to PSh	Cream to yellow; late spring to summer	Often a short-lived perennial
D. × mertonensis (pink foxglove)	6–8	2–3'	PSh	Yellowish pink; late spring to summer	
D. thapsi	5–8	1½–2½'	S to PSh	Purple and red; late spring to summer	Often a short-lived perennial
Dipsacus spp. (teasel)	4–8	5–7'	S to PSh	Pale lilac; summer	Two similar species; garden curiosities
Echium plantagineum	8–10	1–2'	S	Purple, blue, aging to pink; late spring to summer	Often grown as an annual
E. vulgare (viper's bugloss)	6–8	2–3'	S	Bluish purple, aging pink or white; late spring to summer	Cv. 'Blue Bedder' matures to 15 inches tall; flowers bell shaped, blue
Eschscholzia californica (California poppy)	6–8	1–2'	S	Typically yellow-orange; spring to summer	Often short-lived perennial, usually grown as annual
Hesperis matronalis (dame's rocket)	3–8	2–4'	S to PSh	Lilac, white, or purple; late spring to summer	Several double-flowered cultivars
Ipomopsis aggregata (skyrocket)	7–9	1–3'	S to PSh	Red and yellow; summer	Several color variants: yellow, salmon, magenta
I. rubra (standing cypress)	8–10	4–7'	S to PSh	Red and yellow; summer	Usually unbranched; *Gilia rubra* in some catalogs
Isatis tinctoria (dyer's woad)	7–9	2–3'	S	Yellow; summer	*I. glauca*, a perennial, is a better garden plant
Lunaria annua (silver dollar, money plant)	7–9	2–3'	S to PSh	Red-violet or white; spring	Grown for dried pod septa; several cultivars
Matthiola incana (Brompton stock)	8–10	2–3'	S	Purple, red, pink, or white; summer to fall	Usually offered in mixed colors
Michauxia tchaihatcheffii, syn. *Mindium tchaihatcheffii*	7–8	4–6'	S to PSh	Lilac buds, opening to white; summer	Flowers 4 to 5 inches in diameter

Name	Zones	Height	Exposure*	Flower Color and Bloom Time	Comments
Oenothera acaulis (Chilean evening primrose)	5–8	6–9"	S to PSh	White to rose, or white; late spring to summer	Stemless; often a short-lived perennial
O. albicaulis (Mississippi evening primrose)	5–8	6–12"	S to PSh	White to pink; late spring to summer	Often a short-lived perennial
O. argillicola (Appalachian evening primrose)	5–8	3–5'	S to PSh	Yellow, aging red-orange; late spring to summer	Sprawling, ascending habit
O. biennis (common evening primrose)	4–8	2–6'	S to PSh	Yellow, aging reddish brown; summer	Several large-flowered cultivars
O. caespitosa (pink evening primrose)	4–8	1–2'	S to PSh	Pink or white; late spring to summer	Mat forming; often perennial, can be invasive
O. laciniata var. *grandiflora* (cut-leaf evening primrose)	3–7	2–3'	S to PSh	Yellow and red; late spring to summer	Sometimes a short-lived perennial
Onopordum acanthium (Scotch thistle)	6–8	4–9'	S to PSh	Purple or white; summer	Gray white foliage; intensely prickly
O. nervosum (Arabian thistle)	6–8	4–9'	S to PSh	Purple; summer	Similar to *O. acanthium;* sometimes listed as *O. arabicum*
Onosma pyramidale	7–9	1½–2'	S to PSh	Yellow; late spring to summer	Other species with purple or blue flowers
Silybum marianum (holy thistle)	7–9	3–4'	S	Purple; summer	Prickly, white-veined leaves
Smyrnium olustrum (black lovage)	9–10	3–5'	S to PSh	Yellow; spring	Aromatic foliage edible
Viola tricolor (Johnny-jump-up)	4–8	9–15"	S to PSh	Violet; lavender, yellow, and white; spring to summer	Usually grown as an annual
V. × wittrockiana (pansy)	6–8	6–10"	S to PSh	Varicolored; spring to early summer	Usually grown as an annual

* S, full sun; Sh, shade (no direct sun); PSh, partial shade (sun exposure only part of the day); LSh, light shade (e.g., the shade of tall, open trees, with little or no exposure to direct sun).

Scotch thistle (*Onopordum acanthium*)

Standing cypress (*Ipomopsis rubra*)

Variegated Silver Dollar (*Lunaria annua* 'Variegata')

19

Roses

Revised by Stephen Scanniello,
Rosarian at the Brooklyn Botanic Garden

Since ancient times, the rose has held a very special place in the hearts of people throughout the world. Because of its significance as a symbol of purity and faith; because of the many associations, legends, and traditions surrounding it; and because of its sheer beauty, the nearly omnipresent, sometimes vicious thorns notwithstanding, it has been loved and revered by countless generations. The romance of the rose has come down to us in song and story, and it is interwoven into the very fabric of our history. The Greek poetess

A climbing rose trained on a white board fence imparts a note of rural simplicity to a suburban backyard.

Sappho sang of its beauty as far back as the sixth century B.C. The Roman matron of the first century A.D. took pride and pleasure in arranging her roses for the flower shows of her day. The symbols of the two factions contending for supremacy in strife-torn England during the fifteenth century were the white rose of York and the red rose of Lancaster, and "The War of the Roses" ensued.

One of the first flowers to be domesticated, the rose has been faithfully protected, treasured, and planted wherever civilization has spread. Universal in its appeal to the spirit of humanity, it is equally at home over the cottage doorway and within the proud gates of royal palaces.

Since the dawn of science and its application to the study of plants, no other flower has received as much attention as the rose. Plant explorers and botanists have discovered and named more than 200 species, all naturally occurring in the northern hemisphere. After more than a century of intensive plant breeding, we now have many thousands of varied cultivars. When we compare the wealth of material available to us today with the limited number of cultivars and types that were available only a few generations ago, we realize what a debt of gratitude we owe our modern plant hybridizers.

Today there is a rose for every place and purpose: for formal beds and borders; for arbors, trellises, and fences; for hedges; for ground covers on steep banks; for edgings; for accent plants in perennial borders; for use as specimen shrubs and decorative features in portable containers on terrace and patio; and even for planting in little rose bays along crowded streets in the heart of great cities. Roses are one of the most versatile and exciting plant groups with which to work in creating landscape compositions.

ROSE GARDEN DESIGN

Partly because of the special esteem in which the rose is held, partly because the cultural requirements of the rose differ from those of other flowers, and partly because the rose lacks the fullness of growth of many other cultivated plants and, therefore, needs special compositional arrangement, a separate garden or planting area or bed for roses is the most satisfactory method of planting. Such a specialized garden may seem to be too great an undertaking for the average gardener, but it is not impossible to attain even on a

Where space permits, a rose hedge allowed to grow out and sprawl makes a magnificent display.

Where garden space is limited, roses my be combined with clematis along a boundary fence, both offering floral beauty simultaneously.

small property and where resources are limited. A rose garden need not be large in scale or lavish in details of construction.

In planning a traditional rose garden, a few essential considerations should be borne in mind: an enclosure that is not too close and airless yet gives adequate shelter from the wind and provides a background against which the blooms may be seen to the best advantage; a geometric pattern to give the design definite form, so that the garden will have a beauty of its own quite independent of the flowers; and paths of some material such as brick, flagstone, or turf that will be in harmony with the surroundings.

In a rose garden of contemporary design the composition will be more casual and varied, and will permit greater freedom. Such rose beds may be designed to create an interesting and dramatic pattern within the surfaced area of the patio, or roses may be planted in raised beds against the free-sweeping curve of the patio wall. Planted in tubs, roses may also be used as specimen or accent plants to highlight a planting composition.

If the grounds of a suburban home or apartment dwelling are too limited to permit the development of even a very small garden, roses may still be grown and enjoyed—perhaps as a single lovely bush beside the door, or a few floribundas or miniature roses planted in a group near the corner of the house, or some of the graceful, climbing roses on a low fence or high wall. Few flowers bring such touches of warmth and graciousness, of color, and beauty to any home—be it large or small—as does the rose in any form.

CULTURAL REQUIREMENTS

The factors that contribute to success in growing roses of fine quality include a suitable location; a fertile, friable soil;

good drainage; the selection of vigorous, disease-free plants; correct planting procedures; and good cultural practices—pruning, fertilization, mulching, winter protection, and the control of insect pests and diseases.

Location

To produce good bloom, roses require a minimum of six hours of sun during the day. Shade during the afternoon is preferable to morning shade. In fact, some afternoon shade is desirable, as the blooms tend to retain their color for a longer period. Roses will not bloom in situations where the shade is too dense, and they should not be planted in close proximity to trees, shrubs, or hedges that are heavy surface feeders. Under such conditions, the roses will be deprived of both nutrients moisture.

Air circulation is also important. Roses do not make satisfactory growth in closely confined areas where there is insufficient circulation of air.

A sunny arbor covered with climbing roses offers a memorable passage through the garden.

SOIL REQUIREMENTS

The drainage capacity and pH of the soil are very important. Roses will thrive in both fairly heavy clay and sandy loam soils, provided the requirements of drainage and pH are met. The ideal soil is a good garden loam that is well supplied with organic matter and is slightly acidic.

Drainage

Good drainage is absolutely essential. While roses require large quantities of water for their best growth, they are seriously injured by an excess of standing water in the soil. They will not thrive in soils that do not drain readily or where the water table rises to within a few feet of the surface at any time of the year.

If the natural drainage is not adequate to take care of surplus water, the beds may be underdrained with either tile or crushed stone or cinders.

One choice is to use 4-inch agricultural tile, laid end to end at the bottom of a 2-foot trench. The tile joints should be covered with strips of tar paper to keep the soil out of the tile while the trench is being refilled. Whatever material is used, there should be a fall of at least 3 inches in every 50 linear feet. While agricultural tile is traditional, concrete-asbestos perforated pipe, which is available in 8-foot lengths, is easier to handle. Even easier and much less expensive is corrugated PVC drain, which is flexible. If crushed stone or cinders are used, a 6-inch layer placed at the bottom of the trench will usually be sufficient to provide adequate drainage.

An alternative solution to solving poor drainage problems is to construct raised beds. Railroad ties, logs, bricks, and any sort of stone are all ideal materials for building a raised bed. A bed about 18 inches high should be sufficient.

Acidity of the Soil

Roses perform best in a slightly acidic soil, with a pH ranging between 5.5 and 6.5. If the soil is too strongly alkaline or if it becomes too acidic roses have a tendency to become chlorotic—a condition indicated by a characteristic mottling of the leaves: the veins remain dark green and the leaf areas between the veins turn yellow or, in extreme cases, almost white. In addition, the growth of the rose shrub will be stunted and the blooming frequency greatly diminished. When such conditions become evident, the soil should be tested to determine whether the trouble is due either to too much acidity or alkalinity or to a lack of available iron (see the index for the use of iron chelate). If the chlorosis is caused by too high a degree of acidity, the condition may be remedied by an application of lime (see "Rate of Application of Lime to Decrease Soil Acidity" on page 764). In preparing new beds, the soil should be tested and a pH between 5.5 and 6.5 established.

PREPARATION OF THE SOIL

It is important that the soil for roses be well prepared; the roots of a vigorous rosebush will extend to a depth varying from 15 to 20 inches. The best time to improve the fertility and texture of the soil is *before* planting.

If the soil is decidedly sandy, its texture may be improved and its water-holding capacity greatly increased by adding clay loam, compost, and other organic materials to it. Similarly, the texture of extremely heavy clay soils may be improved by the addition of sand, compost, strawy manure, or some comparable material.

The methods of preparing soil for rose beds will depend to a considerable extent on the desires of the owner. If means are limited, the old English practice of "double-digging" will give satisfactory results. Double-digging is a simple, undeniably arduous, but very efficient method of soil preparation. It consists of removing the top spadeful of soil from one end of the bed and placing it at the other end of the bed, ready for later use. A generous layer of well-rotted cow manure or rich compost, to which a few handfuls of superphosphate have been added, should then be worked well into the lower stratum of soil that is left exposed after the top spadeful is removed. The next layer of topsoil is then spaded forward on this lower stratum, and the process is continued until the end of the bed has been reached. The pile of topsoil removed from the first trench is used to fill the last trench. Organic matter should be applied at the rate of 5 to 6 bushels per 100 square feet of area.

After the organic material is thoroughly mixed in, the enriched soil is then returned to the bed and allowed to settle before planting. Depending on the results of a soil test, it may be advisable to add a couple of handfuls of superphosphate to the soil used for backfill when individual rose bushes are planted in the newly prepared bed.

Essentially the same procedure may be followed when individual holes are being prepared for specimen roses.

If the roses are to be planted in the spring, it is best to prepare the beds the previous autumn. The preparation of the bed should be completed at least three weeks before planting so that the soil will have time to settle. Have the final level of the rose bed about 2 or 3 inches above the surface of the surrounding area.

Rose Soil Sickness

It is not recommended to plant a new rose bush in the same site, or hole, where another rose plant had been growing.

There seems to be a detrimental effect on a newly planted rose if planted in the same exact spot as an old plant. The new bush never attains the vigor it should and may die prematurely. Among rosarians, this is referred to, rather unscientifically, as "rose soil sickness."

To prevent rose soil sickness, remove the old soil (2 feet deep and 2 feet wide) and refill with a fresh, organic mix. You can do this with entire beds or with individual holes. But only do all this work if you are replanting where roses were growing for more than five years.

Maintenance of Soil Fertility

Roses have heavy nutrient requirements and must, therefore, have a soil well supplied with the essential elements of fertility. An adequate supply of nitrogen is necessary to promote rapid, vigorous growth and good foliage. Phosphorus induces good root development, stimulates flower bud formation, and increases the size and color of the blooms. Potassium is essential in that it gives strength to the cell walls, increases the resistance of the plant to disease, and aids in the ripening and hardening of the wood in the autumn.

In planning a program for the maintenance of soil fertility, the following points should be taken into consideration: the time of application, the formulation or analysis of the fertilizer to be used, and the method and rate of application. To obtain vigorous growth and abundant bloom, applications of fertilizer should be made on a monthly basis during the growing season of the rose. The first application should be made in the spring, after the pruning has been done. Generally speaking, if your region experiences a winter dormancy due to cold (freezing) weather, the last application of fertilizer should be about one and a half months, before the first expected frost. In zone 7, for example, the first application of fertilizer should be made in March, the last in mid-August.

Many rose growers use a complete, commercial granular fertilizer such as 10-6-4. Often, fertilizers with this ratio have an organic base and contains trace elements. The soil should be fairly moist when the application is made. The fertilizer should be sprinkled on the soil about the plant and worked in lightly with a hand cultivator. Unless a rainfall occurs shortly afterward, the soil should be watered to get the fertilizer into solution and available for absorption by the roots. The foliage of the plants should be dry at the time the application is made and granular fertilizers should not come into contact with the leaves or the canes as it may cause severe burning, particularly if the foliage is wet.

Foliar fertilizers can be used as a supplement to any fertilizing program. The rate of application is given in the directions for the individual fertilizers and should be observed. These soluble fertilizers can be applied as frequently as every other week throughout the growing season.

It's very important to point out that all fertilizer programs should be based on the results of a soil test. A complete soil profile should be studied before *any* soil improvement and planting begins. Incorrectly formulated fertilizer can be damaging to the roses, and excessive amounts are not only wasteful but contribute to pollution of reservoirs and ground water.

SELECTION OF STOCK

The importance of purchasing good stock from a reliable source can hardly be overemphasized. It is poor economy to purchase cheap rose bushes or "bargain" stock. Such plants are almost invariably of inferior quality and rarely make vigorous growth or bloom satisfactorily.

For the protection of the buyer, roses are graded into several standard classes. The top grade is listed as no. 1. To be graded no. 1, a bush must have three or more vigorous canes, and if carefully planted, it is almost certain to develop into a satisfactory plant.

TIME OF PLANTING

Roses may be planted any time of the year, as long as there is no imminent danger of a severe freeze. The timing of planting depends on the way the rose is bought—bare-root or potted.

Generally, bare-root roses are the best choice. These arrive at your home in a dormant state, without soil. Depending on where you garden, the correct planting time for a bare-root rose is in autumn, winter, or early spring. Certain nurseries in California and Texas will ship bare-root roses in mid to late winter, while most other nurseries will ship roses bare-root in the autumn or spring. The nurseries know the best time to ship roses to your area and will advise you accordingly. Two good rules to remember:

1. Bare-root roses should not be planted when the ground is frozen or when a hard freeze is imminent.
2. Roses should be planted bare-root only when dormant.

Nurseries dig their roses from the growing fields in the autumn. At this time they can either ship them or put them into storage for spring shipments. Many of the larger nurseries now send bare-root roses to home gardeners in the autumn.

It's beneficial to plant roses in fall. The soil is conducive to root growth for some weeks, and this initial growth will support full foliar development in the spring. In addition, there is a wider choice of cultivars available in the fall. Hard to find roses or especially popular ones are often sold out before spring shipments are made. Moreover, those who place fall orders have the best possible choice of superior stock.

Orders for fall shipment should be placed in August. To delay is to risk a narrower choice of cultivars. Most mail-order nurseries refuse orders after October 1 and make shipments over the ensuing weeks (usually in mid-November in zone 7).

Should it not be possible to properly plant roses that arrive in a fall delivery, they may be buried in a deep trench for the winter, with only the uppermost inch or two protruding, and then be set in their permanent positions in spring, when the danger of freeze has passed.

As some nurseries do not ship in the fall, it is best to check the catalog or inquire before placing an order. Just as with fall shipments, it is important to find out when spring deliveries may be expected in your area, and to have made necessary preparations the previous fall so that the roses will be planted without delay.

Whether planting in the fall or spring, it is advisable to soak the roots in water for a day before planting in muddy water. Leave the roses soaking until you are ready to plant them.

Container-grown roses are sold dormant or actively growing in various types of pots, boxes, or wrappers. If carefully removed from their containers, without disturbing the roots, they may be planted anytime from spring to fall, even when in full flower. Indeed, when flower color is particularly important, specimens in bloom help facilitate selection, especially when a last-minute replacement is needed for a critical location. Prices of potted roses usually lower as the season advances. Thus bargains can sometimes be found among the leftovers when retailers clear their stock in the fall.

In most cases, retail nurseries and garden centers do not grow their own roses; rather, they purchase them from growers, pot them up, and force them to bloom precociously. If done carefully, there is no harm in this, but carelessly handled stock, with roots forced into undersize pots, leads to weakened plants, disappointing performance, and reduced winter hardiness. It is prudent, therefore, to check the reputation of the retailer before buying potted roses. Local rose societies are a good source of such information.

Own-rooted Versus Budded Roses

Roses are widely available to the home gardener either growing on their own roots or having been propagated by grafting a bud of one cultivar onto a stock or stem of another. Most popular roses have been budded, but most miniature roses are grown on their own roots. When you buy a budded rose, whether bare root or potted, it already has a history. Two years before, in the grower's fields, a dormant bud from the selected cultivar was attached to the rooted stem of a different rose. In North America, the most commonly used root stocks are the cultivar 'Dr. Huey', a red-flowering climber; *Rosa multiflora*, a white species; or, for warm climates only, the cultivar 'Fortuniana', a white-flowered climber. These roses are referred to as the rootstock and the stem. The point where the bud was attached to the stem is called the bud union. Roses that are not budded but are growing on their own root system are known as own-root roses. They are grown from cuttings taken from a mature plant. Today many commercial retail sources offer both budded and own-rooted roses.

METHOD OF PLANTING

Spacing among roses depends most on the class of rose involved in the planting. Those with a vigorous, shrubby habit, such as old garden roses (hybrid perpetuals, gallicas, damasks, hybrid Chinas, etc.) and modern landscape shrubs (English roses, Meidiland, Canadian Explorer roses, etc.) should be set 3 feet apart. Hybrid teas, floribundas, grandi-floras, polyanthas, teas, and Chinas, on the other hand, are best spaced about 2 feet apart.

It should be borne in mind that these general recommendations are not inflexible; many cultivars perform idiosyncratically according to local factors, especially climate. Local botanic gardens and rose societies are good sources of information about the cultural peculiarities of various roses.

Never let the roots be exposed to sun or wind before planting. If possible, plant roses under calm, cloudy conditions, keeping the roots in a bucket of muddy water, or wrapped in wet paper or wet sphagnum moss, until the planting hole is dug and the backfill soil is ready.

At the instant of planting, all injured or broken roots should be carefully pruned away, a clean, slanting cut being made. Any long, straggly roots should be cut back sufficiently so that they will not have to be twisted or bent when the plant is set. A hole of ample size should be dug for each plant. If the loose soil is mounded slightly in the bottom of the hole, the roots can be placed in a natural position, extending both out and down.

Planting depth depends in large part on the plant-hardiness zone in which you are located. In zone 7 and north, budded roses should be planted so that the bud union lies 1 to 3 inches below the soil level—roughly 1 inch in zone 7,

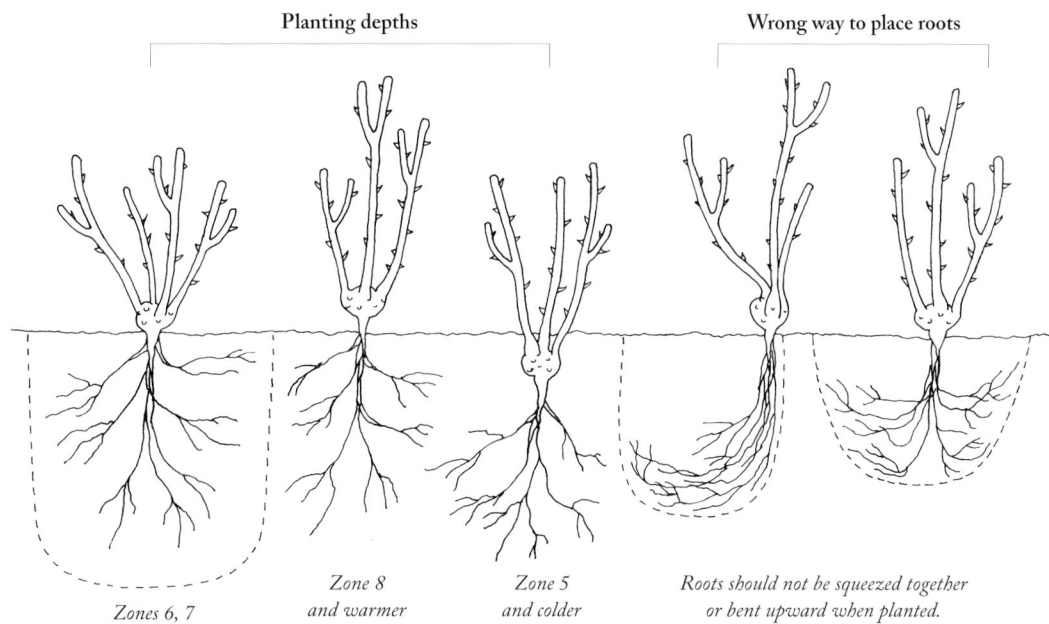

Planting depths

Wrong way to place roots

Zones 6, 7

Zone 8 and warmer

Zone 5 and colder

Roots should not be squeezed together or bent upward when planted.

2 inches in zone 6, and 3 inches farther north; from zone 8 south, the bud union should be above ground. An own-rooted rose should be planted at a depth that securely anchors the plant.

After the plant is in place, the soil should be packed firmly about the roots. Many failures are caused by loose, careless planting, and if success is to be ensured, it is necessary that a few simple rules be observed. Press the soil around the roots with your hands, making sure you press firmly. When the hole has been filled almost to the top, the plant should then be watered thoroughly. Ample watering is as necessary for roses planted in the autumn as it is for those planted in the spring. Immediately after this first watering, the soil should be mounded up about the plant. In the case of roses planted in the autumn this will serve as a winter protection for it, and the beds may then be mulched in the usual way. When roses are planted in the spring, this hilling up of the soil is equally advisable, as it protects the canes from the drying effects of sun, late frosts, and wind while new roots develop that will, later in the season, supply the moisture the plant requires. With spring-planted roses, temporary mounds may be left about the plants for three or four weeks, at which time the soil may then be gradually worked back into the beds.

WATERING

Roses make their best growth during moderately cool weather when the soil is well supplied with moisture. Although roses resent a soil that is too saturated or a water table that has risen above the level of the roots, they require an adequate and fairly abundant supply of moisture throughout the growing season. During periods of drought, roses should be watered thoroughly once a week. The bed should be soaked until the water has penetrated into the soil to a depth that covers all of the roots. Frequent light waterings are of little value and may do more harm than good.

It is most important that all watering be finished several hours before sunset. The plants should be dry in the evening. Plants left wet overnight encourage the development and spreading of black spot and powdery mildew, two pervasive diseases of roses.

The best time to water the rose garden is at daybreak. Overhead watering is recommended on occasion to wash the foliage clean of any fungus spores that might have settled there during the evening. Overhead watering can also wash off dust and grime from the foliage of roses growing in city gardens.

To deter the spread of foliage diseases and to conserve water, alternate methods of irrigation should be considered. Possible approaches include soaker hoses, drip systems, underground irrigation, and aboveground sprinklers that direct a strong circular spray below the leafy branches of the rose plants. For control of diseases and insect pests, see Chapter 34.

MULCHES

As with most garden plants, roses benefit greatly from a mulch. A good mulch not only reduces soil evaporation and insulates roots from intense summer heat but gradually improves soil structure and adds nutrients. It should also discourage weeds and improve the appearance of the rose bed.

Among the materials to be considered, some of the most successful with roses are ground corncobs, shredded sugarcane fiber, shredded cedar bark, wood chips, shredded tobacco stems, eel grass (seaweed), shredded tree leaves, and pine (or other conifer) needles (see Chapter 32). Also useful are moist, well-rotted manure, which will release nutrients; compost, with the same virtue and caveat; and grass clippings—all of which should be applied and maintained at about 1 inch to 2 inches thick. Any nitrogen losses caused by the rapid decomposition of such mulches as manure, compost, and grass clippings will likely be adequately compensated for by the 10-6-4 fertilizer earlier recommended.

The soil should be wet at the time the mulch is applied. Try to schedule a fertilizer application just before putting down mulch. Future applications of fertilizer can be scratched into the mulch.

CUTTING ROSES

When roses are cut for decorative purposes, many of the same principles may be applied that are used in the pruning of the plants. A clean, sharp, slightly slanting cut should be made, approximately ¼ inch above a leaf bud. The symmetry of the bush may be maintained by cutting immediately above an outside bud, thus ensuring that future growth will be outward.

To get the longest lasting blooms and the best fragrances, roses should be cut early in the day. The fresh-cut bloom should be put immediately into a bucket of water, while still in the garden. Immediately recut the stem of the rose, under water. In the house, recut the flower stem—again while submerged in water. To keep the blooms fresh and long lasting, each morning change the water in the vase and recut the stems (always while submerged in water).

WINTER PROTECTION

The need and extent of winter protection depends on three factors: the severity of the climate, the exposure of the rose garden, and the natural hardiness of the cultivars selected. Winter injury is usually attributable either to the actual freezing of the twigs and roots, which breaks down the cell tissues, or to the loss of moisture from the twigs caused by excessive evaporation. Winter injury is quite as likely to be caused by strong, drying winds and by brilliant sunshine as by extreme cold. Throughout the winter, the roots continue

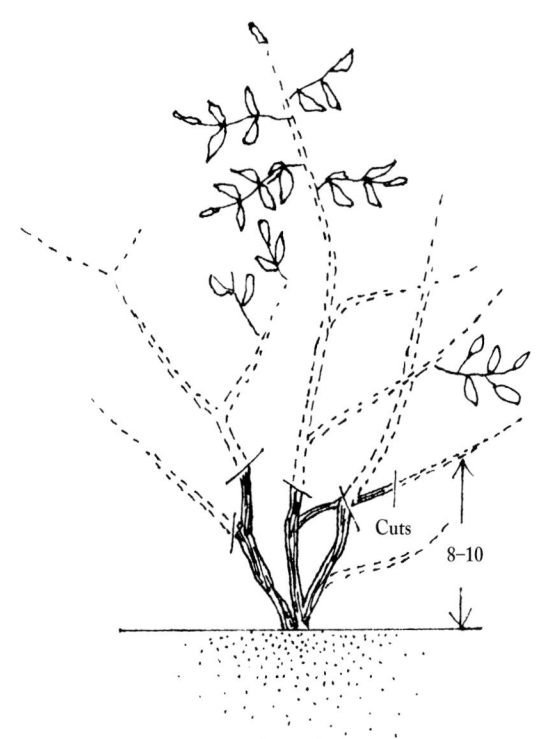

Hybrid tea rose pruned for bloom.

to absorb water from the soil and a slow evaporation of moisture occurs from the canes. If an undue amount of wind and sunshine increase evaporation beyond the point at which the roots can supply sufficient moisture to the twigs, the canes will begin to shrivel and if the process is prolonged, the plant will die, even though no actual freezing of the plant tissues has taken place. One of the first preparations for winter, therefore, should be to see that the soil is well supplied with moisture. The normal autumn rains will often provide for an adequate storage of moisture, but if the autumn season is deficient in rainfall, supplemental watering should be done before the ground freezes.

In the South, i.e., from zone 8 south, roses require little or no winter protection. From zone 7 north, where temperatures regularly fall below minus 10°F or stay well below freezing for sustained periods, it is a good idea to provide adequate protection for some roses, especially those that were planted that autumn. In Brooklyn (zone 7), the rose types needing winter protection are Chinas, teas, and Noisettes. Hybrid teas and other modern types will survive the winter without protection. However, farther north it is necessary to protect even these roses.

In a normal season, the early frosts of autumn will harden and ripen the wood, and the plants will gradually become dormant. It is a prudent precaution to rake and destroy all fallen leaves and bits of twig to prevent them from harboring bacterial and fungus diseases.

Once the ground has frozen, dry soil, dry compost, or dry sand may be mounded around stem bases to a height of 10 or 12 inches. It is very important that this material be as dry as possible when applied so that stem decay not ensue. This mound will afford considerable protection about the crown of the plant and will also prevent the wood and buds of the lower portion of the stem from drying out. It is important that the mulch not be applied until after the ground has frozen. The purpose of the mound is not to exclude cold but rather to stabilize the temperature in and under the mulch zone, thereby minimizing the damaging effects of freeze-thaw cycling. In addition, a mulch of compost or well-rotted manure may be spread over the beds. As this blanket decomposes, the mulch releases nutrients to the soil for spring.

Various climatic conditions contribute to the winter killing of roses, conditions over which we have little control. For example, a prolonged spell of unseasonably warm weather in fall may prevent stems from becoming hardened sufficiently to withstand the rigors of a severe winter. Under such conditions the bushes will have a tendency to continue growth until late in the autumn, and the new shoots will be so soft and succulent that considerable dieback may result and require extensive pruning out in spring. It is recommended in colder climates to give the roses an application of granular potash in the autumn to help harden off the plants.

Protection for Climbers and Standard Roses

Some of our most beautiful climbers, such as 'Sombreuil' and 'Alister Stella Gray', are not able to survive the extreme severity of a northern winter unless given sufficient protection. It has been found that cornstalks and evergreen boughs, while affording satisfactory protection, often harbor field mice and rabbits to such an extent that considerable damage may be done to the bush. Burlap is not good because it holds too much moisture. The most approved method, especially from zone 5 north, consists of removing the canes from the trellis or support early in October while they are still supple, and allowing them to remain procumbent on the ground, where the grass will grow up among them and where the falling leaves that are blown in on them will afford natural protection. Soil is then mounded up about the base of the plant, and after the ground has become frozen, a mulch of salt hay or straw is placed over the mound of soil. To hold the canes in a procumbent position, two strong pieces of wood may be driven into the earth at right angles to each other, forming a wedge to hold the canes in place. This method of protection has proved so satisfactory that even during several winters when the temperature reached −20°F, no injury resulted. Early in the spring, after danger from frost is over, the mounds of soil may be gradually removed from the base of the plant, and the canes then easily refastened to their supports. At the Brooklyn Botanic Garden (zone 7), no winter protection is given climbing roses.

Standard or tree roses grown in zone 6 and north require careful winter protection. One side of the plant should be dug up and loosened and a trench dug on the other side so that the entire stem and top can be bent down into the trench and covered with dry compost and soil. Standard roses at the Brooklyn Botanic Garden (zone 7) are left upright, but it is advisable to protect the bud union (near the top of the unbranched trunk, where the branches originate) with a wrapping of salt hay, applied rather like a thick bandage, through the winter.

If the standard has been grown in a portable container, the plant in its container should be shifted to a garage, shed, or cool basement once nights become frosty. Freezing temperatures cause no harm during this period of storage so long as the temperature remains relatively stable and does not cycle above and below the freezing point. The soil should be kept moist, but there is no requirement for sunlight until the buds swell in spring, by which time the standard should be placed outdoors.

CLASSIFICATION OF ROSES

Until about 1980, roses were grouped into the following seven categories: hybrid teas, floribundas, grandifloras, miniature roses, climbers, old-fashioned roses, and shrub roses. The last category included any miscellany not accommodated in one of the other groups. Gardeners today, inspired by the Heritage Rose Foundation and the many new rose nurseries specializing in unique roses, have refined the rose classification system.

MODERN ROSES (10 CLASSES)	
Hybrid tea	Climbing
Floribunda	Shrub
Grandiflora	Hybrid musk
Miniature	Eglantine hybrids
Polyantha	Rugosa hybrids

One general rule to remember: A *modern rose* is a rose that belongs to a classification (hybrid tea, floribunda, etc.) that has evolved since 1867. That year is the universally accepted date of the introduction of the first hybrid tea rose. An *old garden rose* (antique rose, old-fashioned rose, old rose, or grandma's rose) is one that was included in a classification in existence before 1867. The current classification system may be summarized as seen right ("Modern Roses" and "Old Garden Roses").

For the formal patterns of beds and borders in the rose garden, traditionally hybrid teas, floribundas, and grandifloras are the favorites. Polyanthas, miniatures, teas, and Chinas make interesting alternatives and companions to these.

Climbing roses and ramblers are logically the first choice for covering arbors, lattices, pergolas, and walls. However, any tall-growing shrub, including many of the English roses and Canadian Explorer roses can be used in this fashion. Many species (e.g., *R. rubiginosa*, *R. setigera*, and *R. canina*) can also be used as climbing roses. And for warmer climates, there are Noisettes, teas, and Chinas that are beautiful climbers.

Roses suitable for climbing on supports also make excellent choices for ground cover roses. Shrub roses such as those of the Meidiland series (e.g., 'Red Meidiland', 'Scarlet Meidiland', 'White Meidiland') are an exceptional choice for covering steep, rocky slopes.

For massed shrubbery plantings, for hedges, and for beautiful specimens, the eglantines (species and hybrids), rugosas (species and hybrids), alba roses, all shrub roses (especially Griffith Buck's cultivars and the Canadian Explorer series), and all species roses are standouts. But also consider woody climbers left to grow without physical support; they make beautiful hedges.

OLD GARDEN ROSES (15 CLASSES)	
Species	Noisette
Gallica	Bourbon
Alba	Hybrid China
Damask	Hybrid Bourbon
Centifolia	Hybrid Noisette
Moss	Portland
China	Hybrid perpetual
Tea	

PRUNING

To understand how one can use roses in the garden and, more important, how the different roses should be pruned, it is necessary to become familiar with the many different groups and their individual pruning needs. Pruning tips are given with each class description. Lists of varieties and cultivars of merit are also provided.

ROSES FOR GARDEN BEDS AND BORDERS

Hybrid Tea, Floribunda, and Grandiflora Roses

The hybrid tea, floribunda, and grandiflora roses are probably the most familiar of the rose groups to gardeners. They are generally upright-growing, rather stiff-looking plants that benefit greatly from an annual pruning. They look best when grown in beds, with similar colors and heights grouped together. Roses in these groups give a very satisfactory continual bloom throughout the season, especially in colder climates.

Roses in these three groups should be pruned in the spring or late winter, while they are still dormant. Hybrid teas particularly benefit from a severe pruning, i.e., all but four canes should be removed, and these four cut back to about 6 inches.

It is a general rule that the lower you prune these roses, the larger their flowers will be. Floribundas and grandifloras, on the other hand, do not require such severe pruning; some canes should be removed, though, so that subsequent growth will be open enough to allow good light penetration and air circulation. The remaining canes should be cut back to about 1 foot.

HYBRID TEA ROSE CULTIVARS OF MERIT

'Anna Pavlova': tall; flowers pink; very fragrant.

'Carmen': medium; flowers dark red; very fragrant.

'Casanova': tall; flowers high centered, yellow.

'Century Two': medium; flowers high centered, pink.

'Chrysler Imperial': 2 to 3 feet tall; good form; flowers dark red; outstanding fragrance; 1953 All-American winner.

'Dainty Bess': medium; flowers attractive, five petaled, pink; sweet fragrance; everblooming.

'Dainty Maid': vigorous, bushy habit; foliage dark, leathery; flowers single, cerise opening to silvery pink.

'Double Delight': 2 to 3 feet tall; flowers unique red and white; delightful fragrance; above average hardiness; 1977 All-American winner.

'Electron': medium; compact, bushy habit; foliage attractive, dark green; flowers bright pink with a glow; 1973 All-American winner.

'Fountain Square': medium to tall; foliage attractive, large, glossy; flowers breathtaking, large, white.

'Fragrant Cloud': 5 to 6 feet tall; vigorous habit; foliage glossy, dark; flowers well formed, large, coral red; old rose fragrance.

'Granada': tall; flowers blends of orange, yellow, and pink; fragrant; 1964 All-American winner.

'Heirloom': medium to tall; flowers clear, decorative, lilac; buds attractive, pointed oval; intensely scented; abundance of bloom on single stems.

'Helen Traubel': medium; vigorous habit; flowers large, borne singly, pink blended; mild fragrance; 1952 All-American winner.

'Innocence': 4 to 5 feet tall; flowers five petaled, white; hard to find, a real beauty.

'Irish Elegance': 4 to 5 feet tall; flowers peach to salmon; hard to find, a real beauty.

'Irish Fireflame': bushy habit; foliage dark, glossy; flowers large, single, crimson; very fragrant.

'Kordes Perfecta': 3 feet tall or higher; vigorous habit; flowers creamy white edged with carmine; very fragrant.

'Maid of Honour': 4 to 5 feet tall; flowers apricot; free of diseases.

'Mrs. Herbert Stevens': 4 feet tall; flowers nodding, pure white; tea rose fragrance.

'Mr. Lincoln': 5 to 6 feet tall; upright, vigorous habit; flowers striking, dark red; delightful frangrance; 1964 All-American winner.

'Soeur Thérèse': medium; flowers 8 to 10 petaled, yellow with faint streaks of orange.

'Stephen's Big Purple': tall; flowers high centered, many petaled, purple red; very fragrant.

'Swarthmore': tall; vigorous habit; flowers held on long stems; deep pink; buds classic hybrid tea; sweet fragrance.

'Sweet Surrender': 4 feet tall; flowers nodding, pink; very fragrant; 1983 All-American winner.

'Tiffany': 5 feet tall; vigorous, good habit; flowers striking, pink with a yellow glow at the base; buds outstanding, tapering; highly fragrant; 1955 All-American winner.

'Tropicana': 5 to 6 feet tall; flowers long lasting, hold their color exceptionally well, borne on strong sturdy stems, brilliant orange; free blooming; 1963 All-American winner.

'White Wings': 5 feet tall; vigorous, bushy, upright habit; foliage dark, leathery; flowers single, white; buds long, pointed; fragrant.

'Yankee Doodle': tall; vigorous habit; flowers showy, large, long lasting, pinkish yellow; delightful fragrance; 1976 All-American winner.

 Double Delight

 Chrysler Imperial

 Sweet Surrender

 Maid of Honour

 Fragrant Cloud

 Electron

 Heirloom

 Mr. Lincoln

 Granada

Throughout the blooming season, remove faded blooms by cutting the stems of the blooms just above an outward-facing leaf. This leaf should be composed of at least five leaflets. Cutting at this point along the stem will promote a satisfactory rebloom. This practice is known as "deadheading." In climates that have cold winters (zone 7 and north), deadheading should be discontinued about a month and a half before frost (in conjunction with the last fertilizer application).

Queen Elizabeth

Iceberg

Regensberg

Tamango

Sun flare

Polyantha Roses

Polyantha roses are low-growing shrubs, maturing 2 to 3 feet tall, with clustered flowers. These roses are the direct ancestors of floribunda roses. In the Victorian era, when they were first introduced, they were known as sweetheart roses. Thin out all twiggy growth from the centers in the spring while the plants are still dormant.

Miniature Roses

Miniature roses have had a rapid rise in popularity since the introduction of the first commercially successful cultivar 'Tom Thumb' in 1936. Miniature roses are just that: in all respects they are roses

GRANDIFLORA CULTIVARS OF MERIT

'Montezuma': 5 feet tall or higher; foliage handsome; flowers long lasting, coral or pink; buds attractive, pointed.

'Pink Parfait': 5 feet tall or higher; flowers attractive, pink blend; buds unusual; above average hardiness; 1961 All-American winner.

'Queen Elizabeth': tall; erect habit; foliage handsome; flowers superbly formed, unusually long lasting, lovely clear pink; fragrant; 1955 All-American winner; excellent cut flower.

'Rosalynn Carter': 5 to 6 feet tall; flowers coral orange; very fragrant.

'Roundelay': 5 to 6 feet tall; flowers velvety, intense red.

FLORIBUNDA CULTIVARS OF MERIT

'Columbus': 3 to 4 feet tall; flowers large, very double (35+ petals), pink; excellent cut flower.

'Escapade': 3 to 4 feet tall; flowers five petaled, clustered, magenta pink; excellent hedge rose.

'Eutin': 3 feet tall or higher; flowers in huge clusters, double, red; excellent hedge rose.

'Fabergé': 2 feet tall or lower; bushy habit; foliage dark, leathery; flowers profuse, beautifully formed, pink with white and yellow.

'Fred Loads': more than 6 feet tall; flowers in huge clusters, five petaled, vibrant orange; excellent hedge rose; can be used as a climber.

'Helga': 4 to 5 feet tall; flowers in clusters, large, white; excellent disease resistance.

'Iceberg': 2 to 3 feet tall; flowers medium, decorative, white; fruitlike fragrance.

'Regensberg': short; flowers pink with hints of white striping, white eye.

'Sun flare': medium; flowers 12 to 15 petaled, yellow; very fragrant; 1983 All-American winner.

'Tamango': 2 to 3 feet tall; flowers decorative, lasting, deep cherry red; slight fragrance.

'Woburn Abbey': moderate habit; foliage dark, leathery; flowers well formed, yellow and orange; free bloomer.

POLYANTHA CULTIVARS OF MERIT

'Cameo': flowers tiny, borne in great profusion, a lovely tone of shell pink, shading to orange-salmon.

'Gloria Mundi': flowers in clusters, an unusual scarlet orange.

'Perle d'Or': flowers delicate, starburst, golden apricot.

'Yvonne Rabier': flowers white; strong fragrance; excellent disease resistance.

MINIATURE ROSE CULTIVARS OF MERIT—SHRUB TYPES

'Cinderella': flowers tiny tightly petaled pompoms, less than ½ inch across, white; one of the smallest of the miniatures.

'Cupcake': flowers hybrid tea type, pink.

'Gourmet Popcorn': spreading habit; flowers pompom type, white.

'Jim Dandy': tall; flowers hybrid tea type; orange-red; fragrant.

'Little Linda': very tiny; flowers formal, loosely arranged, yellow.

'Minnie Pearl': flowers hybrid tea type, pink; fragrant.

'Rainbow's End': flowers hybrid tea type, yellow-orange-red blend; good fragrance.

'Sweet Chariot': spreading habit; flowers pompom type, magenta; very fragrant.

in miniature. Dozens of new cultivars are introduced each year, overwhelming the home gardener. Not only are there shrub forms in miniature but there are also climbing miniature roses (described separately in "Climbing Miniature Roses" on page 499). Although miniature roses are especially suited to culture in pots, they are very effective in the garden as bedding plants, as edgings for beds of larger roses, as accents in rock gardens, and to scramble along fences or against buildings.

A simple annual cutting back, best done in early spring while the stems are still dormant or, alternatively, during a lull in blooming, should focus on the thinning or opening of cluttered centers.

Gourmet Popcorn

ROSES FOR ARBORS, PERGOLAS, AND WALLS

Climbing Roses

Many different types of roses are included in the climbing roses, a somewhat arbitrary group. Generally speaking, any tall rose with flexible, arching canes can be trained as a climbing rose. As roses have no special adaptations for climbing—i.e., no tendrils or twining stem tips—they must be tied to a support in order to climb. The roses that work best as climbers are those that send up long canes (10 feet or more) each season.

The fashion in which the canes are trained or the position they take when tied to a support will determine the extent of growth and the quantity of blooms each season. When training canes on a wall or fence, it is best to create a fan pattern, i.e., with all the canes arranged in successive or mirrored curves with their extremities horizontal. On posts, arches, or pillars, the canes may be wrapped in spiral fashion around the support, but again with the extremities trained along horizontal structures. Attention to this aspect of training climbing roses is important, because the greater the number and extent of canes brought into horizontal position, the greater the number of flowers that will be borne. A well-trained climbing rose will bear flowers densely and produce ever-longer replacement canes year after year.

Ramblers and Climbers (Strictly Defined)

As with all specialized interests, a peculiar vocabulary has evolved among rosarians to characterize roses and to distinguish among them, sometimes to the consternation of amateurs. The terms *climbing rose* and *rambler rose* are examples. Ramblers have thin canes relative to their length, and these canes are flexible enough to be wrapped around a support, even in the second year. In climbers, by contrast, the canes are thicker, less pliant, and become quite rigid.

Beyond these distinctions in growth, most ramblers flower once each season, usually between May and July, and present a great flush of bloom. Climbers, especially the newer, increasingly popular cultivars, not only flower maximally in late spring but continue through the summer and into fall.

As for pruning, neither ramblers nor climbers should be pruned at all the first two years (before they flower), other than to remove dead parts or perhaps a shoot grown out of bounds.

Ramblers

Although most of the new canes of ramblers originate at the base of the plant, some develop along older canes. With

Evangeline

RAMBLER CULTIVARS OF MERIT

'Alberic Barbier': foliage very glossy; flowers large, often quartered, white; sometimes a repeat bloom in the autumn.

'Etain': strong grower; flowers large, apricot yellow.

'Evangeline': very strong grower; foliage prone to mildew, but still worthwhile; flowers in enormous clusters, single, soft pink; lovely fragrance.

'Phyllis Bide': graceful; flowers small, buff yellow, buds exquisitely formed, pale gold and pink.

'White Dorothy': pure, white counterpart of the common pink 'Dorothy Perkins'.

this in mind, it is best to prune a rambler just after flowering and to remove as much wood that has just flowered as possible, thereby preventing the formation of a tangled thicket that can be daunting to rejuvenate. Such major pruning is best performed annually.

If, however, you decide to leave some of the older canes, the laterals that have formed along their length should be pruned back to 2 or 3 inches after flowering. All remaining canes, old and new, should be neatly arranged and securely tied to their supports.

Climbers

More rigid than ramblers and often woodier, climbers require a different regimen. Most new canes originate on older wood rather than from the base, hence the importance of being conservative in removing old wood. In climber cultivars that bloom just once each season, remove about one-third of all stems, taking the oldest first, after blooming. This will not only encourage new growth but also allow room for it to develop fully. In cultivars with attractive hips (the fruitlike structure within which are borne the one-seeded fruit), laterals may be left intact until the hips have fallen. Otherwise, laterals should be shortened during the annual thinning of canes.

In climbers that flower all season, the laterals should be deadheaded immediately after flowering to encourage new blooms. In midseason, preferably during a lull in blooming, older, less productive canes should be culled to make room for elongating new canes, which usually terminate in a flower cluster. Not only should these new canes have room but they should be tied in before they become too rigid for training. In late winter or early spring, roughly one-third of all canes (the oldest) should be removed.

Other Climbing Roses
Climbing Sports

The climbing sports, mutants of shrub-type roses, make up a unique group of roses ideal for climbing situations in warmer climates. The following groups—climbing hybrid teas, climbing floribundas, climbing grandifloras, and climbing polyanthas—are simply climbing versions of the original

---

CLIMBER CULTIVARS OF MERIT THAT BLOOM ALL SEASON

'Blaze': vigorous habit; foliage dark, leathery, flowers in great clusters, brilliant red; moderate recurrent bloom.

'Compassion': foliage dark, leathery, flowers hybrid tea type, borne on on long stems, apricot and pink blends; fragrant.

'Dr. J. H. Nicholas': vigorous habit; foliage rich, dark, leathery; flowers large, double, pink; fragrant.

'Golden Showers': medium vigorous habit; foliage dark, glossy; flowers daffodil yellow; fragrant; 1957 All-American winner.

'High Noon': upright vigorous habit; foliage glossy, leathery; flowers lemon yellow; very fragrant; moderately hardy; 1948 All-American winner.

Blaze

Compassion

CLIMBER CULTIVARS OF MERIT THAT BLOOM ONCE A SEASON

'Albertine': flowers 15 to 20 petaled, apricot; very fragrant; no hip display.

'City of York': flowers 15 to 20 petaled, white; very fragrant; good hip display.

'Dr. Van Fleet': flowers large, many petaled, pleasant fragrance; nice hip display.

'Silver Moon': flowers large, 8 to 10 petaled, prominent yellow stamens, white; good hip display.

Albertine

CLIMBING SPORTS CULTIVARS OF MERIT

HYBRID TEAS

'Climbing Crimson Glory': very vigorous habit; flowers deep crimson; very fragrant; hardy to zone 7; good repeat bloomer.

'Climbing Peace': very vigorous habit; flowers yellow, pink, and orange blend; susceptible to freeze damage; occasional repeat bloomer.

FLORIBUNDAS

'Climbing Iceberg': flowers in many clusters, pure white; cold hardy.

'Climbing Sun Flare' or 'Climbing Yellow Blaze': not very vigorous habit; flowers yellow; fragrant; prone to black spot.

GRANDIFLORAS

'Climbing Queen Elizabeth': very vigorous; flowers pink; tends to get very woody; very hardy; occasional repeat bloomer.

'Climbing Sonia': flowers pink; questionable hardiness.

POLYANTHAS

'Climbing Cécile Brünner': very vigorous habit; flowers pink; sometimes a repeat bloomer.

'Climbing Summer Snow': not very vigorous; flowers white; not a repeat bloomer.

shrubby cultivars. In colder climates, they are a bit unreliable when it comes to blooming. Most of them need to retain as much wood as possible from the previous season's growth. Severe winters usually kill the wood that would have produced the next season's blooms. This makes many of them useless in gardens from zone 7 north.

When pruning, treat them as repeat-blooming climbers.

Climbing Miniature Roses

Climbing miniature roses are cultivars, not sports. They flower all season, and so should be pruned as repeat-blooming climbers. Hardy and trouble free, this group includes some notable performers.

In addition to the climbing roses discussed above, a number of old garden roses are suitable for use as climbers. For example, in mild climates, Noisettes, Bourbon roses, and some tea roses can be used as climbers.

CLIMBING MINIATURE ROSES OF MERIT

'Hi Ho': 8 to 10 feet tall; flowers hybrid tea type, magenta red.

'Jeanne Lajoie': very rampant habit; flowers hybrid tea type, pink.

'Pink Cascade': very rampant habit; flowers hybrid tea type, pink.

'Red Cascade': sprawling habit; flowers pompom type, bright red.

Climbing Iceberg

Climbing Sun Flare

Jeanne Lajoie

SHRUB ROSES

Although the term *shrub rose* is redundant (since, strictly speaking, all roses are shrubs), the American Rose Society recognizes shrub roses as a distinct group, albeit a heterogeneous one. All are upright and often quite vigorous shrubs.

In this mixed lot of cultivars are some notable subgroups. Buck's roses refer to a group bred by Dr. Griffith Buck to survive the zone 4 winters of Iowa, they remain underrated and underutilized. Other groups include English roses, bred by David Austin in England, Meidiland landscape roses, carefree shrubs from the house of Meilland in France; Canadian Explorer and Parkland series roses, bred in Canada for cold- hardiness; and Kordesii hybrids, developed by Wilhelm Kordes in Germany. Heights and habits vary from 2-foot mounds to erect stems 12 to 15 feet high.

How a shrub rose is to be pruned depends in part on its placement and use in the garden landscape. If grown as a hedge, a specimen shrub, or as a component of a mixed-shrub planting, the stems of a shrub rose should be thinned each spring while still dormant to make room for new growth. Overlong canes should be shortened at this time and again later in the season during a lull in blooming.

Golden Wings

SHRUB ROSE CULTIVARS OF MERIT *

'Abraham Darby' (Austin): tall growing; spreading habit, can be used as a climber; flowers large, apricot pink; fragrant; everblooming.

'Adelaide Hoodless' (Parkland series): medium; spreading habit; flowers in clusters, small, red; nonrepeating.

'Autumn Sunset': tall; spreading habit; flowers large, 8 to 10 petaled; orange and yellow blends; everblooming; sport of 'Westerland'.

'Bonica 82' or 'Meidominic' (Meilland): tall; upright habit; flowers pink; little fragrance; everblooming; beautiful hip display; 1987 All-American winner.

'Carefree Beauty' (Buck): tall; upright habit, spreading branches; flowers in clusters, large, pink; very little fragrance; everblooming; great hip display.

'Carefree Wonder' (Meilland): medium; upright habit; flowers in clusters, pink and white; little fragrance; everblooming; 1991 All-American winner.

'Folksinger' (Buck): tall; upright habit; flowers in clusters, apricot; fragrant.

'Goldbusch' (Kordesii): tall; can be used as a climber; foliage apple scented when crushed; flowers 8 to 15 petaled, golden yellow; occasionally repeating.

'Golden Wings': medium to tall; large, upright habit; flowers 5 petaled, yellow; fragrant; everblooming; hip display.

'Hawkeye Belle' (Buck): tall; upright habit; flowers blush pink; little fragrance; everblooming; long stems ideal for cutting; must be deadheaded.

'Honorable Lady Lindsay': tall; spreading habit, can be used as a climber; flowers large, blush pink; fragrant; nonrepeating.

'John Cabot' (Canadian Explorer series): very tall; can be used as a climber; flowers large, magenta; some repeating.

'Mabelle Stearns': tall; spreading habit; flowers large, pink; fragrant; everblooming.

'Martin Frobisher' (Canadian Explorer series): tall; flowers full, pale pink, sometimes with a button eye; fragrant; everblooming.

'Morden Blush' (Parkland series): short; flowers pink; long blooming period.

'The Prioress' (Austin): tall; upright habit; flowers large, pink; very fragrant; repeating.

'Scarlet Meidiland' (Meilland): medium; spreading habit; flowers in clusters, small, red; repeating in the fall.

'Westerland' (Kordesii): tall; spreading habit; flowers in clusters, large, orange-apricot; fragrant; some repeating in the fall.

*Name of series or breeder is listed in parentheses.

Abraham Darby

Bonica 82

Carefree Wonder

John Cabot

Hawkeye Belle

Carefree Beauty

HYBRID MUSK ROSE CULTIVARS OF MERIT

'Clytemnestra': medium; spreading habit; flowers star-burst, small, apricot; fragrant; everblooming.

'Cornelia': medium; spreading habit; flowers star-burst, small, pink; fragrant; everblooming.

'Felicia': tall; spreading habit; flowers medium size, pink apricot; fragrant; everblooming.

'Thisbe': tall; spreading habit, can be used as a climber; flowers pompom, small, yellow; sometimes repeating in the fall; good hip display.

Felicia

RUGOSA CULTIVARS AND HYBRIDS OF MERIT

'Agnes': coppery yellow; flowers double, pale amber gold, tall; buds very fragrant; no hips.

'Belle Poitevine': medium; flowers semidouble, lavender pink, crinkled; clove fragrance; large hips; intermittently blooming.

'Doctor Eckener': tall; flowers large, semidouble; beautiful coppery rose blended with yellow; very fragrant.

'Flamingo': 4 to 5 feet tall; hardy, vigorous habit; buds pointed; flowers in clusters, single, five petaled, flamingo pink, deeping through the season; long blooming period.

'Frau Dagmar Hartopp': low growing; rugged and hardy habit; flowers single, ruffled petals, silvery pink; long blooming period; thrives on poor, sandy soil; good under seashore conditions.

'Max Graf': medium; flowers in sprays, large, single, clear pink; nonrepeating; ideal for covering hillsides or embankments.

Belle Poitevine

Hybrid Musk Roses

During the early twentieth century, the Reverend Pemberton, an Englishman, created many cultivars of clustered flowered shrubs that were ideal as climbers or attractive shrubs. For some reason unclear to many, he named them hybrid musk roses. Nevertheless, these roses are the most popular of the large group of shrub roses. They should not be confused with *R. moschata*, the species musk rose, which is not a prototype. Pruning is the same as for shrub roses (see page 500).

Cornelia

Rugosa Hybrids

R. rugosa is a species rose familiar to many gardeners and is valued as much for its adaptability to difficult environments (littoral dunes, for example) and freedom from disease as it is for its inherent beauty, in and out of flower. During the late nineteenth and early twentieth centuries, rosarians developed a number of cultivars that have proven valuable under various garden conditions. Rugosa hybrids vary from spreading 2-foot mounds to erect, 8-foot-tall shrubs. Pruning is the same as for shrub roses (see page 500).

Frau Dagmar Hartopp

Agnes

Eglantine Hybrids

During the late nineteenth century, Lord Penzance of England introduced a wonderful group of shrub roses. All of his hybrids were bred from *R. rubiginosa* (formerly *R. eglanteria*), commonly known as the eglantine or sweetbrier rose. Pruning is the same as for shrub roses (see page 500).

(see page 500).

EGLANTINE HYBRIDS OF MERIT

'Anne of Geierstein': tall; flowers red with a white center.
'Brenda': Fragrant, tall; flowers single, light peach pink.
'Lady Penzance': tall; foliage sweetly scented; flowers bright, copper; one of the most desirable of the group.
'Lord Penzance': tall; foliage sweetly scented; flowers exquisite, single, delicate fawn tint, shading to ecru.
'Meg Merrilies': tall; very vigorous habit; flowers single, rosy crimson; fragrant.
'Rose Bradwardine': tall; foliage heavily scented; flowers clear rose pink.

OLD GARDEN ROSES

Old garden roses can be conveniently divided into two groups: repeat bloomers and nonrepeat bloomers.

Nonrepeat Bloomers

Nonrepeat bloomers have one period of bloom, usually in late spring or early summer. Old garden roses that are non-repeat bloomers include the following subgroups: species roses, gallicas, damasks, albas, centifolias, moss roses, hybrid Chinas, hybrid Bourbons, and hybrid Noisettes.

Minimal pruning is best for all old garden roses. However, stems should be thinned as crowding becomes apparent, which should be done after flowering is over, though it may be deferred to winter, when the absence of foliage reveals stem structure more clearly and facilitates identification of the oldest, most rigid stems for removal. Pruning should be especially light with hybrid Chinas, hybrid Bourbons, and hybrid Noisettes.

Species Roses

Although species roses are often described as those occurring wild under natural conditions, not all wild roses qualify as species roses in the horticultural sense. Some are not adaptable to garden conditions or lack qualities that recommend them to the garden environment. Those that are so considered usually have single, five-petaled flowers (though *R. sericea* ssp. *omeiensis* is four petaled). Taken as a lot, there is scarcely a locality from the subarctic to the tropics that cannot support the culture of one or more species roses.

Sericea ssp. *omiensis*

Gallica Roses

Except for the species roses, gallica roses have the longest history of cultivation. Likely native to continental Europe, they were quickly spread throughout the Old World and the the New World. Prized for their rich, dark floral colors and pronounced fragrance, gallica roses were originally grown specifically for medicinal uses (a legacy of which is a lingering common name, the apothecary's rose). Most gallica cultivars are best grown in regions having pronounced winter cold; they are hardy to zone 5.

NONREPEAT BLOOMING SPECIES ROSES OF MERIT

R. canina (dog rose): tall; flowers small, 5 petaled, pale pink; blooms early summer; large red hips in late summer and autumn; strong arching canes; hardy north to zone 3.

R. pendulina: 3 to 7 feet tall; variable habit; flowers 5 petaled, pink; blooms late spring; large, elongated hips; hardy north to zone 5.

R. rubiginosa (eglantine, sweetbrier): tall; foliage emits scent of green apples when crushed or heavy with dew; flowers 5 petaled, small, pink; blooms around same time as the hybrid teas; flowers nearly void of fragrance; hardy north to zone 4.

R. sericea ssp. *omeiensis*: medium; flowers 4 petaled, small, yellow; blooms very early (approximately one month before hybrid teas or in early May in New York Zone 7); small red hips; arching canes bear red, translucent prickles that can grow to 6 inches across at the base; hardy north to zone 6.

R. wichuraiana (memorial rose): prostrate habit, can be used as ground cover; foliage shiny, turns yellow in the fall; flowers 5 petaled, small, white; blooms early to mid summer (July in New York, zone 7); canes very long, close to the ground; hardy north to zone 5.

NONREPEAT BLOOMING GALLICA
CULTIVARS OF MERIT

'Anais Segales': low growing; flowers with dense petals, purple-pink.

'Apothecary's Rose': medium; spreading habit; flowers 8 to 10 petaled, red-pink; very fragrant; source of ancient medicinal cures.

'Nestor': low; spreading habit; flowers very full, quartered, dark cherry crimson.

'Perle des Panachées': low growing; flowers blush pink to white with stripes.

'Tuscany': compact habit; flowers 12 to 15 petaled, velvety texture, deep crimson.

NONREPEAT BLOOMING DAMASK
CULTIVARS OF MERIT

'Ispahan': spreading habit; buds high centered; flowers in loose clusters, bright pink.

'Leda': spreading habit; buds dark pink; flowers densely petaled; white; fragrant.

'Mme. Hardy': tall; flowers pure white, occasionally tinged with pink; one of the most beautiful and most fragrant of the damask roses.

'Marie Louise': medium; flowers double, rich, deep pink.

'Triginitipetala' (Kazanlik rose): tall; flowers 8 to 10 petaled, pink; very fragrant; used to make attar of roses.

NONREPEAT BLOOMING ALBA
CULTIVARS OF MERIT

'Chloris': tall; spreading habit; flowers small, ivory blush, darker pink near the center, buttoned eyes.

'Felicité Parmentier': low growing; flowers very full, light pink, darker near the center.

'Mme. Legras de St. Germain': spreading habit; flowers very double, large, creamy white; very fragrant.

'Maiden's Blush', 'The Blushing Thigh of an Emoted Nymph': tall; flowers many petaled, blush pink.

Felicité Parmentier

Tuscany

Damask Roses

Although damask roses are probably as venerable as gallicas, there remains considerable uncertainty about their origin. At least some prototypes are believed to have occurred naturally in the Middle East and along the Mediterranean coast of Europe. Much prized for their fragrance, damask roses grow best where there a well-defined cold period and exhibit hardiness as far north as zone 4.

Mme. Hardy

Marie Louise

Alba Roses

Some rosarians suspect that the first alba roses resulted from crossing gallicas, damasks, and the species *R. canina*. Whatever their origin, these beautiful roses are ideal for cold-climate gardeners. Not all albas are white. There are some wonderful variations of shades of pink, too. Most of the varieties in this class are either tall or spreading shrubs. The albas are hardy to zone 4.

Mme. Legras de St. Germain

Centifolia Roses

The centifolia, or cabbage, roses are multipetaled beauties of uncertain origin. It is very likely that these shrubs originated in northern Europe through natural hybridization. The large, globular blooms were made famous in the oil paintings of the early Dutch masters. The centifolia roses are excellent choices for cold-climate gardens and are hardy to zone 4.

Rose de Meaux

Petite de Holland

Moss Roses

Moss roses are of two types: sports of centifolia roses and sports of damask roses. The flower bud (the calyx and pedicel) is entirely covered with a dense, fragrant "mossy" growth. Sports of centifolias have a very soft moss, while the damask roses have a stiffer, or bristly, moss.

Gloire de Mousseux

Old Pink Moss

Hybrid China, Hybrid Bourbon, and Hybrid Noisette Roses

During the 1800s hybrid Chinas, hybrid Bourbons, and hybrid Noisettes were very popular. These roses are the result of hybridizing some of the nonrepeat bloomers discussed earlier (gallica, alba, damask, and centifolia) with the ever-blooming, tender China roses, Bourbon roses, and Noisette roses. The first generation that resulted from these crosses was made up of roses that were very vigorous in growth but not repeat bloomers. They were cataloged as either hybrid China, hybrid

---

NONREPEAT BLOOMING CENTIFOLIA CULTIVARS OF MERIT

'Burgundian Rose': low growing; foliage small; flowers tiny, dark pink purple; good as an edging plant.
'Petite de Hollande': low growing; spreading habit; flowers very double, tightly wrapped petals, pink.
'Robert le Diable': low growing; flowers very double, quartered blooms, mauve red.
'Rose de Meaux': 4 feet tall; spreading habit; foliage small; flowers tiny, pink.

NONREPEAT BLOOMING MOSS ROSE CULTIVARS OF MERIT

'Blanche Moreau': medium; vigorous habit; buds heavily mossed; flowers in clusters, double white tinged with pink; fine flowering.
'Crested Moss': medium; flowers large, full, bright rose pink; an offshoot of the Provence rose, first discovered in 1827 growing in the crevice of a wall in Fribourg, Switzerland.
'Gloire De Mousseux': tall; flowers carmine salmon pink, produced in great abundance; one of the finest of this group.
'Old Pink Moss': medium; buds heavily mossed; flowers pale rose pink; one of the oldest of this group.

Crested Moss

Bourbon, or hybrid Noisette, according to the source class. Since the progeny varied in such floral traits as size, form, and color from the cold-hardy parents, the genetic influence of the tender parents is clear.

These roses remained very popular until the advent of hybrid perpetual roses, especially for training on pillars and arches. They are now enjoying a resurgence, although they are sometimes wrongly offered as simply as cultivars of the nonrepeat blooming groups (gallicas, centifolias, etc.), without acknowledgment of their complex hybrid origin.

There is only one cultivar of merit of nonrepeat blooming hybrid Noisette roses available in the United States. 'Mme. Plantier' is of medium height and spreading habit. Its flowers are held in clusters and are ivory white.

NONREPEAT BLOOMING HYBRID CHINA
ROSES OF MERIT

'Brennus': tall; arching habit; flowers in clusters, very double, purple rose.
'La Ville de Bruxelles': tall; arching habit; flowers large, quartered centers, pink.
'Madame Zöetmans': compact habit; flowers very double, small petals, pink.
'Malton': tall; arching habit; flowers large, full, buttoned eye, rose red; can be used as a climber.

NONREPEAT BLOOMING HYBRID BOURBON
ROSES OF MERIT

'Charles Lawson': tall; spreading habit; flowers very double, lavender pink.
'Paul Ricaut': tall; spreading habit; flowers very double, large, maroon red; good hip display; can be used as a climber.
'Variegata di Bologna': spreading habit; flowers large, globular, pink with red stripes; can be used as a climber.
'Variegata di Bologna Rouge': tall; flowers magenta; sport of 'Variegata di Bologna'.

REPEAT BLOOMING CHINA CULTIVARS OF MERIT

'Comtesse Du Cayla': medium; buds coppery orange, flowers semisingle, reddish orange and yellow.
'Mme. Laurette Messimy': medium; flowers rose pink, tinted with yellow.
'Old Blush': medium; flowers bright pink, darkening with age; the original China rose, introduced in 1796.

Variegata di Bologna | Madame Zöetmans

La Ville de Bruxelles

Repeat Bloomers

Repeat bloomers of the old garden roses group should be pruned in early spring, while still dormant. The shorter branches and laterals should be cut back to a spot where the remaining cane has the thickness of that of an ordinary (#2) pencil. Some of the classes in this group do not form distinct laterals (for example, China, tea, and Noisette). For these roses, simply remove all twiggy, crowded growth.

As the plants age, you will need to remove about one-third of the established growth. This is also best done in early spring, before growth begins. If possible, spread the longer canes horizontally or wrap them around a pillar (if they are long enough). After the first flush of bloom has faded, shorten all the laterals and remove any twiggy growth and crossing branches to prevent later clutter.

China Roses

First introduced into Europe from southwestern China in the late eighteenth century, China roses brought a trait hitherto unknown among roses: continuous bloom throughout the growing season. Almost immediately, hybridizing was undertaken with the hardier, often showier, but only briefly flowering roses then grown, in an attempt to combine these traits with the China rose's extended season of bloom. These experiments eventually led to some of the cultivars listed below. On their own, China roses are unreliably hardy at temperatures below 20°F.

Old Blush

Mme. Laurette Messimy

Noisette Roses

The first Noisette rose was developed in Charleston, South Carolina. In 1811, John Champneys crossed a musk rose with a China rose ('Old Blush'). These new, clustered-flowering, everblooming roses were further expanded by the Noisette family in France, hence the name.

Some Noisette roses are more cold hardy than others; but in general, they do best in warmer climates, i.e., from zone 8 south.

Tea Roses

Tea roses were discovered in the Orient around the same time as the China roses were. Some of the originals of these ever-blooming roses were shipped out of China in tea crates, hence the name tea roses. The cultivars listed below are but a small representation of the great number of tea roses available. Most were created in a frenzy of breeding by French and English rosarians.

Bourbon Roses

Bourbon roses evolved from a rose discovered in the Ile de Bourbon (now Réunion Island) in the Indian Ocean. The newly discovered, everblooming rose with large, clustered flowers is thought to have been a natural cross between a damask rose and a China rose. This parentage has never been proven, but the Bourbons owe part of their heritage to seeds from a rose found on the Ile de Bourbon.

Portland Roses

The origins of the Portland roses are difficult to trace. Many of these are often sold as "damask perpetuals," a name given to them because they appear to be repeat-blooming damask roses. It is very likely that they are the result of multiple crossings between damask roses and China roses. Whatever their origin, Portland roses are beautiful, cold hardy to zone 5, and very fragrant.

Marchesa Boccella

Comte de Chambord

REPEAT BLOOMING NOISETTE CULTIVARS OF MERIT

'Alister Stella Gray': tall; spreading habit; flowers very double, pale yellow, fading to white; can be used as a climber.
'Fellenberg': tall; very vigorous habit; flowers in clusters, cherry red; excellent climber.
'Maréchal Niel': tall; flowers double deep golden yellow; fragrant; not hardy in the North; one of the most beautiful of all roses.
'Rêve d'Or': tall; very vigorous habit; flowers double, soft buff yellow; fragrant.

REPEAT BLOOMING TEA ROSE CULTIVARS OF MERIT

'Lady Hillingdon': medium; buds beautifully pointed; flowers clear saffron yellow.
'Mlle. Franziska Kruger': medium; compact habit; flowers very double, coppery yellow and pink.
'Maman Cochet': medium; flowers large, carmine pink; fragrant.

REPEAT BLOOMING BOURBON CULTIVARS OF MERIT

'Adam Messerich': arching, spreading habit; flowers clear rose pink; fragrant; long stems.
'Louise Odier': tall; flowers very double; pink; very fragrant; will repeat if planted in full sun.
'Souvenir de la Malmaison': about 3 feet tall; flowers pinkish écru; very fragrant.
'Souvenir de St. Anne's': medium; flowers 8 to 10 petaled, pink; beautiful in clay pots; sport of 'Souvenir de la Malmaison.'

Souvenir de St. Anne's

Louise Odier

Souvenir de la Malmaison

Rose de Rescht

REPEAT BLOOMING PORTLAND CULTIVARS OF MERIT

'Comte de Chambord': low; compact habit; flowers with tightly wrapped petals that reflex as they unfurl; large, pink.
'Duchess of Portland': compact habit; flowers semidouble, bright red; not a reliable repeat bloomer at the Brooklyn Botanic Garden (zone 7).
'Marchesa Boccella': spreading habit; flowers pompon type with tightly packed petals, buttoned eyes, pink; excellent repeat bloomer.
'Rose de Rescht': tall; spreading habit; flowers multipetaled, large, crimson maroon; very fragrant; excellent repeat bloomer.

REPEAT BLOOMING HYBRID PERPETUAL ROSE CULTIVARS OF MERIT

'Arrillaga': medium; buds large, glowing, pink; flowers immense, vivid pink with a golden glow at the base of the petals; fragrant and long-lasting.

'Baronne Prevost': tall; spreading habit; flowers flat with tightly wrapped petals, magenta pink; good repeat bloomer.

'Frau Karl Druschki': tall; flowers beautiful form, large, pure white; long, strong stems are unexcelled for cutting; no fragrance; considered the best white rose in cultivation, often called "the white American Beauty."

'Paul Neyron': tall; flowers very large, deep pink.

'Ulrich Brunner': tall; vigorous habit; flowers brilliant scarlet crimson; very hardy.

REPEAT BLOOMING MOSS CULTIVARS OF MERIT

'James Vetch': low; spreading habit; flowers large, compact, maroon red; very fragrant.

'Mousseline', 'Alfred de Dalmas': tall; spreading habit; flowers large, flat, white tinged with pink.

'Salet': tall; spreading habit; flowers very double, buttoned eye, pink.

'Soupert et Notting': medium; vigorous habit; flowers globular, quartered, pink.

Soupert et Notting

Hybrid Perpetual Roses

The hybrid perpetual roses were the last group of old garden roses developed. After the creation of the hybrid Chinas, hybrid Bourbons, and hybrid Noisettes, rosarians continued further breeding and mixing the genes of all their roses. What resulted, almost accidentally, were the hybrid perpetuals, roses that rebloom and are mostly cold hardy to zone 6, or possibly to zone 5, and produce large if not gaudy blooms.

Although the flowers are large, the stems are short. Hence the desire to create an everblooming rose with a long, elegant stem. This was achieved when a French rosarian crossed a hybrid perpetual rose with a tea rose. His new, everblooming, elegant-looking rose is called 'La France'. From this, the hybrid tea roses came into being.

Frau Karl Druschki

Baronne Prevost

Arrillaga

Moss Roses

Although there are few cultivars of repeat blooming moss roses, all are worth growing. Very likely the combination of China roses with moss roses resulted in this small group of unusual, everblooming old garden roses. These moss roses are hardy to zone 8.

James Vetch

Mousseline

III
Special Habitats

20

Prairie and Meadow

PRAIRIE

From Indiana to the Rockies, from Saskatchewan to Texas, there once existed the great American prairies. These grasslands differed from one region to another according to climatic and soil variations, but the presence of grass and the absence of trees throughout these vast areas distinguished them from adjacent forested regions. In addition to these naturally occurring grasslands of America's Midwest, there

*An autumnal floral blanket of black-eyed Susan (*Rudbeckia hirta*), yarrow (*Achillea millefolium*), New England aster (*Aster novae-angliae*), fall aster (*A. puniceus*), and common goldenrod (*Solidago canadensis*), all in flower, with the shrubby smooth sumac (*Rhus glabra*) in fruit and fall foliage.*

are myriad similar sites, some of natural origin and some the result of human activity, which cannot technically be called prairies. Such areas are called meadows and exhibit the same characteristic absence of trees and presence of grass and other herbaceous vegetation. From a landscape standpoint, and ecologically as well, prairies and natural meadows are intrinsically valuable because they are prime habitats for many sun-loving wildflowers. Both vegetational types also offer landscape opportunities for the creation of vistas, "open space," woodland borders, and dramatic foregrounds and backdrops for architectural structures.

Early explorers and settlers frequently described the American prairie as an awesome vastness, which reminded them of almost endless oceans. "A swell and swale reminiscent of the seas" and "an ocean of grass" were common analogies. Indeed, the wagons of the pioneers were even called "prairie schooners," intimating that they plied the prairies as though sailing the oceans. The tall grasses of these prairies waved in rhythm with the wind, whose unbroken currents were not buffered by trees as they are in the forested regions.

Prairies are separated into several rather distinct geographic types across the continent, according to the availability of moisture. The continental distribution of rainfall determines the existence of short-grass prairie in the rain shadow of the Rocky Mountains, mid-grass prairie in the Great Plains, and tall-grass prairie in the eastern reaches of the Midwest. Where rainfall exceeds 30 inches annually, deciduous forest becomes the dominant vegetational type. Throughout this vast prairie region prairie eco-types are also determined by local soil moisture regimes, and these can be characterized as wet (lowland), mesic (upland), and dry (steep hillside and hilltop). Each of these vegetational types has its characteristic flora and its unique beauty. In addition to these distinct prairie types, there are various associations with other vegetational types, such as oak openings (prairie interspersed with oaks), pine barrens (pine and prairie), and savanna (prairie interspersed with occasional solitary trees).

The vast, seemingly endless prairie of yesteryear, with its bison herds and mounted American Indians, has all but disappeared; it exists today only in the form of occasional relicts, preserved by chance from the ubiquitous "cow and plow" of the pioneer and now assiduously conserved. Areas unsuitable for farming, such as steep hillsides or undrainable wetlands, have here and there remained inviolate; likewise

A wildflower meadow reduces lawn area and adds welcome color and natural informality to offset the unnatural expanses of roof and concrete.

old settlers' cemeteries and some railroad and highway rights-of-way also still harbor the indigenous prairie grasses and wildflowers.

Although the prairie as a continental ecosystem has largely been replaced by corn, wheat, and European pasture grasses, the concepts of prairie as a landscape architectural form and of prairie grass species as range forage have made astonishing progress in recent years. The use of the major prairie grass species in restoring midwestern and western range lands emerged from the catastrophic era of the Dust Bowl in the 1930s, which was precipitated by appalling ignorance and by the wanton misuse of land through improvident farming practices and overgrazing of the Great Plains. The U.S. Soil Conservation Service and various midwestern universities carried out pioneering research on the little-known native grasses, many of which are now available commercially and are in wide use. This commercially available stock of native grasses and wildflowers has also found much use along roadsides, on reclaimed strip mines, around industrial and commercial sites, and in suburban home landscapes.

Prairie preservation has become an important aspect of land management for national, state, and local agencies. The reestablishment of prairies—on suitable sites and with appropriate kinds and numbers of grasses, wildflowers, and legumes—is now a major conservation focus throughout the original prairie region. Nearly every major midwestern land-grant university has undertaken prairie restoration projects, and prairie has been accepted as a popular design feature in landscape architecture. But re-creating a prairie is a complicated undertaking at best, and a reconstruction can never be more than an approximation of the original entity. The approximation will vary in complexity according to the expertise and goals of those planning such reconstruction. The universities of Wisconsin and Iowa, among others; the Morton Arboretum in Lisle, Illinois; and the Boerner Botanical Garden in Milwaukee, Wisconsin, have done notable work in intricate prairie restorations.

Even as the original prairies of the old West conjured up a sense of vastness, of oceans of grasses, so too the larger restorations can re-create this same mood. On the other hand, the smaller restorations and relicts owe their popularity to another aspect of the prairie—its surprisingly complex diversity. The prairie is a climax community, a stable self-perpetuating community of plants of ancient lineage, developed to its fullest extent, with every possible ecological niche occupied by one or more kinds of plants and animals duly adapted to it through millennia of evolution. Many of the plants are now traditional garden perennials, which were originally collected from the prairie. Among these are the purple coneflower (*Echinacea purpurea*), sunflower (*Helianthus*

spp.), goldenrod (*Solidago* spp.), coneflower (*Rudbeckia* spp.), lead plant (*Amorpha canescens*), and wild indigo (*Baptisia* spp.). The gardener who knows these prairie wildflowers as familiar perennial border plants will readily perceive that these old friends are transcendent species between prairie and what are now termed meadow, field, or roadside flowers in the once wholly forest-covered eastern United States.

MEADOW

A meadow is a specialized habitat that depends on full sun and the absence of woody vegetation and contains many of the same species as does a prairie. It does not represent, however, a climax community, and in the absence of human intervention, it would soon proceed through natural plant succession to woodland. Not being a re-creation or relict of

*A cheery expanse of oxeye sunflower (*Heliopsis helianthoides*) and wild bergamot (*Monarda fistulosa*) blankets an abandoned farm field.*

a specific natural community, as the prairie is, the meadow's components may contain herbaceous plants from any ecosystem that will adapt to it, as well as horticultural plants, various alien weeds, and tree seedlings. These components can be utilized architecturally in much the same way as prairie: as open space, providing and maintaining vistas; as a foil for woodland background; or to blend with formal lawns. An important ecological aspect of both meadow and prairie is their role as habitat for ground-nesting birds and small mammals, which in turn fosters the return of hawks, owls, foxes, and other predator species. This increase in diversity of animal and bird populations is aesthetically as important as the visual aspect of such landscapes.

Meadow and prairie also share similarities in the maintenance methods necessary to perpetuate them. To maintain a meadow, woody vegetation such as trees and shrubs must be repelled. Mowing the area once a year will accomplish this task without damage to the herbaceous species. In fact, meadows mowed once a year will actually increase in the diversity of sun-loving herbaceous perennials, given a nearby natural seed source, or their introduction, and selection of a time for mowing after seeds have matured. Herbicides have also been used to reduce woody plant competition, but this is usually self-defeating from an aesthetic viewpoint, since most herbicides are either nonselective or may eradicate wildflowers while favoring grasses.

Maintenance of Existing Prairies and Meadows

The management of relict prairies and existing meadows is relatively straightforward, once the basic principles are understood. Establishing a new prairie or meadow is a more complex venture. A lawn mowed several times a year is still a lawn; a lawn unmowed will undergo secondary succession, leading eventually to woodland in the forested regions of America. Lawn mowed once in the fall, or burned periodically where possible, will become meadow. Mowing or burning, thereby repelling woody vegetation, encourages the establishment of sun-loving wildflowers such as sunflowers, goldenrods, asters, milkweeds, and so on. Meadow grasses will have an entirely different aspect from mowed lawn. Even bluegrass will attain heights of 1 foot or more, and seasonal color changes and wind motion will be evident. Meadow can be enriched by adding suitable horticultural species or by collecting and introducing wildlings, either by transplanting or direct seeding.

Prairie restoration is a more intellectual endeavor, for it requires site analysis and careful species selection. It must always be understood that the objective is to re-create an ecosystem, insofar as possible, and that the beauty depends not only on architectural expression and horticultural selection but also on the diversity of the components and the functioning of the biotic community. An existing relict can be carefully enriched by adding members to the community, either by direct seeding or with transplants. Areas with no prairie species can be seeded directly after preparation of the seedbed in much the same way as for standard lawn grasses. Seed can be obtained from commercial seed houses or from universities, botanical gardens, and nature centers, especially in the Midwest. Perhaps the most rewarding method of prairie restoration is to search out local prairie remnants and obtain permission to collect seed. Seed mixtures sown and raked lightly into almost any reasonably fertile topsoil will produce seedlings during the first growing season, providing they have either been subjected to winter cold by seeding in the fall or artificially cold-treated and sown in the spring. During the first year or two prairie plants are minuscule and characteristically produce more root than top growth. This is a critical period, and the new prairie should be either hand weeded (which takes considerable expertise at identifying seedlings) or mowed at a height of 6 inches with a rotary mower, which will discourage the weeds but not harm the tiny prairie seedlings. The novice will not see the mature "prairie" until the third or fourth year, when the plants will indicate their presence by their beautiful blooms. Seed of prairie plants can also be successfully sown in flats and then stratified. The seedlings are grown in a greenhouse or coldframe until transplantable. This method produces excellent results, but it does presuppose proper equipment and ample hand labor.

The above account of prairie establishment procedures is necessarily abbreviated, but there is ample literature on techniques for particular prairie ecotypes and locations, and the serious amateur will want to consult them before undertaking any such project.

More than 60 years ago, as scientists and naturalists across the nation decried the devastation of the Dust Bowl and mourned the passing of the prairie ecosystem, it was impossible to foresee the rebirth of interest in this indispensable aspect of the American biota that has taken place today. This phenomenon, coupled with the understanding of meadows and their usefulness, has opened up new vistas, in a literal sense, on the North American landscape.

Prairie, although a natural climax vegetational community, is in a constant state of flux with the forest border, particularly in its eastern reaches or elsewhere where rainfall over extended periods is sufficient to encourage forestation. During historical drought cycles the prairie has encroached on forest, and during periods of plentiful moisture the forest has advanced into the prairie. Prairie wildfires have been significant as a factor selecting against woody vegetation and perpetuating prairie. Fires were often deliberately set by the Plains Indians as a means of hunting game and perhaps for other reasons as well. In addition, lightning or accidents frequently ignited such fires. With the advance of settlement, however, fire was suppressed, and many prairies then developed into brush and ultimately forest. In light of these historical facts, fire has become a common and even necessary modern prairie management tool.

In addition to woody vegetation, the prairie has another nemesis: Kentucky bluegrass. Bluegrass forms a dense sod in response to continual mowing or heavy grazing and is highly competitive with the bunchgrasses native to prairie. Bluegrass sod precludes the establishment of wildflowers, and once it invades an area, it is extremely persistent. Bluegrass is a cool-season grass, growing vigorously in early spring while native prairie vegetation is still dormant. Burning a prairie at this juncture not only destroys woody vegetation but seriously weakens the bluegrass sod. If burning is not feasible, prairies, like meadows, must be mowed once a year; but fire is the best tool for managing the prairie and is equally beneficial to the meadow.

ESTABLISHING A NEW MEADOW

Meadow gardening has gradually found wide acceptance, especially in parts of the country where brush does not quickly invade fields. It has fewer devotees in suburbia, however, where trim gardens and tidy lawns reign, but elsewhere the natural appearance that meadows create and the reduced maintenance involved have much appeal. The maintenance that is required is mainly an annual fall mowing—to cull tree and shrub seedlings and help with reseeding—and hand pulling of aggressive weeds or spot treatment of them with rapidly degrading herbicides. Many perennial wildflowers cope successfully with the competition of other kinds, but seedlings do best if competition is limited in the first year or two.

Success in meadow establishment depends in large measure on location and on the time and effort you can give it, especially in the seminal years. In general, meadow gardening is not difficult on the relatively dry, windy American prairie, where most trees are not easily established without care in their initial years. In the eastern states and the Pacific Northwest, however, higher, more evenly distributed rainfall favors woody species. There the meadow gardener must work harder. Wherever practiced, meadow gardening appeals especially to those who are sensitive about the conservation of petroleum-based products used in other aspects of horticulture, such as lawn mowing, field and garden

fertilization, and disease and pest control. It is also important in the conservation of water, especially in drier areas where lawns are inappropriate.

Before launching a project, it is best to first see an area already given over to prairie "reconstitution" for some years. Allowing for the idiosyncratic character, possibilities, and problems of any site, there are nevertheless various generalizations to be drawn and that will have regional validity. The astute observer can learn from the experience of others.

Surely one of the generally agreed-on points is to start small. Many worthwhile meadow-gardening projects are abandoned in the first year because the energy of the gardener in August heat does not live up to the aspirations of the preceding April. It is best to start with a limited area and simply not mow it until the the following autumn. Often pleasant surprises will come to light, such as summer-blooming yarrow or, later on, perennial asters. During this period, it is well to watch for invasive perennial weeds, such as bindweed (*Calystegia sepium*) or dock (*Rumex* spp.), or the biennial thistles (*Cirsium* spp.), all of which should be repeatedly cropped to the ground. A light but firm yank will usually dislodge first-year tree seedlings, especially after a rain.

Stable plant communities are aspects of the natural ecosystem and are not human artifacts. Where land is disturbed, as when a patch of ground has been dug, a surprising range of plants will appear—some unknown, many unwanted—unless your land is in an arid part of the country or is a gravelly slope or sand dune. The intent in establishing a meadow is to guide the development of a desirable, reasonably stable plant community, one with aesthetic appeal and that, over the long run, will require little maintenance. It can be an uphill battle in some areas, however; a struggle in which the bulldozer is no help and one that requires even some old gardening shibboleths be cast aside.

It is a cardinal principle, for example, to disturb the soil no more than absolutely necessary. This does not mean that scattering seeds from a packet or can of a wildflower mixture will magically bring a riot of floral color, as some advertising ploys assure. Some soil preparation and plant tending are unavoidable if plants are to be grown from seed sown on site. Even if young plants grown elsewhere are set out on the site in the spring, care, especially watering, will be needed the first year. A 2- to 3-inch mulch of pine needles, shredded leaves, or fine wood chips will conserve moisture and discourage weeds. If in doubt about the character of the soil, have it tested, especially for pH. For most meadow species, a pH of 6.0 to 6.5 is best, although many are relatively uncritical of this factor. If the surface puddles after heavy rains or during the winter, care must be taken to choose species adapted to those conditions.

The area around the intended meadow should also be analyzed, for this is where future trouble may originate, especially in those parts of the country where woods and forests are the climax vegetation. If oaks, maples, and ash are present, their seedlings may be expected, the seeds borne by wind, birds, or small mammals. Ailanthus (*Ailanthus altissima*), black cherry (*Prunus serotina*), and black locust (*Robinia pseudoacacia*) are especially troublesome and should be removed if at all feasible. Norway maple (*Acer platanoides*), introduced from Europe and naturalized in much of the Northeast, is a particularly aggressive invader of disturbed sites. Its saplings, left unattended, quickly choke out all other vegetation, forming a dense, dark thicket. Aggressors among shrubs include arrowwood viburnum (*Viburnum dentatum*) and meadowsweet (*Spiraea latifolia*) in the East, and ocean spray (*Holodiscus discolor*) and Scotch broom (*Cytisus scoparius*) in the Northwest. Rather than resorting to chemical brush killers, many of which act unevenly or are quite ineffective, large invading shrubs can be cut to the ground and their flush stumps covered with a 1- or 2-foot square of black plastic, lightly covered with soil or litter for concealment, to prevent basal sprouting.

A heavy growth of evergreens surrounding an intended meadow can be advantageous, as their dense, continuous shade discourages undergrowth and thus acts as a barrier to potential invaders. Although the conifers themselves may shed seed into the meadow, the yearly mowing will easily control their seedlings.

Another way to stabilize peripheral areas is to encourage natural ground covers, such as hay-scented fern (*Dennstaedtia punctilobula*) on partially shaded ground or certain goldenrods (*Solidago* spp.) in sunny places. Their dense root systems keep out many invaders, although they themselves can sometimes prove troublesome in the meadow.

The range of plant species appropriate for meadow culture is extensive and varies widely from place to place. While such familiar subjects as Queen Anne's lace (*Daucus carota*) and chicory (*Cichorium intybus*) are easily established and make a fine combination almost anywhere, most species have narrower ecological amplitude and must be chosen for their suitability to the site. Local native plant and wildflower societies are sources of much valuable information on species useful in meadows.

Throughout much of the country, a number of species have proven successful in meadow culture under varying conditions, and may be considered primary candidates. None will succeed everywhere; in some locations, certain species may tend to dominate or even overwhelm. Hence the need for care in selecting the mix for your site.

EASILY GROWN, VIGOROUSLY SELF-SEEDING SPECIES FOR MEADOWS

Name	Zones*	Height †	Flower Color and Bloom Time	pH	Comments
ANNUALS					
Centaurea cyanus (cornflower)	7–9	1½–3'	Blue; spring to early summer	6–7	Cultivars with pink, lavender, or white flowers
Clarkia spp. (farewell-to-spring, godetia)	7–9	1–4 (6)'	Red to white; spring to early summer	6–7	Flowers best in cool weather
Cleome hassleriana (spider flower)	7–9	3–5'	Pink, aging to white; summer	6–7	Long slender pods; cultivars with purple, rose, or white flowers
Consolida spp. (larkspur)	(6) 7–9	1½–3'	Purple, pink, or white; spring to early summer	6–7	May winter over as seedlings
Coreopsis tinctoria (calliopsis)	6–9	2½–3'	Yellow and red-brown; spring to summer	6–7	May winter over as seedlings
Cosmos bipinnatus (tall cosmos)	7–9	3–6'	Red, pink, or white; summer to fall	6–7	Flowers very showy
Helianthus annuus (sunflower)	(6) 7–9	4–8'	Yellow; summer to fall	6–7	Very drought tolerant; thrives in heat
Malva sylvestris (annual mallow)	7–9	2–6'	Lavender to purple; summer to fall	6–7	Highly variable; sometimes biennial
Nicotiana spp. (flowering tobacco)	6–9	2–6'	White; summer	6–7	Cultivars with red to pink flowers
Nigella damascena (love-in-a-mist)	7–9	1–1½'	Purple to white; spring to summer	6–7	Attractive seed pods
Papaver rhoeas (Shirley poppy)	7–9	1½–2½'	Red to white; spring to summer	6–7	Flowers best in cool weather
Phlox drummondii (annual phlox)	7–9	1–2'	Purple, red, pink, or white; spring to early summer	6–7	May winter over as seedlings in South

Name	Zones*	Height †	Flower Color and Bloom Time	pH	Comments
Verbena bonariensis (purpletop, tall verbena)	8–9	2½–5'	Purple; summer	6–7	Often perennial in zones 8 and 9
Viola cornuta (horned viola)	7–9	6–12"	Yellow; spring to early summer	6–7	May winter over as seedlings
Viola tricolor (Johnny-jump-up)	6–9	6–12"	Purple, yellow, and white; spring, often again in fall	6–7	Flowers best in cool weather

BIENNIALS

Name	Zones*	Height †	Flower Color and Bloom Time	pH	Comments
Alcea rosea (single-flowered hollyhock)	(6) 7–9	4–8 (12)'	Red to white; summer	6–7 (7.5)	Single-flowered forms shed abundant seed
Daucus carota (Queen Anne's lace)	4–8	5'	White; summer	6–7 (7.5)	Ubiquitous colonizer of disturbed soil
Digitalis purpurea (common foxglove)	7–9	4–6'	Purplish pink; spring	6–7 (7.5)	Cool, damp summers promote seed germination
Hesperis matronalis (dame's rocket)	6–9	3–5'	Lavender or white; spring to early summer	6–7 (7.5)	Often short-lived perennial
Oenothera spp. (evening primrose sundrops)	6–9	6–72"	Yellow, often aging to reddish; spring to summer	6–7 (7.5)	Much variation among several species
Verbascum spp., except *V. thapsus* (mullein)	5	3–8'	Mostly yellow; summer	6–7 (7.5)	Usually spirelike habit

PERENNIALS

Name	Zones*	Height †	Flower Color and Bloom Time	pH	Comments
Anthemis tinctoria (golden marguerite)	4–9	2½' (2½')	Yellow; summer	6–7	Tolerates heat and drought; short lived on clay
Aster spp. (wild perennial aster)	4–7	4' (1')	Purple to white; early fall	4–7	Thrives on moist, sandy soil
Baptisia tinctoria spp. (wild indigo)	7–9	3' (2')	Yellow; summer	6–7	Thrives on dry, sandy soil
Chrysanthemum leucanthemum (oxeye daisy)	3–8	3' (1')	White; summer	5–7	Succeeds in most any soil
Dicentra eximia (fringed bleeding heart)	5–8	8" (6")	Pinkish; spring to summer	5–6	Does best in partial shade of taller plants
Echinacea purpurea (purple coneflower)	3–8	4' (2')	Purple; summer	5–7	Tolerates heat; best on sandy soil
Echinops ritro (globe thistle)	4–9	4' (2')	Steel blue; summer	6–7	Thrives in summer heat, drought
Eupatorium dubium (joe-pye weed)	4–8	8' (3')	Pink; summer	5–6	Does best in damp climates
Lychnis coronaria (rose campion)	5–9	3' (2')	Reddish magenta or white; summer	5–7	Flowers occasionally white; foliage gray
Malva alcea (hollyhock mallow)	5–8	3' (3')	Lavender pink; summer	5–7	Short lived, freely reseeding
Phlox paniculata (summer phlox)	4–8	4' (1½')	Pinkish lavender or white; summer	5–7	Thrives on moist, sandy or clay soil

* For annuals and biennials, the zones refer to seed hardiness.
† For perennials, spread is given in parenthesis.

Striped mallow (*Malva sylvestris* 'Zebrina')

Johnny-jump-up (*Viola tricolor*)

Summer phlox
(*Phlox paniculata*)

New England aster
(*Aster novae-angliae*)

Purple coneflower
(*Echinacea purpurea*)

Calliopsis
(*Coreopsis tinctoria*)

Rose campion
(*Lychnis coronaria*)

Oxeye daisy
(*Chrysanthemum leucanthemum*)

Dame's rocket (*Hesperis matronalis*)

Ozark sundrops (*Oenothera macrocarpa*)

OTHER PERENNIAL SPECIES

Name	Zones	Height (by spread)	Flower Color and Bloom Time	pH	Comments
Achillea millefolium (common yarrow)	2–9	2½ × 2'	White; summer	5–7.5	Thrives on dry, sandy soil
Acorus calamus (sweet flag)	6–9	2½ × 1'	Green; late spring	4–5	Requires wet soil
Actinomeris alternifolia syn. *Verbesina alternifolia* (wingstem)	5–8	6 × 3'	Yellow; late summer	5–6	
Agrimonia parviflora (agrimony)	5–8	2 × 1'	Yellow; late summer	5–6	Best on sandy soil in partial shade
Aletris farinosa (unicorn root)	7–9	2 × 1'	White; early summer	4–5	Requires wet soil
Allium canadense (wild garlic)	4–8	1¼ × ½'	White; late spring	5–6	Thrives on humusy soil
A. cernuum (nodding wild onion)	4–8	2 × ½'	Pale pink; summer	5–7	Tolerates some shade
Amianthium muscitoxicum (fly poison)	4–8	3 × 1'	White; late spring	4–5	Best on sandy soil
Amorpha canescens (lead plant)	4–8	3 × 1'	Purple; early summer	5–7.5	Tolerates drought
Amsonia tabernaemontana (bluestar)	8–10	2½ × 1½'	Blue; late spring	5–6	Thrives on humusy soil
Anaphalis margaritacea (pearly everlasting)	3–8	1½ × 1'	White; late summer	4–5	Thrives on sandy or gravelly soil
Anemone canadensis (windflower)	3–7	2 × 1'	White; spring to summer	5–6	Tolerates partial shade
A. cylindrica (thimbleweed)	5–8	1½ × 1'	White; early summer	5–6	Best in full sun
A. patens syn. *Pulsatilla patens* (pasqueflower)	4–7	8 × 4"	Blue; spring	4–5	Thrives on gravelly soil
A. quinquefolia (wood anemone)	7–9	3 × 12+"	White; spring	4–5	Thrives on sandy soil in partial shade
A. virginiana (thimbleweed)	4–8	2½ × 1'	White; early summer	5–6	Thrives on humusy soil in partial shade
Angelica triquinata (filmy angelica)	3–7	3 × 2'	White; late summer	5–6	Thrives on humusy soil
Antennaria neglecta (pussy toes)	4–8	1 × 3+'	White; late spring	4–5	Tolerates prolonged drought
Apocynum androsaemifolium (dogbane)	4–8	4 × 2'	Pink; late summer	4–5	Adapts to partial shade
A. cannabinum (Indian hemp)	4–8	3 × 1'	White; summer	4–5	Best on sandy soil
Aquilegia canadensis (rock columbine)	4–8	1¼ × 1'	Red and yellow; late spring	5–6	Best on sandy or gravelly soil
Arabis laevigata (rock cress)	5–8	6 × 6"	White; spring	5–6	Best on sandy or gravelly soil
Aralia nudicaulis (wild sarsaparilla)	4–8	2½ × 1½'	Green; early summer	5–6	Best on sandy or gravelly soil in sun or partial shade
Arethusa bulbosa (swamp pink)	3–7	8 × 4"	Pink; late spring	4–5	Requires wet soil
Arisaema dracontium (green dragon)	4–8	1½ × 1'	Green; late spring	5–6	Best on humusy soil in partial shade
Artemisia caudata (beach wormwood)	4–8	3 × 1'	Greenish bronze; fall	5–7	Gray foliage; best on sandy or gravelly soil
A. stelleriana (gray wormwood)	3–7	1½ × 3+'	Yellowish; late summer	4–6	Gray foliage; best on sandy or gravelly soil
Aruncus dioicus (goatsbeard)	4–7	5 × 3+'	White; early summer	5–6	Best on humusy soil in partial shade
Asclepias amplexicaulis (sand milkweed)	4–8	2½ × 1'	Pinkish green; early summer	5–6	Thrives on dry, sandy soil
A. incarnata (swamp milkweed)	3–8	3 × 2'	Pink; summer	5–6	Best on wet soil
A. purpurascens (purple milkweed)	5–9	2½ × 1'	Purple; early summer	5–6	Best on dry, sandy or clay soil
A quadrifolia (four-leaf milkweed)	5–9	2 × 1'	White; late spring	4–5	Best on dry; sandy soil
A. syriaca (common milkweed)	3–9	3 × 3+'	Pinkish lavender; summer	5–7	Adapts to wide range of soils
A. tuberosa (butterfly weed)	3–8	2½ × 1'	Orange; summer	4–6	Thrives on dry, sandy soil
A. verticillata (whorled milkweed)	4–8	1½ × 1'	White; summer	5–6	Best on sandy-humusy soil
Aster ericoides (heath aster)	3–7	3 × 1'	White; fall	4–6	Thrives on sandy or clay soils
A. laevis (smooth aster)	4–8	4 × 1'	Blue-violet; fall	5–6	Thrives on sandy or clay soils
A. linariifolius (narrow-leaf aster)	4–8	2 × 1½'	Lavender; fall	4–5	Best on dry, sandy soil
A. macrophyllus (large-leaf aster)	3–8	4 × 1½'	Bluish lavender; fall	4–5	Best on moist, sandy soil in partial shade
A. oolentagiensis, syn. *A. azureus* (azure aster)	5–8	3 × 1'	Blue-violet; fall	5–6	Best on sandy soil
A. patens (spreading aster)	4–7	2½ × 1½'	Blue; fall	4–5	Best on dry, sandy or clay soil

(continues)

OTHER PERENNIAL SPECIES (continued)

Name	Zones	Height (by spread)	Flower Color and Bloom Time	pH	Comments
A. ptarmicoides (stiff aster)	3–7	2 × 1'	White; late summer	4–6	Best on dry, sandy or gravelly soil
A. sericeus (western silvery aster)	4–8	2 × 1'	Purple; fall	6–7	Thrives on dry to moist, sandy or clay soil
A. spectabilis (showy aster)	4–7	2 × 2'	Lavender; fall	4–5	Best on dry, sandy or clay soil
Baptisia australis (blue false indigo)	6–8	3 × 3'	Blue and white; late spring	5–7	Best on dry, sandy or clay soil
B. bracteata, syn. *B. leucophaea* (cream wild indigo)	5–8	2½ × 2'	Cream; early summer	6–7	Best on dry, sandy or clay soil
B. lactea, syn. *B. leucantha* (white wild indigo)	5–8	3 × 2½'	White; early summer	6–7	Best on dry to moist, sandy or clay soil
Boltonia asteroides (false chamomile)	7–9	4 × 2'	Lavender; late	4–5	Best on dry, sandy or clay soil
Calla palustris (wild calla)	4–7	8 × 4"	White; summer	4–5	Requires wet soil
Calopogon tuberosum (grass pink)	3–10	24 × 4"	Magenta; early summer	4–5	Best on moist, sandy soil
Caltha palustris (marsh marigold)	3–8	10 × 8"	Yellow; spring	5–6	Best on moist; humusy soil in partial shade
Camassia scilloides (eastern camass)	7–9	18 × 6"	Blue; late spring	5–6	Best on moist, sandy soil
Campanula rotundifolia (harebell)	3–8	12 × 6"	Blue; early summer	5–6	Best on dry, sandy or clay soil in partial shade
Cardamine bulbifera (spring cress)	6–8	12 × 6"	White; late spring	5–6	Best on moist, humusy soil in partial shade
Chamaecrista fasciculata, syn. *Cassia fasciculata* (partridge pea)	5–8	3 × 1'	Yellow; summer	4–6	Best on dry, sandy soil
C. nictitans, syn. *Cassia nictitans* (sensitive pea)	5–10	1½ × 1'	Yellow; late summer	5–6	Best on dry, sandy soil
Chamaelirion luteum (devil's bit)	4–7	2½ × 1'	White; late spring	6–7	Best on moist, humusy soil in partial shade
Chelone glabra (white turtlehead)	3–7	3 × 2 +'	White; late summer	5–6	Best on wet, loamy soil in partial shade
Chrysogonum virginianum (golden knee)	6–8	8 × 12"	Yellow; late spring	5–6	Best on dry, sandy soil
Chrysopsis mariana (golden aster)	4–8	1½ × 1'	Yellow; summer	4–6	Best on dry, sandy soil
Cichorium intybus (chicory)	3–8	4 × 1½'	Blue; summer	5–7	Thrives on dry, sandy or clay soil
Cicuta maculata (water hemlock)	4–7	4 × 2'	White; summer	5–6	Requires wet soil
Cirsium discolor (field thistle)	5–8	6 × 3'	Purple; late summer	5–6	Best on moist, sandy or clay soil
Clintonia umbellata (speckled wood lily)	4–7	10 × 8"	White; late spring	5–6	Best on moist, humusy soil in partial shade
Collinsia verna (blue-eyed Mary)	5–8	12 × 4"	White; spring	5–6	Best on dry, sandy or clay soil in partial shade
Collinsonia canadensis (horse balm)	4–8	3 × 2'	Yellow; late summer	5–6	Best on dry, sandy or clay soil in partial shade
Coreopsis lanceolata (tickseed)	5–8	2 × 1'	Yellow; early summer	5–6	Thrives on dry, sandy or clay soil
C. palmata (tickseed)	4–8	3 × 1½'	Yellow; early summer	5–6	Thrives on dry, sandy or clay soil
C. tripteris (tall coreopsis)	4–8	6 × 2'	Yellow; late summer	5–6	Best on moist, humusy soil
Corydalis sempervirens (rock harlequin)	6–9	2 × 1½'	Red; late spring	6–7	Best on moist, sandy or clay soil
Cunila aurea, C. flavula (yellow harlequin)	6–9	12 × 6"	Yellow; spring	5–6	Best on dry, sandy soil in partial shade
C. origanoides (common dittany)	6–8	1 × 1'	Lavender; fall	5–6	Best on dry, sandy soil
Cynoglossum virginiaticum (wild comfrey)	4–7	2 × 1'	Blue; late spring	6–7	Best on moist, humusy soil in partial shade
Cypripedium acaule (purple lady's slipper)	5–7	15 × 6"	Pinkish lavender; late spring	4–5	Best on moist, sandy soil in partial shade
C. calceolus (yellow lady's slipper)	5–7	2 × 1'	Yellow; late spring	5–7	Best on moist, sandy soil in partial shade
Dalea gattingeri (purple prairie clover)	6–7	2 ½ × 1'	Purple; summer	5–6	Best on dry; sandy or clay soil
Dalibarda repens (star violet)	5–7	4 × 36+"	White; early summer	4–5	Best on moist, sandy soil in partial shade
Delphinium tricorne (dwarf larkspur)	4–7	15 × 6"	Purple; late spring	6–7	Best on moist, humusy soil
Desmodium canadense (tick trefoil)	3–8	3 × 1'	Rose purple; summer	5–6	Best on moist, sandy soil
Dicentra canadensis (squirrel corn)	5–8	8 × 6"	White; spring	6–7	Best on moist; sandy or clay soil in partial shade

Name	Zones	Height (by spread)	Flower Color and Bloom Time	pH	Comments
Dodecatheon meadia (shooting star)	3–8	2 × 6"	White and/or pink; late spring	6–7	Best on moist, humusy soil in partial shade
Drosera intermedia (sundew)	6–10	3–6 × 2"	White; summer	4–5	Requires wet soil or boggy
Elephantopus carolinianus (elephant's foot)	7–10	2 × 1'	Lavender; late summer	5–6	Best on dry, sandy soil
Epigaea repens (trailing arbutus)	2–7	4 × 36 +"	White; spring	4–5	Best on moist, sandy soil in partial shade
Epilobium angustifolium (fireweed)	3–7	3 × 1'	Rose pink; late summer	4–5	Best on moist, sandy or clay soil
Erigeron strigosus (daisy fleabane)	3–7	2 × 1'	White; spring to fall	5–6	Best on moist, sandy or clay soil
Eryngium yuccifolium (rattlesnake master)	4–8	4 × 2'	White; summer	5–6	Best on moist, sandy or clay soil
Eupatorium coelestinum (mist flower)	5–8	2½ × 3 +'	Blue; late	5–7	Best on moist, humusy soil
E. fistulosum (Joe-pye weed)	4–8	6 × 3'	Pink; fall	5–6	Best on moist, humusy soil
E. perfoliatum (boneset)	3–8	4 × 2'	White; fall	5–6	Best on moist, sandy or clay soil
E. rugosum (white snakeroot)	5–8	3 × 1½'	White; fall	5–7	Best on moist, humusy soil in partial shade
Euphorbia corollata (flowering spurge)	4–8	2 ½ × 1'	White; summer	5–7	Best on dry, sandy soil
Filipendula rubra (queen of the prairie)	2–7	3½ × 1½'	Red; early summer	5–6	Best on moist, humusy soil in partial shade
Fragaria virginiana (wild strawberry)	3–8	8 × 36 +"	White; spring to early summer	5–6	Best on moist, sandy or clay soil
Gentiana andrewsii (bottle gentian)	4–7	2 × 1'	Blue; fall	4–5	Best on moist, sandy soil in partial shade
G. clausa (bottle gentian)	4–7	2 × 1'	Blue; fall	5–6	Best on moist, humusy soil in partial shade
G. crinata (fringed gentian)	4–7	18 × 8"	Blue; fall	6–7	Best on wet, sandy or clay soil
G. linearis (narrow-leaf gentian)	3–7	1 × 1'	Blue; late summer	4–5	Best on moist, sandy soil in partial shade
G. saponaria (soapwort gentian)	5–8	1½ × 1'	Blue; fall	4–5	Best on moist, sandy soil in partial shade
Geranium maculatum (wild geranium)	4–8	2 × 1'	Rose purple; late spring	5–6	Best on moist, sandy soil in partial shade
G. robertianum (herb Robert)	6–8	1 × 1'	Red-violet; late spring	6–7	Best on moist, humusy soil in partial shade
Geum aleppicum (yellow avens)	3–7	15 × 6"	Yellow; early summer	4–5	Best on moist, sandy or gravelly soil in partial shade
Gillenia trifoliata (bowman's root)	4–8	3 × 2'	White; summer	5–6	Best on dry, silty clay soil in partial shade
Habenaria blephariglottis (white fringed orchis)	5–8	2½ × 1'	White; early summer	4–5	Requires wet, boggy ground
H. ciliaris (orange fringed orchis)	5–8	15 × 6"	Orange; summer	4–5	Requires wet, boggy ground
Hedeoma pulegioides (American pennyroyal)	5–8	12 × 4"	Lavender purple; late summer	5–6	Best on dry, sandy or clay soil
Helenium autumnale (sneezeweed)	3–8	4 × 1'	Yellow; late summer	5–6	Best on moist, humusy soil
Helianthemum canadense (frostweed)	7–8	12 × 6"	Yellow; late summer	4–5	Best on dry, sandy soil
Helianthus giganteus (giant sunflower)	4–7	8 × 3'	Yellow; late summer	5–6	Best on dry, sandy or gravelly soil
H. grosseserratus (sawtooth sunflower)	4–7	10 × 3'	Yellow; summer to fall	5–6	Best on moist, sandy or clay soil
H. × laetiflorus var. *rigidus* (showy sunflower)	4–8	6 × 2'	Yellow; summer to fall	5–6	Best on dry, sandy or clay soil
H. occidentalis (western sunflower)	4–8	5 × 2'	Yellow; summer to fall	5–6	Best on dry, sandy or clay soil
H. strumosus (rough sunflower)	4–8	6 × 2'	Yellow; summer	5–6	Best on dry, sandy or clay soil in partial shade
H. tuberosus (Jerusalem artichoke)	4–8	8 × 2'	Yellow; summer to fall	5–7	Best on moist, humusy soil
Heliopsis helianthoides (oxeye sunflower)	4–7	5 × 1½'	Yellow-orange; summer	5–6	Best on dry, sandy or clay soil
Heracleum sphondylium (cow parsnip)	5–7	10 × 5'	White; summer	5–6	Best on moist, humusy soil
Heuchera americana (alumroot)	4–7	1 ½ × 1'	Green; late spring	5–6	Best on dry, clay soil in partial shade
H. richardsonii (alumroot)	5–8	3 × 1½'	Yellow-green; late spring	5–6	Best on dry, clay soil

(continues)

OTHER PERENNIAL SPECIES (continued)

Name	Zones	Height (by spread)	Flower Color and Bloom Time	pH	Comments
Hibiscus moscheutos (marsh mallow)	5–8	5 × 3'	Pink; summer	5–6	Best on moist, sandy soil
Hieracium venosum (rattlesnake weed)	3–7	18 × 6"	Yellow; early summer	4–5	Best on dry, sandy soil
Houstonia caerulea (Quaker ladies)	6–8	4 × 4"	Lavender; spring	5–6	Best on moist, humusy soil in partial shade
H. purpurea (bluet)	6–8	1½ × 1'	Bluish lavender; late spring	5–6	Best on moist, humusy soil in partial shade
H. serpyllifolia (thymeleaf bluet)	6–8	2 × 36+"	Lavender; early summer	4–5	Best on moist, sandy soil in partial shade
Hypericum ascyron (great St. John'swort)	3–8	5 × 2'	Yellow; early summer	5–6	Best on moist, humusy soil
Hypoxis hirsuta (star grass)	5–10	8 × 4"	Yellow; late spring	4–5	Best on dry, sandy soil in partial shade
Impatiens capensis (jewelweed, touch-me-not)	2–8	4 × 2'	Orange; summer	5–6	Best on wet, humusy soil in partial shade
I. pallida (pale jewelweed)	2–8	4 × 2'	Pale yellow; late summer	5–6	Best on wet, humusy soil in partial shade
Iris cristata (dwarf crested iris)	5–7	8 × 36+'	Blue; late spring	5–6	Best on moist, humusy soil
I. prismatica (slender blue flag)	5–8	1½ × 1'	Bluish lavender; early summer	4–5	Requires wet soil or boggy ground in partial shade
I. pseudacorus (yellow flag)	4–8	2½ × 1½'	Yellow; late spring	5–6	Requires wet soil or boggy ground
I. verna (dwarf iris)	6–8	6 × 3"	Purple; late spring	4–5	Best on moist, sandy soil in partial shade
I. versicolor (blue flag)	4–8	2½ × 1'	Blue; late spring	5–6	Best on wet, humusy soil in partial shade
I. virginica (southern blue flag)	6–8	3 × 1¼'	Blue-violet; late spring	4–5	Best in wet, humusy soil
Jeffersonia diphylla (twinleaf)	5–8	12 × 8"	White; spring	6–7	Best on dry, sandy soil in partial shade
Krigia biflora (dwarf dandelion)	4–8	18 × 8"	Orange; early summer	5–6	Best on dry, sandy soil in partial shade
Kuhnia eupatorioides (false boneset)	3–8	4 × 2'	White; late summer	5–6	Best on dry, sandy soil
Lathyrus venosus (wild pea, vetchling)	4–7	36 × 6"	Purple, early summer	5–6	Best on moist, sandy or clay soil
Lepedeza capitata (bush clover)	4–8	3 × 1'	Cream; late summer	4–5	Best on dry, sandy soil
Liatris aspera (Kansas gayfeather)	5–8	4 × 1'	Rose purple; late summer	6–7	Best on moist, humusy soil
L. graminifolia (grass-leaf gayfeather)	3–8	36 × 6"	Reddish lavender; late summer	4–5	Best on dry, sandy or gravelly soil
L. scariosa (blazing star)	3–8	3 × 1½'	Red-violet or white; late summer	6–7	Best on dry, sandy or clay soil
L. spicata (gayfeather)	3–8	2½ × 1'	Reddish lavender; late summer	5–6	Best on dry, sandy or clay soil
Lilium canadense (meadow lily)	5–8	5 × 1'	Orange; early summer	5–6	Best on moist, humusy soil
L. michiganense (Michigan lily)	4–7	5 × 1'	Red-orange; summer	4–7	Best on moist, humusy soil
L. philadelphicum (wood lily)	4–7	24 × 6"	Red-orange; summer	4–6	Best on dry, sandy or clay soil
L. superbum (Turk's-cap lily)	3–7	6 × 1'	Orange; summer	5–6	Best on moist, humusy soil in partial shade
Lithospermum canescens (hoary puccoon)	3–8	12 × 6"	Yellow; late spring	6–7	Best on moist, sandy or clay soil
Lobelia cardinalis (cardinal flower)	3–7	4 × 1'	Red; late summer	5–6	Best on moist, humusy soil in partial shade
L. siphilitica (great blue lobelia)	5–8	4 × 1½'	Blue; late summer	6–7	Best on moist, humusy soil in partial shade
L. spicata (pale lobelia)	4–7	36 × 6"	Blue or white; summer	6–7	Best on moist, sandy or clay soil in partial shade
Lupinus perennis (wild lupine)	4–8	2 × 1½'	Blue, aging to pink; late spring	4–5	Best on moist, sandy or clay soil
Lysimachia punctata (yellow loosestrife)	5–8	2 × 1½'	Yellow; early summer	5–6	Best on moist, humusy soil
L. quadrifolia (whorled loosestrife)	5–8	2½ × 3+'	Yellow; early summer	5–6	Best on moist, humusy soil in partial shade
Marshallia grandiflora (Barbara's buttons)	5–8	1½ × 1'	Lavender; early summer	5–6	Best on moist, humusy soil in partial shade
Meehania cordata (Meehan's mint)	4–7	6 × 36+"	Lavender; late spring	5–6	Best on moist, humusy soil in partial shade
Mimulus ringens (monkey flower)	3–7	2½ × 1'	Blue-violet; summer	4–5	Requires wet soil or boggy ground in partial shade
Mitella diphylla (coolwort)	3–7	12 × 4"	White; late spring	6–7	Best on dry, sandy or clay soil in partial shade

Name	Zones	Height (by spread)	Flower Color and Bloom Time	pH	Comments
Monarda didyma (bee balm)	4–8	4 × 1'	Red; summer	5–6	Best on moist, humusy soil in partial shade
M. fistulosa (wild bergamot)	4–8	4 × 1½'	Pinkish lavender; summer	5–7	Best on dry, sandy or clay soil
M. punctata (horsemint)	6–8	24 × 8"	Lavender; late summer	5–6	Best on dry, sandy or clay soil
Oenothera fruticosa (sundrops)	4–7	2 × 1'	Yellow-orange; early summer	5–6	Best on moist, humusy soil
O. macrocarpa (Ozark sundrops)	5–8	1 × 1½'	Yellow; early summer	5–6	Best on dry, sandy or clay soil
O. perennis (sundrops)	5–8	2 × 1'	Yellow; early summer	5–6	Best on moist, humusy soil
Opuntia calcicola (hardy prickly pear)	7–8	1 × 2'	Yellow; early summer	6–7	Best on dry, sandy soil
O. compressa (hardy prickly pear)	7–8	1 × 2'	Yellow; early summer	5–6	Best on dry, sandy soil
Osmorhiza claytonii (sweet cicely)	6–9	24 × 8"	White; early summer	5–6	Best on moist, humusy soil in partial shade
Panax trifolius (dwarf ginseng)	3–7	8 × 5"	White; spring	6–7	Best on moist, humusy soil in partial shade
Parnassia palustris (grass of Parnassus)	4–8	12 × 8"	White; late summer	6–7	Best on wet, clay soil
Parthenium integrifolium (wild quinine)	3–8	4 × 2½'	White; late summer	4–5	Best on dry, sandy or clay soil
Peltandra virginica (arrow arum)	5–8	18 × 8"	Green; late spring	5–6	Requires wet soil or boggy ground
Penstemon barbatus (beardtongue)	3–8	4 × 2½'	Red; early summer	5–6	Best on moist, humusy soil in partial shade
P. digitalis (beardtongue)	3–8	5 × 2½'	White; summer	5–6	Best on moist, sandy or clay soil
P. grandiflorus (beardtongue)	3–8	2½ × 1'	Lavender; early summer	6–7	Best on dry, sandy or clay soil
P. hirsutus (beardtongue)	3–7	1½ × 1'	Lavender; late spring	5–6	Best on dry, sandy or clay soil
Phacelia dubia (scorpion weed)	4–8	6 × 4"	Lavender; early summer	6–7	Best on dry, sandy or clay soil
Phlox divaricata (blue phlox)	4–7	15 × 8"	Bluish lavender; spring	5–6	Best on moist, humusy soil in partial shade
P. maculata (wild sweet William)	5–7	2½ × 1'	Pink, purple, or white; early summer	5–6	Best on moist, humusy soil in partial shade
P. ovata (mountain phlox)	5–7	12 × 6"	Lavender; early summer	6–7	Best on dry, sandy or clay soil in partial shade
P. pilosa (prairie phlox)	6–7	2 × 1'	Red to purple; spring to early summer	5–6	Best on dry, sandy or clay soil
P. stolonifera (creeping phlox)	4–7	6 × 36+"	Lavender to purple; late spring	5–6	Best on moist, humusy soil in partial shade
P. subulata (mountain pink)	3–7	4 × 36+"	Red, lavender, or white; spring	5–6	Best on dry, sandy or gravelly soil
Physostegia virginiana (obedient plant)	4–8	2½ × 1½'	Red-violet; late summer	5–6	Best on moist, sandy or clay soil in partial shade
Pogonia ophioglossoides (nodding pogonia)	3–7	18 × 6"	Rose to white; early summer	4–5	Requires wet soil or boggy ground
Polemonium reptans (Jacob's ladder)	4–7	1 × 1'	Bluish lavender; late spring	5–6	Best on moist, sandy or clay soil in partial shade
Polygala lutea (yellow milkwort)	6–8	10 × 4"	Orange; early summer	4–5	Requires wet soil or boggy ground
P. paucifolia (fringed milkwort)	2–7	3 × 36+"	Rose purple; late spring	5–6	Best on dry, sandy or clay soil in partial shade
P. senega (Seneca snakeroot)	4–7	18 × 6"	Greenish white; late spring	5–6	Best on dry, sandy or clay soil
Pontederia cordata (pickerelweed)	3–8	2 × 1'	Lavender blue; summer	5–6	Requires wet, sandy soil or boggy ground
Potentilla fruticosa (shrubby cinquefoil)	3–8	3 × 3'	Yellow; summer	5–8	Best on dry to moist, sandy or clay soil
P. tridentata (three-tooth cinquefoil)	3–7	6 × 36+"	White; early summer	4–5	Best on moist, sandy soil
Pycnanthemum virginianum (mountain mint)	4–7	2 × 1'	White; summer	5–6	Best on moist, sandy or clay soil
Ranunculus septentrionalis (swamp buttercup)	3–7	1 × 3+'	Yellow; late spring	5–6	Requires wet soil or boggy ground in partial shade
Ratibida pinnata (yellow coneflower)	3–7	3 × 1'	Yellow; summer	5–7	Best on dry, sandy or clay soil
Rhexia mariana (meadow beauty)	6–8	24 × 8"	Lavender purple; late summer	4–5	Best on moist, sandy or gravelly soil in partial shade

(continues)

OTHER PERENNIAL SPECIES (*continued*)

Name	Zones	Height (by spread)	Flower Color and Bloom Time	pH	Comments
R. virginica (meadow beauty)	5–8	2 × 1'	Rosy purple; late summer	4–5	Requires wet soil or boggy ground
Rosa blanda (prairie rose)	2–7	6 × 3'	Pink or white; summer	5–8	Best on dry, sandy or clay soil
R. carolina (pasture rose)	4–7	4 × 3'	Pink; spring to early summer	5–7	Best on dry, sandy or clay soil
Rudbeckia fulgida (coneflower)	4–7	2½ × 1½'	Yellow and brown; summer	5–6	Best on moist, sandy or clay soil
R. hirta (black-eyed Susan)	4–8	3 × 1½'	Yellow and brown; summer	5–6	Best on moist, sandy or clay soil
R. laciniata (golden glow)	3–8	6 × 2'	Yellow; late summer	5–6	Best on moist, sandy or clay soil
R. triloba (small coneflower)	5–8	4 × 2'	Yellow and brown; late summer	5–7	Best on moist, sandy or clay soil
Ruellia strepens (wild petunia)	6–9	1 × 1'	Lavender purple; summer	5–6	Best on moist, sandy or clay soil
Sagittaria latifolia (arrowhead, duck potato)	7–9	2½ × 1'	White; summer	5–6	Requires wet soil or boggy ground
Salvia lyrata (cancer weed)	5–8	24 × 8"	Purple; early summer	5–6	Best on moist, sandy or clay soil
Sanguinaria canadensis (bloodroot)	3–7	12 × 8"	White; spring	6–7	Best on moist, humusy soil in partial shade
Sanguisorba canadensis (Canadian burnet)	4–7	3½ × 1½'	White; late summer	4–5	Requires wet soil or boggy ground
Sarracenia flava (yellow pitcher plant)	7–9	2½ × 1'	Yellow; early summer	4–5	Requires wet soil or boggy ground
S. purpurea (purple pitcher plant)	6–9	1 × 1'	Dark red; late spring to early summer	4–5	Requires wet soil or boggy ground
Saururus cernuus (lizard's tail)	6–8	2 × 1'	White; summer	5–6	Requires wet soil or boggy ground in partial shade
Scrophularia lanceolata (figwort)	5–8	3 × 1½'	Yellow; early summer	5–6	Best on moist, sandy or clay soil in partial shade
Scutellaria elliptica (hairy skullcap)	5–8	24 × 6"	Bluish lavender; early summer	6–7	Best on dry, sandy or clay soil in partial shade
S. incana (hoary skullcap)	5–8	2½ × 2'	Bluish to pinkish lavender; summer	5–6	Best on dry, sandy or clay soil in partial shade
Sedum telephioides (tall stonecrop)	6–8	1½ × 1½'	Pink; late summer	6–7	Best on dry, sandy or clay soil
S. ternatum (wild stonecrop)	6–8	4 × 36+"	White; late spring	5–6	Best on dry, sandy or clay soil in partial shade
Senecio aureus (golden ragwort)	3–7	2 × 1'	Orange; early summer	5–6	Best on dry, sandy or clay soil in partial shade
S. obovatus (ragwort)	7–9	2 × 1'	Yellow; late spring	6–7	Best on moist, humusy soil in partial shade
Senna hebecarpa (wild senna)	5–8	4 × 2½'	Yellow; summer	5–7	Best on moist, sandy or clay soil
S. marilandica (Maryland senna)	4–7	4 × 2½'	Yellow; summer	5–6	Best on moist, sandy or clay soil
Seriocarpus linifolius (white-topped aster)	5–7	15 × 6"	White; summer	4–5	Best on dry, sandy or clay soil
Silene caroliniana (Carolina catchfly)	5–8	6 × 6"	Pink; late spring	4–5	Best on dry, sandy or clay soil
S. stellata (starry campion)	5–8	2 × 1'	White; summer	5–6	Best on dry, sandy or clay soil in partial shade
S. virginica (fire pink)	5–8	1 ½ × 1'	Red; late spring	5–6	Best on moist, sandy or clay soil in partial shade
Silphium laciniatum (compass plant)	4–7	6 × 2½'	Yellow; summer	6–7	Best on moist, sandy or clay soil
S. perfoliatum (cup plant)	4–8	6 × 4'	Yellow; summer	6–7	Best on dry, sandy or clay soil
S. terebinthaceum (rosinweed)	4–7	5 × 2'	Yellow; summer	5–6	Best on moist, sandy or clay soil
Sisyrinchium angustifolium (blue-eyed grass)	3–7	12 × 4"	Blue; late spring	5–6	Best on moist, humusy soil
S. campestre (blue-eyed grass)	5–6	12 × 6"	Blue; late spring	5–6	Best on moist, sandy or clay soil
Solidago bicolor (silverrod)	4–8	24 × 6"	White; late summer	4–5	Best on dry, sandy or clay soil in partial shade

Name	Zones	Height (by spread)	Flower Color and Bloom Time	pH	Comments
S. caesia (blue-stem goldenrod)	4–8	2½ × 1'	Yellow; late summer	5–6	Best on moist, sandy or clay soil in partial shade
S. canadensis (Canada goldenrod)	3–7	4 × 1½'	Yellow; late summer	5–6	Best on moist, sandy or clay soil
S. graminifolia (narrow-leaf goldenrod)	3–7	5 × 1½'	Yellow; late summer to early fall	5–6	Best on moist, sandy or clay soil
S. nemoralis (old-field goldenrod)	3–7	3 × 1'	Yellow; late summer to early fall	5–6	Best on moist, sandy or clay soil
S. puberula (downy goldenrod)	3–7	2 × 1'	Yellow; late summer	4–5	Best on moist, sandy or gravelly soil
S. rigida (stiff goldenrod)	4–7	4 × 1½'	Yellow late summer to early fall	5–6	Best on dry, sandy or clay soil
S. sempervirens (seaside goldenrod)	4–7	4 × 1½'	Yellow; fall	4–6	Best on moist, sandy soil
S. speciosa (showy goldenrod)	5–8	5 × 1½'	Yellow; late summer to early fall	5–6	Best on moist, humusy soil
Specularia speculum-veneria (Venus's looking-glass)	5–8	10 × 6"	Lavender blue; early summer	5–6	Best on moist, sandy or humusy soil
Spiraea alba (meadowsweet)	5–7	5 × 2⅓'	White; summer	4–5	Requires wet soil or boggy ground
S. tomentosa (steeplebush)	3–7	4 × 2'	Pink; summer	4–5	Requires wet soil or boggy ground
Spiranthes cernua (nodding lady's tresses)	3–8	24 × 6"	Cream; late summer	4–5	Requires wet soil or boggy ground
Stenanthium cramineum (feather bells)	6–9	2 ½ × 1'	White; summer	4–5	Requires wet soil or boggy ground
Stokesia laevis (Stokes aster)	7–9	1½ × 1½'	Blue; early summer	4–6	Best on dry, sandy or clay soil in partial shade
Talinum teretifolium (fameflower)	8–10	8 × 4"	Bluish purple;early summer	5–6	Best on dry, sandy or clay soil
Tephrosia virginica (goat's rue)	4–7	1½ × 2'	Pink and white; early summer	4–5	Best on dry, sandy or gravelly soil in partial shade
Thalictrum dasycarpum (purple meadow rue)	6–8	4 × 1½'	Light purple; early summer	5–6	Best on moist, sandy soil in partial shade
T. dioicum (early meadow rue)	6–8	2½ × 1'	Purple; late spring	5–6	Best on moist, humusy soil in partial shade
T. polygamum (tall meadow rue)	6–8	5 × 1½'	Cream; early summer	5–6	Best on moist, humusy soil in partial shade
Thermopsis villosa (bush pea)	6–8	4 × 1½'	Yellow; early summer	5–6	Best on moist, humusy soil in partial shade
Tradescantia ohioensis (spiderwort)	7–9	2½ × 2'	Pink, blue, or rose; summer	5–6	Best on moist, sandy soil
T. virginianum (snakeweed)	7–9	2 × 1'	Blue; early summer	5–6	Best on moist, humusy soil
Trichostema dichotomum (bastard pennyroyal)	6–8	10 × 4"	Purple; late summer	4–5	Best on dry, sandy or clay soil
Trillium erectum (stinking Benjamin)	4–7	12 × 8"	Garnet; spring	5–6	Best on moist, humusy soil in partial shade
Triosteum aurantiacum (wild coffee)	4–8	3 × 1'	Maroon; early summer	6–7	Best on moist, humusy soil in partial shade
Trollius laxus (spreading globeflower)	4–7	1½ × 1'	Yellow; early summer	6–7	Requires wet soil or boggy ground
Typha latifolia (common cattail)	3–10	6 × 3'	Brown and cream; early summer	5–6	Requires wet soil or boggy ground
Uvularia grandiflora (merrybells)	3–7	2 × 1'	Yellow; late spring	6–7	Best on moist, humusy soil
Veratrum viride (white hellebore)	3–7	4 × 2'	Green; late spring	5–6	Best on moist, humusy soil in partial shade
Verbena bipinnatifida (Dakota verbena)	3–7	1½ × 2'	Lavender purple; early summer	6–7	Best on dry, sandy or clay soil
V. hastata (blue vervain)	3–7	3½ × 2'	Purple to blue; late summer	5–6	Best on moist, humusy soil
V. stricta (blue vervain)	4–8	3 × 1'	Bluish purple; summer	5–6	Best on moist, sandy or clay soil
Vernonia noveboracensis (ironweed)	5–8	5 × 2'	Purple; late summer to early fall	5–6	Best on moist, humusy soil
Veronicastrum vircinicum (Culver's root)	3–7	3½ × 2'	White to pale blue; summer	5–6	Best on moist, humusy soil in partial shade
Vicia americana (American vetch)	4–7	3 × 2'	Bluish purple; summer	5–6	Best on moist, sandy or clay soil

(continues)

OTHER PERENNIAL SPECIES (*continued*)

Name	Zones	Height (by spread)	Flower Color and Bloom Time	pH	Comments
Viola lanceolata (eastern water violet)	6–7	6 × 4"	White; late spring	4–5	Requires wet soil or boggy ground
V. obliqua (blue marsh violet)	5–7	6 × 4"	Bluish violet and white; late spring	5–6	Requires wet soil or boggy ground
V. pedata (bird's-foot violet)	4–7	4 × 3"	Purple; late spring	4–5	Best on dry, sandy or gravelly soil
V. primulifolia (primrose-leaved violet)	4–7	8 × 5"	Lavender; late spring	4–5	Requires wet soil or boggy ground in partial shade
V. sagittata (arrow leaf violet)	5–8	8 × 4"	Purple; late spring	4–5	Best on dry, sandy or clay soil
V. striata (cream violet)	4–7	6 × 6"	Cream; spring	5–6	Best on moist, humusy soil in partial shade
Waldsteinia fragarioides (barren strawberry)	3–7	4 × 8"	Yellow; late spring	5–6	Best on moist, humusy soil in partial shade
Xanthorhiza simplicissima (yellowroot)	4–8	3 × 1½'	Brown-violet; late spring	6–7	Best on moist, humusy soil in partial shade
Xyris caroliniana (yellow-eyed grass)	7–9	18 × 6"	Yellow; summer	4–5	Requires wet soil or boggy ground
Zizia aurea (golden Alexander)	3–8	2 × 2'	Yellow; late spring	5–6	Best on moist, humusy soil

Wild geranium
(*Geranium maculatum*)

Jacob's ladder
(*Polemonium reptans*)
with **Dandelion**

Compass plant
(*Silphium laciniatum*)

Marsh mallow
(*Hibiscus moscheutos*)

Pink wild sweet William (*Phlox maculata* 'Alpha')

Bottle gentian (*Gentiana clausa*)

Pasture rose (*Rosa carolina*)

Boneset (*Eupatorium perfoliatum*)

Sneezeweed
(*Helenium autumnale*)

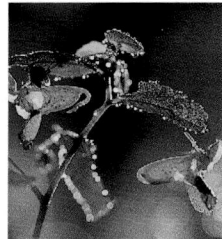

Touch-me-not
(*Impatiens capensis*)

Blue flag
(*Iris versicolor*)

Wild sarsaparilla
(*Aralia nudicaulis*)

Cow parsnip
(*Heracleum sphondylium*)

Chicory
(*Cichorium intybus*)

Common cattail
(*Typha latifolia*)

Roadside strip of wild flowers

Fireweed (*Epilobium angustifolium*)

Hybrid goldenrod
(*Solidago* 'Crown of Rays')

Common milkweed
(*Asclepias syriaca*)

Bird's-foot violet
(*Viola pedata*)

Yellow coneflower
(*Ratibida pinnata*)

Golden ragwort
(*Senecio aureus*)

Wood lupine
(*Lupinis perennis*)

Wood lily
(*Lilium philadelphicum*)

*A late-summer patch of gayfeather (*Liatris spicata*), along with white snakeroot (*Eupatorium rugosum*), goldenrod (*Solidago sp.*), and, on the right, the often invasive purple loosestrife (*Lythrum salicaria*).*

Cream wild indigo
(*Baptisia bracteata*)

Spiderwort
(*Tradescantia virginianum*)

Black-eyed Susan (*Rudbeckia hirta*)
with **Fleabane** (*Erigeron annuus*)

Obedient plant
(*Physostegia virginiana*)

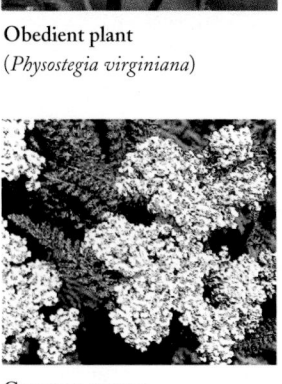

Common yarrow
(*Achillea millefolium*)

Bee balm (*Monarda didyma*)

Whorled milkweed
(*Asclepis verticillata*)

Partridge pea
(*Chamaecrista fasciculata*)

PERENNIAL MEADOW GRASSES

Name	Zones	Height (by spread)	Foliage Color	Season of Interest	pH	Comments
Andropogon gerardii (big bluestem)	4–8	6 × 2'	Red-brown after frost	Late summer	5–6	Best on dry to moist, sandy or clay soil
A. scoparius (little bluestem)	4–8	4 × 2½'	Orange-brown after frost	Late summer	5–6	Best on dry to moist, sandy or clay soil
Bouteloua curtipendula (side oats grama)	6–10	3 × 2'	Green, then tan	Summer	5–7	Best on dry, sandy or clay soil
Calamagrostis canadensis (bluejoint reed grass)	2–8	4 × 2"	Purplish florets	Summer	5–6	Requires wet soil or boggy ground
Elymus canadensis (Canada wild rye)	3–8	3 × 1½'	Tan seed heads	Summer	5–6	Best on dry to moist, sandy or clay soil
Panicum virgatum (switch grass)	5–10	4 × 2'	Red-brown fall foliage	Summer	5–7	Best on dry to moist, sandy or clay soil
Sorghastrum nutans (Indiana grass)	5–8	5 × 2'	Purple, bronze fall foliage	Late summer	5–7	Best on dry to moist, sandy or clay soil
Spartina pectinata (cordgrass)	5–9	5 × 2'	Brown fall foliage	Summer	5–6	Requires wet soil
Sporobolis heterolepis (prairie dropseed grass)	5–8	2½ × 1½'	Green to tan	Late summer	5–6	Best on dry to moist, sandy or clay soil
Stipa spartea (needlegrass)	5–8	3½ × 1½'	Green to tan	Early summer	5–7	Best on dry, sandy or clay soil in partial shade

Switch grass (*Panicum virgatum*)

Indiana grass (*Sorghastrum nutans*)

Side oats grama (*Bouteloua curtipendula*)

Big bluestem (*Andropogon gerardii*) with **Coneflower** (*Ratibida pinnata*)

21

Gardening by the Sea

SEASIDE ENVIRONMENTS HAVE LONG LURED MULTITUDES of vacationers in the summer, but less well known is the fact that a substantial and steadily increasing number of people make their year-round homes in littoral locations. For those wishing to garden, there are special challenges to be met—and many satisfying rewards for those who take the trouble to understand the differences between the coastal zone and more familiar inland environments. For example, certain general conditions prevail, such as sandy, excessively drained,

North America's most important dune stabilizer, American dune grass is easily established and spreads by subsurface runners.

nutrient-deficient soils and, frequently, strong, gusty winds, sometimes bearing salt spray that can damage or kill susceptible garden plants. Soil pH may vary widely, even in small areas, depending on the underlying rock strata, prevailing vegetation, and the frequency of storm-borne salt spray or wave overwash.

Fortunately, a large number of decorative plants have evolved in the various seaside zones around the world and are more or less adapted to similar environments elsewhere. Some require little or no intervention, while for others some augmentation of soil nutrients, some means to increase soil moisture retention, or a way mitigate the wind may be required.

Another point to remember is the moderating effect of the sea on the climate of immediately adjacent land. Large water bodies respond slowly to changes in air temperature, and the resulting retention of heat in the fall protects coastal areas from the extremes of winter cold. Similarly, the slow warmup of the ocean in the spring is reflected in the absence of searing heat along the coast in summer. Thus milder winters than occur in nearby inland areas afford special gardening opportunities (such as growing camellias on Cape Cod and eucalyptus in southwestern coastal Oregon), and so do cooler summers (making it possible to have heat-sensitive calendulas and sweet peas in flower throughout the summer months).

Seaside gardens also may offer special design opportunities. Where the ocean or a bay or estuary is visible, for example, it should be incorporated into the garden plan and not be diminished or obliterated by carelessly placed shrubs or trees. Hedges are often employed in seaside gardens not only to define garden space but to provide protection from wind. Their selection and placement should be made with care, especially when a maritime vista is to be preserved.

Whether starting with a well-established house and garden or with bare ground, it is important to draw up a plan that focuses attention on the relationships in space and time among the various garden components. A house appropriate to the site affords niches for unusual plants and innovative plantings, chosen and designed for the idiosyncracies of wind and sun exposure. Ideally, a garden by the sea intensifies consciousness of the special attributes of the site, yet offers respite from wind and relief from glare. Just as with gardening elsewhere, ideas can be gleaned from the gardens of others, in respect to things worth considering and things to avoid.

Certain gardening guidelines apply most anywhere in coastal areas; 12 are listed below.

1. Use indigenous or naturalized materials as much as possible, especially for major framework plantings, as these are best adapted to local conditions and require little or no intervention or maintenance.

2. In keeping with the importance of the horizon, stress the horizontal, especially along the immediate coast, and make use of mat-forming plants or low, rounded shrubs that can resist wind.

3. Informal garden design is usually more harmonious in environments dominated by the dunes, low hills, and cliffs that prevail along the coast than the rigid, formal arrangements suitable in cities and other places dominated by the works of humankind.

4. Mitigate high winds with hedges, walls, or fences carefully chosen and constructed for staunchness and aesthetic harmony.

5. Make any increases in soil nutrient levels by using compost and well-rotted manure or slow-release commercial fertilizers. In thin, sandy soils, excess nitrate soon percolates beyond the reach of roots and pollutes both coastal wetlands and ground water.

6. Avoid making changes in land form that will be difficult to stabilize or maintain. It is important to vegetate sloping bare spots as these are especially subject to erosion, which, once begun, is often difficult to contain.

7. To reduce water demand and cut maintenance, consider developing a xeriscape—a landscape designed with drought-tolerant plants, most of which are adapted to sandy soils and arid conditions.

8. Do not plant trees on steep embankments, since all but the most densely vegetated slopes erode over the years. The inexorable loss of soil eventually leaves tree roots exposed, hastening instability and uprooting. Instead, use grasses, ground covers, and low shrubs.

9. Minimize lawn area, as most popular lawn grasses, to remain green, must have supplemental irrigation and, where soil nutrients are severely leached, regular applications of fertilizer. Where lawn is necessary, favor fescues and other drought-tolerant kinds in preference to rye grass or bluegrass types. Frequent small applications of organic, slow-release fertilizer will reduce the rapid leaching and downward percolation of nutrients beyond root range and their accumulation to polluting concentrations in the underlying aquifer and nearby wetlands.

10. Include a buffer strip at least 10 feet wide around the periphery of the property or surrounding a lawn area to limit erosion, provide wildlife habitat, and reduce human impact. The buffer zone should consist of native trees, shrubs, wildflowers, and grasses, all self-maintaining and requiring no regular attention.

11. In sites subject to frequent strong winds off the sea or a bay, wind buffers can be planted using multiple and

staggered rows of wind-tolerant trees, such as those listed below. Species with the lowest maximum height should be planted on the windward side of the buffer, those that mature taller on the leeward. In time, such a buffer planting becomes a dense, sloping, wind-shaped, thicketlike hedge that directs most wind upward and over the area immediately downwind.

12. On waterfront properties, access to the shore, whether for bathing, boating, or beachcombing, should be carefully restricted to a well-thought-out route, especially if a dune or coastal bank is involved. Regulations vary and should be determined from local authorities before any digging or construction is undertaken. By bordering a path, boardwalk, or stairway with thorny shrubs, such as autumn olive (*Eleagnus umbellata*), rugosa rose (*Rosa rugosa*), or sea buckthorn (*Hippophae rhamnoides*), the route not only becomes obvious and attractive, but pedestrians will keep to it.

PLANTS SUITED TO EXPOSED SEASHORE AREAS
Subject to strong wind and occasional salt spray.

Name	Zones	Height	Comments
TREES			
Acer pseudoplatanus (sycamore maple)	4–7	40–60'	Very salt tolerant; often self-sows
Ailanthus altissima (tree of heaven)	4–8	25–50'	Suckers from roots, forming copses; self-sows (females)
Araucaria araucana (monkey puzzle)	8–9	40–75'	Evergreen; coarse habit
A. cunninghamii (hoop pine)	10	40–75'	Evergreen; open, tufted habit
A. heterophylla (Norfolk Island pine)	9–10	25–60'	Evergreen; pagodalike habit
Casuarina spp. (Australian pine)	9–10	40–75'	Evergreen; freely self-sows
Crataegus phaenopyrum (Washington hawthorn)	3–8	15–30'	Very thorny; white flowers in the spring, red fruit in the summer
Cupressus macrocarpa (Monterey cypress)	8–9	20–35'	Evergreen; scale-leaf foliage; flat topped with age
Eleagnus angustifolia (Russian olive)	2–7	12–15'	Gray foliage; often thorny
Juniperus virginiana (eastern red cedar)	2–9	15–30'	Evergreen; dark, scale-leaf foliage; conical habit
Lagunaria patersonii (Queensland pyramid tree)	9–10	25–35'	Evergreen; contact with pods causes skin irritation
Maytenus boaria (mayten)	8–10	12–30'	Evergreen; ornamental fruit in the summer and fall
Melaleuca leucodendron (punk tree, cajeput tree)	9–10	25–50'	Evergreen; shaggy bark
Picea asperata (dragon spruce)	6–8	20–40'	Evergreen; conical habit
P. glauca (white spruce)	2–7	25–50'	Evergreen; small cones
P. rubens (red spruce)	2–7	25–50'	Evergreen; best used north of zone 5
Pinus clausa (sand pine)	9–10	12–25'	Evergreen; open, irregular habit
P. contorta (shore pine)	7–8	15–30'	Evergreen; often shrubby, especially on poor soil
P. halepensis (Aleppo pine)	8–9	25–50'	Evergreen; open crown with age
P. muricata (bishop pine)	8–10	25–50'	Evergreen; narrow, columnar habit
P. parviflora (Japanese white pine)	6–8	25–50'	Evergreen; many dwarf cultivars
P. pinaster (maritime pine)	7–9	25–50'	Evergreen; rounded habit with age
P. radiata (Monterey pine)	8–9	25–50'	Evergreen; dense, dark foliage
P. rigida (pitch pine)	4–7	15–40'	Evergreen; often branched to ground; trunk sprouts new shoots (tillers)
P. thunbergii (Japanese black pine)	6–7	20–40'	Evergreen; very irregular habit
P. torreyana (Torrey pine)	8–9	20–40'	Evergreen; long needles
Pittosporum tenuifolium	9–10	15–25'	Evergreen; twigs gray black
Populus alba (white poplar)	3–8	25–60'	Foliage downy white beneath; suckers from roots, forming copses
Prunus serotina (black cherry)	3–9	25–50'	Often deformed by cankers; white flowers; self-sows

(continues)

PLANTS SUITED TO EXPOSED SEASHORE AREAS (*continued*)

Name	Zones	Height	Comments
Quercus ilex (holly-leaf oak)	7–9	25–50'	Evergreen; glossy foliage
Q. ilicifolia (scrub oak)	5–7	10–20'	Often remains shrubby
Q. velutina (black oak)	3–9	30–60'	Large, glossy foliage; tap rooted, hence difficult to transplant
Q. virginiana (live oak)	7–9	25–50'	Evergreen; crown often broader than it is high
Robinia pseudoacacia (black locust)	3–8	25–50'	Suckers from roots, forming copses; young stems thorny; white flowers in the spring

SHRUBS

Name	Zones	Height	Comments
Amelanchier canadensis (shadbush)	3–8	6–15'	White flowers in the spring; purple fruit in the summer
Aronia melanocarpa (black chokeberry)	3–8	3–8'	White flowers in the spring; shiny black fruit and purple foliage in the fall
Baccharis halimifolia (groundsel bush)	3–9	3–10'	Very salt tolerant
Chaenomeles spp. (flowering quince)	4–8	3–8'	Thorny stems; flowers orange, pink, or white in the spring
Cytisus spp. (broom)	5–8	1–8'	Green twigs; flowers mostly yellow in the spring
Eleagnus multiflora (cherry eleagnus)	5–7	6–10'	Flat-topped habit; silvery foliage; red fruit in the fall
E. pungens (thorny eleagnus)	6–9	10–15'	Evergreen; thorny stems; fragrant whitish flowers in the spring
E. umbellata (autumn olive)	3–8	8–15'	Silvery foliage; self-sows
Hippophae rhamnoides (sea buckthorn)	3–7	8–15'	Thorny stems; females bear persistent orange berries in the fall
Ilex glabra (inkberry holly)	3–7	6–8'	Evergreen; black berries in the fall
Itea virginica (Virginia sweetspire)	5–9	3–5'	White flowers in the summer; red fall foliage
Iva frutescens (marsh elder)	3–7	5–10'	Inhabitant of salt marshes
Juniperus chinensis 'Pfitzeriana' (Pfitzer juniper)	8–9	6–8'	Evergreen; ascending habit; blue-green foliage
J. chinensis 'Sargentii' (Sargent juniper)	3–9	1–2'	Evergreen; prostrate habit; spreading 6 to 8 feet
J. communis 'Depressa' (sand juniper)	2–7	3–4'	Evergreen; blue-green foliage discolors in the winter
J. conferta (Japanese shore juniper)	6–8	1–1½'	Evergreen; spreads 6 to 8 feet; blue-green foliage; several cvs.
J. horizontalis (creeping juniper)	3–9	1–2'	Evergreen; spreads 4 to 8 feet; blue-green foliage; many cvs.
Ligustrum spp. (privet)	3–10	6–15'	Evergreen or half-evergreen; glossy foliage
Myrica california (California wax myrtle)	7–8	8–20'	Evergreen; females bear purple berries in the fall
M. cerifera (southern wax myrtle)	8–9	8–12'	Evergreen; females bear gray berries in the fall
M. pensylvanica (bayberry)	2–7	3–10'	Semievergreen; females bear gray berries in the fall
Prunus maritima (beach plum)	3–7	4–8'	White flowers in the spring; red-violet fruit in late summer and fall
P. tomentosa (Nanking cherry)	2–7	6–10'	White flowers in the spring; scarlet fruit in the fall
Robinia fertilis (rose acacia locust)	5–7	6–10'	Suckers from roots, forming copses; pink flowers in the spring
Rosa blanda (smooth rose)	2–7	3–6'	Pink flowers in the spring; red fruit in the fall
R. multiflora (multiflora rose)	5–8	4–10'	Freely self-sows; white flowers in late spring; abundant small red fruit in the fall
R. rugosa (rugosa rose)	2–7	4–6'	Forms dense thickets; pink or white flowers in late spring and summer; large red-orange fruit (hips) in the fall
R. setigera (prairie rose)	4–8	6–10'	Pale pink flowers in late spring; red fruit in the fall
R. virginiana (Virginia rose)	3–8	4–6'	Pink flowers in late spring; red fruit in the fall
R. wichuraiana (memorial rose)	5–8	2–3'	Prostrate habit; spreads 8 to 15 feet; white flowers in late spring and early summer; red fruit in the fall; can be used as a ground cover

Name	Zones	Height	Comments
Santolina chamaecyparissus (lavender cotton)	6–9	1–2'	Evergreen; spreads 2 to 4 feet; fine silvery foliage; yellow buttonlike flowers in the summer
S. virens (green lavender cotton)	6–9	1–2'	Similar to *S. chamaecyparissus* but has green foliage
Viburnum cassinoides (withe rod viburnum)	5–9	5–8'	White flowers in the spring; black berries in the fall
V. dentatum (arrowwood viburnum)	2–8	6–12'	Cream flowers in the spring; black berries in the fall
V. tinus (laurustinus)	8–9	6–12'	Evergreen; white flowers in the spring; black berries in the fall
Xanthorhiza simplicissima (yellowroot)	3–9	2–3'	Suckers from roots, forming dense stands

CLIMBERS

Name	Zones	Height	Comments
Clematis paniculata (sweet autumn clematis)	5–8	8–15'	Climbs by hooked leaf stalks; white flowers in late summer
Hedera helix (English ivy)	4–9	25–50'	Evergreen; climbs by aerial rootlets; black berries in the winter
Parthenocissus quinquefolia (Virginia creeper)	3–10	25–50'	Climbs by tendrils with adhesive discs; blue-black berries in the fall; red fall foliage

GROUND COVERS

Name	Zones	Height	Comments
Arctostaphylos uva-ursi (bearberry)	2–7	6–12"	Woody evergreen, spreads to form dense mats 8 feet or more across; red berries in the fall
Artemisia frigida (fringed wormwood)	4–7	1½–2'	Forms clumps about as wide as it is high; silky gray foliage
A. pontica (Roman wormwood)	4–8	2–2½'	Forms patches 4 to 6 feet across; gray foliage
A. schmidtiana (silvermound wormwood)	4–7	about 1'	Forms clumps about 1½ feet across; silvery foliage
A. stelleriana (beach wormwood)	3–7	1½–2'	Forms mats 4 to 6 feet across; silvery foliage
Calluna vulgaris cvs. (heather)	4–7	6–24"	Evergreen; matures as wide or wider than it is high; flowers mostly rose pink in late summer and fall
Hedera helix (English ivy)	4–9	6–12"	Evergreen; forms rampant mats; climbs trees and walls
Hudsonia ericoides (false heather)	6–8	6–12"	Forms clumps 1 to 1½ feet across; fine textured; heatherlike
H. tomentosa (poverty grass)	6–8	6–12"	Similar to *H. ericoides* but finer and downy whitish
Juniperus spp. (juniper)	3–9	3–12"	Evergreen; spreads 3 to 8 feet; bluish scalelike foliage

PERENNIALS

Name	Zones	Height	Comments
Aster spp. (wild perennial aster)	3–8	1–4'	Purple to white flowers in late summer to early fall
Chrysopsis falcata (golden aster)	6–7	1–2'	Yellow daisylike flowers in mid to late summer
Eryngium amethystinum (sea holly)	4–8	1½–2'	Metallic blue flowers in the summer
Hemerocallis fulva (tawny daylily)	4–9	2½–4'	Orange flowers in early summer
Hibiscus moscheutos (rose mallow, marsh mallow)	5–8	3–6'	Large red, pink, or white flowers in the summer
Lathyrus japonicus (beach pea)	3–7	2–3'	Scrambling habit; rose pink flowers in the summer
Saponaria officinalis (bouncing Bet, soapwort)	4–8	1½–2½'	Forms clumps or patches 5 to 10 feet across; pale lavender pink flowers in the summer
Solidago sempervirens (seaside goldenrod)	4–7	3–6'	Yellow flowers in the fall

PERENNIAL GRASSES

Name	Zones	Height	Comments
Ammophila breviligulata (American dune grass)	7–8	2–3'	Spreads, forming extensive stands; unrivaled sand binder
Eragrostis curvula (weeping love grass)	8–9	3–5'	Good sand binder in hot regions
Spartina alterniflora (marsh grass)	2–8	1–4'	Common in salt marshes
S. patens (salt meadow grass)	2–8	1–3'	Carpets salt marshes
S. pectinata (prairie cordgrass)	5–8	4–6'	Good soil binder in wet ground

Live oak
(*Quercus virginiana*)

Beach pea
(*Lathyrus japonicus*)

Rugosa rose
(*Rosa rugosa*)

Shadbush (*Amelanchier canadensis*)

Japanese black pine (*Pinus thunbergii*)

Eastern red cedar (*Juniperus virginiana*)

Beach plum (*Prunus maritima*)

American dune grass (*Ammophila breviligulata*)

PLANTS SUITED TO PARTIALLY SHELTERED SEASHORE AREAS
Subject to wind but little or no salt spray.

Name	Zones	Height	Comments
TREES			
Abies homolepis (Nikko fir)	4–7	35–50'	Yellowish bark
A. veitchii (Veitch fir)	3–7	35–50'	Unusually hardy
Acacia spp.	9–10	15–30'	Evergreen; usually thorny; yellow flowers in heads or spikes mostly in late winter and spring
Acer platanoides (Norway maple)	3–7	35–50'	Casts dense shade; often self-sows
A. rubrum (red maple, swamp maple)	3–9	25–50'	Red fall foliage; red flowers in the spring
A. saccharinum (silver maple)	3–9	35–60'	Extremely tolerant of poor soil; brittle branches
Aesculus hippocastanum (horse chestnut)	3–7	35–50'	Leaves turn brown in drought; white flowers in the spring
Albizia julibrissin (mimosa, silk tree)	6–9	15–25'	Finely divided leaves; heads of pink flowers in the summer; short lived
Betula papyrifera (canoe birch, paper birch)	2–7	35–50'	Single trunk, with white peeling bark; long lived
B. populifolia (gray birch, white birch)	3–7	15–30'	Multiple trunks; light grayish bark; short lived
Carya tomentosa (mockernut hickory)	4–8	30–50'	Wide spreading; rough, shaggy bark with age
Catalpa spp. (Indian bean)	4–8	25–40'	White flowers in early summer; persistent beanlike pods; late to leaf out
Crataegus crus-galli (cockspur thorn)	3–7	15–25'	Branches have long sharp thorns; white flowers in the spring; red fruit in the fall
Cryptomeria japonica (Japanese cedar)	6–9	35–50'	Evergreen; turns bronzy in the winter
Fagus spp. (beech)	3–9	35–50'	Broad crown; *F. grandifolia* suckers from roots, forming copses
Fraxinus americana (American ash)	3–9	35–50'	Late to leaf out; many pests and diseases
Gleditsia triacanthos var. *inermis* (thornless honey locust)	3–9	30–50'	Usually develops low, wide crown; long, curved, flat pods on some trees
Ilex opaca (American holly)	5–9	15–30'	Evergreen; prickly-leaf foliage; females bear red berries in the fall
Liriodendron tulipifera (tulip tree)	4–9	35–50'	Orange and green flowers held on upper branches in the spring
Maclura pomifera (Osage orange)	4–9	20–40'	Thorny branches; females bear large wrinkled fruit in the fall
Magnolia grandiflora (southern magnolia)	7–9	30–40'	Evergreen; large, white, fragrant flowers in the spring
Malus spp. (crab apple)	3–8	15–25'	Wide spreading; white, pink, or red flowers in the spring; red or yellow fruit in the fall
Morus alba (white mulberry)	4–8	25–40'	Weedy, coarse; self-sows; females bear white to purple fruit in the summer
Nyssa sylvatica (black gum)	3–9	30–50'	Red fall foliage; deep taproot
Olea europaea (olive)	8–9	15–25'	Evergreen; grayish foliage; source of edible olives
Paulownia tomentosa (empress tree)	5–9	25–35'	Large leaves late to appear; lilac flowers precede leaves
Picea abies (Norway spruce)	2–7	35–50'	Evergreen; pyramidal habit
P. pungens (Colorado spruce, blue spruce)	2–7	30–50'	Evergreen; foliage dull green to steel blue
Pinus banksiana (jack pine)	2–6	25–50'	Evergreen; often shrubby; flat topped; intolerant of heat
P. cembra (Swiss stone pine)	4–7	30–40'	Evergreen; picturesque habit; slow growing
P. densiflora (Japanese red pine)	3–7	30–40'	Evergreen; open habit; red-brown bark
P. nigra (Austrian pine)	4–8	35–50'	Evergreen; stiff foliage; good for windbreaks
P. sylvestris (Scotch pine)	2–7	30–50'	Evergreen; picturesque habit; red-brown bark
Platanus × *acerifolia* (sycamore, London plane)	4–8	35–50'	Wide spreading; mottled, peeling bark

(continues)

PLANTS SUITED TO PARTIALLY SHELTERED SEASHORE AREAS (*continued*)

Name	Zones	Height	Comments
Prunus serrulata (Japanese flowering cherry)	6–8	20–30'	Single or double pink or white flowers in the spring
Quercus agrifolia (California live oak)	8–9	20–40'	Evergreen; often shrubby
Q. alba (white oak)	3–9	35–50'	Wide spreading; slow growing
Q. marilandica (blackjack oak)	5–8	15–30'	Often shrubby; slow growing
Q. rubra (red oak)	4–8	40–50'	Large glossy foliage; faster growing than most oaks
Salix spp. (willow)	2–9	15–50'	Twiggy; soft wooded; best in wet ground
Sassafras albidum	4–8	30–40'	Three leaf shapes; often suckers from roots, forming copses
Thuja occidentalis (eastern arborvitae)	2–7	20–35'	Evergreen; pyramidal habit
Tilia cordata (littleleaf linden)	3–7	35–50'	Pyramidal habit; small nuts borne on green wings
Ulmus americana (American elm)	2–9	35–50'	Gracefully wide spreading; very adaptable but subject to fatal diseases
U. parvifolia (Chinese elm)	4–9	25–40'	Tough, durable under harsh conditions
U. procera (English elm)	4–7	35–50'	Broad, high crown; subject to Dutch elm disease
U. pumila (Siberian elm)	4–9	35–50'	Fast growing; branches easily broken in high winds

SHRUBS

Name	Zones	Height	Comments
Aronia arbutifolia (red chokeberry)	4–9	6–10'	Tends to legginess; red berries in the fall
Berberis spp. (barberry) late summer	4–8	3–8'	Some species evergreen; most are thorny; red or black berries in and fall
Buddleia davidii (butterfly bush)	6–9*	8–12'	Fast growing; purple, lavender, or white flowers in summer
Caragana arborescens (pea bush)	2–7	10–15'	Very tough; yellow flowers in the spring
Carissa macrocarpa (Natal plum)	10	6–15'	Evergreen; spiny stems; fragrant white flowers in the spring and summer; fruit red to violet black in the fall and winter
Caryopteris × *clandonensis* (blue-mist bush)	7–9*	1½–2'	Blue flowers in late summer
Clethra alnifolia (sweet pepperbush)	3–9	3–8'	Forms clumps; fragrant white flowers in the summer
Comptonia peregrina (sweet fern)	2–7	2–4'	Forms clumps; aromatic foliage
Coprosma baueri (mirror bush)	9–10	10–15'	Evergreen; orange berries in the fall and winter
Cornus spp. (shrubby dogwood)	2–8	6–12'	Some species have red or yellow stems; white or yellow flowers in the spring; purple, red, blue, or white fruit in the fall
Cotoneaster spp.	4–8	1–10'	Some species wide spreading; white flowers in the spring; red or black fruit in the fall
Erica spp. and cvs. (heath)	5–9	1–4'	Evergreen; fine textured; flowers mostly rose pink or white in late winter and spring, sometimes in the fall
Euonymus alata (burning bush)	3–8	6–10'	Corky wings on twigs; red fall foliage
Forsythia spp.	(4) 6–8	2–10'	Wide spreading; yellow flowers in early spring
Halimodendron halodendron (salt tree)	2–6	3–5'	Twiggy habit; pinkish purple flowers in the summer
Hebe elliptica, H. speciosa	8–9	3–6'	Evergreen; purple, pink, or white flowers in the summer
Hibiscus syriacus (rose of Sharon)	5–8	8–12'	Lavender, pink, or white flowers in mid to late summer
Hydrangea paniculata 'Grandiflora' (peegee hydrangea)	3–8	10–20'	White flowers in mid to late summer, then purplish, and finally tan in fall, held in large clusters
Hypericum spp. (shrubby St. John'swort)	3–8	1–5'	Yellow flowers in the summer
Ilex crenata (Japanese holly)	5–7 (8)	5–10'	Evergreen; lustrous foliage; females bear black berries in the fall
I. verticillata (winterberry)	3–9	6–8'	Females bear red berries in the fall and winter; good on wet or dry ground
Jasminum nudiflorum (winter jasmine)	6–10	3–6'	Yellow flowers during mild periods in the winter; may be used as a climber

Name	Zones	Height	Comments
Kolkwitzia amabilis (beauty bush)	4–8	5–10'	Pale pink flowers in the spring
Laurus nobilis (sweet bay)	8–9	6–15'	Evergreen; large glossy foliage
Leiophyllum buxifolium (sand myrtle)	5–7	1–2'	Pink buds and white flowers in the spring
Lespedeza bicolor (shrubby bush clover)	(4) 6–7	6–8'	Purplish pink flowers in the summer
Lonicera spp. (bush honeysuckle)	(2) 4–8	2–10'	Red, yellow, or white flowers in early to late spring; red or black berries in the summer
Mahonia spp. (hollygrape)	4–8	2–6'	Evergreen; yellow flowers in the spring; gray black berries in the fall
Nerium oleander (oleander)	8–10	6–10'	Evergreen; red, pink, or white single or double flowers in the summer and fall
Pinus mugo (mugo pine)	2–7	2–8'	Evergreen; multistemmed; rounded habit
Potentilla fruticosa (shrubby cinquefoil)	2–7	1–4'	Rounded habit; yellow or white flowers in the summer
Prunus laurocerasus (cherry laurel)	6–8	3–10'	Evergreen; spikes of white flowers in the spring; black fruit in the fall
Pyracantha coccinea (firethorn)	(5) 6–9	6–15'	Evergreen (semievergreen in the North); thorny stems; white flowers in the spring; persistent red or orange berries in the fall and winter
Raphiolepis umbellata (Indian hawthorn)	7–10	4–6'	Evergreen; white flowers in the spring; persistent black berries in the summer and fall
Rhododendron viscosum (swamp azalea)	3–9	3–8'	White clove-scented flowers in summer; best in wet places
Rhus aromatica (fragrant sumac)	3–9	2–5'	Forms large clumps; orange to red fall foliage; good soil binder
R. copallina (shining sumac)	4–9	6–15'	Forms large copses; deep red fruit and foliage in the fall
R. glabra (smooth sumac)	2–9	6–12'	Forms large copses; bright red fruit and foliage in the fall
Rosa spp. (wild rose)	4–9	4–10'	Usually forms dense thickets; stems thorny; pink flowers in late spring to summer; red fruit in the fall
Rosmarinus officinalis (rosemary)	(7) 8–10	4–6'	Evergreen; grayish green aromatic foliage; blue flowers in late winter and spring
Salix purpurea 'Nana' (purple osier)	5–8	5–8'	Twiggy willow shrub; good in wet places
Spiraea spp. (spiraea)	3–9	3–8'	Pink or white flowers in the spring or summer
Symphoricarpos albus (snowberry)	3–7	3–6'	White fruit in the fall, persisting into winter
S. × chenaultii (Chenault coralberry)	4–7	3–6'	Pinkish fruit in the fall, persisting into winter
S. orbiculatus (Indian currant)	2–7	2–5'	Spreads by stolons, forming large copses; purplish red fruit in the fall, persisting into winter
Tamarix ramosissima (tamarisk)	2–8	6–12'	Loose, open, twiggy habit; rose pink flowers in early summer
Taxus spp. (yew)	(2) 4–8	3–15'	Evergreen; dark green foliage; females bear red berries in late summer and fall; many cultivars
Vaccinium angustifolium (lowbush blueberry)	2–5	1–2 (3)'	Forms extensive colonies; blue-black fruit in the summer; red fall foliage
V. corymbosum (highbush blueberry)	3–7	8–12'	Wide spreading habit; blue-black fruit in the summer; bronzy fall foliage
Viburnum spp.	3–8	3–12'	Many species and cultivars; most with white flowers in the spring; red or black fruit in the fall
Vitex negundo (chaste bush, summer lilac)	(5) 6–9	3–12'	Bluish lavender flowers in late summer; may die back in the winter in zones 6 and 7
Weigela florida	5–8	6–10'	Some cultivars have variegated leaves; red, pink, white, or varicolored flowers in late spring to summer

(continues)

PLANTS SUITED TO PARTIALLY SHELTERED SEASHORE AREAS (continued)

Name	Zones	Height	Comments
WOODY CLIMBERS			
Akebia quinata (five-leaf akebia)	4–8	15–30'	Semievergreen; forms large thickets; purplish flowers in the spring followed by sausagelike fruit in the summer and fall
Ampelopsis brevipedunculata (porcelain berry)	4–8	10–20'	Fast growing by way of tendrils; varicolored fruits maturing blue
Celastrus scandens (American bittersweet)	3–8	20–30'	Twiner; females bear yellow and orange fruit in the fall; less rampant than *C. orbiculata*
Clematis spp.	3–8	5–20'	Climbs by twisted leaf stalks; purple, pink, or white flowers in the summer
Euonymus fortunei (winter creeper)	(4) 5–8 (9)	10–30'	Evergreen; glossy foliage; much variation in habit and foliage among cultivars
Hydrangea anomala 'Petiolaris' (climbing hydrangea)	4–7	10–30'	Climbs by rootlets; white flowers in early summer
Jasminum nudiflorum (winter jasmine)	6–10	3–5'	Yellow flowers in mild periods in the winter, especially if exposed to sun and protected from wind
Lonicera spp. (climbing honeysuckle)	4–9	10–25'	Semievergreen; vigorous habit; twiner; red, pink, yellow, and/or white flowers
Passiflora spp. (passion flower)	6–10	10–20'	Many species evergreen; tendril climber; large bicolor or multicolor flowers in the summer
Wisteria spp.	4–9	20–30'	Vigorous twiner; lilac, blue-violet, red-violet, or white flowers in the spring; pods velvety, green, maturing brown in the fall
GROUND COVERS			
Achillea spp. (yarrow)	4–8	1–4'	Forms clumps about as wide as it is high; finely cut foliage; red, pink, yellow, or white flowers in the summer
Aegopodium podagraria 'Variegata' (variegated goutweed)	4–8	1–1½'	Quickly spreads; forms mats 10 feet or more across; green and white foliage
Ajuga spp. (bugle)	4–8	about 6"	Semievergreen, forms mats 3 to 6 feet across; purple flowers in the spring
Arenaria spp. (sandwort)	4–7	about 6"	Forms fine-textured mats 1 to 2 feet across; pink or white flowers in the spring
Armeria maritima (sea pink)	4–7	6–12"	Forms clumps or mats 1 to 2 feet across; pink or white flowers in the spring
Aurinia saxatilis (basket-of-gold)	4–7	6–12"	Semievergreen, spreads 1½ to 2 feet; gray green foliage; yellow flowers in the spring
Cerastium tomentosum (snow-in-summer)	4–8	6–12"	Forms mats 2 to 6 feet across; silvery gray foliage; white flowers in the summer
Convallaria majalis (lily-of-the-valley)	4–7	6–12"	Forms mats 3 feet or more across; fragrant white flowers in the spring
Cotoneaster spp. (creeping cotoneaster)	4–8	1–3'	Some species evergreen; woody; spreads 3 to 8 feet; white flowers in the spring; red or black berries in the fall
Epimedium spp. (barrenwort)	5–8	about 1'	Slowly spreads; forms mats 1 to 2 feet across; red, pink, yellow, or white flowers in the spring
Euonymus fortunei (winter creeper)	(4) 5–8 (9)	6–12"	Evergreen; woody; forms extensive mats 10 to 15 feet across
Hosta spp. (plantain lily)	4–8	1–2½'	Forms dense clumps 2 to 4 feet across; lavender or white flowers in the summer; some shade advisable
Hypericum spp. (creeping St. John'swort)	5–8	1–2'	Some species semievergreen; forms clumps or mats 2 to 4 feet across; yellow flowers in the summer

Name	Zones	Height	Comments
Iberis sempervirens (evergreen candytuft)	4–8	6–12"	Evergreen; forms mats 1 to 2 feet across; white flowers in the spring
Liriope muscari (big blue lilyturf)	7–8	1½–2'	Evergreen; forms clumps or mats 1½ to 3 feet across; lilac purple flowers in late summer
L. spicata (creeping lilyturf)	5–8	about 1'	Evergreen; forms clumps or mats 1 to 2 feet across; lilac to white flowers in late summer
Ophiopogon spp. (lilyturf)	7–9	6–36"	Evergreen; forms dense mats up to 3 feet across; violet to white flowers in late summer
Pachysandra terminalis	3–8	6–12"	Evergreen; forms dense mats 2 to 4 feet across; foliage lustrous; best in shade
Phlox spp. (creeping phlox)	4–8	3–18"	Mostly forms mats 1 to 3 feet across; showy flowers in various colors in the spring
Polygonum japonicum var. *compactum* (Japanese knotweed)	4–7	2–3'	Forms dense mats 3 to 6 feet across; white flowers in late summer; good soil binder
Sedum spp. (creeping sedum)	4–8	3–6"	Forms mats 1 to 3 feet across; red-violet, pink, yellow, or white flowers in the spring or summer
Thymus spp. (thyme)	4–7	3–6"	Forms dense twiggy mats 2 to 3 feet across; foliage fine, aromatic; purple, red, pink, or white flowers in the spring or summer
Veronica spp. (creeping speedwell)	4–7	6–18"	Forms clumps or mats 1½ to 3 feet across; blue, pink, or white flowers mostly in the spring
Vinca major (large periwinkle)	(7) 8–9	1–1½'	Evergreen; forms mats 2 to 4 feet across; often with variegated foliage; lavender purple flowers in the spring
V. minor (creeping myrtle)	(3) 5–8	3–6"	Evergreen; forms mats 1 to 2 feet across; glossy foliage; purple to white flowers in the spring

PERENNIAL GRASSES

Name	Zones	Height	Comments
Andropogon virginicus (Virginia beard grass)	8–10	2–4'	Tolerates very low nutrient levels
Deschampsia spp. (hair grass)	4–7	1½–2'	Clusters of green to purplish flowers, held above foliage, in the summer
Ehrharta erecta (veldt grass)	8–9	2–3'	Requires moderate soil fertility
Elymus arenaria (blue wild rye)	4–7	2–3'	Good soil binder
Erianthus ravennae (plume grass)	5–8	10–12'	Useful as specimen plant
Festuca ovina var. *glauca* (blue fescue)	5–9	6–12"	Forms silver blue clumps
Miscanthus sinensis (eulalia)	5–8	6–8'	Useful as screen or specimen
Molina coerulea (purple moor grass)	5–8	1½–2'	Good soil binder
Schizachyrium scoparium, syn. *Andropogon scoparius* (little bluestem)	5–8	3–6'	Bronzy foliage; thrives on dry sand
S. scoparium var. *littorale*, syn. *Andropogon littoralis* (seaside bluestem)	5–8	2–4'	Similar to *S. scoparium* but smaller
Uniola paniculata (sea oat)	8–9	2–8'	Good for stabilizing dunes

FERNS

Name	Zones	Height	Comments
Asplenium platyneuron (ebony spleenwort)	5–10	1–1½'	Grows best in shaded, alkaline soil
Dennstaedtia punctilobula (hay-scented fern)	3–8	2–3'	Forms dense mats; best in partial shade
Osmunda cinnamomea (cinnamon fern)	3–9	3–6'	Forms dense clumps; best in wet places
Pteridium aquilinum (bracken)	6–9	2–3'	Ubiquitous and very hardy, but invasive

* Occasional dieback to base in winter north of zone 8 does not impede flower in the following summer.

Chinese elm (*Ulmus parvifolia*)

Tamarisk (*Tamarix ramosissima*)

Rose of Sharon
(*Hibiscus syriacus*)

Shrubby cinquefoil
(*Potentilla fruticosa*)

Winterberry
(*Ilex verticillata*)

Indian bean (*Catalpa bignonioides*)

American holly (*Ilex opaca*)

Blue fescue (*Festuca ovina* var. *glauca*)

Evergreen candytuft (*Iberis sempervirens*)

ORNAMENTAL SHRUBS AND PERENNIALS NATIVE TO LITTORAL CALIFORNIA

Suitable for cultivation in coastal areas (zones 8 and 9) with cool, moist winters and warm, dry summers, especially on clay soils with pH 6.5 to 7.5.

Name	Height	Comments
Artemisia californica (California sagebrush)	2½–4'	Shrub; forms extensive stands; gray green foliage
A. pycnocephala (soft sage)	1½–2'	Subshrub; silky foliage; small, inconspicuous flowers
Baccharis pilularis (coyote brush)	2–5'	Resinous shrub; forms extensive stands; small whitish flowers in the summer
Chlorogalum pomeridianum (soap plant)	2–10'	Leaves held in basal rosette; white flowers borne on tall leafless stalks in the summer
Erigeron glaucus (beach aster)	6–12"	Tufted perennial; purple to lilac flowers in the summer
Eriogonum arborescens (Santa Cruz buckwheat)	2–8'	Much-branched shrub; white woolly leaves; small inconspicuous flowers in the summer
E. latifolium (chalk buckwheat)	6–24"	Foliage basal, woolly; clustered small, whitish flowers in the summer
Eriophyllum staechadifolium (lizard tail)	1½–3'	Diffusely branched subshrub; white felty leaves; yellow flowers from spring to fall
Eschscholzia californica (California poppy)	about 1'	Biennial or short-lived perennial; finely cut blue-green foliage; orange flowers in the spring
Lavatera assurgentiflora (tree mallow)	4–10'	Shrub; maplelike leaves; pink flowers from summer to fall
Lupinus chamissonis (San Francisco lupine)	1–2'	Shrub; blue or lavender flowers from summer to fall
L. variicolor (varicolored lupine)	6–12"	More or less creeping perennial; purplish, yellowish, or white flowers in the spring and summer
Mimulus aurantiacus (bush monkey flower)	2–4'	Evergreen shrub; cream to salmon flowers in the spring and summer
Oenothera cheiranthifolia (beach evening primrose)	1–1½'	Tufted perennial; spreading stems; yellow flowers in the spring and summer
Penstemon heterophyllus (blue penstemon)	1–2'	Narrow-leaf perennial; purple to blue flowers in the summer
Rhamnus californica (coffeeberry)	4–6'	Evergreen shrub; small white flowers in the spring; red berries that mature black in the fall
Sisyrinchium bellum (blue-eyed grass)	1–1½'	Clumps of grasslike foliage; blue flowers, yellow at base within, in the summer

Common yarrow (*Achillea millefolium*)

Cinnamon fern (*Osmunda cinnamomea*)

Blue penstemon (*Penstemon heterophyllus*)

22

The Woodland Garden

Oᴏɴᴇ ᴏꜰ ᴛʜᴇ ᴍᴏꜱᴛ ʙᴇᴀᴜᴛɪꜰᴜʟ ᴇxᴘʀᴇꜱꜱɪᴏɴꜱ ᴏꜰ ʟᴀɴᴅꜱᴄᴀᴘᴇ art is to be found in the woodland garden. Here the ideals are not those of the flower garden, where perfection of bloom or variety in horticultural forms is the goal, but rather a selection of species as they occur in the wild. Wildflowers should prevail, and they should be given a setting closely resembling in appearance and physical condition that of their natural habitat. Since such a woodland is fundamentally a garden, it is not a copy or reproduction of nature but is a

Blue-green Hosta *cultivars contrast with distinctive adjoining erect clusters of astilbe, arching stems of great Solomon's seal, and other plants suited to woodland culture.*

545

place which wildflowers grow in their accustomed way. It may be, as nearly as possible, an association of plants—trees, shrubs, and perennials, perhaps with climbers and ferns—in a preserved woodland habitat that is altered only to allow and limit human access to carefully defined paths. As a less likely alternative, it may be a somewhat degraded wooded tract that still has major trees and some shrubs and lower vegetation but has suffered from frequent and random trampling, cutting, refuse disposal, etc. As long as the soil remains largely intact and access can be controlled, such a tract may well provide the basis of a woodland garden.

Purists may wish to cultivate in their woodland garden only plants that are native to the local area or to a particular geographic region. Those with more eclectic tastes or different interests may bring plants into the woodland garden that come from varied, often distant sources, but are nonetheless near relatives or have cultural requirements that are very similar to those of the natives.

THE SITE

The owner of property containing a mature woodland has the ideal situation for a garden of woodland flowers. Indeed, the development of such a tract into a woodland garden is just as logical and natural as is the development of open sunny spaces into gardens of herbaceous flowers.

For many centuries, gardeners and plant breeders have been developing sun-loving plants for various garden habitats, but it is only within recent decades in this country that serious effort has been made with the flora of the forest. It is a distinct facet of gardening and has its own subjects and techniques, to say nothing of an expanding cadre of devotees.

THE DESIGN

The limitations of a woodland area should be recognized in the very beginning, and every effort should be made to turn into assets those features of the place that might otherwise be regarded as liabilities. A woodland garden must necessarily be developed along naturalistic lines. The informal grouping of the trees themselves determines, to a very large extent, the nature of the design.

There is a general impression that an informal design in planning any type of garden is a much simpler and less rigorous practice than a formal scheme. On the contrary, the opposite is usually true. There is usually something very straightforward and quite obvious about the design of a formal garden, whereas the design of an informal area, if studied, possesses subtle quality and charm that are difficult to define.

A woodland clearing enhanced with tubbed plants and scattered benches in the dappled sunlight invites tarrying and contemplation.

Planning the woodland garden does not necessarily require exact plotting of ground areas or the spacing out of plants on a predetermined planting plan. But there should be forethought in the planning of major masses of foliage and flowers for the sake of good composition and balance and for the separation of the plants into groups that are congenial and require similar soil conditions, drainage, and light intensity. If the site includes areas of dissimilar soil conditions, the plants must be assigned to the spaces where they naturally belong and in which they will develop to their fullest potential. Thus a certain tract might have thin, dry soil on the upper levels; neutral, loamy soil in a large area; acidic clay where oak trees stand; and wet, mucky soil along a stream course or bordering a pond. Whether the plan is actually committed to paper or not, it should be sufficiently definite to keep the plants in the situations where they thrive best and to allot the more difficult conditions to those plants that are best able to withstand them.

Woodland Paths

A woodland path has the potential to create a mood unlike any other in the garden. Flower beds may excite the eye with bright colors and a shrub border with bold forms, but a sylvan path is relaxed and subdued. It is shaded and enclosed, yet can offer remarkable scenic variety: a mossy boulder here, a lichen-encrusted trunk there, a carpet of brilliant leaves in fall, an expansive view of distant hills. One moment you may be in a pool of bright light, the next in the cool dimness of deep shade. The shapes and textures of plants, from tiny mosses to tall, wide-spreading shrubs, as well as bark patterns and root buttresses of trees, all take on a special aesthetic role as you stroll through a woodland. As Thoreau put it, "I went to the woods because I wished to live deliberately, to front only the essential facts of life, and see what it had to teach, and not, when I am to die, discover that I had not lived."

The paths in a woodland area should be as natural in appearance as possible, yet be easily traversed. The surface should be kept free of encroaching growth, sharp stones, small stumps, and snags of all kinds. A natural surface of fallen leaves is pleasant, but if the paths are walked frequently, a more permanent surface may be desirable.

The person who is a novice in the art of gardening with wildflowers will find that it is possible to develop very attractive groups of plantings by using some of the more easily grown bulbs and perennials that adapt themselves readily to woodland conditions. For example, with masses of pale lavender blue phlox (*Phlox divaricata*) under a group of white birches in early spring; English primroses (*Primula vulgaris*) and wood anemones (*Anemone* spp.) blooming

An elevated walkway with railings provides safe, easy passage through woodland and brings minimal adverse impact.

along a woodland path; and foxgloves (*Digitalis purpurea*) lifting their stately spires against a background of deep forest green— such delightful pictures may be obtained with a moderate expenditure of time and money. While it is in the shade of trees that subtle differences in plant form and in the hue, glossiness, and overlap patterns of leaves become more fully apparent, plants with variegated foliage, placed judiciously, can add special focal points of longer term interest. Such plants as plantain lily (especially *Hosta* 'Frances Williams' or *H.* 'Piedmont Gold'), Solomon's seal (*Polygonatum odoratum* 'Variegatum'), lungwort (*Pulmonaria saccharata* 'Janet Fisk'), and dead nettle (*Lamiastrum galeobdolon* 'Variegatum') offer degrees of relief from pervasive green.

However, the experienced gardener, not content to limit attention to the more easily grown woodland plants, will attempt to naturalize some of the more fastidious woodland flowers. An adventure of this sort is full of interest and delight.

The materials best suited for such a purpose are pine needles, bark chips, and wood chips. Tanbark is also readily available in many areas of the country and makes a very satisfactory surface. It is a reddish, woodsy brown, and provides a soft, springy surface on which to walk. Tanbark also has the advantage of drying out very quickly after a rain

A massed planting of mixed hostas makes an interesting theme-and-variations display along a shaded path.

and never becoming soggy. Since tanbark will, in time, disintegrate and need to be renewed, it is a wise practice to add a small amount each season. Pine needles are always attractive but often disintegrate quickly and will give comparatively short service, unless a thick layer is used. And unless you are within easy range of a pine grove, they may be difficult to locate. Bark chips are easily spread and form a very attractive surface. Wood chips are usually available at small cost but are somewhat less attractive than other materials. This objection may be overcome by applying a light covering of bark chips or pine needles over the wood chips. Most wood chips decompose very slowly, thus affording good service for a number of years.

SMALL-SCALE WOODLAND GARDENING

It is not necessary to have an extensive tract of natural woodland to enjoy wildflowers and other indigenous vegetation. Often, even in a small suburban property, there is a semishaded patch or corner under trees where some woodland plants can be accommodated. In such an area, various shade denizens, such as wood anemone (*Anemone quinquefolia*), spring beauty (*Claytonia virginica*), liverleaf (*Hepatica americana*), dogtooth violet (*Erythronium americanum*), jack-in-the-pulpit (*Arisaema triphyllum*), Solomon's seal (*Polygonatum commutatum*), Virginia bluebell (*Mertensia virginica*), bloodroot (*Sanguinaria canadensis*), white wake-robin (*Trillium grandiflorum*), wild blue phlox, and other woodland plants can often be naturalized quite easily.

And small though the area may be, you can have the joy of watching for the first flowers of spring—the lovely, glistening white flowers of the bloodroot, which turn always to catch the rays of sunlight, and the exquisite blooms of the liverleaf nestling in the leafy litter. Later in the spring, the delicate lavender blue of wild phlox and the gleaming white of wake-robins will make a lovely visual harmony.

DEGREES OF SHADE

It is difficult to characterize shade in the woodland precisely, because it varies so widely—from place to place according to the extent, density, and motion of the overhead foliage, and from one season to the next as the leaves of deciduous trees come and go. In the summer, the open, airy quality of shade under tall, mature oaks is quite different from the gloom cast by a spreading, low-headed red maple; yet neither casts significant shade when out of leaf. Some perennial wildflowers require spring sunshine before tree leaves expand, then thrive in shade the rest of the season. Indeed, few wild plants endure the constant, year-round dense shade of evergreens, buildings, and canopies. In addition to casting shade, overhanging trees may compete with their roots, in some cases to the exclusion of most or even all competitors. Beech (*Fagus* spp.) and walnut (*Juglans* spp.) secrete allelopathic substances into the soil that suppress the growth of many other kinds of plants; the roots of Norway maple (*Acer platanoides*) desiccate and impoverish the soil surface while the ample foliage above dims the sun for six or seven months, often to the exclusion of virtually all lawn and garden plants beneath.

As a rule of thumb, it is useful to define three categories of shade.

1. *Dense or full shade.* Includes sustained year-round shade cast by evergreens and the continuous season-long shade beneath densely leafed deciduous trees; also the largely unrelieved shade on the north side of buildings and walls; few garden plants survive the dim light and often dry soil under such conditions.
2. *Light or high shade.* Sometimes called filtered sunlight; includes the shade found beneath tall woodland trees,

where little direct sunlight reaches the ground except as patchy dappling; many woodland plants thrive in light shade.

3. *Partial or half shade*. Includes sites receiving three to four hours of direct sun (not more than six) and light shade or even dense shade for the remainder of the day; common on the east or west sides of buildings, under well-spaced, densely shading trees, or along a woodland margin; a wide range of woodland plants thrive in partial shade.

SOIL REQUIREMENTS

Woodland plants vary greatly in their soil requirements; in their native habitats, they are found growing where the soil and other conditions best meet their needs. Some woodland plants require soils that are alkaline or nearly neutral in reaction, others thrive best in moderately acidic soils, a few grow only in soils that are intensely acidic, and some are indifferent to soil conditions. The moisture conditions of the soil are also a matter for consideration, as some plants must have moist or even wet soil, while others grow only in soil that readily dries out. It is, therefore, important to become familiar with the soil requirements of the plants you wish to grow and to provide conditions for them that are congenial and will be favorable for their best development.

Most natural woodland soils, especially those of deciduous hardwood forests, are rich in humus near the surface because of the continuous decomposition of fallen leaves and branches. It is in such woodlands, where sun and shade are dappled and the soil is humusy and only mildly acidic (pH 5.5 to 6.5), that most woodland flowers thrive. These are the flowers that may be grown in a home woodland area and that, once well established, will often spread, as they require only their natural conditions.

However, when one undertakes to develop a small wild garden under trees that have only recently been planted, it may be found that the soil lacks the qualities of a natural woodland soil. It may be heavy in texture and lacking in humus, for example. In such a case, it should be carefully prepared before any planting is done. Generous quantities of rotted leaf mold and compost should be spread and worked into the soil so that it will provide the well-aerated, moisture-retentive, nutrient-rich, humusy conditions for the woodland plants that are to make it their home.

Some of our best-known and most beautiful woodland plants, such as the pink lady's slipper (*Cypripedium acaule*), trailing arbutus (*Epigaea repens*), and some of the lovely native azaleas and rhododendrons, will thrive only in areas where the soil is quite acidic. It is useless to attempt to grow plants in this group unless conditions can be provided to meet their specific needs. This may be done by providing soil that is rich in humus and strongly acidic and by monitoring it and maintaining the correct degree of acidity from year to year (see Chapter 31).

Increasing the acidity of the soil is important, but it is not always the only conditioning process that is necessary. For many rhododendrons and azaleas, as well as mountain laurel (*Kalmia latifolia*), certain orchids (especially lady's slipper), and most ferns, the soil should be moist but also porous and well drained.

Clearly, success in woodland gardening depends on accurately determining the nature of the soil at hand by testing and learning the requirements of the plants to be grown in it. Ideally, plants should be matched to unamended soil, but if they cannot be, the soil must be altered accordingly.

SHRUBS AND SMALL TREES FOR THE WOODLAND

In almost every natural woodland an undergrowth of native shrubs and small trees will be found. Some of these are of great beauty and should be carefully preserved, while others are weedy in character and should be kept under control or removed entirely.

If some of the more desirable woodland shrubs are not available in a piece of woodland, they may be purchased from any nursery that makes a specialty of native plant materials. Such shrubs will add greatly to the beauty and interest of the planting.

Among the native shrubs most worthy of a place in a woodland planting, because of the beauty of their foliage, fruit, or flowers, are red chokeberry (*Aronia arbutifolia*); native azaleas, such as flame azalea (*Rhododendron calendulaceum*), pinxterbloom (*R. periclymenoides*), and the beautiful pink-shell azalea (*R. vaseyi*); spicebush (*Lindera benzoin*), with its yellow flowers in very early spring and its aromatic foliage; mountain laurel, the glory of many an oak-shaded hillside woodland in late spring; and the beautiful low-growing Carolina rhododendron (*R. carolinianum*) and the larger Catawba rhododendron (*R. catawbiense*) and rosebay (*R. maximum*), if space permits. The witch hazels, including the native fall-flowering *Hamamelis virginiana* and winter-flowering *H. vernalis*, as well as the showier Chinese witch hazel (*H. mollis*), Japanese witch hazel (*H. japonica*), and hybrid witch hazel (*H. × intermedia*), are other large shrubs that are at home in the woodland garden.

There are also a number of small trees that should be considered, if they are not already growing in the woodland, such as eastern dogwood (*Cornus florida*), which is one of our most beautiful small native trees, but threatened by disease in the Northeast; redbud (*Cercis canadensis*), bearing deep pink flowers in spring; silver bell (*Halesia carolina*), with its gracefully arrayed bell-like flowers; and shadbush or serviceberry (*Amelanchier canadensis*), bridelike when covered in spring bloom.

PROTECTED PLANTS

Before digging any plants in the wild, gardeners should check with the local cooperative extension, conservation organization, or botanic garden for lists of plants protected by state regulations and the federal Endangered Species Act. Such measures simply reflect the fact that many of our beautiful native woodland wildflowers are becoming increasingly rare as their habitats continue to be destroyed by the onward march of suburbanization. Each year more forest is lost to housing developments, industrial and shopping complexes, and highway projects. Efforts to establish wildflower sanctuaries in densely populated urban areas often fail to preserve populations of rare plants in

sufficient numbers to ensure their continued existence over large portions of their natural range. Digging plants from the woods to bring into the garden can only serve to complicate this serious problem. Moreover, many plants that are dug in the wild fail to survive transplanting into the garden unless done by an expert. Such transplanting, if at all permissible, should be attempted only as a rescue effort when native plants are being threatened with eradication, and even then it should be done only with extreme care. Even with the utmost care, such woodland wildflowers as the pink lady's slipper orchid almost never survive transplanting. Moreover, those that are offered for sale are collected from the wild, which, unless destined for development, is left impoverished of its slipper orchids, with little or no lasting gain for the woodland garden that receives them.

Most wildflowers can be propagated by means of seeds, cuttings, or divisions. Many of the better wildflower nurseries have considerable expertise in these methods. Those wildflower nurseries that clearly state it is their policy not to dig plants in the wild (except as a rescue effort, which many nurseries actually do) are by far the most responsible and usually the best sources of wildflowers for the garden.

NATIVE WOODLAND FLOWERS OF SPECIAL MERIT

Name	Zones	Height	Exposure*	pH	Soil
Anemone quinquefolia (wood anemone)	6–8	4–6"	LSh to PSh	4.5–6	Moist
Aquilegia canadensis (rock columbine)	5–7	1–2"	PSh	about 7	Dry in summer
Arisaema triphyllum (jack-in-the-pulpit)	5–8	1–3"	LSh to PSh	5.5–6.5	Humusy, moist
Cimicifuga racemosa (snakeroot, black cohosh)	5–7	3–8'	LSh to PSh	4–9	Moist
Claytonia virginica (spring beauty)	5–8	8–10"	LSh to PSh	6–8	Moist in spring, then dry
Cypripedium acaule (pink lady's slipper)	5–7	8–10"	Sh, LSh, PSh, or S	3.5–5	Fairly moist to dryish
C. calceolus var. *pubescens* (yellow lady's slipper)	5–8	1–1½'	LSh to PSh	5.5–7	Fairly moist to dryish
Epigaea repens (trailing arbutus)	4–8	2–3"	LSh	3.5–4.5	Moist
Erythronium americanum (eastern dogtooth violet)	4–8	4–10"	LSh to PSh	6.5–7.5	Moist in spring, then dry
E. oregonum (western dogtooth violet)	5–6	10–15"	PSh to S	6.5–7.5	Moist
E. revolutum (western dogtooth violet)	5.6	10–15"	PSh to S	6.5–7.5	Moist
E. tuolumnense (western dogtooth violet)	5–6	10–15"	PSh to S	6.5–7.5	Moist
Hepatica americana (liverleaf)	5–8	2–3"	PSh	6–8	Humusy, moist
Mertensia virginica (Virginia bluebell)	6–8	12–15"	LSh, PSh, or S	6.5–7.5	Moist
Phlox divaricata (wild blue phlox)	5–8	10–12"	LSh to PSh	6–8	Moderately moist
Sanguinaria canadensis (bloodroot)	4–8	3–6"	LSh to PSh	4–9	Humusy, moist
Trillium grandiflorum (white wake-robin)	5–7	1–1½'	LSh	6.5–7.5	Moist to fairly dry

* S, full sun; Sh, shade (no direct sun); PSh, partial shade (sun exposure only part of the day); LSh, light shade (e.g., the shade of tall, open trees, with little or no exposure to direct sun).

Jack-in-the-pulpit
(*Arisaema triphyllum*)

Spring beauty
(*Claytonia virginica*)

White wake-robin
(*Trillium grandiflorum*)

Virginia bluebell (*Mertensia virginica*)

Yellow lady's slipper (*Cypripedium. calceolus* var. *pubescens*)

NATIVE WOODLAND FLOWERS OF SPECIAL MERIT

Flower Color and Bloom Time	*Comments*
White; spring	Difficult to transplant; use container-grown material
Red and yellow; spring	Often self-sows; thrives in correct soil and exposure
Green and purplish; spring	Usually self-sows; forms clumps; red berries in late summer
White; mid to late summer	Divided foliage; impressive spires; best grown in clumps
White to pink; early spring	Self-sows; forms patches; foliage vanishes in early summer
Pink; spring	A challenge to cultivate; soil quality critical; use dormant container-grown material; summer mulch necessary; usually fails
Yellow and brown; spring	Not difficult; adapts to various soils; use container-grown material; grow in clumps
White; spring	Delicate creeper; difficult to establish; use container-grown material
Yellow; spring	Purchase dormant bulbs; spotted foliage vanishes after flowers
White and yellow; spring	See *E. americanum*
Pink and yellow; spring	See *E. americanum*
Yellow and green; spring	See *E. americanum*
Lilac to white; early spring	Evergreen; best grown in clumps; fairly adaptable
Pink buds, blue flowers; spring	Foliage vanishes in early summer; combines well with ferns
Lavender blue; spring	Adaptable; forms mats, covering large patches; good with spring bulbs
White; spring	Easily established; forms large clumps
White, aging to pink; spring	Easily established; plant dormant tubers in fall; best arranged in groups

OTHER PERENNIALS FOR THE WOODLAND GARDEN

Name	Zones	Height	Exposure*	pH	Soil
Actaea alba (doll's eyes)	5–7	2–2½'	LSh to PSh	4–9	Humusy, moist
A. rubra (red baneberry)	5–7	1–2'	LSh to PSh	4–9	Humusy, moist
Alchemilla mollis (lady's mantle)	4–7	1–2'	LSh, PSh, or S	5–7	Moist to fairly dry
Anemone canadensis (Canada anemone)	3–7	1–2'	LSh to PSh	4–9	Low, moist places
A. sylvestris (snowdrop windflower)	5–7	8–12"	LSh to PSh	5–6	Sandy-humusy
Anemonella thalictroides (rue anemone)	4–7	5–9"	LSh to PSh	4–9	Sandy-humusy
Aquilegia caerulea (Rocky Mountain columbine)	3–8	2–3'	LSh, PSh, or S	4.5–6.5	Sandy, or gravelly, moist
Astrantia major (masterwort)	5–7	2–3'	LSh to PSh	5–7	Moist, especially in summer
Bergenia cordifolia	3–8	10–12"	LSh to PSh	5–8	Moist
Campanula rotundifolia (bluebell)	3–7	6–18"	LSh, PSh, or S	6–8	Sandy or gravelly
Chrysogonum virginianum (golden star)	5–7	4–6"	LSh to PSh	5–7	Moist, especially in summer
Clintonia borealis	3–7	8–10"	LSh to PSh	3.5–5	Moist
Convallaria majalis (lily-of-the-valley)	3–8	6–9"	LSh, PSh, or S	4–9	Moist
Corydalis lutea (golden corydalis)	5–7	12–15"	LSh to PSh	5.5–7	Sandy-humusy
Cypripedium reginae (showy lady's slipper)	4–7	1½–2'	LSh to PSh	6–8	Wet ground
Dicentra canadensis (squirrel corn)	5–7	8–12"	LSh to PSh	5–8	Sandy-humusy; dryish
D. cucullaria (Dutchman's-breeches)	5–7	5–9"	LSh to PSh	6–8	Sandy or gravelly, dryish
D. eximia (fringed bleeding heart)	5–7	1–1½'	LSh to PSh	5–8	Sandy or gravelly
D. spectabilis (old-fashioned bleeding heart)	4–7	1½–2½'	LSh to PSh	5.5–6.5	Humusy, moist
Digitalis purpurea† (common foxglove)	6–8	3–6'	PSh to S	5.5–7	Sandy-humusy
Dodecatheon meadia (shooting star)	3–7	8–20"	LSh to PSh	6–8	Humusy, moist
Doronicum columnae (leopard's-bane)	5–7	1½–2'	LSh to PSh	5.5–6.5	Sandy-humusy
Galax urceolata	5–8	1–2'	PSh to S	4–6	Sandy, moist
Gaultheria procumbens (wintergreen, checkerberry)	4–7	2–5"	LSh to PSh	4–6	Sandy, dryish
Gentiana andrewsii (bottle gentian, closed gentian)	6–8	1–2'	LSh to PSh	6–8	Humusy, moist
Gentianopsis crinita (fringed gentian)	3–7	1–3'	LSh, PSh, or S	5.5–7	Humusy, wet
Geranium macrorhizum (cranesbill)	5–7	1½–2'	LSh to PSh	6–8	Sandy-humusy
Gillenia trifoliata (bowman's root)	5–7	2–4'	LSh to PSh	5–6	Humusy, moist
Habenaria ciliaris, syn. *Platanthera ciliaris* (yellow fringed orchis)	7–8	1½–2'	PSh to S	5.5–6.5	Sandy, moist
H. grandiflora, syn. *H. psycodes* var. *grandiflora* (large purple fringed orchis)	7–8	2½–5'	LSh to PSh	4–8	Wet, mucky ground
Hepatica acutiloba (liverleaf)	4–7	2–3"	LSh to PSh	6–8	Humusy, moist
Heuchera americana (alumroot)	4–8	1½–2'	LSh to PSh	4–9	Sandy, moist
H. sanguinea (coralbells)	3–7	1–2'	LSh, PSh, or S	4–9	Moist, especially in summer
Houstonia caerulea (Quaker ladies, bluets)	6–8	3–6"	PSh to S	4–6	Sandy, moist
Iris cristata (crested iris)	4–7	3–6"	LSh to PSh	4–9	Humusy, moist
I. verna (dwarf iris)	6–8	4–8"	LSh to PSh	3.5–5	Humusy, moist
Lobelia cardinalis (cardinal flower)	5–8	2–4'	LSh to PSh	5–7	Humusy, moist to wet
L. siphilitica (great blue lobelia)	5–8	2–4'	LSh to PSh	5–7	Humusy, moist
Lupinus perennis (blue lupine)	4–7	1–2'	PSh to S	4–9	Sandy, moist
Mitchella repens (partridgeberry)	3–7	2–3"	LSh to PSh	4–6	Humusy, moist
Mitella diphylla (bishop's cap)	3–8	8–12"	Sh to LSh	6–8	Humusy, moist
Myosotis laxa (forget-me-not)	6–8	6–12"	PSh to S	4–9	Sandy, moist
M. scorpioides (forget-me-not)	5–7	6–12"	PSh to S	4–9	Sandy, moist
Orchis spectabilis (showy orchis)	5–8	5–10"	LSh to PSh	4–9	Rocky, moist

OTHER PERENNIALS FOR THE WOODLAND GARDEN

Flower Color and Bloom Time	Comments
White; late spring	Decorative white berries in the summer
White; spring	Best in open woods; red berries in the summer
Yellow-green; spring	Forms clumps or mats; decorative foliage
White; spring to summer	Eventually forms large stands
White; spring	Attractive cut foliage
White or pale pink; spring	Forms patches in thin woodland
Blue and white; spring	Self-sows; relatively shortlived
Rose and pink-green; spring to summer	Bold foliage; thistlelike flowers
Pink; spring	Evergreen; large glossy foliage; forms clumps
Light purple; spring to summer	Forms clumps
Yellow; spring to summer	Interesting triangular leaves
Cream; spring	Requires very acidic ground
White; spring	Forms mats; very adaptable; fragrant flowers
Yellow; spring to summer	Finely cut gray green foliage
White with red; early summer	Requires permanently wet location
Greenish white; spring	Forms patches
White, yellow-tipped; spring	Forms clumps
Pink; spring	Forms clumps; often self-sows
Pink and or white; spring	Forms clumps; foliage vanishes by midsummer
Purple to white; spring to summer	Often self-sows; best grown in clumps
Pink and white; spring	Forms patches
Yellow; spring	Earliest daisy to flower
Yellow; spring to fall	Forms patches
White; late summer	Evergreen; red berries through winter
Violet blue; late summer to fall	Flowers scarcely open; good near ponds and streams
Blue; fall	Best in bogs and damp meadows
Magenta to white; spring	Foliage sticky, hairy; aromatic
White and dark red, summer	Leaves three parted
Orange-yellow; late summer	Best in wet meadows
Lilac pink; summer	Thrives in wet woods and swamps
Lilac; spring	Forms patches
Greenish white; late spring to summer	Forms clumps
Pink or white; spring to summer	Slender flower stalks rise above foliage
White with purple blush; spring to fall	Forms extensive stands in open areas
Purple with orange; spring	Forms dense clumps; winter protection advisable in North
Purple with orange; spring	Forms dense clumps
Red; summer	Thrives near ponds and streams
Blue; summer	Often forms extensive stands
Violet blue; late spring	Best in woodland borders and open areas
White and pink; late spring	Best in open woods and woodland borders
White; spring	Best in deep, damp woods
Blue; spring to early summer	Flowers small but numerous; good on stream banks
Blue; spring to early summer	Flowers larger than *M. laxa*
Rosy lavender and white; late spring	Thrives in rocky woodland

(continues)

OTHER PERENNIALS FOR THE WOODLAND GARDEN (*continued*)

Name	Zones	Height	Exposure*	pH	Soil
Podophyllum peltatum (mayapple)	4–8	1–1½'	LSh to PSh	4–9	Humusy, moist
Polemonium reptans (Jacob's ladder)	4–7	8–12"	LSh to PSh	6–8	Sandy, dryish
Polygonatum biflorum (Solomon's seal)	3–7	1½–2½'	LSh to PSh	4–9	Humusy, moist
P. commutatum (great Solomon's seal)	3–7	3–5'	LSh to PSh	4–9	Humusy, moist
Primula polyantha, P. vulgaris (primrose)	5–7	6–18"	LSh to PSh	6–8	Humusy, moist
Rodgersia pinnata	5–7	3–4'	LSh to PSh	5–7	Wet ground
Smilacina racemosa (false Solomon's seal)	4–8	2–3'	LSh, PSh, or S	6–8	Humusy, moist
Tricyrtis hirta (toad lily)	7–8	2–3'	LSh to PSh	6–8	Humusy, moist
Trillium sessile (toadshade)	5–7	10–12"	LSh to PSh	5–7	Humusy, moist
T. undulatum (painted trillium)	5–7	10–12"	LSh to PSh	5–7	Humusy, moist
Uvularia grandiflora (bellwort)	5–8	1½–2½'	LSh to PSh	6–8	Humusy, moist
Viola blanda (sweet white violet)	2–7	3–5"	LSh to PSh	6–8	Moist to dry
V. canadensis (Canada violet)	3–7	5–15"	LSh to PSh	6–8	Sandy, moist
V. conspersa (dog violet)	4–8	3–5"	LSh to PSh	4–9	Humusy, moist
V. palmata (common blue violet)	4–8	3–7"	LSh, PSh, or S	4–9	Humusy, moist to wet
V. pedata (bird's-foot violet)	4–7	4–8"	LSh, PSh, or S	4–6	Sandy, dryish

* S, full sun; Sh, shade (no direct sun); PSh, partial shade (sun exposure only part of the day); LSh, light shade (e.g., the shade of tall, open trees, with little or no exposure to direct sun).

Masterwort (*Astrantia major*)

Liverleaf (*Hepatica acutiloba*)

Bellwort
(*Uvularia grandiflora*)

Partridgeberry
(*Mitchella repens*)

False Solomon's seal (*Smilacina racemosa*)

OTHER PERENNIALS FOR THE WOODLAND GARDEN

Flower Color and Bloom Time	Comments
White; spring	Forms extensive stands
Blue-violet; spring	Forms clumps
Greenish white; spring	Forms clumps; flowers pendent along arching stem
Yellow-green; spring	Forms clumps; pendent purple berries in fall
Various colors; spring	Stalked flowers held above foliage; summer moisture needed
Pink; spring to summer	Best near pond or stream
Cream; spring	Showy red berries in the fall
White, speckled purple; fall	Arching stems; attractive foliage
Maroon to yellow-green; spring	Pungently fragrant flowers
White or rose; spring	Petals wavy; fruit capsule red in the fall
Yellow; spring	Forms clumps
White, purple veined; spring	Adaptable to wide range of conditions
White, tinged purple, late spring	Best in open upland woods
Pale blue-violet; spring	Best used in woodland borders
Purple; spring	Requires constant moisture
Lilac and purple; spring	Thrives in open thin woodland

Golden corydalis (*Corydalis lutea*)

Cardinal flower
(*Lobelia cardinalis*)

Canada violet
(*Viola canadensis*)

Great Solomon's seal
(*Polygonatum commutatum*)

Wintergreen
(*Gaultheria procumbens*)

Dutchman's-Breeches
(*Dicentra cucullaria*)

Showy orchis (*Orchis spectabilis*)

SHRUBS FOR THE WOODLAND GARDEN

All succeed in soil with pH 6.0 to 7.0, unless acidic (pH 5.5 to 6.5) soil is noted.

Name	Zones	Height	Exposure*	Soil
Acanthopanax sieboldianus (five-leaf aralia)	4–8	8–10'	Sh to LSh	Most any well-drained soil
Aesculus parviflora (bottlebrush buckeye)	4–8	8–12'	LSh	Well drained, moist
Amelanchier canadensis (shadbush)	4–9	6–20'	PSh to S	Dryish to wet
Aronia arbutifolia (red chokeberry)	4–9	6–9'	LSh to PSh	Well drained, moist
A. melanocarpa (black chokeberry)	3–8	4–6'	LSh, PSh, or S	Wet to dryish
Aucuba japonica (Japanese laurel)	7–10	6–8'	LSh to PSh	Well drained, moist
Berberis triacanthophora (three-spine barberry)	5–8	2–5'	PSh	Well drained, moist
B. verruculosa (warted barberry)	6–8	3–6'	PSh	Well drained, moist
Camellia japonica (common camellia)	7–9	6–12'	LSh to PSh	Well drained, moist
C. sasanqua (fall camellia)	7–10	6–12'	LSh	Well drained, moist
Ceonothus americanus (New Jersey tea)	4–8	3–4'	LSh	Sandy, dry
Clethra alnifolia (sweet pepperbush)	3–9	4–9'	LSh to PSh	Sandy or peaty, moist to wet
Cornus alba 'Sibirica' (red-stem dogwood)	2–8	5–10'	LSh to PSh	Well drained, moist to dry
C. amomum (silky dogwood)	5–8	6–10'	LSh to PSh	Well drained, moist to dry
C. racemosa (gray dogwood)	4–8	10–15'	LSh to PSh	Well drained, moist to dry
C. sericea 'Flaviramea' (yellow-stem dogwood)	2–8	6–8'	LSh to PSh	Well drained, moist to dry
Corylopsis pauciflora (buttercup winter hazel)	6–8	8–15'	LSh to PSh	Well drained, moist
Diervilla sessilifolia (southern bush honeysuckle)	4–8	3–5'	LSh to PSh	Sandy, dry
Dirca palustris (leatherwood)	4–9	3–6'	LSh to PSh	Wet, boggy ground
Enkianthus campanulatus (redvein enkianthus)	5–7	8–15'	LSh to PSh	Well drained, moist
Hamamelis × intermedia (hybrid witch hazel)	5–8	10–20'	PSh	Well drained, moist
H. japonica (Japanese witch hazel)	5–8	8–15'	PSh	Well drained, moist
H. mollis (Chinese witch hazel)	5–8	10–20'	PSh	Well drained, moist
H. vernalis (winter witch hazel)	5–8	6–12'	PSh	Well drained, moist
H. virginiana (autumn witch hazel)	3–10	15–25'	LSh to PSh	Well drained, moist
Hydrangea arborescens 'Grandiflora' (hills-of-snow)	3–9	3–5'	LSh to PSh	Well drained, moist
H. quercifolia (oak-leaf hydrangea)	5–9	4–6'	LSh to PSh	Well drained, moist
Hypericum prolificum (shrubby St. John'swort)	4–8	3–6'	LSh to PSh	Well drained, moist to dry
Ilex glabra (inkberry)	4–9	6–8'	LSh to PSh	Moist to wet
I. verticillata (winterberry)	3–9	6–10'	PSh to S	Moist to wet
Itea japonica (Japanese sweetspire)	5–9	2–2½'	LSh	Humusy, moist
I. virginica (Virginia sweetspire)	5–9	3–5'	LSh	Humusy, moist
Kalmia latifolia (mountain laurel)	4–9	6–15'	LSh to PSh	Moist to wet
Kerria japonica (sovereign bush)	4–9	4–6'	LSh to PSh	Well drained, moist
Leiophyllum buxifolium (sand myrtle)	5–7	1–1½'	PSh to S	Sandy, moist to dry
Leucothoë fontanesiana (drooping leucothoë)	4–7	3–5'	Sh to LSh	Humusy, moist
Lindera benzoin (spicebush)	5–8	6–12'	Sh to LSh	Humusy, moist
Lonicera fragrantissima (winter bush honeysuckle)	4–8	6–10'	PSh to S	Moist to dry
Mahonia aquifolium (Oregon hollygrape)	5–8	4–5'	LSh to PSh	Well drained, moist
Myrica pensylvanica (northern bayberry)	2–7	5–10'	LSh, PSh, or S	Moist to dry
Osmanthus heterophyllus (holly osmanthus)	7–9		LSh to PSh	Well drained, moist
Paxistima canbyi (cliff green)	3–8	about 1'	PSh to S	Well drained, moist to dry
Philadelphus coronarius (sweet mock orange)	4–8	10–12'	PSh to S	Well drained, moist
Pieris floribunda (fetterbush)	4–7	2–5'	LSh to PSh	Well drained, moist

SHRUBS FOR THE WOODLAND GARDEN

Flower Color and Bloom Time	Comments
Greenish; spring	Deciduous; very adaptable; thorny stems
White; summer	Deciduous; forms wide-spreading clumps
White; early spring	Deciduous; yellow fall foliage; fruit red, aging to violet black in late summer
Pinkish; spring	Deciduous; red fall foliage; fruit red
White; spring	Deciduous; red fall foliage; fruit black
Inconspicuous	Evergreen; females bear red berries in the fall
Yellow and red; spring	Evergreen; open habit; black berries in the fall
Yellow; spring	Evergreen; densely leafy; violet black berries in the fall
Red to white; spring	Evergreen; several cultivars hardy in zone 7
Red to white; fall	Evergreen; flowers smaller than in *C. japonica*
White; summer	Deciduous; thrives in dry summers
White; late summer	Deciduous; yellow fall foliage; flowers sweetly fragrant
Cream; late spring	Deciduous; bluish white berries in the fall; reddish stems in the winter
White; late spring	Deciduous; clusters of blue berries in the fall
Cream; late spring	Deciduous; clusters of pale blue to white berries in the fall
White; spring	Deciduous; white berries in the fall; yellow stems in the winter
Yellow; early spring	Deciduous; may bloom in late winter in South
Yellow; summer	Deciduous; thrives in dry summers
Yellow; early spring	Deciduous; flower small but effective on leafless twigs
Pinkish green; spring	Deciduous; red fall foliage
Yellow; late winter to early spring	Deciduous; lemon yellow fall foliage
Yellow to bronze; late winter to early spring	Deciduous; lemon yellow fall foliage
Yellow; late winter to early spring	Deciduous; lemon yellow fall foliage
Yellow; late winter to early spring	Deciduous; lemon yellow fall foliage
Yellow; fall	Deciduous; lemon yellow fall foliage coincides with flowers
White; summer	Deciduous; forms spreading clumps
White to pink; summer	Deciduous; red, orange, or purple fall foliage
Yellow; summer	Deciduous; unaffected by summer drought
Inconspicuous	Evergreen; black berries held through winter
Inconspicuous	Deciduous; red berries held through winter
White; summer	Deciduous; spreading habit
White; summer	Deciduous; red fall foliage; flowers fragrant
White to pink; late spring	Evergreen; thrives on rocky hillsides to pond borders
Yellow; spring to summer	Deciduous; forms clumps; green stems in the winter
Inconspicuous	Evergreen; fine-textured foliage
Whitish; spring	Evergreen; forms dense mound
Yellow; early spring	Deciduous; foliage fragrant when bruised, yellow in fall
Cream; early spring	Deciduous; lemon-scented flowers, appear well before leaves
Yellow; spring	Evergreen; glossy, prickly foliage; gray black berries in late summer and fall
Inconspicuous	Deciduous in early winter; foliage aromatic; females bear gray berries in the fall and winter
White; fall	Evergreen; foliage spine edged; flowers fragrant; fruit rare
Reddish; spring	Evergreen; good ground cover on steep slopes
White; spring	Deciduous; flowers fragrant
White to pink; spring	Evergreen; flower buds visible in winter

(continues)

SHRUBS FOR THE WOODLAND GARDEN (*continued*)

Name	Zones	Height	Exposure*	Soil
Prunus laurocerasus (cherry laurel)	6–9	6–12'	LSh to PSh	Well drained, moist
Rhododendron arborescens (sweet azalea)	4–8	9–12'	LSh to PSh	Humusy, moist, acidic
R. calendulaceum (flame azalea)	5–8	8–12'	LSh to PSh	Humusy, moist, acidic
R. canadense (rhodora)	2–7	2–3'	LSh to PSh	Moist, acidic
R. carolinianum (Carolina rhododendron)	5–8	6–9'	LSh to PSh	Humusy, moist, acidic
R. catawbiense (Catawba rhododendron)	4–8	6–18'	LSh to PSh	Humusy, moist, acidic
R. maximum (rosebay rhododendron)	4–8	15–30'	Sh, LSh, or PSh	Humusy, moist, acidic
R. minus (Piedmont rhododendron)	5–8	6–10'	LSh to PSh	Humusy, moist, acidic
R. periclymenoides (pinxterbloom)	3–8	8–10'	LSh to PSh	Humusy, moist, acidic
R. prinophyllum (rose-shell azalea)	3–8	2–8'	LSh to PSh	Sandy, moist
R. vaseyi (pink-shell azalea)	4–8	10–12'	LSh to PSh	Humusy, moist, acidic
R. viscosum (swamp azalea)	3–9	6–10'	LSh to PSh	Moist to wet, acidic
Rhodotypos scandens (jetbead)	4–8	3–6'	Sh, LSh, or PSh	Well drained, moist
Ribes alpinum (alpine currant)	2–7	3–6'	LSh to PSh	Well drained, moist
Sambucus canadensis (elder)	3–9	5–10'	LSh to PSh	Humusy, moist
Skimmia japonica (Japanese skimmia)	7–8	2–4'	LSh to PSh	Well drained, moist
S. reevesiana (Reeves' skimmia)	7–8	1½–2'	LSh to PSh	Well drained, moist
Taxus canadensis (Canadian yew)	2–6	3–6'	LSh to PSh	Well drained, moist
T. cuspidata (Japanese yew)	4–8	8–15'	LSh, PSh, or S	Well drained, moist
Tsuga canadensis 'Sargentii' (weeping hemlock)	3–7	6–12'	LSh, PSh, or S	Well drained, moist
Vaccinium angustifolium (lowbush blueberry)	2–7	1½–2'	LSh, PSh, or S	Sandy or rocky, dry
V. corymbosum (highbush blueberry)	3–7	6–12'	PSh to S	Moist to wet, acidic
V. vacillans (dwarf late blueberry)	6–8	1–2½'	LSh to PSh	Dry, acidic
Viburnum acerifolium (dockmackie)	3–8	5–8'	PSh	Dry, acidic
V. cassinoides (witherod viburnum)	3–8	6–10'	PSh	Moist to wet, acidic
V. dentatum (arrow-wood viburnum)	2–8	10–15'	LSh to PSh	Well drained, moist
V. lentago (nannyberry)	2–8	12–20'	PSh	Well drained, moist
V. prunifolium (plum-leaf viburnum)	3–9	10–15'	PSh	Well drained, moist

* S, full sun; Sh, shade (no direct sun); PSh, partial shade (sun exposure only part of the day); LSh, light shade (e.g., the shade of tall, open trees, with little or no exposure to direct sun).

Japanese skimmia (*Skimmia japonica*)

Mountain laurel (*Kalmia latifolia*)

SHRUBS FOR THE WOODLAND GARDEN

Flower Color and Bloom Time	Comments
White; spring	Evergreen; glossy foliage; black fruit
White; early summer	Deciduous; red fall foliage; requires summer moisture
Yellow to red; late spring	Deciduous; very showy flowers
Rosy purple; spring	Deciduous; very hardy but only marginally ornamental
White to pink; late spring	Evergreen; relatively small leaves
Rosy lilac; spring	Evergreen; large leaves roll up tightly in cold
White to pink; early summer	Evergreen; more shade tolerant than most rhododendrons
Rosy pink; early summer	Evergreen; summer moisture required
Pink; spring	Deciduous; often wider than it is tall
Pink; spring	Deciduous; thrives in neutral or even alkaline soil
Pink to orange; spring	Deciduous; very showy flowers
White to pink; early summer	Deciduous; best grown on permanently wet ground
White; spring	Deciduous; small black fruit; held in fours, in late summer and fall
Yellow-green; spring	Deciduous; densely leafy
White; early summer	Deciduous; purple fruit in late summer
Red in bud, opening white; spring	Evergreen; females bear red berries in the fall and winter
White; spring	Evergreen; open habit; females bear red berries in the fall and winter
Inconspicuous	Evergreen; spreading habit; females bear red berries in the summer
Inconspicuous	Evergreen; ascending habit; females bear red berries in the summer
Inconspicuous	Evergreen; branches spread and droop; attacked by adelgid in the Northeast
White; spring	Deciduous; red fall foliage; blue-black berries in the summer
White; spring	Deciduous; red fall foliage; blue-black berries in late summer
Purple; spring	Deciduous; red fall foliage; blue-black berries in the summer
White; late spring	Deciduous; black berries and pinkish foliage in the fall
White; spring	Deciduous; black berries in the fall
White; late spring	Deciduous; blue-black berries in the fall
White; spring	Deciduous; black berries in the fall
White; early spring	Deciduous; black berries in the fall

Sweet pepperbush (*Clethra alnifolia*)

Bottlebrush buckeye
(*Aesculus parviflora*)

New Jersey tea
(*Ceonothus americanus*)

Oak-leaf hydrangea (*Hydrangea quercifolia*)

SMALL DECIDUOUS UNDERSTORY TREES FOR THE WOODLAND GARDEN
All succeed with soil pH ranging from 5.5 to 7.0.

Name	Zones	Height	Comments
Acer circinnatum (vine maple)	5–7	15–30'	Long horizontal branches; red or orange fall foliage
A. griseum (paperbark maple)	4–8	20–30'	Three-parted leaves; attractive peeling orange-brown bark
A. palmatum (Japanese maple)	6–8	15–25'	Very adaptable; cultivars with reddish to purple leaves
A. pensylvanicum (striped maple)	3–7	15–20'	Stems green, eventually white striped
Amelanchier arborea (downy serviceberry)	4–9	15–25'	Hanging clusters of white flowers in early spring before leaves
A. × grandiflora (apple serviceberry)	4–7	15–25'	Leaves purplish when expanding; pink buds open as white flowers in early spring
A. laevis (Allegheny serviceberry)	4–8	15–25'	White flowers in spring as bronzy foliage expands
Carpinus carolinianum (American hornbeam)	2–9	20–30'	Fluted "muscular" swellings develop on expanding trunk
Chionanthus virginicus (fringe tree)	3–9	12–20'	Abundance of pendant white flowers in late spring; often stays shrubby
Cornus alternifolia (pagoda dogwood)	3–7	15–25'	Layered branching; 2½-inch-wide heads of cream flowers in the spring
C. florida (flowering dogwood, eastern dogwood)	5–9	20–30'	Showy white four-bracted flower heads in the spring before leaves; older trees subject to anthracnose
C. kousa (Japanese dogwood)	5–8	20–30'	Flower heads surrounded by four cream to white pointed bracts in late spring, after leaves expand; immune to anthracnose
Crataegus laevigata (English hawthorn)	4–7	15–20'	Thorny; white flowers in spring
Halesia carolina (silver bell)	4–9	20–30'	Pendant, white, bell-shaped flowers in the spring
Magnolia × soulangiana (saucer magnolia)	4–9	20–30'	Large purplish to white flowers in the spring before leaves expand
Ostrya virginiana (hop hornbeam)	3–9	25–40'	Nuts borne in winged hoplike enclosure
Oxydendrum arboreum (sorrel tree)	5–9	25–30'	Orange to purple fall color, especially in partial shade; multitude of andromedalike flower clusters in the summer;
Styrax japonicus (Japanese snowbell)	5–8	20–30'	Hanging, white, bell-shaped flowers in early summer
S. obassia (fragrant snowbell)	5–8	20–30'	Drooping clusters of fragrant white flowers in the spring

FERNS FOR THE WOODLAND GARDEN
Except where noted, soil should be acidic (pH 5.0 to 6.5).

Name	Zones	Height	Exposure*	Soil	Comments
Adiantum capillus-veneris (southern maidenhair fern)	7–9	1½–2'	LSh to Sh	Well drained, moist	Deciduous
A. pedatum (northern maidenhair fern)	3–8	1½–2'	LSh to Sh	Moist to wet	Deciduous
Asplenium platyneuron (ebony spleenwort)	5–10	6–12"	LSh to PSh	Rocky, moist	Evergreen
A. rhizophyllum (walking fern)	6–8	6–12"	Sh to LSh	Rocky	Evergreen; best on limestone outcrops or cliffs
A. trichomanes (maidenhair spleenwort)	2–6	6–12"	Sh	Rocky	Evergreen; thrives in soil-filled clefts; becomes tattered in late summer
Athyrium felix-femina (lady fern)	2–9	2–3'	LSh, PSh, or S	Humusy, well drained	Deciduous
A. pycnocarpon (narrowleaf spleenwort)	7–8	2–3'	LSh to PSh	Humusy, well drained	Deciduous
Botrychium virginianum (rattlesnake fern)	6–10	1–2'	LSh to PSh	Well drained	Deciduous; best in open woodland
Cystopteris bulbifera (berry bladder fern)	3–8	1–2'	Sh to LSh	Moist to wet	Deciduous
Dennstaedtia punctilobula (hayscented fern)	3–8	1½–2'	LSh to S	Well drained, moist	Deciduous; can be invasive
Dryopteris clintoniana (Clinton shield fern)	4–8	2–3'	LSh to Sh	Well drained, moist	Evergreen

FERNS FOR THE WOODLAND GARDEN *(continued)*

Name	Zones	Height	Exposure*	Soil	Comments
D. cristata (crested shield fern)	3–7	1–2'	Sh	Wet	Deciduous in zones 3 to 5, evergreen in zones 6 and 7; best on permanently wet hummocks in grassy bogs
D. dilatata (mountain shield fern)	5–8	1½–2'	Sh		Evergreen; best on steep slopes
D. intermedia (toothed wood fern)	3–8	2–3'	Sh to LSh	Well drained, moist	Evergreen
D. marginalis (marginal shield fern)	3–8	2–3'	LSh to PSh	Well drained, moist	Evergreen
Gymnocarpium dryopteris (oak fern)	3–8	about 6"	Sh to LSh	Well drained, moist	Deciduous
Lygodium palmatum (climbing fern)	5–8	3–4'	PSh	Well drained, most	Deciduous; best in woodland borders; climbs by twining elongating leaves
Matteuccia pennsylvanica (ostrich fern)	4–8	4–8'	LSh to PSh	Well drained, moist	Deciduous
M. struthiopteris (ostrich fern)	2–7	4–6'	LSh to S	Moist to wet	Deciduous
Phegopteris connectilis, syn. *Thelypteris connectilis* (narrow beech fern)	5–8	6–12"	Sh	Wet	Deciduous; good for stream banks
P. hexagonoptera, syn. *Thelypteris hexagonoptera* (beech fern)	5–8	about 1'	LSh	Humusy, moist, well drained	Deciduous

* S, full sun; Sh, shade (no direct sun); PSh, partial shade (sun exposure only part of the day); LSh, light shade (e.g., the shade of tall, open trees, with little or no exposure to direct sun).

Ostrich fern
(*Matteuccia pennsylvanica*)

Sorrel tree
(*Oxydendrum arboreum*)

Climbing fern
(*Lygodium japonicum*)

*Hay-scented fern (*Dennstaedtia punctilobula*) makes a fresh green carpet in partial shade, but often to the exclusion of less competitive species.*

Crested shield fern (*Dryopteris cristata*)

GROUND COVERS FOR THE WOODLAND GARDEN

Name	Zones	Height	Exposure*	pH	Comments
Ajuga reptans (bugle)	4–7	4"†	PSh to S	5–9	Forms mats; glossy foliage; violet blue flowers in the spring; can be invasive in lawns
Asarum europaeum (European ginger)	5–7	4–6"	LSh to PSh	5.5–6.5	Evergreen; forms mats; glossy foliage
Convallaria majalis (lily-of-the-valley)	4–8	6–8"	LSh to PSh‡	5–9	Fragrant white flowers in the spring
Cornus canadensis (bunchberry)	2–7	3–9"	PSh	4–6	Forms mats; diminutive dogwood; white-bracted flowers in early spring; difficult except where summers are cool
Epimedium spp. (bishop's hat)	5–8	8–12"	Sh to LSh	5–7	Foliage persists to late fall or early winter; red, yellow, or white flowers in the spring
Galium odoratum (sweet woodruff)	5–8	4–6"	LSh to PSh	4.5–8	Fine-textured foliage; white flowers in the spring
Gaultheria procumbens (wintergreen)	4–7	4–6"	LSh to Sh	4.5–6	Thrives on sandy soil
Hedera canariensis (Canary ivy)	9–10	6–12"	Sh to S	4–8	Evergreen; forms extensive mats; glossy foliage; will climb trees
H. helix (English ivy)	4–9	4–8"	Sh to S	3–9	Evergreen; forms extensive mats; dark green foliage; many foliar cultivars; will climb trees
Hosta spp. (plantain lily)	4–8	6–12"	PSh to LSh		Forms large clumps; leaves ribbed, glossy; many foliar cultivars; lavender or white flowers in summer or early fall
Lamiastrum galeobdolon 'Variegatum' (yellow dead nettle)	5–8	6–12"	LSh to S	5–7	Drought tolerant; variegated foliage, retained into winter; yellow flowers in the spring
Lamium maculatum (spotted dead nettle)	4–7	6–10"	PSh	5–8	Variegated foliage (especially in some cultivars); pink or white flowers in the spring
Liriope spicata (creeping lilyturf)	5–9	8–10"	LSh	5–8	Evergreen; forms clumps; narrow, leathery foliage; spikes of lavender flowers in the summer
Lysimachia nummularia (creeping Jenny, creeping Charlie)	4–7	2–3"	PSh to S	4–9	Prostrate habit; yellow flowers in the spring; good around stepping-stones or along paths; can be invasive in lawns
Mahonia repens (creeping mahonia)	5–8	2–4"	LSh to PSh	5–8	Evergreen; diminutive Oregon hollygrape
Mazus reptans (creeping mazus)	3–7	2–4"	PSh	5–7	Forms mats; violet blue flowers in the spring; good along paths
Mitchella repens (partridgeberry)	3–7	1–2"	Sh to LSh	4.5–6	Evergreen; dark green foliage; cream flowers in the spring, followed by persistent red berries
Ophiopogon japonicus (mondo grass)	7–10	8–12"	Sh to LSh	5–8	Evergreen; forms mats; dark foliage; thrives on moist to wet ground; lilac to white flowers in the summer
Pachysandra procumbens (Allegheny pachysandra)	7–8	6–9"	LSh to PSh	5–7	Foliage dies down in the winter; cream flowers in the spring
P. terminalis (common pachysandra)	5–8	6–9"	Sh to PSh	5–7	Evergreen; forms dense mats; glossy foliage; best on moist, humusy soil; small cream flowers in the spring
Vinca minor (creeping myrtle)	3–8	4–6"	LSh to PSh	5–8	Evergreen; forms dark green mats; lavender blue flowers in the spring
Xanthorhiza simplicissima (yellowroot)	3–9	1–3'	Sh to PSh	5–6	Forms mats; shrub; attractive cut foliage, turns yellow to purple in the fall

---

* S, full sun; Sh, shade (no direct sun); PSh, partial shade (sun exposure only part of the day); LSh, light shade (e.g., the shade of tall, open trees, with little or no exposure to direct sun).

† In flower, height is 6 to 12 inches.

‡ In the South, best in light to dense shade.

WOODY CLIMBERS FOR THE WOODLAND GARDEN

Name	Zones	Height	Exposure*	pH	Comments
Akebia quinata (five-leaf akebia)	4–8	20–40'	LSh to PSh	4–8	Foliage retained well into winter; maintenance free; forms dense thickets in shrubby undergrowth
Ampelopsis brevipedunculata (porcelain vine)	4–8	15–25'	LSh to S	4–9	Fast-growing tendril climber; clustered blue berries in the fall
Aristolochia durior (Dutchman's-pipe)	4–8	20–30'	PSh	5–7	Twiner; large, circular, overlapping leaves
Celastrus scandens (American bittersweet)	3–8	15–30'	PSh to S	4–9	Vigorous twiner; females bear three-lobed fruit with red seeds in the fall; preferable to the invasive *C. orbiculata*
Clematis spp. and cvs.	3–8	10–15'	LSh to PSh	5–7.5	Climbs by clasping leaf stalks; flower color and bloom time vary with cultivar
Euonymus fortunei (wintercreeper)	5–9	40–70'	Sh to S	4–9	Evergreen; rootlet climber; foliage lustrous
Hedera spp. (ivy)	4–10	20–50'	Sh to PSh†	3–9	Evergreen; rootlet climber; glossy foliage; clustered black berries in the winter
Hydrangea anomala ssp. *petiolaris* (climbing hydrangea)	4–7	20–50'	LSh to PSh	5.5–7	Rootlet climber; peeling red-brown bark; white flowers in early summer; slow to establish
Parthenocissus quinquefolia (Virginia creeper)	3–10	25–50'	Sh to S	4–9	Tendril climber; red fall foliage; clustered blue-black berries in the fall
Polygonum aubertii (silver-lace vine)	4–7	25–35'	PSh to S	5–7	Vigorous twiner; white flowers in the summer
Vitis riparia (frost grape)	2–8	25–75'	LSh to S	5–7	Fast-growing tendril climber; black fruit in late summer
Wisteria spp.	4–9	20–30'	PSh	5–8	Twiner; best in woodland margin where flowers can be seen; pendent clusters of lavender or white flowers in the spring

* S, full sun; Sh, shade (no direct sun); PSh, partial shade (sun exposure only part of the day); LSh, light shade (e.g., the shade of tall, open trees, with little or no exposure to direct sun).

† Will tolerate full sun in the North.

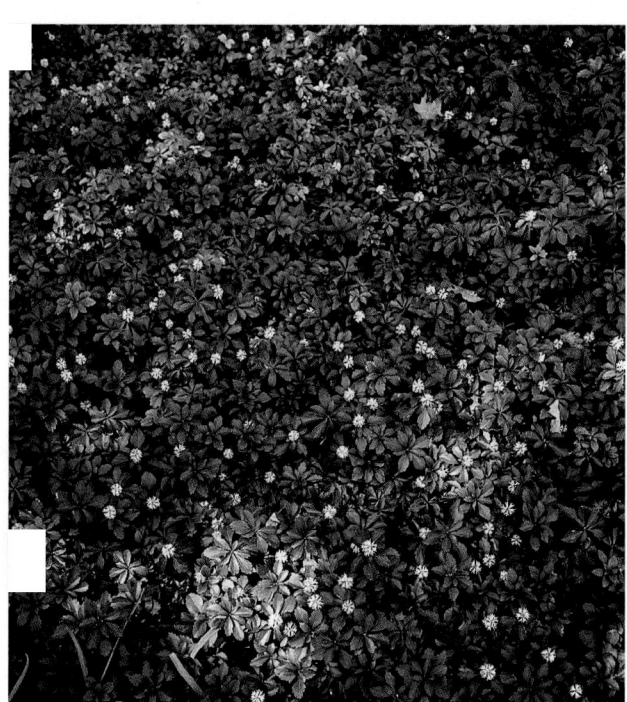

Allegheny pachysandra (*Pachysandra procumbens*)

Plantain lily
(*Hosta* sp.)

Bunchberry
(*Cornus canadensis*)

Spotted dead nettle
(*Lamium maculatum*)

Virginia creeper (*Parthenocissus quinquefolia*)

23

Water and Bog Gardens

A BODY OF FRESH WATER, WHETHER POOL, POND, STREAM, brook, or bog, offers a dimension to gardening that enriches the entire plant-growing experience. Since plants that grow in or close to water rarely occur elsewhere, the catalog of kinds is unique, and it includes many jewels of horticulture.

Naturally occurring, self-maintaining water bodies are easiest to include in the overall garden picture, since many of the basic plant materials are likely already in place: the major trees, shrubs, and various wild perennials and water plants

Even the smallest stream can be an excellent starting point for rudimentary water and bog plants.

565

that require saturated soil. In the case of a stream or brook, allowance must be made for seasonal variation in water flow, including occasional (or even regular) flooding. Gardening under such conditions may focus on one or more points of access, with vistas and paths developed to lure the eye (and ear) to the water itself and to the special plants nearby, both native and introduced.

In a setting cleared of trees, however, the body of water is already preeminent. Designing a garden here may involve framing the focal point with suitable trees, shrubs, and smaller plants or simply providing touches of color and texture to grace the setting and lend seasonal interest. Still water, as in a pool, pond, or dam-impounded creek, offers a reflective surface, mirroring everything that grows nearby and doubling the effect of a tree in full bloom, bed of summer annuals, or a woodland border in full foliar finery.

In a bog or swamp, the natural filling in of a one-time pond or lake has reached an advanced stage, with most of the water displaced by soil and root mats. But these sodden, often strongly acidic conditions are a substrate for yet another suite of specialized plants, some highly ornamental and not to be found or cultivated elsewhere.

For most gardeners, however, a body of water is a special garden appurtenance that must be planned and constructed (see Chapter 8). This chapter deals with gardening opportunities presented by various aquatic sites, both naturally occurring and specially made.

WATER-LILIES

It is often assumed that so exquisite a flower as a water-lily is difficult to grow and that it requires special care. Actually, once it is established, the hardy water-lily thrives with little attention. Some of the species are native to this country and are common in the quiet waters of inland ponds. The tender tropical kinds, including the Egyptian lotus (*Nymphaea caerulea*), need more care and may simply be grown as annuals and replaced each year or removed to a greenhouse for the winter. A possible alternative is a heated pool, which can substantially extend the outdoor season for tender species.

It is commonly believed that water-lilies require abundant space and that there must be a pond of considerable size in which to raise them. While the larger species spread to a circle about 6 feet across, the dwarf species, with small leaves and exquisitely small flowers, are suitable for garden pools little more than 3 or 4 feet in diameter. Such pools can be created from the same kind of heavy polyethylene sheeting that is used in backyard swimming pools, or variously shaped fiberglass pools can be purchased (see Chapter 8).

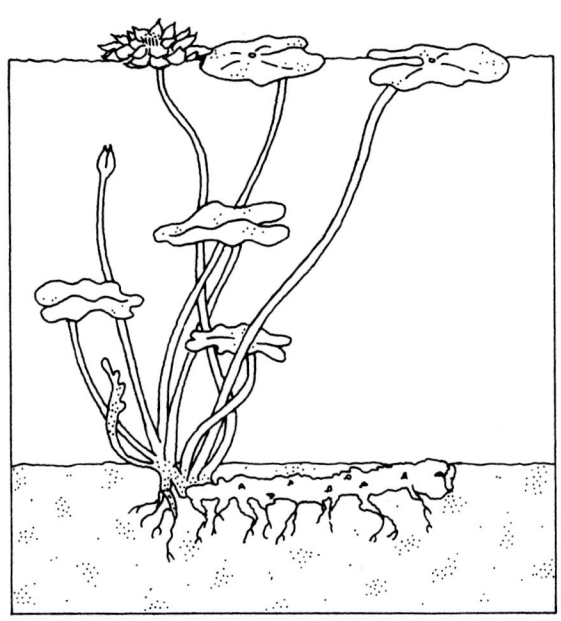

Water-lily habit, showing the rooted horizontal stem or rhizome, its tip bearing the typically circular, cleft leaves and showy flowers, both borne on elongating stalks.

Hardy Water-lilies of Merit

The fragrant water-lily, or fragrant pond lily (*Nymphaea odorata*), is the common white-flowered pond lily of the northern states and is perfectly hardy (zones 3 to 8) and dependable. The floating leaves are dark green, and the flowers, also floating, are about 4 inches across, with white upcurved petals surrounding the central mass of yellow stamens.

Equally useful are any of several naturally occurring varieties, including the following.

N. odorata var. *caroliniana:* leaves up to 1 foot across; flowers rose pink.
N. odorata var. *minor:* leaves small; flowers about 2½ inches across, white.
N. odorata var. *rosea* (Cape Cod water-lily): flowers pink.

Many hybrid cultivars of *N. odorata* are also readily available and deservedly popular.

'Aurora': flowers yellow, aging to red.
'Helen Fowler': flowers 4 to 6 inches across, deep pink, fragrant, held above the water.
'Yellow Pigmy': flowers 3 inches across, yellow.

Other hardy hybrid cultivars include the following.

N. × 'Gladstoniana': flowers 6 to 8 inches across, pure white.

Nymphaea × marliacea *var.* chromatella, *deservedly one of the most popular hardy yellow water-lilies.*

N. × *marliacea* var. *albida:* flowers held above the water, white with the outermost petal-like sepals flushed pink.
N. × *marliacea* var. *chromatella:* flowers canary yellow with deeper yellow stamens.
N. × *marliacea* var. *rosea:* flowers pink.
N. × 'Pink Opal': leaves bronzy, flowers pink to coral red.

Meritorious hybrids of other (sometimes unknown) parentage include the following. All are day blooming.

'Aquarius': flowers red, the outer petals white tipped.
'Attraction': flowers garnet red.
'Commanche': leaves purple when young; flowers rose to apricot.
'Gonnere': 'Crystal White', or 'Snowball': flowers white.
'Helvola': leaves blotched brown; flowers yellow.
'Paul Harriet': flowers yellow, aging to red.
'Pink Sensation', flowers pink, fragrant, held above the water.
'Rose Arey': leaves reddish; flowers rose pink, anise scented.

Some tropical day-blooming water-lily cultivars offer unusual colors and shades, such as purple in 'Mrs. M. E. Randig' and blue in 'August Koch', 'Henry Shaw', and 'Mrs. Edwards Whitaker' (which has lavender blue flowers that age to silver blue). Night-blooming tropical hybrids are available in red and pink, but only the white-flowered forms, such as 'Missouri', 'Sir Galahad', and 'Wood's White Knight,' are effective in dim light.

N. 'Aquarius', a hardy hybrid water-lily in which some of the red petals are white-tipped.

Nymphaea *'Evelyn Randing'*

Cutaway showing structure of a water-lily tub made from a half barrel. Tubs of plastic or fiberglass serve equally well.

Propagation by Seed

Sow the water-lily seed in pans of sand. Cover the seed lightly with screened sand and place the pan in water at a temperature of 70° to 80°F in such a way that the surface of the sand is above the water but in contact with it. After soaking them all day, submerge the pans to a depth of 18 inches or more. After the plants have formed the first floating leaf, usually within two or three weeks, they may be transplanted to flats with 2 inches of soil containing well-rotted cow manure. Thereafter the young plants should be potted as they develop and require more space.

Cultural Requirements

The requirements for water-lily culture are quiet water with a trickling inlet and outlet and full sunshine. The soil may be a mixture of two parts ordinary garden soil and one part well-rotted cow manure or, if natural sources are available, a mixture of equal parts garden soil and pond muck. If neither manure nor muck is obtainable, ½ quart of bone meal per plant may be mixed with the soil.

For convenience in keeping the pool neat, the soil should be placed in tubs, half barrels, or boxes. Perforated plastic or fiberglass is lighter and longer lasting than the cedar or cypress containers previously favored. The soil bed should be about 1 foot deep and so placed that its surface is 1 to 1½ feet below the surface of the water. In planting, the tub is half-filled with soil, and the tuber placed on the soil so that the growing end is pointed upward and about level with the rim of the tub, being held in this position while more soil is filled in around it. The upper 1 or 2 inches should consist of sand. When planting water-lilies in a natural pond, squeeze the tubers down into the muck of the bottom. If the muck does not hold them and they float instead, the tubers should

Section through a dug water-lily pool, showing the stepped terraces for potted and tubbed aquatics, and covered with a plastic liner that is trimmed and weighted with coping stones.

be pinned down with a curved wire. A suitably sized wire or plastic basket is an ideal planting container for natural ponds. Such baskets hold the plants in place, yet at the same time give the roots an opportunity to grow outward into the soil. The best time for planting is early spring.

Winter Care

Once established, hardy water-lilies require no special care. To carry hardy water-lilies through the winter, the only protection necessary is the muck and the water above them. If the ice does not freeze to the bottom where the tubers are, no harm will be done to them.

The pool itself may be protected against ice pressure in several ways. If it is small, it may be covered with boards, logs, or blocks of Styrofoam. This will not only offset the often destructive effects of ice pressure on vertical or nearly vertical pool walls but, if overspread with an insulating blanket of dry leaves and evergreen boughs, will limit the depth of ice and thus minimize any loss of water-lily tubers and rhizomes to freezing. As severe winter weather abates, and well before normal spring growth begins, such insulation should be removed as it can induce premature growth that cannot survive ordinary early spring frosts.

Tropical water-lilies are usually treated as annuals and replaced each year. If greenhouse space is available, however, they may be lifted in their pots or tubs, moved indoors, and immersed in a shallow pool or improvised bathtub for the winter in a sunny location. The water temperature should be kept at 70°F.

OTHER AQUATIC PLANTS

Other aquatic plants that are ornamental in pools or at the margins of ponds and that complement water-lilies include floating heart (*Nymphoides peltata*), primrose willow (*Ludwigia longifolia*), water hyacinth (*Eichhornia crassipes*), and umbrella palm (*Cyperus alternifolius*). Plants that help keep water clear by oxygenating it include cabomba (*Cabomba caroliniana*), water weed (*Elodea callitrichoides*), and water milfoil (*Ceratophyllum demersum* and *Myriophyllum* spp.).

The shore and adjacent shallow water of a pond become very ornamental when graced with groups of such plants as arrowhead (*Sagittaria* spp., especially *S. latifolia*), pickerelweed (*Pontederia cordata*), yellow flag (*Iris pseudacorus*), and blue flag (*Iris versicolor*), especially if backed with ornamental waterside shrubs.

Water hyacinth (*Eichhornia crassipes*)

FLOATING AQUATICS

Roots, when present, are suspended in the water. The leaves and flowers are at the surface. Best grown in full sun or partial shade.

Name	Zones	Flower Color and Bloom Time	Comments
Azolla caroliniana (mosquito fern)	7–8		Small, disclike foliage; survives winter as minute buds; can be invasive
Ceratopteris thalictroides (water fern)	10		Foliage polymorphic (in various forms)
Eichhornia crassipes (water hyacinth)	10	Lavender purple and yellow; summer	Floats by inflated leaf stalks; invasive in the Southeast; should be containered in zones 9 and 10
Lemna minor (duckweed)	4–8	Inconspicuous	Tiny discs quickly multiply and cover water surface in the summer; can be invasive
Pistia stratiotes (water lettuce)	10	Inconspicuous	Rosette of ribbed leaves; best in full sun with water temperature 60°F or higher and pH 6.5 to 7
Salvinia spp.	10		Discs with modified rootlike leaves hanging beneath in water
Utricularia spp. (bladderwort, hardy aquatic species)	2–10	Yellow; summer	Finely dissected, submerged leaves; minute bladders that capture tiny water animals

PERENNIALS FOR WET PLACES

Pond borders, stream banks, and similar locations, with permanently moist to wet acidic soil, sometimes subject to periodic or occasional flooding.

Name	Zones	Height	Exposure*	Flower Color and Bloom Time	Comments
Acorus calamus (sweet flag)	3–7	3–5'	S to PSh	Yellow; late spring to summer	Bold, aromatic, irislike foliage; few flowers when not in water
A. gramineus 'Variegatus' (striped sweet flag)	5–8	1–2'	S to PSh	Yellowish; late spring to summer	Glossy, sedgelike variegated foliage
Arisaema triphyllum (jack-in-the-pulpit)	4–8	1½–2½'	LSh to PSh	Green to brown-violet; spring to early summer	Forms colonies; two three-parted leaves; clustered red fruit in late summer
Asclepias incarnata (swamp milkweed)	3–7	3–5'	S to PSh	White to pink; early summer	Swollen silk-filled seed pods
Astilbe × arendsii	5–8	1½–4'	PSh	Deep red-violet to white; late spring to summer	Forms clumps; best when massed
Caltha palustris (marsh marigold)	3–7	6–12"	S to LSh	Yellow; spring	Dies back to roots in summer
Carex stricta 'Aurea' (golden sedge)	8–10	1–2'	LSh to PSh	Inconspicuous	Yellow foliage; *C. morrowii* 'Evergold' is similar
Chelone glabra (turtlehead)	3–8	2–3'	S to PSh	Deep rose; summer	Spreads, forming clumps
C. lyonii (white turtlehead)	3–8	2–3'	S to PSh	Pinkish to white; summer	Spreads; forming clumps
Darmera peltata (Indian rhubarb, umbrella plant)	6–7	4–6'	LSh to PSh	Pink to white; spring	Forms mats; large leaves; best in cool-summer areas
Dodecatheon spp. (shooting star)	3–7	1–2'	LSh to PSh	Pink or red and/or white; spring to early summer	Very effective when massed
Drosera linearis (narrow-leaf sundew)	3–7	3–6"	LSh to PSh	White; summer	Best in sandy pond borders; the annual *D. rotundifolia* is similar
Eupatorium dubium (joe-pye weed)	4–8	5–8'	S to PSh	Pinkish purple; late summer	*E. fistulosum* and *E. purpureum* are similar
Filipendula palmata (meadowsweet)	2–7	2–3'	S to PSh	White and red; summer	Several cultivars with all-white to deep rose flowers
F. ulmaria (queen of the meadow)	2–7	4–6'	S to PSh	Cream; summer	Some cultivars with yellow or variegated foliage
Helenium autumnale (sneezeweed)	3–8	2–6'	S	Yellow to bronzy; fall	Height varies with cultivar
Hibiscus coccineus (scarlet rose mallow)	7–9	6–8'	S to PSh	Deep red; summer	Tolerates fairly dry soil in summer
H. moscheutos (rose mallow)	5–8	3–8'	S to PSh	Red, pink, or white; summer	Several dwarf, large-flowered cultivars
Hypericum anagalloides (creeping St. John'swort)	7–10	3–6"	S to PSh	Yellow; summer	Creeping; forms mats; best in cool-summer areas
Iris ensata (Japanese water iris)	5–8	2–3'	S to PSh	Purple and yellow; summer	Many cultivars with deep purple to white flowers
I. laevigata (late water iris)	5–8	2–4'	S to PSh	Blue-violet and yellow; summer to early fall	Some cultivars with purple to white flowers; cv. 'Variegata' has white-and-green striped foliage
I. × 'Louisiana hybrids' (Louisiana iris)	(6) 7–9	3–4'	S to PSh	Yellow to black-violet; late spring to summer	Many cultivars with wide range of flower colors and combinations
I. prismatica (narrow-leaf blue flag)	4–8	2–3'	S to PSh	Blue-violet and whitish; late spring to summer	Similar to *I. versicolor* but more slender
I. pseudacorus (yellow flag)	5–8	4–6'	S to PSh	Yellow; summer	Cv. 'Variegata' has cream-and-green striped foliage
I. versicolor (blue flag)	3–7	2–3'	S to PSh	Blue-violet and yellow; summer	Flowers best in full sun
Juncus effusus 'Spiralis' (spiral rush)	4–8	4–6'	S to PSh	Greenish, inconspicuous; summer	Grown for corkscrew growth habit

Name	Zones	Height	Exposure*	Flower Color and Bloom Time	Comments
Kosteletzkya virginica (salt marsh mallow)	(7) 8–10	3–4'	S to PSh	Pink; summer	Thrives in brackish marshland
Ligularia dentata (ragwort)	3–8	3–4'	S to PSh	Yellow; summer	Bold foliage wilts in summer sun; cvs. 'Desdemona' and 'Othello' are similar
L. przewalskii (tall ragwort)	3–8	4–6'	S to PSh	Yellow; summer	*L.* 'The Rocket' is similar
Limnocharis flava (water poppy)	10	1½–2'	S to PSh	Yellow; summer	Neutral or mildly acidic medium (pH 6.5–7) is best
Lobelia cardinalis (cardinal flower)	3–7	2–3'	PSh to LSh	Scarlet; late summer to early fall	Short lived; self-sows
L. siphilitica (great blue lobelia)	4–7	2–3'	S to PSh	Blue or white; summer	More tolerant of temporarily dry conditions than *L. cardinalis*
Lysichiton americanum (yellow skunk cabbage)	6–7	1½–3'	LSh to PSh	Yellow; early spring	Flowers before leaves, emits skunky odor
Lysimachia clethroides (gooseneck loosestrife)	4–8	2–3'	S, PSh, or LSh	White; summer	Forms extensive clumps or patches
L. nummularia (creeping Jenny, creeping Charlie)	4–8	prostrate	LSh to PSh	Yellow; spring	Rampant mat-forming creeper
L. punctata (yellow loosestrife)	4–8	2–3'	S to PSh	Yellow; late spring to early summer	Forms extensive clumps or patches
Matteuccia struthipteris (ostrich fern)	2–7	3–7'	LSh to PSh		Forms dense colonies
Mimulus lewisii (purple monkey flower)	5–7	1½–3'	S to PSh	Magenta; summer	Flowers occasionally white
M. moschatus (musk flower)	7–9	1–2"	S to PSh	Yellow; summer	Forms extensive stands; usually with musky scent
Mitella spp. (bishop's cap)	(3) 5–7	6–24"	LSh to PSh	Green to yellow; late spring to summer	Self-sows, forming patches
Myosotis scorpioides (perennial forget-me-not)	5–8	1–2'	S to PSh	Blue; spring to summer	Long blooming period; tolerates summer drought
Onoclea sensibilis (sensitive fern)	4–8	1½–2½'	S to PSh	Brown spore-bearing fronds; summer through winter	Carpets large areas; persistent spore fronds
Orontium aquaticum (golden club)	(7) 8–9	about 1'	S to PSh	Yellow; late spring to summer	Forms dense colonies at water's edge
Osmunda cinnamomea (cinnamon fern)	3–10	3–6'	S to PSh	Light brown spore-bearing fronds; spring to summer	Forms clumps and elevated hummocks
O. claytoniana (interrupted fern)	3–8	2–3'	PSh to LSh		Spores borne on special divisions of fronds; tolerates dry summer conditions
O. regalis (royal fern)	2–8	3–6'	S, PSh, or LSh		Best in continuous wetness; very variable
Primula beesiana (candelabrum primrose)	5–7	1–2'	PSh to LSh	Red and yellow; spring	Flowers densely grouped on stalks above basal foliage
P. bulleyana (Yunnan primrose)	6–7	1½–2½'	PSh	Orange; spring	Parent with *P. beesiana* of *P.* × *bulleesiana* hybrids
P. florindae (Himalayan primrose)	6–7	2–2½'	PSh to LSh	Yellow; spring to summer	Several orange- or red-flowered cultivars
P. japonica (Japanese primrose)	5–7	1½–2'	PSh to LSh	Red to white; late spring	Intolerant of summer heat
P. pulverulenta (slender primrose)	6–7	2–2½'	PSh to LSh	Red and purple; summer	Pastel shades in cv. 'Bartley' hybrids
Ranunculus repens 'Flore Pleno' (creeping double buttercup)	3–7	1–1½'	S to PSh	Yellow; spring	Spreads rapidly; can be invasive

(continues)

PERENNIALS FOR WET PLACES (continued)

Name	Zones	Height	Exposure*	Flower Color and Bloom Time	Comments
Rodgersia pinnata (featherleaf rodgersia)	5–8	3–4'	S to PSh	Red to white; late spring	Foliage ages bronzy; R. aesculifolia is similar but larger
Sanguisorba canadensis (great burnet)	3–7	3–6'	S to PSh	Cream; fall	Tolerates drier soils
Sarracenia flava (yellow pitcher plant)	7–9	3–4½'	S to PSh	Yellow; summer	Strongly erect yellow-green tubular insect-trapping leaves
S. purpurea (purple pitcher plant)	6–9	8–12"	S to PSh	Dark red; summer	Spreading pitcherlike foliage, blotched purple
Saururus cernuus (lizard's tail)	5–7	2–4'	S to PSh	White; late summer	Forms dense stands
Symplocarpus foetidus (purple skunk cabbage)	4–7	1½–2½'	PSh to LSh	Yellow-green and purplish brown; late winter to early spring	Leaf rosette 3 to 5 feet across; flowers emit skunky odor
Tellima grandiflora (fringe cup)	6–8	2–3'	PSh to LSh	White, aging to reddish green; summer	Forms colonies; flowers best seen close up; can be invasive
Tiarella cordifolia (foamflower)	3–7	about 6"	PSh to LSh	White; spring	Forms dense colonies; can be invasive
Tolmiea menziesii (piggyback plant)	7–8	6–8"	PSh to LSh	White; late spring to summer	Plantlets often develop at base of leaf blades
Trollius × cultorum (hybrid globeflower)	5–7	1½–2'	S to PSh	Cream to orange; late spring to early summer	Best in open, sunny meadows
T. europaeus (European globeflower)	5–7	1½–2'	S to PSh	Lemon yellow; late spring to early summer	Various cultivars of larger habit
T. ledebourii (late globeflower)	5–7	2–3'	S to PSh	Orange; mostly late summer	Especially suited to permanent wetness
Veratrum viride (false hellebore)	3–7	4–6'	S, PSh, or LSh	Yellow-green; summer	Bold appearance; several other spp. with whitish flowers
Vernonia fasciculata (swamp ironweed)	3–7	3–6'	S to PSh	Purple; late summer to early fall	Does best in open locations
Woodwardia virginica (chain fern)	4–9	1–2'	PSh to LSh		W. areolata is similarly hardy; both best near running water
Zantedeschia aethiopica (white calla)	8–10	3–5'	S to PSh	White; late winter to spring	Tallest in shaded, frost-free areas

* S, full sun; Sh, shade (no direct sun); PSh, partial shade (sun exposure only part of the day); LSh, light shade (e.g., the shade of tall, open trees, with little or no exposure to direct sun).

SUBMERGED AQUATIC PERENNIALS

Rooted in mud or sand beneath the water's surface. The stems and all or most of the leaves are submerged. The flowers and some leaves (which are often different from the submerged leaves) are on the surface.

Name	Zones	Water Depth	Flower Color and Bloom Time	Comments
Cabomba caroliniana	5–10	1–3'	White to pink; Summer	Submerged leaves filamentous, floating leaves undivided; hardiest of several species
Callitriche hermaphroditica (water starwort)	6–9	1–3'	Inconspicuous	Evergreen; best in cool, running water; C. heterophylla is somewhat hardier but deciduous
Ceratophyllum demersum (water milfoil)	8–10	1–3'	Greenish to white; to summer	Foliage filamentous
Elodea callitrichoides (water weed)	7	1–2'	Inconspicuous	E. canadensis is similar but often invasive
Isoetes engelmannii (quillwort)	3–7	6–12"		Evergreen; quill-like foliage
Myriophyllum spp. (water milfoil)	(3) 6–10	1–3'	Inconspicuous	Submerged leaves are more divided than floating leaves; similar species vary in hardiness and acidity requirements
Potamogeton spp. (pond weed)	4–10	1–4	Inconspicuous	P. coloratus and P. gramineus are less invasive than most species

Rose mallow (*Hibiscus moscheutos*)

Yellow skunk
cabbage
(*Lysichiton americanum*)

Purple skunk
cabbage (*Symplocarpus
foetidus*)

Gooseneck
loosestrife
(*Lysimachia clethroides*)

Yellow Flag (*Iris pseudacorus*)

Royal fern
(*Osmunda regalis*)

Foamflower
(*Tiarella cordifolia*)

Marsh marigold
(*Caltha palustris*)

Joe-pye weed (*Eupatorium purpureum*)

Yellow pitcher plant
(*Sarracenia flava*)

Cinnamon fern (*Osmunda cinnamomea*)

Swamp milkweed (*Asclepias incarnata*)

EMERGENT AQUATIC PERENNIALS

Rooted in mud or sand beneath the water's surface. The stems and all or most of the leaves are submerged, with
flowers and some leaves at or above the surface; best grown in full sun or partial shade.

Name	Zones	Water Depth	Flower Color and Bloom Time	Comments
Acorus calamus (sweet flag)	3–7	2–6"	Yellow, late spring to summer	Bold, irislike foliage; aromatic flowers
Alisma plantago-aquatica (water plantain)	6–9	2–6"	Purplish white; summer	Leaves about 1 foot long; sunny location best for flowers
Aponogeton distachyus (water hawthorn)	9–10	1–2'	White; summer	Flowers aromatic, 1 inch across in some cultivars
Cyperus alternifolius (umbrella palm)	10	2–6"	Greenish; summer	Height 2 to 3 feet; 10 to 25 leaflike bracts atop each stalk; good tub plant
C. papyrus (papyrus)	10	2–6"	Greenish; summer	Up to 5 feet tall; historic source of paper; best grown in tubs
Iris pseudacorus (yellow flag)	5–8	2–6"	Yellow; summer	Forms dense clumps at pond borders
I. versicolor (blue flag)	3–7	1–3"	Blue-violet and yellow; summer	Forms dense clumps at pond borders
Ludwigia longifolia (primrose willow)	8–10	2–6"	Yellow; summer	Similar to *L. alternifolia*, which is hardy to zone 4
Nasturtium officinale (watercress)	6–9	2–6"	White; spring to summer	Thrives in clear, gently flowing water in sun to partial shade; spreads rapidly; often biennial
Nelumbo lutea (American lotus)	4–8	1–2 (3)'	Pale yellow; summer	Leaves and flowers held high above water; flowers 6 to 12 inches across lowers
Nuphar advena (spatterdock)	3–10	1–3'	Yellow; summer	Tolerates more shade than *Nymphaea* spp.
Nymphoides peltata (floating heart)	6–8	2–3'	Yellow; summer	*N. cordata* similar but has white flowers
Orontium aquaticum (golden club)	(7) 8–9	2–6"	Yellow; late spring to summer	Forms dense colonies
Phragmites australis (common reed)	5–10	2–6"	Tan; summer	Stems 8 to 12 feet tall; forms dense, exclusive colonies; usually spreads invasively, hence best grown in tubs
Pontederia cordata (pickerelweed)	3–10	2–6"	Blue to white; summer	Forms dense colonies
Sagittaria latifolia (arrowhead)	7–9	2–12"	White; summer	Several other species hardy to zone 6
Saururus cernuus (lizard's tail)	5–8	2–6"	White; late summer	Forms dense colonies
Thalia dealbata (water canna)	9–10	2–18"	Violet; summer	Bold effect wrought by large leaves and high flower clusters
Trapa natans (water chestnut)	5–8	2–12"	White; summer	Widely naturalized; nut edible when boiled
Typha spp. (cattail)	3–10	2–12"	Brown; summer	Roots form dense mats, eventually excluding most other vegetation; best grown in tubs
Zizania aquatica (wild rice)	6–8	2–6"	Green; summer	Matures at 12 feet tall; luxuriant self-sowing annual grass

Pickerelweed (*Pontederia cordata*)

Watercress (*Nasturtium officinale*)

Arrowhead (*Sagittaria latifolia*)

BOG GARDENS

In nature, a bog is the result of thousands of years of plant succession and is a very special habitat. Normally, it represents the final vestiges of a glacial lake before ordinary dry-land vegetation takes over. The original lake has been slowly filled in by accumulations of decaying aquatic vegetation and debris from nearby woodlands. The sunken debris has then gradually raised the lake bottom.

Most bogs are characteristically cold, permanently wet, and markedly acidic. They are inhabited by plant species that have evolved to succeed and even thrive under these nutrient-deficient conditions. A gardener who has such a habitat should realize the good fortune at hand and take seriously the responsibility to be its steward.

On the other hand, the gardener with a degraded bog, with some or most original plant cover removed, or even just a poorly drained low spot, can create a bog garden that approximates a natural one. The two essentials are a continuous supply of water and a soil capable of retaining the moisture. The first is best served by water pipes drilled with tiny holes every 2 or 3 feet, and buried 2 or 3 inches deep. The second requisite calls for equal portions of sand and peat moss with generous amounts of humus forked in. The mixture should be deep, ideally at least 18 inches, and overspread with a 1-inch layer of peat moss. To obtain and maintain a highly acidic condition (pH 4.5 to 5.5) it may be necessary to incorporate oak humus.

A bog garden can also be constructed de novo in a well-drained site simply by excavating an 18-inch depression in a naturally low area, spreading a heavy reinforced plastic tarpaulin, and laying the perforated water lines as the depression is filled with soil mixture.

A small bog garden may contain only a few herbaceous plants; a large area offers opportunities for trees and shrubs as well. The lower plants should be in the center—representing the middle of the one-time lake—surrounded by the taller woody species.

As for maintenance, it is advisable to test annually for acidity and to take steps to keep the soil at low pH. Removal of weeds and interlopers is an ongoing task, but not usually onerous.

Wisconsin, or Niobe, weeping willow (*Salix × pendulina*)

TREES FOR BOGS

Permanently wet ground with strongly acidic soil, subject to periodic or occasional flooding.

Names	Zones	Height	Comments
Acer rubrum (red maple)	3–9	60–75'	Very shallow, platformlike root system; red fall foliage; red flowers in early spring; red samaras in late spring (in female trees)
Alnus spp. (alder)	2–7 (8)	50–60'	Roots enrich soil; appearance undistinguished
Betula nigra (river birch)	4–9	50–60'	Peeling reddish brown to gray bark
B. populifolia (gray birch, white birch)	3–7	25–30'	Multistemmed: gray to white bark
Carpinus caroliniana (American hornbeam)	2–9	20–25'	Usually multistemmed; smooth "muscled" bark
Fraxinus tomentosa (pumpkin ash)	5–8	75–90'	Swollen, buttressed trunk base develops with age
Larix laricina (eastern larch, tamarack)	1–5	40–60'	Not easily established; intolerant of prolonged summer heat
Nyssa sylvatica (black gum, sour gum)	3–9	50–60'	Deep taproot complicates transplanting; scarlet fall foliage
Picea mariana (black spruce)	2–6	30–40'	Evergreen; spirelike form
Quercus nigra (water oak)	6–9	50–60'	Slow-growing in the North
Q. palustris (pin oak)	4–8	50–75'	Graceful form; subject to disfiguring thorn gall
Salix spp. (willow)	2–9	25–75'	Many species, some with pendent branches, most with narrow glossy foliage

SHRUBS FOR BOGS
All best grown in full sun or partial shade.

Name	Zones	Height	Flower Color and Bloom Time	Comments
Andromeda glaucophylla (bog rosemary)	2–6	1–3'	White to pale pink; late spring to early summer	Difficult to establish; intolerant of prolonged summer heat
Aronia melanocarpa (black chokeberry)	3–8	3–8'	White; spring	Black berries and reddish foliage in fall
Cephalanthus occidentalis (buttonbush)	6–10	6–20'	White; summer	Long season of bloom; flowers held in spherical heads
Chamaedaphne calyculata (leatherleaf)	7–9	3–4½'	White; summer	Cv. 'Nana' about half size
Clethra alnifolia (sweet pepperbush)	3–9	4–8'	White; late summer	Flowers fragrant
Holodiscus discolor (ocean spray)	5–8	10–15'	Cream; summer	Wide spreading; arching habit
Kalmia angustifolia (sheep laurel, lambkill)	2–7	3–5'	Purplish rose; late spring to early summer	Evergreen; forms clumps; easily established
K. polifolia (bog laurel)	2–7	1–2'	Pink to rose purple; late spring to early summer	Evergreen; forms dense clumps in seasonally dry sites
Ledum groenlandicum (Labrador tea)	2–5	2–4'	White; spring	Intolerant of prolonged summer heat
Myrica gale (sweet gale)	(7) 8–9	10–15'	Inconspicuous	Aromatic foliage; females bear yellow-brown conelike fruit clusters in the fall
M. pennsylvanica (northern bayberry)	2–7	5–9'	Inconspicuous	Aromatic foliage; females bear gray berries in the fall and winter
Rhododendron canadense (rhodora)	2–7	3–4'	Rosy purple; spring	Twiggy habit; deciduous
R. viscosum (swamp azalea)	3–9	3–8'	White; summer	Flowers clove-scented; deciduous
Rosa palustris (swamp rose)	5–8	4–6'	Pink; late spring to early summer	Persistent red fruit
Sambucus spp. (elder)	3–9	6–10'	White; late spring to early summer	Red or black berries in late summer
Spiraea alba (meadowsweet)	5–8	3–5'	White; summer	Flowers held in pyramidal clusters
S. douglasii (western steeplebush)	5–7	6–10'	Pink and white; summer	Ssp. *menziesii* about half as tall
S. tomentosa (eastern steeplebush, hardhack)	3–7	3–5'	Pink; summer	Flowers held in columnar clusters
Vaccinium corymbosum (highbush blueberry)	3–7 (8)	10–12'	Pinkish white; spring	Edible blue-black berries in summer; orange to red fall foliage
V. macrocarpon (American cranberry)	2–7	about 6"	Pale purple; summer	Mat-forming shrublet; edible red fruit in late summer and fall
Viburnum cassinoides (arrowwood viburnum)	3–8	6–10'	White; spring	Fruit red, then blue, maturing to black in fall

PERENNIALS FOR BOGS

Name	Zones	Height	Exposure*	Flower Color and Bloom Time	Comments
Arethusa bulbosa (swamp pink)	3–7	6–12"	S	Purple; summer	Hardy orchid
Calopogon tuberosum (bog orchid)	3–9	1–2'		Rose to magenta; spring	Good in sheltered locations
Cypripedium acaule (pink lady's slipper)	5–8	1-1½'	LSh to PSh	Purplish pink and brown; spring	Slowly forms patches; requires elevated site; difficult to establish
C. reginae (showy lady's slipper)	5–8	3–3½'	PSh to LSh	Pink and white; spring	Very ornamental, especially in groups
Eriophorum angustifolium (cotton grass)	4–7	1–3'	S	White to cream tufts; summer	Several other similar species
Helonias bullata (swamp pink)	7–9	2–3'	S	Pink; spring	Flowers fragrant
Menyanthes trifoliata (buck bean)	3–6	about 1'	S to PSh	White to pale pink; summer	Forms dense patches at edges of shallow water
Narthecium americanum (American bog asphodel)	6–8	1–2'	S to PSh	Yellow; summer	*N. californicum* is similar but red flowered
Osmunda cinnamomea (cinnamon fern)	3–10	3–6'	S to LSh	Spore-bearing light brown fronds; spring to summer	Forms clumps and elevated hummocks
O. regalis (royal fern)	2–8	3–6'	PSh to LSh		Spores borne on specialized divisions of leafy fronds

* S, full sun; Sh, shade (no direct sun); PSh, partial shade (sun exposure only part of the day); LSh, light shade (e.g., the shade of tall, open trees, with little or no exposure to direct sun).

24

Rock, Wall, and Trough Gardens

Although rock gardening as a well-established specialty does not have a long history in horticulture, its roots may be traced back to ancient China and to the hanging gardens of Babylon. Today, many rock gardeners have organized themselves into local, regional, and national organizations and may meet informally to exchange tips and surplus plants or to participate in formal rock plant conferences or study sessions.

The colorful and resilient plants of the rock garden can transform just about any gardener into a rock garden enthusiast.

In many such groups, the adjective *alpine* best describes the geographic scope of members' interests. For others, the focus is on dwarf plants with disproportionately bright, showy flowers, arranged in small landscapes that mimic the environments in which the plants occur naturally. Such environments include rocky ledges and cliffs with pockets and crevices filled with soil, steep unstable slopes covered with sharp-angled pieces of rock and underlain by gritty soil, alpine meadows with moist, humusy soil and often studded with outcrops or scattered large rocks, moist peat beds with a constant source of water contributing to acidic conditions, and open woodland, also with emergent outcrops or heaps of loose rocks.

It is under these conditions that rock garden plants grow naturally, but the variation among these environments is such that no single species occurs in all of them.

In 1864, the Austrian botanist Kerner Von Merilaun decided to try a pioneering experiment. He collected thriving alpines from his native Alps and attempted to grow them in the lowlands. To accomplish this, Von Merilaun constructed a garden on a slope covered with rubble stones, boulders, and stone chippings. This scree, which he built at the Royal Botanical Gardens in Innsbruck, was designed to represent in miniature the "Steingeroellhalde" of the valleys in the Tyrolean Alps. This unique "garden" was then—and is still today, more than a century later—the most successful demonstration of what a rock garden should be and how alpine plants may be grown successfully in an artificially created habitat simulating the original.

Since the rock garden does not have the same tradition-bound history as the Japanese or Chinese garden, public opinion in this country is still divided about its popularity. As a result, this type of gardening has passed through many ups and downs in its century-plus history, probably reaching a low during the early 1900s. Directors of botanical gardens throughout Europe originally started the construction of rock gardens because of the increasing scientific interest in the plants themselves, rather than to produce rock garden showcases. These alpine plant collections, or "alpinums," as they were called, were the forerunners of our present rock gardens. The imaginative alpinums were usually constructed in the shape of miniature mountains and stone hills, or even in the form of volcanoes. The plant material was collected from the wild: in alpine meadows, on screes, and among rocks above the timberline. Since these plants were moved from high to low altitudes, they had a short lifetime and were replaced quite frequently. Propagating from seed or cutting was not perfected until the early 1920s.

However, this new garden style soon became very popular, with the result that the rocks and plants lost their original

An extensive outcrop at the base of an angular, blocky rock face offers an unusual natural setting for a rock garden, embraced by mixed woodland.

significance and the alpinum its intent. Unfortunately, all that remained was a conglomerate of miniature mountains, planted with trees that soon grew completely out of scale. The rock gardens, during these early years, did not have the privacy that is so much desired, as they were quite often built on street corners to discourage short-cuts by passers-by and frequently were even badly ornamented with miniature mountain huts, mountain goats, and dwarfs. This prostitution of purpose and debasement of the original rock garden standards and concepts continued into the early 1930s.

ROCK GARDENS

The first and most fundamental consideration in constructing a rock garden is the relationship of individual plants and plant groups to the overall composition. Without an awareness of this relationship, the amateur can easily become bewildered by the very abundance and diversity of species from which to choose. As a result, it is easy to make poor choices, and the mistakes may not appear until several years have passed.

The designer, in attempting to visualize the ultimate appearance of the rock garden, should be greatly influenced by both the site and the locality. The interrelation of mass, texture, form, color, and detail is the product of the exercise of the rock gardener's adherence to this principle of composition.

Scale

A basic principle to bear in mind is that the garden must relate to the human scale. (No miniature Matterhorns!) We have to reduce the overpowering size of the universe and bring it down to more comfortable proportions in a small, private world. Since most rock gardens are human made, they also must have a definite unity of design with certain aesthetic and utilitarian functions. After all, a garden is not nature but rather a work of art. It is something created artificially that merely makes use of natural components and processes to form a different, though harmonious, picture. More variations of plant material can be shown on a smaller scale than can be found in nature. In one sense, a rock garden

Perspective view of patio area landscaped with rock garden plants

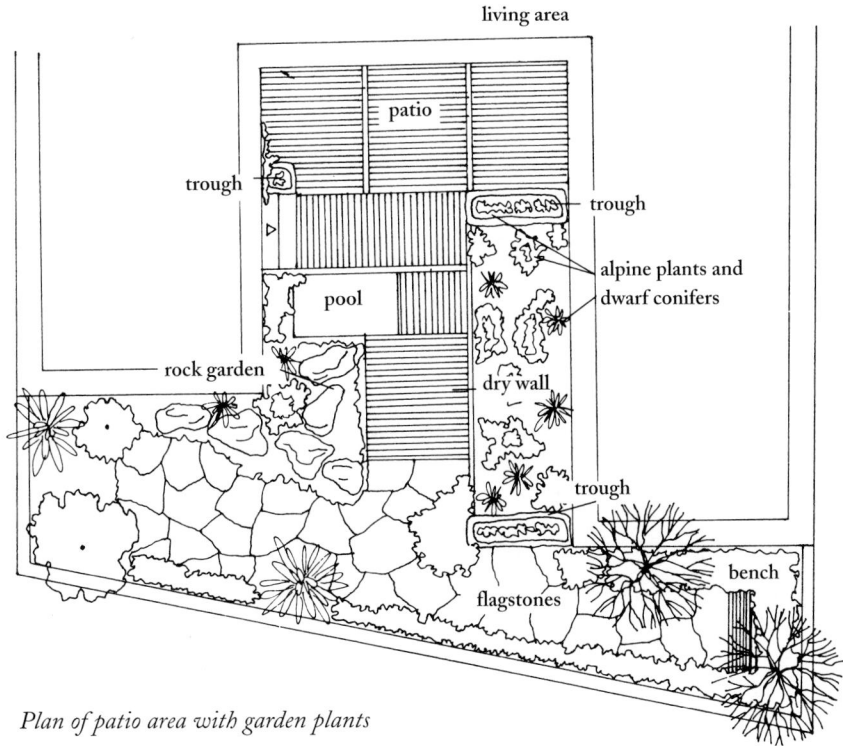

Plan of patio area with garden plants

is a synthesis or condensation of the rocky alpine landscapes of great mountains. When well done, it is believable.

By choosing highly cultivated and hardy plants for difficult locations and by grouping them together aesthetically, we often can create new plant communities that may be superior in effect to the communities of natural plants themselves.

Choice of Site

The particular effect to be developed in any rock garden depends largely on the condition of the site to be used. Quite often, the first choice for a rock garden is a site that is not needed for any other purpose or one that proves to be difficult to tie in with the general design of the garden as a whole. Though all these reasons may seem valid, they are expedient, and such a site may not necessarily be the best one for the purpose.

Generally speaking, most rock gardens can be classified as informal, with the plants and nonliving elements placed and associated as in nature, or, less commonly, formal, with the materials geometrically arranged. Within these design concepts, we can more readily visualize which kind of rock garden will best fit into the existing landscape with which we have to work.

Before deciding on a site, observe the sun exposure at sunrise, sunset, and high noon and also determine the main wind direction. Although a southern exposure ensures the maximum amount of sunlight for sun-loving plants, it also exposes them to prolonged summer heat and to the injurious

Beyond the dark, leaf-strewn pond, somber rocks capped with snow and interspersed with brightly fruited cotoneasters create an interesting winter scene.

effect of the alternate freezing and thawing action in winter. An eastern or even a northern exposure is generally preferable for a diversity of plants.

Avoid a site that cannot be drained properly. Bear in mind that although alpines grow under widely different aspects and factors, they generally do not tolerate strongly acidic, badly drained soil. In addition, alpines will not grow when exposed to drought or to cutting winds. Do not build a rock garden under the overhanging branches of trees or between buildings where drafts and shade will discomfort or inhibit most any plants selected to grow there.

A factor that may indirectly affect the choice for a rock garden location is the provision of water for pools and streams. Water is found in its natural bodies only in a few gardens, and if desired in others, it usually must be brought in artificially. A watercourse is not necessarily essential in a rock garden, but its presence is surely an enhancement.

In selecting a spot for a rock garden, there is one point to remember that, at first glance, may seem of secondary importance: ease of access for the bulky and often heavy material and equipment that will be required in the course of construction. Difficult access can add considerably to the cost of the rock garden, not only in the time and labor involved but also because of the damage done to already established lawns or other parts of the garden.

No work should be started before a suitable site has been selected and the decision made from which direction the garden most likely will be seen to its best advantage. Foreground and background as part of the composition must be considered in choosing the site. On most small properties a suitable background planting will be needed. Such a backdrop will also serve as a frame to keep the eye from straying afield of the garden itself. The informal rock garden can be used to conceal extraneous or distracting objects.

The immediate foreground, also important in the overall design, is the perfect place for an alpine lawn, with stepping-stones set among the plants for easy access to rock outcrops behind. In a hot, sunny location, ground covers such as creeping mazus (*Mazus reptans*), snow-in-summer (*Cerastium tomentosum*), Irish moss (*Sagina subulata*), and mountain pink (*Phlox subulata*) can be used. A small pond or a stretch of closely trimmed turf also can serve as foreground for a rock garden. Turf brought up to the planting areas, and occasionally even to and around the rocks, can provide a neat and pleasing appearance.

Construction

A natural rock garden is usually better placed some distance from the more formal part of the garden, which, as a rule,

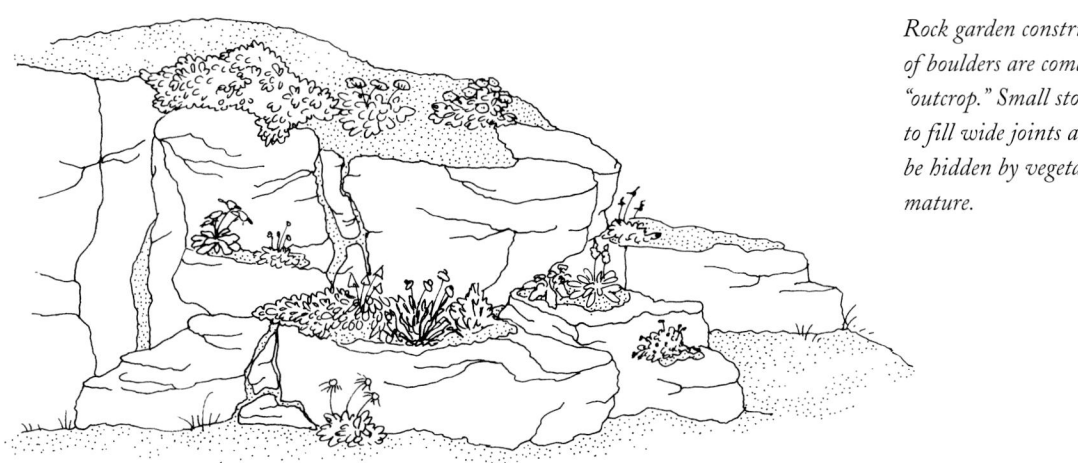

Rock garden construction: Large pieces of boulders are combined into a massive "outcrop." Small stones have been used to fill wide joints and will eventually be hidden by vegetation as plantings mature.

Cliff face consists of a number of separate stones skillfully combined.

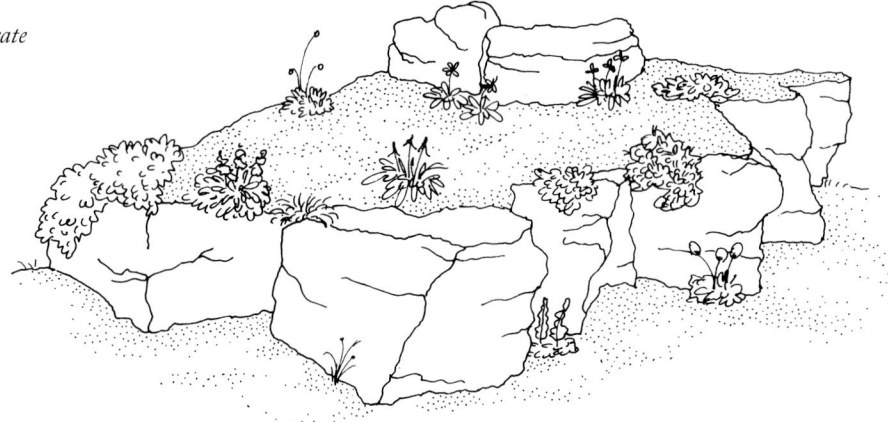

surrounds the house. A prime consideration in building a rock garden should be the rocks themselves, which, after all, determine the garden's character. No garden builder can ignore this basic fact. The aim, of course, should be to select and arrange the rocks in such a manner that each appears as a natural deposit that was there originally and has not been disturbed. A rock garden is not a meaningless jumble of rocks, mixed as to geographical type, showing drill marks and glaring newly exposed surfaces. Nor should the rocks be set up in an unnatural, shaky, or unaesthetic position.

The best stone for the rock garden is one of local origin. Porosity is a factor of considerable importance because the stone stores moisture and is always cool underground. Alpine plants thrive in association with stone and will press their roots as closely as possible to its sides. In this respect, the sandstones and limestones are the best material for rock gardens. Though granite is also good, it is hard and yields an acidic reaction to the soil that limits plant choice. Quartz is too hard and too conspicuous.

Unstratified and Stratified (Sedimentary) Rock

Boulders and hardheads (igneous rocks such as basalt, trap, and granite that weather to round boulders) should not be used to make a stratified outcrop. Instead, their place is on a rugged, boulder-strewn slope. Some may be scattered, while others are arranged in dense, steep clusters. On a rather steep slope the dominance of the rock should give the effect of a stream-cut bank, with the softer material laying bare the outcrop boulders. Stream valleys and pond areas are excellent locations for rock gardens. The size of the rocks used should be determined by the scale of the garden. Large stones give the effect of strength; however, a big boulder in a small garden makes the area seem smaller, while too many small stones create an artificial and weak effect. Only weathered boulders should be selected, and these should be embedded in the soil to their weathered line or to the level of their widest diameter.

It is necessary to understand the jointing of stratified or sedimentary rock to obtain a natural effect. The lines of

A modified outcrop bordering woodland provides rooting spaces for sedums and other sun-seeking creepers in foreground as well as for shade-requiring ferns.

A limestone formation is especially suitable for most informal garden effects. Where this type of stone occurs naturally, it would be difficult to find a better or simpler rock for the garden. And if the limestone is porous, irregular in form, and already weathered to a rather neutral color, the rock gardener is fortunate indeed.

Sandstone is another stratified rock that is widely used. It, too, has a large water-holding capacity and is easy to move around.

Moraine and Erratic Rock

Millennia ago, glaciers and water transported the erratic blocks of rock southward from distant places. Frost, rain, and wind then combined to change granite, feldspar, and porphyry into round, smoothed-off, and dome-shaped rocks. No one stone ever matches another in size or shape.

This individual expression of the solitary stone must be worked out in the construction of the moraine. Erratic blocks in a rock garden cannot be used the same way as stratified or sedimentary rocks; they must rest on the ground. They have to be embedded as if they had been resting there forever. To do this is not an easy task, either aesthetically or physically. The individual stones all must face a common main direction. If the moraine lies against a stone wall, then the main direction is parallel to the wall. In that case the joints of a paving would be diagonal to the main direction.

stratification are traceable throughout the entire formation. In the garden, it does not matter at what angle the strata are inclined, so long as this angle is consistently maintained throughout the placed stonework. A backward tilt to each elevation has the advantage of holding some of the rainfall and conducting it into the soil. This stone material offers the ingenious gardener ample opportunity to create a variety of crevices and planting spots, some in full sun and others where it is cool and shaded behind a bend or beneath an overhang.

1.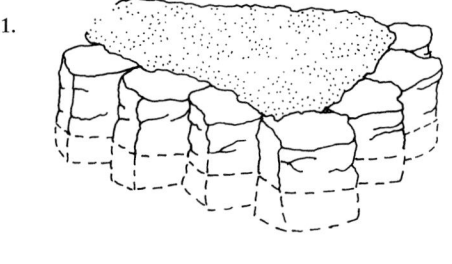

2.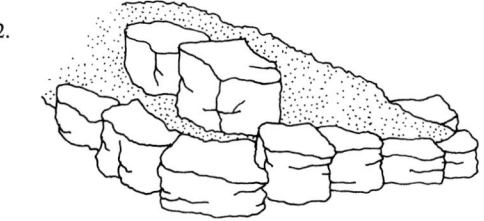

3.

4.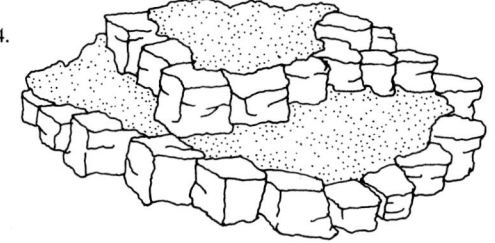

CONSTRUCTION OF A ROCK GARDEN WITH QUARRIED STRATIFIED ROCKS— 1. First planting pocket is completed. The stones are buried to one-third or one-fourth of their total height, and each one slightly overlaps the stone behind it. 2. Begin the next elevation with the corner stone touching the stone below it. 3. The baseline of the next elevation shapes the planting pocket of the lower bed into a roughly triangular form. 4. The finished product is stepped planting.

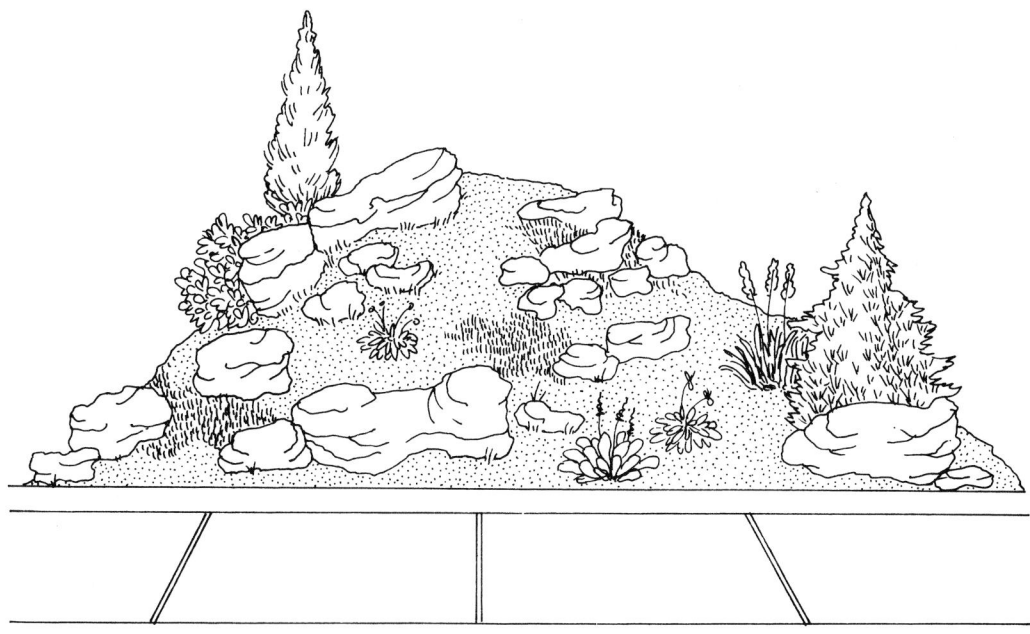

Moraine— This garden emulates the debris left after a glacier recedes.

The mound rises from one side of the field evenly to the opposite side. Here the largest stone will dominate. The surface of the stones must have all the same inclined plane to the lowest point. This order in direction to the side and top is the architectonic element that avoids confusion.

Drainage and Staking

An important consideration in planning a rock garden is drainage. Alpine plants thrive in cool, moist, gritty, humusy soil. Water should drain past the roots and not accumulate. Stagnant conditions are fatal. If wetness predominates, it is best to build the rockery entirely of imported soil made up to specification. An ideal mixture is equal proportions of rough sand with gravel, sphagnum peat, and friable loam. The subsoil should be loosened deeply before it is covered with the new soil mix.

After the contours of the surface have been roughly shaped according to the plan, the site should be staked out to reveal the various natural features the gardener wishes to emphasize. These stakes will indicate such points as the major rocks, a waterfall, or possibly a bend in the walk. In this early process a newspaper pattern suggesting stones is often easier than stakes to help visualize the final result. To indicate the walkway, sawdust or lime may be used. Some particularly large rock may show promise of becoming the dominant part of the ridge or cliff. In certain situations such a rock can be the main attraction of the entire composition, yet still remain in harmony with its surroundings. When placing the stones, it is best to start from a central group and work outward.

Pathways

Once the stones are in place, the approach to the garden is the next consideration. A rock garden should be arranged so that the visitor will view and study the grounds slowly and deliberately, just as he or she would do while climbing a mountain. As in the mountains, one can see the modest beauty of the little cliff and scree dwellers best only if one climbs slowly, step by step.

A trail through the interior parts of a rock garden should be so designed that it links the most interesting views. The path should be lower than the surrounding planting beds, since it also has to serve as a drainage canal for heavy rains, besides helping to regulate the flow of water.

Bold groupings of stones should be placed on curves, suggesting a natural reason for the bend. A dwarf tree or shrub will provide the same effect. Follow the more gradual contours and interrupt them by steps only when some higher elevation must be crossed. It is important that these steps blend into the natural strata line. Although the approach to the garden should be convenient, it must never monopolize the entire scene.

Basic Rock Garden Principles

In summary, there certain basic principles that, if respected, will result in a rock garden of maximum beauty throughout the year. Among them, the following are especially important.

1. The rock garden should be as open and uncluttered as possible and offer a natural visual progression from one

area to the next. It is not desirable that all of it be visible from a single vantage. Rather, it should consist of a gradually unfolding series of tableaux of rocks with plants arranged to capture interest but in a spirit of restraint.

2. The size and placement of rocks should be bold and generous and thus allow for the reducing, softening effect of plants while at the same time easing the movement of pedestrians and garden equipment.

3. Rocks should be significant rather than numerous. They should appear settled and be harmonious in color and texture.

4. Rock gardens function best if they border or are surrounded by an uncluttered, homogeneous vista, whether it be water, lawn, meadow, or a distant horizon.

5. Be analytical of the site before placing a single rock or planting a single perennial. Especially important is the removal of young trees that will cast increasing shade if left. Larger trees nearby may require pruning.

6. Avoid overplanting. The crowding that results will not only obscure the rock framework and sacrifice the individual character of the plants, but will also cause the dying out of many kinds in a short time.

7. Don't forget accent plants—those especially distinctive in color, texture, or form—but, to avoid a clamor of contrasts, use them in moderation and be strategic in placing them.

8. Start with kinds of plants that are of easy culture and known hardiness in your area. As experience accrues, success with more difficult subjects will increase.

9. Find out as much as possible about kinds of plants under consideration before acquiring and planting them. Check on height, spread, and likely life span, not just on flower color and season of bloom.

10. Be careful to avoid kinds of plants that can become weedy problems in years ahead. Grape hyacinth (*Muscari botryoides*) is a charming spring bulb, but its tendency to rampant self-seeding may result in unwanted carpeting of the garden site, and removal proves difficult. Even more pernicious (and immortal) is the common bellflower (*Campanula rapunculoides*).

11. Minimize or avoid altogether the use of such synthetic materials as concrete, brick, rectangular slates, landscape ties, and plastic. Use natural rock wherever possible.

12. To stabilize the surface and obviate the invasion of weeds, use muted mulches, especially those likely to be found naturally in the setting created.

13. Include in rock garden planning a nearby but out-of-sight coldframe and, if possible, a small nursery area, in which plants may be started from seed and grown on before being placed in a permanent location. Give away surplus plants; put nothing in the rock garden simply because you have it.

14. Avoid studding the rock garden with distracting labels. Use small metal tags, or small numbered bits of aluminum (keyed to a list of plants represented), in preference to labels large enough to be read 6 or 8 feet away. Often such labels are as large as the plants they identify, or, in the case of ephemerals, stand most of the year in solitude.

Selection of Shrubs

Together with the rocks, small shrubs and slow-growing conifers form a setting or skeletal framework in which the more colorful and variable herbaceous material creates its pattern. Such woody plants will be at their best in winter when the rest of the garden lies dormant.

Among the conifers are many universally liked dwarfs that exist in a range of forms. Hardiness and lack of boldness make these ideal plant material when they are used either singly or in groups. They are free of most insect pests and fungal diseases. Once they are rooted, these plants will rarely need any maintenance. Since the goal of most rock gardens is to reproduce an "alpine" atmosphere, anything formal should be avoided. For this reason, the globose forms and others of geometric outline are least useful.

Prostrate junipers (*Juniperus* spp. and cvs.) should be used sparingly because they eventually spread over a large area that could be better occupied by alpines. It is important to use the greatest care in the choice of suitable species on the higher parts or tops of the outcrops. Anything with an upright or pyramidal habit would be out of place in such locations. In nature, there might be a tree either gnarled or dwarfed by wind; a windswept veteran with substantially exposed stem and branches is, therefore, most desirable in the higher parts of the rock garden.

Before actual planting begins, stakes are used again, as they were for the placement of the rocks. It is a good idea to write the name of the element on the stake, such as: "pine," "spruce," "faucet," "stone," and so on. More important features are sometimes indicated by heavier stakes or by colorcoded stakes. From a distance the stakes can be studied in their positions, and if there is any dissatisfaction with the plan, the design can be changed before actual planting starts.

DWARF CONIFERS OF SPECIAL MERIT

The species discussed below include examples of the most common groups of slow-growing conifers, all of which are suitable for the rock garden. Their rates of growth, though slow, vary from one kind to another. The foliage of a dwarf cultivar is usually the same as that of the typical full-size species, but because of lack of the characteristic apical dominance in growth, a true central trunk either fails to develop or soon branches. Thus the dwarf is usually densely branched and very compact. With few exceptions, dwarf forms are genetic mutants or have been propagated from abnormal growths such as witches'-brooms (stems with multiple branching from a common point, sometimes resembling an upturned broom) or from juveniles of those kinds whose seedling foliage differs from that of mature individuals. The following dwarf forms are widely available and are more easily established over a number of hardiness zones than most. All are best grown in full sun or partial shade.

ABIES BALSAMEA
VAR. HUDSONIA
(Dwarf balsam fir)

Zones 3–5 (7)

A truly dwarf form of our native balsam fir, dwarf balsam fir forms a flat-topped, deep green bush. It reaches approximately 2½ feet high and 4 feet wide in about 30 years.

CEDRUS LIBANI *'SARGENTII'*
(Dwarf weeping cedar of Lebanon)

Zones 6–9

An attractive miniature weeping treelet or shrub, dwarf weeping cedar of Lebanon reaches 12 to 14 inches before the branches start to weep.

CHAMAECYPARIS
LAWSONIANA *'ELWOODII'*
(Dwarf Lawson cypress)

Zones 5–7

Dwarf Lawson cypress has a slender, spirelike pyramid shape and intensely blue, needlelike leaves. In 15 years, it reaches a height of about 4 feet by about 10 inches wide.

CHAMAECYPARIS OBTUSA
'NANA'
(Dwarf Hinoki cypress)

Zones 4–8

A must in the rock garden, dwarf Hinoki cypress is a low, flat shrub with horizontal branches. The dark green leaves resemble thick, twisted moss. At 30 years of age, the plant is only 10 to 15 inches high and 15 to 20 inches wide at its base.

CHAMAECYPARIS PISIFERA
'FILIFERA AUREA'
(Dwarf weeping yellow Sawara cypress)

Zones 3–8

Dwarf weeping yellow Sawara cypress is a broadly conical shrub. Its horizontal branches bear pendulous, bright yellow branchlets, except where shaded. In about 30 years, it reaches a height of 8 to 15 feet.

CRYPTOMERIA JAPONICA
'VILMORINIANA'
(Vilmorin Japanese cedar)

Zones (5) 6–9

A truly dwarf plant, Vilmorin Japanese cedar forms a dense, dark green globe that becomes deep reddish bronze in the winter. It reaches 20 to 30 inches high after 30 years.

JUNIPERUS COMMUNIS
'COMPRESSA'
(Dwarf common juniper)

Zones 2–7

A gem among dwarf conifers, dwarf common juniper is a columnar shrub that rarely exceeds 3 feet in 30 years. The small needlelike leaves spread to reveal their glaucous inner surface.

JUNIPERUS COMMUNIS
'ECHINIFORMIS'
(Hedgehog juniper)

Zones 2–7

The hedgehog juniper makes a tiny, prickly hummock, 1 to 2 feet high and about as wide, in 20 years.

JUNIPERUS PROCUMBENS
'NANA'
(Dwarf Japanese juniper)

Zones 3–8

A compact plant with short branches, dwarf Japanese juniper forms a prostrate mat. Its spiny leaves are a deep blue-green. After 20 years, the plant will reach 12 to 15 inches high and 3 to 3½ feet wide.

PICEA ABIES *'INVERSA'*
(Dwarf weeping Norway spruce)

Zones 2–8

Slow growing, the dwarf weeping Norway spruce has completely pendulous branches. With age, it becomes a rounded mound about 3 feet tall, striking in its fine texture.

Bird's-nest spruce (*Picea abies* 'Nidiformis')

PICEA ABIES *'NIDIFORMIS'*
(Bird's-nest spruce)

Zones 2–8

Bird's-nest spruce is a dense spreading bush with ascending branches that form a series of tight layers. Its needles are rather thin and narrow. At 20 years, it is about 20 inches high and twice as wide.

PICEA GLAUCA *'CONICA'*
(Dwarf Alberta spruce)

Zones 2–7

Dwarf Alberta spruce is one of the really perfect, slow-growing dwarf conifers, making a symmetrical cone. At 20 years, it is about 4 feet high and 2 feet wide. It is subject to attack by red spider in regions that have hot, humid summer weather.

PINUS STROBUS *'NANA'*
(Dwarf white pine)

Zones 2–8

Dwarf White Pine is a low-spreading variant of the eastern white pine, with crowded branchlets and bluish green needles. At 20 years, it reaches 24 inches in height and a bit more in width.

THUJA PLICATA *'ROGERSII'*
(Dwarf western arborvitae)

Zones 5–7

Dwarf western abovitae has a very attractive, compact pyramid or cone shape. Its foliage is exposed to the sun and displays a lovely old gold color during the growing season. After 20 years, it reaches about 3 feet high and 2 feet across.

THUJOPSIS DOLOBRATA *'NANA'*
(Dwarf Hiba arborvitae)

Zones 5–8

A low, spreading plant with slender branches, dwarf Hiba arborvitae has lustrous green scale leaves. It is usually less than 2 feet high and about as wide in 20 years.

TSUGA CANADENSIS *'BENNETT'*
(Dwarf spreading hemlock)

Zones 3–7 (8)

A flat-topped plant, dwarf spreading hemlock has branches that spread horizontally. Its terminal shoots are fanlike with weeping tips. At 20 years, it reaches about 20 inches high and 3 feet wide. This species, whatever the cultivar, is not recommended for areas where hemlocks are subject to infestation by the woolly adelgid.

OTHER SHRUBS SUITABLE FOR THE ROCK GARDEN

All of the following species thrive in ordinary well-drained soil in full sun or partial shade, unless otherwise indicated.

BERBERIS WILSONIAE
(Creeping barberry)

Zones 6–8

Creeping barberry is a spreading, almost prostrate shrub that grows no more than 1 foot high. Its very small leaves are a dull, pale green, becoming a brilliant scarlet in the autumn. Its branches are very spiny, and the abundant fruit ripens salmon red in the fall.

CALLUNA VULGARIS
(Heather)

Zones 4–7

Many cultivars of heather, some quite dwarf, are well suited to the rock garden. They vary in foliage and flower color and in blooming season as well as in habit and ultimate size. All thrive in gritty or sandy, perfectly drained, acidic soils.

COTONEASTER ADPRESSUS
(Creeping cotoneaster)

Zones 4–8

A gem for the rock garden, creeping cotoneaster is a compact, wide-spreading shrub, 1 to 1½ feet high. In the fall, it displays bright red fruit and scarlet leaves.

CYTISUS DECUMBENS
(Prostrate broom)

Zones 5–8

Prostrate broom grows no more than 6 inches high. It has green twigs that suggest a small broom. Bright yellow flowers appear in late spring.

DABOECIA CANTABRICA
(St. Daboec's heath)

Zones 6–8

One of the most charming and useful of dwarf shrubs, St. Daboec's heath produces long racemes of very showy, rose purple, cup-shaped flowers from early summer to mid or late fall. Its maximum height is about 2 feet. Winter protection is advisable north of zone 7.

DAPHNE CNEORUM
(Daphne or Garland flower)

Zones 4–7

Garland flower is a small shrub, seldom growing taller than 1 foot. It is a great favorite because of the sweet fragrance of its flowers. Its needlelike leaves are evergreen. The rose pink flowers are borne in small clusters at the end of the branches in the spring. Patience is required, as garland flower is usually difficult to establish.

ERICA CARNEA
(Winter heath, Spring heath)

Zones 4–7

Winter heath is a dwarf shrub that forms hummocks or mats less than 1 foot high. It has fine-textured evergreen foliage. Flower color ranges from rosy red to purple to white. The flowers are borne from winter to spring. There is a multitude of heath cultivars, all lime tolerant.

JASMINUM PARKERI
(Dwarf jasmine)

Zones 7–9

A prostrate shrub, dwarf Jasmine normally forms a low mound of densely crowded greenish stems not more than 6 inches high. It bears small, divided leaves and tiny yellow flowers in the summer.

LEIOPHYLLUM BUXIFOLIUM
(Sand myrtle)

Zones 5–7

Sand myrtle is an evergreen shrub with very small, glossy foliage. It succeeds best in an open sunny position and a moist, sandy soil of high acidity. The clusters of white flowers, which open in mid to late spring, are borne at the branch tips.

POTENTILLA FRUTICOSA
(Shrubby cinquefoil)

Zones 2–7

A low shrub of dense, somewhat irregular growth, shrubby cinquefoil averages 1½ to 2 feet in the smaller cultivars. Flowering is fullest in late spring but often continues or recurs intermittently until fall. Flowers range from yellow-orange to white and even red.

RHODODENDRON FERRUGINEUM
(Alpen rose)

Zones 5–8

Alpen rose is a spreading 3- to 5-foot-tall shrub, with reddish leaves that are

scaly beneath. Rose red flowers appear in late spring. Alpen rose is a rock garden treasure, but like the following *Rhododendron* species, it is often difficult to establish.

RHODODENDRON IMPEDITUM
(Yunan rhododendron)

Zones 6–8

A 1- to 1½-foot-tall shrub, Yunan rhododendron has tiny leaves. Its purplish blue flowers appear in the spring.

RHODODENDRON IMPERATOR
(Burma rhododendron)

Zones 8–9

Burma rhododendron has a creeping habit and reaches 1½ feet tall. Its flowers are pink, appear in spring, and are borne even on very small, young plants.

RUBUS PENTALOBUS
(Dwarf flowering raspberry)

Zones 9–10

A creeping, mat-forming, glossy-leaf evergreen, dwarf flowering raspberry reaches only a few inches high. It has tip-rooting stems and white flowers in the spring. A fine-textured, refined ground cover, it is often sold erroneously as *R. calycinoides*.

Spring heath (*Erica carnea* 'Springwood Pink')

Selection of Herbaceous Perennials

A rock garden is a very distinctive type of flower garden, which should be characterized not only by rocks and plants but more particularly by such kinds of plants as are generally associated with rocky conditions. There are no fixed rules defining an alpine plant; however, it is best described as one that flourishes within the alpine zone. Strictly speaking, true alpines live above the treeline and are mostly of dwarf stature. Saxatile plants are those that do best and look most natural growing among rocks, though they may be found in either sun or shade at lower elevations also.

Alpines can generally be grouped in two categories. The lime-loving types include, with a few exceptions, all dwarf pinks (*Dianthus* spp.), aubretias (*Aubrieta* spp.), and rock cresses (*Arabis* spp.) as well as the vast majority of saxifrages (*Saxifraga* spp.). The other category is made up of plants that do better in acidic soil, such as members of the heath family (Ericaceae), including dwarf rhododendrons and azaleas (*Rhododendron* spp.), heaths (*Erica* spp.), and heathers (*Calluna vulgaris* cvs.). Most alpines thrive in a mixture of peat, pine needle mold, and sand in equal parts. The addition of small quantities of bonemeal and charcoal chippings is all that is needed. For lime-loving plants, some granulated limestone should also be added. A simple pH test, using a home soil-testing kit, will help you prepare the soil mix best suited to the plants chosen for culture. During the growing season, an occasional application of a liquid organic fertilizer will help maintain vigor.

Place individual plants where they will show to their best advantage. For a correct arrangement and effect, find out as much as possible about candidate plants'—size, flower color, period of bloom—before purchasing and placing them. Equally important are growth rate and habit as well as hardiness.

Some perennials are most effective in the rock garden when massed. These include basket-of-gold (*Aurinia saxatilis*), rock cress (*Arabis caucasica*), evergreen candytuft (*Iberis sempervirens*), and mountain pink (*Phlox subulata*).

Others are grown for their overall beauty, but as they may not display bold splashes of color, such plants are best grown near paths and, where possible, close to eye level. In this category are woolly yarrow (*Achillea tomentosa*), fall cyclamen (*Cyclamen purpurascens*), spring cyclamen (*C. repandum*), eastern douglasia (*Douglasia laevigata*), Turkish draba (*Draba polytricha*), spring gentian (*Gentiana acaulis*), and grayleaf sedum (*Sedum dasyphyllum*).

Plant Arrangement

Form, color, height, and texture are but a few of the characteristics to be taken into consideration when selecting suitable plant partners. The unbelievable number of types and species of plants should neither be placed in rank-and-file order nor be casually or frivolously be scattered. Every opportunity should be utilized to plant them according to their known ecological demands, so that they can establish themselves permanently. For example, in early spring when the grass paths are still partly moist, we find in the bright sun the warmth-loving grape hyacinth (*Muscari* spp.), spring-flowering crocus (*Crocus* spp.), and puschkinia (*Puschkinia* spp.). Thriving in cool, moist places, mostly in the shade of shrubs, are such bulbs as snowdrop (*Galanthus* spp.), squill (*Scilla* spp.), glory-of-the-snow (*Chionodoxa luciliae*), and winter aconite (*Eranthis hyemalis*). These bulbs do best in solitary patches or masses, uncrowded by other vegetation.

Heathers (*Calluna vulgaris* cvs.) tie in easily with dwarf conifers and with such undemanding perennials as pink pussy toes (*Antennaria rosea*), hawkweed (*Hieracium* spp.), and thyme (*Thymus* spp.). A complete ground cover showing the full beauty of these plants is sometimes all that can be developed in sandy soil that is poor in nutrients. Wildflowers brought into the rock garden are most successful where they are in association with plants of the same habitat, and where they can grow undisturbed together and form a plant carpet.

In selecting plant material and choosing positions, it is important to be sure that each plant is in harmony with the rest of the planting, and that the individual beauty of a plant will not be lost or overwhelmed in the larger group. The loveliest and most precious perennial may seem a weed if not planted in the right location and community.

The distance between plants in a group depends mainly on their rate of growth during the growing season. As a rule, plants used as ground cover grow quickly, and the choice is generally a question of how the plants will compete with each other. For groupings, you should consider how many individuals to plant together or whether to plant one individual and let it spread. Such a decision should be determined largely by the way the species concerned occur in nature. A plant that usually occurs alone, such as Carline thistle (*Carlina acaulis*), should not be grouped in the garden. Similarly, small groupings of three to five plants each are most appropriate when using yellow adonis (*Adonis vernalis*) or alpine anemone (*Anemone alpina*). However, mountain sandwort (*Arenaria montana*), heather (*Calluna vulgaris* cvs.), and mountain avens (*Dryas octopetala*) are most effective when massed.

Care and Maintenance

The maintenance of a rock garden is primarily a matter of weeding only. Weeds, of course, should be destroyed as soon as they appear. Do not allow them to become established, as they are then more difficult to remove and are likely seriously to weaken delicate plants and injure them when pulled. A mulch of stone chips around the plants helps to control the weeds. Stone chips also have the added advantages of keeping the soil from washing off slopes and preventing the soil surface from baking and forming a crust. Furthermore, the soil below the chips stays cooler and water will not evaporate as readily. No mud will splash onto the plants, and the foliage, resting on stone chips, will dry faster.

Winter protection of the rock garden is rarely necessary, though it helps to cover some of the more tender plants with evergreen branches. This should be done only after the ground is frozen 1 to 2 inches deep. Otherwise the plants may not harden sufficiently, with the result that they will go into the winter with soft growth and will be winter killed. In areas where regular snowfall can be expected, snow fencing may be erected around the rockery. The fence not only will act as a windbreak but will help to retain more snow on the planted area. Snow is the best and most natural winter protection for alpines.

In the spring the established rock garden will require some attention. An early inspection will reveal where plants have been heaved out of the soil by frost action, or where soil has been washed away. Plants that have been heaved out should be promptly reset, firmed in, and mulched with soil and stone chips. The lost soil should also be replaced. Some alpines appear to grow their way out of the soil naturally, and these require mulching every year with fresh oil and stone chips.

Wall Gardens

Wall gardens, among the most practical and useful forms of rock gardens, can be created in "dry walls," i.e., walls built without mortar or concrete. The wall is constructed in such a way that it holds plants which, in the wild, grow in the crevices of cliffs. This type of gardening is very low in maintenance and suitable plants more often thrive in such situations better than in the soil of the rock garden. At the same time, they can be admired more readily since they can easily be seen at eye level.

Construction

Dry walls are built without any of the frostproof foundation usually required for masonry walls. A low wall up to about 2 feet high can be built directly on the ground. For taller walls, however, it is better to place a layer of fairly large rocks 18 to 20 inches beneath the surface of the ground, or a trench

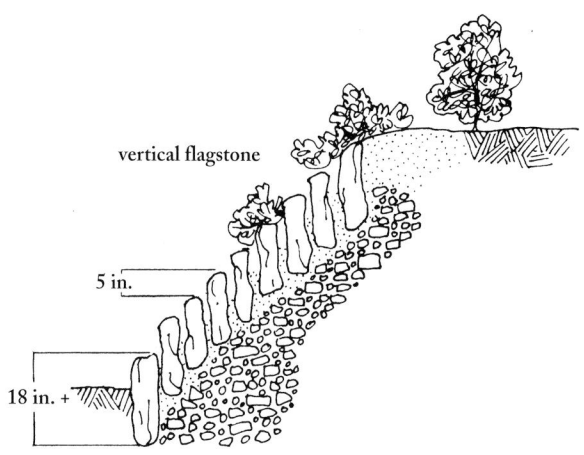

Cyclopean wall (cross section)

can be dug as wide as one-third of the height of the wall, and about 12 inches deep. This trench is filled to ground level with 2 to 3 inches of crushed stone.

As in the rock garden, large rocks are preferred, and the soil mix, which takes the place of mortar, is the same as in the rock garden, i.e., equal proportions of rough sand and gravel, peat moss, and friable loam. Every device for holding the stones together should be used: joints should be overlapped, larger openings should be filled with smaller stone chips, and long tie stones should be used to anchor the wall to the existing bank (see the illustration). Stones with round surfaces should be avoided.

The individual pieces of rock should slope toward the base and rear of the wall. This will help prevent rocks slipping or falling from the wall as a result of frost action and will also direct rainwater into the soil-filled spaces. The face of the wall should slope backward about 2 inches for every vertical foot. The thickness of the base of the wall should be equal to one-third the wall's height. Experience has shown that wall gardens should not be built higher than 4 or 5 feet. When greater heights are involved, it is better to make several walled terraces than one very high dry wall. However, if a high single wall is unavoidable, the size of the rocks should be increased to ensure greater stability.

In laying the rocks, each layer should be more or less horizontal. The prepared soil is placed over the top of this first layer of rocks, and crushed stone or stone chips from the trimmed stones are packed behind each layer of stones. This will give the wall greater stability and ensure better drainage behind it. The stones in the second layer are then laid so that their joints do not coincide with those of the layer below. This process is repeated until the desired height is reached. Every so often a long rock should reach from the face of the wall back to the solid bank. This tie stone will give the wall extra strength.

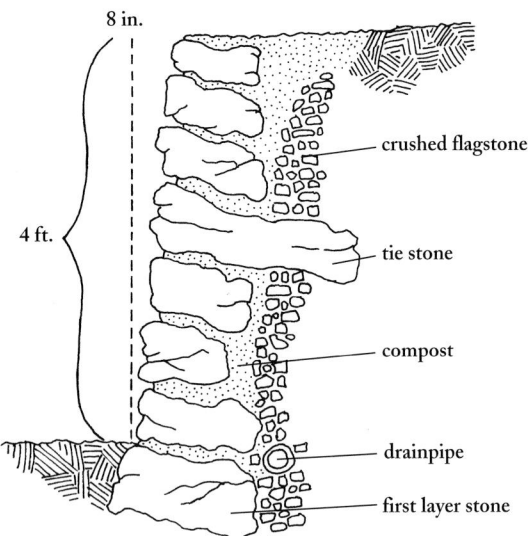

Dry wall (cross section)

Planting Techniques

The most practical method of planting the wall is to set the plants in place as the wall goes up. The rootballs of the potted plants are loosened, and the roots disentangled and stretched as far back as possible on top of the stones and between the joints. Before the next rock is placed on top, some fine soil or peat should be sifted over the roots and then watered well. In walls that have already been established, the planting procedure is somewhat more complicated. In this situation, plants must be taken out of small pots and tucked securely into the crevices. To hold them in place and keep them moist for a longer period, wet sphagnum moss should be wedged around the plants, and the wall should then be sprayed frequently. On a sunny, drought-prone south side, it is best during the first summer to hang sheets of cheesecloth over the planted wall, which, if kept wet, help retard drought stress until the onset of fall rains.

The types of plants that can be used in a wall garden vary tremendously. Take advantage of the many possibilities and grow some of those plants that are difficult to cultivate in an ordinary rock garden. Because of the better drainage, plants will live longer and be less likely to rot.

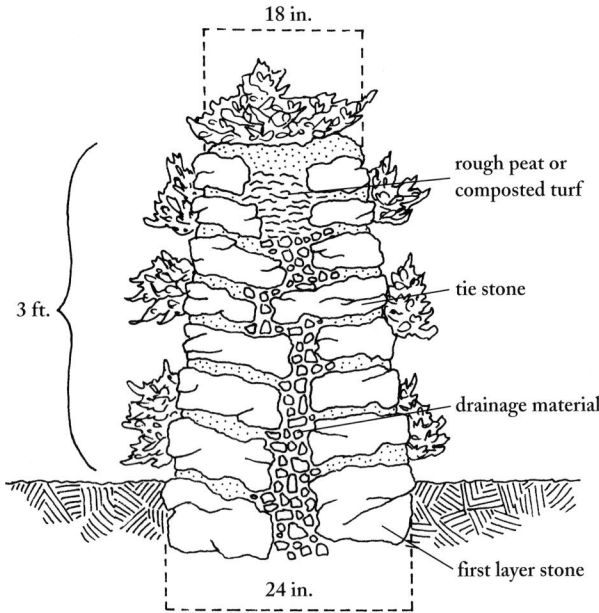

Double dividing wall (cross section)

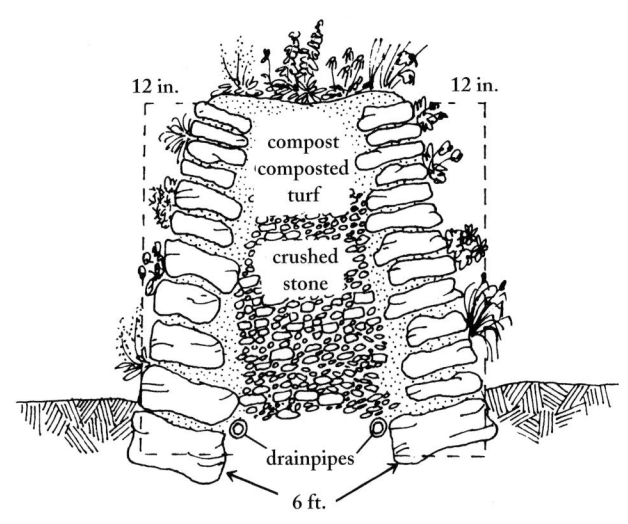

Wall mound (cross section)

PERENNIALS OF RELATIVELY EASY CULTURE FOR ROCK AND WALL GARDENS

Name	Zones	Height	Soil pH*	Exposure†	Flower Color and Bloom Time
Achillea clavennae (silver alpine yarrow)	3–7	4–12"	Al	S	White; late spring
A. tomentosa (woolly yarrow)	3–7	4–8"	Al	S	Yellow; summer
Adonis amurensis (Amur adonis)	3–7	4–12"	Al to N	S	Yellow; early spring
A. vernalis (spring adonis)	3–7	4–12"	Al to N	S	Yellow; early spring
Aethionema × warleyense (Persian candytuft)	7–8	4–6"	Al	S	Pink; early summer
Ajuga reptans (bugle)	6–8	4–6"	N	S to LSh	Blue; spring
Androsace sarmentosa (rock jasmine)	3–7	4–6"	Al to N	S	Pink; late spring
Aquilegia canadensis (rock columbine)	3–8	8–12"	Al to N	S to LSh	Red and yellow; late spring
A. flabellata (Japanese fan columbine)	3–6	8–12"	N	S	White; spring
A. saximontana (Colorado columbine)	4–6	3–4"	N	S	Blue and yellow; spring
Arabis albida (wallcress)	5–8	4–6"	Al to N	S	White; early spring
A. caucasica (Caucasian rock cress)	4–7	6–15"	Al to N	S	White; spring
A. sturtii (shining rock cress)	4–7	3–4"	Al to N	S	White; spring
Arenaria grandiflora (showy sandwort)	5–8	3–4"	N	S	White; summer
A. montana (mountain sandwort)	4–7	4–6"	N	S	White; summer
Armeria caespitosa (thrift)	8–9	3–4"	N	S	Pink; early summer
A. maritima (thrift, sea pink)	6–8	4–6"	N	S	Pink or white; early summer
Aster alpinus (rock aster)	3–7	8–10"	N to Ac	S	Blue-violet; late spring to early summer
Aubrieta deltoidea	7–9	6–8"	Al	S	Purple; late spring
Aurinia saxatilis (basket-of-gold)	3–7	8–12"	N	S	Yellow; spring
Bornmuellera cappadocica	7–8	3–4"	Al to N	S	White; spring
Bruckenthalia spiculifolia (spike heath)	5–7	4–6"	N to Ac	S	Pink; summer
Calluna vulgaris cvs. (heather)	4–8	8–10"	Ac	S	Reddish violet to white; summer
Campanula carpatica (Carpathian harebell)	3–7	6–8"	Al to N	S	Purple or white; summer to fall
C. cochleariifolia (fairy thimbles)	6–8	6–9"	Al to N	S	Blue to white; summer
C. elatines var. *garganica* (Adriatic bellflower)	6–8	6–9"	Al to N	S	Blue to white; summer
C. portenschlagiana (Bavarian bellflower)	4–7	4–6"	Al to N	S	Blue; summer
C. poscharskyana (Poscharsky bellflower)	3–7	9–12"	Al to N	S	Purple to white; summer to fall
Carlina acaulis (Carline thistle)	4–6	4–6"	Al to N	S	Purplish to white; spring
Ceratostigma plumbaginoides (blue leadwort)	5–8	6–12"	N	S to LSh	Blue; late summer
Chrysogonum virginianum (golden star)	5–8	6–9"	N	S to LSh	Yellow; summer
Corydalis lutea (golden corydalis)	6–8	8–10"	N	S to LSh	Yellow; spring to summer
Dianthus alpinus (alpine pink)	3–7	6–9"	Al	S	Red and white; early summer
D. deltoides (maiden pink)	3–7	6–8"	Al	S	Rose pink; spring to fall
D. gratianopolitanus (cheddar pink)	3–7	3–6"	Al	S	Rose pink; summer
D. pavonius (tufted pink)	4–7	6–9"	Al, N, or Ac	S	Red to pink; summer
Draba aizoides (moss draba)	4–8	3–6"	Al to N	S	Yellow; early spring
D. dedeana (Pyrenees draba)	7–8	3–4"	Al to N	S	White and lavender; spring
D. sibirica (trailing whitlow grass)	1–7	2–3"	Al to N	S	Yellow; spring
Festuca ovina var. *glauca* (blue fescue)	3–8	4–6"	Al to N	S to LSh	Blue-gray foliage
Gentiana acaulis (spring gentian)	3–7	2–5"	Al	S	Blue; spring
G. scabra (Chinese gentian)	5–8	10–15"	Al	S	Blue; summer to fall
G. septemfida (Ural gentian)	3–7	10–15"	Al	S	Blue; summer

(continues)

PERENNIALS OF RELATIVELY EASY CULTURE FOR ROCK AND WALL GARDENS (*continued*)

Name	Zones	Height	Soil pH*	Exposure†	Flower Color and Bloom Time
Geranium dalmaticum (dalmatian geranium, cranesbill)	5–8	4–6"	Al to N	S	Rose; late spring
G. sanguineum var. *strictum* (Lancaster geranium)	5–8	6–9"	Al, N, or Ac	S to LSh	Pink with red veins; summer
Globularia cordifolia (shrubby globularia)	6–8	4–5"	Al	S	Grayish blue; late spring to early summer
Gypsophila cerastioides (Himalayan baby's breath)	5–7	3–6"	N	S	Lilac to white; summer
G. repens (creeping baby's breath)	4–7	3–4"	N	S	Pink to white; spring to fall
Haberlea rhodopensis (tufted haberlea)	6–8	3–4"	N	LSh	Lavender; spring
Helianthemum nummularium (sunrose)	5–8	6–8"	Al	S	Yellow; late spring
Heuchera sanguinea (coralbells)	3–7	10–15"	N	S to LSh	Red to white; late spring to early fall
Houstonia caerulea (bluets)	3–8	4–8"	Al to N	S to LSh	Blue to purple; spring
Hutchinsia alpina (chamois cress)	7–8	6–8"	N	S to LSh	White; spring to summer
Hypericum calycinum (large-flowered shrubby St. John's wort)	6–8	1–1½'	N	S to LSh	Yellow; summer
H. olympicum (dwarf shrubby St. John's wort)	6–8	6–8"	N	S	Yellow; summer
Iberis saxatilis (compact evergreen candytuft)	6–8	4–6"	Al	S	White; spring
I. sempervirens (evergreen candytuft)	4–7	6–8"	Al, N, or Ac	S	White; spring
Iris cristata (crested iris)	4–8	4–6"	N	S to LSh	Lilac blue; late spring
I. pumila (dwarf Crimean iris)	3–8	6–10"	N	S	Lilac, blue, or yellow; late spring
I. verna (vernal iris)	7–8	3–4"	N	S to LSh	Lilac blue; spring
Lavandula angustifolia dwarf cvs. (dwarf lavender)	7–9	8–10"	N	S	Blue or white; summer
Leontopodium alpinum (edelweiss)	5–7	4–6"	Al	S	Yellowish gray; late spring to summer
Lewisia cotyledon (bitterroot)	6–8	8–10"	N to Ac	LSh	Pink; spring
L. rediviva (bitterroot)	4–7	2–3"	N to Ac	S	Pink; late spring
Linum flavum (yellow flax)	5–8	10–12"	N	S	Yellow; summer
L. perenne ssp. *alpinum* (alpine flax)	7–8	6–8"	N	S	Blue; late spring to early fall
Lychnis alpina (alpine campion)	5–7	4–6"	Al to N	S	Pink; spring
L. × haageana (hybrid catchfly)	6–8	8–10"	N	S	Red; early summer
Nepeta × fassenii (catmint)	3–7	1–1¼'	N	S	Blue; summer
Oenothera caespitosa (evening primrose)	4–7	6–8"	N	S	Yellow, aging to pinkish; summer
Papaver nudicaule (Iceland poppy)	2–7	6–14"	Al to N	S	Pink to yellow, white; summer
P. radicatum (tufted poppy)	3–7	5–10"	Al to N	S	Yellow or white; summer
Penstemon davidsonii (matted penstemon)	6–7	3–5"	Al to N	S	Purple; summer
P. glaber (smooth penstemon)	3–6	1½–2'	Al to N	S	Blue to white; late summer
P. hirsutus 'Pygmaeus' (pygmy penstemon)	3–8	4–7"	Al to N	S	Purple; late summer
P. menziesii (Pacific beardtongue)	7–8	6–8"	N to Ac	S to LSh	Purple; summer
P. newberryi (mountain pride)	8–9	1–1¼'	N to Ac	S to LSh	Rose pink; summer
P. pinifolius (pine-leaf penstemon)	8–9	1–1½'	N to Ac	S to LSh	Red; summer
Petrorhagia saxifraga (tunic flower)	5–8	4–6"	N	S	Pink; summer
Phlox bifida (prairie phlox)	6–8	4–6"	N	S	Lilac blue; spring
P. divaricata (blue phlox)	4–7	6–8"	N	S to LSh	Lilac blue; early spring
P. stolonifera (creeping phlox)	4–8	4–6"	N	S to LSh	Purple to lavender; spring

(continues)

Basket-of-gold (*Aurinia saxatilis*)

Evergreen candytuft
(*Ibers sempervirens*)

Creeping phlox
(*Phlox stolonifera*
'Bruce's White')

Thrift
(*Armeria caespitosa*)

Wooly thyme (*Thymus pseudolanuginosus*)
with *Impatiens walleriana*

**Japanese fan
columbine**
(*Aquilegia flabellata*)

Sunrose (*Helianthemum nummularium*)

Blue leadwort (*Ceratostigma plumbaginoides*)

Hen and chickens (*Sempervivum tectorum*) **surrounded by
Golden creeping Jenny** (*Lysimachia nummularia* 'Aurea')

Pasque flower (*Pulsatilla vulgaris*)

PERENNIALS OF RELATIVELY EASY CULTURE FOR ROCK AND WALL GARDENS (*continued*)

Name	Zones	Height	Soil pH*	Exposure†	Flower Color and Bloom Time
P. subulata (mountain pink)	3–7	3–4"	N	S	Lavender, red, pink, or white; early spring
Potentilla alba (silky cinquefoil)	5–8	3–4"	N	S	White; early spring
P. crantzii (alpine cinquefoil)	5–7	1–2"	Al to N	S	Yellow; spring
P. fruticosa dwarf cvs. (dwarf shrubby cinquefoil)	6–8	1–2'	Al, N, or Ac	S	Yellow, pink, or white; summer
P. tridentata (three-tooth cinquefoil)	4–8	6–10"	Ac	S to LSh	White; early summer
Primula auricula (auricula)	3–7	6–8"	Al	S to LSh	Yellow; spring
P. denticulata (drumstick primrose)	5–7	10–12"	N	S to LSh	Pink or white; spring
P. marginata (rosulate primrose)	7–8	3–6"	Al to N	S to LSh	Lavender blue; spring
P. sieboldii (Siebold primrose)	5–7	10–12"	N	S	Rose pink or white; spring
Pulsatilla vulgaris (Pasque flower)	5–7	10–12"	Al	S to LSh	Violet to lilac; early spring
Saponaria ocymoides (rock soapwort)	4–7	8–10"	N	S	Pink; spring to summer
Saxifraga paniculata (lifelong saxifrage)	2–7	3–8"	Al to N	LSh	White; spring
Sedum acre (gold moss, live-forever)	5–8	2–3"	N to Ac	S	Yellow; late spring to early summer
S. dasyphyllum (grayleaf sedum)	8–9	2–4"	Al to N	S	Pink; summer
S. middendorfianum (narrowleaf sedum)	7–9	6–14"	Al to N	S	Pink; summer
S. sieboldii (late sedum)	6–8	1–2'	Al, N, or Ac	S	Red-violet; late summer
Sempervivum spp. (hen and chickens, houseleek)	5–8	4–6"	Al to N	S	Red to yellow; late spring to early summer
Silene caroliniana (wild pink)	5–8	3–4"	Ac	S to LSh	Pink; early summer
S. schafta (creeping pink)	6–8	4–6"	N	S to LSh	Purple to pink; late summer
Thymus pseudolanuginosus (woolly thyme)	6–8	1–2"	Al, N, or Ac	S	Pink; summer
T. serpyllum (mother of thyme)	5–8	3–4"	N	S	Rose pink to purple; late spring
Veronica prostrata (cliff speedwell)	5–7	6–8"	N	S	Blue or white; summer
V. spicata 'Alpina' (dwarf speedwell)	3–7	6–8"	N	S	Blue; summer
Viola pedata (bird's-foot violet)	5–7	2–6"	N	S	Purple and lilac; spring

* Al, alkaline; N, neutral; Ac, acidic.

† S, full sun; Sh, shade (no direct sun); PSh, partial shade (sun exposure only part of the day); LSh, light shade (e.g., the shade of tall, open trees, with little or no exposure to direct sun).

TROUGH GARDENS

While many gardeners are bewitched by the charm of miniature alpine landscapes in nature, the question often arises whether it is possible to replicate such a landscape in the home garden. Conditions of soil, aspect, and exposure at hand must be compared with the environmental conditions required by the alpine plants under consideration for garden culture. In cases requiring more intervention and site preparation than are practicable, the trough garden is a substitute that has many virtues of its own. In small compass, conditions can be artificially produced to suit the requirements of many delightful dwarf plants. At the same time trough gardening can provide a new means of gardening even for city dwellers, whose sole available space usually consists of a few yards of paving or concrete slabs. Troughs and miniature gardens also look delightful flanking a lawn or arranged on a terrace. This type of gardening is primarily for the hobby gardener, the elderly, or the admirer of the smallest and rarest plants.

Unfortunately, a number of alpines are not easy to grow in the rock garden because of our varied climate and temperature extremes. However, in a trough, where growing conditions are more under the control of the gardener, the majority of alpine minatures can be grown successfully over a number of years.

Unless placed with great care, dwarf, slow-growing conifers often outgrow the rock garden. In the trough, however, they add that touch of character that is so necessary and desirable in this type of gardening and the root restriction that the trough imposes helps the plants retain their dwarf stature. All dwarf trees grown in trough gardens should be on their own roots (i.e., not grafted).

Another aspect of this method of gardening is that each miniature trough or sink is in itself an artistic creation; but unlike a painting, it is a living thing, providing a series of enchanting pictures that change with each passing season.

There are more practical sides to trough gardening. Many elderly people who are unable to cope with the physical aspects of gardening still have an active "green thumb." These people frequently find trough gardening very satisfying because troughs, arranged on stilts of stone or wood to suit the gardener's height, eliminate the necessity of strenuous bending. And last, but not least, this type of gardening will also keep off that arch enemy of all rock plants, the slug.

One of the most charming plant containers is the old antique stone trough, though the prices for these today are rising rapidly because each is unique. However, very attractive inexpensive troughs can be made of concrete or bricks. A lightweight, more portable but equally good container can even be made of a mixture of equal parts of fine peat, fine perlite, vermiculite, and cement. The inside of the 1-inch-thick walls of these containers is reinforced with chicken wire. For drainage, wooden dowels can be pressed through the wet concrete mixture and pulled or drilled out later.

The most important aspect of trough and table gardens is neither the material nor the form of the container. Far more important is good drainage. Alpines are utterly intolerant of badly drained soil. Wherever they are grown, it is essential to make certain that water does not stagnate around their roots. Alpines like plenty of water and are accustomed to growing in places where, especially during spring and early summer, vast amounts of water from melting snow and ice

flow past their roots. Yet they will not endure having their roots surrounded by perpetually soggy soil.

Soil

Since trough gardening does not depend on existing on-site soil, preparation of the soil mix is entirely in the hands of the gardener. A light moss or pine needle humus makes an ideal base. Any loose, partly decayed material in the humus should remain, as this will help augment the root growth medium in years ahead and reduce the need for frequent soil changes.

Provision for the essential good drainage must be made before the container is filled. A layer of coarse ash, gravel, or stone chips at the bottom of the container is sufficient. Over this, spread a layer of some rough organic material such as semidecayed leaves or coarse peat. This will prevent the finer compost that is used on top from filtering into and obstructing the drainage. With the drainage arranged for, fill the container to the brim with whatever compost has been chosen and prepared. It should be moist but not wet when used. The soil will settle somewhat in time.

A light, portable frost-proof container. This container can be easily made out of equal parts cement, sphagnum, peat, and perlite. For reinforcement it is wise to sandwich a 1-inch mesh chicken wire within the concrete.

Natural stone trough. Old horse and pig troughs are excellent planters for rock garden plants.

Alpines on Tufa

Blocks of the light, porous rock known as tufa can be used as the rooting base for a wide range of small alpines. Ornamental in their own right, tufa chunks can be purchased from most garden centers. Rooted cuttings or seedlings of alpines can be planted in existing holes in the tufa, or extra holes can be drilled in with a screwdriver. The stone is so porous that it remains moist for long periods, and fine soil and roots readily penetrate into the material.

Thus tufa is ideal for making miniature alpine gardens, not only as a substrate but also as an aesthetic setting for cliff-dwelling rock plants, such as saxifrages (*Saxifraga* spp.) and hen and chickens (*Sempervivum* spp.), that can often be overwhelmed in the ground-sited rock garden.

Round table garden. This garden is made of a large concrete drainpipe, 3 to 4 feet in diameter, buried up to 30 inches above ground level.

Plants Suitable for Troughs

In selecting plants for troughs, leaf and flower forms should be carefully studied from the aesthetic point of view, because the trough should be pleasing to look at throughout the year. Plants that are fast growing or rank in habit should be avoided, as should plants that are not winter hardy. Bear in mind that, contrary to a normal planting in a garden, the influence of frost comes not only from above the container but also from all sides. Of course, the type of plant material is determined by the location of the trough. Ideally, a sunny place should be selected. However, saxifrages and some heaths and their relatives (the family Ericaceae) succeed best on the shady side of a building but away from any overhanging branches of trees.

Plants that dwell in higher mountain regions and cliffs generally have narrower ecological amplitudes than lowland species, i.e., in the horticultural sense, alpine plants have rather precise cultural requirements. Often, a place in the garden cannot be found that is suitable for the culture of alpines. Hence the importance of troughs, which offer the opportunity for more intervention and habitat adjustment than an in-ground garden, and if the trough is portable, the opportunity to reposition the entire setting as seasons change. Trough gardening thus offers the possibility of growing the "fussiest" of alpine plants with reasonable prospect of success.

Plants such as dwarf conifers that form a superficial root mat benefit from midday shade, especially in summer heat. Protection from strong winds is also advisable, both in summer and winter, since, besides waterlogging, desiccation of the soil medium and the plants themselves can lead to failure.

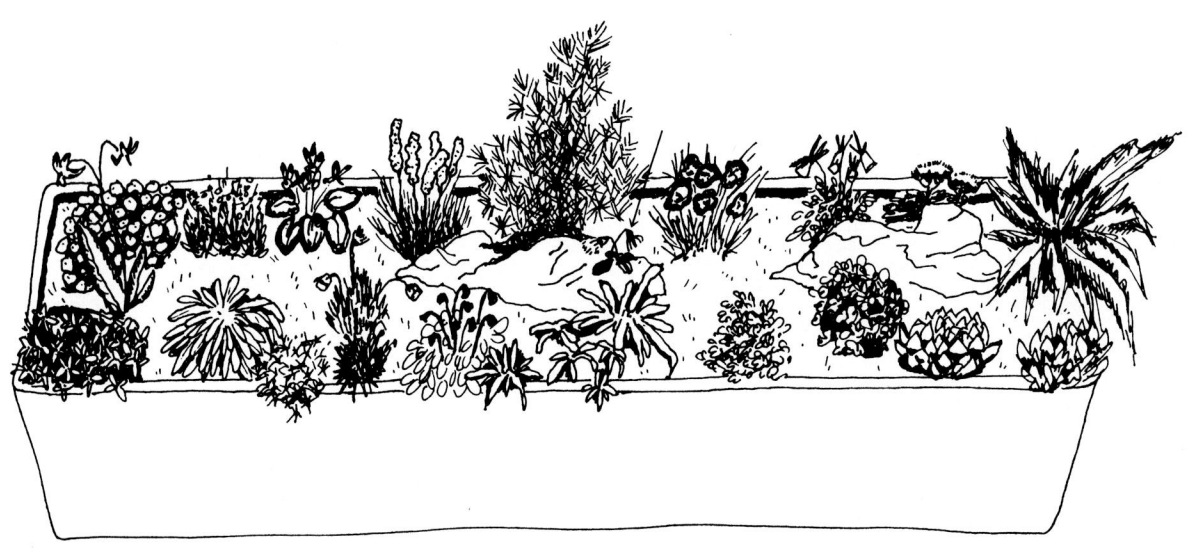

In a large trough, diverse dwarf plants grouped around rocks and a dominant central subject, such as Picea abies *'Pygmaea',* *might include* Aquilegia jonesii, Cyclamen europaeum, Dianthus simulans, Helichrysum milfordii, Hypericum coris, Petrophytum hendersonii, *and* Soldanella alpina.

SLOW-GROWING DWARF CONIFERS SUITABLE FOR TROUGH GARDENS

Name	Zones	Annual Growth
Abies balsamea 'Nana', *A. balsamea* 'Hudsonia' (dwarf balsam fir)	2–8	½"
Cedrus libani 'Nana' (dwarf conical cedar of Lebanon)	(6) 7–9	1"
Chamaecyparis obtusa 'Compacta' (compact Hinoki cypress)	4–8	¼"
C. obtusa 'Minima' (minimal Hinoki cypress)	4–8	¼"
C. obtusa 'Nana' (dwarf Hinoki cypress)	4–8	1"
Cryptomeria japonica 'Nana' (dwarf Japanese cedar)	6–9	¾"
C. japonica 'Vilmoriniana' (Vilmorin Japanese cedar)	6–9	¾"
Juniperus communis 'Compressa' (dwarf common juniper)	2–6 (7)	½"
J. communis 'Echiniformis' (hedgehog juniper)	2–6 (7)	½"
Picea abies 'Humilis' (dwarf Norway spruce)	2–7	¼"
P. abies 'Pygmaea' (pygmy Norway spruce)	2–7	1"
Pinus nigra 'Hornibrookiana' (dwarf Austrian pine)	4–7	⅛"
P. parviflora 'Brevifolia' (dwarf shortleaf Japanese white pine)	4–7	½"
P. sylvestris 'Beauvronensis' (dwarf Scotch pine)	2–7 (8)	1"
Taxus baccata 'Pygmaea' (dwarf small-leaf English yew)	(5) 6–7	½"
Thuja orientalis 'Minima Glauca' (dwarf glaucous Oriental arborvitae)	(5) 6–9	½"

PERENNIAL ROCK PLANTS AND DWARF SHRUBS SUITABLE FOR TROUGH GARDENS

All thrive in full sun or, at most, a brief period of shade, and require gritty, humusy, perfectly drained soil.

Name	Zones	Height by Spread	Soil pH*	Flower Color and Bloom Time
Androsace carnea (rock jasmine)	5–7	3 × 4"	Al	Pink; early summer
A. chamaejasme (rock jasmine)	5–7	2 × 3"	Al	White; early summer
A. sempervivoides (rock jasmine)	5–7	2 × 6"	Al	Pink; summer
A. villosa (rock jasmine)	4–7	2 × 4"	Al	White; summer
Anemone baldensis (dwarf windflower)	6–8	3 × 6"	Ac	White; summer
Aquilegia jonesii (Jones's columbine)	3–6	3 × 4"	Ac	Blue; spring to summer
Arabis androsacea (Cilician rock cress)	6–7	1 × 4"	Ac	White; summer
Arenaria tetraquetra (Pyrenees sandwort)	6–7	2 × 6"	Ac	White; summer
Armeria caespitosa 'Bevans Variety' (compact thrift)	8–9	2 × 6"	Al to Ac	Pink; spring
Artemisia glacialis (mountain wormwood)	5–7	1 × 6"	Al to Ac	Silvery gray; summer
Astilbe × crispa (dagalet)	6–8	6 × 8"	Al to Ac	Rose; summer
Campanula alpestris (alpine bellflower)	5–8	2 × 8"	Al to N	Purple; summer
C. chamissonis (Pacific bellflower)	2–6	4 × 6"	Al to N	Pale blue; summer
C. elatines (Adriatic bellflower)	6–8	3 × 8"	Al to N	Violet; summer
C. piperi (Olympic bellflower)	7–8	6 × 6"	Al to N	Lilac blue; summer
C. rainieri (Rainier bellflower)	6–8	3 × 6"	Al to N	China blue; summer
C. zoysii (Italian bellflower)	6–8	2 × 4"	Al to N	Pale blue; summer
Cassiope lycopodioides (iwa-hige)	3–6	1 × 4"	Ac	White; spring to summer
C. mertensiana (white heather)	5–7	9 × 6"	Ac	White; spring
C. selaginoides (white heather)	4–6	3 × 6"	Ac	White; spring

(continues)

PERENNIAL ROCK PLANTS AND DWARF SHRUBS SUITABLE FOR TROUGH GARDENS (continued)

Name	Zones	Height by Spread	Soil pH*	Flower Color and Bloom Time
Corydalis cashmiriana (Kashmir corydalis)	5–7	4 × 4"	N to Ac	Blue; summer
Cyclamen purpurascens (fall cyclamen)	6–7	4 × 6"	Al to Ac	Red; late summer to fall
C. repandum (spring cyclamen)	7–8	6 × 6"	Al to Ac	Deep pink; spring
Cytisus andoinii † (cottage broom)	7–8	4 × 8"	Al to Ac	Yellow; spring
Daphne petraea † (Italian daphne)	6–8	4 × 6"	Al to Ac	Rose pink; late spring to summer
Dianthus glacialis (Carpathian pink)	5–7	2 × 6"	Al to N	Deep pink; summer
D. pavonius (alpine pink)	4–7	4 × 6"	Al to N	Rose; summer
D. simulans (Orvilos pink)	7–8	3 × 6"	Al to N	Deep pink; summer
Douglasia laevigata (eastern douglasia)	5–7	2 × 6"	Al	Rose red; summer
Draba dedeana (Pyrenees draba)	7–8	1 × 4"	Al to Ac	Yellow; late spring to summer
D. mollissima (Caucasus draba)	6–8	2 × 6"	Al to Ac	Yellow; spring to summer
D. polytricha (Turkish draba)	7–8	2 × 4"	Al to Ac	Yellow; spring to summer
D. rigida var. *bryoides* (Armenian draba)	7–8	2 × 4"	Al to Ac	Yellow; late spring to summer
Dryas octopetala (mountain avens)	2–6	2 × 6"	Al to N	White; summer
Edraianthus pumilio (grassy bells)	6–7	2 × 6"	N	Lavender; spring to summer
Erigeron compositus (Canadian fleabane)	5–7	2 × 6"	Al to Ac	Lavender; summer
Erinus alpinus (alpine balsam)	6–8	3 × 6"	Al to Ac	Lilac; summer
Gentiana dalmaticum (pink gentian)	6–8	6 × 6"	N to Ac	Pink; summer
G. farreri (Tibetan gentian)	5–7	6 × 6"	N to Ac	Light blue; fall
G. verna (spring gentian)	5–7	3 × 4"	N to Ac	Blue; spring to summer
Globularia cordifolia (globe daisy)	6–8	2 × 6"	Al to N	Lavender; summer
Gypsophila aretioides (cushion baby's breath)	5–7	1 × 6"	Al	White; summer
Helichrysum milfordiae (dwarf strawflower)	7–8	1 × 6"	N to Ac	White; spring
Hypericum cerastioides (dwarf St. John'swort)	6–8	4 × 8"	Al	Yellow; summer
Iberis saxatilis (rock candytuft)	6–8	3 × 6"	Al to N	White; summer
Ilex crenata 'Mariesii'† (dwarf Japanese holly)	6–7	8 × 4"	Al to Ac	Inconspicuous
Iris pumila (dwarf iris)	5–8	2 × 8"	N	Lavender blue; spring
Kalmiopsis leachiana† (Oregon laurel)	7–8	9 × 6"	Ac	Rose pink; spring
Leiophyllum buxifolium 'Nanum'† (dwarf sandbox)	5–7	9 × 12"	Ac	White; late spring to early summer
Lewisia brachycalyx (tufted lewisia)	5–7	1 × 3"	N to Ac	White; summer
L. rediviva (bitterroot)	4–7	2 × 4"	N to Ac	Pale pink; summer
Lychnis alpina (alpine campion)	5–7	4 × 4"	N to Ac	Rose; spring
Oxalis adenophylla (sauerklee)	5–7	3 × 6"	N to Ac	Rose; late spring to early summer
Papaver alpinum (Pyrenees poppy)	5–7	6 × 6"	Al to N	Red-orange, yellow, or white; summer
Penstemon davidsonii (creeping beardtongue)	6–8	3 × 8"	N to Ac	Lilac; summer
P. rupicola (rock penstemon)	7–8	4 × 8"	N to Ac	Crimson; late spring to summer
Petrocallis pyrenaica (rock beauty)	4–6	2 × 5"	Al	Lavender; spring
Petrophytum caespitosum (rock spiraea)	3–6	1 × 6"	Al	White; summer
Phlox bryoides (mossy phlox)	3–6	1 × 6"	N	White; late spring to early summer
P. douglasii (Douglas phlox)	5–7	2 × 6"	N	Lilac; spring to early summer
Phyteuma comosum (purple rock campion)	6–8	3 × 6"	Al to Ac	Lilac; summer
P. pauciflorum (blue rock campion)	6–8	2 × 6"	Al to Ac	Blue; summer

Name	Zones	Height by Spread	Soil pH*	Flower Color and Bloom Time
Polygonum tenuicaule (dwarf Japanese knotweed)	6–8	2 × 5"	Al to Ac	White; spring to summer
Potentilla crantzii (alpine cinquefoil)	5–7	1 × 6"	Al to N	Yellow; spring
Primula allionii (alpine primrose)	7–8	2 × 4"	Al	Rose red; early spring
P. farinosa (farinose primrose)	4–6	2 × 3"	Al to N	Pink; spring
P. marginata (rosulate primrose)	7–8	4 × 6"	Al to N	Lavender blue; spring
P. minima (dwarf primrose)	5–7	2 × 4"	Al to N	Rose; late spring
P. rosea (rosy primrose)	6–7	4 × 6"	N	Redish blue; summer
Pulsatilla vernalis (featherleaf Pasque flower)	4–6	4 × 6"	Al to N	White with violet black; spring to summer
Rhododendron impeditum† (blue rhododendron)	4–7	6 × 9"	Ac	Lavender; spring
R. uniflorum var. *imperator*† (one-flowered rhododendron)	4–7	6 × 9"	Ac	Pale purple; spring
Rhodothamnus chamaecistus†	6–7	9 × 6"	Al	Bright rose; spring
Saponaria caespitosa (dwarf soapwort)	7–8	2 × 6"	N to Ac	Pale pink; late summer
S. ocymoides 'Rubra Compacta' (rock soapwort)	4–7	1 × 6"	N to Ac	Carmine; spring to summer
Saxifraga small and compact spp. (saxifrage)	4–7	Various	Al to Ac	Mostly pink, yellow, or white; spring to summer
Sempervivum spp. (hen and chickens, houseleek)	5–8	Various	Al to Ac	Mostly red to white; summer
Silene acaulis (moss campion)	2–7	2 × 6"	Al to Ac	Rose pink; summer
S. alpestris (alpine campion)	5–7	2 × 4"	Al to Ac	White; early summer
Soldanella montana (alpine soldanella)	6–7	4 × 6"	N to Ac	Lavender; early spring
Talinum okanoganense (Okanogan fameflower)	6–7	1 × 3"	N to Ac	White; spring to early summer
Townsendia excapa (Easter daisy)	3–8	2 × 4"	N to Ac	Lavender blue; early summer
Vitaliana primuliflora	5–7	1 × 6"	Al	Yellow; summer

* Al, alkaline; N, neutral; Ac, acidic.

† Shrub.

Alpine cinquefoil (*Potentilla fruticosa*)

Mountain avens (*Dryas octopetala*)

White heather (*Cassiope mertensiana*)

25

Inviting Birds and Other Wildlife to the Garden

MOST AMERICANS DWELL IN CITIES, TOWNS, AND SUBURBAN settings, and these places are blessed with a surprising diversity and abundance of wildlife that was preadapted to or has gradually accommodated to the ways of modern humans. Birds and other wildlife in the garden are much more than seemingly trivial aspects of nature that entertain us. They are in fact constant reminders of the inner, often hidden complexities of the interdependence of all living forms and of our responsibility to help maintain conditions that promote their well-being.

A hovering hawkmoth hard at work.

BIRDS IN THE GARDEN

Almost all species of songbirds and game birds seek insects as food. For example, warblers, flycatchers, thrushes, creepers, thrashers, mockingbirds, woodpeckers, and grackles are busy most of the time eating insect eggs and larvae and mature insects.

Beyond their unending preoccupation with food—necessitated by high metabolic rates—birds periodically seek nesting sites, the character of which varies according to kind. Nests range from the very specific to the vaguely generic; from the elaborate, artful, swinging sack fashioned by the oriole to the rearrangement of a few stones or a mere scrape in the sand done by shorebirds. If we provide suitable habitat, we will have quantities of resident birds and many of the migrants as well. The most important considerations are water, an open area of lawn or meadow, a thicket of shrubs, some trees, and freedom from aggressive predators, especially pet cats. Water is essential, even if it is only a small pool with an inlet that can be opened periodically to keep the water fresh. A meadow or lawn and a nearby copse of bushes for cover, for berries, and for nesting places will satisfy many ground birds. A few tall trees in a grove will attract such twig-inspecting birds as vireos, warblers, thrushes, woodpeckers, and titmice who feed on insects, borers, and young buds. The meadowlarks, quails, field sparrows, goldfinches, and bobolinks need pastures and hay fields. Bluebirds, nuthatches, downy woodpeckers, and flickers inhabit old orchards that offer broken or hollow branches for nesting places. Many kinds of songbirds are content to live close to our homes, especially if there are mature trees and shrubs and gardens nearby. Phoebes, robins, catbirds, cardinals, and various wrens and sparrows all nest in confidence as our close neighbors. For winter shelter, large evergreens are particularly important and should be an integral part of any plan to invite the birds.

When habitats are developed for as many different species of birds as possible, the beautiful and exciting predatory species of hawks and owls may occasionally visit the sanctuary, enhancing immeasurably the birdwatcher's pleasure as smaller birds and mammals quickly disappear seeking cover. In providing bird habitat, the home owner is providing suitable habitat for interesting mammals and insects as well. Chipmunks, squirrels, fireflies, butterflies, and moths all should be welcome visitors in the natural landscape created to attract birds.

Milkweed flower heads, water-lily pads, sunflower seedheads, and petunia blooms offer food and shelter for a diversity of wild creatures in the garden and add much to its interest.

Bird feeders are infinite in design, ranging from such natural materials as a suspended hollow log with knothole openings (c.) and a lopped-off coconut husk (g.) to a perforated plastic cylinder with perches (b.) and a plastic sphere with a rain shield (e.). Windowsill seed trays (a., d., h.) lure many small birds and entertain those viewing from within, while a more distant suet cage (f.), holiday tree ornamented with various feeders (i.), and pole-mounted swivel feeder (j.) bring other, often larger, birds and enliven a winter vista.

A constant and varied food supply is as important as good locations for nests. If you plant the trees and shrubs and garden flowers that provide birds with the various foods they seek, you will have many birds. In the year-round life of birds, many species of trees and shrubs seem attractive in one way or another. The lists beginning on page 606 include plants that have noteworthy associations.

Winter Feeding

Winter feeding, if faithfully practiced, ensures continuous presence of both winter residents and migratory birds. A feeding tray, or a tray with a hopper from which the seeds pour out as they are needed, set well off the ground and protected by a stovepipe collar or otherwise designed to exclude cats and squirrels, will provide a safe spot for the birds to gather. To merely cast crumbs and seed on the snow from time to time is inadequate and wasteful.

The suite of birds that frequent home grounds and visit feeders varies from region to region and according to season. In the eastern states, feeding station visitors include the junco, nuthatch, bluejay, downy and hairy woodpeckers, and various finches and sparrows, to say nothing of the ubiquitous starling and pigeon. When the food supply is suddenly discontinued, stress ensues as the birds seek alternative sources. In severe winter weather, especially during and after late-season snows, many may die as fruit- and seed-bearing shrubs and trees have shed or been stripped of their crops.

Among fruit-bearing woody plants of interest to winter birds, the Washington thorn (*Crataegus phaenopyrum*), winterberry holly (*Ilex verticillata*), and various cotoneasters (*Cotoneaster* spp.) are especially favored. It should be remembered that woody plants valued for retention of brightly colored ornamental berries through the winter are obviously not significant food sources for wildlife. Beyond fruits and seeds, bags of suet hung in loose mesh bags or secured in containers of hardware cloth are especially attractive to woodpeckers, chickadees, and nuthatches.

Nesting Sites

Nesting houses are also a means of attracting birds, especially the species whose habitual home sites have been destroyed or curtailed by modern housing developments. Many birds are adaptable to surrogate circumstances. For example, purple martins will nest in colony houses mounted on tall poles. Barn swallows will occupy ledges under a porch roof. Phoebes, which seek running water, often build their nests under bridges or beneath a roof's eaves. House wrens often choose birdhouses, especially if the hole is just their size. Other wrens look for sheltered ledges or even hanging planter baskets. Bluebirds, now scarce over much of their range, favor a hollow branch stub in a low tree but will accept a deep nesting box on a 6-foot post, with the entrance facing south or southeast and furnished with a peg for perching.

Breeding birds are understandably very wary of cats. However attractive the nest box may be, stalking cats will cause birds to look elsewhere. A post densely clothed with the thorny stems of a climbing rose usually deters cats and other mammalian marauders, and so may entice birds to nest.

One further precaution: leave natural places natural. While some birds have become familar to us because of their adaptability to human habitats, the majority keep to less disturbed areas. Woodpeckers, for example, carve out nest holes in branch stubs and holes in tree trunks, often returning to the same hole year after year. Stubs and holes should be left for them. Red-winged blackbirds, marsh wrens, and whippoorwills nest in swampy places. If you have such a site, make it an outstanding asset not only by attracting special birds but by planting some of the equally special trees, shrubs, and perennials that require sodden ground. Herons and ducks need secluded ponds and quiet streams. Rather than clearing trees from a pond border, make a path into the area that offers a "blind" or secluded observation point. Preserve upland woodland for hermit thrushes, vireos, wood thrushes, ovenbirds, ruffed grouses, and woodcocks. Keep all these natural areas as sanctuaries for the birds.

Flowers Attractive to Birds

Few garden flowers are specifically attractive to birds, but those that are often bring the colorful hummingbirds. These remarkable miniature birds hover beside tubular blossoms and reach their bills down to the base for nectar. Favorite flowers include columbine (*Aquilegia* spp.), flowering tobacco (*Nicotiana* spp.), coralbells (*Heuchera sanguinea*), petunia (*Petunia* × *hybrida*), phlox (*Phlox* spp.), vesper iris (*Iris dichotoma*), butterfly weed (*Asclepias tuberosa*), and trumpet creeper (*Campsis radicans*).

Seed heads of garden plants attract a different group of birds. Goldfinches pick out the seeds in mature sunflower head, and they along with others take the seeds of hollyhock (*Alcea rosea*) and orange cosmos (*Cosmos sulphureus*) as well as of goldenrod (*Solidago* spp.) and thistle (*Cirsium* spp.) in the wild garden.

TREES WITH FRUIT AND SEEDS ATTRACTIVE TO BIRDS

Abies spp. (fir)
Alnus spp. (alder)
Amelanchier spp. (serviceberry)
Arbutus menziesii (madrona)
Betula spp. (birch)
Celtis spp. (hackberry)
Cornus spp. (dogwood)
Corylus spp. (hazelnut)
Crataegus spp. (hawthorn)
Disopyros spp. (persimmon)
Fagus spp. (beech)
Fraxinus spp. (ash)
Ilex spp. (holly)
Juniperus virginiana (red cedar)
Larix spp. (larch)
Liquidambar styraciflua (sweet gum)
Liriodendron tulipifera (tulip tree)
Morus spp. (mulberry)
Picea spp. (spruce)
Pinus spp. (pine)
Prunus spp. (cherry)
Quercus spp. (oak)
Sabal palmetto (palmetto)
Sorbus spp. (mountain ash)
Ulmus spp. (elm)

European elder (Sambicus nigra)—*native species of elder in fruit are equally attractive to birds.*

SHRUBS AND WOODY CLIMBERS WITH FRUIT AND SEEDS ATTRACTIVE TO BIRDS

Arctostaphylos spp. (bearberry, manzanita)
Aronia spp. (chokeberry)
Buxus spp. (box)
Cornus spp. (bush dogwood)
Cotoneaster spp.
Eleagnus spp. (Russian olive, autumn olive)
Ilex spp. (inkberry, winterberry)
Juniperus spp. (juniper)
Myrica spp. (bayberry, sweet gale)
Parthenocissus quinquefolia (Virginia creeper)
Pyracantha coccinea (firethorn)
Rhamnus spp. (buckthorn)
Rhus spp. (sumac)
Rosa spp. (rose)
Rubus spp. (blackberry, bramble)
Sambucus spp. (elder)
Shepherdia spp. (buffalo berry)
Smilax spp. (catbriar, bullbriar)
Symphoricarpos spp. (snowberry, coralberry)
Symplocos spp. (sweetleaf)
Vaccinium spp. (blueberry, huckleberry)
Viburnum spp.

ANNUALS AND PERENNIALS WITH SEEDS ATTRACTIVE TO BIRDS

Amaranthus spp. (amaranth, love-lies-bleeding)
Calendula officinalis
Callistephus chinensis (China aster)
Campanula spp. (bellflower)
Centaurea cyanus (cornflower, bachelor's button)
Chrysanthemum leucanthemum (oxeye daisy)
Cirsium spp. (thistle)
Consolida spp. (larkspur)
Coreopsis spp. (calliopsis, tickseed)
Cosmos spp.
Delphinium spp.
Dianthus spp. (pink)
Eschscholzia californica (California poppy)
Gaillardia spp. (Indian blanket)
Helianthus spp. (sunflower)
Mirabilis jalapa (four o'clock)
Myosotis spp. (forget-me-not)
Petunia × *hybrida*
Phlox spp.
Portulaca spp. (purslane)
Rudbeckia spp. (coneflower, black-eyed Susan)
Scabiosa spp. (pincushion flower)
Tagetes spp. (marigold)
Verbena × *hybrida*
Zinnia spp.

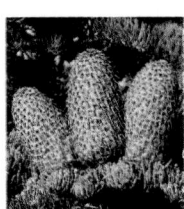

Red fir
(*Abies magnifica*)

Smooth sumac
(*Rhus glabra*)

Eastern Dogwood
(*Cornus florida*)

Disarticulating seed cone of tulip tree (*Liriodendron tulipifera*)

Parachuted seeds disseminating from thistle (*Cirsium* sp.)

OTHER VERTEBRATE ANIMALS
Rabbits and Other Rodents

Although their amusing antics arouse affection, the browsing and burrowing of rabbits, squirrels, woodchucks (or groundhogs), gophers, chipmunks, mice, and voles can sometimes result in considerable garden damage. Damage is often most severe in early spring when there is relatively little available food provided by native plants. Rabbits often decapitate tulips and consume quantities of seedling vegetables. Extermination rarely solves the problem, as the vacuum is soon filled from nearby populations. Exclusion of rabbits by 1-inch mesh woven-wire fencing, dug in about 6 inches and standing 3 to 4 feet high, is still the most effective approach. Elsewhere, sapling trees, often subject to bark stripping and girdling in winter, can be protected with individual wire mesh enclosures.

Squirrels and chipmunks are for the most part relatively harmless, but they do mine bulbs, especially tulip and crocus, and rummage through beds of newly planted seeds and seedlings, which can be protected, at least temporarily, with ½-inch mesh hardware cloth cut to size and set on or just over the newly planted bed. Further remedial measures for these and other garden rodents are discussed in Chapter 34.

Small Carnivores

Such nocturnal carnivores as raccoons and skunks, if present in small numbers, have long been regarded as interesting members of the local fauna and even beneficial, as they hunt mice and voles. However, in suburban locations, where they have become increasingly common, defensive or exclusionary measures may be required if their behavior proves annoying or damaging. In some parts of the country, raccoons have become afflicted with rabies, in which case they should be avoided and sightings of them reported to to the appropriate authorities.

Bats

Bats are often present in both suburban and rural areas, but are seldom noticed. They may be seen flying about at dusk, erratically swooping in search of insects, especially mosquitoes—their chief source of food. Persistent tales to the contrary, the bats occurring in the United States do not prey on humans. Wherever found, they should be encouraged.

Amphibians

Toads and frogs, whether resident on the ground, in ponds, or in trees, are helpful consumers of a wide array of insects,

At the ready, a leopard frog waits motionless on a water-lily pad for a flying insect to pass within range of its long, front-hinged, sticky tongue.

yet they are regarded with suspicion by many who are repelled by their slimy or warty appearance. All are harmless to humans and should be welcomed. Regrettably, these environmentally sensitive creatures have suffered a serious decline in numbers in recent years for reasons not yet fully understood.

Reptiles

Among snakes, the common garter snake and milk snake not only are harmless but are demonstrably beneficial, as they prey on such rapidly reproducing animals as mice and voles as well as frogs and toads. These snakes also eat insects. Numerous other snakes are equally beneficial but may inflict a nasty bite if cornered or surprised. Still others—the rattlesnakes, copperhead, water moccasin, and coral snake—are uncontestably dangerous, but unfortunately, the reputation of these few poisonous kinds has provoked the prevailing, unthinking, often emotional but wholly unjustified prejudice against snakes and reptiles in general. It is equivalent to condemning the entire plant kingdom because of the toxicity of poison ivy and certain mushrooms.

When not sunning themselves on logs or rocks, turtles seek aquatic insects for food.

In addition to most snakes, a number of harmless lizards are also very effective predators on insects and small rodents. Tortoises and turtles, representing another reptilian group, are usually regarded with curiosity and even affection. For the most part, turtles are aquatic and carnivorous,

whereas tortoises are terrestrial and herbivorous. It is important, then, to learn which reptiles frequent your area, to become acquainted with their characteristics and habits, and to respond accordingly.

Water Animals

In garden pools, ponds, brooks, and streams, it is well to encourage fish and frogs as well as turtles. They not only add interest to the scene but also they consume quantities of insects, including mosquito larvae.

Deer

Throughout the United States, gardeners, among many others, have a love-hate attitude toward deer. We are at once charmed by their grace and beauty but enraged by their voracious feeding on garden treasures. We are also wary of the transmission of Lyme disease by the ticks they harbor. In rural areas, deer have long proved troublesome marauders of gardens, especially in early spring. Short of being excluded by high fences, they have been difficult to control, especially in the absence of effective predators. As their numbers have risen, deer have also invaded suburbs in many regions, ravaging plantings of yew, holly, rhododendron, tulip, and hosta, among others. Their exact menu depends on extremes of hunger as well as on time of the year and size of the herd.

Various repellents have been tried, such as mesh bags of human hair hung in shrubs or Milorganite incorporated in the soil. In general, plants with aromatic foliage tend to repel deer. Where deer are especially prevalent and damaging, and the construction of exclusionary fencing unwanted, the best course is to cultivate plants known to be unappealing to them.

PLANTS REPORTED TO BE SPARED BY DEER

SHRUBS AND WOODY CLIMBERS
Amelanchier canadensis (shadbush)
Aruncus dioicus (goatsbeard)
Caryopteris × *clandonensis* (blue mist; treat as a perennial north of zone 7)
Myrica pensylvanica (bayberry)
Rosa rugosa (rugosa rose)
Wisteria spp.

PERENNIALS
Achillea spp. (yarrow)
Ajuga spp.
Artemisia spp. (wormwood)
Convallaria majalis (lily-of-the-valley)
Coreopsis spp.

(continues)

PLANTS REPORTED TO BE SPARED BY DEER
(*continued*)

PERENNIALS
Echinops ritro (globe thistle)
Gaillardia × grandiflora (perennial gaillardia)
Monarda didyma (bee balm)
Polemonium caeruleum (Jacob's ladder)

BIENNIALS
Digitalis purpurea (foxglove)
Verbascum spp. (mullein)

ANNUALS
Ageratum houstonianum
Centaurea cyanus (cornflower)
Cleome hassleriana (spider flower)
Heliotropium arborescens (heliotrope)
Lantana camara (shrubby in zone 10)
Mirabilis jalapa (four o'clock; often perennial south of zone 7)
Salvia spp. (annual sage)
Verbena × hybrida

INVERTEBRATE WILDLIFE
Butterflies and Moths

Among the many kinds of butterflies and moths, the monarch and swallowtail butterflies are especially appreciated as garden visitors. It must be remembered that each individual is preceded by a caterpillar, which is essentially an eating machine, often very specific (and sometimes harmful) in its food requirements. Monarchs lay their eggs on the various species of milkweed (*Asclepias* spp.), whose bitter juice, when consumed by feeding caterpillars, makes them distasteful to predatory birds. In the adult butterfly stage, monarchs seek nectar in the flowers of goldenrod (*Solidago* spp.), cosmos (*Cosmos* spp.), thistle (*Cirsium* spp.), lantana (*Lantana* spp.), and butterfly bush (*Buddleia davidii*), among others.

Swallowtail caterpillars are most frequent on members of the carrot family (Umbelliferae) such as Queen Anne's lace (*Daucus carota*), parsley (*Petroselinium sativum*), cow parsnip (*Heracleum* spp.), and angelica (*Angelica* spp.). As adult butterflies, swallowtails are attracted to thistle (*Cirsium* spp.), phlox (*Phlox* spp., especially *P. drummondii* and *P. paniculata*), hybrid loosestrife (*Lythrum salicaria* cultivars), and clover (*Trifolium* spp.).

In general, butterflies come most frequently to sunny gardens sheltered from wind, as on the south side of a building or within a shrub enclosure. In addition to the plants listed above, butterflies show a preference for lavender (*Lavandula* spp.), heliotrope (*Heliotropium arborescens*), daisy (*Chrysanthemum leucanthemum*), lilac (*Syringa* spp.), and honeysuckle (*Lonicera* spp.). Annuals that are particularly favored include

*The massed tubular florets of butterfly bush (*Buddleia davidii*) attract a nectar-seeking monarch butterfly.*

calliopsis (*Coreopsis tinctoria*), zinnia (*Zinnia* spp.), ageratum (*Ageratum houstonianum*), annual candytuft (*Iberis umbellata*), impatiens (*Impatiens walleriana* and other flat-flowered species), verbena (*Verbena × hybridum*), and snapdragon (*Antirrhinum majus*).

Egg-laying females often seek other very specific kinds of plants on which to deposit their eggs. These include hardy asters (*Aster* spp.) and violets (*Viola* spp.) as well as some of the others indicated above. These plants may occur nearby and not necessarily in the garden itself.

Most moths are small, inconspicuous, and nocturnal. The sphinx or hawkmoth, however, not only is the size of a hummingbird but mimics it in flight, including hovering and flying backward with rapidly beating wings, and in its pursuit of floral nectar. Moreover, it flies in daylight hours.

Bees

Many gardeners feel ambivalent toward bees, the fascination about their social habits tempered by fear of being stung. Of great importance is the fact that these insects are likely the most effective pollinators of flowers in north temperate regions, rivaled only by wind. Particularly important is the honeybee, which, thanks to humankind, is widely distributed almost throughout the world. Their complex social structure and behavior are much studied, especially as these aspects are closely entwined with the structure, color, fragrance, and seasonality of the flowers of many kinds of plants. Vital in the culture of commercial fruits, honeybees adapt quickly to flowers that are colorful, contrast well with their background, and have a central ultraviolet nectar guide. Bee-pollinated flowers are open during the day, offer nectar or pollen or both, and very often emit a distinct fragrance. The most favored colors are purple and blue, with yellow and orange next. Red is not discerned unless it includes ultraviolet. After visiting a flower patch several times, a honeybee can usually find the same patch unerringly for the rest of its life. Information gained on scouting trips is passed on to other members of the hive through an elaborate dance, which indicates the distance, direction, and quality of the source. Depending on the dance, other bees may or may not choose to investigate.

Nectar and pollen, two very important bee foods, are found only in insect-pollinated flowers. Wind-pollinated flowers, such as those of grasses, seldom tempt honeybees as they offer little nutrition. Nectar is transformed into honey by the addition of an enzyme. Worker bees then fan the honey to remove the water, leaving it sufficiently thick and concentrated to deter any growth of yeast or bacteria.

For those interested in home bee-keeping, various informative books have been written, both for the tyro and the experienced apiarist.

INSECT-POLLINATED FLOWERS ESPECIALLY ATTRACTIVE TO HONEYBEES

Alcea rosea (hollyhock)
Asclepias spp. (milkweed)
Aster spp. (hardy aster)
Chamaecrista spp. (partridge pea)
Cucumis spp. (cucumber, melon)
Cucurbita spp. (squash, gourds)
Epilobium angustifolium (fireweed)
Eryngium spp. (sea holly)
Hedera helix (English ivy)
Lythrum salicaria cvs. (loosestrife)
Melissa officinalis (lemon balm)
Rhus spp. (sumac)
Robinia spp. (locust)
Scabiosa spp.
Solidago spp. (goldenrod)
Tilia spp. (linden)
Vaccinium corymbosum (highbush blueberry)
Trifolium spp. (clover)
Vicia spp. (vetch)

26

Container Gardening

In villages, towns, and cities throughout much of the world, perhaps most notably in Europe, and dating at least as far back as ancient Egypt, flower boxes, urns, tubs, and other plant-filled containers have contributed almost as much to the charm of the community as do sculpture and architecture. Today they may be seen everywhere—beneath windows, on balconies, on lampposts, even between gas pumps at filling stations and on railroad station platforms. Containered plants adorn not only private homes but also

Colorful diminutive plants complement the varied cylindrical ceramic containers set in a path of crushed stone.

public buildings, hotels, hospitals, banks, office buildings, and shops. Even in poorer districts, material poverty is commonly disguised with floral beauty and living greenery, often grown in discarded cans and boxes, making it appear that this communion with nature has overcome any poverty of the spirit on the part of those who live there.

In our own country, recent decades have seen a tremendous upsurge of interest in the technique and art of growing plants in containers outdoors. Plants in window boxes and wayside planters more and more frequently grace city offices and houses and apartment buildings, as well as homes and public places in outlying areas. Many a porch, terrace, and patio is made bright with plants in containers, ranging from conventional flower boxes, hanging baskets, and planters to ceramic urns, half-barrels, and strawberry jars. Some favor such old-fashioned, rather quaint containers such as retired wood wheelbarrows, rowboats, and even open horse-drawn carriages; others invent novel applications, such as mining-railway ore cars, farmers' milk cans, and military boots. Container gardens are limited only by the gardener's imagination. A hollowed tree stump, a cast-aside birdcage, a leaky bucket, a discarded steamer trunk—even a plain bushel basket—can all serve as containers in which to grow plants, at least for a season or two, and add special grace and charm to the home and garden environment. Especially valued today are portable containers, since these can be shifted from time

to time through the season and thus create miniature gardens of maximum beauty in places where they will be most appreciated. Indeed, portable containers, if planted with wisely selected materials, can be a constant source of joy throughout the year.

To provide the most favorable growing conditions for the plants, a number of points should be considered: the material of which the container is made, provision for drainage as well as for slowing evaporation, composition of the soil mix, selection of plants best suited to the exposure, and the program of general maintenance.

SIZE AND TYPE OF CONTAINER

Determining the size of a flower box or other container is of major importance. Small containers have several disadvantages. They tend to dry out very quickly, and in extremely hot weather the soil may become overheated. When this occurs, the plants suffer seriously, as it is difficult for them to obtain the nutrients from the soil that they need. Overheated soil is the cause of frequent failures in maintaining flower boxes in good condition. On the other hand, large boxes become extremely heavy when filled with soil, and hanging them properly from a window or balcony may become a problem. The advantage of commercial planting mixes—

Ornamental grasses and flowers grown in large tubs and urns capture attention and add a note of intimacy to a broad, open public sidewalk.

Attractive containers contribute as much to the final result as the plants grown in them.

those that have been lightened with perlite—is obvious here as compared to the weight of garden soil. For window or porch containers, the most satisfactory dimensions are 32 to 48 inches in length, depending on the length of the exterior window sill; a minimum width of 10 inches; and a minimum depth of 8 inches (interior measurements).

Although it is theoretically possible to grow most any garden plant in a suitably placed container of adequate size, relatively few kinds respond well to such culture.

Root development in flower boxes and other containers is necessarily very restricted, and there is considerable competition among the plants for available nutrients. In boxes that are too narrow or too shallow, plants fail to make good growth unless watering is frequent, supplemental nutrients are provided, and a generous layer of mulch blankets the soil mix.

For terraces and patios, and in penthouse gardens, planting boxes may be built according to dimensions that are suited to the location and best meet the specific needs of the plants to be grown. It is also possible to mount flower boxes on the outside edge or directly atop porch railings, using specially made attachments for such a location.

Materials

The material of which a flower box is made has an important bearing on the growth and vigor of the plants it will contain. Metal boxes often have decided limitations. Steel containers rust out after a few years and must be replaced. Moreover, since most metals are good heat conductors, the soil in such boxes may become seriously overheated on hot summer days, resulting in substandard growth and disappointing floral displays.

The plastic and fiberglass containers most commonly seen today offer many advantages. They are lightweight, do not rust or crack, are extremely durable, provide good insulation

against heat and cold, are resistant to acids and chemicals, and the color does not fade. In addition to their use at windows, these plastic flower boxes can also be used as easily movable, decorative features on terraces and patios. Moreover, they may be used as readily indoors as out.

Wood is also an excellent material for plant boxes. If a suitable wood is selected and the box is well made and is of pressure-treated or naturally rot-resistant wood, it should give service for many years. Woods that possess remarkable natural ability to resist decay are cedar and cypress. Both are expensive, but containers made of them last for decades. Redwood should be avoided for conservation reasons. Exterior-grade plywood is also extremely useful for containers. Its advantages are strength and freedom from warping. A disadvantage is the appearance of cut ends, but this can be overcome by design.

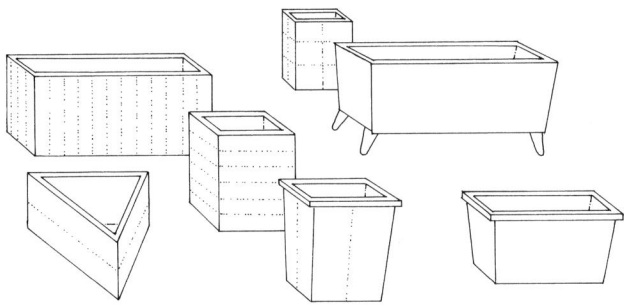

Basic shapes for wooden planting boxes.

Construction

There is a great difference between a really well built container and one that has been carelessly put together. As the sides of a container must resist surprisingly great pressure, this alone argues for good materials, carefully assembled. Boards at least ¾- or ⅞-inch thick are required. Rust-resistant screws are more likely to remain seated in place than nails. Corners should be reinforced with with galvanized or nonferrous angle irons attached inside near the top. They strengthen the box and prevent the boards along the front and rear from pulling away from the end pieces. Holes to permit the drainage of surplus water should be bored in the bottom. The holes should be about ½ inch in diameter, and spaced about 6 inches apart.

In hot climates or wherever boxes will be exposed to long hours of hot sun, an insulated type of box can be constructed that will prevent the soil from becoming seriously overheated. The simplest approach is to make the container somewhat larger than planned and line the interior with panels of ¾-inch- to 1-inch-thick Styrofoam. Impervious to water, this material has excellent insulating value.

If the finished container is to be painted, the interior surfaces should be treated with a sealer to deter absorption of moisture by the wood. A decorative molding is often useful in concealing plywood ends and can further strengthen joints.

A self-feeding, self-watering window box may be built if desired. Such a box has a double bottom. The lower portion, which should be approximately 3 inches in depth, provides a space for a removable metal tray that contains the nutrient solution. Wicks made of glass wool carry the nutrients to the plants. Perlite, vermiculite, or a mixture of either or both with peat moss should be used in the box instead of soil. The plants should be taken from their pots and planted, with the ball of earth surrounding their roots, directly in the mixture.

There should be a row of holes in the bottom of the box approximately 9 inches apart and the wicks should be about 9 inches long. Approximately 5 inches of wick should extend downward through the hole in the box into the metal tray. The remaining portion of the wick should be slit down into four sections, each section being spread out over a 1-inch bed of vermiculite in the bottom of the box. Both the vermiculite and the wicks should be wet with the solution before installation. The remaining vermiculite should be moistened with the solution and placed in the box, which is then ready for planting.

The tray should be kept filled with the nutrient solution. Beyond this, no further feeding or watering is required.

It is important that adequate provision be made for drainage in all types of containers. Unless this is done, the soil in the boxes becomes completely saturated, especially after heavy rain; under such conditions most plants become starved for oxygen and eventually die. Before soil is put in the box, a 1-inch layer of crock (small pieces of broken clay

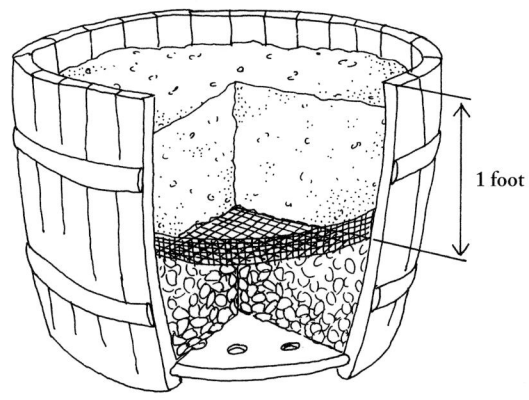

Half-barrels, once drilled for drainage, make very serviceable and attractive planters for the patio. A fine screen separating soil and gravel further assures good drainage.

flower pots) or crushed stone should be spread over the bottom. Above this, a piece of wet burlap, a piece of fine mesh plastic or nylon screening, or a thin layer of thoroughly moistened sphagnum moss should be spread to prevent the soil from sifting down into the drainage area.

SOIL MIXTURE

A commercial potting mix fortified with nutrients is ideal for container gardening because it is relatively light in weight and is free of the pests usually present in garden soil. A combination of such a mix and well-rotted compost or leaf mold also can be used. It is important to incorporate in the soil mix adequate humus for retention of moisture and to ensure aeration and certain drainage. A soil with a pH between 6.3 and 7.0 will be satisfactory for nearly all plants that are commonly grown in containers. The box should be filled within about 1 inch of the top, allowing space for mulch. When vegetables, such as tomatoes, cucumbers, or bush squash are grown in containers, it is especially important to apply fertilizer at one-month intervals as vegetables have very high nutrient requirements.

If desired, the flower box may be filled with moist peat moss, vermiculite, or perlite in which clay pots containing the plants may be sunk. This procedure has several advantages. It makes it easy to change the plants from season to season or to replace a plant that is not doing well, and it obviates the necessity of obtaining soil mix in quantity, which can be costly and, in urban areas especially, difficult to manage. The filler used among the pots should be kept moist at all times and the potted plants should be watered whenever the soil appears dry on the surface. The disadvantage is the expense involved. Plants in clay pots cost considerably more than those grown in plastic pots or cells. Moreover, it is increasingly difficult to find such popular container plants as edging lobelia (*Lobelia erinus*), sweet alyssum (*Lobularia maritima*), and French marigold (*Tagetes patula*) in pots. Clay pots are preferred over plastic pots in this instance, because they absorb moisture from the surrounding filler, or release it if overwatered.

MAINTENANCE

Care of plants in containers involves three essentials: watering, fertilizing, and grooming.

Since the soil in flower boxes dries out much more rapidly than the soil in garden beds, the plants need more frequent watering. A mulch of peat moss on the surface of the soil that helps conserve moisture will be of great benefit. The peat moss should be moistened well before it is used, and it should be allowed to dry out thereafter as it will form a water-repellent crust. A mulch, about 1 inch in depth, is usually sufficient for such purposes. Watering the boxes is best done in the late afternoon or early evening, but to deter fungus diseases it is preferable to allow time for foliage and flowers to dry before nightfall. In extremely dry, hot weather it may be necessary to water boxes that have a southern or southwestern exposure early in the morning and again during the middle of the day.

As in other types of gardening, too much water is just as serious as too little. Since few plants can thrive in saturated, waterlogged soil mix, watering must be carefully regulated, and in cool, cloudy weather it should be suspended altogether until the surface appears dry once again.

To encourage vigorous growth and abundant flowering, supplemental fertilizing is recommended. Beginning about a month after planting, a weekly application of a high-analysis, water-soluble fertilizer that also contains the various trace elements should be made, being mixed at the rate of 1 teaspoonful to 1 gallon of water. A small portion may be sprayed over the foliage if desired (see foliar feeding in the index), or it may all be applied directly to the soil.

If such plants as petunia, pansy, lantana, verbena, and marigold are to be kept in continuous bloom throughout the season, it is necessary to remove the faded flowers to prevent the formation of seed. The removal of dead flowers also greatly improves the appearance of the flower box. Some plants, such as pansies, will give a second period of bloom in late summer if cut back severely and allowed to develop a new growth of vigorous young shoots.

In hanging baskets grown in partial shade, few plants rival hybrid fuchsia (*Fuchsia* × *hybrida*). Whether your choice is the very popular double red-and-white-flowered cultivars 'Swingtime' and 'White Eyes' or the somewhat more subdued 'Lord Byron' and 'Cascade', fuchsias require daily or even twice daily watering in hot, dry weather but little or no watering in cool, damp weather. Limp foliage in direct sun is not a reliable indicator of need; the soil mix should be felt. To maintain flowering, the berrylike fruit should be removed and the basket shifted, if necessary, to ensure some sun exposure each day. Reduced number and size of flowers usually betray insufficient light, the need for which varies somewhat according to cultivar. Supplemental weekly fertilizing with a liquid 20-10-20 preparation also helps maintain optimal flowering.

PLANNING FOR SUCCESSION OF BLOOM

It is possible to have bloom in outdoor containers from earliest spring to late fall. In early spring, boxes containing pansy, English daisy, viola, forget-me-not, and wallflower are appealing heralds of the season, especially if combined with a few pots of Siberian squill, dwarf narcissus, species tulip, or other small spring bulbs. Large pots of red tulips with a carpeting of dwarf blue forget-me-not, or cream tulips with purple-black pansies, truly gladden the eye.

Later in the spring, geranium, petunia, verbena, edging lobelia, lantana, and others, all started indoors in late winter, will come into flower and, with adequate care, will continue performing until fall.

Lobelia erinus 'Cascade'—a trailing cultivar of edging lobelia

In late summer, fall-flowering crocus (*Crocus* spp.) and autumn crocus (*Colchicum* spp.) may be planted near the front or edge of the container. These will provide color when the annuals are removed to make way for the compact chrysanthemums, which will carry the season of bloom well into the fall.

During the winter, small evergreens, such as very small box bushes, may be planted in the containers. Alternatively, they may be decorated with sprigs of decorative fruit, such as holly (*Ilex opaca* or *I. aquifolium*), winterberry (*I. verticillata*), or bayberry (*Myrica pennsylvanica*), or with leafy cone-bearing branchlets of pine (*Pinus* spp.), perhaps interspersed with bittersweet (*Celastrus scandens*). These will be removed before planting again in early spring.

HERBS AND VEGETABLES SUITED TO CULTURE IN OUTDOOR CONTAINERS

Basil
Chives
Creeping rosemary
Cucumber
Marjoram
Oregano
Parsley
Squash (nonvining bush cultivars)
Thyme
Tomato (especially low, determinate cultivars)

Basil

PLANTS SUITED TO CULTURE IN OUTDOOR CONTAINERS

Name	Zone	Height	Exposure*	Flower or Foliage Color, and/or Bloom Time
ANNUALS				
Ageratum houstonianum cvs. (dwarf ageratum)	—	4–6"	S	Blue, also pink or white
Antirrhinum majus cvs. (dwarf snapdragon)	—	6–12"	S to PSh	Various
Begonia semperflorens-cultorum (wax begonia)	—	6–16"	PSh to LSh	Red, pink, or white; some with bronzy foliage
B × tuberhybrida (tuberous begonia)	—	8–15"	PSh to LSh	Red, pink, yellow, or white
Browallia speciosa cvs.	—	8–10"	PSh to LSh	Blue or white
Coleus × hybridus cvs. (dwarf coleus)	—	9–12"	PSh to LSh	Multiple and elaborate foliage variegation
Fuchsia × hybrida (hybrid fuchsia)	—	1–3'	PSh	White, pink, red, and/or purple
Heliotropium arborescens (heliotrope)	—	1–1½'	S to PSh	Purple, lavender, or blue
Iberis umbellata (annual candytuft)	—	8–15"	S	Purple, red, pink, lavender, or white
Impatiens 'New Guinea' hybrids (New Guinea impatiens)	—	10–15"	S to PSh	Purple, red, pink, lavender, or white
I. walleriana cvs. (dwarf common impatiens)	—	4–6"	PSh to LSh	Shades of red or pink, also white or bicolor
Lantana camara (common lantana)	—	1–1½'	S	Yellow, aging to orange to red
L. montevidensis (creeping lantana)	—	6–12" (×2–3')	S	Rose lilac to violet
Lobelia erinus (edging lobelia)	—	4–6" (×12")	S	Deep blue to white
Lobularia maritima (sweet alyssum)	—	4–8"	S	White, also lavender to rose violet
Nemesia strumosa	—	8–14"	S	Various
Nicotiana alata 'Nicki' (dwarf flowering tobacco)	—	10–18"	S to PSh	Red, lavender, pink, or white
Nierembergia hippomanica var. *violacea* (cupflower)	—	6–9"	S	Blue to purple, also white
Pelargonium × hortorum (common geranium)	—	10–20"	S	Red, pink, or white
Phacelia campanulata (California bluebell)	—	8–18"	S	Blue
Phlox drummondii cvs. (dwarf annual phlox)	—	6–8"	S	Various
Portulaca grandiflora (common portulaca)	—	2–4" (×12")	S	Various
Salvia splendens cvs. (dwarf annual salvia)	—	8–12"	S	Purple, lavender, red, pink, or white
Tagetes patula (French marigold)	—	8–12"	S	Yellow, orange, and/or mahogany
Torenia fournierii (wishbone flower)	—	8–12"	PSh	Purple, lavender, pink, and/or white
Tropaeolum majus cvs. (dwarf nasturtium)	—	6–12"	S	Red, orange, or yellow
Verbena × hybrida (garden verbena)	—	10–12"	S	Various
SPRING-BLOOMING AND EARLY-SUMMER-BLOOMING BIENNIALS				
Bellis perennis (English daisy)	(4) 5–8	2–6"	S to PSh	Red, pink, or white
Erysimum cvs. (wallflower)	(6) 7–8	6–12"	S to PSh	Dark red, orange, yellow, or cream
Myosotis alpestris (dwarf biennial forget-me-not)	5–8	6–12"	S to PSh	Pale blue, rose pink, or white
M. sylvatica (tall biennial forget-me-not)	5–8	1–1½'	S to PSh	Pale blue, pink, or white
Viola × wittrockiana (pansy)	6–8	6–10"	S	Various bicolors and tricolors
PERENNIALS AND SHRUBBY PLANTS				
Aucuba japonica 'Variegata' (gold-dust bush)	7–9	1–2' (pruned)	PSh to LSh	Spotted evergreen foliage
Aurinia saxatilis 'Compacta' (dwarf basket-of-gold)	4–7	6–12"	S	Yellow
Buxus spp. (boxwood)	6–9	6–12"	S to LSh	Glossy evergreen foliage
Carissa macrocarpa (Natal plum)	10	1–2' (pruned)	S	White
Chrysanthemum × morifolium cvs. (dwarf chrysanthemum)	5–8	1–1½'	S	Various
Coniferae (dwarf coniferous evergreens)	3–9	1–2' (pruned)	S, PSh, or LSh	Evergreen foliage
Echeveria crenulata (wavy-leaf crassula)	9–10	4–6 (20)"	S	Pink and yellow
Fuchsia magellanica (hardy fuchsia)	(6) 7–9	2–4' (pruned)	S to PSh	Red
Hydrangea macrophylla (common hydrangea)	(6) 7–9	3–6'	S to PSh	Blue (pH 5–5.5) or pink (pH 6–6.5)

Name	Zone	Height	Exposure*	Flower or Foliage Color, and/or Bloom Time
Osmanthus heterophyllus (holly osmanthus)	7–9	2–3' (pruned)	S to PSh	White (hidden but fragrant)
Primula vulgaris (common primrose)	(4) 5–8	6–12"	PSh to LSh	Various
Rosmarinus officinalis (rosemary)	8–10	1–3' (pruned)	S	Blue

BULBS

Name	Zone	Height	Exposure*	Flower or Foliage Color, and/or Bloom Time
Agapanthus hybrids (African lily)	8–10	1½–3'	S	Blue; summer
Colchicum spp. (autumn crocus)	5–8	6–12"	S to PSh	Purplish pink to white; fall
Crocus spp. (spring crocus, fall crocus)	4–8	2–6"	S to PSh	Yellow, purple, or white; spring or fall
Hyacinthus orientalis (hyacinth)	5–8	9–12"	S	Various; spring
Lilium auratum (gold-banded lily of Japan)	5–8	3–6'	S	White, red, and yellow; summer
Muscari spp. (grape hyacinth)	4–9	6–9"	S to PSh	Blue or white; spring
Narcissus spp. and cvs. (daffodil, jonquil, preferably small spp. and evs.)	5–9	6–12"	S to PSh	Yellow, orange, pink, greenish, and/or white; spring
Rhodohypoxis baurii (red star)	8–10	3–6"	S	Red to deep pink; late spring
Scilla siberica (Siberian squill)	5–8	3–6"	S to PSh	Deep blue or white; spring
Tulipa spp. (species tulips and smaller hybrids)	5–7 (8)	6–18"	S	Various; spring

CREEPERS, TRAILERS, OR PLANTS WITH LONG PENDENT STEMS

Name	Zone	Height	Exposure*	Flower or Foliage Color, and/or Bloom Time
Cissus rhombifolia (grape ivy)	10	1–4"	S to PSh	
Hedera canariensis (Algerian ivy)	(8) 9–10	2–6"	PSh to LSh	
H. helix (English ivy, many dwarf cvs.)	4–9	1–6"	S, PSh, or LSh	
Lantana montevidensis (creeping lantana)	10	2–3"	S	Rose lilac to violet
Pelargonium peltatum hybrids (ivy-leaved geranium)	10	2–4"	S	Purple, pink, or white
Saxifraga stolonifera (strawberry geranium)	6–8	9–12'	PSh to LSh	White
Thunbergia alata (black-eyed Susan vine)	10	3–6"	S to PSh	Orange, usually with black-brown center
Tropaeolum majus (climbing nasturtium)	10	3–6"	S	Various
Vinca major (large periwinkle)	8–10	2–4"	PSh to LSh	Blue

* S, full sun; Sh, shade (no direct sun); PSh, partial shade (sun exposure only part of the day); LSh, light shade (e.g., the shade of tall, open trees, with little or no exposure to direct sun).

Tuberous begonia (*Begonia* × *tuberhybrida*)

Strawberry geranium
(*Saxifraga stolonifera*)

Dwarf box
(*Buxus microphylla*
'Kingsville Dwarf')

**Dwarf common
impatiens**
(*Impatiens walleriana* cvs.)

African lily (*Agapanthus* hybrids)

Hybrid fuchsia (*Fuchsia* × *hybrida*)

IV
Flavor and Fragrance

27

The Home Vegetable Garden

Growing vegetables in the home garden offers much personal satisfaction for the gardener as well as a supply of high-quality, flavorful produce that is seldom equaled in commerce. For youngsters, vegetable gardening provides hands-on instructive experience with plants that yields tangible results. For adults, vegetable gardening helps work off tensions in a productive way, keeps us in touch with the natural world, provides aesthetic delight, and if the garden is well designed and managed, can lower the grocery bill.

Surface evaporation among well-spaced crop plants is minimized by a blanket of dried lawn clippings several inches thick.

From the purely biological point of view, the kinds of plants we grow as vegetables are botanical oddities. Few if any occur in the wild in a form familiar to us. Instead, they have been selected over the centuries for their production of nutritious, palatable food, often concentrated in root, stem, leaf, fruit, or seed, and reselected, generation after generation, for heavier food production. Latterly, as plant genetics became understood, many vegetables were bred (i.e., genetically manipulated) to produce still higher yields. The high concentration of nutrients that accumulates in the plant parts we harvest requires higher levels of soil nutrients than for other garden plants. Moreover, the food-making process basic to the growth of all green plants, photosynthesis, is even more critical in vegetable culture, since in most cases it is the excess food stored in enlarged structures that we value. Production of this excess depends heavily on daily exposure to at least six hours of sunlight. Water, the solvent that renders soil nutrients available to plants, is also essential to photosynthesis and for the transport and concentration of organic compounds in the plant organs we value for food. Thus vegetables have heavy demands for soil nutrients, sun exposure, and water to grow the abnormally large roots, stems, leaves, fruits, or seeds that we harvest for the table.

Because these nutritious structures are unnaturally large, plentiful, and concentrated in a small area (the garden), it is not surprising that they are also attractive to other creatures—birds, mammals, insects, fungi, and various other competitors—whose ravages can reduce or annihilate crops. Dealing with these invaders in ways that do not degrade the environment is a major challenge in breeding vegetable crop plants as well as in home-garden culture.

Another characteristic of vegetable crops is their intolerance of root competition and shading by weeds. Although weeds can be very difficult to control in large-scale farming, it is possible through garden design and management to minimize their presence in ways that are environmentally benign and that spare the gardener the often daunting chore of hand-weeding.

With all these desiderata in mind, the ideal site for a vegetable garden is a sunny, moist, well-drained, gently sloping, southwest-facing, wind-sheltered plot of deep, humus-rich ("organic") soil of pH 6.3 to 6.8 near a source of supplemental water. Few have such a site that is not already preempted for other purposes. Hence the need for intervention—and compromise. Primacy must be given to exposure to sun, although some crops perform creditably with as little as four hours' sun exposure. Less important are soil, which is mutable, and moisture, which can be augmented when necessary.

Another important aspect in vegetable gardening is the gardener's attitude. Seed catalogs and much garden writing

Salad greens and low-growing annuals combine harmoniously in a sinuous informal border.

stress perfection, which is seldom attainable. Most blemishes on garden vegetables are superficial puckers, insect tracks, and chewed perforations that have no effect whatever on flavor or nutritional value. Also, extraordinary earliness in crop ripening matters only where growing seasons are brief. Yet every year considerable press space and much gardener effort go into getting the first tomato of the season. Great size, as in tomatoes and pumpkins, is often achieved at the expense of the yield of vegetable units per plant. To adopt an experimental approach to vegetable gardening is beneficial, for the gardener then learns through experience which vegetables grow well under the conditions at hand and which cultivars of each yield the best returns. By also growing some new, hitherto untried crops each year, the choice is increasingly refined and tuned to the idiosyncracies of site, style of gardening, and personal taste.

With careful site selection, necessary initial preparation, analytical crop selection, a good plan (both for garden size and for efficient use of the space through the season), diligent care, and realistic expectations, a vegetable garden can be a joy

Productive and interesting, staggered beds within landscape ties define crops and are accessible by weed-free, plastic-covered paths.

Late-season bloom adorns a bounteous informal garden of mixed produce, with scarlet runner bean and red amaranth gracing a wood chip path opposite the angular thrusts of goldenrod.

to the senses—whether in the plot, in the basket, in the kitchen, or on the table. It can generate produce in variety not only for immediate use throughout the entire growing season but also enough surplus for freezing, canning, or storage.

The following points should help the gardener achieve these goals.

1. Plan and plant the garden so that it will be a pleasure. Figure out how much of each vegetable you wish to have fresh and how much for preserving. Keep simple records of production and use them as a guideline in successive years. Check with gardening neighbors and nearby friends about the vegetables that do best (specific to cultivar, if possible) and those that have been disappointing. New cultivars, however intensely publicized, will not necessarily thrive under your garden circumstances. Most of the old cultivars still on the market continue to be offered because they have proven adaptable and reliable.

Calendula and cleome, though self-seeding interlopers, add lively notes to a raised-bed vegetable garden heavily fenced to exclude horses. Parsley serves as edging in the foreground.

2. Figure out how much ground you can properly care for. It is better to have a small garden properly maintained than to plant so much that you will be discouraged with it by midsummer. A mixed-crop garden of 600 square feet (say, 30 feet by 20 feet) is generous for a family of four, as is 850 square feet for six. If space is short, many space-saving techniques are available to reduce the area required, such as wide row or band planting (i.e., abandoning traditional rows for dense random planting in a 2- or 3-foot-wide band or patch) and intercropping and succession planting (discussed later in this chapter). Trellis or fence culture saves space with vine crops. Based on yield per square foot, value per pound, and time required from seed to harvest, tomatoes are most space-efficient when grown on supports, followed by leaf lettuce, summer squash, snow peas, onions, beans (especially pole types), and beets; least efficient are sweet corn, melons, and pumpkins.

3. In ground not previously planted to vegetables, it has long been traditional to fork or rototill the area the previous fall or in the spring just before planting, laying out the rows in a north to south orientation. The chief reasons to turn soil are to incorporate manure, compost, and/or fertilizer and to improve aeration. The chief reasons for the rows are to facilitate access for planting, cultivating, weeding, and harvesting. While these traditional practices may suit the needs of commercial, mechanized farming, the backyard vegetable garden need not be bound by them.

If the garden is organized into beds 4 feet wide, alternated with paths 18 inches wide, all the work in the beds can be done from the paths. In this way, a major gardening problem—soil compaction—is averted altogether, and the need to dig or till each year to promote soil aeration is obviated. Similarly, the incorporation of organic matter and other amendments can be achieved by raking in or at most shallow forking from adjacent paths, without deep digging. Seeding, transplanting, weeding, and harvesting can also be done from the paths, without setting a foot in the beds.

Where soils are heavy and slow to drain, or where slopes are too steep to be stable, it is beneficial to construct 4-foot-wide beds that will stand 6 to 8 inches above grade. Loamy soil mixed with well-rotted manure or compost should be used to raise the beds to

Boxed beds 3 feet high are convenient for intensive cultivation and easy harvesting of a small number of vegetables in limited variety.

Leafy vegetables neatly arranged in raised beds, if near the kitchen door, may be harvested and prepared at the moment of need.

Enclosed, raised beds facilitate garden organization and ease maintenance. Fencing helps protect crops from strong wind and marauding wildlife.

the desired height. Enclosing such beds with wood (preferably rot-resistant or pressure-treated*), stone, brick, or concrete will increase stability and ease maintenance, and also reduce the need for supplemental summer irrigation.

In light, sandy, rapidly draining soils that dry out quickly, especially in summer, soil evaporation can be slowed by blanketing the surface with compost, well-rotted manure, straw, or even soil-weighted newsprint three or four sheets thick. Equally important, these materials will admit rain or irrigation water (which plastic sheeting will not, unless perforated) and eventually enhance the soil as they decompose.

Paths can be kept reasonably weed free by spreading wood chips, bark chips, or gravel over black five-mil plastic sheeting, perforated with a fork after installation. Less satisfactory for the long term is corrugated cardboard or newspaper. Some gardeners use sections of discarded carpet, but the colors often conflict with garden tones.

---

* According to studies carried out at Cornell University, and contrary to fears expressed in the garden press, pressure-treated wood poses no danger in vegetable gardens as the substances conferring rot resistance are not absorbed by the plants.

By averting soil compaction and minimizing regular deep digging, earthworms are encouraged, and their tunnels and activities do much to mix soil components and promote drainage. By using surface mulches that are as free of weed seeds as possible, weeding is kept to a minimum, and if used throughout the year, such mulches mitigate the compacting effect of raindrops. And by avoiding the ritual use of soil cultivators, crop plants develop fuller root systems and yield more bountiful harvests.

When ground limestone or other amendments are used to adjust soil pH, the soil should be tested in alternate years to be sure the desired level has been maintained. A pH of 6.3 to 6.8 is best for most vegetables. Ground limestone or dolomite, an inexpensive amendment, if spread at the rate of about 5 pounds per 100 square feet, and raked in about 2 inches deep, should raise readings about one pH point. As ground limestone is slow in action, it is best applied in fall for effect in the ensuing season. To acidify alkaline soils, various sulfur preparations are available (see the table on page 763).

4. If at all possible, choose a site exposed to at least six hours of full sun each sunny day. In partly shaded sites, i.e., where exposure is limited to perhaps four hours daily from June to September, the use of raised beds overspread with reflective foil as a mulch helps to mature crops earlier than might otherwise occur. The earliest possible planting of seedlings, started even earlier under lights indoors, will similarly help with yields, as added time in the garden will compensate for a briefer period of sun exposure each day. Even so, yields are usually smaller and tardier with less daily sun time. These measures are nevertheless worthwhile for some crops, such as Chinese cabbage, kale, common cabbage, leaf lettuce, New Zealand spinach, and endive among the greens and bunching onion, leek, beet, carrot, and radish among root crops. Zucchini and butternut squash do reasonably well with less daily sun time, as do peas, beans (both bush and pole), and tomato. Spinach sown early and directly in the garden also produce well. Among other salad greens arugula and parsley are usually successful sown early, as are the herbs basil, dill, and thyme.

Crops intolerant of reduced light are cucumber, melon, eggplant, and pepper, all of which must have long hours of sun exposure to bear well.

If the compost pile or bin is in a sunny position, garden space can be saved by allowing such vine crops as zucchini and other squash, including pumpkin, to sprawl over these often unattractive enclosures and

PRODUCTIVITY OF POPULAR VEGETABLES IN THE HOME GARDEN

Vegetable	Total Production per 10 Feet of Row per Season
Asparagus	2½–4 lb
Bean, bush snap	5–10 lb
Bean, pole snap	15–20 lb
Beet	8–12 lb
Broccoli	8–10 lb
Brussels sprouts	4–6 lb
Cabbage	15–20 lb
Cabbage, Chinese	6–10 lb
Carrot	8–10 lb
Cauliflower	8–10 lb
Celery	50–100 stalks
Cucumber	10–15 lb
Eggplant	5–10 lb
Lettuce, head	10–12 heads
Lettuce, leaf	4–8 lb
Onion	4–8 lb
Pea, edible pod	7–12 lb
Pea, shell	2–5 lb (shelled)
Pepper	25–40 peppers
Potato	10–15 lb
Pumpkin	15–150+ lb
Radish	5–10 lb
Rhubarb	8–12 lb
Spinach	3–5 lb
Squash, summer	10–15 lb
Squash, winter	15–25 lb
Sweet corn	10–15 ears
Swiss chard	10–20 lb
Tomato	10–25 lb

ripen their produce out of the way while the compost matures below.

5. During the early or late winter months, before it is possible to plant outside, plan your garden on a piece of graph paper to save time and avoid the mistakes often made at planting time. To plan with reasonable accuracy, it is well to know how much produce may be expected from each 10 feet of planted row or equivalent. The table above argues for diversifying crops and sowing small amounts of seed at intervals of three or four weeks, especially of fast-growing kinds, to ensure a steady, manageable supply through the season, instead of a brief glut followed by nothing. For example, broccoli is usually planted in the spring and yields a crop in the

SEED VIABILITY OF POPULAR VEGETABLES

Vegetable	Approximate Number of Years of Expected Viability*
Bean, all types	3
Beet	6
Broccoli	4
Brussels sprouts	4
Cabbage	4
Cabbage, Chinese	4
Carrot	2
Cauliflower	4
Celery	2
Cucumber	6
Eggplant	4
Lettuce, all types	6
Onion	2
Pea	3
Pepper	4
Pumpkin	4
Radish	4
Spinach	3
Squash, all types	4
Sweet corn	5
Swiss chard	6
Tomato	6

*Assuming seed is stored under cool, dry conditions, with a slow, gradual decline in percentage of viable seed.

summer, but if sown again in early summer, before the first crop is ready, a second crop will mature in early fall. Similarly, leafy crops resown in midsummer will continue to be harvestable until hard frost.

Another aspect of good garden planning is succession cropping, in which each bed or row is kept in constant production throughout the season. One key to effective succession planting is to start early with the right crops. Seeds require not only moisture to germinate but also—with wide variation according to kind—the right temperature. In cold, moist soil, most seeds will absorb water, but the embryo will fail to grow, resulting in seed rot.

Insofar as possible, it is best to order seed of cultivars known to succeed in your area. Regional seed companies often specialize and fine-tune their offerings to specific climate and soil conditions, while national seedhouses purvey a wide range of cultivars, most of which are adaptable to diverse conditions. Owing to the vagaries of weather, especially rainfall, and of pests and diseases, all of which vary from year to year, one

season's success with a particular cultivar is no guarantee of like performance the next year. Hence the advisability of growing several cultivars of each type of vegetable in any year and noting the results obtained. Seed orders are best placed as soon after catalogs arrive as possible, to ensure maximum choice.

While it is advisable to sow fresh seed for maximum germination, the seed of most vegetables retains viability for at least a few years (see the table at left), providing it is stored under cool, dry conditions, as in a glass jar with a screw cap kept in a cool basement. Seed of open-pollinated, nonhybrid cultivars may be collected from the garden and used, but home-collected seed of hybrids usually results in reversion to inferior crops.

6. When planning the garden and making seed orders, the following points should be borne in mind.

A. Gauge the length of the growing season. Although the use of frost-protective caps, cloches (low tunnels of clear plastic sheeting), waterwalls, and other devices placed over seedlings may advance the spring planting season somewhat, and lightweight plastic shrouds may ward off the effects of an early frost in the fall, it is wise to formulate the gardening season according to the average dates of last spring frost and first fall frost in your area, as may be determined from the local cooperative extension or other agricultural authority. One or two weeks' advance on the spring season and a similar extension in fall should be looked on as an occasional bonus and not as a basis for regular garden planning.

B. Timing is important. Schedule planting for the time of year at which each vegetable grows best. The small, quick-maturing varieties of radish do best when planted in the spring and fall and should not be planted to mature during hot summer weather. They mature in 25 to 30 days. Indeed, it often surprises gardeners how many vegetables produce best in cool weather (i.e., with maximum temperatures below 75° to 80°F). Among the most popular crops, only bean, corn, cucumber, eggplant, pepper, pumpkin, squash, and tomato produce maximally under hot conditions. The beets, on the other hand, may be planted as soon as the ground is workable in the spring and planted until midsummer. Most beet cultivars mature in 60 days.

Two crops that grow especially well in cold ground in late winter or earliest spring, once frost is out of the ground but well before the last killing frost, are peas and fava beans, sometimes called Windsor beans.

A few weeks later, but still one or two weeks before the last spring frost, lettuce, spinach, Swiss chard, onion, and white potato may be planted. Broccoli, cauliflower, cabbage, and Brussels sprouts may also be sown, but many gardeners prefer to start these crops indoors under lights, and then—after one or two weeks in a coldframe to harden them off—plant the seedlings at about the time of the last spring frost.

Just at or slightly before the last spring frost, sow beet, carrot, and radish.

Finally, when temperatures remain above 50°F on clear, still nights, it is time to plant warm-weather crops, such as beans, celery, sweet corn, cucumber, squash, melon, pumpkin, and sweet potato. Other popular heat-loving crops such as tomato, pepper, and eggplant, should be started indoors under lights about two months before set-out time or purchased as transplants. As crops are consumed or decline in productivity, succession or follow up plantings should be made. For example, romaine lettuce, bush bean, beet, Swiss chard, Chinese cabbage, broccoli, kohlrabi, dill, fennel, and radish, if planted around midsummer, will yield harvests well before fall frost.

Even after fall frost, several vegetables remain harvestable or even improved by the cold: carrot, beet, leek, Swiss chard, kale, Brussels sprouts, parsnip, and arugula.

In zones 9 and 10 (i.e., along much of the Pacific Coast of California), cool-season crops sown in mid to late summer reach maximum productivity in the fall and into winter. These include lettuce, carrot, beet, turnip, cabbage, broccoli, and cauliflower. Further north, in zone 8 (especially along the Pacific Northwest coast), many of these same crops bear well through the fall until hard frost in early winter.

C. Determine the length of the period in which each vegetable may be harvested. For example, sweet corn may be harvested over a period of 10 to 14 days, while radish may last for only 7 days if the weather is hot and the soil quite dry. Tomato is harvested over a period of two months.

In this large, well-planned garden of raised beds, soaker-hose irrigation minimizes waste by directing water at controlled rates to target plants.

D. Consider the relationship between growth habit and position in the vegetable garden. For example, asparagus and rhubarb are perennials and for that reason should be planted at one end of the plot, where they will not interfere with soil preparation each year.

E. Reduce the distance between plants in beds to be hand weeded (rather than machine tilled, as on farms). For example, broccoli, cauliflower, and cabbage are usually set 2½ feet to 3 feet apart in the farm row, but in the home garden, a 2-foot or even 1-foot interval may suffice if hand weeding is to be practiced, depending on the ultimate size of the crop plants.

F. Keep crops from shading each other. Grow tall-growing crops at one end (preferably the north end) of the garden where they will not shade lower ones. Pole bean, tomato, and sweet corn, for example, should be grouped away from other crops.

G. Keep related vegetables together to ease pest and disease control. Cabbage, broccoli, Brussels sprouts, collard, and kohlrabi—collectively known as coles—are all variants of a single species, *Brassica oleracea*, and are, therefore, susceptible to attack by the same pests and diseases. By planting these vegetables in close proximity, they may be monitored and treated more easily and efficiently than if scattered. The same principle applies to eggplant, pepper, potato, and tomato, all members of the nightshade family, Solanaceae, as well as to squash, cucumber, melon, and pumpkin, collectively known as cucurbits, being members of the family Cucurbitaceae.

H. Intercrop or alternate a fast-maturing crop between rows or among individuals of a longer term crop. For example, radish may be intercropped or actually mixed with carrot, and leaf lettuce may be intercropped with leek. The main reason for intercropping is to make the fullest use of available garden space. By selecting kinds that differ in manner or rate of growth, competition can be minimized.

I. Practice crop rotation. Some vegetables give better results if not planted in the same place each year. It is poor practice to plant cabbage or any of its close relatives after the early crop has been removed, as the buildup of soil-borne diseases may reduce the quality and size of the next crop.

J. Keep much-used herbs accessible. If parsley and other frequently used, low-growing herbs are planted, have them on the outside edge next to the house so you won't have to walk through the entire garden to get to them.

STORAGE OF SURPLUS PRODUCE

As surplus produce often accumulates rapidly, sometimes by plan, sometimes despite plans to the contrary, it is well to consider beforehand how to deal with the excess. For short-term storage, vegetables may be stored in plastic bags placed among bags of ice in a large cooler chest. Kept in a shaded, protected spot, most produce will stay fresh for three days or more. If freezing or canning is contemplated, supplies and equipment should be at hand well ahead of need. Some crops, such as carrot, beet, turnip, and leek, may be left in the ground and, with the onset of cold weather, be mulched with straw or leaves and pulled as needed during the winter.

As a refinement over leaving root crops in the ground for winter harvest, the root cellar (or cold cellar, cold chamber) can be a great convenience, especially if located near the kitchen. An existing space that is unheated, ventilated, and humid (but not wet) may prove suitable for winter storage of relatively nonperishable produce. Otherwise, a chamber can be constructed inexpensively in a shaded, out-of-the-way corner of the property.

Productive and interesting, staggered beds within landscape ties define crops and are accessible by weed-free, plastic-covered paths.

GUIDELINES FOR THE STORAGE OF VEGETABLES

Bean: Wash, blanch, dry, and freeze.

Beet: Mulch and harvest as needed in the winter or store, unwashed, in bins of moist sand in a root cellar.

(continues)

GUIDELINES FOR THE STORAGE
OF VEGETABLES (continued)

Brussels sprouts: Leave on the plant and harvest as needed in the fall to early winter.

Cabbage: Wrap in paper and store in ventilated bags in a cool place.

Carrot: Same as for beet.

Eggplant: Freeze or transplant to pots for culture in in a greenhouse or sunny window to ripen immature fruit.

Garlic: Braid dried tops and hang on the wall in a root cellar or lay out on screen shelves.

Jerusalem artichoke: Same as for beet.

Kale: Same as for Brussels sprouts.

Kohlrabi: Remove the leaves from the plants and hill up the stem tubers for protection from early frost; after frost, pull up the stems, wrap them in newspaper, and store in a root cellar up to three months.

Leek: Mulch stem bases and harvest as needed through the winter.

Onion: Same as for garlic; consume white and Bermuda onions as soon after harvest as possible.

Pepper: Same as for eggplant.

Pea: Wash, blanch, dry, and freeze or allow to dry out for dry storage.

Potato: Dig up carefully (to avoid breaking the skin) before hard frost, spread out to dry, and then store in a root cellar in shallow layers or in mesh bags that hold 10 pounds or less (i.e., in amounts that measure less than 1 foot thick).

Pumpkin: Store in a cool, dark place after first curing for one week at about 80°F to dehydrate somewhat and allow the skin to harden.

Sweet potato: Dig up before frost, spread out to dry, cure in a humid place at 80° to 85°F, then store in a ventilated place at 55° to 60°F.

Tomato: Harvest all fruit, ripe and unripe, before frost; store unripe fruit in a dark place at 55° to 70°F and use as they ripen.

Turnip and rutabaga: Same as for beet.

Winter squash: Same as for pumpkin; do not cure acorn squash.

SOWING SEEDS IN FLATS

To be successful in vegetable gardening, it is necessary to learn how to sow seed and grow seedlings, both indoors and out. While and corn and beet, for example, are sown directly in the garden, some of the most important crops—tomato, eggplant, and pepper as well as cabbage and its relatives (broccoli, kohlrabi, cauliflower, and Brussels sprouts)—are best started indoors under fluorescent lights or in a greenhouse and later set out as advanced seedlings.

Soil Mixes

Because vegetables require moist, fertile, porous soil to grow quickly and reach maximum productivity, various amendments are commonly made to improve soil quality both in

the flat and in the row. Among those most frequently employed are the following.

1. *Sand.* Small rock grains 0.05 to 2 mm in diameter, preferably sharp angled.
2. *Peat.* Partly decomposed remains of wetland vegetation; high water-holding capacity; contains some nitrate; because it is a diminishing resource, with demand far exceeding natural formation, peat should be used conservatively or replaced with compost.
3. *Sphagnum.* Partly decomposed remains of acidic bog mosses and other vegetation; lightweight; relatively sterile; holds 10 to 20 times its weight in water.
4. *Vermiculite.* Micaceous mineral heated to 2,000°F; forms small, porous, spongelike kernels; sterile; lightweight; absorbs large amounts of water.
5. *Perlite.* Gray white volcanic mineral; properties similar to those of vermiculite.
6. *Compost or leaf mold.* Decomposed vegetable matter; contains nutrients; a retains moisture; may harbor seeds of weeds and other garden plants.
7. *Well-rotted manure.* Animal wastes; free of ammonia, often nutrient rich, moisture retaining, sometimes (especially if from horses) contaminated with live weed seeds.
8. *Sawdust.* Moisture retaining, absorbs some nitrate; should be well rotted.

Seed Flats and Seed Pans

A seed flat is a shallow box used for germinating seeds and sometimes for growing on seedlings to set-out size. Wood flats, measuring 16 by 22½ inches, have largely been replaced by inexpensive lightweight plastic flats, 10½ by 21 inches and from 2 to 2½ inches deep. Seed pans, also usually made of plastic, measure 5 by 7 inches (so that six may be accommodated in a flat) and are usually 2½ inches deep. Both flats and pans have perforated bottoms to facilitate drainage and sloping sides for efficient stacking. Pans are used in preferance to flats when small amounts of a particular kind of seed are to be germinated. It is best to sow only one kind per pan or flat, and each sowing should be labeled as to kind, cultivar, source, and date.

Proportions for Use in Seed Flats
or Seed Pans

A popular, much-used mix, called 2-1-1, consists of two parts ordinary garden soil, one part peat moss, and one part sand. However, any of the media listed above can be used in various combinations with existing soil.

Steps in Preparing Seed Flats and Pans

The following steps should be followed for successful germination.

1. If the flat has an open mesh or slatted bottom, cover the inside with paper.
2. Fill the flat or pan with soil mix and firm it into the corners and around the edges.
3. Smooth the mix with a ruler or other straightedge so that it is level with the top of the flat. Firm slightly with a wood block.
4. Make furrows with a ruler, spacing 1½ to 2 inches apart.
5. Sow seed thinly by passing the open packet over the furrow and tapping it lightly with the other hand. Distribute seed as evenly as possible, and avoid piling it at row ends. In most cases 8 to 12 seedlings per inch is ideal spacing. Old seed may be sown more thickly as a portion of it may no longer be viable.
6. Cover seed one to two times its thickness with fine sand, ground vermiculite, or ground sphagnum. Very fine seed or seed requiring light to germinate should be merely dusted with very fine peat moss.
7. Firm the surface with a flat block or board before watering.
8. Water gently, using a mist nozzle. Avoid puddling, as seed may float to the surface. Adequate ventilation and a pinch of fungicide added to the water will prevent damping off, a fungus disease that can quickly annihilate entire flats of seedlings.
9. Cover the flat with a glass pane or clear plastic wrap pulled tightly to avoid contact with the soil mix.
10. Label the flat or pan with the name of the vegetable, the cultivar, source of seed, and date planted.
11. Place in a warm location (70° to 75°F is best for most vegetables) but out of direct sunlight, as the space between the soil mix and cover will overheat.
12. Remove the cover as soon as germination has occurred and place the flat or pan in sunlight or under indoor lights. Check daily and water when the surface begins to dry.
13. When large enough to handle, transplant the seedlings to cell packs or small pots, using 2-1-1 or other soil mix. Transplanting should be done quickly, out of direct sunlight, and away from wind. Minimize the exposure of the roots to air. Moving one seedling at a time helps cut losses.
14. At least one week before transplanting seedlings to the garden, place in a coldframe or in a protected place outdoors to harden off (i.e., become accustomed to outdoor conditions). Daily or twice daily watering may be required.

CHARACTERISTICS OF SUPERIOR VEGETABLE GARDEN SOIL

1. Warms early in spring; friable, well-drained soils warm more quickly than heavy, wet clays.
2. Retains moisture; humus or manure content helps slow evaporation.
3. Is easily raked to a fine tilth for planting.
4. Drains quickly, without puddling.
5. Does not bake, pack, or crack in summer heat; soils that do require lightening with sand and organic matter.
6. Retains fertility; excessively drained sandy soils leach nutrients beyond the reach of crop roots; lateral runoff from heavy soils results in similar nutrient loss.
7. Retains corrected pH or is easily adjusted.
8. Is free of heavy metals; in urban areas, it is prudent to have garden soils tested, especially for lead (peeled or scraped paint from older houses is a major lead source, as was gasoline); lead arsenate, previously much used in orchards, is also a source.*

*Most lead accumulates in leaf crops, less in roots, least in fruits. Mental retardation and behavior anomalies in children can be caused by lead in the diet.

REASONS FOR INCORPORATING ORGANIC MATTER IN GARDEN SOILS

1. Improves physical structure, facilitating root growth.
2. Eases water penetration and augments moisture retention.
3. Improves aeration, especially in heavy clay soils.
4. Reduces surface crusting and clod formation.
5. Encourages the growth and diversity of beneficial soil organisms.
6. Assists in making soil nutrients available for uptake into the plants.

BASIC TOOLS AND EQUIPMENT FOR THE VEGETABLE GARDEN

A trowel is useful in transplanting seedlings, while a scuffle hoe is best used in weeding and a common hoe is helpful in making rows. Other useful equipment includes stakes and cord to make rows straight, a rake, and a hand weeder.

In most regions, supplemental irrigation is required, especially in late spring and in the summer, and usually involves hoses and spraying devices. Infrequent heavy waterings, delivering about 1 inch of water per week, are preferable, especially where heavy clay soils prevail, to frequent light sprinklings. No water delivery method is ideal for gardens. Soakers waste the least water but irrigate only limited areas. Capillary irrigation is the most efficient but the equipment is expensive to buy and install, and in time often requires intensive maintenance. Overhead oscillating sprayers water large areas but much water is lost as mist. Rotary sprayers or reciprocating sprayers that deliver large drops lose little water as spray but the heavy drops contribute to soil compaction, especially in heavy clay soils deficient in organic matter. Watering by hand with adjustable nozzles is seldom even or adequate and wastes much time.

The best method in any instance depends on soil quality and the area to be covered as well as the frequency of need. Much time can be saved if the vegetable garden is served by one or more auxiliary standpipes with faucets, from which hoses can be run to pole-mounted sprayers. The number and location of the sprayers is determined by garden area and their individual ranges. All outdoor faucets and exposed piping must be drained before the onset of freezing weather; hoses and sprayers are best stored indoors over the winter.

FERTILIZING THE VEGETABLE GARDEN

Fertilizers of any sort, whether "organic" or commercially prepared, add nutrients to the soil, and these are taken up in solution and contribute to plant growth. Well-rotted manure and compost are generally preferable to commercial preparations, because they improve the physical consistency of the soil and release nutrients at rates that do not exceed root absorption. Commercial fertlizers are preferred by many, however, because they are convenient to use and to store and, in most instances, are formulated with precision that can be matched to actual plant requirements. If used injudiciously, however, excess nutrient escapes and contributes to the pollution of aquifers, rivers, and wetlands. Moreover, the soil's physical quality deteriorates.

The three elements in soil nutrients most essential for garden crops are nitrogen, phosphorus, and potassium. Although their functions in plant physiology are complex, nitrogen promotes leaf and other vegetative growth, phosphorus facilitates root growth and hastens maturity, and potassium increases staunchness and disease resistance.

A complete fertilizer is one that contains all three elements in soluble form and is usually described by the percentage of each element in the product. A bag of 5-10-5 fertilizer, for example, contains 5 percent nitrogen, 10 percent phosphorus, and 5 percent potassium. For leafy crops, such as lettuce, spinach, and Swiss chard, a nitrate-rich fertilizer, such as 10-5-5, will augment foliar development. For vegetables that are structurally fruits (snap bean, edible-pod pea, squash, cucumber, pepper, eggplant, etc.) and seeds (dry beans, lima bean, fava bean, pea, etc.), a phosphorus-rich fertilizer such as 5-10-5 is best. Root crops, such as radish, turnip, beet, and carrot, do best with a fertilizer rich in both phosphorus and potassium, such as 5-10-10.

In the germination stage of plant growth, the seed absorbs moisture, which, when given heat, changes the concentrated food contained in the seed to a simple form. This food is sufficient to make a sprout appear through a surface of soil. When the first true leaves expand, and until flowers open, the plant is in the vegetative state. From the time that flowering first occurs, the plant is in the fruiting stage.

Since plants such as lettuce and spinach are eaten in the vegetative stage, and tomato, pepper, and eggplant in the fruiting stage, it is easy to understand that fertilizer requirements vary greatly. When placed in the soil, both phosphorus and potassium are available to plants over a long period. On the other hand, nitrogen has various forms that differ widely in the rates at which they become available. Compounds of nitrogen may be classified into three types.

1. *Inorganic.* Available as soon as it is dissolved in water; an example is nitrate of soda, which is available in all soil conditions.
2. *Organic.* Must undergo complete decompostion before it is available; an example is dried blood, which becomes available in about a month if the soil is warm (the bacteria that promote decay are not otherwise active).
3. *Halfway between inorganic and organic.* Must be changed to the nitrate form; an example is ammonium sulfate, which becomes available in one or two weeks after being applied.

Inorganic fertilizer is used early in the spring when the soil is cold and can also be used at other times for quick results. The effect of an application lasts only two or three weeks. For continuous quick growth over a long period, all three should be mixed together and applied.

Many complete fertilizers are on the market. Some have fancy trade names; others use the firm name and describe the contents with numbers.

Where fertilizers, whether organic or commercial, have been applied for the first crop of the season, it is usually not necessary to apply more for the second crop. Once the soil in a new garden has been tested and conditioned with appropriate amendments, organic fertilizer is best spread on the surface and worked in shallowly, with a rake or cultivator. A mulching effect is thus achieved, while at the same time the contained nutrients become available. Commercial inorganic fertilizer is most efficiently applied by using a suitable attachment on a seed planter or by filling shallow furrows dug parallel to the row about 4 inches from the plants, and then covering them with soil. The soluble nutrients will percolate into the root zone. It should be noted that commercial fertilizers have a desiccating, corrosive effect on living tissue and should, therefore, not be concentrated around germinating seeds or left on foliage.

Overhead watering covers a large area with droplets that lose their force and fall as gentle rain. The sprayer head should generate drops, not mist.

COVER CROPS

In zone 8 and north, a late planting of legumes, such as vetch or clover, adds nitrate to the soil. Grasses, such as winter rye, winter wheat, or oat, add masses of organic matter. Either legumes or grasses can carpet garden soil that is otherwise bare and erosion prone in winter; when they are combined, the soil gets the highest benefit.

Cover crops should be sown four to six weeks before hard frost. In an existing vegetable garden, supplemental fertilizer is usually unnecessary; in a new garden, prepare the soil as for first vegetable crops. In any case, legumes will require no additional nitrate. Sowing rates are ½ pound of grass seed, ¼ pound legume seed, or ⅜ pound of mixed grass and legume seed per 100 square feet.

Dry soil must be watered frequently until seedling cover crops are well established. Sometimes some early hand weeding is required. Birds may devour some young plants; if this loss becomes significant, bird netting may be needed.

In early spring, the cover crop may be turned under if no higher than 3 inches. A taller crop is best mowed, then shredded, after which the tops (called green manure) and stubble are tilled into the soil. Cover crops should not be allowed to set seed, as their seedlings will be weeds in the next season's garden. It may take several weeks for grasses to decompose, less time for legumes. All the nutrients in the cover crop tissues are returned to the soil, along with beneficial humus and, in the case of legumes, supplemental nitrate.

CONTROL OF VEGETABLE DISEASES

In many cases when vegetables have been started early in coldframes or hotbeds instead of in the garden, diseases will appear after transplanting them into the open. The causes can often be traced to insufficient care in preparing the seedbed. A number of diseases are able to winter over in old seedbeds and gardens. Many of the more damaging diseases are carried over by the seed, such as early and late blights of celery; leaf blights and fruit rots of cucumber, eggplant, melon, and squash; black rot and black leg of cabbage, turnip, and cauliflower; early blight and bacterial canker of

Barley, a grass, and vetch, a legume, grown together in broad rows as a soil-enriching cover crop, will be turned under in early spring.

tomato; leaf spot of tomato and greens; and others. Therefore, it is highly important to use clean seed and to clean the seedbed soil when starting the crop.

Investment in good seed justifies safeguarding the crop in the seedbed. While the use of disease-free seed and clean seedbed soil are important steps in producing strong healthy plants, so too is good seedbed management. Healthy plants in seedbeds help ensure a disease-free crop in the garden.

Since many serious diseases of garden vegetables get their start in the seedbed or coldframe, even in spite of the precautions already mentioned, it is prudent to guard against infection from outside sources. Sanitary and protective steps consist of the following.

1. Avoid overfrequent and excessive watering of beds; instead, water more heavily at longer intervals; water only in the morning and ventilate well to hasten drying as soon as possible. Proper watering, heating, and ventilating of beds not only ensures sturdy, vigorous-growing plants but also provides conditions that are not favorable for damping off and other diseases.

2. Discard spotted, wilted, and otherwise diseased plants, for they are starters of infection. Do not put diseased plants in the compost, as the diseases will often recur in garden areas where infected compost is used.

3. Avoid introducing old plant debris and contaminated soil into seedbeds and coldframes.

Remember that thorough protection of the vegetable crop against diseases may be accomplished easily while it occupies so limited a space. For more on pests and diseases, see Chapter 34.

CULTURAL DIRECTIONS FOR POPULAR VEGETABLES

ASPARAGUS
(Asparagus officinalis)

Known as a food plant in the Mediterranean region and Europe for more than 2,000 years, asparagus has been grown in America since colonial times. It is a long-lived perennial reliably hardy from zones 4 to 9. The crop consists of clustered, young, rapidly lengthening stems whose pointed tips are clothed with rudimentary leaves.

Asparagus succeeds on most any soil, but growth and development are adversely affected in heavy soils that remain wet. A moist, sandy, fertile, well-drained soil yields the largest crops. Also, as sandy soil warms up more rapidly in spring, production of spears is hastened.

It is preferable to plant one-year-old crowns, i.e., dormant roots radiating from a central knot of buds, than to grow from seed or older roots. As root growth is extensive, deep, thorough soil preparation is important. Allow about 12 crowns per asparagus-eating person. If there will be more than one row, the rows should be spaced about 3 feet apart, as the summer growth is often 5 to 8 feet tall and diffusely branched. Crowns should be planted about 18 inches apart in the row. Lay planks between the rows to prevent soil compaction.

Asparagus shoots

The row should be forked or tilled at least 18 inches deep and have generous amounts of well-rotted manure and/or compost worked in. For every bushel of this organic material, add 1 pound of commercial 5-10-5 fertilizer, along with whatever ground limestone is required to achieve pH 6.5 to 7.0. Then, in the prepared row, dig a trench 6 inches deep and 1 foot wide, setting aside and saving the soil. Each crown should be set with the roots carefully spread on the surface in the trench and covered with 2 or 3 inches of the saved soil. Firm the soil gently, as the fleshy asparagus roots are brittle. Water thoroughly. When the slender shoots emerge, add more backfill; continue until the trench is refilled. Do not harvest any spears the first year. When the shoots have reached about 1 foot in height, the beds should be bermed with a mulch of loose compost or straw to conserve moisture and deter weeds.

Early the following spring, the beds should be topdressed with well-rotted manure and/or compost. A light harvest may be taken over a two-week period of any 4- to 8-inch-long spears that are at least ½ inch in diameter. Thereafter, allow all stalks to grow. In the third year, the harvest period may be extended to 4 weeks, and in succeeding years to 8 weeks. Cut spears just below the soil surface. Annual applications of manure and/or compost or, failing them, of 5-10-5 fertilizer will help ensure continued maximum production. Over the years, the buildup of organic matter will result in a permanent berm, which eases harvesting, as minimal digging will be required to cut the spears.

If garden space is limited, young asparagus may be interplanted the first year or two with such rapidly maturing crops as radish, lettuce, and spinach. After the third or fourth year, asparagus should yield 25 to 40 pounds of spears per 100 feet of row each year.

If fully blanched asparagus is desired, the beds should be boxed in and filled with soil about 1 foot above grade. A few plants left out of the enclosure can serve as indicators for the time to harvest blanched spears.

Asparagus plants are either male or female. Normally, purchased crowns are of male plants only, as their spears are heavier. Any plants that produce berries should be dug out, discarded, and replaced, since these female plants will always produce slender spears. Alternatively, some female plants may be transplanted to the rear of a sunny flower bed, as the red berries are ornamental. Berried branches may be cut and dried for use in winter bouquets.

One of the principal enemies of asparagus is the asparagus beetle, which causes black spots where it chews spear tips. It may be controlled with Rotenone. Rust disease discolors and often deforms above ground parts. It is best avoided by planting rust-resistant cultivars. For more information see Chapter 34.

Among the relatively few asparagus cultivars offered commercially, 'Mary Washington' is very adaptable and widely available. 'Jersey Giant' bears heavily, especially north of zone 8; 'UC 157' is a heat-tolerant counterpart for the South. All are rust resistant.

BEANS

There are many kinds of beans, as the multitude of English common names reflects: bush bean, pole bean, green bean, wax bean, snap bean, string bean, lima bean, scarlet runner bean, yard-long bean, fava bean, purple-hulled speckled bean, etc. All cultivated beans but the scarlet runner are annuals, and all but the fava are tender tropical American species that require hot weather to produce the pods and seeds that we value for food.

First cultivated about 500 years ago, the climbing string or green bean (*Phaseolus vulgaris*) was soon followed by the climbing lima bean (*P. lunatus*). After much selection and hybridization, the bush string bean (*P. vulgaris* var. *humilis*) and its latter-day tender-podded derivative, the bush snap bean, have become favorite beans for home-garden production. Yellow-podded (wax bean) and purple-podded variants are also grown. Similar refinements in pod quality, and considerable variation in pod form, are seen in modern cultivars of the climbing string bean, known collectively as pole snap beans. The wild climbing lima bean is best known to home gardeners through its low-growing, nonclimbing form, the bush lima. The scarlet runner bean (*P. coccineus*) is a

Green bean 'Visoki Zelen'

Scarlet runner bean *(Phaseolus coccineus)*

climbing species as much grown for its decorative red flowers as for its edible pods. The yard-long bean (*Vigna unguiculata* ssp. *sesquipedalis*) is also a twiner, bearing slender cylindrical pods, usually about 18 inches long.

Quite apart from all the foregoing, the fava bean or broad bean is a cool-weather, nonvining crop from the Mediterranean region that has long been grown for its seeds, which in Europe are harvested either green or mature.

As culture varies somewhat among the various types of bean, they will be treated separately.

Bush Snap Bean

Because bush snap bean bears heavily for a short time in six to eight weeks from seed, it is best to make several small sowings two to three weeks apart from spring to midsummer. Such succession sowings ensure a steady, manageable supply of beans for table use instead of a one-time glut. On the other hand, a large crop may be preferred for freezing or canning.

Bush snap bean is less demanding of high soil nutrient levels than most vegetables; indeed, exuberant foliage and a low pod set betray an excess of nitrate. Such an excess can easily occur as bush beans, like all other beans and peas and most other legumes, have root swellings in which bacteria grow and deposit nitrate

Bush snap bean 'Jade'

into the soil. Hence the advisability of making only light applications of fertilizer, preferably 5-10-5 or 5-10-10. Bush bean thrives in warm days (80° to 90°F), with night temperatures no lower than 50°F. A moist, sandy, well-drained, moderately fertile, loamy soil yields best results. Good harvests may be expected within a pH range of 5.5 to 6.5.

Seed sown 1 to 2 inches deep sprouts within a week if the soil temperature is at least 60°F. Spacing should be 4 to 6 inches, allowing the individual plants maximum sun exposure, ensuring an optimal crop. Pods should be harvested as soon as full length is achieved and while turgid enough to snap when bent. Overaged pods are leathery and swollen over the enlarging seeds. Haricot or filet bean is best harvested very immature, when only 3 or 4 inches long.

Approximately ½ pound of seed is sufficient for a 50-foot row and will yield a total of 35 to 50 pounds of beans, depending on the cultivar and garden conditions. Two or three pickings over a three-week period may be expected, after which the yield quickly declines and plants should be pulled. Seed dusted before sowing with rhizobial innoculant powder may result in enhanced yields, especially in new garden areas where native legumes (members of the family Leguminosae), such as clover or vetch, did not grow. The roots of these plants, and most other legumes, harbor bacteria that deposit nitrate in the soil.

Wax bean 'Butter Crisp'

Care should be taken to keep wetness of foliage and pods to a minimum by avoiding late-afternoon or night watering. Such wetness promotes anthracnose, bean mosaic virus, and mildew, any of which can be serious, especially in areas where beans have been grown successively, year after year. Crop rotation is advisable in such areas.

Although continuous breeding programs bring new bush snap bean cultivars onto the market almost every year, a number of long-standing cultivars are widely available and have proven reliable under diverse conditions. Moreover, they are reasonably resistant to common bean diseases. Among them are 'Blue Lake 274', 'Derby', and 'Roma II'. Others with special characteristics include 'EZ Pick' and 'Provider', which are less cold sensitive than most; 'White Half-runner', a semiclimber that grows to 3 feet; 'Jumbo', which has very long (up to 10 inches) flattened pods on plants that bend to the ground under the weight of the crop; and 'Bush Romano', also with flattened pods.

In wax or yellow bush snap beans, the pods fail to develop green color and are generally of milder flavor than green-podded types. There is little difference among the half-dozen cultivars commonly offered. Purple-podded bush snap beans mature a striking deep purple, which aids their being found among the foliage for harvest, but, as the pigment is lost in cooking, they are especially favored uncooked in salads.

Pole Snap Bean

The pod characteristics of pole snap bean are mostly equivalent to those of bush snap bean, but the plants have elongating, twining stems. The plant is best supported on teepees of poles; on cords suspended from a single pole, such as a discarded television antenna mast; or for large plantings, on 6-foot-high, wide-mesh wire fencing supported on steel stakes. Poles or fencing should be arranged and spaced to prevent shading. Thus supported, pole snap beans are easier to harvest than bush snap beans, and the pods are kept drier and out of contact with the soil. As long as picking is frequent, the pole snap bean bears over a long period and need not be sown in succession plantings.

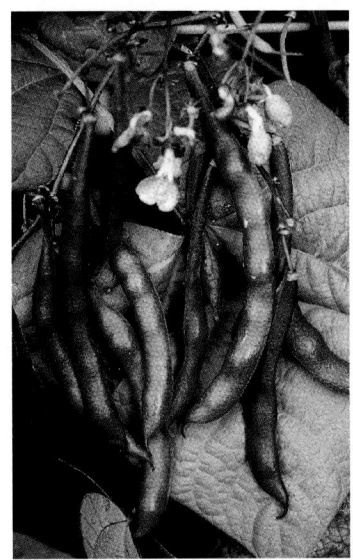

Purple pole bean

Teepees of poles should be spaced 4 feet apart, with each teepee consisting of four to six 7- or 8-foot poles lashed together at the top and spaced about 18 inches apart at the base; sink the poles about 1 foot into the ground. Television antenna masts should also be set at 4-foot intervals. The pole and tripod supports should be partly submerged for stability, and the pole should be strung with three heavy cords from the pole at the limit of reach down to each of the three basal legs. Fencing should be supported by steel stakes or wood posts set at 6-foot intervals. Other support devices can be substituted, such as a bicycle wheel mounted horizontally atop a pole,

with numerous cords stretched from the rim to stakes driven into the ground. Commercially manufactured "bean towers" are also available.

Soil preparation and time and depth of sowing are the same as for bush snap bean (see previous page). Sow three or four seeds at the base of each pole or cord, or at 4- to 6-inch intervals along a fence. In the latter instance, ½ pound of seed will plant 100 feet of fence and may be expected to yield a season total of 150 pound to 200 pounds of produce. The first beans are ready for picking in about two months.

Davis purple pole bean

Among the various green-podded cultivars, 'Kentucky Wonder', 'Kentucky Blue', and 'Blue Lake FM-1' are reliably productive on as wide a range of soils as the most adaptable bush snap bean. In most, the pods are cylindrical, but those of 'Romano' are flattened. Cultivars with yellow, purple, or mottled pods are also available.

As with bush snap beans, excess nitrate augments foliage and diminishes pod formation. Late-day watering, while not advisable, is less serious as the diffuse vines dry more quickly.

Bush Lima Bean

Lima bean is grown for its large flat seeds, which should be harvested when full size but before they harden. Bush lima bean requires about ten weeks from sowing to first picking and bears best in hot summer weather. Once night temperatures dip below 60°F, pod set ceases.

Soil requirements are the same as for bush snap bean (see page 638). Allow 2 to 3 feet between rows, or about 18 inches in raised beds. Sow seed 3 inches apart and as deep. Germination requires warm soil (not below 70°F); at lower temperatures, germination is spotty or fails altogether. Best results are had when the seed eye is planted downward. Plant 15 to 20 feet of row per person.

Of the several cultivars, 'Fordhook' and 'Fordhook 242' are superior large-seeded types; 'Geneva' is a small-seeded form that is more cold tolerant than most; and 'Jackson Wonder' and 'Butterpea Speckled' bear buff seeds that are mottled reddish purple.

Pole Lima Bean

As with pole snap bean, the pole lima bean twines and, therefore, requires similar support. The pole lima requires hot summer weather to bear maximally. Three months is usually required from seed to first harvest. It succeeds best from zone 7 south. On a square-yard basis, pole lima bean yields considerably more than bush lima.

Once the weather becomes dependably warm, sow two or three seeds at each pole or cord, or 4 to 6 inches apart along fencing.

Among the few cultivars, 'Burpee's Best' and 'King of the Garden' are widely grown. In 'Large Speckled Christmas', the greenish white seeds are speckled dark red.

Bush Dry Bean (Shell Bean)

Bush dry bean grows as a low, sprawling plant and is cultivated primarily for the mature, hardened seeds. The seeds are harvested all at once after the pods have dried and most leaves have dropped, about three or four months after sowing. In some cultivars, young pods may be used as snap beans. Each plant should yield about ¼ pound of dried beans. The seeds may be harvested green for immediate table use.

Culture is the same as for bush snap bean (see page 638). Harvesting involves pulling up the whole plant with the pods still attached. The seeds may then be removed by opening the individual pods or shells by hand or, where quantities are substantial, by flailing several podded plants at a time inside a barrel. The plants may also be stuffed into a burlap bag and flailed or even trod on. Once separated, the beans should be stored in a cool, dry place. If tiny holes appear, indicating the presence of weevils, subject the beans to several hours of freezing temperatures.

Among the many cultivars, best known are the following.

'Black Turtle': dark brown seeds.
'Jacob's Cattle': white seeds with reddish speckles.
'Maine Yellow-eye': white seeds with a yellow-brown spot.
'Pinto': deep pink, speckled seeds.
'Red Kidney': large, reddish brown seeds.

Scarlet Runner Bean

Scarlet runner bean is a very adaptable 8- to 12-foot twining climber. Although it is a perennial in zones 9 and 10, it is usually grown as a long-season annual for its immature pods. Culture is the same as for bush snap bean (see page 638), with support as for pole snap bean. Adequate summer moisture is required for maximum pod set.

Sow the large purplish seeds 2 to 3 inches deep in well-prepared soil after night temperatures stay above 50°F. The broad pods, which follow the very attractive red, bee-pollinated flowers, are borne continuously until night temperatures drop below 50°F in the fall. Pods should be harvested while immature, i.e., about 6 to 8 inches long. Once they are full size (about 12 inches long), they become leathery, the strings tough, and the seeds hard.

Few cultivars are available in the United States. 'Enorma' and 'Liberty' bear unusually long pods; 'White Dutch Runner' also produces edible tuberous roots; and 'Hammond's Dwarf' and 'Pickwick Dwarf' are semierect, nontwining forms that bear earlier than usual twiners.

Yard-long Bean

Also called asparagus bean, yard-long bean, a twiner, bears smooth, slender, curved pods that may be used as snap beans, especially if picked while still immature, i.e., 12 to 18 inches long (mature length is 24 to 30 inches). Culture is the same as for bush snap bean (see page 638), with support as for pole snap bean, but since yard-long bean requires hot weather (daytime temperatures above 85°F) to begin twining and a long season to bear creditably, it is best grown south of zone 7.

Most cultivated yard-long beans are green podded, but a purple-podded variant is notable in that the purple pigment persists through cooking.

Fava Bean (Broad Bean)

Although summer conditions in most of the United States are too hot for fava bean culture, it may be grown from zone 7 north as a spring and early summer crop, when daytime temperatures range between 65° and 80°F. The crop consists of seeds, varying in size according to cultivar, which are borne four to six together in fleshy 4-inch pods. They are usually harvested while still green.

Sow seed very early in a well-prepared plot, as soon as the soil can be worked and well before the last spring frost. Planting depth is 1 to 1½ inches, and spacing is 4 to 6 inches apart in rows 1½ to 24 feet apart. The bushy plants reach about 3 feet in height. Fava bean is usually ready for harvest within three months from seed, and in any case ceases bearing by midsummer. Plants should then be pulled out to make room for a succession planting of a different crop. Wet, soggy ground diminishes the harvest, as does drought. A phosphate-rich fertilizer, such as a commercial 5-10-5 preparation or superphosphate, will help improve yields.

Among the more heat-tolerant, disease-resistant cultivars are the following.

'Broad Windsor Long-pod': young pods are also edible.
'Equina': small seeds.
'Ipro': particularly heat tolerant.

BEET
(Beta vulgaris)

Originating in the Mediterranean region, the beet was cultivated in classical Greece and Rome and has been an important root crop ever since.

The beet is usually thought of as a deep red, globular root, but in fact the many cultivars collectively exhibit wide variation in color ranging from red to orange, yellow, or white, and in form, ranging from the usual spherical shape to carrot shaped. Garden beet offers not only the edible roots but equally edible leaves or "tops." Close relatives include the sugar beet and mangel-wurzel, as well as Swiss chard.

Although tolerant of varied weather conditions, beet is best handled as a fast-growing, cool-season crop in most of the United States, flourishing when daytime temperatures range between 60° and 70°F. Sharp fluctuations in weather result in zoning, or rings, in root slices. Loose, sandy-humusy soil is best for root development. Since the "seed" is actually a dried few-seeded fruit, it should be sown sparingly, say at 1-inch intervals, ¾ to 1 inch deep, and the seedlings thinned to 3 to 4 inches apart. The first sowing should be made a week or so before the last spring frost; the second, planted 1½ to 2 inches deep, in midsummer. Germination is often spotty but may be compensated for by transplanting, making sure the slender taproot is positioned straight down. "Monogerm" types have fruit with a single seed, hence offer somewhat more predictable spacing. Crops are ready in 40 to 80 days, depending on the cultivar and garden conditions. It is important to sustain soil moisture throughout the growing period, as temporarily drought-checked plants often fail to develop usable roots. The roots are best harvested when 2 to 3 inches in diameter. Older, larger roots become dense and eventually woody.

Beet greens should be collected when the plant is pulled for the root or from thinned seedlings. Removal of leaves from actively growing plants slows root formation.

About 15 feet of row per person is a good allocation of space initially, with adjustments made in successive years according to use.

A nitrate- and potassium-rich fertilizer, such as a 10-5-10 commercial preparation, is advantageous for maximum production, the nitrate especially for foliage or tops, the potassium for the root.

Cultivars with red, globular roots best grown early or or late in the season include 'Crosby's Egyptian', 'Early Wonder',

Heirloom beet collection

'Edmund's Blood', and 'Little Ball'. Among long-season types, especially suited to zone 6 and north, are 'Long Seasons' and 'Ruby Queen'. One of the most adaptable, durable cultivars is 'Detroit Dark Red'. Among hybrid beets, which are increasing in popularity because of their versatility and crop uniformity, 'Red Ace' is one of the best known.

Specialty beets include the following:

'Chioggia': roots pink, zoned white (contrast tends to be lost in cooking).
'Cylindra': roots carrot shaped, 8 by 1¾ inches.
'Formanova': roots carrot shaped, 6 by 2½ inches.
'Golden': roots yellow; sow densely, as it has a low germination rate.

Cultivars traditionally grown primarily for greens include 'Early Wonder Tall-

top', which has green-and-red foliage, and 'Lutz Green-leaf', which has green-and-white foliage. All other cultivars yield tops of equal utility, but may be more subject to blemishes by insects or disease and also tend to become very soft when cooked.

'Golden' and 'Chiogga' cultivars of beet

BROCCOLI
(Brassica oleracea, Italica group)

'Romanesco' broccoli

In contrast to the other cole, or cabbage-related, crops, broccoli has become a popular table vegetable only in the last century. The crop consists of thickened, fasciated green stalks covered with masses of unopened flower buds. In most of the United States, the key to successful broccoli culture is starting seeds early indoors under lights or in a greenhouse, or purchasing seedlings later, so that the plants are sufficiently advanced when set out to produce a crop before the onset of hot summer weather. Intense heat causes the buds to go to flower quickly. Plan on six to eight weeks from set-out to harvest. Indoor sowing should be done six to eight weeks before the last spring frost, and after a week's hardening off in a coldframe, the seedlings should be planted in the garden about the time of the last frost. About 12 plants per person should meet usual table needs.

To avert transplanting shock, and if space permits, plant the seed in 2½- to 3-inch plastic pots or other drainable containers of comparable size, the number of containers equaling the number of broccoli plants desired for the garden. Fill each pot with potting mix and arrange in a flat or tray. Sow three or four seeds ½ to 1 inch deep in each. Keep the mix moist but not wet, and the temperature at 60° to 65°F. Seedlings should be given maximum sunlight exposure or be placed directly under fluorescent lights for at least 14 hours a day. By the time the seedlings

are 2 inches tall, thin to one plant per pot by snipping off (not pulling) the weaker plants. Avoid cold drafts, but keep the day temperatures in the 60s (°F), and about 10° less at night.

In a coldframe, plants will be subjected to wider temperature extremes, but these should be controlled by opening the frames on sunny days to prevent heat buildup and by closing them on cold nights. Lattice shading may be needed the first few days and watering must be carefully checked each day. Ideally, fully hardened plants should be 4 to 6 inches tall at set-out time.

Alternatively, seed may be sown in flats or seed pans, seedlings transplanted to cell packs, and ultimately shifted to pots. But because transplanting shock often delays the crop a week or more, the whole process should be started that much earlier.

For later crops in cool-summer areas, seeds may be sown directly in the garden

1 to 2 inches apart (requiring ⅛ to ¼ ounce of seed for each 100 feet of row), and later thinned to stand about 1 foot apart. The discarded seedlings make good table greens.

In regions with hot summers, a crop for fall harvest may be started in mid-summer, preferably in pots in a coldframe, lattice-shaded from hot sun, especially in midday. Set the seedlings out in the garden as the shorter days and cooler nights of late summer become evident. As with spring crops, the heads should be harvested when young, compact, and the buds unopened. Harvest continues until well after first frosts. Expect 75 pounds or more from each 100 feet of row. Most cultivars develop small secondary or even tertiary heads after the large central head has been cut.

A side-dressing of well-rotted manure or compost is advantageous before the heads

Row of broccoli

form, especially in sandy, excessively drained soils, both to maintain nutrient levels and to conserve moisture. Commercial 10-10-10 fertilizer may also serve, if used at the rate of 8 ounces per 10 square feet, lightly cultivated into the top 2 inches, and watered well. In this case a summer mulch, such as salt hay or straw, will help retard evaporation.

Hybrid broccoli cultivars tend to produce heads of uniform size that are ready for harvest at the same time. By growing two or more cultivars, and by planning early and late plantings, the harvest period may extend from early summer to mid or late fall. Among the most adaptable hybrids, suited for both early and late crops, are 'Early Emerald', 'Emperor Hybrid', 'Green Comet', and 'Packman'. As early crops only, 'Calabrese' and 'Spartan Early' are widely grown, as is 'Waltham 29' as a late crop. Where heads varying in maturation time are desired and uniformity of size is unimportant, the nonhybrid 'De Cicco' is a good choice.

Romanesque or Romanesco broccoli is a specialty type, particularly useful in salads, having geometrically spiraled, peaked heads. The cultivar 'Minaret' is successful as either an early or a late crop.

BRUSSELS SPROUTS
(Brassica oleracea, Gemmifera group)

Believed to have been first cultivated in the nineteenth century in Belgium, Brussels sprouts are another variant of the cabbage theme, in this case having well-developed cabbagelike buds, 1 to 2 inches, in diameter, borne laterally along the tall, leafy, unbranched stem. The crop is usually raised for fall harvest, but through choice of cultivar, it may be gathered from mid or late summer until the following spring. It is marketed either as defoliated stems with the budlike sprouts still attached, or with the buds removed and packaged. Frost as severe as 15°F causes no harm as long as the sprouts are thawed slowly; indeed, cold improves the flavor. Whole stems with sprouts attached may be stored in a cold, even freezing, place for several weeks after harvest.

Brussels sprouts are most bountiful in regions having cool summers and mild winters. It is a long-season crop that from zone 8 north is best started in the spring and grown for harvest in six to nine months. Seedlings may be started indoors as for broccoli (see page 642), a procedure recommended north of zone 7. Allow about a dozen plants per person in an initial planting. If only one or two dozen plants are to be set out, it may be best to purchase hardened-off transplants. In the garden, seedlings should be spaced about 18 inches apart. Maximum height is normally 3 to 4 feet. Elsewhere, seed may be sown directly in well-prepared soil in the garden, also as for broccoli (see above). Thin the seedlings, allowing 90 to 120 days for the crop to mature before the onset of frosty nights. Supplemental fertilizer, such as a topdressing of well-rotted manure or a 10-10-10 or 10-5-5 commercial fertilizer, will help maximize yield.

As the small buds become evident at the base of the lowest leaf stalks, the adjacent leaf blades should be clipped to expose the sprouts to more light. Because the sprouts usually mature from the lower stem upward, the lowest of them, once of sufficient size, may be harvested from all stems, leaving the rest to continue growing and be harvested later. In late summer or early fall, removal of the leafy top will hasten development of the sprouts. The young inner leaves of the top make excellent table greens, rather like collards but with the flavor of Brussels sprouts. It is best to harvest Brussels sprouts while still young and somewhat undersize, as older ones harden, develop a strong flavor, and can become insect infested or develop decay.

Cultivars that mature in about 90 days include 'Jade Cross', 'Oliver', and 'Prince Marvel'. Longer-season types, maturing in about 120 days, often somewhat more prolific, and harvestable through mild winters, include 'Catskill' and 'Widgeon'. Also a long-season form, but with reddish sprouts, is 'Rubine Red'.

CABBAGE
(Brassica oleracea, Capitata group)

Originally grown in the Mediterranean region, where it is presumed native, cabbage has been cultivated as a food crop for at least 4,000 years. The crop is a great terminal bud, or head, of closely adhering, partly developed leaves, which varies, according to cultivar, in color, texture, and shape. Garden conditions greatly affect the ultimate size of the head. Best adapted to cool conditions, cabbage has been bred and selected for a wide diversity of conditions, and among the many extant cultivars, some perform well in brief long-day subarctic summers, others on midelevation tropical mountainsides and highlands.

In most of the United States, cabbage is grown principally for fall harvest, but many cultivars respond well to accelerated spring culture and yield by early summer. As a wide selection of cultivars is available, some developed for specific cultural conditions, care should be taken to choose appropriate ones for your garden conditions and climate, and for time of harvest. Although garden-grown cabbage is usually superior in quality to commercially raised produce, the space required—up to 1 square yard per plant for well-grown larger types—should should be recognized, especially where space is limited and various other crops may be excluded. Yields average 150 to 200 pounds per 100 feet of row.

For early cabbage crops from zone 8 north, seed should be started indoors, as for broccoli (see page 642), about eight weeks before the last spring frost. Sow seeds in cell packs, two or three seeds per cell, or in flats at the rate of three or four seeds per inch. Seedlings should be grown on in cell packs, thinned to one plant per cell, in intense light (as in a greenhouse) or directly under fluorescent tubes kept illuminated 14 to 16 hours per day. Legginess betrays inadequate light intensity. Germination is rapid (often in two or three days) if the soil is heated to about 75°F, and seedlings grow best if the air temperature is kept at 60°F immediately following germination and circulated gently, as with a small nearby fan. After four or five weeks, subject the seedlings to 7 to 10 days of hardening off in a coldframe, and then transplant them into the garden about two weeks before the last frost. Hardened cabbage seedlings can endure temperatures as low as 20°F without damage. Spacing depends on cultivar, but 1 to 1½ feet between plants is a reasonable minimum. Interplanting with a fast-maturing crop such as radish makes productive use of intervening spaces. In midseason, after any interplanted crops have been removed, a topdressing of well-rotted manure or 10-5-5 commercial fertilizer will help late-maturing cabbage develop fully. It is important that soil moisture be as carefully maintained as possible once head formation begins, as a sudden soaking after a dry period can cause the heads to split or crack.

In zone 9 and in milder areas of zone 8, seed may be sown directly in the garden in early spring, about four seeds together at 1-foot intervals. The seedlings are later thinned, leaving the strongest one to mature.

For fall harvest, so-called midseason, late-season, or storage cultivars perform best. Seeds may be sown outdoors, as outlined above, at about the time of the last spring frost or a bit later, when bright spring sunshine warms the soil surface during the day. Seedlings should be thinned to stand 1½ to 3 feet apart, according to head size and leaf spread at maturity.

To deter or at least minimize the commonest and potentially most serious of the numerous diseases that afflict cabbage (and other cole crops), it is advisable to rotate cabbage so that at least three years elapse before it is grown again in the same row or plot. Use of sterile soil for indoor starting culture and of a fungicide in irrigation water for seedlings usually prevents growth of the damping-off fungus. Prompt removal of fallen leaves and of diseased plants from the garden also helps deter the spread of disease. As for common pests, stem-girdling cutworms can be kept at bay by surrounding each seedling with a heavy paper collar about 2 inches in diameter and about as high, gently pressed ½ inch into the soil. Transparent plastic cloches or floating row covers exclude flea beetles and root maggots. Hand picking or an occasional application of Dipel will control leaf-eating cabbage worms or loopers. See Chapter 34 for control of other diseases and pests, but it is best to keep in mind that some infestation is inevitable and that most are transitory, leaving blemishes that have no effect on food quality.

In addition to the usual early and mid or late season green-headed cultivars, red cabbage belongs to a class of long-season, late-maturing types that have red-violet outer leaves and reddish veining on the inner blanched leaves. Savoy cabbage, with crinkled, textured, green or purplish leaves, is particularly hardy, and varies from early to late season, according to cultivar.

Of the numerous early green-headed cultivars, the conical 'Early Jersey Wakefield' is widely planted in the United States. 'Dakri Hybrid' and 'Golden Cross' are relatively small headed but are harvestable only six weeks after set-out; 'Puma' and 'Earliana' are similar but are harvested slightly later.

Savoy and 'Midway' cabbage

Midseason, late-season, or storage cultivars range from the 3- to 5-pound 'Perfect Ball' to the 10- to 12-pound 'Premium Late Flat Dutch'. Several, including 'Apex' and 'Custodian', are notably tolerant of freezing weather in the fall.

Of the long-season cultivars especially suited to zone 9, 'Early Dutch Round' and 'Tropic Giant Hybrid' are of merit, the latter developing heads weighing 10 to 15 pounds.

Red cabbage cultivars in the 2- to 4-pound range include 'Lasso', Red Acre', 'Red Rookie Hybrid', and 'Ruby Perfection'. 'Regal Red' has heads weighing 5 pounds or more.

Green Savoy cabbage cultivars range from the small, early-maturing 'Blue Max' and 'Spivoy' to the larger, later 'Savoy King Hybrid'. 'January King' has purplish leaves.

Green Savoy cabbage

Red cabbage 'Ruby'

CABBAGE: CHINESE, NAPA
(Brassica rapa, Pekinensis group),
CHINESE WHITE,
AND BOK CHOY
(B. rapa, Chinensis group)

Chinese, Napa, Chinese white and bok choy cabbages are biennials native to Europe but long cultivated in the Orient. They are usually grown as annuals and are valued for their large, mild-flavored leaves that often form heads and, in some cases, thick, white leaf stalks. Both leaves and leaf stalks are eaten raw in salads or cooked.

These cabbages are important greens in southeastern Asia, where selection has led to a wide range of forms suited to culture in mild climates. However, a number of cultivars do well under cooler temperate-zone conditions, and these have gained marked popularity in recent decades throughout the United States.

For early crops, seed of both the Pekinensis and Chinensis groups should be started indoors under fluorescent lights or in a greenhouse about eight weeks before the last spring frost. Seedlings should be grown in cell packs and, about a week before being set out in the garden, hardened off in a coldframe. It is best to delay this final transplanting until night temperatures drop no lower than 45°F. For later crops, seed may be sown in a seedbed outdoors or directly where the plants are to grow. Seedlings should be planted or thinned to stand 12 to 16 inches apart. If spaced more closely, harvest alternate plants early, allowing those remaining to achieve full size. About a dozen late-maturing plants per person should provide adequate yield.

Best results are achieved on humusy, moist, well-drained soil that is rich in nitrate. Where soils are heavy and poorly drained, good results may be had using raised beds. Topdressings of well-rotted manure or rich compost applied every two or three weeks stimulate large leaf size and also conserve soil moisture. Soil pH may range between 5.5 to 7.0. Harvestable crops are usually ready seven to 10 weeks after transplanting seedlings to the garden in the spring or after germination in the summer.

Pak Choi

Smooth-leaved cabbage

Chinese hybrid cabbage

Head-forming cultivars (derived from Chinese or Napa cabbage) include 'Wong Bok', 'Springtide', 'Blues', 'Orient Express', and 'Two-season Hybrid'. Loose or open heads are formed by 'Lettucy' and 'Spoon Cabbage'. 'Lei Choi' and 'Crispy Spears', both derived from Chinese white cabbage, are grown mainly for their large white leaf stalks.

Hybrid Chinese cabbage

CARROT
(Daucus carota ssp. *sativa)*

A variant of the well-known wild carrot or Queen Anne's lace and first discovered in Afghanistan, the familiar orange carrot was first cultivated in the West in fifteenth-century Holland. Soon thereafter it became a vegetable crop of importance throughout the inhabited temperate-zone regions and ultimately in many tropical areas as well. Beta-carotene, a precursor of vitamin A, accounts for the orange color. In wild forms, the roots vary from white to violet black and have a rather strong flavor. In orange-rooted carrots, most of the popular shapes—long (7 inches or more), tapered or cylindrical with blunt ends; half-long (5 to 7 inches), also tapered or cylindrical; mini (3 to 4 inches); and spherical (1½ to 2 inches)— appeared early in the carrot's cultural history. Although cultivar names are varied, the shapes have continued essentially unchanged.

In the garden, carrots, especially the deep-rooted cultivars, require deeply prepared soil that is well drained, rock free, friable, and moderately fertile. A sandy-humusy medium promotes optimal root development, and the best crops are grown in regions having relatively cool summers, i.e., in the 60° to 80°F range. A potash-rich fertilizer, such as a 5-5-10 commercial preparation, ensures maximum root development.

Seed should be sown directly in the garden row or plot. For late spring or early summer crops, sow carrot seed when peas are started until about one week before the last frost. Seed for fall or winter crops is sown in midsummer, in either case allowing two to three months from germination to maturity. Germination is often spotty, but may be improved by sowing seed relatively thinly and evenly and by keeping the seeded rows or beds continuously moist. A ⅛-ounce packet of seed, thoroughly mixed with 1 cup of dry sand, will adequately plant about 25 feet of row or a 4-foot-square bed. If coated or pelleted seed is used, the granules should be spaced about ½ inch apart. Seed should be covered with a 50-50 mixture of dry sand and sifted compost spread ⅛ to ¼ inch deep and tamped firmly. A large cloth covering, such as a discarded sheet or

lightweight bedspread, should then be carefully arranged to cover the seeded ground and weighted along the edges with soil or boards. This and the soil beneath need to be kept moist by watering every day or two in the spring (more frequently in the summer) until the first seedlings appear, usually in about 10 days in the spring, or half as long in the summer. The covering should then be removed. About a week after germination is complete, seedlings should be thinned to stand about 1 inch apart. If left in clumps, the plants will compete and develop undersize, deformed roots. As the roots develop, harvest alternate plants for use, allowing those remaining to grow on to full size, allocating 8 to 12 feet of row per person.

Fall carrot crops may be harvested as late as mid or late winter if the ground is adequately mulched to prevent the soil from freezing. Any plants left in the spring will quickly bolt to flower and seed, a process that consumes the roots.

Carrot greens are irresistible to rabbits and deer. Their browsing is not lethal, but it slows the maturation of the roots. Neither animal is known to pull or dig the roots from the ground. Repellents, such as naphthalene (moth balls) or dried blood, may suffice, but the surest protection is 1-inch mesh woven-wire fencing, 18 inches high, for rabbits, and 4-inch mesh fencing, 6 feet high, for deer.

Among the cultivars with long roots 'Royal Chantenay' is probably the best known of those that are tapered. 'Kuroda', similar in form, is notable for its large size, weighing as much as 1 pound. Hybrid cultivars that are and more or less cylindrical with blunt ends are 'Toudo', with uniform roots (more important in commercial production than in the home garden); 'Ingot' and 'A-Plus', both reputedly with higher beta-carotene content than most; and 'Nandor', up to 10 inches long.

Of half-long carrots with tapered roots, 'Oxheart' has been on the market for decades. Those of more cylindrical, blunt-ended form include the ever-popular 'Nantes Half-long', maturing to about 5 to 7 inches long and 1 to 1½ inches thick; 'Nantes Scarlet', about 6 inches long and 1½ to 2 inches thick; and 'Danvers

Half-long', about 7 inches long and up to 2½ inches thick.

Mini carrots, stumpy-conical in shape, are recommended for spring cultivation on heavy soils. 'Kinko' matures about two months from germination to a length of 3 to 4 inches 'Sucram', only 2½ to 3 inches long, is more cylindrical in form.

Spherical types, also recommended for heavy or rocky soils, seldom exceed 2 inches in diameter, and include the long-cultivated 'Thumbelina", a favorite for salads and hors d'oeuvres.

CAULIFLOWER
(Brassica oleracea, Botrytis group)

A close relative of broccoli, cauliflower is also grown for its low, thickened, fasciated flower stalk, which, however, is usually white or cream colored and covered with a multitude of tiny buds at time of harvest. One of the many mutant coles, or cabbage, derivatives, cauliflower was apparently first cultivated in the Mediterranean region in classical times, but seems not to have been widely grown as a food crop until the eighteenth century.

The primary factor affecting the growth and development of cauliflower is temperature, and cultivars vary considerably as to the temperature optimal for the formation of heads, or curds. For most, cool temperatures—not higher than 75°F—result in maximal development, but as summer readings in most of the United States far exceed this level, the breeding of heat-tolerant forms has been a major focus for hybridizers. It is important to choose cauliflower cultivars known to be suited to local weather conditions.

Also important are soil pH, which should be between 6.4 and 7.4, and moisture, which should be generous throughout the season for satisfactory head formation. As a rule, garden conditions favoring cabbage and broccoli should yield satisfactory cauliflower crops. Depending on the cultivar, heads are ready for harvest 50 to 90 days after setting out in the garden. Superphosphate helps stimulate curd formation.

Seed germination and treatment of seedlings are as for broccoli (see page 642). It is important to provide cells or pots large enough to maintain steady seedling growth, as pot-bound plants whose growth has been checked seldom resume normal growth in the garden. At least 18 inches should be allowed between plants for the development of full-size heads. Crowding encourages premature formation of undersize heads, which may be desired, especially if a different late-season successor crop is planned. In general, however, cauliflower is grown for large heads, the largest of which develop in long-season cultivars harvested in late summer or fall. Allow 6 to 12 plants per person. Normally, each 100 feet of row yields 80 to 100 pounds of produce.

To ensure an even whiteness, the large leaves, surrounding each head may be tied together as a tent once head formation has begun. Heads left exposed to the sun usually mature somewhat yellowish, but this has no effect on flavor or texture. On the other hand, intense late-summer heat may result in heads becoming loose and somewhat fibrous.

Cultivars best grown for early or mid summer harvest, all white-headed, include 'Early Snowball' and 'Snow Crown', as well as the small-headed 'White Corona' (heads 3 to 4 inches across, maturing four to six weeks after setting out). So-called self-blanching cultivars that mature early include 'Alert' and 'Early White'. The innermost leaves of these cultivars are erect and easily tied over the developing head. Early-maturing cultivars are also suitable for succession cropping and late-season harvest.

Long-season, white-headed cultivars usually grown for late-summer or fall harvest include 'Dominant' and such self-blanching forms as 'Andes' and 'Ravella'. Purple-headed cultivars, such as 'Purple Giant' and 'Violet Queen', and greenish-headed ones, such as 'Alverda' and 'Romanesco', are all late maturing.

CELERY
(Apium graveolens var. dulce)

Grown for its thickened, crisp leaf stalks, celery has been known since classical times, and was first cultivated in Italian lowlands in the sixteenth century. Though biennial in nature, it is now grown as an annual thoughout the temperate-zone world and is valued both cooked and raw in many cuisines.

Celery requires maximum light to grow quickly and does best on humusy, continuously moist soils where summers remain relatively cool. In hot weather, growth slows perceptibly. A soil pH between 6.6 and 6.8 is ideal. Although sometimes still grown in 1-foot-deep trenches or between wide boards to reduce light and blanch the stalks, self-blanching celery is more commonly grown today, and there is an increasing preference for mild-flavored green-stalked celery for most purposes. The more fertile the soil, the larger and milder tasting the celery stalks. Enrichment with well-rotted manure is ideal; alternatively, use 10-5-5 commercial fertilizer. If, when the celery is harvested, the innermost stalks are left intact, the plants soon recover and yield further crops. First-year roots survive most winters, but the plants produce smaller leaves and stalks the second spring and soon bolt to flower and seed.

Because the young plants react adversely to cold spring weather, celery should be started indoors, under fluorescent lights or in a greenhouse, about 12 weeks before transplanting into the garden, at the time that tomatoes are set out. Seed should be sown thinly and barely covered in pans or flats kept at about 70°F, and the seedlings grown on at 60° to 65°F. Thinning and transplanting to cell packs is eventually followed by hardening off outdoors or in a coldframe kept above 55°F before setting out in the garden. Whether self-blanching or green, celery should be spaced 6 to 8 inches apart and, in the home garden, is particularly well suited to culture in small, densely planted beds. Plant 5 to 8 feet of row per person. Mature celery is unaffected by light frost and, with a protective mulch of light straw and a covering of white polyethylene plastic, will continue to yield well into winter. In most instances, 25 feet of row or a bed measuring 4 feet square is sufficient and may be had from 1/16 ounce of seed. Any surplus seed will remain viable for about two years.

In most areas, pests and diseases of celery in the home garden are few. Inadequate water may lead to blackened inner stalks.

Cold spring weather can cause premature bolting. Leaf blight can be controlled by crop rotation. Dwarf plants with mottled leaves and twisted stalks are usually indicative of aphid infestation (see Chapter 34). Any weeding should be done by hand, as celery roots are fibrous and shallow, hence easily damaged by hoe or cultivator.

Among the relatively few cultivars on the market, 'Giant Pascal', 'Utah 52-70', and 'Lathom Self-blanching' are all white stalked, and the last is notably bolt resistant. Others include 'Ventura', with green stalks; 'Golden Self-blanching', with yellow stalks; and 'Giant Red', with reddish to red-violet stalks.

CORN, SWEET
(Zea mays var. rugosa)

Sweet corn is a warm-season crop derived from the Mexican grass teosinte. Its immature seeds (kernels) are much valued, especially in summer fare, and sweet corn is strongly promoted in most seed catalogs, even though it offers relatively small return for the space and time required. Moreover, sweet corn ears prove so irresistible to raccoons and birds such as grackles that, left unprotected, a sizable stand can be stripped in hours. Still, gardener interest in growing sweet corn remains high because fresh-picked ears are usually far sweeter than those available commercially, since, once an ear is picked, the sugar in the kernels converts to starch, sometimes in just a few hours. Prompt chilling slows the process; freezing halts it. Thus whether to devote the space and time and to risk the ravages of marauding wildlife becomes a matter of judgment, especially in the small vegetable garden. Efficiency in space use can be heightened somewhat by intercropping young sweet corn with quickly maturing items such as radish, looseleaf lettuce, or bush bean or with a compatible sprawling vine crop such as pumpkin. Protection from raccoons is sometimes had with 4-foot wire-mesh fencing, providing the bottom 6 inches are dug into the ground; electric fencing is more secure but costly. Repellents, such as moth balls and aluminum foil pennants, may deter birds, but 1-inch nylon mesh fish-netting is surer, if less convenient.

Depending on the cultivar, sweet corn requires 60 to 100 warm days from planting to harvest. In regions having short growing seasons, seed may be started indoors under fluorescent lights (12 to 14 hours per day) or in a greenhouse in pots, then hardened off and planted outdoors once night temperatures remain above 50°F. In most areas, however, seed is sown directly in the garden at a depth of ¾ to 2 inches or more, depending on seed size. It is usual to plant seed in groups, or "hills," of three or four, the groups spaced about 1½ feet apart. Alternatively, seed may be sown in single-file rows and spaced about 9 inches apart. In most cases, a minimum of four rows arranged in a block facilitates the wind pollination necessary for kernel set and ear development.

Ordinarily, sweet corn seed sprouts erratically when the soil temperature falls below 65°F and will not germinate at all below 55°F. Better germination results may be had by using seed treated with a fungicide to control seed rot, especially where late-spring cool spells are likely. In any case, well-drained soil enriched with well-rotted manure or compost yields the best crop. Sandy soil that warms quickly in spring is best for early crops; heavier soil should be planted to late-season cultivars.

As the plants have a high requirement for sunlight, sweet corn is best grown in rows oriented north-south and spaced 3 to 4 feet apart. Protection from strong wind is desirable. Mounding, or berming, soil against the bases of stalks helps prevent toppling. Where growing seasons are long and space permits, successive sowings may be made at two-week intervals through early summer to extend the harvest. Ears should be harvested once the silk begins to brown and while the kernels are turgid with milky juice. Well-grown sweet corn normally yields two or three ears per stalk.

Four classes of sweet corn hybrids are recognized, each with certain cultural idiosyncracies.

1. *Standard open-pollinated cultivars.* Standard cultivars come true from seed regardless of the nearby presence of other cultivars. However, hybrid sweet corn, which first appeared in the 1930s, offers much larger ears of sweet, tender kernels and so has almost completely eclipsed these one-time mainstays, now grown out of historic interest. Surviving cultivars include the yellow-kerneled 'Golden Bantam' and the bicolor 'Double Standard'.

2. *Normal sugary hybrids.* The normal sugary types have more sugar in the kernels than do the standards, but the amount varies according to cultivar and quickly converts to starch after harvest. It is advisable to isolate any cultivar in this group from other groups as cross-pollination results in at least some tough, starchy kernels in each ear. This isolation is achieved by a corn-free zone of 100 to 150 feet or more between plantings or by staggering the sowing of seed by two weeks. In several cultivars, such as the yellow-kerneled 'Earlivee' and 'Seneca Chief', ears mature very early, often in 60 to 70 days from germination—an advantage where the growing season is short.

3. *Sugary-enhanced hybrids.* The sugary-enhanced types differ from the normal sugary hybrids mainly in improved kernel tenderness and in somewhat slowed conversion of kernel sugar to starch. Isolation from normal sugar hybrids is not necessary. Desirable cultivars include 'Kandy Korn E.H.',

Super-sweet corn

'Miracle', and 'Sugar Buns', all with yellow kernels; the white-kerneled 'Platinum Lady'; and the bicolor 'Seneca Gold 'n Pearl'.

4. *Super-sweet hybrids.* The super-sweet types are increasingly popular not only because of the much sweeter kernels but also because the sweetness is retained for hours or even days after harvest, especially if the ears are kept cool. However, isolation from other sweet corn classes is necessary for a high-quality crop. The seed, smaller than in other classes, should be planted only ¾ inch deep, in warm (70° to 75°F) evenly and generously moist soil for full, uniform germination. Among the many yellow-kerneled cultivars available, 'Early Xtra-sweet', 'Illini Xtra-sweet', and 'Northern Xtra-sweet' are especially well suited to zone 7 and south, as is the white 'How Sweet It Is' and the bicolor 'Honey 'n Pearl'.

CUCUMBER
(Cucumis sativus)

Native to the lower elevations of the Himalayas in China, the cucumber is a scandent, or climbing, tendril-bearing annual that requires 60 to 100 days or more from germination to produce the large, immature, dark green, white-fleshed fruit that is much valued for summer salads. Small, incompletely developed cucumbers, called gherkins, are often pickled.

Where space allows, cucumber vines are usually planted in groups, or "hills," of three or four. The groups should be spaced 3 to 4 feet apart, and the plants allowed to sprawl, the fruit ripening on the ground. In small gardens, space may be saved by growing cucumbers on wire-mesh fencing 4 to 6 feet high, with the plants spaced about 1 foot apart. If multiple rows are grown, allow space between fences equal to their height, and if possible, orient the fences north to south. Fence-grown cucumbers are uniformly green and straight; ground-grown ones are pale beneath and sometimes curved. A fence planting 25 feet long will yield 25 to 30 pounds of cucumbers over a harvest period

of five to six weeks. A more recent innovation, also useful in the small garden, is the bush cucumber, whose stems are usually less than 3 feet long.

Success with cucumber, however grown, depends especially on exposure to warm sunlight and on adequate and sustained soil moisture. Shade depresses flower formation (as does failure to promptly harvest the fruit) and drought causes young fruit to abort. Well-drained, friable, slightly acidic (pH 6.0 to 6.5) soil of average fertility is ideal as long as copious compost or well-rotted manure is dug into the top 3 inches to help conserve moisture.

For early harvest, or to accommodate long-season cultivars, especially north of zone 7, seed may be started indoors in cell packs, two seeds per cell (the weaker one later clipped out), and grown under fluorescent lights (14 to 16 hours per day) or in a greenhouse four to five weeks before the last spring frost. Taking care not to disturb the roots, seedlings may be set out in the garden once night temperatures fall no lower than 50°F. The same temperature is the absolute minimum for successful cucumber germination in the garden; 70°F is best. Seed should be sown about ½ inch deep where the plants are to grow and later thinned to the recommended interval. A topdressing of well-rotted manure or other organic fertilizer, or ½ cup of 10-10-10 commercial fertilizer for each three or four plants just as the stems begin to elongate helps sustain nutrients on light, sandy soils. Daily harvesting is important for maintaining fruit set. Overaged cucumbers become bitter.

By spreading black plastic on the soil surface before stems elongate and covering the plants with floating or ventilated (slitted) row covers, early crops can be induced. Whenever possible, choose cultivars resistant to such serious cucumber diseases as anthracnose, angular leaf spot, bacterial wilt, cucumber mosaic virus, downy mildew, powdery mildew, and scab. Pests, such as the various cucumber beetles, may be deterred with floating row covers; their depredations are usually less serious than the destructive diseases they carry.

Among the cultivars producing superior slicing or salad cucumbers, most of which

are best harvested when 7 to 9 inches long, are 'Burpee Hybrid II', 'Marketmore 86', and 'Supersett', the last notably disease resistant. In 'Chinese Long', 'Suyo Long', and 'Sweet Success' hybrid, the fruit is best harvested at 12 to 14 inches. The last of these, as well as 'Green Knight' and 'Tasty Green' hybrid, are "burpless," i.e., they cause little or no gastric distress in those sensitive to other cucumbers. Compact or "bush" cultivars, with stems mostly 2 to 3 feet long, include 'Bush Champion', 'Spacemaster', and 'Salad Bush' hybrid, the last especially disease resistant. In 'Sweet Alphee', a cultivar adapted to cultivation in clear plastic tunnels, most (but not all) flowers are female, resulting in an unusually heavy fruit set. 'Armenian', a cultivar with particularly well-developed tendrils, is a good choice for trellis culture, especially where summers are long and hot.

English forcing or European cucumbers, with very long (up to 3 feet), slender, few-seeded, and nearly spineless fruit, are better suited to greenhouse culture than as a garden crop. However, 'Rollinson's Telegraph', 15 to 18 inches long, and 'Euro-American', about 1 foot long, perform well outdoors.

Cultivars developed for heavy production of 4- to 5-inch gherkins include 'Bush Pickle', 'Northern Pickling' hybrid, and 'Early Russian'. Especially prolific is 'Pickle-dilly' hybrid. Some cultivars, such as 'Saladin' and 'Burpless Tasty Green No. 26' hybrid, are suitable for both slicing and pickling. The latter of these is not only burpless but bears fruit that can reach 24 inches in length and still be useful in salads.

Small pickling, or Kirby, cucumbers, such as 'Cornichons', have curved, knobby fruit that should be harvested when 1 to 3 inches long for the preparation of bread-and-butter pickles and small dills.

EGGPLANT
(Solanum melongena)

A slow-growing plant native to tropical Asia, the eggplant is also known as aubergine, brinjal, and boulanger, which in part reflect the remarkably varied shapes, colors, textures, and flavors of the fruit.

Collection of eggplants

Eggplant, as a common name, almost certainly referred originally to the ovoid white-fruited form, but was somehow transferred to the very large, purple-fruited mutant that has become so popular in the United States. Other eggplant types, many commonly grown in the tropics, bear fruit that matures pinkish lavender, red-violet, green, or varicolored, and ranges from mild flavored and elongate to bitter ½-inch berries.

Whatever the character of the fruit, all eggplants require a long, hot growing season; full exposure to sun; and a well-drained, moisture-retentive, humusy soil of moderate fertility and pH of 5.5 to 6.8. In all areas except zones 9 and 10, eggplant must be started indoors under fluorescent lights (14 to 16 hours per day) or in a greenhouse at least eight weeks before the last spring frost. Seed should be sown in pans or flats, about ¼ inch deep and as far apart, and kept at 80° to 90°F to hasten germination and then grown at about 70°F. Seedlings should be transferred first to 2-inch cell packs or pots and later, as growth advances, to 4- or even 6-inch pots. After 7 to 10 days in a coldframe to harden off, and one or two weeks after tomato plants have been set out, when night temperatures are not likely to drop below 55°F, it is time to plant eggplant in the garden. The larger the young plants, the easier their adjustment to the garden environment will be. Small eggplant seedlings are especially cold sensitive and once chilled may fail

to recover and bear. Cultivars with the usual large, ovoid fruit are more cold sensitive than those with smaller cylindrical or spherical fruit.

Spacing in the garden should be about 18 inches. Floating row covers are advisable in cool, cloudy spells in late spring or when an occasional cool night is forecast. Pinching the erect central shoot will induce branching and heavier flowering. Large-fruited cultivars may require staking to keep the ripening fruit above the ground or to allow long fruit to mature straight. Fruit should be removed promptly (by clipping it off, not pulling) upon reaching full size and before the contained seeds turn from white to brown. Old fruit turns mealy and, left unpicked, it inhibits flowering and further fruit set.

Plants should be inspected frequently for the orange egg masses of potato beetles, which should be hand picked and crushed. Young eggplant transplants are especially susceptible to flea beetles, which perforate leaves and damage the stems; control with pyrethrum, rotenone, or sabadilla dust. Verticillium wilt is best controlled by crop rotation, allowing three or four years to elapse before growing eggplant in the same bed or row.

Among the popular large, ovoid, purple-skinned eggplant cultivars are 'Black Beauty', 'Burpee Hybrid', and 'Early Bird Hybrid', all requiring at least seven weeks after setting out for the first fruit to mature. 'Dusky', a pear-shaped, purple cultivar, is also a long-season form. Cultivars with

club-shaped or cylindrical purple fruit include 'Ichiban' hybrid, 'Millionaire', and 'Orient Express', harvestable about one week sooner. Somewhat earlier still are 'Bambino', with spherical purple fruit about 1½ inches across, and 'Pirouette', with purple egg-shaped fruit up to 4 inches long.

White-fruited, mild-flavored cultivars include the ovoid 'White Egg' or 'Easter Egg', with fruit about 3 by 2 inches; 'Baby White Tiger', similar but with smaller fruit; and 'Casper', with pear-shaped fruit to 6 inches long. Two cylindrical types are 'Dourga', with fruit to 6 inches and 'Long White Sword', with 9-inch fruit. Rose purple or pinkish purple forms include the ovoid 'Rosa Blanca', with fruit to about 5 inches long; the cylindrical 'Neon', with fruit up to 6 inches long; and the cylindrical 'Pingtung Long', with fruit to 1 inches. Green-fruited cultivars range from the cylindrical 'Thai Green', with 9-inch fruit, and the spherical 'Snake Eye', with fruit about ½ inch across. Both are mild flavored. 'Emerald Prize' has bitter ¼-inch fruit.

LETTUCE
(Lactuca sativa)

The most popular of the salad greens, lettuce is of uncertain origin, but it is believed to be derived from a wild species (*L. serriola*) of the eastern Mediterranean region and has been known as a food plant for millennia, dating from ancient Egyptian times. Known only as a non-heading plant until the 1500s, lettuce is today known by a large number of cultivars arranged in four groups according to growth habit, leaf shape, and coloring. Lettuce is grown the world over in temperate and tropical regions. In the United States, looseleaf cultivars are most popular in home gardens, followed by butterhead and romaine types. Most heading, crisphead, or iceberg lettuce is grown commercially.

Lettuce grows best in cool weather, i.e., in the 50° to 70°F range of daily high temperatures. Hot conditions inhibit head formation and in all types induce stem elongation, bolting to flower, and the development of bitterness in the leaves. The wide range of cultivars available makes

European and heirloom lettuce cultivars

it possible to have lettuce crops almost all year long throughout the South and along the Pacific Coast. Even in zones 6 and 7, glassed coldframes facilitate lettuce culture in all but the coldest weather. In summer, especially from zone 7 south, open-weave fabric, such as cheesecloth, may be used to filter the sunlight and thus reduce the tendency to bolt.

Lettuce reaches full size most quickly on sandy, well-drained, moderately fertile, moisture-retentive soils enriched with compost or well-rotted manure. Soil pH is not critical, but drought can be devastating. From zone 7 northward, early lettuce crops should be started indoors under fluorescent lights (14 to 16 hours per day) or in a greenhouse in seed pans or flats three to four weeks before the last spring frost date. The seed should be sown thinly, about ¼ inch apart and as deep, and the seedlings transplanted to cell packs. Allow the young plants to harden off a few days in a coldframe before setting them out in the garden. In the South, and for later crops elsewhere, seed should be sown directly in the garden two to four weeks before the last spring frost. Pelleted seed facilitates thin sowing and less thinning. Any plants removed in thinning should be saved for table use.

Ultimate spacing in the garden depends on the growth characteristics of the cultivar. High-density planting of looseleaf and butterhead cultivars extends the return from limited space; set about 4 inches apart, initially harvest alternate plants, and

Netting over lettuce

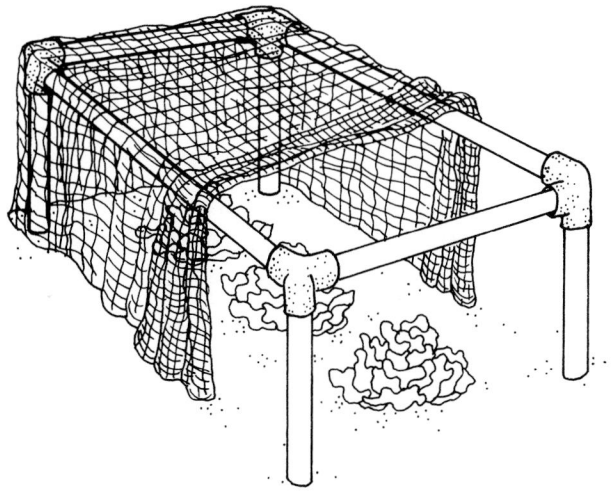

Lettuce shading may be supported by a portable pipe-frame rack.

allow those remaining to achieve full size. Romaine and heading types need 9 to 12 inches between plants. Heading is inhibited if the plants are crowded. Since lettuce is a short-season crop, usually ready for harvest in six to eight weeks, successive sowings should be made at two- or three-week intervals until late summer. Late spring and summer seedbeds should be lightly shaded, for example with cheesecloth, to conserve soil moisture. If lettuce is harvested by cutting above the ground and leaving 1-inch stumps in place, a second somewhat smaller crop is usually ready in another four to six weeks.

By avoiding late-day and night watering, various bacterial and fungal diseases can be minimized, and slugs and snails will be less active. Prompt weeding helps deter the spread of virus diseases carried by certain weeds. Where virus outbreaks seriously affect lettuce, resistant cultivars should be chosen. Hot, dry weather in late spring may lead to attack by cutworms; paper collars around the young plants and 'Slobolt' (a virus-resistant cultivar). Somewhat darker and more bolt resistant are 'Grand Rapids' and 'Prizehead', and still darker green and also bolt resistant are 'Green Ice' and 'Royal Oakleaf'. 'Saladbowl', with light green leaves, is best grown only as a spring crop. Especially suited to coldframe culture in winter is 'Plastique', a French cultivar.

Looseleaf cultivars with red or red-flecked foliage include the reddish bronze 'Red Sails', the burgundy 'Red Saladbowl' (virus resistant), the reddish green 'Ruby', and the red-spotted 'Speckles'. All are best grown as spring or fall crops.

Butterhead and Boston lettuce cultivars have diffuse, fanlike heads; the loosely folded leaves are yellow or white only at the base. Green-leaf cultivars best grown as spring or fall crops include 'Burpee Bibb' and 'Buttercrunch'; 'Kagran Summer', 'All-Year-Round', and 'Ermosa' (virus resistant) are more bolt resistant, hence often do well in summer, especially if lightly shaded. 'Selma-Wisa', a Swiss cultivar, is especially good as a winter coldframe crop. Red-leaf butterhead cultivars include 'Pirat', which is fairly bolt resistant, and 'Redcap', which is bronzy and suitable for spring or fall culture.

Romaine, or cos, lettuce has upright heads of loosely packed, often wrinkled leaves, the inner ones are blanched. Green-leaf cultivars include 'Parris Island', with light to medium green heads 10 to 12 inches high; 'Valmaine', similar but dark green and requiring 10 weeks to mature; and 'Little Gem', with medium green heads only 5 inches high. 'Rosalita', with 10-inch-high heads, has reddish leaves. All romaine cultivars are best grown as spring or fall crops.

Among the spherical heading or crisp-head cultivars suited to home garden culture are 'Burpee Iceberg' and 'Great Lakes', both with light green outer leaves, requiring about 12 weeks to mature and displaying fair heat tolerance. 'Cerise', a virus-resistant cultivar with red-tipped leaves, requires about 9 weeks.

ONION
(Allium cepa)

A biennial grown as an annual for its pungently flavored bulb, the onion is unknown in the wild but is likely to have originated in the region now occupied by Iran and Pakistan. It is known to have been an important food plant in ancient Egypt, India, Greece, and Rome. Today, thanks to a diversity of cultivars, onions are grown throughout the world in both temperate and tropical climates.

Although most onions grow best in regions having cool, damp spring weather and hot, relatively dry summers, many cultivars are suited to more humid conditions and some also to prolonged coolness. Cool spring weather, with temperatures not exceeding 80°F, promotes rapid early

Onion braid

growth. The long days in late spring and early summer stimulate bulb formation. Once temperatures exceed 85°F, growth slows, the bulbs hardening and maturing by late summer or early fall. Onion crops are harvested when the tops bend over and begin to dry. If bulbs are harvested with the foliage intact, the leaves may be serially braided and the strings of bulbs hung up for long-term storage. Dried, cured bulbs may also be stored loose in mesh bags in a cool, dry, well-ventilated place. Immature bulbs, including mini onions and green onions, should be used soon after harvest and not stored.

Japanese bunching onion
(*Allium fistulosum*)

The easiest way to grow onions in the home garden, especially where the growing season is short or the soil is poor, is to plant immature hardened bulbs called "sets." Planted at the rate of 1 pound per 50 lineal feet, sets grow into mature onions sooner than seed-grown plants and are less prone to disease. They may be planted in early to mid spring 2 to 3 inches apart with their tops at the soil surface. Some seedhouses also offer small bare-root transplants which, if set out promptly upon receipt, soon resume growth. By harvesting alternate partly grown bulbs during the summer, space is left for the rest to mature into a final crop of full-size onions for fall harvest and winter use.

For larger crops, and for a wider range of cultivars, onions are grown from seed. Whether grown from sets or seed, onions require maximum sun exposure and a garden soil that is well drained, friable, and as rock free as possible. A pH lower than 6.0 results in poor crops. Sandy, mildly acidic soils with a generous incorporation of compost or well-rotted manure are ideal. Alternatively, 2½ to 3 pounds of commercial 10-10-10 fertilizer per 100 square feet, worked into the top 2 to 3 inches, will serve. Monthly side dressings of organic or commercial fertilizer are beneficial until midsummer. Because heavy clay soils are slow to warm in the spring and are often too dense to accommodate bulb expansion, onion crops grown on them are often disappointing. The addition of sand and organic matter helps alleviate the problem.

To have crops of full-size onions from zone 7 north, onion seed should be started indoors under fluorescent lights (14 to 16 hours per day) or in a greenhouse six to eight weeks before the last spring frost. In seed pans or flats, seed should be sown thinly ½ to ¾ inch deep. Because onion seedlings are very susceptible to damping off and collar rot, it is advisable to use seed pretreated with a fungicide and to add fungicide to the irrigation water. At the two-leaf stage, the seedlings should be carefully lifted and transplanted into cell packs, one per cell, and grown on. Transplanting to the garden should be preceded by a week in a coldframe protected from temperatures lower than 55°F and higher than 80°F. Once night temperatures in the garden fall no lower than 55°F, the seedlings may be set out, spaced about 4 inches apart. Closer spacing may result in root competition and reduced bulb size. Approximately 10 pounds of onions may be expected from each 25 feet of row. Depending on the cultivar, 60 to 125 days (or more) are required for the crop to ripen.

In zones 8 and 9, seed of short-day cultivars is usually sown in the fall for harvest late the following spring or during the summer. Several of the long-day cultivars grown in the North also do well in the South and may be sown in the fall or spring.

It is important to remove weeds while still small, as onions have filamentous, superficial root systems that are easily damaged or dislodged when large nearby weeds are pulled. Root competition and shading from weeds severely depress bulb growth.

Onion and such closely related crops as leek and shallot are subject to numerous bacterial, fungal, and viral diseases, many of which can be locally severe and for which there are no effective or acceptable controls. Certified virus-free onion sets and seed may help prevent the onset of trouble, but where crops become infected in two successive seasons, it is prudent to suspend the culture of onion and its relatives, including ornamental *Allium* spp., for at least several years.

The cultivar most commonly grown from sets is 'Ebenezer', available in yellow-, white- and red-skinned forms.

Among full-size, seed-grown types, there are several long-day or medium-day cultivars best planted from zone 7 north in the spring for late-summer harvest and up to six months' storage.

'Ailsa Craig Exhibition': yellow skinned; suitable for short-term storage (two to three months).
'Buffalo': yellow skinned; matures in 12 weeks (three to four weeks earlier than most); does well in zones 8 and 9.
'Copra': yellow skinned; suitable to extended, long-term storage.
'Southport Red Globe': red skinned; superior cultivar.
'Southport White Globe': white skinned; superior cultivar.

White Bermuda onions

'Spartan Banner 80' hybrid: yellow
    skinned; persistently pungent.
'Sweet Sandwich': yellow skinned; at
    first quite pungent, becoming milder
    with storage.
'Walla Walla Sweet': yellow skinned;
    grown commercially; does well in
    zones 8 and 9.

Short-day full-size cultivars, suitable for
spring sowing in zones 8 and 9, include
the yellow-skinned 'Granex Hybrid', the
white-skinned 'White Bermuda', and the
red-skinned 'Red Granex Hybrid P.R.R.',
all requiring about 12 weeks from seed to
harvest.

Mini or pickling onions, ready for harvest
in eight to nine weeks, include 'Crystal
White Pickling', with white skin, and
'Purplette', with red skin.

Green onions, also called bunching
onions or scallions, are all white skinned
and harvestable in about eight weeks.
Cultivars include the pungent 'Evergreen
Long White Bunching' and the milder
'White Lisbon'. If left unharvested for a
year, green onions often form a clump that
becomes self-perpetuating if only partially
harvested in each successive year.

PARSLEY
(Petroselinum crispum)

A biennial of southern Europe usually
grown as an annual for its deeply dissected,
aromatic leaves, parsley is used mostly as
a garnish or dried for use as a seasoning.
But fresh leaves make a flavorful complement in salads and soups, and may be
substituted for basil in pesto. Some types,
especially the the turnip-rooted variety
(P. crispum var. tuberosum), are also grown
for their fleshy whitish roots, which are
nutty in flavor when cooked and prized
in soups.

Harvested from early summer until early
winter, parsley continues growth in cold
weather if potted up and placed in a coldframe or brought indoors to a sunny
windowsill. Grown in full sun or partial
shade and adaptable to a wide range of
well-drained soils, if rotted manure or
compost has been incorporated. If only
a small number of plants is required, the
most common cultivars are available in

cell packs from nurseries and garden centers.
For larger crops or unusual cultivars, seed
should be acquired and planted directly
in the garden in the spring after the last
frost. Sow about ¼ inch deep and ½ inch
apart, and thin seedlings to stand ultimately
about 4 inches apart. Soaking seed for a
day or freezing moistened seed overnight
hastens germination. Late-season and early
spring crops are best had from seed sown
in midsummer. Early crops may also be had
by sowing seed indoors, as for celery (see
page 647). It is best to allow 8 to 10 weeks
before making the first picking. Side
dressing plants in late fall with well-rotted
manure or compost and, at the onset of
severely cold weather, lightly mulching
with salt hay help ensure good winter
survival and prompt growth in spring.

Among the curly-leaf cultivars are the
following:

'Extra Curled Dwarf': more compact;
    suitable for edging.
'Forest Green': more or less erect leaves,
    which are less spattered with soil.
'Paramount': a popular cultivar.
'Triple Curled': very decorative, tightly
    curled leaves.

Cultivars of flatleaf, or Italian, parsley
include the commonly grown 'Italian
Dark Green' and the markedly larger
'Giant Italian', which has 3-foot-long
leaves and requires a much wider spacing
in the garden.

Root parsley cultivars include 'Hamburg',
with distinctly flavored, parsnip-shaped
roots that are harvestable in about 13 weeks
from seed, and 'Short Sugar', with stumpy
4-inch roots of milder flavor.

PEA
(Pisum sativum)

A tendril-climbing annual, peas are
grown for their spherical, sometimes
wrinkled seeds and, in some increasingly
popular cultivars, for the pods as well.
Although now unknown in the wild, peas
were cultivated in ancient Greece and
Rome, and pea seeds have been found in
archaeological sites dating back to 5000 B.C.

Peas are a cool-weather crop that
should be grown for spring or fall harvest, with an optimal temperature range

'Corgi' pea

for growth and pod set between 50° and
75°F. Preparation of the garden bed is
important, as peas root deeply and require
phosphorus and potassium for generous
production of pods and seeds. Wood
ashes are a useful source. Care should be
taken not to raise nitrate levels unduly,
as peas, along with many other members
of the legume family, fix atmospheric
nitrogen by means of nodule-inhabiting
bacteria on their roots. Treatment of
the soil with a bacterial innoculant helps
stimulate nodule formation and maximize the crop. Excess nitrate, however,
results in exhuberant foliage and poor
pod set. Best results are had on sandy-
humusy, well-drained soils with a pH
between 6.0 and 7.5.

Pea vines may be supported on cut
brush, but harvesting is easier if the plants
are allowed to climb staked 4-foot wire-
mesh fencing. Rows for full-size vines
should be 3 to 4 feet apart, oriented north
to south if possible, and alternated with
planks to reduce soil compaction.

For spring crops, seed should be sown
as soon as the soil can be worked, well
before the last spring frost, and placed
about 1 inch deep and 1½ inches apart.
One pound of seed sows 100 to 125 feet
of row, and should yield 50 to 75 pounds
of vegetable. Germination occurs when
soil temperature reaches 45° to 50°F.
Prolonged dormancy of planted seed in
cold, wet weather may cause seed rot. Seed
should be planted where the plants are to
grow, as peas do not tolerate transplanting.

In regions where cool weather normally extends into early summer, a second sowing may be made about three weeks later to extend the harvest. Crops for fall harvest should be planted eight to ten weeks before the average date of first fall frost.

Ordinary shell peas should be harvested as soon as the seeds fill the pod. Once removed, the peas should be promptly used, frozen, or canned. The edible-pod snow peas are of best quality if picked as soon as the pods are full size but before the contained seeds swell. On the other hand, the edible-pod snap peas should be harvested when both pods and seeds are full size, and while the pods still break with a snap when bent.

Premature browning of foliage from the ground up betrays the presence of pea root rot, a common disease. Crop rotation helps control its spread. Powdery mildew, appearing as a dusty gray coating on foliage, is usually more serious with fall crops, and may be avoided by choosing resistant cultivars.

Shell pea cultivars that climb to normal heights include the following.

'Lincoln': more heat resistant than most, for a late spring or early summer crop.
'Maestro': 9 to 11 peas per pod, disease resistant.
'Tall Telephone': to 6 feet tall; bears heavily.
'Wando': cold resistant; heat resistant.

Dwarf cultivars usually grow no taller than 2 feet and often require no support. Hence they are sometimes called bush peas. Cultivars include 'Green Arrow', which has 9 to 11 peas per pod, and 'Improved Laxton's Progress' and 'Little Marvel', each with 7 or 8 peas per pod. Petits pois, or tiny peas, are a specialty among shell pea fanciers. Cultivars include 'Argona', 'Giroy', and 'Petit Provençal'.

Among the edible-pod peas, the outstanding snow pea cultivar is 'Oregon Sugar Pod', which is resistant to virus diseases and powdery mildew. Among edible pod snap peas, 'Sugar Snap' grows to 6 feet and bears heavily; lower-growing cultivars include 'Sugar Daddy' and 'Sugar Bon', both about 2 feet tall and both resistant to powdery mildew.

PEPPERS
(Capsicum annuum)

A slow-growing short-lived perennial usually grown as an annual, this species offers uncommon variation in the size, shape, color, and pungency of its fruit. Although commonly separated into sweet and hot categories, pepper cultivars are divisible into five major groups and range from the familiar large, green, mild-flavored bell pepper that ripens red, to the habañero, or Scot's bonnet, whose little red-orange fruit resemble tiny tam-o'-shanters and are of incendiary pungency. In general, the smaller and riper the pepper, the hotter the flavor. Paprika is prepared from the dried red fruit of various pungent cultivars. Although the prototypic pepper is unknown in the wild, it is believed to have been native to tropical America, and from there has spread and diversified in all moist, tropical regions and is grown in many temperate-zone areas as well.

Peppers are warm-weather crops and thrive when temperatures rise to 80° or 85°F and fall no lower than 60°F. At higher temperatures, pollen may lose viability, resulting in low fruit set. Sustained cold depresses growth and flower development, lowering fruit set and arresting maturation of immature fruit. In addition to warmth, peppers requires unfailing moisture in the soil, which should be well-drained, humusy, and with a pH of 5.5 to 5.8. Inadequate moisture causes growth-arresting leaf drop and leads to

sun scald of the fruit; waterlogging, on the other hand, is fatal. Pepper plants should be grown in a sheltered location exposed to full sun and shielded from strong cool wind.

A 25-foot row or a 4- by 6-foot bed of 20 to 24 plants should yield 75 to 90 large bell peppers through the season. If fewer plants are needed, it is best to buy transplants. For larger crops, or for specialty types, start peppers indoors under fluorescent lights (14 to 16 hours per day) or in a greenhouse. Approximately eight weeks before set-out time sow seed about ¼ inch deep and about as far apart in pans or flats kept at 75° to 80°F after germination, keep at 70°F during the day and 60°F at night. Transplant seedlings at the three-leaf stage to cell packs, and, as growth advances, to pots. Sweet, or bell, peppers can be induced to bear more heavily if the three-leaf seedlings, just after transfer to cell packs, are subjected to cool night temperatures (53° to 55°F) for one month, with daytime temperatures of 65° to 70°F, followed by a constant 70°F day and night until set out. As growth will be slowed during the cool-temperature period, the seed should be sown about two weeks earlier. The larger the young plants are at set-out time (just after tomato and with eggplant), the easier the transition to garden conditions and the sooner bearing will begin. Seedlings grown in excessive heat or with dim light become leggy and will not bear well. Plants that are stocky and well-branched at set-out

Selection of peppers

time make superior performers. Hot peppers require no special pretreatment, but the larger the seedlings are at set-out time, the sooner they bear.

Premature flowering with little or no fruit set in young pepper plants just after setting out often signals insufficient soil nutrients and should be remedied with a topdressing of well-rotted manure or a commercial fertilizer rich in phosphate. Use of clear plastic slitted row covers and black plastic mulch accelerates growth in cool weather.

Prompt harvest of full-size green peppers will stimulate flowering and greater fruit set than if the fruit is left on to turn color and mature. If, with the threat of frost at season's end, pepper plants are still laden with immature fruit, the plants may be lifted, potted, and grown on in a greenhouse for some weeks while the remaining fruit reaches usable size.

Cutworms can be kept from girdling the stems of young pepper plants by use of paper collars. Most other harmful insects can be kept in check with Rotenone or Pyrethrum. By following crop rotation, avoiding soil compaction, and keeping the soil moist but not wet, most diseases will be deterred. In regions where tobacco mosaic virus is common, resistant cultivars should be selected.

Among the scores of sweet pepper cultivars, large-fruited ones with the familiar green "bell" shape, eventually maturing red, include the standard, widely grown 'California Wonder', which is average in dimensions and flavor, and 'Ace' and 'New Ace Hybrid', both of which resist the blossom drop and low fruit set that occur under unfavorable conditions. 'Bell Tower' and 'Northstar' are resistant to the often troublesome tobacco mosaic virus. 'Peto Wonder Hybrid' bears a relatively light crop of extraordinarily large (7½ by 4½ inches) fruit, 'Sweet Pimento' produces a small fruit, which we know as the common pimiento. The fruit of 'Permagreen' holds its immature green color longer than most.

Among bell peppers of other colors are a number of yellow-fruited cultivars, such as 'Orobelle', widely grown commercially, and 'Gypsy hybrid', which is resistant to tobacco mosaic virus. 'Corona' has orange fruit, 'Purple Beauty' deep purple fruit, and 'Sweet Chocolate' purplish brown fruit. In 'Islander' and 'Lilac Belle Hybrid', the fruit color changes from yellow to lavender. All of them ripen to red.

Sweet peppers with narrowly tapered fruit include the popular 'Cubanelle', which passes from green to red, and 'Sweet Banana', which changes from light yellow-green to red.

Best known of the spherical cherry peppers is 'Large Cherry' (or 'Large Red Cherry'), which bears a multitude of 1½-inch fruit that ripes red and is hot in flavor. Outstanding among the cone- or top-shaped types is 'Poblano', with long, slender, green fruit maturing red-brown and carrying a mild flavor; when dried, its fruit is known as ancho peppers.

There are many cayenne, or chili, pepper cultivars, which are especially popular in the South, in Latin America, and in the Caribbean. Among those performing well as far north as zone 6, the following bear slender, green fruit that matures red, requiring 70 to 80 days to harvest. 'Anaheim TMR 23' is widely grown, mildly pungent, and is somewhat more intensely pungent, and 'Jalapeño M' and 'Super Chili' are moderately hot. Very hot cayennes include 'Long Red Cayenne' and 'Early Jalapeño', while 'Serrano Chili' is fiery in pungency. In 'Hungarian Yellow Wax', a moderately hot cultivar, the fruit is yellow before maturing red.

POTATO
(Solanum tuberosum)

Selection of heirloom potatoes

Native to the middle slopes of the Andes in northern South America, the potato is a short-lived perennial grown as an annual for its tubers. It is one of the world's most important food crops. Historically, the wild potato was cultivated by the Incas for at least two millennia before Spanish explorers took it to Europe in the sixteenth century. There it soon became a staple crop and spread to all temperate-zone countries. Today, thanks to assiduous selection and breeding, it is grown almost throughout the inhabited world.

Although the space required and the cultural techniques and equipment involved in the large-scale cultivation of ordinary, all-purpose potato cultivars are scarcely suited to the home garden,

Heirloom hot peppers

Heirloom potatoes

small-scale potato growing, particularly of specialty cultivars, offers rich rewards. Beyond the usual brown-skinned, white-fleshed keeping potatoes and the red-skinned early potatoes are a wide range of cultivars, some early, some long season; some sporting purple, pink, yellow, or russet skins; and some with flesh of like shades or of entirely different colors. Some have long, slender tubers instead of the usual ovoid shape. Some are suited to boiling or steaming, others are better baked. With this multifaceted diversity, the potato is no longer an ordinary staple crop but one of high visual interest.

In general, potatoes grow best in relatively cool latitudes, i.e., where summer heat in excess of 85° or 90°F is episodic rather than sustained. Air temperatures between 70° and 80°F favor rapid early growth, and soil temperatures of 60° to 70°F favor tuber formation. At higher temperatures, growth slows, and at lower readings tuber formation and growth are erratic. Potato foliage tolerates no frost.

Propagation is mostly by using tubers ("seed" potatoes), which are usually cut into sections, each with at least one dormant bud (called an "eye"). The cut surface is allowed to dry for a few days before planting. Very small tubers (less than 1½ inches long) are best planted uncut. Depending on the number of eyes per tuber, between 5 and 8 pounds of seed potatoes are required for each 100 feet of row, and should yield 120 to 150 pounds of produce. Because potato diseases may

be transmitted by infected tubers, it is wise to plant only those certified disease free. Some growers also certify that they produce seed potatoes without use of synthetic pesticides or fertilizers.

Seed potatoes are planted one or two weeks after the last spring frost in friable, well-drained soil of pH 5.0 to 6.0 and moderate fertility. The seed pieces are set 10 to 14 inches apart and 2 to 3 inches deep in rows 30 to 36 inches apart. When young plants are about 6 inches high, the soil between the rows should be mounded or hilled up several inches to keep the sun off the developing tubers. Tubers that turn green from sun exposure become poisonous. Early-maturing, or new, potatoes are ready for harvest seven to nine weeks from planting; late-season, or keeping, types 10 to 12 weeks. Early potatoes are best used as they are harvested. They may be left in the ground until needed but must be removed before frost penetrates. Late potatoes may be harvested all at once, allowed to dry, and stored in a cool, dry, preferably dark place.

Potato foliage should be checked frequently for the yellow eggs of the potato beetle; all should be crushed. Control larvae and adult beetles by hand picking or with 5 percent Rotenone dust. Potato scab disease can be averted by keeping the soil continuously moist.

Among the standard cultivars, all with tan to russet skins and white flesh, is the well known, widely grown, late-season 'Kennebec' as well as the similar 'Butte'

and 'Green Mountain', the last more tolerant of cold conditions than most. Early-maturing cultivars in this class include 'Onaway' and 'White Cobbler'.

Those with yellow skin and yellow flesh include 'Bintje' and 'Yukon Gold', both midseason, and 'Yellow Finn' (or 'Finnish'), which ripens late.

Cultivars with red skin and white flesh are numerous, the best known of them being 'Red Pontiac', a midseason variety that stores well. Others include the early-maturing 'Caribe' and 'Red Dale', and the mid to late season 'Acadia Russet', 'Dark Red Norland', and Désirée'. Red-skinned, yellow-fleshed cultivars include 'Red Gold' and 'Urgenta'. In 'Blossom', the skin and flesh are pinkish; in 'All Blue' and 'Peruvian Blue' (or 'Peruvian Purple'), the skin and flesh are purple; and in 'Old Spanish', the purple-and-white skin covers white flesh.

Fingerling cultivars include 'Russian Banana' and 'Yellow Fingerling', both with yellow skin and flesh, and 'Ruby Crescent', with reddish skin and yellow flesh.

RADISH
(Raphanus sativus)

In the United States, the radish is usually cultivated as a spring or fall crop for the swollen, red, peppery roots that are harvested young and eaten raw. Its cultivars, however, are remarkably varied in the size, form, color, and flavor of the root. Some of these are valued elsewhere, especially in Europe and Asia, as a cooked vegetable or pickle; for the spicy seed pods; and for the young leaves, which are eaten as greens.

The prototypic form was native to the eastern Mediterranean region, and by 2000 B.C. the radish had become an important crop in Egypt. It spread thereafter to China and Japan and is now grown throughout the temperate zones and in higher elevations of the tropics.

For the customary salad use, cultivars with small round roots should be grown quickly in cool spring or fall weather and harvested within a month of sowing. Delay in harvesting leads to dense, increasingly woody roots that become bitter. An open, unshaded site with sandy, well-drained soil at pH 6.0 to 7.0 and generously fortified with well-rotted manure or compost is ideal. Critical to rapid root formation is unfailing soil moisture. Hot, dry weather results in pithy roots and premature bolting.

Seed should be started in the garden at about the time of the last spring frost. Whether grown in beds or rows, seed should be sown thinly, preferably ¾ to 1 inch apart, and about ½ inch deep. Since the crop matures quickly, successive sowings should be made every 10 to 14 days until about one month before the onset of hot summer weather (with high readings above 85°F). Sowings may resume at the conclusion of intense summer heat and continue until three or four weeks before the first frost of fall. Radish may be interplanted in rows among slow-growing long-season crops, such as leek, onion, or eggplant.

Pests of radish include flea beetles, which perforate leaves but without effect to the roots; slugs, which defoliate or completely decapitate young plants and should be controlled with repellents; rabbits, which should be excluded with wire-mesh fencing; and root maggots, which tunnel into roots and sometimes destroy the crop and may be controlled by crop rotation or, if severe and recurrent, by use of diazinon (see page 799).

Standard red-skinned, white-fleshed cultivars include 'Early Scarlet Globe' and 'Sparkler' whose roots grow to 1 inch across and mature in about four weeks. 'Cherry Belle' has ¾-inch roots and matures in three weeks. 'Easter Egg' blend is a mixture of red-, pink-, and white-skinned types, all with white flesh. In 'Valentine' the colors are reversed: The skin is white, and flesh is red.

Less frequently grown but equally meritorious for use in salads and as raw sticks are Long French radishes, whose slender, tapered, 2- to 4-inch-long roots are usually red with a white tip, and somewhat more pungent than the globular sorts. Culture is the same, but 'Long French' cultivars must be pulled promptly at about three weeks from seed, as their quality soon deteriorates. Among the favored cultivars are 'French Breakfast', 'D'Avignon', and 'Flamivil'. Others include 'Navet', which is 6 to 8 inches long and pink skinned, and 'White Icicle', which is 4 to 6 inches long and entirely white.

Long White or Daikon radishes

Long White, or Daikon, radishes are cylindrical or gently tapered and mature at 6 inches or more in length. Quite peppery and useful either raw or cooked, they require about eight weeks from seed to harvest. Seedlings should be thinned to stand about 4 inches apart. Cultivars include 'Miyashage', with stumpy, white, green-shouldered roots; it is best grown as a fall crop. 'Summer Cross No. Three', has 6- to 14-inch-long roots and is also for fall harvest. 'April Cross Hybrid' has roots up to 18 inches long and 3 inches across and is for late summer or fall harvest. 'Spring Leader' is an early-season type.

Black radishes

Fall or winter radishes, long popular in Europe and Asia, vary from red or black globes, 3 to 6 inches in diameter, to long red, black, or white tapers, up to 24 inches long. Immature roots may be eaten raw, but when full size, they are usually cooked. In the United States, most commonly grown in this class are 'Round Black Spanish', whose roots are 3 to 5 inches across, with black skin over white flesh; and 'China Rose' (or 'Chinese Rose'), which has tapered pink-skinned, white-fleshed roots, up to 5 inches long.

Oriental radishes are long-season, white-rooted, mild-flavored types that are largely unaffected by hot weather. They vary in size and shape and are popular in Oriental cooking. Of the few cultivars available, 'All Seasons' and 'Tokanashi' have tapered roots, up to 18 inches long, and are the most frequently grown.

RHUBARB
(Rheum × cultorum)

A large-leaf perennial grown for its thick, red, succulent leaf stalks, rhubarb is a complex hybrid of unclear origin and is unknown in the wild. Although long an article in the ancient Chinese pharmacopeia, rhubarb first achieved culinary value in eighteenth-century Europe and is now widely grown in temperate-zone regions and at high elevations in the tropics. It is hardy from zone 3 to 8.

Sensitive to day length, rhubarb dies back to the root crown as days shorten in late summer and must have a cold winter period, the requisite length of which varies by cultivar, before new leaves are borne in the spring. Early crops are had from cultivars requiring a shorter cold period than later sorts. For late-winter crops, dormant crowns may be lifted and tubbed in the fall, left outdoors for exposure to winter cold, then brought into a greenhouse and forced (often blanched under black plastic). Crowns so treated are best discarded after harvest. In the garden, leaf stalks are cut in the spring and early summer. All leaf-blade tissue should be cut away as it contains soluble oxalates and a poisonous glycoside that are not neutralized by cooking. To ensure continued vitality of the root crown, four to six leaves per crown should be left on during the harvest period.

So long as it is exposed to full sun in the spring and soil drainage is certain, rhubarb is reliably long lived and undemanding. Moist, sandy-humusy, slightly acidic (pH 6.5) soil yields the largest crops. On heavier soils, especially where drainage is slow, raised beds serve well. Since mature plants can develop a leaf spread of 6 feet, wide spacing is advisable. Competition from weeds should be avoided. Flower shoots should be removed as they appear.

Seedhouses and nurseries usually offer rhubarb as pieces or divisons of crowns, each with at least one strong bud. These should be planted in early spring before the last spring frost about 3 feet apart, with the buds just below the surface. Since the plant is a deep-rooting perennial, it is wise to prepare the soil at least 2 feet deep beforehand. An old, well-established crown may be lifted in the fall, divided, and the divisions replanted. To facilitate root growth, no crop should be taken the first season after planting.

Commercially grown seed of a few cultivars is sometimes available, but three to five years are required for seed-grown plants to reach harvestable size. Propagation by garden-collected seed is not recommended as seed-grown plants produce crops of varying and usually lower quality. In the home garden, 6 to 12 plants are usually sufficient. The harvest period may be extended by growing a few plants each of early-, mid-, and late-season cultivars.

Widely grown, reliable cultivars that bear early crops include 'Cherry Red' and 'Valentine'; midseason cultivars are 'Canada Red' and 'MacDonald'; and one late cultivar is 'Victoria'.

SPINACH
(Spinacia oleracea)

An annual grown for its edible leaves, which are eaten cooked or raw, spinach is of uncertain native provenance but likely to have originated in southwest Asia, whence it spread to China by the seventh century. It is now cultivated in temperate regions the world over.

Spinach grows best in cool weather. Warm-weather substitutes include New Zealand spinach (*Tetragonia tetragonioides*), mountain spinach (*Atriplex hortensis*), and basella, or Malabar, spinach (*Basella alba*). Because they are unrelated to each other and require different culture regimens they are treated separately in this chapter.

Spinach seed should be started directly in the garden as soon as the soil has thawed and well before the last spring frost. Cool soil facilitates germination; indeed, seedlings are unaffected by episodic frost as low as 15°F and grow best when temperatures range between 40° and 65°F. Well-drained, sandy-humusy soil with a near-neutral pH (6.5 to 7.5) yields best results. Except for the pH requirement, spinach nevertheless performs creditably on a wide range of soil types. Seed should be sown 1 to 2 inches apart, about ½ inch deep, and in rows 12 inches to 18 inches apart. Seedlings should be thinned to stand 4 to 6 inches apart; thinnings may be saved for table use. When leaves reach full size, the crop should be harvested by cutting the short plant stem at the soil surface just below the lowest leaves. As day length increases and temperatures rise, successive leaves are smaller and plants bolt to seed. Expect about 25 pounds of spinach per 50 feet of row. To maintain a continuous supply of early spinach, make successive sowings at 10-day intervals until about six weeks before the onset of hot summer conditions.

For fall crops, begin sowing seed in late summer and make successive sowings until about six weeks before low temperatures reach about 25°F. Seed should be sown more densely when soil temperatures are above 80°F, as warm soil inhibits the germination of a substantial percentage.

Spinach 'Space'

Spinach 'Bloomsdale'

Spinach Sigmaleaf

Spinach 'Hojo' (prickly cultivar)

In zones 5 to 7 (or 8), seed sown in cool fall weather may remain dormant until early spring and then provide a very early crop. In zone 9 and the milder parts of zone 8, spinach may be sown in the fall and grown as a winter crop. Leaves often grow to be quite large and may be harvested individually, leaving the growth point intact and capable of regenerating.

Extended periods of high humidity, especially in warm weather, may encourage downy mildew and other fungus diseases. Where such conditions are common, resistant cultivars should be selected. Leaf spot can be minimized by not watering in late afternoon and at night. Birds, which sometimes shred foliage, may be excluded with nylon or wire mesh.

Savoyed, or crinkle-leaf, cultivars are best grown as spring crops. Cultivars include 'Bloomsdale Long-standing' and 'Indian Summer', both with upright (less mud-spattered) foliage; 'Cold-resistant Savoy', particularly suited to early spring germination; and 'Tyee F_1', which is more heat tolerant than most. Smooth leaf cultivars, preferred by some because the leaves are more easily washed, include 'Space', which has an upright habit, and 'Nordic', which is heat tolerant and disease resistant.

Cultivars best suited for fall crops include 'Virginia Blight-resistant Savoy', 'Giant Noble', and 'King of Denmark'. Others, such as 'Giant Winter' and the disease-resistant 'Melody' hybrid, do well as both spring and fall crops. 'Bloomsdale Dark Green' is a good winter cultivar in the South.

SQUASH
(Cucurbita pepo, C. maxima, C. moschata)

Cultivated for their colorful, edible, mild-flavored, highly varied fruits, the cultivars of *C. pepo, C. maxima,* and *C. moschata* are tendril-bearing, climbing annuals that are usually allowed to sprawl and ripen their often large, heavy fruit on the ground. Native to tropical and subtropical America, these species have spawned a diverse array of variants that are grown all year round in warm climates and in the summer throughout the temperate zones. So-called bush squash cultivars have a compact, nonvining, densely leafy habit and tend to bear earlier but somewhat less prolifically than vining or sprawling types.

Cultivars of *C. pepo* that are raised primarily for their immature fruit are called summer squash in the United States and include zucchini, yellow, and scallop squashes. Those cultivars whose fruit is normally grown to maturity and allowed to harden are called winter squash and include acorn cultivars (derivatives of *C. pepo*), hubbard (derivative of *C. maxima*), and butternut (derivative of *C. moschata*) squashes. Winter squash may be stored for some months after harvest. In England, squash is called vegetable marrow, and those harvested immature are courgettes.

All squashes require moist, warm or even hot conditions for optimal growth and prolific crops. From zone 6 north, and wherever the annual period of hot summer weather averages less than three months, squashes, especially winter types, should be started indoors under fluorescent lights (14 to 16 hours per day) or in a greenhouse in 3-inch pots about one month before set-out time (with tomato plants). Seed should be sown two or three together, ½ to 1 inch deep, in a loose soil mix at 70° to 80°F. When true leaves appear, thin (by clipping, not pulling) to one plant per container. Transplant to 4-inch pots in two to three weeks to encourage maximum early growth. Young plants should be hardened off for several days in a coldframe before being set out in the garden. Whenever squash plants are transplanted, care should be taken to avoid disturbing the roots, as transplanting

shock can seriously delay the resumption of growth. Plants should be grouped three together, the groups spaced about 5 feet apart for vining types, 3 feet apart for bush cultivars. In cool, windy, wet weather, the young plants should be protected with clear polyethylene plastic caps or shields.

From zone 7 south, or wherever hot summer weather extends for three months or more, squash seed, especially of summer squash, may be sown directly in the garden in groups, or "hills," of five or six seeds. The hills spaced about 3 to 5 feet apart, depending on plant habit, and the seedlings are later thinned to three plants per hill.

Loose, sandy-humusy, moisture-retentive soils of pH 6.5 to 7.0 and moderate fertility result in heavy fruit set. Excess nitrate stimulates vegetative growth at the expense of fruit. Generous, sustained soil moisture is required for maximum fruit size.

In all squashes, each of the large yellow flowers is male or female. The male, or pollen-bearing, flowers appear earlier and are more numerous than the shorter-stalked, fruit-forming female flowers. Small dark beetles usually invade the flowers and are the main pollinating agents. The young fruit aborts and turns black if pollination has failed. In summer squashes, it is important to harvest usable fruit promptly, as further fruit set is depressed by the retention of vine-ripening fruit.

Large stem-boring grubs cause leaf wilt and premature death of squash plants unless the invaders are killed by carefully

Unusual heirloom squash

slitting the stems longitudinally or by inserting a wire, followed by covering the affected stems with soil to stimulate supplemental root formation. Sabadilla, Rotenone, or Pyrethrum dust may also be used to control borers as well as squash bugs, cucumber beetles, and aphids. Crop rotation helps control mosaic virus. Fungicides may be needed to control downy mildew, which can prove serious in cool, damp weather, and powdery mildew, which often appears in hot, humid weather toward the end of the growing season.

Squash cultivars are very numerous, as ongoing breeding programs continue to deliver new variants almost every year. The following review is, therefore, more indicative of the various categories or groups of squashes than an exhaustive enumeration of cultivars available.

Among summer squashes, all derived from *C. pepo* and all reaching first harvest in about seven weeks from seed, the green-skinned, cylindrical zucchini has long been a favorite, with 'Black Zucchini' and 'Rickgreen Hybrid' being well-known vining cultivars. 'Burpee Hybrid' is a bush type. In 'Cocozelle', a vining cultivar, the fruit is striped light and dark green; 'Gourmet Globe Hybrid' is similar but of bushy habit. 'Zahra' has short, pale green fruit. Yellow-skinned zucchini include 'Burpee Golden Zucchini' and 'Gold Rush'.

Yellow summer squash, equally popular, is mostly tapered or bottle shaped, and includes such straight-neck cultivars as 'Butterstick' and 'Seneca Prolific', both vining, as well as 'Seneca Butterbar', a bush type. Among vining cultivars that bear curved-neck fruit are 'Yellow Crookneck' and 'Early Garden Summer Crookneck', both with a warted skin, and 'Pic-n-Pic Hybrid', a smooth-skinned type. 'Dixie Hybrid' is a smooth-skinned crookneck of bushy habit.

Scalloped summer squash cultivars have circular, flattened, wavy-edged fruit. In 'Peter Pan Hybrid', 'Patty Pan', and 'Benning's Green Tint', the fruit is light green; in 'Butter Scallop' and 'Golden Scallop' it is yellow; and in 'Sunburst Hybrid' it is yellow with green ends.

Winter squashes derived from *C. pepo* mostly have dark green skins and orange flesh, and take 10 to 12 weeks to ripen. Those with fluted, spherical, or blunt-ended fruit are called acorn squash. 'Ebony Acorn' and 'Sweet Mana' are vining acorn cultivars, and 'Bush Acorn Table King' and 'Table Ace Hybrid' are bush types. 'Cream of the Crop' matures yellow skinned. Also derived from this species is 'Spaghetti', with a mass of slender strands within each yellow 6- to 12-inch fruit (requiring about 12 weeks to ripen). 'Delicata' a 7- to 9-inch cylinder, and 'Sweet Dumpling', 4-inch sphere, have cream colored skins with dark stripes.

Winter squashes derived from *C. maxima* are known collectively as hubbards and buttercups, have leathery skins, yellow to deep orange flesh, and for the most part, require 12 to 15 weeks to mature. Among the largest and best keeping is the vining, long-season 'Blue Hubbard', whose fruit is 20 pounds or more, while

Winter squash collection

Heirloom winter squash

Winter squash (space-saving in garden)

at the other extreme is 'Gold Nugget', a bush type which produces 5-inch fruit weighing 1½ to 2 pounds in about 12 weeks. 'Buttercup' has large, flattened, green-skinned (with a grayish end), orange-skinned fruit on vining plants; 'Bush Buttercup' is similar but of compact habit.

Winter squashes derived from *C. moschata* are the butternuts, which bear stumpy, flaring, yellow- or buff-skinned fruit that has orange flesh. The seeds and pulp are only in the flare. The best cultivars are 'Waltham Butternut', a vining plant, and 'Burpee Butterbush', a bush type. Both ripen in 10 to 12 weeks.

SWISS CHARD
(Beta vulgaris ssp. *cicla)*

Swiss chard 'Ruby Red'

Swiss chard is a biennial that is closely related to the garden beet, but it has much larger, often crinkled leaf blades and thickened leaf stalks and lacks the swollen root. Swiss chard is an important source of salad and cooked greens through much of the year but is especially valued in the summer when spinach and lettuce are often in short supply. Although it probably originated from the prototypic beet in the Mediterranean region, Swiss chard had long been cultivated in Europe before spreading to temperate-zone regions elsewhere and to many highland tropical ones as well. It is best grown as an annual with the expectation that the leaves may be harvested well into fall in

zones 5 and 6 and even into early winter in zones 7 and 8.

Chard "seed" is actually a dried, shriveled, few-seeded fruit and should be started directly in the garden in the spring just after the last spring frost. Sow 1 to 1½ inches apart and about ½ inch deep in rows 18 to 24 inches apart. At the first thinning, seedlings should be left to stand about 3 inches apart; a few weeks later a second thinning should leave the young plants about 6 inches apart; after a final midseason thinning, those remaining should be about 1 foot apart. Each thinning produces greens for table use. This procedure maximizes early crop production while allowing the diminished number of remaining plants to grow to full size and yield heavily through to the end of the season. Chard leaves remain usable until temperatures fall below 20°F. Harvest leaves from mature plants by carefully breaking or cutting the stalk bases of the outermost few from each plant, leaving the central immature leaves to expand for eventual harvest.

Swiss chard grows best in full sun or, in midsummer, in partial shade, and it thrives on deep, well-drained, humusy soil of pH 6.5 to 7.5, which has been enriched with well-rotted manure. Where nitrate is deficient, add a high-nitrate fertilizer supplement as a side dressing at monthly intervals until late summer. Continuously maintained soil

moisture is important, as drought induces premature bolting.

Various chewing insects that perforate chard leaves usually cause insignificant harm, but they can be excluded with fine-mesh cloth or nylon screening if necessary. In locations where fungus and virus diseases of beet and chard are serious, crop rotation or even periodic cessation of beet and chard culture may be necessary.

Among the relatively few cultivars on the U.S. market, 'Fordhook Giant' and 'Lucullus' have crinkled, or savoyed, leaf blades with thick, broad, white stalks, and 'Large White-ribbed Geneva' is similar but with smooth, flat leaf blades. 'Rhubarb' and 'Ruby Red' have crinkled blades with red veins and stalks, and in 'Rainbow' the leaf stalks are variegated red, yellow, and white.

TOMATO
(Lycopersicon esculentum)

A short-lived perennial grown as an annual for its juicy, acidic, thin-skinned, usually red fruit, the tomato is native to the slopes of the Andes in Peru and Ecuador. It was taken to Europe in the sixteenth century by returning explorers, where it was long believed to be poisonous (as indeed the foliage is) and grown only as an ornamental curiosity. In the nineteenth century, however, the fruit was accepted as

Rainbow Swiss chard

edible and has since become an important commercial crop the world over and the most popular of home-garden vegetables. The genetic plasticity of the tomato is reflected in the great variation in the size, form, color, and flavor, of the fruit and in the unending parade of cultivars brought onto the market.

Thanks to years of intensive breeding and experimental culture, tomato culti-vars have been developed not only for ordinary in-ground garden culture in all hardiness zones in the United States but also for container cultivation, for green-house crops, for hydroponics, and for humid tropical conditions, among others. The main limiting factor in temperate-zone regions is the number of days that minimum temperatures fall no lower than 50°F; in the humid tropics, the ceaseless onslaughts of pests, diseases, and weeds are the most serious obstacles.

In the home garden, tomatoes often take priority over all other vegetables; indeed, if only one is grown, it is usually the tomato. The tomato adapts to a wide range of climates and soil conditions, but requires no less than three months of warm weather to bear creditably and tol-erates no frost. The optimal temperature range for most cultivars is 70° to 80°F during the day and 60° to 70°F at night. Temperatures higher than 100°F render pollen infertile and destroy embryos; hence fruit set is suspended. Readings lower than 50°F usually slow growth and thus reduce the production of flowers and fruit. By choosing both early and mid season cultivars, the harvest season may be extended, especially from zone 7 south. Crop-reducing pests and diseases can be limited by crop rotation.

A site sheltered from wind is impor-tant, as is exposure to at least five hours of sunlight per day. A friable well-drained, moderately fertile, moisture-retentive soil in the pH range 5.5 to 7.0 is best. Well-rotted manure or compost will help with water retention and furnish most of the requisite nutrients; soil tests may indicate a need for supplemental phosphate, which is necessary for full fruit development. Soil preparation should be 6 to 8 inches deep and extend at least 3 feet away from the planting site, as tomato roots are wide

Caged tomato

ranging. Excess soil nitrate will stimulate lush growth but little fruit set; too little nitrate, on the other hand, causes pale foliage. Insufficient water and calcium deficiency together cause blossom-end rot in ripening fruit; the sudden addition of excess water, as by a summer down-pour, often causes ripening fruit to crack. Fruit not shaded by the tomato plant's leaves may develop pale or whitish areas, a condition called sun scorch.

When choosing cultivars for the home garden, some consideration should be given to the relative merits of determi-nate and indeterminate growth habits. In determinate cultivars, each stem or branch ends in a fruit cluster, and thus grows no further. This results in compact plants (some not exceeding 1 foot tall), often with no need for staking or other support, and thus well suited to container culture. Fruit set is limited, but all ripen together or within a few weeks of each other. Because of the limited number of leaves on determinate tomato plants, care must be taken not to remove any until they yellow. The preponderance of tomato cultivars, however, are of indeterminate growth, with fruit clusters borne laterally along stems that continue elongating all season and, if left unsupported, will sprawl. Fruit ripens over a long period and total yield is potentially greater than with determinate sorts.

If only a few tomato plants are desired, it may be best to purchase transplants.

They should be 6 to 12 inches tall, have well-developed, rich green foliage, and need not be in flower when planted. Cultivar choice is often very limited. For a substantial crop, however, or to grow any of the less common cultivars, it is necessary to start tomatoes from seed. Seed should be started indoors under fluorescent lights (14 to 16 hours per day) or in a greenhouse about six weeks before plants can be safely set out; i.e., only after temperatures on clear, still nights fall no lower than 50°F. Because tomatoes require intense light, prolonged indoor culture usually results in legginess, unless the plants are grown in a green-house. Sow in a loose, peat-based, nutrient-fortified soilless starting mix, either in flats with the seeds 1 inch apart and ¼ inch deep, or in cell packs or individual 2- or 3-inch plastic or peat pots, with two or three seeds per unit. Ideal germination temperature range is 75° to 85°F, after which 65° to 75°F is best for growing on. The medium should be kept constantly moist but not saturated or soggy. When the seedlings develop two true leaves, thin to one plant per pot. Later, when the plants reach about 4 inches in height, increase the pot size and the space around the plants to accommodate growing roots and prevent shading.

About one week before set-out time, the young plants should be hardened off in a coldframe. Some time may be gained in spring by using an enclosure of clear

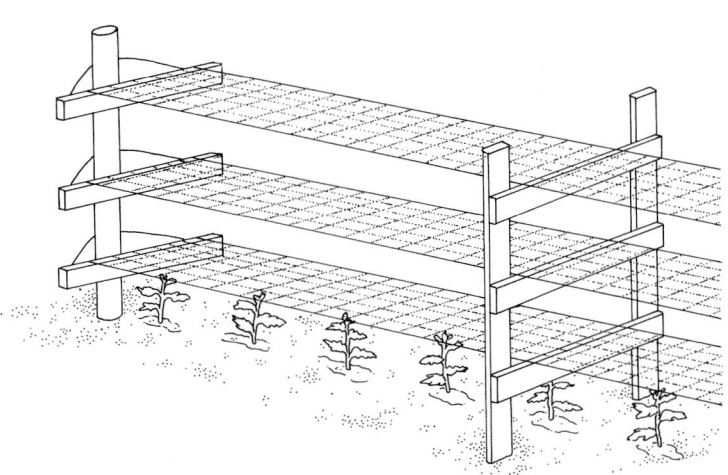

Tomatoes grown through horizontal courses of wide-mesh wire fencing are supported, keeping fruit off the ground and easily harvestable.

plastic water-filled cylinders around each plant to moderate falling temperatures at night, but even with such a device it is inadvisable to set plants out until night temperatures remain above 45°F. Any check of growth in young tomato plants, whether by cold temperatures, insufficient water, low light, or undersize containers, can result in stunted growth in the garden and meager fruit yield. On the other hand, setting out very large transplants already in fruit is no guarantee of bountiful harvests, since temperature, soil moisture, nutrients, and light are the critical factors affecting total yield. Pot-bound, leggy transplants are often slow to resume growth under garden conditions. However, recovery is surer if leggy plants are buried with all but the leafy tip below the surface, thus inducing the lanky stem to produce supplemental roots.

Before plants are set out, arrangements should be made to support them, especially if the cultivars are of indeterminate habit. Although individual plants usually set more fruit if allowed to sprawl, much more garden area is required and ripening fruit that rests on the ground is often invaded by soil organisms. Also, harvesting can be difficult if the plants are tangled together. A wire-mesh cage 6 to 8 feet high and 1½ feet in diameter made of a rolled-up section of fencing and secured in place with one or two posts, will support two or three plants and will also serve as a temporary composter for pulled weeds

and other garden waste, which, while decomposing, helps conserve soil moisture around the tomato roots. Individual 8- to 10-foot stakes set 2 feet deep, or three- or four-post teepees are also easily erected. Stem ties made of polyethylene plastic, discarded pantyhose, or soft cloth are preferable to cord or wire, which can cut into stems. Manufactured wide-mesh "towers" are also available, but these are often not tall enough for vigorous indeterminate cultivars.

As tomato plants begin their rapid growth, it is beneficial, especially with large-fruited indeterminate cultivars, to prune out secondary or lateral shoots (often mistakenly called "suckers"). Removal of all branch shoots as they develop in the angle between leaves and main stem results in just that one stem remaining, and leads to a tall, narrow plant bearing a relatively small number of tomatoes, all reaching maximum size. The more laterals that are permitted to develop, the greater the total fruit yield, but with somewhat smaller individual tomatoes. A common compromise between the single-stem pruning and no pruning at all is to limit the plant to three or four stems, i.e., the main stem and two or three laterals, and to prevent any other branches from developing. Pruning is unnecessary for indeterminate cherry tomatoes and other small-fruited cultivars.

As the season progresses, it is important to maintain soil moisture during any dry periods. Mulching with a mixture of compost, peat moss, grass clippings, and/or salt hay not only reduces soil evaporation but deters weeds. In prolonged drought, even a well-mulched planting requires occasional thorough,

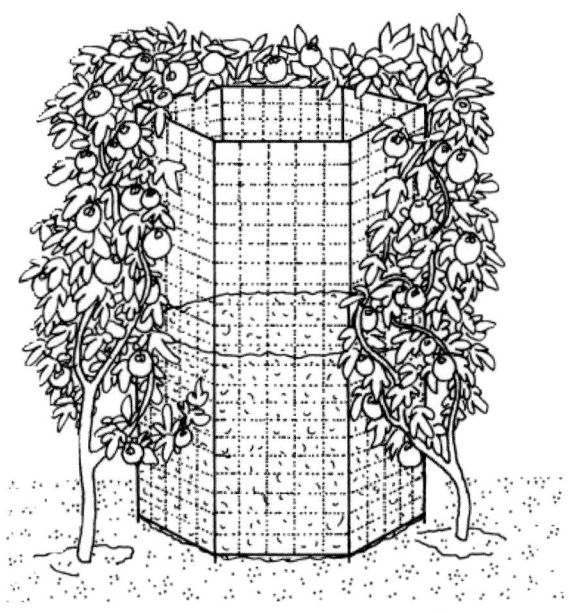

A collapsible hexagonal tomato cage keeps fruit accessible and also serves as a small composter for pulled weeds.

deeply penetrating waterings. Also beneficial, at monthly intervals, are applications of supplemental nutrients, as may be had from liquified seaweed or manure "tea." The nutrients will induce greater fruit set; the water will help maturing fruit reach full size.

Toward season's end (about six weeks before the average first-frost date), all green fruit may be induced to ripen by clipping off all stem ends, thus truncating further growth and flower development. Failing this, all green fruit may be removed at threat of frost, spread thinly in empty seed flats, and placed indoors to ripen. None will increase in size, but most will take on ripe color in the ensuing weeks, whether kept in light or darkness. The cooler the location, however, the more gradual will be the ripening. Flavor will be somewhat blander than with normally ripened fruit.

Tomato is subject to numerous pests and diseases. Fortunately, however, many cultivars show degrees of resistance to such serious diseases as fusarium wilts, verticillium wilt, alternaria blight, alternaria stem canker, gray leaf spot, and tobacco mosaic virus, as well as to nematodes (see Chapter 34), and to cold temperatures. The relative incidence of these problems in your area constitutes a criterion to be used in selecting cultivars for your garden. All cultivars, however resistant, are subject to other invaders, such as flea beetles, which can damage young transplants and should be checked with Rotenone; Colorado potato beetles, which attack foliage and should be picked off by hand or dusted with sabadilla, Rotenone, or Pyrethrum; and tomato horn worms, which are very large, green, hairless caterpillars that usually appear one or a few at a time but nevertheless can quickly strip a tomato plant of nearly all foliage; they are easily hand picked or may be controlled with Dipel (*Bacillus thuringiensis*). Prompt removal of disease-ridden plants and of any dead or yellowed foliage helps deter further disease attacks.

Tomato is available in a great diversity of cultivars that vary not only in fruit traits but also in growth habit, mature height, bearing period, and disease resistance. Those discussed below are mostly well-established cultivars that illustrate the extent of variation. New cultivars are offered almost annually; nearly all of them will fit into one of the three categories described here.

I. Cultivars of Indeterminate Growth

In determinate cultivars with moderately large fruit (4 to 6 ounces) that ripen red and early (in 55 to 65 days after being set out in the garden) include the very popular, disease-resistant 'Early Cascade', which tolerates lower temperatures than most, and 'Early Girl', which bears heavily until fall. Especially favored in home gardens are the larger fruited, later-to-ripen (70 to 80 days) cultivars, ranging from 'Celebrity' hybrid and 'Floramerica', with individual fruit ripening from 8 to 12 ounces through 'Big Boy' hybrid and 'Better Boy' hybrid, with fruit to about 1 pound. 'Beefmaster', 'Bragger', and 'Oxheart' can bear fruit weighing to 2 pounds or more if pruned carefully.

Indeterminate cherry tomato

Cultivars of merit with moderate fruit that ripens in midseason include those that bear fruit ripening to other colors.

'Golden Queen': orange.
'Lemon Boy' hybrid: yellow.
'Ponderosa Pink': rose pink.
'Purple Calabash': purple.
'Taxi': yellow.
'Valencia': orange.
'White Beauty': creamy white.

In general, orange, yellow, and white tomatoes are of a milder, sweeter flavor than red ones. 'Yellow Stuffer' is a yellow form with hollow fruit, and 'Evergreen' remains green even when ripe.

Cultivars with small red fruit range from the versatile 'Danny', with a generous, early-ripening initial crop of 3½- to 4-ounce fruit, to such popular cherry tomatoes as 'Super Sweet 100', 'Sugar Lump', and 'Gardener's Delight', all producing a plenitude of mostly 1- to 1½-ounce fruit from mid-season to fall. One of the smallest-fruited tomatoes is *L. esculentum* var. *pimpinellifolium* 'Red Currant', with red spherical fruit ¼ to ⅓ inch in diameter, borne in clusters of 15 to 20.

II. Cultivars of Determinate Growth

Moderately large (6 to 8 ounces) and red-fruited cultivars of determinate growth include the early-ripening, disease-resistant 'Daybreak' and the later 'Celebrity'. Smaller-fruited cultivars, especially suited to containers, range from 'Patio Prize', and 'Red Express', both about 2 feet tall, to 'Red Robin', a dwarf not exceeding 6 inches and productive in pots. All bear 4- to 6-ounce fruit. Among the red-fruited cherry tomatoes in this group are the disease-resistant 'Pixie II' hybrid: the cold-tolerant 'Cheerio' and 'Washington Cherry', and the tiny (½ inch across) but prolific 'Gem State'. 'Whippersnapper' is a pink-fruited cherry tomato, and 'Gold Nugget' a cold-tolerant yellow cherry. 'Yellow Pear', also diminutive, bears, as it name implies, yellow pear-shaped fruit.

III. Cultivars for Special Purposes

A number of tomato cultivars have been developed to ripen with dense, rather dry flesh, making them suitable for making tomato sauce and paste. Among these are 'Belle Star', 'Nova Paste', and 'Roma' (disease resistant). 'Long Keeper', with medium fruit that ripens to a greenish red-orange, can be stored safely for several weeks after ripening, especially if kept cool. 'Buffalo' bears 6- to 7-ounce fruit, and 'Sierra' bears 8- to 10-ounce fruit. Both are recommended for off-season greenhouse culture.

OTHER VEGETABLES

AMARANTH
(Amaranthus caudatus, A. cruentus, A. tricolor)

Of the *Amaranthus* species, the so-called leaf amaranths (*A. caudatus* and *A. tricolor*), while best known in the United States as ornamental annuals, are occasionally grown for their edible foliage, which is used in salads or cooked as greens, uses for which they have long been well known in the Asiatic tropics. Known as tampala, caraloo, and (confusingly) Chinese cabbage, it is available in several variegated cultivars.

Grain amaranth (*A. cruentus*) is a vigorous plant growing 4 to 7 feet tall and has green to reddish purple foliage and seed heads. The loose clusters of dry fruit contain sesamelike seeds that are protein rich. Seeds are extracted from dry chaff by rubbing the seed heads on a screen and winnowing the bits of chaff with a fan. The seeds are used in cereals and baked goods or may be popped. Culture is essentially as for ornamental amaranths.

Cultivars used as greens include love-lies-bleeding (*A. caudatus*), and 'Early Splendor', 'Flaming Fountains', 'Joseph's Coat', 'Molten Fire', 'Red Stripe Leaf', and 'Tampala' (all of *A. tricolor* and all but the last two best known as ornamentals). Grain cultivars (all of *A. cruentus*) include 'Golden Giant', 'Green Top', 'Intense Purple', 'Manna', and 'Pygmy Torch'.

ARTICHOKE
(Cynara scolymus)

Unknown in the wild but long cultivated in the eastern Mediterranean region and subsequently in southern and western Europe, the artichoke, or globe artichoke, is a perennial, 4 to 6 feet tall, that bears large thistlelike flowers that, in the bud stage, have fleshy scales, or phyllaries, that are cooked and much prized for table use. Although the best produce is had from selected cultivars that are propagated vegetatively, yields of good quality may also be had from a few seed-grown cultivars, such as 'Green Globe' and 'Purple Sicilian'.

The large-leaf plants require 2- to 3-foot spacing and bear lightly the first year, more heavily the second and third, after which they are usually replaced. Heads must be prepared and used within a few days of harvest. Most productive in areas having cool summers, artichokes require a sheltered site with a well-drained, fertile soil rich in organic matter. Seed of such cultivars as 'Green Globe' and 'Purple Sicilian' may be started indoors under fluorescent lights (14 to 16 hours per day) or in a greenhouse six to eight weeks before the last spring frost. Sow seed thinly in pans or flats, cover with 1 inch of fine mix, transplant to cell packs to grow on, harden off in a coldframe a week or more, and then set out in midspring. Expect the first harvest in two or three months. Although hardy to zone 6, artichoke crowns are best mulched with salt hay during periods of freezing weather. Gray and powdery mildews are occasionally serious diseases.

ARTICHOKE, CHINESE
(Stachys affinis)

Native to eastern Asia and known also as crosnes du Japon, chorogi, and knotroot, Chinese artichoke is a perennial, about 18 inches tall, and is grown for its white, beaded tubers. These develop just below the soil surface and may reach 3 inches long.

Propagation is by planting small tubers about 9 inches apart and about 3 inches deep in the bed or row. Tubers should be harvested in the fall; some may be left to overwinter in the ground (zone 5 and south) and start the next season's crop.

ARTICHOKE, JERUSALEM
(Helianthus tuberosus)

A native perennial sunflower that grows 6 to 10 feet tall and occurs in large clumps or patches in sunny, damp places in the wild, Jerusalem artichoke is cultivated for the nutty 4- to 6-inch potatolike tubers that form in late summer, often some distance from the stem base. They are best dug after the foliage has been killed by frost. Often called sunchoke or girasole, the tubers are eaten raw in salads or cooked. Because any bit of tuber left in the ground after harvest will sprout the following spring, and since a patch of Jerusalem artichoke spreads 1 or more feet each year, it is prudent either to contain the cultivation inside a root barrier, such as plastic curbing or a concrete block wall, that extends at least 8 inches deep and isolates several square yards or to establish it well away from the garden, as on a sunny embankment or as a lawn island, where its inexorable spread will not prove troublesome or can be limited by mowing.

Propagation is by whole or cut tubers, which are planted in the fall 4 to 6 inches deep and 9 to 12 inches apart. Heavy clay soils yield the largest harvests, but in lighter, humusy soils, the tubers are more easily dug without being bruised or broken. Harvested tubers should be stored in very slightly damp sand or peat moss and kept in a cool or cold place, such as an unheated garage, for winter use. In the spring, any remaining tubers will sprout and soften, and may be planted.

Cultivars with the large, whitish, knobby tubers characteristic of the wild type include 'French Mammoth White', which has mature tubers that weigh ¼ to ½ pound. 'Stampede' and 'Sugarball' form tubers in mid to late summer, some weeks before most other cultivars. 'Fuseau', a light skinned type, is smooth (without knobs), as are 'Smooth Garnet' and 'Long Red', both with reddish skins. In 'Golden Nugget', the yellowish tubers are long and tapered.

ARUGULA
(Eruca vesicaria)

Much valued as a salad green, arugula, or rocket, is a European annual grown as a very short-season crop for its peppery leaves, the harvest best limited to young foliage. Older leaves become tough and bitter, and once warm weather causes the plants to bolt to flower, they should be discarded.

Arugula

Hence, it is best to grow arugula in the spring and fall, sowing seed well before the last spring frost and again in late summer, with the expectation that fall harvests may continue until temperatures drop below 20°F. Cloche or coldframe protection or greenhouse culture further extends off-season harvests. A light mesh shade (as used for lettuce) helps retard bolting in early summer. Successive small sowings every two weeks ensure a continuing supply of young, tender, flavorful leaves. Seed should be sown about ½ inch deep and 1½ to 2 inches apart.

There are no cultivars.

BASELLA
(Basella alba)

Malabar spinach

A twining perennial of the Old World tropics, basella, or Malabar spinach, is grown as an annual for its smooth, glossy, dark green leaves that are used as a spinach substitute in the summer.

Seed may be started indoors under fluorescent lights (14 to 16 hours per day) or in a greenhouse at 65° to 70°F about four weeks before the last spring frost. Grown the seedlings in cell packs at 60° to 65°F, and set out at tomato-planting time.

South of zone 7, seed may also may be sown directly in the garden about 1 inch deep and 3 inches apart, with coarse mesh fencing 4 to 6 feet high in place for support and ease of harvest. During rapid growth in hot weather, soil moisture must be maintained. The first picking may be taken in 80 to 90 days after sowing.

There are no cultivars.

BEETBERRY
(Chenopodium capitatum, C. foliosum)

Annuals of Europe and North Africa that have become naturalized in parts of the United States, both beetberry species grow to about 2½ feet tall and bear small, red, berrylike fruit that makes an attractive enhancement to fruit salads.

Seed should be sown about ½ inch deep directly in the garden after the last spring frost and the seedlings thinned to stand 12 inches apart. In most areas, the crop reseeds itself year after year.

There are no cultivars.

BITTER MELON
(Mormordica balsamina, M. charantia)

Tropical perennial tendril-climbers that are grown for their warty immature fruit, bitter melons are variously called balsam apple (*M. balsamina*) and balsam pear, bitter gourd, bitter cucumber, Foo-Kwa, or La-Kwa (*M. charantia*). Solitary yellow cucumberlike flowers are followed (females only) by 4- to 8-inch fruit that is picked green and much valued in Oriental cooking. Left to ripen, the fruit turns bright orange and splits to reveal red-coated seeds.

Requisite of 10 to 12 weeks of hot weather from seed to first picking, bitter melon is best grown from zone 8 south. Farther north it is sometimes cultured in greenhouses. Germination is the same as for cucumber (see page 649).

There are no cultivars.

BROCCOLI RAAB
(Brassica oleracea, Italica group)

Similar to common broccoli, the broccoli raab variant bears small, loose clusters of flower buds rather than large dense heads. Its flavor is somewhat peppery, suiting both the heads and young surrounding leaves for use in salads and as cooked greens. If kept picked, the crop renews itself from midsummer until frost.

Culture is the same as for broccoli (see page 642) but with a spacing of about 6 inches. In the cultivar 'Spring Raab', high-quality heads and foliage are harvestable about six weeks after setting out. Flea beetles and cutworms can be troublesome with young transplants.

BURDOCK
(Arctium lappa)

Burdock is a coarse, leafy biennial from Europe, not to be confused with the weedy common burdock (*A. minus*), grown occasionally for the stout taproot that, if harvested the first year from seed, is of substantial size yet still tender. In second-year plants, the root may become fibrous and woody. The roots have a sweet, piquant flavor and are used in soups, stews, and stir-fries. Young leaves are also suitable for salads, and the leaf stalks, when peeled, are cooked as a vegetable.

Seed should be started as early as possible in the spring, well before the last spring frost. Sow about 1 inch deep and 2 inches apart, and thin in stages (harvesting leaves for table use) until the remaining plants are about 2 feet apart. Later sowings will yield crops in the fall or early the following spring. Although burdock adapts to a wide range of soils, a deeply prepared, friable, well-drained medium facilitates maximum root growth and eases harvest.

Among the few cultivars, 'Gobo', ready in about 3 months, is best grown as an early crop; 'Takinogawa Long', with very long roots (to 2 feet) and requiring four and one-half to five months to reach harvestable size, is for late-season use.

CANTALOUPE
(Cucumis melo ssp. melo, Reticulatus group)

Also known as muskmelon, cantaloupe is a sprawling or creeping annual grown for the large orange-fleshed fruit with a corky netted rind. As commercially grown cantaloupe must be harvested unripe for shipment, vine-ripened fruit from the home garden is prized for its usually greater sweetness and flavor. Although most cultivars require substantial garden space for their rampant growth and a long season to ripen, some very compact ones have been developed, as have others that ripen in as little as 10 weeks from set-out time or direct seeding.

Cantaloupe is most successful where summers are long, warm, and dry, but where occasional irrigation is possible. Humid conditions promote leaf diseases. For the best quality fruit, soil pH should be between 6.0 and 7.0, and the medium should be well drained, friable, humusy, and deeply worked.

North of zone 8, seed of most cultivars is best started indoors in cell packs as for cucumber (see page 649), with 85°F advised for germination and about 75°F for growing seedlings. Care should be taken not to disturb the roots in the transfer to the garden. Short-season cultivars may be seeded directly in the garden from zone 7 south, and long-season ones from zone 8 south. Seed should be planted about ½ inch deep in groups of eight. Thin the groups, or "hills," to four seedlings each, with groups about 3 feet apart in rows about 6 feet apart. Cultivars of compact growth may require only half as much spacing. Row covers are advisable if temperatures fall below 50°F, and opaque black plastic mulch helps stimulate early fruit set from zone 6 north. Harvest fruit when the gray green rind begins to yellow and firm finger pressure on the fruit at the stem end causes separation of the fruit from the stem. Cucumber beetles spread bacterial wilt and should be controlled with sabadilla, Rotenone, or Pyrethrum. Early cold in late summer or fall can cause irreversible wilt and no further ripening.

Cultivars with the first fruit ripening about 10 weeks from set-out include 'Sweet Granite' and 'Earligold', both of which are more cold tolerant than most, and the mildew-resistant 'Luscious Plus Hybrid' and 'Sweet 'n Early Hybrid'. Also early are the compact cultivars 'Sweet Bush Hybrid' and 'Minnesota Midget', with 4-inch fruit borne on compact stems no longer than 3 feet. The longer-season cantaloupes, with fruit first maturing in about 12 weeks, include the popular 'Musketeer', with fruit weighing 2 to 2½ pounds; 'Burpee' hybrid, fully spreading with fruit 3½ to 4 pounds, and 'Ambrosia' hybrid, a mildew-resistant, fully spreading form with fruit 4 to 5 pounds.

CARDOON
(Cynara cardunculus)

Somewhat more popular in Europe than in the United States cardoon is a perennial closely related to the artichoke and is grown for its fleshy leaf stalks; which are usually blanched to increase their succulence. It is a large, coarse plant, at least 6 feet tall, and harvests are made in the spring as the shoots begin to elongate or in fall when the tender stem ends are taken. In either case, it is used in salads or prepared as a cooked vegetable. Cardoon is hardy to zone 6.

Cardoon (creeping zinnia in front)

Seed should be sown after the last spring frost. Sow three or four seeds together 1 to 1½ inches deep, the groups about 18 inches apart. The soil should be well drained, humusy, and well prepared with well-rotted manure added. Seedlings should be thinned to one per group. Any exposed to temperatures below 40°F may bear undersize leaves and bolt. From zone 5 north, seedlings may be started indoors, as for artichoke (see page 666) and set out in spring. Tying the leaves together in a wrapper of black plastic achieves blanching.

'Gigante de Romague' is one of the few named cultivars; most often, the cultivar is not indicated.

CAULI-BROC
(Brassica oleracea, Italica group)

More a cauliflower than broccoli, cauli-broc develops heads that are light green and have an intermediate flavor.

The crop matures in 9 to 10 weeks. Culture is the same as for cauliflower (see page 646).

CELERIAC
(Apium graveolens var. rapaceum)

A biennial native to coastal areas of Europe, celeriac, or knob celery as it is sometimes called, is cultivated as an annual for the thickened, celery-flavored root that may be cooked alone or combined with other vegetables, such as potato. A long-season crop, celeriac roots are dug from the fall until well into winter.

In regions where winter temperatures fall below 10°F, i.e., from zone 8 north, they should be deeply mulched or lifted and stored in containers of sand in a cool place. Culture of celeriac is the same as for self-blanching celery (see page 647). Removal of side shoots in late summer helps encourage the formation of large roots. Leaves may be used like those of celery in soups or salads.

There is little distinction among the roots of the relatively few cultivars. In 'Brilliant', the roots are somewhat smooth, hence more easily peeled, and in 'Prague', they mature larger than most.

CELTUCE
(Lactuca sativa var. asparagina)

A 3-foot-tall biennial, celtuce has long been grown in China and Southeast Asia. Celtuce, or stem lettuce is a non-heading lettuce so named for its crisp, thickened, young stems and lettucelike leaves. It is grown as an annual primarily for the stems, which, if harvested while still young, may be eaten raw, cooked in soups, steamed, or incorporated into stir-fries. The immature leaves are also used in salads.

Culture is the same as for looseleaf lettuce (see page 650), with the ideal summer temperature range from 68° to 80°F. The crop is particularly successful on the Pacific coast.

Celeriac

CHICORY
(Cichorium intybus)

A versatile biennial or short-lived perennial from Europe, chicory, in its varied cultivars, furnishes such crops as endive, escarole, radicchio, and witloof as well as Italian "dandelion." The wild blue-flowered form is a widely distributed weed, occurring almost throughout North America.

Young, deep green chicory leaves harvested in the spring as Italian dandelion from plants grown like looseleaf lettuce are used in salads and as a cooked vegetable. Endive, also called escarole, is a densely leafy form much prized for salads. Its crisp, pungent, inner, self-blanched leaves are tender and can also be eaten as a cooked vegetable. Radicchio is a slow-growing, broadly looseleaf or somewhat heading variant with attractive red-violet leaves of somewhat bitter taste (less so when harvested after light frost) that make an appealing component of salads.

The culture of endive and radicchio is the same as for looseleaf lettuce (see page 650).

For witloof, or Belgian endive or sugar-loaf chicory, roots are dug in the fall, stored in damp sand or soil in pots or boxes at just above freezing, and forced in the dark between October and March at 60°F. The blanched buds enlarge to form "chicons," which resemble white romaine lettuces and reach about 6 inches

long in three to four weeks. The chicons are harvested for use in salads or as a cooked vegetable. After harvest, the roots are discarded. In chicory intended for use as a coffee additive, the harvested roots are roasted and ground.

The cultivar most used for spring shoots is 'Catalogna'. For endive, 'Green Curled' and 'Salad King', ready in seven to eight weeks from seed, are deep green and curled, rather like kale. 'Nina' is smaller and harvestable about 10 days earlier.

Escarole, with broad, smooth, self-blanching leaves, is best known through the cultivar 'Nuvol', and is ready for harvest in about eight weeks. Radicchio is available in several cultivars, of which

'Giulio', with loose, intensely red-violet heads is especially favored, while 'Alto' and 'Augusto', both somewhat larger, are more frost tolerant. All are harvestable from midsummer to hard frost.

Among witloof cultivars, 'Flash' is reliable in sand, without soil. Roots are ready for storage in about four months from seed. Chicory cultivars grown for roots to be roasted include 'Large Rooted Magdeburg'.

COLLARDS
(Brassica oleracea, Acephala group)

Collards 'Flash' in winter frost

Also known as looseleaf cabbage or smooth kale, collards are grown as annuals for greens and are especially valued for their sweet flavor and high vitamin content as well as for their cold hardiness. Harvest usually begins in late summer and continues into or even through (from zone 7 south) the winter months. The unbranched stem grows 3 to 6 feet

Radicchio and Chinese cabbage

tall. Leaves are picked individually, with the stem left to continue growth.

For late-season harvest, start seed directly in the garden about 10 weeks before the first fall frost. Seed should be sown about ½ inch deep and 2 inches apart, and seedlings progressively thinned until the remaining plants stand 8 to 12 inches apart. Thinnings should be saved for table use. For earlier crops, particularly north of zone 7, seed may be started indoors and seedlings treated the same as broccoli seedlings (see page 642). Except for cutworms in the spring, pests and diseases are seldom serious.

Cultivars ready for harvest in about nine weeks from seed include 'Vates', which reaches about 4 feet tall, and the more compact 'Champion'. Longer-season cultivars, harvestable initially in about 12 weeks, include 'Georgia Blue-stem', about 3 feet tall, and 'Hicrop' hybrid, a heat-tolerant form that does not exceed 15 inches.

CORN SALAD
(Valerianella locusta)

Widely distributed in Europe and escaped from cultivation elsewhere, corn salad, also called lamb's lettuce or mafache, makes a flavorful if diminutive cool-weather salad green. Entire rosettes of clasping leaves are usually harvested and served as a unit rather than reduced to individual leaves.

From zone 7 south, start seed in the fall before hard frost for an early spring crop, or anywhere in early spring before the last spring frost for a late spring harvest. Sow seed shallowly about 1 inch apart, thinning to 2 to 3 inches apart, and harvest while still immature, beginning in about eight weeks.

Among the several cultivars available, 'Fetticus Broad-leaved' and 'Vit' are both mildew resistant.

CRESS

Several unrelated plants are included under the term *Cress*, all grown for greens that have a peppery flavor. Best known is watercress (*Nasturtium officinale*), a perennial hardy from zones 6 to 8, usually grown in shallow, gently running water. It responds however, to cultivation on relatively wet soil, where seed may be sown in early to mid spring, ¼ inch deep and ½ inch apart. In sunny or partially shaded locations, harvest should begin in about eight weeks and continue into fall.

Upland cress (*Barbarea verna*), with leaves having much the same flavor as watercress, is a biennial hardy to zone 6 and thrives on drier soil. Seed should be sown about ¼ inch deep and 1½ inches apart in the spring about the time of the last frost. Plants should be thinned to stand about 6 inches apart, with the thinnings saved for table use. Young leaves picked before they have reached full size have the best flavor. A steady and abundant supply of young leaves is ensured by making successive small sowings at two-week intervals until late summer. In the cultivar 'Cressida', the leaves are ready for harvest in three to four four weeks.

Curled cress or pepper grass (*Lepidium sativum*) is a circum-temperate dryland annual that reaches 1 to 2 feet tall. It is grown for its curly, pungent leaves. Intolerant of heat, it is best grown as a spring and fall crop. Sow its seed shallowly in early spring before the last spring frost and at two-week intervals thereafter until about three weeks before the onset of hot weather. Plants should be thinned to stand about 4 inches apart and harvests should be taken beginning two to three weeks after germination. Late-summer sowings provide fall harvests until night temperatures drop to about 25°F.

The cultivar 'Curled' is especially favored.

EGYPTIAN ONION
(Allium cepa var. aggregatum)

Also called tree onion, Eygptian onion, a variant of the common onion, is a perennial hardy to zone 5 and is grown for the small, elongated bulbs borne in place of flowers atop 3-foot scapes, beginning the second year.

The bulbs may be planted in the fall 4 inches apart in 2 inches of soil at the bottom of a trench about 8 inches deep. The trench should be gradually filled the following spring as the leaves elongate. Young bulbs may be lifted from spring to early or mid summer and used as green onions. Some should be left to establish a propagation clump, from which small scape-borne bulbs can be taken to plant for future crops.

FENNEL
(Foeniculum vulgare)

Fennel is a biennial or short-lived perennial from Europe that grows 4 to 6 feet tall and is valued for the anise-flavored seed; dill-like leaves; and thick, overlapping leaf stalk bases. Especially popular in the United States is the very large, fleshy, white leaf stalk base of Florence fennel, or finocchio (*F. vulgare* var. *azoricum*), which forms a bulblike swelling that is harvested and used in salads or as a cooked vegetable. Florence fennel, treated as an annual, grows to about 2 feet and is best cultivated from zone 5 south in well-drained, fertile soil.

Since any disturbance of the roots during active growth tends to induce bolting, it is best to start seed directly in the garden. Sow seed about 2 weeks after the last spring frost about ¼ inch deep and 2 inches apart, and thin seedlings to stand about 8 inches apart. Leaves of discarded seedlings may be dried and used as a kitchen herb. First harvest of the bulbous leaf bases begins in about 10 weeks. Mounding soil around the plant base helps blanch the crop. Nitrate-rich fertilizer, such as a commercial 10-5-5 preparation, stimulates development of large leaf bases.

Recommended cultivars of leaf, or sweet, fennel include 'Bronze' and the slow-to-bolt 'Perfection'. Among cultivars of Florence fennel are 'Zefa Fino', also slow to bolt, and 'Finnochio'.

GARLIC
(Allium sativum)

A perennial from central Asia hardy to zone 8 and closely related to onion, garlic is grown for its segmented, aromatic, oily bulbs, which impart a distinctive aroma and flavor to cooking. In addition to the bulb segments or "cloves," garlic is also valued for its leaves, which may be chopped and used in salads or as a garnish.

Garlic is propagated by the cloves, which are planted 1½ to 2 inches deep and 4 to 6 inches apart in the fall in well-drained, fertile, humusy soil. Spring planting yields a smaller crop. Winter mulch is advisable to prevent heaving. Garlic may also be grown from seed, but a seed-grown crop requires about five months to ripen, hence may not be harvestable until late fall or the following spring. Culture from seed is the same as for onion (see page 652). Whether grown from cloves or seed, garlic should be harvested before growth resumes the second spring, after which the plants soon bolt and consume the bulbs. Harvested bulbs should be strung together by their braided tops, or spread out in trays, in a cool (not freezing) place.

Among the several cultivars, 'New York White' is especially hardy and adaptable. Artichoke garlic is an early-maturing, purple-skinned variant with overlapping cloves; 'Early Italian' is a recommended cultivar. Rocambole, or serpent, garlic (*A. sativum* var. *ophioscorodon*) forms cloved bulbs and, atop the sometimes curling flower stalk, bulblets, either of which may be planted for further crops. Maturation to harvestable size may take two years. Elephant garlic (*A. scorodoprasum*), with larger, less pungent bulbs, may be used itself as a cooked vegetable. Culture is the same as for ordinary garlic.

GOOD KING HENRY
(*Chenopodium bonus–henricus*)

Also called wild spinach, Good King Henry is a European perennial that grows to 3 feet tall and is hardy to zone 5. It is grown for the lush young leaves that are usually harvested from spring until late summer and used as cooked greens. The flavor is suggestive of that of asparagus.

Seed is sown at about the time of the last spring frost in well-drained fertile soil and set about ¼ inch deep and 2 inches apart. The seedlings are progressively thinned until the remaining plants stand about 12 inches apart. The first harvest can be made in about eight weeks.

Closely related is the ubiquitous weedy annual, lamb's quarters or pigweed (*C. album*), which, while usually too rank and invasive to consider for cultivation, nevertheless has foliage that makes an admirable summer substitute for spinach.

HORSERADISH
(*Armoracia rusticana*)

Horseradish is a rank, coarse, 3-foot perennial that is native to Europe and long valued as a medicinal plant but is now a pernicious weed both there and in much of the United States from zones 5 to 8. Horseradish is nevertheless grown in the home garden for its fleshy, peppery tap root, which is ground to make horseradish sauce.

Although no viable seed is borne, any fragments of root left unharvested will sprout. Hence the desirability of limiting culture to a perforated steel drum or other large drainable container sunk to its rim in a sunny out-of-the-way place to keep the horseradish from competing with other crops and from spreading out of control. Propagation is by root cuttings, which should be planted horizontally or on a slant 2 to 3 inches deep, in ordinary, moist, stone-free garden soil. Rocks, and also excess nitrate, cause roots to fork. Harvest roots after a hard frost in the fall, preferably by digging them out with a long-bladed tree spade. Replant some for next year's crop, and wash the rest for use. Cleaned roots may be refrigerated in plastic bags or stored in a root cellar, ideally at close to freezing. Harvest may be deferred until early spring, but must occur before new growth begins if the next crop is to develop properly. The few cultivars, including 'Bohemian', Maliner Kreb', and 'New Bohemian', are scarcely distinguishable from the wild type.

JELLY MELON
(*Cucumis metuliferus*)

Also called African horned cucumber or jelly sack, jelly mellon is a tropical African annual tendril climber that is grown for the ovoid to pear-shaped, fleshy, cucumberlike fruit that is covered with blunt, fleshy spines ("horns"). Best grown on a trellis or wire-mesh fence, jelly melon is harvested when the rind turns orange. The lime green, banana-flavored flesh is eaten raw like melon. Once harvested, jelly melon may be stored up to six months in a cool, dry place.

Culture is essentially the same as for cucumber (see page 649).

KALE
(*Brassica oleracea, Acephala group*)

Kale mixed cultivars

An erect, usually unbranched, hardy biennial from Europe, kale is usually grown as a long-season annual and is valued for its young leaves, which are prepared as cooked greens, eaten raw in salads, or used as a garnish. More adaptable to temperature extremes than most other cabbage relatives, kale thrives in summer heat and survives winter chill as cold as 0°F. The flavor of the crop improves after fall frosts, and leaves of many cultivars may be harvested well into winter. From zone 8 south, kale may be picked throughout the winter and into the following spring when new growth begins, furnishing greens before most other vegetables are ready.

Although kale performs creditably even on relatively poor soil, the best quality foliage is developed on friable, well-drained, humusy, fertile soil. For fall and winter crops, start seed directly in the garden about three months before the first fall frost. Sow about ½ inch deep and 1 inch apart, and thin plants in stages to ultimately stand 8 to 12 inches apart. The thinnings should be kept for table use. Harvests from mature plants usually begin about two months from seed. For spring crop in the South, kale may be sown about two weeks before the last spring frost and harvested in six to eight weeks. For a spring or early summer harvest in the North, sow seed indoors or in a greenhouse as for broccoli and transplant hardened-off seedlings into the garden at about the time of the last spring frost. A nitrate-rich soil, occasionally fortified with a topdressing of well-rotted manure, yields the largest leaves. Although pests are few, it is prudent to rotate kale in the garden in successive years. Cutworms can be excluded by using paper collars around the stems of seedlings; cabbage worms can be controlled with the bacterium (*Bacillus thuringiensis*); gray aphids need only be dispersed with a strong stream from a hose or may be washed off after harvest.

Full-height cultivars, eventually reaching about 3 feet, include the following:

'Konserva': loosely curled, dark green foliage, curls more tightly after frost.
'Red Russian': flat, uncurled, purplish green foliage; more tender and milder flavored than most.
'Winterbor': tightly curled, blue-green foliage.

Especially suitable where garden space is limited, 'Dwarf Blue Curled Vates' bears blue-green foliage on stems scarcely more than 1 foot tall.

KALE, SEA
(*Crambe maritima*)

A denizen of sandy or gravelly sea coasts in Europe, sea kale adapts readily to the garden environment and is grown for the blanched young stems and leaf stalks, which are harvested in the spring and cooked as a delicacy. A long-lived perennial hardy to zone 5, sea kale usually requires three years to reach harvestable size. Clothed in large cabbagelike leaves, the stems may reach 3 feet and in time become woody at the base.

Seed should be sown directly in the garden after the last spring forst about ¼ inch deep and 2 inches apart, with seedlings transplanted to stand about 2 feet apart. Ordinary well-drained soil

Sea kale

of moderate fertility and near neutral pH suffices.

An unnamed form whose leaves have white stalks and midribs is especially attractive.

KOHLRABI
(*Brassica oleracea, Gongylodes group*)

Kohlrabi

A biennial of the cabbage clan, kohlrabi is grown for its swollen, spherical, tuber-like stem, which, whether eaten raw in salads or cooked as a vegetable, has a flavor suggestive of that of turnip. Although it thrives in mild weather, kohlrabi is quite heat tolerant. On the other hand, an unseasonal chill of 50°F or lower during the growing season may cause it to bolt

without the stem having fully thickened. From zone 8 south, kohlrabi may be grown as a late-season or winter vegetable; elsewhere it is a summer or early fall crop.

For very early crops, seed should be started indoors under fluorescent lights (14 to 16 hours per day) or in a greenhouse, as for broccoli, about six to eight weeks before the last spring frost. Grow the seedlings in cell packs, hardened off in a coldframe, and set out at about the time of the last spring frost. Recommended spacing between plants is 6 to 8 inches. Young hardened-off plants are reliably frost tolerant. Direct sowing in the garden, ¼ inch deep and 1 inch apart, may begin four weeks before the last spring frost. Prompt harvest of the swollen stems in about seven weeks, when they are about 2 inches thick, will avoid the fibrous pithiness that often develops in larger, older stems. Successive sowings at three-week intervals until about six weeks before the first fall frost will ensure a continuous supply. Paper stem collars will exclude cutworms from young transplants. Overaged stems may split or crack—another reason for early harvesting.

The various cultivars have either pale green ("white") skins or purple-green ("purple") skins; all have white flesh. White-skinned cultivars, traditionally favored as early crops, include 'White Vienna' and 'Grand Duke', which are harvestable about seven weeks from seed; 'Express Forcer' and 'Kolpac' are ready about one week sooner. Purple-skinned cultivars, somewhat more resistant to cracking, include 'Purple Vienna', 'Blaro', and 'Rapid', all harvestable in about seven weeks.

LEEK
(*Allium ampeloprasum* var. *porrum*)

Leeks

A close relative of onion, leek is a biennial grown mostly as a long-season annual for the tight cylinder of leaf bases and the relatively small bulb. Milder and sweeter flavored than onion, leek is used in soups and as a cooked vegetable. Harvest period extends from late summer to the following spring.

A slow-growing crop, leek is best started indoors under fluorescent lights (16 to 24 hours a day) or in a greenhouse about eight weeks before the last spring frost. Sow seed ¼ inch deep and ½ inch apart in flats at about 70°F (not above 80°F). Then grow the seedlings in individual cell packs at 60° to 70°F, harden off in a coldframe when about 1 foot tall, and set out in the garden about 4 inches apart roughly two weeks after the last spring frost. Garden soil should be well drained and deeply prepared—to about 1 foot— and have a pH of 6.5 to 7.0. A generous amount of well-rotted manure should be worked in. The larger the transplants and the more fertile and well prepared the soil, the larger the leeks will be at harvest. Transplants should be set 4 to 6 inches deeper in the garden soil than the young leeks were in the cell packs, i.e., with only

the leaf tips showing. This allows the desired blanching of the cylinder of leaf bases as growth advances. With later crops sown directly in the garden, blanching is achieved by hilling up the soil several times during the growing season, each time a little higher. Where rows are close, planks may be set on edge on either side and parallel to each row and the space between filled with compost. This not only achieves blanching but also protects the quality of the crop in severe winter weather. A loose mulch on top facilitates harvesting through the winter.

By growing a number of cultivars that ripen at different times, the harvest period may be extended. Long-season, winter-hardy cultivars include 'Broad London', 'Elefant', 'Longina', 'Unique', and 'Winter Giant' all requiring at least 20 weeks before harvest. Less winter hardy and recommended for fall harvest are 'French Summer', 'King Richard', 'Pancho', and 'Titan Summer', ripening in 10 to 15 weeks. 'Varna', ready for harvest in seven or eight weeks from seed, may be thickly sown (four seeds per inch) and harvested like bunching onions for use in salads.

LOVAGE
(*Levisticum officinale*)

A 6-foot-tall, easily grown European perennial of the carrot family and hardy to zone 5, lovage is usually considered an herb, but young leaf stalks may be blanched and used as celery. In addition, the fresh root may be grated and used raw in salads or prepared as a cooked vegetable.

Seed should be sown directly in the garden, ¼ inch deep and 1 inch apart, about four weeks after the last spring frost, and the seedlings thinned to stand about 2 feet apart in a location where they may grow undisturbed for years. The soil should be well drained and moderately fertile. By cutting some of the stems back to the ground from time to time during the summer, a fresh supply of young leaves is kept coming; hilling up will blanch the stalks. Roots may be dug at any time. Home propagation is by dividing roots in early spring or by harvesting ripe seed in summer. Shoots affected with leaf miners should be cut out and disposed of (not

composted). Lovage can escape cultivation; it is well naturalized in much of the United States. There are no cultivars.

MANGEL-WURZEL
(*Beta vulgaris*)

Mangel-wurzel is the name applied to a group of beet variants whose swollen roots have brown to orange-brown skins and yellow to orange flesh and usually reach a great size (10 pounds or more) by the end of the growing season. If harvested while still small, mangel-wurzel is very similar to garden beet in flavor and texture, but it becomes fibrous and coarse if allowed to mature. It is grown mainly in Europe for stock feed. Culture is as for beet. No garden cultivars of mangel-wurzel are available. For most, a yellow-rooted beet cultivar, such as 'Burpee's Golden', is a better choice than mangel-wurzel as a table vegetable.

MELON
(*Cucumis melo*)

Discussed in this section are melons other than cantaloupe and watermelon: the green- and yellow-fleshed honeydew and crenshaw cultivars.

Culture is essentially the same as for cantaloupe (see page 667), except that these melons are all sprawling in habit and require 4- to 6-foot spacing between hills. Honeydew skin turns from the unripe greenish white to light yellow or yellow-brown when ripe. In the crenshaw, the dark green skin turns yellow-green at maturity.

Honeydew and crenshaw cultivars of merit include the following. The small-fruited melons (1 to 4 pounds at maturity) are distinctive by their bright yellow skin and white flesh.

'Amber': fruit 10 pounds, ripens in 11 to 12 weeks from seed.
'Burpee Early Crenshaw': fruit 12 to 14 pounds, ripens in 12 to 13 weeks from seed; the largest of the standard melon cultivars.
'Earli-Dew': fruit 4 to 6 pounds, ripens in 11 to 12 weeks from seed.

'Early Silver Line': fruit 1 to 2 pounds, ripens in 10 to 11 weeks from seed.

'Limelight': fruit 7½ pounds, ripens in 13 to 14 weeks from seed.

'Passport': fruit 4 to 6 pounds, ripens in 10 to 11 weeks from seed.

'Sunrise': fruit 3 to 4 pounds, ripens in 12 to 13 weeks from seed.

'Venus': fruit 4 to 6 pounds, ripens in 12 to 13 weeks from seed.

MINER'S LETTUCE
(Montia perfoliata)

Also called winter purslane or Cuban spinach, miner's lettuce is a bright green, succulent-leaf annual of the Pacific Coast that is sometimes grown as a salad plant and included in salad mixtures called mesclun greens. It does best in zone 8 regions where summers are cool (seldom above 80°F) and winters mild. In such areas the paired, basally united leaves may be harvested almost throughout the year, and they confer a somewhat acidic flavor to salads.

Seed should be sown directly in the garden at about the time of the last spring frost, planted about ¼ inch deep and ½ inch apart, and the seedlings thinned in stages to ultimately stand 4 to 6 inches apart. A second sowing is advisable in mid to late summer. Harvests begin about six weeks from seed.

MUSHROOM

Increasingly popular in cooking and salads, mushrooms have gained in importance as objects for home culture. Of the dozen or so species most preferred for table use, the common button mushroom (*Agaricus bisporus*) accounts for most commercial production and is virtually the only one attempted by home gardeners.

The tyro is advised to gain initial experience with a prepared mushroom-growing kit, as is offered by various seedhouses. It is essentially a box filled with humusy substrate that has been inoculated with live "spawn" (a mycelium, or mass of fungus threads) that, when instructions are carefully followed, will grow and, in about four weeks, begin to yield a small crop that usually continues for a further four-week period. For ordinary home culture, any larger installation becomes a major undertaking that yields crops far in excess of table needs. Culture on such a scale usually involves putting up structures designed to facilitate the careful control of such factors as light, temperature, humidity, and air composition. It also involves finding commercial outlets for the periodic crops—which must be packaged by the grower.

MUSTARD
(Brassica juncea)

Mustard cultivars that are variously known as mustard greens, mustard cabbage, Chinese mustard, and so on are discussed here, not the species *B. hirta*, grown for oilseed, or *B. nigra*, grown for seed used to prepare the condiment mustard.

Cultivation of the annual mustards is the same as for Chinese cabbage (see page 645). Crops are most successful if seed is sown in early spring for harvest beginning, with most cultivars, in about six weeks, and again in late summer with harvest continuing until hard frost (25°F). Spacing should be about 6 inches between plants. Leaves may vary in flavor from mild to pungent, according to cultivar, and are most popular as salad components. Removal of flower stalks helps extend the harvest period in summer.

Cultivars with smooth green leaves that are mild in flavor include 'Green-in-Snow', a very hardy form; 'Burpee's Fordhook Fancy', more heat tolerant and slower to bolt than most; and 'Savanna', which offers harvestable leaves in three to four weeks from seed. 'Tendergreen' has curly, green, mild-flavored foliage, while in 'Mizuna' and 'Kyona' the green, mild-tasting leaves are deeply dissected and the midrib is white. Green-leaf cultivars with a pungent, peppery taste include 'Florida Broadleaf', with smooth leaves, and 'Southern Giant' and 'Green Wave', both with curly leaves. In 'Osaka Purple', the smooth, mild-flavored green leaves have purplish veins, and in 'Red Giant', the leaves are crinkled, pungent, and reddish green.

OKRA
(Abelmoschus esculentus)

A coarse tropical perennial that grows to 6 feet or more, okra is usually grown in the United States as an annual and is valued for the immature green pods that are cooked in soups, stews, stir-fries, and gumbo.

From zone 7 north, seed should be started indoors under fluorescent lights (14 to 16 hours per day) or in a greenhouse in cell packs, two seeds per cell, about six weeks before set-out time (with tomato plants). Sow ¼ inch deep and, after snipping out the weaker seedling and when roots become crowded, move to 3-inch pots, preferably of peat. Daytime temperatures of 80° to 90°F facilitate prompt germination; thereafter, 65° to 70°F temperatures aid rapid early growth. Harden off young plants in a coldframe for a week before planting in the garden. Seed may be sown directly in the garden from zone 8 south, and in any case, plants should stand about 12 inches apart. Disturbance of roots in transplanting, thinning, cultivating, or weeding will result in undersize plants and low yield. Soil should be well drained, fertile, and deeply prepared with well-rotted manure. A pH of 6.0 to 6.7 is recommended. Supplemental phosphate may be required for maximum yield. Generous soil moisture is essential; even so, foliage normally wilts in hot sun. When 3 to 4 inches long, pods should be harvested. Prompt harvest of immature pods is necessary for a continuing crop. In zone 9 and in warmer regions of zone 8, old stems may be cut back to stimulate basal sprouting and a second crop.

Cultivars for temperate-zone conditions include 'Clemson Spineless' and 'Perkins Mammoth Long Pod', both with pods still tender at 8 inches long. In 'Candelabra Branching', stems are basally self-branching, hence about 18 inches is required between plants. 'Dwarf Green Long Pod' and 'Lee' remain low, usually less than 3 feet, and bear densely. 'Annie Oakley' is more cold tolerant than most, hence better suited to northern culture. More ornamental than most, 'Burgundy' has reddish purple pods (that turn green when cooked), and in 'Red Okra' the pods and foliage are red.

PARSNIP
(Pastinaca sativa)

An aromatic biennial of Europe and temperate Asia, parsnip is grown as an annual for its tapering, whitish root. It is a long-season crop, normally harvested in the fall and winter and served as a cooked vegetable. Although most cultivars are slow growing, some mature early enough to be lifted in late summer. It is preferable to leave roots in the ground until needed.

For production of well-formed roots, soil must be well drained, friable, prepared at least 1 foot deep with well-rotted (not fresh) manure or compost, and free of stones and tree roots. As germination of seed is usually spotty and erratic in cold soil, and can fail altogether if the soil surface dries, gardeners in zone 6 and north may opt to start parsnip in deep 2- to 3-inch peat or plastic pots indoors under fluorescent lights (14 to 16 hours per day) or in a greenhouse about six weeks before set-out time (with tomato plants). Seed should be sown about ½ inch deep, three seeds to a pot, with the weaker two seedlings snipped out. After being hardened off in a coldframe, the young plants should be transplanted very carefully to the garden and spaced 3 inches apart. This method is especially useful with cultivars having short, half-long roots. Elsewhere, seed may be sown directly in the garden about 1 inch apart once the soil has warmed. Germination can take as long as three weeks, during which time the sown area must be kept continuously moist. Thin seedlings to 3 inches apart.

Of the relatively few cultivars, 'Hollow Crown', much grown commercially, and 'Lancer', a canker-resistant form, have mature roots up to 12 inches long and 3 inches in diameter. Both do best on loose, sandy soils. Cultivars with stumpy, half-long roots include 'Cobham Improved Marrow' and 'Harris Early Model', both of which succeed on relatively heavy soils.

POKE
(Phytolacca americana)

Although seldom cultivated for culinary purposes, poke, also called skoke, garget, and pokeweed, is sought after or even grown for its young, thick, asparaguslike shoots just after they emerge from the soil. They are cooked and eaten as a spring vegetable, especially in the South. Hardy to zone 4, this native perennial is usually encountered as a rank weed in waste places, where it sometimes reaches 8 feet. The violet black berries, eaten by various wildlife, contain hard seeds that are randomly dropped unaffected. Care should be taken not to include any part of the large, carrotlike root when harvesting poke, as this, and to a lesser extent the berries, contains a bitter, acidic saponin and the alkaloid phytolaccine, both of which are poisonous. If grown from seed, poke requires three or four years before the succulent shoots are large enough to harvest. It is preferable to transplant the dormant roots of young wild plants, spacing them about 1 foot apart in the row, than to start poke from seed.

POPCORN
(Zea mays)

A variant of field or grain corn, in which the stalks are allowed to mature and dry before the ears are harvested, popcorn is a long-season crop. After the cobs are picked and spread indoors to cure for several weeks, the glossy, hard kernels are stripped off. When subjected to high heat, they explode and increase 20 to 40 times their original mass.

Culture is the same as for sweet corn (see page 647). Ears are usually ready for harvest in 15 to 18 weeks from seed. Cultivars include the yellow-kernel 'Japanese Hull-less', 'Purdue 410', 'South American', and 'Robust 20-70'. Ripening its kernels in 10 to 15 weeks is the small-eared 'Tom Thumb'. Several small-eared ornamental corn cultivars also bear kernels suitable for popping: 'Miniature Colored' and 'Miniature Indian Ornamental' both have varicolored kernels, and 'Strawberry' has reddish brown kernels arranged in very short, rounded ears.

PUMPKIN
(Cucurbita spp.)

Two species produce fruit that is popularly called pumpkin (two others may also qualify, at least for culinary purposes) and are rank-growing, annual tendril climbers that are usually allowed to sprawl, especially in corn fields. In general, pumpkin is a large (sometimes enormous), somewhat flattened, more-or-less fluted winter squash that usually matures orange throughout and is used in baking and as a cooked vegetable as well as for autumnal decoration. Secondarily, the large yellow-orange flowers are included in various dishes, raw or cooked, and the edible seeds are roasted.

Culture is as for winter squash (see page 660), except that in the case of the very large-fruited cultivars, 6 to 8 feet should be left between hills, since crowding and mutual shading will compromise the mature size of individual fruit. Maturity is reached in 15 to 20 weeks, by which time the vines have usually died.

Parsnip

Cultivars of *C. pepo* include 'Connecticut Field' and 'Jack O'Lantern', much grown commercially and reaching as much as 25 pounds; 'Ghost Rider' and 'Triple Treat' are somewhat smaller; and 'Jack Be Little' and 'Baby Bear' are both quite flat and, at 3 to 6 inches in diameter, lilliputian among pumpkins. Smaller fruited cultivars produce greater numbers of pumpkins than larger fruited ones. Also derived from the same species is 'Bushkin', which bears 10-pound fruit on compact vines less then 6 feet long, and 'Lumina', a white-skinned form.

Cultivars of *C. maxima* include the record-large 'Atlantic Giant', which can be induced to bear fruit (one per plant) maturing at more than 300 pounds; 'Big Moon' at more than 200 pounds; and 'Big Max' at more than 100 pounds. Such cultivars of *C. moschata* as 'Landreth Cheese', 'Magdalena Big Cheese', and 'White-rind Sugar', if not stereotypically pumpkinlike externally, have flesh that is unquestionably pumpkinlike. As much can be said of 'Green-striped Cushaw', a cultivar of *C. mixta*.

QUINOA
(Chenopodium quinoa)

Also called quinua, quinoa is a 5-foot-tall annual that is native to the Andes and grown there for the seed, which is a staple grain. Although mostly a curiosity in the United States, quinoa grain, resembling sesame seeds, makes an interesting inclusion in bread and with cooked beans. The crop develops in the shortening days of late summer and early fall.

Culture is the same as for Good King Henry (see page 671).

RUTABAGA
(Brassica napus Napobrassica group)

Rutabaga, also called Swedish turnip or Swede, is a European biennial variant of rapeseed, which is grown for the large, thickened, purple-topped, yellow-fleshed, distinctly flavored root that is used as a cooked vegetable as well as in soups and stews.

Easily grown in a wide range of soils, rutabaga requires adequate potassium, phosphorus, and boron to develop solid,

well-formed roots. An excess of nitrate will sponsor lush foliage but substandard roots. A pH of 6.0 to 7.0 is best. Soil testing will help determine any needs. For customary fall and winter crops, sow seed directly in the garden 14 to 16 weeks before intended harvest. Sow ½ inch deep and about 2 inches apart, and thin seedlings to stand about 6 inches apart. Harvest should be preceded by several hard frosts to develop flavor. Harvested rutabaga may be stored like carrots (see page 646) or, after trimming, dipped in hot paraffin and stored in a cold, dry place, preferably at 35° to 40°F, where it should last for several months. Regular crop rotation and disposal of (not composting) any diseased plants will help control such potentially serious diseases as black leg, black rot, and turnip mosaic. All roots should be dug up in the fall or early winter.

Cultivars include the widely grown 'American Purple Top' and 'Laurentian Purple Top' as well as the somewhat hardier 'Canada Gem' and 'Pike'.

SALSIFY
(Tragopogon porrifolius)

Known also as oyster plant and vegetable oyster, salsify and the closely related scorzonera (*Scorzonera hispanica*), both European biennials with milky juice and hardy to zone 5, are grown for their taproots and young foliage. The roots are served as a cooked vegetable, and the leaves and shoots of overwintered plants are eaten either raw in salads or cooked. The whitish root of salsify is peeled after cooking; that of scorzonera is black and not peeled. Frost improves the flavor of both.

Seed should be sown in spring directly in the garden about ½ inch deep and 1 inch apart. Most any soil suffices so long as it is well drained and stone free. Seedlings should be thinned to stand 2 to 3 inches apart. Roots may be harvested all together and stored in damp sand in a cold place, or may be left in the ground, mulched, and dug as needed. For spring shoots and leaves, crowns should be mulched at the onset of severe winter weather.

'Gigantia' is a cultivar of salsify with stout, cylindrical roots.

SHALLOT
(Allium cepa)

Although shallot is commercially pricey, its culture is no more difficult than growing onion from sets. Of unknown but likely European origin, the shallot is hardy to zone 5 and is grown for the segmented bulbs that impart a distinctive flavor to salads or when cooked with other foods.

Shallot is propagated by naturally formed bulb segments, rather like those of garlic. North of zone 8, the bulb segments should be planted in early spring, about the time of the last frost, with the tops slightly above the soil surface and about 6 inches apart. Each segment should develop into a bulb with 8 to 10 segments. When the leaves begin dying back in the late summer or fall, the bulbs may be pulled, the tops braided, and hung to dry as for onions, or left in the ground to be harvested as needed. Winter mulch should be used to prevent deep freezing and facilitate winter harvesting. From zone 8 south, shallot is planted in early fall. For spring green onions or scallions in the North, shallot segments may be planted in the fall and mulched in winter, or forced indoors for winter harvest.

The cultivar 'French Shallot' has pinkish bulb flesh when cultivar is unspecified, the bulb color is usually yellow.

SKIRRET
(Sium sisarum)

Long grown as a winter vegetable in Europe and temperate Asia, skirret is a perennial that develops a thickened grayish root that, when cooked, has a flavor variously likened to that of carrot, parsnip, and parsley—all of which are fairly close relatives. The woody root core, whose extent varies from plant to plant, should be removed before cooking.

When propagated from seed, skirret culture is the same as for parsnip (see page 675). Root quality is best after frost, and the roots, hardy to zone 6, may be harvested through the winter as needed or pulled in fall and stored in a cold but frost-free place in damp sand. Root cuttings taken in spring before active growth begins may be used to grow future crops. Although wild populations of skirret are found chiefly in wet places, it adapts readily to ordinary garden conditions so long as the soil is consistently moist.

There are no cultivars.

SORGHUM
(Sorghum bicolor Saccharatum group)

More a curiosity than a serious crop for the home garden, sorghum, an annual grass that reaches 8 feet, has thick stems that contain a greenish sugary juice that is pressed out and concentrated over heat for use as a mild-flavored syrup. A plant of many other uses, sorghum is especially valued for its seed, which is used as feed grain for stock animals, in bird seed mixtures, and ground into cereal. Stems are used to make paper and their branched tops are made into brushes and brooms; the whole plant is used as fodder.

Seed is sown in the spring or, south of zone 8, in the fall; culture is the same as for sweet corn (see page 647).

Among the several cultivars, 'White African' yields a dark syrup, while that of 'Mennonite' is light. 'Keller' is tolerant of cool temperatures and is, therefore, advised for culture in the North.

SORREL
(Rumex acetosa)

Also called sour dock, sorrel is a long-lived perennial, is found around the world in the north temperate zones, and is hardy to zone 3. It produces basal clumps of light green leaves from early spring to late fall. The youngest of these are used sparingly in salads but generously in soups and

Sorrel

sauces, in all cases for their distinctive lemony acidic flavor.

Easily grown, sorrel should be started from seed sown directly in the garden in spring after the last frost about ¼ inch deep and 2 inches apart. Thin by stages until the remaining plants are 6 to 8 inches apart. Propagation may also be effected by dividing older clumps in early spring. Bolting commonly occurs in summer, but this has no affect on the production of basal leaves.

SOYBEAN
(Glycine max)

Apart from its importance as an oilseed; as the source of such highly proteinaceous foods as soy milk, soy ice cream, soy sauce, and tofu; and as forage and a cover crop, soy is grown for the flavorful green seeds, which are steamed or boiled as a vegetable, rather like lima beans. Better suited to northern latitudes and more productive, green vegetable soybeans average twice the protein content of limas. Pods are harvested and cooked as is when the contained two to four seeds are plump; after brief cooking the seeds are popped out by hand and cooked further before being served. Native to southern Asia and Australia, soybean has spawned several cultivars for green vegetable production.

Soybean is propagated by seed that is sown after the last spring frost about 1 inch deep and about 4 inches apart. Plants grow to 2 feet or a bit more. Either sandy or clay soil is suitable as long as it is well drained, includes substantial moisture-retaining organic matter, and has a pH of 5.7 to 6.2. Depending on soil test results, phosphorus and potassium supplements may be required.

In the cultivar 'Envy', the green beans are ready for harvest in 10 to 11 weeks, while 'Butterbean' is ready in 12 or 13 weeks. Vegetable soybeans may also be grown to maturity for hard or dry beans, and then cooked alone or with other vegetables. 'Black Jet', a black-seeded cultivar that ripens in about 15 weeks, is especially prolific.

SPINACH, MOUNTAIN
(Atriplex hortensis)

Known also as orach or German spinach, mountain spinach is an erect, rangy annual that grows to 8 feet or more. It is native to temperate Asia and locally naturalized in the United States. It is cultivated for the mildly acidic-flavored, triangular leaves, 3 to 4 inches long, and cooked as a distinctive spinach substitute in the summer or eaten raw in salads. The acidity can be diminished by adding sorrel.

In garden cultivation, it is best to prune out the seed heads as they form and to harvest the shoot tips frequently, thus maintaining a maximum height of about 3 feet. A plant or two allowed to go to seed, however, will furnish the next year's crop. Seed should be sown directly in the garden after the last spring frost about ¼ inch deep and 2 inches apart. Seedlings should be gradually thinned to ultimately stand about 18 inches apart (the thinnings harvested for table use).

The typical green-leaf form is favored for cooked greens, while the ornamental purplish leaved red orach (*A. hortensis* var. *rubra*) is used mostly in salads. There are no cultivars.

SPINACH, NEW ZEALAND
(Tetragonia tetragonioides)

New Zealand Spinach is a sprawling tropical perennial usually grown as an annual for its crisp, succulent foliage, which is eaten raw in salads or cooked as a spinach substitute in the summer.

The "seed"—really a dried fruit containing several seeds—is best softened in water for a day before being sown ½ inch deep and 3 inches apart, after danger of frost. Later, thin the seedlings to 12 inches apart. Harvest of leaves and shoot tips usually begins eight to ten weeks from seed. New Zealand spinach is most successful from zone 7 south, where at least three months of long, hot days and mild nights stimulate growth and permit continued picking.

The few named cultivars closely resemble the wild type.

SUNFLOWER
(Helianthus annuus)

For culinary purposes, sunflower, a native American annual, is grown for the large vitamin-rich seeds that are borne maximally in both size and number in cultivars that produce a single, immense, nodding or pendent flower head. The mature seeds are eaten raw, toasted, or sprouted. These and other cultivars are sources of sunflower oil, furnish nectar valuable to apiaries, and are valued for fodder.

A coarse plant growing 6 to 10 feet tall, sunflower will quickly reach full height if grown in well-drained, fertile soils that include generous amounts of well-rotted manure and have a pH of 6.7 to 7.5. Where exposed to wind, these top-heavy plants require staking. Sow seed directly in the garden after the last spring frost, setting them 1 inch deep and about 12 inches apart. Harvest is ready in 12 to 14 weeks.

Among the large-headed cultivars, 'Gray Striped' forms heads up to 20 inches in diameter, and 'Russian' up to 12 inches. 'Sundak', maturing in 10 to 11 weeks, is noted for its large seeds and disease resistance.

SWEET POTATO
(Ipomoea batatas)

A tropical, perennial, twining climber related to the morning glory, sweet potato is grown in the United States as an annual for its starchy root tubers, which, in its native haunts, if left unharvested, will grow for years and reach a great size. Although most cultivars have yellow or orange tuber flesh, skin color ranges from purple through reddish brown to yellow.

Propagation is usually by rooted stem cuttings, or sometimes by small tubers, planted in the spring after all danger of frost. Spacing should be about 3 feet between the usual long-stemmed plants, which most often are allowed to sprawl, but to save space, they may be supported with wire-mesh fencing. An interval of 18 inches is sufficient for compact "bush" types. For most cultivars, 13 to 15 weeks of warm weather is required to produce a crop of 15 to 30 tubers per plant. Hence, cultivation is most successful from zone 8 south. Optimal yields are had on well-drained, moist, sandy, organically enriched soil of pH 5.5 to 6.5. Soil deficiencies of such elements as calcium, magnesium, and boron can depress yield. Soil testing is advisable beforehand. Tubers should be carefully dug before hard frost, as bruising soon leads to decay, and frost is fatal. After curing for a week in warm, humid air, tubers may be stored for several months at about 60°F in 80 to 90 percent humidity.

Cultivars include the following:

'Beauregard': purplish skin; orange flesh.
'Bush Porto Rico': copper brown skin; red-orange flesh; a short-stemmed, nontwining bush cultivar.
'Centennial': orange skin; orange flesh; commercially popular.
'Georgia Jet': red skin; orange flesh.
'Sumor': yellow-brown skin; ivory to white flesh.
'Vardaman': orange skin; orange flesh; a short-stemmed, nontwining, bush cultivar.

The yam, superficially similar to the sweet potato, is actually the tuber of an unrelated plant, *Dioscorea batatas*. The yam is native to Southeast Asia and cultivated mostly in the tropics.

TOMATILLO
(Physalis ixocarpa)

Physalis ixocarpa

Known also as husk tomato or jamberry, the tomatillo is a subtropical annual from Mexico and grown throughout much of the United States for its cherry to egg-size fruit, which is encased in a papery husk. The fruit, which ripens yellow, is much prized in Mexican cooking, especially for salsa.

Left unpruned, the erect plants become rangy and diffuse as they approach their 3- to 5-foot maximum height, but they may be trimmed back somewhat without affecting the crop. Fruit production is normally generous and continuous from midsummer to frost. Culture is the same as for tomato (see page 662). The cultivar

'Toma Verde' is especially suited to zones 5 through 7.

TURNIP
(Brassica rapa Rapifera group)

Originating in Europe, turnip is a biennial grown as an annual throughout temperate regions and the highland tropics for its swollen root, which ranges from long and slender to flattish spherical and has a white skin (often with purple shoulders) and white to yellow flesh. It is eaten raw in salads or used as a cooked vegetable.

Although cool, moist summers are best, cultivars that tolerate hot weather are also available. Turnips should be started directly in the garden from early spring, about the time of the last frost, to midsummer, preferably at three-week intervals. Sow seed about ½ inch deep and 1 inch apart, thinning seedlings (which soon develop radish-size roots) in stages to ultimately stand about 4 inches apart. Turnip is flavorful and not woody if harvested small and young, i.e., in seven to nine weeks from seed and while 2 to 3 inches in diameter. Turnip is also grown for its foliage, which is harvested when the leaves are about 6 inches long and used like spinach. A well-drained, friable, moisture-retentive soil enriched with well-rotted manure or compost and a pH of 5.5 to 6.5 is ideal. Sustained soil moisture is essential to full root development. Root maggots can reduce crop quality and may require treatment of the soil. Flea beetles can be controlled with Pyrethrum.

Cultivars grown primarily for roots include the very popular commercial favorite 'Purple-top White Globe' as well as 'Royal Crown', which both have purple shoulders. 'Market Express', 'Presto', 'White Egg', and 'White Lady' are all white and harvestable in five to seven weeks. Red skinned, white fleshed, and suggestive of large radishes are 'Scarlet Queen' and 'Ohno Scarlet'. In 'Longue de Caluire', the roots are long with black skin and white flesh, and in 'Amber Globe', best grown as a late-season crop, the roots are yellowish. Among cultivars grown primarily for greens, 'All Top' is especially satisfactory.

WATERMELON
(Citrullus lanatus)

Watermelon is an annual tendril climber or creeper from sub-Sahara Africa and has wide-ranging stems. It is grown in most all warm temperate and tropical regions for its large, edible fruit and it enjoys much popularity in the United States. In form, the fruit varies from spherical to oblong, with skin coloration ranging from solid dark green or yellow to mottled or striped light and dark green. The flesh ranges from pink to red and even yellow.

To grow watermelon from zone 6 north is often difficult because of an insufficient growing season. Cultivation is the same as for cantaloupe (see page 667). Criteria for harvest readiness, which is usually reached in 9 to 11 weeks from seed, include a dull thud when the fruit is thumped with the fingers, a color change of the shade patch, or resting surface, of the fruit from white to yellow, and the browning of the stem tendril nearest the fruit.

Cultivars with wide-ranging habit and 8- to 10-pound oval or oblong fruit with solid green skin and red flesh include 'Park's Whopper' and the similar but mottled or striped-skinned 'Sweet Favorite'. Also similar but bearing spherical fruit with solid green skins is 'Sugar Baby'. Small-fruited, compact or "bush" cultivars include 'Garden Baby', with mottled skin, and 'Bush Baby', with solid green skin. Seedless (actually few-seeded) cultivars include 'Dixie Queen', 'Honey Red Seedless', and 'Nova', all of which must be grown with normal black-seeded plants of another cultivar to fruit. 'Golden Crown', a full-seeded type, is distinctive with yellow skin over red flesh. Among the larger fruited, green-skinned, red-fleshed cultivars are 'Winter Melon', which has 15-pound fruit; 'Sangria', which has 25-pound fruit; and 'Cobb Gem', which has 50-pound (or heavier) fruit. Watermelon cultivars with yellow-fleshed fruit and mottled or striped green skins include 'Moon and Stars', 'Sunshine', and 'Yellow Baby'.

28

Fruits and Nuts in the Home Garden

THE FRUIT GARDEN

A carefully planned and well-maintained fruit garden can be a constant source of satisfaction to the home owner. Beyond yielding a bountiful and varied supply of fruit during the growing season, fruit trees and bushes can play an important part in the overall home landscape, and a healthy and thriving fruit garden around one's house can add immeasurably to gardening pleasure, to say nothing of increasing the value of the property. Moreover, given adequate space, fruit

Where space is limited, as in most home gardens, bearing grapes may be trained to grow on perimeter fences.

production that exceeds your household needs can be a source of supplemental seasonal income.

Many choice cultivars bear fruit, often far superior in quality to what is grown commercially, that may be produced in the home garden. When fruit is to be shipped a great distance, harvesting takes place long before the fruit is fully ripe, and much of its potential sweetness and flavor never develop in consequence. Fruit grown in the home garden may be harvested at its finest stage of ripeness and will possess a quality usually unobtainable in the commercial market.

In addition to their purely utilitarian uses, most fruit trees have a decidedly decorative value. Few garden subjects are more beautiful than an apple tree in full bloom, and both pear and apple trees can be very picturesque at any season. They may be used as shade trees on the terrace or lawn; they may grace the driveway; or they may be espaliered, trained to grow in a geometric pattern against a wall.

An espalier is a trellis or open support on which a vine or a woody plant may be trained. Espaliered trees are usually trained to a given number of branches (see illustration), and they should preferably be grown on a wall facing southeast. Espaliered fruit trees have long been traditional in English and French gardens and have become increasingly popular in this country. Apples, pears, peaches, plums, nectarines, and quinces may be readily induced to grow in this way. Espaliered fruit trees are especially useful where space is limited, as in a small urban garden or on a rooftop.

As a principle, it should be clear that wherever and however fruit (and nut) trees are grown, they require varying degrees of special care to bear full crops.

Since most fruits are borne on long-lived woody plants, the planning, selection, and planting—especially of the trees and large shrubs—are not likely to be repeated and hence should be done as carefully as possible. It is wise to determine which fruits grow and bear well in your area. It helps to discuss successes and problems that others have had growing various fruits in your locale. The local state extension service should also be consulted, especially about locally prevalent pests and diseases of fruit crops, about repelling or excluding deer, about controlling rodents, and about any local difficulties with unassisted pollination.

Where space is limited, fruit trees may be espaliered against walls, fences, or buildings by training selected branches of young trees on support wires. Fruit set is reduced, but size is often above average.

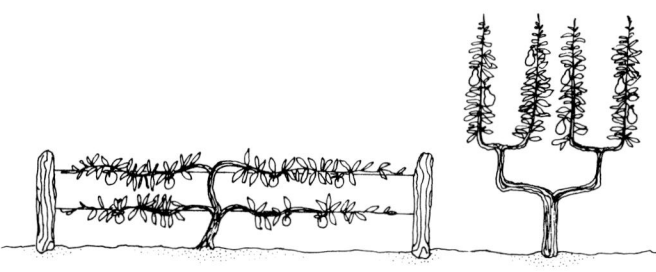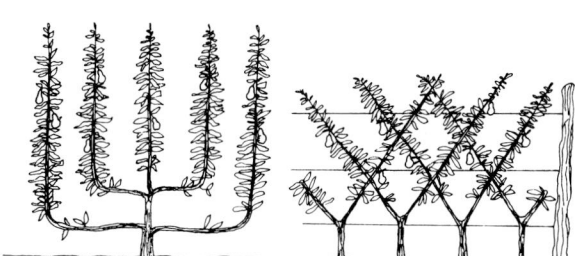

Four examples of espaliered fruit trees

It is necessary first to decide and plan what fruits you want for your garden. The space available, climate, exposure, and your personal taste are the primary determinants. When these decisions have been made, the order for stock should be placed well in advance of planting time. There are many dependable mail-order catalog companies that provide the home gardener with good quality and a wide choice of materials. If ordering is delayed, fulfillment may be slowed by the rush season, and supply of certain cultivars exhausted. Therefore, by ordering early and stating the desired shipping date, the stock will arrive in ample time for best planting. It is ideal to to plant stock as soon as the frost is out of the ground and before growth has begun.

Before any planting takes place, however, be sure to have the soil tested, at least to determine its pH, since this factor affects the availability of soil nutrients to the fruit trees and bushes. For most, the soil must be well drained (though this is not the case for tall blueberries); sandier soil is better for peach and nectarine, heavier for apple and cherry. Pear and plum succeed on a wide range of soils, but not if it is soggy. For most fruit trees, a pH between 5.5 and 6.5 suffices, but for apple the range is 6.0 to 7.0. Bush fruits do well on a wide range of well-prepared garden soils, and, for the most part, with a pH between 6.0 and 7.0. Blueberries stand alone in requiring strongly acidic soils—pH 4.5 to 5.0 is ideal—and thrive in mucky, boggy ground. Grapes should be grown exposed to full sun in sandy, humusy, slightly acidic soil (pH 6.0 to 6.5).

Choosing Cultivars

In preparing an order, the home gardener must specify the cultivars or "varieties" wanted in each of the fruit categories chosen, making sure that the desired cultivars are hardy under local conditions. Most hardy fruit cultivars are dependable in zones 5 through 8, but there are numerous exceptions.

Tree Fruits

Trees are graded according to their height and thickness of trunk and are priced accordingly. Fruit trees are offered in two or three sizes of one- and two-year-old stock. The A, or best, grade usually costs little more than a smaller tree. It seems to be a matter of preference as to whether one- or two-year-old stock is planted. However, there is no doubt that the best grade should be purchased, regardless of age.

Keeping in mind that fruit trees are usually sold bare-root, i.e., dug while dormant and sold or shipped without soil, the main advantages in purchasing one-year-old trees are the following.

1. Not as many roots are cut or broken in transplanting.
2. The tops are more easily pruned to a desired height.
3. As they are usually unbranched, there is less likely to be damage to the top.
4. You can make your own selection of branching pattern as growth proceeds.
5. Because they are smaller than two-year-old or older transplants, they are more easily handled and planted.

Dwarf Trees

Where space for tree fruit culture is limited, as on many urban and suburban properties, dwarf fruit trees have a special appeal. Dwarfing of fruit trees is achieved by grafting a standard cultivar on a dwarfing rootstock. This rootstock causes the tree to make less annual growth and remain smaller throughout its life than would be the case if the standard cultivar remained on its own roots. These dwarf trees are better suited to many home grounds not only because they occupy less space but also because they begin bearing at an earlier age, bear fruit that is more easily reached for harvest, and are easier to prune and otherwise maintain.

Dwarf fruit trees are available in two basic sizes: the very dwarf, which are often trained for espalier (but need not be so grown) and often stay lower than 8 feet, and the so-called no-ladder trees, which mature at 10 to 12 feet. Very dwarf apples, for example, are grafted onto Malling IV rootstock (named for the agricultural research station in England that developed this grafting system to control apple tree size), while no-ladder types are on Malling VII rootstock.

When planting grafted dwarf trees, be sure that the point of the graft or union is left above ground. If it is covered with soil, roots may form, causing a dwarf cultivar to grow on to standard dimensions.

In addition to single-cultivar grafts, multiple-cultivar grafts are also grown, especially in dwarf apples, usually as a curiosity than for substantial production. They do, however, offer great diversity in a small space, although at considerable initial cost. Regrettably, the individual grafts seldom have equal life expectancy, and so in time they tend to weaken and die, one by one.

Bush Fruits

Popular fruits that are borne on shrubs are called bush fruits. Bush fruits are preferred by many because they are more easily handled at all stages than trees and obviously occupy much less space. Moreover, they can be more readily integrated into the vegetable garden or used as ornamental subjects elsewhere on the grounds.

For the purchaser, two sizes are usually offered: one-year-olds and two-year-olds. A well-grown two-year-old bush will give excellent results and possibly produce fruit sooner and in larger quntities than a one-year-old bush. The only reasons to buy one-year-old bushes are to reduce initial cost and, in marginal habitats, to lessen transplanting shock.

Care of Bare-Root Stock

Often the stock is received before planting conditions are satisfactory. The site may not yet be prepared or the soil may be too wet. Other growing materials arriving at the same time of year may cause a delay in planting.

As soon as the stock is received, it should be removed from the package and its roots immersed in a bucket of water. If there is to be a delay of more than one or two days in planting at the chosen site, the material should be planted temporarily in a long shallow trench (i.e., "heeled in"), preferably away from bright sun and wind or, if this is unavoidable, tipped southward to about 45° to minimize the possibility of trunk and branches being sun scorched. Alternatively, bare-root material may be kept in a cool, damp cellar for several days. In any case, the roots should not be permitted to dry out, and final planting should take place before the buds begin to open. The roots should have a chance to grow before the weather warms and active top growth begins. For this reason, the earlier the stock is planted in the spring, the greater the chance it will have to establish its root system before the buds begin to swell. This will result in greater shoot growth the first season than if planting occurs later.

Nursery stock may also be planted in the fall. In some cases, fall planting may be advisable, especially if the soil is heavy clay and apt to be too wet at planting time in early spring. Weather conditions are generally more stable in the fall and the soil may be in better condition for planting. On the other hand, the advantages of spring planting are that the stock makes considerable top and root growth before winter, and thus is better able to resist dieback the first winter.

Laying Out and Planting an Orchard

Well-defined planting distances are recommended for each type of fruit. As these recommended intervals are the product of much experimentation and experience, they should be carefully observed. The distances in most cases may seem excessive, especially for standard tree fruits, but it should be borne in mind that they are determined by the likely branch spread of the mature tree. If fruit trees are planted too close, the tops eventually grow together, casting shade on lower branches, causing the tops to grow abnormally high, reducing fruit yield, and often causing the fruit to be borne near the top of the tree.

If unlike fruit trees, such as apples and cherries, are to be planted in adjacent rows, the recommended intervals for each should be added together and the sum divided in half. This figure is the interval to be used in spacing the unlike kinds.

When digging a hole for a fruit tree, lay aside the darker topsoil and keep it separate from the often lighter subsoil. If the soil is dense and firm, loosening it with a fork will ease planting and facilitate root growth. Make the hole wide enough to spread out the roots. Crowding roots into an undersize hole will not only result in substandard growth but often leads to toppling years later. In sandy soils, make the hole deep enough to set the tree 2 to 3 inches deeper than it was in the nursery (except in basally grafted trees, such as dwarf apples); if the soil is heavy clay, the planted tree can be set slightly higher than the nursery depth. By digging the hole so that the sides are vertical, the roots can be spread deeply, allowing an even depth of topsoil to be backfilled over the roots. This soil should be tamped lightly and watered before the subsoil is spread over the top of the hole, and again tamped and watered. No manure or other fertilizer should be incorporated with the backfill at planting time. Instead, a mulch or topdressing of well-rotted manure or compost should be spread around the tree after planting is completed, both to provide supplemental nutrients by slow percolation and to help conserve soil moisture during the critical first summer.

Where advisable, as when newly planted trees have disproportionately small roots or slender trunks, staking should be employed, following the instructions given in Chapter 11. Care should be taken to remove stakes after one or two years to avoid chafing or girdling of trunks or limbs. Fruit-laden limbs of older trees may require temporary props to prevent breakage.

Pollination of Fruit Trees

Pollination is the transfer of pollen grains from the saclike anther tip of the stamen to the stigma or receptive surface of the female part of the flower that, once pollinated and its contained ovules or rudimentary seeds fertilized, becomes the fruit. In many fruit trees and bushes, the pollen is borne in small quantities and is too heavy and sticky to be carried far by the wind. Instead, it is inadvertently picked up and carried on the bodies of insects attracted to the flowers by their color or scent and nectar. Some of this adhering pollen is accidentally dusted on the stigmas of other flowers as the insects continue their flower-by-flower search. When pollination is effective and the ovules are fertilized, the fruit begins to grow. Ineffective pollination results in aborted fruit.

In some cultivars of fruits, the pollen is capable of fertilizing the ovules of the same cultivar, while others must receive pollen from a different cultivar to effect fruit set. Failure of fruit set may result from any of the following:

1. Lack of viable pollen.
2. Discharge and receipt of pollen at a time when the stigma is not receptive.
3. An insufficient amount of viable pollen produced (a problem in certain cultivars).
4. Too great a physical separation of male and female flowers when flowers of each sex are borne on separate plants.

In most fruit trees and bushes, the male and female structures in a flower mature at different times, thus favoring cross-fertilization over self-fertilization and illuminating the importance of pollination vectors—chiefly bees—in fruit culture.

Originally, fruit trees were grown from seed. This practice resulted in wide variation in the fruit quality of the progeny, most of which was inferior. Little was understood about pollination and fertilization. So many different variants were planted together that cross-pollination took place naturally. Once it was learned that superior individuals could be propagated vegetatively, with each new tree producing fruit exactly like those of the tree from which it came, fruit growers concentrated on fewer but better types. These cultivars were propagated by cuttings or grafting, which not only ensured unvarying perpetuation of the desired fruit qualities but also permitted mass-planting of any cultivar. But when an orchard, or a tree, of one cultivar is planted too far from trees of another cultivar whose pollen is required for fruit set, corrective measures must be taken. There are two common methods.

The quickest method is to place bouquets of flowers of another cultivar in the tree at blooming time. These bouquets should be placed in pails of water so that the flowers will last some days, and should be hung in the uppermost part of the tree. This method depends on adequate numbers of bees or other pollinating insects. In large orchards where wild bee populations may be insufficient, rented hives of honeybees are placed nearby to help ensure effective pollination.

The second method is to top graft a different cultivar into the tree. Usually three or four years are needed to get results from this approach. Meanwhile, bouquets of picked flowers should be used to maintain fruit production.

Before choosing any fruit tree cultivars, it is prudent to check with your county cooperative extension agent for any recommendations or caveats.

Growth and Fruiting in Popular Fruit Trees

There is often considerable variation in the time that two different cultivars of the same fruit type will come into flower and even between two individuals of the same cultivar. Usually, this reflects genetic differences between cultivars or simply idiosyncrasies of the location. Differences between fruit types or species are to be expected; for example, some cultivars of apple require eight years before the first crop is produced, while most peach and sour cherry cultivars begin bearing within three years.

Until a fruit tree begins to produce flower buds, it usually makes vigorous vegetative growth, sometimes as much as 4 or 5 feet a year. As a tree prepares to bear flowers and fruit, some of its buds are larger and more plump; these buds contain rudimentary flower parts; the smaller buds contain rudimentary foliage. In time, short spurlike lateral twigs develop on the straighter vegetative twigs of apple and pear trees. Similar changes take place on cherry and plum trees. Peach buds become noticeably larger, with two large floral buds flanking a central vegetative one. As the tree matures, terminal vegetative growth slows down to 12 to 18 inches a year, or even less, with flower buds predominating and fruit production increasing.

Apples and pears are borne terminally on spurs, most of which occur laterally along vegetative branches and twigs. The flower bud is actually mixed, usually containing five (though varying from three to eight) flowers surrounding a cluster of leaves. Spurs grow irregularly, as compared to the straight vegetative axes. When a spur fruits, a small bud forms to one side, and this will bear only leaves the next season but will be succeeded by a flower bud that will open the following spring. Thus each spur produces fruit no oftener than alternate years. When a tree bears a heavy crop one year and none the next, this is often because all of its spurs have borne the first year, and thus it is a biennial bearer until some spurs break the pattern, resulting in the normal production of fruit each year. Fruit spurs in apple and pear trees usually continue producing for 10 to 12 years and seldom exceed 8 or 12 inches in length. Successor fruit spurs develop on new vegetative twigs.

In plum and cherry trees, flower buds are borne on spurs, and each bears two to four flowers. Smaller leaf buds also appear on spurs; the tip or terminal bud is always vegetative. Peach trees bear their fruit from lateral buds borne along the previous season's growth, usually two on either side of a vegetative bud. Quince bears its flowers on shoots of the season; i.e., on side shoots that grow quickly in the spring, each terminating in a single flower.

Grapes, while not trees, have distinctive flowering habits. In nature, each vine of a wild species bears either male (staminate) or bisexual flowers; in grape cultivars, however, all flowers are bisexual. Flower buds develop on the current season's growth. If some are damaged by frost, others develop and bloom. The buds grow in clusters and if, on female vines, they are effectively pollinated, fruit ensues.

Pruning Fruit Trees

Although each type of fruit tree has its own idiosyncracies, as indeed does each individual tree, there are, nevertheless, some basic principles that apply to all. In general, pruning is best done in late winter. Depending on the size of the twig, branch, or limb to be cut, you will need pruning shears, loppers, or a pruning saw.

1. Dead, broken, and diseased branches should be removed promptly, at any time of year. In winter, dead branches are brittle, have shriveled and eventually shredding bark, and have hard, undersize buds that easily break off.
2. High branches should be removed to prevent their shading more accessible lower ones.
3. Unproductive branches, such as fast-growing, erect suckers, or "water sprouts," should be removed as they appear.
4. Low, hanging, shaded, unproductive branches should be removed.
5. Thin, weak, overcrowded spurs that bear little fruit should be removed.
6. Any large limbs to be removed should be cut in stages or sections to avoid damaging nearby branches. The final cut should be flush with the trunk or nearest large limb. An undercut through the bark and sapwood before a final cut from above will prevent the bark from tearing when the limb falls.

CULTURAL INSTRUCTIONS FOR FRUIT TREES

APPLE
(Hybrids between Malus pumila and M. sylvestris)

Historically, the hybrid apple originated naturally in southwest Asia, probably in or near the Caucasus, and was known in ancient Egypt, Greece, and Rome. It has since been introduced throughout the temperate-zone world and also in the highland tropics. The need for extended cold dormancy is the principal limiting factor to its further spread.

Planting Age
One- and two-year-old trees are best for planting, as they recover very quickly from transplanting shock, are lowest in price, and are easily handled. Older trees may be planted but only if sufficient soil is moved with the roots—an operation that can be costly and risky.

Time of Planting
Apple trees may be planted during the late fall or early spring months when they are in a dormant condition. North of zone 8, early spring planting is preferable to fall planting as a precaution against winter dieback. Bear in mind that the root system of a tree is active long before noticeable top growth has begun to take place. Therefore, late fall or early spring planting is most desirable so that the root system will have begun growth before the buds swell and open. A tree that is well established on its root system before top growth actually begins will make more vigorous growth the first season.

Soil
A deep, well-drained, loamy soil, well supplied with organic matter, and free of hardpan and shelf rock, will give good results. Heavy clay soils that tend to waterlogging should be avoided. On the other hand, adequate moisture in summer is vital.

Planting Distance
Standard apple trees should be planted 40 feet apart in all directions. They may, however, be set as close as 30 feet apart each way if space is extremely limited and the cultivars are not of the most vigorous growth. Full dwarfs may be spaced about 10 feet apart; half-dwarfs, or no-ladder trees, about 15 feet.

Method of Planting
To plant a fruit tree, dig a hole just large enough to receive the roots without crowding and deep enough to set the tree deeper (except in the case of grafted dwarfs) or shallower, according to the soil type (see page 684). When removing the soil, keep the sides of the hole vertical so that it is as wide at the bottom as at the top.

Trim off any broken, injured, or excessively long roots to within the bounds of the hole, and place the tree in the hole. Put the topsoil in first and firm it around the roots. Then put the subsoil in and firm it again.

Pruning Newly Planted Trees
The purpose of pruning and determining the branching of young trees is to establish

For the small property, dwarf apple cultivars stay in bounds and ripen all fruit within reach.

a strong framework of branches, which will satisfactorily carry the future load of fruit.

The top of a one-year-old apple tree should be cut back to a height of 36 inches from the ground after it has been set out.

Two-year-old trees may contain many branches. In this case it is essential to choose the branches for the framework and remove the others when the tree is planted. Choose three or four branches making at least a 45° angle with the trunk, and about 6 inches apart. Of course, they should not diverge on the same plane and should be spaced uniformly around the tree for balance. The lowest branch should be at least 18 inches from the ground. Those that are less vigorous may be removed. However, it is best to leave some branches that are not too thick or that do not directly compete with each other, as they materially aid in increasing the total growth.

Time of Pruning Young Trees

Pruning may be done any time the trees are in a dormant condition. However, as winter killing begins at the tip of a branch, pruning should not be done until the coldest part of the winter is past and not later than the time at which the buds begin to swell.

Pruning Young Prebearing Trees

Pruning should be as light as possible until the tree reaches its bearing age. This age varies greatly according to the cultivar. Remove one of two closely parallel branches; one of two crossing branches; and branches that are weak, cause crowding, or appear diseased. Do not remove any branch that may not be interfering at present just to get rid of it. Such branches are a great help to the tree for several years. Do not allow any of the rapidly heightening, so-called scaffold branches to grow beyond the leader or main central stem. This will necessitate some cutting back each year as the leader should be several inches longer than the others. Always cut back to buds on one-year-old wood or to lateral branches on older wood. Permit some branches to fill in the center of the tree without overcrowding.

Pruning Young Bearing Trees

It is normal for initial crops in young trees to be light. Pruning should be minimal during this period, as drastic changes may cause bearing to be interrupted for several years.

Pruning Older Bearing Trees

Pruning is beneficial for a bearing apple tree, but it may be overdone if you do not understand the principles involved. It is preferable to watch someone with experience demonstrate this pruning for you. Less damage is caused by lack of pruning than by pruning done the wrong way. Correctly pruned, an apple tree can be kept in a high state of production for many years.

When a tree begins to bear and form fruit-producing points, it becomes less vegetative and vigorous than it was previously. The amount of terminal growth is less and is made in the spring within a period of three to four weeks. Fruit spurs are formed, which will bear the fruit. Inept pruning at this stage can cause fruit production to stop.

The procedure for pruning is as follows:

1. Study the tree from a distance of 15 to 20 feet. Try to visualize how it should look when properly pruned.
2. First remove all dead and diseased wood as well as any suckers or water sprouts.
3. If any large branches must be removed, make your decision on the ground and not up in the tree. Branches look entirely different from these two points of view. One is justified in removing a large branch if it is
   • Rubbing against another.
   • Running parallel to another only a few inches away.
   • Heavily shaded by a branch above it.
   • Growing up through the center of the tree through many other branches.
   • Too close to the ground.
   • Growing back toward the center and interfering with other branches.
   • Broken or diseased.
   • Long, spindly, and weak.
4. Thin out the remaining branches by removing
   • Those that are crossing, crowding, parallel, broken, or diseased.
   • Those that are weak and spindly.
   • Those that are growing in the wrong direction.
5. If the branches are extra long and growing out of bounds, cut them back to within the same range as the others. Always cut back flush to a lateral branch on wood more than one year old. The intent is to promote bushier lateral growth.
6. Scrape any loose bark off with the back of the saw, hoe, or tree scraper. This will remove hibernating places for the codling moth, scale, and other insects.

Duration of Fruit-bearing

Many apple cultivars bear fruit 4 or 5 years after planting and reach their full bearing at 12 to 15 years, while some do not begin to bear until they are at least 8 years old. Some cultivars live much longer than others. Although factors such as soil, fertilization, insect pests, and diseases will affect any tree. However, with good cultural methods, a tree should bear over a period of 40 years.

Overcoming Failure to Bear

The principal causes of failure to bear fruit are the following.

1. Insufficient soil nitrogen.
2. Severe or improper pruning.
3. Lack of pollinating insects.
4. Wrong cultivars for the location.
5. Lack of pollen supply at the time needed (as may occur during prolonged rain at flowering time).

Cultivation

Weeds compete with trees for nutrients and water. This competition can be most harmful when the trees are newly set or are just about to bear. By keeping weed growth suppressed, the tree is able to make a better and faster start. Cultivation should consist of removing weeds immediately around the young trees and mowing the weeds between the rows. Cultivation should cease four to six weeks before fall

An apiary near an orchard helps supply the bees needed for pollination and also furnishes honey for the table or for sale.

Any fertilizer should be spread to the tree's dripline, i.e., the reach of the tree's outer branches. It is not necessary to fork or rake such supplements into the soil. Deep forking or spading can easily damage or sever many roots.

When trees are growing on a lawn, the best method is to make holes with a stick or bar under the outer branches 12 to 18 inches apart, 1½ inches in diameter, and about 6 inches deep. Fill them almost to the top with fertilizer. It is not necessary to cover these holes with soil or other material. Using this method, the fertilizer soon dissolves and percolates to where the roots can absorb the nutrients.

Fertilizing Bearing Trees

In general, bearing trees should be fertilized regularly. In addition to producing a crop of fruit, a bearing tree should make about 1 foot of terminal growth each year. Many bearing trees are biennial bearers, which means that they bear a heavy crop one year and few if any fruits the following year. However, fertilization should be just as regular as with an annual bearer, since no fruit spur will bear two years in succession and each type of tree requires about the same supply of nutrients overall. Fertilizers help stimulate the formation of flower buds for the next year's crop. For a full-grown tree, 100 pounds of well-rotted manure or 5 to 7 pounds of a complete commercial fertilizer is sufficient.

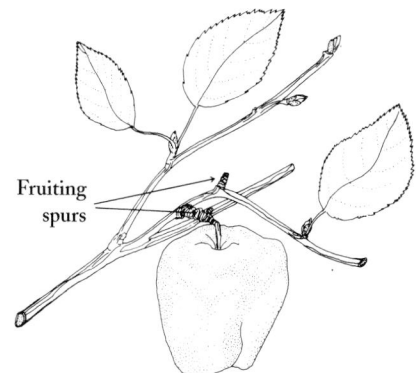

Fruiting spurs

Fruiting spur of an apple tree

begins, so the trees will be hardened off and in good condition to withstand the cold winter months.

If cultivation is not possible, as is the case on lawns, the next best treatment is to keep the weed or grass growth cut. Two cuttings per season is usually sufficient. If possible, these cuttings should be used as a mulch under the tree.

Fertilization
Fertilizing Prebearing Trees

Prebearing trees are those that have not reached bearing size. The importance of supplying nutrients for development of a large bearing framework for future years is obvious. If a tree makes 12 to 18 inches or more of terminal growth each year, supplemental fertilizer is not indicated. If, however, such a tree makes less than 12 inches of growth, fertilizing the site is not only justifiable but important to the tree reaching bearing condition.

A high-grade complete fertilizer or some form of organic supplement should be used. For best results, the nitrate in the fertilizer should be available to the young tree as soon as growth begins.

The amount of fertilizer applied is determined by the tree's size and age. A two-year-old tree should receive about 25 pounds of well-rotted manure or about 6 ounces of 10-10-10 commercial fertilizer; these amounts are gradually increased as the tree grows.

Thinning

When a tree has set an overabundance of fruit, some should be removed to prevent branches from breaking and to increase the size of the remaining fruit. Thinning should be practiced four to five weeks after the fruit has begun to form. Only one apple should be left in a cluster, and individual apples should be 6 to 8 inches apart on a limb or branch. If one side of a tree has practically no fruit and the other side is heavily laden, good-size fruit will develop with little thinning. To prevent breaking the spur, snip the stalk near the apple when harvesting so that its base remains attached to the spur.

With early-ripening cultivars, thinning may be delayed until six weeks after the blossoms have set fruit. Then the fruit to be removed is large enough and soft enough to use for pies and applesauce.

Apples should be harvested when the mature fruit color, specific to the cultivar, has developed and before any significant fruit drop has begun. Fallen fruit is often past its prime and soft, hence subject to bruising and unsuited to storage.

Minimizing the Use of Pesticides and Fungicides

Apples are subject to numerous pests and diseases, some of which can be serious and even devastating to the crop. Thanks to assiduous efforts in recent decades to develop disease-resistant cultivars, it is possible to grow apples without ritual resort to poisonous sprays. In addition to choosing resistant cultivars, the home apple grower will find that the following procedures help ease the travail that was once associated with apple culture.

1. Smother young San José scale and the eggs of red mites and various aphids with horticultural oil, a nontoxic preparation sprayed on dormant apple trees in early spring, just as the leaves emerge about ½ inch from the buds.

2. Remove sources of pests and diseases, especially any dead, dying, or abandoned apple, pear, or hawthorn trees within 200 yards. These are sources of leaf rollers and codling moths. Active infestations of these pests can be controlled with Bt or Dipel (*Bacillus thuringiensis*) which is toxic only to their larvae.

A drench of horticultural oil in early spring helps control a range of pests that overwinter on dormant fruit trees.

3. Control plum curculio (betrayed by crescent-shaped scars on young fruit that drops prematurely in early summer) and other fruit and foliage pests by spraying phosmet (Imidan), which is the safest of the synthetics and is, in this case, far more effective than natural preparations or botanicals. Mixed with a sticking agent (such as Nufilm), the first spraying is made at the very first sign of scars on young fruit. Daily inspection after flowering is vital, as the curculio adults swarm in quickly, especially on mild, damp evenings. The second spraying is made whenever new wounds appear.

4. Trap the flies whose larvae are destructive apple maggots by using any more or less apple-size red spheres as decoy apples. Cover them with a sticky polybutane preparation such as Tangle-Trap and hang them at 3-foot intervals in fruit-bearing branches from early July until harvest time.

5. Gather up and remove fallen fruit to prevent or at least limit the development and spread of such pests as apple maggots, codling moths, and leaf rollers.

6. Where apple trees are in grassy areas not subject to regular mowing, keep the grass and weeds down,

A decoy apple covered with a sticky attractant traps flies whose maggots invade ripening fruit.

either by spreading salt hay beneath the trees or mowing once a month. Remove mulch and accumulated clippings in early fall and mow the area very low to discourage bark-gnawing mice over the winter. Protect trunks of young trees with vented plastic collars.

7. Hang bars of scented toilet soap, several per tree, from low branches to repel deer.

8. Elevate above the highest branches a large plastic balloon painted with

large "scare eyes," which simulate those of owls, to frighten away birds that might otherwise peck at ripening fruit.

Apple Cultivars for Home Cultivation

Although scores of cultivars are offered commercially, many with ardent devotees, the relatively few listed here, all hardy from zones 5 to 8, are notable not only for superior flavor, texture, other fruit qualities, and broad adaptability but also for differential resistance to serious apple maladies.

'Dayton': very resistant to apple scab; moderately resistant to cedar-apple rust, powdery mildew, fire blight.

'Jonafree': very resistant to apple scab; moderately resistant to cedar-apple rust, powdery mildew, fire blight.

'Liberty': immune to cedar-apple rust; quite resistant to powdery mildew, fire blight.

'Red Free': immune to cedar-apple rust; very resistant to fire blight; moderately resistant to powdery mildew.

'William's Pride': immune to cedar-apple rust; resistant to powdery mildew, fire blight.

Other cultivars, such as the well-known 'McIntosh', 'Red Delicious', 'Granny Smith', 'Jonathan', 'Winesap', 'Cortland', and 'Northern Spy', among many others, have undeniably appealing qualities, and some have long been in cultivation here and in Europe. Their susceptibility to apple disorders, however, involves the grower in a spraying regimen that increasingly compromises their appeal for home-garden culture.

Crab apples are small-fruited species and cultivars, some of which are grown for their tart-flavored fruit which is used for jelly. Most crab apples are subject to the same suite of pests and diseases as full-size apples, but some, such as the cultivars 'Dolgo', with crimson fruit, and 'Hyslop', with yellow-and-red fruit, have meritorious fruit that may justify the work necessary to keep pests and diseases in check. Most crab apples are best grown for their ornamental flowers.

CHERRY
(*Prunus* spp.)

Cultivated cherries are derived mainly from two European species, *P. avium*, which is the prototype of the sweet cherry cultivars, and *P. cerasus*, of the sour or pie cherries. Duke cherries (*P. × effusus*) are intermediate in flavor, as befits their origin—hybrids of *P. avium* and *P. cerasus*. Other species producing edible cherries include the Asiatic *P. tomentosum* and the native western sand cherry (*P. besseyi*). Cherry pits have often been found in ancient Roman ruins and crops were believed to be harvested in Asia Minor as long ago as 800 B.C.

As their prototypic species are quite unlike, sweet cherries and sour cherries have somewhat different cultural requirements. Although hardy from zone 5 through 8, sweet cherry cultivars react poorly to long, unbroken periods of sub-zero cold in the winter and of summer heat exceeding 90°F. They thrive best in such regions as the Hudson Valley, the Great Lakes, and the Pacific Northwest. Sour cherries, by contrast, may be expected to produce well most anywhere from zones 3 or 4 to 8 or 9. Although soils are less determinative, sweet cherries produce best on deep, well-drained, sandy, or gravelly loams, while sour cherries succeed as well on heavy clays as on sandy soils and also endure summer drought.

Sweet cherries become larger trees—up to 60 feet tall and as wide if not pruned—and bear for 40 years or more, whereas the lower, often shrubby, sour cherries seldom exceed 20 feet and bear for about 20 years. In other respects, the various cherries are managed similarly.

Selection of Cultivars

Cherries grown for fruit are usually propagated by grafting onto seedlings of the wild mazzard (*P. avium*) or mahaleb (*P. mahaleb*). Those grafted onto mahaleb come into bearing earlier and grow larger than those grafted onto mazzard. On the other hand, cherries grafted onto mazzard are longer lived and of lower height at maturity, a factor of note with sweet cherries, as it eases harvesting.

It should also be borne in mind that most cultivated sweet cherry cultivars, and Duke cherries too, are not self-fertile and hence must be accompanied by a nearby tree of another cultivar for effective pollination and fruit set. Sour cherries, however, are all self-fertile; thus even one tree alone will set a good fruit crop.

Planting and Maintaining Prebearing Trees

In general, procedures are the same as for apple (see page 687). Sweet cherries should be spaced 30 feet in all directions, sour cherries at 20 feet, and Duke cherries at 25 feet. Pruning should be minimal after the major limb structure has been established in young trees and should be undertaken after the last spring frost.

Care of Bearing Trees

Bearing usually begins in four to six years. Little pruning is needed beyond the occasional removal of vigorous, erect "scaffold branches" and, in sweet and Duke cherries, keeping the head low enough to permit harvesting. Enhancing soil fertility with fertilizers should be done as for apple (see page 689). Thinning the fruit crop is unnecessary.

Cherries should be picked when the fruit has taken on the mature color specific to the cultivar. To avoid tearing the skin, it is best to harvest them with the stalks attached.

Pests and Diseases

Depending on location, whether cherry orchards exist nearby, and on the controls employed wherever cherries are cultivated, pests and diseases can be serious and even daunting. Use of horticultural oil spray in late winter or early spring to suffocate overwintering eggs and larvae will help control some pests, such as aphids. Leaf spot, which may cause partial or complete defoliation in summer, requires gathering and destroying infected leaves (not composting them) and adding a potassium supplement to the soil. Brown rot can be limited, if not controlled, by separating and destroying all fruit that has softened and developed brown areas. On small trees, birds can be kept from stripping the fruit by draping nylon mesh over the top well before the cherries ripen. Consult your cooperative extension agent for recommendations concerning these and other disorders.

Cherry Cultivars for Home Cultivation

As self-pollinating sweet cherries obviate the need for separate pollinating trees, they should be given serious consideration where space is limited. Red-fruited cultivars include 'Stella' and 'Starkcrimson'. Among standard sweet cherry cultivars that require pollinators, the deep red commercial favorite is 'Bing', which unfortunately often cracks in wet weather. Other cultivars include 'Black Tatarian', which has very dark red fruit and is successful as far south as zone 9; 'Hedelfinger' and 'Van', which have bright red fruit; and 'Lambert', whose flowers are more frost tolerant than most. Catalogs usually indicate cultivars recommended as pollinators (which themselves bear crops); for other suggestions, consult your local cooperative extension.

Yellow-fruited cherries are generally less subject to bird attack than red-fruited ones. Yellow-fruited sweet cherry cultivars include 'Gold Sweet' (or 'Golden Sweet'), which succeeds as far south as zone 9; 'Royal Ann' (also sold as 'Napoleon'), which has yellow fruit with a red cheek and is much grown commercially; and 'Rainier', which is similarly bicolor and is productive in the Deep South.

Sour cherries include two red-fruited, self-pollinating Duke cultivars: the very popular 'Montmorency' and the earlier to ripen 'Early Richmond'. No-ladder sour cherry cultivars, which do not exceed 10 feet, include 'Meteor' and 'North Star'.

Best known of the dwarf, or bush, sweet cherries, is 'Black Beauty', which matures to 3 to 6 feet tall and bears deep red fruit. A yellow-fruited cultivar in this class is 'Golden Boy'.

Cultivars of the shrubby, silver-leaf *P. tomentosa* include 'Hansen's', which has dark red fruit, and 'Nanking', which has bright red fruit. Neither exceeds 8 feet.

PEACH *AND* NECTARINE
(Prunus persica)

The peach originated in China and spread westward by means of ancient trade routes through Asia to Europe. It was a prized fruit tree in classical Greece and Rome. Today its various cultivars are grown in most temperate-zone regions and in some subtropical areas as well. Although the peach and the nectarine, its smooth-skinned variant, are sensitive to prolonged periods of subzero temperatures, they do require a period of cold dormancy each year. Hot conditions in the growing season are advantageous. Both are well suited to home garden culture because of their relatively small size and ease of management. Standard cultivars reach about 20 feet at maturity, while those grafted or budded on dwarfing stock (called "no-ladder" cultivars) top out at 10 to 12 feet.

Planting Sites and Soil

Because peach and nectarine crops can be damaged or devastated by late spring frost, hillsides above frost-prone valley bottoms are preferable. A well-drained, moderately fertile, sandy loam is the best soil. Heavier soils, however, give creditable results as long as drainage is adequate. Young trees benefit from an annual top-dressing of well-rotted manure or a nitrate-rich commercial fertilizer such as 10-5-5. It is best to maintain a pH of 6 to 7.

Method of Planting

Planting is essentially the same as for apple (see page 687), except that it is best not to grow peaches and nectarines in lawns; open, mulched beds free of compaction yield the best results. Spacing for standard cultivars should be about 20 feet in all directions and for dwarf no-ladder cultivars, 8 to 12 feet. Planting may be done in the fall in zones 8 and 9, but elsewhere spring planting is safer.

Pruning
Pruning Prebearing Trees

If purchased stock has been prepruned at the time of sale, and three or four evenly spaced side branches have been established at roughly a 45° angle from the trunk axis, further pruning should have as its goal the development of a bowl-shaped framework of diverging limbs that will bear the relatively heavy fruit load evenly and within reach of a low ladder. By removing any strongly vertical shoots that tend to form shade-casting "scaffold" branches and by keeping the interior relatively open, a well-shaped tree will result.

In the case of whips (very young, unbranched, rapidly growing trees), the growth of low branches should be induced

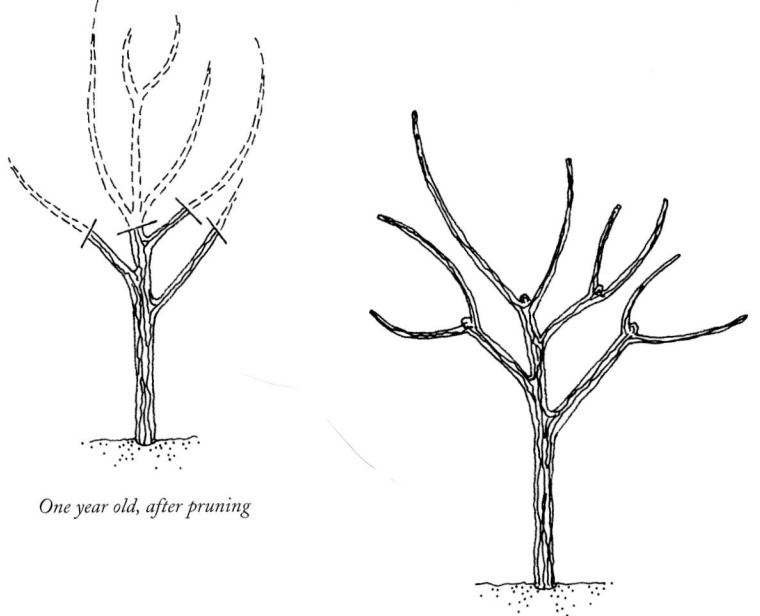

Young peach trees

One year old, after pruning

Two years old, after second pruning

by topping the whip back to about 3 feet and allowing only three or four side branches to develop at different levels along the main stem and more or less evenly spaced around it. All pruning should be done in the spring after the last frost and before growth begins. Both peaches and nectarines adapt well to espalier training. Flowering and fruit bearing should begin the third or fourth year after planting.

Pruning Bearing Trees

Peaches and nectarines are borne on growth of the previous season. As the intention is to have a good supply of flowering and fruiting wood each season that will be staunch enough to carry the fruit load, some annual cutting back is essential. If peach and nectarine trees are not pruned, the fruit is borne at the ends of the twigs, which often causes the twigs to break. A maximum height of 14 to 16 feet is a good goal for a standard cultivar.

Specifically, the pruning procedure is as follows.

1. Cut out all dead, diseased, and broken branches.
2. Thin out crossed, parallel, and weak branches.
3. Keep the center relatively open, and prune out any water sprouts (sometimes called suckers).
4. Cut back any strong growth to about 15 inches to induce lateral branching.
5. Keep the tree within height limits.

If a healthy tree fails to grow vigorously after it has begun bearing, all twigs should be cut back severely to a lateral branch. This will stimulate new growth much more effectively than a heavy application of fertilizer.

A well-maintained peach or nectarine will bear heavy crops for 20 to 25 years, and sometimes to 40 years. Dwarf cultivars often have a shorter bearing life.

Overcoming Failure to Bear

Spring frosts, long periods of killing winter temperatures, and insufficient nutrients are the main causes of low or no fruit production. The first two may be minimized by planting cold-tolerant cultivars, and nutrients may be supplemented with well-rotted manure or a suitable commercial fertilizer. With the exception of the clingstone cultivar 'Indian Blood', very few peaches or nectarines fail to bear when grown alone.

Fertilization and Cultivation

Maintaining or improving the nutrient content of the soil is done generally as for apple (see page 689), except that about half as much fertilizer is needed by peaches and nectarines. Cultivation should be directed to limiting the growth of large weeds and to maintaining a 2-inch blanket of organic mulch throughout the year.

Thinning

When about the size of a walnut, young peaches and nectarines should be thinned to about 4 inches apart, or so there will be 30 to 50 leaves per fruit. This reduction will result in larger, higher quality fruit. When a tree is overloaded with fruit, the volume of flesh will be less in each, but the size of the pit will be the same. Thus thinning increases the proportion of flesh to pit in the remaining fruit.

Harvesting

Fruit should be harvested when the skin and flesh have turned from green to their ripe tones, usually in late summer. Unlike most fruit, peaches and nectarines do not improve in flavor once taken from the tree; hence they should not be picked until quite ripe.

Pests and Diseases

Even under ideal conditions, peaches and nectarines are relatively short lived; and when weakened by chronic disease or insect

A dwarf peach, carefully pruned for maximum yield, shows much promise in full bloom.

attack, they seldom perform satisfactorily and often die prematurely. Borers invading the trunk and major limbs physically weaken the tree structurally and may reduce sap flow. In some regions, root nematodes can be troublesome. Common diseases include peach leaf curl, in which large red blisters and blade deformity impede the leaves' food-making function; beyond picking off and destroying diseased leaves, there is no effective control. Brown rot can be controlled by destroying all fruit showing soft brown areas. Consult your cooperative extension agent for locally acceptable measures to control these and other maladies that affect peaches and nectarines.

Peach and Nectarine Cultivars for the Home Garden

Most of the many peach cultivars on the market are sold both as standards and as no-ladder dwarfs and have red and yellow, velvety-skinned fruit with freestone pits, which are easily separated from the yellow flesh. Among the most popular and reliable are 'Elberta' and 'Hale Haven'. Also in this class is 'Reliance', which is especially prized for its cold tolerance (to zone 4), late flowering, and early ripening—important attributes for successful cropping in higher latitudes. All three are grown commercially. Other cultivars include the following.

> 'Belle of George': skin red; flesh white.
> 'Champion White': skin yellow; flesh white.
> 'Golden Jubilee': skin yellow; flesh yellow.
> 'Polly': skin yellow; flesh white.
> 'Red Haven': skin red, nearly hairless; flesh yellow; grown commercially.

Peach cultivars requiring only brief, relatively mild winter cold include 'Desert Gold', which is suited to zones 8 and 9; 'Gulf Queen', which is a standard that is successful in zones 9 and 10; and 'Garden Sun', which is a dwarf (only 4 to 5 feet tall) that is suited to tub culture in zones 7 to 9. The only clingstone peach still widely grown is 'Indian Blood', which has red skin and red flesh and is especially favored for canning. Unfortunately, it requires another tree of a different cultivar for pollination.

Nectarines, mostly hardy from zone 7 to 9 and often grown in the Deep South in place of peaches, include 'Delicious', 'Crimson Gold', 'Sunglo', and 'Red Gold', all with red skins and yellow flesh. 'Honeyglo', a dwarf (6 feet tall), bears similarly colored fruit. 'Gulf Pride' is suited to zones 9 and 10.

Some growers offer multiple cultivars on a single stock.

PEAR
(Pyrus communis)

The great majority of pear cultivars grown in the United States are derived from *P. communis*, a species occurring wild in much of Europe and western Asia. The still popular 'Kiefer' is a natural hybrid of this species and the Asiatic *P. pyrifolia*. Derivatives of *P. pyrifolia* and *P. ussariensis* are known collectively as Asiatic pears. Historically, pears were grown in classical Greece and Rome. Today it is an important fruit crop in temperate-zone regions the world over.

Planting and Soil

Culture is essentially the same as for apple (see page 687), except that the architecture of pear trees is distinctive and requires somewhat different treatment. Also, most pear cultivars are neither reliably winter hardy north of zone 5 nor successful south of zone 8, especially if summers have long periods with temperatures above 90°F. As pear trees flower early—before the leaves expand—care must be taken to site them away from frost pockets. Similar to apples, most pear cultivars are self-sterile, hence compatible or mutually interfertile cultivars must be grown in fairly close association. Pears lend themselves to espalier training. Many pear cultivars are available both as standard-size trees and as no-ladder dwarfs. Multiple grafts, sold as three-in-one or five-in-one trees, mostly on dwarfing stock, can be useful where space is limited, but grafts vary in their longevity. Standard cultivars should be spaced 20 feet apart; no-ladder dwarfs about 10 feet apart.

Soil should be well-drained, fairly moist, and only moderately fertile. Excessively

moist, rich soil stimulates lush vegetative growth, which is particularly subject to fire blight, a serious bacterial disease.

Pruning Young Prebearing Trees

Pears should be pruned in the spring just after the last frost and before active growth begins. Earlier pruning can result in dieback from entry of fungal diseases.

A one-year-old pear tree should be pruned back to a height of about 3 feet. Usually, it is sold as a straight, unbranched whip. If lateral branches are present, they should be pruned back to about 6 inches, or if they appear weak, they should be removed altogether.

In a two-year-old tree, four or five branches are selected as main limbs for the future framework of the tree. The reason for having more main limbs on a pear tree than on an apple tree is that fire blight can result in the loss of one or two limbs. By training several branches to serve as main limbs, the loss of one or two will not be fatal to the tree.

Once the desired framework is established, only light pruning is necessary until bearing begins. Compared with apples, pears take a long time to come into bearing, often 7 to 10 years or more after planting. As the habit of growth varies somewhat according to cultivar, it is best to allow growth to advance fairly naturally, subject only to a little thinning and heading back from time to time.

Pruning Bearing Trees and Overcoming Failure to Bear

Follow the procedures outlined for apple (see pages 688).

Fertilizing

The amount of fertilizer to add annually, whether in the form of well-rotted manure or commercial product, is the same as for apple (see page 689), with reduced amounts for dwarfs or immature trees. Since overfertilization can be counterproductive, it is best to have the soil tested periodically and to adjust soil amendments accordingly. Surface cultivation is not necessary and most pears grow and bear well on lawns. Elsewhere, rank weeds should be mowed occasionally, especially around dwarfs or young tress.

Harvesting

Pears develop their best flavor if not allowed to ripen fully on the tree. They should be picked as they begin to turn yellow or when they part easily from the spur. They should be sweet, juicy, and free of graininess or grit. A few days after picking, they will be at their most flavorful.

Pests and Diseases

There are many pests that attack pears, but these are not generally specific to the pear and are seldom serious (see Chapter 34). The most damaging enemy of pears is the disease fire blight, in which leaves, flowers, and fruit (any actively growing tissue) suddenly wilt and turn black but remain attached to the tree. Cankers develop on the branches. All affected branches should be removed by cutting at least 6 inches below the diseased tissue. Pruned branches and all dead parts should be burned, buried, or taken off the site, and the blades of all tools used should be dipped in a bacteriocide, such as alcohol or household bleach (sodium hypochlorite). Your cooperative extension agent should be contacted for other locally acceptable control procedures.

Pear Cultivars for Home Cultivation

The most durable, venerable, and currently popular cultivar by far is 'Bartlett', which was originally the French cultivar 'Williams Bon Chragetien' that was renamed when introduced in the United States. Like most of the following cultivars, 'Bartlett' is available both as a standard and as a dwarf. 'Moonglow' and 'Comice' are similar to 'Bartlett' but blight resistant and usually earlier than Bartlett to bear (often in five years). 'Clapp's Favorite' has a red-cheeked, yellow skin, and 'Duchess' is self-pollinating. 'Collette', available only as a standard, has an extended period of flowering, with fruit ripening over a period of two months. 'Kieffer', also sold only as a standard, is blight resistant and bears within five years. 'Seckel', grown as a standard or a dwarf, ripens later than most. In 'Red Sensation', 'Red Bartlett', and 'Red d'Anjou', the ripe fruit has a red skin. 'Beurre Bosc', available only as a dwarf, has russet-skinned fruit. 'Douglas'

is notably precocious, bearing fruit just one or two years after planting.

The following Asiatic pears are self-pollinating and bear spherical, almost apple-shaped fruit, which, in contrast to ordinary pears, should be allowed to ripen on the tree. 'Turnbull', a standard, and 'Giant Asiatic', a dwarf, produce relatively few pears but each may weigh as much as 3 pounds at maturity. 'Hosui', 'Twentieth Century', and 'Shinseiki', all available as standards or dwarfs, bear smaller fruit, and 'Chojuro', available as a dwarf only, has yellow fruits that are speckled with red at maturity.

PLUM
(Prunus × domestica and other spp.)

Most plums grown in the United States are cultivars that are variants of the European plum (*P. × domestica*), which was grown in ancient Rome and which itself is believed to be a natural hybrid of *P. cerasifera* and *P. spinosa*, two species of Turkey and adjacent regions of Europe and Asia. These cultivars include greengage plums and purple-skinned prune plums. Damson plums are derived from the bullace (*P. × domestica* ssp. *institia*), cherry plums from the myrobalan (*P. cerasifera*), and Japanese plums from the variable *P. triflora*. Several North American species of *Prunus*, particularly *P. americana*, have been crossed with some of the less adaptable Old World species to develop plum cultivars suited to zone 4 and also to zones 9 and 10. Thanks to assiduous breeding programs in recent decades, plums today are of complex lineage, with fruit color varying from violet black to yellow, and are suited for cultivation in all temperate-zone regions.

Culture, Soil, and Maintenance

Culture of plum cultivars varies somewhat according to parentage, but in general, procedures are the same as for apple (see page 687). Spacing ranges from 30 feet in all directions for the larger European and Japanese cultivars to 20 feet for those developed from the shrubby, low-headed bullace. No-ladder plums

(developed by grafting standard cultivars on dwarfing stock) should be spaced 10 to 12 feet. The onset of bearing varies widely among cultivars and is considerably influenced by site factors, but it usually occurs within five to 10 years of planting.

Soils are best if of fairly heavy clays of pH 6.0 to 7.0 and enriched with organic matter or a nitrate-rich commercial fertilizer. Annual mulching with well-rotted manure is beneficial. Soil testing will reveal whether supplemental potassium is indicated.

Young trees should be pruned to develop three leaders, which will grow on and branch to form a rounded head. Branches should be thinned annually to remove any that are too close or are crossed, and to keep the top relatively open.

Most cultivars of the European plum offered on the retail market are self-fertile, and so are especially suited to grounds where only a single plum tree can be accommodated. Many of these are, in fact, only partially self-fertile and will set heavier crops when near a pollinator tree. All Japanese plums require separate pollinators. The bearing period of most standard cultivars is 20 to 30 years; for no-ladder dwarfs it is 12 to 15 years.

Thinning

Once the fruit set has begun to grow and after the "June drop" (when a portion of the young fruit normally aborts and falls), the remaining fruit should be thinned so that none is touching another. This not only obviates bruising and scabbing but also ensures a crop of full-size fruit at maturity. Thinning is especially desirable with Japanese plums; left unthinned, the crop will ripen, but each plum will be undersize and have relatively little flesh enveloping the full-size pit.

Harvesting

Fruit of European plum cultivars should be harvested only when fully ripe, which requires care to avoid bruising or tearing the thin fruit skin. Japanese plums ripen soft and are especially subject to damage, hence they are often picked while still firm and allowed to ripen off the tree. Damson plums last longer once picked than most others.

Pests and Diseases

Most pests and diseases affecting plum are the same as those that affect cherry and peach, except that woody swellings, or galls (called "black knot"), caused by a fungus, can strangle twigs and diminish the crop. The galls and affected twigs should be promptly pruned out and destroyed. The plum curculio, a weevil whose legless larvae feed on ripening fruit, can seriously reduce the harvest. For these and other enemies, see Chapter 34, and consult your cooperative extension agent for control measures approved in your area.

Plum Cultivars for Home Cultivation

European plum cultivars that are hardy from zone 5 through 8, are available as standards and no-ladder dwarfs, bear purple-skinned, yellow-fleshed, freestone fruit, and are at least partially self-fertile include the following. 'Stanley' is one of the most widely grown. 'Fellemberg', 'Mount Royal', and 'Blue Ribbon' are similar to it but have clingstone fruit. 'Yellow Egg' is a freestone cultivar with wholly yellow fruit, and 'Greengage' is a clingstone cultivar in which the ripe fruit has green skin and yellow flesh. The Damson group is known primarily by the self-fertile, clingstone, standard-size cultivar 'Damson', which has purple-skinned, yellow-fleshed fruit.

Japanese plums all require pollinators, are all clingstones, and are mostly tolerant of more cold and sustained heat (zones 4 or 5 to 9 or 10). Cultivars include the wholly red-fruited 'Santa Rosa', available as a standard and a no-ladder dwarf; 'Burbank Red Ace', dwarf only; and 'Ozark Premier', also dwarf only. 'Superior', available as a standard and dwarf, and 'Kaga' and 'Waneta', available as standards only, have red skins and yellow flesh. 'Shiro', available as a standard and dwarf, bears wholly yellow fruit.

OTHER FRUIT TREES

APRICOT
(Prunus armeniaca and other spp.)

Native to China and grown in Europe since classical times, apricot cultivation in the United States is limited by the occurrence of damaging spring frosts after flowers have opened and, especially in the East, by pests and diseases. Although commercial production of apricots is mostly in California, this fruit is hardier than the peach, and some cultivars can be grown as far north as zone 3. The key to success in the home garden is location, which is preferably on sloping ground on the south side of a building (ideally against the chimney), where protection from spring frost can make the difference between regular full crops and light, erratic ones. Locations near large, temperature-moderating bodies of water (a lake, bay, or ocean) are especially favorable. Late flowering in some cultivars helps ease the problem.

In general, culture is the same as for cherry and peach, but it is important to select cultivars suited to the climate and resistant to likely enemies in your area. Consult your cooperative extension agent for guidance. Cultivars grafted onto peach roots are more nematode resistant in sandy areas than self-rooted trees. So-called self-pollinating cultivars bear more prolifically if a suitable pollinator is also planted. So long as the soil is well-drained, consistently moist in the growing season, and at a pH of 6.5 to 7.5, its character is not critical, although heavier soils are more productive. Spacing should be 20 to 25 feet for standard cultivars, 10 feet for dwarfs.

The pruning of young trees is the same as for peach, with emphasis on keeping the top low to facilitate harvesting. Fertilizing the soil around bearing trees calls for restraint, as excess nitrate can diminish fruit production. Thinning fruit to 4 inches apart is beneficial. Fruit should be picked only when ripe; the flavor of fruit ripened off the tree is usually pallid. Bearing usually begins in about five years after planting. Pests and diseases are the same as for peach.

Among the cultivars available as standard trees (maturing 15 to 20 feet tall) and as dwarfs (mostly 6 to 12 feet), 'Goldcot' is a disease-resistant, self-pollinating type with freestone fruit, while 'Moongold' and 'Sungold', both hardy to zone 3, require pollinators (they are mutually compatible). 'Henderson' and 'Sureset' both require pollinators and perform well in zones 4 through 9. Of the dwarf-only cultivars, all bearing within three to four years, 'Moorpark', which reaches 8 feet, and 'Manchurian Bush', which grows to 10 feet and is hardy to zone 3, are both self-pollinating, while 'S.H. Chinese Golden', which grows to 10 feet, is especially tolerant of sustained cold to zone 5.

FIG
(Ficus carica)

The sole temperate-zone representative of a great assemblage of tropical trees, shrubs, woody climbers, and stranglers, the fig was originally native to mountain valleys in southwest Asia and has been in cultivation for more than 2,500 years. Over the last few centuries, selections hardy to zone 8 and, with winter protection, zone 7, have been isolated and propagated for home garden culture. The fig itself is a curiously enlarged pouch with minute flowers within, which, once pollinated by tiny wasps, develop into seeds as the enveloping "fruit" enlarges. The center of commercial production in this country is California, where 'Smyrna' and other cultivars are grown to produce dried figs and 'Kadota' and some others are grown for canning.

In the home garden, figs are generally grown to be eaten fresh, and the cultivars used do not require pollination to develop. Depending on set-out size and site conditions, the onset of fruit bearing usually occurs within five years. In home garden plantings, spacing varies from 10 or 12 feet between small cultivars to 20 to 25 feet between standard types. Pruning of young, newly planted trees is done to maintain a single trunk and to develop a branching framework that will afford sun exposure to all branches. In regions with long growing seasons, many cultivars will renew growth and set a second crop in the same season if branch ends are pruned back after the first crop has ripened. Dead or failing branches should be removed whenever discovered.

In regions where temperatures occasionally fall below 15°F, figs may be safely grown if located on the south side of a building or wall and, when severe weather threatens, the trees are wrapped in straw or heavy paper and covered with roofing paper or heavy polyethylene sheeting to shield them from cold, drying wind. The wrapping must be waterproof to be effective and must be removed in early spring before growth begins. Ordinary well-drained, consistently moist soil suits figs so long as the pH is between 6.0 and 7.5. Full sun is essential for bountiful crops.

Cultivars suited to the East include the white- (actually yellow- or light green-) skinned 'Osborn's Prolific' and the black- (purple-) skinned 'Brown Turkey', 'Brunswick', and 'Blue Celeste'. 'Tena' and 'Alma' are white-fruited cultivars for the Gulf Coast. 'White Genoa' and 'Desert King' do well in the Northwest, and 'Green Ischia' and 'White Adriatic' are white figs that bear well in coastal and parts of interior California, as do the black cultivars 'Violette de Bordeaux', 'Black Mission', and 'Bourjassote Noire'.

KAKI PLUM *OR* JAPANESE PERSIMMON
(Diospyros kaki)

The kaki plum is the familiar tomato-like persimmon sold in markets. For centuries it has been an important fruit in the Orient, where many cultivars are recognized, but only in recent decades has it been grown in the United States, where it is suited to cultivation in zone 9 and, with winter protection, in zone 8 and milder parts of zone 7.

Kaki plum must be handled with care, even as a young, spring-planted treelet only 2 feet tall, as damage to the long taproot can be fatal. Ultimate height is

25 to 40 feet, with an equal spread. It is advisable to plant several together, spaced about 40 feet apart, as the sexes are usually on separate trees. Depending on size of sapling and site conditions, bearing seldom occurs sooner than 10 years from set-out time. Ordinary well-drained soil in an open position suffices; pests and diseases are not problems. Fruit should be harvested when it achieves the mature color characteristic of the cultivar.

The cultivar 'Tanenashi' will bear if grown alone and produces seedless fruit with yellow to red-orange skin and yellow flesh. 'Eureka' is similar but requires a pollinator, and the fruits contain a few seeds.

Closely related are the date plum (*D. lotus*), an Asiatic species with ½-inch, egg-shaped, sweet-flavored fruit that turns from yellow to black when ripe, and the American persimmon (*D. virginiana*), a larger tree, up to 50 feet or more, native to the eastern United States. Female American persimmons bear intensely and at first inedibly tart fruits, 1 to 2 inches long, that turn orange, very soft, and deliciously sweet once ripened by early frosts. Neither is commonly grown.

MULBERRY
(Morus spp.)

Native to western Asia, the black mulberry (*M. nigra*, in contrast to the east Asian white mulberry, *M. alba*, whose foliage is important in silkworm culture) was cultivated in ancient Mesopotamia, Greece, and Rome. In more recent times, breeding and selection have led to large-fruited, few-seeded cultivars that have found favor in the Old World. They are infrequently grown in the U.S. South (zone 7 to 9), however, partly because the very soft fragility of the ripe fruit precludes commercial handling. The fruit is used primarily in jellies, jams, and wine.

The native red mulberry (*M. rubra*) is similar but hardier (zones 6 to 9) and bears small purple fruit that is seedier and equally fragile when ripe. The fruit is much sought after by birds, whose purple droppings can stain outdoor furniture and pavement and cause unwanted seedlings to appear in hedges, shrubbery, and gardens.

Both species are of easiest culture and thrive on virtually any well-drained soil, eventually reaching a height and spread of 35 to 50 feet, but easily kept lower with annual pruning.

PAPAW, PAWPAW
(Asimina triloba)

The only temperate-zone member of the large tropical Annona family, the native papaw (not to be confused with the unrelated *Carica papaya*, which bears the large melonlike papaya or papaw of the lowland American tropics) is a small, low-headed, large-leaf tree or shrub, about 20 feet tall and as wide, that bears pungently fragrant three-parted, brown-violet flowers in the spring before the leaves. The flowers are followed by clusters of curved, bananalike fruit (hence such local common names as Kansas banana, Missouri banana, and poor man's banana) that reach 3 to 5 inches long. They ripen yellow-green in late summer or early fall and by then lose their disagreeable astringency to become pleasantly aromatic with sweet custardlike flesh. Although it is nutritious, the fruit of wild trees varies considerably in flavor and size at maturity.

Papaw is usually found forming thickets or copses in the understory of damp woods in the South and Midwest. But, for maximum fruit production, young container-grown trees are best planted in open ground on well-drained, consistently moist soil from zone 5 to 9. If the planting is surrounded by lawn, root suckers can be controlled by mowing. Only small trees, 2 to 3 feet tall, should be planted, as any disturbance of the roots, especially of the taproot, is likely to prove fatal. To ensure adequate sun exposure (especially important in zones 5 to 7 for maximum fruit production), space papaw at least 20 feet from the nearest shading trees or buildings. Once established, papaw thrives with little or no care, and bearing should begin in six to eight years. Since pollination is by carrion-seeking flies, it is useful to hang scraps of turned meat in plastic mesh bags in the flowering branches as attractants. An annual topdressing of compost will help retain soil moisture in summer.

Cultivars include the self-fertile 'Sunflower', with large (to 7 inches) few-seeded fruit, and the large-fruited 'Overleese' and smaller-fruited 'Davis', both requiring wild trees or other cultivars for pollination and bearing fruit with two rows of hard, flat seeds.

QUINCE
(Cydonia oblonga)

A small, broad-headed tree or large shrub, 15 to 20 feet tall, the quince is closely related to apple and pear, and bears astringent, applelike fruits that are usually longer than broad, strongly aromatic, ripen yellow, and are used primarily for jellies and in pies. Although it is widely cultivated in Europe, western Asia, and temperate South America, where, in addition to its culinary value, the fruit is used in herbal medicine, quince is little grown in the United States.

Hardy and productive from zone 7 to 4, quince is best planted in spring as a two-year-old treelet in well-drained, moderately fertile soil. Fruit is produced best in open positions, and trees should be spaced 15 to 20 feet apart. Culture is essentially the same as for apple (see page 687), with emphasis on developing a low, open head to facilitate fruit harvest. Fruit should be gathered when fully ripe in mid to late fall, before frost, and may be stored two to three months in a cool, frost-free place,

preferably away from other produce (which might otherwise be tainted by the quince aroma). Pests and diseases are the same as for apple and pear.

Of the several natural varieties, *C. oblonga* var. *maliformis*, with apple-shaped fruits, performs better in zones 4 and 5 than other quince variants. Several cultivars are also available, all distinguished by fruit traits. Depending on set-out size and site conditions, initial bearing usually occurs in 5 to 10 years.

SERVICEBERRY
(Amelanchier spp.*)*

The genus *Amelanchier* is best known by the native shadbush, shadblow, or serviceberry (*A. canadensis*), a small bushy tree occurring in the eastern United States in habitats as dissimilar as dry woods and swamps. The fruit, eaten overripe when it is black-violet, is usually collected in the wild in early to mid summer. Fruit of this and other species of *Amelanchier* may also be stewed, used for jam, or dried for use in place of currants or raisins. Virtually any soil, well drained or not, suits serviceberry. Fruit set is best in open locations. Prune the top annually to keep the fruit within reach. Young trees, scarcely 3 or 4 feet high, begin flowering, but significant fruit set is usually deferred for several years. Space trees 15 to 20 feet apart.

WILD TREE CHERRIES
(Prunus spp.*)*

In addition to the widely grown cultivars of the European sweet cherry (*P. avium*) and sour cherry (*P. cerasus*), a few native tree cherries are occasionally grown in gardens for their fruit. Principal among these is chokecherry (*P. virginiana*), which is seldom taller than 25 feet and about as wide, often has several trunks, and is hardy from zone 7 to 2. In spite of its being subject to the defoliating attacks of tent caterpillar, it is especially valued north of the hardiness limits of other cherries. The pea-size fruit is borne in elongated clusters of 20 to 30 and ripen deep red to black-violet, at which point it loses much of its tartness and may be used for preserves.

Of similar if infrequent use is the black, or rum, cherry (*P. serotina*), which grows to 60 feet or more and as wide. This species is a very common invader of disturbed habitats in eastern North America from zone 8 to 3, and its ripe, black-violet fruit (smaller than the chokecherry) may also be used in jams. Seeds are spread by birds, which freely consume ripe fruit.

In both species, trees located in sunny positions begin bearing when 8 to 12 feet tall. Crops vary from year to year, as in nearly all fruit trees, according to the presence of weather-sensitive pollinating insects—chiefly bees—during the flowering period.

BUSH FRUITS

BLACKBERRY
(Rubus spp.*)*

Blackberry refers to several wild, mostly native species—some erect or arching, some trailing (known mostly as dewberries)—as well as to derived hybrids (such as boysenberry, loganberry and youngberry) and cultivars, mostly distinguished by their glossy "berries," each a tightly adhering cluster of one-seeded fruit surrounding a central core, generally maturing black-violet. As trailing blackberries must be trained or tied to wire fencing or trellis,

erect or highbush types are preferred for home cultivation, especially those that are thornless.

Although less hardy than raspberry, most blackberry cultivars are hardy and productive from zone 8 to 5, and some succeed to zone 10. In northerly regions, it is best to plant blackberries where they will be protected from drying winter wind and away from frost pockets. Deep, sandy-humusy soil is ideal, but good results may be had on most any well-drained soil of pH 5.5 to 7.0 that has been prepared (rototilled) 8 to 10 inches deep, with well-

rotted manure or compost generously incorporated. An open, sunny location is best, but even with a few hours' shade each day crops are still creditable. Planting may be done either in early spring or early fall. Trailing cultivars should be spaced 4 to 6 feet apart below the support wires in rows 3 to 4 feet apart. Upright cultivars should be set 2 to 3 feet apart; these, too, are more easily managed if trained to supports.

Pruning and thinning canes of upright blackberry cultivars are vital to full berry production. Each cane lives two years; it grows the first, remaining unbranched

A bower of ripening blackberries promises delicious bounty in a few days.

unless pinched or tip-pruned, then develops flowering branches and bears fruit the second year, after which it dies. New canes are produced each year, ensuring a crop each summer once bearing has begun. New, fast-growing, vegetative canes of the year should be tip-pruned during the summer at about 3 feet to induce side branching. In the fall, all canes that have fruited during the summer should be cut back to the base, leaving only mature, laterally branched, one-year canes. In the late fall or early winter, select the four to six strongest of these one-year canes and remove all others. This will ensure strong development of flowering and fruiting shoots the following spring.

Canes of trailing blackberries have the same two-year cycle, but once a plant begins to bear, it is best to separate second-year bearing canes from first-year vegetative ones. This is done by tying up mature one-year canes to the support wires in early fall after cutting out all two-year canes that have just finished bearing. In the following season, the tied canes will bear, while new vegetative canes grow out from the base. These new canes should be trained to sprawl on the ground parallel to the support wires until season's end, when they will be tied up as the old bearing canes are removed.

In dry summer weather, the adequacy of soil moisture will determine berry size at maturity. Mulching helps conserve soil moisture, but irrigation may be needed. All suckers arising from roots away from the crowns should be pulled up. Avoid cultivation, as most roots are shallow and easily disturbed or severed.

Fertilizer, preferably well-rotted manure with compost, should be applied as a topdressing and only in the spring as the canes leaf out. If put down in summer, new canes will continue growing until frost and unhardened growth will be winter killed. If put down in the fall, much nitrate will have leached away before resumption of growth in spring.

Choice of certified disease-free plants of cultivars known to be reasonably trouble-free in your area is the best defense against disease. An equally desirable prophylaxis, but in some locations virtually impossible to attain completely, is the removal of all wild blackberries from a 100-foot zone around the blackberry planting, primarily to discourage the occurrence of blackberry rust, a perennial fungus disease. Patches of bright orange on leaf undersurfaces betray its presence; the only control is to dig out all infected plants and burn them or bag them for disposal off-site. Contact your local cooperative extension service for recommended cultivars and for approved measures of pest and disease control.

Among cultivars with upright canes are the commercially popular 'Darrow', especially suited to the Northeast, and 'Dirksen' and 'Ebony King', both rust-resistant forms; all are hardy from zone 5 to 10. Better suited to the South (zones 6 to 10) are 'Cheyenne' and 'Shawnee', and to the Gulf Coast (zones 9 and 10), 'Brazos'. 'Illini' is hardy through zone 4. Thornless upright cultivars include 'Perron Black', 'Chester', and 'Free 'n Easy', all suitable for zones 5 to 8.

Trailing blackberry cultivars include 'Cascade', an early-season, heavily bearing form best grown on the Pacific Coast; the prolific 'Boysen' (commonly called boysenberry), whose raspberrylike flavor suggests its hybrid blackberry-raspberry origin. 'Logan' (loganberry) also has a hint of raspberry flavor and is much grown on the Pacific Coast, as is 'Tayberry', a true blackberry that has cylindrical fruits up to 2 inches long. Among thornless trailing cultivars are 'Lucretia', especially suited to the Pacific Northwest; 'Black Satin', suited to the East and Midwest; and 'Olallie', suited to California and the Gulf Coast.

BLUEBERRY
(*Vaccinium* spp.)

Three species account for most blueberry production in the United States, and from these, numerous hybrids and cultivars have been developed, a fraction of which are important commercially and also suitable for the home garden. The most important species is the highbush blueberry (*V. corymbosum*), a large shrub, 12 feet tall and as wide in the wild, that inhabits acidic freshwater marshes in the eastern United States. Its cultivars are usually smaller in habit, bear larger fruit, and adapt to somewhat drier terrain, as long as the soil is strongly acidic. Its counterpart in the Southeast is the southern highbush blueberry, or rabbit eye (*V. ashei*), an even larger, more prolifically fruiting shrub that performs well on soils of pH 5.5 to 6.5 and is tolerant of periods of summer drought. Lowbush blueberry (*V. angustifolium*), the last of the trio, is a spreading ground cover shrub, often only 1 foot tall, that forms extensive stands or mats in dry, open or partly shaded ground, thriving especially on acidic sandy soil.

Hybrid blueberries suited to the home garden are mostly derived from the very variable highbush blueberry and have been bred and selected primarily for larger fruit than is borne by wild shrubs. They grow best from zone 5 to 8. The basic requirements for successful cultivation and maximal fruit bearing are a consistently moist soil with a pH of 4 to 5 (readings up to 6.0 may be lowered by annually adding aluminum sulfate; elsewhere tub culture is an option, as with the compact cultivar 'Dwarf Tophat'), generous supplements of compost, a yearly total of at least 700 hours of cold below 40°F, and exposure to at least six hours of sunlight each clear day in the growing season.

Although blueberries are self-fertile, heavier crops are set when two or more cultivars are planted together. In any year, total yield will depend on the weather during the flowering period; cold, wet, windy weather discourages the pollinating bees and may result in a light crop. It is best to plant young shrubs, 1 to 2 feet tall (usually about four years old), in early spring, spacing them about 5 feet apart in all directions. Care should be taken to arrange the roots so that they are not deeper than 6 inches. An organic mulch will help maintain soil moisture and keep out weeds. Any fertilizer supplement should include ammonium sulfate or urea, not the ammonium nitrate found in most commercial fertilizers. At the time of planting, 1 ounce per bush is sufficient followed by three additional 1-ounce applications at monthly intervals.

Little pruning is needed until bearing begins, usually within three years, at which time it is best to select the four to six strongest stems and prune out the rest. Crops gradually increase as the shrubs grow larger. Depending on the characteristics of the cultivar, it may be advisable to thin the young fruit crop or "head back" the shrubs to prevent a branch-breaking overload of fruit. In any case, shrubs are best kept lower than 6 feet. On any bush, fruit will usually ripen over a period of several weeks, and as there is much variation in ripening period among cultivars, it is possible to have at least a two-month season of harvest.

Well-grown hybrid highbush blueberries have few diseases. The principal pests are marauding birds, which can strip a laden bush very quickly and hence should be excluded from ripening crops with ¾-inch-mesh nylon netting.

Cultivars of highbush blueberry are numerous; those of particular merit are grouped according to hardiness. Especially suited to zones 3 to 5 are the following.

A young hybrid blueberry bush bears fewer but much larger berries than wild shrubs.

Blueberries ripen over a period of four to six weeks in most cultivars.

'Northland': about 4 feet tall; somewhat spreading habit; frost-tolerant flowers.

'Patriot': 4 to 5 feet tall; large berries.

'Saskatoon': less demanding of strongly acidic soil.

Among the many cultivars that produce best in zones 4 to 9 are the early season (early to mid July) 'Early Bluejay', 'Blueray', and 'Ivanhoe'; midseason cultivars (mid to late July) include 'Atlantic', 'Jersey', and 'Bluecrop'; and late season cultivars (early to mid August) include 'Herbert' and 'Elliot'. For zones 7 to 10, the following early-ripening cultivars are recommended, mainly because they are ready about one month before the earliest rabbit-eye harvest: 'Sharpblue', for zones 9 and 10, and 'O'Neal', a very large-fruited form for zones 7 to 9. Midseason cultivars include 'Avonblue' and 'Georgiagem', both best in zone 9. 'Blue Chip' is another very large-fruited form, for zones 7 and 8.

Rabbit-eye blueberry cultivars bear black fruit (with little or no bluish bloom) that is somewhat less flavorful and mostly later to ripen. The shrubs have less exacting requirements as to soil moisture and pH and require less winter cold. Hence they are more easily grown than highbush cultivars in localities where temperatures fall no lower than 0°F. They succeed best from zones 7 to 9. Cultivars include the early-flowering (with risk of frost damage) and early-ripening 'Climax', which has a wide-spreading habit, and 'Premier', which

has an upright form. The midseason 'Woodard' is wide spreading and suited to zones 8 and 9; 'Briteblue' is upright and does best in zones 7 and 8. The late-season 'Tifblue' has berries that remain quite tart until fully blue-black.

Lowbush blueberries are seldom planted, but extensive natural stands are sometimes managed for commercial production. The berries are generally smaller but ripen sweeter than the highbush and rabbit-eye types. Although there is some natural variation in berry size, it is much less than in the other species. The popular cultivars 'North Country', 'Dwarf Northblue', and 'Northsky' grow especially well in zones 3 and 4. Although they are of mixed parentage, they have the spreading habit of the wild lowbush blueberry.

CURRANTS
(Ribes spp.)

Less commonly grown in the United States than in their native Europe, currants are small-berried bush crops that ripen red, white, or black. Cultivation of black currant (*R. nigrum*) is prohibited in much of the country because it serves as alternate host to the white pine blister rust, a disease that devastates white pine and other pine species. Other *Ribes* species are locally proscribed as well. Check with your local cooperative extension office before planting any currants.

Wild red currant (*R. silvestre*), the white currant (a genetic variant of red currant that lacks red skin pigment), and a few other European species are the parents of modern red currant and white currant cultivars. All are 4- to 6-foot-tall shrubs that are easily cultivated in areas having cool summers (mostly from zones 3 to 7) and on a range of well-drained, moderately fertile soils with pH readings between 6.5 and 7.0.

The planting of one-year-old rooted cuttings may be done in fall or early spring, with planting sites prepared as for apple (see page 687). Allow about 4 feet between plants. Bearing usually begins within three years and gradually increases as the plants grow.

For maximum production, all old stems (older than three years) should be removed,

but in the home garden, where a few or perhaps as many as six shrubs are grown, unpruned shrubs usually bear adequately. However, any dead or borer-infested stems should be removed promptly.

An application of well-rotted manure or commercial 5-10-5 fertilizer, spread well beyond the reach of the branches, helps maintain or even improve yields. Harvesting the strings of berries is usually done by hand in midsummer.

A covering of ¾-inch-mesh nylon netting will keep birds from harvesting ripe fruit. Diseases are numerous but seldom serious, with the exception of leaf spot, which can cause premature defoliation and, where serious, may call for a regular fungicide spray schedule. It is also important to rake up and remove all fallen leaves. Leaf spot is not to be confused with browned leaf edges, a symptom of potassium deficiency, which is easily corrected by working hardwood ashes into the soil around each bush early in the spring.

The principal red currant cultivars are 'Red Lake', which has large crops of ⅛-inch fruit, and 'Wilder', which has fruit up to ¼ inch in diameter. 'White Imperial' is a white-fruited form.

GOOSEBERRY
(Ribes hirtellum, R. uva-crispa)

Never as popular in the United States as in Britain and northern Europe, gooseberry cultivation, as with that of black currant, has been prohibited in areas where white pine and other five-needle pine species are important forest trees. This is because gooseberry is an alternate host to the white pine blister rust disease. Your cooperative extension agent will let you know whether gooseberry can be grown legally in your area.

In the United States, most gooseberry cultivars are derived from the American gooseberry (*R. hirtellum*), while some, the so-called English gooseberries, are derived from the wild European gooseberry (*R. uva-crispa*). Both species are rounded shrubs that grow to about 3 feet tall and have thorny stems. American gooseberry cultivars bear small, pea-size fruit; English gooseberries have larger, more flavorful fruit, but the bushes are subject to downy mildew, a defoliating fungus disease, to which American cultivars are resistant. A number of disease-resistant, nearly thornless, hybrid cultivars variously combine attributes of both parent species and make worthy candidates for the home garden.

Gooseberries, like currants, grow best in full sun in cool-summer regions, mainly from zone 3 to 7, in well-drained, sandy, acidic (pH 6 to 6.5) soil to which much compost or well-rotted manure has been added. In addition to nitrate, soil potassium and magnesium often require supplementation (in the form of potassium sulfate and magnesium sulfate) and may be indicated, especially for sandy soils, if leaf margins turn brown and crops are light. As gooseberry roots are shallow, a summer mulch is advisable to conserve soil moisture. Shrubs should be spaced 3 to 4 feet in all directions. Bearing usually begins within three years of set-out.

For maximum fruit production, annual pruning in winter is necessary and consists mainly of removing all old (three-year-old or more) stems, all horizontal branches that are low to the ground, and the arching tips of long stems that might bend to the ground under a load of fruit. The goals of pruning are to keep young shoots coming, as these bear the most fruit, and to keep the crop above the ground.

Flowers appear in the spring and are frost sensitive, a limitation that affects choice of planting site. Maturing fruits, usually ready by early summer, attract marauding birds, as do (though to a lesser degree) winter buds. Both may be protected with a year-round enclosure of ¾-inch-mesh galvanized wire fencing, installed so that the top may be removed for harvesting.

The most commonly grown cultivar is the nearly thornless 'Pix-well', in which the light green pea-size fruits mature pinkish to purplish green and are much prized for pies and jellies. 'Welcome', also nearly thornless with pinkish fruits at maturity, does particularly well in partial shade. 'Colossal' and 'Jumbo' bear green fruit that grows up to 1 inch long.

RASPBERRY
(Rubus spp.)

Raspberries are closely related to blackberries, but are distinctive not only in flavor and the gray bloominess of the fruit but also in the retention of the core on the bush when the caplike fruit is harvested. The European red raspberry (*R. idaeus*) and the American red raspberry (*R. idaeus* ssp. *strigosus*) are the prototypes of red-fruited and yellow-fruited cultivars. The native black-cap raspberry (*R. occidentalis*) has violet black fruit, and various hybrids of this and the American red raspberry bear purple fruit. Several other species yield edible fruit, of which one, *R. albescens*, native to tropical Asia, is grown in zones 9 and 10, mainly in Florida.

Most raspberry cultivars, however, do best from zones 4 to 7 and in regions where summers have only occasional periods of heat exceeding 90°F and where there is pronounced winter cold. Shelter from spring frost and high wind is beneficial. Well-drained, sandy-humusy loam of moderate fertility, with a pH of 6.0 to 6.5, and a generous supplement of well-rotted manure—mainly to maintain soil moisture in the summer—is ideal, and should be forked or rototilled to a depth of at least 8 inches. Weed control is especially important, as raspberries perform poorly when crowded or shaded by intruders.

For most families, 15 to 20 bushes suffice. Raspberries are best planted in the fall, arranged in rows oriented north to south, and trained on horizontal wires

Pruning a raspberry

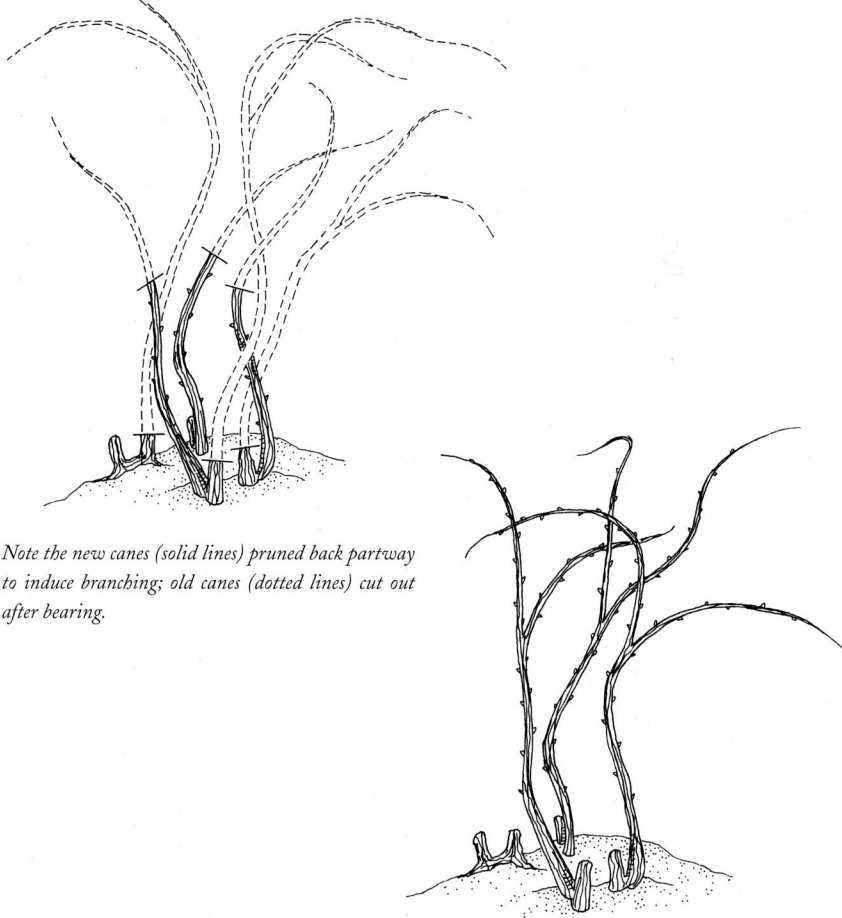

Note the new canes (solid lines) pruned back partway to induce branching; old canes (dotted lines) cut out after bearing.

New canes after branching, ready to fruit next year.

set 15 to 18 inches apart on 5-foot posts. Posts and wires should be set before planting.

Space one or two bare-root red raspberry plants about 2 feet apart, and all others 3 feet apart. Cut back all canes to about 6 inches. Spread the roots as widely as possible in the hole, and plant 2 to 3 inches deeper than the soil line indicates they had been in the nursery. Use of mulch will afford winter protection and will both conserve soil moisture and discourage weeds the following season. Raspberry canes are biennial, and the pruning regimen for them is essentially the same as for blackberry (see page 698). Bearing usually begins the second year after planting, but it takes another year or two to reach maximum levels. Ripened fruit should be harvested frequently but only when dry, take care to avoid bruising. Place picked berries out of direct sun or chill them as soon as possible after picking.

In zone 3, most cultivars require winter protection, as with burlap shields or by bending the canes to the ground and covering them with sod or soil. In nutrient-deficient soils, make annual applications of a high-potassium fertilizer (such as 7-10-10 or 7-12-10) in the spring to help keep up fruit yield. Mix the fertilizer well with a topdressing of compost or well-rotted manure to maintain soil moisture through the summer.

As pests and diseases are numerous and often cumulative in effect, relocation of rows or renewal of plantings every three to five years may be required to control diseases as well as weeds. In regions where aphid-spread virus diseases are serious, aphid-resistant or -immune cultivars should be chosen. Consult your cooperative extension station for names of and controls for locally important disorders; when possible, select resistant or tolerant cultivars. See Chapter 34 for more on pest and disease control.

Cultivars are numerous and vary in performance according to soils, climatic extremes, and pest and disease susceptibility. Seek information from experienced local gardeners or the local cooperative extension station before selecting. The red raspberry cultivars 'Latham', hardy to zone 3, and 'Heritage', hardy to zone 4 and "everbearing" (bearing two successive crops each season), are widely grown commercially but are not reliably virus resistant; they bear well under varied conditions as far south as zone 7. 'Canby', a nearly thornless form best grown from zone 5 to 8, is aphid immune and hence little troubled by virus disease. Others, all more or less susceptible, include 'Bababerry' and 'Indian Summer', both bearing two crops a season; 'Hilton', with 3- to 4-foot canes that require no support; and 'Dormanred', which requires less cold and is tolerant of more heat than most cultivars and hence is useful in zones 8 and 9.

The best yellow-fruited raspberry is 'Fall Gold', which is hardy to zone 4 and bears two crops a year; except for fruit color, it is generally similar to 'Heritage'. The purple-fruited 'Royalty' is rather less flavorful than red and yellow raspberries and is also hardy to zone 4. It is aphid immune as well as resistant to most other pests.

Black raspberries, because of their categorical susceptibility to virus, should be grown 300 feet or more away from virus-prone red- and yellow-fruited cultivars. 'Cumberland' is much grown commercially and 'Black Hawk' is somewhat virus resistant.

OTHER BUSH FRUITS

BEACH PLUM
(Prunus maritima)

Beach plum is a densely twiggy, somewhat thorny native shrub that grows to 6 feet tall. It is found mostly in coastal areas from New Brunswick (zone 3) to Virginia (zone 7) and is rarely cultivated as a fruit crop because production is very erratic and unpredictable. The fruit varies from ½ to ¾ inch in diameter and ripens in late summer from deep red to purple; it is covered with a waxy gray bloom and contains a small freestone pit. Most fruit is harvested from wild shrubs found on littoral dunes and nearby sandy areas and is used to make preserves or liqueur. When cultivated elsewhere on richer soil, the shrubs tend to become larger and rangier—even treelike—but seldom bear reliably or heavily.

Fruit set, which can be heavy, depends on the activities of pollinating bees at flowering time. In the cool, wet, windy weather that can occur during the brief flowering period, bees often remain away, accounting for the often skimpy crops. In any case, full exposure to sunlight on sandy, acidic soil is essential.

Several cultivars have been named, mostly on the basis of fruit size exceeding that of wild shrubs. These include 'Eastham', 'Hancock', 'Premier', and 'Squibnocket', all with fruit suitable for eating fresh when ripe as well as for preserves. A yellow-fruited variant is also known.

ELDERBERRY
(Sambucus canadensis)

Of the various American and Old World species of elder, the native sweet elder or American elder is preferred for elderberries in the United States. It is a large, fast-growing shrub that grows to about 12 feet tall and as wide and occurs naturally on stream banks and in moist woodland borders from zones 3 to 9 east of the Mississippi. Elder is easily cultivated under ordinary garden conditions. Damp ground in full sun results in the largest yields. The small white flowers borne in large, flat clusters in late spring are followed by small glossy berries that ripen black in late summer. The ripe fruits are used for preserves, pies, and wine. In addition, blanched young leaves are included in salads, flower clusters are dipped in batter and prepared as fritters, and half-ripe berries are especially suitable for jelly as no supplemental pectin is required. Bearing usually begins within three or four years of set-out. Prune out dead or weak stems each spring as the leaves expand.

The naturally occurring variety, *S. canadensis* var. *maxima*, has fruit clusters up to 18 inches in diameter that cause the branches to bend low as the berries mature. Temporary propping may be required to prevent breakage. In the selected cultivars 'Adams', 'Nova', and 'York', the individual berries are up to ⅜ inch in diameter, or about 50 percent wider than in wild bushes.

The blue elder (*S. caerulea*), a large shrub or small tree of the West, bears fruit that matures blue-black, the European elder (*S. nigra*) bears a black fruit. Both are also sometimes grown for their fruit.

JOSTABERRY
(*Ribes × nidigrolaria*)

A horticultural hybrid resulting from a cross made in the 1950s between the black currant and gooseberry, jostaberry (pronounced *yo'-sta-ber-ry*) is a vigorous, thornless shrub that grows to 8 feet. It is hardy from zone 3 to 8 and bears clusters of glossy black fruit. Each berry is ½ to ¾ inch across and has the flavor of gooseberry with a hint of currant. Ripened fruit is used like gooseberries in jams, jellies, and pies.

As jostaberry does not serve as alternate host for the white pine blister rust, it should generally be legally permitted for culture, except perhaps in regions where all species of *Ribes* are banned. Consult your local cooperative extension agent before planting. It is also resistant to powdery mildew and a range of pests of currants and gooseberries.

Culture is the same as for gooseberry (see page 701). Adequate summer moisture is necessary for full fruit development, hence the advisability of a 4- to 6-inch-thick summer mulch. Except in poor soils, fertilizer supplements are unnecessary. Winter pruning to remove older, less productive wood augments the crop. Crops from mature shrubs total 6 to 12 pounds per season and usually have fully ripened by early summer.

The cultivars 'Yostagranda', 'Jostaki', and 'Yostina' are scarcely distinct, but, if available, two or more grown together ensure optimal cross-pollination and maximal fruit set.

PRICKLY PEAR
(*Opuntia* spp.)

Of the very large and diverse cactus genus *Opuntia*, several species are grown for their edible fruit. Most notable is the so-called Indian fig (*O. ficus-indica*), which grows in dry regions in zones 9 and 10 from southern Texas to southern California. Shrubby or even treelike, the Indian fig has spiny pads bordered with showy yellow flowers that are followed by fleshy, pear-shaped fruits (called *tuna*) that reach 2 to 3½ inches long, maturing red to purple. These are eaten raw or are skinned and prepared as preserves. The boiled, strained juice may be fermented (*colonche*) or further concentrated to become a thick paste (*melcocha*). Ground seed and pulp are the basis of tuna cheese (*queso de tuna*). In addition, young, partly grown pads are used as a cooked vegetable or made into candy.

Well-drained calcareous soil and a position exposed to full sun are the principal cultural requirements.

Of the many natural variants, the nearly thornless 'Burbank' is most favored for cultivation. Other native species with edible fruit include the Lindheimer prickly pear or nopal (*O. lindheimeri*), which is hardy in central Texas north to zone 8 and also

has a thornless form, and the Engelmann prickly pear (*O. engelmannii*), a usually thornier species growing in the wild to zone 7 in Utah.

SAND CHERRY
(*Prunus besseyi*)

Also called bush cherry, western sand cherry, or Rocky Mountain cherry, sand cherry is a densely branched, spreading shrub that grows to 3 to 6 feet tall and as wide. It has abundant white flowers in the spring, which are followed by glossy fruit, ⅝ to ¾ inch across, that ripens black-violet in late summer. The fruit is eaten raw or made into preserves.

Hardy from zone 3 to 6, sand cherry is best grown from container stock. Once established and kept adequately watered for one or two years, it needs little regular care. Space about 4 feet apart in a sunny location. It is particularly suited to cultivation on neutral or slightly alkaline soils (pH 7 to 7.5) and requires no pruning, other than the removal of weak or dead stems.

Among the cultivars, 'Hansen's' bears flavorful fruit ¾ to ⅞ inch across, and 'Black Beauty' bears heavy crops of ⅝-inch fruit. Expect the initial crop within three years of set-out.

SHRUBBY CHOKECHERRY
(*Prunus virginiana* var. *demissa*)

Better suited to the acidic soils of the East, shrubby chokecherry is a diminutive natural variety of the common chokecherry that stays lower than 8 feet and, after its white flowers appear in the spring, bears a multitude of ⅓-inch fruit that turns red and finally ripens black-violet in mid to late summer. The fruit is used for sauces, preserves, and wine. Culture and behavior are otherwise the same as for chokecherry.

The cultivar 'Xanthocarpa' has fruit that matures yellow.

VINE FRUITS

GRAPE
(*Vitis* spp.)

Cultivated in what are now Turkey and Syria as long ago as 5000 B.C., the grape has been prominent throughout history, principally as the source of wine. Today, grapes are grown worldwide both in gardens and vineyards, wherever climate permits, for winemaking, as a table or dessert fruit, for grape juice, and for preserves.

The European wild grape (*V. vinifera*) accounts for most production, especially outside the United States. Its cultivars are favored for winemaking and are much grown in the Mediterranean region, South Africa, California, southern South America, and Australia. Such hardy native American species as the summer grape (*V. aestivalis*), the muscadine (*V. rotundifolia*), and the fox grape (*V. labrusca*), when hybridized with *vinifera* cultivars, have extended the range of wine grape culture to cooler areas, such as interior New England, Upstate New York, the Midwest, and the Northwest. Other hybrids are grown primarily for table grapes. Derivatives of the muscadine are favored in the South for table fruit, grape juice, and preserves.

In general, grape culture requires adequate space, attention to annual pruning, and sufficient warm weather to vine-ripen the crop. The usual procedure is to plant one- or two-year-old vines in early spring before leaf out. Most any well-drained, moderately fertile soil suffices, but deep soils are best, because grape roots penetrate as much as 10 feet. The vines should

be spaced 6 to 8 feet apart along a two-wire fence installed before planting, with the lower wire about 2 feet above the ground and the upper one 2 feet higher. If more than one fence is built, the courses should be about 6 feet apart and oriented north to south. Each vine should be set in a hole that has been previously dug about 1 foot deep and as wide, and one-quarter to one-third filled with compost-enriched soil. Roots are spread on this medium (with any excessively long ones pruned) and then covered with enough of the same soil to fill the hole. The soil should be lightly tamped and watered.

For maximum fruit production, grapes must be pruned annually in early spring. Young, newly planted, dormant vines should be cut back to two buds. In the first season, the stronger of the two shoots growing from these buds should be allowed to grow up to the top wire and then be cut off at that level; any other growth is removed. This stem becomes the trunk, and it will bear buds along its length. In the second year, the two buds nearest the lower wire and the two nearest the upper wire are allowed to produce lateral arms, or canes, and these are tied to the wires as they grow. All other shoots are removed. Buds formed on these four laterals become the bearing shoots in the third season. In the next pruning, at the beginning of the fourth season, the previous season's bearing shoots are cut back to about four buds, since only vigorous new growth will flower and bear fruit. By repeating this process each spring, vines are kept small and pro-

ductive until senescence sets in, anywhere from 10 to 30 years, when production begins to diminish and severe cutting back or the replacement of vines becomes necessary.

Many gardeners prefer growing grapes on an arbor rather than on fence wires, training the vines to grow up and across a flat-topped frame, usually about 8 feet high, providing not only an easily harvested fruit crop but also summer shade. If pruning is neglected, less fruit will be produced year by year and the vines frequently outgrow the arbor and ascend nearby trees and buildings. The best procedure is to plant young vines about 4 feet apart around the periphery of the arbor and in the first year allow the most vigorous one or two shoots to grow to the top of the arbor, there to be cut off. In the second year, three or four branch shoots from each of these trunks are allowed to grow across the top of the arbor. In early spring of the third year, each of the thickest canes of the previous year's growth is cut back to three or four buds. Any slender canes (less than a pencil's thickness) are pruned out entirely. By repeating this annual cutting back and thinning, the vines will remain productive, cast the desired shade, and stay in bounds.

It is important to note that however grapes are grown, the fruit must be left on the vine until fully ripe, i.e., when they are most sweet and flavorful. Once removed, the fruit will not continue ripening.

Pests and diseases of grapes are numerous and sometimes serious. Root disorders are largely averted by grafting cultivars

Growth and pruning of a grapevine

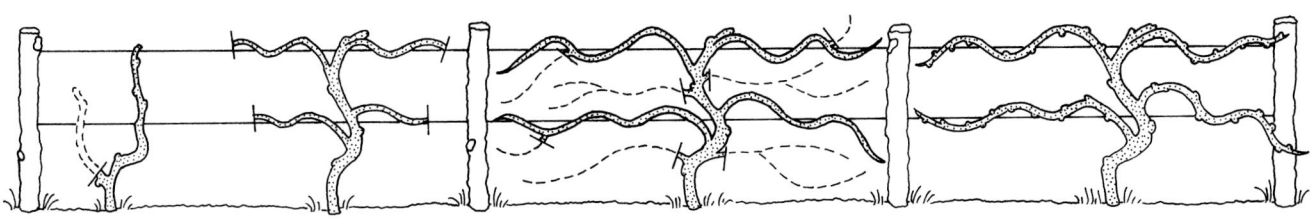

1. Prune off weaker shoot.

2. Prune off all but four shoots. Allow horizontals to grow.

3. Prune back stragglers.

4. Pruned vine with buds.

onto resistant roots of native species. Pests range from deer and birds, against which fencing or netting is the surest defense, to flea beetles and sap-sucking phylloxerid bugs. Among the more common diseases are powdery mildew of leaves and black rot of fruit. For control of such insects and fungi, it is best to consult your local cooperative extension station for currently acceptable preparations and procedures.

Grape cultivars are numerous and vary particularly in presence or absence of seeds, time of ripening, pest and disease resistance, and hardiness. The cultivars listed below are intended more as an indication of the range of diversity that is commercially available than as specific recommendations. Such recommendations are best obtained locally from your cooperative extension agent, your state agricultural university, or local gardeners experienced in grape culture.

White (actually green) seedless table grape cultivars are dominated by 'Interlaken', a highly productive but relatively tender (hardy only to zone 7) type that ripens in August and is subject to bird damage, and 'Himrod' (hardy to zone 5), which ripens in early September. Other seedless whites as well or better suited to home gardens and hardy to zone 5 are the following.

'Lakemont Seedless': disease resistant; ripens in August.
'Ontario': disease free; ripens in mid-September.
'Romulus': ripens in late September.

Among seeded white grape cultivars are 'Scuppernong', a muscadine well suited to the South that ripens in early September, and 'Golden Muscat', which ripens in late September.

Red seedless table grapes include the popular, disease-resistant cultivars 'Canadice' and 'Suffolk Red Seedless', which are hardy to zone 5 and ripen in early September. 'Saturn', hardy to zone 6, and 'Reliance Seedless', hardy to zone 5, ripen in mid to late August. 'Delaware', a seeded type hardy to zone 5, ripens in late September. Among purple (or blue-black) seedless table grapes are the disease-resistant 'Venus

Seedless', a cultivar suited to the South, and 'Mars Seedless', which ripens in August. The less disease-resistant 'Glenora' and 'Concord Seedless' (not to be confused with the commercially dominant 'Concord', a seeded cultivar), ripen in early September. All are hardy to zone 5 except for 'Venus Seedless', which is best south of zone 7.

Seeded purple table grapes are mostly hardier (to zone 3) and are believed by some to be more fully flavored. Cultivars include 'Van Buren' and the disease-free 'Worden', both ripening in early September; 'Alden', the ever-popular 'Concord', and the disease-free 'Buffalo' and 'Steuben'. All ripen in late September. 'Sheridan' ripens in late September to early October.

Wine grapes suited to home cultivation include the white-fruited cultivars 'Aurora', a hardy (to zone 5) seeded type that ripens in early September but is subject to bird damage, and the commercially very popular 'Niagara', a seedless type (hardy to zone 6) that ripens in mid-September. Grape cultivars for red wines include 'Foch', which ripens in early September and is subject to bird damage. The very popular 'Fredonia', and the disease-resistant 'Baco Noir' both ripen in mid to late September. 'Catawba', ripens from late September to early October. All are hardy to zone 5.

KIWIFRUIT
(*Actinidia* spp.)

In addition to the various species grown as ornamental climbers (see page 278), at least two species of *Actinidia* are grown in the United States for their edible fruit. Better known is the commercially grown, brown-bristly, large-fruited kiwifruit (*A. deliciosa*), also called cape gooseberry, which is a vigorous woody twiner of southeast China that has juicy green-fleshed, egg-size fruit. Long cultivated in China (as *yang-tao*), it is an export crop in New Zealand and has more recently been grown commercially in California and elsewhere in the South, mostly in zones 8 and 9. The other species, the

hardy kiwifruit or tara vine (*A. arguta*) is also from China but is hardy to zone 4. It is a similarly vigorous woody twiner and is increasingly grown in home gardens for its smooth, emerald green fruit 1¼ to 1½ inches long.

Kiwifruit vines are dioecious, i.e., each plant bears either male or female flowers. Hence, for fruit crops, it is necessary to plant both male and female vines, usually at a ratio of one to eight. Some cultivars, however, are self-fertile—a distinct advantage where space is limited. The large-fruited kiwifruit is successful in regions having at least 600 hours of temperatures below 45°F each year, but no lower than 10°F, and a long (eight months or more), hot summer to ripen the fruit. The smaller-fruited, hardy kiwifruit endures winter temperatures as low as −25°F and requires a five- to six-month growing season.

Culture for either involves a strongly built arbor, trellis, or fence up to 8 feet high in full sun or partial shade and a well-drained, deeply prepared, moderately fertile soil, preferably of pH 6.5 to 7.5, with generous incorporation of well-rotted manure or compost. A location protected from strong wind will help avert bruising of the fruit. For maximum fruit production, vines should be spaced 8 to 10 feet apart. Where space will accommodate only one vine, a female plant with a male branch grafted on may be obtained or a self-fertile cultivar may be used. One- or two-year-old bare-root or container-grown vines are planted in the spring, with the expectation of a small yield in two or three years and full production—up to 5 gallons per female vine per season—after five years and continuing for decades. Except in those parts of zones 8 and 9 where mixed fruit crops have long been grown, kiwifruit is free of pests and diseases. Occasional pruning of excessively long shoots will help keep vines in bounds.

The best cultivar of the large-fruited kiwifruit for home garden culture is the self-fertile 'Blake', with fruits ripening in zone 8 conditions. The comparably self-fertile hardy kiwifruit cultivar is 'Issai', also with fruit ripening in late summer to early fall.

HERBAL FRUITS

STRAWBERRY
(Fragaria × ananassa)

Of all the fruit bearers commonly grown in the home garden, strawberries bear soonest after planting, require the least space, are thornless, and never soar out of reach. To grow this perennial crop successfully, however, it is important to understand the idiosyncracies of the various types and to appropriately culture those you choose.

Until the twentieth century, strawberries were picked in the wild or from wild plants grown in gardens. Hybridization of several small-fruited European species and two American ones in England in the 1800s led to the first large-fruited but somewhat blander-flavored hybrids, of which there were several in cultivation by 1900. Since then, continued breeding there and in the United States has resulted in today's diversity of large-fruited, June-bearing cultivars, many of which are suited to particular climate regimens and soil conditions and are variously resistant to aphid-borne viruses and other diseases. By crossing the European alpine strawberry (*F. vesca* var. *semperflorens*) with certain large-fruited cultivars, remontant, or "everbearing," cultivars were developed, in which the usually heavy June crop is followed by a weakly synchronized second crop in late summer or early fall. Further crossing, especially of *F. virginiana* ssp. *glauca*, whose fruit production is unaffected by day length and is, therefore, continuous through the growing season, with large-fruited cultivars resulted in the so-called day-neutral class, in which three often vaguely synchronized crops are borne successively on relatively small plants.

For home garden cultivation, each of these classes has virtues and caveats. Day-neutral strawberries are easiest to grow, require less space, and bear medium-size fruits over a long period. Everbearing types are mostly larger plants, usually larger fruited, and offer two main crops with a scattering of fruit in the warm summer weather between them. The largest and most numerous fruits are produced by the June-bearing cultivars, but beside their brief season, they require more cultural attention. In addition to these three classes, alpine strawberries include several cultivars bearing small (½ to 1 inch long), richly flavored fruits from late spring until frost, but plants spread quickly and thus need frequent thinning.

In general, it is important for the tyro to limit initial choice to about 25 plants of one cultivar (either day-neutral or everbearing) and perhaps 25 more of a June-bearer (especially if preserving is intended) and to choose disease-resistant cultivars from reputable growers. Your local cooperative extension service can advise about which cultivars are best suited to conditions in your region and which are best avoided. For example, early-fruiting cultivars are risky in areas subject to midspring frosts, as a freeze will kill flowers and preclude a crop.

Strawberries of any class do best on well-drained, humusy, fertile soil of pH 6 to 6.5. Full sun is best in the North; partial shade may be advisable in the South. Soil for strawberries should be rototilled or forked well ahead of planting, preferably the previous season, and left fallow long enough to be sure that all perennial weeds have been removed. Root competition from weeds or disturbance of strawberries by uprooting them can seriously diminish the crop.

Most strawberries are propagated by slender, horizontal runners that grow out in all directions from the parent plant and sprout "daughter" plants that strike root and become independent. Management of runners varies according to type of cultivar.

Planting year-old bare-root stock (rooted daughters) is best done in early spring, i.e., as as soon as the soil is frost free and workable. Whether received in the mail or purchased at a nursery, crowns should be planted immediately. Alternatively, the package may be stored in the refrigerator a few days or, if the delay is to be longer, the crowns heeled-in temporarily in the garden. Immediately before planting, apply 10-10-10 commercial fertilizer at the rate of 25 pounds per 1,000 square feet of bed.

Day-neutral Cultivars

Day-neutral cultivars should be planted about 6 inches apart in two staggered rows in a bed 12 to 15 inches wide and, if two or more parallel beds are planted, about 30 inches between beds. It is important to keep the roots of all the crowns moist as planting proceeds. For each crown, dig a wide, shallow hole that will permit the roots to be spread downward and outward. It is especially important that, once the hole is filled, the crown be at ground level, with all roots covered and all buds showing. If crowns are just ½ inch too low or ½ inch too high, fruit yield will be much reduced. Not long after the leaves appear, flowers will develop. All of these early flowers should be pinched off to allow plants to develop vegetatively and strengthen. After about six weeks, flowers may be left to open and develop fruit. Any runners that appear should be removed throughout the first season.

To conserve soil moisture, deter weeds, and avert heat buildup in the soil, mulch beds with at least 3 inches of straw or other neutral weed-seed-free material. To help maintain fruit set, add 1 pound of 10-10-10 to every 50 feet of bed each month. Drip or soaker-hose irrigation is preferable to sprinklers, as it minimizes the possibility of fruit rot that can occur when strawberries are wet for long periods. In late fall or early winter, as low temperatures approach 20°F, the beds should be mulched with 6 inches of straw or pine needles; this covering should be removed from crowns about one month before the date of the usual last spring frost.

From the second year onward, the fruit harvest will reach maximum yield, which can be as much as 2 pounds of fruit per plant for the season. Yield is usually heaviest in June, lightest in hot weather (especially from zone 7 south), and moderate in the fall. As day-neutral plants usually remain productive for years, continued removal of runners is advisable, except if replacement plants are needed or an expanded planting of the same cultivar is desired. The more runners that are allowed to grow, the sparser the fruit harvest. In time, weeds and/or pests and diseases mount and crops diminish, necessitating renewal and relocation of the planting.

Everbearing and June-bearing Cultivars

Everbearing strawberries, though heavily promoted, have eluded popularity, partly because they are not truly everbearing and also because their total seasonal yields are no greater than those of June-bearing cultivars. When choosing cultivars in either of these classes, it is best to focus on those that start bearing in mid to late June (to avoid frost damage to flowers) and on those with medium fruit (as the very large fruit is usually bland in flavor). Beds for everbearing and June-bearing cultivars should be about 4 feet wide and long enough to accomodate three staggered rows of plants set 18 inches apart for June-bearing types, 12 inches for everbearing. The greater interval allows runners space to develop and root; this is especially necessary for June bearers, because it is the daughter plants that yield fruit the following season, not the plants originally set out.

In June-bearing cultivars, all flowers should be removed from the original plants to stimulate early runner development; there is no fruit crop the first year. Moreover, only one or two daughters should be permitted to develop on each runner. Runners should be guided with sticks so that each daughter will strike root no closer than 6 inches to any other. In everbearing cultivars, original plants may be allowed to bear late; i.e., flowers may be left in place to form fruit after the first week or two of July, thus ensuring at least a small crop in the first season.

In June-bearing cultivars, once the crop has been harvested, the planting is "renovated," first by removing all foliage, either by hand or, in large, level beds, by using a rotary lawn mower set at least 1½ inches high to remove the leaves without damaging the crowns. Then, 20 pounds of 10-10-10 fertilizer should be spread per 1,000 square feet of bed (this should not be done in spring, as it would stimulate lush foliage at the expense of flowers and fruit). Old plants (and weeds too) are dug out and the remaining daughters are thinned to stand no closer than 6 inches apart. A topdressing of well-rotted manure or compost and a thorough watering complete the process. Everbearing cultivars do not require such drastic treatment, and runner production is not as prolific. However, thinning, careful weed removal, and fertilizing are necessary.

Alpine Cultivars

Alpines are treated like day-neutrals (of which they are a prototype), but require less winter protection and more assiduous thinning. Old plants that have clumped can be lifted and divided in the fall or early spring. Alpines may be grown from seed, with the expectation of a first small crop the second year.

Winter Protection

A winter mulch of wheat, rye, or oat straw, pine needles, or salt hay spread 3 to 4 inches thick after hard frost but before temperatures drop below 20°F helps control freeze-thaw cycling, which often kills strawberry roots and causes the crowns to be lifted or "heaved" out of the ground. Alternatively, fallen tree leaves may be used, except those that form a compact, soggy mass (such as Norway maple, *Acer platanoides*) or that acidify the soil (such as oak, *Quercus* spp.). Crushed corncobs or buckwheat hulls are other acceptable substitutes. In the spring, as growth resumes, most of the winter mulch should be gently raked out of the beds but a light residual covering will help prevent mud from splashing on the fruit, slow soil moisture evaporation, and discourage weed growth.

Pests and Diseases

Whatever the type of strawberry, it is important to promptly harvest all ripe and damaged fruit to prevent the development of black rot, which can rapidly infect and devastate a planting. The other principal diseases, especially red stele disease, are avoided by choosing resistant cultivars. Crop rotation is advisable when replanting. Birds can be excluded by using ½-inch mesh nylon netting, especially if it is held somewhat above the plants.

Strawberry Cultivars for Home Cultivation

There are relatively few cultivars of day-neutral strawberries, bearing from June to frost.

'Selva': disease resistant; bears prolifically; large fruit; bland flavor.
'Tribute': similar to 'Tristar'; somewhat more disease resistant and cold tolerant (to zone 4).
'Tristar': very adaptable from zone 5 to 8; bears medium fruit; good flavor.

Everbearing cultivars, bearing mainly in June and again late in the season, include the disease-resistant and prolifically bearing 'Ozark Beauty', a commercial leader, as well as 'Ogallala', which is more drought tolerant than most. 'Fort Laramie' is hardy to zone 3. 'Ostara' and 'Streamliner' are prolific and have uniform fruit, a consideration in commercial production or when preserving. 'Shortcake' produces a large late-season second crop, and 'Ever Red' is noted for large fruit size. Except for 'Fort Laramie', all are hardy from zone 4 to 8.

Among the numerous cultivars of June-bearing strawberries, mostly hardy from zone 4 to 8, and all noted for a single heavy crop in late spring or early summer that favors this class for preserving as well as for table use are the following. 'Earliglow' matures early (early to mid June), 'Guardian' matures in midseason (mid to late June), and 'Red Chief', also matures in midseason and is hardy to zone 3. All are notably disease resistant. Particularly favored for commercial production are the disease-resistant, midseason cultivars 'Honeoye' and 'Surecrop', and the late-season 'Sparkle'. Early-season 'Cardinal' and 'Dunlap' perform well in a wide range of soils. 'Trumpeter' and 'Kent', also early-season, are hardy to zone 3. 'Big Red' and 'Fairfax' are early-season cultivars, 'Allstar' and 'Catskill' are midseason cultivars, and 'Robinson' is a late-season cultivar. 'Spring Giant', which bears 3-inch-long fruit, must be grown with another cultivar for pollination.

Of the alpine strawberry cultivars available in the United States, the deep red fruited 'Ruegen Improved' is the most widely grown. 'Pineapple Crush' and 'Yellow Wonder' are yellow fruited, and the natural variety *F. vesca* var. *albicarpa* has fruit that matures white.

WONDERBERRY
(Solanum spp.)

Also called sunberry, or annual wonderberry, a few low-growing species of the large, diverse, primarily tropical genus *Solanum* are sometimes grown in the United States for their edible fruit. Among the best known of this group is the wonderberry (*S. × burbankii*), a hybrid developed and promoted by Luther Burbank early in the century. It grows to 1 to 1½ feet tall and bears ½-inch currantlike fruit that matures black or orange. The garden huckleberry (*S. melanocerasum*, not to be confused with *Vaccinium* spp. and *Gaylussacia* spp., both shrubby groups) reaches 1½ to 2 feet tall and bears black fruit that matures to ½ to ⅝ inch in diameter. Less commonly grown for its fruit is the black nightshade (*S. nigrum*), a weedy plant that varies in habit from prostrate to upright and (2½ feet tall) and bears ¼-inch berries that must ripen to black to be edible (the unripe green fruit is poisonous). Ripe berries of all three species are used in fruit salads and in making preserves.

Ordinary well-drained, moderately fertile soil suits these plants. Sow seed directly in the garden. Thin seedlings to stand 1 foot apart.

THE NUT GARDEN

Although the term *nut* has a precise botanical meaning (a one-celled, one-seeded fruit with a bony outer covering, as in the acorn), many other fruits with woody, leathery, or fibrous husks are popularly called "nuts." Those that are edible and suited to home garden cultivation are discussed here.

ALMOND
(Prunus dulcis)

Closely related to the peach, the almond (or more correctly the sweet almond) is a bushy tree, 20 to 25 feet tall, which is grown for its soft-shelled seeds. Although culture is essentially the same as for peach (see page 692), the almond's very early blooming habit suits it for productive cultivation only in southern California, where the comparatively brief and mild chilling requirement is met and the flowers are not threatened by early spring frosts. Elsewhere in the United States, although the almond is hardy to zone 6, nut crops are seldom reliable. At maturity, the fruit turns leathery, splits along one side, and reveals the nut, which should then be harvested.

'Hall's Hardy' is the cultivar most commonly grown outside the commercial growing area in California. 'All-in-One', a hybrid with the peach and grafted onto peach rootstock, flowers later and hence is successful to zone 7.

CHESTNUT
(Castanea spp.)

Since the virtual demise of the American chestnut (*C. dentata*) as a nut-bearing species by chestnut blight in the early 1900s, the chestnut trees currently grown in the United States are Chinese chestnuts (*C. mollissima*), wide-spreading trees that reach about 60 feet tall and are hardy from zone 4 to 8. and Much less commonly grown is the Japanese chestnut (*C. crenata*), which reaches about 30 feet and is hardy from zone 5 to 8. Both are resistant to chestnut blight. Imported chestnuts harvested in Europe are usually from the Spanish chestnut (*C. sativa*), which is not adapted to prolonged hot summer weather and is susceptible to chestnut blight. Hence it is little grown in the United States.

Chinese chestnut and its various hybrids thrive on well-drained, even droughty, acidic soils of average or low fertility. Trees should be spaced about 40 feet apart, with the first crop usually appearing in five to seven years. As chestnuts are mostly self-sterile, nut crops are best if representatives of two clones or cultivars are grown together. Nut size is largest in those trees in which all but one nut in each burr are suppressed. Few diseases afflict cultivated chestnuts when grown in the garden. The crop matures in early fall and is ready for harvest when the spiny burrs split open, revealing the nuts within.

Although numerous cultivars of Chinese chestnut are available, the large-nutted trees grown in the United States are usually sold without designation. Where available, 'Abundance', 'Kuling', 'Meiling', and 'Nanking' are adaptable, productive cultivars. Among hybrids (mostly of *C. mollissima* × *C. dentata*), 'Miller's Manchurian', 'Dunstan' hybrid, and 'Revival' are reliable if, again, two or more trees are grown together, preferably of different cultivars.

FILBERT, HAZELNUT
(Corylus spp.)

Filbert, or hazelnut, cultivars are small, low-headed trees (20 feet tall) that are derived from the European hazel (*C. colurna*), the American hazel (*C. americana*), and the giant filbert (*C. maxima*).

Filbert cultivars are grown from zone 4 to 9 and will succeed in most any well-drained soil, thriving where soil pH is 6 to 7. Light shade is beneficial, especially in zones 4 and 5, where winter conditions can be harsh. It is necessary to plant two or more trees of different cultivars in proximity for good nut set. Space the trees no closer than 15 feet apart. To maintain full production, suckers should be removed from trunk bases. Bearing usually begins the third or fourth year after planting. Nuts should be harvested from the yellowing husks in late summer; if not, they fall to the ground.

Squirrels are often serious pests, sometimes stripping entire crops. They are effectively controlled only by erecting a 1-inch-mesh wire enclosure around and over each tree. Where such protection is required, annual pruning is practiced to keep trees about 8 feet high.

Numerous cultivars exist. 'Barcelona' and 'Royal', both commercially important in the Pacific Northwest, bear heavy crops of large nuts. 'Butler', which, in addition to bearing creditable nut crops, is an effective pollinator for 'Barcelona' and 'Royal' cultivars. In addition, a number of named interspecific hybrids are grown, including 'Hazelbert' (*C. avellana* × *C. americana*), 'Filazel' (*C. avellana* × *C. cornuta*), and 'Trazel' (*C. avellana* × *C. cornuta*). These hybrids have, in turn, spawned other cultivars with superior nut characteristics.

PEANUT
(*Arachis hypogaea*)

Also known as goobers and groundnuts, peanuts are very important commercially, especially in tropical and subtropical regions, but seldom grown as a nut crop in gardens in the United States. Their long-season requirement makes success unpredictable north of zone 8. The peanut is a spreading annual legume whose yellow sweet-pea-like flowers are borne on elongating stalks (called "pegs") that push the developing ovaries into the soil where the pods develop, each with two to five seeds (the peanuts). When the seeds have matured, the entire plant yellows and dies.

Ordinary creeping peanuts require 20 weeks to mature; short-stemmed "bunching" cultivars mature in somewhat less time. Seed should be sown indoors under fluorescent lights (14 to 16 hours per day) or

in a greenhouse in individual 2½-inch pots four to six weeks before the last spring frost. After hardening off in a coldframe, set the seedlings in the garden about 8 inches apart once night temperatures stay above 50°F. Well-drained, humusy soil, exposure to full sun, and generous soil moisture through the blooming period are requisites. Weed control is also important. Whole plants with pods still attached should be lifted when brown and air-dried for one or two weeks in a frost-free place before the pods are removed and opened.

Among the cultivars best suited to home-garden culture, all of compact bunching habit, are 'Pronto', which has small seeds that ripen in about 15 weeks; 'Valencia Tennessee Red', whose seeds ripen in about 17 weeks; and 'Virginia Jumbo', which has large seeds, mostly two or three per pod, that ripen in about 20 weeks.

PECAN
(*Carya illinoensis*)

A long-lived species of hickory that can reach 100 feet in its native south-central U.S. range, the pecan is now grown over much of the United States, but nut crops are most prolific in zones 8 to 10. Among the various cultivars, there is considerable specialization for varied climates and soils; it is best, therefore, to consult your local cooperative extension agent or your states agricultural university for recommendations in your area.

Deep, well-drained, loamy soil favors the pecan. As the nuts are gathered from the ground after they have fallen naturally, there is no advantage in keeping trees low headed. Transplanting trees from the wild seldom succeeds, as pecan has a deep taproot. It is best to plant young nursery-grown stock, preferably containered, in the fall, using grafted or budded cultivars, which are sometimes available with several cultivars grafted on a single trunk. An annual application of nitrate-rich fertilizer stimulates maximum production of large nuts. Bearing usually begins within 7 to 10 years.

Among the more adaptable cultivars are the following.

'Colby': seldom exceeds 50 feet; zones 5 to 9.

'Giant Mehan': large, thin-shelled nuts; zones 7 to 10.

'James Hican': nuts are larger than most; hybrid of pecan and shagbark hickory (*C. ovata*); hardy to zone 5.

'Mullahy': very productive cultivar; hardy to zone 4.

'Perque': thin-shelled nuts; zones 5 to 9.

'Stuart': begins bearing while still quite young; zones 7 to 10.

Because of self-sterility in many cultivars, it is best to plant at least two trees, each of a different cultivar. Spacing should be generous—60 to 75 feet between trees—to encourage full top development and maximum production per tree.

Other hickory species suited to home cultivation for nut crops include big shellbark (*C. laciniosa*) and little shellbark, or shagbark (*C. ovata*), each reaching 100 feet in the wild but usually much lower in cultivation. There are many thin-shelled, prolifically bearing cultivars of each species.

PISTACHIO
(*Pistacia vera*)

Pistachio is an evergreen tree that reaches about 30 feet tall and is native to the Mediterranean region. It is grown commercially in the United States in zones 9 and 10 in southern California and Arizona, but it will survive winter temperatures to 15°F, suiting it for the warmer parts of zone 8, including southern New Mexico and south-central Texas east to coastal South Carolina. Hardiness in this zone is ensured when pistachio is grafted on the roots of the hardier but inedible Chinese pistachio (*P. chinensis*).

Nut crops are best in areas with low humidity, long, hot summers, and poor soil. Trees are planted about 25 feet apart, with one male tree planted per five to seven females. Nuts are ready for harvest when the reddish fruits become wrinkled. Consult your cooperative extension service for cultivars best suited to your area.

WALNUT
(*Juglans* spp.)

All of the fifteen species of walnut produce edible nuts, but the highest quality are those of various cultivars of English walnut (*J. regia*), a tree that reaches 100 feet in its native Europe and Asia, but it is kept much lower by annual pruning when grown for nuts. As with the pecan, numerous cultivars of English walnut have been developed for a wide range of conditions, and some are quite specific in their tolerances and requirements. Hence the desirability of consulting local information sources, such as the cooperative extension service, before planting.

Except for pruning, culture is the same as for pecan (see page 710). English walnut succeeds best in neutral to slightly alkaline soils (pH 7 to 7.5) and, if grown in deep soils, is tolerant of considerable summer drought. To avoid substantial sap loss ("bleeding"), pruning should be done in early fall through winter but not when the trees are actively growing or bearing. The aim should be to develop a diverging vase- or cup-shaped framework of major limbs that will eventually support a top of about apple tree dimensions.

As most English walnut cultivars fail to bear well in areas subject to hard freezes once spring growth has begun, commercial production is largely limited to California and the South. Better suited to northerly areas (to zone 4) is the Carpathian walnut (*J. regia* var. *orientis*), which not only is very cold hardy but is late to flush and flower. Such cultivars as 'Lake', 'Hansen', and 'Rodhouse' bear reliably in zones 4 to 9 if two or more trees, preferably of at least two cultivars, are planted together. Spacing should be about 60 feet, and young trees should be pruned to a single leader until 8 to 10 feet tall. Significant bearing usually begins in about 10 years as long as weeds are controlled. A mature tree should yield 3 or more bushels of nuts each year. If not harvested as the shells split in late summer, the ripe nuts fall to the ground.

Black walnut (*J. nigra*) is a tall tree native in zones 5 to 9 in the eastern United States. It bears hard-shelled nuts with sweet kernels, often in profusion (15 bushels or more per tree). In numerous cultivars, such as 'Kwik Krop' and 'Thomas', the shell is thin enough to be easily cracked and the kernel is larger than in wild trees.

Both black walnut and English walnut trees secrete allelopathic substances into the soil that inhibit the growth of a wide range of plants, including apple, tomato, and other vegetables, white pine, and rhododendron and azalea and their relatives (the family Ericaceae). Thus such plants should not be grown near these trees, nor should fallen walnut leaves be used to mulch them.

Other walnut species sometimes cultivated for their nuts include butternut (*J. cinerea*) and heartnut (*J. ailanthifolia*), both known by numerous cultivars with heavy yields, thin shells, and/or larger kernels than in wild trees. The buartnut (*J. × bixbyi*) is a hybrid of these two species.

29

The Herb Garden

Historically, the herb garden was one of the earliest expressions of garden art, dating back to classical times. It was especially prominent during the Renaissance. Throughout Europe, physic gardens were found within the cloistered walls of monasteries and from these gardens were dispensed a variety of medicinal herbs, in an effort on the part of the monks to alleviate the suffering and distress of their people. It was an era when the enjoyment of plants for their beauty alone, while not entirely forgotten, was largely

Many herbs, such as garlic chive (foreground), shiso (center), and basil (upper left), are not only valuable culinary herbs but also useful ornamentals.

A large, formal herb garden accessible by brick paths combines colors and forms in an appealing palette.

subordinate to more practical uses. Besides food, people were interested primarily in growing plants for medicinal purposes, for flavorings in cookery, for dyes to color fabrics and leather, and in some cases for fragrance alone. An intimate knowledge of such plants was general throughout the countryside, as is evidenced by the wealth of common plant names in most European languages. The superstition and folklore regarding these plants were passed on from generation to generation; indeed, some herbs were even grown for their poisonous principles.

Herb gardens in the Middle Ages were laid out in formal patterns with quaintly geometric beds, narrow paths, and prim edgings. During the Elizabethan era in England, the herb garden was an important feature of garden design, and the patterned beds on the broad terraces surrounding the manor houses became more and more intricate in design.

The early colonists brought with them to this country knowledge and understanding of the use of herbs, and it was not long before many of the old, familiar plants were flourishing in the dooryard gardens of New England; others were better suited to Virginia. Herbal uses of native plants, in some cases learned from aboriginal Indians, were added to those long known in England and continental Europe.

During the nineteenth century, the interest in herbs declined steadily, and the herb garden became an almost forgotten thing of the past. After World War II, however, there was a great reawakening of interest in the culture of herbs, and their popularity continues.

THE SMALL HERB GARDEN

Although one occasionally sees a new herb garden with intricate, ingeniously knotted beds reminiscent of earlier days, most herb gardens today are simple affairs. Sometimes herbs are relegated to the vegetable garden, or are used as a foreground planting in a shrub border where many of them adapt very readily. Some gardeners who have no other available space tuck them in at random among perennials in garden beds and borders.

One of the best locations for a small herb garden is a sunny space near the kitchen door. Such a space may be made very attractive and can have a definite charm if a simple design is evolved and if materials are selected with care. Where space permits, some old weathered bricks could be used to make a small terrace bordered with herbs. Two small

Sample geometric patterns for small herb gardens.

Where garden space is limited, selected herbs may be grown in ornamental pots, preferably near the kitchen door.

A formal knot garden of shrubby herbs, such as thyme and germander, symmetrically arranged and closely sheared to form geometric patterns.

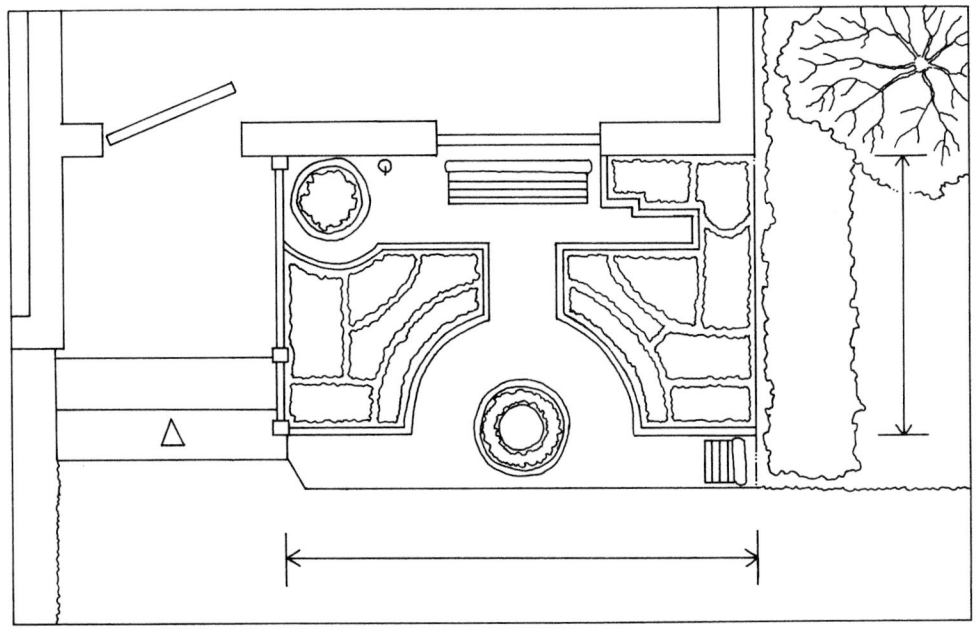

A small circular herb garden, especially if convenient to the kitchen, serves as a living larder of flavors as well as a decorative landscape focus.

Layout for a small formal herb garden convenient to the kitchen door.

bay trees in tubs and a few pots of rosemary and a bench can lend additional interest. If there is no available space for even a small terrace, perhaps a walk can be bordered with narrow herb beds, or space found for a little herb patch beside the door, bordered with parsley and marjoram, with tarragon, basil, pineapple sage, and lavender planted close against the house wall. Just a few feet of sunny space—that is all that is needed for an effective and pleasing herb garden.

While working in the kitchen one can derive a great deal of pleasure from slipping out for a moment to pluck a few fresh sprigs from the herb bed and so add flavor or embellishment to whatever food is being prepared. And few plants will give so generously in return for the time and labor expended on them as will the herbs.

The selection of herbs to be grown in a small herb garden depends to a considerable extent on personal preference. The variety of different herbs need not be large—a half dozen or so will suffice to give a subtle tang to many a dish. And no matter how small the garden, a few fragrance herbs, such as English lavender and lemon verbena, should be included for their special contribution.

Herbs are usually divided into several categories, although there is considerable overlap among them: aromatic herbs are grown primarily for fragrance; culinary herbs are used for flavors in cookery; medicinal herbs continue to be important in pharmacy (although some are poisonous and should be treated with caution); and herbs grown for pigments yield some of our most beautiful dyes.

Among the herbs most generally grown for culinary use are the following.

Basil	Oregano
Chives	Parsley
Coriander (cilantro)	Rosemary
Dill	Sage
Lavender	Summer savory
Marjoram	Tarragon
Mint	Thyme

CULTURAL REQUIREMENTS

Most herbs may be grown very easily from seed, but when only small numbers of plants are needed, they may be purchased from a garden center or nursery or obtained through a friendly exchange of cuttings and divisions among gardeners.

Some of the plants commonly grown in the herb garden require frequent division to keep them within bounds and from crowding others. The various mat-forming mints are

Parsley surrounds a patch of lettuce, offering greens frequently needed in the kitchen.

especially aggressive and are best grown in a container sunk to its rim, its bottom knocked out or perforated to facilitate drainage. Clump-forming kinds, such as chives, benefit from being lifted and divided every year or two.

Most herbs thrive in full sun and in sandy, well-drained loamy soil. If the medium is overfertilized, foliage will be luxuriant, but at the expense of fragrance and flavor.

As is indicated in the table below, a few herbs do best in partial shade or light shade, and a few need wet ground instead of well-drained soil.

If the foliage is to be used for fragrance or flavoring, the herbs should be cut just as the flowers are about to open, for it is at this stage that the essential oils are most abundant in many herbs. The most favorable time for cutting is in the morning, after the dew has dried but before the plants have been touched with hot midday sun. When herbs are to be cut for flowers, as in the case of lavender and chamomile, they should be cut when in full bloom. If the seeds are to be used, the seed heads should be cut when they are no longer green. Those herbs that are harvested for their roots should be dug in the autumn after growth has ceased.

Some herbs can be grown on a sunny window sill during the winter months, where they offer a welcome bit of green as well as flavorings. Basil, mint, rosemary, and parsley are among those that will thrive if favorable conditions are provided. They may be grown either in pots or in small window boxes in soil that is more fertile than in the outdoor herb garden. Sandy loam enriched with compost is best, as is exposure to the sun in a southern or southeastern window, preferably with cool (55° to 65°F) temperatures.

HERBS FOR THE HOME GARDEN

Because a very large number of plant species are (and historically have been) grown for various herbal purposes and because uses vary regionally and by cultural tradition, this table includes not only well-known culinary herbs but also an assortment of species presently or formerly grown for fragrance, dyes, and pharmaceuticals. Species known to be hazardous if taken internally are so indicated.

Name	Plant Type	Zones	Height	Exposure	Flower Color and Bloom Time	Comments
Aconite (*Aconitum napellus*)	Perennial	6–8	2–4'	S to PSh	Purple; late summer	Roots: *toxic* alkaloids depress nervous system, reducing heartbeat and sensation
Agrimony (*Agrimonia eupatoria*)	Perennial	6–8	4–5'	S to PSh	Yellow; summer	Leaves: astringent, used historically in poultices, lotions, and teas to soothe throat and heal sores
Alkanet (*Anchusa azurea*)	Perennial	3–7	4–5'	S	Blue-violet; summer	Flowers: edible, used in salads; source of red dye
Aloe (*Aloe barbadensis*, syn. *A. vera*)	Perennial	10	1–2'	S to PSh	Seldom flowers	Leaves: gel has anaesthetic, antibacterial, and tissue-restorative properties; used in lotions and creams
Ambrosia (*Chenopodium botrys*)	Annual	—	2–4'	S	Yellow-green; summer	Flowers: used in potpourris and sachets
American hellebore (*Veratrum viride*)	Perennial	3–8	4–6'	LSh	Greenish yellow; summer	Requires moist soil; alkaloids reduce heartbeat and stimulate blood flow to organs and extremities; *all parts poisonous to eat*
Angelica (*Angelica archangelica*)	Biennial	4–8	5–6'	S	Greenish white; spring and summer	Requires moist soil; used as diuretic and antiseptic; historically used for calming teas; fruits, seeds, and roots: used to flavor teas and and liqueurs; fragrance used in potpourris, soaps, ointments, perfumes, and tobacco; *suspected carcinogen*
Anise (*Pimpinella anisum*)	Annual	—	1½–2'	S	Yellowish white; summer	Protect from wind; used in teas to promote digestion; seed oil: flavors food and liqueurs; fragrance used in toiletries
Anise hyssop (*Agastache foeniculum*)	Perennial	8–10	3–4'	S	Violet or white; summer	Leaves: used in teas

Name	Plant Type	Zones	Height	Exposure	Flower Color and Bloom Time	Comments
Arnica (*Arnica montana*)	Perennial	6–9	1–2'	S to LSh	Yellow-orange; summer	Flowers: anaesthetic used in ointments to relieve pain; *all parts poisonous to eat*
Artemisia: *see Mugwort*						
Autumn crocus (*Colchicum autumnale, C. speciosum*)	Perennial bulb	5–9	1–1½' (foliage); 6–9" (flowers)	S to PSh	Lavender to white; late summer to early fall	Alkaloid colchincine: used to alleviate gout; used to inhibit cell division in plants; *all parts highly toxic to eat*
Barberry, common (*Berberis vulgaris*)	Shrub	3–8	6–8'	S to LSh	Yellow; spring	Bears red berries in the fall; alkaloid berberine used as a sedative, regulates heart rate; fruit: used in cookery; root: source of yellow dye
Basil, sweet (*Ocimum basilicum*)	Annual	—	1–2'	S	White; summer	Leaves: aromatic oil is antibacterial; used in cookery and liqueurs; fragrance used in potpourris, sachets, soaps, and toiletries
Bay, poet's laurel (*Laurus nobilis*)	Shrub or tree	8–10	8–12 (50)'	S to PSh	Greenish yellow; spring	Bears black berries in the fall; leaves: oil used for treating internal disorders; used in ointments, soaps, and perfumes; used in cookery
Bayberry (*Myrica pennsylvanica, M. cerifera*)	Shrub or tree	2–7 (6–9)	3–10 (35)'	S	Yellowish; early spring	Berries: wax used in candles and soaps; historically used in tonics and stimulants; *suspected carcinogen with internal use*
Bearberry: *see Uva-ursi*						
Bedstraw (*Galium verum*)	Perennial	3–8	1–2'	S to PSh	Yellow; summer	Flowers source of yellow dye
Bee balm (*Monarda didyma*)	Perennial	4–9	2–3'	S	Red; summer	Requires moist to wet soil; fresh leaves: flavor food and wine; dried leaves: used in teas and potpourris; oil: historically used as an antiseptic (available as a synthetic)
Bergamot (*Monarda fistulosa*)	Perennial	4–8	1½–2'	S	Pinkish lavender; summer	Oil: flavors food; fragrance used in potpourris
Betony (*Stachys officinalis*)	Perennial	5–9	2–3'	S	Red-violet; summer	Astringent tannins: used to soothe throat irritations; used to flavor teas
Belladonna (*Atropa belladonna*)	Perennial	6–9	2–4'	S	Purplish green; summer	Alkaloid atropine: depresses parasympathetic nervous system, increasing heartbeat and body temperature and dilating pupils; can cause delirium; *all parts poisonous to eat*
Birch, cherry (*Betula lenta*)	Tree	3–8	25–50'	S	Small yellowish catkins; spring	Requires moist to wet soil; bark and leaves: methyl salicilate used as analgesic and counterirritant in creams and liniments; used for birch beer
Bistort (*Polygonum bistorta*)	Perennial	4–8	1–2'	S to PSh	Rose or white; summer	Dried roots: contain astringent
Black hellebore, Christmas rose (*Helleborus niger*)	Perennial	3–8	6–12"	PSh	White or pink; late winter	Historically used in exorcisms; glucosides helleborin and helleborein: can irritate skin, *very toxic if taken internally*
Bloodroot (*Sanguinaria canadensis*)	Perennial	3–8	6–12"	PSh	White; early spring	Root: source of red or rust brown dye; alkaloid sanguinarine: used as stimulant in cancer therapy

(continues)

HERBS FOR THE HOME GARDEN (*continued*)

Name	Plant Type	Zones	Height	Exposure	Flower Color and Bloom Time	Comments
Blue cohosh (*Caulophyllum thalictroides*)	Perennial	7–9	1–3'	PSh	Yellow-green; spring and summer	Historically used as a medicinal herb; caulosaponin: vasoconstrictor; *poisonous to eat*
Boneset (*Eupatorium perfoliatum*)	Perennial	3–8	2–4'	S	White or purplish; late summer	Historically used as a medicinal herb; now believed to cause kidney or liver injury; *all parts poisonous to eat*
Borage (*Borago officinalis*)	Annual	—	1–2'	S	Blue; summer	Self-sows; fresh and dried leaves: used in cookery
Broom (*Cytisus scoparius*)	Shrub	5–8	3–6'	S	Yellow; spring	Flowers: source of yellow dye; shoot tips: source of volatile sparteine, which affects the heart and other organs; *all parts poisonous to eat*
Burdock (*Arctium lappa*)	Biennial	3–8	2–4'	S	Red-violet; summer	Displays clinging seed heads after flowering; roots, young leaves, and shoots: used in Japanese cookery; historically used medicinally for blood disorders and to cure skin diseases (unsupported scientifically)
Burnet: *see Salad burnet*						
Calamint (*Calamintha sylvatica*)	Perennial	6–9	1½–2'	S	Pink, spotted purple; summer	Dried leaves: used in teas and potpourris
Calendula, pot marigold (*Calendula officinalis*)	Annual	—	1–1½'	S to PSh	Orange; summer	Flowers: edible and source of yellow dye; historically highly valued for use in tonics and for its curative properties (unsupported scientifically)
Camomile: *see Chamomile*						
Caper (*Capparis spinosa*)	Shrub	8–10	1–2"	S	White; spring and summer	Flower buds: pickled and used in cookery
Caraway (*Carum carvi*)	Annual or biennial	3–8	1–2'	S to PSh	White; spring	Seeds: used in cookery; aromatic oil: used in mouthwashes, perfumes, and soaps; all parts edible
Cardamom (*Elettaria cardamum*)	Perennial	10	6–8'	PSh	White with yellow and blue; summer	Can be used as a tub plant; seeds: used in cookery
Cascara sagrada (*Rhamnus purshianus*)	Shrub	7–9	5–10'	S to PSh	Greenish yellow; spring	Bark: ground and dried used in laxatives; extracts flavor foods and liqueurs
Castor bean (*Ricinus communis*)	Shrub, perennial, or annual	(8) 9–10	6–12'	S	Greenish to red; summer	Bears three-seeded capsules after flowering; seeds: source of lubricants and ricin, a blood-coagulating protein with cathartic effects when diluted; *seeds poisonous to eat*
Catnip (*Nepeta cataria*)	Perennial	3–9	1–2'	S	White and purple; spring and summer	Nepta-lactone: feline aphrodisiac; leaves: used in cookery; leaves and flowers: used in teas
Cat thyme (*Teucrium marum*)	Perennial or annual	9–10	1–1½'	S	Purple; summer	Dried leaves: attractive to cats; used in teas
Cayenne pepper (*Capsicum annuum*, 'Longum' group)	Annual	—	1–2'	S	White; summer	Bears slender red fruit (the pepper): capsaicin: stimulates saliva and gastric secretions; used in cookery, liniments, and poultices
Celery (*Apium graveolens*)	Biennial or annual	7–9	1–2'	S	White; summer	Seeds: oil flavors food and liqueurs; fragrance used in soaps and toiletries

Name	Plant Type	Zones	Height	Exposure	Flower Color and Bloom Time	Comments
Chamomile, German (*Matricaria recutita*)	Annual	—	1–2'	S	White and yellow; summer	Flowers: oil has antiinflammatory, antispasmodic, and antiinfective properties; used in ointments, lotions, and repellents; fragrance used in potpourris
Chamomile, Roman (*Chamaemelum nobile* 'Treneague')	Perennial	4–8	3–6"	S	No flowers	Creeping habit; has same uses as German chamomile; tea retains too little oil to be effective; leaves: used for outdoor fragrance
Chervil (*Anthriscus cerefolium*)	Annual	—	1–2'	PSh	White; summer	Leaves and stems: used for cookery; historically used as a medicinal herb (unsupported scientifically)
Chicory (*Cichorium intybus*)	Biennial or perennial	3–9	3–4'	S	Blue; summer	Leaves and roots: used in cookery; lactucin and lactucoprin: have a mildly sedative effect when used in coffee; roots: used for coffee substitute
Chives (*Allium schoenoprasum*)	Perennial	5–8	1–1½'	S	Purple to white; spring	Leaves: used in cookery
Clary sage (*Salvia sclarea*)	Biennial or perennial	5–9	2–3'	S	Blue or white; spring and summer	Nerol: antispasmodic properties; leaves: used in cookery; flowers: used in potpourris, perfumes, soaps, and food flavorings
Coffee (*Coffea arabica*)	Shrub	10	3–6 (40)'	PSh	White; spring and summer	Bears red berries after flowering; caffeine: acts as analgesic and stimulant; may cause nervousness and insomnia
Coltsfoot (*Tussilago farfara*)	Perennial	3–8	4–8"	S	Yellow; spring	Leaf stalks and roots: contain mucilage, which was historically used as an expectorant; leaves: once used in cookery; *suspected carcinogen; best regarded as poisonous if eaten*
Comfrey (*Symphytum officinale*)	Perennial	5–8	2–3'	S to PSh	Blue, yellow, pink, or white; spring	Leaves: source of brown dye; allantoin: used in ointments and creams to promote tissue growth and healing; used in toiletries; *internal use is controversial*
Coriander, cilantro (*Coriandrum sativum*)	Annual	—	1½–2½'	S	White; spring and summer	Seeds, leaves, and roots: used in cookery; whole plant: used in potpourris; oil extracts: used in perfumes and to mask medicinal flavors
Corsican mint (*Mentha requienii*)	Perennial	6–9	½" or less	S to PSh	Lilac; summer	Prostrate habit; leaves: used to flavor food and beverages
Costmary (*Tanacetum balsamita*)	Perennial	6–9	2–3'	S	Yellow; spring	Leaves: used to flavor food and beverages; fragrance used in potpourris; historically used as a medicinal herb (unsupported scientifically)
Cumin (*Cuminum cyminum*)	Annual	—	10–15"	S	White or pink; summer	Seeds: oil contains cuminaldehyde; used in cookery; used as a fragrance
Curry plant (*Helichrysum italicum* ssp. *serotinum*)	Perennial	8–10	12–15"	S to PSh	White; summer	Leaves: used in cookery
Dandelion (*Taraxacum* spp.)	Perennial	5–9	3–12"	S	Yellow; spring	Roots: historically used for medicinal purposes; used in coffee and teas and as coffee substitute; leaves: used in cookery; flowers used for wine and as a garnish

(continues)

HERBS FOR THE HOME GARDEN (continued)

Name	Plant Type	Zones	Height	Exposure	Flower Color and Bloom Time	Comments
Deadly nightshade (*Atropa belladonna*)	Perennial	7–9	2–3'	PSh	Purple; summer	Extracts: used medicinally for disorders of the nervous system, eyes, and mucous membranes; depresses effects of some poisons; *all parts poisonous to eat*
Dill (*Anethum graveolens*)	Biennial	8–10	2–3'	S	Yellow; summer	Leaves: often called dillweed; used in cookery; seeds: used in cookery and insecticides
Dittany of Crete (*Origanum dictamnus*)	Shrublet	7–10	9–12"	S	Pink or purplish; summer	Flowers: used in teas; leaves: used historically for medicinal purposes (unsupported scientifically)
Dock (*Rumex acetosa, R. sanguineus*)	Perennial	3–7, 6–9	1–4'	S	Greenish yellow or reddish; summer	Dried roots: extract used as a purgative; young leaves: used in cookery
Echinacea (*Echinacia angustifolia*)	Perennial	3–8	1–2'	S to PSh	Purple; summer	Roots: contain caffeic acid glycoside, facilitates healing; is mildly antibiotic
Elder (*Sambucus caerulea, S. canadensis, S. nigra*)	Shrub	3–9	5–15 (30)'	S to PSh	White; spring to summer	Bears black berries; flowers: used in teas; berries: used in cookery and for wine; berries and leaves: source of dyes; roots, stems, and leaves: *contain poisonous cyanogenic glucosides*
Elecampane (*Inula helenium*)	Perennial	5–8	4–6'	Sh	Yellow; summer	Dried root: used to treat respiratory disorders; used to flavor food
Epazote (*Chenopodium ambrosioides*)	Annual	—	2–4'	S	Green; summer	Flowers: used in cookery and teas, used in potpourris and sachets
Ephedra, joint fir (*Ephedra* spp.)	Shrub	4–7	6–36"	S	Greenish; summer	Chinese species: source of ephedrine; used as a decongestant and diuretic; American species: used to make Mormon tea
Eucalyptus (*Eucalyptus* spp.)	Tree	—	15–100 (400)'	S	Various colors; spring or summer	Leaves, bark, and roots: contain eucalyptol, used in cough medicines; fragrance used in potpourris
Eyebright (*Euphrasia officinalis*)	Annual or short-lived perennial	6–9	2–8"	S	White or purple; summer	Historically used to make tea and ointments to treat eye disorders (unsupported scientifically)
Fennel (*Foeniculum vulgare*)	Perennial	5–8	3–4'	S	Yellow; summer	Leaves and stems: mildly stimulating, used in cookery; seeds: used in cookery; flowers and leaves: source of dyes; fragrance and oils used in soaps, creams, and perfumes
Fenugreek (*Trigonella foenum-graecum*)	Annual	—	1–2'	S	White; summer	Seeds: used in cookery; source of yellow dye; nut-flavored mucilage used as laxative and in poultices
Feverfew (*Tanacetum parthenium*)	Biennial	6–8	1–2'	S to PSh	White and yellow; summer and fall	Leaves: extract used for treating migraines; relaxes smooth muscles; source of dye
Flax (*Linum usitatissimum*)	Annual	—	1–1½'	S to PSh	Blue; summer	Linseed oil: mucilage is used in medicinal teas, cough medicines, and poultices; stems: fiber is source of linen fabric; seeds: used in cookery; young seed capsules: contain cyanogenetic nitrates and the glucoside linamarin, *both in toxic concentrations*

Name	Plant Type	Zones	Height	Exposure	Flower Color and Bloom Time	Comments
Foxglove (*Digitalis purpurea, D. lanata*)	Biennial	6–8	3–6'	PSh	Lavender and white; spring and summer	Leaves: contain low concentrations of the glycoside digitoxin, stimulates heart contractions; *self-medication can be fatal*
French sorrel (*Rumex scutatus*)	Perennial	6–9	1–1½'	S	Pinkish green; summer	Leaves: used in cookery
Garlic (*Allium sativum*)	Perennial	8–9	2–3'	S	White or pink; summer	Used in cookery; aromatic allicin is a potent antibacterial (sometimes rivaling penicillin)
Garlic chives (*Allium tuberosum*)	Perennial	7–9	1–1½'	S	White; summer	Leaves: used in cookery
Gentian (*Gentiana lutea*)	Perennial	5–8	3–4'	S to PSh	Yellow; summer	Roots: contain appetite stimulant; used to flavor bitters and vermouth
Germander (*Teucrium chamaedrys*)	Shrublet	5–8	1–2'	S to PSh	Red-violet; summer	Residue of steeped leaves: historically used for medicinal purposes (unsupported scientifically)
Ginger (*Zingiber officinale*)	Perennial	10	2–4'	PSh	Yellow and purple; summer	Rarely flowers in cultivation; used in cookery and in teas
Ginseng, American (*Panax quinquefolius*)	Perennial	6–8	9–15"	PSh	Greenish; summer	Root: extracts used to treat anemia, atherosclerosis, diabetes, and hypertension; historically used as an aphrodisiac (unsupported scientifically)
Goldenrod (*Solidago nemoralis, S. odora, S. virginiana*)	Perennial	4–8	3–4'	S	Yellow; summer	Leaves: used in teas; flower heads: source of yellow dye; historically used as a medicial herb (unsupported scientifically)
Goldenseal (*Hydrastis canadensis*)	Perennial	3–8	6–24"	Sh	Greenish white; spring	Sap: source of yellow dye; hydrastine: in low concentrations acts as a mild antiseptic, affects muscle tone; canadine: mild sedative and muscle relaxant, used to treat stress
Great mullein (*Verbascum thapsus*)	Biennial	3–8	3–6'	S	Yellow; summer	Historically has had many uses; source of hair dye; leaves: used as foot pads; dried flower stalk: can be dipped in tallow and used as a torch
Grindelia (*Grindelia camporum*)	Short-lived perennial	8–10	2–3'	S	Yellow; spring	Resinous component: used as expectorant and antispasmodic; used in ointments and solutions to treat rashes and burns
Hawthorn, English (*Crataegus laevigata*)	Tree	5–8	10–20'	S	White; spring	Extracts treat circulatory disorders effectively; historically used as a medicinal herb for other treatments (unsupported scientifically)
Henna (*Lawsonia inerma*)	Shrub	9–10	15–20'	S	White or rose; spring	Leaves: source of henna dye; extracts have antibiotic and contraceptive properties
Hop (*Humulus lupulus*)	Perennial twining vine	5–8	15–20'	S	Greenish; summer	Stems: fibers used for basketry and cloth; bitter juice: used for beer; humulone and lupulone: act as sedatives and antiseptics
Horehound (*Marrubium vulgare*)	Perennial	3–7	1½–2'	S	White; spring and summer	Marrubiin used for cough suppressants and purgatives; used to flavor beverages

(continues)

HERBS FOR THE HOME GARDEN (*continued*)

Name	Plant Type	Zones	Height	Exposure	Flower Color and Bloom Time	Comments
Horseradish (*Armoracia rusticana*)	Perennial	5–8	2–3'	S	White; summer	Roots: mustard oil used in poultices and as a diuretic; used in cookery
Horsetail (*Equisetum* spp.)	Perennial	2–9	1–2'	PSh	Straw-colored cones; spring	Requires moist soil; liquid from crushed stems used historically for treating digestive and urinary disorders (unsupported scientifically)
Hyssop (*Hyssopus officinalis*)	Perennial	3–8	2–3'	S to PSh	Blue-violet; summer	Leaves: used to flavor food and liqueurs; fragrance used in perfumes; tea used as a mild expectorant; historically used for other medicinal purposes (unsupported scientifically)
Indigo (*Indigofera tinctoria, I. suffruticosa*)	Shrub	10	2–3'	S	Purple or white; summer	Sap: historical source of indigo dye (now available as a synthetic)
Jasmine, poet's (*Jasminum officinale*)	Shrubby climber	7–10	10–25'	S to PSh	White; spring	Flowers: used in teas; aromatic floral oil: used in perfumes, toiletries, and soaps
Jimsonweed (*Datura stramonium*)	Annual	7–9	3–5'	S	White to blue-lavender; summer	Seeds: atropine, hyscamine, and hyoscamine display hallucinogenic properties; used in commerical pharmaceuticals for treating muscular, circulatory, respiratory, and topical disorders; *all parts poisonous to eat; the hallucinogens are toxic*
Juniper (*Juniperus communis*)	Shrub	6–8	2–6'	S	Bluish berries; summer	Berries: used in cookery and for gin; oils can cause a severe diuretic reaction
Lady's bedstraw (*Galium verum*)	Perennial	5–8	1–2'	S to PSh	Yellow; summer	Flowers: source of yellow dye; roots: source of red dye; historically used to ease pain and induce sleep (unsupported scientifically)
Lavender (*Lavandula angustifolia* and other spp.)	Shrublet	5–8	1–2'	S	Light purple; late spring and early summer	Used in cookery and to flavor wines and teas; oils: sedative, spasmolytic, antiseptic, and carminitive properties; used in perfumes; flowers: used in potpourris
Lavender cotton (*Santolina chamaecyparissus*)	Shrublet	7–9	1–2'	S	Yellow; late spring and early summer	Leaves: used in potpourris and sachets; source of yellow dye; historically used as vermifuge
Lemon balm (*Melissa officinalis*)	Perennial	4–8	1–2'	S to PSh	White; summer	Leaves: used in cookery and to flavor teas and liqueurs; oil: mild sedative and antiseptic properties; fragrance used in potpourri
Lemon grass (*Cymbopogon citratus*)	Perennial	9–10	2–3'	S	Greenish; summer	Used in cookery; lemony aldehyde citral used in teas; used in insect repellents
Lemon verbena (*Aloysia triphylla*)	Shrub	8–10	3–5'	S	Lavender; summer	Leaves: used in cookery and teas; oil extract: used in perfumes, toilet water, and soaps
Licorice (*Glycyrrhiza glabra*)	Perennial	8–10	3–4'	S to PSh	Red-violet; summer	Rhizomes: glycyrhizin is somewhat poisonous but is 50 times sweeter than sugar and is used as a commerical sweetener, used to flavor tobacco, food, and drugs; used in toiletries
Lily-of-the-valley (*Convallaria majalis*)	Perennial	(2–)3–7(–8)	4–6"	PSh	White; spring	Flowers: source of glycosides used as heart stimulant; *poisonous to eat*

Name	Plant Type	Zones	Height	Exposure	Flower Color and Bloom Time	Comments
Lobelia (*Lobelia inflata*)	Biennial or annual	5–8	2–3'	S to PSh	Blue; summer	Lobeline and other alkaloides: stimulate then depress central nervous system; used in antismoking preparations
Lovage (*Levisticum officinale*)	Perennial	4–8	3–4'	S to PSh	Yellow; late spring and early summer	Seeds: used in cookery; seed oil: used to flavor candies and liqueurs; root oil: used in teas; used in perfumes and soaps
Lungwort (*Pulmonaria officinalis*)	Perennial	6–9	1–1½'	Sh	Pink in bud, opening blue; spring	Leaves: historically used for treating respiratory ailments (unsupported scientifically)
Madder (*Rubia tinctoria*)	Perennial	6–9	3–4'	S	Cream; summer	Roots: source of red dye (available as a synthetic); extracts used in bone-growth research
Marjoram (*Origanum majorana, O. vulgare*)	Perennial	7–10	6–12"	S	Pink; summer	Leaves and flowers: used in cookery; used in potpourris and soaps; extract has mild antioxidant and fungicidal properties
Marsh mallow (*Althaea officinalis*)	Perennial	3–7	4–6'	S	Pale bluish rose; summer	Requires moist to wet soil; roots: used in candies; leaves: used in cookery; demulcent extract used to treat digestive disorders; used as binder in the manufacture of pills
Mayapple (*Podophyllum peltatum*)	Perennial	4–7	1–1½'	LSh	White; spring	Fruit: sometimes eaten; historically used as medicinal herb; podophyllin in roots *now deemed unsafe for internal use*
Mexican marigold (*Tagetes lucida*)	Annual	—	1½–2½'	S	Yellow; summer	Leaves: used in cookery; fragrance used in potpourris, sachets, and repellents
Mint (*Mentha* spp.)	Perennial	3–8	1–2'	S to PSh	Purple, pink, or white; summer	Menthol (mainly from *M. × piperita*): used as a carminative and antispasmodic, especially in antacids; peppermint and spearmint (*M. spicata*): used in cookery; used in teas and tobacco; fragrance used in potpourris and sachets
Mint, American mountain (*Pycnanthemum pilosum*)	Perennial	4–8	2–3'	S	Pink; summer	Leaves: used in teas
Mint, Korean (*Agastache rugosa*)	Perennial	8–10	4–5'	S	Violet to rose; summer	Leaves: used in teas; used in potpourris
Mistletoe (*Phoradendron serotinum* and other spp.)	Semiparasitic shrub	6–10	1–2'	PSh	Green; summer	Viscin a resin used as an anesthetic and to treat cancer; amines: act as vasoconstrictors, raise blood pressure; phoratoxins: dangerous hallucinogens; *all parts poisonous to eat*
Mugwort (*Artemisia vulgaris*)	Perennial	3–8	4–6'	S to PSh	Greenish; summer	Invasive weed; leaves: used in herbal pillows and bath powders; oils: used in repellents
Mustard (*Brassica hirta, B. juncea, B. napus, B. nigra, B. rapa*)	Biennial	7–10	2–4'	S	Yellow; spring and early summer	*B. nigra* seeds: glycoside sinalbin and enzyme myrosin used in mustard plasters; *B. hirta, B. juncea,* and *B. nigra* seeds: used in cookery; leaves of *B. juncea* cultivars: used in cookery; *B. napus*: source of birdseed rape

(continues)

HERBS FOR THE HOME GARDEN (continued)

Name	Plant Type	Zones	Height	Exposure	Flower Color and Bloom Time	Comments
Muster John Henry, giant marigold (Tagetes minuta)	Annual	—	5–8'	S	Yellow; early fall	Leaves: used medicinally; used in cookery
Myrrh, garden: see Sweet cicely						
Myrrh, resin (Commiphora myrrha)	Shrub	9–10	4–8'	S	Greenish; summer	Oily resin: astringent and antiseptic, especially on mucous membranes; carminative; used in soaps, perfumes, and fumigants
Myrtle (Myrtus communis)	Shrub	8–10	8–15'	S	Cream; spring	Leaves: used in potpourris; flowers: traditionally used in garlands and bridal wreaths
Nasturtium (Tropaeolum majus)	Perennial or annual	10	1–2(6)'	S	Red, orange, or yellow; summer	Leaves and flowers: used in cookery; buds: can be pickled; historically used as an insect repellent (unsupported scientifically)
New Jersey tea (Ceanothus americanus)	Shrub	4–7	2–3'	S to PSh	White; late summer	Acidic tannin historically used as a stringent and blood coagulant; used to flavor beverages
Onion (Allium cepa)	Biennial bulb	5–9	2–4'	S	White to purple; late and spring summer	Sap: mildly antiseptic; extracts: inhibit blood clotting and reduce cholesterol; skin: source of dyes
Oregano (Origanum vulgare)	Perennial	5–8	1–2'	S	Rose violet to white; summer	Leaves: infusions used for gastric distress and headache; poultices used for muscle pain; used in cookery; used in toiletries
Oregon grape (Mahonia aquifolium)	Shrub	5–8	3–6'	PSh	Yellow; spring	Stems and roots: sources of yellow dye; berry: used in cookery, rich in viatmin C; alkaloid berberine used to treat skin disorders
Orris (Iris × germanica var. florentina)	Perennial	6–8	1–2'	S	Spring; purple and yellow or white	Rhizome: used in potpourris and violet blends; historically used to treat internal disorders (unsupported scientifically)
Painted daisy: see Pyrethrum						
Parsley (Petroselinium crispum)	Biennial	6–9	1–1½'	S to PSh	Greenish yellow; spring	Leaves: used in cookery; leaf oil: parsley camphor of medicinal value; seed oil: used in perfumes and soaps
Passion flower (Passiflora incarnata)	Perennial tendril climber	6–9	10–20'	PSh	White with purple; summer	Floral extract: mildly narcotic; used in tranquilizers and sedatives; used in bath powders
Pennyroyal (Mentha pulegium, syn. Hedeoma pulegioides)	Perennial or annual	6–12"	7–9'	S	Bluish lilac; summer	Sap: repels insects; pulegone used as abortifacient; used in minute amounts in teas; toxic
Pepper: see Cayenne pepper						
Perilla, lemon (Perilla frutescens var. nankinensis)	Annual	—	2–3'	S to PSh	Purplish; summer	Leaves: used in Japanese cookery
Periwinkle (Catharanthus roseus)	Perennial usually grown as annual	10	1–1½'	S to PSh	Magenta; summer	Sap: vinblastine sulfate used to treat Hodgkin's disease; alkaloid vincristine used to treat cancer
Pipsissewa (Chimaphila umbellata)	Dwarf shrub	4–7	6–10"	PSh	White; and spring summer	Leaves: infusion used as diuretic for urinary disorders; extract used for root beer

Name	Plant Type	Zones	Height	Exposure	Flower Color and Bloom Time	Comments
Plantain (*Plantago major*)	Perennial	5–8	1'	S to PSh	Greenish; spring and summer	Foliage prostrate; sap: used to treat bee stings; whole plant: source of yellowish dye; leaves: used in cookery
Pokeweed (*Phytolacca americana*)	Perennial	4–9	4–8'	S to PSh	White; summer	Bears purple berries after flowering; berries: source of dyes; young shoots: used in cookery; root, fruit, and seeds: *poisonous to eat*
Poplar (*Populus* spp.)	Tree	2–9	25–75'	S	Catkins; early spring	Buds: salicylates act as an analgesic (related to aspirin); contain antioxidant used in toiletries; leaves and twigs: sources of gray, brown, and yellow dyes
Poppy (*Papaver somniferum*)	Annual	2–3	2–3'	S	Purple, mauve, or white; summer	Opium, derived from latex, is a powerful narcotic
Pot marigold: *see Calendula*						
Potentilla (*Potentilla* spp.)	Perennial	3–8	3–12"	S to PSh	Yellow; spring and summer	Roots: source of reddish dye; several species have tannins and other astringents; used topically and in lotions and soaps; sometimes taken internally
Pyrethrum (*Tanacetum coccineum*)	Perennial	5–8	1–1½'	S	Red to white with yellow; summer	Flowers: used for the botanical insecticide Pyrethrum
Rose (*Rosa* spp.)	Shrub	4–8	1½–6'	S	Mostly pink to white; late spring to early summer	Hips: rich in vitamins; used in cookery and teas; petals: used in cookery; used in tonics, soaps, creams, and potpourris
Rosemary (*Rosmarinus officinalis*)	Shrub	8–10	2–6'	S	Pale blue; winter to early spring	Leaves: used in cookery; source of yellow-green dye; used in liniments and antibacterial preparations; fragrance used in soaps and perfumes
Rue (*Ruta graveolens*)	Subshrub	5–8	1–3'	S	Yellow-green; summer	Historically used as a contraceptive and abortifacient; *now deemed ineffective or unsafe*
Safflower (*Carthamus tinctorius*)	Annual		1–3'	S	Yellow-orange; summer	Oil: used in cookery; flowers: source of red dye
Saffron (*Crocus sativus*)	Perennial corm	6–9	4–8"	S	Red violet, lavender, or white; early fall	Stigmata: used in cookery; source of dye; floral oil: historically used as a medicinal herb (unsupported scientifically)
Sage (*Salvia clevelandii, S. fruticosa, S. officinalis, S. pomifera; S. columbariae, S. elegans, S. glutinosa, S. leucantha, S. hispanica, S. viridis*)	Shrub, perennial, or annual	5–10	1–4'	S	Pink, purple, red, blue, or white; summer	Oils and leaves: used in cookery and teas (fascomiglia); used in tonics (chia); used in insect repellents and bee attractants; used in toiletries; tannins and volatile oils: used in antiperspirants, astringents, and antiseptics
St. John'swort (*Hypericum perforatum*)	Perennial	3–8	1–2'	S to PSh	Yellow; summer	Sap: source of yellow to red dye; used as an antidepressant; oil and tannin used in food preservatives
Salad burnet (*Sanguisorba minor*)	Perennial	5–8	1–3'	S to PSh	Pinkish; spring	Leaves: used in cookery
Sassafras (*Sassafras albidum*)	Tree	5–8	35–50'	S	Yellow-green; spring	Root oils: historically used in root beer and teas; used in liniments and lotions; *root oils contain a carcinogenic*
Savory, summer (*Satureja hortensis*)	Annual	—	1–1½'	S	White or pale pink; summer	Leaves: used in cookery and teas; used as an astringent and mild antiseptic

(continues)

HERBS FOR THE HOME GARDEN (continued)

Name	Plant Type	Zones	Height	Exposure	Flower Color and Bloom Time	Comments
Savory, winter (*Satureja montana*)	Perennial	6–8	6–12'	S	White or lilac; summer	Leaves and oils: used in cookery
Scented geranium (*Pelargonium* spp.)	Shrub, usually grown as annual	10	1–3'	S	Purple, red, pink, or white; summer	Leaves and flowers: used in perfumes, soaps, potpourris, sachets, and insect repellents; used in cookery and tea
Sesame (*Sesamum indicum*)	Annual	—	3–5'	S	Rose or white; summer	Seeds and seed oil: used in cookery; seed oil used for medicinal preparations
Shiso (*Perilla frutescens*)	Annual	—	2–3'	S	White and purple; summer	Leaves: used in Japanese cookery
Silphium (*Ferula assa-foetida, F. moschata, F. narthex*)	Perennial	8–10	4–6'	S	Yellow; summer	Historically used as a medicinal herb; ferujol oil acts as a contraceptive in laboratory rats
Soapwort, bouncing Bet (*Saponaria officinalis*)	Perennial	4–7	1–2'	S to PSh	White to pale pink; summer	Roots and leaves: saponin used in soaps and lotions to control eczema and acne
Sorrel, garden sorrel (*Rumex acetosa*)	Perennial	3–7	1–2'	S	Greenish; summer	Leaves: used in cookery
Southernwood (*Artemesia abrotanum*)	Shrub	4–8	3–4'	S	Yellowish; summer	Leaves: oil absinthol used in repellents and soaps; stems: source of yellow dye
Spanish thyme (*Plectranthus amboinicus*)	Perennial	10	2–4'	PSh	Mauve to white; summer	Leaves used to flavor food and beverages
Stinging nettle (*Urtica dioica*)	Perennial	5–8	3–4'	S to PSh	Greenish; summer	Dried leaves: used in bath powders; used in teas; fresh leaves: used in cookery; stems: source of linenlike fiber
Sweet cicely, garden myrrh (*Myrrhis odorata*)	Perennial	5–8	3–5'	PSh	White; spring	Leaves; used in cookery, roots: mildly antiseptic; historically used for other medicinal purposes (unsupported scientifically)
Sweet flag (*Acorus calamus*)	Perennial	3–7	2–3'	S to Sh	Greenish; summer	Requires moist to wet soil; roots: calamus oil used in potpourris and sachets; *unsafe for internal use; carcinogenic*
Sweet woodruff (*Galium odoratum*)	Perennial	5–8	6–8"	PSh	White; spring	Leaves and flowers: coumarin used to flavor wine and teas; used in potpourris and perfumes; stems and leaves: sources of tan dye; roots: source of red dye
Tansy (*Tanacetum vulgare*)	Perennial	4–8	3–5'	S to PSh	Yellow; summer	Leaves: used in lotions; source of yellow or green dye; used as an insect repellent; in small amounts used in cookery; thryone, present in varying concentrations, is *toxic, limiting internal use*
Tarragon (*Artemisia dracunculus*)	Perennial	3–7	1–2'	PSh	Yellow to greenish	Sap: antioxidant and antifungal agents used in food preservation; oil: used in soaps and toiletries; leaves and oils used in cookery and liqueurs
Thyme (*Thymus* spp.)	Perennial	6–8	4–12"	S to PSh	Lilac to pink; spring and summer	Leaves: oil thymol used in soaps, perfumes, and medicines; used in cookery and liqueurs (Benedictine)
Uva-ursi, kinnikinick (*Arctostaphylos uva-ursi*)	Shrub	4–7	3×36"	S to PSh	White; spring	Creeping habit; leaves and berries: tannin and arbutin have astringent and antiseptic properties; leaves: source of green and tan dyes

Name	Plant Type	Zones	Height	Exposure	Flower Color and Bloom Time	Comments
Valerian (*Valeriana officinalis*)	Perennial	5–8	2–3'	S to PSh	Pink; late spring to early summer	Roots: oils flavor tobacco and beverages; used in soaps; valepotriates: used in tranquilizers
Vervain (*Verbena officinalis*)	Perennial	4–8	1–3'	S	Pale violet; summer	Historically used as a medicinal herb (unsupported scientifically); *contains a toxic glycoside*
Victorian box (*Pittosporum undulatum*)	Shrub	9–10	6–8'	S	White; summer	Flowers: used in potpourris
Violet (*Viola odorata* and other spp.)	Perennial	6–8	4–6"	PSh	Violet; spring	Leaves and flowers: antiseptic properties; used in medications; used for violet water; flowers used in cookery
Virginia snakeroot (*Aristolochia serpentaria*)	Perennial	8–10	1–2'	S to PSh	Brown-violet; summer	Roots: borneol, aristolochine, and aristolochin (*all toxic*) historically used for treatment of snakebite (unsupported scientifically); *all parts poisonous to eat*
Wahoo (*Euonymus atropurpureus*)	Shrub	4–7	10–15'	S to PSh	Purple; spring	Historically used as a medicinal herb; bark, leaves, and berries; dangerously emetic and purgative; *all parts poisonous to eat*
Watercress (*Nasturtium officinale*)	Aquatic perennial	6–8	1–2'	S to PSh	White; spring	Leaves: used in cookery; upland cress (*Barbarea verna*) of similar use
Willow (*Salix purpurea* and other spp.)	Shrub or tree	2–10	3"–75'	S to PSh	Silvery or greenish; spring	All tissues contain salicin, a component of aspirin; bark: astringent used in medicinal soaps and lotions
Wintergreen (*Gaultheria procumbens*)	Shrublet	4–7	4–6"	PSh	White; summer	Creeping habit; leaf oil: used as a flavoring; leaves and berries: methyl salicilate used in dilution as a painkiller, *otherwise toxic*
Witch hazel (*Hamamelis virginiana*)	Shrub	5–8	8–15'	PSh	Yellow; fall	Leaves and bark: tannic and gallic acids and volatile oils with mildly astringent properties; used to treat hemorrhoids
Woad (*Isatis tinctoria*)	Biennial	7–9	3–5'	S	Yellow; spring	Leaves: source of blue dye, historically important before the discovery of indigo; astringents once used in poultices *now considered toxic*
Wood betony: *see Betony*						
Wormwood (*Artemisia absinthium*)	Perennial	4–7	2–2½'	S to PSh	Greenish yellow; spring	Thujone (absinthe): convulsant and narcotic when taken internally; used as a topical local anaesthetic and antiseptic; used to treat athlete's foot; used in insect repellents, formerly used in alchoholic beverages (*now illegal*)
Yarrow (*Achillea millefolium*)	Perennial	2–8	2–3'	S	White; summer	Used as a source of dyes; used in toiletries; azulen and other principles have anti-inflamatory, analagesic, and antispasmodic properties
Zatar (*Thymbra spicata*)	Shrub	8–10	1½–2'	S	Pink; summer	Used in North African cookery

* S, full sun; Sh, shade (no direct sun); PSh, partial shade (sun exposure only part of the day); LSh, light shade (e.g., the shade of tall, open trees, with little or no exposure to direct sun).

Garlic
(*Allium sativum*
'Luzern Silver')

Chives
(*Allium schoenoprasum*)

Spearmint
(*Mentha spicata*)

Hyssop (*Hyssopus officinalis*) in bloom

Variegated nasturtium (*Tropaeolum majus* 'Alaska')

Bergamont
(*Monarda fistulosa*)

Lavender (*Lavandula angustifolia*)

Lemon balm
(*Melissa officinalis*)

Pot marigold
(*Calendula officinalis*)

Coriander
(*Coriandrum sativum*)

Fennel (*Foeniculum vulgare*), bearing yellow flowers along with the lavender pink blooms of Joe-pye-weed

Golden marjoram (*Origanum vulgare* 'Aureum') with thyme

Sage (*Salvia officinalis*)

Rosemary (*Rosmarinus officinalis*) in bloom

Sweet basil
(*Ocimum basilicum*)

Tarragon
(*Artemisia dracunculus*)

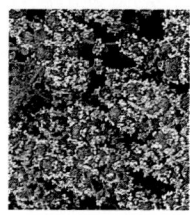

Thyme
(*Thymus* sp.)

Caraway (*Carum carvi*)

V
Cultural Methods and Practices

30

Tools and Garden Equipment

G<small>ARDENING IS A CRAFT. G</small>OOD CRAFTSMEN HAVE GOOD tools. For the greatest efficiency and satisfaction in all gardening operations, good tools are essential. Not only should gardeners know how to select strong and durable tools that will give reliable service over a period of many years but they should also know how to use and care for tools to keep them in good condition.

It is a matter of sound economy to buy well-made tools. A good tool differs from a poor one in the materials used in

A broad, shallow basket is the most convenient carrier for small hand tools.

its manufacture and in the manner of its construction. Good tools stand up to wear better than cheap tools and are usually more efficient. This is particularly true in the case of tools used for cutting, such as lawn mowers, pruning shears, grass shears, and hedge trimmers. If well made and correctly used, such instruments will retain a cutting edge for many seasons and, when sharpening is required, can be readily restored. For example, a good spade should be constructed with steel shanks extending partway up the handle, as these provide additional strength. Spades, shovels, and hoes become significantly more efficient if their leading edges are sharpened at a 35° angle with a hand file or electrically powered rotary stone. Trowels made from a single sheet of steel cut and stamped into shape are never as strong or durable as trowels of forged steel with wooden handles driven into the hollowed shank.

BASIC GARDEN TOOLS AND EQUIPMENT
Long-handled Shovel

The long-handled shovel—the gardener's basic digging tool—is essentially a curved, round-ended blade for rough excavation and a scoop for moving loose earth. The best shovels not only have riveted straps or extensions of the ferrule running part way up the handle but also have the frog, or hollow, in the back of the blade covered with a welded triangle of steel. Short-handled shovels require one to lean forward, but are useful in confined spaces.

D-handled Spade

For digging straight-sided holes and ditches; for slicing through sod and roots; and for just about any chopping, cutting, prying, and turning over, the D-handled spade is the tool of choice. Blade dimensions vary widely according to specialized needs. For example, the tree spade has a blade that is only 5 or 6 inches wide but 18 to 20 inches long, suiting it well for trenching around a tree or shrub to be balled and burlapped for transplanting.

D-handled Garden Fork

The D-handled garden fork is primarily a cultivating tool with flat or squared tines (in contrast to the tapered cylindrical tines of the hay or pitch fork) that are suited for loosening and mixing soil, for gently dislodging and lifting clumped perennials, and for digging root vegetables. Broken or bent tines betray abuse; the fork is not intended to pry rocks or roots.

The forged trowel is a lifetime investment.

Transplanting Trowel

Numerous styles of transplanting trowels are available, but the large, heavy, forged trowel is still the most useful and durable. Since trowels and other small tools are often misplaced and lost in the garden, it is advisable to wrap their handles with brightly colored plastic tape.

Pronged Cultivator

Rather like a small garden fork with the tines set at a 90° angle to the handle, the pronged cultivator also is intended for use in loose ground, generally to maintain tilth and remove small weeds. Small cultivators are useful around seedlings. In the large, conventionally designed vegetable garden, the wheeled cultivator can ease the maintenance of row crops. With increased use of mulches, however, the need for cultivators has diminished.

Garden Hoe

Of the several types of garden hoes available, the most versatile is the prong hoe. This hoe has a single broad blade on one side and one or two pointed prongs on the other, suiting it to heavy-duty weeding and deep cultivation. The prongs are hazardous if left pointing up.

When the scuffle hoe blade is kept sharp, weed control is easy.

Scuffle Hoe

The horizontal rectangular or triangular blade of the scuffle hoe, if kept sharp, does a superb job of decapitating weeds in gardens and unpaved paths. Push-pull types have two cutting edges.

Bow-headed Garden Rake

Intended for finish grading and surface preparation, the bow-headed garden rake may be overturned for leveling. To avert obvious hazard, an unattended rake should always be left with its tines facing down. The bow-headed rake is more versatile and stronger than the straight or T-headed type.

Broom Rake

Ideal for cleaning up fallen leaves, grass clippings, and other lightweight debris, the broom rake has a fan of flexible diverging steel tines and is made in various widths, though, in some types, may be adjustable. Wider fans, intended primarily for raking fallen leaves on lawns, are available in lightweight bamboo. Polished hardwood handles are less likely to raise blisters than unfinished ones.

Pruners

Pruners from the ordinary hand pruner to the cord-activated pole pruner. Cutting heads are mostly either the scissor or the anvil type. In the former, one blade slides past another; in the latter, a sharp, hardened blade presses against a soft, slotted metal bar. Each has its devotees and detractors. Handle design is important if blisters are to be avoided; handles jacketed with plastic or soft rubber are preferable. Since pruner blades are sharp enough to cut wood, it behooves one to treat these instruments with caution. For stems roughly ⅜ to ¾ inch in diameter, the long-handled lopping shear is a useful augmented version.

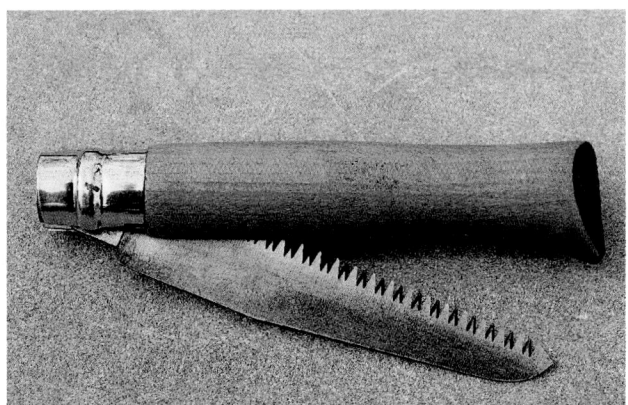

A folding pruning saw has a hinged blade that may be safely concealed when not in use.

Pruning Saws

The smallest of the pruning saws cut on the pull stroke, and the most convenient and safest version may be folded for storage. Larger types with two-stroke blades include tree saws with curved blades and bow saws with straight blades. Chain saws, powered by gasoline or electric motors, speed the cutting of large limbs but are very hazardous in unskilled hands.

Lawn Mower

Discussed more fully in Chapter 10, the ubiquitous gasoline-powered rotary lawn mower is not necessarily the best choice in every case. For those fastidious about their lawns, the reel mower leaves a neater trim, and for small lawns of 1,000 to 1,500 square feet, the highly maneuverable, lightweight push mower is perfectly adequate, and much easier to maintain. In any case, it is worth the additional cost to purchase high-quality equipment that is suited to the type and extent of lawn to be mowed, and it is important to service it carefully.

Garden Hose and Attachments

The garden hose is one of the most indispensable pieces of equipment for lawn and garden. If a well-made hose is used carefully, it should last many years; one of inferior quality will crack and split in a few years' time, even if used only minimally. The lightweight plastic hose has largely replaced the rubber hose. The best types remain supple at low temperatures. The two-ply rubber hose has the longest life, partly because it cannot be kinked, but is heavy to move from place to place. Soil soakers, which are permeable hoses that allow water to gently leak out along their entire length, may be had either in plastic or in canvas and are useful in small areas where a gentle flow of water is to soak into the soil. Puddling or runoff indicates too strong a flow or inadequate soil preparation. Hoses and soakers of all types are best coiled for storage and placed on a dry floor. If they must be hung, the support should be broad and curved to avoid kinking and weakening the fabric cord.

Various hose attachments have made watering less of a problem for gardeners. The fog nozzle gives a very fine, mistlike spray and is excellent for watering newly sown seedbeds and young seedlings. It is also valuable for syringing the foliage of broad-leaved evergreens and for increasing the humidity around tuberous begonias, achimenes, and other plants that thrive best in a moist atmosphere. A hose attachment for applying liquid fertilizers is used by many commercial growers and is another useful piece of equipment for the home gardener. Similar attachments are available for the application of pesticides.

Although automatic timers are available to facilitate regular irrigation without attention, the results are often disappointing. Such devices, unless governed by a soil moisture sensor, do not respond to the idiosyncracies of rainfall, so may saturate the area or provide only a daily superficial sprinkling instead of the occasional deep watering that profits nearly all gardens and lawns. Unless carefully regulated, automatic irrigation can waste much water and harm the very plants targeted for help.

To water transplanted seedlings, the watering can equipped with a removable spray head, or rose, is invaluable.

Cans of galvanized steel or brass will last for decades; plastic substitutes are cheaper but in time often develop fatigue cracks.

Garden Carts and Wheelbarrows

Variously constructed of wood, steel, plastic, and fiberglass, the larger carts and wheelbarrows are furnished with pneumatic tires and can greatly facilitate and ease garden work if carefully chosen for your needs and with the constraints of the site in mind. For example, the large two-wheel cart is of great assistance in moving bulky items, such as bales of peat moss or an assemblage of tools, but where frequently used paths and passages are less than 4 feet wide, a smaller model will be more serviceable. Wheelbarrows are highly maneuverable, but their use generally involves a greater expenditure of energy. Carts and wheelbarrows stored under cover will last many years; if left outside, they should be upended and draped with a tarpaulin to shed rain.

SUPPLEMENTAL TOOLS AND EQUIPMENT
Plant Containers

The active gardener inevitably accumulates a surplus of various pots, flats, cell packs, hanging baskets, and other plant containers that, unless carefully managed, can lead to uncontrolled messiness. By selecting or retaining only the containers actually needed and that can be nested together for efficient storage, such confusion can be minimized. Unwanted standard containers can be offered to other amateur gardeners or even to professional growers.

Bulb Planter

For those who plant bulbs in large quantities in well-prepared ground, the hand dibble, or soil corer, can be a worthwhile investment. Large, deeply planted bulbs call for the long-handled corer.

Fertilizer Spreader

The two-wheeled fertilizer spreader is useful in evenly distributing dried granular or powdered soil amendments over large lawns and gardens. Although such amendments should be made only in response to actual need as determined by soil tests, and not ritually, the spreader can save time and material. It is important to clean the hopper and blades after each use, since most fertilizers and other amendments are corrosive.

Sprayers and Dusters

Increased public consciousness about the hazards of routine or indiscriminate use of various biocides intended to control pests and diseases has led to reduced demand for sprayers, dusters, and related equipment. See Chapter 34 for more information.

POWER TOOLS

The long-traditional half-moon or circle-blade edger, scissor-action grass clipper, and hand-operated hedge shear have gasoline- and electrically powered counterparts that many gardeners prefer, especially on large properties, their substantially higher costs notwithstanding. Gasoline-powered garden tools depend on small engines that tend to be finicky, noisy, demanding of hazardous fuel that emits gases and fumes, and requisite of maintenance. Nevertheless, with proper use and careful upkeep, they quickly accomplish much work and last for years.

Electrically powered tools are quieter, lighter in weight, less immediately polluting, and more controllable, but they limit the user to the length of a power cord or to the charge in a battery and are usually less powerful than their gasoline-driven counterparts.

Whether one's needs justify the cost, upkeep, and storage space for any power tool is a matter of personal judgment. In any case, it is prudent to test any tool under consideration before actually purchasing it.

Trimmer

Among the powered garden tools most frequently seen are string or line trimmers, which cut a horizontal swath 8 to 17 inches in diameter with a piece of nylon cord. Battery-powered units are the most convenient but are suited only to light duty. Gasoline-powered trimmers (using two-cycle engines) are more powerful and versatile. In all types, the nylon cord must be lengthened as it wears away; in some, this is done automatically or when the user taps the machine on the ground. Manual-feed models must be turned off before additional line can be pulled out. Protective goggles should be worn.

Edger

An edger trims on a vertical plane to limit the spread of grass into gardens and over the margins of paths and drives. On small properties, frequent routine edging is easily performed with manual equipment, but if long delayed, trimming may become a substantial project in which power equipment can be a great help. Gasoline-powered edgers turn blades that slice up to 4 inches in depth. Electric edgers are smaller, lighter, and instantaneous in action but less powerful. When operating any power edger, it is especially important to wear protective goggles. With skill, one can also use a line trimmer for light edging.

Grass Shears

Powered with rechargeable batteries, electric grass shears are heavier than the manual versions but can do much in a short time and without causing hand fatigue. As with all power equipment, caution is important; carelessness may result in grievous injury.

Shredder-Chipper

Among the larger, costlier kinds of home garden equipment is the shredder-chipper, a labor-saving machine that converts fallen leaves, twigs, and small pruned branches into more or less homogeneous bits. The shredder part flails leaves, twigs, and stalks into small fragments that will readily decompose into humus; as they are fed in through a chute, branches are cut by the chipper into small pieces that can be used as mulch.

Although much smaller than the familiar trailer-mounted commercial machine used by arborists, the home gasoline-powered shredder-chipper still requires considerable storage space, generates substantial noise and vibration, and has operational limitations that should be considered before purchase. For example, it is difficult to get dry leaves into most shredders; in this case, shredding is more simply accomplished by passing an ordinary rotary lawn mower over the fallen leaves. A mix of dry and wet leaves works better in the shredder but the shredded mass then often clogs the exit chute. Also, while straight, green limbs without side branches chip easily, the more usual dead limbs are slower to chip and if crooked or branched they may be difficult or impossible to get into the typical cylindrical or squared chute, unless manually cut up beforehand. In most chippers, the rated 3-inch maximum diameter should be reduced to 2½ inches. The roar, clatter, and vibration are tiring for most operators, even if one wears the recommended ear plugs in addition to eye-protecting goggles. As impressive as a shredder-chipper may seem in converting unwanted debris into readily usable compost and mulch, it is best to test one before buying, especially as various designs and sizes are available, powered either by gasoline or electricity.

Power Tiller

The increasingly popular two-wheeled rototiller has a horizontal transverse shaft of rotating tines that are powered by a 3- to 6-horsepower gasoline engine and, depending on the density and stoniness of the soil, should physically prepare raw ground for planting. In sandy, friable soil relatively free of rocks and tree roots, the results can be impressive and immediate, even with a small model. But under less ideal conditions, even the most powerful machine will vibrate, lurch, and labor, requiring close and energetic control by the operator and several passes over the same terrain before the full 6- or 8-inch tilling depth is achieved. Whether this goal is more readily met with front- or rear-mounted tines is a matter of debate. In addition to loosening soil, the tiller can be very useful in turning under a cover crop or mixing in fertilizer and other soil amendments. Perhaps the most important question to be considered is whether there will be enough use to justify the purchase cost, maintenance requirements, and storage space. Occasional rental may be a more appropriate option.

Chain Saw

Although the chain saw has replaced the ax almost worldwide, safety consciousness is vital for anyone using this tool, however small it may be. Unless one is trained and experienced, the felling of large trees is best left to well-equipped professionals. Saws with a bar length of 12 or 14 inches seem best for home use: they can fell small trees, cut limbs and small trunks into logs, and reduce waste lumber to fireplace size.

Because of the possibility of kickback—the vicious thrust of the saw upward and back toward the operator when the tip of the rotating chain contacts wood—care should be taken to engage only the long sides of the saw bar when cutting and to always wear a helmet. Safety precautions are especially important when using an older saw that lacks a chain brake or safety tip. It is also advisable to cut logs on a wooden saw buck, to wear heavy shoes and gloves, and if using the machine for an extended period, to use ear plugs.

Chain saws require regular servicing as the two-cycle engines are inherently finicky. Once the chain teeth become dull—often on one side as the result of glancing a rock or nail—the saw tends to cut in an arc and bind. This is a signal that sharpening or a new chain is required. All the dictates of caution and good sense are required when operating a chain saw or when you are near one in use. If you are careful and skillful, however, the chain saw can save much arduous work and quickly add logs to the woodpile. Electrically powered chain saws are easier to control but are less powerful and seem not to hold up under sustained use.

Blowers and Vacuums

Useful in quickly piling up and bagging fallen leaves, grass clippings, and other lawn and pavement debris, blowers and vacuums, which range from small hand-held units to large two-wheeled 5-horsepower models, are successors to the venerable leaf rake. As many combined blower-vacuums generate substantial noise, local regulations may limit their use. Gasoline-powered models are more versatile, while those driven by electric motors are quieter and much less demanding of maintenance.

Because of the wide variation in weight, noise, performance, and power source, it is highly advisable to test the machine before buying. The smaller types are often designed as components of so-called power systems, with fittings that include a trimmer, edger, tiller-cultivator, brush cutter, chain saw, etc. As appealing as these ingeniously designed tools may be, combining such diverse functions inevitably involves compromises that affect performance.

TOOL AND EQUIPMENT STORAGE

Part of the satisfaction to be derived from gardening is to have readily accessible the correct tools and supplies needed for a given task. Yet it is often difficult, especially where space is limited, to find places to store things where they will be out of the way yet easily available when needed. Too often, the car is displaced from the garage by a disorganized accumulation of outdoor items that, with a little care and discretion, could be accommodated without causing inconvenience.

Equipment should be organized and stored by season. Items needed in winter, such as snow shovels, snow stakes, snow blower, and snow fence, should be stored together and apart from the lawn mower, fertilizer spreader, and other garden tools. Often all that is required is to suspend all hand tools and light equipment from hooks and pegboard panels. In other cases, especially on larger properties, a separate gardening workroom or tool shed may be required.

The tool room should be within direct reach of the garden and arranged not only for storing tools but for organizing and storing pots, flats, planting media, and fertilizers. This should also be a place to maintain and repair tools, prepare labels, arrange flowers, construct bird feeders, and keep records, among sundry other chores and projects. If the temperature can be kept cool but constantly above freezing,

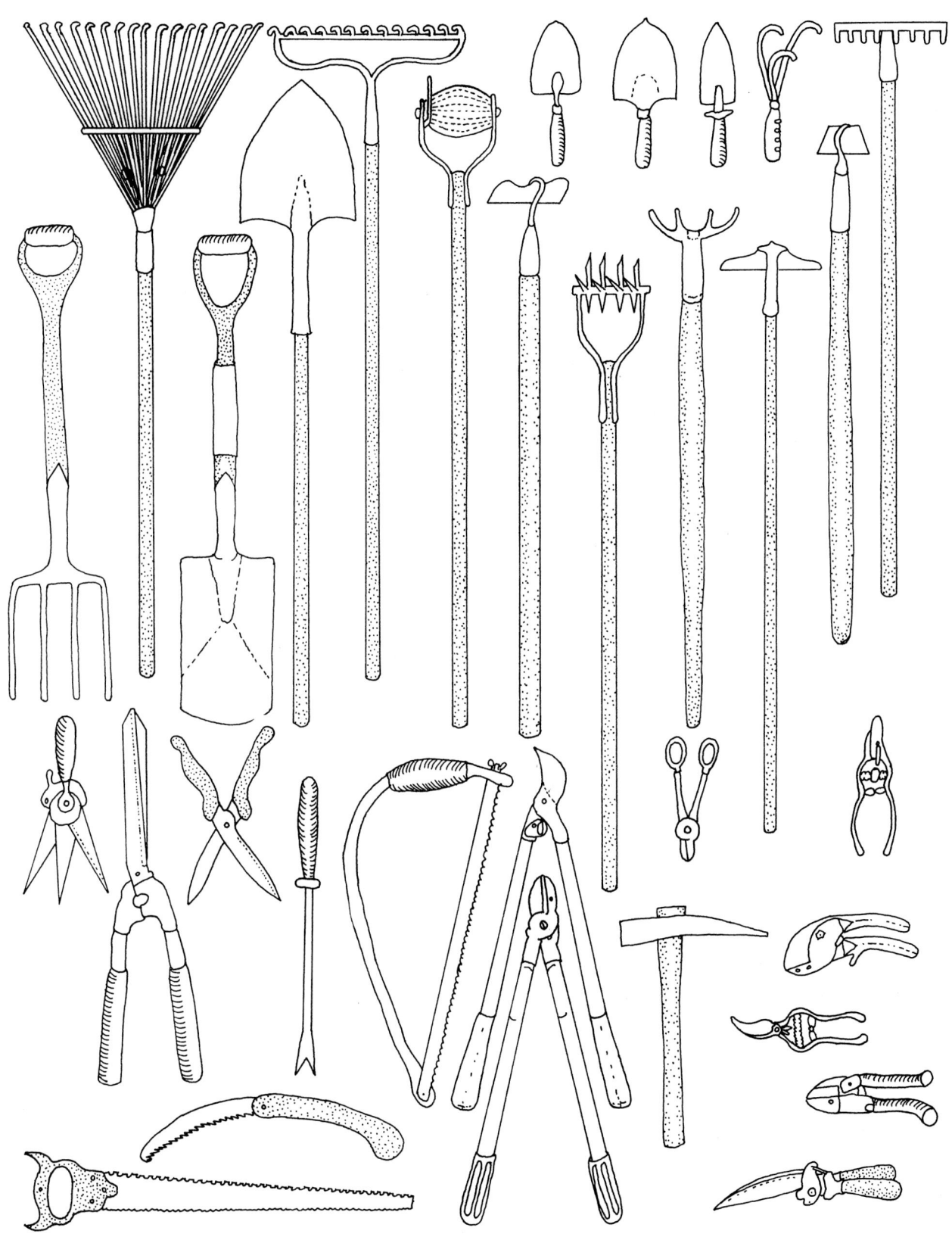

Garden tools stored compactly on a wall are easily found when needed. Pegboard panels facilitate rearrangement or changes.

A spacious garden shed not only accommodates tools but, when furnished with a double door, eases passage of wheelbarrow, cart, and power equipment. Windows and skylights facilitate inside work.

the tool room can be used as the place to store seeds and bulbs (in rodent-proof containers), to mix and store potting soil, and to wash pots and flats.

Failing the space for a tool room in the house or garage, the answer may be an outdoor tool shed. This can be as simple as a prefabricated freestanding or lean-to shelter made of steel, wood, or vinyl, preferably set on a poured 4-inch concrete slab (the preparation of which is not so simple) or on a peripheral footing of mortared concrete blocks, within the confines of which the floor may be constructed of brick, gravel, treated lumber, or other rot-resistant material. In any case, the shed must be anchored to its base, following both the instructions in the kit and any applicable local building codes. Alternatively, the shed may be designed and built professionally or by yourself to suit the idiosyncracies of the setting and mirror or complement the architecture of the house, again respecting any local code regulations.

A useful addition to the tool shed, garage, or tool room is a lath house, which is an airy slatted shelter for houseplants and other plants intolerant of sun exposure; it can also be covered with tough, sun-resistant, clear polyethylene plastic film and, with minimal heating, serve as a cool greenhouse in the winter (see Chapter 40).

Tool Maintenance and Storage
General Cleaning

Ideally, tools should be cleaned immediately after use and before they are returned to their place. It is far easier to remove moist soil from a spade or hoe than when the soil is hard and dry and has become encrusted on the metal. A blunt wood blade of the type used to mix paint is the most convenient thing to use in removing soil from spades and hoes. However, if the soil has been allowed to dry and harden, it may be removed by rubbing the surface vigorously with a wet cloth or with a rag soaked in kerosene.

General Winter Storage

Before tools are put away for the winter, they should first be thoroughly cleaned. Rust can easily be removed with steel wool. A protective coating of wax or grease should then be applied. Ordinary floor wax may be used or almost any type of grease or a light grade of rust-inhibiting oil—a cheap grade of vaseline is excellent, cup grease is entirely satisfactory, or lard may be used. It is wise to ensure that such tools as pruning shears, lawn mowers, knives, and hoes are sharpened before they are put away so that they are ready for use when the rush of spring work begins.

Sprayers

Sprayer heads and tanks should always be throughly rinsed out after each use, as the ingredients are nearly always corrosive. To keep the piston in good working order, the plunger rod and leather or plastic plunger should be oiled at frequent intervals during the spraying season and especially when the sprayer is to be stored for the winter. Before storing, worn washers should be replaced and the hose cleaned with a mild vinegar solution, then rinsed with clear water. During the winter, the sprayer should be stored in a dry place. This is particularly important in the case of ungalvanized steel sprayers to prevent them from rusting.

Fertilizer Spreader

The fertilizer spreader should be thoroughly cleaned after use, and the wheels should be oiled at the axle to prevent rusting. It should be kept in a dry place. Most fertilizers are very corrosive to metal, and the spreader's period of usefulness will be greatly extended if these simple precautions are followed.

Hose

When not in use, the garden hose should be kept on a reel or a mounted fixture in a shaded place. Nothing shortens the life of a plastic or rubber hose more rapidly than to allow it to lie out in the sun day after day. When a hose is put away for the winter, care should be taken to see that it is thoroughly drained and, if hung, is suspended from a rounded support.

Mower and Other Power Equipment

The lawn mower, whatever the type, should be thoroughly cleaned at the end of the season. All grass clippings, dirt, and grease should be removed. A steel brush is excellent for this purpose. Any parts that show evidence of rust should be cleaned with steel wool. All exposed metal parts should receive a coating of oil. All gears and bearings should be oiled.

For power mowers, the oil filter should be cleaned and rinsed in gasoline, and clean oil should be added to a 4-cycle engine. All gasoline should be removed from the tank, as it is liable to leave a gummy residue as it evaporates. Run the engine until all the gasoline in the tank, fuel line, and carburetor is used up. To remove all crankcase sediment, drain the oil while the engine is still warm, and then add fresh oil. Remove the spark plug and pour 1 ounce of no. 20 grade oil into the cylinder. Cover the cooled mower with a plastic, waterproof cover to protect it from dampness and dust.

Similar maintenance should be performed on rototillers, chain saws, and other motorized equipment.

31

Soils and Soil Improvement

No subject is of more fundamental importance to the gardener than soil composition and management. To handle garden soils intelligently, and to maintain if not increase the fertility of the soil, it is necessary to have a thorough knowledge not only of the soil itself but also of the manner in which plants receive their nutrients from the soil. Synonymous with simple "dirt" in the minds of some, the term *soil* seems to imply more complexity and connote greater respect; etymologically, both terms are derived from two ancient unrelated root words for manure.

The secret to soil improvement in all gardens is the conversion of plant remains to friable compost.

No soil is ideal for all cultivated plants (or for wild species, either), but if a careful program of soil management is undertaken, the structure, fertility, and water-retaining capacity of soils of widely varying types can be improved to meet the needs of the vast majority.

There are certain factors affecting plant growth over which a gardener has very little control, such as climate, rainfall, sunshine, and humidity; but over the various factors of soil quality, control can certainly be exercised. Moreover, soil should be considered a heritage from the past. Not only for our own immediate benefit should we conserve, maintain, and increase its fertility; it is our obligation to do so for generations to follow us. To allow soil to degrade is to mortgage their future.

Soil formation is a process that has continued since earliest geologic times when the surface of the earth was composed entirely of rock. The action of sun and frost, wind and water, upon these rock surfaces has resulted in a gradual process of fragmentation and disintegration and the consequent slow formation of soils. Eons ago the first land plants grew in the hollows and crevices of the rocks where this newly formed mineral soil accumulated. As these primitive plants died, they were physically pulverized and acted on chemically by bacteria, fungi, protozoa, and various invertebrate animals, and thus provided nutrients for successor plants. Gradually, as the millennia passed, this decaying organic matter increased and became mixed with granular minerals, supporting ever more vegetation, which in time clothed nearly all exposed land surfaces. The same processes continue today as algae, mosses, and lichens, nature's pioneer plants, gain footholds in the bare rock of glacial and volcanic areas, and gradually break that rock down into primitive soils.

In some of the colder areas of the world where coniferous forest has long abounded, we may find deep, porous soils that are peaty in nature. Such soils are especially characteristic of bogs and are composed almost entirely of partly decayed organic matter. Elsewhere, the world's grasslands produce soils equally rich in organic matter. In other areas we find soils that are classed as mineral soils, composed largely of mineral granules. Between these two extreme types, the peaty soils and the mineral soils, we find many soils of widely varying character.

Most soils, as we find them in our gardens today, are composed of five intermingled components: the mineral substances obtained from the slow disintegration of rock surfaces; humus or decaying organic matter; minute living organisms such as the bacteria, protozoa, and fungi that are usually present in large quantities; water, which holds in solution the dissolved mineral salts; and air. In areas where the soil has been under cultivation for many years or where

soil management has been poor, we often find soils that have lost much of their humus content and that, in many cases, may have become depleted of their mineral elements. It is these soils that present the greatest problems.

TYPES OF SOIL

Soils are generally grouped into three classes according to structure: sand, silt, or clay. These classes are determined by the size of the soil particles. Sand contains 20 particles or fewer to a cubic millimeter, silt 20 to 200 particles, and clay more than 200. A soil of ideal texture is a mixture of sand, silt, and clay, and is usually called garden loam. The structure of the soil has a very direct bearing on its water-holding capacity, on its warming in early spring, on the ease with which it can be worked or handled, and on the penetration of plant roots and the consequent nutrient uptake of the plant.

Clay Soils

Much of the earth's surface consists of clay. A clay soil has a water-holding capacity many times higher than that of a sandy soil because each soil particle is capable of holding a film of water on its surface. Therefore, a specific volume of clay soil, which possesses many more particles per cubic millimeter than sand, is capable of holding many times as much water as the same volume of sand. The water-holding capacity of clay soils may seem an asset in seasons of extreme drought, but it is, on the whole, almost as much of a liability. A heavy clay soil is very slow to dry out in the spring, and all planting operations and general cultural practices must, therefore, be delayed because of its winter wetness,

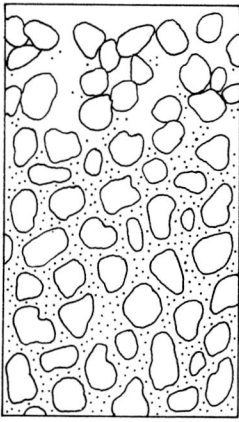

Stylized comparison of silty soil particles (on left) with sandy particles, both with intermingled fine dots representing clay.

high density, and greasy texture. It does not absorb the sun's rays as readily as does a soil of more open structure and, therefore, does not warm up as quickly in the spring, thus delaying the onset of the spring growth of plants. Since its density often inhibits root growth, clay soil may cause dwarfness in some species—a not unwelcome result in some cases, as, for example, in fruit trees.

If left uncultivated too long after a rain, a clay soil will form a hard, baked crust that reduces air penetration and can actually repel water, often forming deep cracks as its surface contracts. On the other hand, if it is plowed or cultivated or otherwise handled when it is too wet, it will form large, hard lumps that are exceedingly difficult to break up. Thus, clay soil is one of the most difficult of all soil types to handle wisely, and every effort should be made to improve its structure. Much may be accomplished by the addition of sand, humus, and compost. It is also advantageous to shallowly fork or rototill clay soils in the fall, leaving the surface rough and uneven throughout the winter. The action of the frost will have a beneficial effect on the close texture of the soil, making it somewhat more friable. If a layer of shredded leaves or other suitably fragmented organic material is spread over the surface before it is forked or tilled, the incorporation of this material will further improve the workability of the soil in spring.

Sandy Soils

Sandy soils possess many of the advantages that are lacking in soils of a decidedly heavy texture, i.e., they warm up quickly in the spring, they are loose or open in structure, and they do not retain moisture. But, because water percolates through so freely, nutrients leach downward beyond the reach of roots, sometimes quite rapidly, and accumulate in surface waters and aquifers, where they can cause serious pollution. Exposed sandy soils also lose moisture through evaporation more readily than heavier soils, and therefore, the plants grown on them require more frequent irrigation. Thus it is quite as important to improve the structure of sandy soils as it is to improve the structure of heavy clay soils. This may be accomplished most successfully by the addition of liberal quantities of compost, well-rotted manure, or other organic matter. In addition, if in preparation the garden has been underlain with several layers of newspaper at a depth of 1 foot, or the individual root balls of tree and shrub transplants are so underlain, the loss of moisture will be slowed. Strips of tarpaper, roofing paper, or even remnants of kitchen floor covering 1 to 2 feet wide set beneath crop rows in the vegetable garden will slow downward percolation and help keep moisture available for root absorption in summer dry spells.

Coarse, unscreened compost makes a valuable summer mulch that conserves soil moisture, deters weeds, stabilizes soil temperature, and gradually releases nutrients.

For the longer term, however, it is important to spread and work in, using a garden fork or rototiller, a 4-inch layer of well-rotted manure—preferably stable manure mixed with straw or fine wood-chip bedding. It is best to do this annually in early spring for the first few years and in alternate years thereafter. Use a weed-free mulch on the soil surface during the summer. These measures will help maintain soil moisture, provide a slow-release nutrient base, deter weeds, and stabilize soil temperatures. Approximately 3 cubic yards of manure, mulch, or a combination is required for each 1,000 square feet of new garden.

Other gardening guidelines that apply in areas with excessively drained soils include the following.

1. Place any commercial fertilizer that is used exactly where it is needed rather than broadcasting it over the entire garden area; supplemental manure or compost should be applied in a 3- to 4-inch-deep layer in a

1-foot-wide band on either side of crops grown in rows or strips.

2. After seeding, tamp the soil by walking on a plank set on the planted row, or if the soil surface is dry, use a garden roller, thereby driving off excess air and increasing seed-soil contact.

3. Plant tomato transplants, just-sprouted dahlia tubers, and gladiolus corms in little depressions up to 1 foot deep; as the plants grow, the depressions should be gradually filled with compost or well-rotted manure, thus ensuring their roots an ample supply of moisture and nutrients throughout the summer.

4. To minimize soil disturbance and the penetration of root-drying air, clip off weeds, especially large ones, at the soil surface, rather than pulling or hoeing them out; cover the weeded area with compost or mulch, but allow a 2-inch clear zone around each plant or along planted rows to discourage attack by diseases and pests.

Loam Soils

The ideal soil for most garden operations is a fertile loam, which is a mixture of sand, silty clay, and humus. It should be porous enough in texture to provide good drainage (i.e., without puddling after a summer rain or a heavy watering) and adequate aeration; it should be spongy enough to retain an ample supply of moisture, it should contain sufficient humus to provide favorable conditions for the growth of beneficial soil microorganisms, it should contain the mineral elements necessary for normal plant growth, and it should have a pH level that renders these nutrients available for uptake by roots. Achieving and maintaining a soil of this type is the goal of every gardener, and with a good program of soil management and an intelligent understanding of the needs of growing plants, much may be accomplished in building a soil that will very nearly approximate the ideal.

HUMUS

An adequate supply of humus in the soil is one of the most important factors in any program of good soil management. Humus, or organic matter in various stages of decay, serves many functions in improving the structure and character of any soil. It increases the water-holding capacity of soils, it modifies the soil structure, it is readily warmed by the sun's rays in spring and stimulates early plant growth, and it prevents the leaching of soluble plant foods. Humus also liberates compounds, which, in turn, act on the chemical elements in the soil, thus making available to the plants mineral nutrients that would otherwise remain complex or in insoluble form. Furthermore, it promotes the bacterial action in the soil to a very marked degree.

The value of humus in increasing the water-holding capacities of soils can hardly be overemphasized. It is unlike the particles of mineral soils in that it does not merely hold the water on its surface; it soaks it up like a sponge. Studies have shown that while 100 pounds of sand will hold 25 pounds of water and 100 pounds of clay will hold 50 pounds of water, 100 pounds of humus will hold 190 pounds of water. Between 20 and 40 percent of the water-holding capacity of soils is due to their humus content; in seasons of prolonged drought soils high in humus content will remain moist in both the upper and lower soil horizons far longer than soils that are deficient in humus. Under such conditions, plant growth is correspondingly greater.

Humus is also of great value in improving the texture of soils, as it has the ability to modify the soil's structure to a very marked degree. A soil that is of open, friable structure, the kind regarded as an ideal garden loam, is made up of crumbs of soil held together in a granule, and it is the humus that furnishes the binding material for these soil particles. A soil of this texture facilitates the ready availability of moisture and plant nutrients. It also permits easy root penetration, which is an important factor, since roots seek the water and nutrients in the soil, not vice versa. When a clay soil is deficient in humus, it becomes tight and compact in structure. The penetration of the roots is, therefore, reduced and the nutrition of the plant is often seriously compromised as a consequence. Such a soil has a tendency to become hard and baked when it is dry, and in that state is far less permeable to water than soil of a more open, granular structure. Not only does the water penetrate the soil less readily but it is also more quickly evaporated. Soils of this type may be greatly improved in texture by the application of liberal amounts of humus. When sandy soils are deficient in humus, many valuable plant nutrients are lost through leaching and plant growth also suffers seriously from lack of moisture in times of drought. It is, therefore, quite as important to see that sandy soils are well supplied with humus as it is to maintain an adequate humus supply in clay soils.

Mineral fertilizers supplement but in no way replace the nutrients in humus. Experiments have proved that mineral fertilizers are much more effective if they are applied either with, or immediately following, an application of humus, than if they are applied alone. At the Maryland Experimental Station, crop yields have shown an increase varying from one-fifth to one-third more when manure and mineral fertilizers were applied together than when double the amount of either was applied alone. This same principle applies to the building up of soil fertility in the garden.

Sources of Humus
Peat

The various forms of peat are excellent sources of humus. Technically, peat is the partially carbonized organic residue of plants, the decomposition of which has taken place in standing water. Peat varies somewhat according to the conditions under which it forms—whether in deep water, marshes, swamps, or bogs. When tree trunks and branches, mosses, sedges, and grasses decay under water, their decomposition is greatly retarded because of the reduced availability of air, and the resulting product, known as peat, differs considerably from the humus that is found in upland forests.

As organic matter, peat is highly absorbent and retentive of moisture, and has the added advantage of being comparatively free from weed seeds and harmful fungi. Peat is usually acidic and should, therefore, be used with discrimination. It is of particular value for use in connection with the planting of broad-leaf evergreens, such as rhododendrons, azaleas, and mountain laurel, and many other acid-loving plants, but it should not be used too liberally in connection with plants that are not acid tolerant. The actual fertilizing value of peat is negligible. It contains some nitrogen, the amount varying from 1 to 3.5 percent, depending on the source of the peat, but it is extremely low in phosphorus and potassium.

Most peat is imported from Canada as pulverized peat moss and comes in tightly packed 6-cubic-foot bales weighing about 200 pounds. It is largely of bog origin, and it is all but devoid of nutrient content. When it is to be incorporated in the soil, or used as a mulch, handling is greatly facilitated if the material is thoroughly soaked before being applied. When dry, the light, fluffy, extremely dusty texture of peat moss makes it hard to manage.

Because of its very slow rate of formation, peat in any form should be treated as a nonrenewable resource and used thoughtfully and conservatively—ideally as a supplement to home-generated compost.

Domestic peat is usually sold with a higher moisture content, is darker in color, and is finer in texture. In general, it is considered a better source of humus than the imported peat, as it may be more evenly worked into the soil and its effect is more lasting. However, it is not readily available.

Leaf Mold

An excellent and sometimes readily available type of humus, leaf mold is highly retentive of moisture, is almost wholly organic, and slowly releases nutrients as it continues to decompose. Leaf mold varies considerably in acidity, depending on the kinds of leaves involved. Oak leaves and, to a lesser degree, pine needles, when decayed, form a leaf mold that is of acid pH. However, the majority of our deciduous trees form a leaf mold that is only very mildly acidic. The best and most abundant source of leaf mold is the natural forest floor. A small but readily available supply may be kept at hand by making a compost of fallen tree leaves each autumn. Many municipalities provide leaf mold to residents, and it is also commercially available in many areas.

MAKING COMPOST

Not only is compost a valuable adjunct to any garden, but generating compost has become a civic responsibility of every thoughtful home owner, one that has long been practiced and advocated by devoted gardeners everywhere. No matter how small the property may be, there are always unwanted organic materials, both from the garden and the kitchen, that can be converted into compost. The end product of the composting process is a soil that is very rich in humus and that offers needed plant nutrients. Such soils are of particular use in the preparation of seedbeds. Compost is

A composting barrel, which, if the contents are turned frequently and kept moist, soon generates useful compost.

also valuable as a topdressing for lawns and in the preparation of the soil in hotbeds and coldframes, and it is used extensively to enrich and improve the texture of the soil in flower gardens and on vegetable plots. Indeed, there are so many uses for a good compost that the supply seldom is adequate to meet needs.

At its simplest, composting may be accomplished by heaping organic debris in a pile. A partially shaded or lightly shaded location is preferable to one in full sun, as it will more readily retain moisture. A pile of convenient, workable size is one 4 to 6 feet in width, 3 to 4 feet in height, and of any desired length. The foundation of the pile should consist of some coarse material, such as inverted sods or weed stalks, and upon this foundation alternating layers of organic refuse and soil should be built up, with stock-animal manures included wherever they are obtainable as they greatly increase the supply of decomposition bacteria. Almost any type of organic material may be used, with the exception of dense wood. Grass clippings, sod, weeds, refuse from the vegetable garden are excellent raw materials, as are vegetable peelings and fruit rinds. Composting converts all into potential wealth for the gardener.

Diseased plants or those infested with pests should not be composted, as the unwanted organisms may persist in the compost and ravage the garden wherever it is spread. Similarly, weeds gone to seed should be excluded; most weed seeds are long-lived and many can survive the high temperatures that sometimes develop in a compost pile.

The decomposition of organic matter is due to the activity of certain organisms, and the rate of decomposition in a compost pile will be greatly accelerated if these microorganisms are present in sufficient numbers. This may be accomplished through the addition of humusy soil to the pile (such a pile teems with microorganisms); through the use of some well-rotted compost from another pile; or through the use of one of numerous commercial compost activators on the market.

Since these organisms, which play such an important part in the decomposition of organic materials, are most active in slightly acidic to neutral conditions, it is advantageous to add an occasional sprinkling of ground limestone to the pile during the process of construction. The moisture content of the pile is also important. The top of the pile should be concave, to catch as much rain as possible, and if dry materials such as hay or straw are used the pile should be thoroughly soaked during the process of building. It should have a moist, spongy consistency at all times. A rounded pile tends to shed water, with the result that decomposition is slow and the interior too dry for composting to proceed. An occasional turning is advisable, rebuilding the pile so that the outer portion is placed in the center of the new pile and thus

accelerating the generation of useful compost. An unturned pile will still generate compost, but only inside where moisture is constant. The undecomposed outer material will become compost after it has been covered with new material.

The time required to convert raw organic materials into a good humus suitable for garden use depends on a number of factors, such as temperature, the moisture content of the pile, the types of materials used, and whether a chemical activator is used. Bacterial action is more rapid in warm climates than in colder regions; green materials will decompose more rapidly than more woody materials, and some of the new commercial activators will speed the process of decomposition to such an extent that it is possible to obtain an excellent humus in just a few mild or warm months.

Where outdoor space is limited for composting, a bin, crib, or corral can be constructed using such ubiquitous materials as wire-mesh fencing, snow fencing, or shipping pallets, or just large plastic garbage containers, the bottoms and sides perforated for drainage and aeration. Manufactured composters are also available, but, while neat and

A compost bin fashioned from stacked posts offers ideal conditions for conversion of garden waste into compost.

convenient and even ingenious in design, they are not inexpensive and their capacity usually quite small.

Another approach is the compost pit, which is usually a trench about 1 foot deep, 2 feet wide, and as long as desired. It has the advantages of being out of sight and having a more or less automatically regulated moisture level that is equivalent to that of the adjacent soil, but it must be dug, the dug soil taken away, and the generated compost used promptly before the roots of nearby trees and other plants invade.

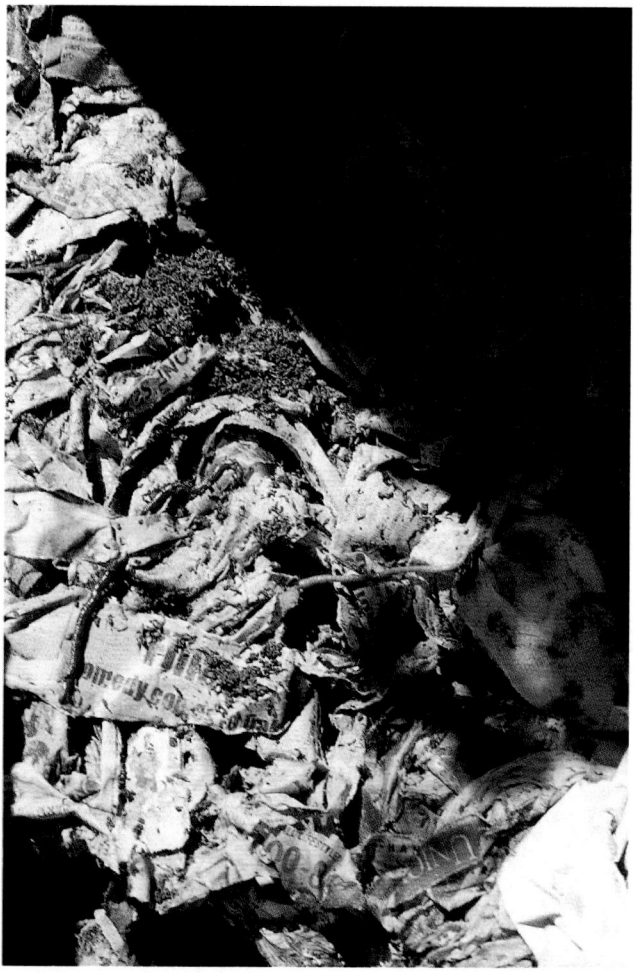

In a compost bin, suitable for indoor use, red worms convert kitchen waste into usable compost.

Untended exposed composting areas may attract rodents seeking nesting sites, and scraps of meat, fish, and other animal material will attract marauding dogs, cats, raccoons, and other carnivores and scavengers unless deeply buried or the area is effectively screened or fenced. To avoid this problem, refrain from discarding such food scraps that will attract unwanted visitors.

Composting may be carried out indoors throughout the year using a lid-covered, perforated box (usually 4 feet long, 2 feet wide, and 1½ feet deep, and divisible into smaller compartments), into which kitchen waste is placed and a supply of purchased red worms is added (about 1 pound of worms per 4 pounds of vegetable waste). Each worm ingests its weight in organic matter daily and produces an equivalent amount of cast, which accumulates as compost and may be removed for future use. A temperature range of 60° to 75°F is best, and adequate moisture must be maintained.

Typical rates for applying compost are ½ to 1 pound per square foot of garden, but no harm is done by using more.

Making Compost Weed Free

When using compost as a topdressing on lawns, or for a seedbed in a coldframe, or for flats in which seeds are to be started, it is a great advantage to have it weed free.

There are various methods of producing compost that will be entirely free of viable weed seeds. One of the methods best adapted to the facilities available to the home gardener is one in which granular calcium cyanimide (Cyanamid) is added. Not only does this substance kill all weed seeds but it also increases the nutritive value of the compost, as Cyanamid contains 20 percent nitrogen and the equivalent of 70 percent hydrated lime.

The process is essentially simple and is best carried out by two people. The compost, which should be well decomposed and moderately moist, should be sifted through a ¼-inch mesh wire screen. It should then be mixed thoroughly with the Cyanamid at the rate of 13 pounds of Cyanamid to each cubic yard of compost. The easiest way to measure a cubic yard is to have a bottomless box that holds 1 cubic yard or an exact fraction thereof. The box may be filled and lifted away and refilled again as many times as necessary. One of the best ways of adding the Cyanamid in the correct proportion, and ensuring that it is well distributed through the compost, is to place the compost in the measuring box layer by layer, adding a proportionate amount of Cyanamid as the layers are built up. If four layers are used, slightly more than 3 pounds of Cyanamid should be sprinkled over each layer. The Cyanamid should never be applied in excess of 13 pounds per cubic yard, as it might result in the burning of turf or plants when the compost is spread.

The mixing may be done by shoveling the material back and forth on a concrete floor or some other level surface. After it has been thoroughly mixed, it should be screened again and then stored under a shelter in a wooden bin or in some place where the pile will not be disturbed.

It usually takes four to six weeks to obtain a complete kill of all weed seeds, provided the weather is mild. It takes considerably longer in cold weather, so the work should preferably be done during the warm months.

Although the above method is more thorough, it should be noted that a properly functioning hot compost pile, which will self-heat to 160°F, can be almost as efficient in eliminating most weed seeds. This can be accomplished by piling compost in a sunny place and covering it with black plastic. If the compost consists mainly of leaves, it will be ready in a few weeks; more fibrous material (such as corn husks) will take longer. However, much nitrogen is dissipated by heat generated in the process.

COVER CROPS

Cover crops are often spoken of as "green manures." The term is applied to crops that are grown for the sole purpose of being plowed or spaded under, to improve the physical texture of the soil, to increase its organic content, and to increase its fertility. Such a procedure is one of the best and also least expensive methods of improving poor soils. It is, on the whole, more suitable for large-scale operations than for use on small areas. It may play a very important part, however, in the initial preparation of the soil for a vegetable garden or a fruit orchard, or for a lawn area.

The most valuable cover crops, from the standpoint of increasing the fertility of the soil, are certain legumes, such as soybeans, alfalfa, clovers, and vetches. Legumes actually increase the nitrate content of the soil through the aid of nitrogen-fixing rhizobial bacteria (*Rhizobium* spp.). These highly specialized bacteria, which have the ability to take nitrogen from the air, are minute, rod-shaped bodies that are found in the soil under certain favorable conditions. When these bacteria come into contact with the roots of certain legume plants, they enter the root hairs, causing the growth of tiny spherical structures called root nodules. The rhizobial bacteria take free nitrogen from the air and supply it to the plant as nitrate. The plant, in return, nourishes the bacteria, which multiply rapidly. This relationship is called symbiosis. Various kinds of rhizobial bacteria colonize the roots of various legumes—one kind living on one group of legumes, another living only on certain other types.

Some legumes, such as alfalfa, are very dependent on the nitrogen-fixing bacteria and the plants are unable to survive unless these bacteria are present in the soil. Other legumes, such as soybeans, are considerably less dependent and will make reasonably good growth on soil where no bacteria are present. When grown under such conditions, however, these crops are no more valuable than a nonleguminous crop, as they do not increase the nitrogen content of the soil unless the bacteria are present. To ensure the presence of these nitrogen-fixing bacteria in the soil, all legume crops (including such vegetables as beans and peas) should be inoculated before planting with a specially prepared inoculant carrying the exact type of bacteria needed for the particular legume to be grown. Such inoculants are obtainable in granular form from any commercial seed house.

The value of legumes as cover crops can hardly be overemphasized. A well-grown leguminous crop that is plowed under at the proper stage of growth will frequently add 100 to 150 pounds of actual nitrogen to the soil per acre. This would practically equal 10 to 15 tons of good animal manure.

The stage of growth at which cover crops are plowed under has a very direct influence on the value of the crop. The nitrogen and mineral content are highest shortly before maturity. Therefore, the crop should be plowed under when it is in a slightly immature stage, i.e., before it flowers.

If cover crops are to be grown on soils of very low fertility, the eventual value of the crop as a soil improper will be greatly increased if the cover crop receives the benefit of an application of commercial fertilizer, and if conditions are made as favorable as possible for good growth. There is little to be gained from growing a cover crop on land that is so poor it can support little in the way of plant growth. Under such conditions, the benefits will hardly justify the cost of seed and labor. Where soil is quite poor in physical structure and deficient in nutrients, it is necessary not only to prepare it as fully as possible before sowing cover crop seed but to commit the area to a year-long growth of leguminous cover crop before attempting to plant vegetables or ornamentals. Thereafter, it may be necessary to rotate vegetable production with cover crops on an alternate-year basis.

It is a generally accepted fact that the crops planted immediately after the plowing under of a cover crop (particularly a nonleguminous crop) will thrive infinitely better if a fairly liberal application of well-rotted manure or a commercial fertilizer is made at the time that the crop is turned under. The same principle applies to the plowing under of a heavy growth of sod. This is because the process of decomposition is carried on by certain of the bacteria in the soil. These bacteria need to use the nitrogen in the soil in order to carry on their activities, and unless a surplus of nitrogen is present the plants suffer in consequence. By applying a highly nitrogenous fertilizer, such a surplus may be ensured.

COVER CROPS OF MERIT

Leguminous Crops
Recommended Procedures for Legumes

Plant legumes in the fall six to eight weeks before hard frost, or in the spring about two weeks before the average date of the last frost. The soil should be free of crop residue and raked smooth.

In most cases, seed should be pretreated with rhizobial inoculant but never with fungicide (which can destroy the inoculant), and sown at the rate of 1 to 1½ cups per 50 square feet. Small seeds (alfalfa, clover) should be premixed with dry sand for even distribution. After broadcasting the seed by hand or with a mechanical spreader, rake to cover. Broadcast larger seeds and tamp or roll-in before watering, or sow in shallow drills. If possible, plant just before a forecast rain. Water thereafter as needed.

For maximum nitrate return, turn under just as flower buds begin opening. If growth is taller than 6 inches, mow before spading or rototilling. Allow the turned-under crop two to three weeks to decompose before planting.

ALFALFA
(Medicago sativa)

A perennial hardy to zone 5, alfalfa requires a longer time to become established than the annual and biennial crops, but there are instances when its use as a short-term cover crop is justified. For example, in open fields that will eventually be put into lawns, no better use can be made of the land than to put it into alfalfa.

Seed should be sown in early spring or late summer at the rate of 10 to 12 pounds per acre. If the field is weedy, late summer sowing is preferable. A well-drained, moderately fertile soil of pH 6.5 to 7.0 yields the best results. Alfalfa hay may be harvested for a number of years. However, when the area is needed for some other purpose, the crop may be turned under in the spring or fall. Tops and roots contain about 2½ percent nitrogen, and as much as 150 pounds of nitrogen per acre may be added to the soil.

ALSIKE CLOVER
(Trifolium hybridum)

Alsike clover is adaptable to cool climates, alkaline soils, and occasional flooding, but it winter kills north of zone 6. Inoculate with *Rhizobium trifolii*. Otherwise, treatment is the same as for mammoth red clover.

FIELD PEA, AUSTRIAN WINTER PEA
(Pisum sativum var. arvense)

Useful under cool, moist conditions, field pea usually winter kills north of zone 8. It performs best on loamy soils and should be inoculated with *R. leguminosaeum*.

HAIRY VETCH
(Vicia villosa)

A winter annual and one of the most effective soil builders, hairy vetch is the hardiest of the cultivated vetches and grows best in cool weather on sandy, well-drained soils having a pH of 6.5 to 7.0.

HUBAM SWEET CLOVER, WHITE SWEET CLOVER
(Melilotus alba)

A tall biennial (reaching 6 feet the second year), Hubam sweet clover is one of the few cover crop legumes that grows well on poor soil. It even does well on subsoil or washed clay, as so long as the pH is 6.5 or higher. Spring planting is best, with seed inoculated with *R. meliloti*, followed by turning under the following spring.

ITALIAN CLOVER, CRIMSON CLOVER
(Trifolium incarnatum)

Reliably overwintering in most of the United States except north of zone 5, Italian clover performs well on any soil but acidic muck. It should be inoculated with *R. trifolii*.

MAMMOTH RED CLOVER
(Trifolium pratense var. sativum)

A biennial or short-lived perennial, red clover should be left in place at least one year. In most situations, it is a splendid soil builder. Sow very early in the spring, preferably with a small temporary grain crop such as oats, at the rate of ¼ to ⅓ pound per 1,000 square feet. Inoculate seed with *R. trifolii*. A moderately fertile soil at pH 5.5 or higher yields the heaviest growth. The crop should be plowed under just as the flower heads emerge.

SOYBEAN
(Glycine max)

One of the most valuable of all cover crops, soybean is a fast-growing annual that should be sown in mid to late spring at the rate of 2 quarts per 1,000 square feet. Soil pH should be higher than 5.0. If poor, the soil should be fortified with a complete fertilizer before sowing. Seed should be inoculated with *R. japonicum*.

YELLOW SWEET CLOVER
(Melilotus indica)

A biennial, yellow sweet clover may be grown in place of Hubam sweet clover. Culture and seed inoculation are the same.

Nonleguminous Cover Crops

Site preparation for nonleguminous cover crops is the same as for legumes, but fall sowing should take place four to six weeks before the first hard frost. No seed inoculation is required. Although nonlegumes do not increase the nitrate content of the soil, they do add more organic matter when turned under than legumes.

RYE
(Secale cereale)

Rye is a winter-hardy annual grass and is considered the most valuable of all nonleguminous cover crops. It should be sown in late summer and succeeds reasonably well on soil of average fertility regardless of pH. It should be plowed under in the spring when it has reached a height of about 10 inches. At this point the plant contains the highest percentage of nitrogen than at any other stage.

SPRING OATS
(Avena sativa)

Also an annual grass, spring oats thrive under cool, moist conditions on most any soil except heavy clay. Planted in late summer, this species winter kills north of zone 6; at these northerly latitudes it should be turned under in late fall, before the soil hardens with frost.

Combination Cover Crops
Of the several combination cover crops that work well and offer the advantages of each component species, the following is the best.

Hairy Vetch and Rye
Hairy vetch and rye are best planted in very late summer at the rate of 1 quart per 1,000 square feet, with the mixture made up of three parts rye to one part vetch. Soil pH should be 6.5 or higher (to meet vetch's requirement), and the crop should be turned under in midspring.

MANURES
Animal Manures

Long before commercial fertilizers were developed, the good qualities of animal manures in improving and maintaining soil fertility were known and appreciated. Not only does animal manure increase the fertility of the soil but it also serves other important functions as well: it increases the organic content of the soil, it improves the physical structure of the soil, and it increases the bacterial activity to a very appreciable degree.

Contrary to popular belief, the actual elements of fertility contained in animal manures are small when compared with those contained in most inorganic commercial fertilizers. The following table indicates the usual percentages found in various types of manure.

Manure Source	Nitrogen	Phosphorus	Potassium
Poultry	1	0.8	0.4
Sheep	0.95	0.35	1
Horse	0.7	0.25	0.55
Cow	0.6	0.15	0.45
Pig	0.5	0.35	0.4

Moreover, only about one-half of the nitrogen, one-half of the potassium, and one-sixth of the phosphorus are readily available for use by the plants. It can be seen, therefore, that the actual fertility added to the soil by an application of manure is low, and that the benefits derived from such an application are those more directly concerned with the physical character of the soil.

The value of animal manure, from a standpoint of fertility, depends to a considerable extent on the way it is treated. If a high percentage of the nutrients it contains as fresh manure are to be conserved, it must be handled with care; if not, it may lose a substantial percentage of its nutrients. The most generally accepted practice is to store manure under cover, constantly moist.

The recommended rate of application of manure is ½ to 1 pound per square foot for horse, cow, or other nonpoultry manures, and roughly 20 percent that amount for poultry manures. A cubic yard of moist manure weighs between 1,000 and 1,500 pounds. If spread and worked in in late summer or early fall, there may be time to sow a cover crop, which will take up and store liberated nutrients; otherwise, especially in sandy soils, they may leach away before crops are sown the following spring.

Fresh manure should never be used where it will come into direct contact with the roots of the plants, as it is liable to cause dehydration or burning. Most gardeners prefer to use manure after it has partially rotted. In this form, the nutrients are more readily available and the danger of any harmful effects is largely mitigated. On large-scale operations, manure is usually spread on the surface of the soil and then plowed or harrowed in. On smaller areas, it is usually forked or rototilled into the soil.

If regularly applied in recommended amounts, animal manures, reinforced with cover crops and/or compost, will supply most of the major and minor nutrients required by garden plants. In some instances, nitrate may be marginal or low, and in the eastern half of the United States magnesium may be deficient. Soil tests will show whether supplements are needed. A high-nitrogen commercial fertilizer or dried blood can rectify the former problem, a high-magnesium limestone, the latter.

One caveat: poultry manure, when used regularly and liberally, can raise the soil pH to detrimental levels, especially in areas with alkaline soils. In such areas, pH should be monitored and the type of fertilizer adjusted accordingly.

In most regions, the following formulation of natural materials will meet the nutrient requirements of nearly all crops and ornamentals on each 1,000 square feet of established garden.

1,000 pounds (25 bushels) of moist, well-rotted stable manure (for nitrogen)

20 pounds (two and one-half 2-gallon pails) of bonemeal or 12 pounds (one and one-half 2-gallon pails) of powdered rock phosphate (for phosphorus)

30 pounds (three and one-half 2-gallon pails) of hardwood ash (for potassium)

Dehydrated Manures

There are various forms of dry, shredded, and pulverized manures on the market. From the standpoint of economy, such manures are a poor investment. During the process of dehydrating, some of the nitrogen is lost, and comparatively little actual fertility is added to the soil. For the same expenditure, far better results may be obtained from the use of moist stock-animal manures, compost, bonemeal, or rock phosphate and wood ash amendments.

Liquid Manures

The type of liquid manure (or manure "tea") still used by many gardeners is made by immersing a bushel of manure in a barrel of water. A newer method consists of dissolving a highly concentrated nitrogenous fertilizer—such as nitrate of soda, urea, or ammonium sulfate—or a well-balanced complete fertilizer in water and then applying it to the plant. This produces a solution that is more constant in nutrient content from batch to batch and, therefore, somewhat more predictable in results. Follow package directions for dilution rate.

Seaside Materials as Fertilizer

In coastal areas, kelp, eel grass, and other marine vegetation often accumulate on beaches and may be available in quantity. If dried somewhat, it is relatively light and easily carried. Most seaweed is relatively low in nitrogen but high in potassium and various trace elements. Ground shells of molluscs and crustaceans are a good source of phosphorus and calcium. Once allowed to be rain-washed of residual salt, these materials may be dug in along with animal manures in the fall. If fish waste is incorporated, immediate burial is imperative, both to limit the odor and to discourage scavengers. Commercially prepared fish emulsions and other fertilizers based on marine life are widely available.

Artificial Manure

Since manure is often difficult to obtain in urban and suburban areas, it is a source of satisfaction to the gardener to be able to make an artificial manure that is similar in every way to the natural product. This may be done by mixing commercial fertilizers and lime with straw, hay, weeds, grass clippings, leaves, or any other garden refuse. It is essential that this work be undertaken in the late spring or early summer, as the decomposition of the material depends on bacterial action, and summer temperatures and abundant moisture are factors of vital importance. To each 500 pounds of straw or other litter, the following ingredients should be added:

15 pounds ammonium sulfate
1½ pounds superphosphate
6½ pounds potassium chloride
12½ pounds ground limestone

The method of making artificial manure resembles that for making compost, previously outlined. Unless the rainfall is unusually heavy, the pile should be soaked daily for a period of a week or more so that the bacterial action may be promoted as rapidly as possible. After the process of decomposition has started, a thorough weekly soaking will usually be sufficient. The sides as well as the top of the pile should be soaked, and the pile should be kept moist at all times. Within three or four months the material should have become sufficiently decomposed, and it will have a composition very similar to a good quality barnyard manure. Note that 1 ton of straw will produce approximately 3 tons of organic material.

ORGANIC AND INORGANIC FERTILIZERS

Plants have definite nutrient requirements that vary somewhat according to species. Whether these needs are met from organic sources, such as manure or compost, or from inorganic, synthetic, or commercial fertilizers is of no account to the plants concerned. If the nutrients required are available in a suitable form when needed, they will be taken up and metabolized and will promote growth and reproduction of the plant; if not, the plant will suffer and may die prematurely.

The main problem that has arisen with long-term sole reliance on commercial fertilizers in gardens (and farms) is that they contribute nothing to the physical character of the soil, which then usually degrades year by year into a subsoil-like medium that is progressively less conducive to root growth. Gardeners often react to the disappointing performance of flowers and vegetables by increasing the application of fertilizers, sometimes to levels far in excess of the roots' absorptive capacity. Such excess fertilizing is at the least wasteful and at worst contributes to nitrate pollution of public water supplies and wetlands. This problem is especially serious in densely settled suburban areas that characteristically have many gardens and extensive lawns.

If commercial fertilizers are required (a need that should be determined by soil testing and the requirements of the plants to be grown), they should be used in conjunction with organic amendments, such as compost, humus, or peat moss, which will improve soil texture and moisture retention, promote root growth, and facilitate nutrient uptake.

For ordinary garden use, slow-release fertilizers, whose nutrients gradually become available over a long period, are preferable to highly soluble formulations, whose nutrients are instantly available, often in excess. Urea-form, a high-analysis, slow-release fertilizer, is made by combining urea (a synthetic nitrogen compound) with formaldehyde (which retards organic breakdown of the urea). In other useful fertilizers, granules of soluble nutrients are pelleted or encapsulated within slowly decomposing organic resins, thus limiting and extending their availability. For trees, fertilizer spikes containing a slow-release nutrient mixture are driven into the soil, the number of spike units determined by the diameter of the tree trunk.

Plant Nutrition

In order to provide for an adequate supply of nutrients in the soil, it is essential to understand something of the method by which plants manufacture their food from the elements obtained from the soil and the air.

There are 15 elements known to be essential for the nutrition of plants. Of these, three elements—carbon, hydrogen, and oxygen—are obtained from water or from the atmosphere. The remaining 12—nitrogen, phosphorus, potassium, calcium, magnesium, boron, copper, manganese, molybdenum, iron, sulfur, and zinc—are normally obtained from the soil. These mineral nutrients in the soil can be utilized by the plant only when they are in solution and can be absorbed through the root hairs. When foliar feeding is practiced there is absorption of the minerals through the leaves.

From these 15 essential elements, a plant is able, in the presence of light, to manufacture sugars, proteins, and other complex organic substances that are food used for the maintenance of existing tissues and for the growth of new tissue. As long as these essential elements are present in sufficient amounts, the plant is able to continue this process of food manufacture. However, if one or more is not available to the plant in sufficient quantity, the production of food becomes limited and the plant displays characteristic symptoms in addition to reduced growth and vigor.

The 12 mineral elements that are essential for normal growth are divided into two general groups: the major elements and the minor, or trace, elements. In the first group, we find nitrogen, phosphorus, potassium, calcium, and magnesium. Since the days of early scientific investigation it has been recognized that these elements are essential for plant growth and that each of them fulfills an important function.

The three elements most likely to be deficient in soils that have been brought under cultivation are nitrogen, phosphorus, and potassium.

Because of the importance of these three elements to plant performance, fertilizers are rated primarily by the proportion of each in the formulation, and in that order. That is, a 5-10-5 fertilizer contains 5 parts of nitrogen to 10 parts of phosphorus to 5 parts of potassium.

Nitrogen

Nitrogen is an essential element for plant growth. Its most important function is to stimulate vegetative development, and it is, therefore, particularly necessary in the production of leaves and stems. If too much nitrogen is applied, however, the undesirable result is an overluxuriant growth of foliage at the expense of flowers and fruit, and maturity will consequently be delayed. The cell walls of the stems will also become weakened and the plant's resistance to disease will be appreciably lowered.

Although nitrogen is the major component of air, it cannot be used by the plant in that state; in the soil, it occurs in compounds with other elements. Soils in temperate-zone regions are usually lowest in available nitrogen during the early spring months, and it is at this season that quickly available nitrogenous fertilizers are of particular value. It also sometimes happens that in prolonged periods of heavy rain during the summer much of the available nitrogen is leached out of the soil, and when such a condition occurs an immediate application of nitrogen may be required.

When applying nitrogen in any of its inorganic forms, the material should not come into direct contact with the foliage of the plant as it may cause severe burning. If it is accidentally dropped onto the foliage, it should be washed off immediately with a strong spray of water.

Sodium Nitrate

The most quickly available form of nitrogen is nitrate of soda, which contains approximately 15 percent nitrogen. Upon application it is almost immediately available to the plant. It is more quickly available in acidic soils than in alkaline. It should be used only on well-established plants that are making active growth, and the soil should be moist when an application is made. Nitrate of soda may be applied in the dry form, the substance being scattered on the surface of the soil at the rate of 1 pound to 100 square feet, or it may be applied in the form of a solution, being dissolved in water at the rate of 1 ounce to 2 gallons of water. In soils where lime is not present, the long-continued use of nitrate of soda may cause a toxic condition because of an undue accumulation of sodium carbonate.

Calcium Nitrate

Calcium nitrate contains 15 percent nitrogen. It is readily available, but leaves a decidedly alkaline residue in the soil and is, therefore, not as useful as sodium nitrate, especially in regions having alkaline soils. The rate of application is approximately the same as for sodium nitrate.

Ammonium Sulfate

A by-product obtained in the manufacture of coal gas, ammonium sulfate contains approximately 20 percent or more of nitrogen in a readily available form. In warm soils, it is often as quickly available as is nitrate of soda, and it has been proven that in alkaline soils its availability is even faster and greater than that of sodium nitrate. When it is used over a period of many years it has a tendency to promote soil acidity, but this may be readily neutralized with lime.

When ammonium sulfate is applied to acidic soils, the results will be more satisfactory if it is used in combination with superphosphate than if it is used alone. The usual rate of application varies from 1 to 2 pounds per 100 square feet or, in the form of a solution, 1 ounce to 2 gallons of water.

Urea

Urea, a synthetic form of nitrogen, is a combination of ammonia and carbon dioxide. It contains 46 percent nitrogen in a form that is quickly soluble, but it is not as quick in its action as nitrate of soda. As it is a highly concentrated form of nitrogen, urea must be used with care and discretion. When applied dry it should be mixed with sand, so that an even distribution may be secured. It is usually applied at the rate of ½ pound per 100 square feet. In the liquid form, it is used at the rate of 1 ounce to 7 gallons of water.

Ammonium Phosphate

Ammonium phosphate obtainable in two forms: as monoammonium phosphate, which contains 10 percent nitrogen and 48 percent phosphoric acid, and as diammonium phosphate, which is more highly concentrated and contains 21 percent nitrogen and 53 percent phosphoric acid. The usual rate of application for ammonium phosphate varies from 1 to 2 pounds per 100 square feet.

Cyanamid

Cyanamid is another useful synthetic product of fairly high concentration; it is composed of calcium cyanamide and calcium hydroxide. Cyanamid contains 20 to 25 percent nitrogen and is highly alkaline in its reaction. The usual rate of application for Cyanamid is approximately 1 pound per 100 square feet.

Urea-form

Urea-form fertilizer releases nitrogen slowly, i.e., over a period of 6 to 12 months, and also eliminates the danger of localized leaf desiccation, or burning, which is one of the principal cosmetic objections to commercial fertilizers, especially when used on young ornamental plants and on lawns. The main source of nitrogen in the urea-form fertilizers is a urea-formaldehyde compound that releases nitrogen slowly and will not cause burning, even under the most adverse conditions.

Another advantage of urea-form is that the nitrogen requirements of a plant for the entire season may be supplied in a single application. In general, the organic forms of nitrogen are less highly concentrated than the inorganic forms and are more slowly available to the plants. This is a factor of considerable importance in the management of large areas of turf and in fertilizing shrub plantings, flower beds, and long-season vegetables. It is of less importance in the case of quickly maturing flower and vegetable crops.

Cottonseed Meal

Cottonseed meal, a byproduct, contains approximately 7 percent nitrogen, which becomes slowly available over a long period of time and is more readily available in warm soils than in cold soils. The usual rate of application varies from 2 to 5 pounds per 100 square feet. There is practically no danger of overstimulation of the plants or of burning when cottonseed meal is used, and in addition to nitrogen it supplies other elements of fertility in small amounts. The usual analysis is 7 percent nitrogen, 2 to 3 percent phosphorus, and 2 percent potash.

Castor Pomace

Very similar to cottonseed meal in general composition, castor pomace contains slightly less nitrogen. The nitrogen content usually averages about 5 percent and a somewhat heavier application is therefore made.

Dried Blood

Dried blood is an excellent organic source of nitrogen, containing 9 to 14 percent. The nitrogen is in a form that is readily soluble and therefore quickly available to the plant. The usual rate of application varies from 2 to 3 pounds per 100 square feet. Some find the odor of dried blood objectionable (though it is effective as a rabbit repellent), but it soon dissipates.

Phosphorus

Phosphorus is an essential element in all functions of plant growth, and it is particularly associated with the production of fruit and seed. It also induces good root development, contributes toward the formation of strong cell walls, and in general, hastens maturity. In addition, phosphorus helps to balance an overabundance of nitrogen in the soil. Phosphorus is fixed in the soil soon after it is applied and it does not leach out. As it does not travel in the soil, it must be absorbed by the plant at the point where it falls. There is practically no danger from excessive applications. It is somewhat more available in slightly acidic soils than in definitely alkaline soils. The presence of ammonium sulfate increases its availability, while the presence of calcium carbonate, sodium nitrate, and iron salts decreases it.

Superphosphate

The most commonly used source of phosphorus, superphosphate is obtainable in various grades: 16, 20, or 45 percent. It is the product that results from treating raw phosphate rock with sulfuric acid. The rate of application varies from 3 to 10 pounds per 100 square feet, according to the needs of the soil.

When superphosphate is applied as a topdressing, its penetration is very slow. It is wise, therefore, to work it thoroughly into the soil whenever possible, either by lightly forking it in or by cultivating it in with a hand weeder or a prong cultivator.

Basic Slag

A by-product in the manufacture of steel, basic slag is sometimes used as a source of phosphorus. It usually contains 10 to 25 percent phosphoric acid and 40 to 50 percent lime. The phosphorus in basic slag is practically all available, as it becomes water-soluble as soon as it is acted on by carbon dioxide. The rate of application is approximately the same as for superphosphate.

Bonemeal

Raw bonemeal is made from finely ground bone and contains 3 to 4 percent nitrogen and 20 to 25 percent phosphoric acid. Although the phosphorus content may seem high, it is held in a tricalcium form and is only very slowly available. The small percentage of nitrogen is quickly available but the phosphorus becomes available so slowly that, in many instances, the use of bonemeal is of doubtful value. Steamed bonemeal is even less valuable than raw bonemeal as some of the nitrogen is lost during the process of steaming. Moreover, the fineness of bonemeal has a direct bearing on the availability of the contained nitrogen, and its availability is restricted until the onset of warm weather. When plants are in need of phosphorus, superphosphate is a better source.

Rock Phosphate

Rock phosphate is the material that is used in the manufacture of superphosphate. It usually contains 66 to 80 perecent calcium phosphate, but because its availability is very low, rock phosphate is not recommended.

Potassium

Potassium is particularly valuable in promoting the general vigor of the plants, and it increases their resistance to disease. Potassium also plays an important part in root formation. In general, it has a balancing influence on other plant nutrients.

Potassium Chloride

One of the most commonly used sources of potassium, potassium chloride contains 48 percent to 50 percent in a readily available form, as it is immediately soluble. The usual rate of application is 1 pound to 100 square feet.

Potassium Muriate

Potassium muriate contains approximately 45 percent potash, i.e., potassium oxide (K_2O), and is applied at the same rate as potassium chloride.

Potassium Sulfate

Another inorganic compound, potassium sulfate contains about 50 percent potash. It is readily soluble, and therefore quickly available to the plant. A rate of 1 pound per 100 square feet is usally adequate.

Wood Ashes

Wood ashes are also a valuable source of potash, although much less highly concentrated than the inorganic forms. Wood ashes vary tremendously in composition. Ash produced from hardwood trees and that has not been leached by exposure to rain often runs as high as 10 percent available potash, while wood ashes produced from softwood or coniferous trees and hardwood ashes that have been exposed to rain may contain less than 2 percent potash. Wood ashes also run high in lime content, sometimes containing as much as 40 percent. The type of wood ash most readily available on the market is a high-grade, unleached hardwood ash. Wood ashes are usually applied at the rate of 50 to 75 pounds per 1,000 square feet.

Trace Elements

The minor, or trace, elements of essential minerals are boron, copper, iron, manganese, molybdenum, sulfur, and zinc.

The term *trace* refers not to the amount of the element in the soil but to the amount needed by the plant. Although these elements are needed only in infinitesimal amounts, they are nevertheless of great importance and may mean the difference between healthy and sickly, stunted growth. A number of plant diseases are caused by a lack of one or more of the trace elements. In certain crops, spectacular increases in yield resulted where the required minerals were supplied to meet the needs of the plants.

Trace elements are usually present in most soils. However, some soils lack one or more of these important minerals, or if present they may be in a form unavailable to the plants.

Many of the complete commercial fertilizers contain the trace elements that are most likely to be deficient in the soil. The manufacturers of high-analysis, quickly soluble fertilizers usually include them in their formulas.

Some organic fertilizers are a poor source of trace elements, while others are a very rich source. Only when the raw materials that are the components of an organic fertilizer contain the trace elements will they be present in the finished product. Thus a good organic fertilizer should contain a variety of organic materials. The best organic sources of trace elements are dried blood and fish emulsion, which contain the major and minor elements in a highly soluble form, and may be effective complements to well-rotted manure.

The development of the chelating agents has made it possible to make certain trace elements, such as iron and zinc, more readily available to plants than has been possible heretofore. (The word *chelate* [pronounced *key'-late*] is derived from the Greek for "claw"; chelates may be likened to two claws that catch and hold metal ions.)

Complete Fertilizers

If commercial fertilizer is used, whether on lawns, or vegetable or fruit gardens, on flower beds, or on trees and shrubs, a well-balanced, complete formulation is the surest way to supply needed plant nutrients. Such a fertilizer is usually based on the ratio of 1 percent nitrogen, 2 to 3 percent phosphorus, and 1 percent potassium, or any desired multiple, such as 2-6-2, 4-12-4, 5-10-5, and 15-30-15, and will also include trace elements. In preparing commercial fertilizers, most reliable firms make it a practice to supply the required amount of nitrogen in two, sometimes three, forms: in a quickly available inorganic form, in a somewhat more slowly available form, and in a very slowly available organic form. Such a practice greatly increases the value of any fertilizer from the standpoint of the gardener, as it means that the nitrogen becomes available for the plant's use over a long period of time.

The time and rate of application of complete commercial fertilizers vary considerably with the individual requirements of the plant and the purpose of the application. The most approved fertilizer practices are discussed in detail in the various chapters on lawns, roses, perennials, greenhouse gardening, and other topics.

Quickly Soluble Fertilizers

The quickly soluble fertilizers are water-soluble salts, to be dissolved in water before use. As the concentrated solutions are uneconomical, because of the costs of packing and shipping large amounts of liquid, it is wiser to use the salts. Directions given on the package should be followed carefully.

Soluble fertilizers contain the same nutrient elements as do the standard complete fertilizers—nitrogen, phosphorus, and potassium—and often in the same proportions, but usually in higher analysis. Some brands contain most of the trace elements and some also vitamins and hormones. These additions are especially advantageous if the solution is to be used for foliar fertilizing.

These high-analysis, rapidly soluble fertilizers can be used to advantage in many ways. They can be applied directly to the soil to promote the growth and vigor of houseplants, flowering plants of all types, vegetables, ornamental trees, and shrubs. As they are in solution, the nutrients become almost immediately available to the plant. They can be applied as a spray to the foliage of the plant (see Foliar Fertilizing later in this chapter). They can be used as a pre-planting dip for seeds to quicken germination and promote a more vigorous growth of the young seedlings. These fertilizers may be used as a dip for leafy, softwood cuttings to develop more vigorous plants. They may be used as a solution in which to soak bulbs and tubers, such as tulips and tuberous begonias, for a few hours just before planting to increase their initial vigor and perhaps the amount and size of bloom. And they may be used very satisfactorily on small lawn areas.

The rapidly soluble fertilizers are not practical on extensive areas of lawn unless application can be made by a commercial outfit that has the necessary equipment. Moreover, because of their high solubility, they should be used conservatively, i.e., in weaker dilution, especially on light, sandy soils; but to compensate, they must be applied more frequently than on heavy clay soils.

It has been found that when young seedlings or rooted cuttings are to be transplanted, or when older plants are to be moved from one location to another, they will suffer less of a setback if given an application of a high-analysis soluble fertilizer. In the case of young plants, best results will be obtained if the fertilizer is applied to the propagating bed, seedbed, or flat in which the plants are growing, about three days before the time of transplanting. The benefits will be greater than if the application is made at the actual time of transplanting. In the case of purchased plants it is, of course, not possible to follow this procedure. When the application is made at the time of transplanting, 1 cup of the solution should be allowed for a small plant, 2 cups for a large plant. The solution should be poured around the plant before the hole has been completely filled.

These starter or booster solutions may be used to great advantage in the vegetable garden when setting out tomato, cabbage, cauliflower, broccoli, pepper, and celery plants, and they are also very valuable when transplanting annuals, biennials, and perennials in the flower garden. But the same caveats apply regarding overuse and the leaching away of excess nitrate.

High-analysis, soluble fertilizers are more expensive per unit of plant nutrient than the standard complete fertilizers, but they are easy to mix and apply; the danger of drying or burning plant tissue is eliminated; they are procurable in small quantities; and there is no waste.

In handling these soluble fertilizers, a number of precautions should be taken. Soluble salts should not be stored in lightweight paper containers because the contained salts will absorb atmospheric moisture and the container will deteriorate. Glass mason jars with screw tops are excellent for long periods of storage. If a solution is to be kept over from one application to another, it should be stored in a glass or earthenware jug, *not* in a metal container, as the salts are corrosive.

Slower release, highly concentrated, readily soluble fertilizer is available in perforated plastic envelopes, which are buried. The packet acts as a reservoir, slowly releasing the nitrogen, phosphate, and potash in correctly controlled proportions. When this method is used there is no danger of injury to tender roots, and it also means a great saving in time and labor. This method is recommended for the fertilization of established trees and for trees at the time of planting, for roses at the time of planting and for established beds, for potted plants, and for perennials.

More recently, pelletized fertilizers that have the same basic effect have been developed, and are proving equally useful in the same applications. Fertilizer sticks and stakes are also useful, the latter particularly recommended for established trees and large shrubs.

Chelates

When chelating agents are applied to the soil, the metal does not combine with other elements to form insoluble compounds but remains free to be taken up and used by the plants. On the other hand, when simple iron compounds are used without chelates, they often combine to make insoluble compounds and thus become unavailable to the plants. This explains why plants sometimes suffer from iron chlorosis or iron starvation when the soil actually contains sufficient iron for normal plant growth, and it also explains why additional applications of simple iron compounds on soils definitely deficient in iron often fail to correct the chlorotic condition. It is their ability to hold the iron in the form in which plants can readily use it that gives the chelates their great importance.

The symptoms of iron deficiency in plants are not difficult to detect. In mild cases, the veins of the leaf appear to be a darker green than the areas between the veins. If the deficiency is pronounced, the areas between the veins gradually become a lighter green, then yellowish in appearance, and, finally, in a severe case of iron chlorosis, the foliage becomes a very pale ivory color. Unless the condition is corrected it will eventually cause the death of the plant.

Iron chelates are used extensively in citrus groves and in the great commercial flower- and vegetable-growing sections of California and Florida and many other areas. In some instances the effects of an application have been little short of miraculous. In one citrus grove, the foliage on orange trees that were suffering from acute iron chlorosis became green again within six weeks and the vigor of the trees was entirely restored.

Iron chelates are also of great value to the home gardener for the treatment of ornamental plants that are suffering from iron starvation, and for use on orchard trees and vegetable crops.

Among ornamental plants suffering from iron chlorosis that have responded well to applications of the iron chelates are azalea, camellia, chrysanthemum, gardenia, gladiolus, hydrangea, magnolia, oak, the rhododendrons, and the roses.

Iron chelates may be applied directly to the soil in either powder or liquid form or may be dissolved in water and applied as a foliar spray. When applied to the soil in powder form, the powder should be spread evenly over the surface of the soil beneath the plant at the recommended rate, and it should then be watered in thoroughly until the soil is moist to a depth of at least 6 inches. It will be easier to obtain an even coverage if the powder is mixed with dry sand or fertilizer. The powder may, if desired, be dissolved in water and either sprayed onto the soil or applied with a watering can.

When a foliar spray is applied, it is important to make sure that all leaf surfaces are thoroughly covered. When foliar sprays are being applied to outdoor plants, there will be less danger of injury if the application is made during the middle third of the growing season. It is not advisable to apply foliage sprays to plants when they are in blossom or in fruit.

Products are also available consisting of small vials of trace elements that can be inserted directly into the xylem, or water-conducting wood, of large trees, by tapping them in with a hammer. The ease of application is a major consideration in choosing this method.

Foliar Fertilizing

Trees, shrubs, roses, many flowering plants, and vegetables respond well to foliar fertilizing, or foliar "feeding," as it is commonly but incorrectly called. It is an increasingly common practice among amateur gardeners as well as among professional horticulturists. Foliar fertilizing is of particular value in supplying trace elements where a deficiency exists, and often on cold, wet soils nitrogen and phosphorus can be made more readily available to the plant through foliar fertilizing than through application to the soil.

Research has shown that at least one-half of the nitrogen in a fully soluble, high-analysis fertilizer enters the leaf directly within a few hours after application and that a substantial percentage of the phosphorus and potassium is also absorbed in this way. In addition to these major elements, many of the trace elements such as iron, zinc, boron, and manganese may also be applied in the form of foliage sprays.

In purchasing soluble fertilizers to be used for foliar fertilizing, it is wise to make sure that they contain these trace elements. In certain soils there may be definite deficiency of some of the trace elements, whereas in other soils they may be present but unavailable to the plant, and one of the most satisfactory ways of supplying them is through foliar fertilizing.

Experiments have revealed that chelated organic forms of some of these trace elements are very effective in overcoming deficiencies when applied as foliar sprays. For example, iron in chelated form has proved very effective in controlling chlorosis of lawns, deciduous fruits, and vegetables, and chelated zinc is effective in controlling a number of conditions attributable to a deficiency of this element.

Some plants can absorb nutrients through their leaves more readily than others. Absorption normally takes place more readily through the lower surface to the leaves than through the upper surface. In leaves possessing a heavily waxed surface, it has been found that the absorption of nutrients is usually very restricted or entirely inhibited.

There are many satisfactory types of applicators on the market suitable for applying liquid fertilizers as foliar sprays. It is important not to use too concentrated a solution, and the manufacturer's directions should be followed carefully.

Excellent results have been obtained from the foliar fertilizing of many kinds of plants. For example, in carefully controlled experiments conducted in the 1950s, various treated rose cultivars produced about 10 percent more flowers than untreated plants of the same cultivars. Greenhouse and indoor plants seem to respond even more dramatically. Orchids, anthuriums, philodendrons. African violets, gloxinias, achimenes, streptocarpus, crotons, ferns, and certain forms of cactus, such as the Christmas cactus, have shown excellent results. In some cases, the increase in the health and vigor of the plants has been spectacular. Young African violet plants that have become yellowish and sickly in appearance, once given a foliar fertilizing, may turn dark green in just a few days. The accepted practice in many greenhouses is to give two or three weekly applications at first, followed by monthly ones. Sometimes one or two applications at a critical time in the life of a plant are all that is necessary.

Certain insecticides may be mixed with foliar fertilizers and applied simultaneously, thus saving time and labor. Check labels for chemical compatibility.

It must be borne in mind that foliar fertilizing supplements and does not replace the uptake of nutrients by roots.

SOIL TESTS

Since it is sometimes difficult to determine deficiencies that are not very obvious yet may be of considerable importance, it is a good idea to have an occasional soil analysis made. Soil samples may be sent to your state agricultural experiment station or to the local cooperative extension service for analysis.

Obtaining Soil Samples

The season when the sample is taken, the method of obtaining the sample, and the preparation of the sample are all factors of importance in soil analysis.

Time of Sampling

The most reliable information concerning the need for fertilization and for the application of lime may be obtained from samples taken either in the early spring or in late fall. During the active growing season, the nutrient level of the soil is affected to some extent by the growth of the plants that occupy the area. Heavy rainfalls also very definitely affect the nutrient level, and low test results are frequently secured after periods of prolonged leaching. Nitrates and ammonia compounds are the most variable, as they are the elements most easily lost by leaching. No single test should be considered definitive and final; repeat testing is advisable.

Method of Sampling

A trowel or spade may be used to make a V-shaped hole, 6 or 7 inches deep. Remove the loose soil from the hole, then cut a thin uniform slice off the straight side of the hole from top to bottom. If the sample is being taken from a lawn area, it should represent the zone of the densest root growth, which will range from 3 to 6 inches deep. If the area to be tested is of considerable size, or if it varies in appearance in any marked degree, it will be necessary to obtain several samples. If there is a decided variance in the general character of the soil, one section being of a sandy texture and another having a more dense structure, the samples should be kept separate. If the soil is uniform in character, the samples may be mixed together, forming a composite sample. Samples should be numbered and labeled and the sender should keep a record of the source locations.

Preparing the Sample

After the sample has been obtained, the soil should be spread out to dry on a clean sheet of paper. Care should be taken to prevent the soil from becoming contaminated with dust, fumes, or chemicals of any kind.

After the soil has dried out thoroughly, it should be packed for shipment.

Soil pH

The relative acidity or alkalinity of the soil is commonly expressed in terms of the symbol pH. The neutral point in the scale is 7. Soil testing below a pH 7 is acidic; soil testing above pH 7 is alkaline.

The pH values are based on logarithms, 10 being the base. Therefore, a soil testing pH 5 is 10 times as acidic as soil testing pH 6, while a soil testing pH 4 is 100 times as acidic as soil testing pH 6. (In going either up or down the pH scale from the neutral point of pH 7, the value of the unit is 10 times greater than the next one approaching 7.)

PH SCALE IN SOIL TESTING

pH 9.5	Intensely alkaline
pH 9	Strongly alkaline
pH 8.5	Definitely alkaline
pH 8	Moderately alkaline
pH 7.7	Slightly alkaline
pH 7	Neutral
pH 6.5	Very slightly acidic
pH 6	Slightly acidic
pH 5.5	Moderately acidic
pH 5	Moderately acidic
pH 4.5	Definitely acidic
pH 4	Strongly acidic
pH 3.5	Intensely acidic

The soil in most regions of the United States is acidic, because ample rainfall tends to make soils acidic. Where there is scant rainfall, as in deserts, soils tend to be neutral or alkaline. The Southwest, the Great Plains, the high western plateaus, and many of the valleys in the Rocky Mountains have neutral or alkaline soils.

The most acidic peat soils are pH 3 (about the same as lemon juice); the most alkaline soils are no more than pH 10 (about the level of seawater). For all practical purposes, garden plants will not grow in soil with a pH below 3.5 or above 8.5. Gardens most likely have soils ranging between pH 4.5 and 7.5.

Most plants grow well in soil having a pH of 6. Soils, however, need not have precisely this value for plants to grow well. Most plants have a wide range of tolerance, and generally speaking, any value between 5.5 and 7 is acceptable. It is only at the extremes of acidity and alkalinity that real problems appear, often nutrient deficiencies. For example, in strongly acidic soils calcium and molybdenum, both necessary for plant growth, are less available. Similarly, boron, copper, iron, manganese, and zinc are unavailable in strongly alkaline soils. Acidic soils with a pH below 5 may, in addition, contain enough aluminum to be toxic to some plants.

The pH in a particular soil can only be determined accurately with a soil test. There are other, more important things to be learned from having soil professionally tested (such as whether or not it contains lead), but pH data are part of the package.

In addition to obtaining a complete soil analysis every few years from a state agricultural university, agricultural experiment station, or cooperative extension service, gardeners should learn to make simple, rapid tests to determine the pH of the soil. There are now many excellent yet inexpensive soil-testing outfits on the market, and such a kit should be considered an essential part of one's equipment. Complete directions accompany each outfit and these should be followed precisely.

Increasing the Acidity of the Soil

It is a comparatively simple procedure either to increase the degree of acidity in the soil or to bring an acidic soil to a more nearly neutral level. Many woodland plants such as the azaleas, mountain laurel, the rhododendrons, trailing arbutus, and the pink lady's slipper require a definitely acidic soil. For such plants a pH ranging between 4.5 and 5.5 is desirable. When such plants are to be grown, the soil should be tested, and if it does not fall within this range, measures should be taken to increase the acidity. This may be accomplished in a number of ways.

Method No. 1

The ideal method, and the one strongly recommended if the existing soil is fertile and of good texture, is to incorporate into the soil certain organic materials that will increase its acidity. The following materials may be used for this purpose:

- Acidic muck from swamps and stream banks.
- Oak leaf mold.
- Peat moss, of the coarse, acidic type.
- Rotting bark and wood, or partly rotted sawdust, preferably of oak or hemlock.
- Sphagnum moss, finely ground.

After the organic materials have been worked thoroughly into the soil, another soil test should be made to determine whether the acidity has been brought to the desired level.

Method No. 2

Where the existing soil is of poor physical quality or where raised beds are to be used, it is advisable to prepare a special soil mixture that will provide the desired amount of humus and the correct degree of acidity. Such a mixture should contain at least 50 percent decayed organic matter. The following mixture is recommended: 50 percent coarse, acidic peat; 25 percent rotted oak leaf mold; and 25 percent sandy loam. If, after testing, this does not provide the desired degree of acidity, a small quantity of a chemical may be added according to the directions given in "Method No. 3."

Method No. 3

There are a number of chemicals that may be applied to the soil to increase its acidity. Among the most satisfactory for this purpose are aluminum sulfate and sulfur. These may be used as a surface application. being spread evenly over the area and watered in thoroughly, or they may be mixed with the soil as the bed is being prepared. The rate of application is given in the following table.

A number of fertilizers such as ammonium sulfate, ammonium phosphate, cottonseed meal, and urea, will acidify soil when applied over a period of years. Therefore, fertilizers of this type should be selected for use on plants that are known to thrive best in acidic soils. Some fertilizer companies offer special mixtures suitable for such plants. Fertilizers that are known to be definitely alkaline in their reaction, such as nitrate of soda, calcium nitrate, Cyanamid, bonemeal, and wood ashes, should not be used on acid-loving plants.

TABLE FOR INCREASING SOIL ACIDITY

Change from pH	Sulfur (pounds per square feet)	Aluminum Sulfate (pounds per square feet)
8–7	2	4.5
8–6.5	3	7
8–6	4	10
8–5.5	5.5	13.5
8–5	7	17.5
7.5–7	1.75	3.5
7.5–6.5	2	5
7.5–6	3.5	7.5
7.5–5.5	5	11.5
7.5–5	6.5	15.5
7–6.5	1.5	2.5
7–6	2	5.5
7–5.5	3.5	9
7–5	5	13
6.5–6	1.5	3
6.5–5.5	2.5	6.5
6.5–5	4	10.5
6–5.5	1.5	3.5
6–5	3	7.5
5.5–5	1.5	4

Source: A. Laurie and V. H. Reis, *Floriculture* (1942), 374.

Reducing Soil Acidity

Lime

Lime serves several important functions. It is of particular value in neutralizing the acidity of the soil; in addition, it also changes the structure of the soil, hastens bacterial action in it, aids the liberation of nutrients that would otherwise remain in the soil in unavailable form, hastens the decomposition of organic matter, and supplies a small amount of calcium (which is one of the essential plant foods).

Lime is usually applied either in the form of ground limestone or as hydrated lime. Hydrated lime is quicker in its action but not as lasting in its effect. Lime should never be used in combination with animal manures or with nitrogenous fertilizers, as this causes the rapid release of ammonia. When lime is applied, it should be spread over the surface of the ground and should then be thoroughly mixed with the upper few inches of soil. It should not be plowed or spaded deeply into the soil.

The rate of application depends entirely on the forms in which the lime is applied, and the texture of the soil. The following table serves as a general guide.

RATE OF APPLICATION OF LIME TO DECREASE SOIL ACIDITY

As it is not advisable to apply more than 50 pounds of hydrated lime or 75 pounds of ground limestone per 1,000 square feet at any one time, it will necessary to make successive applications on strongly acidic soils and raise the pH gradually. It is often detrimental to a plant's growth to make an excessively heavy application of lime at one time.

Soil Acidity (pH)	Hydrated Lime (pounds)		Ground Limestone (pounds)	
	Per 1,000 Square Feet	Per Acre	Per 1,000 Square Feet	Per Acre
LIGHT SANDY SOIL				
4	60	2,610	90	3,915
4.5	55	2,392	82	3,567
5	45	1,957	67	2,914
5.5	35	1,522	52	2,262
6	None	None	None	None
MEDIUM SANDY SOIL				
4	80	3,480	120	5,220
4.5	75	3,263	112	4,872
5	60	2,610	90	3,915
5.5	45	1,957	67	2,914
6	None	None	None	None
LOAM AND SILT LOAM				
4	115	5,002	172	7,482
4.5	105	4,567	157	6,827
5	85	3,697	127	5,524
5.5	65	2,827	97	4,219
6	None	None	None	None
CLAY LOAM				
4	145	6,307	217	9,439
4.5	135	5,872	202	8,787
5	100	4,356	150	6,525
5.5	80	3,480	120	5,220
6	None	None	None	None

Note: A light application of lime at the rate of 25 pounds per 1,000 square feet has proved beneficial on certain soils, even though they have a pH of 6.

An excessive application of lime has a very injurious effect on some plants, causing a condition known as lime-induced chlorosis or yellowing. This is regarded as a physiological disease, and it is due directly to a deficiency of iron in the plant tissues. The symptoms are very marked in most plants, and are apt to appear on young growth in the early spring, although they may be noticed at almost any time during the growing season. The leaves present a characteristically mottled appearance, being either yellow or whitish in color. The midrib of the leaf and the veins remain a very dark green, and the mottling takes place in the areas between the veins.

Iron is absolutely essential for the production of chlorophyll, which is the green coloring matter of the leaf, and when iron uptake falls below a certain level, chlorophyll fails to develop. This deficiency of iron in the plant is very closely associated with the lime content of the soil, as the solubility of iron in the soil depends to a large extent on the degree of soil acidity. Iron is readily soluble in a definitely acidic soil, but as the pH of the soil approaches the neutral point, the iron becomes less and less soluble. In soils that are decidedly alkaline, comparatively little iron or, in extreme cases, no iron at all is available for the plant. Therefore, the long-continued use, or excessive application of lime, bonemeal, wood ashes, and certain inorganic fertilizers tends to increase the alkalinity of the soil to a point where it is not favorable for certain forms of plant growth due to this precipitation of iron, which consequently becomes unavailable to the plant.

In general garden practice, it is well to maintain the soil at pH 6 to 6.5, and not to increase its alkalinity beyond a pH of 7.5, which seems to be the limit of safety for many plants. There are, of course, special plant groups that are definitely more acid or alkaline tolerant, and some that require a decidedly acidic soil; but for the majority of garden plants, a pH slightly below neutral is the safest.

If a condition of lime-induced chlorosis occurs, it may be corrected by the use of the iron chelates.

SOIL CONDITIONERS

Soil conditioners are effective in improving the structure and physical condition of certain types of soil. They should not be used indiscriminately, as it is a waste of time and money to apply them to soils that will receive little or no benefit.

Calcium sulfate (gypsum) is a soil conditioner that displaces those elements, especially sodium, that make a soil sticky and hard to work. Applied at a rate of 9 to 28 ounces per square yard, according to the clay in the soil, it results in better workability within several weeks.

The gardener must bear in mind that soil conditioners are not fertilizers and do not increase the nutrient content of the soil. Soil conditioners have been developed for the purpose of maintaining in porous and loose condition clay soils that are normally heavy and tight in structure. On such soils, which are difficult to handle and which present many problems, soil conditioners have proved of great value. Soils of a light, sandy nature and soils high in organic content show little benefit, and rarely justify the use of such conditioners.

Under tillage conditions, heavy clay soils have a tendency to become more and more compact and to provide poor conditions for plant growth. They contain little pore space and consequently have low air capacity and lack the ability to absorb water readily, making the application of soluble fertilizers difficult they are also extremely difficult to handle when the moisture content is high or low. They are thus problem soils.

If a suitable soil conditioner is used, and if the directions on the package are followed, such soils may be maintained in a fairly crumbly, friable condition throughout the season. Water will percolate freely, there will be sufficient pore space for an adequate supply of oxygen for plant needs, and good response can be obtained from soluble fertilizers. A soil so conditioned can grow thrifty, vigorous plants.

Decaying organic matter is nature's soil conditioner, but such material is not always available to the gardener in sufficient quantity to be effective, and in such cases the chemical soil conditioners fill a long-felt need. Approximately 1 pound of a synthetic soil conditioner is equivalent to several bushels of a natural soil conditioner in improving the structure of fine-particled clay soils. Chemical soil conditioners have several advantages over natural soil conditioners. Results will be obtained more quickly, as within a few days after the application of a synthetic conditioner the soil particles will be crumbly and mellow. Also, this improvement in the soil structure will last over a longer period than will be the case in the necessarily limited use of organic materials.

Soil conditioners can be incorporated into the soil most satisfactorily when the soil is neither too wet nor too dry. The surface of the soil should preferably be slightly dry, with moist soil just below the surface. The soil conditioner should be worked into the soil to a depth of 6 inches, the soil being well pulverized during the process. The more thoroughly the chemical is mixed with the soil, the better the results. After the conditioner has been thoroughly incorporated into the soil, a moderate watering will speed up the chemical reaction. Best results are obtained if seed sowing and transplanting are delayed for several days after application.

It is a simple matter to determine whether or not a certain soil will benefit from an application of a soil conditioner. The following test gives a reliable indication: Take a *small* handful of the soil; add four or five drops of water to the soil, using a medicine dropper; mix the soil and water together thoroughly until every tiny granule of soil crumbles; then roll the soil between the palms of your hands into the form of a cigarette. If the cigarette holds its shape, it is an indication that the structure of the soil will be greatly improved by an application of a soil conditioner. If the soil remains granular and cannot be formed into the shape of a cigarette, it is evident that a soil conditioner is not needed and that the soil will derive no benefit from its use. If a "weak cigarette" is formed, which flops over at the end when lifted, this indicates that the application of a soil conditioner will be of enough benefit to warrant its use.

When used on a large scale, soil conditioners are very expensive; but in preparing soil for house plants, seedbeds, and coldframes and in special limited areas in the garden and on small areas to be seeded to lawn grasses, great benefit will be derived from their use if the soil is a heavy clay one.

In the vegetable and cutting garden treatment may be limited to the actual rows or hills where the plants are to be grown.

32

Mulches

Mulches not only have a very beneficial effect on plant growth but also reduce to a minimum the time and labor required for garden maintenance. On the well-managed home property, mulching becomes a year-round operation.

A good mulch, consisting of suitable materials properly applied at the correct time, serves many functions. The most important of these is the conservation of soil moisture. A good mulch readily permits the penetration of water into the soil. During periods of heavy precipitation it checks the full

A substantial winter mulch of conifer branches tempers freeze-thaw cycling that can heave shallow-rooted perennials in late winter and early spring in northern areas.

force of the rain, lessens the danger of surface runoff, and permits the water to sink gently into the soil. It also protects the soil from the drying effects of sun and wind, thus reducing the evaporation of moisture from the soil surface. On soils protected by a mulch, one never finds a hard, baked crust such as is found all too frequently on soils exposed to the sun's rays. Even during periods of intense summer heat and drought, the soil under a heavy mulch will remain cool and moist. It is usually dark and crumbly, characteristics of a soil that will provide favorable conditions for good root development.

Indeed, it should be remembered that woodland, prairie, and other vegetation are nearly always automatically mulched by fallen leaves, twigs, and other debris, all of which retard surface evaporation as they are decomposed by fungi and other organisms into soluble nutrients, which are in turn taken up by living plants. Thus there is nothing artificial about mulching; on the contrary, to deny a garden mulch is to subject all its components to undue stress.

The application of a mulch is also one of the most effective measures of weed control. There are few weeds that can push up through a heavy mulch, and if they occasionally succeed, they are so straggly that they can easily be pulled out.

A mulch also serves as an insulating material and helps to maintain more even soil temperatures. In summer the soil under a mulch is sometimes as much as 20°F cooler than surrounding soils, and in winter the soil under a blanket of mulch slowly cools and stabilizes, often a few degrees higher than nearby exposed ground. What is most important is that a good winter mulch moderates the freezing and thawing of soil that in late winter and early spring can play havoc with shallow-rooted perennials, often heaving them out of the ground to die in the drying sun and wind. More uniform soil temperatures usually result in better plant growth and, in the case of vegetables, superior quality. Newly transplanted trees and shrubs especially should receive a thorough mulching during the first winter, to prevent frost heaving and root desiccation.

The end result of an organic mulch is that it eventually decomposes and adds humus to the soil. During this process of decomposition, valuable plant nutrients are released that maintain the fertility of the soil. In the course of time, soil under a heavy mulch will become crumbly to the touch, dark in color, and have a clean, woodsy smell. The upper few inches of soil will be full of roots and will be well supplied with earthworms and beneficial soil microorganisms. If plants are kept mulched with organic materials year after year, there will be a constantly replenished supply of humus for their needs.

Thoughtless or careless use of mulches can cause damage and has led some to question their value generally. For example, water-conserving summer mulch can actually slow the growth of tomatoes and other warm-season crops if applied too early, since such a mulch insulates the cool soil from the sun's warmth. Also, a winter mulch applied before the ground freezes may offer protection for mice and voles, encouraging them to feed on roots and bulbs or gnaw the stems and trunks of shrubs and small trees at groundline. Some mulches may carry pests or disease organisms or harbor weed seeds. Dry, inflammable mulches can pose a fire hazard, especially along frequently traveled walkways. A few rapidly decaying mulches, such as sawdust, may cause a temporary nitrate deficiency in the soil, but this is readily corrected or, better yet, prevented by adding or mixing some 10-6-4 fertilizer, sodium nitrate, or urea beforehand.

These points notwithstanding, mulching, when properly carried out, confers benefits that far outweigh any disadvantages. Indeed, the points in favor of mulching are so convincing that the gardener is usually not faced with the problem of whether to mulch or not to mulch but rather with the question of which kind of mulch to use.

SELECTING MATERIALS FOR MULCHES

In selecting materials for mulches, there are a number of factors to be considered: the material's availability, its cost compared with that of other materials, its appearance, its physical effect on the soil, its chemical reaction or pH, its durability, its combustibility, its rate of decomposition, its freedom from weed seeds, and whether it poses a danger of introducing disease or attracting pests through its use. In general, organic mulches are to be preferred to inorganic mulches because of their nutritive benefit to the soil.

Organic Mulches

Since organic mulches decay in time, releasing nutrients into the soil, they are inherently temporary and must be replaced. Inorganic mulches do not decay, and hence do not contribute to soil fertility.

Although most organic mulches do not significantly affect soil pH, some are mildly to moderately acidifying—an advantage when used on acidophilic plants such as rhododendrons, azaleas, mountain laurel, and enkianthus.

Widely Available Organic Mulches
Leaves
Wherever deciduous trees grow, leaves are available for mulch, especially at the time of leaf drop. Although dry leaves tend to be blown about by the wind, there is a way to keep them where wanted. For example, leaves run through a shredder or run over by a rotary lawn mower are reduced to small bits that tend to stay in place. A garden to be leaf

mulched, if first strewn or studded with twigs or with 6-inch stem stubs of perennials left in place, will trap and hold leaves through the winter. Partly composted leaves not only adhere to each other but admit rain to the soil beneath. A thin top layer of compost or manure, perhaps 1 inch thick, will keep a loose layer of leaf mulch in place.

The fallen leaves of various maples, especially Norway maple (*Acer platanoides*), often form a dense, soggy mat in winter that, if left undisturbed in the spring, can impede the growth of bulbs and perennials. This can be averted by mixing in the leaves of other kinds of trees or by loosening the mat with a garden fork in early spring.

Wherever possible, the winter mulch of tree leaves should be left in place to conserve soil moisture during the ensuing summer. If winter mulch must be removed, it should be composted and replaced with a suitable summer mulch.

Grass Clippings

Although it is preferable to leave finely cut, evenly distributed grass clippings on the lawn, collected clippings may be used as mulch elsewhere, providing certain precautions are taken. Clippings over 1 inch long tend to dry on the top of the lawn and detract from its appearance. Clumps or piles can kill the grass beneath, resulting in bare spots. A mulching lawn mower that evenly distributes clippings can avert this problem. All green lawn clippings intended for use as mulch should be mixed with tree leaves or rough compost to facilitate aeration and decay without malodorous putrefaction and the destructive buildup of heat. Permitting lawn clippings to dry, either on the lawn or after being spread on a paved driveway, before composting slows their decomposition enough to prevent heat buildup. The concentration of useful nitrate in grass clippings is high. Hence, the routine collection and removal of grass clippings results in a nitrate deficiency for the lawn.

Peat Moss (Sphagnum Peat)

Attractive, conveniently packaged, long-lasting, and therefore popular, peat moss confers a fine-textured, deep brown color to garden soil. It must be applied with discretion, however. When wetted and then allowed to dry, peat moss particles adhere and form a dense crust that is temporarily impervious to water, thus defeating its water-conserving function. Dry, compacted peat moss will also smolder if ignited. However, peat moss mixed with pine needles remains friable; the combination is especially suitable as a mulch for rhododendrons and azaleas as it is mildly acidifying. When spread, the mulch should be 2 to 3 inches thick.

Shredded wood, somewhat resembling straw but longer lasting, makes a useful, erosion-deterring, year-round mulch in a newly planted shrub bed.

Wood Chips

As chipping machinery is used more widely by arborists and electrical utilities to reduce bulky pruned branches to more easily transported compact bits, wood chips can often be had for the asking. Because of their rather coarse, open texture, wood chips should be spread at least 3 inches thick to be effective in conserving soil moisture, moderating soil temperature, and excluding the light needed for weed seedling growth. Freshly cut chips made from living wood may consume some nitrate as they decay, but this is seldom serious and can be easily offset with a light application of a high-nitrate fertilizer. It is best to leave a small unmulched zone around soft-stemmed plants, such as cucumber and squash, to avert stem rot and other possible diseases. Because of their relative coarseness, wood chips are best used under trees, shrubs, and other large plants.

Bark Chips

Bark chips are made in various grades from the corky bark of timber trees and are sold in bags. The finer sorts are often very attractive, but because of their larger exposed surface area relative to volume, they tend to decay more rapidly than the coarser grades. By and large, bark is inert, and thus its decomposition makes no significant demands on soil nitrate. A layer 2 or 3 inches thick is usually sufficient.

Salt Hay, Field Hay, Straw

Hay and straw are lightweight materials usually sold in compressed bales, and because of the unavoidable unkempt appearance they confer on a garden, they should not be used where appearance is important. A 3- or 4-inch layer around vegetables works well, and by season's end the remains can be turned under. Salt hay is preferable to ordinary field hay, as the latter often includes a multitude of weed seeds.

Straw mulch around young herbs in a raised bed will moderate soil temperature as well as slow soil evaporation and keep out weeds.

Newspaper

Three to five sheets of newspaper, suitably weighted with hay or a light layer of twigs, wood chips, or pebbles can serve as an effective low-cost mulch, especially in parts of the garden where appearance is not a prime consideration. In due course, the paper decays and may be incorporated in the soil. Although some of the inks used in newspapers before the 1970s contained such heavy metals as lead and chromium, these inks are no longer approved by the American Newspaper Publishers Association, and none has been detected in its annual tests since 1985. However, as the treated paper used in magazines and newspaper inserts may still have such harmful inks, they should not be used as mulching for vegetables.

Less Common Organic Mulches
Buckwheat Hulls

Buckwheat hulls, inert, brown, disclike husks, are bagged as a byproduct of buckwheat flour milling; are very fine-textured; and though rather variable in color, confer a handsome finished appearance to rose beds and perennial plantings. As the dry hulls are lightweight and may be blown about in high wind, it is helpful to wet them soon after spreading. Once moistened, they tend to stick together. Slow to decay, buckwheat hulls are effective in a layer 1 to 2 inches thick but should not be used on slopes, as they gradually slide downhill.

Cocoa Hulls

The ground hulls of cacao beans, from which chocolate is prepared, are dark brown and vary considerably in fineness, and thus in the texture afforded the garden. More serious is their tendency to bond together and form a hard crust, as does peat moss, but this can be obviated by incorporating wood chips or other coarser materials with the cocoa hull mulch. The initially strong aroma of chocolate dissipates after a few days. Cocoa hulls release potassium into the soil in concentrations beyond the tolerance of such plants as rhododendrons and azaleas, as well as lilacs, maples, and tomatoes. A 2- to 3-inch-thick layer is usually effective in slowing soil evaporation.

Ground Corncobs and Cornstalks

Although not ideal aesthetically, especially when first spread, ground corncobs, 2 to 3 inches thick, make an effective though initially pale mulch that becomes acceptably darker with age. Corncob mulch decays fairly quickly, often within a year, so should be replaced annually.

Cornstalks, unless ground or shredded, are too coarse for ornamental plantings but can be used to weigh down lighter mulches, such as polyethylene plastic.

Strawberry beds mulched with well-rotted manure benefit from moisture retention and nutrient release. Leafy path mulch also deters soil evaporation and compaction.

Sawdust and Wood Shavings

Sawdust makes a very satisfactory mulch, once it is dampened and not subject to strong wind. Contrary to popular opinion, sawdust neither is poisonous to plants nor acidifies the soil. However, decomposing sawdust mulch may lead to a mild reduction in available nitrate, which is easily restored or averted with a light application of high-nitrate fertilizer. For most purposes, a 1- to 2-inch layer of sawdust will suffice.

Wood shavings are less satisfactory, as they are easily blown out of the garden by wind or floated off by heavy rain. Moreover, when dry they are a fire hazard. Unless uniformly ground to a fine grade, they impart a coarseness that is seldom pleasing. If used, they should be covered with a heavier, denser material.

Pine Needles

Sometimes called pine straw, the fallen dead leaves of pines and other conifers make a uniform, visually pleasing mulch that serves very well. Slightly acidifying, pine mulch is especially valuable under rhododendrons and azaleas. A layer about 2 inches thick is sufficient in most cases and can be overspread with a supplemental layer annually as the mulch slowly decays.

Manure

Providing it has aged long enough for the ammonia to have dissipated, usually 3 to 6 months, and is mixed with straw or wood shavings, stable manure serves well not only as a mulch but as a topdressing fertilizer. *One caveat:* most weed seeds survive equine digestion, but not bovine. Hence, for this reason alone, cow or steer manure is preferable to horse manure—unless the latter has been hot composted, as is the case with a number of commercially available preparations based on horse manure. Depending on the texture of the manure mulch, it may be spread 2 inches deep if dense, or deeper if of a fluffy consistency.

Special or Locally Available Organic Mulches
Hops

Spent hops or brewery residue is water-logged when fresh, emits an objectionable odor for one or two weeks, and is light in color. Such considerations notwithstanding, this material makes a perfectly satisfactory mulch. Usually available free for the taking, hops are notably fire resistant, but if laid down in layers more than 4 inches thick, heat buildup may cause injury to small shrubs and other slender-stemmed ornamentals.

Tobacco Stems

Ground stems of commercial tobacco not only make a very useful mulch but also repel a wide spectrum of insects. However, this material usually remains so loose and unconsolidated that a substantial layer—3 or 4 inches—is required to retard soil evaporation. It is not recommended on or near rose beds, as it often harbors black spot, a serious fungus disease of hybrid roses.

Peanut Shells

Though lightweight, and therefore easily applied, peanut shells are rather too pale to be inconspicuous. Moreover, they float in heavy rain and, once dry, may be set afire. Still, a 3- or 4-inch layer insulates well and allows water to pass through readily.

Cranberry Clippings

In areas where cranberries are grown commercially, substantial amounts of clippings from these low-growing, fine-textured, purplish leaf shrublets are available after the autumn harvest, usually at little or no cost. Spread generously beneath shrubs and on perennial beds after the onset of cold weather, they make an attractive winter mulch.

Begasse

The dried remainder of sugarcane after the sweet sap has been expressed, begasse makes a very useful mulch, especially if spread as a 2- or 3-inch layer beneath azaleas and rhododendrons. Mildly acidifying, it is particularly beneficial for these and related shrubs in the West, where calcareous soils prevail.

Coffee Grounds

Available from coffee-processing plants, coffee grounds, an initially aromatic, dark brown residue, make an attractive mulch. On drying, however, they tend to form a hard crust, which must be broken if air and the water from summer showers or periodic sprinklings are to penetrate to the roots. A 3-inch layer usually suffices.

Mushroom Compost

The spent compost on which mushrooms have been grown commercially is a deep brown manure-rich medium that makes a fine-textured mulch around shrubs and in gardens. It quickly decomposes and has nutrient value. A 2- to 3-inch layer is adequate.

Paper Pulp

The soupy pulp prepared by macerating newspapers with sawdust or wood shavings in water, when spread about 1 inch thick beneath shrubs and around perennials, dries to form a crusty layer about ¼ inch thick. Because of the light color of the crust, the soil beneath remains cool, and earthworms seem much attracted to its undersurface. Despite its firm texture, the mulch readily admits air and water, and in time it turns from ashy white to medium gray.

Seaweed

Various seaweeds, including kelp, rockweed, and eel grass, once washed free of seawater, make a useful mulch that not only conserves water, deters weeds, and moderates soil temperatures but is also believed to repel certain insects and nematodes. Moreover, after decaying, seaweed adds micronutrients to the soil. For all its virtues, seaweed regrettably imparts a rather crude, disheveled appearance to the garden unless overspread with a finer-textured, more homogeneous material. Because of its open texture, 4 to 6 inches are usually required.

Apple Pomace

The pulpy residue left after apples are pressed for cider, pomace is an initially fragrant material that makes a serviceable mulch for some months before disappearing into the soil. When fresh, it attracts bees and other insects, and areas where it is used may sprout numerous seedling apple trees the following spring unless the seeds were crushed or removed. Used repeatedly, apple pomace acidifies the soil. A 2-inch layer per application suffices.

Inorganic Mulches
Black Polyethylene Plastic Sheeting

Readily available in rolls at garden centers and nurseries, black polyethylene is a low-cost, impervious material that has long been used commercially. With discretion and care, it can be useful in the home garden as well, especially if overspread with another mulch, such as wood chips or pebbles, to keep it in place and lend a more pleasing appearance. In the vegetable garden, exposed black plastic advantageously heats the soil beneath it in the spring, but when the weather warms, the plastic should be covered with salt hay or straw and punctured with a garden fork at frequent intervals to admit water.

Stones

Crushed stone or gravel or rounded pebbles, while heavy in bulk, make an attractive mulch. It must be at least 2 inches thick if it is to accomplish the three main purposes of any mulch: soil moisture conservation, weed control, and soil temperature moderation. Although stone mulch is effectively permanent, it traps fine organic litter that eventually forms soil pockets that become contiguous with the underlying soil and can foster weed growth. This can be delayed considerably by underlying stone mulch with perforated plastic sheeting.

Asphalt Paper

Although much valued in agriculture, especially in connection with pineapples and certain other row crops, asphalt paper is seldom employed in home gardens, except when left as house-building surplus. Heavier and firmer than plastic film, it nevertheless must be weighed down, perforated, and as the season warms, covered to prevent excessive heat buildup beneath.

Aluminum Foil

Also employed extensively in agriculture, aluminum foil not only conserves soil moisture and averts excessive heat buildup but also, because of its high reflectivity, intensifies the sunlight that reaches leaf surfaces and thus augments crop yields. It is this very glare, however, as well as its fragility and high cost, that militates against its general use in home gardens. If chosen, it must be carefully weighted to prevent tearing. Rolls 3 feet wide in gauges 0.001 to 0.0015 are the most convenient.

Calcined Clay

Crushed into a fine gravel, calcined clay—a porous, inert material—is familiar to all who maintain cat litter boxes. It is usually pale gray-brown or yellow-brown and makes a useful mulch if applied in 1- or 2-inch layers. It is best employed in places where soil disturbance will be minimal and a fine-textured appearance is desired, as in rock gardens or dwarf conifer displays.

Combination Mulches

Often the most suitable mulch is a combination of materials, each chosen for a particular attribute. For example, manure makes an enriching mulch on bulb beds, and if topped with a layer of sawdust the muddy spattering of flowers in a heavy spring rain is averted. Also, the blowing about of a leafy mulch in fall can be prevented by spreading a thin top layer of manure or compost, which not only contributes nutrients but helps hasten the breakdown of the leaves beneath. In the vegetable garden, salt hay spread over black plastic is a good summer combination. Pine needles over a mulch of corn-cobs, peanut hulls, or salt hay will greatly improve the appearance of the planting, or if it is mixed with peat moss or coffee grounds it will help prevent the caking of these materials.

ADDITIONAL NITROGEN

Certain raw organic materials such as sawdust, wood chips, corncobs, and to some extent, cereal straws, may reduce soil nitrate during decomposition. This is because the soil bacteria that help breakdown raw organic materials into humus require nitrate during the process, sometimes causing nearby plants to suffer. This may be prevented by increasing the supply of nitrogen in the soil when such mulches are applied, so there will be a sufficient amount to meet the needs of both the soil bacteria and the plants. Ammonium sulfate, nitrate of soda, ammonium nitrate, or a complete fertilizer high in nitrogen may be used. The following amounts are recommended for use on soils of average fertility, per 100 square feet: ½ pound of ammonium sulfate or nitrate of soda, or ⅓ pound of ammonium nitrate, or 1 pound of a 10-6-4 complete fertilizer.

On large areas, the fertilizer is usually applied directly to the soil. If it is necessary to apply it after a mulch has been put on, it may be applied on the surface of the mulch and watered in, or it may be dissolved in water and applied to the mulch in the form of a solution.

When small quantities of sawdust are used for mulching individual plants, the fertilizer may be mixed with the sawdust as it is applied.

SUMMER MULCHES

Summer mulches are chosen primarily to conserve moisture and control weeds. They are widely used in flower, vegetable, and fruit gardens as well as around trees and shrubs.

In the Flower Garden

The summer mulch in the flower garden should be applied in the late spring or early summer, after the ground has become thoroughly warm. Buckwheat hulls and peat moss are especially good materials for use on flower beds, as they are weed free, clean, easy to handle, and make a uniformly inconspicuous mulch. A layer 2 inches deep will usually be sufficient. When plants have low, leafy crowns, the mulch should be worked in carefully about the plant to avoid covering the crown. If peat moss is used, it should be thoroughly wet and, if possible, mixed with pine needles before it is applied and should be maintained in a moist, fluffy condition, never being allowed to dry out and form a crust.

Where slugs are troublesome, precautions must be taken in mulching herbaceous plants and annual flowers. A slug repellent or killer should be applied to the soil before the mulch is put on, and careful watch should be kept. If the slug preparation was not applied to the soil beforehand, it may be applied to the surface of the mulch. See Chapter 34 for methods of slug control.

In the Vegetable Garden

A summer mulch in the vegetable garden will reduce to a minimum the labor required and will also appreciably increase yields and improve the table quality of the crops. And if an organic mulch is used, the benefit to the soil will be great. Sawdust, straw, and black plastic may be used.

On Small Fruits

When summer mulches are used on bush fruits, such as raspberries, blackberries, and blueberries, it will result not only in the control of weeds and a consequent saving in labor but also in more vigorous growth and increased production. Sawdust, straw, and hay are excellent mulching materials. A year-round sawdust mulch on blueberries is especially recommended.

On Trees and Shrubs

As most broad-leaf evergreens are shallow rooted, they thrive best under a permanent mulch that should remain undisturbed. As the older layers decompose, new material should be added. This may be done whenever materials such as leaves, especially from oaks, are available. Permanent mulches may also be maintained under deciduous trees and shrubs. Permanent organic mulches of leaves, straw, and/or sawdust should be maintained at a depth of 4 to 6 inches.

WINTER MULCHES
In the Flower Garden

In the North, a winter mulch serves several important functions in the flower garden. It protects roots from extreme cold; by making soil moisture available continuously, it protects the foliage of certain plants from drying winds and brilliant winter sunshine that are apt to sear and scorch tender growth; by stabilizing soil temperature, it prevents plants from starting into growth too early in the spring; and equally important, it prevents the alternate freezing and thawing of the soil that, during the late winter and spring months, is so harmful to many herbaceous plants, heaving the crowns out of the soil and leaving the roots exposed. Young plants whose roots are very near the surface, and shallow-rooted plants, such as columbines, are the most likely to be injured. In many parts of the country, winter kill is more often the result of frost heaving than extremely low temperatures.

A light winter mulch of fir branchlets, as from discarded Christmas trees, traps fallen tree leaves, casts stabilizing shade, and moderates strengthening late winter sunlight.

Materials

A number of materials, such as salt hay and straw, may be used very satisfactorily as winter mulches in the flower garden. If small evergreen boughs are available, they offer excellent material for winter covering, as they are lightweight and permit a good circulation of air. They may also be used to hold leaves, straw, or other light materials in place. Fallen leaves are one of nature's own coverings, but if they are to be used as a winter protection on garden beds, only those kinds should be selected that will not mat and become a soggy mass before spring. Leaves from oak, beech, and sycamore are excellent, while leaves from Norway maple should be avoided.

When to Apply the Mulch

The winter mulch should not be applied until the plants are completely dormant and the ground is frozen. The purpose of the mulch is not for protection against ordinary cold (which, in fact, most plants of the temperate zones must have to grow and reproduce) but rather to protect the plants from the temporary unseasonal warmth of late winter and early spring days, which can be very damaging and even fatal to some herbaceous plants when it is followed by a return to severe weather.

Depth of the Mulch

The depth of the winter mulch will depend on the type of material used and the severity of the winter climate. It is as disastrous to apply too heavy a mulch and smother the plants as it is to apply too light a covering. Care should be taken not to cover the crowns of such plants as foxgloves, Canterbury bells, hollyhocks, heucheras, garden pinks, or anchusas, all of which retain their basal foliage throughout the winter. The mulch should be worked in about the roots, with only a few light wisps of salt hay over the foliage.

Removal of the Winter Mulch

The removal of the winter mulch is always a matter of concern to the gardener. If a fairly heavy mulch was used, it should be removed gradually and the final covering should, if possible, be lifted off on a cloudy day so that any young shoots that have started into growth may not be too suddenly exposed to brilliant sunshine.

It is unwise to leave the winter mulch on too late in the spring, as it will seriously retard the growth of the plants, and shoots that have tried to push through it may be spindly and weak. It is usually safe to begin to remove the mulch as soon as sustained cold weather seems to be over and the early, small bulbs, such as the squills and crocuses, are in bloom. Mulch that does not impede the growth of protected plants may be left in place to continue decomposing and enriching the soil.

On Evergreens

Evergreen shrubs, particularly the broad-leaf evergreens, are greatly benefited by a winter mulch. Under an adequate winter mulch the soil does not freeze as quickly or as deeply as soil that is exposed. This is a matter of considerable importance with evergreens, as they are never completely dormant. They continue to need water during the winter, and are able to obtain it much more readily from heavily mulched soils than from bare, frozen ground. Hence, permanent year-round mulching is especially appropriate for these plants. A 3- to 4-inch-thick layer is most effective.

33

Control of Weeds

I<small>N FORESTS, THERE ARE NO WEEDS. I</small>N <small>PRAIRIES, THERE ARE</small> no weeds. Nor in deserts, on mountaintops, or along shore dunes. These are all natural habitats occupied by plant communities that include a wide array of species, all evolved for the conditions found there, conditions that the plants help to make.

In a larger sense, a weed is a plant out of place: the wrong plant in the wrong place at the wrong time. Perhaps a weed is better defined as an unwanted plant. If this is true, it

Dandelion, the stereotypic weed of lawns and gardens, has spread from Europe to all temperate-zone regions and many tropical mountains.

follows that there are no species of weeds, for a plant that is a weed in one place may in fact be cultivated in another. Pigweed is a pest in agricultural fields, but is grown by some as a spinach substitute. Purslane beleaguers backyard flower gardeners, but in some vegetable gardens it takes its place alongside lettuce, arugula, and mizuna as a salad green. And who has not heard of dandelon wine or chicory coffee?

In the framework of plant community structure, the plants we call weeds are healers of earth laid bare, ever ready to clothe its wounds until trees can take over. In nature, such wounds include landslips, washouts, floods, and sandstorms, which often leave soil too raw and exposed for most plants to gain a foothold. Weeds quickly move in to occupy and stabilize the surface, and in doing so set the stage for their own replacement.

And so, in our gardens one way to deter weeds is to avoid bare ground. By covering exposed soil with any of several mulches or with ground-covering plants, not only will soil be conserved and soil temperature moderated but weeds will automatically come under control. This is one reason knowledgeable gardeners spread salt hay among vegetables, bark chips or buckwheat hulls among flowers, and oak leaves among rhododendrons and azaleas.

In wooded country the encroachment of seedling trees very quickly pushes the margins of the woodlands out into the fields, and a time-honored annual chore of the farmer in such regions is to cut back the young seedlings to maintain the meadows. In a well-balanced agriculture, however, many native weeds are held in check by the very completeness of the use of the land. The annual cutting of a hayfield will usually destroy seedling trees and weeds in their first season of growth, while the cultivation of crop fields eliminates many weeds in an early stage of growth and prevents them from maturing. Thus it is only along the fence-rows and stone walls that separate the fields that seedling trees, shrubs, and weeds survive and are a source of infestation of the farmer's fields. Yet one of the important virtues of these hedgerow thickets is that they provide food and shelter for birds and wildlife.

But on land that has been left idle in that zone that seems to surround so many of our cities, where it is no longer profitable to farm yet where the time for real estate development is not yet ripe, the weeds and weed trees often have a 20-year head start on the ultimate home owner. By the time there is a demand for home sites in such areas, they have all too frequently already become tangles of honeysuckle, sumac, poison ivy, tree of heaven (*Ailanthus altissima*), and multiflora rose. Even on well-established and carefully maintained grounds, it is necessary to exert constant vigilance to prevent the introduction and encroachment of undesirable plants. Many gardeners and property owners alike have lived to regret the day they failed to realize the danger of permitting a few trailing runners of Japanese honeysuckle to form a pleasant mat of green beneath some trees, or to take immediate action against the small patch of poison ivy that had established itself along a fence, or when they failed to dig out the mugwort that suddenly appeared in the flower border.

Some trees and shrubs, such as the tree of heaven, Norway maple, and the sumacs, left to their own devices, form such rank thickets and copses that eradication becomes a daunting undertaking. Certain woody climbers can also become devastatingly rampant if neglected, though if kept within bounds they are of great ornamental value. In this group we find akebia, wisteria, trumpet creeper (*Campsis radicans*), and Oriental bittersweet (*Celastrus orbiculatus*).

There are also the ubiquitous, rank-growing perennials, such as the tawny daylily (*Hemerocallis fulva*), plume poppy (*Macleaya cordata*), and bouncing Bet (*Saponaria officinalis*), which form vigorous colonies on the perimeter of many cultivated areas and can invade gardens. It is, therefore, important for every home owner and gardener to know which trees and shrubs, which vines and herbaceous plants have a tendency to spread and dominate or crowd out the more desirable plants. It is important also that everyone become familiar with approved means of control so that environmental harm can be obviated or kept to a minimum.

As people have become more aware of what constitutes natural plant communities, the concept of "weeds" has expanded to include plants that are alien to any given ecosystem. Thus Norway maples are considered weeds in a sugar maple grove in New England, and the black locust is a weed among the native oaks of Europe. That this concept is valid in a practical as well as a scientific sense is borne out by the fact that, once introduced, it is the alien organism that usually becomes rampant; in its new setting it frequently has no natural controls and has not been restricted to a narrow niche through long evolutionary pressures. It is not surprising that our most common pernicious perennial and woody weeds—species such as kudzu, Japanese bamboo, tree of heaven, and Japanese honeysuckle—are invasive aliens.

Even as the study of weeds has become more complex, so have the methods for their control. Decades ago, legislation outlawed the casual, often cavalier use of such brush killers as 2,4,5-T and Silvex for environmental reasons. Many other commonly used compounds may eventually meet the same fate. Thus knowledge and foresight have become even more necessary tools in the age-old, ongoing battle with weeds.

TREES THAT MAY BECOME WEEDS

Although the popular stereotype of a weed is an unattractive, rank-growing plant of the season, a number of our noxious weeds are woody plants—trees, shrubs, and woody climbers—that grow incrementally and, once of sufficient size, are often resignedly accepted as part of the home landscape. The species described below have attributes that should not only deter the gardener from planting them but raise questions about their acceptability even as mature specimens.

Deciduous Species

ACER NEGUNDO
(Box elder)

A useful maple species on poor soil in difficult sites nearly throughout the United States, box elder is a noxious pest on fertile soil and should be cut out entirely. Female trees set abundant wind-carried seed, which soon results in unattractive thickets.

A. PLATANOIDES
(Norway maple)

Long valued as a street and park tree in much of the United States north of zone 8, Norway maple has escaped from cultivation in many urban and suburban areas, its abundantly produced, wind-borne seed spawning extensive thickets of young trees that exclude all else. Untended hedges, shrub plantings, and gardens soon succumb to the dense shade and shallow, soil-drying root mat of these weedy trees. Prompt felling and removal of volunteer trees is advised. Young saplings are easily pulled in early spring, before the season's root growth begins.

A. PSEUDOPLATANUS
(Sycamore maple)

A valuable salt-tolerant tree in coastal areas, sycamore maple can be nearly as invasive as Norway maple in inland areas, especially on fertile soils. Volunteers should be removed in the same way as described for Norway maple.

A. SACCHARINUM
(Silver maple)

A native tree that has been overused for street and park use in the Midwest, southern California, and other regions, silver maple also generates thickets of seedlings and saplings that should be promptly removed, as with other troublesome maples.

AILANTHUS ALTISSIMA
(Tree of heaven)

Imported from China, tree of heaven outperforms all other trees in its ability to thrive under adverse urban conditions. Generally, it grows very rapidly, with young trees making as much as 6 feet of growth in a single season, and ultimately reaches 50 to 75 feet in height and spread. Although tree of heaven has undeniable value as a tree for city planting, it is too coarse and fast growing to be useful in most suburban home landscapes. Moreover, female trees shed the abundantly borne seed all through the winter, and the young seedlings soon grow into dense thickets of saplings, often at the expense of more desirable materials. Tree of heaven also invades

Acer saccharinum

secondary woodland, as has happened in New England, New York, Pennsylvania, California, and other states, where this species is especially prolific.

Young trees either should be cut down as soon as they appear or should be destroyed by spraying. Fortunately, the wood of the tree of heaven is soft and light and the task of cutting is comparatively easy, but it is a task that should not be postponed. Tree of heaven may also be controlled effectively by spraying with glyphosate or 2,4-D. If sprouts develop from the wide-ranging roots, they should be sprayed while active growth is under way, preferably when about 2 feet high.

BETULA POPULIFOLIA
(Gray birch)

A valuable colonizer of disturbed sites on poor, often dry soil and often forming dense stands, gray birch frequently requires thinning to allow other species to become established and to permit a smaller number of its own kind to mature with substantial trunks that will stand up to snow and ice loads. Selectively removing trees by cutting trunks to ground level will achieve these ends.

MORUS ALBA
(Common mulberry, white mulberry)

Common mulberry is a tenacious, fast-growing tree with tough, rangy, yellow roots and glossy leaves of varying shapes. This Asiatic species, more than the native red mulberry (*M. rubra*), casts dense, gloomy shade, and the female trees bear great quantities of white to purple blackberry-like fruit that is irresistable to birds, who drop the undigested seeds far and wide. Seedlings appear everywhere and, left untended, soon become large enough to make removal difficult. Digging out young trees is the best control; if cut, the stumps should be flush with grade and covered over with 5-mil black plastic to deter suckers.

POPULUS ALBA
(White poplar)

White poplar is useful in seaside settings, where from zone 3 to 8 its foliage, cottony white beneath, tolerates salt spray and its framework withstands high winds (though it often suffers broken limbs). This species, more than other poplars, however, suckers freely from the roots, forming dense copses that eventually extend 30 feet or more from the base of the parent tree. If white poplar is planted as a lawn specimen, mowing will offset the suckering habit, but elsewhere, these unwanted sprouts require frequent removal by lopping, sawing off, or digging. Since the parent tree and all suckers are linked by a common root system, treatment with a systemic herbicide (such as glyphosate) in any substantial part can lead to the death of all.

PRUNUS SEROTINA
(Black cherry)

A commonly seen pioneer tree on disturbed land over much of the eastern United States from zone 3 to 9, black cherry, handsome though it often becomes in age, bears immense crops of black pea-size fruit, each with a rock-hard pit. Thanks to birds of many kinds, the fruit is carried away and the pits dropped. The result is dense stands of cherry saplings and young trees in untended places that soon crowd out all competitors. Young black cherry trees should be dug out, and older ones cut to or just below grade and the stumps covered with 5-mil black plastic to discourage stump sprouts.

ROBINIA PSEUDOACACIA
(Black locust)

Useful in stabilizing and enriching soil in difficult sites and valued as a wind-deflecting shelter-belt tree (especially in Europe) and as a source of strong, rot-resistant timber (useful for fence posts), black locust suckers freely from the roots, to the extent that a single tree can spawn a grove, all the trunks initially interconnected by roots, all genetically identical. Unless regularly mowed or lopped, the thicket of suckers can overwhelm other less aggressive species. Hence the need annually to cut out the unwanted, usually thorny sucker growth.

ULMUS PUMILA
(Siberian elm)

Fast-growing, tolerant of adversity, and unaffected by such elm scourges as Dutch elm disease and phloem necrosis, Siberian elm is nonetheless an undesirable tree for the home grounds. Not only do twigs and branches litter the ground after relatively minor windstorms but the shower of winged, wind-borne seeds in late spring leads to volunteer seedlings popping up in shrubbery, hedges, and ground cover beds, soon overtopping all else and casting dense shade. Such volunteers should be removed annually, either by pulling, digging, lopping, or cutting.

Evergreen Species

Evergreen species that may become weedy include red cedar (*Juniperus virginiana*), Norway spruce (*Picea abies*), pitch pine (*Pinus rigida*), and white pine (*Pinus strobus*) in the East, especially the Northeast, and Douglas fir (*Pseudotsuga menziesii*) in the West, especially the Pacific Northwest. Other species are equally troublesome locally. All shed much seed and develop overcrowded, densely shading groves in disturbed, untended places and require occasional clearing or thinning to admit light and to encourage other species.

WEEDY SHRUBS

As with trees, there are some shrubs that quickly proliferate and encroach where not wanted given the least opportunity. Others are too coarse and rampant in growth to be harmonious in well-designed home landscape. In these two categories we find, among others, the following species.

BERBERIS THUNBERGII
(Japanese barberry)

Much used over most of the United States as a hedge shrub, Japanese barberry, a thorny species, is especially valued for its winter display of red berries. These, however, are consumed by birds and distributed widely in the vicinity, often leading to dense, even impenetrable volunteer growths. Volunteer shrubs should be dug out, preferably while small, or may be treated in summer with glyphosate.

CYTISUS SCOPARIUS
(Scotch broom)

In the Pacific Northwest and parts of coastal New England, Scotch broom, a yellow-flowered leguminous shrub, self-seeds and becomes invasive, particularly in open sites on sandy or gravelly soils. Control is best effected by digging out or flush cutting unwanted shrubs.

ELEAGNUS UMBELLATA
(Autumn olive)

Autumn olive, closely related to Russian olive (*E. angustifolia*), has been planted as a highway divider screen in some areas of the United States and serves its purpose very well. It is dense and tolerant of air pollution, highway salt, and other factors. Unfortunately, it flowers and fruits profusely, and while this is a happy situation for birds, the result is that the seeds are carried long distances and germinate readily wherever dropped. The shrub has thus become a nuisance in some places. To get rid of autumn olive, cut the trunks to the ground and cover the stubs and immediately surrounding area with 5-mil

black plastic. Alternatively, the stubs may be painted with 2,4-D.

HIBISCUS SYRIACUS
(Rose of Sharon)

Valued for its late-summer flower display, rose of Sharon sets much seed, which is scattered by strong winter winds that agitate the gradually splitting seed capsules. In untended nearby shrub borders or hedgerows an ever-increasing thicket of volunteer seedlings and saplings arises, crowding out all else. Out-of-place shrubs should be dug out, preferably when young, or cut off at or just below grade.

HYPERICUM FRONDOSUM
(Shrubby St. John'swort)

A shrub that grows to 3 feet tall, shrubby St. John'swort is not only weedy in nature but seeds so prolifically that large numbers of young plants spring up near and far, making it a doubly undesirable species for the home grounds. It is best to dig out all shrubs of this species and substitute another, such as *H. densiflorum* or *H. kalmianum*, neither of which is invasive.

LONICERA TATARICA
(Tatarian bush honeysuckle)

Tatarian bush honeysuckle is a large, twiggy, gray-barked shrub of rangy habit that reaches 10 feet tall and as wide. This Chinese species has escaped cultivation in much of the East, and thanks to seeds being scattered by berry-consuming birds, it has become a serious weed in many areas, especially in coastal New England. Shrubs too large to dig out should be cut off at or just below grade.

LYCIUM HALIMIFOLIUM
(Matrimony vine)

Matrimony vine, which is in fact a sprawling shrub with slender, drooping branches, is useful as a ground cover on eroded banks, but it should never be used in a shrub border or in other plantings on the home grounds. It spreads rapidly from underground suckers, and in a comparatively short time forms an extensive thicket that is difficult to eradicate as any bit of root left in place soon sprouts suckers. It is, however, very sensitive to glyphosate or 2,4-D and is usually killed by one application.

RHUS GLABRA
(Smooth sumac)

Smooth sumac is a valuable colonizer of droughty banks along highways and railroads over much of the United States, with flaming red fall foliage and, in female plants, conical, deep red fruiting clusters that persist into winter. Because of its thicket-forming habit, the result of wide-ranging, suckering roots, it overwhelms other shrubs. Unwanted sumac should be dug out, or they may be sprayed with glyphosate while actively growing, probably several times in successive summers. Contrary to popular belief, neither this species nor any other red-fruited sumac causes dermatitis.

R. TYPHINA
(Staghorn sumac)

Similar to *R. glabra* except for its larger size and densely hairy stems, staghorn sumac requires the same treatment for removal.

ROBINIA FERTILIS
(Rose acacia)

Often mistaken for the closely related but noninvasive *R. hispida*, rose acacia, a shrubby locust, forms thickets that grow to 6 feet high and bears rose pink, sweet pea–like flowers, which are followed by bristly, purplish green pods. It spreads underground by suckering roots and forms dense colonies, which are useful in stabilizing highway and railroad embankments but can be a menace in the garden. Spraying the blue-green foliage with glyphosate or 2,4-D in early to mid summer is the best control measure, as digging inevitably leaves pieces of root that sprout and reinfest the area.

ROSA MULTIFLORA
(Multiflora rose)

Multiflora rose, a shrubby, festooning rose, was introduced into the United States for use on farms in hedgerows and on roadside embankments to provide dense barriers ("living fences"), to reduce wind erosion in tilled fields, to provide wind protection for vulnerable crops, and to create shelter for wildlife. It soon escaped cultivation and became naturalized in disturbed places throughout the country, and in some regions it is a serious pest. On the home grounds it often springs up in hedges, shrub plantings, and in perennial and ground cover beds. Young plants should be dug out; older ones may be cut off at or just below grade.

Multiflora rose (*Rosa multiflora*)

SYMPHORICARPOS ORBICULATUS
(Coralberry)

A twiggy, small-leaved shrub, 4 to 6 feet high, coralberry spreads by wide-ranging runners that root at intervals and develop into separate shrubs, which in turn send out more runners, thus forming dense, impenetrable thickets that exclude all other shrubs and lower garden plants. Stems and runners should be cut and the relatively shallow roots dug out, or the leafy tops may be sprayed with glyphosate or 2,4-D, preferably while actively growing.

WOODY CLIMBERS THAT CAN BECOME WEEDY

AKEBIA QUINATA
(Five-leaf akebia)

Five-leaf akebia is a slender-stemmed twiner with attractive foliage that is often planted on fences, porches, and pergolas. Unless care is taken to keep its growth within bounds, however, it is capable of spreading over the ground as a dense mat and smothering shrubs and low trees in the vicinity. Five-leaf akebia should be kept strictly within bounds by judicious pruning. If it has been allowed to grow unchecked, it may be eradicated by spraying with glyphosate or 2,4-D.

CAMPSIS RADICANS
(Trumpet creeper)

Unattended, trumpet creeper forms dense thickets that spread by root suckers and eventually dominate large areas. Short of using herbicides, such growths can be very difficult to bring under control. Buildings that support trumpet creeper can be seriously damaged by the shoots invading spaces between shingles, clapboards, and structural members and, as stem girth expands year by year, forcing them apart and allowing moisture and debris to gain entrance. Glyphosate is effective if applied while the plant is actively growing.

CELASTRUS ORBICULATUS
(Oriental bittersweet, common bittersweet)

Although the common bittersweet is a favorite because of its bright yellow-and-orange fruit, it must be kept within bounds, as it rapidly ascends shrubs and trees, smothering them with festooned foliage and strangling their trunks and branches with its winding, ever-thickening stems. The similar but less common native bittersweet (*C. scandens*) is not as invasive. Careful annual pruning is needed to keep Oriental bittersweet under control, and where eradication is desired, it may be cut

Celastrus orbiculatus in a crab apple tree

either at or just below grade, and the stumps and surrounding area covered with 5-mil black plastic to prevent roots from suckering, or the foliage may be sprayed with glyphosate or 2,4-D during active growth in summer.

CLEMATIS PANICULATA
(Sweet autumn clematis)

Given time, and without care, sweet autumn clematis will climb up through shrubs and low trees and spread over low buildings, blanketing all with a dense tangle of debris-trapping stems that, apart from the floral display at summer's end, contribute little aesthetically and can do considerable harm. Unruly growth should be cut back to grade and the stubs and surrounding area covered with 5-mil black plastic to deter the suckering of roots.

HEDERA HELIX
(English ivy)

English ivy, an evergreen climber–ground cover, carpets shaded ground and ascends any vertical surface it contacts by means of aerial rootlets, clothing tree trunks, walls, and buildings with heavy growth. Although it is not parasitic, and thus has no organic contact with supporting trunks and other vegetation, English ivy can smother shrubs; trap debris, which, on wooden buildings, can lead to structural decay; and exclude garden plants from carpeted ground. It is best controlled by pruning and digging out unwanted growth and thereafter by annual shearing and trimming.

LONICERA JAPONICA
(Japanese honeysuckle)

In places, Japanese honeysuckle has become one of our most troublesome and devastatingly destructive weed vines. Because of its attractive appearance and its fragrant flowers, it is still frequently planted by property owners who are completely unaware of the liability they are incurring. When this vine gets out of bounds, it spreads rapidly under trees and in open, sunny areas as well, climbing shrubs and small trees and smothering them with the shade of its matted, semi-evergreen foliage. In some areas, it has destroyed many acres of secondary forest and invaded large areas of cropland. Entire farms have been abandoned because of its devastations. It can, however, be eradicated by spraying with glyphosate or 2,4-D during active growth. It may require two or more applications in successive years.

PARTHENOCISSUS QUINQUEFOLIA
(Virginia creeper)

In mature woodland, Virginia creeper is a compatible, versatile component of the forest ecosystem, but in cultivation it can become a problem plant, particularly if the area is limited and the garden scale is small. It can quickly cover open areas, ascend trees and buildings by means of adhesive-tipped tendrils, and dominate all vegetation below the treetops. Roots and underground stems repeatedly sucker, making effective mechanical control difficult. Buildings ascended by Virginia creeper can be completely covered, and in time suffer deterioration. To control, cut stems at or just below grade (preferably in winter, to avoid the visual blight of persisting dead foliage) and pull away from trees and buildings. Ground-covering growth should be sprayed with glyphosate or 2,4-D while in full leaf and actively growing.

PUERARIA LOBATA
(Kudzu vine)

Introduced as an ornamental climber more than a century ago, Kudzu, a rapacious, extremely fast-growing twiner from China, has become a vicious pest throughout the Southeast. It is extremely difficult to control by mechanical means but may be eliminated by spraying with glyphosate while in full leaf and actively growing. Two or three applications in successive years may be required.

TOXICODENDRON RADICANS
(Poison ivy)

The tremendous increase in the frequency and spread of poison ivy during the past century merely reflects its natural role as a colonizer of disturbed habitats, especially along partially shaded woodland borders and in freshwater wetlands. However unwelcome poison ivy is in the vicinity of human habitation, it nevertheless offers beautiful fall coloration and is valued as a wildlife plant. Undeniably, however, contact with any part of the plant, dormant or actively growing, alive or dead, can bring on dermatitis. Beyond this, poison ivy is a serious menace in orchards and secondary woodlands, and grows rampantly along roadsides, paths in parks, beaches at lakes and ponds, and many other public places, spoiling the enjoyment of the outdoors for those who are susceptible—and very few are immune.

Poison ivy (*Toxicodendron radicans*)

Aerial growth of poison ivy should be carefully cut at ground level, preferably during leafless dormancy, using a pruning saw or loppers and the protection of gloves. On the ground, the foliage may be sprayed or painted with glyphosate or amitrole. With either, repeat applications may be required in successive years. All parts, whether alive or dead, should be buried or disposed of off site, and neither composted, as the poisonous principle is slow to decompose, nor burned, as the poisonous sap vaporizes and is carried in the smoke.

While poison ivy occurs throughout most of the eastern United States, its western counterpart, poison oak (*T. diversiloba*), is limited to a 200- to 300-mile-wide zone from western Washington to southern California. It has hairy leaves that are not glossy and tends to grow in thickets, but otherwise resembles poison ivy and is equally virulent. Eradication procedures are as for poison ivy.

WISTERIA *SPP.*

Although the wisterias are among the most beautiful of all woody climbers, they can become rampant weeds if allowed to get out of bounds. Their capacity to twine ever higher into trees, up buildings, and over arbors, and to pull structures apart, makes them bad neighbors for railings, shutters, downspouts, gutters, and shingles. Another unfortunate characteristic of the wisterias is its habit of spreading by way of long, trailing runners, which root at intervals and form new plants. In this way, a wisteria left unchecked can take possession of a large area very rapidly and and form an almost impenetrable thicket. Pruning shears and pruning saw are the main tools for keeping wisterias in bounds. They are relatively resistant to 2,4-D and even to glyphosate, often requiring several applications at yearly intervals during active growth to be effective.

COMMON PERENNIAL, BIENNIAL, AND ANNUAL WEEDS OF GARDENS AND LAWNS

There are a number of perennial plants that tend to spread rapidly and have the potential to become serious pests in lawns. This occurs when they escape from the confines of the garden itself or from nearby woodlands and less well-cultivated areas. And there are other undesirable perennial plants that are sometimes unwittingly brought into the garden, the owner being entirely unaware of their aggressive characteristics. In some instances, such plants appear suddenly as voluntary invaders in the garden, and unless immediate steps are taken to eliminate them, they will soon gain such headway that the more desirable plantings are overwhelmed and crowded out.

The most common and widely distributed species are listed in the table below. Where possible, they should be pulled, scuffle hoed, or dug out. If herbicides must be used, the summary of relatively safe herbicides at the end of this chapter will provide guidance as to choice and procedure.

COMMON WEEDS OF GARDENS AND LAWNS

In each case, the height given is maximum; under favorable conditions, most weeds flower and shed seed at much lower heights.

Names	Occurrence	Distribution	Characteristics
Abutilon theophrasti (velvet leaf)	Garden	Entire country, except the upper Midwest, Rocky Mountains and Mexican border	Annual; 3 feet tall; erect habit; downy hairy leaves; small yellow flowers; crownlike seed capsules
Achillea millefolium (common yarrow)	Garden and lawn	Entire country; except the desert Southwest	Perennial; 2½' tall; erect habit; forms clumps; finely divided leaves; flat heads of small white flowers
Agropyron repens (quack grass)	Garden and lawn	Entire country	Perennial grass; creeping habit; usually abundant when present
Allium vineale (garlic grass)	Garden and lawn	Entire country, except the western mountains	Perennial; forms clumps; slender, erect aromatic leaves in early spring and fall
Amaranthus blitoides (prostrate pigweed)	Garden	Entire country, except the Gulf Coast and desert Southwest	Annual; prostrate, spreading habit; densely leafy stems; inconspicuous greenish flowers
A. retroflexus (red-root pigweed)	Garden	Entire country	Annual 3 to 6 feet tall; erect habit red taproot; leafy stems; dense heads of small green flowers
Ambrosia artemisiifolia (common ragweed)	Garden	Entire country, except the upper Great Lakes and northern Maine	Annual; 4 feet tall; erect habit; branched; much-divided leaves; spikes of small green flowers (causing pollenosis in some)
Artemisia vulgaris (mugwort, chrysanthemum weed)	Garden	Northeast	Perennial 3 to 5 feet tall; erect habit; forms dense stands; deeply lobed, aromatic leaves; small greenish flowers
Asclepias syriaca (common milkweed)	Garden	East of the Rocky Mountains and north of the Gulf Coast	Perennial; 3 feet tall; erect habit; deep root; milky sap; large blue-green leaves in pairs; spherical clusters of fragrant pink flowers; warty green pods
Barbarea vulgaris (yellow rocket)	Garden	Northeast, Midwest, and Pacific Northwest	Biennial or perennial; 2 feet tall; erect habit; branched; deeply divided leaves; yellow flowers
Bellis perennis (English daisy)	Garden and lawn	Pacific Northwest	Biennial or perennial; forms flat rosettes in clumps; white or pink dandelionlike flowers
Bidens bipinnata (Spanish needles)	Garden	East; except northern New England and Canadian border	Erect Annual 2 to 4 feet tall; habit; deeply divided leaves; yellow flowers; hooked seeds
Brassica nigra (black mustard)	Garden	Entire country, except the upper Midwest	Erect Annual; 2 feet tall; habit; branched; yellow flowers; pods pressed against stem
Bromus secalinus (annual cheat, chess)	Garden and lawn	Entire country, except the upper Midwest	Annual; 4 feet tall; erect habit; flat; rough-hairy leaves
Capsella bursa-pastoris (shepherd's purse)	Garden and lawn	Entire country	Annual; 2-foot branched stems; leaves in small rosette; small white flowers; heart-shaped seed capsules
Cerastium vulgatum (mouse-ear chickweed)	Garden and lawn	Entire country, except North Dakota and the desert Southwest	Annual or perennial creeping habit; sticky hairy leaves; small white flowers
Chenopodium album (pigweed, lamb's quarters)	Garden	Entire country	Annual; 6 feet tall; erect habit; branched; red-streaked stems; gray green leaves (edible); small gray green flowers
Cichorium intybus (chicory)	Garden	Entire country, except the upper Midwest and desert Southwest	Biennial or perennial; 4 feet tall; erect habit; branched, coarsely toothed leaves; brightblue dandelionlike flowers
Cirsium arvense (Canada thistle)	Garden	Northern half of country	Perennial; 4 feet tall; erect habit; spiny foliage; purple flower heads
Convolvulus arvensis (field bindweed)	Garden	Entire country, except the Southeast, South, and Texas, New Mexico, Arizona	Perennial; 3 feet tall; creeping or twining habit; fleshy tuberous root; white or pink funnel-shaped flowers

(continues)

COMMON WEEDS OF GARDENS AND LAWNS (*continued*)

Names	Occurrence	Distribution	Characteristics
C. sepium (hedge bindweed)	Garden	East of the Rocky Mountains and in the Pacific Northwest	Perennial; 10 feet tall; creeping or twining habit; fleshy tuberous roots; white or pink and white funnel-shaped flowers
Conyza canadensis (fleabane, horseweed)	Garden	Entire country	Annual; 4 feet tall; erect habit; branched; small white daisylike flowers
Cuscuta spp. (dodder, love vine)	Garden	Entire country, except northern New England and the northern Great Lakes	Annual; twining habit; leafless yellow to orange parasitic stems; small white flowers
Cynodon dactylon (Bermuda grass)	Garden and lawn	East; the Gulf Coast and Pacific Northwest	Perennial; forms turf mat, very narrow leaves
Cyperus esculentus (nut grass, nut sedge)	Garden and lawn	Entire country, except North Dakota	Perennial; forms clumps; triangular stems; glossy leaves; yellow-brown flowers; spreads by slender white rhizomes
Daucus carota (Queen Anne's lace)	Garden	Entire country, except the upper Midwest	Biennial; 3 to 6 feet tall; rosette first year, tall stem second year; finely divided leaves; small white flowers in a flat cluster; "nest" of seed heads
Digitaria ischaemum (smooth crab grass)	Garden and lawn	Entire country, except southern Florida and desert Southwest	Annual; flat, spreading habit; node rooting; flowers and seed heads in late summer
D. sanguinalis (large crab grass)	Garden and lawn	Entire country, except the upper Midwest	Annual; flat, spreading habit; node rooting; flowers and seed heads in late summer; leaves turn reddish in fall
Echinochloa crus-galli (barnyard grass)	Garden and lawn	Entire country, except Florida	Annual; 1 to 3 feet tall; spreading to erect habit; long, flat leaves; branched flowers; seed heads
Euphorbia corollata (flowering spurge)	Garden	East, except along Canadian border	Perennial 2 to 3 feet tall; erect habit; white sap; upper leaves held in circles; clusters of small white flowers
Galanthus nivalis (star-of-Bethlehem)	Garden and lawn	East and the Pacific Northwest	Perennial from bulb forms clumps; narrow, fleshy, white-banded leaves, flowers clustered, white, open in sun
Galinsoga parviflora (small-flowered galinsoga)	Garden	Entire country, except northernmost states	Annual; 1 foot tall; spreading habit; much branched; leafy; small yellow-and-white flowers
Galium aparine (annual bedstraw)	Garden	Entire country	Annual; spreading habit; weak, bristly stems; diffusely branched; leaves clustered; small white flowers
Hieraceum spp. (hawkweed)	Garden and lawn	Entire country	Perennial; leaves in flat rosettes; 1- to 2-foot branched stalks; yellow or orange dandelion like flowers
Holcus mollis (velvet grass)	Garden and lawn	Northeast Coast Pacific and the Northwest	Annual; erect habit; clumped stems; velvety gray green leaves; whitish flower heads
Hypericum perforatum (St. John'swort)	Garden	East of Rocky Mountains and the Pacific Northwest	Perennial 2½ feet tall; erect; habit; branched; paired, blue-green leaves; yellow flowers
Ipomoea hederacea (ivy-leaved morning glory)	Garden	Entire country, except Maine to Wisconsin, the upper Midwest, and western mountains	Annual Twinning habit; lobed leaves; blue to purple, funnel-shaped flowers
Lactuca serriola (prickly lettuce)	Garden	Entire country, except northern Maine	Annual; 4 to 6 feet tall; erect habit milky juice; prickly leaves on north and south sides of stems; small yellow dandelionlike flowers
Lamium amplexicaule (henbit)	Garden	Entire country, except upper Midwest	Annual; spreading habit; four-angled stems; paired upper leaves joined at bases; pinkish purple flowers
Lepidium spp. (pepperweed)	Garden	Entire country, except the upper Midwest and desert Southwest	Perennial or annual; 1 foot tall erect habit; branched; small upper leaves; small white flowers; flattened, disc-shaped seed capsules
Leucanthemum vulgare (oxeye daisy)	Garden and lawn	Entire country except the northern Rocky Mountains	Perennial; 1 to 3 feet tall; erect habit; forms clumps; toothed, dark green leaves; white and yellow flowers

Names	Occurrence	Distribution	Characteristics
Linaria vulgaris (butter and eggs)	Garden	Entire country	Perennial; 1½ feet tall; forms clumps; narrow blue-green leaves; yellow-and-orange snapdragonlike flowers
Lythrum salicaria (purple loosestrife)	Garden	Northeast	Perennial; 4 feet tall; forms clumps; erect leafy stems; thrives in damp places; red-violet flowers
Malva neglecta (common mallow)	Garden	Entire country	Annual or biennial; spreading habit; taprooted; lobed circular leaves; small, pale lilac flowers
Mollugo verticillata (carpetweed)	Garden and lawn	Entire country, except the upper Midwest	Annual; prostrate habit; branched, clustered leaves; small white flowers
Oxalis corniculata (annual yellow wood sorrel)	Garden and lawn	Entire country	Annual; 1 foot tall; spreading stems; light green cloverlike leaves; small yellow flowers
Oxalis stricta (perennial yellow wood sorrel)	Garden and lawn	Entire country	Perennial; taprooted; spreading 6-inch stems, purplish green cloverlike leaves; small yellow flowers
Physalis heterophylla (clammy ground cherry)	Garden	East of Rocky Mountains	Perennial; 2 feet tall; wide-spreading habit; branched; sticky hairy leaves; yellow-and-purple flowers; berries borne in papery jackets
Phytolacca americana (pokeweed)	Garden	East, except the Great Lakes	Perennial; 8 feet tall; forms clumped stems; thick root; large smooth leaves; long clusters of small white flowers; violet black berries
Plantago lanceolata (buckhorn plantain)	Garden and lawn	Entire country	Perennial; 1 foot tall; narrow, ribbed leaves in flat rosette, flowers in erect heads, brown with cream anthers
P. major (broad-leaf plantain)	Garden and lawn	Entire country	Perennial; 1 foot tall; wide, ribbed leaves in flat rosette; greenish flowers on erect spikes
Polygonum japonicum (Japanese bamboo)	Garden	East and Midwest	Perennial; 6 to 8 feet tall; forms dense clumps and stands; branched; branched clusters of small, white flowers
P. pensylvanicum (annual smartweed)	Garden and lawn	East of Rocky Mountains	Annual; 1½ feet tall; jointed stems; narrow leaves; small red flowers in clusters
P. persicaria (lady's thumb)	Garden and lawn	Entire country, except the desert Southwest	Annual; jointed stems; diffusely branched; heads of small red flowers
Portulaca oleracea (purslane)	Garden and lawn	Entire country	Annual; prostrate habit; succulent stems; small succulent leaves (edible); small yellow flowers
Rumex acetosella (sheep sorrel)	Garden and lawn	East, Midwest and the Pacific Northwest	Perennial; 1 foot tall; forms dense, expanding clumps; spreads by roots; small yellowish red flowers
R. crispus (dock)	Garden	Entire country	Perennial; large rosette, then tall leafy stems; small reddish flowers; brown persisting seed capsules
Saponaria officinalis (bouncing Bet)	Garden	Eastern country	Perennial; 2 feet tall; forms large clumps; leaves paired on knobby stems; flowers white to pale lilac
Sedum acre, S. sarmentosum (creeping yellow sedum)	Garden	Northeast	Perennial; creeping habit succulent; small light green leaves; branched clusters of small yellow flowers
Setaria spp. (annual foxtail grass)	Garden and lawn	Entire country	Annual; 3 feet tall; erect habit; coarse gray green leaves
Sinapis arvensis (Charlock)	Garden	Entire country	Annual; 2 feet tall; erect habit; lobed, toothed leaves; elongated clusters of yellow flowers
Solanum carolinense (horsenettle)	Garden	Entire country, except Rocky Mountains	Perennial 2 feet tall; erect habit; prickly, leafy stems; blue-violet and yellow flowers; yellow berries
S. nigrum (black nightshade)	Garden	East of Rocky Mountains	Annual; 2 feet tall; erect or spreading stems; stalked leaves; small white flowers; black berries
Solidago spp. (goldenrod)	Garden	Entire country, except the desert Southwest	Perennial; forms clumps of tall leafy stems; topped with wands of small yellow flowers

(continues)

Dock (*Rumex crispus*)

Pokeweed (*Phytolacca americana*)

Chicory (*Cichorium intybus*)

Red clover
(*Trifolium pratense*)

Common chickweed
(*Stellaria media*)

Common ragweed
(*Ambrosia artemisiifolia*)

Hedge bindweed
(*Convolvulus sepium*)

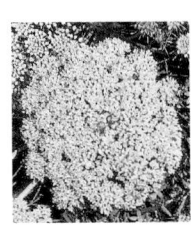

Queen Anne's lace
(*Daucus carota*)

St. John'swort (*Hypericum perforatum*)

Common milkweed (*Asclepias syriaca*)

Horseweed (*Conyza canadensis*)

COMMON WEEDS OF GARDENS AND LAWNS (*continued*)

Names	Occurrence	Distribution	Characteristics
Sonchus asper (spiny sow thistle)	Garden	Entire country	Annual; 3 feet tall; erect habit; reddish stems; lobed prickly leaves, yellow dandelionlike flowers
S. oleraceus (annual sow thistle)	Garden	Entire country	Annual; 3 feet tall; erect habit; green stems; deeply lobed leaves small yellow dandelionlike flowers
Sorghum halepensis (Johnsongrass)	Garden and lawn	East, Gulf states, and Southwest	Perennial; 3 feet tall; perennial diffusely branched; spreads by root stocks; coarse blue-green leaves
Stellaria media (common chickweed)	Garden and lawn	Entire country	Annual; forms clumps or tufts; slender, weak, light green stems and leaves; small white flowers
Taraxacum sp.* (dandelion)	Garden and lawn	Entire country except South Texas and the Imperial Valley, California	Perennial, flat rosette of coarsely toothed leaves; milky sap; yellow flower heads on hollow stalks; seeds airborne
Trifolium pratense (red clover)	Garden and lawn	Entire country, except the desert Southwest	Perennial; 2 feet tall; taprooted; three-parted leaves; rose pink flower heads
Xanthium spp. (cocklebur)	Garden	Entire country, except Northern New England	Annual; 3 feet tall; erect habit; branched; coarsely toothed or lobed leaves; purple flower heads become brown prickly burrs

*Although it is a most common weed, dandelion's correct scientific name remains disputed by specialists.

Methods of Weed Control

In general, and aside from hand weeding in small areas, the most effective measures of control for weeds and other undesirable plants include cultivation; especially scuffle hoeing; smothering by means of an effective mulch; and failing control by these mechanical methods, use of a carefully chosen, correctly applied herbicide.

Cultivation

Many annual weeds in the flower garden, the vegetable garden, and the orchard, as well as some perennial weeds, may be controlled very satisfactorily by shallow cultivation. It is, of course, the age-old method of weed control and will probably continue to be used by gardeners throughout the world for centuries to come. It is the method most frequently used for the control of weeds in the flower garden, where other methods, such as the use of chemical sprays and granules, are usually not feasible. In this connection it should be pointed out that the use of deep mulches is rapidly replacing cultivation in vegetable gardens, and to some extent this is becoming an accepted form of weed control in flower gardens also.

Since deep cultivation inevitably causes some root damage, the removal of young weeds is usually better accomplished by use of the scuffle hoe, which has a horizontal blade for cutting off weeds just below the soil surface. Scuffle hoeing should be timely and thorough. In normal seasons, a hoeing every 10 to 14 days will keep most weeds under control, although in very rainy seasons more frequent cultivations may be necessary. If the hoeing is done in the morning on a bright day, the cut weeds may be left to dry out in the sun. The soil should never be stirred with a cultivator when it is too wet; if wet, the soil is best left to dry a bit before any scuffle hoeing or other cultivation, as lumps and clods may form—a particular hazard with heavy clay soils. If a tightly squeezed ball of soil breaks apart when dropped to the ground, scuffle hoeing is in order; if it remains a solid lump, the soil needs time to lose some moisture.

Mulches

There are various materials that may be used very satisfactorily for mulches (see Chapter 32). The application of a mulch has become an increasingly popular practice among gardeners within recent years, and mulches have proved their value in the flower garden, the vegetable garden, and the orchard. In addition to being a very effective method of controlling weeds, a mulch also helps not only to conserve the soil's moisture but also to maintain a more even soil temperature. These cooler summer soil temperatures create generally more favorable growing conditions for the plants. Moreover, the gradual decomposition of organic mulches contributes to soil quality.

In small areas where weedy grasses spring up so readily from bits of trailing roots and stems, one of the most effective methods of eradication is to smother all growth with a very heavy, impervious mulch. Black plastic, building paper, or even heavy layers of newspapers may be used. At the end of several weeks, both the roots and tops of the weeds will be dead, provided that all light has been excluded. Small patches of Canada thistle, bindweed, and other persistent perennial weeds may also be eradicated in this way.

Herbicides

Chemicals that can be used to kill weeds are called herbicides. Some substances, such as diesel oil, work by direct contact, killing only that part of the plant that is treated with the herbicide; repeat treatments are usually necessary to control perennial weeds. There is very limited residual action. Systemic herbicides, on the other hand, are absorbed by the plant. These herbicides move through the plant by a method called translocation, and they adversely affect the plant internally, frequently causing its death. Most are absorbed through the foliage, but some can be picked up by the roots or even through green bark. Some chemicals applied to the soil prevent seed germination; these are known as preemergence herbicides. These are absorbed by the rootlets of germinating seeds and take effect before the tops appear. Of great importance is residual persistence of the preemergence herbicide in the soil, which determines how long it will be effective. A crop cannot be safely planted until after the herbicide residue has degraded and become neutral or inert.

Herbicides can be applied either as sprays or as granules. Formulations vary in degrees of concentration. It is most important to read the label very carefully for exact amounts to use and methods of application. As with other biocides, the label on a herbicide container is a legal document that obligates the user to follow its instructions scrupulously. Beyond this, ongoing research and development will result in a parade of new herbicidal preparations as well as changes in the status of existing products, necessarily rendering the the listings here as valid at the time of writing.

Types of Herbicide Sprays

The U.S. Department of Agriculture, the state experimental stations, and many large commercial concerns have long carried out extensive studies in an effort to discover and develop effective measures of weed control through the use of chemical and hormone sprays; and after intense research and development, many herbicides, or weed killers, came onto the market, especially during the 1950s to the 1980s. In fact, so great was the progress in developing herbicides that large-scale agricultural operations were revolutionized in this country and around the world. It became possible to eradicate, or least bring under reasonable control, weeds occurring along roadsides, in crop fields, in gardens, and in orchards, while heretofore it had seemed useless even to make an attempt to do so, because measures of control were so limited.

Herbicides that kill certain kinds of plants while leaving others unaffected are called selective; those that kill all contacted plants are nonselective. However, this deceptively simple classification is complicated by the fact that plant susceptibility varies with the plant's age and the time and manner of application.

Whatever herbicides are chosen for weed control, precautions are in order. Most herbicides are toxic if taken internally, and they can also burn the skin. Some degrade with prolonged exposure to light and others degrade even in the dark. It is prudent, then, to acquire herbicides in small quantities, to mix only what is required, to store any surplus in a locked cabinet that is light-free inside, and to restrict each pump sprayer to one kind of herbicide.

Inorganic Herbicides

Historically, brine solutions and ashes suspended in saltwater were used to control weeds in classical times, and copper sulfate came into use in the late 1800s to kill weeds in grain fields. Beyond the various instances in which weed resistance to herbicides have been noted, several inorganic herbicides have been found to persist in the soil for extended periods and in some locations have polluted groundwater. As a result, most inorganic herbicides are restricted or banned by the Environmental Protection Agency (EPA), and none is recommended for use in the home garden. This includes the once widely used ammonium sulfamate (also known as AMS, Ammate X, etc.), which is very injurious to lawn grasses, and the various herbicidal borates, which render soil toxic for years.

Organic Herbicides

The widely publicized damage that was caused by the general use of 2,4,5-T, particularly in the form of Agent Orange in Vietnam, led to its withdrawal by the EPA in 1979 and also to the banning of Silvex. Since then other organic herbicides have been much investigated. Those discussed below are believed safe for use in the home garden. They should be considered last resorts in weed control, however, and are justified only when the magnitude of the undertaking or the tenacity of the weed species concerned makes hand weeding or mechanical methods impracticable. The commercial name, or trademark, of the following herbicides is listed in parentheses after the chemical name.

Amitrole (Aminotriozole, Cytrol, Weedazol)

In plants susceptible to amitrole, a triazine (see the following lists), the vital food-making process, photosynthesis, is inhibited. Aminotriazole is a variant that has certain advantages over amitrole: it does not volatilize and form vapors that might prove harmful to sensitive plants, it dissolves readily in water and is easy to apply, it is nontoxic to humans and animals, it is not a fire hazard, and it is not corrosive to metal spray equipment. It is readily inactivated in heavy soils and, if used at prescribed rates, does not build up a toxic residue in the soil. Nevertheless, because of possible harmful effects, it is illegal to use Aminotriazole on land that will be later used for food crops. Therefore, it is obvious that this (like any herbicide) is not a preferred control measure, only a last resort.

WEEDY PLANTS THAT ARE SENSITIVE TO AMITROLE

Bermuda grass	Quack grass
Buckbrush	Russian knapweed
Canada and sow thistles	Poison ivy
Cattails and tules	Poison oak
Horsetail rush	Prickly ash
Leafy spurge	White ash
Nut grass (sedges)	White, scrub, and red oaks

PLANTS THAT MAY SHOW SOME RESISTANCE TO AMITROLE

At rates required for ordinary control.

Apple	Rhododendron
Creeping myrtle	Sassafras
Dogwood	Smooth sumac
English ivy	Spicebush
Japanese honeysuckle	Viburnum
Lilac	Virginia creeper
Pachysandra	Walnut
Red maple	Wild grape

Benefin (Balan)

Benefin is a dinitroanaline compound used to eradicate annual grasses and broad-leaf weeds in established lawns.

Bensulide (Betasan, Prefar)

An organophosphate that is effective as a preemergence herbicide against germinating grassy and broad-leaf weeds in established lawns, bensulide is not translocated, hence has no effect if sprayed on foliage.

Bromoxynil (Brominal)

Bromoxynil is a substituted nitrile widely used as a nonselective control for weed growth in driveways and paths as well as in industrial sites and vacant lots. It is a fast-acting growth inhibitor.

Dalapon (Dowpon)

Dalapon is an aliphatic acid that attenuates growth and is much used to control perennial weed grasses, especially Johnsongrass and Bermuda grass. It is also effective on cattail, great reed, and rushes.

DCPA (Dacthal)

An arylaliphatic acid, DCPA is used primarily as a preemergence herbicide to control crab grass, annual foxtail grasses, and annual panic grasses, as well as perennial witch grass. It also controls such annual lawn weeds as common chickweed, carpetweed, and purslane. It should not be used in areas with thin, sandy soils as it is water soluble and can pollute groundwater.

Dicamba (Banvel, Tricornox)

Used for both preemergence and postemergence control of broad-leaf weeds, dicamba is translocated through the plant from point of absorption (root or leaf) and lethally accelerates growth. It persists in most soils no more than two weeks, although in cold, heavy clays it may linger for a month or more before being broken down to to a benign state.

Dichlobenil (Casoton)

One of the substituted nitriles, dichlobenil is fast acting in inhibiting growth in a wide range of broad-leaf annual weeds and is especially favored in orchards and nurseries.

Diphenamid (Dymid, Enide)

Diphenamid is substituted amide preemergence weed control that is effective against both grassy and broad-leaf seedlings. It is tolerated by most older vegetation. It persists in the soil for 3 to 12 months.

EPTC (Eptam)

While some carbamates are insecticidal and others are fungicidal (see Chapter 34), EPTC is a physiologically active carbamate compound used mainly to control nut grass in and around woody ornamentals.

Fluazifop-butyl (Fusilade, Grass-B-Gone, Over-the-Top Grass Killer)

Fluazifop-butyl is a butyl phenoxyl propinoate selective herbicide that acts as a systemic herbicide and is used primarily to control grasses. It should not be used in areas with thin, sandy soils as it is very water soluble and can pollute groundwater.

Glyphosate (Clean-up, Round-up)

A potent organophosphate herbicide, glyphosate is nonselective and controls not only a wide range of annual and perennial weeds, both grassy and broad-leaf, but also many woody weeds, including poison ivy and poison oak. It is translocated throughout any target plant when sprayed on young full-size foliage and does not escape into the soil. If applied to soil, it soon degrades to a benign state. Nevertheless, literature reports of eye and skin irritation, dizziness, and digestive upset sustained by agricultural workers handling large quantities of various herbicidal preparations containing glyphosate, incomplete studies on the nature and extent of glyphosate residues in various soils, and the constant possibility of glyphosate-resistant mutant weeds appearing in response to heavy, repeated application of products containing this herbicide argue for cautious, conservative use.

Herbicidal Soap (Sharpshooter)

Consisting of various potassium salts of fatty acids, herbicidal soaps are contact herbicides that are nonselective in action and are used in target spraying weeds around shrubs and in vegetable gardens, where accidental contact with desirable plants can be minimized. Several weedy grasses (such as quack grass) are relatively unaffected.

Oryzalin (Surflan, Dirimal)

A dinitroanaline herbicide, oryzalin is used to control grassy weeds. If watered in before germination, it acts as a preemergent.

Pendamethalin (Prowl)

Another dinitroanaline, pendamethalin is used mainly to control crab grass, barnyard grass, foxtail grasses, and other grassy weeds.

Siduron (Tupersan)

Siduron is a substituted urea preemergence herbicide that is used primarily in the establishment of lawns, where it controls the germination of such annual grassy weeds as crab grass, barnyard grass, and foxtail grass.

Simazine (Princep)

A nonselective triazine herbicide, simazine is used primarily to eliminate weeds from patios, walks, driveways, and other places where vegetation is unwanted.

Trifluralin (Treflan)

Trifluralin is another of the several dinitroanaline herbicides and is used for preemergence control of a wide range of weeds. It is absorbed through rootlets as seeds germinate and inhibits cell division, thus halting growth. Treflan should be used with care, especially in gardens, as it persists in the soil for several months before fully decomposing.

2,4-Dichlorophenoxyacetic (2,4-D)

A phenoxyacetic derivative and the first of the organic herbicides (introduced in 1944), 2,4-D is absorbed and translocated throughout a sprayed plant. It accelerates cell division and overstimulates plant growth to a lethal degree. Like its related compounds 2,4,5-T and Silvex (both now banned in the United States), 2,4-D is used worldwide to control broadleaf vegetation, including woody species, but is relatively ineffective against grasses. Contrary to earlier belief, it is long persistent in the soil, hence should be used with great care.

SUMMARY OF WEED CONTROL IN LAWNS, FLOWER AND VEGETABLE GARDENS, AND SHRUB PLANTINGS

Where feasible, mechanical control is preferable to use of herbicides.

Type of Control	Herbicide	Application
LAWNS		
Nonselective control to clear a future lawn of all weedy vegetation	Glyphosate	Apply in the spring and summer during active weed growth; weed grasses should be moistened before spray is applied
Seedling turf to control broad-leaf weeds	Bromoxynil	Apply after turf grasses have appeared but before broad-leaf weeds have reached three- or four-leaf stage
Young bluegrass and fescue turf		
For preemergence control of		
Barnyard grass, crab grass, and foxtail grass	Benefin, bensulide, oxadizon, or siduron	Apply before crab grass appears
Goosegrass	Bensulide or oxadiazon	Seldom provides more than 75 percent control
For postemergence control of		
Crab grass	Fenoxaprop-ethyl	Apply just as crab grass germinates
Nut grass or nut sedge	Bentazon	Drench foliage; delay mowing for three to five days; reapply in two weeks if needed

Type of Control	Herbicide	Application
Young Bermuda grass turf		
For preemergence control of		
Annual bluegrass (fall germinating)	Benefin, bensulide, dacthal, or trifluralin	Apply in the fall before germination of bluegrass; water after application; do not use if winter lawn is to be planted
Annual grasses (spring germinating, including crab grass)	Benefin, bensulide, dacthal, trigluralin, or siduron	Apply before germination; water after application
Annual broad-leaf weeds (including spurge)	Dacthal	Apply before weeds germinate; water after application; make second application in midsummer if needed
For postemergence control of		
Crab grass seedlings	Fenoxaprop-ethyl	Apply in late spring or early summer; repeat if needed
Established perennial weeds (including nut grass and nut sedge)	Glyphosate	Apply to individuals as a spot treatment; repeat in eight weeks if needed
Annual weed (including spurge)	Bromoxynil	Apply with detergent when weeds are small; repeat if needed; may cause temporary yellowing of nearby Bermuda grass
Established turf		
For preemergence control of		
Crab grass	Benefin, besulide, oxadizon, or siduron	Apply before germination; water after application
For postemergence control of		
Chickweed, dandelion, onion grass, plantain, and red clover	2,4-D spray or granules	Repeat if necessary
Established Diachondra turf		
For postemergence control of		
Grassy and broad-leaf weeds	Diphenamid	Apply to soil in the spring and fall; water thoroughly
GARDENS (FLOWERS AND VEGETABLES)		
For control of biennial and perennial weeds	None recommended	Cut off tops of weeds with a scuffle hoe or pruner; use black plastic mulch covered with straw, wood chips, or other particle material
For control of annual weeds	None recommended	Use mechanical methods such as scuffle hoeing, hand weeding, and mulching
ORNAMENTAL SHRUBS		
For control of annual broad-leaf and grassy weeds	Diquat	Use spray if scuffle hoeing and mulch do not work or area is too large. Spray on weed foliage
For control of perennial broad-leaf and grassy weeds	Dacthal, glyphosate, or trifluralin	Use spray if scuffle hoeing and mulch do not work or area is too large. Apply on soil before weed seeds germinate. Spray on young, full size weed foliage. Spread granules on soil, then water.
For control of Bermuda grass	Dalapon or dichlobenil	Spray on foliage
For control of nut grass or nut sedge	Eptam	Spray on foliage

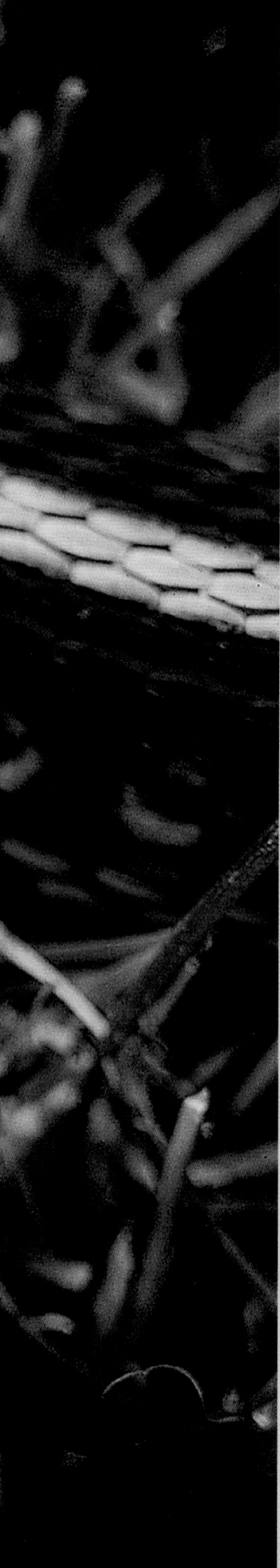

34

Plant Pests and Diseases

In the broadest sense, a plant pest is any organism that causes harm to a valued plant. In ordinary gardeners' parlance, however, the term is restricted to animals and insects—and does not include pathogens (such as the fungi, bacteria, and viruses) that cause plant diseases, or weeds, which are unwanted plant competitors.

The control of pests and diseases in gardens has become a controversial, emotion-laden subject in recent decades. The word *chemical* has become negatively charged because of the

The garter snake, a frequent garden visitor in summer in many areas, should be welcomed as a predator of many harmful insects.

widespread, heavy, and often ritual use of biocides (collectively, all insecticides, fungicides, bactericides, and other agents intended to kill pests and diseases) that, while often effective in achieving the intended results, have in many cases had unanticipated negative impacts on the environment.

The use of biocides, especially the synthetic organic compounds, has been made possible by the great surge forward in biochemistry that began just before World War II. The problem has been a lack of information and appreciation that such synthetic compounds are artificial and have no counterparts in nature and, more important, no natural enzymes to break them down to simpler, benign substances. Hence we have seen the long-term persistence of many of these biocides and their deleterious effects on unintended target species. Moreover, it was not anticipated how very quickly insect pests could adapt to some of these toxic compounds by evolving resistant mutant forms.

Great strides have been made in developing new biocides or "chemicals" for garden use with concern for their environmental impact, both immediate and long term. The very fact that DDT, chlordane, and a host of other materials have been banned from use, and that certain other toxic products may be used only by a trained and licensed pesticide applicator, are evidence of progress. Even so, the ideal in gardening, the paradigm to which all gardeners should subscribe, is to garden without resort to biocides. If a control agent is needed as a fallback, after all else has failed, the biocide should be specific in effect and should rapidly degrade to a benign state.

To minimize recourse to biocides, it is necessary to give priority to growing plant species and cultivars known to be resistant or immune to disease and unattractive to pests. All plants are pest and disease resistant to some degree in their native ranges, but most of our garden plants are exotics, having evolved in other ecosystems that are quite unlike that in the home garden. Others, such as most vegetables and fruits, lawn grasses, roses, and many other popular garden flowers are the creations of plant breeders and do not exist in nature at all. Such displaced or artificially developed plants are often besieged by pests and diseases with which they have had no evolutionary history, hence they lack the natural defenses that wild species have evolved over millions of years in their native habitats. To complicate matters further, people have unwittingly transmitted pest and disease organisms themselves from regions where they exist in balance in the ecosystem and cause little harm, to areas where they were hitherto unknown, where their food-seeking activities can be harmful to plants we value, and where their reproduction and spread proceed unlimited by the natural controls that held them in check in their native provenance.

In a well-documented study, it was shown that the $4 billion spent in 1991 on pesticide controls in the United States may have saved $16 billion in likely crop losses but incurred some $8 billion in evident, codifiable environmental and social costs as well as undetermined costs in damage wrought to wildlife, including birds and other animals, invertebrate organisms, and microbes, and to ground water. The major environmental and public health problems believed to be caused by biocides are at least partly responsible for heightened public concern about pollution attendant to the use of these agents. This awareness has resulted in a research focus on environmentally sound cultural practices, whether in the home garden or on the farm, and on minimizing the use of these control agents.

Today gardeners are exhorted to practice integrated pest management (IPM), including disease and weed management. Not merely a catchy acronym, IPM involves learning the life cycles of pest, disease, and weed species, insofar as possible, and responding to infestations as specifically and benignly as possible. The treatment of weeds is covered in Chapter 33, but the following general principles of IPM apply.

1. Because it usually consists of a concentration of vulnerable plants, the garden is potentially an ideal environment for pests and diseases to attack.

2. To whatever degree possible, the gardener should grow species and cultivars known to be immune or resistant to or tolerant of pests and diseases prevalent in the region.

3. If a particular species or cultivar proves chronically subject to serious attack by a pest or disease, it is better to discontinue its culture and seek a substitute than to attempt control with repeated or heavy applications of biocides.

4. Whatever plants are grown—trees, shrubs, garden flowers, vegetables, fruits, or lawn grasses—should be kept as near peak health as possible, since plants in good condition are far more resistant to attack than those in stress or decline.

5. The gardener should accept the likelihood that some damage by pests and diseases is inevitable but that most of them pass quickly without treatment or do insignificant harm.

6. Where corrective measures are necessary, the gardener should give priority to those that disrupt feeding, growth, or reproduction of causative organisms rather than resort to wholesale annihilation by toxins.

7. When controls are used, they should be applied to specific plants at critical periods in the offending organism's life cycle and never applied ritually to all garden subjects.

As is pointed out in Chapter 31 on soils, good garden soil is the foundation for maximum freedom from pests and diseases. A fairly open or light texture (receptive of air and water),

Mating praying mantises reveal a striking size difference. The impregnated female consumes her diminutive mate. Later, she dies after depositing eggs. Both prey on various insects.

with substantial organic matter (for water retention and nutrient release), and a pH between 5.5 and 7.0 (promoting maximum availability of soil nutrients) are basic requirements for productive garden soil, one that will promote full development of the greatest diversity of garden plants.

Also important is making the fullest possible use of natural and biological controls. Natural controls include abiotic, or nonliving, factors such as weather, temperature, moisture, and wind. For example, raindrops, strong wind, and very high or low temperatures affect the populations of many harmful insects. Biotic, or living, controls are better known to gardeners, and include predators, parasites, and the diseases of pest species. Ladybugs, green lacewings, praying mantis, and garter snakes are familiar naturally occurring predators of a wide range of insects, many of them harmful. Biological controls may also be introduced into the garden; for example, it is possible to augment the ladybug and syrphid fly populations in your garden with purchased insects for better control of mites and aphids. To succeed over the long term, biological controls must control simply by reducing numbers in pest populations and not by eliminating them, since the control insects must continue to have enough food to reproduce and maintain their numbers.

As ladybugs or ladybird beetles prey on aphids and other small insect pests, they should be welcomed and, if necessary, their population augmented by purchase.

In addition, cultural and mechanical controls may be employed to limit the depredations of harmful pests. Choice of pest-free plant materials, such as preadapted, pest-resistant species and cultivars, is an important cultural control, as is the selection of healthy, pest- and disease-free nursery stock. Soil testing and thorough preparation of the planting site and, in the vegetable and fruit garden, crop rotation and prompt removal of diseased plants or parts are also important cultural controls. Maintaining adequate soil moisture through watering and the periodic addition of organic matter or commercial fertilizer are also cultural procedures that help prevent infestations and outbreaks.

Mechanical controls are numerous and sometimes very specific in effect. Just as deer and rabbits can be excluded from gardens with wire-mesh fencing, birds from fruit-bearing trees and bushes with netting, and cutworms from cabbage seedlings by plant collars, various other barriers make useful mechanical controls. Floating row covers (i.e., porous, translucent, lightweight, polypropylene plastic sheeting spread over vulnerable seedlings or transplants and weighted) exclude various harmful, highly mobile insects. Sticky compounds applied to trunks and stems impede the ascent and descent of leaf-eating caterpillars. Diatomaceous earth can isolate target plants from slugs and snails.

Reflective foil mulches repel virus-carrying aphids. All are examples of nonliving mechanical barriers.

Other mechanical controls include pressure spraying infected plants with water to fling or crush soft-bodied insects and mites; frequent hand picking or crushing of large insects such as potato beetles, Japanese beetles, and hornworms; using confusion pheromones or sex attractants that exhaust male moths and other insects before mating takes place. Light traps or bug zappers are not recommended, as they attract and kill a wide range of insects, many of which are harmless or even beneficial (such as green lacewings).

USING CHEMICAL CONTROLS IN THE GARDEN

Chemical toxins are the backup biocides that may be employed when biological, mechanical, and other less aggressive controls have proven ineffective and should never be substituted for good cultural procedures or be used as preventives or be applied routinely. Commonly called pesticides, these are toxic agents that kill insects (insecticides), mites (miticides), slugs and snails (molluscicides), and nematodes (nematicides) as well as disease-causing fungi

In the vegetable garden, floating row covers help protect seedlings from the ravages of flying insects.

Chemical products to control pests and diseases are poisons that should be carefully stored in a cool, dark, dry place beyond the reach of children and pets, preferably under lock and key.

(fungicides) and bacteria (bactericides). They should be stored and used strictly according to their label or package instructions, as many are concentrated and very poisonous.

Some of the oldest pesticides in use are made from inorganic materials, such as Bordeaux mixture, a watery mixture of lime and copper sulfate, and lime sulfur, a solution of sulfur salts; both were used as fungicides in ancient Greece. Other inorganics include sulfur dust and boric acid.

Most pesticides, however, are organic in their chemical nature, i.e., they have the element carbon as a component. Some organic pesticides are made from plant extracts (and therefore are called botanicals) and include, for example, such a well-known preparation as nicotine sulfate, made from nicotine extracted from the tobacco plant (*Nicotiana tabacum*).

These are natural substances that are either harmless to mammals, including humans, or soon break down to a harmless state when exposed to light. Some organic pesticides, especially insecticidal soaps and horticultural oils, are particularly favored because they are selective in action, safe for humans and wildlife, and effective against some pests that are otherwise difficult to control, such as scale insects, spider mites, and aphids. As some plants are adversely affected when actively growing, these soaps and oils are usually applied near the end of winter dormancy. Soaps act quickly by disrupting the cellular functions of target insects and mites and oils by obstructing their breathing pores and by suffocating their eggs. Neither soaps nor oils have any residual effectiveness, and as they kill only those organisms that are actually contacted, they must be applied in a drenching spray.

Microbial controls comprise another class of pesticides. For the most part, these are naturally occurring microorganisms,

the best known of which is the bacterium *Bacillus thuringiensis*, known mostly as Bt and sold in various forms under a variety of trade names. It is used to control harmful caterpillars and leafeating beetles as well as mosquito larvae. Another is *B. popilliae* (Bp), which causes the milky spore disease that affects the Japanese beetle. Although much hailed as panaceas (as DDT was in the 1950s), these bacterial agents should be used with restraint, as repetitive, high-intensity applications will inevitably stimulate resistance in target pests and lead to the development, through genetic mutation, of resistant or immune forms.

Other microbial controls include the protozoon *Nosema locustae*, which debilitates certain grasshoppers, and the parasitic nematodes *Steinernema bibionis* and *Heterorhabditis heliothis*, which control cutworms, crown borers, and root weevils.

The most commonly used pesticides are synthetic organic compounds. These have been formulated in the laboratory, in some cases adapted from naturally occurring compounds, and include such familiar preparations as carbaryl (Sevin), much used to control gypsy moth and other leaf-eating caterpillars; diazinon (Spectracide), used against mites and a wide range of insects; and malathion, which is used to control sucking insects.

Triforine (Funginex) and other systemic fungicides are also in this class, as is the popular systemic herbicide glyphosate (Roundup and Cleanup). In systemics, the active principle is absorbed by the sprayed part of the plant and moved through it to all other parts. Systemic pesticides should be used with great caution, as many are toxic to mammals, including humans, and vary in residual persistence.

Some pesticides are selective—effective in controlling one species or a restricted group of harmful insects—and others are nonselective or broad spectrum—toxic to a wide range of organisms. Generally, selective pesticides are preferable because of their specific, limited effects. Nonselective preparations may be appealing as controls for multiple, simultaneously attacking pests, but they also kill beneficial insects, making their use incompatible with biological control. A number of nonselective, long-persisting pesticides (most notably DDT) have been withdrawn from the U.S. market because of the demonstrable environmental damage they have caused.

Most pesticides, such as Bt, are stomach poisons and must be applied to the plant tissue that the target insect eats in order to take effect. Others, like DDT, are absorbed through the insect's outer surfaces and act as nerve poisons. Still others, such as naphthalene and paradichlorobenzine (PDB), emit gases that are toxic when breathed by the insect. Such fumigants are often used to sterilize soil, but as these can damage or kill desirable plants, this procedure is not recommended.

Cautionary Measures

In view of the fact that nearly all pesticides are poisonous substances that can cause serious injury or harm, the following precautions are germane.

1. The application of pesticides is a serious undertaking and should never be practiced in a casual or frivolous manner.

Bees, important pollinators of most temperate-zone plants, often perish when broad-scale, nonselective pesticides are used over large areas.

2. Pesticides should be carefully chosen for their specificity, effectiveness, and brief period of toxicity; no single pesticide can solve all pest problems; and indeed, relatively few garden problems legitimately call for pesticide use.

3. The label on a pesticide container is not merely a compilation of advisory instructions or hints but is a legal document approved by one or more federal regulatory agencies; misuse of a pesticide is a violation of federal law.

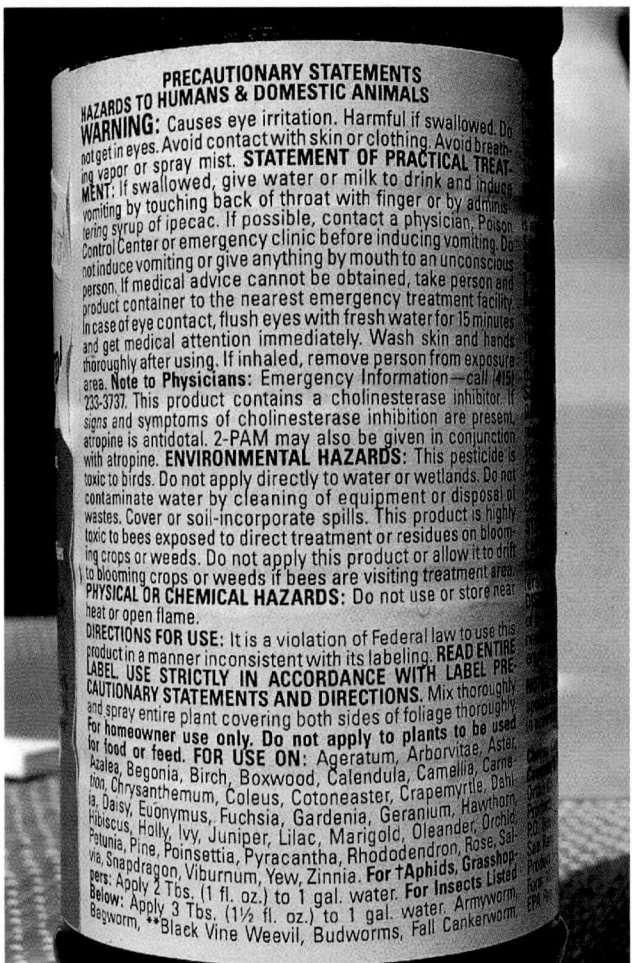

Always read the label on a pesticide container before use, as any harm or injury resulting from inappropriate application is legally the user's responsibility.

4. Failure to read and understand label instructions can lead to unnecessary and avoidable problems, among them:
   - Personal illness or injury, sometimes not immediately apparent, as by toxic residues on fruits and vegetables.
   - Injury or even death of wildlife, pets, or other people.
   - Damage or death of unintended target plants.
   - Lawsuits by persons accidentally affected by toxic sprays.

5. The all-too-common practice of using more pesticide or higher concentrations of a mixture than called for on the label is at the least wasteful and at worst the cause of unintended, often harmful results.

6. Personal exposure to pesticides should be minimized by reserving their use for special disorders not responsive to less traumatic methods; by wearing gloves, dust masks, goggles, long pants, long-sleeved shirts, and hats for personal protection, and by being prepared to take emergency action should an accident occur.

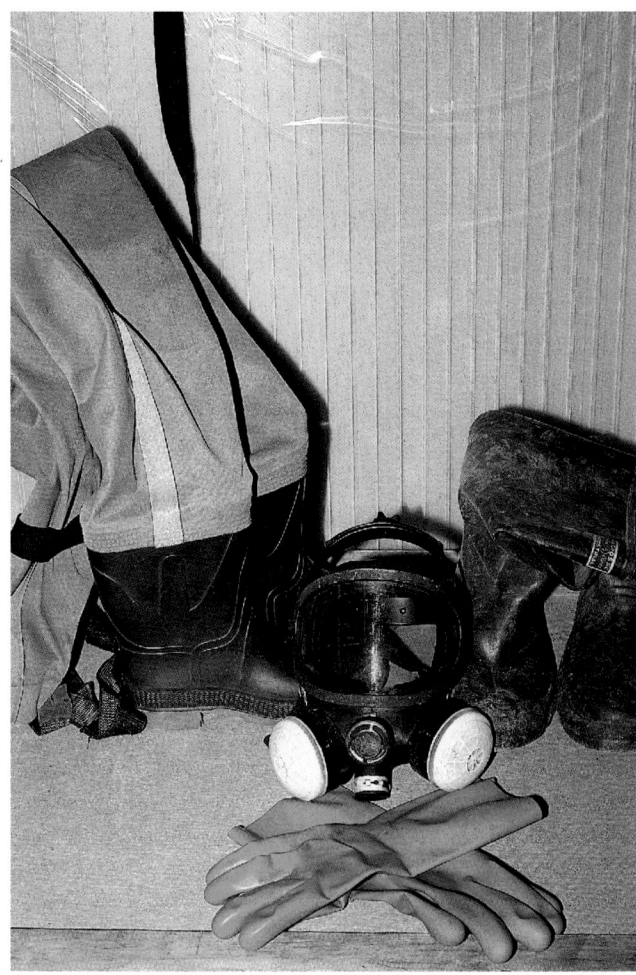

Protective mask, gloves, and boots, required equipment for profes-
sional pesticide applicators, should be donned by any gardener using
these poisonous preparations.

INSECT PESTS IN THE GARDEN

Of the millions of species of insects documented thus far (far more than of all other groups of organisms combined, plant and animal), a relatively small number are garden pests. It is generally little known or appreciated that a far larger number of insect species are directly and indirectly beneficial and quietly carry out valuable environmental services almost unnoticed, such as pollinating flowers and furnishing food to a great array of animals, to say nothing of the aesthetic interest provided by a butterfly or a hawk moth or a katydid. Still, it is true that some insects feed on plants that we value and, when their feeding does damage, we consider them pests.

The best we can and should hope for in our gardens is to keep insect pests under control, and this can be done only by prompt and concerted effort. To care intelligently for our gardens, it is necessary to know something of the life histories and feeding habits of common garden pests and the measures available to control them without harming the plants or other creatures.

Insects begin life from a single cell known as the egg. In most cases the eggs are fertilized by the male and are then deposited in some suitable place by the adult female. In some cases, however, unfertilized eggs develop into living young without mating having occurred. This remarkable phenomenon is known as parthenogenesis, and the most common example is the aphid. Throughout the summer months multitudinous generations (as many as 100) of aphids are produced, consisting entirely of females that have developed from unfertilized eggs. In the autumn, males suddenly appear, and the eggs that are to carry the species over the winter are fertilized.

Most insect eggs are very small. Depending on the species, the number of eggs laid by one female varies from one to as many as one million, with the average probably about a hundred. In some species, the eggs are laid all at one time, while in others they are deposited in successive batches. Instinctively, the female lays her eggs where the young will find suitable food in the quantity and of the quality needed. After the eggs have been laid, the mother's responsibility usually has come to an end (often, she dies in the process). In any case, and with few exceptions, the newly hatched insects are entirely on their own. Except for eggs laid in the fall to winter over, the time each developing insect spends in the egg is usually about two weeks. The life cycle of most insect species is completed within a growing season. Exceptions include ants, honeybees, and wireworms, which live longer than a year, and at the other extreme, some aphids live only a few days and some flies go through their life cycle in a matter of weeks.

In studying the life histories of insects, we find that they are grouped into three classes: those that do not experience a metamorphosis, or sudden major change in appearance and habits; those that undergo a gradual metamorphosis; and those that have a complete, or complex, metamorphosis.

Those insects that do not undergo a metamorphosis constitute a relatively small group, and include such species as spring tails and fish moths that are of little or no importance to the gardener. When the young of these species are hatched, they are perfectly formed and resemble the adults in every respect except size.

In the second group, those having a simple or gradual metamorphosis, we find many of our old acquaintances, such as grasshoppers, squash bugs, the scale insects, and the aphids. In the case of many species in this group, the newly hatched young are very similar to the adults except for the absence of wings. In some species, however, the difference is more noticeable. The immature insects in this group are called nymphs. In general, nymphs have the same feeding

After passing through egg, caterpillar, and pupa stages, an adult butterfly feeds on nectar in the tubular flowers of Mina lobata, *a morning glory relative.*

habits as their parents and are often found together with their parents. They grow in stages, during which their wings develop and they become more and more like the adults.

We find the largest number of insect species in the last group, those that pass through a complete metamorphosis, having four distinct life stages: the egg stage, the larva stage, the pupa stage, and the adult stage. In most cases the newly hatched young in no way resemble the adults and have totally different habits. The immature insect in this class is known as a larva. When the larvae become full grown, they pass into the pupa or chrysalis stage, and later the adult form emerges. All growth is made in the larva stage. No growth ever occurs in the adult stage. Little beetles never grow into big beetles, nor do little butterflies grow into big butterflies.

Growth takes place in a series of molts. An entirely new skin is created within the old skin. When this is ready, a fluid known as the molting fluid is poured forth by certain specialized cells in the body. This cracks and loosens the outer skin, enabling the insect to crawl forth. Ordinarily, four or five (exceptionally 20) molts occur before the nymphs or larvae become full-grown adult insects. In the case of a nymph, the final molt results in a fully developed adult, whereas in the case of a larva the final molt carries the insect into the pupa stage.

The pupa stage is one of the most important in the life of an insect, for it is during this period that it undergoes the wonderful transformation from an often sluggish larva, such as a grub, maggot, or caterpillar, into an alert, highly developed adult—a bee, a moth, a beetle, a fly, according to the species. Larvae generally are instinctively assiduous in seeking a suitable, protected site to pupate, as under bark scales, in debris of some kind, or in long grass blades, or may wrap themselves within a leaf or bury themselves in the ground. In most species, the pupa becomes hard and forms a waterproof and usually airtight case. In some species, the larva spins a cocoon for the protection of the pupa, and in other species it constructs intricate little chambers within the soil. The period of pupation varies greatly. Many species pass the winter in the pupa stage, while others spend only a few days within the pupa case. As insects are such a large, diverse, ubiquitous, and rapidly evolving group, it is not surprising that they exhibit wide variation in life cycles.

From the vantage of feeding habits, insects are grouped into two distinct classes: those with chewing mouth parts and those with sucking mouth parts. In the first group are caterpillars, beetles, grubs, and grasshoppers, among others. These feed largely on the foliage of growing plants; others, such as grubs, feed on roots; and borers invade stems and tubers, both woody and soft. In this group of insects are some of the garden's most formidable enemies: the aster beetle, the iris borer, the rose beetle, the Japanese beetle, the yellow woolly bear caterpillar, the cabbage looper, and many others. The insects in this group chew and swallow solid plant tissues and they may, with very few exceptions, be controlled by the use of stomach poisons.

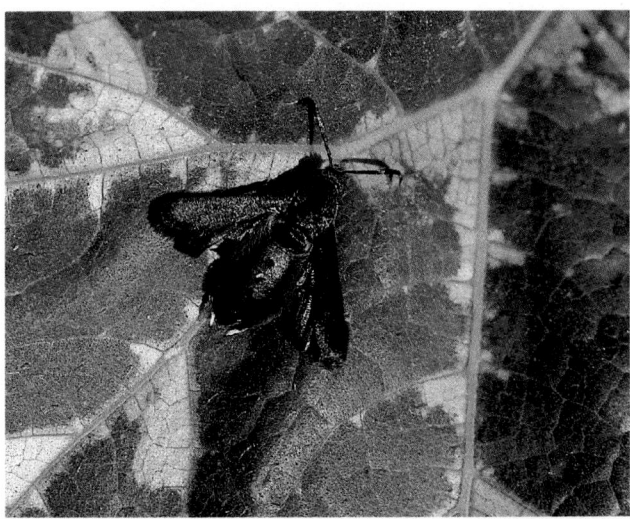

Adult moth of a squash vine borer.

sorts: red spider mites, which appear as reddish specks and attack the leaves of various plants, often causing premature leaf drop; tarsonomid mites, with glistening tan or white bodies, which attack strawberries, narcissus, and amaryllis (*Hippeastrum*), as well as many other greenhouse and houseplants; and gall mites, which invade the buds of the black currant and cause disfiguring but relatively harmless swellings on leaves or stems (e.g., witches-brooms) of various other shrubs and trees.

Mycoplasmas are microorganisms, related to bacteria, that are carried by leafhoppers and invade plant tissues through wounds made by these sucking insects, causing yellows (a general yellowing and the eventual death of the entire plant) in various vegetables, as well as in China aster and other garden flowers.

Nematodes or eelworms are tiny wormlike animals, some of which which invade the roots of tomatoes and potatoes as well as spring bulbs and the leaves of various ornamentals, while others transmit viruses to a number of vegetables, fruits, and ornamentals.

Slugs and snails are soft-bodied molluscs that glide on secreted mucus, mostly in the dark and especially in damp places. Various species attack a wide range of vegetables and flowers, grinding the plant tissue with a filelike tongue, or radula.

PESTS AND DISEASES OF VEGETABLES, FRUITS, AND NUTS

Nearly all commonly grown vegetables are subject to a multiplicity of pests, in large part because we usually grow our crops in exclusion in gardens where they are well nourished, offering pest organisms convenient access to a diversity and substantial supply of appealing nutrients. Since many vegetables have abnormally large roots, stems, leaves, or fruits—the parts we eat—they are even more subject to pest attack. Although most pests of vegetable gardens occur widely throughout the United States, some are restricted to certain hardiness zones. Moreover, their populations often rise and fall from year to year, resulting in varied, uneven, unpredictable occurrence in your garden. For example, bean beetles may ravage that crop one year, then scarcely appear for several years thereafter, but, in the interim, tomato hornworm or cabbage looper may be temporarily prevalent. As with most questions on garden pathology, your cooperative extension agent can advise you of likely pests in your area and the most efficacious, environmentally responsible preventive and corrective measures to take.

Diseases of vegetables occur variably for the same reasons, but are often very host specific and occur at particular times of year under certain conditions. Much progress has

A swallowtail butterfly on sweet William heightens garden interest as it moves from flower to flower, harmlessly sucking sugary nectar and inadvertently pollinating the blooms.

In the second group, those insects having sucking mouth parts, we find such familiar enemies as the aphids, the various scale insects, and the leafhoppers. Instead of being equipped with jaws with which they can cut and chew their food, these insects have delicate tubelike mouth parts with which they are able to pierce through the outer layer of plant tissue and suck the juices within. These long, needlelike beaks are usually jointed and they may point forward, upward, or downward. When not in use they are generally laid back on the breast between the front legs. It is not possible to control the insects in this group by coating the outer surface of the plant with poison dusts or sprays, as they are able to pierce through the poisoned layer and can then draw their nourishment from the plant quite unharmed. It has been found, however, that these sucking insects can be controlled by contact poisons—poisons that come into contact with the body and are absorbed.

Beside insects, several other biological groups include garden pests. Mites, tiny animals related to spiders, with four pairs of legs and sucking mouth parts, are of three principal been made in horticultural research to breed vegetable cultivars that are resistant to common, serious diseases. In general, it is prudent to favor resistant cultivars over those subject to diseases known to be chronic problems in your area. Here, too, the local cooperative extension station can help. Cultural practices, such as crop rotation, influence the frequency and intensity of attack by certain disease organisms.

Vegetables relatively free of serious pests and diseases in most regions of the United States include asparagus, beets, carrots, Jerusalem artichoke, kale, kohlrabi, leek, lettuce, okra, onions, parsley, peas (especially edible pod), radish, rhubarb, spinach, and Swiss chard. Those that are frequently attacked, with crop reduction a consequence, include cucumbers, melons, peppers, squash, sweet corn, tomatoes, and watermelons. With these vegetables, it is particularly important to choose disease-resistant cultivars known to grow well in your region, adopt preventive measures, and be watchful for attack symptoms.

Much the same is true for fruits, except that in tree and bush fruits relatively little research has been devoted to pest and disease resistance. Strawberry breeding, however, has focused on disease resistance. Before deciding on which fruit crops to plant—whether you have in mind a a few trees or bushes, or a sizable bed or orchard—it is best to consult your local cooperative extension station for a review of locally prevalent pests and diseases of these crops and of the environmentally acceptable preventive and remedial measures necessary to control them.

This also applies to nuts, especially almonds, chestnuts, filberts, peanuts, pecans, and walnuts.

COMMON PESTS AND DISEASES OF VEGETABLES, FRUITS, AND NUTS

Crop	Pests	Diseases
COMMONLY GROWN VEGETABLES		
Asparagus	Asparagus beetle	Rust
Beans (all except fava bean)	Mexican bean beetle	Anthracnose, bacterial blight, mildews, rust, virus mosaic
Beets	Aphids, flea beetles, leaf miners, webworms	Leaf spot (caused by *Cercospora*), others according to region (consult your cooperative extension agent)
Broccoli	Aphids, black flea beetles, caterpillars (including cutworms, loopers), harlequin bugs, root maggots	Bacterial black rot, clubroot, tip burn, yellows
Brussels sprouts	Same as for broccoli	Same as for broccoli
Cabbage	Same as for broccoli	Same as for broccoli
Carrot	Caterpillars, carrot rust fly; deer, rabbits	Carrot yellows, leaf blight, others according to region (consult your cooperative extension agent)
Cauliflower	Same as for broccoli	Same as for broccoli
Celery	Carrot rust fly, celery worm, tarnished plant bug	Blackheart, early blight, late blight, leaf spot
Chinese cabbage	Same as for broccoli	Same as for broccoli
Corn, sweet	Corn ear worm (same as tomato fruit worm), European corn borer, southern corn root worm (larva of spotted cucumber beetle)	Bacterial wilt (Stewart's disease), corn smut
Cucumber	Aphids, borers, spider mites, spotted cucumber beetle, striped cucumber beetle	Angular leaf spot, anthracnose, bacterial wilt, downy mildew, mosaic, powdery mildew, scab
Eggplant	Aphids, caterpillars, Colorado potato beetle, flea beetles	Fruit blight, leaf blight, verticillium wilt
Lettuce	Cutworms, rabbits, slugs, snails	Tip burn, yellows
Onion	Onion maggot	Downy mildew, smut, others according to region (consult your cooperative extension agent)
Peas	Aphids, birds	Powdery mildew, root rot, wilt

Crop	Pests	Diseases
Peppers	Aphids, cutworms, flea beetles, leaf miner, pepper maggot, pepper weevil, stem borers	Anthracnose, bacterial leaf spot; blight (caused by *Phytophthera*), blossom-end rot, fungal leaf spot, ripe rot, sun scald, tobacco mosaic
Potato	Colorado potato beetle, potato aphid, potato flea beetle, white grubs, wireworms	Black leg, fusarium wilt, late blight (caused by *Phytophthera*), rhizoctonia, scab
Radish	Birds, cabbage root maggot, flea beetles, plant lice	White rust
Rhubarb	Rhubarb curculio	Foot rot
Spinach	Aphids, flea beetles, leaf miner	Leaf spot
Squash	Aphids, borers, squash bug, striped cucumber beetle	Bacterial wilt, leaf mosaic, powdery mildew
Swiss chard	Same as for beets	Same as for beets
Tomato	Aphids, Colorado potato beetle, cutworms, flea beetles, nematodes, red spider mites, tomato fruit worm (same as corn ear worm), tomato hornworm	Alternaria blight, alternaria stem canker, anthracnose, blossom-end rot, fusarium wilt, grayleaf spot, tobacco mosaic, verticilum wilt

LESS COMMONLY GROWN VEGETABLES

Crop	Pests	Diseases
Amaranth	Black flea beetle	Clubroot, leaf spot
Artichoke, Chinese	None serious	None serious
Artichoke, globe	Aphids, caterpillars	Gray mildew, leaf spot, powdery mildew
Artichoke, Jerusalem	Stem borers	None serious
Arugula	Flea beetles, plant lice	None serious
Basella	None serious	None serious
Beetberry	None serious	Leaf spot
Bitter melon	Same as for cucumber	Same as for cucumber
Broccoli raab	Same as for broccoli	Same as for broccoli
Burdock	None serious	None serious
Cantaloupe	Same as for cucumber	Same as for cucumber
Cardoon	Same as for globe artichoke	Same as for globe artichoke
Cauli-broc	Same as for broccoli	Same as for broccoli
Celeriac	Same as for celery	Same as for celery
Celtuce	Same as for lettuce	Same as for lettuce
Chicory	None serious	None serious
Collards	Same as for broccoli	Same as for broccoli
Corn salad	None serious	None serious
Cress, upland	Same as for broccoli	Same as for broccoli
Egyptian onion	Same as for onion	Same as for onion
Fennel	Same as for celery	Same as for celery
Garlic	Same as for onion	Same as for onion
Good King Henry	Same as for beetberry	Same as for beetberry
Horseradish	Horseradish flea beetle	Curly top virus, clubroot
Jelly melon	Same as for cucumber	Same as for cucumber
Kale	Same as for broccoli	Same as for broccoli
Kohlrabi	Same as for broccoli	Same as for broccoli

(continues)

COMMON PESTS AND DISEASES OF VEGETABLES, FRUITS, AND NUTS (*continued*)

Crop	Pests	Diseases
Leek	None serious	None serious
Lettuce, miner's	None serious	None serious
Lovage	Same as for celery	Same as for celery
Melons	Same as for cucumber	Same as for cucumber
Mushrooms	None serious	None serious
Mustard	Flea beetles, plant lice	Yellows
Okra	None serious	Fusarium wilt, yellows
Parsley	Celery worm, parsley caterpillar (larva of swallowtail butterfly), parsley-stalk weevil	None serious
Parsnip	Carrot rust fly, celery worm, parsnip webworm, parsley caterpillar	Celery blight, leaf spot
Poke	None serious	None serious
Popcorn	Same as for sweet corn	Same as for sweet corn
Pumpkin	Same as for squash	Same as for squash
Quinoa	Same as for beetberry	Same as for beetberry
Rutabaga	Flea beetles, root maggot, turnip aphid	Black rot, clubroot
Salsify	None serious	None serious
Sea kale	None serious	None serious
Shallot	Same as for onion	Same as for onion
Skirret	Same as for parsley	Same as for parsley
Sorghum	None serious	None serious
Sorrel	None serious	None serious
Soybean	Same as for beans	Same as for beans
Spinach, mountain	None serious	None serious
Spinach, New Zealand	None serious	None serious
Sunflower	Same as for Jerusalem artichoke	Same as for Jerusalem artichoke
Sweet potato	Aphids, blister beetle, leafhoppers, sweet potato weevil, tortoise beetle	Black rot, foot rot, fusarium stem rot, scurf, soft rot (in storage), Texas root rot, others according to region (consult your cooperative extension agent)
Tomatillo	Same as for tomato	Same as for tomato
Turnip	Same as for rutabaga	Same as for rutabaga
Watermelon	Same as for cucumber, especially aphids	Anthracnose, blossom-end rot, ground rot, stem-end rot

COMMONLY GROWN TREE FRUITS

Apples	See page 690 (consult your cooperative extension agent)	See page 690 (consult your cooperative extension agent)
Cherries	See page 691 (consult your cooperative extension agent)	See page 691 (consult your cooperative extension agent)
Crab apples	Same as for apple	Same as for apple
Nectarines	Same as for peaches	Same as for peaches
Peaches	See page 693 (consult your cooperative extension agent)	See page 693 (consult your cooperative extension agent)
Pears	See page 695 (consult your cooperative extension agent)	See page 695 (consult your cooperative extension agent)
Plums	See page 696 (consult your cooperative extension agent)	See page 696 (consult your cooperative extension agent)

Crop	Pests	Diseases
LESS COMMONLY GROWN TREE FRUITS		
Apricot	Same as for peaches	Same as for peaches
Fig	Nematodes, scale, rust mites	Anthracnose, leaf spot, rust, fruit rot
Kaki plum, Japanese persimmon	None serious	None serious
Mulberry	Birds, scale, whitefly	Bacterial blight
Papaw	None serious	None serious
Quince	Same as for pears	Same as for pears
Serviceberry	Birds, otherwise none serious	None serious
Wild tree cherries	Birds, tent caterpillar, otherwise same as for cherries	Same as for cherries
COMMONLY GROWN BUSH FRUITS		
Blackberries	Aphids, beetles, borers, caterpillars, scale, spittle bugs, weevils, white flies	Anthracnose, crown gall, mosaic, wilt
Blueberries	Birds, flea beetles, fruit fly maggot, leaf rollers, spittle bugs, squirrels, thrips	Mildews, rose bloom disease, rust
Currants	Currant aphid, currant borer, currant worm, four-lined plant bug	Anthracnose, cane blight, white pine blister rust
Gooseberries	Borers, currant aphids	Gooseberry mildew
Raspberries	Same as for blackberries	Same as for blackberries
LESS COMMONLY GROWN BUSH FRUIT		
Beach plum	Same as for plums	Same as for plums
Elderberry	Birds, blue beetle borers	None serious
Jostaberry	Same as for currants	Same as for currants
Prickly pear	Birds, maggots, worms	None serious
Rugosa rose	None serious	None serious
Sand cherries	Same as for cherries	Same as for cherries
Shrubby chokecherry	Same as for cherries	Same as for cherries
Wonderberry	Leaf-eating insects	None serious
PERENNIAL AND ANNUAL FRUIT		
Strawberry	Aphids, birds, beetle grubs, mites, nematodes, strawberry weevil, strawberry crown borer	Black rot, botrytis or gray mold, red stele disease, verticillium blight
NUTS		
Almond	Same as for peaches	Same as for peaches
Chestnut	Weevils	Chestnut blight (especially American chestnut), stem canker
Filbert, hazelnut	Caterpillars, crown gall, Japanese leafhopper, scale	Black knot, blight, leaf spot
Peanut	Consult your cooperative extension agent	Consult your cooperative extension agent
Pecan	Aphids, caterpillars, lacebugs, leaf rollers, mites, scale, webworm, weevil	Anthracnose, bunch disease (witches'-broom), canker, leaf blotch, leaf spot
Pistachio	None serious	None serious
Walnut	Same as for pecan	Same as for pecan

Plant Diseases

Plant diseases may be grouped into three general classes: those caused by fungi and bacteria; those caused by viruses, mycoplasmas, and viroids; and those caused by unsuitable environmental conditions.

In the first group we find the majority of the common diseases of garden plants. Disease-causing fungi are minute, usually threadlike in habit, mostly too small to be seen by the naked eye, and differing from familiar plant life by lacking the green pigment known as chlorophyll. Disease fungi are parasites, unable to live except by invading and taking their nourishment from other life forms, in this case our garden plants. Some disease fungi have many different kinds of garden plants as their targets or hosts, while others are specifically parasitic on just one kind. Some are short-lived, in some cases only for a few days, while others persist in woody plants or in the soil for years. Most fungi, at a certain stage in their development, liberate minute, one-celled bodies known as spores. The dustlike spores are readily carried from plant to plant, mostly by wind, the agent that facilitates the spread of fungal disease. When supplied with sufficient moisture at the right temperature on a suitable surface, the spores germinate and, with the correct host at hand to invade, produce new fungi. Since moisture is especially critical to their germination, it is clear why so many fungus diseases are prevalent during and just after wet spells.

Bacteria are even more minute than fungi, and usually exist as colonies or masses of detached cell-like bodies that, when parasitic, collectively consitute an infection. They secrete substances that digest plant tissue, and they absorb the products of this process and excrete other substances, some of which are poisonous to the host. To be spread from host to host, bacteria generally depend on some unparasitized living agent, such as insects or human hands, or on nonliving media, such as garden tools, the splashing of raindrops from leaf to leaf, or the spattering of soil by rain or sprinklers.

Viral infections affect a great range of garden plants. The viruses themselves are ultramiscroscopic and chemically consist of protein and nucleic acid. Although they may be crystalized, viruses replicate, mutate, and otherwise behave like true organisms. The cause of many plant diseases, viruses are spread about in the garden by contaminated pruners and knives, by insects, and by infected seeds and cuttings. Some of the most common symptoms of viral infection are the curling of leaves, the development of irregular mottling or variegation, and excessively branched or bushy growth habit of host plants.

Mycoplasmas seem to be intermediate between bacteria and viruses, both in size and behavior, and are the cause of such disorders as aster yellows and some witches'-brooms or abnormal bunchy branching in certain trees and shrubs.

Viroids are small molecules of infectious ribonucleic acid, each a mere one-fiftieth the size of a virus, that lack a protein coat. Such diseases as chrysanthemum stunt and chrysanthemum chlorosis mottling, formerly thought to be caused by viruses, are in fact caused by viroids.

Finally, in the environmentally caused diseases, we find plants suffering from an inadequacy of soil nutrients, an excess of one or more nutrients, or from excess soil acidity or alkalinity, which, in turn, affects the availability of soil nutrients to the plant. Whatever the cause, the symptoms commonly include retarded, subnormal growth; yellowed foliage; and poorly developed roots. To remedy environmental causes, refer to Chapter 31.

The Garden Medicine Cabinet

Just as it is necessary to have a basic understanding of the life cycles, structure, and behavior of various types of pests and disease organisms, it also wise for the gardener to become familiar with some of the standard biocides used in the garden and to keep a sufficient quantity, correctly stored, for use when needed. A well-located, locked cabinet for such supplies will not only ensure their availability for appropriate use but will also keep these toxic preparations away from children and pets.

Aside from the basic products described below, a selection of which you may wish to have on hand, comparatively little equipment is needed. A 1-gallon container, a 1-quart measure, a set of graduated measuring spoons, a simple sprayer, and a dust gun (all dedicated to biocide use only) are the chief items. The size of the sprayer and duster will be determined by the extent of your garden and the kinds of plants being grown; for a small garden, a 1-quart plastic bottle with a finger pump may suffice, whereas a large garden may require a knapsack sprayer or a two wheeled tank sprayer.

Insecticides and Miticides

To be effective and at the same time appropriate for garden use, insecticides and miticides must meet certain criteria:

They should not repel target pests and cause them to disperse.
They should be fast acting.
They should adhere well to plant surfaces.
Once applied, they should quickly degrade to a benign state and not persist in the environment.
In storage, they should maintain potency.
They should have little or no toxicity for untargeted organisms, such as mammals (including humans), other wildlife, and plants.
If in concentrated form, they should be accompanied by clear instructions and should be easily diluted.

Ongoing research and development in the field of agricultural and horticultural biocides result in the frequent introduction of new products. In general, it is better to keep track of these new preparations, and reports of their intended and unintended impact, by subscribing to one or more reliable gardening periodicals than to rely on promotional literature from producers. The more closely an insecticide or miticide conforms to the basic criteria given above, the more appropriate it is for backup use in the home garden.

As most pesticides and miticides gradually lose their effectiveness in time, they should be dated when purchased and not stored indefinitely. Except for malathion and methoxychlor, which do retain potency indefinitely, the period of effectiveness for the relatively safe compounds discussed later in this chapter ranges from two to four years, and then only if liquids are kept from freezing and dusts and granular preparations are kept dry. Disposal of outdated biocides should be carried out according to your local regulations (check with your cooperative extension agent) and not washed down the sink, buried, or put in the garbage.

Stomach poisons are used as a control for insects with chewing mouth parts, while contact insecticides are used to control sucking insects. To be effective, most contact insecticides must come into direct contact with the body of the insect, as they kill the insect either by clogging up the breathing tubes or by entering the body and causing a chemical reaction within the body tissues. As some contact sprays are effective against certain sucking insects and not effective against others, it is important that the proper spray or dust is selected for use. Some of the newer chemicals are effective as both contact and stomach poisons.

Relatively Safe Insecticides and Miticides

Of the biocides available for the control of harmful insects and mites in home gardens, the following conform most closely to the criteria listed on page 808. This is not to say that these preparations lack poisonous properties or that misuse of them will not be accompanied by harm or damage. If used strictly according to label instructions for severe infestations, they should provide the intended control without risk of personal harm or environmental damage. The trade names of the biocides are listed in parentheses after the generic term.

Bacillus thuringiensis (Dipel, Thuricide, MVP, Bactospeine, M-One, Agritol, Bakthane L-69, Biogard, Biotrol, Larvatrol)

A naturally occurring bacterium effective as a stomach poison in controlling many kinds of caterpillars, *B. thuringiensis* (Bt) is also available in more potent forms that are effective controls for larvae of the Colorado potato beetle and adults of the elmleaf beetle as well as for mosquito larvae. Bt is also effective in controlling cabbage worms, cabbage loopers, tomato hornworms, and corn ear worms.

Bt is sold in four formulations: a wettable powder, a liquid concentrate, a dust, and granules. The formulation and concentration to be used depends on the pest. In general, sprays prepared from the liquid concentrate and mixed with a spreader-sticker (such as liquid dishwashing soap, to promote even distribution and retention of the spray on all plant surfaces) are more effective than dusts. Borers in squash stems and other vine crops can be controlled by injecting a Bt solution into the lower stem. Bt granules are used mostly to control corn ear worm and are sprinkled onto the emerging silks every three or four days for two weeks. Bt should be used with restraint as some pests (such as the caterpillar of the diamondback moth) have already shown resistance, and others will likely follow. It shows no toxicity to mammals, including humans and pets, to wildlife, or to untargeted insects.

Dimethoate (Cygon, DeFend, Rogor)

Safest of the systemic organophosphate synthetic preparations, dimethoate is an effective stomach poison against a wide range of insects and mites that attack ornamentals, vegetables, and some fruits (apples, pears, melons, citrus, etc.). It is particularly effective against leaf miners, scales, and mealy bugs. Label instructions indicate lapse time between application and harvest according to crop. Dimethoate should not be used on Chinese holly (*Ilex cornuta*), including its cultivars and hybrids; on azaleas, hydrangeas, chrysanthemums, or ferns; or on such indoor plants as *Schefflera*, *Brassaia*, *Gloxinia*, or African violet (*Saintpaulia* spp.), as these may be injured.

Dormant Oils or Horticultural Oils

The oils are petroleum-based compounds used in sprays to damage the protective coatings of overwintering insects, cause suffocation, and disrupt or prevent the development of insect eggs. They are considered environmentally safe because they break down within days of application to a benign state. They are particularly effective against aphids, mealy bugs, scales, and mites. Once limited to use on deciduous woody plants while in leafless dormancy, new formulations may be applied to most plants throughout the growing season, even on evergreens, providing the correct dilution is used on sensitive species. Dormant oil sprays have diminishing effectiveness at temperatures lower than 45°F and must be applied so that undersurfaces are as thoroughly covered as the tops. As there is no residual effect, only those insects actually sprayed are killed.

As an alternative to commercially produced oils, the following home preparation is useful, especially for aphids, whiteflies, and spider mites: to 1 cup of vegetable oil add 1 tablespoon of liquid detergent; shake; then add 1 tablespoon of this mixture to 1 cup of water for a spray.

Horticultural Soaps or Insecticidal Soaps (Safer's, Sharpshooter)

Soaps, long-used preparations, contain water-soluble potassium salts that are effective in controlling various small chewing and sucking insect pests of ornamentals, vegetables, and fruits. Although they were at one time uneven in quality and often damaging to a wide range of plants, improvements in manufacture have narrowed the list of sensitive plant species without loss of insecticidal and miticidal effect. Japanese maple (*Acer palmatum*); mountain ash (*Sorbus* spp.); and the young, tender growth of coniferous evergreens should not be sprayed; neither should such garden annuals as coleus, nasturtium, sweet peas, or zinnia. Hard water reduces the effectiveness of these preparations, but calm, cloudy, humid weather increases effectiveness by extending the period that sprayed surfaces remain moist. Horticultural soaps have no effect on mammals (including humans and pets) or wildlife, hence require no lapse time between application and harvest on crops. As with dormant oils, only those insects actually sprayed are killed; hence, to be effective, the spray must thoroughly cover all plant surfaces.

Imidan (Prolate)

Imidan, a wettable powder, has long been used as a stomach poison to control major fruit tree pests and has proved very effective against the gypsy moth. It is less toxic to mammals, including humans, than most other organophosphates and, once applied, quickly breaks down to inert, nontoxic residues. Several days' lapse time between application and harvest is advisable. Imidan is toxic to fish, so should not be sprayed near pools, ponds, or streams.

Malathion (Cythion)

An organophosphate often mixed into combination pesticides, malathion is effective against many chewing insects in addition to aphids and mites that attack ornamentals, vegetables, and fruits. It shows low to moderate toxicity to mammals, and more to birds, but degrades in one or two days to a benign state. Depending on formulation, a brief waiting period between application and harvest may apply to crops; check label instructions. Effectiveness against spider mites is low because of increasingly common resistant strains. A nonsystemic with an unpleasant odor, malathion may injure aspen (*Populus* spp.), viburnum, and some species of juniper, especially if the foliage is young and tender. It can also damage paint finishes.

Methoxychlor

A chlorinated hydrocarbon often combined with malathion, methoxychlor is most frequently used to control the bark beetles that attack the American elm (*Ulmus americana*) and English elm (*U. procera*) and also for control of various pests of fruit trees and vegetables. Although it degrades to a nontoxic state fairly rapidly, it should not be used on vegetables and fruits within three weeks of harvest. Toxicity to mammals (including humans and pets) is very low.

Mexacarbate (Zectran)

Mexacarbate is a synthetic carbamate used as a stomach poison to control scales, mealy bugs, leaf-eating caterpillars, and mites as well as slugs and snails infesting ornamentals. Because of its toxicity and persistance, it is not for use on vegetables or fruits.

Neem Extract (BioNeem, Margosan-O, Neemisis)

Neem extract is a botanical insecticide prepared from the seeds of *Azadirachta indica*, a tree native to India. Its primary active ingredient is azidarachtin, long used pharmaceutically in Asia, especially as an antidecay agent in toothpastes. As an insecticide, neem extract controls such leaf-eating insects as caterpillars, loopers, and leaf beetles as well as aphids, mealy bugs, whiteflies, leafhoppers, and thrips. It disrupts the insects' hormonal balance (thereby interfering with development and molting), suppresses the drive to feed, and repels insects from sprayed surfaces. Toxicity to mammals, including humans and pets, is very low, but neem is toxic to fish, and so should not be sprayed near pools, ponds, or streams. It is not registered for use on vegetables and fruits.

Oxydemetonmethyl (Meta-Systox-R)

Oxydemetonmethyl is a systemic pesticide that can be absorbed through the leaves or roots of the sprayed plant and translocated in the sap in sufficient concentration to kill chewing and sucking insects. It is especially effective against aphids, birch leaf miner, leafhoppers, whiteflies, and pine needle scale as well as certain mites.

Pyrethrins (Nature's Insecticidal Spray, Pyrenone)

Extracted from the flowers of the daisy *Tanacetum cinerariifolium*, grown in east Africa and in Ecuador, pyrethrins are fast-acting contact insecticides against most any target insect and are often combined with other ingredients in aerosol sprays or dusts for use on ornamentals and vegetables and fruits. Because of their very low toxicity to mammals (including humans and pets) and wildlife, they are among the safest insecticides available. Vegetables and fruits sprayed with pyrethrins may be eaten the next day. They break down rapidly in light, and residual toxicity usually lasts no more than one day.

Rotenoids (Rotenone)

Originally used by aboriginal tribes in South America as a fish poison, the rotenoids used in the United States are extracted from the roots of wisterialike climbers (*Lonchocarpus* spp., called *cubé* in Peru). Effective as both a contact and a stomach poison, rotenoids are used to control pests such as caterpillars, beetles, true bugs (of the insect order Hemiptera, with a flattened, usually somewhat triangular body, often green, sometimes emitting an aromatic repellent), cutworms, and army worms as well as aphids, thrips, whiteflies, and spider mites. Sprayed or dusted insects cease feeding immediately and die within one or two days. Because rotenoids quickly degrade to inertness, especially in bright sun and usually within a week, the Environmental Protection Agency has permitted use of rotenoids on a wide range of vegetables and fruits. Initially, they are moderately toxic to mammals, hence the importance of carefully following label instructions as to the lapse time between application and harvest. Because of the acute sensitivy of fish and other aquatic wildlife to these compounds, they should not be used near pools, ponds, or streams.

Ryania, Ryania Dust

Although it has been difficult to obtain, ryania—an alkaloid prepared from the dried, pulverized roots of the tropical American shrub *Ryania speciosa*—is a promising botanical used alone or in combination with other pesticides to control caterpillars, loopers, thrips, aphids, beetles, and other harmful insects on vegetable and fruit crops as well as on ornamentals. Because it is harmless to mammals (including humans) and birds, it is exempt from the usual waiting period between application and harvest. Ryania is relatively slow in its action, initially causing target insects to stop feeding but not killing them for 12 to 24 hours. Depending on light, temperature, and rain, its residue can remain insecticidal for several days. With increased supplies and lower cost, ryania could become an important control agent in the garden.

Sabadilla, Sabadilla Dust

Prepared from the ground seeds of the tropical American plant *Schoenocaulon officinale*, of the lily family, sabadilla acts as both a contact and a stomach poison against such chewing insects as caterpillars, beetles, and true bugs (of the insect order Hemiptera) well as thrips. It is ineffective against aphids and mites. It is used mainly on vegetables, especially squash, cucumbers, melons, potatoes, peanuts, and various leaf crops. Sabadilla loses its effectiveness in bright light (but retains potency if stored in darkness); one day should elapse between application and harvesting. Toxicity to mammals (including humans and pets) is low, but the dust can provoke violent sneezing in some individuals.

Tetradifon (Tedion)

A synthetic organic sulfur preparation, tetradifon is a stomach poison used primarily against mites; it is ineffective against aphids and other insects and does not affect mammals and birds. It is applied on ornamentals, vegetables, and fruits, and is effective against the eggs, young, and adults of all mites. There is no waiting period between application and harvest of crops.

Pesticides and Miticides Not Recommended for Garden Use

The trade names of the biocides are listed in parentheses after the generic term.

Acephate (Isotox, Orthene, Orthonex)

Acephate is an organophosphate used to control aphids, caterpillars, thrips, and other insects on ornamentals but not on crops. Acephate is too toxic and persistent for ordinary garden use.

Carbaryl (Savit, Sevin, Sevinol)

A briefly persisting carbamate (usually one to three days), carbaryl is a stomach poison used to control chewing insects, caterpillars in particular, on most ornamentals, vegetables, and fruits and also on turf grasses. While benign to mammals (including humans and pets) and birds, it is highly toxic to honeybees and earthworms and injurious to such ornamentals as clematis and Virginia creeper.

Diazinon (Knox-Out, Spectricide)

Diazinon is an organophosphate used as a contact and a stomach poison to control soil pests, especially on root vegetables and turf grasses. It is, however, extremely toxic to birds and is persistent for 7 to 10 days after application, thus its use is restricted or prohibited in many localities.

Dicofol (Kelthane)

At one time used as a miticide, dicofol, a chlorinated hydrocarbon preparation, has become suspect because of contamination with the prohibited insecticide DDT during manufacture. Moreover, persistence may extend to 30 days.

Disulfoton (Bug Dart, DiSyston)

Usually sold as a plant stake or in granular form, disulfoton is an extremely toxic organophosphate systemic that slowly dissolves and is absorbed by plant roots. The active principle is translocated to leaves and growth points. It is especially hazardous for mammalian pets (dogs and cats), who may drink poisoned water in receptacles beneath pots.

Endosulfan (Endocide, Thiodan)

Endosulfan is a chlorinated hydrocarbon widely used in agriculture to control chewing insects on aboveground vegetables and ornamentals, but its broad-spectrum activity can kill a wide range of unintended insects. In addition, it is proscribed for use on root crops because residues can concentrate in underground plant organs.

Lime Sulfur
A calcium polysulfide used in controlling mealy bugs, aphids, and mites, lime sulfur can damage plants if used when temperatures exceed 80°F in the 24 hours after application. It also corrodes painted surfaces.

Nicotine Sulfate (Black Leaf 40, Tender Leaf Insect Spray)
A botanical insecticide prepared from the tobacco plant (*Nicotiana tabacum*), nicotine sulfate is used to control sucking insects, such as aphids and spider mites, on most ornamentals (not roses) and also vegetables and fruits, but not within seven days of harvest. It is a nerve poison that quickly paralyses target insects, especially in bright light at high temperatures. When mixed with an alkali, such as soaps, the insecticidal effect intensifies. Although nicotine sulfate, whether alone or in mixtures, quickly breaks down to an inert state, especially in hot, sunny weather, it has been banned for home garden use in some states. Even if permitted in your area (check with the cooperative extension station), nicotine sulfate should be used with great care, as it is toxic to mammals (including humans and pets) and birds; spillage on skin and inhalation of mist should be avoided by use of gloves and masks.

Sulfur
The world's oldest insecticide and miticide (since classical times), sulfur causes injury to too many plants to be useful. Sensitive kinds include squash, cucumbers, melons, and spinach as well as apricot and many kinds of nut trees. Viburnum is also sulfur sensitive. Because some people suffer skin irritation, it may be necessary to wait a day after applying sulfur before returning to the garden.

Trichlorfon (Dylox)
Trichlorfon is a chlorinated organophosphate used to control armyworms, bagworms, webworms, leaf-mining bugs, tarnished plant bugs, and other pests, especially in agriculture. It is injurious, however, to such garden ornamentals as zinnias, hydrangeas, and carnations and is generally too hazardous for use in home gardens.

Garden Fungicides
The purpose of any garden fungicide is to kill disease-causing fungi or to prevent their growth. Although bacteria are biologically distinct, the plant diseases they cause and the controls for them are usually treated with those of fungi. The best fungicides to use in the garden are those with a rapid, specific effect that have little or no deleterious effect on the host plants and that do not linger in the environment. Hundreds of commercially prepared fungicides (and a lesser number of bactericides) are on the market, some offered under varying trade names, with new formulations announced each year while others are quietly withdrawn— all contributing to a confusing situation for the gardener. As with pesticides, the use of fungicides should be conservative, and any preparation should be administered strictly according to label directions. Fungicides are poisons and should be accorded appropriate cautions in handling, preparation, and use. As with pests, the best response to chronic disease in most kinds of garden plants is to cease growing them and to substitute other species and cultivars, preferably those known to be resistant or immune.

With fungicides, the timing and mode of application are critical to achieving the desired result. Control of many plant diseases, such as various rusts and the black spot disease of hybrid roses, depends on preventing the fungal spores from germinating and the parasitic threads from penetrating plant tissues rather than attempting to garner control after symptoms appear. Thus preventive applications may be necessary in cases involving the almost certain affliction of certain plants by ubiquitous diseases. Such preventive steps, however, should never be ritually applied to other plants, as this not only is wasteful and contrary to the principles of biological control and integrated pest (and disease) management but can cause harm to affected plants. Moreover, it is often advisable to alternate or rotate fungicides that must be used frequently, as in controlling black spot on roses, as a way of discouraging the mutation of disease fungi into resistant forms.

As no one fungicide will prevent or control all plant diseases, the gardener should gain familiarity with at least the principal ones by generic name and the diseases against which they are differentially effective in order to intelligently select any that may be needed. Fungicides should not be combined by the gardener without expert advice, as the chemical compounds may not be compatible and can lead to unwanted results, ranging from no control of the disease fungi to death of the sprayed plants.

Principal Fungicides for Garden Use
Although most fungicides are toxic primarily to targeted fungi, it is advisable to wash all vegetables and fruits to remove any fungicide residue before use. The trade name appears in parentheses following the generic term.

Anilazine (Dyrene)
Anilazine is a triazine compound that has marked fungicidal action (other triazines are used primarily as herbicides). It is widely used commercially to control leaf spot on potato and

tomato as well as various lawn diseases. As anilazine is non-systemic in action, tomatoes or other crops that have been treated may be simply washed clean of any residue before use.

Benomyl (Benlate, Dupont Systemic Fungicide, Lignasan, Miller's Systemic Fungicide)

One of the benzimidazoles, benomyl is a systemic fungicide that controls a wide spectrum of diseases, including powdery mildews, scabs, leaf spots, blotches, blights, and rots. It is variously applied to and absorbed by leaves, fruits, roots, and seeds of a wide range of ornamentals, vegetables, and fruits. Although initially used only on commercial crops, benomyl and other systemic fungicides, under an increasing number of trade names, have become available for home garden use. Of these, triforine (Funginex) is especially valued for control of black spot in roses and is more reliably effective if applications are alternated with ferbam, folpot, or maneb. Oxycarboxin (Plantvax, VitaVax) is effective against cedar-apple rust and hawthorn rust. No lapse time is required between application and harvest of treated crops.

Bordeaux Mixture (Acme Bordeaux Mixture, Black Leaf Bordeaux Powder, Copper Hydro Bordow)

One of the oldest fungicides and bactericides, Bordeaux mixture is a combination of copper hydroxide and calcium sulfate. It is used to combat a diversity of diseases, including botrytis blight, cankers, leaf spot, and bacterial wilt. However, it is relatively ineffective against powdery mildew and various rusts. It is, on the other hand, repellent to such insect pests as leafhoppers, flea beetles, and the potato psyllid. Bordeaux mixture may be purchased premixed, or it may be safely prepared by throroughly dissolving 3 ounces of copper sulfate in 3 gallons of water and then mixing in 5 ounces of hydrated lime. Because of its corrosive action, Bordeaux mixture should not be stored in metal containers. Wash all treated produce before use.

Captan (Orthocide)

Captan is one of the carboximide fungicides and is extensively used to control a wide array of plant diseases, including scab, blotch, rot, and mildew in ornamentals, vegetables, and fruits. It is applied as a spray or a dust, or as a slurry for the fungicidal treatment of seeds. Treated seed usually carries a colored residue. Like carboximides in general, captan is very safe to handle, hence is one of the mainstay fungicides for garden use. Wash residues from crops before use.

Copper Fungicide Compounds (Basi-Cop)

The copper fungicide compounds are inorganic compounds that contain copper salts. As copper is toxic to all plant cells, the various copper-based fungicides release copper ions at low levels—enough to kill the fungi but not enough to harm the host. The relative insolubility and stability of the salts in copper fungicide compounds result in their residues being retained on leaf surfaces for extended periods and, after repeated use, the accumulation of these substances in the soil, sometimes to the detriment of future crops or other plantings.

Beside Bordeaux mixture, the following compounds and their uses suggest the utility of this group:

Copper carbonate	Many fungal diseases
Copper dihydrazine sulfate	Powdery mildew; black spot of roses
Copper oxide	Powdery mildew
Copper oxychloride	Powdery mildew
Copper oxychloride sulfate	Many fungal diseases
Copper sulfate	Seed treatment
Copper-zinc chromates	Diseases of potato, tomato peanuts, citrus, and cucurbits (squash, cucumber, melons, etc.)

In all cases, it is advisable to wash treated crops before use.

Dinocap (Karathane, Mildex)

Useful both as a fungicide, especially to control powdery mildew, and as a miticide, dinocap is a dinitrophenol, which has been in use since before World War II. It prevents spore germination on various ornamentals as well as on vegetables and fruit crops. However, it can damage plants when applied under hot, humid conditions, i.e., when temperatures exceed 85°F and relative humidity is 70 percent or higher. Treated vegetables and fruit should be washed before use.

Dodine (Cyprex)

A disease-specific nitrogen compound that is rapidly taken up by target fungi, dodine is effective in controlling such fruit diseases as scab in apple, pear, and pecan; cherry leaf spot; leaf diseases of strawberry; and leaf curl and bacterial leaf spot in peaches. It is also used against leaf blight in sycamore (*Platanus* spp.) and black walnut (*Juglans nigra*). Wash treated fruit before use.

Ferbam (Carbamate, Coromate, Fermate, Karbam Black)

One of the long-used (since the 1930s) dithiocarbamates, ferbam is among the most popular fungicides. It is preferred by many for the treatment of black spot of roses, especially when alternated with triforine (see Benomyl, above), folpet, or maneb. It provides effective control of such diverse diseases as rusts in carnations and snapdragons, various blights (such as botrytis and anthracnose), black rot of grapes, and numerous other diseases of fruits. Many of these diseases, however, may be averted altogether by growing specifically disease-resistant cultivars. Treated fruit should be washed before use.

Folpet (Phaltan)

A complex organic compound, folpet is effective against many fruit tree diseases as well as chrysanthemum leaf spot and powdery mildew and black spot of roses. For black spot, alternate with another fungicide, such as triforine (see page 813), ferbam, or maneb. Spray residue on fruit should be washed off before use.

Lime Sulfur

Lime sulfur, another inorganic compound used as a fungicide as well as an insecticide, is not recommended for garden use, as too many garden plants are sensitive to it and can be seri-

ously harmed. Its effectiveness in combatting powdery mildew is at least matched by benomyl and triforine, both of which have little or no detrimental effect on sprayed plants.

Maneb (Dithane M-22, Chem-Neb, Manzate)

Another dithiocarbamate that has been long in use, maneb is preferred by some for control of black spot in roses, especially if applied well before the appearance of symptoms. Maneb is also effective against cercospora leaf spot, downy mildew, various blights, and most other common fungal diseases of vegetables and fruits. Wash all sprayed produce before use.

Pentachloronitrobenzene (Terrachlor)

Also long in use (since the 1930s), Pentachloronitrobenzene (PCNB), originally used as a seed sterilant, but it is also effective against wilts and other foliage diseases as well as root rot (especially in sweet peas) and clubroot in cabbage. Any treated vegetables should be washed before being eaten.

COMMON GARDEN PESTS

Pest Name	Description	Plants Affected
Adelgid	Woolly tufted insects, suck plant juices	Various conifers, eastern hemlock most seriously affected, usually dying prematurely
Aphids	Small, soft-bodied, black, green, red, or whitish sucking insect; deposit honeydew; often increase rapidly by parthenogenesis (asexually)	Many kinds, including roses, vegetables, and houseplants
Bagworm	Small larva; constructs 2-inch hanging nest that harbors eggs over winter	Conifers, especially arborvitae, false cypress, fir, juniper
Bark beetle	Numerous ⅛-inch beetles construct tunnels, introducing fungi (including Dutch elm disease)	Elms, conifers, fruit trees
Berry midge: *see Gall midge*		
Bird	Many kinds, including sparrows, jays, starlings, crows	Leaf and seed vegetables, fruit trees and bushes, lawn grasses
Blister beetle	Reddish yellow to dark green, soft-bodied, ½ to ¾ inch long; briefly abundant	Bedding annuals, chrysanthemum, clematis, potato and other vegetables
Borer	Variable; mostly larvae of beetles and moths; betrayed by sawdustlike frass	Wide range of trees and shrubs, including birch, rhododendron, lilac, peach, apple, and dogwood; squash and relatives; iris
Bulb flies, bulb maggot	Variable, ¼ to ⅗ inch long, beelike; lay eggs in bulb neck; maggots move to base	Bulbs, especially narcissus, hyacinth, amaryllis, and snowflake

Streptomycin (Agrimycin, Agri-Strep, Phytomycin)
In common with other antibiotics, streptomycin is produced by a microorganism, in this case an actinomycete. In very dilute concentration it will inhibit the growth of or destroy other microorganisms, including those causing such bacterial diseases as leaf blights of fruit trees, soft rot of vegetables, and leaf spot of cucumber. Other horticulturally employed antibiotics include aureomycin for seed sterilization and cyclohexamide (Actidione Ferrated) for control of cedar-apple rust and various turf diseases. Spray residue is best washed off before treated produce is consumed.

Terrazole (Truban)
Terrazole is a thiazole compound that is much used to sterilize soil for seed germination and seedling growth as well as for greenhouse use. It is also used for the control of many turf diseases and for treating seeds, especially of those crop plants whose seedlings often succumb to damping off.

Thiram (Arasan, Thylate)
A dithiocarbamate, thiram is used especially to control rusts and scabs of apple and crab apple. Wash treated fruit before use.

Zineb (Dithane Z-78, Parzate)
Zineb is another long-used dithiocarbamate that is very popular because of its effectiveness in controlling such diverse diseases as botrytis blight or gray mold of geranium; anthracnose of sycamore and maple, stem rot of clematis; and leaf spots and rusts of various trees, shrubs, and smaller garden ornamentals. It is much used to prevent the rot of "seed" potatoes (i.e., pieces of tuber planted for propagation) and tomato blight. Any residue on crops should be washed off before use.

COMMON GARDEN PESTS

Structures Affected and Symptoms	Controls		
	Biotic	Mechanical	Chemical
Discolored leaves; stunted growth; gall formation; branches die upward in hemlock	None known	Remove affected hemlocks	Dormant oil slows hemlock decline; for others none required
Mostly leaves, roots, and young stems; often deformed and undersize	Predatory insects, such as tiny braconid wasps, chalcid wasps, hover-fly larvae, green lacewings, and lady bugs	Remove or crush with strong water spray	Dormant oil, insecticidal soaps, systemic insecticides such as imidan, or stomach poison such as neem
Foliage eaten by larvae in spring	None known	Hand pick bags in winter	Spray in early spring with insecticidal soap, later with contact insecticide such as sabadilla or a systemic such as dimethoate
Sapwood beneath bark, especially of weak, dying trees	Promote healthy growth of susceptible species	Remove and destroy affected branches or trees	Trap beetles with aggregation pheromones; spray with stomach poison, especially methoxychlor
Ripening fruits and vegetable seedlings pecked; corn ears and pea pods stripped; sown seed eaten	Predatory birds (raptors), cats, and dogs	Use ½-inch nylon mesh; scarecrows, glitter strips, glare eyes, and humming tape are seldom reliable	Prepared repellents are erratically and differentially effective at best
Foliage eaten in brief period in late summer	None known	None known	Contact insecticide such as rotenoids or sabadilla
Stems, trunks, branches, roots, tubers, especially of weak or unhealthy subjects	Promote healthy growth of susceptible species	Remove diseased or dying subjects; insert wire into tunnels; slit squash stems	Apply toxic paste; spray with systemic insecticide such as dimethoate or with nicotine sulfate
Maggots enter bulb base and hollow out interior	Replace affected species with resistant ones	Dig out and burn infested bulbs; cover ripening foliage of susceptible bulbs with fine-mesh row cover	Dust soil surface with contact insecticide such as rotenoid

(continues)

COMMON GARDEN PESTS (*continued*)

Pest Name	Description	Plants Affected
Caterpillar (including armyworm, inchworm, looper, and those of gypsy moth and grape berry moth)	Elongate, hairy or smooth, minute to 3 inches, usually numerous; armyworm moves in files or ranks	Wide range of ornamentals, vegetables, and fruits
Cats	All types	Dry-surfaced, smoothed soil, especially in spring
Chinch bug	The 1/16-inch nymphs mature into 1/5-inch adults	Lawn grasses, corn, grains; especially in hot, dry spells
Codling moth	Small brown moth; lays eggs on fruit into which caterpillars burrow; cause premature fruit drop	Apples, pear, quince
Cucumber beetle	Small, yellow, black-striped beetle	Cucumber, melon, squash, and relatives
Curculio: *see Weevil*		
Cutworm	Overwintered gray-brown caterpillarlike larvae of various moths	Vegetable transplants, especially cabbage and relatives, lettuce, and onion; also strawberry and bedding annuals
Deer	Principally white-tail deer, both sexes, all ages	Various ornamentals, especially rhododendron; yew, various young trees; and strawberry
Dog	All types	Trees, lawns, bedding plants
Earwig	Shiny, brown, 1/2 to 3/4 inch long, with terminal pincers; feeds nocturnally, hiding by day in dark places such as flower buds	Various vegetables and double-flowered ornamentals, especially dahlia and chrysanthemum
Flea beetle	Tiny yellow and black or metallic blue-green beetle; jumps when disturbed	Cabbage and relatives, grape
Fruit fly	Small two-winged, yellow-brown fly	Cherry, plum, apple, pear, currant, gooseberry
Gall midge	Various, host specific, 1/8-inch flies, lay eggs on fruit and leaves	Pear, chrysanthemum, honey locust
Gall mite	Tiny, two-legged, maggotlike, white or yellow	Various evergreen and deciduous trees (especially apple); tomato

COMMON GARDEN PESTS

| Structures Affected and Symptoms | Controls | | |
	Biotic	Mechanical	Chemical
All parts, but especially young foliage	Preparations containing *Bacillus thuringiensis*	Hand pick if accessible and not too numerous	Aggregation pheromones, contact insecticide such as imidan (on ornamentals), stomach poison such as mexacarbamate
Seed beds, newly seeded lawns, rows of vegetables, beds of annuals	None known, except tethered dogs	Keep seed beds moist; cover with wire mesh or hardware cloth	Repellents largely ineffective (e.g., quassia and pepper dust)
Leaves attacked, leading to brown patches in lawns	Replace damaged lawn with resistant species, such as tall fescue	Flood area of suspected infestation to see if insects ascend grass blades; if so spray with chemical compounds listed to the right	Stomach poison such as methoxychlor, neem, rotenoids, or sabadilla
Maturing and ripe fruit	For isolated trees, lure and trap male population with pheromones	None known	Spray with contact insecticide such as imidan, rotenoids, or sabadilla at appropriate time when eggs hatch, in early summer
Young shoots in the spring and early summer	Grow wilt-resistant cultivars	Cover transplants with cheesecloth or row covers until flowers appear	None effective
Stems girdled, especially of young plants; also strawberry fruit	Remove weeds, as they encourage egg-laying	Encircle transplants with 1-inch collar of weatherproof paper or plastic; hand pick larvae	Spray seedlings with stomach poison such as methoxychlor, neem, rotenoids, or sabadilla
Foliage of evergreens, bark of trees, especially in late winter; strawberry in the spring	Avoid growing susceptible species where deer are numerous	Strong wire-mesh fencing 6 to 8 feet high	Various repellents have little long-term effect (e.g., eggs, soap, kerosene, dried blood, and human hair)
Root and foliar damage, especially by urination and scratching	None known	Fencing, to site valuable plants away from dog access; high-frequency sound	Repellents may discourage ritual visits (e.g., red pepper, naphthalene flakes [mothball flakes], and tobacco dust), the last two toxic to pets and wildlife
Flower petals eaten; buds and tightly packed leaves of expanding shoots eaten	None known	Remove hiding places; shake insects out of susceptible plants; set inverted flower pots as lures	Spray target plants with residual contact spray such as rotenoids
Leaves perforated with small, round holes; buds and young leaves of grapes skeletonized	None known	Keep seedlings well watered	Use disinfected seed; spray attacked plants with malathion, neem, rotenoids, or sabadilla
Eggs laid on ripe or decaying fruit; maggots burrow into flesh	Plant cornflower and thistle nearby as larval food lure	Harvest fruit promptly	Spray adults with contact poison such as rotenoids or sabadilla
Young fruit drops; galls form on leaves	None known	Hand pick galled foliage and destroy	Spray with systemic insecticide such as dimethoate or contact poison such as rotenoids; time spraying to avoid pollinating insects on pear
Foliage with small red galls or blisters, or deformed, or abnormally pigmented; fruit undersize; development of witches-brooms	Discontinue cultivation of afflicted kinds	Remove and burn infested portions of plants	Spray with dormant oil, then with systemic insecticide such as dimethoate or with imidan, methoxychlor, tetradifon, or (for ornamentals only) mexacarbamate

(continues)

COMMON GARDEN PESTS (continued)

Pest Name	Description	Plants Affected
Gall wasp	Small, ¼-inch wasp; lays eggs that cause growth of galls (e.g., oak apples)	Various trees and shrubs, especially oaks, roses
Gopher, ground squirrel	Burrowing rodent with long-clawed front feet; mostly in South and West	Lawns and gardens; soil heaped around burrow openings
Grasshopper, locust	Green to brown; flying and jumping; often very numerous	Wide range of ornamentals, vegetables, and fruits
Gypsy moth: *see Caterpillar*		
Inchworm: *see Winter moth*		
Japanese beetle	Green and copper adults; lays eggs in soil; grubs burrow until following spring	Various, especially fruit trees and bushes, roses, dahlia, hollyhock, and other ornamentals; lawns
Lacebug	Lacy forewings, ¼ inch long, flattened	Japanese andromeda, rhododendron, azalea
Leaf beetle	Mostly small, variously colored; include larval ladybug	Potato, bean, asparagus, squash and relatives, elm, willow, grape
Leafhopper	Mostly green, ⅕ inch long; hop from leaf to leaf when disturbed	Roses, geranium, potato, grape, apple, blackberry, strawberry, beech, hornbeam
Leaf miner	Minute burrowing larvae of various moths, beetles, and flies	Various trees (holly, birch, hawthorn), shrubs (azalea, box), perennials (columbine, chrysanthemum), vegetables (cabbage and relatives, tomato), and fruits (apple, cherry)
Leaf roller	Various caterpillars, adult weevils, gall midges, sawflies, and mites	Wide array of ornamentals and fruit trees and bushes
Mealy bug	Female white to pink, covered with waxy "meal"; male tiny, winged; in dense colonies; excrete honeydew	Wide range of ornamentals, especially in protected locations (as in houses)
Mole	Small burrowing mammal; seldom seen but betrayed by ridges made as it seeks worms and insects	Lawns, gardens
Mouse, rat, vole	Small mammal; usually nocturnal; nests in debris or burrows	Bulbs, especially crocus, tulip, lily; also peas, beans, corn
Nematode, nema, eelworm	Very small, wormlike; some vectors of virus diseases, others predatory on insect pests	Wide range of garden plants, including clematis, box, phlox, narcissus, tomato, potato, onion

COMMON GARDEN PESTS

Structures Affected and Symptoms	Controls Biotic	Mechanical	Chemical
Leaves, twigs, thorns	Relatively harmless; none needed	None needed	None needed
Bulbs, roots, seeds, and insects eaten	None known	Spike or scissor traps; carbon monoxide gas (in auto engine exhaust, conducted by hose to animal run)	Repellents (e.g., 2 ounces castor oil and 1 ounce liquid detergent mixed with 2 quarts water, poured sparingly in opened tunnels)
Foliage, especially of wilted, dying, or stressed plants	*Nosema locustae*, a protozoon parasite	Remove nearby weeds; rototill affected areas to expose eggs to birds and winter cold	Pheromone traps; commercially prepared poison bran
Leaves and flowers eaten by adults; grass roots eaten by grubs	Milky spore disease (*Bacillus popilliae*) and parasitic nematode (*Neoplectaria hoptha*) attack grubs; also parasitic wasps	Hand pick adults	Adults lured into baited traps placed downwind; spray neem or sabadilla on foliage; drench soil with pyrethrins
Leaf undersurface eaten by spiny, dark gray larvae, resulting in pale, mottled effect and weakening of plant	Avoid cultivation of affected species	Hand prune infested leaves or branches and destroy	Systemic insecticides such as oxydemetomethyl or contact insecticides such as rotenoids or sabadilla
Mostly leaves; also roots of grape	Parasitic nematodes; spined soldier bug or stink bug	Hand pick, especially when on vegetables	Residual contact insecticides such as rotenoids or methoxychlor with pre harvest interval for crops; nicotine sulfate soil drench for grapes
Undersurfaces of leaves eaten, causing pale zones and providing entry for pathogenic viruses	Control usually unnecessary unless transmitted disease develops	None known	Systemic insecticide such dimethoate or oxydemetomethyl, or contact spray such as imidan, rotenoids, or sabadilla
Tunnels into or eats out green cells between upper and lower leaf epidermis, sometimes causing premature leaf drop	Damage often superficial, usually requiring no control	Pick off and destroy infested leaves	Systemic insecticides such as dimethoate or oxydemetomethyl
Leaves rolled into a cylinder or cone, often bound with silk, then eaten in part, usually dying prematurely but not dropping	None known	Cut out and destroy rolled leaves	Dormant oil or insecticides such as imidan, methoxychlor, neem, rotenoids, or sabadilla (effective if applied before rolling begins)
Leaves, young shoots, roots	Ladybug; parasitic wasps	Quarantine newly acquired plants; wipe off insects with brush dipped in 70 percent rubbing alcohol	Systemic insecticides such as dimethoate or stomach poisons such as mexacar bamate, neem, rotenoides, or sabadilla; dormant oil on trees and shrubs
Roots not eaten, but whole plants thrust up in serpentine ridges	Weasels and raptors help control surface-walking young adults	Smoke, flooding, spring traps, and electric repellents variable in effectiveness	Commercially prepared poisoned earthworms
Recently planted bulbs and seeds	Mouser cats; raptor birds	Plant bulbs deep, tamping firmly, or in wire baskets; baited snap traps; remove protective fitter or debris	Anticoagulant poison bait (keep away from pets and wildlife); seeds and bulbs treated with fungicides usually unpalatable
Infest roots and leaves, leading to yellowing of foliage, early leaf drop, decline, and death	Cease cultivation of susceptible kinds; difficult to control	Crop rotation; remove and destroy infested plants; quarantine newly acquired plants; water with soaker hose; brief hot-water treatment for dormant roots and bulbs	Frequent application of dimethoate on trunks and stems in the spring and early summer

(continues)

COMMON GARDEN PESTS (*continued*)

Pest Name	*Description*	*Plants Affected*
Phylloxerid	Small, aphidlike sucking insect	Grape, oak, pecan
Pillbug, sowbug	Grayish, segmented crustacean, ½ inch long; in damp places; roll up when disturbed	Wide range of seedlings and transplants
Plum curculio: *see Weevil*		
Psyllid, or sucker	Small, active; host-specific; true bug, with flat-bodied nymphs (suckers)	Apple, pear, box, tomato, potato
Rabbit	Vegetarian; inhabits burrows; forages day and night	Wide range of bedding ornamentals and vegetables; bark of young trees
Raccoons	Omnivorous climbing mammal; mostly nocturnal; difficult to control	Vegetable and fruit crops; young plants uprooted during search for worms and soil insects
Red spider mite	Tiny sucking mite: usually red but may be green or yellow	Wide range of ornamentals (especially conifers), vegetables, and fruits (especially apple and plum)
Root aphids	Tiny, host-specific sucking insects; accompanied by ants; change hosts as life cycle advances	Various ornamentals, vegetables (lettuce, carrot), and fruits (strawberry)
Root fly, root maggot	Houseflylike adult; lays eggs in soil; maggot burrows downward to roots	Cabbage, onions, beans, carrots
Sawfly	Black or yellow-brown flylike adult; host-specific caterpillarlike larvae	Pine, birch, maple hazel, apple, cherry, currant, gooseberry, raspberry, various perennials
Scale insect	Female an immobile shield or shell, often covering eggs; male a small winged bug; nymphs always mobile	Wide range of ornamentals and fruit trees
Slugs, snails	Unsegmented, soft, glide on secreted mucus; feed with filelike tongue, mostly at night and in damp weather	Wide range of ornamentals, especially seedlings; also young growth of tulip, hyacinth, lily, hosta, pinks, strawberry

COMMON GARDEN PESTS

Structures Affected and Symptoms	Controls Biotic	Mechanical	Chemical
Fatal galling of roots of grape; yellowing and early leaf drop in oak; galling of foliage and nuts in pecan	Graft susceptible grapes on resistant roots	None known	Systemic insecticides used for aphid control such as oxydemetomethyl
Seedlings decapitated	None known	Lure with dark plastic, newspaper, or boards and destroy	Apply malathion around plants
Expanding buds and flowers attacked by nymphs; foliage deformed or killed; crops reduced	None known	None known	Insecticidal soap or insecticides used for aphid control such as imidan, methoxychlor, neem, rotenoids, or sabadilla
Seedlings and young shoots, leafy vegetables, especially in early spring; tree bark in winter	Cats, raptors; plant susceptible plants in beds of other kinds (e.g., lilies in daffodils)	Trapping, shooting, and gassing where legal; check your local regulations; 1-inch wire mesh fencing, 2 to 4 feet high and sunk 1 foot in the ground	Repellents (e.g., 7 pounds rosin in 1 gallon water painted on tree trunks or thinned with water and sprayed) sometimes effective; poisons often illegal
Mostly large, heavy produce such as corn, squash, pumpkins, apples, pears	None known; may infect dogs and cats with rabies	Wire-mesh fencing deters; only sturdy enclosures—complete or electrified—fully protect; hence resort to hunting and trapping (where legal, check your local regulations)	Dog repellents largely ineffective
Foliage often turns bronzy or yellow, curling and prematurely dropping	Predatory mites (useful especially in greenhouses)	Frequent misting with water; weekly spray with water and detergent or other mixtures (e.g., 1 tablespoon flour mixed with 1 tablespoon buttermilk in 1 gallon water)	Spraying trees and shrubs with dormant oil; toxic compounds not advisable as many resistant strains exist
Roots attacked, often resulting in wilting and debilitation	Choose resistant cultivars	None known	Drench soil with nicotine sulfate
Maggots attack and often kill seedlings; older plants have reduced crop yield	Delay planting to evade most injurious first generation; encourage predatory rove beetle; a serious pest not easily controlled	Row covers to exclude egg-laying females	Granular or powdered insecticides such as neem, rotenoids, sabadilla
Foliage, young fruit	None known	Hand picking larvae	Insecticidal soap or insecticides used to control ordinary caterpillars such as imidan, neem, rotenoids, sabadilla
Leaves, stems	Syrphid fly larvae, ladybugs	Scrape off small infestations, especially from houseplants, with cotton swabs or facial sponges	Dormant oil, insecticidal soap, systemic insecticides such as dimethoate, oxy-demetomethyl, or stomach poisons (for ornamentals only) such as mexa-carbamate
Leaves, roots, young stems, immature fruits	Preyed on by frogs, snakes, thrushes, lizards, and rabbits; parasitized by rove beetles, certain maggots, and other molluscs	Attracted by decayed organic matter; capture overnight in citrus skins or cabbage leaves and kill in saltwater; repel with wood ashes; exclude by enclosing vulnerable plants, as in empty plastic bottles with	Beer in shallow cans sunk flush with surface; prepared molluscicides (toxic to pets and wildlife); stomach poisons such as mexacarbamate (ornamentals only)

(continues)

COMMON GARDEN PESTS (*continued*)

Pest Name	Description	Plants Affected
Squirrel	Climbing rodent; gray or red-brown, active all year harvesting and digging	Apples, pears, peaches, nuts, sycamore, beech, corn, various bulbs, lawns
Tarsonemid mite	Glossy, white or tan; 1/10 inch long; drops off plant if disturbed	Various ornamentals such as begonia, chrysanthemum, perennial aster, gerbera, cyclamen, ferns; strawberry; many greenhouse plants
Tent caterpillar, webworm	Dense, silky webs in branch crotches, from which young emerge to feed	Various trees, especially cherry, apple, and relatives
Thrips	Brown, yellow, or black; 1/10 inch long; usually winged, with rasping and sucking mouth parts; often very numerous in hot, dry weather	Wide range, including onion, cabbage and relatives, tomato, cucumber, peas; fruit trees; lilies, iris, dahlia, chrysanthemum
Tortrix moth (including codling moth, eye-spotted moth, Nantucket tip moth)	Small, with leaflike wings; green caterpillars with dark heads; often hidden in silk-bound leaves	Peas, apple and other tree fruits (*see Codling moth*), grapes, pines
Wasp	Usually solitary or a few together, but part of large hive	Principally fruit trees and bushes
Weevil (including curculio)	Adult has snout and chewing mouth parts; eggs laid in incisions made by adults, where whitish brown-headed, legless grubs feed	Many crops, including grains, cotton, root vegetables, tomato, peas, beans, various tree fruits and nuts; numerous ornamental trees and shrubs
Whitefly	About 1/12 inch long; usually all stages, including flying adults; translucent eggs; scalelike larvae; excretes honeydew	Wide range, including flowering maple, begonia, chrysanthemum, coleus, dahlia, geranium, poinsettia; also squash and relatives, tomato
Winter moth (including inchworm and looper)	Tawny or brown adult; active in spring or fall; lay eggs in trees; caterpillars feed, then descend on thread to pupate in soil	Fruit trees, beech, dogwood, elm, hawthorn, linden, maple; also firethorn, rhododendron, roses
Wireworms	Soil-inhabiting larva of click beetles; 1/2 inch long; feeds on subterranean plant parts	Many ornamentals, including carnation, chrysanthemum, dahlia, gladiolus; also beans, beets, cabbage and relatives, lettuce, onions, corn, potatoes, tomatoes, and strawberry
Woodchuck	Large, burrowing rodent	Various low plants, including vegetable transplants, especially in the spring

COMMON GARDEN PESTS

Structures Affected and Symptoms	Controls		
	Biotic	*Mechanical*	*Chemical*
		top open and bottom cut out or by flanged wooden or metal enclosure	
Fruit, nuts, bulbs, buds, bark	Raptors, cats	Enclose vulnerable shrubs and beds with wire mesh or hardware cloth; trapping and shooting (where legal, check your local regulations)	Repellents largely ineffective; poisons often illegal
Leaves, flowers often distorted and undersize	None known	Carefully remove bag, and destroy infested plants	Dormant oil; stomach poisons such as mexacarbamate (ornamentals only), rotenoids, and tetradifon; or systemic insecticides such as dimethoate
Young leaves	*Bacillus thuringiensis*; some predation by birds	Hand picking; band trunks with sticky substance; burning or smoking out nests may damage or kill branches	Stomach poisons such as methoxychlor or rotenoids, but usually unnecessary
Silvery flecking of affected leaves, flowers, and pods	Infestation often very brief, requiring little or no control	None known	Insecticidal soap; systemic insecticides such as dimethoate; or contact insecticides such as imidan, rotenoids, and sabadilla
Leaves, young shoots (especially pine), flowers (grape), fruit	*Bacillus thuringiensis*; insect parasites	Pieces of corrugated cardboard or burlap to lure caterpillars	Pheromone attractants; contact poisons such as imidan or sabadilla; or systemic insecticides such as dimethoate
Holes eaten in ripe, overripe, or damaged fruit	Predatory insects such as dragonflies	Destroy nest if too close to habitation; otherwise disregard or avoid	Attractants (such as vinegar), in which wasps drown
Mainly fruits (often prematurely dropping), nuts, roots	Parasitic nematodes	Spread white cloth beneath fruit trees, shake, and destroy collected weevils	Contact poisons such as imidan, ficam, or sabadilla, precisely timed for full effectiveness according to compound
Densely colonize undersides of leaves, which are often distorted and drop early	Whitefly parasite, a small parthenogenetic wasp that lays eggs on scalelike larvae	Suspended yellow sticky boards (yellow cardboard coated with Tanglefoot)	Dormant oil, insecticidal soap; alternate or rotate such contact insecticides as rotenoids with such systemic insecticides such as dimethoate, neem, or oxydemetomethyl
Leaves, buds, flowers, young fruit	*Bacillus thuringiensis*	Sticky band on tree trunk prevents walking moths from ascending and laying eggs in leafy branches	Biosoap (a degradable soap with nicotine extract); neem, or sabadilla
Roots and lower stems, mainly of seedlings; also potato tubers and gladiolus corms, causing wilting, toppling, and death	Plant corn here and there to lure wireworms away from other crops	Thorough weeding; separation of garden from lawns to discourage egg laying; prompt harvesting of root crops	Seed disinfection; nicotine sulfate soil drench; or granular insecticides such as sabadilla
Foliage	Dogs and cats	Buried fencing; live-trapping (use a trap 10 inches high, 12 inches wide, and 32 inches long); shooting (where legal, check your local regulations)	Carbon monoxide gassing (using hose to connect auto exhaust pipe to woodchuck burrow); chemical poisons illegal in many localities

Young tent caterpillars spin dense webs and skeletonize newly expanded leaves of pear, thereby reducing or aborting the fruit crop.

Woven-wire fencing, its height and mesh interval determined by size and habits of the animals to be excluded, is an effective barrier against such ground dwellers as rabbits and deer.

Common to most species of aphids, flying adults are preceded by several stages of ever larger, wingless nymphs, but, like adults, have piercing, sucking mouth parts.

A gopher at the opening to its burrow. These omnivorous rodents are serious garden pests in warmer parts of the country west of the Mississippi, especially on the Pacific Coast.

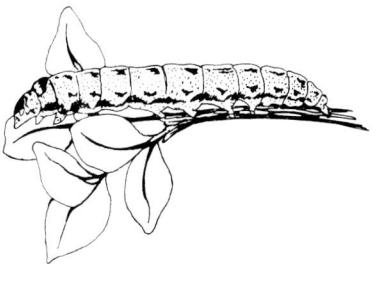

Hosta leaves perforated by slugs, usually at night or in wet weather. Of the many control measures, luring with beer in shallow cans recessed in the soil is safe and effective.

Caterpillar is the larval stage in the four-step life cycle of a moth or butterfly: egg, larva (caterpillar), pupa, adult (flying moth or butterfly).

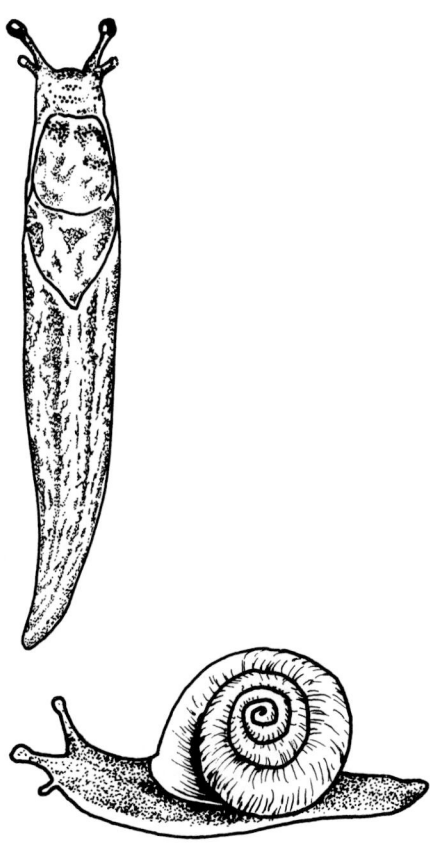

Slugs differ from snails by lacking shells but otherwise are similar in structure and habits and inflict the same harm to garden plants.

Grasshoppers are more toublesome in agriculture than in gardens but may invade from nearby farms.

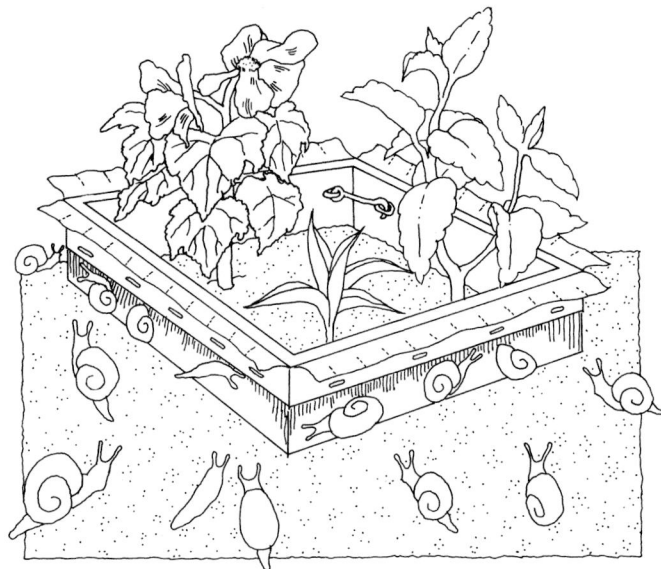

Plants vulnerable to attack by slugs and snails enclosed within collapsible flanged box.

Slugs and snails glide on their own mucus secretions, which may be reduced or stopped with dry sand, diatomaceous earth, or salt.

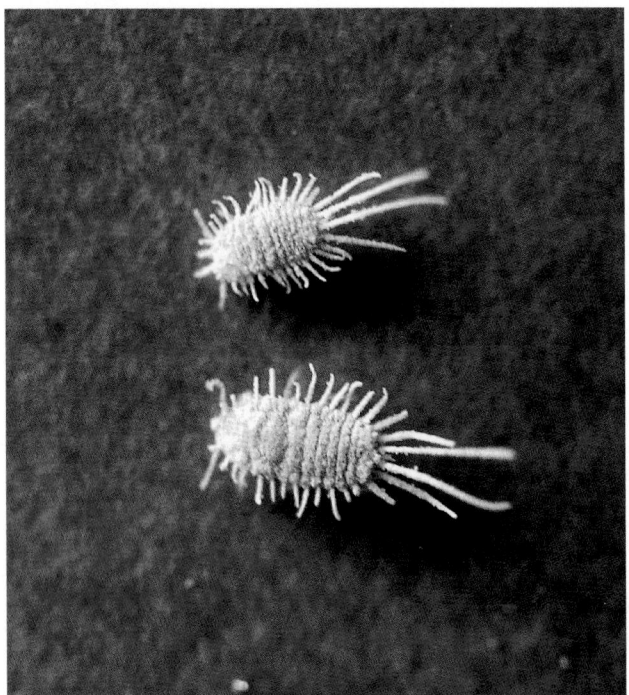

Female mealy bugs, these two not yet invested in waxy white secretion, often attack house plants in winter and can persist in stem crevices, on roots, and in soil from year to year.

*Adelgid on hemlock, appearing as white woolly tufts at bases of needles on young twigs and harboring tiny sucking insects that have devastated eastern hemlock (*Tsuga canadensis*) in much of the Northeast.*

Colorado potato beetles, usually very numerous when present, can seriously reduce the potato crop. In gardens hand picking or spraying with rotenoids is the usual control.

Aphids, sucking sap from a rose bud and flower stalk, can soon number hundreds on a single bud as the result of rapid asexual reproduction. A strong water spray can crush or fling away these soft-bodied pests.

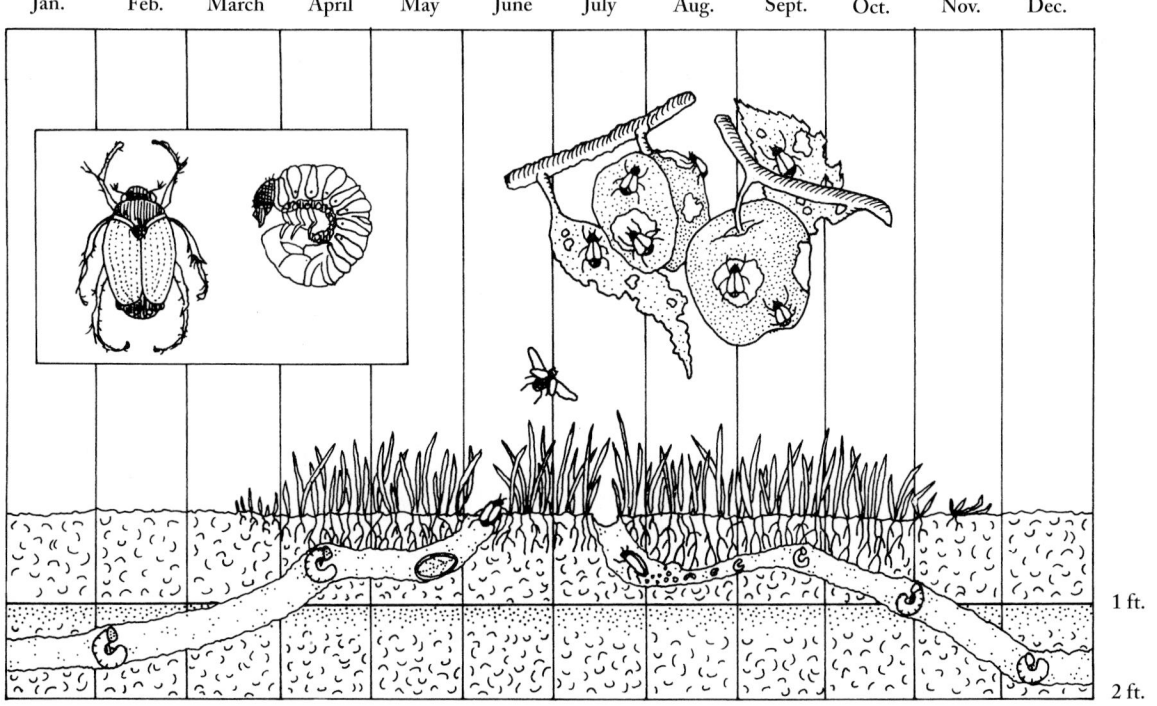

Japanese beetles, less serious as a garden pest than fifty years ago, still damage lawns, especially in spring as the burrowing grubs feed heavily on grass roots before emerging as flying adults.

Japanese beetle adults emerge in early summer to feed on leaves and flowers of roses and many other orna-
mentals as well as crop plants; their grubs consume the roots of lawn grasses from fall to spring.

Adult whiteflies, with translucent larvae and nearly
invisible eggs, suck leaf juices and cause stunting in a
wide range of garden plants.

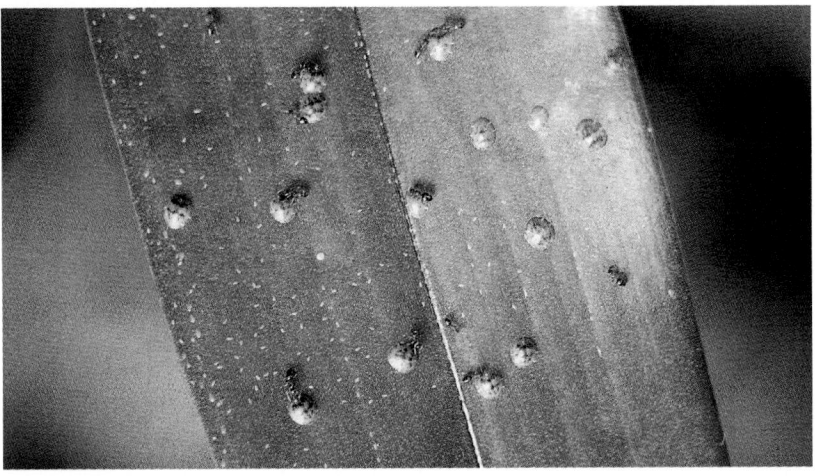

Female scale insects, surrounded by immatures, shield eggs as they suck plant juices. Honeydew secretions
are collected by ants.

Spider mite, 25 times actual size, usually forms large
populations and spins cobwebby film on host leaves and
sucks juices of increasingly weakened host.

Powdery mildew often infests zinnia foliage in hot, humid summers,
killing lowest leaves, slowing growth, and diminishing bloom.

Black spot is most commonly seen on foliage or hybrid roses; left unchecked, it can cause
complete defoliaton. Several fungicides are best used in rotation.

Corn smut, once a serious disease, is now largely avoided by use of resistant cultivars. Grossly enlarged, discolored kernels contain masses of black spores that, once liberated, are carried by wind to nearby corn plants.

*Cankered trunks of dogwood (*Cornus florida*) betray dogwood crown canker, a serious, usually fatal disease of older trees in much of the Northeast and of the western dogwood (*C. nuttallii*) of the Pacific Northwest.*

Bacterial wilt of cucumber is usually fatal, but can be avoided by growing resistant cultivars.

Leaf spot commonly afflicts tomato, especially in protracted wet spells; if serious, control with copper-based fungicides, such as copper carbonate.

COMMON GARDEN DISEASES

Disease	Hosts	Symptoms
Anthracnose	Foxglove, hollyhock, snapdragon (especially in greenhouse), beans, cucumber, tomato, leafy mustards; sycamore, maple, and privet	Blackening and death of young shoots; black spots on fruit
Apple canker	Apple and pear	Recessed areas on branches expose interior wood; serial death of branches
Apple scab	Apple and pear	Dark green or brown spots on leaves; blistered shoots; corky patches on fruit
Armillaria root rot	Various shrubs and trees, especially conifers, willows, and birch, hawthorn, lilac, in or near woodland	Progressive dieback of limbs; premature fall foliage coloration; rapid decline and death because of insufficient roots
Bacterial canker	Cherry, peach, plum, citrus, poplar, and tomato	Oozing depressions in bark; serial dieback of branches, then death of whole tree or plant
Bacterial wilt, bacterial blight	Squash, cucumber, melon, and poppy	Wilting foliage, especially of young plants, then death
Black knot	Mainly cherry and plum	Spindle-shaped swelling on twigs stunts and kills branches
Black spot	Hybrid roses	Spots on leaflets radiate and coalesce; affected foliage yellows and drops
Blight	Various ornamentals and crops	Rapid decline and death of part of or entire plant
Brown rot	Tree fruits, especially apple and peach	Maturing fruit turns brown, with concentric yellowish or gray zones appearing
Bulb rot	Ornamental bulbs, especially tulips	Poor emergence; soft rotting shoots; gray areas on bulbs
Canker	Wide range of ornamentals, including roses, box, dogwood, gardenia, maple, sycamore, and conifers; also cabbage and relatives, parsnip, grape, and tree fruits	Sunken lesions in stems and roots; often lethal
Clubroot	Cabbage and relatives, wallflower, and stock	Swollen, misshapen roots; slow, stunted growth; pale, undersize foliage that wilts in sun
Crown gall	Various trees and shrubs, especially fruit trees and conifers; also various vegetables, bush fruits, and bedding plants	Soft tumorlike galls at ground level eventually rot (in soft-stemmed species) or become woody (in shrubs and trees); conifers most seriously affected

COMMON GARDEN DISEASES

Cause	Controls		
	Biotic	Mechanical	Chemical
Parasitic host-specific species of the fungus *Colletotrichum*	Use resistant cultivars	Remove garden debris and infected plants or structures	Copper-based fungicides; dithiocarbamates
Parasitic fungus *Nectria galligena*, whose spores enter wounds	Use resistant cultivars	Prune out affected branches; remove all pruned branches and fallen fruit	Systemic fungicides such as anilazine
Parasitic fungus *Venturia inaequalis*	Use resistant cultivars	Prune and destroy scabby twigs; rake up and destroy fallen leaves	Copper-based fungicides
Parasitic fungi, especially *Armillaria mellea*, the shoestring or honey fungus	Use resistant species	Remove and destroy affected trees (including stumps); delay replanting trees or shrubs for at least one year	Disinfect soil before replanting
Various pathogenic bacteria specific to host groups	Use resistant cultivars	Cut out infected branches or entire trees and destroy offsite	Copper-based fungicides
Bacillus (bacterium) *Erwinia tracheiphila*, which is transmitted by cucumber beetle	Parasitic nematodes; repellent companion plantings of mint or wormwood (*Artemisia* spp.); use resistant cultivars	Cover plantings with cheesecloth to exclude cucumber beetles; remove and destroy infected plants	Rotenoids, neem, or streptomycin
Pathogenic fungus *Apiosporina morbosa*	Use resistant cultivars or other fruits	Cut out and destroy knotted twigs	Ferbam or a copper-based fungicide such as copper carbonate
Diplocarpon rosae, the black spot fungus	Use differentially resistant cultivars	Remove and destroy all fallen diseased foliage; mulch rose bed in the spring to prevent splashing of spores onto young foliage	Copper-based fungicides such as copper dihydrazine sulfate; ferbam, triforine, folpet, or maneb, preferably alternating two
Airborne pathogen, usually fungal, bacterial, or viral	Use resistant immune species or cultivars	Remove and destroy infected plants; rotate crops	Various, according to causes, vectors, and hosts (*see Bacterial wilt, Fire blight, Potato blight*)
Rot fungi *Monilinia fruticola*, *M. fructigena*, and *M. laxa*, perhaps others	Use resistant cultivars	Destroy all dead or cankered branches and dried up or fallen fruit	Systemic fungicides such as benomyl, or captan or maneb
Asexual parasitic fungus *Rhizoctonia tuliparum*	Use resistant cultivars from reputable sources (disease usually introduced on newly planted bulbs)	Promptly dig out all infected bulbs (including, if possible, any failing to grow) with soil and discard off site; discontinue bulb culture for at least five years	None known
Various pathogenic fungi, often transmitted by insects	Use resistant species	Prune or dig out and destroy infected plants, then disinfect tools by immersing in household bleach solution	Systemic fungicides such as anilazine
Parasitic fungus *Plasmidiophora brassicae*, which enters through root hairs	Grow seedlings in sterile, soilless mix rather than acquire transplants grown elsewhere	Adjust soil pH to 7.0	When transplanting seedlings, wet roots and soil with benomyl
Host-specific strains of the pathogenic bacterium *Agrobacterium tumefaciens*, which stimulates cancerlike galls in host stems	Use resistant species or cultivars (especially of conifers)	Improve drainage if soil is heavy and excessively wet	Dip roots of transplants in Bordeaux mixture

(continues)

COMMON GARDEN DISEASES (*continued*)

Disease	*Hosts*	*Symptoms*
Damping off	Young seedlings of a wide range of plants, especially snapdragon, geranium, petunia, periwinkle, impatiens, eggplant, cabbage and relatives, and peas	Seedlings wilt and topple while germinating or shortly after
Dieback	Wide range of woody plants, especially ornamental shrubs, roses, and fruit trees	Shoots slowly die back from tip
Downy mildew	Vegetables such as cabbage and relatives, squash and relatives, peas, spinach, onions, beets, and lettuce; also grape, rose, and other ornamentals	Glistening white or purplish downy growth on undersides of leaves, which wither and die
Dutch elm disease	Principally American and English elms	Sporadic yellowing and death of branches, followed by general decline and death of tree
Fire blight	Mainly pear; also apple, quince, hawthorn, and firethorn	Blackened flowers, leaves, and fruit; cankered branches that ooze in the spring
Gall	Wide range of ornamentals, vegetables, and fruits	Tumorlike swellings on leaves, stems, and roots; often superficial and insignificant
Gray mold, botrytis mold	Many vegetables and fruits; diverse ornamentals, especially chrysanthemum, dahlia, hydrangea, impatiens, geranium, poppy, sunflower, rose, and rhododendron	Fluffy gray coating on stems, leaves, flowers, and soft fruits, occurring especially on stressed plants or on produce in storage
Leaf scorch	Wide diversity of cultivated plants	Drying and death of leaf margins
Leaf spot	Virtually all plants, especially on aging leaves	Blotches, spots, rings, or holes ("shot holes," where dead tissue has fallen away)
Mosaic: *see Virus*		
Neck rot, stem rot	Onion, narcissus, gladiolus, and crocus	Decay develops at base of leaves or stalk and or top of bulb or corm, proceeds downward, destroying structure
Peach-leaf curl	Peach, nectarine, and almond	Young leaves yellowish, undersize, puckered, curled, thickened; turn red and prematurely drop
Phloem necrosis	Various trees, especially American elm	Symptoms of Dutch elm disease
Potato blight	Potato and tomato	Brown patches develop and spread on leaves, leading to premature leaf drop; tuber rot, especially in storage
Potato scab	Potato	Rough, scaly, superficial patches on tubers

COMMON GARDEN DISEASES

Cause	Controls		
	Biotic	*Mechanical*	*Chemical*
Various parasitic host-specific fungi	No cure, hence must be prevented; start seeds (except peas) indoors in well-drained, sterile, soilless mix	Use pretreated seed and clean seed pans and cell packs; sow seed thinly; pull and discard diseased, toppled seedlings	In seed pans showing initial outbreak, apply captan or thiram to unaffected surviving seedlings; use garlic spray (one ground clove per 1 quart of water) as preventive
Various parasitic host-specific fungi	None known	Cut out all dead and dying shoots and destroy; improve drainage if soil is heavy and excessively wet	Rotenoids, neem, streptomycin
Various closely related, parasitic, host-specific fungi	Use resistant cultivars	Gather infected foliage and destroy; dig out and remove heavily diseased plants	Spray with Bordeaux mixture or other copper-based fungicides or with zineb
Parasitic fungus *Ceratocystis ulmi*, transmitted by elm bark beetle	Use resistant hybrids (such as 'Urban Elm' or 'Sapporo Autumn Gold')	Promptly remove and destroy any trees showing symptoms	Systemic fungicides, such as benlate or Arbotect 20-S, may slow decline but do not arrest it
Bacterial pathogen *Erwinia amylovora*	Use resistant cultivars; remove nearby hawthorns	Prune out infected limbs and destroy; remove badly infected trees	Spray susceptible subjects with strepto-mycin as preventive
Various host-specific fungi and pathogenic bacteria; also caused by various insects	Use resistant species and cultivars	Disfigured crops may be removed; other action usually unnecessary	Control insect vectors, such as midges, also mites
Ubiquitous, weakly parasitic fungus *Botrytis cinerea*	Use resistant cultivars; promote maximum vigor of plants	Remove debris, such as crop residue; avoid overcrowding (which may restrict air circulation)	Spray with benomyl only as a last resort, as numerous resistant strains already exist
Various diseases, environmental factors (drought, salt, wind, frost, etc.)	Use resistant cultivars	Irrigate; mulch; protect plants from adverse environmental forces; apply antidessicant such as Wilt-Pruf	Fungicide or bactericide, according to cause
Various plant pathogens, especially associated with prolonged surface wetness	Use resistant cultivars	Gather infected leaves, remove, and destroy	Copper-based fungicides and dithiocarbamates
Parasitic fungi *Botrytis allii* on onion, *Fusarium oxysporum* on narcissus, and various fungi on gladiolus and crocus	Thoroughly dry harvested bulbs and corms before storage	Destroy all infected bulbs and corms	Onion seed and sets should be disinfected by vender
Parasitic fungus *Taphrina deformans*, which favors cold, wet spring weather	Use resistant cultivars	Promptly gather infected leaves, destroy and remove	Spray Bordeaux mixture on dormant trees in early spring.
Mycoplasma transmitted by elm-leaf hopper	Avoid use of American elm	Remove infected trees	Methoxychlor to slow decline
Parasitic fungus *Phytophthora infestans*, which thrives in warm, wet weather	Use resistant cultivars	Remove and destroy all infected leaves, stems, and fruits; inspect stored potatoes and remove infected tubers	Spray Bordeaux mixture or other copper-based fungicide on infected plants (early in season)
Various pathogenic bacteria and fungi, especially active in dry, sandy soil	Use resistant cultivars	Use well-rotted manure and/or compost to improve soil quality	Essentially a "skin-deep" problem, seldom requiring chemical control

(*continues*)

COMMON GARDEN DISEASES (*continued*)

Disease	Hosts	Symptoms
Powdery mildew	Diverse ornamentals, especially rose and lilac; vegetables, especially cabbage and relatives, squash and relatives, and peas; fruits, especially apple, peach, grape, gooseberry, and strawberry	Grayish film on leaves and fruits, especially in hot summer weather, sometimes accompanied by stunted growth (especially in vegetables)
Root rot	Root vegetables, fruit trees and bushes, and various ornamentals	Soft spots in vegetables; wilting and yellowing of foliage; blackening of stems, then death
Rust	Diverse kinds, such as apple, quince, currant, blackberry grain crops, juniper, pine, holly grape, barberry, chrysanthemum, snapdragon, carnation, and hollyhock	Rusty orange (or yellow or white) eruptions on foliage and/or stems, weakened, often stunted or irregular growth, sometimes accompanied by galls
Shot-hole fungus: *see Leaf spot*		
Smut	Mostly corn, other grasses, cereals, and some perennials and vegetables	Swollen plant parts bear great quantities of black dustlike spores
Sooty mold	Tulip tree, conifers, and others, including various houseplants, on whose leaves insect honeydew has been deposited.	Sooty black, often unsightly coating on upper surfaces of leaves, especially in hot summer weather
Tar spot	Mainly maples, sycamore, holly, and willow	Pale leaf spots become black and haloed; premature leaf drop in American holly (*Ilex opaca*)
Tulip fire	Tulips	Delayed emergence of sickened leaves and flowers; underdeveloped roots; death of bulb
Virus	Wide range of ornamentals, vegetables, and fruits	Various symptoms: leaf mosaic or mottling (often benign); leaf curl; stunting, often followed by decline and death
Wilt: *see Bacterial wilt*		
Witches'-broom	Peach, plum, cherry, hornbeam, sycamore, and numerous other trees	Abnormal proliferation of shoots from a common point; often concurrent with or subsequent to another disease
Yellows	Various garden ornamentals (such as hyacinth and gladiolus) and vegetables (cabbage and relatives)	Yellowing and death of foliage

COMMON GARDEN DISEASES

Cause	Controls		
	Biotic	*Mechanical*	*Chemical*
Various related, host-specific parasitic fungi	Use resistant cultivars	Remove and destroy badly infected plants; spray antitranspirant (such as Wilt-Pruf) to inhibit spore germination	Dormant oil (may be mixed with sodium bicarbonate); systemic fungicides such as benomyl or triforine (to which some of the infecting fungi are resistant)
Various parasitic fungi, often aggravated by waterlogged soil	Use resistant cultivars	Remove and destroy infected individuals; lighten heavy soils with organic matter and sand	None known; must be prevented
More than 6,000 species of parasitic fungi, most host-specific, with complex life cycles (some alternating between two hosts)	Use resistant species and cultivars	Remove and destroy infected plants and alternate hosts	Thiram, zineb, and triforine (to which many rust fungi are resistant)
Various pathogenic fungi	Use resistant cultivars	Remove and destroy all infected plants	For leaf smut, treat as for leaf spot
Various nonparasitic fungi that blanket leaf surfaces, exclude light, and cause premature leaf drop	Avoid growing plants that attract aphids, such as roses, nasturtium, plum and tulip trees; mealy bugs, whiteflies, and other sucking insects	Wash off mold on small plants	Use appropriate pesticides to control sucking insects
Several host-specific fungi	If serious in your area, use resistant cultivars	Collect and destroy all infected leaves on tree and from the ground	Copper-based fungicides such as copper carbonate
Host-specific parasitic fungus *Botrytis tulipae*	Discontinue tulip culture where disease is severe	Dig out and destroy infected bulbs, roots, and shoots	Soak dormant bulbs in fungicide such as captan or benomyl
Obligate parasitic pathogens live within host cells and disrupt normal functions	Use resistant cultivars; control virus-transmitting aphids; time crops to avoid vectors	Crop rotation; destroy infected plants; remove crop debris; disinfect tools, clothing, and hands	None known; cannot be eliminated
Pathogenic fungi such as *Taphrina* spp. or rust fungi; mites; mycoplasmas; plant parasites (such as mistletoe)	None known	Prune out growths when objectionable	Control known vectors with appropriate biocides
Various parasitic fungi, pathogenic bacteria, and mycoplasmas	Use resistant cultivars	Dig out infected plants and adjacent soil and remove from site	None known; dip replacement bulbs and corms in benomyl

COMMON DISEASES AND PESTS OF SELECTED TREES AND SHRUBS

Name	Diseases and Pests*
Abies spp. (fir)	Various cankers; spruce budworm, woolly aphid
Acer palmatum (Japanese maple)	Canker
A. platanoides (Norway maple)	Anthracnose, verticillium wilt
A. pseudoplatanus (sycamore maple)	Canker
A. rubrum (red maple)	Leafhoppers
A. saccharinum (silver maple)	Anthracnose, canker, leaf spot, powdery mildew; aphids, borers, gall mites, leafhopper, nematodes, whitefly
A. saccharum (sugar maple)	Leaf scorch, verticillium wilt; thrips
Aesculus glabra (Ohio buckeye)	Anthracnose, canker, leaf blotch, leaf scorch, leaf spot, powdery mildew; bagworm, borers, Japanese beetle, mealy bug, scale
A. hippocastanum (common horse chestnut)	Same as for *A. glabra*
A. pavia (red buckeye)	Leaf blotch
Ailanthus altissima (tree of heaven)	Canker, shoestring root rot, verticillium wilt
Albizia julibrissin (mimosa, silk tree)	Wilt; webworm
Alnus spp. (alder)	Canker, powdery mildew; lacebug, leaf miner, tent caterpillar
Amelanchier spp. (shadbush, serviceberry)	Fire blight, leaf blight, powdery mildew, rust; borers
Amorpha fruticosa (bastard indigo)	Canker, leaf spot, powdery mildew, rust
Ampelopsis brevipedunculata (porcelain grape)	Japanese beetle
Berberis spp. (barberry)	Anthracnose, leaf spot, rust (especially *B. vulgaris*; not *B. thunbergii*), wilt; aphids, nematodes, scale
Betula spp. (birch)	Canker, powdery mildew, rust; aphids, borers, leaf miner
Broussonetia papyrifera (paper mulberry)	Canker, dieback, leaf spot, root rot; nematodes
Buddleia davidii (butterfly bush)	Nematodes (zone 8 and south)
Buxus spp. (box)	Blight, canker, leaf spot, root rot; mealy bug, leaf miner, mites, psyllid, scale, webworm
Callicarpa spp. (beauty-berry)	Leaf spot, black mold
Calluna vulgaris (heather)	Japanese beetle, mites, scale
Calocedrus decurrens (incense cedar)	Heart rot
Camellia spp.	Canker, leaf gall, leaf spot, molds, root rot; mealy bug, nematodes, scale, thrips, weevils
Campsis radicans (trumpet creeper)	Blight, leaf spot, powdery mildew; leafhoppers, scale
Carpinus caroliniana (American hornbeam)	Canker, leaf spot; scale
Castanea mollissima (Chinese chestnut)	Canker; weevils
Catalpa spp.	Leaf spot, powdery mildew, root rot, twig blight, verticillium wilt; mealy bug, midges
Ceanothus americanus (New Jersey tea)	Leaf spot, powdery mildew
Cedrus spp. (cedar)	Root rot; scale, weevils
Celastrus scandens (American bittersweet)	Crown gall, leaf spot, powdery mildew, stem canker; aphids, scale
Celtis occidentalis (common hackberry)	Leaf spot, powdery mildew, witches'-broom; scale
Cercis spp. (redbud)	Canker, leaf spot, verticillium wilt; caterpillars, leafhoppers, scale
Chaenomeles spp. (flowering quince)	Leaf spot (causes premature defoliation)
Chamaecyparis lawsoniana (Port Orford cedar)	Root rot (caused by *Phytophthora lateralis*)
Clematis hybrids	Leaf spot, stem rot; borers, mites, nematodes, scale
Cornus spp. (shrubby dogwoods)	Crown canker, leaf blight, leaf spot, root rot, twig blight; borers, leaf miner, scale
C. florida (flowering dogwood)	Anthracnose; most of those pests affecting shrubby species of the genus *Cornus*
Corylus spp. (hazel, filbert)	Blight; crown gall; Japanese beetle, leafhopper, scale
Cotoneaster spp.	Canker, fire blight, leaf spot; borers, lacebugs, mites, scale
Crataegus spp. (hawthorn)	Fire blight, leaf blight, leaf spot, powdery mildew, rusts, scab; aphids, borer, lacebugs, leaf miner, mites, scale, tent caterpillar
Cytisus spp. (broom)	Blight, leaf spot

Name	Diseases and Pests*
Daphne spp.	Canker, crown rot, leaf spot, twig blight; aphids, mealy bug, scale
Deutzia spp.	Leaf spot; aphids, leaf miner
Eleagnus angustifolia (Russian olive), *E. umbellata* (autumn olive)	Canker, crown gall, leaf spot, rusts, verticillium wilt; aphids, scale
E. pungens (thorny eleagnus)	Spider mites (in dry weather)
Erica spp. (heath)	Mites, scale
Eriobotrya japonica (loquat)	Fire blight
Euonymus spp. (especially evergreen)	Anthracnose, crown gall, leaf spot, powdery mildew; aphids, scale, thrips
Fagus spp. (beech)	Canker, leaf spot, powdery mildew; aphids, borers, caterpillars, scale
Forsythia spp.	Crown gall, leaf spot; nematodes, spider mites, weevils
Franklinia alatamaha	Wilt (caused by *Phytophthora cinnamomii)*
Fraxinus spp. (ash)	Cankers, dieback (cause unknown), leaf spot, rusts; gall mites, leaf miner, scale, webworm
Gardenia jasminoides (Cape jasmine)	Canker, powdery mildew; aphids, mealy bug, mites, nematodes, scale, thrips, whitefly
Gleditsia triacanthos (honey locust)	Canker, leaf spot, powdery mildew; aphids, caterpillars, mealy bug, mites, scale
Hedera helix (English ivy)	Canker, leaf spot, powdery mildew; aphids, caterpillars, mealy bug, mites, scale
Hibiscus syriacus (rose of Sharon)	Blight, canker, leaf spot, rust; aphids, Japanese beetle, nematodes, scale, whitefly
Hydrangea arborescens (hills-of-snow), *H. macrophylla* (big-leaf hydrangea), *H. paniculata* 'Grandiflora' (peegee hydrangea)	Bacterial wilt, blights, leaf spot, powdery mildew, rust; aphids, mites, nematodes, rose chafer, scale
Ilex crenata (Japanese holly)	Black knot (in the South); nematodes (in the South), spider mites
I. opaca (American holly)	Leaf drop, leaf rot, leaf spot, powdery mildew, tar spot; berry midge, leaf miner, mites, scale, whitefly
I. verticillata (winterberry)	Leaf spot, powdery mildew, tar spot
Juglans spp. (walnut, butternut, heartnut)	Bacterial blight, canker, leaf spot, witches-broom; aphids, caterpillars, lacebugs, mites, scale
Juniperus spp. (juniper)	Rust, twig blight, wilt; aphids, bagworm, bark beetle, midges, mites, scale, webworm
Kalmia latifolia (mountain laurel)	Blights, leaf spot; borers, lacebug, scale, whitefly
Kerria japonica	Blight, canker, leaf spot, root rot
Koelreuteria paniculata (goldenrain tree)	Canker, leaf spot, root rot
Laburnum × *watereri* (golden chain tree)	Leaf spot, twig blight; aphids, mealy bug
Lagerstroemia indica (common crape myrtle)	Black spot, leaf spot, powdery mildew, root rot, twig blight; aphids, scale
Larix spp. (larch)	Canker, rusts; aphids, caterpillars, Japanese beetle, sawfly
Ledum groenlandicum (Labrador tea)	Anthracnose, leaf gall, leaf spot, rust
Leucothoë spp.	Leaf spot
Ligustrum amurense (Amur privet), *L. vulgare* (European privet)	Anthracnose, galls, leaf spot, powdery, mildew, root rot, twig blight; aphids, leaf miner, mealy bug, mites, nematodes, scale, weevils, whitefly
Liquidambar styraciflua (sweet gum)	Leaf spot; caterpillars, scale, webworm
Liriodendron tulipifera (tulip tree)	Canker, leaf spot, powdery mildew, root rot, verticillium wilt; aphids, scale
Lonicera spp. (honeysuckle)	Leaf blight, leaf spot, powdery mildew; aphids, flea beetles, loopers, mealy bug, plant hopper, sawfly, scale, webworm
Magnolia × *soulangiana* (saucer magnolia)	Canker, dieback, leaf blight, leaf scab, leaf spot, mildews; scale
× *Mahoberberis* spp.	Same as for *Mahonia*
Mahonia spp. (hollygrape)	Leaf spot, rusts; aphids, scale, whitefly
Malus spp. (apple, crab apple)	Canker, fire blight, rust, scab; aphids, borers, scale
Metasequoia glyptostroboides (dawn redwood)	Canker; Japanese beetle
Microbiota decussata (Siberian carpet)	Wilt
Morus spp. (mulberry)	Bacterial blight, canker, leaf spot, powdery mildew; mites, scale
Nerium oleander (oleander)	Caterpillars, mealy bug, scale

(continues)

COMMON DISEASES AND PESTS OF SELECTED TREES AND SHRUBS (*continued*)

Name	*Diseases and Pests**
Nyssa sylvatica (black gum, tupelo)	Canker, leaf spot, rust; leaf miner, scale
Oxydendrum arboreum (sorrel tree, sourwood)	Leaf spot, twig blight
Pachysandra terminalis (common pachysandra)	Leaf blight; mites, scale
Paeonia suffruticosa (tree peony)	Canker, leaf blight, stem wilt; scale
Parthenocissus spp. (Virginia creeper, Boston ivy)	Canker, downy mildew, leaf spot, powdery mildew, wilt; Japanese beetle, leafhopper, scale
Paxistima canbyi (rat-stripper)	Leaf spot; scale
Philadelphus spp. (mock orange)	Canker, leaf spot, powdery mildew, rust; aphids, leaf miner, nematodes
Photinia spp.	Fire blight, leaf spot, powdery mildew; scale
Picea spp. (spruce)	Canker, root rot, rust; aphids, bagworm, borers, budworm, caterpillars, leaf miner, sawfly, scale, spider mites, weevils
Pieris japonica (Japanese andromeda)	Dieback (caused by *Phytophthora*), leaf spot, lacebug, mites, nematodes, scale
Pinus spp. (pine)	Blister rust, canker, dieback, rusts, tip blight, needle blight; bark beetles, borers, European and Nantucket tip moth caterpillars, miners, nematodes, sawfly, scale, spittlebug, webworm, weevils
Pittosporum tobira (Japanese pittosporum)	Leaf spot; mealy bug
Platanus spp. (sycamore)	Anthracnose (with witches'-broom), canker, leaf spot, powdery mildew; bagworm, borers, lacebug, scale
Polygonum aubertii (silver-lace vine)	Japanese beetle
Populus spp. (poplar)	Branch gall, canker, dieback, leaf blister, leaf spot, powdery mildew rust; borers, caterpillars, scale, willow beetle
Potentilla fruticosa (shrubby cinquefoil)	Spider mites
Prunus spp. (evergreen cherry laurels)	Leaf spot, shot-hole fungus
P. avium (sweet cherry), *P. cerasus* (sour cherry)	Bacterial canker, brown rot, crown gall, leaf curl, leaf scorch, powdery mildew, root rot, scab, shot-hole fungus, witches'-broom; aphids (with honeydew that supports sooty mold), caterpillars, fruit flies, leaf weevils, saw flies, scale
P. persica (peach)	Same as for cherries, plus earwigs, spider mites, wasps
P. sargentii (Sargent cherry)	Dieback, leaf curl, leaf spot, shot-hole fungus, witches'-broom; aphids, caterpillars, Japanese beetle
P. serrulata (Japanese flowering cherry), *P. subhirtells* (Higan cherry), *P. × yedoensis* (Yoshino cherry)	Same as for *P. sargentii* plus cherry black fly (causes sooty mold, distorted leaves, and reduced growth), borers
Pseudotsuga menziesii (Douglas fir)	Cankers, leaf blight, twig blight, witches'-broom; aphids, bark beetle, budworm, caterpillars, gypsy moth, pine moth, scale
Ptelea trifoliata (hop tree)	Leaf spot, rust
Pyracantha coccinea (firethorn)	Fire blight, leaf blight, root rot, scab; aphids, lacebugs, scale
Pyrus communis (common pear)	Bacterial blight, canker, crown gall, fire blight, leaf curl, powdery mildew, root rot, scab; aphids midges, mites, psyllids, saw flies, scale, thrips
P. spp. (other pear species)	Mostly same as for *P. communis*, plus tip dieback
Quercus spp. (oak)	Anthracnose, canker, leaf blister, leaf spot, powdery mildew, rust, shoestring rot, wilt; borers, caterpillars, insect galls (especially on *Q. palustris*, pin oak and *Q. virginiana*, live oak), leaf miner, mites, scale, weevils
Rhamnus spp. (buckthorn)	Leaf spot, powdery mildew, rust; aphids, scale
Rhododendron spp. (including azalea)	Canker, crown rot, dieback, galls, leaf spot, powdery mildew (especially in deciduous azaleas), rust, shoestring root rot, shoot blight; aphids, birds (especially woodpeckers), borers, lacebugs, leafhoppers, mealy bug, mites, nematodes, scale, thrips, whitefly
Rhus spp. (sumac)	Leaf spot, rust; aphids, mites, scale
Ribes spp. (currant)	Anthracnose, cane blight, leaf spot, rust; aphids, mites, scale
Robinia pseudoacacia (black locust)	Canker, leaf spot, powdery mildew; borers, leaf miner, scale

Name	Diseases and Pests*
Rosa spp. (hybrid roses, various species roses)	Black spot, canker, powdery mildew, rust; aphids, beetles, borers, leafhoppers, mites, slugs, thrips, etc.
Salix spp. (willow)	Same as for *Populus* spp.
Sambucus spp. (elder)	Canker, leaf spot, powdery mildew; borers
Sassafras albidum	Canker, leaf spot, powdery mildew, root rot, wilt; Japanese beetle, scale, weevils
Sherpherdia canadensis (russet buffalo berry)	Leaf spot, powdery mildew, rust
Sophora japonica (Japanese pagoda tree)	Canker, powdery mildew, twig blight, witches'-broom; leafhopper
Sorbus spp. (mountain ash, rowan)	Canker, crown gall, fire blight, leaf rust, scab; aphids, borers (especially in weakened trees), leafhopper, saw flies, scale
Spiraea spp.	Fire blight, leaf spot, powdery mildew, root rot; aphids, caterpillars, leaf roller, root-knot nematode, scale
Symphoricarpos spp. (coralberry, snowberry)	Anthracnose, fruit rot, leaf spot, powdery mildew, rust, stem gall; aphids, scale, whitefly
Syringa spp. (lilac)	Bacterial blight, fungal blight (*Phytophthora*), leaf blight, leaf spot, powdery mildew, witches'-broom; borers, caterpillars, leaf miner, scale
Tamarix spp. (tamarisk)	Cankers, powdery mildew, root rot; scale
Taxodium distichum (bald cypress)	Twig blight; gall mites, spider mites
Taxus spp. (yew)	Needle blight, root rot, twig blight; deer, gall midge, mealy bug, nematodes, scale, weevils
Thuja spp. (arborvitae)	Canker, leaf blight, tip blight; aphids, bagworm, canker, leaf miner, mealy bug, scale, spider mites
Tilia spp. (linden)	Anthracnose, canker, leaf blight, leaf spot, powdery mildew, verticillium wilt; aphids, borers, caterpillars, Japanese beetle, lacebugs, leaf miner, mites, saw flies, scale
Tsuga canadensis (Canadian hemlock, eastern hemlock)	Canker, leaf blight; rust; bagworm, borers, gypsy moth, leaf miner, loopers, saw flies, scale, spider mites, woolly adelgid (fatal in the northeastern United States)
T. caroliniana (Carolina hemlock)	Same as for *T. canadensis*, but somewhat resistant to woolly adelgid
T. diversifolia (Japanese hemlock)	Same as for *T. canadensis*, but quite resistant to woolly adelgid
Ulmus americana (American elm), *U. × hollandica* (Dutch elm), *U. procera* (English elm), *U. rubra* (slippery elm)	Bacterial wilt, canker, Dutch elm disease (transmitted by bark beetles), leaf curl, leaf spot, phloem necrosis, powdery mildew, verticillium wilt; aphids, bark beetles, borers, elm-leaf beetle, Japanese beetle, galls, gypsy moth, leaf miner, mites, scale
U. alata (winged elm)	Powdery mildew; resistant to Dutch elm disease and phloem necrosis; otherwise same as *U. americana*
U. parvifolia (Chinese elm), *U. pumila* (Siberian elm)	Same as for *U. americana*, but resistant to Dutch elm disease, elmleaf beetle, and Japanese beetle
Vaccinium corymbosum (highbush blueberry)	Birds, deer, leaf roller, rabbits, squirrels
Viburnum × burkwoodii (Burkwood viburnum)	Anthracnose, crown gall, leaf spot, powdery mildew, rust; aphids
V. carlesii (Korean spice viburnum)	Leaf spot, powdery mildew
V. lentago (nannyberry)	Powdery mildew (especially in shade)
V. opulus (European cranberry viburnum)	Aphids
Vinca minor (creeping myrtle)	Blight, canker, dieback, leaf spot, root rot
Vitex spp. (chaste bush)	Leaf spot, root rot
Vitis spp. (grape)	Anthracnose, bacterial blight, black rot, crown gall, downy mildew, gray mold, powdery mildew; birds, cutworm, deer, flea beetle, greenfly, leafhopper, nematodes, phylloxerids, rabbits, red spider mite; wasps, weevils, whitefly
Wisteria spp.	Canker, crown gall, leaf spot, mosaic, powdery mildew, root rot; Japanese beetle, leaf beetle, mealy bug, scale, webworm, weevils
Zelkova spp.	Canker, leaf spot, powdery mildew; aphids, borers, leaf miner (resistant to Dutch elm disease, phloem necrosis, elm-leaf beetle, and Japanese beetle)

*Diseases are listed first; then pests.

COMMON DISEASES AND PESTS OF GARDEN PERENNIALS, BIENNIALS, ANNUALS, AND BULBS

Name	Diseases and Pests*
PERENNIALS	
Acanthus spp. (bear's-breeches)	Slugs, snails
Achillea spp. (yarrow, except *A. tomentosa*)	Powdery mildew, rust, stem rot
Aconitum spp. (monkshood)	Crown rot, mosaic, powdery mildew, verticillium wilt; mites
Aegopodium podagraria (bishop's goutweed)	Leaf blight (in hot, humid weather)
Ajuga spp. (bugle)	Crown rot (especially when overcrowded)
Anchusa azurea (Italian alkanet)	Crown rot
Aquilegia spp. (columbine)	Crown rot; aphids, borers, leaf miner, leaf spot
Arabis spp. (rock cress)	Clubroot, downy mildew, white rust; aphids
Arenaria spp. (sandwort)	Leaf spot, powdery mildew, rust
Artemisia spp. (wormwood)	Leaf rust
Aster spp. (perennial aster)	Mildews (especially in dry soils), rust; Japanese beetle
Astilbe spp.	Powdery mildew, wilt
Belamcanda chinensis (blackberry lily)	Borers
Campanula spp. (perennial bellflower)	Slugs, snails
Centaurea dealbata (Persian cornflower)	Aster yellows, rust, stem rot
C. hypoleuca 'John Coutts' (Coutts' bluet)	Aster yellows, rust, stem rot
C. montana (mountain bluet)	Aster yellows, rust, stem rot
Chrysanthemum × *morifolium* (garden mum)	Aster yellows, bacterial blight, leaf spot, powdery mildew, rust, wilt; aphids, borers, leaf miner, mites
C. × *superbum* (Shasta daisy)	Same as for *C.* × *morifolium*
Cimicifuga spp. (bugbane, snakeroot)	Leaf spot, rust
Clematis spp. (perennial clematis)	Stem rot; blister beetle, tarnished plant bug
Convallaria majalis (lily-of-the-valley)	Anthracnose, leaf spot, stem rot
Coreopsis lanceolata (common coreopsis)	Leaf spot, powdery mildew, rust; aphids, plant bugs, spotted cucumber beetle
Delphinium elatum (tall delphinium)	Blights, canker, crown rot, leaf spot, powdery mildew; aphids borers, leaf miner, mites
Dianthus spp. (perennial pinks)	Bacterial wilt, botrytis blight, leaf spot, root rot, rust, stem rot; aphids, cabbage looper, cutworm, mites
Dicentra spp. (bleeding heart)	Stem rot, wilt; aphids
Digitalis spp. (perennial foxglove)	Leaf spot, powdery mildew
Doronicum spp. (leopard's-bane)	Powdery mildew; aphids, saw flies
Echinacea purpurea (purple coneflower)	Leaf spot; Japanese beetle
Erigeron spp. (fleabane)	Downy mildew, leaf spot, powdery mildew, rust; aphids
Eschscholzia californica (perennial California poppy)	Bacterial blight, leaf mold, powdery mildew
Eupatorium coelestinum (hardy ageratum)	Powdery mildew; aphids, leaf miner
Filipendula spp. (dropwort, queen of the meadow, queen of the prairie)	Powdery mildew
Gaillardia × *grandiflora* (perennial gaillardia)	Aster yellows, leaf spot, powdery mildew; leafhopper, plant bugs
Galega officinalis (goat's rue)	Powdery mildew; aphids, cutworms
Geranium spp. (perennial cranesbill)	Rust; leaf spot, plant bugs
Gypsophila paniculata (perennial baby's breath)	Aster yellows, botrytis blight; leafhoppers
Helenium autumnale (sneezeweed)	Leaf spot, rust; snout beetle
Heliopsis helianthoides	Aphids
Helleborus spp. (Christmas rose, hellebore, lenten rose)	Black spot, crown rot

Name	Diseases and Pests*
Heuchera sanguinea (coralbells)	Stem rot; mealy bugs, root weevils
Hibiscus coccineus (scarlet mallow)	Blights, canker, leaf spot, rust; aphids, Japanese beetle, scale, whiteflies
H. moscheutos (rose mallow)	Same as for *H. coccineus*
Inula ensifolia (sword-leaf inula)	Mildews
Iris cristata (crested iris)	Slugs, snails
I. ensata (Japanese iris)	Thrips
I. hybrids (bearded iris)	Borers
I. pallida (orris)	Borers
Lamiastrum galeobdolon var. *variegatum* (yellow dead nettle)	Slugs, snails
Lavandula angustifolia (English lavender)	Leaf spot, root rot; caterpillars, root knot nematode
Liatris spp. (blazing star, gayfeather)	Root nematodes (zone 8 and south)
Linum spp. (flax)	Cutworm, grasshoppers
Lupinus spp. (perennial lupine)	Powdery mildew, rust; aphids, plant bugs
Lychnis spp. (catchfly, Maltese cross)	Leaf spot, root rot, rust, smut; whiteflies
Macleaya cordata (plume poppy)	Anthracnose
Malva alcea (pink mallow)	Japanese beetle
Mirabilis jalapa (four o'clock)	Leaf spot, root rot, rust; Japanese beetle
Monarda spp. (bee balm, bergamot)	Powdery mildew, rust
Myosotis scorpioides (perennial forget-me-not)	Powdery mildew; red spider mite
Oenothera spp. (perennial evening primrose, sundrops)	Root rot
Paeonia lactiflora hybrids (peony)	Botrytis blight, phytophthora blight
Pelargonium × *hortorum* (perennial garden geranium)	Bacterial leaf spot, black leg, botrytis blight, root rot, rust, stem rot; caterpillars, mealy bug, mites
Penstemon spp. (beardtongue)	Leaf spot, rust
Phlox spp. (perennial phlox)	Crown rot, leaf spot, powdery mildew; flea beetles, mites, rabbits
P. subulata (mountain pink)	Rust; spider mites
Physalis alkekengi (Chinese lantern)	Cucumber beetle, flea beetle
Physostegia virginiana (obedient plant)	Rust
Polemonium caeruleum (Jacob's ladder)	Leaf spot, powdery mildew, rust, wilt
Primula spp. (primrose)	Bacterial leaf spot, rusts; aphids, flea beetles, red spider mite
Ricinus communis (perennial castor bean)	Bacterial leaf spot, bacterial wilt, blights, gray mold, stem rot; armyworm
Rudbeckia hirta (black-eyed Susan)	Downy mildew, powdery mildew, rust; aphids, saw files
Salvia spp. (perennial sage)	Damping off, powdery mildew; scale, whitefly
Saxifraga spp. (saxifrage)	Aphids, rust
Scabiosa caucasica (perennial scabiosa)	Slugs, snails
Sempervivum spp. (hen and chickens, live-forever)	Crown rot, rust
Sidalcea malviflora (checkermallow)	Japanese beetle
Teucrium chamaedrys (germander)	Downy mildew, leaf spot, powdery mildew, rust; mites
Thalictrum spp. (meadow rue)	Powdery mildew, rust, smut
Tradescantia spp. (spiderwort)	Botrytis blight; caterpillars
Trollius spp. (globeflower)	Powdery mildew
Veronica spp. (speedwell)	Downy mildew, leaf spot
Viola spp. (violet)	Anthracnose, crown rot, downy mildew, leaf spot; cutworm, slugs, snails

(continues)

COMMON DISEASES AND PESTS OF GARDEN PERENNIALS, BIENNIALS, ANNUALS, AND BULBS (*continued*)

Name	Diseases and Pests*
BIENNIALS	
Alcea rosea (hollyhock)	Anthracnose, leaf spot, rust; Japanese beetle, spider mites
Bellis perennis (English daisy)	Powdery mildew
Campanula medium (Canterbury bell)	Crown rot, leaf spot, powdery mildew, rust; aphids, slugs, snails
Dianthus barbatus (sweet William)	Bacterial wilt, botrytis blight, leaf spot, root rot, rust, stem rot; aphids, cabbage looper, cutworm, mites
Digitalis purpurea (common foxglove)	Leaf spot, powdery mildew, root rot, stem rot; aphids, Japanese beetle, mealy bug
Erysimum cultivars (wallflower)	Bacterial wilt, clubroot, gray mold, white rust
Myosotis alpestris (biennial forget-me-not)	Powdery mildew; red spider mite
M. sylvatica (biennial forget-me-not)	Same as for *M. alpestris*
Viola × wittrockiana (pansy)	Anthracnose, crown rot, downy mildew, leaf spot; cutworm, slugs, snails
ANNUALS	
Abutilon spp. (flowering maple)	Whitefly
Ageratum houstonianum	Powdery mildew, root rot
Amaranthus spp. (Joseph's coat, love-lies-bleeding)	Root rot; stem borers
Antirrhinum majus (snapdragon)	Downy mildew, gray mold, leaf blight, rust, wilt; aphids, mites
Arctotis venusta (African daisy)	Leaf blotch, leaf spot, root knot, root rot
Asclepias curassavica (bloodflower milkweed)	Aphids
Begonia Semperflorens-Cultorum hybrids (fibrous-rooted begonia)	Botrytis blight, leaf spot, powdery mildew, stem rot; mealy bug, thrips
Brassica oleracea Capitata group (flowering cabbage)	Cabbage looper
Browallia speciosa	Fusarium wilt; leafhoppers, whitefly
Calendula officinalis	Aster yellows, leaf spot, powdery mildew, root rot; stem rot; cabbage looper
Callistephus chinensis (China aster)	Aster yellows, stem rot; aphids, spider mites
Celosia argenteum (cockscomb, plume celosia)	Leaf spot, stem rot; mites
Centaurea cyanus (cornflower, bachelor button)	Rust, stem rot, wilt
Coleus × hybridus	Leaf spot; aphids, mealy bug, mites, whitefly
Cosmos spp.	Bacterial wilt, canker; aphids, Japanese beetle
Cuphea spp. (cigar plant, firecracker flower)	Whitefly
Dahlia hybrids (bedding dahlia)	Mosaic virus, smut, wilt; aphids (virus vectors), borers, caterpillars, earwigs, mites, slugs, snails, tarnished plant bug, thrips
Dianthus spp. (annual pinks)	Bacterial wilt, botrytis blight, leaf spot, root rot, rust, stem rot; aphids, cabbage looper, cutworm, mites
Dimorphotheca sinuata (African daisy)	Aster yellows, blights, downy mildew, rust; leafhoppers
Dyssodia tenuiloba (Dahlberg daisy)	Aster yellows
Eschscholzia spp. (California poppy)	Bacterial blight, leaf mold, powdery mildew
Fuchsia × hybrida	Botrytis blight, rust; aphids, Japanese beetle, mealy bug, mites, scale, thrips, whitefly
Gomphrena globosa (globe amaranth)	Damping off
Gypsophila elegans (annual baby's breath)	Aster yellows, botrytis blight; leafhoppers
Helianthus annuus (sunflower)	Leaf spot, powdery mildew, rust, stem rot; aphids, cutworm, midges
Helichrysum bracteatum (strawflower)	Stem rot (especially on wet ground)
Impatiens spp. (balsam)	Damping off; mealy bug, slugs, snails, whitefly
Limonium sinuatum (annual statice)	Root rot

Name	Diseases and Pests*
Linaria spp. (toadflax)	Downy mildew, powdery mildew, root rot, stem rot; aphids, flea beetles, nematodes
Lobularia maritima (sweet alyssum)	Damping off; curculio
Lupinus spp. (annual lupine, blue bonnet)	Powdery mildew, rust; aphids, plant bugs
Matthiola incana 'Annua' (stock)	Bacterial blight, root rot; flea beetles
Molucella laevis (bells of Ireland)	Crown rot
Nicotiana spp. (flowering tobacco)	Colorado potato beetle, flea beetles
Ocimum basilicum (sweet basil)	Slugs, snails
Pelargonium × *hortorum* (garden geranium)	Bacterial leaf spot, black leg, botrytis blight, root rot, rust, stem rot; caterpillars, mealy bug, mites
Petunia × *hybrida*	Botrytis blight, stem rot, tobacco mosaic; aphids (vector for mosaic), flea beetles
Phlox drummondii (annual phlox)	Crown rot, leaf spot, powdery mildew; flea beetles, mites, rabbits
Ricinus communis (castor bean)	Bacterial leaf spot, bacterial wilt, blights, gray mold, stem rot; armyworm
Rudbeckia trifida (late coneflower)	Downy mildew, powdery mildew, rust; aphids, saw flies
Salpiglossis sinuata (painted tongue)	Wilt; nematodes
Salvia spp. (annual sages)	Damping off, powdery mildew; scale, whitefly
Schizanthus pinnatus (butterfly flower)	Leaf gall, powdery mildew, root rot, wilt; aphids
Tagetes spp. (marigold)	Gray mold; Japanese beetle, leafhoppers (vector for aster yellows), slugs, snails, spider mites
Tropaeolum majus (nasturtium)	Leaf spot, wilt; aphids, cabbage looper, mites, thrips
Verbena × *hybrida* (garden verbena)	Damping off
Zinnia elegans (common zinnia)	Damping off, gray mold, root rot, seedling blight; cutworm, earwigs, Japanese beetle, nematodes

BULBS†

Name	Diseases and Pests*
Acidanthera bicolor (peacock orchid)	Bacterial blight, botrytis leaf spot, crown rot, fusarium yellows, leaf blight, mosaic, scab, smut, wilt; aphids, mealy bug, spider mites, tarnished plant bug, thrips, wireworms
Allium giganteum (giant allium, giant onion)	Bulb rot (*Sclerotium cepivorum*)
Anemone blanda (Grecian windflower)	Rhizome rot
Begonia × *tuberhybrida* (tuberous begonia)	Botrytis blight, leaf spot, powdery mildew, stem rot; mealy bug, thrips
Canna × *generalis*	Aster yellows, bud rot, mosaic; Japanese beetle
Chionodoxa luciliae (glory-of-the-snow)	Nematodes, rodents (especially chipmunks and mice)
Colchicum spp. (autumn crocus)	Leaf smut
Crinum spp. (crinum lily)	Bulb rot, red-spot fungus (leaf scorch); nematodes, slugs, snails
Crocus spp.	Rot, scab; mice squirrels
Cyclamen hederifolium (hardy cyclamen)	Cats, mice, squirrels
Dahlia hybrids	Mosaic virus, smut, wilt; aphids (virus vectors), borers, caterpillars, earwigs, mites, slugs, snails, tarnished plant bug, thrips
Fritillaria imperialis (crown imperial)	Bulb rot, leaf spot, mosaic, rust
Gladiolus × *hortulanus*	Same as for *Acidanthera bicolor*
Hymenocallis spp. (spider lily)	Basal rot, red-spot fungus (leaf scorch), tomato spotted wilt (insect-borne virus); spider mites
Iris reticulata (netted iris)	Fusarium basal rot, ink spot
Lilium spp. (lily)	Bulb rot; aphids (vectors of lily mosaic), deer, rabbits
Narcissus spp. (daffodil)	Bulb rot
Scilla siberica (Siberian squill)	Crown rot
Tulipa spp. (tulip)	Basal rot, gray mold, stem rot; deer, rabbits
Zantedeschia spp. (calla)	Bacterial soft rot, cucumber mosaic, leaf blotch, phytophthora root rot, tomato-spotted wilt

*Diseases are listed first; then pests.

†Including corms, rhizomes, and tubers and without regard to frost tolerance.

TREES AND SHRUBS SELDOM ATTACKED BY PESTS AND DISEASES

Abelia grandiflora (glossy abelia)
Abeliophyllum distichum (white forsythia)
Abies concolor (white fir)
A. fraseri (Fraser fir)
Acanthopanax sieboldianus (five leaf aralia)
Acer spp.
Actinidia spp. (hardy kiwifruit, tara vine)
Aesculus parviflora (bottlebrush buckeye)
Akebia quinata (five-leaf akebia)
Aralia spp. (Hercules' club)
Aronia spp. (chokeberry)
Asimina triloba (papaw)
Aspidistra elatior (cast-iron plant)
Aucuba japonica (Japanese laurel, gold-dust bush)
Bignonia capreolata (cross vine)
Caragana spp. (pea bush)
Carpinus betulus (European hornbeam)
Carya spp. (hickory)
Caryopteris spp. (blue-mist bush)
Cedrela sinensis (Chinese cedrela)
Cephalanthus occidentalis (buttonbush)
Cercidophyllum japonicum (katsura tree)
Chamaecyparis spp. (false cypress, except *C. lawsoniana*)
Chimonanthus praecox (winter sweet)
Chionanthus spp. (fringe bush)
Cladrastis lutea (American yellowwood)
Clerodendrum trichotomum (harlequin glory-bower)
Clethra spp. (summersweet)
Cleyera japonica (Japanese cleyera)
Colutea arborescens (bladder senna)
Comptonia peregrina (sweet fern)
Cornus kousa (Japanese dogwood, kousa)
C. mas (cornelian cherry dogwood)
Corylopsis spp. (winter hazel)
Corylus colurna (Turkish filbert, hazel)
Cotinus spp. (smoke tree)
Cryptomeria japonica (Japanese cedar)
Cunninghamia lanceolata (China fir)
× *Cupressocyparis leylandii* (Leyland cypress)
Cyrilla racemiflora
Davidia involucrata (dove tree)
Diervilla spp. (bush honeysuckle)
Diospyros spp. (persimmon)
Dirca palustris (leatherwood)
Disanthus cercidifolius
Elliotia racemosa (Georgia plume)
Elsholtzia stauntonii (Staunton elsholtzia)
Enkianthus spp.
Eucommia ulmoides (hardy rubber tree)
Evodia danielii (Korean evodia)
Exochorda spp. (pearlbush)
Fatsia japonica
Feijoa sellowiana (pineapple guava)
Firmiana simplex (parasol tree)
Fothergilla spp.
Gaultheria spp. (checkerberry, wintergreen, salal)
Gaylussacia brachycera (box huckleberry)
Gelsemium sempervirens (carolina yellow jessamine)
Genista spp. (woadwaxen)
Ginkgo biloba (maidenhair tree)
Gymnocladus dioicus (Kentucky coffee tree)

Halesia spp. (silver bell)
Hamamelis spp. (witch hazel)
Hippophaë rhamnoides (sea buckthorn)
Hovenia dulcis (Japanese raisin tree)
Hydrangea anomala ssp. *petiolaris* (climbing hydrangea)
H. quercifolia (oak-leaf hydrangea)
Hypericum spp. (shrubby St. John'swort)
Ilex aquifolium hybrids (English holly cvs.)
I. glabra (inkberry)
I. pedunculata (longstalk holly)
I. vomitoria (yaupon)
Illicium spp. (anise tree)
Indigofera kirilowii (Kirilow indigo)
Itea spp. (sweet spire)
Jasminum spp. (jasmine)
Kalopanax pictus (castor aralia)
Kolkwitzia amabilis (beauty-bush)
Leycesteria spp. (Himalaya honeysuckle)
Lycium spp. (boxthorn, matrimony vine)
Maackia amurensis (Amur maackia)
Maclura pomifera (Osage orange)
Magnolia spp. (except *M.* × *soulangiana*)
Melia azedarach (Chinaberry)
Menispermum canadense (moonseed)
Michelia figo (banana shrub)
Nandina domestica (heavenly bamboo)
Neillia chinensis (Chinese neillia)
Neviusia alabamensis (snow wreath)
Osmanthus heterophyllus (holly osmanthus)
Ostrya spp. (hop hornbeam)
Parrotia persica (Persian parrotia)
Parrotiopsis jacquemontia
Phellodendron amurense (Amur cork tree)
Pistacia chinensis (Chinese pistachio)
Podocarpus spp.
Poncirus trifoliata (hardy orange)
Prinsepia sinensis (cherry prinsepia)
Pseudolarix kaempferi (golden larch)
Pterocarya fraxinifolia (Caucasian wingnut)
Pterostyrax hispidus (epaulette tree)
Punica granatum (pomegranate)
Raphiolepis umbellata (Indian hawthorn)
Rosa banksiae (Lady Banks' rose)
R. multiflora (multiflora rose)
R. rugosa (Japanese rose, rugosa rose)
Ruscus aculeatus (butcher's broom)
Santolina chamaecyparissus (lavender cotton)
Sapindus drummondii (western soapberry)
Sapium sebiferum (Chinese tallow tree)
Sciadopitys verticillata (umbrella pine)
Skimmia japonica (Japanese skimmia)
Sorbaria spp. (false spiraea)
Staphylea spp. (bladdernut)
Stephanandra incisa (lace bush)
Stewartia spp.
Stranvesia davidiana (Chinese stranvesia)
Styrax spp. (snowbell, storax)
Symplocos spp. (sweetleaf)
Taxodium adscendens (pond cypress)
Thujopsis dolobrata (false arborvitae, Hiba arborvitae)
Trachyspermum spp. (star jasmine)

Tripterygium regelii (Regel's three-wing nut)
Viburnum acerifolium (maple-leaf viburnum)
V. macrocephalum (Chinese snowball)
V. cassinoides (withe rod viburnum)
V. davidii (David viburnum)
V. dentatum (arrowwood viburnum)
V. dilatatum (linden viburnum)
V. lantana (wayfaring tree viburnum)
V. plicatum f. *tomentosum* (double-file viburnum)
V. prunifolium (black haw viburnum)
V. rhytidophyllum (leatherleaf viburnum)

V. sargentii (Sargent viburnum)
V. setigerum (tea-leaf viburnum)
V. trilobum (American cranberry viburnum)
Weigela florida
Xanthoceras sorbifolium (yellowhorn)
Xanthorhiza simplicissima (yellowroot)
Yucca filamentosa
Y. glauca (soapweed)
Zanthoxylum spp. (prickly ash)
Zenobia pulverulenta (dusty zenobia)

PERENNIALS, BIENNIALS, ANNUALS, AND BULBS SELDOM ATTACKED BY PESTS AND DISEASES

PERENNIALS

Abelmoschus spp. (perennial flowering okra—
    perennial from zone 8 southward)
Achillea tomentosa (woolly yarrow)
Acorus gramineus (Japanese sweet flag)
Actaea spp. (baneberry)
Adenophora spp. (ladybell)
Adiantum spp. (maidenhair fern)
Adonis spp. (pheasant's-eye)
Aethionema spp. (stonecress)
Alchemilla mollis (lady's mantle)
Alopecurus pratensis 'Aurea' (golden foxtail grass)
Amsonia tabernaemontana (blue stars)
Anaphalis triplinervis (pearly everlasting)
Anemone × *hybrida* (Japanese anemone)
Anemone pulsatilla (pasque flower)
Antennaria rosea (rose pussy toes)
Anthemis tinctoria (golden marguerite)
Armeria maritima (sea pink, thrift)
Arrhenathemum elatius 'Variegatum' (variegated oat grass)
Arum italicum (painted arum)
Aruncus dioicus (goat's beard)
Arundo donax (giant reed)
Asarum spp. (wild ginger)
Asclepias tuberosa (butterfly weed)
Asphodeline lutea (yellow asphodel)
Asplenium ebenoides (dragontail fern)
Astrantia major (great masterwort)
Athyrium spp. (lady fern, painted fern)
Aubrieta deltoidea (false rock cress)
Aurinia saxatilis (basket-of-gold, yellow alyssum)
Baptisia australis (blue indigo)
Begonia grandis (hardy begonia)
Bergenia spp.
Bletilla striata (hardy orchid)
Boltonia asteroides (white boltonia)
Briza media (quaking grass)
Brunnera macrophylla (Siberian bugloss)
Buphthalmum salicifolium (oxeye, wheel daisy)
Calamagrostis acutiflora 'Stricta' (feather reed grass)
Callirhoë involucrata (winecups)
Caltha palustris (marsh marigold)

Carex morrowii 'Aurea Variegata' (variegated Japanese sedge)
Carlina acaulis (stemless carline thistle)
Centaurea macrocephala (globe centaurea)
Centranthus ruber (red valerian)
Cerastium tomentosum (snow-in-summer)
Ceratostigma spp. (plumbago)
Chasmanthium latifolium (northern sea oats)
Chelone spp. (turtlehead)
Chrysanthemum coccineum (painted daisy, pyrethrum)
C. nipponicum (Montauk daisy, Nippon daisy)
Chrysogonum virginianum (golden star)
Coreopsis verticillata (threadleaf coreopsis)
Cortaderia selloana (pampas grass)
Corydalis lutea (golden corydalis)
Cystopteris bulbifera (bulblet bladder fern)
Dennstaedtia punctilobula (hay-scented fern)
Deschampsia caespitosa (tufted hair grass)
Dictamnus albus (gas plant)
Disporum spp. (fairybell)
Dodecatheon spp. (shooting star)
Dryopteris spp. (shield fern)
Echinops ritro (globe thistle)
Elymus arenarius (blue Lyme grass)
Epimedium spp. (barrenwort)
Equisetum spp. (horsetail, scouring rush)
Eremurus spp. (foxtail lily)
Erianthus ravennae (plume grass)
Eryngium spp. (sea holly)
Euphorbia spp. (perennial spurge)
Galium odoratum (sweet woodruff)
Gaura lindheimeri (white gaura)
Gazania ringens (perennial from zone 9 southward)
Gentiana spp. (gentian)
Gerbera jamesonii (perennial Transvaal daisy)
Gillenia trifoliata (bowman's root)
Hakonechloa macra 'Aureola' (golden variegated hakonechloa)
Helianthemum spp. (rockrose)
Helianthus spp. (perennial sunflower)
Helictotrichon sempervirens (ornamental oats)
Hemerocallis spp. (daylily)
Heuchera americana (alum root)

(continues)

PERENNIALS, BIENNIALS, ANNUALS, AND BULBS SELDOM ATTACKED BY PESTS AND DISEASES (continued)

Holcus mollis 'Variegatus' (variegated velvet grass)
Hordeum jubatum (squirrel-tail grass)
Houttuynia cordata
Iberis sempervirens (perennial candytuft)
Imperata cylindrica var. *rubra* 'Red Baron' (Japanese blood grass)
Iris pseudacorus (yellow flag)
I. sibirica (Siberian iris)
I. versicolor (blue flag)
Kniphofia hybrids (red-hot poker)
Koeleria glauca (blue June grass)
Lamium maculatum (pink dead nettle, spotted dead nettle)
Lathyrus latifolius (perennial sweet pea)
Leontopodium alpinum (edelweiss)
Ligularia spp. (goldenray, ragwort)
Limonium spp. (perennial statice, sea lavender)
Liriope spp. (lilyturf)
Lobelia cardinalis (cardinal flower)
L. siphilitica (great blue lobelia)
Lychnis coronaria (red campion)
Lysimachia spp. (loosestrife)
Lythrum salicaria cultivars (garden loosestrife)
Matteucia pensylvanica (ostrich fern)
Mertensia virginica (Virginia bluebell)
Mimulus spp. (perennial monkey flower)
Miscanthus spp. (eulalia, silver grass)
Molinia caerulea 'Variegata' (variegated purple moor grass)
Nepeta × *fassenii* (catmint)
Omphalodes cappadocica (navelwort)
Opuntia compressa (hardy prickly pear)
Osmunda spp. (cinnamon fern, interrupted fern, royal fern)
Panicum virgatum (switch grass)
Papaver orientale (Oriental poppy)
Pennisetum spp. (perennial fountain grass)
Perovskia atriplicifolia (Russian sage)
Petrorhagia saxifraga (tunic flower)
Phalaris arundinacia var. *picta* (ribbon grass)
Phlomis russeliana (Jerusalem sage)
Phyllitis scolopendrium (hart's-tongue fern)
Platycodon grandiflorus (balloon flower)

Polygonatum spp. (Solomon's seal)
Polygonum spp. (bistort, fleeceflower, Japanese bamboo, knotweed)
Polystichum spp. (Christmas fern, holly fern)
Potentilla spp. (cinquefoil)
Prunella grandiflora (heal-all)
Pulmonaria spp. (Bethlehem sage, lungwort)
Ranunculus spp. (buttercup)
Rodgersia spp.
Romneya coulteri (matilija poppy)
Roscoea spp.
Rudbeckia nitida (coneflower)
Ruta graveolens (rue)
Sagina subulata (pearlwort)
Sanguisorba spp. (burnet)
Santolina spp. (lavender cotton)
Saponaria spp. (bouncing Bet, soapwort)
Schizostylis coccinea (crimson flag)
Sedum spp. (stonecrop)
Senna hebecarpa (hardy senna, hardy cassia)
S. marilandica (hardy senna, hardy cassia)
Silene dioica (rose campion)
Smilacina racemosa (false Solomon's seal)
Solidago spp. (goldenrod)
Sorghastrum avenaceum (Indian grass)
Spartina pectinata (cordgrass)
Spigelia marilandica (Indian pink)
Stachys spp. (betony, lamb's ear)
Stipa pennata (feather grass)
Stokesia laevis (Stokes aster)
Strobilanthes atropurpurea (Mexican petunia)
Symphytum spp. (comfrey)
Thermopsis spp.
Tricyrtis hirta (toad lily)
Tritonia crocata
Unvularia grandiflora (bellwort)
Valeriana spp. (valerian)
Verbena rigida (vervain)
Waldsteinia fragarioides (barren strawberry)
Xanthisma texana (star of Texas)

BIENNIALS

Hesperis matronalis (dame's rocket)

Verbascum spp. (mullein)

ANNUALS

Abelmoschus spp. (flowering okra)
Adonis spp. (pheasant's-eye)
Aethionema spp. (stonecress)
Alternanthera ficoidea (garden alternanthera)
Bassia scoparia f. *trichophylla* (Kochia, summer cypress)
Brachycome iberidifolia (Swan River daisy)
Brassica oleracea Acephala group (flowering kale)
Capsicum annuum (ornamental pepper)
Catananche caerulea (Cupid's dart)
Catharanthus rosea (annual periwinkle)
Cleome hassleriana (spider flower)
Convolvulus tricolor (bush morning glory)
Coreopsis tinctoria (annual coreopsis, calliopsis)

Euphorbia cyathophora (annual poinsettia)
E. marginata (snow-on-the-mountain)
Eustoma grandiflora (lisianthus, prairie gentian)
Gaillardia pulchella (annual gaillardia)
Gazania ringens
Gerbera jamesonii (Transvaal daisy)
Heliotropium arborescens (heliotrope)
Hunnemannia fumariifolia (tulip poppy)
Hypoestes phyllostachya (polka-dot plant)
Iberis umbellata (annual candytuft)
Ipomoea spp. (morning glory)
Lavatera trimestris (bush mallow)
Lobelia erinus (bedding lobelia)

Lonas annua (yellow ageratum)
Melampodium cinereum (butter daisy)
Mimulus spp. (annual monkey flower)
Nierembergia hippomanica var. *violacea* (cupflower)
Nigella damascena (devil-in-a-bush, love-in-a-mist)
Papaver spp. (annual poppy)
Pennisetum spp. (annual fountain grass)
Polygonum spp. (bistort, knotweed)

Portulaca grandiflora
Sanvitalia procumbens (creeping zinnia)
Scabiosa atropurpurea (annual scabiosa)
Thunbergia spp. (angel wings, black-eyed Susan vine)
Tithonia rotundifolia (Mexican hat, torch flower)
Torenia fournierii (wishbone flower)
Zinnia angustifolia (narrow-leaf zinnia)

BULBS*

Agapanthus spp. (African lily)
Allium christophii (star of Persia)
A. moly (golden garlic)
A. senescens (ornamental onion)
A. tuberosum (garlic chives)
Caladium × *hortulanum* (fancy-leaf caladium)
Crocosmia cvs. (montbretia)
Eranthis hymale (winter aconite)
Erythronium spp. (avalanche lily, dogtooth violet, trout lily)
Fritillaria meleagris (checkerlily, Guinea flower)

Galanthus nivalis (snowdrop)
Gloriosa superba (climbing lily)
Hyacinthoides spp. (wood hyacinth)
Hyacinthus orientalis (hyacinth)
Leucojum spp. (snowflake)
Lycoris spp. (hardy amaryllis, naked lady)
Muscari spp. (grape hyacinth)
Ornithogalum spp. (chincherinchee, star-of-Bethlehem)
Polianthes tuberosa (tuberose)

*Includes corms, rhizomes, and tubers and without regard to frost tolerance.

PESTS AND DISEASES OF HOUSEPLANTS

While growing plants indoors is a special joy for many gardeners, especially those in city apartments with no access to an outdoor plot or yard, it must be remembered that indoor environments, however carefully they are maintained, are nevertheless so unlike the natural conditions in which our various houseplant species evolved that the plants are usually under considerable stress and thus often in less than optimal physiological condition. Stressed plants in substandard condition are especially prone to attack by pests and diseases. Hence the primary importance of choosing the kinds of plants best suited for cultivation under the varied conditions, room by room, that your home offers (see Chapter 38); of choosing individual plants that are pest and disease free and otherwise in a superior physiological state; and of caring for those you have chosen in a manner that as nearly as possible meets their genetically determined requirements.

Although respecting these criteria will minimize the occurrence of pests and diseases on your houseplants, outbreaks will happen, and these must be dealt with promptly, appropriately, and effectively if the pest or disease is to be contained and quelled, and damage minimized. To do so, the following steps are recommended:

1. Identify the pest or disease as accurately as possible.
2. Take steps to interrupt its life cycle, thereby bringing it under control.

3. Favor mechanical or cultural measures over intervention with chemical biocides.
4. If biocides are necessary, choose those that are quickly effective, are as specific as possible and soon become benign (i.e., do not leave a toxic residue).

Whatever substances are employed to effect control, it is the user's responsibility to follow label instructions scrupulously, to isolate plants under treatment from other plants (which may be sensitive to one or more of the biocide's components); and to keep other people and any pets away until the toxic principles have neutralized.

Common Pests of Houseplants
Aphids

Aphids are small (the size of a sesame seed), soft-bodied, often pear-shaped insects that are green, pink, red, white, gray, or black. Their populations commonly become very large, owing to their capacity to proliferate from unfertilized eggs. Aphids weaken plants by sucking their juices and, secondarily, by often transmitting pathogenic viruses. Aphid infestations are usually found on young stems and leaves, which are variously misshapen or undersize, but may also occur on roots. Light infestations aboveground can be controlled by washing the insects off with a strong water spray or by using a cotton swab dipped in alcohol. Larger or persistent infestations may call for a systemic pesticide, such as neem (see page 810). A soil drench of malathion will control root aphids.

Mealy Bugs

Mealy bugs are usually first detected as whitish, cottony tufts or masses, characteristically grouped in the angles between leaf stalks and stems, among crowded rudimentary leaves at shoot tips, and on the undersurfaces of leaves. These are sucking insects whose numbers soon increase, spreading the infestation, weakening the affected plant(s), and because of the sugary honeydew they excrete, attracting ants and coating all surfaces beneath with a sticky gum that eventually supports the growth of an opaque black sooty mold. Control mealy bugs first by wiping them off with an alcohol-dipped cotton swab and drowning them in alcohol. Next spray the areas of infestation with an oil detergent solution: mix 1 tablespoon of dishwashing detergent with 1 cup of vegetable oil; add 2 teaspoons of this mixture to 1 cup of tepid water in a mister or pump-spray bottle. One hour after spraying, wash off the residue with clear water. If necessary, repeat in 10 to 14 days, but no sooner. If the infestation persists, spray with tobacco tea, made by soaking one whole cigarette (or the equivalent in butts, one cigar butt, or 1 teaspoon of pipe tobacco) overnight in 1 cup of water. Strain to remove the tobacco bits and add ¼ teaspoon vegetable oil (preferably olive) and ¼ teaspoon of detergent. Mix thoroughly before spraying infested areas. Exposure to sunlight will hasten the breakdown of the poisonous nicotine to a harmless state. Repeat at weekly intervals until there is no further recurrence. Note: Let no one ingest this mixture; quickly wash off any of the tobacco tea that spills on the skin; do not use on food crops.

Scale Insects

Scale insects are first detected as small tan or brown, glossy, hard-shelled oval bumps or lumps, often about as wide as a peppercorn, on young stems and on the veins of leaves. These creatures usually increase rapidly and form dense colonies on stems and weaken the plant by sucking its juices. The scales themselves do not move, but the nearly invisible young are mobile, chiefly at night. Honeydew is excreted, with the same results as with aphids and mealy bugs.

Adult scales may be scraped off plant surfaces with a dull knife and drowned in alcohol. After scraping, the infested plant areas should be gently rubbed with an alcohol-soaked swab to dislodge minute eggs (often concealed by adult scales) and nymphs or immature insects. It is usually necessary to repeat the scraping and swabbing at weekly intervals until there is no recurrence. Persistent infestations may be treated with lemon oil on a swab.

Spider Mites

Spider mites, most often the red spider mite, are first detected by the damage they cause: premature dropping of abnormally yellowish or bronzy leaves peppered with minute yellow dots, easily seen against a dark background, and caused by a soaring population of tiny brown, red, pink, greenish, or yellowish mites the size of pin points, which form cottony webs where they suck plant juices and, left uncontrolled, severely weaken an infested plant, often beyond redemption.

Spider mites are deterred by moist conditions; misting plant surfaces with water, especially in the winter when the relative humidity indoors is often 20 percent or less, will usually prevent spider mites from gaining a foothold. To combat an active infestation, however, an oil-detergent spray (see page 809) or, where possible, a dip in a bowl full of the oil-detergent solution, is the preferable initial treatment. It may be followed by tobacco-tea spray (see Mealy Bugs) if the infestation persists.

Whiteflies

Whiteflies are small (about the size of celery seeds), white, sucking insects that quickly take to wing in clouds when an infested plant is shaken. Eggs are laid in great numbers, often in circles, on leaf undersurfaces, and the legless larvae, resembling tiny oval discs, remain attached to the leaf by their sucking mouth parts until they mature into flying adults. Large amounts of honeydew are excreted, leading to the sticky coating and sooty mold that accompany infestations of aphids, mealy bugs, and scale.

Whiteflies are not easily controlled, partly because of their increasingly frequent resistance to various commonly (and often overly) used pesticides, and partly because of their prolific reproduction and the differential susceptibility of the various growth stages to treatment. Flying adults may be lured and trapped with yellow sticky boards, such as Vapona strips, which should be carefully positioned to obviate any hazard to children or pets. Control of immature insects may be possible using oil-detergent spray or, failing that, tobacco tea (see Mealy Bugs) or a systemic pesticide such as neem (see page 810). Rotenoids and malathion are also used but are of diminishing effectiveness against increasingly resistant whitefly populations.

Other Pests

Other pests are of occasional occurence or cause minimal harm. Thrips are tiny, fast-moving insects that suck juices from flowers and young leaves and cause streaked areas that are dotted with black excrement. They may be controlled with oil-detergent spray (preferably with a dip), with tobacco tea (see Mealy Bugs), or with rotenoids.

Most other houseplant pests are nuisances rather than perpetrators of real harm. Ants will depart once honeydew-producing mealy bugs, scale, and whitefly have been eliminated. Pillbugs, centipedes, and millipedes usually gain entrance into pot soil when houseplants are summered out of doors. Their diet is primarily decaying organic matter. Repotting with clean soil averts the problem—if indeed there is any.

Earthworms, however valuable in the garden, can interfere with root growth in small pots by constantly burrowing and churning the soil in their search for the humus they favor as food. Knock root balls out of pots before transferring houseplants indoors and remove the earthworms as they appear.

Diseases of Houseplants

Of the relatively few diseases suffered by houseplants, powdery mildew is the most serious and is fostered especially by poor air circulation in warm, humid conditions. It is a fine white mold that covers leaf surfaces with a whitish or grayish powder and is particularly a problem with begonias, sometimes causing a general leaf drop. A systemic fungicide such as benomyl or triforine is recommended.

Basal rot often results from overwatering. Rerooting unaffected tops can sometimes salvage the situation, but usually rotted plants are total losses.

35

Coldframes and Hotbeds

COLDFRAMES

A coldframe is an indispensable adjunct, even to the smallest garden. It is, as the name implies, an unheated box whose bottom is open to the soil on which the frame rests, and whose top is a transparent, removable panel exposed to the sun. Thus it is an enclosure that passively protects its contents from the most severe winter ravages and serves as a growing chamber in spring, especially for hardening off seedlings started indoors before they are set out in the garden.

Coldframes are ideally made of brick or treated lumber, tilted to the South, and covered with a single unpartitioned, wholly transparent pane, but a serviceable, if temporary, unit can be fashioned from a variety of discarded materials.

Coldframes are also valuable as propagating chambers, both for starting seeds in flats in spring and for vegetative propagation at various times of the year. Indeed, an enterprising gardener will find that the frames are in use during every month of the year—that there is never a time from one season's end to another when they lie fallow.

Uses of Coldframes in Early Spring: Hardening Off Plants

During late winter or early spring, depending on the climate in your region, coldframes may be used to harden off seedlings that have been started under lights or in a greenhouse. Hardening off is of considerable importance as young seedlings often suffer a serious setback or may even perish if moved directly from indoor protection to the garden. The coldframe provides an ideal transition, as the plants may be protected from sudden drops in temperature, from cold rain or even snow, and from drying wind while their pigmentation deepens and cell structure firms. When pots or flats are moved to the frames, they should be placed on a bed of gravel to ensure adequate drainage.

Uses of Coldframes in Spring and Summer
Seed Sowing

A coldframe also offers very satisfactory facilities for the starting of young seedling plants throughout the spring and summer months (see Chapter 36 for seed sowing). The hardy and half-hardy annuals may be sown in the frames early in the spring, many weeks before seed can be sown in the open ground; perennials also may be sown in the spring, and the young transplanted seedlings may be grown on in open frames until they are ready to be moved to the nursery rows or to their permanent place in the garden; biennials may be sown during the summer months and potted up. As many of them, such as foxgloves, Canterbury bells, and wallflowers, need winter protection in cold climates, they may be carried on in the frames until spring.

Propagation by Cuttings

During the late spring and summer months a coldframe may be converted into a propagating case, the soil being temporarily replaced with sand or peat moss or some other medium satisfactory for the rooting of cuttings (see Chapter 36).

Uses of Coldframes in Fall: Seed Sowing

Most perennials and some annuals may be sown very successfully in late summer and fall, and there are many benefits to be gained if such a practice is followed. With some

kinds, the object is to have young seedling perennials develop more than they would in the open garden and thereby be better able to withstand winter cold. With others—particularly those kinds whose seeds require a cold period before germination can take place—it is not to secure germination during the autumn, but to have the seeds remain dormant during the winter months. They will then germinate very early in the spring, and the young seedlings will have a vigor that usually exceeds those grown from spring-sown seeds. A higher rate of germination is also frequently secured.

A coldframe offers ideal conditions for autumn sowing. The seed may be sown either in a well-prepared seedbed or in flats. It is essential that good drainage be provided, and if flats are used, they should be placed on a layer of gravel. The seed should not be sown until just before the onset of winter, when the ground begins to freeze. There will then be no danger of having the seed germinate before spring. At the time of sowing, the soil should be watered so that it is moderately damp but not excessively wet. Periodic checks should be made, and if the soil becomes dry during the winter a light watering should be given, preferably during a spell of mild weather, when the state of soil moisture can be better estimated (since, when frozen, damp soil often resembles dry soil) and any water added will be absorbed rather than shed. After the seed has been sown, the sash should be placed over the frames, which are raised slightly to provide adequate ventilation.

Since a reasonable degree of temperature stability is another goal in the winter maintenance of coldframes, it is often advisable to limit or exclude the penetration of winter sunshine (which is of no value to dormant, defoliated plants), and this may be accomplished by placing a lath sash over the glass. This slat shade should be removed very early in the spring so that the soil may warm up as rapidly as possible and early germination and growth be induced. As soon as the soil in the frame has begun to thaw, the seed should be given the usual care, i.e., the soil should not be allowed to dry out, adequate ventilation should be provided, and the sash should be removed on mild, sunny days to prevent overheating.

Uses of Coldframes in Winter
Protection of Marginally Hardy Plants and Tender Bulbs

Not only are coldframes useful during the winter months for the protection of the less hardy plants (i.e., those reliably hardy in the next hardiness zone south of [milder than] yours) and of newly started perennials but they also make it possible to grow some of the tender bulbs, which cannot be grown in the open ground in areas where the winters are of extreme severity. In zone 7, for example, this category includes Dutch iris, various gladioluses, and St. Brigid anemone. If planted in the fall in coldframes, and thus protected in winter, these bulbs provide abundant bloom when warmth returns.

Storage of Bulbs and Plants for Forcing

Coldframes may also be used for the storage of bulbs and plants that are later to be forced indoors. Bulbs such as crocus and hyacinth, as well as certain narcissus and tulip cultivars, and perennials such as astilbe, bleeding heart, lily-of-the-valley, and Virginia bluebell may be handled very successfully in this way. Chrysanthemum plants that are of dubious hardiness may be lifted from the garden in in the fall after flowering and carried over the winter in the frames, and cuttings may be made from these stock plants in the spring.

Location

It is best to place coldframes on gently sloping ground (for certain drainage) that faces south or southeast (for maximum sun exposure). The frames should be placed with the high end (about 6 inches higher than the low end) toward the north and with the sash sloping toward the south so that full benefit may be obtained from the rays of the sun and to facilitate runoff of rain from the transparent cover. Whenever possible, a sheltered spot should be chosen with a wall or hedge on the north to afford protection against winter winds. If a sheltered spot is not available, however, a temporary winter windbreak may be constructed of corn stalks, or evergreen boughs braced against a section of snow fence. If a gravel walk is laid immediately in front of the frames, it will greatly facilitate easy access in wet weather and will prove a significant convenience. Sufficient space should be left at the rear of the frames for the comfortable removal of the sash. The frames should be easily accessible and running water should be conveniently available.

Construction

Four criteria should be kept in mind:

1. *Keep it simple.* Automatic openers, whatever their appeal, are finickly devices subject to failure; special hinges, latches, and hooks accomplish little that cannot be done with simple blocks of wood; moreover, hinges of any type are not only unnecessary but can impede the frequent necessity to remove the coldframe cover.
2. *Use recycled materials.* Used lumber, old bricks, and discarded window sash can be incorporated into your coldframe.
3. *Plan to complete the project in a few hours.* Most measurements can be rough; a hammer and saw and perhaps a drill and a T-square are the principal tools.
4. *Keep it inexpensive.* Little if anything is gained by spending lavishly on a coldframe that, with a little ingenuity and some determined searching, can be built for next to nothing.

Of the many materials that are suitable, scraps of treated wood and secondhand bricks and concrete blocks are the most satisfactory for the construction of coldframes. Stone, new brick, concrete, and various metals also may be used, but while they may be very durable, the additional expense is hardly justifiable.

Wood is the least expensive material and if pretreated to prevent rot, wood frames will last for many years. Untreated wood will serve as well functionally, but boards in contact with the soil will have to be replaced after a few years. Wood frames are very easily constructed, and as they do not require highly skilled workmanship, they may readily be made at home.

It is also possible to purchase precut frames commercially from some of the major seedhouses and greenhouse construction companies. These are shipped disassembled and are easily put together. Such commercial frames are often very satisfactory and offer the distinct advantage of being easily moved from one section of the garden to another if a change in the general arrangement of the working area should be desired or if you move to a new property. These ready-made frames may be obtained in various sizes, the smallest of which are particularly suited for use in suburban gardens.

Frames constructed of concrete blocks are more permanent than wood frames, but they are not easily moved from one location to another. The initial cost may be considerably higher than for wood frames, but it is a one-time cost, as no replacement will be necessary. The concrete blocks should extend into the ground a few inches below the frost line for the locality and should be laid with mortared joints. The appearance of the frames will be greatly improved and frost damage to mortared joints reduced if a cement-sand mortar finish is applied as a surface coat over the concrete blocks.

The front of the frame may vary in height from 6 to 12 inches. If the frames are to be used as a seedbed and to winter small plants such as pansies and English daisies, a height of 6 inches will be sufficient. If large plants such as foxgloves and Canterbury bells are to be wintered over in the frames, a height of 12 inches will be needed. Cross-ties usually extend from the back of the frame to the front at intervals of every 3 feet in order to provide additional support for the sash. These ties should be dovetailed into the walls of the frame; a longitudinal rib along the center of each cross-tie will keep the sash from slipping out of position.

The standard size for coldframe sash used by practically all commercial growers and by most large-scale private gardeners is a side-to-side width of 3 feet and a front-to-back depth of 6 feet. For the usual home garden, however, where operations are on a limited scale and where convenience is a matter of considerable importance, a smaller size is often more satisfactory. Small sash, measuring 2 by 4 feet, or 3 by 3 feet, may be obtained from various firms, and they have many advantages. They are much lighter and, therefore, easier to handle than the standard-size sash. In addition, the entire area within the frame can be reached from the front with comparative ease, which greatly facilitates such operations as seed sowing and transplanting.

Most coldframe sashes are made of wood, and they may be purchased either glazed or unglazed. The process of glazing is a rather simple one and considerable expense may be saved if this is done at home. Transparent or translucent plastic sheeting is also used in place of glass. Although the initial cost is less than glass and the weight is minimal, plastic must be replaced every few years.

Coldframe sash may also be made of fiberglass, which has the advantage of allowing the penetration of ultraviolet rays. Sash made of fiberglass is lighter in weight than glass sash and, because it is unbreakable, is easier to handle. It is, however, less transparent, and does not provide as much protection against extreme cold as does sash made of glass. It is also possible to make economical use of discarded storm windows, which, if framed in aluminum, are very easy to raise and lower, but will require securing by latches or ties to prevent their being blown off in strong wind. Even lighter is acrylic plastic, such as Plexiglas, which is also not subject to breakage (a factor to consider if the coldframe is located beneath eaves from which heavy snow or ice may fall in winter). Also useful, but perhaps too heavy for some to manage, are discarded patio sliding glass doors or shower doors. With these materials, the dimensions of the coldframe will be determined by the length and width of their frames.

When not in use during the summer months, coldframe sashes should be neatly stacked, preferably under cover where they will not be exposed to the weather. It is a matter of sound economy to keep the coldframe sash in good condition. All cracked or broken panes of glass should be replaced and wood sashes should be kept well painted. If attention is given to these details, coldframe sash should last for many years.

Management

There are a few general rules that should be followed in the management of coldframes. The most important factors to be considered are ventilation, watering, protection against extreme cold, and protection against extreme heat.

Ventilation

During the late winter and early spring, the sash should be partially raised for a brief period on clear, sunny days, when the temperature ranges above 45°F, the object being to maintain as even a temperature as possible. As the season advances, the sash may be raised for a longer period each day, and on warm days it may be removed entirely during the middle of the day. The sash should be lowered or replaced before the temperature begins to drop in the afternoon, to conserve as much heat as possible. On windy days, the sash should be raised on the opposite side from the direction of the wind, to protect the plants from a cold or drying draft. With the approach of warm weather, the sash may be removed entirely. When sashes are to be raised slightly, small blocks of wood may be placed between the edge of the frame and the sash. A block measuring approximately 1 by 4 by 6 inches is excellent for this purpose, as it permits the size of the opening to be easily varied.

Watering

It is an accepted rule among gardeners that, to prevent the outbreak of diseases, plants grown under glass, either in greenhouses or in frames, should be watered when the temperature is rising rather than when it is falling. It is, therefore, advisable, and particularly so early in the season, to water the frames in the morning so that the foliage of the plants may be dry at night. In cold, cloudy weather water should be withheld as much as possible, again to deter the growth of various fungus diseases.

Protection against Extreme Cold

During periods of extreme cold, additional protection should be given to the coldframe. Insulated mats, such as sheets of bubble plastic cut to size, small quilted tarpaulins, or lightweight building insulation bats cut to fit inside waterproof garment bags may be used for this purpose. In mild climates no protection other than the sash itself is necessary.

Summer Shade

In the summer months, some provision must be made for protecting the seedbeds and the young seedling plants in the frames from intense sunshine. Lath sashes are very satisfactory for this purpose. They are light and easy to handle, permit a free circulation of air, and allow filtered sunshine to reach the plants. Panels of loose-weave burlap or plastic greenhouse screening mesh tacked onto lath frames also make a very satisfactory shade.

HOTBEDS

Hotbeds differ from coldframes in that they are supplied with some form of artificial heat. They may be heated by the old method of fermenting manure, or by the more modern method of specially devised, shallowly buried electric cables with thermostat controls. In occasional instances where hotbeds are located in close proximity to a greenhouse, they may be heated with hot-water pipes as part of the greenhouse heating system. More feasible in most instances is to extend a loop of pipe from the hot-water system of a dwelling and furnish it with a separate pump and thermostat. The construction and management of the hotbed will usually be determined by the type of heating to be used.

Uses of Hotbeds

Since the soil in a hotbed is maintained at a warm and fairly constant temperature, it provides excellent facilities for the germination of most seed and for the growing of a wide variety of young seedling plants. Some plants with a short season of growth, such as lettuce, may be carried through to maturity in the hotbed, although the majority of plants started in the hotbed are later transplanted to the garden or field. Seed may be sown in the hotbed several weeks before it is advisable to make use of the coldframes, and the young seedlings will make much more rapid growth. Later in the season when there is no longer any need for supplemental heat, the hotbed may serve as a coldframe and be used to fulfill the same functions. The hotbed is especially useful for gardeners who are lacking suitable indoor space to start seeds and raise seedlings under fluorescent light.

Types of Organic Hotbeds
Manure Hotbeds

A pit approximately 2½ feet deep is necessary if manure is to be used, the dimensions for width and length being determined by the size of the frames and the number of frames desired. If the earth walls of the pit are firm, no inside wall need be constructed. If, however, there is any danger that the earth walls may crumble, it will be necessary to construct supporting walls. Walls made of wood will be of only temporary value, as they will lack durability in such a location, but materials such as concrete block, stone, and brick are excellent. The upper part of the frame is similar in construction to that of a coldframe.

Manure-heated hotbeds should be started in early March, and it is necessary to use fresh horse manure obtained from stables where straw has been used for bedding. Approximately 4 cubic yards of manure will be required for a single-sash hotbed measuring 6 by 3 feet.

The manure should be piled near the hotbed, and every three or four days the heap should be turned, throwing the outside toward the center. When the entire pile has begun to heat evenly, which is evidenced by steam arising from the pile, the manure may be placed in the pit. It should be spread evenly in 6-inch layers, each layer being firmly tramped and packed. After the manure has been placed in the pit to a depth of 2 feet, a thin layer of straw should be spread over it and the soil should then be added. The depth of soil may vary from 4 to 6 inches, and it should be of a mixture suitable for a seedbed. A soil thermometer should be placed so that the mercury extends well down into the soil and the sash should remain tightly closed. For the first few days the thermometer will register a high temperature, usually well above 90°F. When the soil temperature has cooled down to 75°F, the bed is ready for use and the seed may be sown.

In extremely cold climates it is well to bank manure about that portion of the bed which extends above the surface of the ground, as this will increase the warmth within the frame to a very appreciable extent.

Hotbeds Filled with Raked Leaves

Raked leaves can be used in place of fresh horse manure, and the procedure is the same. The leaves should be spread evenly, in successive 6-inch layers, then each layer firmly tramped and packed, and immediately covered with topsoil. The temperature within the frame will not rise as high as with horse manure, but raked leaves are a good substitute where manure is either unobtainable or too expensive.

Hotbeds with Wood Chips

Wood chips, often used as a mulch or in walkways, can be used successfully in any of the above-described deep frames. A generous sprinkling of unslaked lime (quicklime) should be placed on top of each 6- to 8-inch layer of firmly packed wood chips. This should be repeated until a depth of about 30 inches is reached. A thin layer of leaves or pine needles should then be placed on top, to prevent the topsoil from being washed into the chips.

When cleaning out an organic hotbed each year, the half-rotted medium can be mixed with topsoil and sand for use as an excellent compost in the garden and for potting.

Artificially Heated Hotbeds
Electric Hotbeds

Various types of electric units have been especially designed to heat hotbeds. One of the most satisfactory is the insulated electric cable, which may be buried in the soil and will provide uniform heat. The procedure for the construction of such a bed is as follows.

A pit approximately 12 inches deep should be excavated. It should be about 2 feet longer and 2 feet wider than the dimensions of the frame that will be set on top of the filled pit. The pit should be filled with 6 inches of gravel. The frame may be placed directly on this bed. The outside of the frame should be banked with soil to provide insulation against the penetration of cold air. A layer of burlap or of sphagnum moss should be placed over the gravel and 1 inch of sand spread over the surface of the bed. The electric cable is then laid on the sand in uniform loops so that the heat will be evenly distributed. Approximately 60 feet of flexible, heavily insulated 110-volt cable will be required for a two-sash hotbed (6 feet square). This will provide for 10 coils spaced about 7 inches apart. The ends of the cable should be connected to a thermostat.

The thermostat should be installed on the inside of the frame with the switch box on the north side of the bed and should be regulated so that a uniform temperature is maintained. Tender plants will require a temperature ranging from 60° to 75°F; half-hardy plants will prefer a temperature of 50° to 60°F; and those that are truly hardy will thrive well in a temperature ranging from 45° to 60°F.

Approximately 400 watts will be required to provide heat for a two-sash hotbed in zone 6 or 7. Electricity required will usually average 1 kilowatt hour per square yard of hotbed per day.

The soil that is to be used for the seedbed may be placed over the cable to a depth of 6 inches. If flats are to be used, 3 inches of sand may be spread over the cable and the flats may be placed on the sand.

The one great disadvantage of an electric hotbed is that the current may fail because of a severe storm or some other emergency. In such a case, the plants are apt to suffer serious injury, and every effort should be made to protect them, through the use of straw mats, old blankets, or other materials that will provide temporary insulation.

Hot Water or Steam Pipes

One of the most satisfactory and also most economical ways to provide heat for the hotbeds is to install a system of pipes that may be connected with the heating system in the dwelling house or greenhouse. The pipes may be placed around the top of the frame on the inside or they may be placed beneath the soil. As a second option, such a system provides for a uniform heat, which may be maintained at a minimum of expense and labor. Installation should include a separate thermostat, pump, valves to isolate the system from the main heating system of the dwelling, and a drain cock.

Management

The management of a hotbed is similar in most respects to the management of a coldframe. There is, however, more danger from damping off, as the plants are somewhat more susceptible to attack because of the greater degree of heat and humidity. Every precautionary measure should be taken to control an outbreak of this disease. (See page 872 for the control of damping off.)

Since artificial heat is provided, the plants grown in a hotbed are more tender than those grown in a coldframe and more sensitive to sudden fluctuations in temperature. So ventilation and watering must be done with care. Plants started in a hotbed that are intended for garden use should be hardened off before being set out.

A COLDFRAME CALENDAR

Schedule for zones 6 and 7; to be adjusted for colder or milder zones

Month	In an Unheated Frame	In a Heated Frame (45–50°F, with a thermostated soil cable)
October	Pot up hardy spring-flowering bulbs (tulips, daffodils, hyacinths, crocuses) for winter-forcing, sinking pot rims 3" below ground surface	Sow lettuce at 10- to 14-day intervals
November	Sink potted hydrangeas; bury hardwood cuttings (*see Chapter 36*); transplant from garden perennials not reliably hardy but requisite of cold dormancy	Harvest and sow lettuce
December	Mulch perennials with loose material, such as pine needles or wood chips	Harvest and sow lettuce
January	Keep frame closed except during mild periods	Harvest and sow lettuce; begin to force potted hydrangeas and hardy bulbs
February	Keep frame closed except during mild periods	Harvest and sow lettuce; continue forcing potted bulbs
March	Begin loosening or removing mulch as weather moderates; ventilate frame on mild sunny days to avoid heat-induced premature growth	Harvest lettuce; sow radish, arugula, and coriander, as well as lettuce; ventilate when interior temperature exceeds 70°F
April	Start cool-weather flowers and vegetables; daytime ventilation is critical	Start tender flowers and vegetables; force strawberries; daytime ventilation is critical
May	Transplant seedlings to garden; harden off seedlings started indoors under lights; sow seed of perennials and biennials	Discontinue nighttime heat; start hardwood cuttings stored the previous November
June	Transplant perennial and biennial seedlings to nursery bed; use empty open frames to grow vine crops such as cucumber	Root and pot up daughter strawberry plants taken from new runners
July	Root softwood cuttings (*see Chapter 36*)	Clean out frame and check heat cable; make structural repairs; restore or replace soil
August	Clean out frame if empty; restore or replace soil	Make late sowings of perennial and biennial seeds
September	Sink potted strawberries rooted in June	Begin sowing lettuce at 10- to 14-day intervals

36

Propagation

THERE ARE FEW SUBJECTS OF MORE VITAL INTEREST TO the avid gardener than propagation. Although the art of propagation dates to the very origin of plant cultivation, more progress has been made by scientists within the past few decades than had occurred over many previous centuries. As a result, though many of the old and established practices may still be followed with good results, recent advances have revolutionized some of the techniques of propagation.

Among the most stately of garden perennials, Russell lupines *are easily raised from seed.*

Plant propagation falls into two main categories: (1) sexual propagation, or the use of seed to produce new plants, and (2) asexual or vegetative propagation, which includes producing new plants by one of the following methods.

Cuttings, the formation of roots on detached stems or leaves.
Division of root clumps and other plant parts.
Specialized reproductive structures, such as bulbs, corms, tubers, or offsets.
Layering, the induced formation of roots on attached stems.
Grafting or budding.
Spores, the asexually produced reproductive cells of ferns sown in much the same manner as seed.
Tissue culture, the growth of plants from cells or tissues in an artificial growing medium under sterile conditions.

Originally, tissue culture was done only in laboratories, but it is now increasingly used for the commercial propagation of orchids and other groups that grow very slowly from seed.

The success of a large proportion of the plant propagation methods discussed in this chapter depends on the creation of special environments in which temperature, humidity, light, and ventilation are controlled. The home greenhouse offers great flexibility in artificial environmental control, but beside the considerable initial cost and operating expense that a greenhouse involves, it also requires more time and occupies more space than most home gardeners are prepared to commit. Hence the popularity of the more prosaic alternatives described here.

PROPAGATING UNITS
Containers for Propagation

Flowerpots, small planter boxes, greenhouse flats, and discarded aquariums and terrariums may all be converted into very satisfactory propagating cases for seeds or cuttings.

Seed

When only a few seeds are sown, a 3- or 4-inch flowerpot or a narrow open plastic box that fits on a windowsill will give good results and can be easily cared for, even in small homes or cramped quarters. An aquarium or terrarium is even better, as the cover facilitates the buildup and control of internal humidity. To simultaneously germinate larger amounts of seed, larger chambers are required, and these usually involve the provision of fluorescent light.

Cuttings

When only a few cuttings are to be rooted, the double flowerpot is one of the most satisfactory devices. A small 3- or 4-inch pot is placed within a 4- or 5-inch pot, the hole in the bottom of the small pot being tightly closed with a cork. The rim of the small pot should be level with the area of sand in the large pot. The intervening space below and about the sides should be filled with sand or with a sand and peat moss mixture. The small pot should be kept filled with water, and the gradual seepage through the porous clay of the pot will keep the rooting medium uniformly moist. If a large glass jar is inverted over the pot, or a clear plastic bag tied around the pot, it will prevent an excessive evaporation of moisture and will provide very favorable conditions for the rooting of the cuttings.

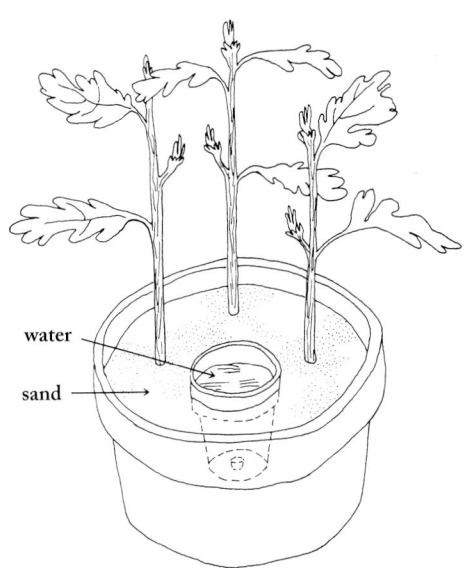

water
sand

Propagating pot

If many seeds are to be sown or cuttings rooted, and if space permits, a plastic greenhouse flat will accommodate both seeds and cuttings. When cuttings are to be rooted, it is important to conserve moisture and maintain high humidity. A simple system for covering cuttings in a flat entails slipping two wire hangers over either end of the flat and draping a small sheet of plastic across the top or, more simply, slipping the whole unit inside a plastic bag and tying the end of the bag closed.

Fluorescent Lighting

Fluorescent lights offer the gardener whose dwelling has low natural light sources an excellent opportunity to propagate plants indoors. An inexpensive unit may be constructed, using paired fluorescent lighting tubes designed especially for this purpose. To provide a full spectrum of light, one tube should be rated "daylight" and the other "natural." An ordinary industrial or shop unit with reflectors and suspension chains is well suited to the purpose. The units are hung over the young plants at a height of about 3 inches and are raised (or the plants lowered) as growth proceeds. Home temperatures are usually adequate for this purpose, and humidity may be easily controlled by using pebble trays filled with water beneath the pots, flats, or other propagation containers. For more on fluorescent-light gardening, see Chapter 38.

Coldframes and Hotbeds

As discussed in Chapter 35, the standard coldframe is simply a large open-bottom box with a transparent or translucent cover that can be removed for temperature regulation and to facilitate access. Ideally, the coldframe faces south and is about 6 inches lower in the front so that the sash slopes downward. The bottom or floor of the frame should be prepared in accordance with what is to be grown in it, i.e., pot plants can be hardened off by placing them in a 3-inch bed of gravel, whereas plants or cuttings grown in situ require additional soil preparation. In the summer, lath or shade cloth placed across the top of the sashes reduces the light reaching the cuttings below.

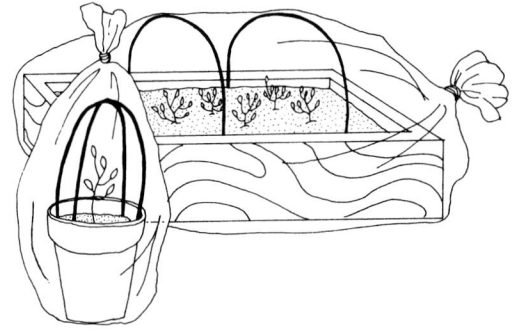

Wire coat hangers are bent to provide framework over which plastic is wrapped and sealed.

Since the coldframe will probably become a permanent structure, it is best to use durable materials such as treated wood, brick, or concrete block (if available).

The addition of electrical heating cables to a coldframe, while usually not requiring excessive modifications, expands a frame's usefulness immeasurably, especially if care is taken to minimize heat loss.

Windowsill and Lean-To Greenhouses

The most versatile and certainly the most attractive propagating unit is the home greenhouse. Among the most popular home greenhouses are the relatively inexpensive windowsill units and the attached walk-in "lean-to" types. Normally, these are both constructed of lightweight aluminum framing with glass panes against a south- to east-facing window or door, and since they are both attractive and practical, they soon become an integral part of the home.

Plastic Greenhouses

With the development of improved plastics, it is possible to construct an inexpensive and very satisfactory home propagating unit. The use of plastic materials for this purpose enables the home gardener to obtain the desired degree of temperature, humidity, and adequate ventilation without incurring the high expense involved in building and maintaining the traditional glasshouse. However, there is one major drawback to such greenhouses—since the plastic covers slowly deteriorate on exposure to the sun, they must be replaced every few years. It is, therefore, advisable that such a greenhouse be sited and built to make that replacement as easy as possible.

So many types of greenhouses are available that it is important to analyze fully the eventual use for which your greenhouse is intended. Local extension services offer information about minimum structural requirements, taking into account snow load, winds, and temperatures. Helpful booklets outlining current structural and operating costs and recent advances in the entire field are also available.

Greenhouses that are primarily intended for plant propagation should contain a special bench area reserved specifically for starting plants. The propagating bench has an enclosed base that is filled with sand, perlite, and other propagating media, and may provide bottom heat as well as overhead mist. The complexity of the installation will be determined by the range of materials to be propagated and the frequency of use.

Work Areas

A greenhouse should contain or be adjacent to an area that is reserved for such activities as potting up plants and making cuttings. Ideally, this area should be located so that it will not interfere with the propagating unit. It should contain ample room to store tools, pots, soil mixes, and frequently used chemicals, and it should also provide a flat, raised surface for work. With careful organization and adequate storage space all supplies and materials will be at hand for any greenhouse project, including sowing seed, rooting cuttings, potting up seedlings, watering, controlling pests and diseases, and mixing various rooting media. Nothing is more frustrating for a conscientious gardener than to begin a project, only to realize halfway through that a major search must be made for a particular item.

IMPORTANCE OF DISEASE PREVENTION

In propagation, as in all aspects of horticulture, it is better to prevent outbreaks of disease and attacks by pests than to attempt control them after they have become evident. So-called decontamination or sterilization of tools, containers, and rooting media is useful in minimizing disease and pest transmission, but as bacteria and fungal spores are airborne, such measures as baking soil in an oven, boiling pots and other containers, and scouring tools with disinfectants achieve only relative and short-lived sterilization. Nevertheless, as germinating seeds and young seedlings are most susceptible to the ravages of diseases and pests, and to consumption by foragers, it is at this stage that sanitation measures, however transitory in effect, are particularly valuable. Also helpful are fungicides that, when used in irrigation water as preventives, help suppress the growth of such devastating seedling diseases as damping off.

PROPAGATING MEDIA AND SOIL MIXTURES

A variety of materials may be used to germinate seeds and to root cuttings. In addition to being sterile (i.e., pest and disease free), a medium should meet these criteria:

1. It should be firm and dense enough to hold cuttings or seeds in place during rooting or germination.
2. It should not alter its bulk substantially whether wet or dry, since excessive shrinkage while drying causes root damage, and separation from the container wall makes rewetting difficult.
3. It should drain freely yet retain enough moisture so that repeat watering will not be necessary more often than once daily.

Rooting Media Components

Perlite

Used to increase the aeration in a rooting medium, perlite is a type of volcanic rock that is ground and processed into light, porous, sterile particles that hold many times their own weight in water.

Vermiculite

Made from a micalike ore that is composed of myriad layers that attract and hold water, vermiculite is used to increase the water-holding capacity of a rooting medium.

Sphagnum Moss

Sphagnum moss, a dried preparation, is used to increase the water-holding capacity of a rooting medium. It is prepared from the bog moss *Sphagnum* and usually has been shredded. It may be used either as the sole medium, as a fine topping over another medium, or as a component in a mixture.

Peat Moss

Used in heavy mixtures to lighten and increase porosity, peat moss is dried, pulverized peat—the partly decomposed remains of various bog and aquatic plants. It absorbs and retains many times its dry weight in water.

Sand

Sand is granular rock and is used to add body to and promote drainage in a rooting medium. It is also excellent when used alone for rooting cuttings.

Germinating and Rooting Media Mixtures

The following four media combinations are the most frequently and successfully used to germinate seeds or root cuttings. It should be borne in mind that no single formulation suits all propagation purposes. The combinations that best suit your purposes will be discovered through experimentation and experience.

> (1) 1 part sterilized garden loam + 1 part coarse sand or perlite + 1 part moist peat moss
> (2) 1 part vermiculite + 1 part sphagnum moss
> (3) Sphagnum moss, alone
> (4) Coarse sand, alone

Prepackaged Sterilized Soils

Sterilized soils can readily be purchased in a wide variety of mixes and quantities, and this is probably the easiest way to be ensured of a sterile medium, especially if small quantities are required. Alternatively, separate ingredients may be purchased and combined to create a customized medium. Local nurseries often mix their own soils and may be prepared to sell small amounts to the home propagator.

GROWING PLANTS FROM SEED

Although it is easier to purchase living plants for the garden, the selection available commercially is usually very limited, and if more than a few plants are desired, the cost can be considerable. Beyond this, there is unrivaled joy and satisfaction

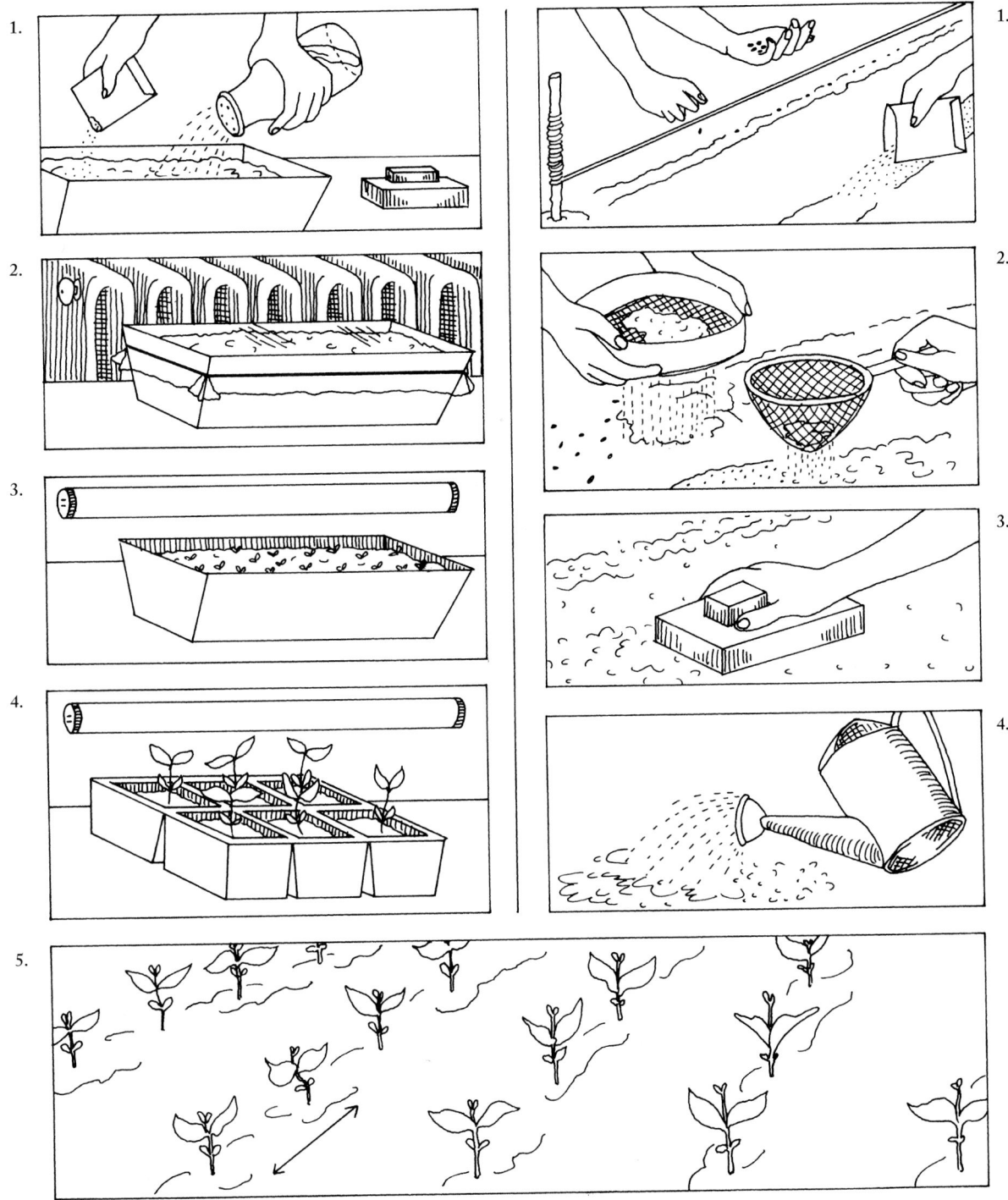

Indoors, many perennials, biennials, and annuals may be started from seed sown (1, on left) in seedpans and tamped firm with a block, (2) kept covered near a heat source to hasten germination, (3) then the young seedlings grown on uncovered under fluorescent light until being (4)transplanted singly into cell packs before (5) transfer to the garden.

Outdoor seed sowing is usually later, (1, on right) often in rows or (2) in patches or bands and covered with fine soil, then (3) tamped firm, and (4) watered carefully and often until germination begins, after which (5) seedlings are transplanted to the garden.

to be experienced in watching seeds become seedlings and grow on to maturity as flowering plants in the garden. The process of seed germination has been fundamental to civilizations through time everywhere, since most every society must propagate and grow plants for subsistence. Hobby gardening is a latter-day extension of that legacy. Moreover, growing plants from seed is an inexpensive way to diversify and expand a collection, and frequently it is the only way to acquire unusual kinds.

A seed is the product of sexual reproduction in flowering plants and consists of an embryonic plant, a supply of concentrated, partly dehydrated food, and a protective coat. To sprout, dormant seed must have moisture and a suitable temperature and, immediately upon germination, light and a medium suitable for root growth. Although the seed of most garden plants needs to be only lightly covered with warm, moist soil to a depth equal to twice its diameter, some seed has specific germination requirements or must be stored in certain ways before germination can occur. For example, some kinds, especially subtropical annuals, must have an extended dry period; others, particularly those native to temperate zones, must experience a period of pronounced cold while dormant; in some others, the seed coat must be nicked or scratched before water can penetrate. While most seeds are indifferent to light while sprouting, some will do so only in the dark (hence must be well covered with soil), and others require light (hence must be left uncovered on the soil surface). These are inherited strategies to restrict germination in nature to the most favorable period for initial growth.

Although nature the loss of many or even most seed and the death of all but a small number of seedlings is of little biological consequence, the aim in horticulture, especially when the seeds available for each kind are relatively few and the importance of individual plants is high, is to have as many seeds as possible germinate, and to do so simultaneously. Hence the usefulness in learning the idiosyncracies of the various kinds being grown and in taking the steps necessary to break seed dormancy.

Sowing Seed Indoors

As noted earlier, various premixed media are available commercially, or one may be mixed from basic ingredients. Each has certain advantages and certain limitations.

Soil Mixtures

As a medium for seed germination indoors, a soil mix must be loose and crumbly in texture and must drain well but also retain moisture between waterings. Supplemental sand and organic matter are often beneficial. The soil should be as free as possible of weed seeds, since it may be difficult to distinguish weed seedlings from those of desired kinds. To minimize root damage in the seed bed, weed seedlings should be snipped off, not pulled. Left unchecked, weeds can easily overwhelm a seed bed and smother the seedlings of planted kinds.

Fill the pots, seedpans, flats, or whatever container will best serve the purpose. Level the mixture and press firmly with a flat block of wood or similar object that serves as a tamper. This should bring the surface of the soil to within ½ inch of the rim. When pots or seedpans are used, the seed is usually sown broadcast over the surface of the soil. The seed should be sown as thinly and evenly as possible. Heavy seeding should be avoided, as it will result in spindly, weak plants with intertwined roots. When very fine seed is sown, no covering may be needed, except, perhaps, for the merest sprinkling of dust; the seed may be pressed gently into the soil with a block of wood or a small tamper. Larger seed should be covered with a finely sifted layer of the soil mixture or with sand. When flats are used, the seed may be sown either broadcast or in shallow drills, the rows being spaced 1½ to 2 inches apart. The soil should be firmed lightly after the seed has been sown.

To prevent heavy seeding in drills, hold the open seed packet over the drill with one hand, tilt it gently, and tap your wrist with the other hand as you move the packet along the drill. The aim is to have the seeds fall into the drill one at a time. Small seeds may be mixed with sand to further ensure thin, even distribution. In certain kinds of small-seeded plants, the seed is available as more conveniently handled pellets or may have been affixed to paper tapes at appropriate intervals. Each tape, with its attached seeds, is planted as a unit.

As soon as sowing has been completed, the flats or seedpans should be watered. The most satisfactory method, particularly in the case of very fine seed, is the subirrigation method. The seedpan or flat should be placed in a pan of water and allowed to remain until the surface of the soil has become dark and moist in appearance. It should then be removed and any surplus water allowed to drain off. This method is far superior to the overhead method. If, however, the overhead method is employed, a very fine spray should be used, such as a fog nozzle. Irrigation with large droplets will cause the seeds to be dislodged and to clump in depressions, resulting in overcrowding. A rubber bulb-sprinkler, of the sort used to dampen clothes for ironing, is very satisfactory for the purpose if only a small number of pots are being handled. At no time should the seed boxes be allowed to dry out, and they should be kept carefully shaded until the seed has germinated. Shading will greatly facilitate the conservation of moisture and will hasten germination. Drying of the medium during germination is fatal in nearly all kinds of garden plants. A pane of glass or acrylic (such as Lucite) covered with newspaper or open-weave burlap is very good. Once germination has begun, it is essential that some provision be made for ventilation, as by propping the cover open about ½ inch. Failure to ventilate can lead to an outbreak of damping off.

Germination will be hastened if the pots or flats are set in a warm place, the ideal temperature ranging from 60° to 70°F. In a greenhouse, the seed boxes are sometimes placed along the heat pipes underneath the benches, and in the home a radiator may be used to serve the same purpose. As soon as the seeds have germinated, seedlings must be placed in full light. If the seedpans or flats are placed in a sunny window, they should be turned every two or three days, as the seedlings will grow toward the light. Watering should be done both regularly and carefully. The seed boxes must never be allowed to dry out, but an excess of moisture must also be avoided. Improper watering can lead to runtiness, which, in some plants (e.g., *Amaranthus* and *Celosia*) is irreversible and results in poor flowering.

Milled Sphagnum Moss with Vermiculite

A mixture of milled sphagnum moss and vermiculite makes an excellent soilless, sterile medium for seed germination. Various commercially prepared mixtures are fortified with nutrients for initial growth, but in a few weeks after germination a dilute nutrient solution is required when watering young seedlings.

Because vermiculite alone frequently becomes a sticky, poorly aerated, almost greasy medium, it should always be used in combination with another material.

When sowing seed on sphagnum moss with vermiculite, the procedure is very simple. The medium should be moistened slightly to increase the ease of handling, and the flat or seedpan should be filled until it is level. The surface should then be firmed until the medium is ¼ to ½ inch below the rim, and it should be watered thoroughly. As this firm, smooth surface is favorable to the growth of green algae, it has been found advisable, after the flat or pot has been allowed to drain for a few minutes, to add an additional layer of finely shredded moss about ⅛ inch in depth. This should be given a light sprinkling and the seed should then be sown either broadcast or in drills. When sowing fine seeds no covering is necessary, but with larger seed, such as zinnias and marigolds, it is advisable either to press them down into the medium or to add a light covering of the shredded moss. After the seed has been sown, a light sprinkling of water should be given; a fine, mistlike spray from an atomizer is ideal. The flat or seedpan should then be covered with a pane of glass or with a sheet of plastic that has been formed around the container. Except in the case of those kinds whose seed requires light for germination (such as *Impatiens*), the seed boxes need not be exposed to direct sunlight or fluorescent lights until after the seeds have germinated. Little watering is necessary, merely enough to keep the medium moist. As soon as germination has taken place, the covering should be removed, and from this time on, considerable care must be taken to see that the sphagnum does not dry out.

Seedling plants that are to be transplanted while still quite small may be grown very satisfactorily in this medium without the use of supplemental nutrient solutions. If, however, the seedlings are to be held for any length of time beyond the cotyledon, or seed-leaf stage, it will be found advisable to apply a well-balanced solution to obtain vigorous growth. The solution should be applied at intervals of every few days in a quantity sufficient to saturate the moss. A commercially prepared mixture may be used, but a very satisfactory mixture may be made at home by using either of the following formulas:

---

(1) 2 teaspoons of 12-12-6 fertilizer + 1 gallon of water
(2) 2 tablespoons of 4-12-4 fertilizer + 1 gallon of water

By withholding the nutrient solution, seedlings of most kinds may be held for some time in an arrested state of development without suffering any permanent setback. When transplanted from the flat or seedpan they will resume normal growth.

One of the greatest advantages of growing plants in sphagnum is the ease with which they may be transplanted. If removed carefully, there is usually much less disturbance to the root system than when seedlings are grown in soil.

One of the most important advantages of all, however, is that any loss from damping off is infrequent, in sharp contrast to the often heavy toll that is sustained when seedlings are started in nonsterile media.

Sand

Seed may also be germinated very successfully in pure sand. If the sand is sterile, all danger of damping off will be eliminated. Sand of a somewhat coarse grade is preferable to very fine sand. If seedlings are to be held for any length of time, however, a nutrient solution must be applied. Many growers using this method feel that it is advisable to apply a nutrient solution before the seed is sown. This may be done by placing the pot or seedpan in a pan of the solution and leaving it in place until the surface has become moist. The nutrient mix is commonly used at the rate of 1 cupful of solution to 1 quart of sand. The usual procedures for germinating seed in sand are the same as those for sowing seed in other media.

Seed Dormancy

There are several forms of dormancy.

1. Dormancy regulated by the external seed coat even though the internal seed is nondormant.
2. Dormancy caused by an immature seed embryo.
3. Dormancy caused by the internal physiology of the seed.
4. A combination of internal and external dormancies.

Obviously, the home propagator must know how to treat the many different types of seed in order to produce a wide variety of plants. Many seeds will germinate under widely varying conditions of temperature and light. However, some seeds have special requirements and maximum (or even any) germination depends on these requirements being met.

Methods of Removing Seed Coat Dormancy

Several methods of ending or "breaking" dormancy caused by a hard, impervious seed coat are available.

Method 1: Soaking

Some seeds are soaked in water to soften hard seed coats, dissolve inhibitors, and/or reduce germination time. This is especially important with the seeds of woody members of the legume or bean family (Leguminosae or Fabaceas), such as mimosa or silk tree (*Albizia julibrissin*), yellowood (*Cladrastis lutea*), broom (*Cytisus* spp.), honey locust (*Gleditsia triacanthos*), Kentucky coffee tree (*Gymnocladus dioicus*), golden chain (*Laburnum* × *watereri*), Chinese scholar tree (*Sophora japonica*), and wisteria (*Wisteria* spp.).

The length of soaking time will vary considerably. Some seeds require only 24 hours; other seeds require several weeks. As a general rule, the seed should be soaked until it begins to swell. After the seed has been soaked, it should not be allowed to dry out before sowing, and the soil should be moist but not excessively wet at the time that it is sown. If the process is continued for more than a few days, the mass of seed should be stirred and aerated occasionally. Natural growth inhibitors can be dissolved by soaking the seed for a short period, rinsing them repeatedly and then blotting them dry. Frequently, seed soaking not only reduces the time required for germination but ensures that all or most seeds will germinate simultaneously.

Method 2: Scalding

In the case of some very dry, hard-shelled seeds, such as the seeds of the Kentucky coffee tree (*Gymnocladus dioicus*), scalding water may be used with considerable success. Boiling water is poured over the seed and allowed to cool gradually. Once again, this process should be used only when absolutely necessary, since exposure to the high temperature of boiling water may destroy the seeds' viability.

Method 3: Mechanical Scarification

The germination of some seed is greatly increased if it is scarified before sowing. Mechanical scarification—a process that scratches the surface of a hard seed coat, making it more permeable to water—is commercially performed by specially designed machines. However, mechanical sophistication is not necessary to scarify seeds. Successful results may be had simply by scratching or nicking the surface of the seed coat with a file. Care should be taken not to damage the inner parts of the seed during this process. Morning glories, canna, and hard-seeded members of the bean family, including acacia, bladder senna (*Colutea arborescens*), Chinese scholar tree (*Sophora japonica*), honey locust (*Gleditsia triacanthos*), partridge pea (*Chamaecrista fasciculata*), sensitive plant (*Mimosa pudica*), and and the true sennas (*Senna* spp.), all germinate eratically unless the seed coat is filed or chipped so that moisture can enter freely.

Nicks filed in hard-coated seeds facilitate prompt, simultaneous germination.

There are also a number of other mechanical procedures that may be employed very successfully. For example, in the case of some extremely large seeds, a minute hole may be bored to hasten the penetration of moisture.

Method 4: Chemical Scarification

Sulfuric acid is used commercially to scarify hard seed coats, but because of the hazard involved, this approach is not recommended for home gardeners.

Moist-Chilling Stratification for Simple Dormancy

Simple dormany of the embryo (the minute rudimentary plant contained in each seed) may be broken by the procedure known as moist-chilling stratification. This treatment, which is used with many species of trees and shrubs that are native to temperate-zone regions, exposes seeds for a prescribed period of time to low temperature and prescribed humidity. For seed with a very hard seed coat, stratification should be preceded by a moist, warm treatment period to break down the seed coat. After soaking the seeds in warm water for 24 hours (if necessary), drain off the water and mix the seeds in a moist but not wet medium of one part sand and one part milled sphagnum moss, then wrap the mixture in a plastic bag. The ratio of medium to seed should be about three to one. Store the seeds at 40°F. To maintain a consistent temperature, store the seed in your refrigerator and check the package periodically to make sure the medium is still moist. This process is known as "after-ripening" and usually requires about three months' time. At the end of this period, the seed should be planted immediately and germination allowed to proceed at a relatively cool temperature (50° to 60°F).

The seeds of some woody plants of temperate-zone regions will germinate as soon as they are sown after ripening. Alternatively, these seeds, most of which are very small, may be collected when ripe; stored in a cool, dry location; and sown in the spring. Among the plants included in this group are those listed below.

WOODY PLANTS WHOSE SEEDS HAVE SIMPLE DORMANCY
Requiring moist-chilling stratification.

Name	Stratification Time Required (months)
Abies (fir)	2–3
Acer (maple)*	3
Berberis (barberry)	3
Betula (birch)	3
Carya (hickory)	4
Cedrus (cedar)	2
Chamaecyparis (false cypress)	3
Clematis	3
Cornus (dogwood)	3
Fagus (beech)	3
Fraxinus (ash)	2–3
Liquidambar (sweet gum)	3
Magnolia	3–4
Malus (apple, crab apple)	3
Nyssa (tupelo)	3
Picea (spruce)	2–3
Pinus (pine)	2–3
Prunus (cherry, plum, peach)	3
Pyrus (pear)	3
Sorbus (mountain ash)	3
Thuja (arborvitae)	2
Tsuga (hemlock)	3

* Most species.

WOODY PLANTS WHOSE SEEDS REQUIRE NO DORMANCY PERIOD

Acer (maple)*	*Hydrangea*
Alnus (alder)	*Kalmia* (mountain laurel)
Calluna (heather)	*Kolkwitzia* (beauty-bush)
Catalpa (catalpa, Indian bean)	*Leucothoë*
Cercidiphyllum (katsura tree)	*Philadelphus* (mock orange)
Clethra (sweet pepperbush)	*Pieris* (andromeda)
Deutzia	*Potentilla* (cinquefoil)
Enkianthus	*Rhododendron* (azalea)
Erica (heath)	*Spiraea* (spirea)
Evodia	*Weigela*

* Species with spring-ripening seed, such as red maple or swamp maple (*A. rubrum*).

Warm Stratification for Double Dormancy

Seed characterized by double dormancy normally requires two years to germinate. This time span can be significantly reduced by the following procedure. In the fall, clean, dry seed is set in a mixture of equal parts of sand and moist peat moss. This should then be placed in a plastic bag and set in an area with a constant temperature range of 65° to 75°F. After a period of three months, the seeds and moist medium are transferred to the refrigerator for an additional three months. At the conclusion of the cool period, the seeds should be sown, as described in the moist-chilling procedure. The initial warm, moist treatment is essential to break down hard seed coats. Although this process may be carried on outdoors, it may prove difficult because weather conditions are so variable, and rodents are inevitably attracted to the seed mixture.

WOODY AND PERENNIAL PLANTS WHOSE SEEDS HAVE DOUBLE DORMANCY
Requiring warm stratification.

Cotoneaster	*Juniperus* (juniper)
Crataegus (hawthorn)	*Paeonia* (peony)
Halesia (silver bell)	*Stewartia*
Hamamelis (witch hazel)	*Taxus* (yew)
Helleborus (hellebore)	*Viburnum*
Ilex (holly)	

Dry Storage

Seeds of most cultivated annual, biennial, and perennial garden plants originally native to temperate-zone or highland tropical regions fail to germinate until after prolonged (several weeks to several months) storage at 45° to 50°F. On the other hand, plants native to lowland tropical regions (such as marigolds and the common impatiens) require no period of dry storage but do not suffer if stored some months or even years under cool, dry conditions.

Growing Annuals from Seed

The annual flowers and vegetables that can be grown readily from seed may be grouped into three general categories:

1. *Hardy.* Those that may be sown in the open early in the spring, before the last spring frosts, as soon as the soil is workable.
2. *Half-hardy.* Those that may be sown in the open once all danger of frost is over.
3. *Tender.* Those that not only tolerate no frost but suffer at temperatures below 45°F, hence are usually started in a greenhouse, under fluorescent lights, on a warm windowsill, or in a hotbed and are set out only after night temperatures are reliably mild; also included here are those whose initial growth is too slow for them to be started outdoors with the expectation of flowering satisfactorily.

If early bloom is desired, many annuals may also be started indoors. The rapidly growing kinds such as zinnia and marigold should not be sown more than 6 weeks before time for transplanting to the garden, as they will become spindly and leggy if held too long indoors. Slow-growing annuals such as lobelia, petunia, snapdragon, salpiglossis, and verbena may be sown 8 to 10 weeks before the time for transplanting to the open.

Raising Biennials from Seed

Nearly all popular biennial flowers may be grown very easily from seed. The seed is usually sown in coldframes during late spring or summer. When the seedlings have reached sufficient size, they are transplanted and are usually grown on in the frame or in a nursery bed until fall. Those that are not reliably hardy are wintered in the frames, while those that are hardy may be transplanted to the open ground. For details regarding time of sowing and method of handling, see Chapter 18.

Raising Perennials from Seed

Many perennials can be raised very successfully from seed. In general, especially for hybrids and cultivars, it is best to use commercially obtained seed rather than home-collected seed, as the latter tends to produce wild-type offspring whose flowers are frequently smaller, fewer, and/or less colorful than those of genetically altered cultivars. Other perennials develop so slowly when grown from seed that it is far more practical to resort to the division of old clumps or to some other means of vegetative reproduction.

PERENNIALS COMMONLY PROPAGATED BY SEED

Achillea (yarrow)	*Geum* (avens)
Aconitum (monkshood)	*Gypsophila* (baby's breath)
Amsonia (bluestar)	*Helenium* (sneezeweed)
Anchusa (bugloss, alkanet)	*Helleborus* (Christmas rose)
Aquilegia (columbine)	*Hesperis* (dame's rocket)
Arabis (rock cress)	*Heuchera* (coralbells)
Arenaria (sandwort)	*Iberis* (perennial candytuft)
Artemisia (mugwort)	*Linum* (flax)
Asclepias (butterfly weed, milkweed)	*Lobelia* (cardinal flower, great blue lobelia)
Aubrieta (purple rock cress)	
Aurinia (alyssum, basket-of-gold)	*Lupinus* (lupine)
Baptisia (false indigo)	*Macleaya* (plume poppy)
Boltonia	*Monarda* (horsemint, bee balm)
Campanula (bellflower)	*Myosotis* (forget-me-not)
Centaurea (knapweed)	*Oenothera* (evening primrose, sundrops)
Centranthus (red valerian)	
Cerastium (especially *C. tomentosum*) (snow-in-summer)	*Penstemon* (beardtongue)
	Physostegia (false dragonhead)
Chelone spp. (turtlehead)	*Platycodon* (balloon flower)
Cimicifuga (black cohosh, snakeroot)	*Primula* (primrose)
Conoclinium (especially *C. coelestinum*) (mist flower, hardy ageratum)	*Salvia* (sage)
	Scabiosa (pincushion flower)
Coreopsis (tickseed)	*Sedum* (stonecrop)
Delphinium	*Tanacetum* (especially *T. coccineum*) (pyrethrum, painted daisy)
Dianthus	
Dicentra (bleeding heart)	
Dictamnus (gas plant)	*Thalictrum* (meadow rue)
Digitalis (perennial foxglove)	*Veronica* (speedwell)
Gaillardia (blanketflower)	*Viola* (violet)

Seed Viability

Some seeds retain their vitality for many years, whereas others must be planted as soon as they are ripe if good germination is to take place. The seeds of most of our commonly grown annual and perennial flowers retain their vitality for at least a year and some of them for two years or even longer.

With the majority of garden flowers we can expect a percentage of germination ranging from 75 to 85 percent, and in some cases an even higher percentage may be obtained if the seed has been carefully graded and germination conditions are optimal.

If seed has been carried over from one season to the next, or if there is any reason to doubt its viability, it is wise to do a germination test before the seed is sown. A number of methods can be used in testing seed, one of the simplest being the paper towel method. The seeds are placed between two sheets of paper towel, which are kept constantly moist in a covered dish (laboratory Petri dishes are ideal) and at a temperature ranging between 65° and 70°F. If several kinds of seed are to be tested, the paper may be marked off into small squares, with one square for each kind. The percentage of germination may be easily determined by dividing the number of seeds that have sprouted by the total number tested. Using 10 seeds (or multiples) for each kind will make calculating percentages easier.

When the seeds are to be held in storage for any length of time, they should be kept in a dry place with a range of temperature varying from 45° to 50°F. The viability period depends mainly on the kind of seed, but storage conditions are major determinants in preserving seeds successfully within that period.

GERMINATION PERIOD AND SEED LONGEVITY FOR POPULAR PERENNIAL AND ANNUAL FLOWERS

Species (Common Name)	Period of Germination (Days)	Approximate Longevity (Years)
Achillea (yarrow)	14	4
Ageratum (floss flower)	14	4
Agrostemma (corn cockle)	14–21	4
Alcea (hollyhock)	14–21	2–3
Amaranthus (annual poinsettia, amaranth)	14–21	4–5
Ammobium (everlasting)	14	1–2
Anagallis (pimpernel)	21	4–5
Anchusa (bugloss)	14–21	3
Anemone (windflower)	28–40	2
Anthemis (chamomile)	14	2
Antirrhinum (snapdragon)	10–14	3–4
Aquilegia (columbine)	30–50	2
Arabis (rock cress)	21	2–3
Armeria (thrift)	21	2
Aster	14	1–2
Aubrieta	25	2
Aurinia (basket-of-gold)	21–28	4
Bellis (daisy)	10–14	2–3
Boltonia	20	5
Brachycome	10	3–4
Browallia (bush violet)	28–40	2–5
Calendula (pot marigold)	14	5–6
Campanula (bellflower)	14	3
Catharanthus (periwinkle)	14	1–2
Celosia (woolflower, cockscomb)	6–10	4
Centaurea (cornflower, sweet sultan)	20	1–2
Chelone (turtlehead)	20–30	1–2
Chrysanthemum (annual mum)	11–18	4–5
Clarkia (godetia)	14	2–3
Cobaea (cup-and-saucer vine)	21	2
Coleus	14	2
Coreopsis (tickseed)	21	2
Cosmos	10–14	3–4
Cyclamen	50	4–6
Cynoglossum (hound's tongue)	14	2–3

Species (Common Name)	Period of Germination (Days)	Approximate Longevity (Years)
Dahlia	10	2–3
Datura (thorn apple)	15–21	3–4
Delphinium (larkspur)	15–21	1
Dianthus (pink)	6–10	4–5
Digitalis (foxglove)	15	2
Erigeron (fleabane)	14	2
Erysimum (wallflower)	14	2–3
Eschscholzia (California poppy)	10	2
Euphorbia (spurge)	21–28	3
Gaillardia (blanket flower)	15–20	4
Gerbera	14	1
Geum (avens)	21	2
Gypsophila (baby's breath)	10–14	4
Helianthus (sunflower)	10–14	2–3
Helichrysum (strawflower)	7	1–2
Heliotropium (heliotrope)	21	1–2
Hesperis (rocket)	18	3–4
Hibiscus (rose mallow)	15–30	3–4
Hunnemannia (Mexican tulip poppy)	14	2–3
Iberis (candytuft)	14	2–3
Impatiens (balsam)	15	2
Ipomoea (morning glory)	10	5
Kniphofia (torch flower, red-hot poker)	21	2
Lathyrus (sweet pea)	21	3–4
Lavatera (bush mallow)	14–35	4–5
Lilium (lily)	21	1
Limonium (sea lavender)	14–21	2–3
Linaria (toadflax)	15	2–3
Linum (flax)	21–30	1–2
Lobelia	10–15	3–4
Lobularia (sweet alyssum)	10–12	4
Lunaria (money plant)	14–21	1–2
Lupinus (lupine)	10	2
Lychnis (catchfly, campion)	21–30	2–3
Matricaria (german chamomile)	11–14	2–3
Matthiola (stock)	14	5
Mesembryanthemum (ice plant)	14	3–4
Myosotis (forget-me-not)	14	2
Nemesia	18–21	2–3
Nepeta (catmint)	17	2–3
Nicotiana (flowering tobacco)	10	3–4
Nigella (love-in-a-mist)	14	1–2
Oenothera (evening primrose)	31	2
Osteospermum (African daisy)	15–21	1
Papaver (poppy)	12	3–5
Pelargonium (geranium)	30–40	1
Penstemon (beardtongue)	17	2
Petunia	10	2–3
Phlox	10–15	1–2
Physostegia (false dragonhead)	25	2–3

(continues)

GERMINATION PERIOD AND SEED LONGEVITY FOR POPULAR PERENNIAL AND ANNUAL FLOWERS

(continued)

Species (Common Name)	Period of Germination (Days)	Approximate Longevity (Years)
Platycodon (balloon flower)	12–15	2–3
Polemonium (Jacob's ladder)	20	2
Portulaca (moss rose)	14	3
Ranunculus (buttercup)	30–40	6–7
Reseda (mignonette)	11–14	2–4
Rudbeckia (coneflower)	21	2–3
Salpiglossis	14	6–7
Salvia (sage)	14	1
Saponaria (soapwort)	10	2
Scabiosa (pincushion flower)	14–21	2–3
Schizanthus (butterfly flower)	21	4–5
Senecio (groundsel)	10	2–3
Stokesia (Stokes aster)	28	2
Tagetes (marigold)	7	2–3
Tanacetum (painted daisy, tansy)	21	1
Thalictrum (meadow rue)	30	1
Thunbergia (black-eyed Susan vine)	14	2
Tithonia (Mexican hat)	25	2
Torenia (wishbone flower)	14	1–2
Tropaeolum (nasturtium)	10	6–7
Verbena (vervain)	14	1
Viola (violet, pansy)	14	1
Zinnia	5–10	6–7

Meeting Special Requirements

Although seeds of most garden plants germinate under a wide range of conditions, some require special treatment and attention to ensure maximum germination. As is shown in the lists on pages 870 to 873, seeds of certain flowers will not germinate well if the temperatures at the time of sowing are too high; other seeds will not germinate well if the temperatures are too low. For most garden plants, the optimum temperature range within which seeds will give the best germination is about 70°F, other conditions being favorable. Seeds with definite temperature requirements for maximum germination will, with a few exceptions, sprout under less favorable temperature conditions, but the percentage of germination will become increasingly lower as the temperature varies from the optimum, and the period of germination will be erratic.

For seed requiring low temperatures, every effort should be made to provide conditions that are as nearly ideal as possible to secure high, simultaneous germination. Such seed should be sown during cool weather whenever possible, or the seed flats should be placed in as suitably cool a location as is available. For seed in the very low temperature group, the following procedure is recommended for best results: The seed should be mixed with damp, sterile sand and moist peat moss and placed in the crisper compartment of the home refrigerator. As soon as the seed has begun to germinate, the sand, peat moss, and just-sprouted seed may be sown in drills in a flat, coldframe, or seedbed, and from this point on they may be handled in the usual manner.

Seed in the high temperature range should not be sown outdoors until the soil is thoroughly warm and will not fall below 55° or 60°F at night. If started early indoors, the seed pans or flats should, if possible, be placed in a location where a temperature above 68°F can be maintained.

Pansy seed has rather unusual requirements, as it often fails to germinate well unless there are wide fluctuations in temperature. When sown where a constant temperature is maintained, with no fluctuations whatsoever, pansy seed will sometimes not germinate at all. It will sprout with moderate variations in temperature. But, in general, the wider the fluctuations the better the germination. This explains why pansy seed usually germinates best in the early autumn when hot days alternate with cool nights.

Some seeds pass through alternating periods of dormancy. They will germinate well when fresh, then, a few months later, will become completely dormant and will appear to have lost viability. Six months later they will again show a high percentage of germination. Primrose seed is in this class. Perennial seed that does not sprout yet remains firm and shows no signs of rotting may be passing through such a period of dormancy and should be left in the seedbed.

It has been found that some seeds will germinate best in the dark, while other seeds will give the highest percentage of germination in the light, other conditions being favorable. In most species, the seeds are indifferent to light intensity, and will germinate equally in dark or light.

GARDEN PERENNIAL AND ANNUAL SPECIES WHOSE SEED REQUIRES CHILLING TO GERMINATE

Antirrhinum (snapdragon)	*Lobularia* (sweet alyssum)
Aurinia (basket-of-gold)	*Lupinus* (lupine)
Dianthus (pink)	*Matthiola* (stock)
Iberis (candytuft)	*Phlox*
Lathyrus (sweet pea)	

POPULAR GARDEN PLANTS ARRANGED BY LIGHT REQUIREMENTS FOR SEED GERMINATION

SEED REQUIRES LIGHT TO GERMINATE
Press into soil but do not cover.

Achillea spp. (yarrow)

Ageratum houstonianum (floss flower)

Agrostis nebulosa (cloud grass)

Anethum graveolens (dill)

Antirrhinum majus (snapdragon)

Aquilegia spp. (columbine)

Arabis spp. (rock cress, wallcress)

Arctotis spp. (blue-eyed African daisy, Cape daisy, monarch of the veldt)

Aurinia saxatilis (basket-of-gold)

Begonia spp.

Browallia speciosa

Calceolaria spp. (pocketbook plant, pouch flower)

Campanula spp. (bellflower)

Capsicum spp. (pepper)

Chrysanthemum spp. (annual mum, perennial mum)

Coleus × *hybridus*

Coreopsis spp. (calliopsis, tickseed)

Cortaderia selloana (pampas grass)

Crossandra infundibuliformis (firecracker flower)

Cuphea spp. (cigar flower)

Daucus carota (carrot, Queen Anne's lace)

Dizygotheca elegantissima (false aralia)

Doronicum spp. (leopard's-bane)

Exacum affine (German violet, Persian violet)

Ficus spp. (fig)

Fuchsia × *hybrida*

Gaillardia × *grandiflora* (blanketflower)

Gerbera jamesonii (Transvaal daisy)

Grevillea robusta (silk oak)

Helichrysum bracteatum (strawflower)

Hesperis matronalis (dame's rocket)

Impatiens spp. (garden balsam, impatiens)

Justicia spp. (flamingo flower, king's crown, plume flower)

Kalanchoe spp.

Lactuca sativa (lettuce)

Lagerstroemia indica (crape myrtle)

Leontopodium spp. (edelweiss)

Lobularia maritima (sweet alyssum)

Lychnis spp. (campion, catchfly, Maltese cross)

Matthiola spp. (stock)

Molucella laevis (bells of Ireland)

Nicotiana spp. (flowering tobacco)

Papaver orientale (Oriental poppy)

Perilla frutescens (beefsteak plant, shiso)

Petunia × *hybrida*

Physalis alkekengi (Chinese lantern)

Platycodon grandiflorus (balloon flower)

Primula spp., except *P. sinensis* (primrose)

Punica granatum (pomegranate)

Reseda odorata (mignonette)

Saintpaulia ionantha and cvs. (African violet)

Salvia coccinea, S. splendens and other red-flowered spp. (scarlet sage, red sage)

Sanvitalia procumbens (creeping zinnia)

Satureja spp. (savory)

Sinningia speciosa (gloxinia)

Solanum pseudocapsicum (Christmas cherry, Jerusalem cherry)

Streptocarpus spp. (Cape primrose)

Tithonia rotundifolia (Mexican hat, torch flower)

SEED REQUIRES DARKNESS TO GERMINATE
Cover with a layer of fine soil equal to twice the seed's diameter.

Asparagus spp. (asparagus fern, smilax)

Borago officinalis (borage)

Calendula officinalis (pot marigold)

Catharathus roseus (periwinkle)

Centaurea spp. (bachelor's button, cornflower, sweet sultan)

Consolida spp. (larkspur)

Coriandrum sativum (cilantro, coriander)

Cyclamen spp.

Cynoglossum amabile (Chinese forget-me-not)

Delphinium spp.

Foeniculum vulgare (fennel)

Gazania cvs. and hybrids (treasure flower)

Lathyrus odoratus (sweet pea)

Lonas annua (golden ageratum)

Mesembryanthemum spp. (ice plant)

Mimosa pudica (sensitive plant)

Myosotis spp. (forget-me-not)

Nemesia strumosa

Papaver spp., except *P. orientale* (poppy)

Phlox spp. (mountain pink)

Primula sinensis (Chinese primrose)

Psylliostachys suworowii (sea lavender, statice)

Salpiglossis sinuata (painted tongue)

Saponaria spp. (bouncing Bet, soapwort)

Schizanthus spp. (butterfly flower)

Trachymene coerulea (blue lace flower)

Trifolium spp. (clover, shamrock)

Snapdragons are easily grown in quantity from seed spread on and gently pressed into the surface of moist soilless mix, but left exposed to light.

Common garden impatiens is propagated from seed that must be exposed to light to germinate. Infertile double-flowered cultivars are propagated from stem cuttings.

Wax begonias for bedding are grown from the dustlike seed spread on the surface of fine, moist, soilless mix 10 or 12 weeks before setting out. Individual plants may be propagated from stem cuttings or division.

Begonia seedlings

Preventing Damping Off

One of the greatest handicaps in sowing seed in soil is the prevalence of the fungi that cause the damping off of young seedlings. Therefore, when seed is sown in coldframes, hotbeds, or indoors, every possible precaution should be taken to prevent the growth and spread of these fungi, which attack the young seedlings either before they emerge or at a later stage, causing the stem to rot and shrivel at the ground level. The loss of one or two plants may not seem serious, but it is a danger signal that should be carefully heeded, as the fungus spreads very rapidly and hundreds of plants may become infected in just a few hours. Unfortunately, the very conditions that are most favorable for the germination and growth of young seedlings also favor the growth and spread of the fungi that cause the destructive damping off. These fungi are dormant in dry soil, but under conditions of warmth and moisture they develop rapidly. Consequently, the disease is apt to be more serious in damp, cloudy weather than it is in bright, sunny weather; and it is more serious where there is inadequate ventilation than where there is good circulation of air. The overcrowding of young seedlings tends to aggravate the spread of the disease.

To minimize damping off, the rooting medium and containers may be heat treated and the seed treated with fungicide. Once germination has begun, ventilation is important.

Seed Treatment

The treatment of the seed is very simple and will ensure the preemergence control of damping off. This protection of the seeds has become an accepted practice by many commercial greenhouse growers and seed purveyors, and it should be adopted by home gardeners, as it is a very important factor in the successful control of the disease. The most effective means of protecting seed is to dust it at the time of sowing with a fungicide such as ferbam, benomyl, or captan. These protectants provide effective control against not only damping off but also seed decay and various seedling blights. Some seed firms now offer seed that has already been treated with a protectant.

OPTIMUM TEMPERATURE RANGES FOR BEST GERMINATION FOR SELECTED GROUPS OF GARDEN PLANTS

High (68° to 85°F)

Ageratum (floss flower)	*Nicotiana* (flowering tobacco)
Aquilegia (columbine)	*Salvia* (sage)
Cleome (spider plant)	*Tagetes* (marigold)
Dahlia	*Verbena* (vervain)
Ipomoea (morning glory)	*Zinnia*
Lobelia	

Low (55° to 68°F)

Antirrhinum (snapdragon)	*Lobularia* (sweet alyssum)
Aurinia (basket-of-gold)	*Torenia* (wishbone flower)
Calendula (pot marigold)	*Viola* (violet)
Chrysanthemum	

Very Low (42° to 55°F)

Consolida (larkspur)
Lactuca (lettuce)

Indifferent

Aster
Phlox

Varying

Petunia
Viola (esp. *V.* × *wittrockiana*) (pansy)

Transplanting

When the first or second pair of true leaves has developed, young seedlings should be transplanted to prevent overcrowding and to induce better root development. It is best to transplant them into individual containers, such as 4- or 6-unit cell packs or separate 2½- or 3-inch pots. If the young seedlings are strong and vigorous and if weather conditions are favorable, they may also be transplanted into the coldframes, or if cold-hardy, they may even be planted in open ground.

A mixture of one part loam, one part peat moss, and one part sand or perlite is a good blend for transplanting into containers. The mix should be moist enough to form a ball when pressed together in your hand, yet dry enough to crumble when the ball falls to the ground. The young plants, whether in containers, in coldframe beds, or in the open, should be spaced 2 to 3 inches or even further apart in all directions, depending on their habit, size, and vigor.

To minimize root injury, seedlings should be carefully loosened when lifted from the seedbed. The pointed end of a small label is excellent for this purpose. If the small seedling plants are massed together in a clump, as so often happens when seeds have been sown thickly, the soil should be shaken gently from the roots and the individual plants carefully separated from the group. Only a small number of seedlings should be removed at a time, because no more than a few moments should elapse between the time when the young plants are lifted from the seedbed and when the operation of transplanting is completed. If the roots are exposed for any length of time they may dry out, causing the plant to suffer a serious setback. The roots should be kept covered with soil as much as possible during the operation, protected from wind, and shielded from direct sunlight.

Long, straggly roots should be pinched back to induce a vigorous, well-branched, fibrous root system. A hole large enough to receive the roots without crowding them should be made with the pointed end of a label, small stick, or pencil point. The roots of the plant should be placed in the hole, and the soil should then be pressed firmly about the roots and stem so that they cannot be easily dislodged. In transplanting delphinium or similar seedlings, care must be taken not to cover the crown with soil as these plants are very subject to rot unless the crown is slightly above the surface of the soil.

Most seedlings are easily handled, being picked up by the leaves with the thumb and forefinger. In the case of very tiny seedlings, such as begonias and primroses, it is sometimes more convenient to use a small pair of forceps.

Seedlings should be handled by their leaves, which are replaceable if damaged, not by their single stems, which at this stage may not recover if damaged. Even a small crimp in the delicate stem of a young seedling will usually result in the weakening or destruction of its internal anatomy, preventing the translocation of water and nutrients.

When transplanting seedlings into cell packs, pots, or other containers, it is most helpful to have all supplies at hand before starting and to conduct the entire procedure on a conveniently elevated surface—which, if you are standing, should be about 40 inches high, or the height of a carpenter's workbench.

To avert serious wilt, newly transplanted seedlings should be watered promptly. Transplanting is at best a severe shock to young seedling plants, as many of the tiny root hairs that supply moisture and nutrients to the plant are inevitably injured or destroyed, and can recover only with prompt watering. Furthermore, to prevent rotting of the seedlings' tender stems it is a good idea to add weak fungicide solution to the water at this time. Use a fine spray or fog nozzle when watering, and then shade the new transplants for a few days until damaged roots have been restored. The ideal weather for transplanting is cloudy (even drizzly) and calm, when humidity is high and direct sunlight absent.

Seed Sowing in the Open

The seed of many annual flowers may be sown directly in the garden where they are to bloom. Some of the perennials and biennials, as well as many annuals, may be sown in outdoor seedbeds, being transplanted to their permanent position in the garden after they have made some growth in the nursery bed. The disadvantages of sowing seeds in the open ground are that it is not possible to fully control temperature and moisture and it is more difficult to keep out marauding insects, birds, and small mammals. Heavy rains often cause the soil to become firmly compacted before the seeds germinate and may also seriously injure the delicate young seedlings. Long hours of hot sunshine may cause the soil to dry out too rapidly and, especially on heavy clay soils, to form a hard crust unless frequent attention is given to watering; but in spite of all these handicaps, seed sowing in the open can be done successfully in the majority of cases if careful attention is given to a few essential details. A well-prepared seedbed will do much to offset the vagaries of nature, and initial growth proceeds unimpeded.

The time of sowing depends, to a large extent, on the kind of seed. From zone 8 south, a few of the very hardy annuals, such as snapdragon, poppy, cornflower, larkspur, balsam, cosmos, and calliopsis may be sown in the autumn where they are to flower. The secret of success in autumn sowing lies in the fact that the seeds should not be sown until late in the season, well after the first fall frosts, when most nights are cold. They will then lie dormant in the soil throughout the winter and germinate with the first warm days of spring, many weeks before the soil is in condition for the sowing of seeds. These autumn-sown seedlings are unusually sturdy and vigorous and will give an abundance of early bloom, much more than plants from spring-sown seed.

For the more tender annuals spring sowing is preferable, and it is wise to wait until the soil is warm and workable. It is unwise to attempt the sowing of seed when the soil is wet and heavy and sticky. Seed of most annuals will not germinate well and plants tend to do poorly in heavy, saturated soil. Unless the soil will crumble readily after it has been pressed firmly in the hand, it is best to wait for it to dry further.

If the soil is a friable loam, you need not be greatly concerned about the preparation of a special seedbed, particularly in the case of kinds with sturdy seedlings, such as lupines, zinnias, and marigolds. If, however, you are dealing with a heavy soil that will have a tendency to form a hard, baked crust, it is necessary to prepare a special seedbed. This may easily be done by working compost, sand, and moist, finely pulverized peat moss into the upper 6 inches of soil. This will make the soil looser and more retentive of moisture and, most important of all, will prevent it from forming a hard crust through which the young seedlings cannot penetrate. In the case of very fine seed, such as petunias and ageratums, it is advisable to sift the top 1 inch of soil and the final light dusting to cover the seed. With larger seed, this precaution is not necessary. The depth of sowing depends on the size of the seed. In general, seed should be sown at a depth corresponding to twice its diameter. Large seed such as that of lupines and sweet peas should be planted about ¾ inch deep; zinnias and marigolds about ¼ to ½ inch; while petunia, nicotiana; and ageratum seeds are so fine that they need only be barely covered with a light sprinkling of sand or dust.

Ageratum (*Agertum houstonianum* 'Blue Danube')

After the seed his been sown, the soil should be watered with a very fine spray and should not be allowed to dry out until the seed has germinated and the young plants have become well established. Providing some light shade during germination will help retain moisture. If the seed has been sown in the garden where the plants are to flower, shading is usually not feasible, but in an outdoor seedbed in the nursery, it is possible. A lath frame forms a very satisfactory shade as it permits free circulation of air and admits some direct sunshine. Inexpensive shades may be easily made by tacking pieces of burlap or plastic mesh on 2 by 2-inch wood strips or other lightweight lumber.

In preparing a seedbed in the nursery, it is essential to select a well-drained location. In low-lying locations, or where soils are heavy clays, adequate drainage is ensured by raising the nursery bed about 6 inches above grade.

The easiest method of propagating geraniums is by stem cuttings, which, once rooted, should be individually potted up and grown on.

VEGETATIVE REPRODUCTION
Stem Cuttings

Stem cuttings may be grouped into three separate classes: softwood cuttings; cuttings made from half-ripened wood; and hardwood cuttings, which are those made from hard or dormant wood. Nearly all greenhouse plants and all herbaceous perennials as well as some shrubs may be propagated by softwood cuttings. Many shrubs and woody climbers, and some trees, are propagated by cuttings made from half-ripened wood, while others are most successfully propagated by hardwood cuttings.

Rooting Media and Propagating Units

Experimentation will reveal which of several rooting media should be used when propagating with cuttings. The medium used usually depends on the type of plants to be propagated and the sophistication of the propagating facilities. Regardless of whether the propagating unit is a modest 3-inch flowerpot or an elaborate automatically misted greenhouse bed, remember that the aim is to conserve moisture and maintain high humidity.

Several media are suggested below. Do not be tempted to root cuttings in water. Roots may very well be formed, but water induces a distinct type of root tissue to develop (usually lacking root hairs) and it is difficult to transplant rooted cuttings successfully with this type of root growth to soil. The following rooting media are suggested.

1. Moderately coarse, sterile sand.
2. One part coarse sand, one part peat moss.
3. One part coarse sand, one part perlite.
4. One part coarse perlite, one part medium perlite.

As conditions that favor the rooting of cuttings also provide excellent conditions for the growth of fungi, it is advisable initially to water in the cuttings with a dilute preparation of a fungicide and this should be followed with a fungicide spray every 10 to 14 days. Captan 50 W, used at a concentration of 2 teaspoons per gallon of water, is an effective fungicide for this purpose.

Substances that Promote Root Formation

Root-forming compounds known as plant hormones have a very direct influence on plant growth and hasten the root development of succulent, softwood, and hardwood cuttings.

There are a number of excellent commercial preparations on the market, and detailed instructions are provided by the manufacturer. The directions should be followed with care since some hormones are too strong for certain plants, not only causing damage but also actually stunting the rooting process or even killing the cutting. These plant hormone substances may be used with a wide variety of cuttings. They mark a distinct advance in the technique of propagation, as root formation can be stimulated on many plants, such as magnolias and certain dogwood species, which are otherwise difficult to propagate.

In general, rooting hormones are available in three concentrations: no. 1 for soft tissue (houseplants), no. 2 for semiripened wood (many shrubs), and no. 3 for ripened wood (most trees).

Softwood Stem Cuttings of Herbaceous Plants

Stem cuttings are sometimes referred to as "slips," the term being frequently applied to small shoots that are pulled or "slipped" from a plant for the purpose of propagation.

PERENNIALS PROPAGATED BY STEM CUTTINGS

Achillea (yarrow)	*Gaillardia* (blanketflower)	*Myosotis* (forget-me-not)
Arabis (rock cress)	*Geum (avens)*	*Oenothera* (evening primrose, sundrops)
Artemisia (silver mound)	*Gypsophila* (baby's breath)	*Penstemon* (beardtongue)
Aster	*Helenium* (sneezewort)	*Phlox*
Aubrieta	*Helianthus* (perennial sunflower)	*Physostegia* (false dragonhead)
Aurinia (basket-of-gold)	*Heliopsis* (orange sunflower, oxeye)	*Platycodon* (balloon flower)
Campanula (bellflower)	*Hesperis* (sweet rocket)	*Potentilla* (cinquefoil)
Centaurea (cornflower)	*Heuchera* (coralbells)	*Rudbeckia* (coneflower)
Chrysanthemum	*Iberis* (perennial candytuft)	*Salvia* (sage)
Coreopsis (tickseed)	*Linum* (flax)	*Saponaria* (bouncing Bet, soapwort)
Delphinium (larkspur)	*Lobelia*	*Sedum* (stonecrop)
Dianthus (pink)	*Lychnis* (campion)	*Silene* (catchfly, campion)
Dicentra (bleeding-heart)	*Lupinus* (lupine)	*Teucrium* (germander)
Dictamnus (gas plant)	*Lythrum* (loosestrife)	*Veronica* (speedwell)
Eupatorium (mist flower)	*Monarda* (bee balm, bergamot, horsemint)	

Time of Making Cuttings

Softwood stem cuttings of herbaceous perennials such as delphiniums, phloxes, and chrysanthemums are best taken in the spring just as the plants are starting into growth, although they may be taken at any time during the growing season when young, nonflowering shoots are obtainable. Cuttings of blue phlox (*Phlox divaricata*), mountain pink (*P. subulata*), rock cress (*Arabis* spp.), and perennial candytuft (*Iberis sempervirens*) are most successful if taken in late spring or early summer, well after their flowering season is over.

Making the Cuttings

The parent plants from which the cuttings are taken should be vigorous, healthy, and preferably well branched. The cuttings should usually be taken from the terminal growth, preferably from nonflowering shoots. Growth that is too soft and succulent should be avoided, as cuttings taken from such shoots are apt to rot before root formation can take place. Instead, shoots that are somewhat older and are brittle enough to snap when bent double should be selected. Old, hardened stems are unsatisfactory as they root very slowly and have a tendency to produce inferior plants. In some cases, old plants can be headed back to induce a growth of new lateral shoots suitable for cuttings.

Softwood cuttings usually range from 2 to 4 inches long. Using a very sharp knife, a clean diagonal cut should be made a short distance below a joint or node (the point at which a leaf is joined to the stem). After the cuttings have been taken, it is advisable to plunge them in cold water or to wrap them in damp newspaper for about a half hour or more to prevent them from wilting. This practice does not apply to geraniums or to plants that exude milky juice, such as crown of thorns (*Euphorbia milii*). Cuttings from such plants should be sprinkled lightly with water and spread out

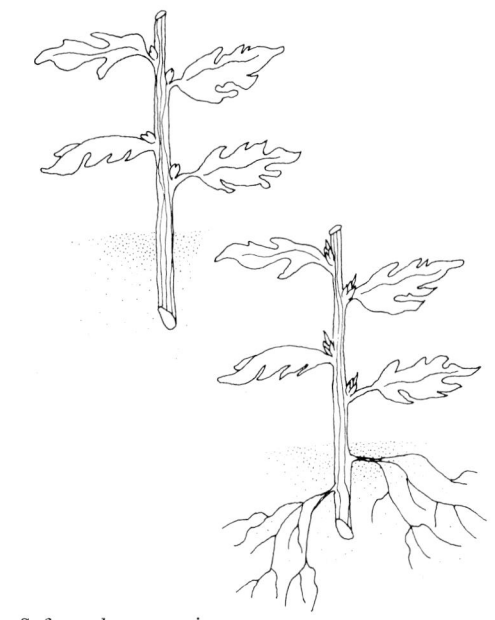

Softwood stem cutting

on a surface where they will be exposed to the air for several hours. This will give the bleeding cells an opportunity to become sealed and there will be less danger of rot after the cutting is placed in the propagating case.

In preparing the cutting, all flower buds should be removed and the leaf area should be slightly reduced. The leaves should be removed from one or two nodes at the base of the cutting with a sharp knife, not pulled or stripped off. The leaf area at the top should not be reduced unless there is an excessive amount. In the case of coleus and a few other plants with large, succulent foliage a portion of the leaves may be removed, but as a general practice it is well to leave as much leaf area near the tip of the cutting as possible, since leaves of a softwood cutting manufacture food for the plant and thus have an important part to play in the development of the new root system.

Planting the Cuttings

After the cuttings have been prepared, they should be inserted in the propagating medium. The depth will vary somewhat with the type of cutting but, in general, it should be such that one or two nodes are buried. The rooting medium should be pressed firmly about the cuttings and thorough watering should be given after the cuttings are in place. Shade the bed for the first few days at least. As to the degree of sun exposure thereafter, be guided by the condition of the foliage. The leaves should be firm and should never be allowed to show any appearance of wilting. Plants differ greatly in this respect. As the roots begin to form, it is important that full sunlight be provided.

Temperature

For the majority of plants, a temperature ranging between 65° and 75°F is ideal, although some plants require somewhat lower or a much higher degree of heat. Root formation is usually greatly stimulated if bottom heat is provided. If possible, the temperature of the rooting medium should be 5° to 10° warmer than the surrounding air. In greenhouses the bottom heat is supplied by the pipes that comprise the regular heating system or by an automatically controlled electric heating cable. In a hotbed it may be supplied by an electric soil cable or by fresh manure, while in the house it may be supplied by a soil cable or by radiator pipes if they are accessible.

Moisture and Air Circulation

An adequate supply of moisture and sufficient circulation of air are also important factors. For the majority of plants a moderate degree of moisture is desirable. The sand of a rooting medium should never be allowed to dry out completely, nor should it be allowed to become wet to the point of saturation. Cacti and other succulents require a relatively dry environment, while a few of the large-leaved greenhouse plants require a high level of humidity. Success with cuttings thus depends on selecting the rooting medium that will best maintain requisite moisture levels as well as the correct humidity.

There should be sufficient circulation of air so that moisture does not remain on the leaves constantly or for too long a time. However, direct drafts should always be avoided, as they are desiccating and, therefore, usually very harmful to young cuttings.

Potting Up

Depending on the time of year, about two to four weeks will be required for the rooting of most softwood cuttings. Evidence of root formation will usually be indicated by the beginning of new top growth. When the roots are well developed and have reached a length of ½ inch or more, the cuttings should be carefully removed from the sand. They may then be potted up in small pots or planted in flats or frames. A sandy loam with a small proportion of leaf mold is ideal for this first potting. After the young plants have become well established, they may adapt to other soils.

Softwood and Half-ripened Stem Cuttings of Shrubs and Trees

Many shrubs and trees may be propagated by softwood and half-ripened stem cuttings. Softwood cuttings are generally taken during the late spring or early summer, while half-ripened stem cuttings should be taken during the late summer months, the exact time depending on the kind of plant and its growth habit.

The cuttings should be taken from the tip end of the shoots and the wood should be just brittle enough to snap off when bent double. Avoid soft, fast-growing suckers as well as old hardened, brittle growth.

When making cuttings, take special care to limit transpiration or water loss. Choose cloudy weather or the early morning of a day when you will have time to insert them in the rooting medium. During the interim, the cuttings should be kept wrapped in damp burlap or newspaper, placed in a plastic bag, and kept out of the sun. The cuttings should vary in length from 4 to 6 inches and be taken with a clean cut made below a node. The leaves should be clipped from the lower portion of the cutting and the base dipped in the appropriate rooting hormone before inserting the cuttings in the propagating unit. For each hormone-dipped cutting, a hole should be made with a pencil or dowel, the cutting placed in the hole, and the medium pressed firmly around it. Do not thrust the cutting into the medium, as this will strip off the hormone coating.

Selecting the right time to take these cuttings is most critical and can dramatically affect the percentage of successful rooting, as well as the length of time it takes for the cuttings to produce roots. In general, softwood and half-ripened stem cuttings are taken from deciduous trees and shrubs as well as from broad-leaf evergreens.

Mist Sprays for Softwood Cuttings

Mist spraying is a great aid to propagators. It is a practice widely used by commercial growers and can also be adapted for use by the home gardener who wishes to propagate plants by softwood cuttings on a fairly large scale.

Mist spraying of softwood cuttings has many advantages. At no point in their development do the cuttings dry out, as the foliage is kept constantly moist. Since shade is not necessary when mist spraying is used, the plants receive ample sunlight and the danger of having the cuttings suffer from lack of sufficient air circulation is greatly lessened. As a consequence, there is less opportunity for disease to gain headway. A high percentage of rooting is usually obtained with mist spraying, and resultant growth is healthy and vigorous. By this method it is also possible to root cuttings of larger size. This, of course, is a decided advantage when propagating trees and shrubs, as it is often possible to save several years of growing time. Mist spraying, especially when combined with the application of rooting hormones, has also made it possible to propagate plants that were hitherto extremely difficult to grow from cuttings, such as most evergreens.

The procedure is simple and can be adapted for use in greenhouses, in coldframes, and outdoor propagating beds. However, it is essential that there be good drainage where mist spraying is used. Pipes containing a series of nozzles that give off a very fine mist are installed above the propagating area. The mist spray is usually regulated automatically by a clock, or by an "electronic leaf" (described below). If misting frequency is determined by a clock, the number of applications required depends mostly on the weather and on the judgment of the operator. Constant mist will supply far more water than is needed and is definitely detrimental to most cuttings. A clock may be set to regulate not only the frequency of mist delivery but also the length of each misting period.

The most satisfactory mist control is had through use of an "electronic leaf," a device consisting of two carbon contact points, embedded in a small block of plastic that is on a short stand. This is inserted in the rooting medium with the cuttings. The surface of the plastic dries off a little more rapidly than do the leaves of the cuttings. When there is no longer a film of moisture covering the plastic, the contact is broken and the mist spray is automatically turned on, going off again as soon as the leaves are thoroughly moist. When cuttings are first inserted in the medium, the "leaf" is placed at its farthest point from the jets. As the cuttings begin to root it is gradually moved closer to the jets, which reduces both the frequency and quantity of mistings. After the cuttings are rooted, the application of mist should gradually cease and lath shade should be provided. The cuttings should then be hardened off before being transplanted to grow on.

Hardwood or Dormant Stem Cuttings

Many deciduous trees and shrubs may be propagated very readily by means of dormant or hardwood cuttings. These cuttings should be taken in the autumn after the leaves have fallen, in the winter, or the very early spring. In the case of a few shrubs, such as rose of Sharon (*Hibiscus syriacus*) and

bush honeysuckle (*Diervilla* spp.), only branch tips should be used. With the majority of shrubs and trees, however, the branches may be cut into sections varying from 6 to 10 inches in length. The cuttings should be made from normal, healthy shoots of the current season's growth.

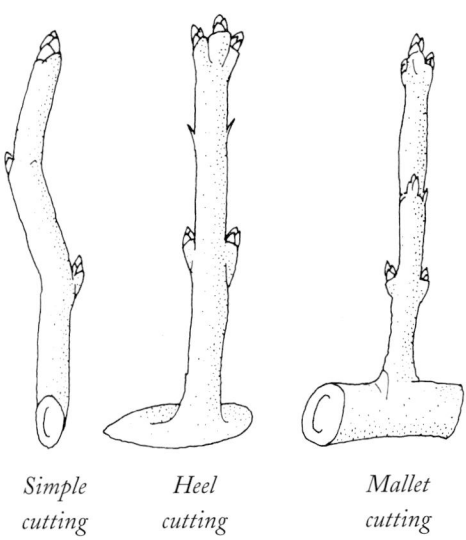

Simple cutting   *Heel cutting*   *Mallet cutting*

Since these cuttings are made when temperatures are very low, be careful not to cause tissue damage by bringing frozen cuttings into a warm work area. If you must work in a heated area, allow the cuttings to warm slowly in the sun first. In most cases, there should be at least three or four buds on each section of stem used as a cutting.

A clean, slightly diagonal cut should be made just below a bud at the bottom of each cutting. Be sure to use a sharp knife when taking these cuttings; pruning shears or other dull tools will almost certainly mash the bases of the cutting, creating an ideal site for disease to set in and consequently limiting your success.

After the cuttings have been made, they should be tied in bundles of convenient size with the lower or butt ends even and the cuttings facing in the same direction. A label should be attached to each group and the bundles should then be buried in slightly moist sand, soil, peat moss, or sawdust. A cool cellar with a temperature ranging between 40° and 45°F provides an ideal storage place for hardwood cuttings during the winter months. If such a place is not available, however, the bundles of cuttings may be buried below the frost line in a well-drained spot outdoors in sand or in light, sandy soil. During this period of storage a callus will form over the butt ends of the cuttings. In the spring when the ground is workable, the cuttings may be removed from storage and planted out in nursery rows. By autumn, the cuttings should be well rooted and the young plants may then be shifted to more ample quarters in the nursery.

Two other types of specialized hardwood cuttings are the "heel" and "mallet" forms. The heel cutting is usually a straight twig, most of which is the most recent season's growth but the basal portion, furthest from the tip, also includes about ½ inch of the previous year's growth. The mallet type is a lateral shoot that includes a ¼-inch section from the previous year's vertical growth. Both types give the same results as a simple tip cutting and are usually reserved for use with coniferous, or narrow-leaf, evergreen cuttings.

Hardwood cuttings are usually used in propagating deciduous woody plants and coniferous evergreens. Certain evergreens, such as spruces (*Picea* spp.), hemlocks (*Tsuga* spp.), firs (*Abies* spp.), pines (*Pinus* spp.), and some junipers (*Juniperus* spp.), are however more easily propagated by air layering methods (discussed later in this chapter).

TREES AND SHRUBS PROPAGATED BY HARDWOOD STEM CUTTINGS, LISTED BY GENUS OR GROUP

Berberis (barberry)	*Hamamelis* (witch hazel)
Buddleia (butterfly bush)	*Ilex* (holly)
Buxus (boxwood)	*Kerria*
Cercis (redbud)	*Kolkwitzia* (beauty-bush)
Chaenomeles (flowering quince)	*Ligustrum* (privet)
Chamaecyparis (false cypress)	*Lonicera* (bush honeysuckle)
Clethra (sweet pepperbush)	*Philadelphus* (mock orange)
Cotoneaster	*Pieris* (andromeda)
Deutzia	*Syringa* (lilac)
Elaeagnus	*Taxus* (yew)
(Russian olive, autumn olive)	*Viburnum*
Euonymus (burning bush)	*Weigela*
Forsythia	

Leaf Cuttings

Among the more commonly grown houseplants, several may be very easily propagated by leaf cuttings, the methods varying according to kind. In general, plants with thick, fleshy leaves may be most readily propagated this way, as such leaves have a reserve supply of food and moisture.

African violet (*Saintpaulia ionantha*), gloxinia (*Sinningia speciosa*), peperomia (*Peperomia* spp.), and rex begonia (*Begonia* 'Rex Cultorum' hybrids) may be propagated by removing an entire leaf from the plant and inserting the petiole, or leaf stalk, in the rooting medium. Snake plant (*Sansivieria* spp.) may be increased by cutting the leaves into pieces 3 to 5 inches long and inserting them partway into the medium in the propagating case. With kalanchoe (*Kalanchoe* spp.), the leaf should be removed from the plant, laid flat on the sandy medium, and weighted with pebbles. The new plants are produced from latent buds in the inden-

tations along the margins of the leaves. Often these young plantlets begin to grow while the leaf is still attached to the parent plant. To propagate rex begonia and Cape primrose (*Streptocarpus* spp.), the usual practice is to make a slight cut through the main veins of the leaf just below the point where they fork. The leaf is then placed flat on the sand or other rooting medium, being pinned in place with small wire hairpins or weighted with pebbles. Another method of propagating begonias is to trim the leaf into the shape of a V, each piece containing a large vein. The point of the V is then inserted in the sand and the new plant will develop at this point.

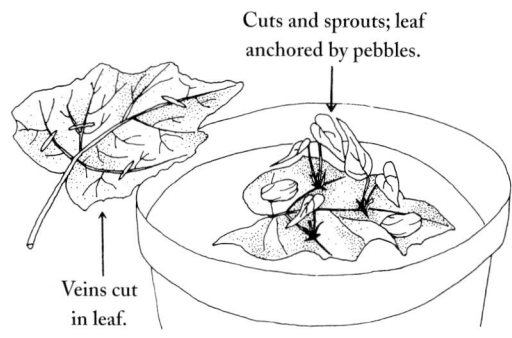

Begonia: *whole leaf cutting*

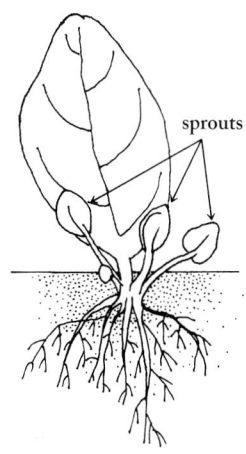

Saintpaulia: *leaf cutting*

Root Cuttings

After the plants have been lifted, the roots of certain kinds may be cut into pieces 2 to 3 inches long. These pieces of root should then be planted in greenhouse flats or frames, being placed in a horizontal position at a depth of approximately 1 inch. Pure sand, sand, and peat moss in mixture, or a light sandy soil will give equally satisfactory results as a rooting medium.

If the cuttings are taken in the autumn, they may be carried over the winter in the coldframe, and by spring the new plants will be ready to set out in the nursery. If the cuttings are given mild bottom heat in the greenhouse propagating bench, the development of new roots and top growth will be very rapid.

In many cases, root cuttings may be taken at almost any season of the year, but the most favorable time will usually be indicated by the plant's natural habit of growth. Oriental poppy (*Papaver orientale*), however, is best propagated in mid to late summer, after the foliage has yellowed in anticipation of dormancy. Since the foliage soon vanishes and the individual taproots are surprisingly slender, it is well to mark each plant with a label in the spring. Japanese anemone (*Anemone × hybrida*), which flowers in late summer or early fall, propagates best if lifted late in the season after the blooming period is over. Tall summer phlox (*Phlox paniculata*) may be propagated by root cuttings anytime after flowering.

PERENNIALS PROPAGATED BY ROOT CUTTINGS

Anchusa azurea (bugloss)
Anemone × hybrida (Japanese anemone)
Asclepias tuberosa (butterfly weed)
Ceratostigma plumbaginoides (blue leadwort)
Dicentra spectabilis (bleeding heart)
Dictamnus albus (gas plant)
Echinops spp. (globe thistle)
Gypsophila paniculata (baby's breath)
Macleaya cordata (plume poppy)
Oenothera spp. (evening primrose)
Papaver orientale (Oriental poppy)
Phlox paniculata (summer phlox)
Polygonatum commutatum (Solomon's seal)
Romneya coulteri (canyon poppy)
Stokesia laevis (Stokes aster)
Thermopsis caroliniana (false lupine)
Trollius × cultorum (globeflower)
Yucca filamentosa (Adam's needle)

Propagation by Division
Clumps
The division of old clumps is one of the simplest of all methods of propagation. Many perennials and a few shrubs may be propagated very successfully in this way.

The plants should be lifted from the soil and pulled apart with care to minimize injury to the roots and crown. In cases where crowns have become tough and hard, two spading forks inserted back to back may be used to loosen them. In occasional instances where no alternative seems possible, a clean cut can be made with a sharpened spade, a sharp machete, or a strong butcher's knife.

For certain herbaceous perennials the frequent division of clumps is desirable from the standpoint of good cultural procedure; in other cases it is employed only when there is a desire to increase the stock. For example, hardy asters and chrysanthemums progressively deteriorate if left undisturbed over a period of years and should, therefore, be systematically lifted and divided every two or three years, whether new plants are desired or not. On the other hand, peonies should not be divided more frequently than once in seven or eight years and they may often be left undisturbed indefinitely with no apparent reduction in performance. Bleeding heart (*Dicentra spectabilis*) should be left undisturbed unless an increase of stock is desired, as the plants will naturally increase in size and beauty as the years pass.

The season of the year most favorable for the division of old clumps varies according to the plant's natural habit of growth. Hardy asters and chrysanthemums should be divided during the early spring just as growth starts. Phlox is best divided in the early autumn after the period of bloom has passed, but may be divided successfully at almost any season. If bleeding heart must be divided, it should be dug in the late summer or fall, after the foliage has yellowed; digging in the spring will diminish or abort flowering that season. Similarly, peonies should be lifted, divided, and replanted in the fall, if they must be disturbed at all.

Rhizomes
A rhizome is a specialized horizontal underground, or partially underground, stem that, in most cases, produces roots, shoots and leaves. A rhizome may be distinguished from a root by the presence of nodes. A true root has no nodes. The rhizomes of some plants penetrate quite deeply into the soil; while in the case of certain irises, the rhizomes rest on or just beneath the surface of the ground, being only partially subterranean. Plants of this type may be readily propagated by a division of the rhizomes. In the case of bearded iris, the plant may be lifted from the soil and the rhizomes gently separated, each rhizome having two or three sprouts for new growth (see the illustration on page 881). The rhizomes of some plants bear no prominent shoots. In such cases, the rhizome may be cut into short pieces, which are temporarily planted in sand until they have rooted. The majority of rhizomatous plants should be propagated when dormant. In the case of the bearded iris, however, the most favorable time is during the summer after the blooming period.

Tubers
Tubers are thickened underground stems bearing conspicuous buds or eyes. Among flowering plants, the dahlia is the most prominent member of this group, while the ordinary white potato and the Jerusalem artichoke are well known

PERENNIALS PROPAGATED BY DIVISION OF CLUMPS

Achillea spp. (yarrow)	*Chrysanthemum* spp.	*Lupinus* spp. (lupine)
Aconitum spp. (monkshood)	*Cimicifuga* spp. (black cohosh, snakeroot)	*Macleaya cordata* (plume poppy)
Ajuga spp. (bugle)	*Clematis* spp. (perennial clematis)	*Mertensia virginica* (Virginia bluebells)
Amsonia tabernaemontana	*Conoclinium coelestinum* (mist flower)	*Monarda* spp. (bee balm, bergamot, horsemint)
Anchusa azurea (Italian alkanet)	*Coreopsis* spp.	*Oenothera* spp. (evening primrose)
Aquilegia spp. (columbine)	*Delphinium* spp.	*Paeonia × lactiflora* (peony)
Arabis spp. (rock cress, wallcress)	*Dianthus* spp. (pink)	*Penstemon* spp. (beardtongue)
Artemisia spp. (dusty miller, silver mound)	*Dicentra* spp. (bleeding-heart)	*Phlox paniculata* (summer phlox)
Aster spp. (hardy aster)	*Doronicum* spp. (leopard's-bane)	*Physostegia* spp. (false dragonhead)
Astilbe × arendsii	*Echinops* spp. (globe thistle)	*Primula* spp. (primrose)
Aubrieta deltoidea (purple rock cress)	*Euphorbia* spp. (spurge)	*Rudbeckia* spp. (coneflower)
Aurinia saxatilis (basket-of-gold)	*Filipendula* spp. (meadowsweet)	*Scabiosa caucasica*
Baptisia australis (false indigo)	*Gaillardia* spp. (blanketflower)	(perennial pincushion flower)
Boltonia asteroides	*Helianthus* spp. (perennial sunflower)	*Sedum* spp. (stonecrop)
Campanula spp. (bellflower)	*Hemerocallis* spp. (daylily)	*Tanacetum coccineum*
Centranthus ruber (valerian)	*Heuchera sanguinea* (coralbells)	(painted daisy, pyrethrum)
Cerastium tomentosum (snow-in-summer)	*Hosta* spp. (plantain lily)	*Thalictrum* spp. (meadow rue)
Ceratostigma plumbaginoides (blue leadwort)	*Iris* spp.	*Trollius* spp. (globeflower)
Chelone spp. (turtlehead)	*Linum perenne* (perennial flax)	*Veronica I'cronica* spp. (speedwell)

Daylily clumps are best divided and the divisions replanted in late summer or early fall.

among the vegetables. The tubers may be cut into sections, as in the case of the potato, or they may be planted whole, as in the case of the dahlia. It is essential that each tuber have at least one healthy bud. When dahlias are propagated by tubers, a small portion of stem should be attached to each tuber.

Propagation of Bulbs and Corms
Bulbs, Bulblets, and Bulbils

There are numerous bulblike structures, popularly called bulbs, that in reality may be tubers, rhizomes (as described above), or corms. In the more precise botanical sense, bulbs are modified stems, leaves, and buds that grow at least partly submerged in the ground. Most are composed largely of fleshy, scalelike leaves or leaf bases and contain large quantities of stored plant food.

There are two principal types of true bulbs: the tunicated type, which is covered with close-fitting layers of leaf tissue that forms a dry husk, as in hyacinths and tulips; and the scaly type, which is composed of thick, loose, overlapping scales, as in true lilies.

Many bulbs are readily increased by natural separation. A fully matured bulb, known as a "mother bulb," will, under favorable conditions, produce one or more bulbs of flowering size and a number of small bulblets. These should be removed when the mother bulb is dug and should be planted in flats or in nursery plots, as they will usually require several years to reach blooming size. Commercial growers dismember bulbs or cut them into segments. When planted in nursery beds, the pieces gradually grow, and after several seasons each becomes a full-size bulb.

Certain lilies, such as the tiger lily (*Lilium lancifolium*), produce enlarged, deeply pigmented buds or bulbils in the angles of the upper leaves after flowering. These bulbils detach and drop to the ground in fall, strike root, and after several years, develop flowering plants. The bulbils may be detached in late summer or early fall, planted in flats with a sandy humusy soil, wintered in the coldframe, and grown on in the open nursery before being set out in the garden.

The hardy begonia (*Begonia grandis*) also produces bulbils (or tiny tubers) on its upper stems in late summer; these may be treated like lily bulbils, except that culture should be in light shade.

Corms and Cormels

A corm is a round, swollen, fleshy, underground base of a stem. It is solid, being composed almost entirely of undifferentiated stem tissue, and is unlike a bulb in this respect. Among the most familiar examples of plants grown from corms are the crocus, cyclamen, gladiolus, ixia, and tritonia. Each year one and in some cases several new corms of flowering size are formed on top of the mother corm, which deteriorates at the end of the growing season. Many small cormels are also usually formed at the base of the new corm. When the plants are dug in the autumn, the new, flowering-size corms may be separated and stored for spring planting. In general practice, these corms are planted the following season to produce bloom. If, however, a very rapid increase of stock is desired, as in the case of a new or very expensive variety, these large corms may be cut into sections so that more plants may be produced. The tiny cormels should be stored until planting time in the spring. They may then be planted in rows, being treated very much like seed, and they will reach blooming size in one to three years, their flowers being exactly like those borne by the corm on which they developed.

Propagation by Specialized Shoots
Layering

Layering is one of the simplest and most dependable methods of propagation, although it is adapted only to those plants that possess a characteristic habit of growth and that root readily when their arching or spreading branches come into contact with the soil. It is of especial value in the propagation of some of the broad-leaf evergreens, such as certain cultivars of rhododendron and magnolia. Cultivars of forsythia and daphne may also be propagated by layering. There are several different types of layering: tip layering, simple layering, serpentine layering, mound layering, and air layering.

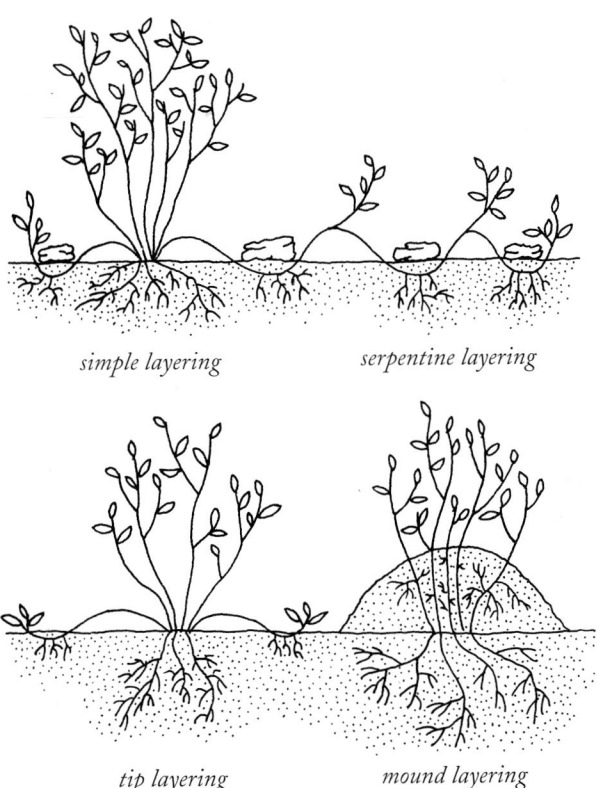

simple layering   *serpentine layering*

tip layering   *mound layering*

Tip Layering

Tip layering is the propagation method commonly used with blackberries, raspberries, and other plants with arching stems. In late summer, the supple canes are bent over and their tips shallowly anchored in the soil. A new plant will soon form, often in a month, which may then be severed from the parent plant and transplanted to any desired position.

Simple Layering

Usually done during the spring and summer months, simple layering involves rooting a branch behind its tip. If the branch is woody, a cut should be made partway through it about 18 inches from the tip. The cut should be propped open with a match or some very small piece of wood or a notch may be cut out. The branch should then be bent over to the ground, and the portion with the cut or notch covered with soil. Any leaves may be removed from that portion of the stem that is to be buried, with the leafy tip end of the branch left exposed. If necessary, the branch may be pegged down with a forked stick, or it may be weighted with a stone.

After the layer has rooted, it may be severed from the parent plant and, when well established, transplanted, preferably the following spring.

Serpentine Layering

A method frequently used in the propagation of vines with long flexible stems, serpentine layering enables one to obtain a large number of new plants (see the illustration). In serpentine, or continuous, layering the entire shoot except the tip is covered with soil. Continuous layering can be used only with a rather limited group of plants, as many types will not send up shoots from buds that are buried in the soil. This method is of particular value in the propagation of ivy (*Hedera* spp.) and various willows (*Salix* spp.).

Mound Layering

Plants of a characteristically bushy habit of growth may frequently be propagated successfully by mound layering. This method is of particular value in the propagation of hydrangea (*Hydrangea* spp.), cotoneaster (*Cotoneaster* spp.), flowering quince (*Chaenomeles* spp.), Carolina allspice (*Calycanthus florida*), and currant (*Ribes* spp.). The plants should be pruned back severely, preferably a year before the layering is to be done, to encourage the production of new shoots at the base. Soil should be mounded up about the entire base of the plant in the spring and these new basal shoots will strike root at the nodes. This method of propagation is somewhat slow, as it will frequently require one, two, or more years for the new plants to become well established.

Air Layering

Although used more than 2,000 years ago by the Chinese, air layering was largely limited in the United States to the propagation of a few greenhouse plants, such as the India rubber plant (*Ficus elastica*) and certain dracaenas (*Dracaena* spp.) Today, however, thanks to new techniques and plastic materials that hold moisture, air layering is much more widely used. For example, professional and amateur gardeners have found it an excellent method of propagating such shrubs as holly (*Ilex* spp.), rhododendron, and azalea (*Rhododendron* spp.).

The most favorable time for air layering hardy materials is just as growth starts in the spring. A stem or branch of the previous season's growth should be selected. A cut should be made ½ to 2 inches long, extending approximately one-third of the way through the stem. The cut should be made with a sharp knife and may be made either toward or away from the tip. The flap of bark made by the cut should be entirely removed. The cut should then be dusted with a rooting hormone such as Hormodin no. 3 using a small paintbrush. Fine sphagnum moss, which has either been horticulturally milled or rubbed through a ½-inch screen, should be used to bind the wound. The moss should be thoroughly moistened and then squeezed until no water drips from it. Moss that is soggy when it is applied may cause fermentation and

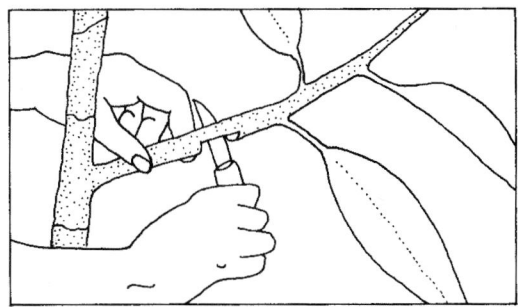

One-in. length of stem is trimmed to induce new growth.

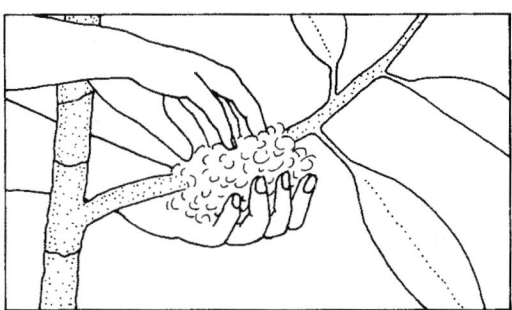

Damp sphagnum moss is clustered around open area.

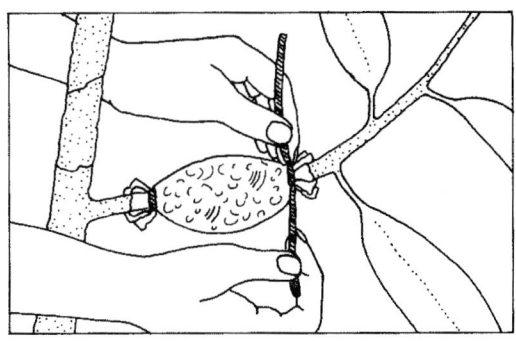

Plastic secures the moss and is tied firmly at each end.

discourage rooting. After the moss has been moistened and the excess water squeezed out, it should be rolled into a ball and then cut in half. These two pieces should be bound around the wounded area on the stem. A 6 by 6-inch piece of polyethylene or vinyl plastic should then be wrapped tightly around the ball of moss and sealed at both top and bottom with waterproof tape. The strips of tape should completely seal the plastic and be bound several times around the stem of the plant. It is important that a complete seal be made to prevent rainwater from seeping in and to keep interior moisture from escaping.

When roots have formed at the point where the cut was made, the branch should be severed from the parent plant. The plastic covering is then removed, and the newly rooted plant is either potted up or planted in a nursery bed.

TREES AND SHRUBS THAT CAN BE ROOTED BY AIR LAYERING

Acer (maple)	*Malus* (apple, crab apple)
Betula (birch)	*Populus* (poplar)
Carya (hickory)	*Prunus* (cherry, plum, peach, and
Catalpa	almond, both ornamental and fruiting)
Cercis (redbud)	*Rhododendron* (azalea)
Cornus (dogwood)	*Salix* (willow)
Crataegus (hawthorn)	*Syringa* (lilac)
Enkianthus	*Taxus* (yew)
Ilex (holly)	*Tsuga* (hemlock)
Magnolia	*Viburnum*

Suckers

Some plants may be propagated by means of suckers, which are fast-growing leafy shoots produced from adventitious buds on the underground parts of a plant. Certain apple and crab apple cultivars (*Malus* spp.) and cherry, peach, and plum cultivars (*Prunus* spp.) produce suckers generously. Lilac (*Syringa* spp.) may also be propagated by this method. If the tree or shrub that is to be propagated has been grafted, it is important to make certain that the sucker has been produced from a bud above the graft. If it has developed from a bud below the graft, it will be similar to the stock on which the tree or shrub was grafted and will not possess the desirable characteristics of the grafted plant. Certain species of willow (*Salix* spp.) and poplar (*Populus* spp.) are easily propagated by means of suckers.

Runners

Some plants, such as strawberry (*Fragaria* spp.), Boston fern (*Nephrolepis exaltata* 'Bostoniensis'), and strawberry geranium (*Saxifraga stolonifera*), may be readily propagated by means of runners. In plants of this type the stems creep along the surface of the ground and strike root at the widely spaced nodes, producing new plants that continue to receive nourishment from the parent plant until they are well established. The connecting stem may be severed at any point between the old plant and the new plant, and the new plant may then be moved to a new location.

Stolons

A stolon is a slender branch that, under favorable conditions, will take root. Stolons may be produced either above ground or below ground, the new plant being produced from the bud at the end of the stolon.

Some shrubby plants take root very naturally by means of stolons and may be readily propagated in this way. In this category we find red-stem and yellow-stem dogwood (*Cornus stolonifera* cvs.), most willows (*Salix* spp.), and certain old-fashioned roses, such as 'Harison's Yellow'.

Among turf grasses, some of the bents (*Agrostis* spp.) are very readily increased by planting stolons. The sod is broken into small pieces. The stolons are then strewn on the surface of a well-prepared seedbed and covered with approximately ½ inch of soil. The soil must be kept continuously moist until growth has started.

Grafting

Grafting involves taking a piece of the upper or above-ground part of a plant, called the scion, which is usually a carefully removed bud or a twig or young branch of a tree or shrub, and uniting it with the lower part of another plant, called the stock, which is often just a rooted stub. Although the scion may be much smaller than the stock, both must be from closely related plants. A successful graft requires that there be direct contact between the cambium layers of both scion and stock, i.e., the thin, growing layer beneath the bark or epidermis and outside the woody interior. Budding is a type of grafting in which the scion is a bud with some associated stem tissue.

Fruit trees do not come true from seed, as most of our orchard cultivars are hybrids. In order to perpetuate such a cultivar or variety, vegetative propagation or a vegetative union is necessary. Grafting and budding are the two common methods of propagating fruit trees. A strongly rooting but otherwise undesirable tree may be replaced by a more desirable one by grafting. Pollination success can be ensured by grafting the proper cultivar on one branch of a tree that fails to set fruit, because the presence of another cultivar will promote cross-fertilization and the formation of fruit. Where garden space is limited, two or more cultivars of the same fruit tree species may be grafted on a common stock.

Bridge Grafting

When the trunk of a tree has been girdled, as by the gnawing of rodents, especially in winter, the remedial bridge-grafting procedure is as follows.

1. Remove the soil from around the trunk of the tree until the live bark at the trunk base or on the root buttresses is exposed.
2. Trim off the rough edges of the bark with a sharp knife at the base of the tree and also on the root.
3. Take a piece of a strong dormant branchlet (one year old, or the previous season's growth) and it cut to a length equal to the gap to be bridged plus 2½ inches, which allows 1¼ inches for the top side and 1¼ inches for the bottom, or root, side. All cuts should be made with a sharp knife.

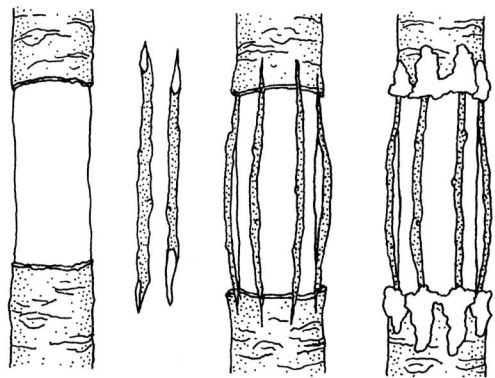

Steps in bridge grafting

4. Cut out a piece of bark above and below the girdled area, into which the ends of the scion should fit snugly.
5. Make a slanting cut, 1¼ inches long, on each end of the scion and place each end in the part where the bark was removed.
6. Space the scions about 2 inches apart around the trunk.
7. Two small brads without heads should be used to hold the scion firmly in place at each end. They should be nailed through the middle two-thirds of each scion, each end of which is properly fitted above and below the girdled area.
8. Apply grafting wax over the united areas to isolate them from air and thus avert their drying out.

Whip Grafting

Whip grafting is used to propagate nursery material and may be carried out in midwinter when most other garden operations are at a standstill. One-year-old, well-rooted stock should be used. They may be grown from seed or purchased from nurseries that make a specialty of growing stock material. The procedure is as follows.

1. Cut the top off a selected well-rooted stock whip, leaving a 3-inch stub. Discard the top.
2. Make a long, clean, slanting cut across the stub, and then cut a vertical notch on the surface of the cut.
3. Select a 3- to 6-inch section of scion whose diameter approximates that of the stock and that bears several plump buds.
4. Cut one end as described in Step 2, but leave a tongue to fit into the notch of the stock as an anchor.
5. Join the scion to the stock and be sure that green or cambium tissue beneath the bark of the scion contacts the comparable tissue of the stock.
6. Wrap the graft tightly with waxed string and store in moist sand or leaves in a damp, cool place with a temperature of approximately 45°F until the pieces have united.
7. As soon as the soil can be prepared in the spring, set the plants 6 inches apart in rows 3 feet apart. Set deep enough to cover all but the top bud. Remove the string before planting.

This method may also be practiced on young trees in the nursery row that are not over one year old. If older, the smaller branches may be successfully grafted in this way.

Cleft Grafting

Cleft grafting is used to improve the top growth of fruit trees and is especially helpful when the stock limb to receive the scion is considerably larger than the scion itself. Usually, the receiving or stock limb is ½ to 2 inches in diameter. This type of grafting is most successful if done early in the spring when the bark is loose, before growth has made much progress. It may be done after that, however, if the scions are dormant. The procedure is as follows.

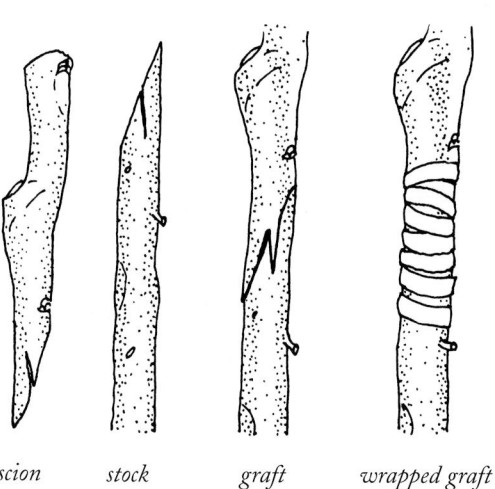

scion   stock   graft   *wrapped graft*

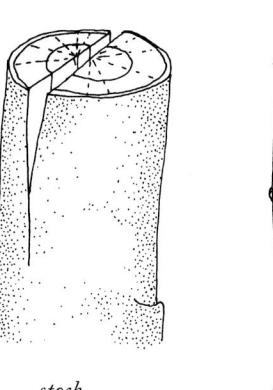

stock

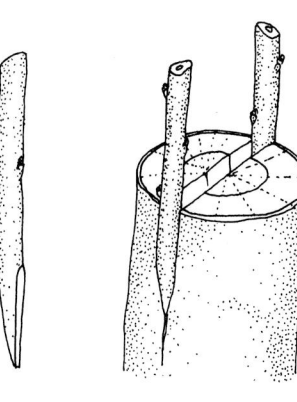

scion   *Scion inserted in stock. All cut surfaces require thorough waxing.*

A.

C.

1. (A) Saw or prune the limb off at the point chosen to make the graft.
2. (B, C) With a sharp knife smooth the edges so the cambium layer may be easily seen.

3. Carefully split the stub, using a knife or, if the stub is thick, drive a grafting chisel, to a depth of 3 to 4 inches.
4. (D) The scion of the desired subject should have been taken from the terminal growth of a bearing tree, which should be the previous season's growth.

B.

D.

E.

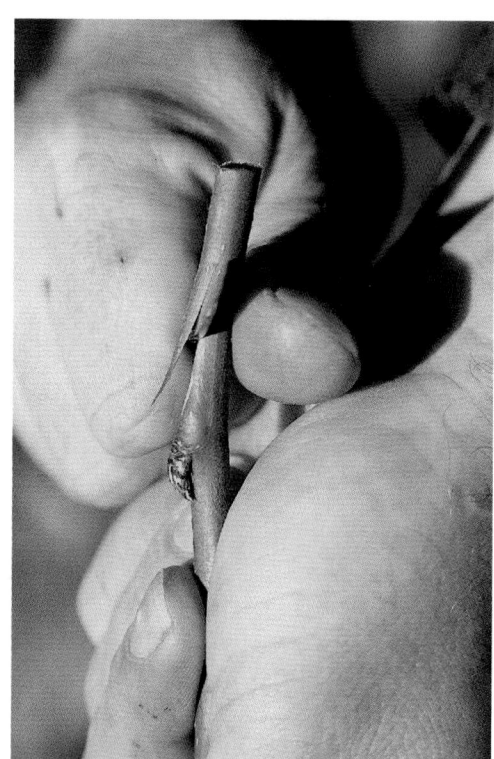

5. The tip of the scion should be cut off, and the second cut is made 1½ inches below the third bud.
6. (E, F) That part of the scion below the third bud is cut to make a wedge. The side with the bud should be slightly thicker than the side that will be in toward

G.

the center of the stub. This wedge should be 1¼ inches in length.

7. (G) The cleft is opened with the end of a wedge-shaped chisel, and the scion is inserted so that its cambium layer is in direct contact with that of the stock.

F.

H.

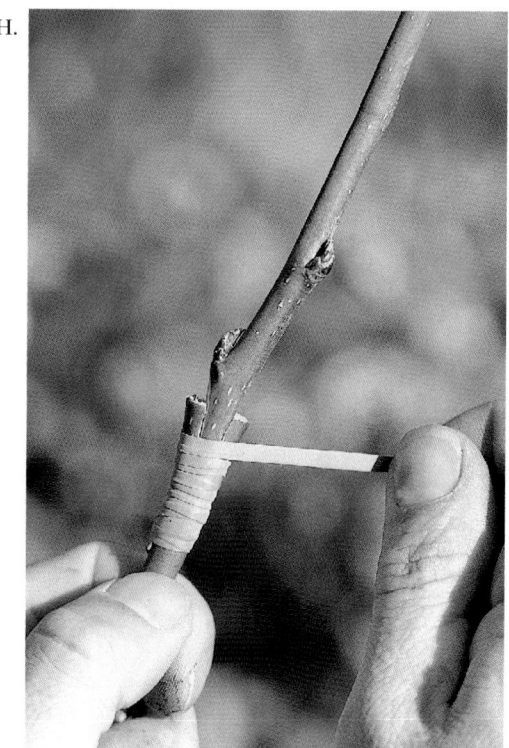

I.

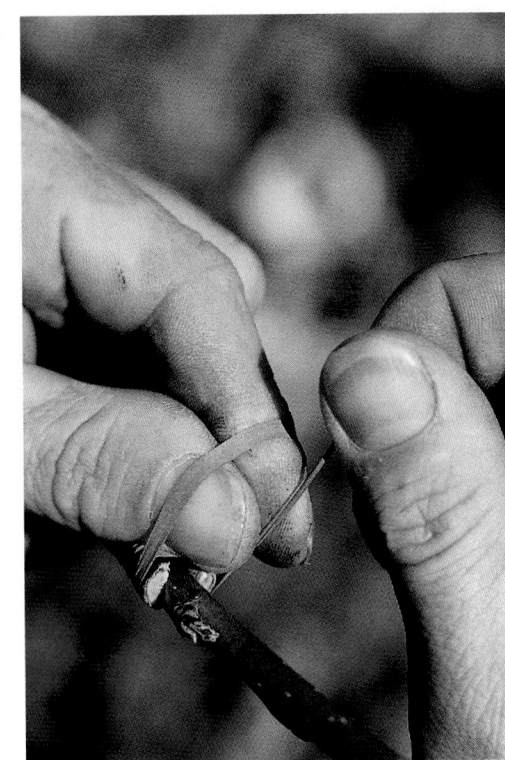

One scion is inserted on each side of the stock if it is more than 1 inch in diameter, and the chisel is removed. The pressure from the sides of the split stock holds the scions firmly in place. Keep in mind that the scions should be uniform in size so that they fit well and have equal pressure from both sides of the stock.

J.

K.

8. (H, I, J, K) Wrap the graft with raffia or rubber bands, and cover the entire exposed area immediately with grafting wax to prevent drying out and to inhibit the entrance of disease organisms and the accumulation of excess moisture.

An extra large branch may be cleft grafted by making two clefts at right angles to each other. In this case four scions are necessary. Small wedges of wood are best put in each cleft to prevent the scions being crushed, since great pressure is exerted by the wood in a larger limb.

When the grafting of an individual limb is finished, the entire exposed area should be waxed over to prevent drying out, to inhibit the entrance of moisture, and to inhibit disease organisms. The grafts should be checked occasionally to make sure that the wax is properly protecting it. When grafting is done after considerable growth has been made, it is best to cover the entire scion with wax, which keeps it in a dormant state a little longer while the scion is uniting with the stock.

Cleft grafting is very satisfactory on apples and pears but is difficult on plums and cherries and almost impossible with peaches.

Budding

Budding is done during August or in the early part of September when the bark slips easily. Its main use is to propagate young trees of a desired cultivar. It is also used extensively to propagate hybrid roses. The procedure is as follows:

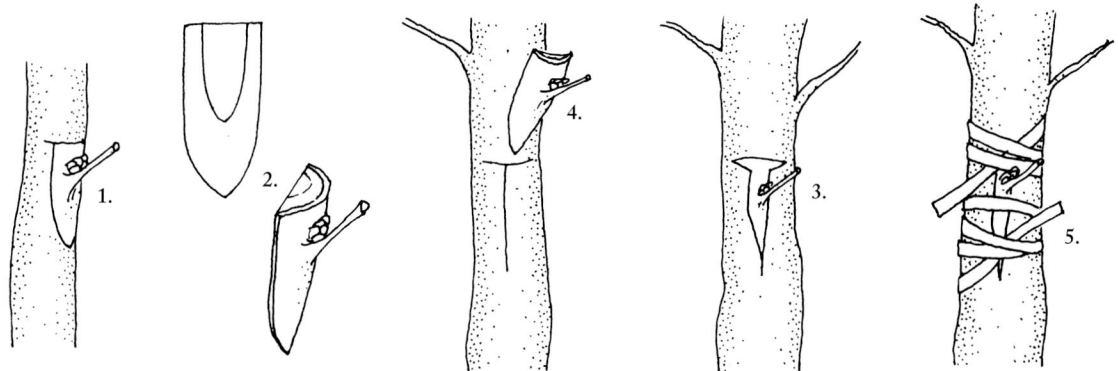

Steps in budding: 1. Cut out bud with bark triangle. 2. Back and side views of bud. Note that sliver of wood must be removed before insertion in stock. 3. Cut and insertion on stock. 4. Bud inserted. 5. Protective raffia wrapping holds bud in place.

1. At the point where the budding is to be done, as close to the ground as possible, make a cut in the shape of a T: its vertical distance should be ¾ inch and the horizontal distance ½ inch.
2. The bud to be used is selected from the terminal growth on the current season's growth. Be sure that the bud is well developed. Remove the leaf next to the bud, but leave part of the leaf stalk attached.
3. Using a sharp knife, remove the bud with some of the wood and bark attached to it. When properly removed it looks like a shield.
4. Carefully loosen the corners of the T-shaped cut in the stock and slip the bud in under the corners.
5. Wind raffia, rubber bands, or waxed string above and below the bud to establish good contact.
6. Within two weeks, the bud should be united.
7. The bud remains dormant until the following spring,

at which time the stock should be cut back to the bud, which develops into the desired limb.

Pruning and Training of Grafts

Grafts, especially those on large limbs that have been cleft grafted, must be properly managed. If two or more grafts are made on a stub, only one should be allowed to fully develop. The best one should be selected before next season's growth starts. It is cut back to promote lateral branches. The other is cut back to two or three buds, the purpose being to keep it alive so that it will help to heal over the stump but not compete with the graft selected. The principle used to train grafts until maturity or bearing is the same as with young trees planted in the ground.

It is best to graft only one side of a tree if it is more than eight years old. The other side can be grafted the following year.

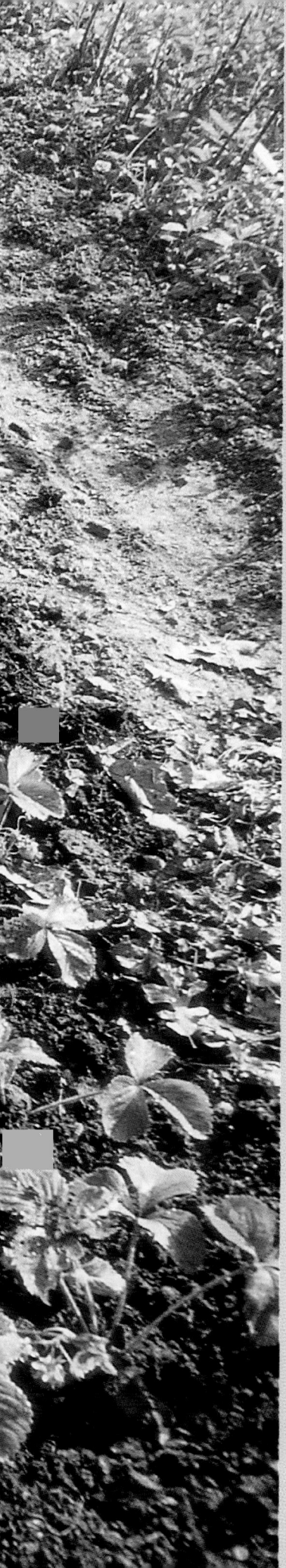

37

Garden Practices

A GOOD GARDEN PROGRAM INCLUDES SUCH GENERAL practices as soil preparation, cultivation, watering, fertilizing (popularly called feeding), pruning, deadheading, staking (when needed), winter protection, frost protection, preventing transplanting losses, and controlling pests and diseases. It also requires tailoring the size and complexity of the garden, as well as the selection of plant materials, to the time and resources available. All too often, the maintenance aspect of gardening is overlooked when a new planting is made, and

Leafy compost and well-rotted manure combine to make a nutrient-rich mulch for strawberries.

this can lead to frustration and disappointment. If in doubt, it is best to start with a small, easily kept garden and gradually expand to an extent you perceive as manageable.

Fundamentally, gardening involves the choice and arrangement of various kinds of plants for ornament or for the produce they provide, and the alteration and management of the environment to suit their requirements. Some garden plants, especially the majority of woody kinds, are grown essentially as they occur in the wild, while others, most notably vegetables, have been genetically altered to bring out certain traits and may have been so changed as to be viable only with continuous human intervention, i.e., only in a garden.

The challenge before gardeners is to manage their gardens and home grounds in as environmentally benign ways as possible. Because of the increasing scarcity of certain resources, such as freshwater, and the hazards of pollution, especially of groundwater and air, it has become a civic responsibility for gardeners to conserve water, minimize fertilizer and pesticide use, compost organic waste, and

Stepping stones distribute body weight more widely than shoes, hence cause less compression, a common garden problem , especially on heavy clay soils.

choose kinds of plants that require the least intervention—especially if that intervention may be harmful or wasteful. Whenever possible, garden design and practices should favor maintenance that does not involve the routine use of air-polluting machinery, such as gasoline-powered lawn mowers; the repeated application of highly soluble or fast-release water-polluting fertilizers; or the use of biocidal preparations to control pests and diseases that may stimulate the generation of resistant mutants.

SOIL PREPARATION

The arduous and venerable practices of double digging and trenching, in which soil is dug and mixed with manure in two stages to a depth of 2 feet in well-ordered rows from one end of the garden to the other, have long since given way to somewhat shallower soil preparation, using the garden fork or the rototiller. Deeper digging and enriching is now generally limited to specific sites, for example, where a tree or large shrub is to be planted. Most vegetables, garden flowers, and lawn grasses require soil preparation no deeper than 1 foot. The older practices of deep preparation are useful in loosening—and thus aerating and improving drainage of—heavy soils, but elsewhere they lead to the mixing of topsoil and subsoil, which contributes little to nutrient availability and even lowers the soil quality by reducing its moisture retention. On thin, sandy soils, especially where the topsoil zone is shallow, such deep digging virtually destroys soil quality.

In general, the less digging, the better. The soil compaction that often prompts annual digging may be minimized by designing gardens to restrict foot traffic to mulched paths, stepping-stones, or planks. Soil quality can be improved year by year by adding well-rotted manure, compost, and organic mulches, all of which release nutrients as they decompose and form a loose, friable soil.

Shallow forking or rototilling may be necessary each year in the vegetable garden and in beds used for annuals, but elsewhere, soil amendments are best applied as topdressings and left on the surface, where they help control weeds, reduce evaporation, and stabilize soil temperature. Released nutrients percolate downward or are taken below by earthworms as they consume organic detritus.

SOIL CULTIVATION

Traditionally, soil cultivation is said to serve several important functions: It destroys weeds, breaks the crust that forms on clay soils after rains, aerates the soil, and creates a moisture-conserving dust mulch on the surface. Careful study has shown, however, that routine cultivation is unnecessary on soils already loosened with organic amendments and blanketed with mulch. Indeed, cultivation can be detrimental to plants with shallow root systems. Heavy clay soils, so often difficult to work, are best lightened and improved with well-rotted manure, compost, sand, and peat moss, not by ritual cultivation. Weed control, when required, is best effected by severing tops from roots with a scuffle hoe whose cutting edge is kept sharp by filing.

Various types of small hand weeders are available for use in flower beds and borders, in rock gardens, and in nursery plots. For a more extensive planting, such as a large vegetable garden, a wheel hoe fitted with a sharpened horizontal scuffle blade is very efficient in clearing young weeds.

WATERING

Soil nutrients become available to plants only when dissolved in water. Therefore, soil moisture is a garden necessity. Factors that contribute to soil drying, besides inadequate rainfall, are soil percolation (the movement of water through soil), exposure to sun and wind, particle size, uptake of water by plant roots, evaporation of water from the surface, and air and soil temperature. Bare, unmulched, sandy soil that lacks organic matter and supports a large number of shallowly rooted plants (such as lawn grasses) will soon go dry in hot, windy weather. Mitigation of any of these factors will slow the drying and thus reduce the need for supplemental irrigation.

In general, the most favorable times for watering are late afternoon and early evening. The evaporation of moisture is considerably less at such times, and the plants are consequently able to derive more lasting benefit from the application. The major exception to this generalization is the vegetable garden, where late watering and the consequent overnight wet conditions can sponsor the outbreak of fungal or bacterial diseases. Thus early morning watering is best for this garden area. Young seedling plants, whether ornamental or vegetable, must never be allowed to suffer a lack of moisture, even briefly, as irreversible stunting can result.

The method of watering will vary according to the kinds of plants being serviced, the type of soil involved, and, to some degree, on the extent of your gardening operations. One of the best ways of maintaining a constant, uniform supply of moisture in the soil, especially for trees and shrubs, is to sink 1-foot lengths of 4-inch clay drain tile in the ground, one open end being level with the surface of the soil. If these pieces of tile are kept filled with water, there will be a gentle and very gradual seepage of moisture throughout the soil.

The usual method of supplying supplemental water is by a garden hose fitted with any of a wide range of attachments that form and distribute droplets. An adjustable nozzle, either hand held or set in a holder, can send out water in a fine spray; a fan of droplets; or a narrow, forceful stream.

Rose attachments similar to those used on watering cans are useful where a steady, gentle spray is desired. More commonly seen are various types of rotary or oscillating sprinklers that cover large areas and relieve the tedium of hand watering. Whatever the sprinkler device, it should be left in place until an area is thoroughly soaked and should then be moved on to another section of the garden or lawn. A special device particularly useful for watering shallowly rooted shrubs and small trees is a water sword, which may be attached to a hose and plunged deeply into the ground. Rate of water flow through the sword and the length of the watering period will depend on soil porosity, i.e., whether sandy or clayey, as well as on dryness of the soil, size of the tree, and so on.

There is comparatively little danger of too liberal applications of water when watering is done episodically, but during prolonged periods of heavy rain, or if an in-ground, clock-governed automatic irrigation system delivers water too frequently or for extended periods, the soil may become so saturated with moisture that plant growth may suffer in consequence. Under such conditions, much of the available nitrate in the soil is leached beyond the reach of roots, and plants are unable to make normal growth. Moreover, in water-logged ground, air penetration is minimal, which impedes root growth and further weakens affected plants. Even large trees may show ill effects, as may happen when drainage patterns are changed as a result of construction. If trees begin to suffer from such a condition—by displaying an unseasonal yellowing or browning of the leaves and a general thinning of foliage—holes should be bored beneath the spread of branches and some distance beyond to facilitate air penetration to the roots.

Gardens in dry regions, even if planted with carefully selected drought-tolerant species, often require supplemental irrigation. In such regions, however, water is usually in short supply and too costly to apply broadcast. Hence the increasing popularity of drip irrigation, an efficient delivery system consisting of a network of plastic tubes or pipes laid on the surface through the garden at fairly close intervals and from which water dribbles through pores or emitters. Emitter size and frequency, along with valves, regulate the flow.

Various refinements, such as porous soaker hoses and drip tapes, also direct irrigation water to points of need and eliminate loss by mist formation. For isolated trees and large shrubs, small sprinklers may be used, especially those that direct a nonmisting, large-droplet spray downward from an elevated spray head. All such devices, if left in place, and even if they are equipped with filters, need occasional cleaning to remove sediment and algae. Irrigation systems using water drawn from ponds and lakes are especially apt to require frequent cleaning.

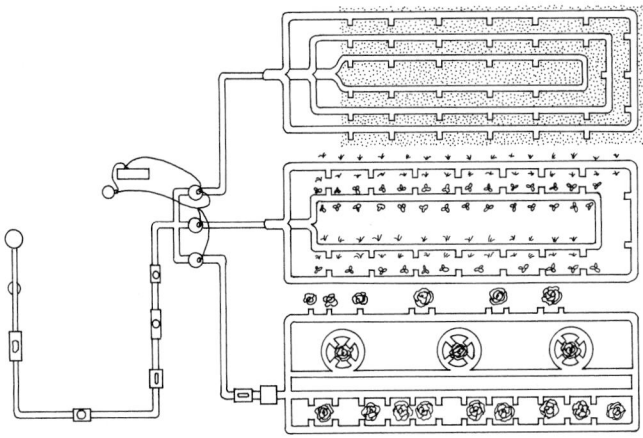

Plan of an in-ground drip irrigation system, designed for lawn (top), row plantings (middle), and scattered specimen trees and shrubs (bottom).

Even in relatively well-watered or mesic regions, it is increasingly desirable and, in some localities, necessary to design gardens using plants that have evolved to conserve water and are tolerant of occasional or periodic droughts. The term most commonly applied to this kind of gardening, wherever practiced, is "xeriscaping," which, however, is best limited to the use of cacti, succulents, and other notably drought-resistant plants in very dry or desertous areas, such as the Southwest, where long periods elapse between rains and where dew is an important source of moisture for plants. Elsewhere, where rainfall is sufficient to support a wide diversity of ordinary leafy plants, but where drought may occur from time to time, gardening practiced with maximal water conservation in mind is more correctly called "mesiscaping."

Whatever the designation and wherever it is applied, this commendably responsible approach is in contrast to the usual practice of selecting garden plants just for their appearance, and then, once they are in place, to intervene as necessary, with watering, fertilizing, pruning, and pest and disease control. All these measures betray the plants' unsuitability in that environment. The better suited a species is for your garden conditions, the less intervention it will require.

Fertilizing

All plants depend on 17 naturally occurring chemical substances for growth and development. Compounds of nitrogen, phosphorus, and potassium are of primary importance and must be present in the soil. For these compounds to be available to a plant, the soil must have a degree of pH (acidity or alkalinity) that governs the form in which these compounds occur. If the pH is too high or too low, the plant may not succeed because one or more soil-borne nutrients are not in

a form suitable for uptake by that species. Thus, depending on the nutrient requirements of the kinds of plants being grown, garden soil may require an adjustment of pH, or supplemental nutrients, or both. In addition, the physical condition of the soil greatly affects root growth.

Compost improves any soil by increasing its water retention while promoting drainage, by returning nutrients, by improving aeration, and by varying particle size. A detailed discussion of the value of soil tests, the mineral nutrients needed for plant growth, and the form in which these nutrients may be applied, can be found in Chapter 31 and in various other chapters dealing with special plant groups.

There are, however, a few fundamental principles that should be observed in the application of fertilizers. Under no condition should water-soluble commercial fertilizers be allowed to come into contact with seeds at the time that they are sown or with the roots of trees, shrubs, and smaller garden plants at the time of planting. The germination of most seeds will be seriously reduced if commercial fertilizers are used in the drill, or shallow furrow, at the time of sowing. This is because they include concentrated salts that draw water from anything they contact so that they may liquify and go into solution. Thus, unless well mixed with soil, fertilizers can desiccate or "burn" living plant tissue, and if this tissue is delicate, as it is in growing roots, it can cause the death of the affected part or even the entire plant.

The most approved method of supplying nutrients to young plants is to place the fertilizer in drills 3 or 4 inches away on each side of the row. The drills should be 2 to 3 inches deep and the fertilizer should be covered with a small quantity of soil. This method is especially recommended for vegetables and for flowers in the cutting garden that are grown in rows.

The best way to apply fertilizer to garden beds and borders is to broadcast it over the surface of the soil at the prescribed rate and to cultivate it in very lightly. The soil should then be thoroughly watered so that the fertilizer may dissolve and become available to the plants. If individual plants within the border are to be fertilized, a shallow furrow in the form of a ring may be made several inches from the crown of the plant and the fertilizer placed in the furrow. Care must be taken to keep the fertilizer from coming into contact with the foliage, as this too may cause severe burning. For most purposes, pelletized, slow-release fertilizers are preferable to highly soluble, fast-acting preparations.

Pruning

It is important that every gardener acquires a knowledge of the fundamental principles of pruning. You should understand when pruning is advisable or even necessary, and at what season of the year it should be done. You should also become familiar with the most approved pruning practices. The primary purposes of pruning are to maintain or restore a balance between root absorption capacity and transpiration by the leaves, especially at the time of transplanting; to remove injured, diseased, or dead wood; to increase both the quantity and quality of flowers and fruit the plant bears; to control the structure of a tree or shrub and to guide its growth; to improve the appearance and symmetry of a plant; to maintain a plant, especially a hedge shrub, at a certain size; and to aid in the rejuvenation of old trees, shrubs, or vines.

To prune a tree or shrub intelligently, it is necessary to understand that in all plants there is a definite relationship between root growth and top growth. If there is a reduction in normal root growth, there must be a compensating reduction in top growth. This is why the judicious pruning of trees and shrubs at the time of transplanting is important. In bare-root and ball-and-burlap transplanting, it is almost inevitable that some if not most of the roots will be severed and shortened. Therefore, to compensate for this reduction in root growth, the top must be pruned. Under the best of circumstances, any tree or shrub dug out of the ground will suffer shock and will require time, sometimes years, to reestablish itself. As such, a plant will be unable to sustain vigorous top growth during the period of shock and recovery, severe pruning is usually recommended.

On the other hand, container-grown material will sustain little or no root disturbance during transplanting, but as containered roots are often severely crowded, they should be loosened somewhat at the time of planting. This will encourage their diffuse growth away from the artificially dense ball and hasten establishment.

Although each species has a genetically determined growth habit, symmetry and appearance may be modified to varying degrees by intelligent pruning. No attempt should be made, however, to change radically the shape or form of a plant, except for such specific applications as topiary, bonsai, and hedge trimming. Pruning should aid in developing strong limb patterns. Any top pruning of pines, spruces, firs, and other more or less geometrically growing conifers with relatively few growth points should be done with special care, as clipping these growth points may permanently alter the form of the tree or shrub. After ornamental trees have attained their full development and have been trained to the desired form, comparatively little pruning is necessary.

Systematic yearly care includes the removal of broken branches and any dead or diseased wood and the cutting away of any branch that may be interfering with the development of other branches. In the case of shrubs the same general principles hold true: In many cases, old or failing stems should be cut away entirely to stimulate vigorous new

growth. The pruning requirements of trees and shrubs are discussed in Chapters 11 and 12 as well as in sections of Chapter 28.

Just as the removal of roots necessitates the reduction in top growth, so does the severe pruning of top growth disturb the equilibrium of the normal function of the roots, and balance is restored by the growth of new shoots and branches. In many cases, this is the goal with fruit trees and flowering shrubs, where the production of vigorous, young, flowering and fruiting stems is desirable. Some species bear flowers and fruit on new growth, and such growth may be encouraged by the annual pruning out of old wood. Many of our flowering shrubs, most roses, the small bush fruits, and the grapevines may be found in this group.

Such pruning is also associated with the rejuvenation of old, deciduous trees and shrubs that have become weak or senescent. Invariably, vigorous pruning is followed by an increase in top growth, but moderation must be practiced. This is particularly true in the rejuvenation of old trees. If very severe pruning of large trees seems necessary or advisable, the process should be extended over a period of several years. If excessively heavy pruning of top growth is attempted at one time, it will usually stimulate the formation of much rank

Removal of high limbs can involve climbing, rope rigging, and chainsaws, and is best left to trained professionals.

growth in the form of suckers and water sprouts, which often fail to survive the first winter. Moreover, these rampant shoots compromise the form and appearance of the tree. Not only should they be removed if they occur, but their production should be controlled by pruning.

It should be noted that at some point in age, woody plants, most noticeably trees, inevitably go into a slow decline that culminates in death. This natural, irreversible decline usually extends over several years or even decades, but may accelerate under stress, as when the pruning of live limbs is severe or when changes occur in soil moisture or pH. It is at such a stage that pests and diseases often strike and hasten the decline.

Pruning Practices

To make a neat, clean, close cut, and to avoid injury to the bark, pruning shears should be held with the blade next to the portion of the twig or branch that is to remain on the plant. A ragged cut, crushed stems, and torn, mutilated bark indicate regrettable carelessness by the person responsible for the pruning. In cutting back small branches, the cut should be made at a slight angle, just above a bud (see the illustration on page 213). If the cut is made above an outside bud, the growth will be directed outward and the form will be open and spreading. If a more compact, upright growth is desired, the cut should be made above an inside bud. When branches have opposite or paired rather than alternate or solitary buds, one of the buds may be removed, and the growth may thus be guided in any desired direction.

If large branches are to be removed, the final cut should be made as close to the main trunk as possible so that the wound may heal rapidly and there may be no disfiguring stump. If the limb is comparatively large, more than one cut may be advisable. The first cut should be made from below, about 1 foot from the main trunk, and it should extend no more than halfway through the branch. The second cut should be made from above, at a distance 3 or 4 inches farther out on the branch, and it should sever the limb entirely. The final cut should consist of the removal of the stub as close to the trunk as possible.

The once-common practice of painting or "dressing" cut surfaces where tree branches or limbs have been removed is now largely discontinued. Studies have shown that the compounds used to paint wounds usually crack and leak in time, thus not only allowing entry of moisture but impeding its evaporation and thereby increasing the likelihood of heartwood decay and the weakening of the tree. Harsh petroleum-based fungicidal or bacteriocidal tree-wound preparations can be toxic to the very trees they are intended to protect. The best way to facilitate the healing of pruned surfaces or other tree wounds is to leave them flush, smooth, and unpainted.

However beautifully freezing rain decorates the landscape, the added weight of ice can disfigure trees and shrubs with broken limbs, especially if they have not been pruned to reduce structural weakness.

Pruning Equipment

Elaborate pruning equipment is not usually necessary. Most pruning may be accomplished efficiently with three or four tools—a pair of good pruning shears, a pair of lopping shears with extended handles, one or two pruning saws, and a pole pruner usually are the only tools necessary. Pruning shears, whether of the scissor or anvil type (see Chapter 30), are effective in cutting woody twigs and branches up to ⅜ to ½ inch in diameter (depending on the hardness of the wood), lopping shears up to ¾ to 1 inch in diameter, and pruning saws for thicker branches. The pole pruner, useful for trimming branches beyond reach, is essentially a pruning shear (sometimes also with an optional saw blade) mounted on one or an interlocking series of poles and is actuated by a long cord. In each case, it is essential that shears be sharp, as dull cutting blades crush tissue which then dies. Pruning shears should always be correctly tightened and adequately oiled.

STAKING

Certain garden perennials, biennials, and annuals, such as delphiniums, hollyhocks, and cosmoses, usually require support if they are not to topple or break apart in wind or rain. In nature this support is provided by adjacent vegetation, but in the garden, where plants are allowed more room, it must be provided by the gardener, and is usually done by tying stems to slender stakes. Stakes are especially effective

Done with care and sensitivity, staking should be unobtrusive yet preserve natural habit, as with theses delphiniums and lilies.

as supports for the narrow, spirelike growth of hollyhocks, foxgloves, and delphiniums, but for beds of more diffusely branched or multiply stemmed plants, such as cosmos, Mexican hat (*Tithonia rotundifolia*), and peony, it is more effective to staple a section of 4- or 6-inch-gauge wire fencing horizontally onto to predriven 3-foot-high posts before the need arises and to allow the plants to grow up through the mesh, which then becomes their support. In the vegetable garden, this is also a useful procedure for tomatoes.

The best material for tying stems, especially those of annuals and perennials, is cotton postal twine, as this soft-textured cord is less likely to chafe or girdle stems than manila or nylon cord or wire. Sections cut from panty hose also make good tying material, although exposure to intense sun weakens it. Care should be taken to avoid tying stems so tightly that their natural expansion is impeded. The best procedure is to first tie the cord around the stake tightly with double knots and then to tie the stems loosely but securely, also with double knots. This allows the supported stems some freedom of movement and also expansion room, but averts the cord sliding down a smooth stake.

Plants such as the tomato and the annual blue milkweed (*Oxypetalum caeruleum*) that are sarmentose in growth, (i.e., tend to climb but have neither the twining habit nor clinging appendages such as tendrils or hooks) may be supported by tying their stems to poles or stakes or, for best results, by using a cylinder made of a section of wire-mesh fencing (see page 664). Other garden plants such as peony and Nippon daisy (*Chrysanthemum nipponicum*) that tend to sprawl under the weight of their flowers are kept neatly upright if a suitably large square of coarse (4- to 6-inch mesh) wire fencing is mounted horizontally on posts about 2 feet above the clump in the spring so that the shoots can grow through the mesh openings before flowering.

Whatever the materials and procedure, every effort should be made to preserve the natural disposition of the plants involved and to make the supports and ties as inconspicuous as possible. Black, dark brown, or dark green are the colors most easily concealed.

DEADHEADING

The removal of spent flowers prevents seed formation and often stimulates additional flower-bud formation, sometimes extending the period of bloom well beyond the normal season. This is especially true with annuals. In some cases, as, for example, with columbine, foxglove, perilla, and calendula, deadheading prevents the dispersion of great amounts of winter-hardy seed and the subsequent intrusion of massed volunteers whose blooms or other appealing characteristics are usually considerably less meritorious than those of the originally planted cultivars.

In some garden plants, such as cannas and daylilies, deadheading is primarily done for aesthetic reasons, as the large, shapeless, wilted flowers substantially detract from the beauty of these plants.

SAVING AND STORING SEED OF GARDEN PLANTS

Garden plants that are open pollinated (i.e., are essentially unchanged from their wild forebears) produce seed that is "true," yielding plants with the same floral characteristics as those of the preceding generation. Hence, ripe seed may be collected, dried, and filed in small, labeled envelopes or in capped bottles or vials and kept in a cool place over the winter. For many, the refrigerator (kept at about 40°F) is ideal for such storage.

Among annuals, the following are genetically stable over successive generations and may be grown from garden-collected seed:

Emilia javanica (tassel flower)
Eschscholzia californica (California poppy)
Lobularia maritima (sweet alyssum)
Nigella damascena (love-in-a-mist)
Portulaca grandiflora

Others, such as *Cleome hassleriana* (spider flower), *Consolida ambigua* (larkspur), *Cosmos bipinnata* (tall cosmos), and *Nicotiana* spp. (flowering tobacco) are similarly stable from generation to generation, though variable in flower color. But as their seeds are winter hardy as far north as zone 7, seedlings often appear as garden volunteers, especially if the garden bed remains uncultivated until midspring.

In such biennials as hollyhock (*Alcea rosea*), foxglove (*Digitalis purpurea*), Scotch thistle (*Onopordum acanthium*), and mullein (*Verbascum* spp.), the seed may be collected and sown the following spring, or the plants may be allowed to self-sow. Some perennials are also reliable reseeders, including purple coneflower (*Echinacea purpurea*), globe thistle (*Echinops ritro*), Texas gaura (*Gaura lindheimeri*), Siberian iris (*Iris sibirica*), and lupine (*Lupinus* spp.). As with annuals and biennials, surplus seed, whether home collected or bought commercially, may be safely kept for one or two years in the refrigerator.

WINTER PROTECTION

For a tree, shrub, woody climber, perennial, or first-year biennial to survive winter, it must be hardy, i.e., able to adjust both to the rhythms of climate and to the vagaries of weather. It must be tolerant not only of the steady downward trend of temperatures and reduced hours and intensity of daylight in the fall but also of unseasonable, suddenly imposed cold and of the sustained cold of winter and the occasional absolute low readings which, on average, define the USDA plant-hardiness zones. It must also be unresponsive to unseasonable winter mild spells and also endure the occasional spring freezes that occur as day length increases and temperatures trend upward.

Providing adequate winter protection for trees, shrubs, and flowers is a problem all gardeners must face, especially in northern climes. The type and extent of protection necessary depend on the natural hardiness of the plants, on the severity of the climate, and on their exposure in the garden.

Winter injury to plants is usually attributable to either of two factors: severe cold or loss of moisture from shoots and branches. Excessive loss of moisture, which is quite as frequently a cause of winter kill as is severe cold, is due largely to the effect of strong, drying winds during periods of brilliant winter sunshine. It is a well-known fact that the evaporation of moisture from the twigs, branches, canes, and in the case of evergreens, from the leaves continues at a slow rate throughout the winter, and that to supply this moisture, the roots of the plant must continue to absorb water. When the evaporation is unduly accelerated by prolonged periods of winter wind and sunshine, the roots are unable to supply moisture rapidly enough, especially if they lie entirely in the frost zone, and the branches and canes become dehydrated. If this condition, sometimes called winter burn, becomes sufficiently aggravated, it frequently results in the dying back of a large portion of the plant, or in its death.

Therefore, one of the most important preparations for winter in the case of woody plants, particularly such broad-leaf evergreens as holly (*Ilex* spp.) and rhododendron and evergreen azalea (*Rhododendron* spp.), is to be certain that the soil remains adequately supplied with moisture. If rainfall has been light during the autumn months, it will be necessary to soak the ground thoroughly before it freezes and to provide a thick blanket of mulch. Numerous trees and shrubs may be saved from winter injury if these precautions are taken. Shallow-rooted evergreens, especially the broad-leaf kinds such as holly and rhododendron, are sometimes sprayed in early winter with antidesiccants (for example, WiltPruf) to slow moisture loss, particularly in northern areas where deep frost penetration is usual. For many plants, winter protection against wind and sun is quite as important as protection against extreme cold. This may be effected by erecting a baffle or enclosure of burlap mounted on posts around and over vulnerable shrubs, especially during the first winter or two after planting.

The most reliable practices for providing winter protection for herbaceous perennials, rock plants, roses, trees, and shrubs are discussed in detail in the specific chapters.

FROST PROTECTION

When sudden cold spells occur, plants may be protected from frost in numerous ways. If only a small number of plants needs protection, cover them with pots, baskets, boxes, or lath frames over which burlap, muslin, or sheets of plastic have been spread.

One of the most effective ways of lessening frost damage is through the use of water. If plants can be subjected to a fine, gentle, continuous spray of water during a sudden drop in temperature, satisfactory protection can be obtained in many cases, even where the thermometer drops as low as 20°F. When the air temperature drops below freezing, the water sprayed onto the plants begin to form into ice. During the process of freezing the water gives off heat and enough of this heat is absorbed by the plants to prevent them from freezing, with its resultant breakdown of cell structure. As long as water is applied continuously, the plant will remain above the freezing point. The application of water should begin when the temperature at plant level drops to 34°F. It must be constant throughout the period when the air temperature is below freezing and should be continued until all the ice has melted off the plants.

This method is used by many commercial growers, particularly where sprinkler irrigation systems are available, and often means the saving of an entire crop. Much less water is required than the amount normally used for irrigation purposes, however, as only a fine, light spray is essential. In the home garden a stationary or rotary sprinkler on the end of a hose will give very good results, although it is possible to cover only a comparatively small area in this way unless a number of hoses and water connections are available. When a light frost (to about 32°F) is forecast, sufficient protection may often be obtained by watering the plants with a fine, mistlike spray several times during the evening and again early in the morning, keeping them wet until the temperature has risen above freezing. By using this method, it is possible to maintain at least parts of the garden well past the first few light frosts and, in the vegetatble garden, to extend the harvest period several weeks. In the spring, it is an especially valuable procedure for preserving transplants of tender young annuals that would otherwise succumb to a late frost and also to prevent frost damage to early-flowering fruit trees and bushes and certain ornamentals, such as star magnolia (*Magnolia stellata*).

Tall, slender plants, such as dahlias and gladiolus, are not as well adapted to this method of frost protection as are lower, more bushy types because the weight of the ice buildup on the plant may cause the stems to break. This does not usually happen, however, unless the temperature drops below 27°F.

If a sudden, light frost has caught you unawares and no precautions have been taken, plants can sometimes be salvaged by shielding them immediately from the morning sun, as with baskets or opaque cloth, so that they will thaw gradually. Potted plants can be moved to a completely shaded area for this purpose.

PREVENTING TRANSPLANTING LOSSES

When seedlings are transplanted from flats or the nursery bed, many small roots are cut or crushed, thus temporarily reducing the water-absorbing capacity of the root system relative to the transpiration requirements of the foliage. Unless leaf area is also appreciably reduced, or the transplants are shaded and shielded from wind to reduce transpiration, wilting usually occurs, because the plant is unable to maintain a balance between water intake and outgo. Some plants tend to wilt more rapidly and severely than others and are slower in making a recovery. In cases of very severe wilting there is a complete destruction of the cells and the plant dies.

The usual precaution taken by the gardener is to transplant on a cloudy, calm day, when there is an abundance of moisture in the air, but this is not always possible. Artificial shade may be provided temporarily for newly transplanted stock in the form of tents of newspaper or pruned leafy tree branches.

An alternative method, often used with trees and shrubs, is to spray the foliage with a transparent coating that reduces water loss before they are transplanted. To be effective, such a spray must have the ability to control the amount of water transpired by the leaves without stopping it completely, and it must not interfere with the proper gas exchange. A number of such antidesiccant sprays have been developed that meet these requirements, and these are sold under various trade names. Such sprays can be useful to the gardener, as they help reduce transplanting shock and keep losses to a minimum. Used according to the manufacturers' directions, and applied before transplanting, these sprays facilitate moving deciduous trees and shrubs that are in leaf, as well as evergreens that must be dug under less than optimum conditions.

Such measures may not seem essential with container-grown stock, but their roots are usually abnormally dense and restricted, and, if not loosened at the time of planting, may draw more soil moisture than can be readily replaced by normal rates of water percolation, leading to a dry root ball. Potted azaleas, when planted in the garden, are especially prone to this difficulty, one that can be prevented by loosening the root ball at the time of planting and by spraying the foliage with antidesiccants while root growth extends into adjacent soil.

CONTROLLING INSECT PESTS AND DISEASES

Although the maintenance of plant health is the best way to ward off enemies, constant vigilance on the part of the gardener is needed if diseases and insect pests are to be effectively controlled. It is necessary to recognize the first symptoms of disease or the first manifestation of the presence of injurious insects. The appropriateness and effectiveness of any treatment depend on the promptness, frequency, and thoroughness of the application, if indeed any is required.

The identification and full description of the more common insect pests and diseases as well as the most responsible measures of control and application are given in Chapter 34.

VI
The Indoor Garden

GARDENING INDOORS • GARDENING UNDER ARTIFICIAL LIGHT •

GREENHOUSE GARDENING

38

Gardening Indoors

ONTEMPORARY HOUSES PRESENT THE GARDENER WITH many stimulating new opportunities and challenges for the dramatic and aesthetic use of plants. Great expanses of glass reaching from ceiling to floor, intricate room dividers with specially designed built-in boxes for plants, and walls of brick or stone are all adaptable to the skillful, imaginative use of plants. Many houses have "sunken" floor wells into which large potted plants may be set, and overhead "bubble" skylights make it possible to grow large plants where least

Transitional in summer between the verdure outside and the living space within, house-plants in winter help keep the gardening spirits alive.

expected. When well used, plants add distinction and a very special vitality to indoor living spaces.

Houses built with less extravagant use of glass, and even the conventional apartment or suburban dwelling, can also accommodate a wide selection of plants. Almost every American home, whether large or small, understated or opulent, can provide adequate growing conditions for living plants. By carefully choosing plants and containers to suit particular circumstances and, perhaps, after some trial and error, even the least experienced gardener can usually achieve the effect desired.

Never before has such a wealth of plant material been available for these purposes. For example, since World War II plant explorers have discovered, growing in the dim light of tropical rain forests, many kinds of plants that are admirably adapted to the subdued light of interiors in the modern suburban home and city apartment. Some of these plants, with their huge, glossy, deeply lobed leaves, are exotic and exciting in appearance, while others are valued for their gentler qualities of delicate leaf pattern and iridescent hues on the undersurface of the foliage.

Recently, breeders have developed many new cultivars with interesting leaf forms, with variegated foliage, or with splashes of white and dustings of gold—a kaleidoscope of color and form bringing life and animation to any indoor planting composition. Especially suited to the more traditional type of home are the new cultivars of ivy, begonia, and African violet, all of which add color, warmth, and bloom to the window garden. Few foliage plants are more decorative than some of the new hybrid begonias, for example, and a pebble-filled tray containing pots of a number of kinds with contrasting leaf forms, varied textures, and subtle colorings offers great beauty and distinction—all variations on the begonia theme.

Although lifestyles vary, anyone with even only a latent green thumb can find some time in an actively scheduled life to grow superb houseplants. An important part of such success lies in the careful selection of plants, and another in analyzing the potential in the rooms of each home to support such plants. Then, by assiduously modifying the indoor environment to suit the final choices, the indoor gardener can easily accommodate many kinds of plants. Houseplants are very easily acquired, either from nurseries, florists, and garden centers, from supermarkets (of which two-thirds in the United States offer houseplants), by mail order, or from friends and neighbors. In any year, the best-selling houseplants have been poinsettias, chrysanthemums, azaleas, Easter lilies, and African violets, in that order. Incidentally, the principal producing areas are California, Texas (and adjacent Mexico), and Florida (and the nearby West Indies), as well as Michigan, Ohio, and Pennsylvania.

Another important aspect of gardening indoors is to learn the proper care and nurturing of the plants. For those willing to give plants what they need when they need it—before they begin to languish—the reward is the beauty of well-grown and thriving houseplants.

Although the exposed potted soil and the physiological food-making and respiration processes of houseplants may reduce indoor air pollutants in theory and perhaps to some degree in fact, the actual impact is likely negligible at best, simply because the pollution levels nearly always far exceed the capacity of the plants to make a significant difference. Houseplants should be grown primarily for aesthetic reasons, not for any air-purification effect.

INDOOR ENVIRONMENTS

Because houses and human lifestyles impact the plants we grow indoors, and in many respects are foreign to the evolutionary history of the species concerned, houseplants are often under discernable stress. Whether it be caused by such factors as low light, low humidity, cold or hot drafts, too much or too little water, or alien fumes, stress should be kept to a minimum (recognizing that it can never be entirely eliminated), for it is on such amelioration that success will rest. The most easily grown houseplants have broad ecological amplitude and adjust to a wide range of conditions.

Each room presents opportunities and limitations, and these will vary from season to season through the year. The scientific aspects of growing houseplants are strengthened if you have some knowledge of the field conditions under which each kind grows in its native provenance as well as of a basic understanding of the role of light, nutrients, and water in a plant's physiological economy. Widely distributed species that grow naturally in a diversity of habitats are generally more suited to houseplant culture than those restricted to narrowly defined niche environments. The art of growing houseplants involves placing and combining plants so that they will be decorative, harmonious enhancements to the indoor environment and thus heighten the quality of life of residents and visitors.

In any room, the intensity of the natural light entering windows with different exposures varies, hence different plants will thrive at or near different windows. Sometimes modifications can be made to adjust the environment, making it more suitable for certain plants. For instance, palms, begonias, and geraniums may grow well all winter in an east window with no protection from the sun's rays. However, from April to the end of September a sheer curtain may be required to soften the strong spring and summer sunlight, especially for the palms and begonias. Geraniums, however,

A multilevel bower of colorful houseplants offers a taste of summer verdure in a sunny window.

grow better in full summer sunlight and so should be moved to an uncurtained east window, where they will thrive with a group of succulents that also do best in sunlight with no special shading. Likewise, humidity can be increased somewhat if necessary, and supplemented either with shallow water in pebble trays beneath the pots or by means of electrical humidifiers.

Once you have learned something about the cultural requirements of the plants to be grown and have considered ways the indoor environment can be modified to suit the plants' needs without diminishing its importance as living space, it is possible to enjoy a wide variety of plants. Selections, of course, should be made with care, and the specific requirements of each plant must be met as completely as possible. In any case, it bears repeating that such considerations as light, temperature, ventilation, and humidity are carefully studied so that the most favorable environmental conditions are established for the plants one selects. Each of these factors may be modified, often with very simple procedures, to create an environment conducive to plant life. A good rule of thumb is that if a newly acquired plant lives without declining for three to six months, then it can probably thrive in that situation indefinitely. Of course, there are exceptions to

this general rule, as with Norfolk Island pine (*Araucaria excelsa*), cast-iron plant (*Aspidistra elatior*), snake plant (*Sansevieria fascinata*), and various palms, for example, which are able to survive months in low light but eventually will slowly decline because they lack proper growing conditions.

Light

Light is essential to the growth of all green plants. The leaves serve as manufacturing sites. Here plants use air, water, and nutrients in the presence of chlorophyll and light to make their own food (hence the fallacy in referring to the application of fertilizers as "feeding"). If leaves are deprived of light, they cannot manufacture food, their chlorophyll decomposes, and they die—as does the plant for lack of food.

Though light is a critically important growth requirement for healthy plants, many people often overlook this fact in their eagerness to enjoy plants in interior situations away from windows. Supplemental electric lighting can be very effective in keeping houseplants healthy (see Chapter 39). For example, a simple reading lamp with ordinary incandescent bulbs, set 3 feet or closer to a plant on an end table, may provode that extra bit of light a plant needs to maintain itself. However, it is essential that the homeowner consistently use the same light, perhaps by use of a timer, each evening for it to be effective. If this light becomes part of the usual evening illumination, then it will function both to light the room and to stimulate the nearby plant to manufacture a little extra food.

Fluorescent lights have long been used as supplemental or even primary light sources for plants in the home and, in the absence of greenhouse space, are vital for starting many kinds of garden plants in the North. Success with fluorescent illumination usually requires committing spaces for one or more shelves over which the lighting units are suspended in a manner that permits vertical adjustment of the distance between the light source and the plants. Such an installation can be made inexpensively by using standard shop-light units, or a manufactured stand with lights may be purchased (usually as a cart with casters). Ordinary cool-white fluorescent tubes with white reflectors are suitable for starting seedlings, but a combination of cool-white and wide-spectrum or full-spectrum "grow lights" is best for the long-term culture of houseplants. As sunlight is more intense than any electric

A diverse selection of plants arranged compactly on several levels beneath fluorescent lights.

light, a plant requires more hours of exposure to electric light than to sunlight. Most kinds respond well to about 14 hours of illumination daily. The light source, especially if incandescent bulbs or fluorescent tubes, needs to be relatively close to the plant. The distance must be adjustable, not only to accommodate plant growth or a change of plants but also to compensate for diminished illumination as the light source (especially if fluorescent) ages. A timer facilitates regularity in providing electric lighting and in the hours (the photoperiod) that it is provided each day.

Light for plants in dim interior spaces may also be provided by mercury-vapor or metal halide spotlights designed specifically to stimulate plant growth. These installations, though costly, have revolutionized the range of plants that may be grown and the scope of indoor gardening, especially in large commercial or public spaces. They provide light that is stronger over greater distances than that emitted by incandescent bulbs or fluorescent tubes, but they usually require professional installation. The spotlights will not function on a rheostat, however, so cannot be dimmed, and they are not recommended as reading lamps because of their intensity. Their development is, however, a great step forward in illuminating larger areas to satisfy the needs of plants.

Plants vary tremendously in the intensity of light required for their best development. Many ferns, which in their native habitats often grow in dense woodland shade, require comparatively dim light, though they do demand high humidity. Most foliage plants, particularly those that are native to the tropical rain forests, thrive best in diffused natural light. In the home, a north window will best meet the needs of such plants, and some may even be grown successfully in the interior of the room, away from a window. There are comparatively few foliage houseplants that can tolerate direct sunlight, particularly the afternoon summer sun. Plants with variegated foliage require more light, due to the fact that the cells in the white portion of the leaves contain little or no chlorophyll, and therefore, they are unable to carry on the manufacture of food.

Most flowering plants require full sunlight, or sun for at least the major portion of the day. Such plants thrive best in a window with a southern or southeastern exposure. A few flowering plants, such as achimenes (*Achimenes* cvs.), African violet (*Saintpaulia ionantha*), and Cape primrose (*Streptocarpus* × *hybridus*), do best with limited sun and should be grown in a window with an eastern exposure. Windows with tinted glass do not appreciably reduce the light wavelengths required for plant growth.

When houseplants are left in one position for any length of time, the leaves and stems will inevitably turn toward the light and the growth of the plant will become very unsymmetrical. To prevent such one-sided growth, the pots should be turned at frequent intervals so that all portions of the plant may receive an equal amount of light. The growth will then remain symmetrical and well balanced.

Temperature

Every kind of plant has an optimum temperature range that provides the most favorable conditions for maximum growth and flowering. Some plants suffer seriously when there are fluctuations of temperature much above or below this range, while others are able to withstand wide fluctuations without suffering serious damage. In spite of the best preparations you may make for your houseplants, the major changes sustained by them when brought indoors after a summer outside include not only suddenly lowered light levels and higher, more even temperatures, but also reduced ventilation and lowered humidity. To minimize the trauma, it is wise to make the transfer before night temperatures outdoors fall significantly lower than they will be indoors. Insofar as possible, the shift should be made in stages, as for example to an unheated porch or sun room before being brought into a heated living area.

The majority of houseplants thrive well in a moderate temperature, ranging between 62° and 70°F, with a somewhat cooler temperature at night. Some plants require a very warm temperature, between 75° and 80°, and will not make satisfactory growth unless this requirement is met. Still others will thrive only in a consistently cool temperature, 50° to 60° F; plants in this group are best suited to growing on a cool porch or in a closed-off room that is not occupied.

When plants are grown on window sills or ledges, especially if the window glass is single pane and the installation is double-hung without weather stripping or storm windows, it is a wise precaution to place a heavy layer of newspaper between the plants and the window on severely cold nights. This simple preventive measure will provide excellent insulation for the plant when it needs it most.

Ventilation

Although houseplants require air, they must be protected from strong drafts of cold or hot air. Ventilating should, therefore, be done in such a way that the plants are protected from sudden temperature change. In mild weather the doors or windows of the room may be opened; in severe weather it may be advisable to open the windows in an adjoining room, so that the plants are not subjected to direct drafts. In rooms lacking openable windows, the air should be mechanically circulated.

Ventilation has a direct influence in mitigating the effects of deleterious gas and fumes. Some plants, such as the Jerusalem cherry (*Solanum pseudocapsicum*), are extremely sensitive and even a minute quantity of cooking gas will have a most damaging effect, causing a blackening of the buds, discoloration of the leaves, and in the fruiting stage, premature fruit drop. Most plants, however, react by suspending growth and dropping their oldest leaves.

Gentle air movement and change of air are beneficial in deterring the onset of disease, powdery mildew in particular, as well as in slowing the buildup of light-filtering dust on leaf surfaces.

Humidity

Closely associated with the problems of ventilation and watering is that of humidity. A moist atmosphere is essential to the health and vigor of most leafy plants. Many of the plants we favor for indoor cultivation, especially those suited to relatively low light intensities, evolved as understory plants in tropical rain forests, where high relative humidity prevails throughout the year. Others, such as the dracaenas, are denizens of the dry tropical forest and so can survive protracted periods of the very low relative humidity (often 20 percent or less) that prevails indoors when it is severely cold outdoors. Rain forest plants react to low relative humidity by reducing their total leaf area, often by the yellowing and drying of the oldest leaves, which can lead to legginess, or by the browning of leaf tips and margins. Some heating systems are equipped with humidifying devices, and special water-holding compartments are attached to some types of radiators. If such devices are not already part of the heating system, water pans may be purchased and attached to the radiators. Another easy and effective method of increasing the humidity is to set the plants on metal or plastic trays that have been filled with pebbles and water. The bottom of the pots should rest on dry pebbles above the level of the water. This method may also be used with flowerpot saucers, again making sure that the water around the pebbles does not reach the bottom of the pot, since this would cause the soil to be constantly saturated.

Because of the wide interest in growing plants under fluorescent lights (see Chapter 39), many practical horticultural items are available in garden centers and specialty plant shops that cater to indoor plant growers. It is now easy to obtain rectangular plastic plant trays to hold the pebbles and water that will increase humidity. These trays usually measure 11 by 22 inches, and two of them fit perfectly under a standard 4-foot fluorescent fixture. Perlite, vermiculite, and long-fiber sphagnum moss are sometimes used in place of pebbles. And the molded plastic panels used to cover fluorescent ceiling fixtures, sometimes referred to as "egg crate," can be cut and used instead of pebbles or other material in humidity trays. Water is added almost to the top of the holes in the egg crate panels, and the pots will then remain high and dry. While the humidification effect is the same as if using pebbles, this system is easier to keep clean and is more lightweight than pebbles. The nonwoven capillary matting that is used to water plants automatically from below also functions as a good source of humidity, and increasingly this material is used in plant trays in place of either pebbles or egg crate panels. Any of these methods will increase the relative humidity immediately around houseplants.

Syringing houseplants daily or more often is still often suggested as an ideal method of increasing humidity and cleaning leaf surfaces, but this practice is obviously impracticable when no one is home for extended periods. Admittedly, syringing has an immediate effect on the local environment of plants but its long-range effect, in most homes or apartments, is negligible at best. Many indoor gardeners in recent years have purchased humidifiers for either individual rooms or even the entire house, to the total benefit of their plants and their own health as well.

Raising the humidity of indoor air significantly in cold weather can lead to difficulties, however, especially in houses lacking a vapor barrier in the insulation. If in doubt, it is best to have a professional engineer or knowledgeable builder advise you of the state of the insulation in your house and what precautions and limits to observe should you wish to raise humidity levels. Ideally, relative humidity should be about 50 percent at 70°F, with 30 percent a practical minimum for most houseplants. If you are unable to operate and maintain a humidifier, however, the alternative is simply to concentrate on plants that have proven their ability to survive low humidity (the individual plant listings that follow as well as the table on page 932).

An alternative under such restrictive conditions is to cultivate plants in one or more terrariums, where light, temperature, soil moisture, and humidity can be regulated to suit the plants chosen for culture. These can range from clear glass or plastic bottles to large cases, such as decommissioned aquariums.

Most houseplants benefit greatly from a summer spent outdoors in dappled shade, or with only morning sunlight, or other ideal situations. Although not everyone can move houseplants out for the summer, those who can usually do so willingly because of the wonderful growth a plant accomplishes in several months of favorable conditions. Often the plants that are summered outdoors live easily in houses during the moderate spring and fall months when the harsh, dry air of the heated house or apartment is needed intermittently. The growth achieved in the summer outdoors on either a modest apartment terrace or at ground level may be sufficient to carry a plant through the harder winter months when it is standing in front of a coolish window.

CULTURAL PRACTICES

Most indoor plants are grown in pots or tubs of soil, and many of these containers serve their purposes well, provided they have drainage holes in the bottom. These holes should be covered with a layer of pebbles or pieces of broken clay pots (crock) to keep the soil inside, and yet allow excess water to drain away. It is extremely difficult to use an undrained container for an extended period without harming the plant. For most gardeners, success is easily achieved by using containers with adequate drainage holes. The container in which the plant is growing can be hidden inside a decorative pot or a second container that is undrained. In effect, this is the same as placing the potted plant in a saucer. In both instances, the excess water that drains out of the soil must be emptied so that the plant will not constantly be standing in water; otherwise its roots will die from lack of oxygen in the soil saturated by stagnant water.

From a decorative point of view, many people like to standardize the color and material of the flowerpots they use. A collection of plants all in pots of one color has a pleasing unity even though the plants themselves have varying cultural demands.

Soil Mixtures

Different plants demand different types of soil; deciding what mix to use comes with experience and horticultural common sense. An excellent general-purpose potting mixture consists of one part sand, two parts fibrous loam, and one part organic matter—half of which should be compost, leaf mold, or peat; the other half well-rotted manure (preferably cow manure). This mixture should be combined with a 5-inch potful of ground limestone or bonemeal and thoroughly stirred into each bushel of the mix. The mix should then be screened before using. However, since many gardeners will lack ready access to the components called for in this mix, the following recipe is an alternative:

> 1 quart soil from a well-maintained garden (no clay)
> 1 quart builder's sharp sand (not beach sand) or perlite
> or vermiculite
> 2 quarts peat moss (either sphagnum or Canadian peat)
> 1 tablespoon dolomitic limestone

Commercially prepared potting soil with components approximately in these proportions is also an acceptable substitute.

Soil

Although garden soils vary, all provide substance or weight to the soil mix as well as nutrient salts that help obviate complete reliance on a prepared fertilizer. Moreover, garden soil is a source for the trace minerals necessary for plant growth. Soil body, combined with the sharp sand used for drainage, is important when potting large plants that need soil heaviness for stability. When we mix soil for pot culture, anchoring the plant is important, but aeration and drainage are equally important.

Sand

Sand, which is readily obtained from a builder's supply house, should be as coarse and sharp as possible. In fact, aquarium gravel could even be substituted; it is almost impossible to find sand that is too coarse. Avoid very fine beach sand, or the sand that is used for children's sandboxes, as such fine sand will pack together with other components in the soil mix and will not provide the necessary drainage and aeration. For cacti and succulents, increase the sand to one-half the total mix, then combine it with small pebbles and finely broken brick or flowerpot shards.

Peat Moss

Derived from sphagnum moss and sometimes called "Canadian peat" or "tourbe," peat moss is usually dark brown to reddish in color, depending on the source and moisture content. This material is often acidic (as low as pH 4.5); for most plants, limestone is necessary to bring the pH up to about 6. It may be necessary to add more or less dolomitic limestone, depending on the pH of your water supply. In the northwest and northeast parts of the country, the water is generally acidic, so more limestone will not be detrimental. In Florida, southern California, and much of the Midwest, the water is alkaline and, therefore, requires little or no limestone.

Peat moss that has been derived from sedges and reeds is black. It is usually sold in plastic bags in a slightly moist condition and is sometimes called humus or Michigan peat. It is generally more finely divided than the sphagnum (Canadian) peat. This type of peat moss is very useful in mixes for ferns, begonias, African violets, and other plants that have delicate fibrous roots. Use it to replace half of the Canadian peat.

Lime

Lime is granular or ground, or prepared from dolomite (a combination of calcium carbonate and magnesium carbonate), and is used to bring the pH level of the soil mix nearer to neutral. A tablespoon of agricultural ground limestone per quart of peat moss is usually sufficient.

Perlite

A white volcanic rock that is light in weight, porous, and sterile, perlite may be used as a replacement for sand, and actually aerates soil better than sand. Perlite does not deteriorate, nor does it contain nutrients.

Vermiculite

Made by heating mica until it expands, vermiculite is sold in both a horticultural grade (small particles) and an insulating grade (larger particles). Both types are useful as soil conditioners to aerate soil and to take the place of sand. The horticultural grade is most frequently used and is especially practical for smaller flower pots. Nutrients and water are held in the platelike structure, which contains small amounts of potassium, calcium, and magnesium useful to plant growth. It is sterile when new, but after several years the particles in vermiculite break down and collapse so that it loses its aerating ability.

Mixes Made without Soil

Various mixes are available that contain no soil. These are especially useful to apartment dwellers who may find ordinary garden soil difficult to obtain and inconvenient to handle and store. Soilless preparations are used extensively in gardens under artificial lights.

SOILLESS MIX 1

1 quart sphagnum peat moss
1 quart horticultural vermiculite
1 quart perlite (coarse or medium preferred)
1 tablespoon dolomitic limestone

Soilless mix 1 is ideal for tropical plants that require good drainage and aeration and that have the ability to withstand drying out between watering. For example, it is excellent for bromeliads, wax plants (*Hoya carnosa*), peperomias, philodendrons, dracaenas, snake plants (*Sansevieria trifasciata*), ornamental figs (*Ficus* spp.), rhizomatous begonias, and geraniums (*Pelargonium* spp.).

SOILLESS MIX 2A

2 quarts sphagnum peat
1 quart vermiculite
1 quart perlite
2 tablespoons limestone

SOILLESS MIX 2B

3 quarts sphagnum peat
2 quarts perlite
1 quart vermiculite
3 tablespoons limestone

Soilless mixes 2A and 2B are heavier than mix 1, and mix 2B, which drains especially well, is intended for those indoor gardeners who have had difficulties resulting from overwatering. This mix should be used with plants that have fine root systems, including ferns, begonias, caladiums, coleus, prayer plant (*Maranta leuconeura*), and most gesneriads.

SOILLESS MIX 3

1 quart sphagnum peat
2 quarts perlite
2 quarts vermiculite
1 tablespoon limestone

Soilless mix 3 is especially suited for cacti, succulents, and some dry-land bromeliads (such as *Dyckia brevifolia*).

Since none of the soilless mixes described here contains nutrients, it is necessary to add soluble fertilizer in various dilutions. Some gardeners apply the fertilizer at ½ strength (as directed by the manufacturer) every other watering. Other growers fertilize with ⅛ or ¹⁄₁₀ strength fertilizer at every watering. Both types of applications should be omitted every fifth watering, to allow some of the extra fertilizer to leach out of the soil.

Potting

Houseplants should be repotted only when they will derive very definite benefit, and it has been found that plants vary greatly in their needs for frequent potting. Most flowering plants will, like the geraniums, give better bloom if they are allowed to become somewhat pot-bound. Such plants as amaryllis, the various palms, podocarpus, and schefflera will also thrive well in very small pots, and these seem to suffer no ill effects from becoming extremely pot-bound. Many houseplants may be grown in comparatively small pots if sufficient nutrients are provided in the form of the occasional applications of a complete fertilizer (see "Fertilizing" on page 911).

However, young plants, grown either from seed or from cuttings, must be put into larger pots at frequent intervals to accommodate their more rapid growth. The general practice is to repot such plants as soon as the pots they occupy become well filled with roots. Unless this is done, the plants may become stunted, and will be unable to make normal and vigorous growth and may fail to bloom. A pot ½ to 1 inch larger in size is usually sufficient for the next stage of growth.

When plants are grown in pots, it is essential that ample drainage be provided. In small pots a piece of broken pot (crock) placed over the hole in the bottom of the pot will usually be sufficient. When large pots are used, and particularly if the plant is to remain in the pot for some time, it is wise to place a layer of crock across the entire bottom. This layer should be ¾ inch deep in pots, tubs, or urns that are 18 to 24 inches in diameter.

In potting seedlings or rooted cuttings, the pot may be partially filled with soil. The plant should be held in place, with the roots spread out in a natural position. The remaining soil should then be added and pressed firmly into place with your fingers. In small pots, a space of approximately ½ inch should be left between the surface of the soil and the rim of the pot. In potting rooted cuttings, a soil mixture consisting of two parts sharp sand, one part loam, and one part leaf mold or peat is recommended. For young seedlings in the early transplanting stages a mixture of one part sand, one part loam, and one part leaf mold or peat moss will give excellent results. The pots should be watered thoroughly and shaded from direct sunlight for several days, so that the plants may have an opportunity to become reestablished.

In repotting an established plant, the plant may easily be removed by inverting the pot and, with one hand supporting the soil surface, gently tapping the rim on the edge of a firm surface, such as the edge of a potting bench or a work table. The soil in the pot should be fairly moist so that it does not crumble. A small quantity of soil should be placed over the drainage material and the plant then placed in the center of the new pot. If the pot is only slightly larger than the one in which the plant had previously grown, it will be necessary to remove some soil from the bottom and sides of the ball of earth surrounding the roots. This should be done with care so that the root system is kept as nearly intact as possible. The space between the old ball of earth and the side of the new pot should then be filled with the new potting soil, which should be worked down and firmed into place with your fingers or a small potting stick.

Watering

The watering of houseplants is a task that requires good judgment and common sense. It is quite as serious an error to overwater as it is to fail to provide adequate water. Not only do different species of plants vary tremendously in their moisture requirements, but individual plants vary considerably according to the stage of growth. When plants are making active growth, forming new shoots and flower buds, they obviously require much more water than they do when in the resting, nonflowering stage. Although daily watering is not necessary for all houseplants, it is wise to make a frequent survey to ascertain their needs. When the surface of the soil in the pot is dry to the point of being crumbly to the touch, or if a (clay) pot gives a hollow, ringing sound when it is tapped lightly with the knuckle, the plant needs water. If water is applied to the surface of the soil by means of a watering can, the surplus water will drain out through the opening in the bottom of the pot. If watering is done by placing the pot in a pan of water, it should be allowed to remain in the receptacle until the surface of the soil becomes moist. The pot should then be removed and the surplus water allowed to drain away. This latter method is excellent for those plants that have dense, fuzzy, disease-prone leaves, such as African violet (*Saintpaulia ionantha*) and gloxinia (*Sinningia speciosa*). In any case, pots should never be allowed to stand in saucers that are filled with water, as the soil in the bottom will soon become water-logged and acidic, and the growth and vigor of the plant will be seriously affected. Note that although many plants seem unaffected by cold tapwater, it is best to allow water to stand several hours before use, both to warm and to clear itself of any chlorine.

If houseplants must be left unattended for extended periods (say two or three weeks), the simplest way to prevent soil desiccation is to place each pot in a plastic bag and to tie the neck of the bag around the trunk or stem just above the soil, so that the pot and soil surface are in the bag and the plant's leafy top remains out. Before bagging, the pot should be thoroughly watered and allowed to drain. Placed out of direct sunlight, a potted plant so treated will lose moisture only through the leaves and not from the soil surface or, in the case of clay pots, through the pot wall. The entire plant may be placed in the plastic bag, but condensation of transpired or evaporated water can provide a medium conducive for the proliferation of fungus diseases.

Another method is to spread commercially prepared capillary matting under potted plants and to immerse part of the matting in a reservoir of water. The water absorbed from the reservoir is drawn by capillary action so that the entire mat becomes wet. The soil in pots set on the mat (and the entire pot, if made of clay) slowly absorbs the moisture, which is replenished from the reservoir. The process works best with clay pots, or with plastic pots in which the soil extends all the way down to the drain holes (that is, without crock).

Still another procedure is to tap the rootball of the plant out of the pot, insert one or two wicking cords through the drainage hole(s) at the base and halfway up the inside wall, replant the rootball, thoroughly water the soil and wet the wick(s), and then suspend the the potted plant over a glass or bottle so that the wick is immersed in the reservoir and will slowly conduct water upward into the pot. This procedure is particularly effective with small potted plants.

Before depending on any method during an absence, it is best to test its efficacy beforehand and to monitor results on a day-to-day basis.

Fertilizing

One phase of houseplant culture that requires some understanding is the use of fertilizers. Because the roots of potted houseplants are restricted to a small fraction of the volume of soil they would normally occupy in open ground, that soil can easily become depleted of its nutrient content. Fertilizers are not food, vitamins, or pep pills, but varied formulations of soluble nutrients that are absorbed with water

by the roots and make it possible for a green plant to make its own food, which it then uses to grow and reproduce. Those fertilizers with a 20-20-20 ratio of nitrate, phosphate, and potash best meet the major nutrient requirements of most houseplants and also supply some necessary micronutrients, or trace elements. In general, it is best to use very weak dilutions of fertilizers on houseplants, especially as their diffusion in the soil is limited by the pot. Excessive concentrations of fertilizers can actually dehydrate roots and cause root burn, usually with fatal results.

Applications of fertilizer should be made only when the plants are making active, vigorous growth, such as during the spring and summer or after the flower buds have formed but before the flowers have begun to show color. At this period of growth, a light application of fertilizer may be made at two-week intervals. No application should be made when the plants are in a resting stage during the fall and winter.

There are many excellent, rapidly soluble fertilizers on the market today that are suitable for houseplants, some formulated for particular plant groups. Many gardeners prefer to alternate or rotate applications of different soluble fertilizers.

Fertilizers for houseplants are available in several different forms—liquids, powders, granules, spikes, and tablets—ranging from highly soluble, fast-release preparations to less soluble, slow-release types. It is best to apply any fertilizer concentrate, liquid or dry, either diluted in irrigation water or, in the case of spikes or tablets, by burying them at the edge of the pot. Because of its hygroscopic (drying) nature, dry fertilizer should not be left on the soil surface or on leaves or stems.

Pruning

Beside the usual cosmetic shaping and the removal of dead leaves or branches that most houseplants receive, some may be pruned purposefully to assume geometric shapes, rather like topiary, or to become standards or tree forms. Such training may require some months or years before the desired results are fully achieved, but can lead to a very handsome effect. A standard, for example, can be developed with such familiar houseplants as geranium (*Pelargonium* spp.), azalea (*Rhododendron simsii*), camellia (*Camellia japonica*), fuchsia (*Fuchsia hybrida*), myrtle (*Myrtus communis*), rosemary (*Rosmarinus officinalis*), and sweet bay (*Laurus nobilis*). The process generally works best with small-leaf plants, but good results, especially if a large standard is sought, may be had with flowering maples (*Abutilon* spp.), common geranium (*Pelargonium* × *hortorum*), and princess flower or glory bush (*Tibouchina urvilleana*), among others.

To make a standard, choose a plant with a strong main, vertical stem. Prune away all lower branches, leaving only a few near the top, or, in the case of a large-leaf subject, no branches at all, just the leader. Provide a stake for support. When the main stem reaches the desired height, clip its apex and also those of any surrounding branches to induce the multiple branching that will result in a dense, rounded head. Pruning is repeated whenever shoots grow beyond the head limits. It is important to rotate standards so that they remain symmetrical and balanced. With patience and careful pruning and support, as well as attention to light, water, supplemental nutrients, and summering (outdoors, if possible), a long-lived standard will become a cherished component of the indoor garden.

Other forms may be considered, such as training philodendrons, ivies, or other climbers into window garlands, wreaths, or into miniature ground cover beds beneath larger plants. Some smaller kinds may be used to create miniature scenes including colored pebbles and stones and bits of driftwood.

Selected woody plants, and not necessarily those brought indoors, may be grown as bonsai, the ancient oriental art of container cultivation, inspired by the picturesque dwarfness of trees growing naturally in soil-filled pockets in mountain outcrops. In bonsai, the focus is on reproducing in miniature the natural form of the tree or shrub chosen for treatment. Small-needled or scale-leaf evergreens (especially junipers) are particularly favored because of the diminutive dimensions of their foliar parts. A gnarled habit is induced by restricting root growth and by selective top pruning. Many bonsai styles are recognized and many idiosyncratic cultural procedures are used to keep the plants small and healthy. For more detailed information, see such specialized guides as the following Brooklyn Botanic Garden handbooks: *Dwarfed Potted Trees: The Bonsai of Japan; Bonsai: Special Techniques;* and *Indoor Bonsai.*

Houseplant Hydroponics

A variation of conventional hydroponics, houseplant hydroponics is a culture method in which plants are rooted among porous clay pebbles in a closed pot above a reservoir of water in which nutrients are dissolved. Because the water with nutrients is out of sight, it is necessary to have a float gauge (usually a Styrofoam dowel floating in a short length of PVC pipe) inserted through the pebbles into the water below. The pebbles successively absorb the water and nutrients by capillary action so that all roots are moist but not growing in the reservoir itself. While the uppermost pebbles are nearly dry, those in and just above the reservoir are saturated, and those in between are variously moist. From time to time, it is necessary to transfer the plants to buckets of water and rinse the pots and pebbles of accumulated debris and sediment. Not all houseplants are adaptable to this

medium, but African violet (*Saintpaulia ionantha*) and begonias (*Begonias* spp.) do well, as do ferns, palms, and most other foliage plants. Perlite or vermiculite may be substituted for porous clay. Charcoal helps slow water turbidity.

More elaborate commercially prepared systems are available, including some with electrically circulating aerated water and nutrients. These are sometimes used on a large scale for growing vegetables hydroponically.

GENERAL CARE OF HOUSEPLANTS
Keeping Foliage in Good Condition

Plants transpire through their leaves. When the foliage becomes coated with a film of fine dust particles, or with grease droplets from the kitchen, this natural process may be impeded and the plants suffer as a consequence. To keep houseplants glossy-leaved clean and fully functional, the foliage should be be syringed or rinsed at periodic intervals, preferably once a month. Plants with thick, hairy leaves, however, such as African violets and gloxinias, may be syringed occasionally with tepid water, but in the normal course of growth, older, less efficient leaves are replaced. Water droplets left on their leaf surfaces can cause unattractive spotting.

If only a few plants require attention and they are not too large, they may be placed in the kitchen sink, laundry tub, bathtub, or shower, and syringed with a fine but fairly strong spray of lukewarm water from the faucet. Both the upper and undersurfaces of the leaves should be treated this way. The foliage is best allowed to dry before the plants are placed again in sunlight.

In the case of large plants that cannot be moved easily, the leaves may be wiped with a damp cloth or sponge.

Dividing Houseplants

Many foliage plants benefit greatly from occasional division and replanting. Not all plants can be handled in this way, however, because of their habit of growth. In general, plants that grow in clumps, with several stems rising from below the soil, each with a separate root system, may be divided successfully. Such popular houseplants as fibrous-rooted or wax begonias, Christmas kalanchoe, peace lily (*Spathiphyllum*), and the peperomias are examples.

The procedure is simple. The plant should be removed from the pot. The soil should then be shaken or washed away from the roots, and the sections should be gently pulled apart. It is important that each section have good roots. In some cases it may be necessary to cut the sections off the main stock plant with a sharp knife.

Long, straggly roots should be cut back, and in some cases it may be advisable to remove one or two of the old leaves in compensation, retaining the younger, more vigorous growth only.

Each section should be planted in a pot of sufficient size, using a well-prepared potting mixture. The soil should be worked well about the roots, firmed to fill any air pockets, and watered thoroughly, after which it should be kept in subdued light for several days.

Pest and Disease Control

Because they are kept in relatively still air, unwashed by rain, and inaccessible to insect-eating wildlife, houseplants are subject to attack by various pests. Many pests are acquired with the plants themselves, often as concealed eggs, despite the best sanitation measures by the commercial growers who raise them. Also, plants that are summered outdoors may harbor new pests when brought indoors in the fall. All should be checked carefully before being admitted as indoor subjects.

Some kinds of houseplants are rarely infested and require no special treatment. Others, however, are so susceptible to one or more pests that regular treatment may be required to keep them reasonably pest free.

Though syringing with a fine stream of water every few weeks will help considerably in reducing certain insect populations, this practice alone seldom provides sure control, particularly on the plants that are most often infested with insects and mites.

Houseplants that climb—such as ivy (*Hedera helix*), kangaroo vine or grape ivy (*Cissus rhombifolia*), small-leaf philodendrons, and wandering Jew (*Tradescantia zebrina*)—and those with leaves close to the soil—such as African violet (*Saintpaulia ionantha*)—are difficult to spray thoroughly. Some gardeners find it more convenient to dip such plants into an insecticidal solution. A 1- or 2-gallon container is filled with the diluted insecticide, the flowerpot is inverted, and the leaves and stems dipped into the solution. To prevent the soil from dropping into the insecticide, cover the soil surface with aluminum foil, plastic sheeting, newspaper, or cardboard.

Large plants that cannot be handled this way must be sprayed with the proper insecticide in situ, or moved to the bathroom or outdoors on a mild day and sprayed, whichever is more convenient. The very lightweight and inexpensive disposable plastic 1-mil dropcloths sold in hardware stores are useful for protecting rugs and walls if a plant must be sprayed in place.

Ready-to-use insecticides in spray cans are available in hardware, department, and garden supply stores. These usually contain rotenone, pyrethrum, malathion, and other active ingredients. When using insecticides in spray cans, be sure to hold the nozzle at least 18 inches from the leaves and give them just a light, quick misting, not a drenching. Prolonged wetting may cause injury to the leaves or even death of the plant. When using any biocide indoors, make the application in a well-ventilated place or, in the case of large specimens, open one or more nearby windows. For more detailed information on pests and diseases of houseplants, see page 847.

Troubleshooting Houseplant Problems

As long as houseplants—most of them, at least—hold their own and make a positive contribution to the home environment, an indoor gardener may consider the endeavor a success. But when plants begin to fail, it is well to appreciate, preferably beforehand, the most common causes of trouble, how they may be rectified, and how future disappointment may be avoided. The following are the chief causes of failure of houseplants.

1. Too Little or Too Much Water

Most houseplants (cacti and succulents excepted) will not survive dry soil for long. Wilting of young leaves and bud drop are the first symptoms, followed by the progressive loss of leaves, and finally the shriveling of stems and death. In clay pots, soil desiccation can occur quickly, since evaporation occurs through the pot wall as well as from the soil surface; hence the preference for plastic pots indoors. A rapidly growing houseplant, especially in the spring, may wilt even if the soil moisture is ideal, simply because water uptake through the roots is not equal to the water lost by transpiration through the leaves. Such a plant should not be watered; rather, it should be moved to a less intensely sunny position.

In the main, however, the problem that most houseplants have with water is that it is added too often, resulting in saturated, water-logged soil, with little or no air penetration, which progressively acidifies as roots die. Ironically, the top of a chronically overwatered plant receives insufficient water and can display the same symptoms as one that is inadequately watered. More houseplants die from overwatering than any other single cause. Watering should take place only when the soil surface is dry, not ritually, and then the watering should be thorough, until the excess drains through the bottom holes, and not just a token light sprinkling.

2. Insufficient Air Reaching Roots

It surprises many to learn that roots not only require oxygen but that they absorb it directly from the soil. Fine clay soils compact easily, not admitting enough air to support root growth. In such a soil, excess water can almost completely block air penetration. Soilless mixes based on peat can also become water-logged and cause root death. A light, sandy soil with some organic matter is best for most houseplants, but no one formulation will suit all; cacti and succulents are at the dry extreme, aquatics at the wet extreme, and most other houseplants somewhere in between. The leaves of overwatered, root-dying houseplants characteristically turn yellow and drop or brown; by this time, so much root damage may have occurred that affected plants are beyond redemption. If you grow houseplants in pots of impermeable plastic, metal, or glazed ceramic, especially in large sizes, you may benefit by using water meters with soil probes to determine accurately when water is required.

3. Excess Fertilizer

Most houseplants have low nutrient requirements, especially during winter dormancy when little or no growth occurs. Excess fertilizer can alkalize soil, adversely affecting water uptake, often resulting in leaf scorch or tip burn. Because newly purchased plants are often already overfertilized, it is well to flood the soil ball to flush out the excess fertilizer salts. Discard the drain water. It should be borne in mind that not more than 2 percent of a plant's tissues are composed of nutrients taken up from the soil by the roots. The rest comes from air (mainly carbon dioxide) absorbed by leaves and water as well as by the roots. Nutrients are required in small amounts during periods of growth, but adding fertilizer to perk up dormant houseplants nearly always hastens their demise.

4. Unsuitable Pot

When a houseplant's root system occupies the same pot for years, it gradually fills the space, compressing the soil, and making air and water penetration increasingly difficult, ultimately leading to the death of roots and failure of the entire plant. This is usually preceded by months (or even years) of little or no growth (which may seem desirable) and symptoms of nutrient starvation and/or improper watering. While such pot-bound conditions stimulate flowering in many houseplants (such as *Clivia miniata*), it must eventually be alleviated by shifting the plant to a larger pot and the careful addition of new soil to fill the additional space. This transfer is best done at the close of the dormant period. Repotting should not be undertaken ritually, but only when inspection of the root ball, when tapped out of the pot, shows that it needs more room.

5. Excessively Low Temperatures

By placing a number of inexpensive thermometers on windowsills or in other indoor areas where houseplants are grown, you can easily determine the range of temperature variation. On cold, windy winter nights, the range can be substantial. It is not uncommon for a room heated to 65°F to show readings below 50°F next to windows in the winter, even with storm windows in place. Many houseplants, especially if dormant, are not adversely affected, but some, such as African violets (*Saintpaulia ionantha*) and prayer plant (*Maranta leuconeura*), show sudden, irreversible wilting and browning, leading ultimately to death. You can protect houseplants from windowsill chill by closing the drapes between the plants and the window or by placing plastic sheeting or several layers of newspaper over the window.

6. Pests and Diseases

A careful weekly inspection, perhaps while checking soil moisture and preferably with a magnifying glass at hand, is the best way to detect pests at an early stage. The range of common pests is small and the principal fungus disease is powdery mildew (see Chapter 34). Treatment in most cases is not complicated. Most difficulties can be prevented by good cultural practices, because as for garden plants in any environment, those whose requirements are met will be less stressed and thus less likely to be ravaged by parasites. Special attention should be given to newly acquired plants, as these may harbor pests or diseases that can contaminate the indoor garden. The same attention is due houseplants summered outdoors before transferring them indoors for the winter.

7. Poor Potting Soil

Whether a commercially prepared mix or one formulated at home, potting soil for houseplants should include sharp sand or perlite, about one-quarter by volume, to ensure ready penetration of water and air. If a commercial preparation lacks either, it should be added. The mix should also contain organic matter, mainly to slow the rapid drying out that occurs indoors in the winter (especially in porous clay pots). Color is a poor guide to soil quality; a porous, readily draining medium that stays moist for days or even weeks is the goal. Symptoms of poor potting soil include weak growth, undersize leaves, and little or no flowering.

Summer Care of Houseplants

Most houseplants benefit by being placed outdoors for the summer months, providing certain precautions are taken. By their very nature, plants must grow, and for most kinds, spring and summer are when growth is most active, new leaves replacing the older, less efficient ones. Most foliage houseplants should be summered in the shade when placed outdoors, even if they have spent their indoor period on a sunny windowsill. Solar intensity is much greater outdoors, and leaves suddenly exposed to full sun often scorch yellow or brown and prematurely die. To minimize the shock of relocation to an outdoor position, it is best to wait until night temperatures on clear, still nights fall no lower than about 55°F, or not significantly lower than indoors. Similarly, in late summer or early fall, gradually lowering night temperatures should be the gauge for returning houseplants indoors. Cool-loving plants should go out first and come in last, while tropicals are limited to a briefer outdoor period.

Large-leaf plants and those of slender habit should be placed where they will be protected from strong wind, which can quickly shred leaf blades and bend or break stalks. Some protection is afforded, and maintenance eased, by grouping the plants together, rather than scattering them. Where space allows, a lath house is ideal as a protected environment for summering houseplants.

Watering should be monitored even more carefully outdoors, especially if plants are placed in some remote corner where they can easily be overlooked or forgotten. High temperatures (even in shade) accelerate water loss through leaves as well as from soil in containers. At the same time, the hazards of overwatering houseplants outdoors are just as great as inside. In general, water management and pot stability are eased if pots are sunk to their rims in the garden. Placement of gravel or crock in the bottom of the hole will discourage the growth of roots out through the drain holes. If large plants are to be returned to the same garden sites each summer, empty pots of the same size may be left in the holes over the winter, obviating the need to dig anew each spring. For those houseplants that have clearly outgrown their pots, the shift to the next larger pot size is most easily done when they are taken outside for the summer. It is also a good time to apply supplemental fertilizer, as well as to prune, groom, and guide their growth.

Before taking the plants back indoors, they should be carefully checked for pests. Root balls should be tapped out of their pots and any earthworms removed; the agitation of the root ball will bring them to the surface. The pots themselves may be scrubbed at this point, before the root balls are reset. If a plant summered in the shade is to go to a sunny position indoors, make the transition gradually, from a shaded sill to a brighter one in stages.

Some houseplants seem not to suffer if kept indoors year round, among them most ferns, angel-wing begonias, and such large-leaf aroids as flamingo flower or tailflower (*Anthurium* spp.), dumb cane (*Dieffenbachia* spp.), Swiss cheese plant (*Monstera deliciosa*), and the large, self-heading, nonclimbing species of *Philodendron*. African violet (*Saintpaulia ionantha*) Cape primrose (*Streptocarpus* × *hybridus*), and gloxinia (*Sinningia speciosa*), if placed outside at all, are best set in protected places on a roofed-over porch, away from rain, sun, and wind. Fuchsias, orchids, and bromeliads are especially effective in hanging baskets.

COMMONLY GROWN HOUSEPLANTS

Houseplants are an endless source of pleasure. Their variation is tremendous, ranging all the way from hanging baskets of donkey tail (*Sedum morganianum*) and wandering Jew (*Tradescantia zebrina*), to graceful accent plants like palms, to miniatures like the diminutive peperomias. Some houseplants, such as the fancy-leaf geraniums, also produce the extra bonus of flowers, but most do not overpower us with bloom. While large, old specimens may be exceptionally beautiful in form and foliage, they can eventually outlive their usefulness and welcome by becoming too large. Before this happens, it is well to propagate the plant and have a new one ready and established as a replacement. Still, venerable old houseplants, such as 20-year-old jade plants (*Crassula argentea*) and Christmas cacti (*Schlumbergera* × *buckleyi*), have a special charm not found in young specimens.

About 1,000 species of plants are commercially available for use as houseplants. The list of species that follows includes those that are relatively easy to maintain; attention is called to any special attributes or cultural requirements in each case. If no special needs are indicated, you should provide the basic soil mix, water only when the soil surface has dried, and fertilize as noted earlier in this chapter. Because of the confusing plethora of common names (many of them contrived by vendors), the plants are discussed in alphabetical order by their scientific names.

Cultural Notes for Special Plant Groups
Bromeliads

Many species in the large, diverse family of bromeliads are available commercially, ranging from tiny tufted epiphytes and the filamentous Spanish moss (*Tillandsia usneoides*) to large rosetted plants resembling the commercial pineapple (itself a bromeliad). Bromeliad houseplants require light shade or, in winter, partial shade (i.e., early- or late-day exposure to direct sun). They also need a very porous, organic potting mix of wood chips or osmunda fiber, rather like that for epiphytic orchids. For plants with rosetted leaves, the cup or tank formed by their tightly fitting leaf bases should be kept filled with water, since much moisture absorption occurs through the leaf bases. Flowers normally appear once a year.

Cacti

The cacti make up another large family, most of whose members are native to the Southwest and adjacent Mexico and specialized for warm desert conditions. Many make excellent houseplants. In general, cacti thrive in full sun and sandy, gritty, quickly draining soil. The normal range of indoor temperatures and low-winter humidity suit the great majority. Indeed, in periods of dormancy they need only an occasional watering. Flowering and growth normally occur in the spring and summer.

The principal exceptions to these cactus rules are the Christmas cactus and its relatives (*Schlumbergera* spp., *Hatiora gaertneri*) and the orchid cactus (*Epiphyllum* hybrids), which are derived from rain forest epiphytes and do best in damp organically rich soil mix with limited exposure to the sun.

Gesneriads

Gesneriad is the common name for the plant family Gesneriaceae, which includes some of our most popular houseplants, among them African violet (*Saintpaulia ionantha*), gloxinia (*Sinningia speciosa*), and Cape primrose (*Streptocarpus* spp.). They are popular for both their flowers and foliage. In general, humidity of at least 40 percent, a temperature range of 65° to 75°F, and light shade, (i.e., bright filtered light with only early- or late-day exposure to sun in winter) is the formula for success with the gesneriads.

Orchids

Most cultivated orchids are tropical epiphytes that require warm, humid conditions best met in greenhouses. However, several are adaptable to windowsill conditions and respond well if their sometimes idiosyncratic requirements are met. Best known for success as houseplants are venus's-slippers (*Paphiopedilum* spp.), moth orchid (*Phalaenopsis* spp.), and the smaller members of the genus *Cymbidium*.

Palms

Old favorites for pot and tub culture, palms need light shade on the bright side to thrive, and north of a line extending from Washington, D.C., to Sacramento, California, they benefit from exposure to winter sun. By keeping a palm in the same pot for years, but topdressing the soil to meet nutrient needs, growth will be very slow. Although most palms are natives of the wet tropics, many adapt very well to our usually dry indoor conditions in winter, but do best if summered outdoors.

Succulents

The succulents make up a diverse assemblage of species from several plant families that are native to seasonally dry tropical regions. All are specialized to store water in modified leaves and/or stems, and so are able to withstand (if not actually require) dry soil, especially during dormancy, but do need more or less normal amounts of water when growing and blooming. Beyond the familiar aloe (*Aloe barbadensis*), jade plant (*Crassula argentea*), Christmas kalanchoe (*Kalanchoe blossfeldiana*), and donkey tail (*Sedum morganianum*) are scores of others. Although most cacti are succulents par excellence, they are customarily treated separately.

HOUSEPLANT SPECIES OF MERIT

ABUTILON × HYBRIDUM
(Flowering maple)

A shrubby plant that tends to single-stemmed legginess unless topped and the resulting branches occasionally pinched, flowering maple is best kept less than 3 feet tall (unpruned, it can reach 6 feet or more). It bears large, softly hairy, maple-like leaves, beneath which are suspended a succession of solitary bell-shaped flowers, mostly in shades of brown-violet to salmon. The flowers can also be red, pink, yellow, or white. Exposure to full winter sun results in the most generous bloom, as does partial shade outdoors in summer. Under good conditions, flowering is continuous. Propagate by seed or cuttings.

ACHIMENES *CULTIVARS*
(Hot-water plant)

Achimenes is a group of tropical perennial gesneriads that grow from small scaly rhizomes and develop a clump of slender, leafy stems (usually not more than 1 foot high). They bear solitary or paired flowers, mostly in shades of purple or lavender blue, or in white. The flowers are often spotted. Best grown for summer bloom in baskets, achimenes thrives in humid air in an east-facing window. After flowering, the leaves gradually fade, the stems die back, and the rhizomes become dormant. Water should then be withheld and the baskets stored in a cool, dry place for at least three or four months. To break dormancy, dampen the soil, and more important, keep the air humid;

in humidities lower than 50 percent, achimines will not perform well.

If the stems were crowded during the previous blooming season, i.e., closer than 1 inch apart, the soil should be gently separated from the small, scaly rhizomes, which should be replanted in fresh, organically rich, fluffy, acidic soil about 2 inches deep and as far apart, or plant 6 rhizomes in a 6-inch pot or 10 in an 8-inch pot.

AESCHYNANTHUS LOBBIANUS
(Lipstick plant)

Lipstick plant is a climbing tropical gesneriad, best grown in hanging pots or baskets, where it produces a cascading 2-foot mop of drooping purple stems that bear hairy, purple-veined leaves and clusters of intensely red flowers. Several other species are available, which have red, orange, or yellow flowers.

Unfailing generous moisture and 30 to 50 percent humidity are required when the plant is actively growing and blooming, but both should be reduced during rest periods. Bright shade is indicated, as direct sun causes scorching. Propagated by cuttings, layering, or seed.

AGLAONEMA COMMUTATUM
(Chinese evergreen)

A low-light plant, Chinese evergreen species grows naturally in rain forest shade. As a houseplant it requires minimal care. Whether grown in regular potting soil or kept alive a long time in plain water, this

plant will stay green and presentable in dim light, though it will not increase in size appreciably. When grown in bright shade and in ordinary soil mix, it develops numerous leaves. Although rarely blooming, Chinese evergreen sometimes produces a curious greenish flower resembling a calla lily. A temperature range of 60° to 80°F and constantly moist soil yield best results. Chinese evergreen is propagated by division or stem cuttings.

ALOE BARBADENSIS
(Healing plant)

As with most succulents, aloe thrives where light intensity is high and humidity is low. Since aloe stores water in its thick, succulent leaves, the soil should be allowed to become quite dry between waterings. It grows best in east- or west-facing windows. Even so, if summered outdoors, it is best to place aloe in dappled sunlight or bright shade as the leaves tend to scorch if the transition is too abrupt. As a houseplant, aloe seldom flowers. Propagation is by stem offsets.

ARAUCARIA HETEROPHYLLA
(Norfolk Island pine)

The Norfolk Island pine becomes a massive, 100-foot-tall tree in its native tropical habitat near Australia and elsewhere in outdoor cultivation. It is striking for the radial, tiered symmetry of its spikelike branches in whorls along the trunk. As a houseplant, it tolerates low light levels, but in such illumination, it will grow only very slowly. To flourish, Norfolk Island pine needs bright shade or filtered light, preferably with some direct sun exposure in early morning or late afternoon. It definitely benefits from summers outdoors. Ideal indoor temperatures are 65° to 75°F during the day and 50° to 55°F at night. Lower branches may die if the humidity is too low, temperature too high (as can occur near a radiator), or light too dim. As it is difficult to propagate, oversize specimens are best replaced with new seedlings.

ASPARAGUS SPRENGERI
(Asparagus fern)

The asparagus fern is a tuberous-rooted, drought-tolerant, multiply branched plant that produces slender sprawling or drooping stems, 2 to 3 feet long. It is especially suited to basket culture. Sun exposure is beneficial, although curtain filtering is advisable in the summer months indoors; outdoors, it should be placed in partial shade. Soil should be kept moist when the plant is actively growing, but at other times its large, water-filled tubers allow it to survive weeks or even months without watering. Old stems often drop their light green needlelike leaves when the plant is brought indoors for the winter and subjected to lower humidity. Several other species are available as houseplants. Propagation is by clump division and seed.

ASPIDISTRA ELATIOR
(Cast-iron plant)

Cast-iron plant is a low-light houseplant that stays green and attractive in interior locations for a long time—months, in fact. However, it should be summered outdoors in moderate shade. Cast-iron plant is ideal for rooms that have only a northern exposure, where light is insufficient for anything else; placed in a dim window, cast-iron plant will survive, though it will display little growth. The brighter the indirect light it receives, the better. A temperature range of 60° to 75°F is best, although anywhere from 45° to 85°F is tolerable. Soil should be kept barely moist. Cast-iron plant is propagated by division of clumps.

BEGONIA

Since there is a multitude of begonia species and cultivars with a wide range of growth habits, this group has been divided into the following categories for convenience.

Cane stemmed	Strong, upright stems; includes forms commonly called angel-wing begonias, flowers in late spring to early fall
Shrubby	Thick, upright stems; the main stems develop numerous lateral branches; flowers in late spring to early fall
Swollen base	Thick, but not tuberous, stem bases; flowers in summer
Tuberous	Bulblike rootstock; dormant in winter; requires high humidity while leafy and flowering; flowers often large and doubled, borne continuously in summer
Rhizomatous	Mostly grown for foliage; flowers at various times if given adequate light
Trailing	Long, vinelike stems; thrives in hanging baskets; flowers mostly small, borne when stems are growing
Rex cultorum	Clump forming; low growing; often has large, textured, and/or variegated leaves; multitude of small flowers in late winter; best in bright shade or filtered light
Semperflorens	Fibrous rooted; of easy culture in bright shade or with early morning or late afternoon sun; includes the popular everblooming wax begonias

In general, begonias thrive in bright shade to filtered sunlight throughout the year south of the east-west line linking Washington, D.C.; St. Louis; Denver; and Sacramento. North of this line, a few hours of winter sunlight (November through February) is beneficial in either an east- or west-facing window. Temperatures in the 60s (F) are ideal.

Although soil moisture is important, overwatering begonias is often fatal, especially if the roots begin to rot. The soil mix should include more than the usual portion of humus, peat moss, or compost. Many begonias respond well to artificial light culture and most grow especially well when summered outdoors

Rex begonia in bloom

in light shade with constantly adequate moisture. Depending on habit, begonias are propagated by cuttings or by clump division and, in all cases, by seed.

Species well suited for use as houseplants include the following:

B. bowerae (eyelash begonia): 6 inches tall; rhizomatous; stems and leaves pale green, with long hairs; leaf blades have brown margins; flowers pink, purplish borne in winter and early spring.

B. breviramosa (New Guinea begonia): 2 feet tall; shrubby; stems have rust-red hairs; leaves green with white markings; flowers pink, numerous, borne in late spring to early fall.

B. × cheimantha (Christmas begonia): 6 to 12 inches tall; semperflorens group; leaves heart shaped; flowers red, pink, or white, borne in winter.

B. coccinea (plain-leaf angel-wing begonia): 2 to 4 feet tall; cane-stemmed; leaves are longer than they are wide, often spotted in cultivars; flowers red, pink, or white, borne in large clusters in the spring.

B. dichroa (orange-flowered angel-wing begonia): 8 to 15 inches tall; cane stemmed; flowers salmon pink to orange, borne in summer.

B. dregei (grape-leaf begonia, maple-leaf begonia): 1 to 2 feet tall; tuberous; leaves pale green with purple veins and gray spots; flowers white, borne in summer.

B. × erythrophylla (beefsteak begonia): 1 foot tall; rhizomatous; leaves glossy, green, red beneath; flowers red, borne from winter to spring.

B. foliosa (fern-leaf begonia): can reach 2 feet tall, but usually much shorter; semperflorens group; leaves numerous, very small, two-ranked (in opposite rows); flowers minute, white, borne in spring.

B. goegoensis (fire king begonia): 1 foot tall; rhizomatous; leaves cupped, warted, green with bronze, held on squared stalks; flowers pink, borne from summer to fall.

B. heracleifolia (star-leaf begonia): 1½ feet tall; rex cultorum; leaves 8 to 15 inches across, deeply lobed, bronzy green above, red beneath, have scattered tufts of red hairs; flowers light pink, borne from winter to spring.

B. imperialis (imperial begonia): 1 foot tall; rhizomatous; leaves red-brown with green, hairy; flowers white, everblooming.

B. masoniana (iron-cross begonia): 7 to 10 inches tall; rhizomatous; leaves about 8 inches across, green with pebbly warting and a large brown central zone with irregular arms; flowers pinkish, borne from spring to summer.

B. metallica (hairy-leaf begonia): 6 to 9 inches tall; semperflorens group; leaves metallic green with purple veins and silvery hairs; flowers pink with red hairs, borne summer to fall.

B. prismatocarpa (Guinean begonia): can reach 6 inches tall, but usually shorter; rhizomatous; leaves numerous, about 1 inch long; flowers yellow, everblooming.

B. semperflorens (wax begonia): 6 to 12 inches tall; semperflorens group; leaves glossy, green or bronzy; flowers red, pink, or white, everblooming; very popular, but subject to powdery mildew.

B. subvillosa var. *leptotricha* (woolly bear begonia): 1 to 1½ feet tall; semperflorens group; leaves green with brown fuzz; flowers white, borne mostly in summer.

B. × tuberhybrida (tuberous begonia): 1 to 1½ feet tall; tuberous; leaves large, borne on fleshy seasonal stems; flowers large, sometimes double, red, pink, white, or yellow, sometimes bicolor, borne in summer; subject to powdery mildew.

B. venosa (spice begonia): at least 2 feet tall; semperflorens group; leaves cupped, felty; flowers white, spicily fragrant, borne in summer to winter.

BRASSAIA ACTINOPHYLLA
(Schefflera, umbrella tree)

Schefflera is an adaptable houseplant that is always attractive, whether a small seedling or a large specimen. Given moderate care, a seedling will become a large, handsome plant in several years. Young plants have small leaves with three to five radially arranged leaflets. As the plant matures more leaflets are added, and eventually number up to 16 per leaf, each 2 to 3 inches wide and up to 15 inches long. Schefflera does best if it gets a few hours of direct sunlight each day, although it can also adjust to less light; it is then slower growing. Allow the soil to dry moderately between waterings. Schefflera is propagated by air layering and by cuttings.

BRASSAIA ARBORICOLA
(Dwarf schefflera)

B. arboricola is smaller than *B. actinophylla* in all respects and usually develops numerous branches. The leaflets are round tipped and less glossy. Maximum height is about 4 feet and the plant does best in the shade, without any sun exposure. Propagation is by layering or cuttings.

CALADIUM BICOLOR
HYBRIDS AND CVS.
(Fancy-leaf caladium)

Fancy-leaf caladium, colorful foliage plants, are purchased as bulblike tubers that require a period of winter dormancy. When grown in a bright, curtain-filtered window, they make excellent spring and summer plants, but they usually begin to fade about the time of the fall equinox. Tubers should then be removed and allowed to dry a few days. Store them in dry peat moss or vermiculite for at least three months. They may then be replanted in a light, sandy soil mix with supplemental peat moss and kept at 65°F or somewhat warmer. Tuber offsets are the principal means of propagation.

CAPSICUM ANNUUM
'CONOIDES'
(Ornamental pepper)

Small leaved, low, and generously branched, ornamental pepper is easily grown from seed and is especially suited to grouping in planter boxes on sunny windowsills. The small fiery hot fruits are usually held erect and mature from red to black. The fruit may be picked and used in the kitchen, dried for ornament, or left on the plants where they persist for months. Fruiting occurs in the summer and fall.

CEROPEGIA WOODII
(Rosary vine, string of hearts)

Since rosary vine forms succulent bulb-like tubers that store water, you can occasionally allow the soil to become quite dry. These tubers form along the vining stem, and they may be cut off, with a piece of this stem included, and planted in new pots to propagate the plants. Hang or suspend the vine in a sunny window—it is almost foolproof if given enough light, though it will also tolerate quite low light for months at a time. Neutral or alkaline soil is best.

CHLOROPHYTUM COMOSUM
(Spider plant)

Spider plant is tuberous-rooted plant with a tufted rosette of recurved, often variegated leaves and long, slender, pendent flower stalks that eventually bear plantlets. When the plantlets reach a suitable soil surface, they strike root and eventually detach from the parent plant. When grown in hanging baskets or hanging pots, mother plants will retain these plantlets for months or even years, and the whole assemblage becomes a leafy cascade. Spider plant does best in bright shade or when exposed to early morning or late afternoon sun in the winter. The soil should be allowed to dry between waterings.

CISSUS RHOMBIFOLIA
(Grape ivy)

Given bright light, warmth, and occasional waterings, grape ivy will thrive and may be trained as a rounded mound of foliage or, provided cords or other attachment for its tendrils, may be allowed to climb and frame a window. Several other species are also cultivated; all require similar conditions. Grape ivy endures low light for extended periods but then shows little growth. Neutral to alkaline soil is best. Grape ivy is reproduced by cuttings or layering.

× CITROFORTUNELLA MICROCARPA
(Calamondin orange)

Calamondin orange is cross between tangerine (*Citrus reticulata*) and oval kumquat (*Fortunella margarita*) and is still sometimes offered commercially as *Citrus mitis*. It is a diminutive citrus with 2-inch leaves and 1-inch fruit and is suited well to tub culture in a sunny south-facing window; a temperature range of 55° to 65°F provides for the longest fruit retention. It does especially well if summered outdoors in partial shade. If flowers appear during this period, insect pollination will ensure a good fruit set. Though too acidic to eat raw, the ripe fruit makes a tart marmalade. Propagation is by seed.

CLERODENDRUM THOMPSONIAE
(Bleeding heart vine, glory-bower)

A woody climber that reaches 6 feet or more, bleeding heart vine is usually grown as a greenhouse subject, but it makes an attractive houseplant if given sufficient humidity and a bright, sunny position. The red and white flowers, mostly borne in the spring, are especially

Ceropegia woodii

showy in contrast to the dark green, quilted foliage. Variegated cultivars provide an even showier display. Summering outdoors in partial shade is beneficial. A sandy-humusy soil yields best results. This species is propagated by cuttings.

CLIVIA MINIATA

Grown for its lustrous, strap-shaped leaves and annual display of orange tubular flowers, clivia may be grown in the same pot for years; indeed, being pot bound seems to augment its floral display. It is beneficial, however, to include a soluble fertilizer (5-10-5) in summer waterings. Summering outdoors in filtered sunlight also helps promote the late winter or early spring flowering. When extremely pot-bound plants are moved to the next larger pot size, care should be taken to add rich, humusy soil, well packed with a stick to fill all spaces. As prolonged sun exposure will cause leaf scorch, sun exposure should be limited to about three hours, preferably in the morning, with bright shade for the remainder of the day during the months indoors. Clivia is reproduced by rootstock offsets and by seed.

COFFEA ARABICA
(Coffee)

In its natural environment, coffee is an understory shrub that grows beneath thinly shading trees, thus shielded from intense sunlight, especially in summer. Coffee flourishes as a houseplant if given bright shade with sun in the early morning or late afternoon. Humidity of at least 40 percent is necessary to keep the handsome glossy leaves from browning at the tips and along the edges. Be watchful for spider mites, which commonly infest coffee when grown indoors. New plants may be grown from fresh (unroasted) coffee beans, or the main stem or upright ends of branches may be air layered (see page 883 for instructions). Horizontal shoots, if rooted, tend to grow horizontally, even when potted up separately. Coffee can also be propagated with cuttings.

COLUMNEA × BANKSII

One of a large number of species, columnea, a gesneriad, has numerous long, pendent branches that impart the effect of a cascade. The branches terminate in red and yellow flowers, which are borne from spring to fall. Culture is the same as for *Aeschynanthus lobbianus*.

CRASSULA ARGENTEA
(Jade plant)

Jade plant rewards its grower with masses of thick, glossy leaves arranged on thick, succulent stems that eventually reach 3 to 4 feet in height with an equal spread. Easily grown in a south-facing window getting three to five hours of direct sun each bright day, jade plant also benefits from summering outdoors in a partly sunny location. The shift should be made gradually to avoid scorching the leaves. With sufficient light, jade plant produces an annual crop of white sedumlike flowers in the winter. The plant thrives in low humidity and does well if the soil is allowed to dry between waterings. Propagation is by cuttings.

CYMBIDIUM *SPP. AND CVS.*

Although most orchids amenable to cultivation do best in greenhouses or in controlled chambers under artificial light, some do well on windowsills. Most cymbidiums are too large for such culture in the ordinary home, but some of the grasslike miniatures are small enough to be easily accommodated. It is best to summer them outdoors in bright shade with a little direct sun in early morning or toward the end of the day. Indoors, they should be placed in an east-facing window and kept fairly cool, at around 60°F. Flowering normally occurs in mid to late winter. Every two or three years, or when overcrowded, repot into a larger container, using a sandy-humusy mix that includes a slow-release fertilizer. Humidity should be no lower than 40 percent. To propagate cymbidium, offsets may be taken or the clumps divided.

DIEFFENBACHIA AMOENA, D. MACULATA
(Dumb cane)

Even in the wild, there is much variation in leaf color among *Dieffenbachia* plants. It is, therefore, reasonable to expect great variation in markings and color in the leaves of these plants that are grown horticulturally. Since the leaves are large and the plant eventually reaches 4 to 6 feet, dumb cane is best used to flank windows, especially facing north. With warmth and humidity, leaves are retained longer; dry conditions often result in legginess, with a few leaves atop a tall stem, and cold drafts can be fatal. Of the two species, *D. amoena* is more tolerant of the low light in interior spaces. Both thrive on moist, acidic soil. Propagation is by layering.

The common name, dumb cane, alludes to the tongue-swelling calcium oxalate spicules in the sap, a danger to be considered if you have young children.

DIONAEA MUSCIPULA
(Venus's flytrap)

Because tubers of these plants can be purchased in the most unexpected places—even in drugstores—this should tell you that venus's flytrap is considered an intriguing novelty to most people. But, unfortunately, it does not survive in the ordinary home environment. It requires a temperature of 55° to 80°F, humid air, and a moist peat and sphagnum medium. Thus it is best grown as a terrarium subject (see page 956). Be sure that purchased plants have been propagated from seed or tissue culture and not collected wild, where this species is threatened with extinction. The curiously folded, bristle-edged leaves are arranged in a rosette, from the middle of which a stalk of small white flowers arises in summer. Partial sun is best. Venus's flytrap is propagated by clump division, leaf cuttings, or seed.

DIZYGOTHECA ELEGANTISSIMA
(False aralia)

A warm location with a temperature range of 60° to 75°F and bright shade, preferably including some early-morning or late-afternoon sun (curtain filtered in the summer), will reward the indoor gardener with steady growth of the elegant false aralia. Undersize new leaves and the premature loss of older ones from the bottom up usually indicate insufficient humidity. The soil should be neutral and kept moist. False aralia rejuvenates well when summered outdoors in a sheltered,

Dizygotheca elegantissima

mostly shaded location. The principal pest is scale. False aralia is propagated by cuttings.

DRACAENA FRAGRANS *'MASSANGEANA'*
(Corn dracaena)

A stately, slow-growing, thick-stemmed plant, 5 to 8 feet tall, corn dracaena has long, arching, cornlike foliage, sometimes topped by a cluster of whitish flowers. It is especially adaptable to interior locations with low light and is unaffected by dry air. Other species, also long proven worthy of indoor culture in shade, include the following.

D. concinna (red-edge dracaena): 3 to 6 feet tall, leaves narrow, glossy, margined with deep red.

D. sanderiana (Belgian evergreen): 2 to 4 feet tall; leaves glossy, up to 1 inch wide, longitudinally striped yellow.

D. surculosa (gold-dust dracaena): 1 to 3 feet tall, stems slender, branched; leaves ovate, dark green, spotted yellow.

D. deremensis (striped dracaena): 3 to 6 feet tall, leaves up to 2 feet long, longitudinally striped white; does best in warm, humid conditions.

Dracaenas are propagated by air layering and by cuttings.

EPIPREMNUM AUREUM
(Pothos, ivy arum)

Formerly listed as *Scindapsus aureus*, pothos will succeed almost anywhere indoors, but thrives in dim light, producing glossy, variegated leaves on vining stems that can reach 3 feet. Other than reasonably moist soil, its demands are few. Pothos is propagated by cuttings.

EPISCIA *CVS.*
(Carpet plant)

Carpet plant has a spreading habit and is best grown as a basket plant in an east-facing window. It is a close relative of the African violet and is also called peacock plant and flame violet, alluding to its bright red flowers. Acidic soil, moderate temperatures, and fairly high humidity (30 to 40 percent) are requisites—the last is often difficult to provide in houses. It is propagated is by cuttings.

EUPHORBIA PULCHERRIMA
(Poinsettia)

Poinsettia, the quintessential Christmas holiday pot plant, is a 6- to 12-foot shrub in its native Mexico but is seldom seen more than 3 feet tall in cultivation. Above the smooth, rich green, oaklike leaves is borne a rosette of large red, pink, yellow, or white and spattered or marbled leaflike bracts that surround small yellow flowers.

Kept in bright shade, preferably with some exposure to winter sun, and with consistently moist soil, poinsettia will hold its colorful bracts (and foliage) all winter. In the spring, it may be planted outdoors as a foliage plant for the summer, preferably in partial shade. If it is to be brought indoors to reflower, it should be shifted to a larger pot (preferably clay) before being plunged in the ground; then put it back into a plastic pot when it is brought in for the winter. For instructions on reflowering, see page 950.

× FATSHEDERA LIZEI
(French ivy, shrub ivy)

Easier to grow than the closely related *Fatsia japonica* because of its greater tolerance of dry air and low light, French ivy is the result of a cross between *Fatsia japonica* and English ivy (*Hedera helix*), hence the contrived generic name ×*Fatshedera*. It displays various parental characteristics: The leaves are ivylike but larger and of one shade of green, as in *Fatsia*, and the stems, though upright, are too slender to support plants more than 3 feet tall. Shrub ivy thrives in a cool, shaded, but bright location, in neutral, moderately moist soil. Summering outdoors in shade is beneficial. Layering and cuttings are the means of propagation.

FATSIA JAPONICA
(Aralia)

Aralia is a large-leaved plant, 2 to 6 feet tall, that is usually grown as a single specimen in a pot or tub. It requires moist, neutral to alkaline soil and does best in cool conditions—temperatures from 55° to 60°F at night and 65° to 70°F during the day. *Fatsia* requires two to three hours of winter sun exposure each bright day from zone 7 north to maintain vigor. In this species, propagation is by cuttings.

FERNS

As a group, the ferns suited to indoor culture do best in humid air (at least 30 percent and preferably 40 percent) and away from cold drafts, a combination few homes can provide without containment

in a special room served by a humidifier. The species described here, however, are more tolerant of dry air than most and are not devastated by an occasional cool draft, but they require more light than other ferns.

Complete drying kills most ferns, and even a partial drying out can cause leaves to brown at the edges and new growth to be deformed and undersize. Temperatures below 70°F are best. If summered outdoors, slugs frequently consume new fern growth (see Chapter 34). Many small ferns are very adaptable to terrarium culture (see page 956). Ferns are usually propagated by clump division, but they may also be raised from spores.

Cyrtomium falcatum
(Holly fern)

A cool, partially shaded winter location and summers spent outdoors in shade with the pot (preferably clay) sunk in moist earth is the best procedure for success with the beautiful holly fern.

Davallia fejeensis
(Rabbit's-foot fern)

Rabbit's-foot fern is also known as bear's-foot fern and squirrel's-foot fern, the various common names referring to the fuzzy rhizomes that spread over the soil surface. These rhizomes are especially effective when the fern is grown in a hanging basket. Partial shade and a cool, humid atmosphere yield best results. Several other species, all evergreen, are also available.

Lygodium japonicum
(Japanese climbing fern)

A slender twining vine, 3 to 6 feet high, Japanese climbing fern requires support; exposure to at least three hours of full sun each bright day, especially from zone

8 north; and humidity not below 30 percent. It benefits from summering outdoors in bright shade with some early-morning or late-afternoon sun. This species is especially popular with orchid growers, who use it for greenhouse shade.

Nephrolepis exaltata
(Boston fern)

Boston fern is a favorite basket subject that grows well in partial shade, moderate temperature, and neutral, moist soil. Several other species are available, all of which thrive under relatively cool conditions, as long as there is bright shade with some early or late sun in the winter.

Platycerium bifurcatum
(Staghorn fern)

Staghorn fern, which is rather bizarre, can readily adjust to home conditions if it is provided good light—full winter sunlight and curtain-filtered sunlight during the summer. Allow the potting medium to dry out between waterings, and then water thoroughly in a sink or tub so that the plant can be saturated. Staghorn fern thrives best in long-fiber sphagnum moss, fern fiber medium, or a 50–50 mixture of these two ingredients. The plant produces two kinds of leaves. Shield leaves clasp the pot or the vertical slab that the plant is mounted on. Although they turn brown with age they should not be trimmed away because they keep the acidic rooting medium from drying out too rapidly. These fronds hold water and should be watered whenever the plant is. The second type of leaf is the true staghorn-shaped frond, two or three of which will be produced twice a year—in the spring and fall. Several other species, all similar in habit, are also available.

Nephrolepis exaltata

Polypodium aureum
(Bear's-paw fern, hare's-foot fern)

Bear's-paw fern is one of the most adaptable ferns. If given good light and the usual careful attention, it will reward you with sculptural blue-green new leaves and fuzzy rhizomes that become successively larger and more interesting as the plant ages. But by the same token, "growing older and larger" is one of the plant's chief faults, because it can get too large for many rooms and must, therefore, be divided. This is best done in early spring, just as the new leaves are beginning to grow after the winter's rest period. Acidic, humusy, well-drained soil and partial shade suit it best.

Pteris cretica
(Stove fern)

Because the common name stove fern is confusing to many (as it alludes to the heated greenhouse, or "stove," in England), the Latin generic name is often used instead. Like the Boston fern and holly

fern, this species is among the easiest to grow, as long as bright shade, fairly high humidity (about 30 percent), and cool temperatures (60° to 70°F) are consistently maintained. Summering in the shade outdoors promotes annual growth.

FICUS BENJAMINA
(Benjamin fig, weeping fig)

Tropical fig trees are popular as houseplants because, given moderately bright shade, preferably with some early- or late-day exposure to winter sun, they grow well under ordinary indoor conditions. If moved through a succession of ever larger pots, Benjamin fig will become sizable—likely too large for most rooms. Kept in a small pot, say about 1 foot in diameter, the plant's growth will slow, but the density of roots may call for more frequent watering. Although Benjamin fig responds well to pruning, care is required to preserve the plant's graceful habit. It is important to note that this species is sensitive to sudden changes, as when moved in the fall from an outdoor spot to an overheated indoor room. Some or all the leaves may drop after such a change, but usually new ones soon grow. Specimens grown with braided trunks tend to remain smaller than those with straight trunks. The cultivar 'Exotica', with slender weeping branches, is the variant most commonly seen. In 'Variegata' the leaves are edged with white. Propagation is by air layering or cuttings.

FICUS ELASTICA
(Indian rubber tree, parlor fig)

Attractive with large, glossy, leathery, deep green leaves, Indian rubber tree in time usually outgrows available space. An oversize plant may be replaced by air layering one of its branches (see page 883). As with most figs, this species thrives in bright shade but is likely to scorch if subjected to full sun in the summer. In the cultivar 'Doescheri', the leaves are variegated; in 'Rubra', the midrib and leaf stalk are red and the young leaves maroon. Propagate by air layering or cuttings.

GASTERIA BICOLOR
(Oxtongue plant)

Oxtongue plant, a relative of the popular aloe, has fleshy leaves that may be arranged in rosettes or in two ranks or files opposite each other. Like most succulents, it is easy to grow in sun or partial shade and may be left in the same pot for years. Several other species are also in cultivation. It is easily propagated by division or offsets.

GREVILLEA ROBUSTA
(Silk oak)

Silk oak, an Australian tree, can tolerate both dry soil (between waterings) and dry air very well. It requires good light, however, i.e., it should be exposed to winter sunlight in the early morning or late afternoon and should otherwise be in bright shade. It thrives when temperatures are at 55° to 60°F at night and 65° to 75°F during the day. Summering outdoors is beneficial but may result in a full foot of growth. If kept pot bound, growth will be slower. Silk oak responds well to pruning. It is propagated by seeds, cuttings, or tissue culture.

HATIORA GAERTNERI
(Easter cactus)

Often offered commercially as *Schlumbergera gaertneri* because of its superficial resemblance to *S.* × *buckleyi*

(Christmas cactus), Easter cactus bears red flowers in late winter or early spring. The similar *H. rosea* has pink flowers. Both bear luxuriantly if watered only sparingly in the two months before flowering. Otherwise, culture is the same as for *S.* × *buckleyi*.

HAWORTHIA FASCIATA
(Zebra haworthia)

One of a very large group of succulents, zebra haworthia has a dense rosette of erect, rigid, fleshy leaves that are variously textured and white banded. Older plants of *M. fasciata* and the numerous other species in cultivation produce white, yellow, or pink flowers, usually small and tubular, on slender stalks in the winter. Other than placement in a sunny position and occasional watering, little care is required. A sandy, acidic soil mix yields best results. Propagation is by clump division and offsets.

HEDERA HELIX
(English ivy)

English ivy, especially its small-leaf cultivars, is one of the most useful and adaptable houseplants. It may be allowed to trail outward or downward from a pot, planting tray, or planter box, or it may be trained upward on or through a mesh lattice to frame a window. It can be induced to grow along lattice strips on a well-lighted wall or even on the ceiling. More conventionally, it may be kept to a com-

pact, bushy form. Small-leaf cultivars lend themselves to training on wire-mesh forms in the shape of animals or architectural figures, rather like topiary. Especially handsome are cultivars with variegated foliage. All are very adaptable for indoor culture, adjusting to any exposure, including low-light interior locations. They endure heat but prosper in cool (60° to 65°F) places and do best in neutral soil. English ivy is propagated by layering and cuttings.

HOWEA FORSTERANA
(Sentry palm)

Although the sentry palm becomes lofty outdoors in the tropics, it is known in its 2- to 4-foot juvenile state as a houseplant. It is favored among palms because of its adaptability to low humidity. Also known as kentia palm, this species does best in moderate shade to low light; in warm (65° to 80°F), moderately humid air; and in a moist, neutral soil. It withstands adverse conditions longer than any other houseplant palm. Sentry palm is reproduced by fresh seed.

HOYA CARNOSA
(Wax plant)

The wax plant is a wonderful vine that will literally cover a sunny east- or west-facing window if given enough time and support. While it is comparatively slow growing, within a few years it can amass quite a quantity of vining stems with waxy green or variegated leaves. If wax plant receives sufficient light, it will flower indoors, usually in the winter. Old flower spurs should not be cut off, as they will bear another round of flowers in the next season. Grow wax plant in a cactus soil mix, kept on the dry side; allow the pot to dry out completely between waterings. Be watchful for mealy bug, a common insect pest of wax plant. Several other species are also grown, all similar in cultural requirements. Propagation is by cuttings.

IMPATIENS WALLERIANA

Erroneously listed under such names as *I. holstii* and *I. sultani*, *I. walleriana* is the common bedding impatiens which, under favorable conditions, makes a presentable houseplant through the winter. Most suited for indoor use are dwarf cultivars, which stay under 6 inches and branch freely.

The flowers, mostly between 1 and 1½ inches across, range from purple or red through pastel shades to white. Bicolors are also available. Flowering depends on exposure to several hours of sunlight; on humidity of 30 percent or more; on moderate temperatures without cold drafts; and on a fertile, sandy soil, preferably with considerable organic matter incorporated. Failing any of these requirements, impatiens will survive, though with few or no flowers and often with only a tuft of undersize leaves at the end of each branch. Even under the most favorable circumstances, flowering may fail during and just after a prolonged period of cloudy weather. Mealy bugs and red spider often infest weakened plants. As impatiens tissue is almost entirely water, care should be taken to maintain adequate soil moisture, especially as wilting is often accompanied by loss of leaves and flower buds.

In late winter or early spring, leggy plants should be cut back to induce basal rejuvenation. The cuttings will strike root in damp sand or even in water. Double-flowering cultivars, which set little seed, are best propagated in this way. New Guinea impatiens (*I. hawkeri* hybrids) require higher light levels and are, therefore, best wintered over in a greenhouse. Propagation is usually by seed, but double-flowered and New Guinea impatiens are mostly grown from cuttings.

IPOMOEA TRICOLOR
(Morning glory)

Of the various ornamental species of morning glory, *I. tricolor*, which includes the well-known cultivars 'Heavenly Blue' and 'Pearly Gates', is often successful as a colorful—though usually short-lived—houseplant. It should be grown from seed in a sunny south-facing window, preferably in a window box or large pot; provide support for the twining stems. Although the large bell-shaped flowers face the light and last but a day (longer in cloudy weather), they add a welcome touch of summer to

the bleakness of the winter scene outside. Leaves yellow and drop prematurely in low humidity, and weakened plants become subject to infestation by whitefly or red spider mites. Morning glory is propagated by seed.

JUSTICIA BRANDEGEANA
(Shrimp plant)

Formerly known as *Beloperone guttata*, shrimp plant is a small tropical shrub grown outdoors in southern Florida and southern California; and elsewhere it has long been grown as a houseplant. It usually grows 1½ to 2 feet tall, and its branches terminate in an elongate series of tightly overlapping reddish green bracts (the "shrimp"), between which are borne small, tubular, white flowers. It thrives in a sunny window in the winter and benefits from summering outdoors in partial shade. Leggy plants should be cut back when put outside, so that they may rejuvenate over the summer. Alkaline soil is best. Propagation of shrimp plant is by cuttings.

KALANCHOE BLOSSFELDIANA
(Christmas kalanchoe)

A good basket plant in a sunny position, Christmas kalanchoe is increasingly used in the Christmas trade, for which it is forced into flower in greenhouses. It may flower spottily and intermittently the rest of the winter, after which it is best summered outdoors in partial shade. Given 14 hours of unbroken darkness followed by 10 hours of direct sun or bright light each day from September to early

December, it may be induced to reflower for the next Christmas season. Whether in or out of flower, Christmas kalanchoe has attractive, glossy, succulent foliage. It is propagated by cuttings of stems or leaves.

MARANTA LEUCONEURA
(Prayer plant)

A low-growing foliage plant, prayer plant is a carpeting ground cover in tropical woodlands, but it adapts well to indoor culture. Its flexible leaf-stalk joints position the patterned blades strictly upright each night. In *M. leuconeura* var. *kerchoviana*, the gray green leaf blades have a row of olive green spots on either side of the midrib. The cultivar 'Massangeana', which is the form most frequently seen, has bluish rusty brown leaves that exhibit a jagged silver band along the midrib and silver lines along the lateral veins. Prayer plant grows best in moderate shade to quite low light. It needs moderate (about 30 percent) humidity; temperatures of 65° to 75°F, and moist, acidic soil. Excessive light or low humidity causes the leaves to curl and prematurely die. Propagation is by rooted basal shoots or clump division.

PAPHIOPEDILUM CVS.
(Venus's-slippers)

Although Venus's-slippers, and most other orchids suited to indoor cultivation, are best grown in a greenhouse or under fluorescent lights, this species can be grown on windowsills if certain conditions are met. For one thing, the relative humidity

Paphiopedilum hirsutissimum

must be 50 percent or higher. Bright light is necessary, but the plants must be shaded from direct sun. Night temperatures should be 60° to 65°F, but daytime temperatures should be at least 10° higher, preferably to about 80°F. Several species, including *P. hirsutissimum*, *P. insigne*, *P. spicerianum*, and *P. venustum*, require a cooler temperature regime, with nighttime lows down to 45°F. An open, sandy, acidic soil with plenty of organic material is needed and should be watered every day. The grower is rewarded once each year with a solitary or small cluster of large, saclike flowers with colorful wings, from each rosette.

PELARGONIUM × HORTORUM
(Common geranium)

Pelargonium × Hortorum 'Freckles'

Of the many species of *Pelargonium*, common geranium and its many cultivars are the ubiquitous bedding geraniums that have long been popular as houseplants.

Forgiving of much neglect, geraniums will produce clusters of red, pink, white, or bicolor flowers above their aromatic foliage as long as they are exposed to several hours of sunlight daily. They are best grown in a neutral, sandy soil that is allowed to dry out between waterings. Low humidity will cause older leaves to die, but leggy plants readily rejuvenate if cut back. Favorite plants may be propagated by rooting cuttings in damp sand. Summering outdoors stimulates new growth, which, with occasional pinching of shoots, can be guided, resulting in well-formed plants for indoor use.

PELARGONIUM PELTATUM
(Ivy-leaf geranium)

More slender and rangy in habit than *P. × hortorum*, ivy-leaf geranium has smaller, firm-textured, lobed, ivylike leaves and smaller clusters of flowers. It is especially suited to basket culture and greatly benefits by being placed outdoors in partial shade for the summer. Flower colors include purple, red, pink, and white, and a number of cultivars have variegated leaves.

PEPEROMIA OBTUSIFOLIA
(Baby rubber plant, radiator plant)

In general, peperomias are low-growing foliage plants of easy culture. There are many species and cultivars, differing chiefly in habit and foliage traits. Baby rubber plant has spreading stems that bear relatively large, round, thick, waxy leaves that, in the common cultivar 'Variegata', are marked cream and white. Like most peperomias, *P. obtusifolia* thrives in a north-facing window in neutral to acidic soil. It is dormant but remains leafy throughout the winter season but grows plentiful new foliage when the humidity rises, especially if placed outdoors in the shade and kept moist.

Also meritorious is *P. argyreia* (watermelon begonia), which is symmetrically upright in habit and bears deep green heart-shaped leaves that are marked with silvery stripes. Neither species exceeds 1 foot in height. Both are propagated by cuttings.

PERSEA AMERICANA
(Avocado)

Important as a tropical fruit tree, the avocado makes an easily grown houseplant and is adaptable to a wide range of conditions. Seeds taken from ripe store-purchased fruit should be allowed to dry for a few days, before being set, flat end down, about one-third of their length in pots of damp sand or propped with toothpicks in glasses of water. Germination takes about one month, after which a root descends, followed by a rapidly rising leafy shoot, with all initial growth supported by the food stored in the large seed. With the seed still attached, the young plant should be carefully potted up in ordinary soil mix so that the seed rests on the soil surface. Avocados do best in partial shade and moderate humidity (30 percent or more), but they can survive months in low light at cool temperatures (55° to 65°F). Excessive heat and dry air cause premature dropping of older leaves and marginal browning of other leaves. Summering outdoors stimulates growth and almost complete replacement of the foliage. Placement in the shade is best, although early morning or late afternoon sun causes no harm. Unless pruned, avocados become small trees and make useful additions to the houseplant scene in the winter. Their size and shape can be determined by occasional pruning. The clusters of small

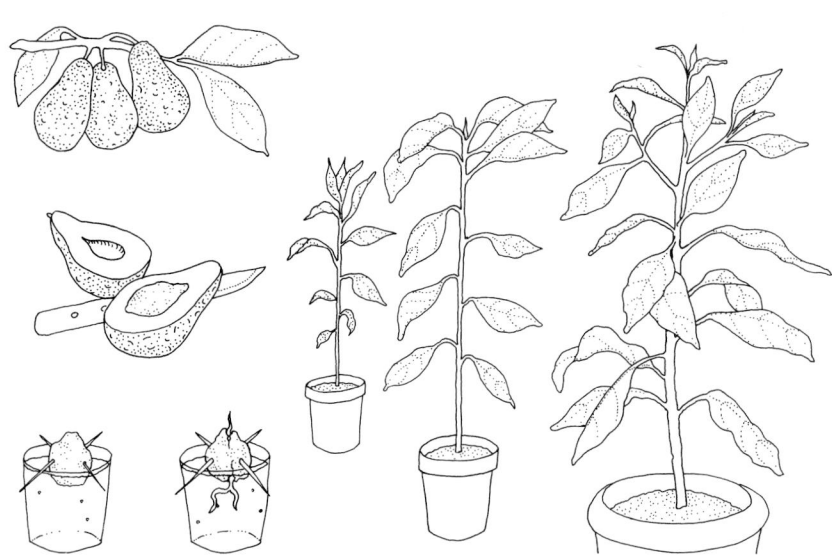

Steps in growing an avocado from a pit. A ripe fruit may be opened, the large seed removed and propped up with toothpicks, its base immersed in water. After sprouting roots and shoot, the young plant should be potted and transferred to ever large pots, with its growth tips pinched to guide size and form.

flowers seldom appear on the houseplant avocado, and in any case, the genetic factor for large fruit size is not inherited. Commercial fruit-bearing avocados are reproduced vegetatively.

PHALAENOPSIS *SPP.* *AND HYBRIDS*
(Moth orchid)

Moth orchids respond well to house culture. Because they are epiphytes that are rooted in the debris that accumulates in tree crotches in the wild, they need only chunks of bark or osmunda fiber as a rooting medium. This should be watered thoroughly, then allowed to dry out before the next watering. Roots should be plump and white; if dark, watering is likely excessive. Moth orchids do best in consistent warmth: 70° to 80°F in the day and about 65°F at night. Humidity should preferably be about 50 percent but no lower than 30 percent. Sun exposure is beneficial, especially in the morning and late afternoon. The care required to grow epiphytic orchids is amply rewarded by the incomparably beautiful and long-lasting blooms, appearing once each year and usually lasting for weeks. Propagation is by clump division or by seed.

PHILODENDRON SCANDENS *VAR*. OXYCARDIUM
(Glossy philodendron)

Philodendron scandens var. *oxycardium* 'Moonlight'

In the very large genus *Philodendron*, some species are of a compact "self-heading" habit, while others are climbers that require support (but in nature ascend by means of aerial roots). Most species grown as houseplants are known only by their relatively small, juvenile leaves; in each case, the adult leaves are much larger and often differently shaped and positioned.

Glossy philodendron, the most commonly grown vining sort, is of easiest culture, thriving in bright shade and moist, sandy soil with some organic matter, but it survives long periods in very low light and rooted in nothing more than water. It has glossy, heart-shaped leaves, as does the similar *P. cordatum* (heart-leaf philodendron), which has somewhat larger leaves. Both are easily propagated by cuttings.

PHOENIX ROEBELENII
(Miniature date palm)

Although the miniature date palm is very adaptable to low interior light, it requires bright indirect light to thrive. Summers outdoors will stimulate fresh new growth, providing sun exposure is limited to the early morning or late afternoon. Consistently moist, neutral soil is best. Propagation is by seed.

PITTOSPORUM TOBIRA
(Japanese pittosporum)

Although the shrubby Japanese pittosporum grows best in full sunlight, it is very tolerant of shade and even of chilly drafts and cool nights. Pittosporum can be used in a well-lighted hall or breezeway. Night temperatures as low as 30°F cause no harm. With judicious pruning from time to time, it may be kept to almost any desired size for many years. The cultivar 'Variegata' has variegated leaves with creamy white markings. This species is propagated by cuttings and seed.

PODOCARPUS MACROPHYLLUS
(Southern yew, Japanese yew)

Not a true yew (*Taxus*), the southern yew shrub is grown outdoors from zone 8 south and elsewhere is valued as a foliage houseplant. It may be grown into a slender column up to 5 feet tall and thus can fit into a narrow vertical space. The 3-inch, dark green, slender leaves are distinctive. This plant is a good candidate for an entry hall because it will tolerate cold drafts. A summer outdoors is necessary if it receives poor light throughout the winter when it is semidormant and not in active growth. Otherwise, bright, indirect light or curtain-filtered sun is important during the spring and summer when it is actively growing. Southern yew is propagated mostly by seed but also by cuttings.

RHAPIS EXCELSA
(Lady palm, bamboo palm)

The graceful bamboo palm is slow growing and, in time, develops slender stems, 4 to 8 feet tall. The leaves are fan shaped. Although it is adaptable to low interior light, it thrives in bright shade, with no exposure to direct sun. The leaf tips brown if the humidity is too low. A clump of this palm in a tub is most decorative and not demanding. *Rhapis humilis* (slender lady palm, reed rhapis) is similar but has even more slender, reedlike stems. Propagation is by rooted suckers, clump division, or seed.

RHODODENDRON SIMSII *CVS.*
(Indian azalea)

The small-leaf evergreen Indian azalea, if placed outdoors in partial shade for the summer months, will flower generously indoors for some weeks during the winter. The flowers are large and range from red to white, with many pastel shades and often with flecks or spots: they may be single or double. Flowering lasts longest on plants placed in east-facing windows and if cool temperatures (below 70°F) prevail. A sandy-humusy, acidic soil mix is required. Propagate by cuttings.

SAINTPAULIA IONANTHA
(African violet)

Few plants have achieved such wide popularity as the African violet, largely because it is a small houseplant that readily blooms indoors. It does best with an eastern exposure, protected from mid-day sun. The African violet is particularly well adapted to growing under lights (see Chapter 39). Temperatures between 65° and 75°F best meet its needs. If placed near a cool window, growth and flowering will stop. Commercially prepared soil for African violets is advisable. Because water, especially if cold, causes yellow spotting of African violet leaves, the plants should be watered from below. Place pots in saucers of water until the soil surface has darkened with moisture then drain off the remaining water. Since humidity must be moderately high (at least 30 percent) for African violets to thrive, a water-filled pebble tray beneath the plants is advisable, especially when low outdoor temperatures result in low interior humidity. African violet is propagated by leaf cuttings and fresh seed.

SANSEVIERIA TRIFASCIATA
(Snake plant)

One of the most common and sturdiest of all houseplants, the snake plant will survive poor growing conditions and amazing neglect. It is often used in combination with other plants in planter boxes as room dividers. The gray green leaves are rigid, erect, and pointed, and are marked with deep green bands. They are usually 1½ to 2 feet tall, but may reach as high as 3 feet. Snake plant is of the easiest possible culture. Although it will readily endure dry air; poor, indifferently watered

Sansevieria trifasciata

soil; and minimal light, it thrives in bright, filtered light with some direct sun exposure in the morning or late afternoon (which may induce blooming) in a moderately fertile soil that is allowed to dry between waterings. Propagation is by clump division and by rooted suckers.

SCHLUMBERGERA × BUCKLEYI
(Christmas cactus)

Often listed as *S. bridgesii* or *Zygocactus bridgesii*, Christmas cactus is a hybrid between two Brazilian epiphytic or semiepiphytic cacti that grow in the leafy debris trapped in the crotches of rain forest trees. As a houseplant, then, it follows that Christmas cactus grows best in a humusy, well-drained soil mix and, unlike

the treatment given most cacti, the soil should be kept fairly moist, especially in the spring and summer when most growth occurs. If watering is reduced during a two-month period in early fall and the plants are given a 14-hour period of uninterrupted darkness each night, a generous flush of flowering will develop for the holiday period. Without this special treatment, flowering will be lighter and spread over a longer period.

Schlumbergera truncata (Thanksgiving cactus), one of the parents of Christmas cactus, is similar except for the sharply toothed pads and earlier flowering period. It flowers heavily if given the same preflowering treatment a month or so earlier.

Both species benefit by being summered outdoors, preferably in hanging pots away from the ravages of slugs and snails. They

should be located in bright shade, with direct sun exposure only in the early morning or late in the day. Propagation of both is by cuttings.

SEDUM MORGANIANUM
(Donkey tail, burro's tail)

A trailing or pendent succulent native to partially shaded canyon walls in Mexico, donkey tail makes an exceptional houseplant, especially if the numerous stems are allowed to spill out of the pot, forming a green cascade. The effect is enhanced by grouping several plants in an 8- to 12-inch pot that is hung in a sunny window. Sandy, acidic soil kept on the dry side is best. Mealy bug is the most common pest.

SINNINGIA SPECIOSA
(Gloxinia)

Gloxinia grows from a tuber or bulblike underground stem. As its native environment, in parts of interior Brazil, is subject to months of prolonged drought each year, gloxinia goes into dormancy after flowering, during which all foliage dies back to the tuber. If kept lightly watered until growth resumes and then provided with a monthly application of African

Schlumbergera truncata

violet fertilizer, flowering resumes, usually in the spring. There are many cultivars with large cup-shaped flowers, ranging from purple or red to white and often spotted. An acidic soil mix and fairly humid atmosphere (30 percent or more) are beneficial. A shallow container with a fibrous, humusy medium that covers the tuber by about 1 inch placed in a location exposed to full sun or partial shade will give the best results. Flowers last longer if blooming plants are kept in the shade. Gloxinia is propagated by tuber division or seed.

SOLANUM PSEUDOCAPSICUM
(Jerusalem cherry)

Jerusalem cherry, a small, treelike shrub, is available as a Christmas plant and may either be kept for several years or grown each year from seed. The plant is best cut back somewhat in the spring, summered outdoors, and then brought back to a well-lighted but cool windowsill in the fall. Since it is not really a long-lived woody plant, it can be counted on for only several years, at which time it can be replaced from seed (saved from one of the "cherries") sown in early spring.

SPATHIPHYLLUM PATINII
(Peace lily)

Good growth under low-light conditions, such as near a north-facing window, make the peace lily an ideal houseplant. As this is a denizen of tropical bogs, the soil should never be allowed to dry out and humidity should be augmented with water-filled pebble trays beneath the pots, especially in the winter. When given sufficient indirect light, peace lily will reward the grower with white, flattish, callalike flowers on stalks rising above the dark, glossy, radiating foliage. This and several other similar species all do well in moist neutral to acidic soil. Peace lily is propagated by clump division.

STAPELIA GIGANTEA
(Giant carrion flower)

The giant carrion flower is a leafless, succulent South African native and a member of the milkweed family. It seldom grows taller than 8 inches and makes an interesting houseplant. If summered outdoors, it will later provide the grower with a 12- to 15-inch flower, which is chartreuse with reddish lines, that commands attention not only by its unusual appearance but also by the carrionlike aroma it emits. The odor can be contained by covering the plant with a clear plastic bag or placing it in a terrarium for the flowering period. As with other foul-smelling flowers (of which there are many in nature), the pollinators are flies. There are numerous other species, all propagated by seed.

STREPTOCARPUS ×
HYBRIDUS
(Cape primrose)

Streptocarpus hera

Like its close relative the African violet, Cape primrose has been hybridized and improved until it is much more showy and reliable in bloom than its wild ancestors. Its flowers are purple, red, pink, lavender, or white. Unlike the African violet, however, Cape primrose thrives in a cool atmosphere; summer heat causes it to cease flowering and decline. Soil requirements, however, are the same as for African violet, i.e., extra humus and constant moisture. Unlike African violet, Cape primrose may be watered from above without hazard to the foliage, which can achieve a spread of 18 inches. Flowering normally occurs in the winter and spring, with as many as a dozen or more blooms open at a time. As flower stalks arise from the leaf bases, only those leaves that have borne flowers should be removed. Cut these leaves lengthwise, remove the midrib, and set the cut edges shallowly in damp sand to produce new plants. With good vegetative growth in the summer and fall, a generous production of flowers is ensured the following winter and spring. Bright, filtered light with some direct exposure in the morning or late afternoon yields best results. Propagation is by leaf cuttings and seed.

SYNGONIUM PODOPHYLLUM
(Arrowhead vine)

Arrowhead vine is a vinelike tropical plant (often sold as *Nephthytis afzelii*) that is very often used satisfactorily in room-divider plantings, especially because it grows well in low interior light. It may be allowed to trail, or it may be trained to ascend a section of tree bark or an osmunda fiber post, clinging by means of aerial roots. There are numerous cultivars with variegated leaves, most of which retain the patterns even in quite low light. Of easiest culture, arrowhead vine, or African evergreen, as it is sometimes called, will grow for months in plain water, but it thrives in moist, acidic soil. Propagation is by division or seed.

TRADESCANTIA ZEBRINA
(Wandering Jew)

An easily grown creeping plant that covers extensive areas in forest shade in Central America, wandering Jew lends itself to culture in hanging pots and baskets. It does especially well in bright shade in fairly warm, moderately humid air. Excessively dry air results in the withering of older leaves and a thin, unkempt appearance. Rejuvenation occurs rapidly if plants are cut back severely and summered outdoors in shade. A sandy, acidic soil is best. Several other species are available, some with attractive flowers. All are easily propagated by cuttings.

OTHER HOUSEPLANTS

Name	Height*	Habit†	Exposure‡	Temperature Range (°F)ǀ Night	Day
Abutilon megapotamicum (flowering maple)	1–2'	Spreading	S to PSh	60	70
Acacia baileyana (Cootamundra wattle)	6–12'	Shrub, tree	S	50	65
Acalypha hispida (chenille plant)	2–4'	Shrubby	S	65	75
Adiantum spp. (maidenhair fern)	6–15"	Forms clumps	PSh to LSh	60	75
Aechmea fasciata	1½–2½'	Forms rosettes	LSh to DSh	65	75
A. fulgens var. *discolor*	1–1½'	Forms rosettes	LSh to DSh	65	75
A. miniata var. *discolor*	1–1½'	Forms rosettes	LSh to DSh	65	75
A. orlandiana (finger of God)	1–1½'	Forms rosettes	LSh to DSh	65	75
Agapanthus cultivars (lily of the Nile)	1–2'	Forms clumps	S to LSh	65	75
Agave americana (century plant)	1–2'	Forms immature rosettes	S	50	70
Allamanda cathartica (Brazilian buttercup)	6–8'	Climber	S	55	75
Aloe arborescens (octopus plant)	2–4'	Shrubby	S to PSh	55	70
A. aristata (torch plant, lace aloe)	About 1'	Forms clumps	S	60	75
A. variegata (tiger aloe)	6–9"	Forms dense clumps	S	60	75
Alstroemeria hybrids (Peruvian lily)	1–2'	From tuberous roots	S	65	80
Alyogyne huegelii (blue hibiscus)	2–4'	Shrub	S to PSh	60	80
Amomum compactum (round cardamom)	1½–2'	Forms upright clumps	PSh	55	70
Amorphophallus rivieri (devil's tongue)	2–3'	Erect stalk rises from large corm	PSh	60	75
Ananas comosus (pineapple)	1–2'	Forms dense rosettes	S	55	75
Anemone coronaria 'De Caen' (DeCaen anemone)	1–1½'	Leafy stems rise from tuber	PSh	65	75
Anisodontea × hypomandarum (African mallow)	4–6'	Shrub	S to PSh	60	75
Annona cherimola (cherimoya)	5–8'	Tree	PSh to LSh	65	75
Anthurium scheuzerianum (flamingo flower, tailflower)	1–2'	Forms clumps	LSh	70	80
Antigonon leptopus (coral vine)	6–12'	Tendril climber	S	60	75
Aphelandra squarrosa (zebra plant)	2–4'	Shrubby	S to PSh	60	75
Ardisia crenata (coralberry)	2–4'	Shrubby	S	55	70
Asarina barclaiana (climbing snapdragon)	5–10'	Twining climber	S	60	75
Asparagus densiflorus Sprengeri group (emerald asparagus fern)	2–4'	Arching	PSh	60	75
A. densiflorus 'Myers' (foxtail asparagus fern)	2–4'	Stiffly erect	PSh	60	75
A. macowanii (Oriental asparagus fern)	3–6'	Arching	PSh	60	75
A. setaceus (lacy asparagus fern)	4–8'	Erect	PSh	60	75
Asplenium nidus (bird's-nest fern)	3–6'	Creeping	S to PSh	60	75
Astrophytum ornatum (star cactus)	About 1'	Globular to columnar	S	60	80
Aucuba japonica 'Varieata' (gold-dust bush)	2–4'	Shrub	LSh to DSh	55	70
Bambusa multiplex (dwarf bamboo)	3–10'	Forms slender canes	S to PSh	65	80
Billbergia nutans (friendship plant, queen's tears)	1½–2'	Forms clumps	PSh	60	75
B. pyramidalis (pyramidal billbergia)	1–1½'	Forms clumps	PSh	60	75
Bougainvillea glabra 'Sanderiana'	3–6'	Shrub	S	50	65
Bouvardia ternifolia	2–3'	Shrub	LSh	55	70
Brassavola nodosa (Queen of the night orchid)	6–12"	Forms clumps	PSh	65	75
Browallia speciosa (sapphire plant)	4–8"	Spreading	S	55	65
Brugmansia suaveolens (angel's trumpet)	3–6'	Shrub	PSh	65	75

OTHER HOUSEPLANTS

Humidity[||]	Soil Requirements[#]	Comments
Moderate	Moist, acidic to neutral	Flowers red to yellow, everblooming
Moderate	Ordinary mix, moist	Foliage blue-green, finely divided; flowers in balls, yellow
Moderate	Moist, neutral	Pendent red tassels, in spring to fall
High	Moist, acidic	Foliage delicate
Moderate to high	Moist, acidic	Flowers blue; bracts pink, borne once a year
Moderate to high	Moist, acidic	Flowers blue-purple; bracts red, borne once a year
Moderate to high	Moist, acidic	Foliage olive, red-brown on back; flowers blue; bracts red, borne once a year
Moderate to high	Moist, acidic	Foliage spotted beneath; flowers yellow; bracts red, borne once a year
Moderate	Moist, neutral	Flowers clustered, blue, on scapes, in summer
Low	Sandy, dry, neutral	Foliage bold; can take lower temperatures in the winter
Moderate	Sandy, moist, acidic	Flowers large, fragrant, yellow, in spring and summer
Low	Sandy, dry, neutral	Foliage forms dense thicket
Low	Sandy, dry, neutral	Foliage heavy, thick
Low	Sandy, dry neutral	Foliage thick, white blotched
Moderate	Sandy, moist, acidic	Flowers pink, salmon, white, varicolor, in summer
Moderate to high	Moist, neutral	Flowers 3½ inches wide, lilac to red-violet, in summer
Moderate to high	Moist, acidic	Foliage aromatic; flowers yellow, borne intermittently
Moderate	Moist, acidic	Flower, malodorous, in winter or spring; followed by large divided leaf on mottled stalk
Moderate to high	Moist, neutral	Foliage rigid blue-green, often variegated
Moderate	Moist, neutral	Flowers red or violet to white in spring
Moderate	Moist, neutral	Flowers numerous red-lilac, in spring and summer
Moderate	Moist, neutral	Foliage large, pendent, aromatic
High	Sandy, moist, acidic	Foliage lustrons; flowers red, borne intermittently
Moderate	Moist, neutral	Flowers, rose pink, mostly in summer
Moderate to high	Moist, acidic	Foliage white veined, flowers yellow, in fall
Moderate	Moist, neutral	Berries long-lasting, red, in fall and winter
Moderate	Moist; neutral	Flowers purple, tubular, in spring and summer
Moderate	Moist to dry, neutral	Foliage light green, needlelike
Moderate	Moist to dry, neutral	Foliage, short, congested, needlelike
Moderate	Moist to dry, neutral	Foliage light green, tufted stems spring; needs room
Moderate	Moist to dry, neutral	Foliage needlelike, in flat sprays; stems thorny
High	Moist to wet, alkaline	Epiphyte; foliage undivided
Dry	Gritty, dry to moist, neutral	Flowers yellow, in spring, on old plants
Moderate	Moist, acidic	Foliage deep green, spotted yellow
Moderate	Humusy, moist, neutral	Foliage scattered blue-green
Moderate	Moist, acidic	Epiphyte; foliage gray green; flowers pendent, in clusters, bluish; bracts pink, in winter
Moderate	Moist, acidic	Epiphyte; flowers in upright clusters, red; bracts pink, in winter
Moderate	Moist, alkaline	Bracts red, purple, pink, or salmon, in summer outdoors
Moderate	Moist, neutral	Flowers rose pink to red, in winter and spring
High	Osmunda or bark, moist	Epiphyte; flowers fragrant at night, greenish white, in fall and winter
Moderate	Moist, acidic	Annual; flowers purple or white, in spring and summer; good in baskets
High	Moist, acidic	Flowers 9 to 12 inches long, pendent, white, yellow, or pink, everblooming

(continues)

OTHER HOUSEPLANTS

Humidity[||]	Soil Requirements[#]	Comments
High	Moist, acidic	Flowers purple to lavender, then white, in winter
Moderate	Sandy, moist, neutral	Foliage oak like, metallic blue sheen
Moderate	Sandy, moist, acidic	Evergreen, foliage small, lustrous
High	Moist, acidic	Foliage long, narrow
High	Moist, acidic	Foliage variously blotched dark green and purple
High	Moist, acidic	Foliage glossy, variegated yellow in lines
High	Moist, acidic	Flowers yellow, orange red, or purple, usually spotted about six months from seed
Moderate	Moist, acidic	Flowers red, pink, or white, in winter to early spring
Moderate	Moist, alkaline	Flowers blue or white, in winter and spring
Moderate to high	Moist, acidic	Fruit small, erect, purple aging to red, in fall and winter
Moderate	Moist, neutral	Flowers fragrant, white, borne intermittently
High	Osmunda or bark, moist	Epiphyte; flowers large, purple, lavender, or white, borne once a year
Low	Gritty, dry, neutral	Covered with shaggy white hairs
Low to moderate	Gritty sand, moist, neutral	Flowers large, nocturnal, white, mostly in spring and summer
Moderate	Moist, acidic	Flowers fragrant, tubular, white, in winter and spring
Moderate	Moist, acidic	Flowers red to red-violet, in winter and spring
Moderate	Moist, acidic	Flowers fragrant, tubular, white, in winter and spring
Moderate	Moist, neutral	Remains small if kept potbound
Moderate	Moist, acidic to neutral	Useful for a few weeks; may rejuvenate in summer outdoors
Moderate	Moist, neutral	Foliage glossy, young leaves reddish
Moderate	Moist, alkaline	Foliage glossy, leathery, undivided
Moderate	Moist, alkaline	Foliage numerous, small five-parted
Moderate	Moist, neutral	Foliage glossy leaves; fruit ornamental, mostly in winter and spring
Moderate	Moist, neutral	Foliage glossy; fruit yellow, mostly winter and spring
Moderate	Moist, neutral	Fast-growing but slow to fruit
Moderate	Moist, neutral	Fruit mostly in winter and spring; bears well if summered outdoors
Moderate	Moist, neutral	Foliage ornamental; fruit usually few, in winter and spring
Moderate	Moist, neutral	Fruit mostly in winter and spring; bears well if summered outdoors
Low	Gritty, dry, neutral	Covered with white bristles; flowers wine red, mostly in spring
Moderate	Moist, neutral	Flowers pink and purple, in spring and summer
Moderate	Moist, neutral	Flowers red, in spring and summer
High	Moist, alkaline	Foliage variously shaped, multicolored
Moderate to high	Moist, neutral	Red or yellow flowers, spring to fall; basket plant
Moderate to high	Moist, alkaline	Leaves maroon, often variegated
High	Moist, acidic	Glossy foliage, red stems; orange flowers
High	Moist, acidic	Red flowers in winter
High	Moist, acidic	Orange to salmon pink flowers in summer; humidity essential
High	Moist, acidic	Leaves purplish, gold-banded, silvery beneath
Moderate	Moist, neutral	Flowers lavender, pink, or white, in summer to fall
Moderate	Moist, neutral	Flowers red to white; winter and spring; dormant in summer
High	Osmunda or bark, moist	Epiphyte; flowers white and green, borne once a year

(continues)

OTHER HOUSEPLANTS (*continued*)

Name	Height*	Habit†	Exposure‡	Temperature Range (°F)⌡ Night	Day
Cymbalaria muralis (Kennilworth ivy)	1–2'	Slender pendent stems	S to Psh	60	70
Cyperus albostriatus (dwarf umbrella plant)	8–12"	Sedge	PSh	65	75
C. alternifolius (umbrella plant)	2–3'	Sedge	PSh to LSh	65	75
Delairea odorata (German ivy, parlor ivy)	3–6'	Twining climber	S to PSh	55	65
Dichorisandra thyrsiflora (climbing spiderwort)	3–4'	Climber	PSh	65	75
Dioscorea batatas (yam)	3–6'	Twining climber	PSh	65	75
D. bulbifera (air potato)	3–6'	Erect	PSh	65	75
Diosma ericoides (breath-of-heaven)	1–1½'	Upright, branched	PSh	60	70
Dracunculus vulgaris (devil's tongue, dragon arum)	1½'	Erect stalks from large corms	PSh	60	75
Drepanostachyum falcatum (sickle bamboo)	3–5'	Forms clumps	S to PSh	65	75
Duranta erecta (pigeon berry, sky flower)	4–6'	Upright	S	60	75
Dyckia brevifolia (dyckia)	6–10"	Forms stiff rosettes	S	60	80
Echeveria setosa (hairy echeveria)	3–5"	Forms rosettes	S	60	70
Echinopsis aurea (golden-lily cactus)	6–12"	Columnar	S	50	70
Epidendrum × o'brienianum (scarlet orchid)	2–4'	Erect canelike stems	PSh	60	75
Epiphyllum hybrids (orchid cactus)	2–3'	Flattened spreading stems	PSh	60	75
E. oxyphyllum (queen of the night)	2–3'	Winged stems	PSh	60	75
Erica melanthera (heath)	1½–3'	Twiggy shrub	S	50	65
Eucharis × grandiflora (Amazon lily)	1–2'	Forms upright clumps from bulbs	S	60	75
Evolvulus glomeratus (blue daze)	1–2'	Slender upright	S	60	75
Exacum affine (Persian violet)	6–12"	Compact	PSh to LSh	55	70
Feijoa sellowiana (pineapple guava)	3–6'	Shrub	S	60	75
Galphimia glauca (gold shower)	3–4'	Shrub	S to PSh	60	75
Gardenia thunbergia (white gardenia)	4–8'	Shrub, treelet	PSh	50	70
Gesneria cuneifolia	6–8"	Compact	PSh	65	75
Gloriosa superba (climbing lily)	4–8'	Tendril climber	S	55	70
Goethea strictiflora	1–2'	Shrub	S to PSh	60	75
Guzmania zahnii	1½–2'	Forms dense, leafy rosettes	Sh	65	75
Gymnocalycium spp. (ball cactus)	4–6"	Globular	S	50	65
Hardenbergia violacea (purple coral pea)	4–6'	Twining climber	S to PSh	60	75
Hatiora salicornioides (bottle cactus, drunkard's dream)	1–2'	Slender stems	S	55	70
Hedychium coronarium (white ginger lily)	4–6'	Forms clumps	PSh	60	75
H. flavescens (yellow ginger lily)	4–6'	Forms clumps	PSh	60	75
H. greenei (red ginger lily)	4–6'	Forms clumps	PSh	60	75
Heliconia psittacorum (parrot flower)	2–5'	Forms clumps	S	65	80
Hermannia verticillata (honeybells)	About 1'	Creeping stems	S to Psh	55	65
Hibiscus rosa-sinensis (Chinese hibiscus)	2–6'	Shrub	S to PSh	60	75
Hoffmannia bullata (corduroy plant, tafeta plant)	2–3'	Shrubby	LSh	60	70
Howea belmoreana (Belmore sentry palm, curly palm)	2–4'	Palm	PSh to DSh	60	70
Hydrangea macrophylla (common hydrangea)	2–3'	Shrubby	PSh	55	65
Hylotelephium sieboldii (creeping pink sedum)	6–12"	Pendent	S	60	70

OTHER HOUSEPLANTS

Humidity[||]	Soil Requirements[#]	Comments
Moderate	Moist, acidic	Flowers lilac and yellow, in summer; good basket plant
Moderate	Moist, alkaline	Like *C. alternifolius* but smaller, do not use water basin
High	Mud, wet, alkaline	Foliage graceful; set pot in water-filled saucer
Moderate	Moist, neutral	Foliage lobed, often variegated, ivylike
High	Moist, sandy, acidic	Flowers blue, yellow stamens, in spring through fall
Moderate	Moist, neutral	Foliage attractive
Moderate	Moist, neutral	Stems bear tubers
Moderate	Moist, neutral	Foliage aromatic, flowers numerous, small, white, in spring
Moderate	Moist, acidic	Flowers malodorous, in winter or early spring followed large divided leaf on mottled stalk
Moderate	Moist, neutral	Foliage blue-green; stems yellow-green
Moderate	Moist, neutral	Flowers purple to white
Low	Gritty sand, dry, neutral	Flowers on 2- to 3-foot spike, yellow-orange
Low	Moist to dry, neutral	Foliage fleshy, spiraled
Low	Gritty, dry, neutral	Flowers large, satiny, yellow, in spring
Moderate	Sphagnum, moist	Epiphyte; flowers red-orange, in spring and summer
Moderate to high	Wood chips, moist, acidic	Epiphyte; flowers large, red, in winter and spring
Moderate to high	Wood chips, moist, acidic	Epiphyte, flowers large, fragrant, nocturnal, whiter in winter and spring
Moderate	Moist, neutral	Flowers pink to white, in spring and summer
High	Moist, acidic	Foliage broad, strap shaped; flowers large, white, in summer and fall
Moderate	Moist, neutral	Flowers small, funnel-like, blue, in spring and summer
Moderate	Moist, neutral to acidic	Flowers blue and yellow, in summer
Moderate	Moist, neutral	Flowers fleshy, purple and white, in winter and spring, fruit green and red
Moderate	Moist, acidic	Foliage leathery; flowers yellow, in winter and spring
Moderate	Moist, acidic	Flowers white, in winter and spring; easier to grow than *G. augusta*
High	Sandy, moist, acidic	Flowers red, orange, pink, and yellow, in spring
Moderate	Sandy, moist, acidic	Flowers yellow and red, in summer
Moderate	Moist, acidic	Foliage large; flowers red to cream, red veins, in spring and summer
High	Bark chips, moist	Epiphyte; foliage red at base, with maroon; flowers cream; bracts yellow to red in summer
Low	Gritty, dry, neutral	Flowers red, pink, yellow, or white, in spring and summer
Moderate	Moist, neutral	Flowers purple, pink, or white; in winter and spring
High	Gritty, moist, acidic	Stems with swellings; flowers yellow to orange, in spring
High	Moist, acidic	Foliage large; flowers white, in spring and summer
High	Moist, acidic	Foliage large; flowers yellow, in spring and summer
High	Moist, acidic	Foliage large, red-green; flowers red, in spring and summer
High	Sandy, moist; acidic	Foliage cannalike; flowers red-orange, in spring and summer
Moderate	Moist, acidic	Flowers pendent; yellow, in summer
Moderate	Moist, neutral	Flowers large red, orange, yellow, pink, or bicolored, in spring to fall
High	Moist, neutral	Foliage greenish brown, deeply impressed veins
Moderate	Moist, neutral	Juvenile form tolerates low interior light
Moderate	Moist, neutral to acidic	Flowers blue or pink; best grown outdoors in summer
Low	Sandy, moist, acidic	Culture same as for *Sedum morganianum*

(continues)

OTHER HOUSEPLANTS (continued)

Name	Height*	Habit†	Exposure‡	Temperature Range (°F)ʲ Night	Day
Hypericum aegypticum (dwarf shrubby St. John'swort)	1–2'	Shrubby	S	60	70
Impatiens hawkeri (New Guinea impatiens)	10–15"	Succulent stems	S to PSh	60	75
I. niamniamensis (Congo cockatoo)	1–2'	Shrubby	PSh	65	75
Iresine herbstii (beefsteak plant, bloodleaf)	2–3'	Forms mats	S to PSh	65	75
Ixora coccinea (flame of the woods)	2–4'	Shrub	S	60	75
Jasminum officinale (common jasmine)	2–4'	Shrub	PSh	50	65
J. polyanthum (climbing white jasmine)	4–8'	Climber	PSh	50	65
J. sambac (Indian jasmine, Arabian jasmine)	4–8'	Climber	PSh	50	65
Justicia carnea (Brazilian plume, flamingo flower)	3–6'	Shrubby	S	60	70
Kaempferia roscoeana (peacock plant)	About 1'	Horizontal	PSh	60	70
Kalanchoe daigremontiana (good-luck plant)	1–2'	Erect, unbranched	S	55	65
K. pinnata (air plant, floppers, leaf-of-life)	2–3'	Erect, unbranched	S	55	65
K. tomentosa (panda plant)	1–2'	Erect, few branches	S	55	65
Kohleria cvs.	1–2'	Erect, from tuber	PSh	60	70
Lachenalia aloides (Cape cowslip)	About 1'	Two leaves, from bulb	S to PSh	60	70
Lantana camara		Shrub	S to PSh	65	80
L. montevidensis (creeping lantana)	1–2'	Spreading	S to PSh	60	75
Laurus nobilis (sweet bay)	4–8'	Shrub	S to PSh	60	70
Ledebouria socialis (silver squill)	4–6"	Forms clumps	S to PSh	60	70
Leea amabilis (velvet leaf)	1–2'	Shrub	PSh	60	70
L. coccinea (West Indian holly)	1–2'	Shrub	Psh	60	75
Lepismium cruciforme	2–3'	Forms elongated pads	PSh	60	75
Leptospermum scoparium (Australian tea rose)	2–4'	Shrub	S	55	65
Licuala spinosa (palas palm)	3–4'	Forms clumps	S to PSh	65	80
Lithops spp. (living stone, pebble plant)	1–3"	Bilobed, stemless	S	65	75
Lotus bertholotii (coral gem, winged pea)	2–3'	Cascading	S	60	75
Ludisia discolor (jewel orchid)	6–12"	Spreading	LSh	65	75
Malpighia coccigera (Singapore holly)	2–3'	Shrub	LSh	60	70
Malvaviscus arboreus (turk's-cap hibiscus, sleepy hibiscus)	2–4'	Shrub	S	60	75
Mammillaria bocasana (powder-puff cactus)	4–6"	Globose, forms clumps	S	65	80
M. bombycina (silken pincushion cactus)	6–9"	Columnar	S	65	80
M. candida (white-ball cactus)	4–6"	Globose	S	65	80
M. elongata (finger cactus)	6–9"	Columnar, forms clumps	S	65	80
M. gracilis (slender finger cactus)	4–6"	Columnar, forms clumps	S	65	80
M. haageana (woolly-head cactus)	4–7"	Globose	S	65	80
M. hahniana (Hahn's mammillaria)	6–9"	Short, columnar	S	65	80
M. plumosa (woolly-head cactus)	4–6"	Globose, forms clumps	S	65	80
M. prolifera (clustered mammillaria)	3–4"	Forms denses clumps	S	65	80
M. zeilmanniana (pincushion cactus)	2–3" × 4–6"	Forms clumps	S	65	80
Mandevilla × amabilis (pink jasmine)	6–8'	Twining climber	S to PSh	60	75
M. sanderi (Brazilian jasmine)	6–8'	Twining climber	S to PSh	60	75

OTHER HOUSEPLANTS

Humidity[||]	Soil Requirements[#]	Comments
Moderate	Moist, neutral	Flowers, yellow, everblooming
High	Moist, acidic	Foliage often variegated; flowers purple, red, and pink, in spring to fall
Moderate	Moist, acidic	Flowers red and yellow, in spring to fall
Moderate	Moist, neutral	Foliage red and purple; good ground cover
High	Moist, neutral to acidic	Flowers red, orange, yellow, or white, in spring to fall
High	Moist, acidic	Flowers, fragrant, white, in summer to fall
High	Moist, acidic	Flowers white, in; summer
Moderate	Moist, acidic	Flowers fragrant, white, in spring to fall
Moderate	Moist, neutral	Flowers pink; in summer and fall
High	Moist, acidic	Foliage two irridescent bronzy leaves; flowers lavender, in summer
Moderate	Moist to dry, neutral	Flowers gray violet; in summer to winter; plantlets on leaf margins
Moderate	Moist to dry, neutral	Flowers reddish green; in summer to winter; plantlets in leaf notches
Moderate	Moist to dry, neutral	Foliage thick, hairy; flowers yellow-green; in summer to winter
Moderate	Moist, acidic	Flowers red, pink, or orange, speckled; in spring
Moderate	Moist, neutral to acidic	Flowers yellow with red or purple; in winter
Moderate	Moist, neutral	Flowers red, orange, yellow and/or pink; in summer and fall
Moderate	Moist, neutral	Foliage musk scented; flowers lilac to purple; in summer and fall
Moderate	Moist, neutral	Foliage large, glossy; very adaptable
Moderate	Moist, acidic	Foliage fleshy, silvery purple in summer; flowers greenish
High	Moist, acidic	Foliage bronzy, white veins, velvety
Moderate	Moist, acidic	Foliage glossy; flower buds red, opening to pink, in spring
Moderate	Compost, moist, acidic	Flowers small, white, borne on pad margins, in winter and spring
Moderate	Sandy-humusy, moist, acidic	Foliage aromatic; flowers white pink, or red; in spring and summer
High	Moist, neutral	Stemless; foliage spine edged
Low	Sandy, dry, acidic	Succulent; flowers white or yellow, in summer to winter
Moderate	Sandy, moist to dry, neutral	Flowers red in summer and tall; superior basket plant
Moderate to high	Compost and bark, moist, acidic	Foliage velvety, red-maroon; flowers white, borne once a year
Moderate	Moist, neutral	Foliage glossy, some spine edged; intermittent
Moderate	Moist, neutral to acidic	Flowers pendent, partly opening, red, in summer to winter
Low	Gritty, moist to dry, neutral	Foliage white hairy, covered with red hooked spines; flowers pale pink, in spring
Low	Gritty, moist to dry, neutral	Foliage white hairy, hooked red spines; flowers pink in spring
Low	Gritty, moist to dry, neutral	Covered with white spines; flowers pink, in spring
Low	Gritty, moist to dry, neutral	Spines yellow to red; flowers light yellow, in spring
Low	Gritty, moist to dry, neutral	Covered with white spines; flowers cream with pink in spring
Low	Gritty, moist to dry, neutral	Foliage usually woolly, ban to dark brown spines; flowers pinkish purple, in spring
Low	Gritty, moist to dry, neutral	Foliage covered with white bristly hairs; flowers deep pink, inspring
Low	Gritty, moist to dry, neutral	Flowers rare, white to pink, in winter
Low	Gritty, moist to dry, neutral	Flowers yellow, often pink tinged, in spring
Low	Gritty, moist to dry, neutral	Flowers pink to purple; in spines white and brown; spring
Moderate	Moist, acidic	Flowers rose pink; in spring and summer
Moderate	Moist, acidic	Flowers pink and yellow; in spring and summer

(continues)

OTHER HOUSEPLANTS (*continued*)

Name	Height*	Habit†	Exposure‡	Temperature Range (°F)ǀ	
				Night	Day
Manettia luteoerubra (firecracker vine)	6–8'	Twining climber	LSh	60	75
Microcoelum weddellianum (Weddell palm)	6–10'	Palm	LSh to DSh	60	70
Miltonia cultivars (pansy orchid)	8–15"	Creeping	S to PSh	60	70
Mitriostigma axillare (African gardenia)	1–3'	Shrub	PSh	55	70
Murraya paniculata (orange jessamine)	4–8'	Shrub	S to PSh	60	75
Musa velutina (dwarf banana)	3–5'	Erect, unbranched	S to PSh	60	75
Myrsine africana (African boxwood)	2–3'	Shrub	S to PSh	60	75
Myrtus communis (myrtle, Swedish myrtle)	4–8'	Shrub	S	55	70
Narcissus cyclamineus 'Tête-à-Tête' (dwarf daffodil)	6–9"	Forms clumps from bulb	S to PSh	60	70
Nautilocalyx lynchii	1–2'	Erect	S to PSh	65	75
Nematanthus wettsteinii	1–1½'	Pendent	S to PSh	65	75
Neomarica northiana (twelve apostles, walking iris)	1½–2½'	Irislike	PSh	55	70
Neoregelia spectabilis (fingernail plant)	2–3'	Forms tight rosettes	PSh to LSh	60	75
Nerium oleander	2–8'	Shrub	S	60	70
Nolina recurvata (bottle palm, ponytail plant)	4–8'	Palm	S	60	70
Ochna serrulata (Mickey-Mouse berry)	3–6'		S to PSh	60	70
Oplismenus hirtellus 'Variegatus' (basket grass)	2–3'	Grass	S to PSh	60	75
Orbea variegata (starfish flower, toad cactus)	4–6'	Forms clumps	S	60	75
Oreocereus celsianus (mountain cactus)	2½–4'	Cylindrical	S	60	70
Osmanthus fragrans (sweet olive, sweet tea)	1–3'	Shrub	S	55	65
O. heterophyllus 'Variegatus' (variegated holly-olive)	2–4'	Shrub	S to PSh	55	65
Oxalis bowiei (giant pink oxalis)	6–12"	Forms clumps	PSh	60	70
O. megalorrhiza (greenhouse clover)	3–6"	Forms clumps	LSh to PSh	60	75
O. ortgiesii (tree oxalis, fishtail plant)	1–2'	Erect	LSh	60	70
O. pes-caprae (Bermuda buttercup)	3–6'	Forms clumps	PSh	60	75
O. purpurea 'Grand Duchess' (purple oxalis)	4–8"	Forms clumps	PSh	60	70
O. rubra (window-box oxalis)	8–12"	Forms clumps	PSh	60	70
O. tetraphylla (lucky clover, good-luck plant)	1–1½	Forms clumps	PSh	60	70
O. vulcanicola (red-velvet oxalis)	1–2'	Erect	S to PSh	60	70
Pachycereus marginatus (organ-pipe cactus)	3–6'	Columnar	S	65	75
Pachypodium lamerei (Madagascar palm)	5–8'	Erect, cactuslike	S	55	70
Pachystachys lutea (lollipop flower)	2–4'	Shrub	PSh	65	80
Pandanus veitchii (screw pine)	2–8'	Shrubby	PSh to LSh	65	80
Parodia aureispina (yellow Tom Thumb cactus)	About 2½"	Globose	S	60	75
P. leninghausii (golden-club cactus)	1–2'	Columnar	S	60	75
P. microsperma (red Tom Thumb cactus)	6–9"	Globose	S	60	75
P. scopa (silver-ball cactus)	1–2'	Globose	S	60	75
Passiflora alatocaerulea (passion flower)	6–10'	Tendril climber	S	60	75
P. graessneri (golden-ball cactus)	6–9"	Globose	S	60	75
P. vitifolia (red passion flower)	6–10'	Tendril climber, rangy	S	65	80
Pedilanthus tithymaloides ssp. *smallii* 'Variegata' (Jacob's ladder bush)	2–3'	Shrub	S	65	80

OTHER HOUSEPLANTS

Humidity[‖]	Soil Requirements[#]	Comments
Moderate to high	Moist, neutral	Flowers red, yellow tipped; in summer and fall
Moderate	Moist, neutral	Fronds long, arching
Moderate	Osmunda fiber, moist	Epiphyte; flowers white, red, pink, or yellow; borne once a year
Moderate	Moist, neutral	Flowers white or pink; in spring
Moderate	Moist, acidic	Flowers white fragrant; borne intermittently
Moderate	Moist, neutral	Foliage grows to 3 feet; flowers white, borne intermittently; fruit ripening pink
Moderate	Moist, neutral	Foliage aromatic; berries blue-violet, in summer and fall
Moderate	Moist, neutral	Foliage aromatic; flowers white to pale pink; in spring and summer
Moderate	Moist, acidic	Flowers small, trumpets, yellow, in 3½ months, last for about three weeks
High	Moist, acidic	Gesneriad; foliage showy; flowers yellow, in spring
High	Moist, acidic	Gesneriad; foliage glossy; flowers orange, in spring
Moderate	Moist, acidic	Flowers borne on tip-rooting stalks; various colors, in spring and summer
High	Moist, acidic	Foliage tipped red; flowers purple; in winter and spring
Moderate	Moist, neutral	Flowers red to white, in summer
Low	Gritty, dry, neutral	Foliage spiky mop; swollen trunk base
Moderate	Moist, neutral	Flowers yellow, berries black on red receptacle; in summer
Moderate	Moist, neutral	Foliage striped white and pink
Low	Sandy, moist to dry, neutral	Flowers pale purplish green; in spring and summer
Low	Gritty, moist to dry, neutral	Covered with brown spines and white hairs; in spring
Moderate	Sandy clay, moist, neutral	Foliage glossy; flowers white, in summer
Moderate	Moist, neutral	Foliage variegated, hollylike
Moderate	Sandy-humusy, moist, neutral	Foliage purplish; flowers rose red, in summer and fall
Moderate to high	Moist, neutral	Flowers yellow, borne on thick stalks; in summer and fall
Moderate	Fertile, moist neutral	Foliage dark; flowers profuse, yellow, in spring to winter
Moderate	Moist, neutral	Foliage bright green; flowers yellow, in spring and summer
Moderate	Moist, neutral	Foliage purple; flowers lavender to white; in fall and winter
Moderate	Moist, neutral	Flowers rose pink, everblooming
Moderate	Moist, neutral	Foliage small, cloverlike, green; flowers small, rose pink, in summer
Moderate	Moist, acidic	Foliage purplish flowers yellow, in summer and fall
Low	Gritty, moist to dry, neutral	Stems stately green, fluted
Moderate to dry	Gritty, moist, neutral	Foliage glossy, dark; flowers white
Moderate	Moist, neutral	Foliage deeply reined; flowers white; bracts yellow, in summer
High	Moist, neutral	Foliage glossy, spiraled, finely saw edged
Low	Gritty sand, dry, neutral	Flowers yellow, in spring and summer
Low	Gritty sand, dry, neutral	Spines yellow-brown; flowers yellow, in summer
Low	Gritty sand, dry, neutral	Flowers blood red; in spring and summer
Low	Sandy-humusy, moist, neutral	Spines silvery; flowers yellow; in summer
High	Moist, neutral to acidic	Flowers purplish green, everblooming
Low	Gritty sand, dry, neutral	Spines golden yellow; flowers yellow; in spring
High	Moist, neutral to acid	Flowers scarlet, in spring and summer
Moderate	Sandy, moist to dry, acidic	Succulent; stems zigzag, foliage two-ranked, variegated, flowers pink, borne intermittently

(continues)

OTHER HOUSEPLANTS (*continued*)

Name	Height*	Habit†	Exposure‡	Temperature Range (°F)ʲ	
				Night	Day
Pelargonium capitatum (rose-scented geranium, attar of roses)	1–2'	Shrubby	S	60	70
P. crispum (lemon geranium)	1½–2½'	Shrubby	S	60	70
P. denticulatum (fernleaf geranium)	3–4'	Shrubby	S	60	70
P. domesticum (regal geranium)	1½–2½'	Shrubby	S	60	70
P. fragrans (fragrant geranium)	1–1½'	Shrubby	S	60	70
P. graveolens (rose-scented geranium)	3–4'	Shrubby	S	60	70
P. nervosum (lime geranium)	1–1½'	Shrubby	S	60	70
P. odoratissimum (apple geranium)	6–12"	Trailing	S	60	70
P. quercifolium (oakleaf geranium, almond geranium)	3–4'	Shrubby	S	60	70
P. scabrum 'M. Minon' (apricot geranium)	2–3'	Shrubby	S	60	70
P. tomentosum (peppermint geranium)	1–1½'	Shrubby	S	60	70
Pellaea rotundifolia (cliff brake)	4–7"	Fern	LSh to DSh	60	70
Pellionia pulchra (rainbow vine)	6–12"	Trailing	LSh	65	75
P. repens (trailing watermelon begonia)	1–1½'	Trailing	LSh	65	75
Pentas lanceolata (Egyptian star)	1–2'	Bushy	S	65	80
Peperomia caperata 'Emerald Ripple' (green ripple pepper)	6–9"	Upright	LSh	65	75
P. cubensis 'Variegata' (Cuban pepper)	1–2'	Creeping	LSh	65	75
P. fraseri (flowering pepper, mignonette pepper)	1–1½'	Upright	LSh	65	75
P. griseoargentea (silverleaf pepper)	8–10"	Upright	PSh to LSh	65	75
P. marmorata 'Silver Heart' (silver heart pepper)	1–1½'	Upright	LSh	65	75
P. orba 'Pixie' (teardrop pepper)	5–7"	Ascending	LSh	65	75
Pericallis × hybrida (florist's cineraria)	1–2'	Bushy	LSh	55	65
Philodendron bipennifolium (fiddlehead philodendron)	5–10'	Climbing	LSh to DSh	65	75
P. bipinnatifidum (tree philodendron)	3–6'	Erect or ascending	LSh	65	75
P. erubescens (redleaf philodendron)	5–10'	Climbing	LSh	65	75
P. domesticum (spade-leaf philodendron)	5–10'	Climbing	LSh	65	75
P. wendlandii (bird's-nest philodendron)	3–6'	Erect or trailing	LSh	65	75
Pilea cadierei (aluminum plant)	1–1½'	Erect to spreading	PSh	65	75
Plectranthus australis (Swedish ivy)	2–3'	Pendent	PSh	60	70
Polyscias filicifolia (fern-leaf aralia)	4–8'	Shrub	PSh	65	75
P. quilfoylei 'Victoriae' (lace aralia)	3–6'	Shrub	PSh	65	75
P. scutellaria 'Balfourii' (Balfour aralia)	4–8'	Shrub	PSh	65	75
Primula vulgaris (English primrose)	4–8"	Forms rosettes	PSh to LSh	55	65
Psychopsis krameriana (butterfly orchid)	2–3'	Form, clumps	S	60	70
Punica granatum 'Nana' (dwarf pomegranate)	1–2'	Twiggy shrub	S to PSh	65	80
Rebutia kupperiana (brown-spine crown cactus)	3–4"	Often forms clumps	S to PSh	65	90
R. miniscula (red crown cactus)	2–3"	Globose	S to PSh	65	90
Rivina humilis (bloodberry)	1–2'	Bushy	S	65	80
Polysticum tsussimense (miniature shield fern)	4–8'	Fern	LSh	60	70
Portulacaria afra (elephant bush)	4–8'	Shrub	S	60	70
Rondeletia odorata (Panama rose)	3–6'	Shrub	LSh	60	75

OTHER HOUSEPLANTS

Humidity[ll]	Soil Requirements[#]	Comments
Moderate	Gritty, moist, neutral	Foliage aromatic; flowers pinkish purple, in spring and summer
Moderate	Gritty, moist, neutral	Foliage aromatic; flowers pink, red veined, in spring and summer
Moderate	Gritty, moist, neutral	Foliage aromatic; flowers pink, purple veined; in spring and summer
Moderate	Gritty, moist, neutral	Foliage rigid; flowers purple to white, large; in spring and summer
Moderate	Gritty, moist, neutral	Flowers white with red; in spring and summer; cultivars with variegated foliage
Moderate	Gritty, moist, neutral	Flowers white to pale pink, veined purple; in spring and summer
Moderate	Gritty, moist, neutral	Flowers rose pink with red; in spring and summer
Moderate	Gritty, moist, neutral	Flowers white with red veins, in spring and summer
Moderate	Gritty, moist, neutral	Flowers purplish pink with darker pink, in spring and summer
Moderate	Gritty, moist, neutral	Foliage glossy, dark; flowers deep rose pink, scented apricot; in spring and summer
Moderate	Gritty, moist, neutral	Flowers white with purple, in spring and summer
High	Moist, acidic	Foliage with circular leaflets
Moderate	Peaty, moist, acidic	Stems and foliage marked with purple
Moderate	Peaty, moist, acidic	Foliage purplish, black veined; good basket plant
High	Moist, neutral to acidic	Flowers red, pink, blue, lavender, or white, in spring to fall
Moderate	Moist, neutral to acidic	Foliage bright green, corrugated
Moderate	Moist, neutral to acidic	Foliage variegated
Moderate	Moist, neutral to acidic	Flower spikes white; in summer
Moderate	Moist, neutral to acidic	Foliage clustered, silvery, heart shaped
Moderate	Moist, neutral to acidic	Foliage silvery between veins
Moderate	Moist, neutral to acidic	Foliage dense
Moderate	Moist, acidic Sandy	Flowers purple, mauve, pink, or white, winter
Moderate to high	Moist, neutral	Foliage lobed
Moderate to high	Moist, neutral	Foliage 2 to 3 feet long, deeply lobed; stems with aerial roots
Moderate to high	Moist, neutral	Foliage coppery purple beneath
Moderate to high	Moist, neutral	Foliage heart shaped, often variegated
Moderate to high	Moist, neutral	Foliage in rosettes
High	Moist, neutral	Foliage variegated; stems leggy in dry air
Moderate	Moist, neutral	Foliage purplish beneath; flowers white, in summer; good basket plant
High	Moist, neutral	Foliage finely divided, often variegated
High	Moist, neutral	Foliage finely and irregularly dissected, variegated
High	Moist, neutral	Foliage compound with rounded white-edged leaflets
Moderate to high	Sandy, moist, acidic	Flowers purple, red, orange, yellow, or white; in spring; short-lived
High	Osmunda, moist, acidic	Flowers yellow, spotted brown, on slender scapes held above the foliage; borne once a year
Moderate to high	Moist, neutral	Flowers and fruit red-orange, in summer
Dry	Gritty sand, dry neutral	Stems purplish; flowers deep red, in spring
Dry	Gritty sand, dry, neutral	Flowers red, borne at base, in spring
Moderate	Moist, neutral	Berries glossy, red, in summer and fall
Moderate	Moist, neutral	Good in bottle gardens and terrariums
Moderate	Moist, neutral	Foliage often variegated; flowers small, pink, in spring and summer
Moderate to high	Moist, acidic	Flowers red-orange, in summer and fall

(continues)

OTHER HOUSEPLANTS (*continued*)

Name	Height*	Habit†	Exposure‡	Temperature Range (°F)ʲ	
				Night	Day
Rosa chinensis 'Minima' (pygmy rose; miniature rose)	1–1½	Shrub	S to PSh	60	70
Rosmarinus officinalis (rosemary)	2–4'	Shrub	S to PSh	65	75
Ruellia graecizans (scarlet ruellia)	1–2'	Bushy	S to PSh	65	75
R. macrantha (Christmas pride)	2–4'	Bushy	S to PSh	65	75
R. makoyana (trailing velvet plant)	1–2'	Creeping	S to PSh	65	75
Sauromatum venosum (voodoo lily)	1½–2½'	Erect, unbranched, from corms	S to PSh	60	70
Saxifraga stolonifera (strawberry geranium)	6–12"	Compact	PSh to LSh	65	75
Scindapsus pictus 'Argyraeus' (satin pothos)	4–8'	Climbing	LSh to DSh	60	70
Selaginella kraussiana (spreading clubmoss)	6–12"	Trailing	LSh to DSh	65	75
S. lepidophylla (resurrection plant)	3–5"	Tufted	LSh to DSh	65	75
S. pallescens (sweat plant, moss fern)	4–7"	Tufted	LSh to DSh	65	75
Senna corymbosa (Argentine senna)	3–6'	Shrub	S	65	75
S. floribunda (shrubby senna)	3–6'	Shrub	S	65	75
Serenoa repens (saw palmetto)	2–3'	Forms rosettes	S	60	70
Sinningia canescens (Brazilian edelweiss)	9–12"	Forms clumps, from tubers	PSh to LSh	65	75
Smithiantha × hybrida (temple bells)	6–10"	Forms clumps	PSh to LSh	65	75
Soleirolia soleirolii (baby's tears, Irish moss)	6–9"	Creeping	PSh	65	80
Stangeria eriopus (Hottentot's head)	1½–2'	Forms rosettes	PSh	60	70
Stapelia pulvinata (carrion flower)	6–8"	Spreading	S	70	80
Stephanotis floribunda (Madagascar jasmine)	4–8'	Twining climber	LSh	60	75
Strelitzia reginae (bird-of-paradise flower)	2–4'	Forms clumps	S to PSh	60	75
Streptocarpus caulescens (tall Cape primrose)	1–2'	Erect	LSh	60	70
S. holstii (tall Cape primrose)	1–2'	Erect	LSh	60	70
S. kirkii (shrubby Cape primrose)	1–1½'	Erect	LSh	60	70
S saxorum (creeping Cape primrose)	1–2'	Trailing	LSh	60	70
Syagrus comosa (babao, pati palm)	4–8'	Slender	LSh to DSh	65	75
Tetranema roseum (Mexican foxglove)	1–1½"	Forms rosettes	PSh	60	70
Thelocactus bicolor (glory-of-Texas cactus)	6–12"	Globose	S	65	90††
T. setispinus (coral cactus, strawberry cactus)	4–6"	Globose	S	65	90**
Tibouchina urvilleana (glory-bush, princess shrub flower)	5–10'	Shrub	S	60	75
Tillandsia cyanea	1–1½'		PSh	65	75
T. lindeniana	1–1½'		PSh	65	75
Tolmiea menziesii (piggyback plant)	6–12"	Forms rosettes	PSh to LSh	55	70
Tradescantia albiflora 'Albovittata' (giant white inch plant)	1–2'	Trailing	LSh	60	70
T. pallida (purple heart plant)	1–2'	Trailing	PSh to LSh	60	75
T. spathacea (Moses-in-the-bulrushes)	1–2'	Forms clumps	PSh to LSh	65	80
Tulbaghia fragrans (pink agapanthus)	1–1½'	Forms clumps	S to PSh	60	70
Veltheimia bracteata	About 1'	From bulbs	S to PSh	60	70
Viola hederacea (Tasmanian violet)	2–3"	Forms clumps	PSh	60	70
Vriesia hieroglyphica	2–2½'	Forms rosettes	LSh	65	75

OTHER HOUSEPLANTS

Humidity[||]	Soil Requirements[#]	Comments
Moderate	Moist, neutral to acidic	Flowers red, pink, or white; in spring and summer
Moderate	Moist, alkaline to neutral	Foliage aromatic; flowers blue, in winter and spring
Moderate	Moist, neutral	Flowers red, in spring and summer
Moderate	Moist, neutral	Flowers rose pink; in spring and summer
Moderate	Moist, neutral	Foliage dense, olive; flowers rose red, in spring and summer
Moderate	Moist, acidic	Flower large, malodorous, yellow and brown in winter or spring, followed by large divided leaf on mottled stalk
High	Peaty, moist, acidic	Foliage variegated; white flowers, in summer and fall
Moderate	Moist, acidic	Foliage variegated with silvery spots
High	Sandy-humusy, moist, acidic	Good in baskets and terrariums
High	Sandy-humusy, moist, acidic	Good terrarium plant
High	Sandy-humusy, moist, acidic	Good terrarium plant
Moderate	Moist, neutral	Flowers yellow; cylindrical pods, in summer
Moderate	Moist, neutral	Flowers yellow; cylindrical pods, in summer to winter
Moderate	Moist, neutral	Foliage spreading, spiny
Moderate to high	Moist, acidic	Flowers violet with pink to red throat, in spring and summer
High	Moist, acidic	Foliage velvety; flowers nodding, red, in spring
High	Sandy, moist, acidic	Best used in bottle gardens and terrariums
High	Sandy-humusy, moist, neutral	Foliage rigid, fernlike
Dry	Gritty, moist, neutral	Succulent; flowers 3 inches across, malodorous, maroon with yellow hairs, in summer and fall
High	Sandy, moist, acidic	Foliage glossy; flowers fragrant, white, in summer
Moderate	Moist, neutral	Foliage blue-green, cannalike; flowers orange and blue, in spring and summer
Moderate to high	Moist, acidic	Flowers purple to lavender; in fall and winter
Moderate to high	Moist, acidic	Flowers purple and white; in winter
Moderate to high	Moist, acidic	Flowers lilac, in winter
Moderate to high	Moist, acidic	Flowers pale lilac and white, in spring and summer
Moderate	Moist, neutral	Good tub palm; several other species available
High	Moist, neutral	Flowers lavender, held above leafy rosette, in summer
Low	Gritty sand, dry, neutral	Spines red and white; flowers pink with orange center, in summer
Low	Gritty sand, dry, neutral	Many hooked spines; flowers yellow, in summer and fall
Moderate	Moist, acidic	Flowers large purple, each lasting one day, in summer and fall
High	Wood chips, moist, acidic	Epiphyte; flowers and bracts pink, held in erect, flattened cluster, in summer
High	Wood chips, moist, acidic	Epiphyte; flowers purple; bracts pink, held on 2½-foot scape, in summer
Moderate	Moist, neutral	Plantlets develop from leaf bases, in spring and summer
Moderate	Moist, neutral	Foliage silver-striped; good as a cascade, in summer
Moderate	Moist, neutral	Foliage purple; flowers lilac, in summer
High	Moist, neutral	Foliage violet beneath; flowers white, everblooming
Moderate	Moist, acidic	Flowers pinkish purple, held in clusters, in summer
Moderate	Moist, neutral to acidic	Flowers pink, held in dense spikes, in spring
Moderate	Moist, neutral	Flowers blue-violet and white everblooming
High	Wood chips, humus, moist, neutral	Foliage with lines; flowers yellow; bracts yellow-green, in summer

(continues)

OTHER HOUSEPLANTS (*continued*)

Name	Height*	Habit†	Exposure‡	Temperature Range (°F)ʲ Night	Day
V. splendens (flaming sword)	2–3'	Forms rosettes	LSh	65	75
Westringia rosmariniformis	2–4'	Shrub	S	55	65
Zantedeschia aethiopica (white calla)	1½–2½'	From rhizome	S to PSh	55	65
Z. elliotiana (yellow calla)	1½–2½'	From rhizome	S to PSh	55	65
Z. rehmannii (pink calla)	1–1½'	From rhizome	S to PSh	50	60
Zingiber officinale (ginger)	1–2'		PSh	60	70

*Heights apply to plants grown indoors. Many become much larger when grown in the garden.

†Note that some species, e.g., philodendrons, change habit and appearance as they pass from the juvenile to the mature state. Habits noted apply to plants grown indoors.

‡S, full sun (at least five hours of direct sun each sunny day); PSh, partial shade (one to three hours direct sun, preferably in the early morning or late afternoon); LSh; light shade (continuous dappled or filtered sunlight or in a north-facing window); DSh, dense shade (continuous unbroken shade or in interior areas with low natural lighting); Sh, shade.

ʲOptimal range; most plants adapt to a wider range but have a shorter life or meager flower display.

‖High, 50 percent or higher relative humidity (difficult to achieve indoors in the winter); moderate, 30 to 50 percent (use pebble-filled trays, humidifiers, or frequent syringing in the winter); low, 30 percent and lower (typical for indoor heated air).

#Wet, frequent heavy watering but not continuous saturation (difficult to maintain indoors in the winter); moist, continuously damp soil surface may appear dry between waterings dry, infrequent watering in the winter (soil should dry out between waterings), damp soil during growth and flowering.

**In dormant periods, temperatures 10° to 15°F lower are advisable.

††In dormant periods, temperatures 15° to 20°F lower are advisable.

Window-box oxalis
(*Oxalis rubra*)

Bird-of-paradise
(*Strelitzia reginae*)

Chinese hibiscus
(*Hibiscus rosa-sinensis*)

Emerald asparagus fern (*Asparagus densiflorus*)

Rosemary (*Rosmarinus officinalis* 'Miss Jessop's Upright')

OTHER HOUSEPLANTS

Humidity[||]	Soil Requirements[#]	Comments
High	Wood chips, humus, moist, neutral	Foliage banded brown; flowers yellow; bracts yellow-orange, in summer
Moderate	Sandy, moist, acidic	Foliage small, silvery; flowers white, in summer
Moderate to high	Moist to wet, neutral	Floral spathe white, in winter and spring
Moderate	Moist, neutral	Floral spathe yellow, in winter and spring
Moderate	Moist, neutral	Floral spathe pink, in winter and spring
Moderate	Moist, acidic	Foliage large, attractive; flowers in rare, in summer

Flowering maple
(*Abutilon megapotamicum*)

Persian violet
(*Exacum affine*)

Turk's-cap hibiscus
(*Malvaviscus arboreus*)

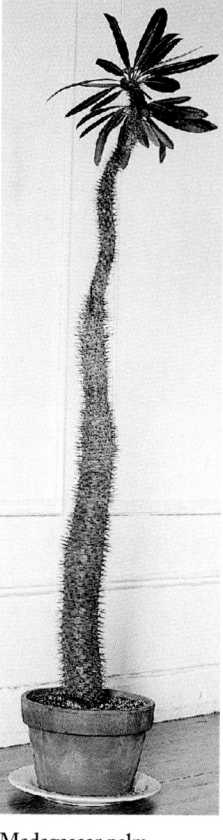

Madagascar palm
(*Pachypodim lamerei*)

Musa velutina (flower cluster and fruit)

Devil's tongue (*Amorphophallus rivieri* [in flower])

Devil's tongue (*Amorphophallus rivieri* [in leaf])

FORCING BULBS INDOORS

Many hardy spring-flowering bulbs may be forced into bloom during winter and early spring, providing welcome color and fragrance at a time that is otherwise often quite drab. To have such a display requires some planning and preparation the previous fall.

The essential step in forcing hardy bulbs to bloom indoors is to expose them to at least 2½ months of cold temperatures averaging 40° to 45°F, preferably starting with the first three or four weeks at 45° to 50°F and ending with the last weeks at about freezing. From zone 7 north, this cold treatment is most easily provided by placing planted pots in an open coldframe and covering them deeply with dry fallen leaves, preferably oak leaves or pine needles as these do not form a soggy mat when wet. The mulch will help stabilize daily temperature fluctuations and deter hard freezing. Where hard freezing is likely before the pots are to be brought indoors, it is best to bury them in a trench with their tops several inches below the surface. Covered with a heavy blanket of mulch, there should be only minimal penetration of frost, thus easing pot removal. The frost is not harmful to the bulbs.

In zones 8 to 10, where cold periods are intermittent and insufficiently intense for bulb treatment, it is advisable to purchase bulbs that have been prechilled for forcing. Alternatively, untreated bulbs may be stored in the refrigerator for the requisite cold period. Whatever the cold treatment method, they should be potted up in mid to late fall and stored outdoors to encourage root growth. Depending on your local autumn temperatures, the potting schedule will require appropriate adjustment.

Bulbs that have insufficient exposure to cold are slow to respond to indoor conditions and have disappointingly weak and erratic growth and may fail to flower.

The type of pot used, whether clay or plastic, is less critical than the size and drainage of the pot and the nature of the rooting medium. A 6-inch-wide bulb pan (a low-shouldered pot) is adequate for six tulips, four hyacinths, or 10 to 12 crocuses; an 8-inch pan accommodates eight tulips, six hyacinths, or 18 to 20 crocuses. The soil medium may be a mixture of one part garden loam, one part sharp builder's sand, and one part peat moss or a prepared nutrient-enriched bulb mix, moistened before use. Before planting, cover the drain hole(s) with curved pot shards (crock) to promote free drainage. Partly fill the pan with soil, place the bulbs, and complete filling to within ½ inch of the rim, with the bulb necks at or just below the surface. In the case of tulips, by planting the bulbs with their flat bases against the wall of the pan, the broad leaves that emerge will encircle the cluster of flowers that rise on their individual scapes in the center.

Planted pots should be thoroughly watered—the most effective method is to set them in a partly filled bucket, tub, or sink and allow them to soak—before being stored outdoors in a coldframe.

By bringing pots indoors a few at a time, the period of bloom can be much extended. Usually four to six weeks must elapse indoors before flowers appear. The longer the period of cold storage, the more rapidly the bulbs will come into bloom. Bulbs in pots placed in a warm, sunny window will respond quickly, but once the flowers are about to open, it is best to keep the plants out of direct sun to extend the flowering period.

Hyacinths respond especially well to forcing, but their flower stalks sometimes fail to elongate, especially if the cold period has been too brief. In such cases, the flowers open in a tight cluster down among the leaves. A 4- or 5-inch-long open-topped cylinder of opaque paper or cardboard inserted between the flower mass and the surrounding leaves may help promote elongation. Tall, large-flowered daffodils often require staking; lower, smaller-flowered ones do not. When selecting bulbs for forcing, it is best to choose cultivars recommended for indoor culture.

In addition to crocuses, lower-growing or "minor" hardy bulbs suitable for forcing include dwarf bulbous iris (Iris danfordiae and I. reticulata) and lily-of-the-valley. The bulblike crowns of the latter, while not bulbs in the strict sense, may be treated like hardy bulbs and be expected to make a fine display alone or in combination with taller narcissus or tulips.

After bloom is over, tap the rooted bulbs out of the pan and plant the mass at the correct depth in a previously prepared hole in the garden. Although tulips often fail to recover, hyacinths, narcissuses, and crocuses usually survive, but may not reflower for a year. Bulbs rooted in water, however, are exhausted by flowering and should be discarded.

To force tender or nonhardy bulbs, such as 'Paper White' narcissus and amaryllis, dormant bulbs are potted and grown indoors after a period of dry dormancy (rather than cold). Those grown in water should be kept in the dark until their roots are well developed, since light depresses root growth. In frost-free areas (parts of zone 10), tender bulbs past bloom that have been soil rooted may be planted in the garden for eventual reflowering. Elsewhere, treatment varies. Narcissuses are discarded, regardless of rooting medium. Amaryllis in its leafy stage is grown on through the summer in partial shade, preferably outdoors. During this period, it is important that maximum leaf growth be encouraged in amaryllis so that the bulb will grow and set embryonic buds for future flowering. Biweekly applications of manure tea or a balanced fast-release fertilizer will help ensure maximum growth. In the fall, when the foliage begins to yellow, pots should be turned on their sides, water with-held, and the bulbs, still in place, given a 2- or 3-month period of dormancy in a cool, dry place, protected from frost. Thereafter, 5 or 6 weeks before bloom is desired, the gradual moistening of the soil will initiate root growth, the elongation of flower scapes, and the enlargement of the buds that were formed the previous summer.

CHRISTMAS TREES AND OTHER HOLIDAY PLANTS
Living Christmas Trees

The artificial Christmas tree has gained much favor, espe-cially in urban areas where cut trees are often inordinately expensive and, unless the butt end is kept in water, soon dry out and begin dropping needles once indoors. The cut tree nevertheless has the charm of naturalness (and, initially, of fragrance) and involves a ritual of acquisition (albeit often by purchase) that is a closer approximation to the hallowed historic practice of taking a tree from the woods than is assembling a manufactured surrogate. With care taken to place the natural tree away from radiators and direct sun-light and to keep up the water level in the reservoir that forms part of the steel base, it should hold its needles and remain limber and be relatively reluctant to support fire for at least two weeks. The argument that to use cut trees con-tributes to deforestation is largely nullified by the long-established tree plantation industry in which nearly all Christmas trees are grown as a crop, in the same way that agricultural produce is raised, harvested, and marketed.

Not all conifers are suited for use as cut Christmas trees. Balsam fir, Douglas fir, and various short-needle pines (such as Scotch pine) retain living qualities longest; spruces, on the other hand, quickly drop needles, sometimes in just a few days; and arborvitae, juniper, and false cypress soon become dry and brittle.

Living trees, dug in the fall and balled and burlapped for indoor use, not only serve the holiday need but may also contribute to the home landscape thereafter, and this latter prospect helps justify their often considerable cost. It is important, however, to discriminate among the kinds of liv-ing trees available and plan where they will be placed out-doors, for while a Colorado blue spruce may be comfortably accommodated on the home grounds in the decades after it is planted, a Norway spruce soon becomes a major tree and will eventually tower to 75 feet or more. A disproportion-ately small root ball augurs for failure, just as dull, brittle needles or shriveled twigs do. Once purchased, a living tree should remain outdoors in the shade as long as possible and

its root ball kept wrapped and moist at all times. If a hard freeze threatens, place the still wrapped root ball in the con-tainer that will hold it indoors, so that it may adopt the con-tainer's shape while the soil is still soft and pliable. Once the tree has been moved indoors, care must be taken to keep the root ball continually moist (but not saturated) and to limit the indoor period to 10 days; if kept longer, buds will begin to expand and, once this begins, they will all be destroyed by winter cold when the tree is returned outdoors—a sure pre-scription for death.

Soon after purchase, and before the tree is taken indoors, the planting site should be chosen and prepared, i.e., the hole should be dug and the backfill piled nearby. If freezing weather threatens before planting time, the hole and back-fill should be heavily mulched with leaves or straw covered with a tarpaulin to keep the soil soft and workable. The tree should be planted promptly after the indoor period, watered well, heavily mulched, and its trunk carefully guyed to two 5-foot stakes (see Chapter 11). The foliage should be sprayed with an antidesiccant. Even with the most diligent care, however, living trees are the object of extreme stress when suddenly subjected to the dry, heated atmosphere of our homes in winter and then just as suddenly returned to winter cold. It is no surprise that many fail to survive.

Christmas Poinsettia

The Christmas poinsettia (*Euphorbia pulcherrima*) is a bushy, long-lived tropical shrub native to open areas in Central America, where it eventually reaches 10 feet and blooms each year during the winter dry season, often with-out its green leaves. Over the years, growers in temperate-zone regions have not only learned how to force poinsettias into bloom for Christmastime, but to do so with small plants, often less than 1 foot tall, and with all leaves intact. These feats are accomplished by artificially regulating day length to stimulate flower formation; by propagating new plants from cuttings; by providing ample moisture during all phases of growth; and by keeping the air humid, within a critical 60° to 70°F range, and free of cold drafts.

In the dry air of our often overheated homes, poinsettias will nevertheless hold both red floral leaves and green foliage leaves as long as the soil is not allowed to dry out and the plant is placed in a bright, sunny window. In fact, it is usual for plants cared for in this way to remain attractive with both red and green leaves until late spring, when houseplants are best moved outdoors.

At this point, you can simply slip the poinsettia out of its pot and plant it in a sunny position, where it will soon grow new green shoots and become a handsome foliage plant, 2 to 3 feet tall, until frost cuts it down the following fall.

On the other hand, if you would like to reflower your poinsettia for the next Christmas, these are the steps to take.

1. Transfer the plant in June to a larger pot—say the next larger size and preferably clay pot—using a rich, humusy soil and placing a stone in the drainage hole to keep roots from growing out.
2. Cut the old plant back to 4 or 5 inches tall.
3. Plunge it, pot and all, in a sunny spot in the garden, with the rim of the pot at ground level.
4. Make sure the soil is kept moist without interruption all summer.
5. Lift the potted plant and take it indoors in August, before nighttime temperatures drop below 60°F.
6. Slip the clay pot into the same size plastic pot to retard evaporation.
7. Starting October 1, cover the entire plant each day at 5:00 P.M. and do not uncover until 8:00 A.M. to maintain the nine-hour days necessary to induce flowering. This can be done with an inverted box or by placing the plant in a dark closet for the extended night period. Most important is the unbroken continuity of darkness, for even one instantaneous interruption will disrupt bud formation.
8. By Thanksgiving, when the uppermost leaves should begin coloring, the plant can again be left continually on a sunny windowsill and enjoyed as the display colors intensify. As the weather cools outside, make sure the windowsill environment drops no lower than 60°F and that your poinsettia gets at least two or three hours of sunlight each bright day.

The cuttings left from the spring pruning can be rooted and, even if only 5 or 6 inches long, will behave just as though they were still attached to the mother plant. Remove all but three or four leaves and place the cuttings in tepid water to staunch the flow of milky sap. Dip the cut ends in a little powdered charcoal and carefully insert halfway down in a pot or tub of damp sand. Cover with clear polyethylene and place in a well-lighted place but out of direct sunlight. Once the cuttings sprout roots, usually within a month, transplant each to a small clay pot, sink in the garden, and treat as described above, transplanting on to larger pots as needed.

Today, with pink, yellow, marbled, and spattered forms added to the traditional red and white, the diversity that can be achieved in poinsettia displays makes them even more suitable for enjoyment not only through the winter but throughout the year.

Other Holiday Plants

Among other popular potted plants used in flower for holiday adornment are chrysanthemums, gardenias, and camellias. All prosper best in mild, humid conditions, witness their greatest success in cool, damp greenhouses. Indeed, potted gardenias are so sensitive to hot, dry conditions that already formed flower buds frequently abort and drop when a plant is taken into the house. In zones 8 to 10, potted camellias should be planted outdoors after the holiday period; elsewhere they may be wintered in a cool greenhouse. Generally, florist's mums are best treated as dispensable, although if kept on a cool, sunny windowsill, they can survive the winter, be placed outdoors in the spring, and be induced to flower again in the fall. They do not endure hard frost, however, and perform best as greenhouse subjects.

Plants that bear colorful fruits are especially valued at holiday time as supplements to the traditional hardy holly. Potted holly shrubs are not suited to extended periods indoors

Hippeastrum cv. 'Apple blossom' with paper white narcissus

as they require cold dormancy to succeed. Dwarf citrus (e.g., orange, lemon, kumquat, and calamondin) are easily cultured indoors as long as they are exposed to several hours of sun each bright day and cool (preferably 55° to 60°F) night temperatures. If summered outdoors, they usually flower and set a substantial fruit crop for the next holiday period.

Coralberry (*Ardisia crenata, A, crispa,* etc.), an adaptable subtropical shrub, is rather hollylike, with dark green, glossy foliage (but without spines) and tight clusters of bright red berries. Potted plants, usually sold when about 1 foot tall, will grow to 3 feet if moved to successively larger pots and will often reflower and set new fruit if summered outdoors. Cool nights (55° to 60°F) indoors are beneficial.

The various Christmas peppers (*Capsicum annuum,* 'Conoides' group), Jerusalem cherry (*Solanum pseudocapsicum*), and winter cherry (*S. capsicastrum*) may be potted up from the garden and brought indoors. But because insufficient light, high heat, and low humidity cause their leaves to yellow and drop and fruit to shrivel, they are generally not satisfactory for long-term culture in the house.

Amaryllis (*Hippeastrum* hybrids), cyclamen (*Cyclamen persicum*), African violet (*Saintpaulia ionantha*), and gloxinia (*Sinningia speciosa*), all treated earlier in this chapter, are traditional holiday plants, as are the Rieger begonias (largely replacing the less adaptable cheimantha and hiemalis begonias), which, however, should be sprayed with a fungicide to prevent the almost certain outbreak of leaf-destroying powdery mildew.

Less commonly seen but of great merit are various bromeliads, such as the Christmas candle (*Tillandsia imperialis*), which bears purple flowers in a spike studded with scarlet bracts; flaming sword (*Vriesia splendens*), which has green- and brown-striped leaves and a red spike bearing yellow flowers; and blushing bromeliad (*Neoregelia carolinae*), which has glossy foliage that turns bright red at flowering time and retains the color for months. See the cultural notes for the bromeliads on page 915.

Blushing bromeliad (*Neoregelia carolinae* 'Tricolor')

39

Gardening under Artificial Light

Many homes and apartments do not provide sufficient window space to accommodate the gardening ambitions of their enthusiastic owners. But since light is the single most important limiting factor to successful indoor gardening, the vast majority of such gardeners grow plants under fluorescent lights. With many kinds of plants suited or preadapted to culture in fluorescent light, the indoor gardener's success has been great, and not least because with

Epiphytic or air-plant orchids are among the most rewarding plants to grow under artificial lights. Although each kind usually flowers only once each year, the long-lasting blooms are arresting in their varied forms and colors, and the great number of species and hybrids assures unbroken succession and unending interest.

artificial light the grower has complete control over all the cultural conditions needed for potted plants. Moreover, new fluorescent tubes have been developed that deliver nearly perfect light for plant growth. With just a little extra effort and expense, anyone can create an enjoyable indoor garden that will provide excellent conditions for a wide spectrum of plants. People who live in small apartments can enlarge their growing space because light gardens can be installed almost anywhere. For example, they may fit on a shelf in a roomy closet. Whole rooms and basements have been given over to light gardens after their owners have become enthusiastically involved in their hobby. Many people have gardens that occupy several different locations throughout the house. Light gardening is also ideal for older people, because it does not involve strenuous activity, yet the rewards are great. With careful selection of plant materials, flowers can adorn your home every day of the year. Indeed, some plants are horticulturally superior when grown under such lights to those produced in a greenhouse or outdoors in nature.

Indoor light gardening is also a practical way to start vegetable and flower seeds for transplanting to the outdoor garden. All the tomatoes, peppers, and marigolds you will need for the entire season can be started in just a few feet of space. And you even can plant the special cultivars usually available only from seed merchants, rather than being limited to the often meager selection at a garden center or nursery.

LIGHT AND SOURCES OF LIGHT

All green plants must have light to flourish and grow. It does not matter where the light comes from, as long as it is of the proper wavelength and intensity for a sufficiently long period each day. In view of the fact that all artificial light creates some degree of heat, which, in excess, can be damaging to plants, fluorescent lights are best because they produce the least heat while at the same time delivering the most light at the lowest cost. While the ordinary fluorescent tubes designed for general household, workshop, or industrial illumination can be used to grow plants, those designated "cool white" or "warm white" are the most efficient and provide the best results for the cost of the installation. So-called grow lights (sold as Gro-lux, Vita-lite, and Agro-lite, etc.) are considerably less efficient but, in some cases, result in larger leaves and slower growth than either cool white or warm white tubes. They are, however, much more expensive.

All fluorescent tubes produce a small amount of heat because of the ballast, which is contained inside the fixture and is necessary for the efficient operation of the tubes. This small heat source is far from a limiting factor, but placement and ventilation of the fixtures are important considerations when a light garden is being planned, especially if the garden is to contain more than just a few fixtures.

The most frequently used fixture to hold the fluorescent tubes is the standard (and least expensive) 4-foot-long, double-tube fixture with a white enamel reflector. Light gardens in large areas often employ standard 8-foot tubes. These gardens are usually built by experienced growers who started with shorter tubes, then expanded their gardening area. Short tubes (20 inches) also are available for smaller spaces such as inside bookcases or other pieces of furniture, or in confined spaces such as closets. The cost of the shorter tubes, relative to the amount of light they emit, is somewhat higher. They are best arranged in parallel sets of two, four, or six.

In building your own light garden, put the lamps on 6-inch centers, i.e., with the center of one fluorescent tube 6 inches away from the center of an adjacent parallel tube. In this way, standard double-tube fixtures will light an area of 4 feet by 12 inches. To light a greater space, use more fixtures with tubes on 6-inch centers.

An ornamental cart features flowering specimens of the bromeliad Aechmea fasciata, *well suited to artificial light culture.*

Light fixtures can be built into stationary plant stands or a semimovable cartlike plant stand. Efficient and attractive ready-made stands can be purchased at most garden stores or from mail-order catalogs. Workshop fixtures can be hung very simply from the ceiling, especially in basements where such installations may be more informal and utilitarian. By hanging fixtures with a chain, the lights can be easily raised as the plants grow. Lightweight but strong plastic link chain is available in garden stores for this purpose, or standard metal chain can be used. A basement installation of several lights over a sturdy table (as can be made from a discarded slab door on sawhorses) is basically all that is necessary to grow your own seedlings for the outdoor vegetable and flower garden.

Engineering a light garden often demands a handyman's touch, but nothing really complicated is involved. Many light gardens are built like bookcases, so that several shelves can accommodate the maximum garden with the minimum sacrifice to living space. In such gardens, of course, the upper shelves will be slightly warmer than the lower ones. Track-mounted adjustable shelves offer maximum flexibility.

Although cool white and warm white fluorescent tubes work well for most light garden plants, under grow lights, orchids and succulents flower better and bromeliads and begonias develop better foliage color. In mixed plantings that include plants of either category as well as others, alternating grow light tubes with standard cool white or warm white tubes in the fixture is a satisfactory compromise.

Amount of Light

Plants grown under lights thrive in 12 to 16 hours of light a day. Some gardeners prefer manually to turn their garden lights on each morning and off each night, but for others, an electrical timer switch performs the service automatically. During the occasional weekends away from home, 24 hours of light a day is not disastrous to the plants (and, indeed, is beneficial to some, such as the African violet), but protracted darkness is.

Fluorescent tubes are brightest when they are new; after about 100 hours of use they dim somewhat, but then level out to produce nearly constant (though very slowly declining) high-intensity light for about a year, thereafter fading into a pale yellowish light before failing altogether. It is a good idea to stagger the replacement of the tubes because new, bright tubes will burn or yellow the leaves of plants if all the tubes are replaced at once. Most growers replace their tubes after about 18 months of use. Tubes that emit broad-spectrum light last longer, but are more expensive than standard cool white or warm white tubes.

Plant species vary in the amount of light they can utilize. Brightness of light is easily controlled by adjusting the distance between the tube and the leaf surface. Some succulents demand bright, intense light. These plants will thrive only when placed 2 to 4 inches from the tubes, under the center of each tube's length. Most plants grow best with less intense light, however, so for them, 8 to 14 inches below the lamps is the optimum distance at the center of the tube. Only ferns and some begonias will thrive farther away from the tubes; 24 inches is about the maximum distance even for these low-light plants.

Since the light intensity decreases from the center to the ends of the tube, bear in mind that some orchids, most succulents, herbs, and geraniums benefit from the central or brightest position under the tubes. On the other hand, gesneriads, low-light orchids, and terrestrial bromeliads thrive near the ends of tubes in multiple-tube systems. But you must be the judge in determining proper distances. The plants indicate, by their growth and appearance, whether they are getting enough light or too much. A plant that produces large leaves with long lengths of stem between individual leaves is not getting enough light. Inadequate light is usually what ails plants under lights, if all other cultural conditions are met. You should either put such light-deficient plants in a central position under the tube or raise them nearer to the tubes.

A plant that grows abnormally, with its leaves curled or flattened against the stem or pot, or that develops an abundance of red pigment, probably is receiving light that is too bright. It should either be moved to the ends of the tubes or be lowered. Seedlings, however, should be placed only a few inches below the tubes so that they will be short and sturdy. As the plants grow, however, either the lights or the seedlings will have to be moved; hence easily adjustable fixtures are needed for seedling culture.

To maximize fluorescent light, a reflector should be installed above the tubes. In this way more light will be directed to the leaves of the plants you are growing. Standard fixtures come with built-in reflectors. White or mirrored surfaces on walls adjacent to light gardens will also increase the amount of light on the plant. By keeping the tubes clean and replacing them at 18-month intervals, you can maintain maximum output of light for your indoor garden.

HUMIDITY AND VENTILATION

Many of the most successful plants grown under lights are those that benefit from the stable environment so easily achieved in this type of gardening. Often overlooked, however, are ventilation and humidity, two closely linked factors of great importance. Ventilation, even when effectively controlled, usually accelerates the drying out of the indoor environment. Not only must soil moisture be closely monitored and replenished as needed but relative humidity should also be checked, especially during the cold winter months, when it may drop below 20 percent indoors. Since it is through leaves that plants lose the most moisture, many species respond to low humidity by reducing their total leaf area, mainly by dropping the older leaves, which contributes to an unattractive leggy appearance in many cases. Hence the need for achieving a balance between the disease-preventive effect of air in motion and the physiological necessity of adequate humidity. Small electric fans are useful in indoor gardens to move air gently around the plants. If these fans are used, it will be necessary to place water-filled pebble trays under the plants to increase the humidity in the immediate vicinity. This is readily achieved under linear fluorescent tubes by using the $11 \times 22 \times 2$-inch plastic trays that fit perfectly under standard fixtures. These may be filled with small pebbles or gravel, or even with perlite if weight is a consideration, then filled with water.

Another product that is useful in helping maintain humidity is the capillary mat material that has long been used on benches in commercial greenhouses where it provides continuous watering of the pots placed on it. This same mat material also augments humidity in indoor light gardens as well as simultaneously and automatically watering the plants from beneath. Short lengths of this matting material may be difficult to obtain, but some local plant societies and specialty plant shops often offer it to the indoor grower. It has been found that many plants that once needed a contained (terrarium) atmosphere can be grown in the open on mats placed in plastic trays and kept constantly moist.

TERRARIUMS AND OTHER CONTAINED ENVIRONMENTS

One of the most rewarding aspects of indoor light gardening is terrarium culture. Many miniature tropical plants (including ferns) thrive in the high humidity that a terrarium provides. The miniature landscape or composition created in a small space can be a constant source of pleasure as plants flower and develop into perfect specimens in their enclosed environment. Such protected conditions are in fact essential for certain uncommon begonias, gesneriads, and other species otherwise unsuccessful in cultivation.

Humidity and Ventilation in the Terrarium

For a terrarium to provide constant high humidity, it must be kept closed most of the time. Sometimes, when located ideally and the plants within are thriving, the terrarium may remain closed indefinitely. Such a circumstance is especially welcome because the plants within will be nearly maintenance free. Usually, several locations must be tried before the ideal one is found. Often, what may be ideal at one time of year proves unsuitable at others.

Most terrariums need some attention, however, especially in hot weather, when the cover is opened slightly to allow limited air circulation and to enable heat to escape. The hottest summer days are the most perilous for a terrarium planting. High temperature and humidity cause the leaves of many plants to turn brown, and for many kinds this can be fatal. It is during such periods that the terrarium fancier must be particularly alert and prepared to move the terrarium to the coolest available location until the adverse conditions abate.

Types of Containers

Various containers of clear glass or plastic make ideal terrariums, but the covers and lids that close these containers vary in convenience. The challenge of a lovely miniature garden inside a bottle with a narrow neck obviously will not appeal to everyone. Such gardens are considered an art form, rather like flower arranging.

Most familiar "working" terrariums are built in unused fish tanks, in wide-mouthed bowls or in specially constructed glass chambers with convenient doors or access through the top of the container, which is usually fitted with a piece of glass. Once the plants become established, the terrarium needs little care. The first few weeks are critical, however, because the plants are adjusting to their new environment and the grower is learning the particular idiosyncrasies of the new terrarium. During this period, if water condensation on the inside of the glass is excessive, the covering will have to be opened to allow the extra water vapor to escape. A small amount of condensation on the glass is no cause for worry. However, most terrariums need to be carefully watered every few months to compensate for the slow, unavoidable loss of water.

Making the Terrarium

The various components for a terrarium are easily found. All that is needed is a suitable clean container with transparent walls and a top (removable), pebbles or gravel for drainage, prepared potting soil, and a selection of plants. It is well to have in mind the growth rates and ultimate size of the plants under consideration, so that none will grow so fast as to overwhelm the slower growers. Put at least 2 to 3 inches of gravel on the floor of the container, add barely moist soil, then use your imagination and creativity to design a miniature landscape with the plants. Small rocks and weathered

TERRARIUM PLANTS

FOR CULTURE IN CLOSED CONTAINERS WITH HIGH HUMIDITY

Begonia imperialis, dwarf vars. and cvs. (imperial begonia)
B. Semperflorens-Cultorum hybrids, dwarf cultivars (wax begonia)
Bertolonia spp. and cvs.
Calathea lietzii (dwarf prayer plant)
C. pavonii (dwarf prayer plant)
C. roseo-picta (dwarf prayer plant)
C. 'Sanderiana' (dwarf prayer plant)
Chamaeranthemum gaudichaudii (dwarf acanthus)
Cissus striata (dwarf grape ivy)
Dionaea muscipula (Venus's flytrap)
Erythrodes nobilis (Brazilian erythrodes)
Ficus pumila (creeping fig)
F. sagittata 'Variegata' (variegated climbing fig)

Fittonia verschaffeltii (mosaic plant)
Koellikeria erinoides
Kohleria amabilis
Lycopodium spp. (ground pine)
Maranta leuconeura (prayer plant)
Nertera granadensis (baby's tears, bread plant)
Polystichum, dwarf spp., young plants (holly fern)
Pteris ensiformis 'Victoriae' (variegated sword brake)
Selaginella kraussiana 'Brownii' (dwarf club moss)
S. pallescens (moss fern)
Sinningia pusilla 'White Sprite' (dwarf white sinningia)
Stenandrium lindenii

FOR CULTURE IN PARTIALLY OPEN CONTAINERS WITH MODERATE HUMIDITY

Adromischus cristatus (crinkleleaf plant)
Aglaonema costatum (spotted evergreen)
Aloe aristata (lace aloe)
A. jucunda (Somalian aloe)
Asparagus densiflorus 'Sprengeri' group, young plants (asparagus fern)
Bambusa multiplex, dwarf cvs. (dwarf hedge bamboo)
Carissa macrocarpa 'Horizontalis' (creeping Natal plum)
Ceropegia linearis ssp. *woodii* (sweetheart vine)
Chlorophytum bichetii (dwarf spider plant)
Citrus spp., seedlings (grapefruit, lemon, lime, orange)
Conophytum minusculum (dwarf ice plant)
C. stephanii (dwarf ice plant)
Crassula excilis (cushion plant)
Cryptanthus acaulis (earth star, starfish plant)
Cyanotis somaliensis (creeping cyanotis)
Cyperus congestus (dwarf sedge)
C. esculentus (chufa)
C. fertilis (dwarf sedge)
Dracaena cincta, syn. *D. marginata* 'Tricolor'
   (dwarf red-banded dracaena)
Echeveria elegans (Mexican gem)
E. × gilva (wax rosette)
Echinopsis, dwarf spp., young plants (cactus)
Euonymus japonicus 'Microphyllus Albovariegatus',
   other variegated small-leaf cvs. (dwarf variegated euonymus)
Euphorbia dwarf succulent spp., young succulent plants
   (succulent euphorbia)

Faucaria tigrina (tiger jaws)
Gasteria bicolor var. *liliputana* (dwarf gasteria)
Gymnocalycium, dwarf spp., young plants (cactus)
Hatiora salicornioides (bottle cactus, spice cactus)
Haworthia, dwarf spp., young plants
Kalanchoe blossfeldiana hybrids (Christmas kalanchoe)
Lithops spp. (living stone)
Mammillaria, dwarf spp., young plants (cactus)
Mitchella repens (partridgeberry)
Monanthes polyphylla (dwarf crassula)
Opuntia, dwarf spp., young plants (prickly-pear cactus, cholla)
Osmanthus fragrans, young plants (fragrant olive)
O. heterophyllas 'Myrtifolius' (dwarf holly olive)
× Pachyveria spp.
Parodia, dwarf spp., young plants (cactus)
Pelargonium × hortorum, dwarf cvs. (geranium)
Portulacaria afra var. *foliisvariegatis* (variegated elephant bush)
Punica granatum 'Nanum' (dwarf pomegranate)
Rebutia spp. (cactus)
Rosa chinensis 'Minima' cultivars (miniature rose)
Sansivieria, dwarf spp. and cvs. (snake plant)
Scindapsus pictus, young plants (ivy arum, pothos)
Sedum, dwarf tropical spp. (stonecrop)
Sempervivum spp. (hen and chickens)
Syngonium spp., young plants (African evergreen, arrowhead plant)
Tillandsia ionantha (dwarf tillandsia)

FOR CULTURE IN OPEN OR CLOSED CONTAINERS

Acorus gramineus 'Pusillus' (dwarf sweet flag)
Adiantum bellum (Bermuda maidenhair)
A. diaphanum (filmy maidenhair)
Alternanthera ficoidea var. *amoena* (joyweed, parrot leaf)
Begonia hydrocotylifolia (pennywort begonia)
B. Semperflorens-Cultorum, dwarf hybrids (wax begonia)
Caladium humboldtii (dwarf angel wings)
Chamaedorea elegans, young plants (good-luck palm, parlor palm)
Episcia spp. and cvs. (carpet plant, lovejoy)
Hedera helix, dwarf cvs. (dwarf English ivy)
Hypoestes phyllostachya, young plants (polka-dot plant)
Impatiens walleriana, dwarf cvs. (dwarf impatiens)
Ledebouria socialis (African squill)
Malpighia coccigera (Singapore holly)
Mentha requienii (Corsican mint)

Pellionia pulchra (rainbow vine)
P. repens (trailing watermelon begonia)
Peperomia, dwarf spp. and cvs.
Philodendron, dwarf spp. and cvs. young plants
Pilea microphylla 'Variegata' (variegated artillery plant)
P. serpyllacea (red artillery plant)
Plectranthus forsteri 'Marginatus' (variegated Swedish ivy)
P. madagascariensis (fragrant mint leaf)
Saintpaulia, dwarf spp. and cvs. (African violet)
Saxifraga stolonifera (strawberry geranium)
Siderasis fuscata (rusty dayflower)
Soleirolia soleirolii (Irish moss)
Tetranema roseum (Mexican violet)
Tradescantia, dwarf tropical spp. (spiderwort)

pieces of wood worked into a mounded, uneven surface all lend interest to the overall plan. A one-sided terrarium will naturally be arranged differently from one that is to be viewed from all sides. The latter type might contain a single dominant plant set in the center of the container, surrounded by smaller plants and diminutive nonliving objects. Once the terrarium is completed, add less water than you think it needs. After one or two days you may determine that a bit more water is required. It is critical to avoid overwatering, since excess water is very difficult to get out without disassembling the entire terrarium, and soggy soil is fatal to most plants.

Pteris ensiformis 'Victoriae', a variegated fern

USING THE INDOOR LIGHT GARDEN TO START VEGETABLE AND FLOWER SEEDS

With readily available materials, many kinds of vegetables and flowers can be started indoors for later use in the home garden. For this purpose, fairly cool temperatures are advisable, as, for example, in the basement or perhaps a heated garage. Temperature and adequate light intensity are the critical factors for the production of sturdy seedlings. Ideally, the seedlings should receive bright fluorescent light in an area with a daytime temperature of 70° to 75°F and a drop of at least 10°F at night—down to 60° or even 55°F.

To hasten germination, a soil temperature of about 75°F is best (and may be had in a warm room or by setting the seed pan or flat over the ballast of a fluorescent unit), but as soon as the seedlings have begun to emerge, they should be moved to the cooler location and be placed 2 to 3 inches beneath the tubes, with the uppermost leaves kept about that far away from the lighting as growth advances.

Kinds of Vegetables and Flowers to Start Indoors

With simple materials, many fine-seeded annuals and perennials that are tiny as seedlings and slow in initial growth may be started under fluorescent lights indoors, and be well advanced by set-out time.

Since space beneath fluorescent tubes is usually at a premium, start only those kinds that will benefit from early indoor germination. For example, it is foolish to start beans and Swiss chard, which are best sown directly in the garden at the proper time. In most hardiness zones, however, tomato, pepper, eggplant, okra, melon, and cabbage and its many relatives, as well as most herbs and many annual flowers (especially small-seeded kinds) profit from an early indoor start. Seedlings of the cabbage clan should be hardened off and planted outdoors early, even before the last spring frosts, while the set-out date for others is later. For maximum germination, use fresh seed, following the instructions discussed later in this chapter.

Preparing Seed Flats

Plan to start preparing the seed flats 10 to 12 weeks before the plants are to be set outdoors. Use standard plastic seed flats, wood flats, or for a small number of plants, small plastic seed pans or discarded aluminum food containers, all with holes for drainage. Fill the flats with commercially prepared soil purchased for this purpose, or use one of the soilless mixes (see page 909).

Sowing

Fill the flats with premoistened soil and tamp it in place. Thinly sow the seed in rows that are 2 to 3 inches apart. Sowing in definite rows allows you to judge easily how well the seeds are germinating. Cover the seed to a depth of twice the diameter of the seed, and gently tamp in place. Very tiny plant seeds, like petunia, should not be covered, but simply gently watered in. See page 871 for a list of garden plants whose seeds require light for germination and hence must not be covered. Label the flat, or each row or section if you have planted more than one type in a flat, with the plant name and date of sowing. Water the planted seeds with warm water thoroughly and carefully, until the water runs out of the drainage holes. Allow the flat to fully drain (for several hours) before covering with a plastic bag or a pane of glass or Lucite. Then place the flat in a warm place to germinate, such as over the ballast of a fluorescent fixture, in a closable germination box with fluorescent fixtures mounted in its hinged lid, or in a sand-filled box kept warm with electrical soil-heating cables.

Most vegetable and flower seeds take 6 to 10 days to germinate, or less if the soil is warm. The flat or pan of seedlings should then be placed 2 to 3 inches beneath the tubes and the transparent cover removed. As the seedlings grow, you must judge whether they are too crowded. If they seem too crowded to grow well, they should be thinned by clipping out the surplus plants, not by pulling them, since this can damage the roots of the seedlings left in place. If the seedlings are not too thickly crowded, however, wait until each has developed at least two true leaves, then transplant the extra plants to other soil-filled flats or to cell packs. The newly transplanted seedlings may wilt after being moved, but usually recover in one or two days.

An alternative to sowing in seed flats or pans is to use compressed peat moss pellets (Jiffy 7), widely sold at garden centers and nurseries. Sow two seeds per moistened peat pellet, and proceed as instructed above. Once the seed germinates and the plants are 4 to 6 inches tall, thin the seedlings to one per pellet, selecting the stronger. At this stage, the individual plants in their pellets should be transplanted to a flat of soil or into individual pots. Plants should be spaced 2 to 4 inches apart and filled in around the Jiffy 7 with soil. Melon, especially, responds to the Jiffy 7 because it is slow to recover from ordinary transplanting.

The transplanting step just described allows you to care more easily for your group of seedlings; since most of the seedling roots will be inside the Jiffy 7, the final shock of transplanting is less than if the plants were directly sown into soil in a flat.

Another choice is to sow directly in four- or six-chambered cell packs. These packs and pots may be nested and stored for reuse.

Damping Off

Careful watering of seedlings in containers is critical. Daily checking is essential, and as much care should be taken to avoid overwatering as to maintain an adequate supply of moisture. The fungus disease known as damping off often attacks and quickly kills seedlings in overwet soil. Allow the surface of the soil to become dry; the plant can actually wilt ever so slightly without undue harm. Then water thoroughly until the water runs out of the drainage holes. Pay particular attention to watering the edges or the sides of the flat; it is here that flats dry out first because of increased air circulation. Apply a weak fertilizer (one-quarter strength) to every second watering.

If seedlings appear girdled and then topple, they have succumbed to damping off. You can try to arrest the spread of the disease through the flat by scooping out affected seedlings and soil, and by using less water on the rest, but such salvage attempts often fail. Damping off is most easily prevented by using a commercially prepared soilless medium, by including a suitable fungicide (such as captan or ferbam) in the water, and by increasing air circulation around the germinating seed.

Hardening Off

Before being planted out in the garden, seedlings grown indoors under lights must be acclimated to outside conditions. This toughening process is called "hardening off." First, on warm spring days, the flats should be moved to a lightly shaded outdoor location, protected from strong, drying winds and from direct sun exposure, and brought in at night if temperatures are forecast to fall below 50°F. After several days of such exposure, the plants should gradually be exposed to more sun, culminating in full sun all day before placing them in a coldframe or similar structure. This need be nothing more than a shallow excavation that will hold the flats and is covered with a slightly opened storm window. After remaining in the coldframe for a week or two, and once all danger of frost is past, the seedlings are sufficiently hardened off to be safely transplanted to the garden.

PLANTS THAT GROW WELL UNDER LIGHTS

Annual plants that are grown under lights from seed to flowering are wonderfully rewarding. Often these may be started in early fall for winter bloom. Although the plants are usually short-lived (an average of six months for most kinds), seed is easily obtained and is an excellent way to have a varied collection at little cost. To achieve constant bloom, replanting must be done at monthly intervals, but since for most kinds commercial packets are generous, you should be able to make many sowings of a few seeds for pot culture. Store extra seed in a screw-top jar in the refrigerator. When buying seed, only dwarf and miniature varieties should be selected since space is so limited in light gardening. Suitable cultivars of the annuals discussed below are especially successful when grown under lights. For best results, the soil should be a commercially prepared, nutrient enriched, sterilized potting mix or, less ideally, a home-prepared medium made up of equal parts of friable garden loam (pH about 6.5), sharp sand, and peat moss. Sterlization reduces the likelihood of pathogens or weeds attacking or competing with the ornamentals.

ANTIRRHINUM MAJUS
(Snapdragon)

Dwarf cultivars of snapdragon such as 'Little Darling', 'Floral Carpet' hybrids, and 'Sweetheart' hybrids are quite small and readily branch from the base. Colors are mixed.

CELOSIA ARGENTEA
(Plumed celosia)

Dwarf plumed celosias make compact pot plants. These include 'Fiery Feather', which is 10 to 12 inches tall and has red plumes; 'Kimono' hybrids, which are 6 to 8 inches tall and have red to yellow plumes; and 'New Look', which is 8 to 10 inches tall and has red plumes.

COLEUS × HYBRIDUS

Any coleus is easily grown under lights, but dwarf cultivars with deeply serrated, strikingly variegated leaves are particularly interesting. Unless the light is quite bright and terminal shoots are pinched, even dwarfs may tend to tall legginess. Leggy plants should be cut back, and the cuttings may be rooted. The best-suited cultivars are 'Carefree' hybrids, 'Fashion Parade', 'Saber' hybrids, and 'Wizard' hybrids; all are less than 10 inches tall.

IMPATIENS WALLERIANA
(Common impatiens)

Dwarf cultivars of impatiens that are best suited to indoor cultivation include 'Accent' hybrids, which have 2-inch flowers in mixed colors; 'Cleopatra' hybrids and 'Mini' hybrids, which have a very compact habit and flowers in mixed colors; and 'Starbright' hybrids which have red to pink flowers with a white central zone on each petal. Excess nitrate and/or inadequate light cause outsize growth and legginess.

Coleus 'Lime Queen'

KALANCHOE BLOSSFELDIANA
(Christmas kalanchoe)

Although it is usually treated as a short-term Christmas plant, kalanchoe performs well under lights throughout the year. Any cultivar is suitable. Individual flowers are small but are borne in dense clusters and in colors ranging from red through pink and yellow to white, according to cultivar.

LANTANA CAMARA

Only dwarf cultivars of lantana are suited to the confines of the indoor light garden. Among them are 'Dwarf Pink', 'Dwarf White', 'Dwarf Yellow', and 'Nana Compacta' (yellow).

PENTAS LANCEOLATA
(Egyptian star)

Dwarf cultivars of Egyptian star are derived from the subspecies *quartiniana*. These include 'California Lavender', 'California Pink', 'Orchid Star' (pinkish lavender), and 'Tu-Tone' (pink and white).

PETUNIA × HYBRIDA

Dwarf cultivars of petunia are very easy to grow under lights if the plants are kept pruned and kept attractive by prompt removal of spent flowers. Among those cultivars most suitable in the floribunda class (the flowers are 2½ to 3 inches across) are 'Celebrity' hybrids (various colors) and 'Ice' hybrids (rose pink to near white with dark veins). In the single grandiflora class (with flowers 3½ to 5½ inches across) are 'Apple Blossom' (pink, fringed), 'Cascade' hybrids (red to lilac pink), and 'Prio' hybrids (purple, red, pink, or white). In the double grandiflora class (the flowers are 3½ to 4 inches across, double, and ruffled) are 'Red and White Double Empress' and 'White Swan'.

SALVIA SPLENDENS
(Scarlet sage)

All of the dwarf scarlet sage cultivars are suitable. Among them are 'Scarlet Pygmy' and 'Salmon Pygmy', both usually less than 6 inches tall.

TAGETES PATULA
(French marigold)

All of the dwarf cultivars of French marigold are adaptable to indoor light culture. The following, all 6 to 8 inches tall, are especially meritorious: 'Boy' hybrids (yellow to red-brown), 'Gypsy Sunshine' (yellow), 'Lemon Drop' (yellow), and 'Pretty Joy' hybrids (yellow to red-brown). The cultivar 'Teeny Weeny' is only 4 to 5 inches tall, has a spreading habit, and bears single red-brown flowers that are mottled with yellow.

ZINNIA ELEGANS

Of the compact zinnia cultivars, the following are especially well suited. 'Peter Pan' hybrids are 8 to 12 inches tall and have 3- to 5-inch flowers in various colors, 'Red Lollipop' is 8 to 10 inches tall and has 2½-inch flowers that are deep red, and 'Thumbelina' hybrids are 4 to 6 inches tall and have 1- to 1½-inch flowers in various colors.

TENDER PERENNIALS THAT GROW WELL UNDER LIGHTS

Except where otherwise indicated, soil for the following plants is the same as that used for annuals.

ANTHURIUM SCHERZERANUM
(Flamingo flower)

A 1-foot-tall relative of the familiar lipstick flower (*A. andraeanum*), flamingo flower blooms more or less continuously if rooted in a porous mix, preferably an orchid mix with extra leaf mold, or sphagnum moss with charcoal added. It must be kept moist at all times, and the aerial roots should be covered with long-fiber sphagnum. Add fertilizer every month.

BEGONIA *SPP.*

Many species and cultivars in the various begonia classes (see page 918) are small enough for culture under lights. By using small pots, a number of begonias that would exceed space constraints for indoor light gardening may be kept small without sacrificing their ornamental attributes.

Suitable for cultivation in 2½-inch pots and growing no taller than 4 inches are *B. bowerae* (including the cultivar 'Nigramarca'), *B.* 'Buttercup', *B.* 'China Doll', *B. prismatocarpa*, *B. rex* 'Peridot', *B.* 'Robert Schatzer', and *B.* 'Smidgins'. The following cultivars can be grown in 4-inch pots and do not exceed 6 inches in height: *B.* 'Baby Perfection', *B.* 'Cathedral', *B.* 'Crispie', *B.* 'Gay Star', *B.* 'Red Spider', and *B.* 'Sun God'. The following *B. rex* cultivars are also suitable for 4-inch pots: 'American Beauty', 'Baby Rainbow', 'Bantam Gem', 'Dew Drop', 'Granny', 'Red Berry', and 'Robin'. The following cultivars reach 9 inches when grown in 4-inch pots: *B. dregei*, *B. floccifera*, *B.* 'Aries', *B.* 'Dancing Girl', *B.* 'Emerald Jewel', *B.* 'English Lace', *B.* 'Sir Percy', and *B. rex* 'Kitty'.

Among the many cultivars of the ubiquitous wax begonia (*B.* Semperflorens-Cultorum hybrids), the smallest, most compact types, such as *B.* 'Ballet', *B.* 'Firefly', and *B.* 'Pink Camellia', are fine as indoor light garden subjects, but these do equally well on the windowsill. The so-called calla types, with white-variegated leaves, are best grown outdoors.

Although cane and shrubby begonias are generally too large to grow under lights, the smallest cultivars are successful. These include *B.* 'Medora', with beautifully spotted leaves but few flowers, and the everblooming cultivars *B.* 'Lenore Olivier', *B.* 'Orange Rubra', and *B.* 'Sachsen'.

The popular winter-flowering Rieger cultivars (*B. hiemalis*) are not recommended for house culture because of their great and often fatal susceptibility to powdery mildew, often in spite of preventive treatment with a fungicide.

BROMELIACEAE
(Bromeliads)

The large, diverse family Bromeliaceae consists of mostly tropical species, and includes many epiphytes, or air plants. In nature, epiphytes grow attached to tree limbs, rocks, or other supports, and their roots derive moisture and nutrients from debris trapped in tree crotches or in rock crevices. Some kinds use the water that accumulates in the cups or tanks that are formed by the closely fitting bases of their rosetted leaves. Those lacking such reservoirs should be generously misted or sprayed with water daily. Perfect drainage and air circulation around the roots are essential for success with epiphytic bromeliads. The plants may be tied or glued to pieces of cork, bark, driftwood, osmunda fiber, or tree fern trunk, with roots of the wetter-growing types wrapped in sphagnum moss. Dry-growing kinds, such as many species of *Tillandsia*, should have their roots left uncovered.

Terrestrial bromeliads require a porous, acidic medium, such as one of the commercially prepared soilless mixes.

Each bromeliad rosette or stem will flower only once, but one or more offshoots or "pups" develop at the base. These may be left to grow in place and bloom the next year, or they may be removed and

Cryptanthus bivi

mounted or rooted separately. Offshoots are usually not removed until they are one-quarter to one-third the size of the mother plant.

Small epiphytic bromeliads suited to indoor light gardens include *Aechmea miniata* var. *discolor*, *A.* × 'Foster's Favorite', and *A.* × 'Royal Wine', all responding well to moderate light intensity. Miniature *Tillandsia* species, such as *T. cyanea* and *T. ionantha*, should be mounted on pieces of bark or driftwood.

Among terrestrial bromeliads small enough to grow under lights are various species, varieties, and cultivars of earth star (*Cryptanthus*), including *C. bivittatus*, *C. bromelioides* var. *tricolor*, *C. fosterianus*, *C. zonatus*, and *C.* 'It', all of which succeed in the relatively dim light at the ends of fluorescent tubes.

Guzmania ligulata and *G.* 'Major', with especially large, colorful, long-lasting spikes, thrive in medium light. The smaller species of *Billbergia*, such as *B. nutans* and *B. zebrina*, require brighter light.

CACTACEAE
(Cacti)
AND OTHER SUCCULENTS

The most successful of cacti—a large, diverse group—when grown under lights are those that are flat, spreading, or compact. Bright light, a gritty, well-drained soil, and cool night temperatures are best for most kinds. The principal exceptions are Christmas catus (*Schlumbergera* × *buckleyi*), Thanksgiving cactus (*S. truncata*), and Easter cactus (*Hatiora gaertneri*), all of which do best in more subdued light, a humusy, though well-drained soil, and moderate, relatively even temperatures.

Other succulents, unrelated to cacti, that are suited to culture under artificial lights include *Aloe barbadensis, Crassula argentea, Gasteria lingua, Haworthia fasciata, Kalanchoe blossfeldiana, Pedilanthus tithymaloides* ssp. *smallii, Peperomia* spp., *Portulacaria afra, Sedum morganianum,* and *Stapelia gigantea,* all of which are treated in Chapter 38.

CALCEOLARIA, 'HERBEOHYBRIDA' GROUP
(Pouch flower, pocketbook flower)

Pouch flower is highly decorative when in flower and blooms for months at a time. It will usually bloom in about three months from seed, and its flowers are mainly in the yellow to orange range, often spotted red or red-brown. Cool temperatures and barely moist soil prolong flowering. Compact cultivars, not exceeding 9 inches in height, are the best choices. Plants past flowering should be discarded.

CROSSANDRA INFUNDIBULIFORMIS
(Firecracker flower)

An everblooming evergreen plant that reaches 1 foot tall and bears salmon-colored flowers, firecracker flower can be grown either from seed or stem cuttings taken at the base. Frequent fertilizing, using one-eighth the recommended dilution, and constant soil moisture are required for continuous bloom.

CYCLAMEN PERSICUM
(Florist's cyclamen)

Aside from requiring generous light, florist's cyclamen must be protected from the heat buildup that often occurs in indoor light gardens. A temperature range of 60° to 70°F is best. All cultivars are 6 to 9 inches tall, and most have large flowers ranging from red-violet to white, in the latter case usually with a red center. Cultivars with more numerous but smaller flowers than usual include 'Dwarf Fragrance' hybrids and 'Little Dresden' hybrids.

Florist's cyclamen (*Cyclamen persicum*)

EXACUM AFFINE
(Persian violet)

Persian violet is a compact, often rather globular plant that produces masses of ½-inch blue (rarely white), yellow-centered flowers almost constantly for several months. It is easily grown from seed, which should be sown every few months as the plants tend to decline after a long period of bloom.

GESNERIACEAE
(Gesneriads)

Many members of the diverse family Gesneriaceae are especially successful when grown under lights. For cultural details, see Chapter 38.

Achimenes *cultivars*
(Hot-water plant)

The compact, floriferous hot-water plant can be brought into bloom at any season. The cultivars *A.* 'Blue Waltz' (purple),

A. 'Charm' (pink), and *A.* 'Tarantella' (pink) are erect but less than 10 inches tall and bear abundant large flowers. Plant the small, scaly tubers ½ inch deep in sandy-humusy soil that is kept moist, as drought induces dormancy.

Aeschynanthus lobbianus
(Lipstick plant)

Lipstick plant is a trailing plant that bears its intensely red flowers irregularly throughout the year when grown under lights. In addition to *A. lobbianus,* several others are also well suited to indoor light culture: *A. ellipticus* (pinkish orange), A. micranthus (small, red, profuse), and *A. obconicus* (maroon and red).

Codonanthe carnosa
(Ant-nest plant)

Ant-nest plant is an epiphyte whose root ball is always inhabited by ants in its native tropical American rain forest habitat. This fleshy leaf, trailing plant bears white or pale pink flowers continuously. There are several other species, all fairly similar to *C. carnosa*, and all best grown in hanging baskets with a light, fluffy, humusy compost that freely admits air and allows rapid drainage.

Columnea repens

Species and cultivars of columnea are particularly rewarding as indoor light garden subjects. An everblooming species, *C. repens* has orange flowers borne on arching stems. The cultivars *C.* 'Early Bird' and *C.* 'Joy', also everblooming, bear yellow and red flowers; *C.* 'Pixie', a small hybrid, has orange flowers.

Episcia dianthiflora
(White carpet plant)

Although all species and hybrids of *Episcia* do best in warm temperatures (above 70°F) and high humidity (50 percent or more), white carpet plant is tolerant of

cooler, drier conditions. It can be grown as a trailer or kept to a single rosette by trimming the stolons. The related hybrid *E.* 'Cygnet' has larger leaves, larger flowers, and is more floriferous, while *E.* 'Cleopatra' has pink-and-white variegated green foliage and bears red flowers. Because it requires high humidity and is sensitive to drafts, it is usually grown as a terrarium subject.

Gesneria cuneifolia

Gesneria must also have the warmth and humidity required by most species of *Episcia* and, in addition, for best results, should be grown in an alkaline medium (pH 7.5 to 8). It bears red, orange, or yellow flowers, according to the clone. Other species, such as *G. christii*, *G. citrina*, and *G. saxatilis*, are especially suited to terrarium culture. The cultivar *G.* 'Lemon Drop' is a more tolerant hybrid, adapting better to ordinary indoor light garden conditions than other gesneriads.

Kohleria cvs.

Kohlerias are rhizomatous plants that can outgrow the usual light garden, but by taking tip cuttings you can check their height. The cultivar *K.* 'Connecticut Belle' is smaller than most, and has mottled foliage and pink flowers.

Saintpaulia ionantha
(African violet)

Most popular of the gesneriads, African violets vary considerably in plant and leaf form and in the color and size of the flowers. Ongoing hybridization yields new cultivars every year. Miniatures and trailing types make good terrarium subjects.

Sinningia speciosa
(Florist's gloxinia)

Although florist's gloxinia may be too large for some indoor light gardens, there are numerous dwarf cultivars and smaller species. Some of the best are *S.* 'Cindy', *S.* 'CindyElla', *S.* 'Coral Baby', *S.* 'Dollbaby', and *S.* 'Snowflake'. *S. concinna* and *S. pusilla* are also suitable.

Smithiantha × hybrida
(Brazilian edelweiss)

Such dwarf cultivars of Brazilian edelweiss as *S.* 'Littleone' and *S.* 'Zebrina' hybrids are better suited to culture under lights than the full-size forms. The flowers, borne in large spikes, range from yellow to red.

HOYA BELLA
(Dwarf wax plant)

While most other species of *Hoya* are too large for ordinary light gardens, dwarf wax plant is a small species with delicate leaves. Flowers appear on short leafless spurs year after year, so do not remove these. It flowers best when allowed to become pot bound in a well-drained mix with some extra lime or bonemeal added.

LEDEBOURIA SOCIALIS
(Silver squill)

Formerly known as *Scilla violacea*, silver squill is a tender bulb with spotted leaves, 2 to 4 inches long. It makes a dwarf, evergreen clump and blooms in the spring with arching sprays of bluish flowers. Its

Codonanthe

real value, however, is its neat foliage. It does best if pot bound and rooted in a gritty soil mix for succulents; let it dry out between waterings and fertilize only sparingly. Propagate by removing the outermost bulbs.

ORCHIDACEAE
(Orchids)

Of the many genera or groups of epiphytic orchids that can be successfully grown under lights, *Paphiopedilum* and *Phalaenopsis* include some of the easiest species and cultivars. However, the range can be considerably expanded with high light intensity and mastery of the more important cultural idiosyncracies. A good basic rooting medium consists of three parts washed, moist bark chips; one part coarse perlite; one part charcoal, horticultural grade; and one part chopped, dried leaves or fibrous peat or chopped sphagnum.

Paphiopedilum *cvs.*
(Venus's-slippers)

The easiest of orchids to grow under lights, Venus's-slippers will bloom reliably year after year if properly handled. Dwarfs especially suited to indoor light gardens include *P. bellatulum*, *P. concolor*, *P. fairieanum*, and *P. niveum* 'Ang Thong'. The notable species *P. glaucophyllum* produces a succession of flowers on the same scape.

Phalaenopsis *spp. and cvs.*
(Moth orchid)

Moth orchids produce beautiful, long-lasting flowers. When they fade, cut their stalks back about three-quarters of the way, leaving several nodes intact. Within one or two months, a new spike will arise and the plant will reflower. During this second flowering, a new spike will grow from the base of a younger leaf, thus ensuring a long period of bloom. The smaller species are easier to grow under lights than the larger hybrids. Especially recommended are *P. amboinensis*, with yellow flowers that are striped brown; *P. equestris*, with an almost continuous succession of small pink to purple flowers; and *P. parishii*, a dwarf with small white flowers.

Other Epiphytic Orchids

Other orchids that are successful under lights are species of *Ascocentrum* (especially *A. ampullaceum* and *A. curvifolium*), *Brassavola* (especially *B. nodosa*), *Goodyeara*, *Lockhartia*, *Masdevallia*, and *Pleurothallis*.

OXALIS *SPP.*
(Wood sorrel)

Wood sorrel, a cormous plant, will go dormant if allowed to dry out. Most growers deliberately dry the plants out once a year, place the pots (with the corms still in the soil) in a refrigerator for several weeks, then restart them with added fertilizer or repot the corms in fresh medium. Among the many cultivated species, *O. regnellii* has triangular leaflets and white flowers and *O. aureoreticulata* has gold-veined green leaflets and rose red flowers.

PELARGONIUM × HORTORUM
(Geranium)

Dwarf and miniature cultivars of geraniums are good subjects under lights, provided they are kept as cool as possible. Zonal geraniums have attractively colored leaves in such variety that it doesn't matter whether they bloom or not. The leaves are banded with green, red, and cream,

and are spectacular under lights. The tricolored varieties are the most desirable, such as *P.* 'Mrs. Henry Cox,' *P.* 'Mrs. Strong', and *P.* 'Skies of Italy'. *P.* 'Alpha' has brilliant red-orange flowers and small apple green leaves. *P.* 'Black Vesuvius' has orange-scarlet flowers and tiny black-green leaves with a red band.

PUNICA GRANATUM *'NANA'*
(Dwarf pomegranate)

The dwarf, fine-textured pomegranate is an excellent subject for bonsai under lights. Try it from seed or cuttings, and you will be pleased with the lovely pendulous red or pink blossoms. The plant will even set fruit. The soil must stay moist and the top should be kept pruned.

ROSA CHINENSIS *'MINIMA'*
(Pygmy rose, miniature rose)

Pigmy roses are dwarfs that suggest quarter-size hybrid tea roses. Most grow 12 to 15 inches tall, but some grow only 5 to 8 inches. They require the same care that outdoor roses do. They must be grown in the garden in the summer, then pruned slightly and sprayed before being taken indoors in the fall. Keep them from becoming straggly, but do not prune them back as drastically as you would hybrid teas.

Oxalis regnellii 'Rubra-alba'

40

Greenhouse Gardening

FOR MANY PEOPLE, GARDENING IS A JOYOUS ADVENTURE, from the precocious flowering of winter jasmine and Chinese witch hazel during winter thaws and the appearance of the first snowdrop and winter aconite in earliest spring to the mums of autumn, with the accompanying blaze of fall foliage in the north, and the absolute last whisper of the season's outdoor floral activity when the modest winter hazel opens its pendent buds around the time of the winter solstice. By then we have been driven indoors and must await the arrival of the

A glass and aluminum lean-to greenhouse of traditional design complements the architecture of the house and blends into the surrounding garden.

seed catalogs to catalyze us toward the next gardening season. For a relatively few very fortunate gardeners, however, the small greenhouse makes it possible to carry on gardening activities all year round. For many others, the dream of having such a facility often looms large.

In this chapter, the focus is mainly on the so-called cool greenhouse, i.e., one kept at 45° to 55°F at night and 10° to 15°F warmer during the day in winter. Such a range favors the cultivation of a wide range of ornamental temperate-zone and subtropical plants. It is also favorable for forcing bulbs for out-of-season bloom and for starting cool-season vegetables and flowers for earlier setout than would otherwise be possible. Maintaining warmer, tropical conditions in the greenhouse through the winter is more costly, especially in the north. Moreover, to treat the great diversity of plants that might be grown under such conditions is beyond the scope of this book.

Until recently, small private greenhouses had long been considered a luxury beyond ordinary means. However, new types that are simple in design and efficient in operation have brought the small greenhouse well within the means of many. It need not be elaborate or expensive: A small lean-to, built against the house, may be constructed for little more than the cost of a television set, and it will offer delightful possibilities for winter gardening. The money thus invested will return big dividends in beauty, in learning, and in satisfying activity. Even an unheated greenhouse offers many opportunities and is a challenge to the skill and ingenuity of the gardener.

If the greenhouse can be attached directly to the house, it may usually be operated on the same heating unit, which substantially reduces the cost of operation. Such a location also has the advantage of providing shelter from strong winds. If a greenhouse is to be attached to the house, it should preferably have a south or southeastern exposure. If it is not attached to the house, it should be located so that it receives a maximum amount of sunshine and is protected, if at all possible, from prevailing winter winds.

A range of commercial greenhouses covered with translucent plastic membrane reveals a modular structure and heating and ventilation technologies that have been widely adapted to home greenhouse use.

Before World War II, most greenhouses were made of glass and wood, with steam heat and manually operated ridge vents. Intensive operating and maintenance requirements made them impractical for home use.

Where the topography of the ground presents no problem, the greenhouse should preferably be oriented so that its length runs north to south, as this will provide for maximum intensity and distribution of sunlight in the winter months.

CONSTRUCTION

The average hobby or home greenhouse is basically a simple structure. If one is handy with tools, precut and prefitted greenhouse kits are available today ready for assembling. These kits include detailed instructions and are, of course, the most economical to erect. Plans for greenhouses are also available from most local cooperative extension services. In any case, there are many details that must be considered in constructing a greenhouse, whether it is to be heated or unheated. It is essential that the house be built of sturdy, durable materials that cast a minimum of shade within, that satisfactory provisions be made for ventilation, that the benches be designed to meet any specially designated needs, and that the heating unit be entirely adequate yet as economical as possible.

A free-standing glass and aluminum greenhouse with wide benches and cut-outs for access. White sand in benches beneficially reflects light upward, retains moisture to humidify the air, and helps support occasionally top-heavy pots.

Aluminum is very durable and does not corrode. Although the initial cost may be higher than for wood, the maintenance costs will be reduced to a minimum as aluminum will require no painting and no restorative repairs and replacements.

The least expensive types of greenhouses are those made of plastic sheeting spread over a frame of aluminum hoops. Polyethylene film, polyvinyl chloride (PVC), clear vinyl, polyester (Mylar), or fiberglass panels are the plastics most frequently used. Such plastic greenhouses are very popular among commercial nurseries and are used today on a very large scale. The cost of a plastic structure is a fraction of the cost of one made of glass, especially if constructed by the owner. For many, a plastic hoop house is the only affordable greenhouse available.

Among the other advantages of plastic greenhouses is that they have greater moisture retention and less heat loss than a glass structure. The light transmission varies from approximately 81 to 90 percent through a single thickness. Actually, some plants thrive better in this lower light intensity than they do in a glass greenhouse. A great saving in heating costs may be realized by using a double plastic skin, the two layers separated by pressurized air, which serves as insulation. The chief disadvantage of plastic greenhouses is that the plastic skin deteriorates under strong sunlight and must, therefore, be placed in two to five years, depending on exposure and the type of plastic involved.

The material for the construction of the benches is usually a matter of personal preference. Wood is the most economical, if the initial cost alone is considered, but it is the least satisfactory under permanently humid conditions, because it will rot and need replacing within a few years. If wood is used, however, and assuming the once preferred cypress or cedar is too costly, the wood should be pressure treated to retard decay. Concrete benches are still preferred by some, but they are very expensive and cannot be moved. One of the most satisfactory, versatile types is an open wire-mesh bench, made with galvanized wire, that is supported on a pipe or angle-iron frame. It provides good ventilation and heat distribution at low cost.

Soil-filled benches, of the type used commercially for cut-flower crops, should be 6 to 8 inches deep. Adequate provision for drainage must be provided in the form of narrow openings between the boards or holes in the panels that form the bottom of the bench. Benches on which potted plants are to be placed should be 2 to 3 inches deep. Such benches, which resemble shallow trays, should be filled with pebbles or cinders on which the pots may rest. This will not only facilitate drainage but will aid in maintaining the desired degree of humidity and help stabilize temperature. Benches should be no wider than your reach; i.e., benches accessible from only one side should be 2 to 3 feet wide, and benches accessible from both sides can be as wide as 6 feet. Most benches stand 30 to 32 inches high, but should be adjusted to suit individual needs and uses.

The greenhouse should be supplied with piped water and a sufficient number of faucets provided at convenient points. The faucets should be threaded so that a hose may be easily attached. In general, it is much more convenient to use short hoses with several faucets than one long, heavy,

A tall, narrow greenhouse adapted to the culture of tropical epiphytes or air plants, with benches and wall panels of wire mesh to support containers and rooting media.

cumbersome hose. One faucet for every 12 lineal feet of greenhouse is recommended.

Concrete makes the most satisfactory walkways for greenhouses, although cinders and gravel are sometimes used where it is necessary to augment humidity, as, for example, in orchid houses. Concrete walks are easy to keep clean, will withstand wear, and are impervious to dampness.

It is very convenient to have a small workroom or potting shed attached to the greenhouse. But if space is not available, or if the various items of expense must be kept to a minimum, the north end of the house may be utilized for this purpose. A bench of convenient height and length should be provided for use in the preparation of soil mixtures, and for such operations as seed sowing, transplanting, and potting, which are an almost daily part of the greenhouse routine. Bins may be constructed underneath the bench for storage of surplus flats, pots, cell packs, and other containers, and to hold the components of soil mixtures. Adequate shelf space should also be provided for insecticides, fumigants, labels, and other small items.

In managing a home greenhouse, the most important considerations are heating, ventilation, and watering.

HEATING

Circulating hot water is the best means of heating the small greenhouse. The heat is more evenly distributed than with the once popular steam heat.

A thermostatically controlled oil or gas furnace is the most satisfactory type of heating unit for greenhouses today, especially if it is an extension of the existing home heating system with a separate heating zone.

Another fairly efficient heating system is forced warm air, but this is often unevenly distributed and can cause high rates of moisture loss in locations near the warm-air draft. In most regions, electric heat, especially for greenhouses of substantial size, is prohibitively expensive. In any case, regardless of the choice, any heating system should be thermostatically operated, since environmental control is vital in greenhouse gardening.

Overall fuel costs for greenhouse heating can be kept to a minimum if the solar heat that accumulates within the structure is retained as long as possible. This can easily be achieved by closing the ventilators earlier each day than one would normally do and also by carefully covering the glass during the night with straw mats or boards. Massive heat-absorbing objects within the greenhouse, such as a thick masonry foundation up to bench height, or a series of water-filled barrels stored under the benches, slowly radiate heat through the night and thus reduce the demand for furnace heat.

If the greenhouse is of sufficient size, it is wise to have it partitioned into at least two sections, and to have the heating system designed with separate thermostats to maintain a moderately high temperature in one section and a much lower temperature in the other section. This will make it possible to grow a wider variety of plants, as some plants thrive in coolness, while others must have a comparatively high temperature. If, however, the greenhouse is small, and it is not feasible to provide for more than one temperature, this need not be too great a handicap. The choice of plant materials will, of necessity, be somewhat more limited, but even the smallest greenhouse, maintained at a rather low temperature, will offer delightful opportunities for winter gardening. Moreover, all greenhouses have cool spots, especially in corners where more heat is radiated through the glass or plastic relative to the adjacent interior air mass. Such differences are easily monitored with thermometers.

Fragile and sensitive to change, the small neotropical orchid Lepanthes lindleyana, *when propagated by division, is best grown in a protective bottle where light, humidity, and temperature can be controlled.*

As a matter of general practice, commercial operators set night temperatures at 40° to 45°F in extremely cool houses to 65° to 70°F in houses where tropical or subtropical plants are grown. During most days, temperatures naturally rise 10° or 15°F higher or even more. Thermometers and thermostats in greenhouses should be placed out of direct sun. In a small greenhouse where but one temperature is to be maintained, a range between 50° and 55°F at night and 60° to 70°F during the day will usually prove a satisfactory compromise. Some plants are able to endure severe fluctuations in temperature, while others are extremely sensitive to such changes. It is wise

for the amateur to choose plants with a wider amplitude for environmental change than the so-called temperamental or fussy plants have. Once you gain experience in greenhouse gardening and can provide conditions that very nearly approximate the ideal, it is possible to grow some of the more exotic greenhouse species but the novice is well advised to start with sturdy types that are less demanding.

A wood-framed greenhouse fitted with single-pane glass offers architectural charm but is more costly to construct and maintain than a double-skin plastic-covered hoop house of the same size. The conveniently located coldframe facilities hardening off seedlings, forcing spring bulbs, and protecting marginally hardy garden plants in winter.

VENTILATION

To reduce heat buildup, facilitate air change, and promote gentle air movement, the greenhouse should be equipped with easily opened ventilating panels and at least one door. Some greenhouses are equipped with ventilators on the sides as well as on the roof, and this is the most desirable type of construction. However, it requires care, skill, and good judgment to control a ventilating system efficiently. As a general practice, the ventilators should be opened in the morning when the temperature is rising. On warm days when there is brilliant sunshine and little wind, the ventilators should be opened to the fullest extent. On very cold days a mere crack may be sufficient. The ventilators should be closed early enough in the afternoon to conserve as much heat as possible. When a strong wind is blowing, it is wise to open the ventilators on the opposite side of the house from the direction of the prevailing wind to prevent a direct draft of air on the plants. Sudden changes in temperature and sudden shifting from brilliant sunlight to dark clouds mean more or less constant attention to the regulation of the ventilators in a greenhouse if the heating unit is to function at its maximum degree of efficiency.

So important is fresh air to the welfare of the plants that on days in early autumn and in the spring when it would be

A free-standing fiberglass and aluminum greenhouse, opened for the summer and furnished with a shading panel.

possible to maintain the desired temperature within the house, provided that the ventilators were kept closed, it is preferable to admit fresh air even if it necessitates keeping the heat on low.

Excellent electronically controlled devices for regulating the ventilators in greenhouses are available and such devices are well worth the extra cost, as they relieve the owner of much care and anxiety. When fluctuations in temperature occur, the ventilators are automatically opened and closed by these thermostatically activated devices. Moderating such fluctuations is especially important in a small greenhouse, as its low cubic content and relatively greater surface area result in the rapid loss and gain of heat.

WATERING

The species of plants grown in greenhouses vary widely in their moisture requirements, and individual plants also vary at different stages of growth and at different times of year. It is essential to good greenhouse management, therefore, that you understand the moisture requirements of the plants you are growing. The requirements of the most commonly grown greenhouse plants are discussed later in this chapter.

There are, however, certain general principles that apply to all kinds. Greenhouse plants should be arranged according to their watering requirements. For example, cacti and succulents do not need the amount of water that moisture-loving plants do. Watering should be done preferably when the temperature is rising, and it is, therefore, part of the usual morning routine in the greenhouse. To secure the best results, the temperature of the soil in the beds and benches

should be approximately that of the surrounding air in the greenhouse. Water absorption by the plant takes place very slowly in cold soils. Greenhouse plants in ground beds frequently fail to do well because of this factor. Such a condition may be remedied, however, by running heating pipes along the sides of the beds, or by placing pipes underneath the beds. Some plants are so sensitive to temperature that it is advisable, whenever possible, to supply them with water that has been warmed to about 70°F. In this group are such plants as poinsettia, gardenia, gerbera, lily, and rose. Tanks or barrels may be kept in the greenhouse for the storage of sufficient water to supply the needs of such plants.

Most plants will make their best growth, other conditions being favorable, in soils that are uniformly supplied with sufficient moisture. For greenhouse plants grown in beds and benches, the optimum moisture conditions may best be maintained by occasional heavy watering. Both the amount and frequency of application will be determined, to a considerable extent, by the age of the plants, the type of root system they possess, and the physical structure of the soil. Large, actively growing plants will require relatively large amounts of water. Plants with fibrous root systems will require larger amounts than those with taproots. Heavy soils will require less frequent applications than light, sandy soils. If greenhouse beds and benches are given a fairly heavy watering at rather infrequent intervals, the plants will make a vigorous root growth that will extend deeply into the soil. If frequent, light waterings are given, the plants will have a tendency to become shallow rooted.

The force with which the water is applied is also a factor to be taken into consideration. A heavy stream of water should be avoided, as it causes the soil to become increasingly compacted, reducing aeration. An adjustable hose nozzle, or a rose nozzle of a size to permit a moderately fine spray, may be attached to the hose. For watering small seedlings and young growing plants, a fog nozzle or a watering can is preferable. The standard greenhouse watering can with a long spout is ideal for this purpose, and a series of rose nozzles of various sizes may be purchased.

Careful attention must always be given to the watering of young seedlings. Fresh-sown seed and young seedlings are most efficiently watered by placing the seed pan or pot in a tray filled about one-third with water. By capillary action the water will soon rise to the surface in the seed pan or pot, at which time it should be removed from the tray. On bright, sunny days it is often necessary to water more than once. Seed flats and young transplanted seedlings should never be allowed to dry out, and they should be kept partly shaded, by, for example, a sheet of newspaper.

The watering of potted plants also requires skill and judgment, as these plants, too, vary widely in their moisture requirements. Some, such as azalea, maidenhair fern, and many begonias, may suffer irreversible harm if allowed to dry out. Many other plants, including poinsettia, fuchsia, calla, and clivia, require a definite rest period, during which watering should be appreciably decreased or, in some cases, entirely suspended, thereby simulating the annual drought period in their native regions. In general, potted plants should be watered only when necessary. Plants that are making active growth, and especially those that are in full flower, will usually require liberal quantities of water, as young leaves and all floral structures transpire water more freely than mature, firm foliage.

For plants in clay pots, an excellent way to determine the need for water is the method used by many experienced English gardeners—tap the pot with the knuckle. If the tap resounds in a dull thud, it is an indication that the plant does not need water. If, however, the tap resounds with a hollow, ringing sound, additional moisture should be supplied. Another method is to lift the pot and test it by weight. It should be remembered that a clay pot is always heavier than a plastic pot, and usually the clay pot will dry out faster. Plunging the pot into some sand or gravel will keep the roots cooler and the pot will not dry out as quickly. It is important that there be sufficient drainage space below the pot.

The majority of plants with smooth leaves may be watered from overhead without any danger of injury to the foliage. Plants with hairy or very fleshy leaves, such as African violet, are best watered in such a way that no moisture comes into contact with the foliage, especially as the usually humid greenhouse atmosphere slows evaporation and thus promotes leaf diseases. A watering can may be used very successfully for this purpose if the rose nozzle is removed. In some cases, it is advisable to place the plants in a pan of water until the surface of the soil in the pot has become moist.

Automatic irrigation systems are valuable for watering single crops in large greenhouses but are less appropriate in small greenhouses with mixed plantings in containers. Drip irrigation is useful in this instance, as long as the emitters can be located where needed and the flow from each can be individually adjusted.

In greenhouses lacking exposed earth and in which plants are potted and grown on wire-mesh benches, the air may become not only hot but also quite dry. Such conditions cause many plants to drop older leaves and also encourage certain pests, especially red spider mite. Where feasible, occasional syringing is useful to elevate humidity, decrease uptake of water by roots, and perhaps most important, prevent or reduce any outbreaks of red spider mite.

During the winter, syringing should be done on bright, sunny days when the temperature is rising. It is not advisable to syringe plants late in the afternoon when the temperature is dropping, as the result will be a condensation of moisture on the foliage, which may prove injurious to the plant. During the summer, however, greenhouse plants may be safely syringed in late afternoon.

In general, plants that have smooth, firm foliage benefit from syringing; those with fleshy or hairy foliage should not be syringed, as the protracted retention of water on their surfaces in the quiet, humid atmosphere of the greenhouse may be more harmful than beneficial.

HUMIDITY

The maintenance of a proper degree of humidity in the greenhouse is a matter of vital importance. Plants vary greatly in their optimum humidity requirements, just as they vary in their moisture requirements. The fact that the optimal humidity for roses is 75 percent while for most members of the cactus family it is less than 50 percent means that these two plant groups must be accorded very different treatment. Every gardener should be familiar with the general humidity requirements of the various plant groups being grown. In some cases, the optimum humidity requirements of specific plants have been very definitely determined, in others it is relatively unimportant.

Humidity is closely associated with the respiration of plants and with the manufacture of food within them. It is a generally accepted fact that high humidity makes it possible for the leaf pores, or stomata, to open wider and to remain open longer than possible when the humidity is low. If plants are grown in an atmosphere in which the humidity is far below optimum, water loss through leaf transpiration will exceed water absorption by roots, causing older leaves to wither and drop, thereby reducing transpiration. However, this usually reduces the growth and vigor, to say nothing of diminishing the decorative appearance, of the plants affected.

For plants, there is a close relationship between humidity and the factors of light and temperature. During prolonged, dull winter periods, high humidity can be detrimental, as it may encourage plant diseases, whereas on bright, sunny days when the temperature is comparatively high, the effect will be decidedly beneficial. It is particularly desirable on bright days in winter when cold outside temperatures keep the heater on for extended periods to maintain the desired humidity inside.

There are various ways in which the humidity in a greenhouse may be increased: by syringing the plants, by wetting down the walks, and by spraying beneath the benches, particularly on the heating pipes. It is possible to maintain a higher degree of humidity in a house where the walks are made of gravel than it is in a house where the walks are concrete. However, most growers prefer concrete because the degree of humidity can be more definitely controlled and the house can be kept dry, except when moisture is artificially applied at times when it may seem desirable to increase the humidity. In orchid houses, where a very high degree of humidity is necessary, a sprinkling or misting system is sometimes installed under the benches.

It is desirable to monitor the degree of humidity in a greenhouse definitively. This may be done by means of a hygrometer, or some similar device designed especially for the purpose.

THE EFFECT OF SUMMER ON THE GREENHOUSE

With the approach of summer, the intensity of the heat in a greenhouse would become unbearable both for the plants and for the gardener if some form of shade were not provided. The ideal device for such a purpose is a roll of small strips of metal, green plastic, cheesecloth, wood, or thin pieces of bamboo wired together to block a percentage of solar radiation, and thus diminish heat buildup. Such screens may be regulated by means of pulleys and rolled up and down at will. It is a decided advantage to be able to roll them up on cool, cloudy days and to lower them on bright, sunny days when the temperature within the house is soaring. If it is not possible to obtain any of the above roller-type shades, the best substitute is a coating of some suitable preparation applied to the outside of the glass. Such shading compounds can be purchased from any reputable garden or greenhouse supplier. They are usually obtained in either powdered or liquid form; they mix instantly with water and are available in white or green.

During the summer months when most of the plants have been removed for an outdoor sojourn, the greenhouse should be given a thorough cleaning. Any necessary repairs or repainting may be done at this time. The soil from the benches may be removed and fresh soil brought in, and the greenhouse may be made ready for the next winter season.

THE EFFECT OF LIGHT INTENSITY

Experiments carried out at state agricultural experiment stations have helped determine the effect of varying light intensities on plant growth. It has been found that plants vary tremendously in their responses to light. In the case of some plants, it is possible to hasten the blooming period and to increase the quantity and quality of the bloom by reducing the nighttime dark period. This adjustment in day length, or photoperiod, is accomplished by means of lights placed above the plants. In the case of other plants the reverse procedure, the shortening of the day, has resulted in the production of early bloom, and this, in turn, is accomplished by shading the plants with black cloth to exclude all light for a portion of the day. Extensive experiments have shown that some plants are not affected by either of these treatments, and in other cases the effect has been so slight that the additional labor and expense involved have not been justified.

Increasing the Length of the Day

Additional light may be supplied for a period varying from four to eight hours either at the beginning or the end of the day. The method most commonly employed by commercial growers is to provide additional light for a period of five hours, beginning at 5:00 P.M. and continuing until 10:00 P.M. The method employed in supplying the light is of considerable importance. If fluorescent tube fixtures are used, they should be placed approximately 18 to 24 inches above the plants. Alternatively, incandescent bulbs may be employed. For the majority of plants a 40-watt bulb may be used with excellent results; for some plants that are unusually responsive to light a 15- or 25-watt bulb will be sufficient. Either clear or frosted incandescent bulbs may be used. Ordinary nitrogen-filled bulbs have, in the majority of cases, proved to be more satisfactory than mercury, neon, or sun lamps. It is essential, however, that reflectors be used. The most desirable type of reflector is one about 8 inches in diameter and deep enough so that only the tip of the bulb extends beyond the rim. The plants should be given an opportunity to become well established in the benches before using extra light.

Reducing the Length of the Day

The usual procedure in shortening the length of the day to induce early flowering is to drape black cloth or some other dark, opaque material over the plants. Closely woven black sateen has proved to be one of the best materials for this purpose, and if proper care is taken it will give good service for several seasons. In most cases a reduction of four or five hours in the length of the day is sufficient. The practice most generally followed is to place the cloth over the plants at 5:00 P.M., allowing it to remain until 7:00 A.M. The time when the short-day treatment should be initiated depends entirely on the normal bud-forming period of the plants.

THE UNHEATED GREENHOUSE

Although an unheated greenhouse has decided limitations, it also offers many satisfying opportunities. In addition to imposing no energy cost, the unheated greenhouse serves purposes different from those of the conventional heated structure. In the winter, it is particularly valuable as a place to protect plants that are only marginally hardy in your region but that nevertheless do require a cold period each year. In the spring, it is a protected environment in which to start and harden off half-hardy and tender annuals and vegetables, ensuring their being ready for the garden sooner than otherwise possible. In the fall, it may be used to store pots planted with hardy bulbs that require some weeks of cold before being taken into the house for forcing. These and many other opportunities present themselves in the unheated greenhouse. Two of the most popular variants are the following: the alpine house and the pit house.

Alpine House

For a collection of rare alpine plants, or for plants difficult to grow outdoors, the unheated greenhouse is the ideal location. With plenty of ventilation near the benches, or even with air-conditioning during the summer months, this type of greenhouse can be used throughout the year for growing alpine plants. The glass or plastic skin will protect the plants from harsh or dry winds, while the amount of water needed also can be more carefully controlled. On sunny winter days the ventilators must be opened to prevent the temperature from rising too much and also to keep the plants in their dormant stage. In the summer, the lath shading is rolled over the glass or plastic, but this shading must be at least 6 inches above to maintain a cooling air current between the glass or plastic and the shading.

Pit House

The pit house can be described as a combination of sunken greenhouse and walk-in coldframe. In effect, it is really a greenhouse that is partially below grade, and its internal temperature is moderated somewhat by that of the surrounding ground, which cools the pit house in the summer and warms it in the winter, diminishing the extremes of temperature outside. Usually only 12 to 24 inches of the gable ends and roof (made of coldframe sash) are above ground. To ventilate the pit house, the sash can be either partially raised or removed completely. The advantage of the pit house over a regulation greenhouse for alpine plants is that the plants are closer to the glass, the temperature can more readily be controlled, and the roof can be removed to expose the plants to the weather. The pit house is also easier and cheaper to install.

North of zone 8, where the climate is severe, it is difficult, if not impossible, to obtain any actual bloom in an unheated greenhouse during the midwinter months. But with the first warm days of spring such a greenhouse may become a veritable garden, and it will offer a wealth of material for flower arrangements in the house. Bulbs of all kinds may be forced into early bloom, and astilbe (*Astilbe* × *arendsii*), bleeding heart (*Dicentra spectabilis*), Virginia bluebells (*Mertensia virginica*), columbine (*Aquilegia* spp.), pansy (*Viola* × *wittrockiana*), and primrose (*Primula* spp.) may all be brought into flower. Snapdragon (*Antirrhinum majus*), calendula (*Calendula officinalis*), larkspur (*Consolida* spp.), and wallflower (*Erysimum* cultivars) may be sown in the early autumn and the young plants carried over the winter in the benches. Although such flowers will make comparatively little growth during the winter, they will develop into sturdy plants with strong, vigorous root systems and will come into flower months ahead of spring-sown seedlings.

It is a decided advantage to have the unheated greenhouse be as protected as possible. Straw mats or burlap frames packed with straw may be used to provide added protection during extremely cold weather.

SELECTION OF PLANT MATERIALS

If the potentialities of a small greenhouse are to be realized to the fullest extent, the plant materials to be grown must be selected with great care. The usual desideratum is to have as much bloom as possible in the greenhouse from early autumn until late spring and to have a wide variety of flowers that are of particular value for cutting and for decorative purposes in the house.

Annuals, perennials, bulbs, and potted plants all have an important part to play, and with careful thought and planning an abundance of bloom may be had throughout the winter months.

Many of the annuals that grow so luxuriantly outdoors during the summer months and are so valuable for cutting may be equally productive in the greenhouse. To this list we are able to add some of the more temperamental annuals, which cannot always be grown so successfully in the garden under the trying conditions of summer temperatures and humidity. To obtain a succession of bloom from autumn until spring, it is necessary to plan a program of work well in advance and to follow the schedule with care.

RECOMMENDED GREENHOUSE PLANTS, ESPECIALLY FOR THE COOL GREENHOUSE, INCLUDING SOIL, CULTURE, AND PROPAGATION

ANTIRRHINUM MAJUS
(Snapdragon)

The snapdragon is among the best of all greenhouse plants and will give a wealth of colorful bloom throughout the winter months. Cultivars suitable for growing in the greenhouse are available in a veritable rainbow of colors: white, yellow, apple blossom pink, rose, apricot, scarlet, deep Indian, red and wine, among others.

If autumn or early winter bloom is desired, the seed should be sown early in June. The young seedlings should be pricked out before they become crowded, and they may be carried on in flats or in pots until they are ready to be benched in late August or early September.

A rather heavy, coarse soil, well supplied with organic matter and of good fertility, is considered ideal, although snapdragons will do well on widely varying soil types. A slightly acidic reaction (pH 6.5) is best; alkalinity often causes yellowing in the leaves. An application of superphosphate, ½ pound per 10 square feet, made at the time of planting, promotes excellent results and obviates the need for additional fertilizer.

When the young seedlings have developed five or six sets of leaves, they should be pinched back. The plants should be spaced 10 inches apart each way in the bench. Snapdragons succeed extremely well if given a night temperature of 45° to 48°F with a rise of 10° to 15° during the day. They are one of the few plants that can be grown with great success in an unheated greenhouse and will give an abundance of bloom during the late winter and early spring months if grown under such conditions. In a heated greenhouse, they often bloom immediately after chrysanthemums and in this way excellent use is made of all available bench space. For a late planting, the seed should be sown in late August and the young seedlings grown on in flats or pots until

the chrysanthemums have been removed and bench space is available. It is a common practice among commercial growers not to water the foliage of snapdragons, merely to water the roots as a precautionary measure against the spread of rust, even though most cultivars are reputed to be rust resistant. If optimal development of flowers is sought, it is necessary to practice disbudding, i.e., to remove any small shoots that appear at the base of the leaves and in the axils of the flower stalks. Snapdragons thrive in a relatively low humidity of 50 to 60 percent.

AQUILEGIA SPP.
(Columbine)

It may be difficult to think of columbine, a popular hardy perennial, as a greenhouse plant, yet it can be forced so easily and the flowers are so exquisite for cutting that a few clumps should certainly be included. Plants that have flowered the previous season in the garden or in the nursery are ideal for greenhouse cultivation. It is well to mark the clumps while they are in bloom, as it is then possible to choose plants that are unusually beau-

Hybrid columbine (Aquilegia 'McKana Giant')

tiful in form or in coloring and will, therefore, be of particular value as cut flowers later on in the season.

Clumps should be lifted and potted up with compost in fall and placed in the coldframe where they will be subjected to necessary cold, but with some slight protection. In midwinter, the dormant plants may be brought into the greenhouse and planted in a bench, or potted in 10- to 12-inch pots. Growth will start within a few days and by March or early April the plants will be in full flower. A cool temperature, ranging between 45° and 55°F, is required, as columbine will not flower well if subjected to excessive heat. After the plants have finished flowering, they may be replanted outdoors.

BEGONIA *SPP.*

For greenhouse culture, begonias may be grouped into four general classes: semituberous rooted, tuberous rooted, foliage group, and fibrous rooted. Although different rooting media are used for propagation in the various groups, the potting mixture for well-rooted plants is essentially the same for all begonias: three parts loam, two parts well-rotted manure, one part peat moss, and one part sand, with 4-12-4 commercial fertilizer worked in at the rate of one full 4-inch pot per 2½ bushels of soil mix.

Semituberous or Rhizomatous Group

The semituberous-rooted begonias include the popular Christmas begonia (*B. cheimantha* cultivars) and the Rieger, or elatior, begonia (*B. hiemalis* cultivars). These and other species and cultivars in this group are most readily propagated by rooting sections or cuttings of the thickened horizontal stem or rhizome. Partially detached pieces strike root wherever they contact soil. Some may also be propagated by leaf stalk cuttings taken from well-ripened, medium leaves in late fall (see Chapter 36). The stalks, or petioles, should be inserted in the propagating case in such a way that the leaf blades do not come into contact with the sand. The formation of roots requires four or five weeks, but the cuttings should not be potted up until new shoots have begun

to develop from the leaf base. However propagation is effected, use a neutral (pH 7) potting mixture of one part loam, one part sand, and one part peat moss, and keep the top of the cutting near the surface.

The young plants may be grown on with a bottom heat of about 70°F, and as they develop they may be shifted into larger pots, ending up with a 6- or 7-inch pot. A humid atmosphere and partial shade are desirable, and pinching should be practiced to produce stocky, well-developed plants. Staking is usually advisable, as the stems are very brittle. During the growing period a night temperature of 58° to 60°F is desirable, with a slightly higher temperature during the day.

Tuberous-rooted Group

The tuberous-rooted begonias are diverse assemblage grouped under the name *B. × tuberhybrida*, the better-known cultivars of which are described on pages 918-19. In this group, propagation is by tuber division, seed, and stem cuttings.

Foliage Group

Begonia 'Fireflush'

Also diverse, especially as to foliar shape, size, vesture, and markings, the foliage group cultivars are considered variants of *B. rex.* Propagation is by means of leaf cuttings. Only well-matured leaves should be selected for propagation. About 1 inch of the leaf margin should be cut away and the remaining portion of the leaf should be cut into triangular sections, with a small section of the leaf stalk at the base and a vein running through the middle. The cutting should then be inserted in the propagating case, the section of petiole being completely covered.

Begonia rex × B. hemsleyana

Fibrous-rooted Group

Begonia Semperflorens-Cultorum hybrid

The very popular, much-grown fibrous-rooted begonias, grouped under the name *B.* Semperflorens-Cultorum hybrids, are valued for their green to purplish, sometimes variegated foliage, their red, pink, or white flowers, and the ease with which they may be grown. They may be propagated by seed, by stem cuttings, and in the case of multistemmed cultivars (such as 'Gloire de Chatelaine'), by division. Seed is best sown in late fall or winter. As they are dust-fine, they must be handled with care (see page 864). Seed should be sown very thinly and the seedlings pricked out and planted in flats or cell packs once they have developed leaves large enough to permit handling. Cuttings may be taken anytime, but they root most readily in early spring.

BOUVARDIA *SPP.*

The waxy, richly perfumed, white, pink, yellow, or red flowers of the bouvardias are a source of constant joy during the months that they are in bloom. The tubular blooms are fine for cutting and emit a fragrance suggestive of orange blossoms.

New plants may be started very readily from cuttings made in late winter or early spring, and the young plants may be grown in pots. Bouvardia may also be propagated by means of root cuttings. The roots should be cut into 1- to 2-inch-long pieces, and these may be planted horizontally in flats containing a mixture of equal parts of sand and peat moss.

To do well, bouvardia requires a very fibrous, friable soil generously supplied with leaf mold or screened compost. The medium should be neutral to slightly alkaline (pH 7 to 7.5). Acidic soil results in the browning of leaf margins or sometimes complete defoliation.

If acquired during the summer, set outdoors, but later transfer into the greenhouse when night temperatures descend below 50°F. Alternatively, they may be kept permanently in the greenhouse. They should be repeatedly pinched back to induce branching. As bouvardias suffer when transplanted, it is best to keep them potted, moving them into larger pots as root density increases.

Bouvardias thrive in moderately cool temperatures, with 55°F at night considered ideal and rising about 10°F in the day. The plants usually begin flowering in early fall and continue for three or four months. When they have finished blooming, they should be cut back and placed under the bench. During this rest period they should be watered little and, finally, in mid winter, not at all. At this point, they may be safely taken from their pots, have the soil shaken from their roots, be repotted with fresh soil, and kept moist. With such treatment, bouvardias usually resume vigorous growth and bloom profusely.

CALENDULA OFFICINALIS
(Pot marigold)

Calendulas are among the most satisfactory of all annuals for the cool greenhouse, and their bright flower heads, in shades of orange, yellow, and gold, are borne profusely throughout the winter months. The plants are of easy culture and repay generously for the little attention required.

Calendulas are easily grown in almost any soil, but they do best in a fairly heavy, fertile loam. In preparing the medium, one part well-rotted manure should be used to every three parts of soil, superphosphate should be applied at the rate of 1 pound per 20 square feet, or ¾ ounce per square foot.

Although calendulas are fairly indifferent to soil pH, a neutral reading (pH 7) is best. Mulching with peat moss or other loose organic matter helps maintain cool soil temperatures.

Plants grown from seed sown in midsummer will begin flowering in midfall; sowings made in midfall will begin bearing in midwinter. Seedlings grow rapidly and, whether grown in pots or greenhouse benches, should be spaced about 1 foot in all directions (or about 6 inches for dwarf cultivars).

Flower size and length and stiffness of the flower stalk are strongly influenced by temperature. To have large, well-supported flowers, the night temperature should be 45° to 50°F, and 60° to 65°F during the day. Higher temperatures will yield earlier, more abundant bloom, but flower size will be smaller and the stems weak.

CHRYSANTHEMUM × MORIFOLIUM CVS.
(Greenhouse mum)

So generous with their bloom, so lovely in form and coloring, and so entirely satisfactory both for cutting and as potted plants, mums should be included in every greenhouse, no matter how limited the space. Many cultivars that are not hardy outdoors in most zones may be grown successfully in the greenhouse, and with careful planning the period of bloom may be extended over several months.

Rooted cuttings of many cultivars may be initially purchased from commercial growers, but after the first season, cuttings may be made from the stock thus obtained. These rooted cuttings should be potted up in early spring; they may be grown on in pots, and shifted to larger pots as the plants develop, or they may be planted in benches.

The soil for mums should be carefully prepared. A 1-inch layer of rotted sod or coarse, strawy manure should be placed in the bottom of the bench and a soil mixture consisting of one part well-rotted manure and three parts sandy loam is recommended. An application of 20 per-cent superphosphate at the rate of 1 pound per 12 square feet, or 1¼ ounces per square foot, may be made at the time of planting. The soil should be very slightly acidic (pH 7.5).

If large flowers borne on tall, single stems are desired, all side shoots and all growth from the base of the plants should be removed, and they should be spaced 8 to 10 inches apart. For normally branched plants, 12 inches should be allowed.

The pompon types of chrysanthemum should be kept pinched back until midsummer to obtain sturdy, well-branched plants, six or eight flowering branches being allowed to develop. Commercial growers usually bench their mums (i.e., transplant them to greenhouse benches) from late spring to early summer, as this enables the young plants to become well established during the summer.

A few weeks after the plants have been benched, a 1-inch mulch of domestic peat moss should be applied. Such a mulch has a dramatic effect on the growth and vigor of the plants, sometimes causing as much as a 50 to 100 percent increase in growth.

When the buds begin to show, weekly applications of ammonium sulfate may be made, 1 ounce dissolved in 2 gallons of water usually being sufficient. Chrysanthemums do best if night temperatures do not exceed 50°F.

After the flowering season is over, the plants may be lifted from the bench and placed in a coldframe and serve as a source of cuttings in early spring.

CLARKIA AMOENA
(Godetia)

The copper-colored stems of clarkia, studded with crisp little whorls of bloom, are very useful for cutting, and a few plants will add welcome variety to flower arrangements. If the flowers are cut just as the buds begin to open, they will last extremely well.

For early bloom, sow seed in latest summer; for later bloom, in midfall. Relatively indifferent to soil conditions, the young plants grow rapidly, whether in pots or benches (where they should be spaced about 1 foot apart). A night temperature of about 50°F helps ensure optimal performance.

CONSOLIDA *SPP.*
(Larkspur)

Some of the cultivars of larkspur, or annual delphinium, are well adapted for greenhouse culture. Grown from seed, the young plants may be grown on in pots or in the bench, and flowering normally occurs three to four months after sowing.

A light, fertile soil, neutral or slightly alkaline (pH 7 to 7.5), yields best results. Decidedly cool temperatures, 50°F at night to 60°F in the day, are most favorable for larkspur. Spaced 8 to 10 inches apart, they offer a wealth of bloom and are available in shades of violet, lavender blue, rose, pink, and white. The tall, stately flower spikes are also exceedingly fine for cutting.

CYCLAMEN PERSICUM
(Florist's cyacamen)

When cyclamens are well grown, they flower abundantly all winter and contribute a jewel-like beauty to the greenhouse garden. For maximum growth and fullest flowering, the temperature should range from 50° to 60°F in the winter.

Cyclamen may be propagated either by seed, or by cutting the corm into sections with one or two leaves attached to each section. The seed should be sown in early fall, with the expectation that these plants will first flower the winter of the following year. A mixture of equal parts friable loam and peat moss makes a good medium for the seedbed, and the seeds should be planted about 1 inch apart. If kept at a temperature ranging between 55° and 60°F, they will germinate in four to five weeks. After several leaves have developed, the plants should be transplanted into 2½-inch pots, with the tiny corm placed so that its top is level with the surface of the soil. At each subsequent repotting, the corm should be placed slightly higher until at the time of the last shift the corm rests on the surface of the soil.

Soil with a pH between 6 and 7 and light in texture should be used for cyclamen plants in the early stages of growth. For plants reaching maturity, the following soil mixture is recommended: three parts friable loam, one part well-rotted manure, ½ part peat moss, and ½ part

Florist's cyclamen (*Cyclamen persicum*)

sand. At the final potting, a 3-inch potful of 4-12-4 commercial fertilizer should be added to each bushel of soil.

During the summer months, the young plants should be kept in a cool, semi-shaded spot, a well-ventilated, partially shaded greenhouse being satisfactory. Frequent syringing of the foliage and the maintenance of high humidity is desirable. The shade should be removed in the fall. If, at this time, the pots are set on shelves or elevated on inverted flowerpots, the development of the plant will be hastened. Cyclamen plants are best grown in clay pots rather than in glazed or plastic containers. Watering must be done with care, with pots being set in a saucer or pan of water until the surface of the soil becomes moist. The plants may be carried over for the next year by resting them after the period of bloom is over, until buds reappear, providing the same treatment as for young plants.

DIANTHUS CARYOPHYLLUS
(Carnation)

Carnations, the ever-dependable and ever-popular greenhouse mainstay, are grown commercially from cuttings. The usual practice is to take the cuttings from vigorous plants in late fall. They may be taken from the axillary shoots, preferably from the lower portion of the flowering

stem. They should range from 3 to 5 inches in length and be inserted in the propagating case with sharp sand as the best rooting medium. Although it was formerly a common practice to remove a portion of the foliage, a higher percentage will root if the foliage is not reduced. Under favorable conditions the cuttings should root in about four weeks, although some cultivars will root more readily than others.

Carnations perform best in sandy-humusy loam, and thrive equally well within a range of pH 5.5 to 8. At the time of planting, superphosphate, applied at the rate of ¾ ounce per square foot, is a useful amendment. Beginning about eight weeks after benching, monthly applications of a 4-12-4 commercial fertilizer may be made at the rate of ⅓ ounce to each square foot. Planting distances vary from 6 to 12 inches apart, according to the cultivar's habit.

Once cuttings are well rooted, i.e., with roots ½ to 1 inch long, they should be potted up in 2½-inch pots, with a mixture of equal parts compost, sand, and peat moss being used. Before becoming pot bound, they should be shifted to larger pots, as carnations suffer from any check of this sort, often irreversibly, the plants becoming hard, yellow, and stunted in appearance. Carnations should not be potted very firmly, and care should, therefore, be taken not to set the plants too deeply. Watering must also be done with care, as overwatering is often fatal.

Soon after the plants have been potted for the first time, they should be pinched back to within about 3 inches. The lateral or auxiliary shoots should be pinched back as they develop, to produce symmetrical, well-branched plants. Pinching should continue until you want the flower buds to mature. For early bloom, pinching should cease in early summer. If late bloom is desired, pinching may be continued until after the plants are benched. It requires 10 to 20 weeks for a newly pinched shoot to produce a flower. The plants may be grown on in pots until they are ready to be benched, or as soon as danger of frost is past, they may be set in the open ground. If field culture is practiced, growth will be more vigorous and greater disease resistance obtained. On the other hand, pot-grown plants yield earlier bloom. The plants are usually benched in late summer. They thrive in soil that is uniformly moist but, as noted above, not saturated.

DICENTRA SPECTABILIS
(Bleeding heart)

White bleeding heart
(Dicentra spectabilis 'Alba') in garden

There are very few hardy garden perennials that can be forced as successfully as bleeding heart, and few flowers are more graceful and appealing. After you have grown them in the greenhouse, you will not want a season to pass without using at least a few plants for decorative purposes both in the greenhouse and for brief periods in the living room.

Two-year-old clumps should be carefully lifted in the fall and heeled-in in a coldframe, where they have exposure to required cold. In midwinter (late January to early February), the plants should be brought into the greenhouse and potted

up in ample 10- to 12-inch bulb pans. They should then be placed in the coolest temperature available and forced slowly. During this period of growth, the plants will require abundant moisture. By late March or early April the pendent, pink-and-white or all-white, heart-shaped flowers will begin to open, and the plants will then remain in bloom for many weeks if they are kept in a moderately cool temperature. After the flowering period is over, the plants may be replanted out of doors, and will show no ill effects from this gentle process of forcing.

ERYSIMUM *CULTIVARS*
(Wallflower)

Still erroneously listed in some catalogs as *Cheiranthus cheiri*, the so-called English wallflowers are prized for their delightful fragrance and quaintly decorative quality, with colors ranging from cream through yellow, apricot, orange, red, rust, and brown. They are of easy culture, and although they are naturally biennials when grown outdoors, they are admirably adapted to the cool greenhouse.

For bloom during the winter months, seed should be sown the previous March. The young seedlings may be pricked out into small pots or into flats as soon as they have made sufficient growth. Humusy soil helps ensure the fullest flowering.

During the summer months, the young plants may be grown on in pots or they may be planted in nursery beds in open ground. To flourish, wallflowers require cool temperatures, ranging at night between 45° and 50°F with the day temperature no higher than 65° or, at most, 70°F. Throughout their growing period the plants require a liberal amount of water. Wallflowers may be grown in pots, in raised benches, or in solid beds; plants should be spaced approximately 12 inches apart.

ESCHSCHOLZIA CALIFORNICA
(California poppy)

The large-flowered cultivars of California poppy make very decorative greenhouse flowers. Seed should be sown a few per pot or thinly in the greenhouse bench

where they are to flower, as this species, in keeping with poppies of all kinds, often fails when transplanted while growing. Plants should be thinned to one per pot or 8 to 10 inches apart in the bench. Flowering begins eight to 10 weeks from sowing and is especially prolific if conditions are kept cool.

California poppy
(Eschscholzia californica)

EUPHORBIA FULGENS
(Scarlet-plume euphorbia)

The brilliant orange-red flowers of the tender, shrubby scarlet-plume euphorbia are strikingly decorative and make a few plants a welcome addition to the small greenhouse, especially when in flower in summer and fall. This species is propagated by softwood cuttings taken from stock plants in midspring or by hardwood cuttings taken in early winter after the parent plants have flowered. The cuttings should consist of two or three nodes, and should be rooted in a medium of equal parts peat moss and sand. Once rooted, plants do best in a rather heavy, slightly acidic (pH 6.5) soil, either in a bench or potted up. Each plant should be pinched back so that three or four stems develop from the lower portion of the plant. The plants should be spaced 10 to 12 inches apart in the bench. A fairly steady growing temperature of about 60°F is preferable. Sudden changes in temperature often cause leaves to drop and flowers to abort. Once rooted, the new plants usually flower within a few months.

Scarlet-plume euphorbia (*Euphorbia fulgens*)

As they grow, poinsettia plants may either be shifted into larger pots or be benched. If well-branched, symmetrical plants are desired, they may be pinched back until early September. The ideal temperature for poinsettias ranges between 60° and 65°F. The temperature should never be allowed to drop below 60°F at night. Beginning in mid-September, the night period should not be interrupted with light, as this may abort the development of the colored bracts. Ideally, the night period should be at least 14 hours long. The plants are also extremely sensitive to cold drafts, to prolonged chill, and to both overwatering and inadequate moisture. Any of these conditions can cause leaves to yellow and drop.

Poinsettia
(*Euphorbia pulcherrima* cultivar)

EUPHORBIA PULCHERRIMA
(Poinsettia)

Poinsettia is the most decorative of all plants for the Christmas season, and if conditions are favorable, it is possible to produce well-grown specimen plants even in the small greenhouse. Poinsettias are propagated by cuttings taken from mature stock plants. After the holiday flowering season is over, the stock plants are usually lifted and placed under a bench for a period of 10 to 12 weeks. The temperature of the greenhouse should range between 50° and 60°F, and the plants should be kept dry, although not dry enough to allow the wood to shrivel. About April 1, the plants should be pruned back severely and potted up or replanted in the bench and watered thoroughly. A rich soil should be prepared for the stock plants, consisting of three parts loam and one part well-rotted manure with a light application of superphosphate. The first cuttings may be taken in early summer. They may be cut at a node or with a slight heel of old wood from the parent stem. As the plants bleed readily, the cuttings should be dropped into cold water for a few moments (not more than five minutes). The cuttings should be trimmed so that only the two top leaves remain, and they should be rooted in a medium of moderately fine, sterilized sand and kept shaded during the day. The cuttings should be well rooted and ready for potting in about three weeks. Poinsettias thrive in a soil of moderate fertility and slightly acidic pH (6 to 7). A mixture of two parts loam, one part sand, and one part well-rotted manure is recommended. For the final potting or benching soil, add one 3-inch potful of superphosphate to each bushel of prepared soil.

FELICIA AMELLOIDES
(Blue daisy, blue marguerite)

Formerly called *Agathaea coelestris*, blue daisy is a subtropical subshrub usually grown as an annual. It serves both as a potted plant and for cutting and is admirably suited to culture in the small greenhouse. The daisylike flowers, of a soft powder blue, with golden centers, are borne in profusion throughout the winter and early spring months. The plants remain in flower over a long period of time, which makes them particularly desirable as potted plants for house decoration.

Blue daisy may be raised either from seed or from cuttings. In plants grown from seed there is some variation in flower color. Cuttings made during the early spring root readily, and the young plants may be grown on in pots to bloom through the summer and into fall.

Blue daisy adapts to a wide range of soils. A light, humusy soil gives best results, however.

In early autumn the plants may be transferred to the greenhouse bench if the flowers are to be used only for cutting. If they are to be grown as potted plants, they may be shifted into 6- or 8-inch pots or bulb pans. The plants thrive in a moderately cool house (50° to 60°F). Flowering resumes in the spring.

FREESIA *CVS.*
(Florist's freesia)

Freesias are exceedingly well adapted for greenhouse culture. They may be obtained in a wide range of colors—mauve, lavender, blue, yellow, orange, pink, and carmine rose. The graceful, one-sided clusters of sweetly scented flowers are valued for cutting.

If bloom is desired throughout the winter months, the bulbs may be planted in succession from August until the middle of December. They may be grown either in pots or in flats. For early bloom only large corms should be used; for later bloom the smaller sizes will be entirely satisfactory. The corms should be spaced approximately 2 inches apart each way in a potting medium consisting of two parts loam, one part compost, and one part sand.

After planting, the corms should be placed in a cool, dark place until the leaves first appear. If planted in the summer the pots or flats may be placed in a coldframe and shaded with lath sash. The pots should be kept moist but not truly wet. As soon as leaf growth has started, the shade should be removed. The pots should be brought into the greenhouse well before danger of frost. A night temperature

between 55° and 60°F is satisfactory, with daytime readings about 10°F higher.

As the flower stalks are very delicate, some support is necessary and very slender bamboo stakes may be used with a number of strings crisscrossed between them. When the plants have finished flowering, water should be gradually withheld and the corms allowed to ripen. After the foliage has begun to yellow, the corms may be taken from the soil and the largest set aside for early bloom the following year. Store all corms through the summer in a cool, dry place.

GARDENIA AUGUSTA

The gardenia adapts well to greenhouse culture and is widely grown commercially. The intensely fragrant blooms make this plant much in demand as a pot-grown item. The flowering period varies according to the climate. When grown in unheated greenhouses or outdoors on the West Coast, a long flowering period is attained, while in other parts of the country it may be comparatively brief, depending on the interval of night temperature that remains below 65°F, with 62° to 65°F the best night range. Daytime temperatures should be at least as high as 70°F. Equally important are high humidity and moist soil. The dry air that prevails in houses during the heating season causes buds to abort and leaves to drop. Dry soil has the same affect. In the greenhouse, the temperature should range from 70° to 75°F in the day to no lower than 60°F at night. Soil should have a pH between 5.5 and 6.5, be sterilized to protect against nematodes and canker, and be kept constantly moist. Flowering usually begins in late fall and continues into spring.

GERBERA JAMESONII
(Transvaal daisy)

A native of Transvaal in South Africa, gerbera is a very popular greenhouse subject. The flowers are unusually fine for cutting and are available in exquisite shades of yellow, salmon, apricot, orange-pink, and cerise. Transvaal daisies are true perennials in their native habitat but are too tender to withstand the rigors of our

Florist's freesia (*Freesia* 'Super Giant Hybrid')

winters north of zone 8. In many areas they are, therefore, greenhouse subjects.

These daisies are readily propagated both by seed and by the division of old established clumps. As gerbera seed loses its viability rapidly, only fresh seed should be used for propagation. The seed should be sown in March, and as soon as four or five small leaves have developed, the seedlings should be transplanted directly into 4- to 6-inch pots or into beds where they are to flower. Established plants may be divided in late spring or early summer.

For display, gerberas are most effective if grown in solid beds. During the summer, the plants should be given a light mulch and kept carefully watered. The plants should be spaced 12 to 15 inches apart. A moderately cool night temperature of 55° to 60°F is best. If given good care, the plants will produce abundant bloom throughout the winter and early spring months.

Gerberas grow best in sandy-humusy, well-drained soil of average fertility and in the pH range of 7 to 7.5. In the fall and spring a weekly application of urea, 1 ounce to 7 gallons of water, is recommended.

GLADIOLUS *CVS.*

Both the large-flowered types of gladiolus and the showy primulinus hybrids (derived from *G. dalenii*) as well as many of the very exquisite dwarf hybrids and cultivars, may be forced in the greenhouse for early spring bloom. The culture of the latter group is, however, quite distinct from the culture of the large-flowered types.

Corms of large-flowered cultivars and the smaller-flowered primulinus types should be specially prepared for forcing by the vendor. These may be planted directly in a bench, preferably in August or September, the rows being spaced 12 inches apart and the corms 4 inches apart in the row, or they may be planted in flats or in pots. The method of planting will usually be determined by the amount of greenhouse space available. When pot culture is adopted, three corms may be planted in a 6-inch pot. In flats, the corms may be spaced 4 inches apart each way.

Gladiolus

The corms should be planted at a depth of approximately 1 inch, and the soil should be at least 1 inch below the rim of the pot or flat to allow for watering. In all other respects, greenhouse culture is practically identical with outdoor culture. The plants should be given full sun, they should be watered adequately, and a moderate temperature (70° to 75°F) is best. If bench space is not available at the time of planting, the pots or flats may be placed beneath the benches for a brief period, until the corms have started into growth and the shoots have obtained a height of about 4 inches. They should then be brought into full light. The primulinus hybrids are particularly well adapted to forcing, and as cut flowers they are preferable to the large-flowered types.

Highly varied and often more exquisite in form and coloring than the large-flowered cultivars, many distinctive small-flowered, winter- and spring-flowering species from South Africa and their hybrids are especially suited to culture in the cool greenhouse. These include *G. cardinalis*, *G. dalenii*, *G. papilio*, and *G. tristis* as well as *G. × colvillei* and such cultivars as 'Comet', 'Elvira', 'Guernsey Glory', 'Impressive', 'Robinetta', and 'The Bride'. As most of these are neither hardy enough to grow outdoors north of zone 8 nor able to flower where growing seasons are short, they can be grown to perfection in the small greenhouse.

Corms of small-flowered sorts should be planted in midfall and stored in a coldframe until early winter, when they

may be brought into the greenhouse and forced under moderately cool conditions (55° to 60°F). The graceful flower spikes will begin to open in early spring. For a succession of bloom during the spring months, the pots should be brought in from storage at an interval of every 10 days.

HELIOPHYLLA LEPTOPHYLLA
(Cape stock, sun-lover)

Cape stock is one of the most attractive of South African annuals suited to greenhouse culture, yet it remains relatively little known. The long sprays of clear blue flowers, similar in coloring to those of perennial flax, are borne in profusion throughout the late winter months, and they are very useful in cut-flower arrangements. The fact that a few plants will produce such an abundance of bloom, and that they may be cut almost continually over a period of several months, makes them of unique value as a greenhouse flower.

Seed may be sown anytime during late summer and early fall, using a sandy-humusy greenhouse soil mix. Cape stock grows best in a moderately cool temperature. The plants may be grown either in pots or in raised benches, the latter being preferred. A distance of 8 to 10 inches between the plants will give ample space for their best development.

IRIS *SPP.*
(Bulbous iris)

Of all the kinds of bulbous irises that may be grown in the greenhouse, Wedgwood iris (*Iris tingitana* 'Wedgwood'), a cultivar of the Spanish iris, is especially meritorious. It is extremely well suited to forcing, and the large, clear blue flowers are of great value for cutting. Other Spanish irises, as well as English and Dutch irises, may also be forced into early bloom very successfully and are available in a wide range of colors.

Plant the bulbs (actually corms) in late summer or early fall in shallow bulb pans or flats, spacing them 1½ inches apart. A soil mixture of one part compost, one part loam, and one part sand is recommended. Water thoroughly to induce root growth. The planted bulbs should be stored in a coldframe until midfall and may then be brought in and placed in a cool greenhouse with a night temperature of 45° to 50°F and daytime readings about 10°F higher. If a succession of bloom is desired, a few pots or flats should be brought in from the frames at 10-day intervals. When the buds begin to show, the night temperature should be raised to 55°F, but the plants should never be subjected to a high temperature, as the quality and longevity of bloom are diminished. Bulbous irises require abundant water during the growing period, but the amount should be reduced when the buds begin to develop. Only the largest bulbs should be used for forcing.

Bulbs that have been especially prepared for forcing are available commercially, and the cultivar 'Wedgwood' may be brought into flower by Thanksgiving. Alternatively, bulbs may be subjected to a temperature of 80°F for three weeks after they are dug in early summer. Then, for a six-week period from mid-August to late September, they should be held at a temperature of about 50°F. At this point, they are ready for potting and forcing.

LATHYRUS ODORATUS
(Sweet pea)

So delightfully decorative are sweet peas for cut-flower arrangements that they are an important crop in the small greenhouse, even when little space can be allotted for them. Some of the winter-flowering types are exquisite both in form and in coloring, the flowers being grouped on long, slender stalks.

Sweet peas are propagated by seed. As the seeds have a hard outer covering, germination may be hastened by soaking them for 24 hours before sowing. The seed may be sown directly in the beds or in the benches where the plants are to flower, or it may be sown in small pots or in flats, and the seedlings later transplanted to their permanent position in the greenhouse. A light soil mixture should be used, consisting of equal parts of sand and loam. The time of flowering will depend to a considerable extent on the date when the seed is sown. Seed of the early or winter-flowering type, sown about the middle of July, will flower from

October through January. This is the type best suited for greenhouse culture. If sown September 1, the flowering period will extend from February to the middle of March, and if sown late in September, the plants will flower in March, April, and May. For early bloom it is, therefore, necessary to start the seed in midsummer.

Sweet peas do best on a sandy-humusy soil at pH 7. Free drainage is essential, as the plants are seriously harmed if roots are deprived of air. To a rich, well-prepared compost, add 0-10-10 commercial fertilizer applied at the rate of 1 ounce per square foot. Excess soil nitrate depresses flower development.

Sweet peas thrive in cool temperatures. During the summer, the greenhouse should be well ventilated, and adequate shade should be provided for the seedlings. Throughout the entire growing period low temperatures should be maintained. In the winter, the night temperature of the greenhouse should be 45° to 50°F, with day temperatures about 10°F higher, never exceeding 65°F, the highest tolerable maximum. Because of their ultimate height, sweet peas are best grown in

ground-level beds rather than in raised benches. The rows may be spaced from 3 to 4 feet apart, double drills being approximately 6 inches apart. The plants should remain thickly in the rows, being spaced hardly more than a few inches apart. As soon as they have become well established, they should be provided with adequate support. Wire or stout twine on wire supports may be used. When the plants come into bloom, all flowers should be picked immediately after fading, as seed pod formation tends to induce the formation of short-stalked flowers and fewer blooms.

LILIUM LONGIFLORUM
(Easter lily)

Several varieties and cultivars of Easter lily are used for forcing, the most popular being *L. longiflorum* var. *giganteum* and *L. longiflorum* 'Erabu', both distinguished by large, white, trumpet-shaped flowers held at right angles to the stem. Bulbs are obtainable in three circumference sizes: 5- to 7-inch, 7- to 9-inch, and 9- to 11-inch. Most commercial growers use the

Easter Lily (*Lilium longiflorum*)

intermediate size. The largest size yields more flowers per stem but is, of course, considerably more expensive. Northern grown bulbs, which produce shorter plants with more blooms per stem than southern grown, are usually preferred for greenhouse culture.

Bulbs should be subjected to four to six weeks of 40° to 50°F chill either before or after planting for best performance. If prechilled bulbs are planted in late November or early December, blooms should appear by Easter, as long as greenhouse temperatures range from 70°F in the daytime to 60°F at night. Some cultivars, such as the popular 'Croft', require about 120 days, so should be planted a month earlier.

Easter lilies grow best in a somewhat heavy but porous soil with a pH ranging between 6 and 7. A soil mixture of four parts fine loam, one part sand, and one part well-rotted manure is recommended. The bulbs should be planted in 6-inch pots, with their tops set 1 to 1½ inches below the soil surface. The potted bulbs should be placed on a bench in a greenhouse where the temperature can be maintained at about 55°F. The potting soil should be only slightly moist and very little water should be given until root growth has started, at which time the temperature of the greenhouse should be increased to 60°F. It is best if the irrigation water is warmed to about 70°F. After active growth has started and the plants have attained a height of 6 inches, biweekly applications of a liquid fertilizer may be given, 1 ounce of ammonium sulfate per 2 gallons of water. The time of bloom may be slightly hastened or retarded by raising or lowering the temperature a few degrees.

LUPINUS CVS.
(Lupine)

Several annual lupine cultivars are well adapted to greenhouse culture. The best are *L. hartwegii* 'Azure Blue', which has flowers of a delicate, almost mistlike blue, and *L.* 'Sutton's Tall Pink', which has flowers in a soft shade of pink.

Lupine seed may be sown either in the bench where the plants are to flower or in flats, and then transplanted into 2½- or

Stock (*Matthiola incana*) with pansy

3-inch pots. For winter and spring bloom, sow seed from August to October and again in January.

A moderately rich soil, well supplied with organic matter, will produce fine bloom. The soil should be neutral or slightly alkaline in its reaction (pH 7 to 7.5).

The plants may be shifted into the benches as soon as space is available, being spaced 12 inches apart. A cool greenhouse with a night temperature of 50° to 55°F gives best results. Daytime temperatures should range 10° to 15°F higher.

MATTHIOLA INCANA
(Stock)

The delicate fragrance of stock adds greatly to its appeal as a cut flower, and it does extremely well under cool greenhouse conditions.

The seed should be sown in flats in early August, the young seedlings being transplanted directly into the benches where

they are to flower or grown on in pots or flats. A light, porous and well-drained soil of good fertility is best.

When the young plants are shifted to the benches, they should be spaced 8 to 10 inches apart each way. The plants, which should be pinched back once to induce branching, will begin to flower late in the winter. The coolest possible temperature is desired, a night temperature of 48° to 50°F being ideal.

NARCISSUS SPP. AND CVS.
(Daffodil, jonquil)

All the members of the genus *Narcissus* may be easily forced into early spring bloom in the greenhouse. With the exception of *N. tazetta* 'Paper White' and Soleil d'Or' (for forcing instructions see page 000), planting should take place in the fall, either in bulb pans or flats, with the top of the bulb about 1 inch below the surface. Place the flats in a location, such as a coldframe, where they will be exposed to cold for a minimum of 12 weeks. The containers should be covered with several inches of leaves or other loose mulch. By bringing a few containers at a time into the greenhouse, a succession of bloom will be maintained for some months. Well-chilled bulbs come into bloom in about three months. If forced at a cool night temperature (50° to 55°F), blooms will be of highest quality and will last longer than if forced at higher temperatures. Bulbs of hardy narcissus, once forced, should not be used for forcing again, since even with the best postflowering care in the greenhouse, the bulbs diminish in size and will not perform. However, with such care, the bulbs may be planted outdoors in the garden in the spring and after a year or two will resume flowering.

ORCHIDACEAE
(Orchids)

Few greenhouse plants arouse more gardener interest than orchids. This is in large part because of the great diversity in plant habit and flower color, size, and form that they offer. Moreover, the blooms of most kinds remain fresh for weeks, and when in flower, the potted plants can be brought into the home for display. When out of bloom, however, orchids are relatively uninteresting and should be returned to the greenhouse to grow and set buds for the next flush of flowering, usually in a year's time.

The vast majority of orchids suited to greenhouse culture are epiphytes, i.e., plants that perch on other plants (usually tree limbs and trunks) or even rocks for support and spread their roots over the surface of the bark or rock, but do not invade or parasitize the support. The debris trapped by their matted roots provides necessary nutrients. Although light and moisture (including humidity) requirements vary according to kind, most epiphytic orchids thrive in filtered light and sustained humidity, and root well in pots (preferably clay) filled with bark chips. Irrigation water is occasionally fortified with a nutrient supplement, which is best obtained as a prepared "orchid food." Growing temperatures for most kinds

should range from 65° to 75°F in the day to 50° to 55°F at night. Many respond well to summering outdoors, their pots set in baskets suspended from tree limbs. As the slow-growing plants tend to spread out of their containers, periodic repotting is necessary. Pests and diseases are few.

PELARGONIUM × HORTORUM
(Geranium)

The popularity of the geranium as a houseplant has endured over many, many years. A century ago, geraniums were among the few flowers grown on windowsills, and they are still beloved there today, their popularity undiminished in spite of the many other kinds of plants now available for various indoor environments. In the greenhouse, geraniums will bloom all year round, given certain easily met conditions.

Geranim 'Dolly Varden'

Although geraniums are extremely adaptable, full sunlight is essential for optimal performance. Equally important for maximum flowering is a daytime temperature of 65° to 70°F, with night temperatures about 10°F lower.

Geraniums are propagated by means of softwood stem cuttings. When winter bloom is desired, cuttings should be made in May. Geraniums may also be grown from seed, but as the seeds are very expensive, this method is generally used for establishing stock plants from which cuttings may be taken.

Geraniums thrive in soil low in nitrate and relatively high in phosphate and

potash. An excess of nitrogen in the soil induces a rank, leafy growth and inhibits flowering. Geraniums will thrive reasonably well in almost any ordinary garden soil. If, however, maximum growth and abundant bloom are desired, the following soil mixture will give the best results when used in the final potting: eight parts friable garden loam to one part well-rotted manure. To each bushel of prepared soil, add one 4-inch flowerpotful of superphosphate and one 3-inch potful of 2-10-10 commercial fertilizer. Thoroughly mix with the soil before potting. The same mixture may be used to repot old plants. If a good potting mixture is used, no subsequent application of fertilizer will be needed, especially in a soil with a pH between 6.5 and 7.5.

Geraniums flower more abundantly when they are allowed to become slightly pot bound, so they should be carried through the winter in 4- or 5-inch pots. Old plants should be grown in 6- and 8-inch pots. During the first summer of growth, the young plants should be pinched back frequently, so that they may become symmetrical and well branched rather than rangy or leggy, and no flower buds should be allowed to develop until late summer. Thus treated, plants should then give ample bloom from October until April. In May, those plants that have bloomed throughout the winter months should be severely pruned back, leaving about three strong shoots, 3 to 4 inches long, on each plant. During the summer, the plants should be placed in a partially shaded place and kept fairly dry. It is important not to encourage new growth during this rest period. In the early autumn, the plants may be repotted in fresh soil and should give abundant bloom during the ensuing winter months.

Geraniums should be watered sparingly; they give better bloom if they are kept somewhat on the dry side. Overwatering and poor ventilation are frequently the cause of a bacterial leaf spot that is very disfiguring to the foliage.

PIQUERIA TRINERVIA
(Stevia)

Sometimes still incorrectly listed as *Stevia serrata*, stevia is valued as a filler in mixed bouquets. The small, white flowers are produced in abundance on long stems that are heavily clothed with deep green foliage.

Stevia is propagated by stem cuttings taken from the stock plants in January. As soon as the cuttings have rooted, they may be potted up in 2½-inch pots using a rich, humusy compost. If a light application of superphosphate is made at the time the plants are brought into the greenhouse, the danger of overly succulent, soft-stemmed growth will be reduced.

As the plants develop, they may be shifted into 4-inch pots, and later into 7-inch pots and are best grown under very cool conditions, ideally 40° to 45°F. As soon as all danger of frost is over, the pots may either be set on a bed of gravel in a coldframe or transferred to nursery rows. During the summer, the plants should be kept pinched back to encourage bushy, symmetrical form. In the autumn, before the first frost, the plants should be brought into a cool greenhouse. They may be grown on in pots or planted in beds or benches, spaced 12 inches apart. The plants will normally come into flower shortly before the Christmas season. The flowering period may be hastened by shading the plants with black cloth for four hours a day for a period of 30 days, beginning September 1.

PRIMULA SPP.
(Primrose)

There are many species of *Primula* that are excellent when grown as potted plants in the greenhouse. They are very decorative when in flower and bloom over a long season.

Primroses are usually grown from seed, which should be sown in late winter or early spring for bloom the following winter. Germination will be hastened if the seed is soaked for a few hours before sowing. When the young seedlings have attained sufficient size for transplanting, they may be moved into flats or small pots filled with a soil mixture of three parts loam and one part well-rotted manure. As the plants develop, they may be shifted into larger pots. Since they have a tendency to wilt badly, primroses should be shaded after each transplanting.

They do best in a slightly acidic soil (pH 6 to 7). The final potting mixture should be three parts loam, two parts well-rotted manure, and one part sand. To each quart of soil, 1 tablespoon of 4-12-4 commercial fertilizer should be added. Because of its tendency to waterlog, peat moss is best omitted from the soil mix. Primroses require consistent moisture, but sogginess is just as fatal as drought. In the summer, the pots may either be kept in a lightly shaded greenhouse or placed on a bed of gravel in a coldframe under lath shade. In the winter, a moderately cool greenhouse, ranging from 50° to 60°F, is ideal.

RHODODENDRON
SPP. AND CVS.
(Azalea)

There are few plants more decorative or rewarding than azaleas when they are in full bloom. Many species and cultivars may be grown very successfully under greenhouse conditions and forced into bloom for Christmas or Easter. Most azaleas are grown from cuttings, but others are usually grafted. As the propagation of azaleas is a highly specialized field, it is advisable for the owner of the small greenhouse to purchase a few plants that have been specifically prepared for forcing. These can readily be obtained from a good garden center or nursery.

To perform well, azaleas require a strongly acidic soil (pH 4.5 to 5.5). The potting soil should consist of a mixture of two parts sandy loam and one part peat moss. Yellowing of the foliage and poor root development are indicative of a lack of available iron, resulting from soil that is too highly alkaline. To correct an iron deficiency, an application of ¹⁄₁₀ ounce of 12 percent chelated iron per 10 square feet of bench area or ¹⁄₂₅ ounce (2 grams) per gallon of water for potted plants will give excellent results.

Azalea plants are usually shipped with their fibrous roots forming a small ball. As soon as they have been unpacked, the ball should be immersed in a bucket of water until it has become thoroughly saturated. It should then be allowed to drain (but not to dry out) before potting.

For the first two or three weeks, the plants should be placed in a cool greenhouse where the night temperature ranges around 45°F. Azaleas require an abundance of water and a moist atmosphere. If the plants are to be brought into flower by Christmas, they should be kept at a temperature of 45° to 50°F until the first week in November (ideally November 5). They should then have a night temperature of 60°F and a temperature of 65°F during the day. If the plants are desired for Easter bloom, they should be kept in a very cool house (45° to 50°F) until six weeks before Easter. All new vegetative growth that appears at the base of the flower buds should be pinched out. If this is not done, the flowers will be small and there will be many blind buds.

After the flowering period is over, the plants should be trimmed back lightly and placed in a warm, moist greenhouse so that vigorous new growth may be encouraged. In June, the pots may be sunk in the open ground or the plants may be shifted to the nursery rows. A soil mixture similar to that of the potting mixture should be used. The symmetry of the plants should be maintained by the occasional pinching back of any rangy shoots. No pinching should be done after the first two weeks of summer. In early fall, the plants may be lifted and brought into the greenhouse.

ROSA CVS.
(Rose)

Many roses are admirably adapted to greenhouse culture and give abundant bloom throughout the winter months.

Greenhouse roses may be propagated by cuttings, by budding, or by grafting. Grafting is the most approved method and the one most commonly employed by commercial growers. As the propagation of roses is a highly specialized practice, it is advisable for the owner of a small greenhouse to purchase only strong, healthy, pot-grown plants that are suitable for forcing.

Roses require a slightly acidic soil (pH 6 to 7) to thrive. A rich soil mix, consisting of three parts friable, sandy loam and one part well-rotted manure will give excellent results.

As to temperature regimen, 55° to 60°F at night and 70° to 75°F in the daytime are the best ranges for roses. These plants may be grown either in raised benches or in solid beds. Good drainage is essential and beds or benches should be narrow, preferably not more than 4 feet wide, as the best blooms are invariably produced on the outside plants. Roses may be set in their permanent position in the greenhouse between the middle of May and July 1, being spaced 12 to 14 inches apart. The plants should be set a little deeper than they were when growing in the pots. During this period when the plants are becoming established, they should be watered thoroughly but at no time should the soil be allowed to become soggy or saturated. To keep up humidity, the walks in the greenhouse should be kept damp and the foliage sprayed several times a day during sunny weather. The temperature should be kept as low as possible and the greenhouse should be well ventilated. To promote winter bloom, flower buds should not be allowed to develop until September.

As the plants grow, wire may be stretched along the side of the benches and wire stakes placed beside the plants to provide support. At the time of flowering, applications of commercial 4-12-4 fertilizer may be made every three or four weeks, being applied at the rate of 1½ ounces per 10 square feet of planted area. Greenhouse roses will usually continue to give good results over a period of three or four years, and sometimes even longer. Plants that are to be carried over in the benches should be given a period of rest during the summer. Beginning about the middle of June water should be withheld gradually, though the plants should not be allowed to become too dry. During this period the plants should be pruned vigorously, the weak stems being pruned even more severely than strong ones. The plants should be cut back to 18 to 20 inches. A few inches of topsoil may be removed, and the bed or bench refilled with compost.

SAINTPAULIA IONANTHA
(African violet)

See page 929.

SCHIZANTHUS PINNATUS
(Butterfly flower)

Seldom at its best in the garden under the heat of the summer sun, the butterfly flower is one of those annuals admirably adapted to the cool greenhouse. Only there does it reach full perfection, and a well-grown pot of this plant is truly a thing of beauty. The small, orchid-shaped flowers in luminous tones of pink, lavender, and white are borne in great profusion and are lovely both for cutting and as potted plants.

Seed is best sown in late summer for early spring bloom, with the plants grown on in pots or in bench beds. A soil mix consisting of two parts humusy loam and one part well-rotted cow manure will give excellent results.

Care should be taken when transplanting seedlings not to snap off the brittle stems that link roots to leaves. Whether grown on in pots or benches, the plants should be spaced about 12 inches apart before coming into flower. They thrive with cool night temperatures in the 45° to 50°F range and 10° to 15°F higher during the day. If the plants are allowed to become somewhat pot bound, the blooming period will be hastened.

SINNINGIA SPECIOSA
(Gloxinia)

Gloxinias are strikingly colorful plants, bountiful with their bloom, and well deserve the popularity they enjoy as greenhouse plants. The large-flowered hybrids have a wide color range, from white, pink, and rose to red and purple, with many intermediate hues, often with spots and blotches in contrasting colors. The showy blooms sometimes reach 6 inches or more in diameter. However, many gardeners prefer the more modest slipper type, with its smaller, more delicate and numerous flowers.

Gloxinias may be grown from tubers or be propagated from leaf cuttings or seed. Plant tubers anytime from late fall to late winter if favorable growing conditions can be provided. If tubers have been shipped, it is wise to plant them as soon after arrival as possible to prevent their shriveling. Flowering is heaviest in the spring. They may be started either in small pots or in trays, with vermiculite or milled sphagnum moss being used as the starting medium. They may also be planted directly in the pots in which they are to flower, using 5-inch pots for small tubers and 6- to 8-inch pots for large tubers. The top third of the tuber should be exposed above the level of the soil in the pot.

Leaf cuttings may be taken from mature, flowering plants during the spring and early summer. The leaf should be cut close to the main stem and be placed in the shade for ½ hour to give the end a chance to dry. The leaf is then inserted in moist sand or vermiculite in the propagating case. Cuttings also root very readily in wet sand, even water. When new growth appears and the original leaf dies, the new plant may be transplanted into a pot. Plants grown from leaf cuttings will bloom the following spring and summer.

Gloxinias may also be easily grown from seed. The seed is very fine, rather like that of begonias, and requires careful handling (see page 864 for details). The seeds germinate in about 10 days and the young seedlings should be transplanted into flats when they have two or three pairs of leaves, then shifted into 5- or 6-inch pots. Seed-grown gloxinias come into flower in 6 to 10 months. Seed sown in early January should produce flowers by midsummer.

For their best development gloxinias require a humid atmosphere, a favorable temperature range, sufficient light, protection from brilliant sunshine, and a congenial soil.

Gloxinias do best in a rich, porous, well-drained soil, with a high content of organic matter. The following mixtures give excellent results:

> 1 part garden loam + 1 part sand + 1 part peat moss
> 1 part garden loam + 1 part leaf mold + 1 part sand

The ideal range of temperature for gloxinias is 68° to 72°F during the day and 62° to 65° at night, although these plants are adapted to somewhat wider fluctuations. If temperatures range much above 75°F, however, growth will tend to suffer. Gloxinias should be given as much indirect or diffused light as possible and need to be shaded from strong sun. Insufficient light, on the other hand, will result in spindly, leggy growth.

Watering must be done with care. The best method is to place the pot in a pan of water and leave it until the surface of the soil appears moist. The plant should not be watered again until the soil begins to look dry. It should never be allowed to stand in water for a long period of time. If overhead watering is practiced, the water should be poured close to the rim of the pot to avoid wetting the leaves or the crown of the plant. When water stands in the crown, it is conducive to crown rot and the spread of gray mold. Ample drainage material should be placed in the bottom of the container at the time of potting, as good drainage is essential for gloxinias.

When the period of bloom is over and the foliage begins to yellow and die down, water should be gradually withheld as the plants become dormant. The pots should be stored in a cool place at a temperature of about 50°F and be watered just enough to keep the tubers from shriveling. If desired, the tubers may be removed from the pot and stored in peat moss in a cool place until their period of dormancy is over. They may then be potted up again in fresh soil in February or March.

Plants that flower in early spring can be cut back to the first pair of leaves and will usually produce an excellent second bloom within 8 to 10 weeks. After the second period of bloom is over, prepare them for dormancy.

TULIPA CVS.
(Tulip)

For use both as potted plants and as cut flowers, tulips add their share to the galaxy of bloom in the greenhouse during the spring months, and with careful management, a succession of bloom may be had over a period of many weeks. Tulip bulbs should be planted in the fall either in bulb pans or flats, using a soil mixture consisting of two parts friable loam, one part leaf mold or compost, and one part sand. Ample drainage is essential, and the top of the bulb should be 1 to 2 inches below the surface of the soil. Unless you are using bulbs that have been especially pretreated for forcing, you need to provide a long period of cold storage so that the bulbs make requisite root growth. They should be stored in a protected place outdoors, such as a coldframe, for 12 to 14 weeks. It is best to cover the containers with leaves, straw, shredded wood ("excelsior"), or other open, light material to keep temperatures cold, to protect any shoots that may develop, and to ease the retrieval of the containers for forcing in the greenhouse. Early-flowering cultivars may be brought in after 12 weeks of storage, later cultivars after 14 weeks. When first brought in, pots are best placed in a cool, semidark place for a few days, as the young shoots may discolor if immediately exposed to direct sunlight. Tulips should be forced at a comparatively low temperature (55° to 60°F) for ideal results. Though a high temperature is conducive to more rapid development, the quality and longevity of the flowers are seriously diminished. After the pots have been placed in full sunlight, they should be turned every few days so that the flowers and leaves may develop evenly.

VIOLA SPP.
(Violet)

Although they are hardy perennials, violets are admirably suited to the cool greenhouse, and if the plants are grown under favorable conditions, they will deliver abundant bloom during the winter months.

Violets are usually propagated by division of clumps in the spring after the flowering season is over, and the young plants are grown on in flats. During the summer, the plants may be kept in coldframes or they may be planted in the open ground. Some growers prefer to transplant the young plants into their permanent position in the greenhouse in the spring. If this practice is followed, adequate ventilation must be provided and the greenhouse must be heavily shaded during the summer.

Violets do best in a well-drained, sandy loam that includes considerable organic matter. They are grown in ground-level beds, in raised benches, or in pots. Most commercial growers prefer ground-level beds, as it is easier to maintain cool, moist soil, and cool conditions are essential for success. Single-flowered cultivars require a night temperature of 45° to 50°F and a daytime temperature no more than 15°F higher. Double-flowered cultivars need temperatures about 5°F lower. Higher temperatures promote vegetative growth at the expense of flowers. Equally important is unfailing soil moisture and adequate ventilation.

ZANTEDESCHIA SPP.
(Calla lily)

Calla lilies are grown for the decorative quality of their blooms when used in cut flower arrangements. Two species are grown in greenhouses: Z. aethiopica (white calla) and Z. elliottiana (yellow calla). Commercially, callas are propagated by removing the small offsets that form around the parent rhizome. Several years of growth are required before these young plants come into bloom.

Callas require a rich soil. A mixture of two parts heavy, humusy loam and one part well-rotted manure will give excellent results. Callas may be grown in solid beds, raised benches, or pots. A night temperature of 55° and a day temperature ranging between 60° and 65°F are necessary. The plants require an abundant supply of moisture throughout their growing period. After the flowering period is over, the plants should be gradually dried off and given a rest period. They may be watered occasionally but all active growth is allowed to cease. In August, the topsoil from the beds may be removed. After the plants have been given a thorough soaking, a heavy mulch of well-rotted manure should be applied. Active growth will soon be resumed, and the plants will begin to flower late in the autumn.

PLANTS THAT MAY BE GROWN IN POTS IN THE GREENHOUSE
FOR TEMPORARY DECORATION IN THE HOUSE

Abutilon × *hybridum* (flowering maple)
Acacia drummondii (Drummond's acacia)
A. paradoxa (kangaroo thorn)
Astilbe × *arendsii*
Begonia spp. and cvs.
Bougainvillea glabra (paper flower)
Browallia speciosa 'Major' (sapphire flower)
Camellia japonica
Chorizema ilicifolia (flame pea)
Chrysanthemum × *morifolium* (greenhouse mum)
Cyclamen persicum (florist's cyclamen)

Dicentra spectabilis (bleeding heart)
Euphorbia fulgens (scarlet plume)
E. pulcherrima (poinsettia)
Felicia amelloides (blue daisy)
Fuchsia spp. and cvs.
Gardenia augusta (Cape jasmine)
Genista canariensis (Canary broom)
G. × *spachiana* (florist's broom)
Hatiora gaertneri (Easter cactus)
Kalanchoe spp. (beach bells)
Lantana camara

Pelargonium × *hortorum* (geranium)
Pericallis × *hybrida* (florist's cineraria)
Primula spp. (primrose)
Rhododendron spp. (azalea)
Saintpaulia ionantha (African violet)
Schlumbergera × *buckleyi* (Christmas cactus)
S. truncata (Thanksgiving cactus)
Sinningia speciosa (gloxinia)
Solanum pseudocapsicum (Jerusalem cherry)
Strelitzia reginae (bird-of-paradise flower)
Streptosolen jamesonii (firebush)

EPIPHYTIC ORCHIDS EASILY CULTURED IN
THE COOL OR MODERATE GREENHOUSE

Brassavola nodosa (lady-of-the-night)
Cattleya skinneri (corsage orchid)
Dendrobium densiflorum (spice orchid)
Encyclia cordigera syn. *Epidendrum atropurpureum* (butterfly orchid)
Epidendrum × *o'brienanum*
Lycaste aromatica
Oncidium ampliatum (dancing lady)
O. tigrinum
Phaius tankervilliae, syn. *P. grandifolius* (nun's-hood orchid)
Stanhopea wardii
Trichopilia tortilis

GREENHOUSE CLIMBERS AND GROUND COVERS

Allamanda cathartica (golden trumpet)
Antigonon leptopus (coral vine)
Asparagus densiflorus (Sprenger's asparagus fern)
Asparagus setaceus (plumose asparagus fern)
Clerodendrum thomsoniae (bleeding heart vine)
Delarea odorata (German ivy)
Ficus pumila (creeping fig)
Hedera helix (English ivy)
Jasminum officinale f. *grandiflorum* (royal jasmine)
Monstera deliciosa (split-leaf philodendron)
Passiflora spp. (passion flower)
Philodendron scandens ssp. *oxycardium* (common philodendron)
Stigmaphyllon ciliatum (butterfly vine, golden vine)
Tradescantia fluminensis (wandering Jew)
Vinca major (blue buttons)

BULBS, CORMS, AND TUBERS SUITABLE FOR
FORCING IN THE GREENHOUSE

Anemone coronaria (windflower)
Convallaria majalis (lily-of-the-valley)
Crocus spp.
Freesia cvs.
Galanthus nivalis (snowdrop)
Gladiolus cvs.
Hippeastrum cvs. (amaryllis)
Hyacinthus orientalis (hyacinth)
Iris spp. (English iris, Juno iris, Spanish iris)
Lilium auratum (gold-banded lily)
L. candidum (madonna lily)
L. formosanum (Formosa lily)
L. japonicum (Japanese lily)
L. lancifolium (tiger lily)
L. longiflorum (Easter lily, trumpet lily)
L. maculatum (spotted lily)
L. pumilum (coral lily)
L. regale (royal lily)
L. speciosum (Japanese lily)
Narcissus spp. and cvs. (daffodil, jonquil)
Ranunculus asiaticus cvs. (greenhouse ranunculus)
Tulipa spp. and cvs. (tulip)
Zantedeschia aethiopica (white calla lily)
Z. elliottiana (yellow calla lily)

GREENHOUSE PALMS

Chrysalidocarpus lutescens (Cane palm)
Howea belmoreana (Belmore sentry palm)
H. forsterana (Forster sentry palm)
Latania lontaroides (red latan)
Livistona rotundifolia (Tan palm)
Microcoelum weddellianum, syns. *Cocos weddelliana,*
   Syagrus weddelliana (Weddel palm)
Phoenix rupicola (Indian date palm)

DECORATIVE FERNS GROWN IN
THE COOL GREENHOUSE

Adiantum raddianum (maidenhair fern)
A. tenerum 'Farleyense' (glory fern)
Asplenium nidus (bird's-nest fern)
Cyrtomium falcatum (holly fern)
Nephrolepis exaltata (sword fern)
Platycerium spp. (staghorn fern)
Pleris cretica (cretan brake)
Polypodium spp. (polypody)

PLANTS FOR THE COOL GREENHOUSE FOR CUT FLOWERS

Antirrhinum majus (snapdragon)
Bouvardia longiflora
Calendula officinalis
Centaurea cyanus (bachelor's button)
Chrysanthemum × morifolium (florist's chrysanthemum)
Clarkia spp. (godetia)
Consolida spp. (larkspur)
Cynoglossum spp. Hound's tongue
Delphinium spp.
Dianthus caryophyllus (carnation)
Erlangea tomentosa (erlangia)
Erysimum cheiri (wallflower)
Eupatorium spp. (thoroughwort)
Euphorbia spp. (spurge)
Gerbera jamesonii (Transvaal daisy)
Gypsophila spp. (baby's breath)
Lathyrus odoratus (sweet pea)
Limonium spp. (statice)
Lupinus spp. (lupine)
Matthiola incana (stock)
Myosotis spp. (forget-me-not)
Nemesia spp.
Osteospermum spp. (Cape marigold)
Piqueria trinervia (stevia)
Salpiglossis sinuata (painted tongue)
Scabiosa atropurpurea (pincushion flower)
Schizanthus pinnatus (butterfly flower)
Streptosolen jamesonii (firebush)
Tanacetum parthenium (feverfew)
Trachymene coerulea (blue lace flower)
Viola spp. (violet)

HARDY SHRUBS THAT MAY BE FORCED IN POTS OR TUBS IN THE COOL GREENHOUSE

Chaenomeles japonica (Japanese quince)
Clethra alnifolia (sweet pepperbush)
Daphne cneorum (garland flower)
Deutzia gracilis (slender deutzia)
Philadelphus × lemoinei (Lemoine's mock orange)
Pieris japonica (andromeda, lily-of-the-valley shrub)
Prunus spp. (shrubby flowering almond, cherry, plum)
Rhododendron spp. (azalea)
Spiraea prunifolia (bridal wreath spirea)
S. thunbergii (Thunberg spirea)

HARDY FLOWERING SHRUBS AND TREES WHOSE CUT BRANCHES FORCE WELL IN THE COOL GREENHOUSE

Alnus spp. (alder)
Cercis spp. (redbud)
Chaenomeles spp. (flowering quince)
Cornus florida (flowering dogwood)
C. mas (cornelian cherry dogwood)
Forsythia spp.
Hamamelis spp. (witch hazel, winter-flowering species)
Jasminum nudiflorum (winter jasmine)
Magnolia stellata (starry magnolia)
Malus spp. (flowering crab apple)
Prunus spp. (flowering cherry)
Rhododendron spp. (azalea)
Salix spp. (pussy willow)
Spiraea thunbergii (Thunberg spiraea)

Pink paper flower (*Bougainvillea glabra* 'Pink Queen')

White paper flower (*Bougainvillea glabra* 'Snow White')

Royal jasmine (*Jasminum officinale* f. *grandiflorum*)

Gloryfern (*Adiantum tenerum* 'Farleynese')

Forster sentry palm (*Howea forsterana*)

VII
Gardener's Miscellany

GLOSSARY

A

ACHENE. A dry, unopening, one-seeded fruit with a thin, often transparent outer wall, as in the buttercup (*Ranunculus* spp.).

ACIDIC. Refers to soil having a pH lower than 7.

ACORN. Nut of an oak with its basal cup.

ADAPTATION. Genetic or behavioral adjustment of a plant to its environment.

AERATION. Penetration of air, especially oxygen, into soil and other rooting media.

AIR LAYERING. Method of asexual or vegetative reproduction in which roots are formed on stems and branches that are still attached to the parent plant.

ALGICIDE. Substance toxic to algae, which are tiny primitive green plants occurring in water or on wet surfaces.

ALKALINE. Refers to soil having a pH higher than 7.

ALLÉE. A formal walk or drive between files of similar, evenly spaced trees or shrubs, usually all of the same kind.

ALLELOPATHY. Production of one or more substances by one plant that inhibit the growth of others.

ALLUVIAL. Refers to soil transported and deposited by water.

ALPINE. A rock garden plant, especially one native to high montane environments.

ANAEROBIC. Conditions lacking oxygen or organisms living under such conditions.

ANNUAL. Plant that grows from seed, flowers, sheds seed, and dies within a year, usually in a few months.

ANNUAL RINGS. Concentric zones of wood deposited during growth periods, as seen in a smooth cross section of a stem, trunk, or root.

ANTHER. Terminal pollen-disseminating chamber of the stamen, or "male," organ.

ANTIDESICCANT. A substance applied to leaves to slow transpiration, especially during and after transplanting or, in the case of evergreens, during extreme winter conditions.

AQUATIC. Any plant growing in water, whether floating or bottom rooting.

ARBOR. A structure built over a walk or patio to support woody climbers.

ARBORETUM. A collection of trees and shrubs organized as a garden or park, usually with each kind labeled.

ARMED. Thorny or prickly.

AROID. A member of the plant family Araceae, which has florets arranged at the base of a columnar spadix, surrounded by a sheathlike, often colored spathe.

ASEXUAL PROPAGATION. Reproduction by cuttings, grafting, division, tissue culture, and other methods rather than by seed.

AUXIN. Growth hormone produced by the plant that promotes the elongating of roots and shoots, the twining of climbers, and the rooting of cuttings; may be augmented by synthetic hormones or be depressed or halted by herbicides.

B

BAG FERTILIZER. Commercially prepared, concentrated, granular nutrient formulation sold in measured amounts.

BALANCED FERTILIZER. A commercial, or bag, fertilizer containing equal parts of nitrate, phosphate, and potash.

BALL. A root mass with associated soil, especially when wrapped and tied in burlap or plastic sheeting or containered for transplanting.

BARE ROOT. Used in reference to plants that are transplanted without soil about the roots.

BARK. Outermost protective, usually corky tissue of tree trunks and shrub stems.

BEARD. A growth of hair in flowers, especially on the falls of certain irises.

BED. An open area, accessible from all sides, intensively planted.

BEE PLANT. Any species that produces abundant pollen or nectar attractive to bees as a food source.

BELVEDERE. A garden house or lookout, often architecturally imposing and the focus of a formal garden.

BERRY. A pulpy or juicy, few- to many-seeded fruit.

BIENNIAL. A plant that matures in two years, i.e., it grows vegetatively the first year and then flowers, sheds seed, and dies the second year.

BILABIATE. Two lipped, as in the flowers of snapdragons.

BIOCIDE. A poison applied to kill or control one or more weeds, pests, or disease organisms.

BISEXUAL. A flower having functional stamens and pistil(s).

BLADE. The flattened, thin portion of a leaf or petal.

BLANCHING. A process in which leaves or stems are made white by excluding light, as is often done with celery, leek, and asparagus.

BLEEDING. The leaking of sap from wounds, especially of trees pruned in the spring.

BLOOM. A fine, powdery, waxy coating, easily rubbed off, especially conspicuous on certain fruits, such as grapes, plums, and blueberries; a flower or flowers, or being in flower.

BOLE. A large tree trunk.

BOLTING. The premature elongation of a stem into a flower stalk, especially in certain vegetables.

BORDER. A long strip of cultivated ground backed by a building, wall, hedge, or other tall backdrop, devoted to flowers or mixed plantings.

BOTANIC(AL) GARDEN. A garden designed to promote the study of plants; specimens or groupings (sometimes synoptically or ecologically arranged) are labeled as to name and provenance; it often includes greenhouses, conservatories, or a museum and offers publications and various services for professionals and amateurs.

BOWER. A shady recess beneath an arbor.

BRACT. A modified leaf, sometimes large and brightly colored, as in poinsettias and certain dogwoods, but usually reduced and scalelike.

BROADCAST. To scatter seed rather than sow it in rows or drills.

BROMELIAD. A member of the family Bromeliaceae, which includes such horticulturally popular genera as *Billbergia* and *Tillandsia* as well as the pineapple.

BULB. A thickened subterranean bud, with a very short, thick stem from which roots grow, and densely layered, thickened leaf bases or fleshy scales; also loosely applied to corms, rhizomes, tubers, and other underground storage organs.

BULBIL. A very small bulb (bulblet), usually developing at the base of leaves (as in certain lilies) or in flower clusters (as in certain onions).

BUSH. A low, densely branched shrub, especially one grown for fruit, such as raspberry, blackberry, etc.

C

CALLUS. The thick new tissue that grows over wounds.

CALYX. The outermost whorl or circle of floral organs, composed of free or united sepals, often green and enclosing the flower bud.

CAMBIUM. The actively growing layer in the stems of a dicotyledonous plant, which adds girth year by year in woody species.

CANE. Biennial stem in certain bush fruits, such as blackberry and raspberry; the jointed, hollow stem of bamboo.

CAPITATE. Headlike, or arranged in heads or capitula.

CAPITULUM. A much-condensed flower cluster, as in clover or the flower heads of daisies and their relatives.

CAPSULE. A dry fruit that opens when ripe to liberate seeds.

CARNIVOROUS. See *Insectivorous.*

CATKIN. A scaly spike of tiny, usually inconspicuous, flowers, as in oak, birch, and willow.

CELL PACK. An open-topped, partitioned container for growing seedlings, usually with four or six chambers.

CELLULOSE. A major constituent of plant cell walls.

CERTIFIED STOCK. Nursery plants of certain identity that are free of pests and diseases at time of certification.

CHECK. To arrest growth.

CHIMERA. A plant organ or whole plant that has tissues of two or more species, as in the tree *Laburnocytisus adamii*, in which the inner stem tissue is of the purple-flowered shrubby broom (*Cytisus purpureus*) and the outer tissue is of the goldenrain (*Laburnum anagyroides*), a yellow-flowered tree; this chimera bears some purple flowers and some yellow.

CHLOROPHYLL. Complex of green plant pigments that absorbs light in photosynthesis.

CHROMOSOME. One of the bodies in the nucleus of each cell, made up of DNA, which carries the cell's genetic information.

CILIA. Hairs forming a fringe, as on the edge of certain leaves.

CLADODE OR CLADOPHYLL. A flattened stem that resembles and functions as a leaf, as in certain species of *Acacia.*

CLAMBERING. Climbing but with no special habit or organs for support, as in the tomato.

CLASS. A major classification unit.

CLAW. The long, narrow, stalklike base of a flower petal or sepal in certain plants.

CLAY. Fine soil particles less than 0.002 mm in diameter; a soil consisting primarily of clay particles.

CLEISTOGAMOUS. Refers to flowers in which pollination occurs in unopening buds, as in certain violets.

CLIMBER. A plant requiring mechanical support to ascend, often having special adaptations in structure or habit; popularly called a vine.

CLONE. A population of genetically identical individuals, as in the offspring of vegetatively propagated plants; an individual so derived.

CLUSTER. A flower grouping or inflorescence, including the raceme, spike, cyme, capitulum, etc.

COLDFRAME. An unheated enclosure with a removable transparent or translucent top, used for plant culture and protection.

COLE. Cabbage and related vegetables, including broccoli, cauliflower, kale, bok choy, mustard, kohlrabi, and turnip.

COLONIZER. A plant species that soon occupies a recently cleared or exposed area.

COMPLEX. A group of related kinds whose relationship to each other is not understood.

COMPOSITE. A member of the daisy family (Asteraceae, formerly Compositae); a structure formed of distinct parts.

COMPOST. Plant remains in various stages of decomposition.

COMPOUND. Consisting of two or more similar parts, as in a compound leaf.

CONCENTRATED FERTILIZER. Containing at least 30 percent nitrate and phosphate and potash in varying proportions.

CONE. A dense, often elongate reproductive structure, consisting of overlapping, often woody scales, that bears seeds or pollen, as is characteristic in most conifers and as fruiting structures in birches, alders, tulip tree, etc.

CONIFEROUS. Cone-bearing woody plants bearing naked seeds, such as pines, spruces, hemlocks, and their relatives.

CONTACT POISON. An insecticide that kills by penetrating the insect's skin or shell, or a herbicide that kills plant tissue wherever the surface is contacted.

CORIACEOUS. Leathery.

CORM. A solid, swollen, modified subterranean stem, often bulblike, as in the crocus and gladiolus.

COROLLA. The inner whorl or second circle of bladelike floral organs, made up of petals and often brightly colored.

CORONA. A circular appendage or series of appendages in a flower, often crownlike, usually arising from the calyx or corolla, as in narcissuses, or from stamens, as in milkweeds.

COTYLEDON. A seed leaf—usually one, as in the onion, or two, as in the radish—which is commonly the first leaf appearing above ground during germination.

COVER CROP. A growth of fast-maturing plants, such as rye or vetch, that are dug into the soil to decompose (also called green manure).

CREEPING. The trailing of a plant on or just beneath the soil surface; the plant often roots at intervals.

CRESTED. With raised, often irregularly toothed ridges.

CRISPED. With curled or ruffled edges.

CROCK. Pieces of broken clay pots placed in the bottom of plant containers to promote drainage.

CROP ROTATION. Shifting crops from place to place in successive years to avoid nutrient depletion and the buildup of pests and diseases characteristic of one kind of plant.

CROSS. A hybrid.

CROSS-POLLINATION. The transfer of pollen from the anthers in the flowers of one plant to stigma(s) in the flowers of another, resulting in cross-fertilization.

CROTCH. The angle between two or more limbs or branches.

CROWN. The plant base, i.e., the union of the stem and roots, the bud-bearing tip of a rhizome, the leafy top of a tree, or a corona.

CUCURBIT. Any member of the family Cucurbitaceae, including squashes, cucumber, melons, watermelon, and gourds.

CULM. The stem of grasses, bamboos, and sedges.

CULTIGEN. A plant of garden origin and known only in cultivation.

CULTIVAR. A cultivated variety, as distinct from a botanical or wild variety; the name begins with a capital letter, is enclosed by single quotation marks, and is not italicized; it is usually in English; abbreviated cv. (plural is cvs.).

CUP. A short or low corona in the daffodil, jonquil, and narcissus.

CUSP. A sharp, often thickened, rigid point.

CYLINDRICAL. Elongate and circular in cross section.

CYME. A flower cluster in which the main axis and each successive branch end in a flower, as in hydrangea, daylily, and St. John'swort.

D

DAMPING OFF. A fungus disease of seedlings.

DAY-NEUTRAL. A plant unaffected by changes in day length.

DEADHEADING. Removing spent or faded flowers.

DECIDUOUS. Not persisting, dropping when no longer functional, as with the petals of most flowers; applied mainly to the leaves of trees and shrubs that detach in the fall, leaving the plant defoliated until spring.

DECOMPOSITION. Decay, as in compost, manure, or other organic residue.

DECUMBENT. Prostrate or creeping, but with the stem tip ascending.

DEHISCENCE. The means by which a capsular fruit or pollen-bearing anther opens to discharge its contents.

DELIQUESCENT. Usually applied to tree architecture in reference to the repeated branching of trunk and branches to form a leafy crown; see also *Excurrent*.

DETERMINATE. Refers to stem growth limited or arrested by a terminal flower that opens before all others.

DIBBLE. Pointed hand tool used in planting bulbs, seedlings, and cuttings.

DICHOTOMOUS. Forking regularly, equally, and repeatedly.

DICOT, DICOTYLEDONOUS. Plant whose seeds have two cotyledons.

DIFFUSE. An open, loosely branched growth habit.

DIMORPHIC. Occurring in two forms, such as the leaves of English ivy, eucalyptus, juniper, and cinnamon fern.

DIOECIOUS. Plants that bear unisexual flowers on separate individuals, as in holly.

DIPLOID. Having two sets of chromosomes.

DISBUDDING. Removal of accessory buds or shoots.

DISC FLOWER. One of the minute flowers that comprise the central head in daisies and their relatives.

DISTICHOUS. Arranged in two distinct rows.

DISTRIBUTION. The geographical range of a plant.

DIURNAL. Opening during the day and closing at night, as in daylily flowers.

DIVIDED. Separated into smaller segments, as in the leaves of roses divided into leaflets.

DORMANT. The period during which a plant makes no active growth and seeds do not germinate, determined variously by water availability, temperature, and internal factors.

DOUBLE. Refers to flowers with additional petals, usually by conversion of some stamens into supplemental petals, as in garden roses.

DRESSING. Any nutrient-yielding material applied dry on the soil surface to enhance plant growth.

DRILL. A narrow furrow made to receive seeds for germination.

DRIPLINE. The approximate circumference around a tree defining the limit of overhead foliage and used as a guide in applying fertilizer.

DROUGHT. The depletion of soil moisture by evaporation and root uptake or, in physiological drought, by the presence of water that is too salty to be absorbed, or has turned to ice.

DRUPE. A one-seeded, usually fleshy fruit in which the seed is enclosed in a bony or woody pit, as in the cherry and peach.

DRYING OFF. The gradual withholding of water from potted bulbs that require dormancy before reflowering, often done by laying pots on their sides, as with amaryllis.

DWARF. A small and/or slow-growing variant.

E

EMBRYO. Tiny rudimentary plant within a seed that, on germination, becomes a seedling.

EMULSION. A suspension of a fatty or oily substance in water, which, on agitation, often appears milky, as in certain pesticides.

ENDEMIC. Naturally restricted to a limited area.

ENTIRE. With a smooth, unbroken edge, i.e., lacking teeth or lobes.

ENZYME. A catalyst in a biochemical reaction.

EPHEMERAL. Lasting a day or less, as in the flowers of the daylily, portulaca, and mallow.

EPIDERMIS. The outer covering or skin of a plant.

EPIPHYTE. A plant growing on another but deriving no nourishment from the supporting plant, as in most bromeliads and orchids (also known as air plants).

EROSION. The often destructive transfer of soil, usually by the gullying or sheeting action of water but in some regions by fine soil becoming airborne in high winds.

ESCAPE. An introduced plant that becomes naturalized.

ESPALIER. A method of training small trees to horizontal, regularly spaced wires or other supports in particular patterns.

ESSENTIAL ORGANS. In a flower, the stamens and pistil(s).

EVERGREEN. A tree or shrub whose older leaves are retained until after new leaves are formed, thus remaining continuously leafy.

EVERLASTINGS. Dried flowers that retain their shape and color and are, therefore, valued in winter arrangements.

EXCURRENT. With a single, predominant growth axis, as in the habit of most spruces and hemlocks.

EXOTIC. Any plant grown outside its natural geographic range.

EXPOSURE. Position in relation to climatic factors, such as wind and sun; degree of access to solar rays, usually expressed in relation to the total daily possible number of hours of sun, ranging from full sun (S), six or more hours; through partial shade (PSh), three to six hours; light shade (LSh), dappled sun and shade, as beneath tall trees; dense shade (DSh), no sun exposure except at dawn and dusk; to shade (Sh), no exposure to direct sun whatever.

EYE. The center of a flower, especially when of a contrasting color; a bud on a tuber, as in the potato.

F

F₁. The first-generation offspring of a cross.

FACULTATIVE. Incidental or not essential; refers to a plant capable of growing in varied habitats.

FALLS. The outer, downward-directed, petal-like components of iris flowers.

FAMILY. An association of genera that closely or uniformly resemble each other more than other genera in general appearance and technical characters; in some cases consisting of a single very distinctive genus, as in horsetails, (*Equisetum*), or even a single species, as in katsura tree (*Cercidiphyllum japonicum*) or maidenhair tree (*Ginkgo biloba*); loosely and incorrectly used in place of genus.

FASCIATED. A malformed, monstrously broadened or thickened stem, often as if several stems are joined side by side; normal in broccoli and cauliflower and occurs occasionally in such woody plants as wisteria and tree-of-heaven.

FASTIGIATE. With all branches directed upward, thus conferring a narrow, upswept habit, as in the Lombardy poplar and numerous conifers.

FERTILIZATION. The application of fertilizer; the union of pollen nuclei with those of ovules to form seeds.

FIBROUS. Having roots with many fine, matted branches.

FILAMENT. The stalk of a stamen, supporting the pollen-bearing anther.

FILIFORM. Long and slender, threadlike.

FLAGS. The inner, upward-directed, petal-like components of an iris flower.

FLAT. A shallow box that, when filled with soil mix, is used to germinate seeds and start seedlings.

FLORET. A tiny flower, especially when occuring in a condensed cluster, as in the disc or head of a daisy.

FLORICANE. The biennial stem of a bush fruit in its second, bearing, and final year, as in the raspberry.

FLOWER. A modified axis or stem bearing one or more whorls of specialized organs, including stamens (pollen bearing) and pistils (ovule containing), usually surrounded by a perianth consisting of a corolla formed of separate or united, often highly colored petals, and a calyx formed of separate or united, often green sepals.

FLUSH. A burst of growth.

FOLLICLE. A dry, one-chambered fruit that opens by one seam or suture to liberate the seeds, as in milkweed.

FORCING. Making plants bloom at a time other than is natural.

FORM, FORMA. A minor subdivision of a species or natural variety, usually distinct by a single genetically trivial characteristic, such as flower color; abbreviated f.

FREE. Separate or distinct, not united or joined, especially in reference to petals and other floral structures.

FRIABLE. Crumbly soil quality.

FROND. The compound leaf of a fern or palm.

FROST DAMAGE. Damage or death of soft or unhardened plant tissues following the formation of ice within them; also caused by sudden freezing, sustained cold, or recurrent freezing and thawing, any of which can kill shoot tips, foliage, and flower buds; it can also split stems and, in evergreens, desiccate foliage, especially when frost penetration in the soil is deeper than the plant's roots.

FROST POCKET. A low, protected site where still, cold air collects, causing frequent severe frosts.

FRUIT. A ripened, seed-bearing ovary, often with accessory parts such as persistent sepals, stamens, styles, etc.

FRUTESCENT, FRUTICOSE. Shrubby, i.e., with numerous woody stems.

FUGACIOUS. Dropping early, as in the scales of the expanding leaf buds of trees in spring.

FUMIGATION. Control of pests and disease organisms by the application of toxic fumes.

G

GAZEBO. A garden shelter designed and placed to command a view.

GENE. A segment of chromosomal DNA that determines a specific trait of a plant.

GENERIC NAME. The first term in a plant's binomial botanical name; the name begins with a capital letter and is italicized; it is usually in Latin.

GENUS, GENERA. A group of closely related species (sometimes only one), having certain characteristics in common and distinct from all other plants, such as oaks, maples, pines, and the ginkgo.

GERMINATION. A complex process by which a seed embryo becomes a seedling.

GESNERIAD. A member of the family Gesneriaceae, which includes such horticulturally important genera as *Achimenes*, *Columnea*, *Saintpaulia*, and *Streptocarpus*.

GIRDLING. The removal of a zone of tree bark, cambium, and sapwood around the entire trunk, resulting in death of the crown if not the whole tree; the expansion of a knot of major tree roots, resulting in strangulation and the death of the tree.

GLABROUS. Hairless, smooth.

GLAND. A secretory structure or surface.

GLAUCOUS. Covered with a powdery bloom.

GLOCHID. A tiny spinelike bristle, often detachable, occurring in tufts in cacti.

GRAFTING. The induced union of a bud or shoot (the scion) detached from one plant and brought into contact with the rooted stem (stock) of another plant.

GROUP. In cultivated plant nomenclature, a series of similar cultivars within a species or hybrid.

GROWING BAG. A soft-sided plastic container used to grow nursery stock and certain vegetables, such as tomatoes.

GROW ON. To promote further growth, especially by changing the container or the garden site.

GUY. A wire or cable, usually installed in twos or threes, to support a transplanted tree.

H

HABIT. The general appearance or proportioning of a plant.

HALF-HARDY. Frost-intolerant annuals that require a long season to mature, hence in most zones require starting indoors in late winter or early spring before being set out.

HARDENING OFF. The gradual adjustment of plants started indoors to outdoor or garden conditions, especially to cold nights and drier soil.

HARDY. Frost tolerant to some degree.

HEAD. A short, dense flower cluster, as in daisies; the leafy portion of a tree above the trunk, or the crown; a dense, tight aggregation of leaves, as in lettuce or cabbage.

HEAVING. The thrusting of plants out of the soil by recurrent freezing and thawing; occurs especially in winter and early spring on heavy soils.

HEAVY. Refers to soil consisting entirely or mostly of clay.

HEDGE. A file of shrubs planted at close intervals, usually of one kind and intended as a screen or for definition.

HEEL. A fragment of a stem with an attached side shoot, the unit used as a scion in certain types of grafting.

HEELING IN. Temporary storage of plants in shallow trenches, usually by laying them on their sides at close intervals, and covering the roots with soil until conditions favor transplanting to a permanent site.

HERB. A plant lacking woody aboveground stems; a plant grown for flavor, fragance, dyestuff, or pharmaceutical properties.

HERBACEOUS. Not woody; dying back to the ground when dormant.

HILLING UP. Mounding soil around the base of a plant to protect marginally hardy materials, such as roses, in winter; in the vegetable garden, to help stabilize top-heavy crops (such as corn), to blanch leaf stalks (as in celery), and to keep sun-sensitive tubers and roots covered (as in potatoes and carrots).

HIP. The fleshy fruitlike torus or floral receptacle of the rose containing numerous one-seeded achenes (the true fruits).

HORMONE. An organic compound produced at one location in the plant and translocated to another place where, in low concentration, it has a specific effect.

HOSE-IN-HOSE. An abnormal tubular flower in which one corolla lies within another, as in certain azaleas.

HUMUS. A complex mixture of organic materials in various stages of decomposition.

HUSK. A general term for an outer covering, as of nuts or corn ears.

HYBRID. A plant or kind resulting from a cross between genetically unlike parents, the name is often preceded by a multiplication sign (×).

I

ILLEGITIMATE NAME. A botanical name that is unacceptable because it was not first published according to the rules of the International Code of Botanical Nomenclature.

INDEHISCENT. Not opening, principally in reference to certain fruits, such as cherries, blueberries, and grapes.

INDETERMINATE. A mode of growth not halted or redirected by a terminal flower or leaf, as in most leafy shoots.

INDIGENOUS. Native to a region.

INFERIOR. Occurring beneath or below, as with the ovary of a squash flower in relation to the other floral parts.

INFLATED. Blown up, distended, bladdery.

INSECTICIDE. A substance toxic to insects.

INSECTIVOROUS. Insect eating, in reference to certain plants specially adapted to lure, trap, and digest various insects and other small invertebrates.

INTERCROPPING. Cultivating rapidly maturing crops, such as radishes, between rows of more slowly maturing crops, such as leeks.

INTERNODE. The part of a stem or twig between nodes or points of leaf attachment.

INTERRUPTED. Not continuous, usually in reference to the sporadic occurrence of leaf-derived structures among true leaves, as in spore-bearing leaf divisions among foliar leaf divisions in the interrupted fern (*Osmunda claytoniana*).

IRREGULAR. Applies to a flower that has a single plane of symmetry, as in the snapdragon, or no plane of symmetry, as in the canna.

ISLAND. A bed of ornamental plants that is visible and accessible from all sides.

J

JOINT. A swollen node, as occurring in four o'clocks or knotweeds.

K

KEEL. A central ridge; the two united, lowermost petals of a legume flower, as in the pea or bean.

KITCHEN GARDEN. A walled garden of vegetables, herbs, and espaliered fruit trees, as well as flowers for cutting, usually located near the kitchen door; more loosely, any garden so situated.

KNOT GARDEN. An intricately patterned formal garden consisting of a curving or angled linear layout of low plants, often herbs, surrounding intervening areas covered with colored gravel or planted with low bedding annuals.

L

LAMINA. A blade or flat, expanded portion, as in a leaf or petal.

LATERAL. Borne at or on the side.

LATEX. Milky sap, as in the milkweed.

LATH HOUSE. A framework covered with spaced lath strips to reduce sun and wind exposure to the plants within.

LAX. Loosely arranged, or widely spaced.

LAYERING. A type of vegetative reproduction in which a shoot produces roots while still fully or partly attached to the parent plant.

LEACHING. The downward or horizontal percolation of nutrients in soil water beyond the reach of roots.

LEAF. A stem attachment that functions as the principal site of the plant's food-making process, photosynthesis, and consists of a usually expanded blade or lamina, which is most commonly supported and positioned by a distinct stalk or petiole.

LEAFLET. One of the blades of a compound leaf, as in the ash or rose.

LEAF MOLD. The fluffy or powdery remains of decomposed vegetation.

LEGUME. A pod or one-chambered fruit opening along both sutures, or along one with the other serving as a hinge, to liberate the seeds, which are usually arranged in a file; a member of the bean or pea family (formerly Leguminosae, now Fabaceae, Caesatpiniaceae, and Mimosaceae).

LIANA. A woody climber, especially of tropical origin.

LIMB. A large tree branch; the spreading rim beyond the throat of a tubular flower.

LIP. One of the two (upper and lower) parts of a bilabiate (two-lipped) flower, as in the snapdragon; a highly specialized part of an orchid flower.

LOAM. Any easily worked soil that contains substantial organic matter.

LOBE. A major segment, especially of a leaf, as in most maples and oaks.

M

MANURE. Organic matter, especially animal dung, usually mixed with straw, sawdust, wood chips, or other stable bedding.

MEDIUM. Soil or other rooting mixture.

MICROCLIMATE. Environmental conditions in a small, limited area.

MIDRIB. The main vein of a leaf, usually dividing the blade into equal halves.

MONOCARPIC. Flowering and fruiting only once, then dying, as in annuals and biennials.

MONOCOT. A plant whose seeds have only one cotyledon, or seed leaf.

MONOECIOUS. A plant with unisexual flowers, but with both staminate (male) and pistillate (female) flowers borne on the same individual, as in squash and cucumber.

MULCH. Loose, bulky, usually organic material applied to the soil surface to conserve moisture, deter weeds, and stabilize soil temperature.

MULTIPLE FRUIT. A fusion of individual fruits arising from adjacent flowers, as in the mulberry or pineapple.

MUTANT. A genetic variant that arises suddenly and is often markedly different from its parent(s).

N

NATURALIZING. Plants arranged to suggest natural wild growth; the establishment and unassisted reproduction of plants outside their natural range.

NECTARY. A gland, usually within a flower, that secretes a sugary substance attractive to bees and other insects, and, in some cases, to hummingbirds.

NITRIFICATION. The sequential steps by which nitrogen is converted into nitrate, in which form it is useful to plants.

NOCTURNAL. Refers mainly to flowers that open at night and close during the day, as in the moonflower and four o'clock.

NODE. A point on a shoot or stem where one or more leaves arise.

NUT. An indehiscent fruit in which the single seed is surrounded by a bony coat, as in the acorn of oaks, or, more commonly but less accurately, a drupe with a relatively thin outer husk and a large stone encasing the single seed, as in the walnut and hickory.

NUTLET. A small nut, rather like an achene but with a thicker, harder wall, as in sage, basil, and other members of the mint family.

O

OBLIGATE. Requiring specific conditions to survive.

OPPOSITE. Borne two at a node, on opposite sides, as in leaves of the maple.

OVARY. The portion of the pistil containing the ovules or eggs; after fertilization, it becomes the fruit.

OVULE. The female sex cell that, after fertilization, becomes the seed.

P

PALMATE. With parts arranged like the fingers of a hand, i.e., arising and diverging from a common point, as in the lobes of maple leaves.

PEDICEL. The stalk of an individual flower held in a cluster.

PEDUNCLE. The stalk of a flower cluster, or of an individual flower borne alone.

PELTATE. Refers to a circular leaf blade with the stalk or petiole attached at or near the center, as in the garden nasturtium.

PEPO. A gourd fruit, i.e., fleshy, with a hard rind, and containing many seeds, as in the melon, squash, and cucumber.

PERENNIAL. Growing for three seasons or more, usually in reference to herbaceous plants that die to the ground when dormant, but also includes woody plants.

PERFECT. Refers to a bisexual flower, i.e., one with both stamens and pistil(s).

PERIANTH. A collective term that includes the calyx (sepals) and corolla (petals).

PETAL. A unit of the corolla, usually brightly colored.

PETIOLE. The leaf stalk.

PETIOLULE. Stalk of a leaflet.

pH. Hydrogen ion concentration, by which soil acidity is measured.

PHLOEM. Conductive tissue that transports manufactured food from leaves to growth points or storage organs.

PHYLLOCLAD. A modified flattened stem serving as a leaf, as in the Christmas cactus.

PHYLLODE. An expanded, flattened, leaflike leaf stalk or petiole with no true blade, as in certain acacia species.

PHYLOGENY. The evolutionary development of a kind or group.

PICOTEE. A flower whose petal margins are of a color that contrasts with the rest of the flower.

PINCHING BACK. The shortening of young shoots to achieve a bushier habit or to enhance flower and fruit development.

PINNATE. With leaflets of a compound leaf arranged like branches of a feather, i.e., along both sides of the axis.

PIONEERS. The first plants to occupy an environment, especially one much disturbed or cleared of vegetation.

PIP. A bud on the root crown, as occurs in the lily-of-the-valley and peony.

PISTIL. Collectively, the female reproductive organs, consisting of the ovary; its outward, often stalked extension, the style; and the pollen-receptive tip, the stigma.

PIT. The stone in a drupe; a partly submerged greenhouse.

PITH. The spongy cylindrical core in the stems of many plants, such as the elder.

PLEACH. To trim the upper branches of parallel hedges so that they will grow together and cover the walkway beneath.

PLUG. A small rooted piece of turf grass used in quantity to establish a lawn.

PLUMOSE. Feathery, plumed, with many upward-directed divisions.

PLUNGE. To sink potted plants into soil.

POD. In general, a dry, dehiscent fruit; more strictly, a legume, i.e., the fruit of most members of the pea family, including beans, lupines, locust, and wisteria.

POLESAW. A pruning saw attached to a pole and used to prune trees.

POLLARD. To cut all branches of a tree back to the trunk, usually each year, to restrict growth and produce strong, straight stems or whips for use as stakes and fencing.

POLLEN. Dustlike grains liberated from the anther, each containing male sex cells.

POLLINATION. The transfer of pollen from anther to stigma, mostly by insects or wind.

POLYGAMOUS. Having both bisexual (perfect) and unisexual (imperfect, i.e., staminate and/or pistillate) flowers.

POLYMORPHIC. Occurring in several forms, as with the leaves of mulberry, or in the growth habit of poison ivy.

POLYPLOID. A plant whose cells have more than the usual two sets of chromosomes.

POME. A fleshy fruit made up of the union of the ovary and its much-expanded receptacle or torus, as in the apple, pear, and quince.

POMPON. A densely doubled flower or flower head, especially of the dahlia and mum.

POT BOUND. A plant whose roots are severely crowded in a container.

POTTING ON. To move a potted plant into a larger container.

POTTING UP. The initial potting of a plant.

PREEMERGENCE. Refers to herbicides applied before the germination of weed seeds, to inhibit embryo growth.

PRICKING OUT. Transplanting seedlings from the germination bed to a place or container for growing on.

PRICKLE. A small, sharp-pointed outgrowth of bark or epidermis.

PRIMOCANE. A biennial cane, especially of the raspberry and blackberry, during its first year.

PROPAGATION. The increase or multiplication of plants.

PROPAGATION BOX, PROPAGATION FRAME. An illuminated, humidity-retaining enclosure for seed germination and the rooting of cuttings.

PROP ROOT. An aerial root arising aboveground from the stem and growing downward into the soil, augmenting support, as in corn.

PRUNING SAW. A serrated blade, usually curved, with the teeth directed toward the handle; therefore it cuts on the pull stroke.

PUBESCENT. Hairy, usually without reference to type, quality, or duration of hair.

PUNCTATE. Marked with tiny pits or translucent dots.

PUNGENT. Of acrid taste; sharp pointed.

PYRENE. A seed with a surrounding bony or woody coat, as in cherry, peach, and other "stone" fruits.

R

RACEME. An elongate cluster of stalked (pedicellate) flowers.

RACHIS. The axis of a flower cluster or of a compound leaf.

RADIATE. Spreading evenly from a common center, as in the petal-like ray flowers of the daisy or sunflower.

RADICAL. Arising directly from the roots, as in the rosetted leaves of the dandelion.

RADICLE. The rudimentary or initial root growing from the embryo.

RANK. A row, as in the two-ranked leaves of the hemlock.

RAY. A ray flower, petal-like, and often arising from the periphery of a head, as in the daisy and sunflower.

RECEPTACLE. The swollen or elongated end of a stem from which the flower parts arise.

RECURVED. Curved downward.

REFLEXED. Sharply curved downward.

REMONTANT. Refers to plants that bloom more than once in a growing season, as in certain daylily and iris cultivars.

REPELLENT. Substances that ward off unwanted insects and other animals.

RESPIRATION. The process by which a plant takes in oxygen, oxidizes matter, releases energy, and gives off carbon dioxide.

RETICULATE. Netted, as in the outer covering or tunic of certain bulbs.

REVERSION. Return to an original state, as in the flower color of successive generations of hybrid cultivars.

RHIZOME. A specialized, horizontal, rooted stem, usually underground; its apex bears leaves and flowers, as in the iris.

RIB. The primary or a major leaf vein.

ROOT PRUNING. Severing a portion of the root system before transplanting or as a means of slowing or reducing growth.

ROOTSTOCK. Rhizome; a specialized subterranean stem.

ROSE. An expanded, perforated cap on the spout of a watering can.

ROSETTE. Leaves radiating from the root crown, as in the dandelion.

RUDIMENTARY. Underdeveloped and nonfunctional.

RUNNER. A slender, trailing stem, usually rooting at the nodes.

S

SAMARA. A winged, wind-dispersed, indehiscent fruit, either single, as in the ash and tree-of-heaven, or double, as in the maple.

SANDY SOIL. Having particles 0.05 to 2 mm in diameter, mainly derived from quartz.

SAP. A solution containing various proportions of water, salts, sugars, and other complex substances, found in all living plant parts and circulating through the vascular system.

SAPROPHYTE. A colorless plant that lives on dead organic matter, such as the Indian pipe and many fungi.

SARMENTOSE. Climbing or ascending, but without specialized means of support, as in the tomato.

SCABROUS. Rough or gritty to the touch, such as elm leaves.

SCAFFOLD BRANCH. In fruit trees, a permanent limb or major branch that supports renewable lateral branches or fruit spurs.

SCALE. A minute, flattened appendage or vestigial leaf; a sucking insect covered with a protective shield.

SCANDENT. Climbing.

SCAPE. A leafless peduncle or flower stalk arising directly from roots or bulb, with no attached foliage, as in narcissus and amaryllis.

SCARIFICATION. Loosening the soil without turning it over; removal of lawn thatch; scratching or nicking hard-coated seeds to hasten germination.

SCION. In grafting, a bud or cutting to be inserted into the rooted stock.

SECUND. One-sided, as in the disposition of flowers in the foxglove.

SEED. A ripened fertilized ovule, containing the embryo.

SEEDLING. A very young plant grown from seed.

SEGMENT. In general, a part or portion of a deeply divided but not compound structure.

SELECTIVE HERBICIDE, SELECTIVE PESTICIDE. A biocide that kills only certain kinds of weeds or pests, leaving other organisms unaffected.

SELF-COLORED. Of one color.

SENESCENCE. Postmaturity decline, eventually leading to death, a process that in trees can span decades.

SEPAL. A unit of the calyx, usually green and sometimes leaflike, covering the unopened flower bud.

SEPTATE. Partitioned.

SESSILE. Stalkless.

SET. An immature bulb or tuber used for propagation, especially of the onion or potato.

SETA. A bristle.

SHARP. Refers to sand in which the grains are angular and promote free drainage.

SHEATH. A tubular structure surrounding another structure, as with the bases of palm fronds surrounding the stem.

SHRUB. In general, a multistemmed woody plant, usually low and often producing successive shoots from the base.

SILKY. Covered with fine, soft hairs.

SILT. Soil particles 0.05 to 0.002 mm in diameter, usually deposited as alluvium.

SIMPLE. Unitary, not compound or divided into secondary parts, as in a willow leaf (but not a rose leaf).

SINUS. The space or indentation between two structures, as between the lobes of an oak leaf.

SLIP. A cutting.

SLOW RELEASE. Refers to fertilizers that are slow to dissolve or that require bacterial decomposition before being absorbed by roots.

SMOOTH. Hairless.

SOAKER. A finely perforated hose from which water trickles or seeps along its entire length.

SOIL. The surface layer of the earth, consisting of mineral particles, organic matter, water, and air, inhabited by microorganisms and functioning as the source of water and nutrients for most plants.

SOIL CONDITIONER. Any material that improves the physical structure of soil.

SOLITARY. Borne singly.

SORUS. A spore-bearing patch ("fruit dot") in ferns, usually occurring on the undersides of the leaves.

SOUR. Refers to soil that is acidic and/or waterlogged.

SPADIX. The thick, fleshy spike bearing minute flowers characteristic of aroids, as in the calla and jack-in-the-pulpit.

SPATHE. A bract or modified leaf surrounding or ensheathing the spadix, as in aroids and palms.

SPECIES. (singular and plural; abbreviated sp., singular, and spp., plural): A group of similar, interfertile individuals, comprising a subdivision of a genus; the second term in a plant's binomial botanical name; the name begins with a lowercase letter and is italicized; it is usually in Latin.

SPIKE. An elongate cluster of unstalked or sessile flowers, as in blazing star or mullein.

SPINE. A strong, rigid, sharp-pointed outgrowth, usually occurring on stems.

SPORE. A one-celled, dustlike, wind-dispersed, asexual reproductive body characteristic of ferns, mosses, and fungi.

SPORT. A mutant.

SPRAY. A nontechnical term for a loose cluster of flowers or for a flower-bearing branchlet; an application of water or biocide in droplet form under pressure.

SPUR. A tubular projection, often nectar-bearing, of a flower, as in the columbine or impatiens; in fruit trees, a short shoot terminating in a flower bud or cluster and bearing fruit.

STALK. In general, an elongate support, as for a leaf (petiole), leaflet (petiolule), or flower or fruit (peduncle or pedicel).

STAMEN. The "male" reproductive organ of a flower, consisting of the pollen-bearing anther, which is usually supported on a stalklike filament.

STAMINATE. Refers to a flower, or to a plant with flowers, bearing only stamens, no pistils.

STANDARD. The uppermost, often broad and bannerlike petal in a legume flower, as in the pea or bean; a flag or erect petal in an iris flower; a normally branched plant trained to, or grafted on, a single elongate stem.

STARTING. Stimulating dormant bulbs, corms, tubers, etc., to resume growth; germinating seeds.

STEM. The axis of a plant that bears leaves and flowers.

STERILE. Lacking sex organs or without flowers, hence bearing no fruits and seeds.

STERILIZATION. The process by which soil or other media are made free of harmful organisms before being used for seed germination or plant culture.

STIGMA. Pollen-receptive tip of the pistil, from which pollen grains grow tubes internally to fertilize the ovules.

STIPE. The stalk of the ovary in some pistils, such as those of the spider flower (*Cleome* spp.); leaf stalk of a fern; stalk of a mushroom.

STIPULE. Appendage at the base of the leaf stalk in some plants, usually paired and small, often temporary, sometimes leaflike, as in peas.

STOCK. In grafting, the plant into which the scion is to be inserted and that will assume the rooting function of the new plant; named plants or seeds of known characteristics; plants used for propagation.

STOLON. A node-rooting, horizontal, or repeatedly arching stem that develops new plants wherever it strikes root, as in the strawberry.

STOMA, STOMATA. Minute pore(s), mostly on leaf undersurfaces, through which water vapor and gases pass.

STONE. The woody or bony covering (pyrene) of the seed in a drupe.

STONE FRUIT. A drupe, as in the apricot, cherry, peach, and plum.

STRANGLE. To impede mechanically a stem's increase in girth.

STRATIFICATION. The storage of seed in cold or warm conditions for prescribed periods to improve germination.

STRESS. Impaired plant functioning, caused by such environmental factors as drought, flood, temperature extremes, unfavorable pH, high wind, chemical pollutants, soil compaction, mechanical injury, being transplanted, etc.

STRIATE. Finely lined or ridged.

STRICT. Rigidly upright, as in the habit of the Lombardy poplar.

STYLE. The usually elongate extension of the pistil, terminating with the stigma.

SUBSHRUB. Strictly speaking, a woody perennial whose stems regularly die back partway in winter, as in the butterfly bush and chaste bush from zone 6 north; loosely, a very small shrub treated as a perennial, such as thyme or perennial candytuft.

SUBSOIL. Soil strata beneath topsoil, usually containing little organic content, low nutrient yield, and poor physical structure.

SUBSPECIES. A major subdivision of a species, intermediate between species and botanical variety, often of distinct geographical distribution in nature and otherwise differing from other subspecies of the often wide-ranging species concerned; abbreviated ssp. (plural is sspp.).

SUBSTRATE. Soil or other rooting medium.

SUCCULENT. A thickened, fleshy, juicy plant part; a plant characterized by succulent leaves and/or stems.

SUCKER. Vegetative growth, characteristically vigorous, arising from tree roots, as in black locust and tree-of-heaven; see *Water sprout.*

SUFFRUTESCENT. Subshrubby.

SUPERIOR. Above, as with an ovary located above the attachment of sepals, petals, and stamens.

SUPERPHOSPHATE. An inorganic fertilizer containing about 20 percent soluble phosphate (or 47 percent in triple-superphosphate), used in liquid fertilizer mixtures.

SUTURE. A seam indicating the line of union, as where a dehiscent fruit opens when mature.

SWARD. An expanse of turf.

SYMMETRICAL. Divisible into equal or similar halves.

SYMPETALOUS. With united or joined petals, as in the morning glory.

SYNCONIUM. The fig, which is a swollen, hollow receptacle whose inner surface is lined with minute flowers and ultimately tiny one-seeded fruits, the whole being popularly regarded as a fruit.

SYSTEMIC. A biocide absorbed by a plant and distributed internally to all parts.

T

TAMPING. Firming freshly loosened soil, usually with a flat object such as block of wood.

TAXON (PLURAL, TAXA). A classification unit of any rank.

TAXONOMY. The science of classification, especially of kinds of organisms.

TENDER. Sensitive or intolerant, especially of frost.

TENDRIL. A slender, twisting extension, either a modified leaf or stem, that contacts and clutches a support, facilitating the ascent of certain climbers, such as peas, gourds, passion flower, and grapes.

TEPAL. A segment or component of a perianth whose sepals and petals are alike, as in the begonia and tulip.

TERMINAL. Occurring at the tip.

TERRESTRIAL. Rooted in soil; a land plant.

TESTA. The outer coat of a seed.

TETRAPLOID. Having four, or twice the usual number of, chromosome sets.

THATCH. Organic debris that accumulates on the soil surface, especially in lawns.

THIN. Refers to a shallow, rapidly drying soil.

THORN. A modified, abbreviate, leafless stem; simple, as in the hawthorn, or branched, as in the honey locust.

THROAT. The opening of a tubular flower.

TISSUE CULTURE. The growth of plant cells or tissues in an artificial medium under sterile conditions, used to propagate orchids and other slow-growing plants.

TOLERANT. Showing little or no effect from adverse conditions, such as disease, cold, pH extremes, etc.

TOMENTUM. A downy mat of short woolly hairs.

TOOTH. A minor projection, usually numerous, as on leaf margins.

TOPDRESSING. Any nutrient-yielding material placed on the soil surface near plants to receive the supplemental nutrients.

TOPSOIL. The uppermost soil layer, often dark with organic matter, varying greatly in depth, especially valuable for plant cultivation.

TORUS. A floral receptacle, especially when unusually large as in the rose or the pome fruits.

TRACE ELEMENTS. Micronutrient salts of boron, copper, iron, manganese, molybdenum, and zinc essential to plant growth but required in only minute amounts; present in most soils.

TRAIN. To manage plant growth in a certain way, as to grow in a particular direction or assume a desired form.

TRANSLOCATION. The movement of water and soluble materials through the vascular system of a plant.

TRANSPIRATION. The loss of water vapor by leaves, usually through the stomata.

TRANSPLANTING. Moving plants from one location to another.

TREE. A woody plant with a single main stem or trunk or bole, and usually with a high crown.

TRELLIS. A structure made of intersecting slats.

TRICHOME. A hair or bristle.

TRIFOLIATE. Having three leaves, as in the wake-robin.

TRIFOLIOLATE. Each leaf consisting of three separate blades or leaflets, as in the clover.

TRIMORPHIC. Occurring in three forms, as in the leaves of sassafras.

TRIPLOID. Having three chromosome sets instead of the usual two.

TRUE. Refers to self-bred plants whose seeds produce progeny very similar to the parent.

TRUNCATE. Abruptly squared off, as in the leaf of the tulip tree.

TRUSS. A compact or dense flower cluster, as in rhododendrons and geraniums.

TUBE. The more or less cylindrical lower portion of a tubular flower, below the throat.

TUBER. A short, thick, swollen storage organ, usually subterranean and either a modified stem with scattered buds ("eyes"), as in the potato, or a root with buds at the top, as in the turnip, or, less commonly, an aboveground stem, as in the kohlrabi.

TUBERCLE. A small, rounded body, or a bump on another organ.

TUFA. An extremely porous, lightweight limestone used in rock gardens.

TUNIC. A loose, membranous or fibrous outer skin, occurring especially on certain corms, as in crocuses, or bulbs, as in onions.

TUNNEL. A strip of clear plastic sheeting spread over wire hoops to protect young plants in rows.

TURBINATE. Top shaped.

TURF. Lawn grass.

TURGID. Swollen with liquid, tumid.

TWIG. A slender, young, woody branch; the growth of the season in shrubs and trees.

U

UMBEL. A flat-topped to rounded flower cluster in which all the individual flower stalks or pedicels arise from a common point, as in Queen Anne's lace or the onions.

UNARMED. Lacking thorns or prickles.

UNDULATE. Wavy, especially in reference to leaves and petals.

UNISEXUAL. Of one sex only, i.e., staminate or pistillate.

UREA. A nitrate-rich organic compound used in liquid fertilizers.

V

VALVATE. With lobes or segments (valves) joined by their edges, as in pea pods.

VARIETY. In amateur gardening used often in the place of the term *cultivar*: in botany, a naturally self-perpetuating subdivision of a species, not sufficiently distinct to constitute a subspecies or separate species, but more distinctive than a form; abbreviated var.

VASCULAR. Pertaining to the conducting and supporting tissues of a plant, i.e., to the xylem and phloem.

VEGETABLE. A plant grown for its edible parts, other than nuts and sweet fruits.

VENATION. The arrangement of veins, especially in leaves (sometimes called nerves).

VERSATILE. Swinging from an attachment in the middle, especially in reference to anthers, as in lilies.

VERTICILLATE. Arranged in whorls or circles around the stem.

VESICLE. An air- or liquid-filled bladder, such as the submerged traps in the bladderwort (*Utricularia* spp.).

VESTIGE. An imperfectly developed, reduced, nonfunctional, degenerate structure, as in the ephemeral, rudimentary, soft green emergences on the young growth of prickly pear cactus.

VESTURE. Hairiness.

VIABILITY. The capacity of seeds to germinate.

VINE. A climber, most appropriately restricted to grape.

VIRGATE. Wandlike.

VISCID. Sticky, gummy.

VIVIPARY. Refers to seeds that germinate in the fruit while it is still attached to the parent plant, as in the mangrove.

VOLUBLE. Twining.

W

WATER POLYMER. A gelatinous substance used to increase water retention in soil media and to keep bare-root stock moist.

WATER SPROUT. A rapidly growing shoot appearing on the trunk or limbs of a tree.

WEED. An unwanted plant, especially when growing in a place needed by desired plants or for other purposes; a freely seeding species of great ecological amplitude, hence often invasive.

WEEPING. Trees and shrubs with pendulous branches.

WHIP. A young unbranched or little-branched tree.

WHORL. A circle or ring of three or more leaves or flowers at a node.

WILD GARDEN. A planting that resembles a natural setting, especially in woodland; a conservation garden.

WINDBREAK. A file or belt of trees and/or shrubs planted to deflect wind; a shelter belt when broad and extensive.

WING. A papery or membranous extension of a fruit, such as a maple samara; a leaf base extending down the stem as a slender ridge, as in burning bush; one of the two lateral petals in a legume flower, as in the sweet pea.

WOOLLY. With a mat of long, soft hairs.

X

XEROPHYTE. A plant occurring in arid, desertous habitats.

XYLEM. The conductive tissue of stems and roots that transports water and dissolved nutrients; it ultimately becomes wood.

Z

ZONE. Plant-hardiness regions determined by the lowest winter temperature; the various zones are separated by 10°F graduations.

USDA Plant Hardiness Zone Map

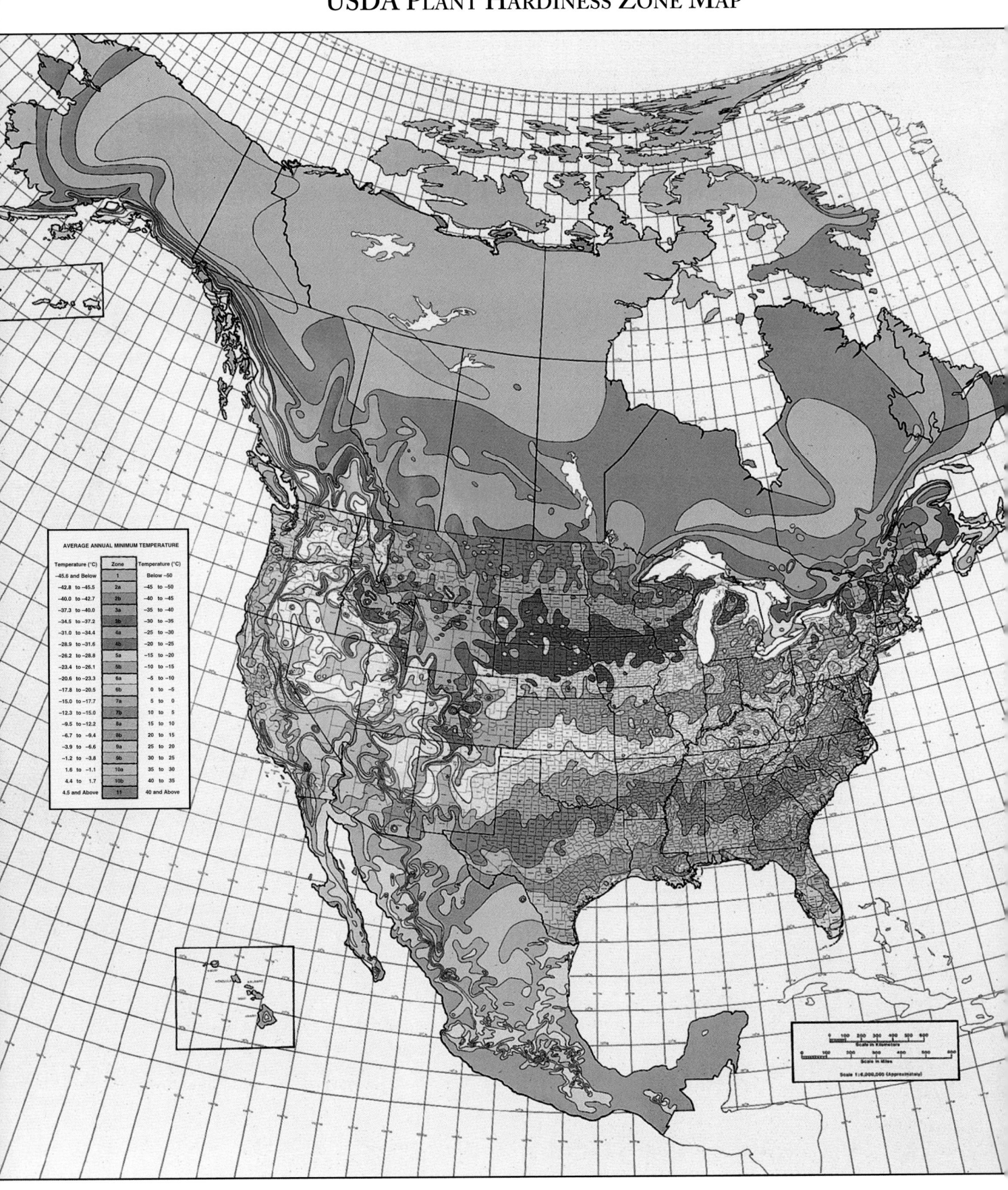

AVERAGE ANNUAL MINIMUM TEMPERATURE		
Temperature (°C)	Zone	Temperature (°C)
-45.6 and Below	1	Below -50
-42.8 to -45.5	2a	-45 to -50
-40.0 to -42.7	2b	-40 to -45
-37.3 to -40.0	3a	-35 to -40
-34.5 to -37.2	3b	-30 to -35
-31.0 to -34.4	4a	-25 to -30
-28.9 to -31.6	4b	-20 to -25
-26.2 to -28.8	5a	-15 to -20
-23.4 to -26.1	5b	-10 to -15
-20.6 to -23.3	6a	-5 to -10
-17.8 to -20.5	6b	0 to -5
-15.0 to -17.7	7a	5 to 0
-12.3 to -15.0	7b	10 to 5
-9.5 to -12.2	8a	15 to 10
-6.7 to -9.4	8b	20 to 15
-3.9 to -6.6	9a	25 to 20
-1.2 to -3.8	9b	30 to 25
1.6 to -1.1	10a	35 to 30
4.4 to 1.7	10b	40 to 35
4.5 and Above	11	40 and Above

PHOTOGRAPHY CREDITS

INDEX

Note: Page numbers in **bold italics** refer to illustrations.

H